Share Valuation Han

Third edition

Share Valuation Handbook

Third edition

David Collison CTA (Fellow), FCA, TEP

Roger Barnard LLB, LLM, FCA, CTA (Fellow)
BKL Weeks Green has contributed Chapter 8 and
the Share Option material in Chapter 5

a Wolters Kluwer business

Wolters Kluwer (UK) Limited
145 London Road, Kingston-upon-Thames
Surrey KT2 6SR
Telephone: +44 (0) 870 777 2906
Fax: + 44 (0) 208 247 1184
Email: customerservices@cch.co.uk
website: www.cch.co.uk

Disclaimer

This publication is sold with the understanding that neither the publisher nor the authors, with regard to this publication, are engaged in rendering legal or professional services. The material contained in this publication neither purports, nor is intended to be, advice on any particular matter.

Although this publication incorporates a considerable degree of standardisation, subjective judgment by the user, based on individual circumstances, is indispensable. This publication is an 'aid' and cannot be expected to replace such judgment.

Neither the publisher nor the authors can accept any responsibility or liability to any person, whether a purchaser of this publication or not, in respect of anything done or omitted to be done by any such person in reliance, whether sole or partial, upon the whole or any part of the contents of this publication.

Telephone Helpline Disclaimer Notice

Where purchasers of this publication also have access to any Telephone Helpline Service operated by Wolters Kluwer (UK), then Wolters Kluwer's total liability to contract, tort (including negligence, or breach of statutory duty) misrepresentation, restitution or otherwise with respect to any claim arising out of its acts or alleged omissions in the provision of the Helpline Service shall be limited to the yearly subscription fee paid by the Claimant.

British Library Cataloguing-in-Publication Data.

A catalogue record for this book is available from the British Library.

Typeset by Columns Design Limited, Reading, UK
Printed in the Netherlands by Alfabase, Alpen aan den Rijn

Contents

Part 2 – Cases

Note: For each case, a commentary is given identifying the points in the case that are important when valuing a shareholding. The judgement of the court is then given in full.

Cases are given in chronological order

In all cases in this volume, the page reference is given at the end of the page as originally published in the source to which reference is made. Thus, the opening words of Lord Hershell in *Birch v Cropper* **case 1** are referenced [1889] 14 AC 525 at 529.

Preface

Virtually every accountant in general practice is required, from time to time, to estimate the value of a shareholding in a private company, when there is, in reality, no likelihood of the shares currently being sold. A valuation is required to calculate the liability to inheritance tax when the estate of the deceased includes a private company shareholding. A valuation is required to calculate a capital gains tax liability when a gift of shares in the family company is made. A valuation is required for the income tax charge when an employee is given shares in the company that employs him. The vast majority of accountants undertake a share valuation exercise rarely.

The intention of this book is to provide a readily assessable, practical and yet authoritative guide to the process of valuing shares in an unlisted company. There are three distinct purposes for which the book may be used:

1. The reader may seek guidance on the valuation of a particular type of share (eg a minority share in a farming company).
2. The reader may need to give case law authority for the method of valuation he has employed.
3. The reader may be required to respond to a Revenue challenge. And Revenue challenges typically quote a case law authority.

The book is structured in two separate parts. Part 1 takes the reader through the techniques of share valuation. Description of the different techniques is cross-referenced to case law authority in Part 2 of the book.

Statute gives hardly any guidance on the manner in which a valuation is to be undertaken. For example, Inheritance Tax Act 1984 simply states that the value is: 'the price which the [shareholding] might reasonably expected to fetch if sold in the open market at that time' (IHTA 1984, s 160). The statutory provision for capital gains tax is similarly short and statute is silent on the method of valuing for income tax (other than for employee share options). On the basis of brief statutory statement, a body of case law has built up. However, the number of cases that actually get to the courts is very small indeed. Businessmen have been able to create companies by a relatively simple process of registration since Companies Act 1844. (Before that Act, to create a company it was necessary to petition the Privy Council for a royal warrant.) From 1844 to 2006 only 48 cases on share valuation for tax purposes had been heard by the courts.

In Part 2 of this book I reproduce the entire decision of the court in each of these 48 cases, plus a further 2 cases arising under Company Law where the decision of the court is particularly relevant, in my view, when there is a valuation for a tax purpose. For each of the 50 cases, I give my commentary on the points arising in the decision that are, I believe, most relevant to the practical business of valuing a shareholding.

In this third edition we have taken the opportunity of thoroughly re-referencing the material. The format of the book is, I believe, more user friendly than the second edition. Secondly, and very importantly, two methods of referencing have been used throughout. Each point arising in Part 1 and each commentary in Part 2 incorporates the form of reference that has become standard in our profession. This will greatly assist the reader who wishes to give a reference in his/her correspondence with HM Revenue & Customs, or who needs to check the context of a case law quotation in a letter received from HMRC Share Valuation. Cases in this book span a period of 117 years. Inevitably, the standard reference system used to index all cases heard in the High Court and above over such a long period has become a little cumbersome. In order to assist the reader moving within this volume, cases have been given a sequential number and the paragraphs within the judge's decision are numbered. This gives a more rapid means of locating a particular reference.

Whilst working on this edition, I was asked why I find tax cases interesting. Re-reading all the share valuation cases in chronological order, which is the order in which they appear in this volume, gives, for me, a fascinating insight in the development of the subject matter of our profession. In 1889, the court is tentatively declaring the principles that apply to a company and has to look to the experience of partnership in order to do so. By 1926, the court is ruling on the relevance of alternative techniques of valuation that have developed. In 1973, Lord Wilberforce in the House of Lords welcomed as 'a sound and rational development of the law' the concept that valuation of company shares should, in certain defined circumstances, be cased on the 'just and equitable' principle that has always been applied to the relationship between partners in a partnership. In 2006, the court reminds us that a company is not, however, a partnership and that a minority shareholder has a holding of less worth than that held by the majority shareholder.

Reading case law also gives insight into people's lives. We have the case where the Special Commissioner rearranged the room so that all verbal statements were made on the side of the taxpayer where he had his good ear, even though the Commissioner had a suspicion that the taxpayer's hearing was, perhaps, selective by virtue of the attractiveness or otherwise of the facts being stated. We have a taxpayer who, in a case heard after 12 years of negotiation with the Revenue, is described by the Special Commissioner as being 'able to recall the good points about his company rather more easily than he could recall the bad'. I am reminded of a client whom I had responsibility for some years ago. When she was widowed she got her finances into a mess. She was happy when we came to an agreement with the Revenue that she would pay her significant arrears of tax in monthly installments. However, a few months after signing this agreement, she read in her newspaper that the British Government was lending money to an African Government of which she disapproved. She wrote to the

Revenue expressing her disapproval of the use to which her tax payments were being put, cancelled her standing order and made no further payments of tax during the rest of her life. The Revenue took no action to collect the tax until she died, when the tax was paid from her estate.

I hope the reader will find this book of interest, as well as instructive.

As with all my books, I am indebted to Emma Beeton, my PA, for patiently dealing with the text. For this edition, I am also particularly grateful to Roger Barnard for his updating of the practical examples and to Sharon Kissonduth for the painstaking work of re-referencing.

The law is stated as at 6 April 2007, the date on which Income Tax Act 2007 is operative. References to Taxes Act 1988 have, thus, been restated to the appropriate sections of Income Tax (Earnings and Pensions) Act 2003, Income Tax (Trading and Other Income) Act 2005 and Income Tax Act 2007.

David Collison
Cambridge, April 2007

Table of Statutes

Table of Statutory Instruments

Table of Cases

Page numbers in **bold** refer to the main discussion of the case.

C

D

E

F

G

H

I

PART 1
Commentary

1 The legal and economic context

1.1 A fiscal valuation and a commercial price

The price a purchaser offers for a shareholding is a reflection of the value the purchaser thinks he will be able to obtain from the shareholding in the future. This applies whether a commercial offer is made for a takeover, or whether a shareholding is valued for a fiscal purpose. The past may be a guide, but the future is what the investor is buying.

In many ways the exercise undertaken in valuing shares for tax purposes is the same as the calculation that a potential purchaser would make before offering to buy a shareholding. The fiscal valuer is valuing the actual shareholding in the company in the real world. He must be aware of the company's track record, the nature of its trade, the future prospects of the company and the prospects for the industry in which it operates, as well as the likely purchasers, for the shares to be valued. The valuer must take the company as he finds it in the same way as a potential investor. The valuer must consider the information that would be available to that potential investor. Clearly, the information required would depend upon the amount of the investment, the size of the holding and other relevant factors. This may mean that information that does not actually exist must be treated as if it were known to the potential investor. (See TCGA 1992, s 273(3) and IHTA 1984, s 168(1) at section **2.6**, being the statutory override of the decision in *Re Lynall deceased* (1971) 47 TC 375 **case 29**.)

The particular characteristics of a fiscal valuation include the following:

- For capital gains tax and inheritance tax purposes (the main instances of fiscal valuations) the requirement is to ascertain the value that would be obtained in the open market. An open market is different from a sale by private treaty, in that all the world is deemed to be in an open market with all the information available relevant to the shares available to every person in that market. Strangely, perhaps, statute describes the information that is deemed to be available as that which would be available if there were a sale by private treaty (TCGA 1992, s 273(3) and IHTA 1984, s 168(1)). This does not change the fundamental point that it is the price for a sale in the open market that must be ascertained, not the price for a sale by private treaty. In a sale by private treaty the seller and purchaser can probably negotiate and adjust the price accordingly. This cannot be presupposed in a sale in the open market.
- A fiscal valuation is required on a given date, such as a death. That date may not be the opportune time to make a disposal. Nevertheless, statute deems there to be a sale on the relevant day, even though in practice in the real world a sale would not have taken place. For example, the company may not have reached the point where its owners would regard it as in a

marketable state. In reality, no one would sell the shares until this has happened. If the business of the company is cyclical, it may be the wrong time in the cycle to make a sale, but again the statute assumes that a sale does take place, even though the company is in the 'wrong' condition.

- In the real world, there may be an earnout so that part of the price is conditional upon performance in the future. This possibility must be disregarded in a fiscal valuation as statute requires outright purchase on a given day without strings attached.
- Moreover, even though in practice a purchaser will be protected by warranties and indemnities, this cannot be so in a fiscal valuation. It must be assumed that the purchase price takes account of all the problems, with a degree of prescience which, perhaps, is not possible in the real world.
- The articles of association may restrict the transfer in such a way that the directors could refuse to register a transfer. For a fiscal valuation, however, it must be assumed that the purchaser will be registered by the company as a shareholder but he takes his shares on the basis that the directors could refuse to register a transfer to a subsequent purchaser.
- In the real world either side can walk away from negotiations and the seller can withdraw the shares from the market if the offers are not adequate. The fiscal valuation is based on a hypothetical sale that happens; there is never any scope for saying that the sale would be aborted.
- Also in the real world, the parties can, and often do, act irrationally, which they cannot be assumed to do in a fiscal valuation.

Nevertheless, despite the differences between a fiscal valuation and a valuation in the real world there is the fundamental similarity between the two. The valuation produced must be the figure that, in the real world, someone would actually pay. If instinct suggests that it is either too low or too high, the valuation process must be re-examined as it may contain a fundamental flaw. The valuer may be able to test this to some degree by a comparison of actual sale of other companies close to the valuation date, particularly on multiples of earnings, with the usual caveat that no companies are identical. If nothing else, if there is a difference in value, it may be possible to identify the main reasons in reconciling the two. Common sense is a major attribute, provided the valuer has the basic level of understanding of business in general and the business of the company in particular.

In practice, it must be admitted that the willingness of the client to pay for the valuer's time is, of necessity, closely linked to the difference the value makes to the tax payable. It is not usually worth considering expensive research and argument with HMRC Share Valuation if the difference between the valuer's price and that suggested by HMRC Share Valuation is not large and particularly so if the tax at stake is not material. Attention must, however, be directed at all the fiscal consequences of a valuation before it is concluded that a value suggested by HMRC Share Valuation should be accepted to avoid further costs. It is commonplace that a value agreed for a capital gains tax matter where the tax at stake is small can then cause considerable embarrassment when a shareholder dies and the value must be ascertained for inheritance tax purposes. In the current fiscal climate, the point may be of more relevance put the other way around. Many valuations agreed for inheritance tax purposes where the tax at stake is small as a result of business property relief are later regretted when the company is sold and a low base cost for capital gains tax is a consequence of the agreed inheritance tax value. In larger cases, though, the valuer may have to make a more in-depth examination in almost the same way as if advising a real investor, including some degree of due diligence.

On any valuation exercise, and particularly when looking at the value of a company as a whole, it is always useful to ask the main shareholders and directors what they consider to be the value. They often have an idea as to what they would accept. Clearly, this is not the open market price as such but it may give a useful figure for comparison. Indeed, posing the question may reveal offers for the company at or about the valuation date. If a valuer's figure and the offer made by the party are a long way apart, the valuer should at least try to work out why his figure is different.

In a commercial valuation, recognition has to be taken in many instances of the principle that a company's shares are to be valued on the basis of it being a quasi partnership, a principle that was established 83 years ago in *Re Yenidje Tobacco Co Ltd* [1916–17] All ER 1050 **case 10** and applied 55 years later by the House of Lords to a minority shareholding in *Ebrahimi v Westbourne Galleries Ltd* [1972] 2 All ER 492 **case 31**. The principle of the quasi partnership has only a very limited place in a fiscal valuation. In the author's view, the fact that the company is a quasi partnership may raise the price a hypothetical purchaser would offer, if he could reasonably be expected to be able to sell the shares on to one of the other 'partners'. What is not acceptable, in the author's view, is the argument that the hypothetical purchaser be treated as if he were, himself, to obtain the rights of a quasi partner. (See further *Strahan v Wilcock* [2006] All ER (D) 106 **case 49**.)

The approach to be taken on a commercial valuation is considered further in Chapter 12.

1.2 The legal background

A company operates under the provisions of company law. A share in a company is a creation of that law. Some points of UK company law that are relevant in share valuation include:

(a) It is critical to read the articles of association of the company whose shares are to be valued to determine the rights of each class of shares. The definition of 'ordinary shares' and 'preference shares' varies from one company to another. It is the rights specified in the company's articles of association that determine the rights that are the subject of the valuation. In some companies, different voting rights are conferred on the different classes of share for different purposes. In *Bushell v Faith* [1970] AC 1099 the weighting of votes varied according to the nature of the motion; certain shareholders had enhanced voting power on appointing directors.

(b) The impact of a shareholders' agreement on the valuation of shares is an interesting area of debate. It is clear that any restrictions contained in the articles are to be taken into account in the sense that the purchaser will in turn be subject to those restrictions. The rights a shareholder has by virtue of the terms of a shareholders' agreement are enforceable against the other individuals who are shareholders; they are not rights in the company. In *Re The Isle of Thanet Electricity Supply Co Ltd* [1950] 1 Ch 161 **case 23**, shareholders unsuccessfully argued that they had rights in a winding-up in addition to rights specified in the articles. The law seems to be clear in that a shareholders' agreement cannot override the articles, from the point of view of the company at least, but personal obligations are imposed on the parties to that agreement. This is the broad effect of the House of Lords decision in *Russell v Northern Bank Development Corporation Limited* [1992] 3 All ER 161. Ordinarily, the purchaser would not be bound by such an agreement but it may be a requirement that on his sale of shares, the purchaser enters into a deed of adherence or its equivalent, so as to be bound by that agreement. Indeed, this could even work to his advantage. This does not make the hypothetical purchaser a party to a shareholders' agreement, but the fact that all the other shareholders are subject to it may have a significant effect on the ability of the hypothetical purchaser to sell his holding. In an extreme case, if the shareholders' agreement states that shareholders will always pay par for shares transferred, it may be very difficult to find an unconnected potential purchaser who would pay more than par, irrespective of the earnings of the company. The author has experience of a shareholders' agreement requiring transfers at par of shares in a farmers' co-operative which had a very large number of shareholders. In the author's view, the effect of the shareholders' agreement was that the only correct valuation of the shares was at par.

(c) Even in the case of a 75 per cent holding, with the ability to alter the articles of association, the controlling shareholder must act bona fide in the interests of the company and not purely to his own advantage. Thus, it cannot be argued that a value of a minority holding, for example, is minimal simply because the controlling shareholder could ride roughshod over his interests, although in practice the amount at stake might not be worth the risk of expensive legal action.

(d) There may be particular legislation that applies to the industry in which the company operates. For example, there may be regulatory requirements in force, which may have a bearing on profitability.

(e) Similarly, there may be legislation introduced or proposed that will affect business in general. For example, regulations come into effect during the next 12 months which will prohibit the use of lead in electronic visual displays. This may make existing designs obsolete, or increase the cost of production by requiring other materials. New safety procedures may be on the cards, which could affect the particular product a company sells.

(f) The economy of other parts of the world could have an effect on a company, particularly if it exports to or imports from regions that are experiencing substantial economic growth. This can work both ways. An increase in economic activity may give higher wages and, hence, higher costs for products produced in that country. However, an increase in wages may increase the market of those able to buy the company's products.

(g) In some industries, there is often a rule of thumb valuation which is not based on profitability. For example, in the funeral business a major factor is the number of funerals, especially in the context of a trade purchase. In other industries the formula is sometimes a multiple of turnover, such as commission. Such multiples are probably more appropriate to smaller businesses being acquired by larger ones, where the latter is interested in buying gross business and can make overhead savings. It is clear that HMRC Share Valuation have full information of the trades where such multiples might apply so this is something that the valuer must bear in mind. In practice, his client should be aware of any trade practice even if the valuer has no knowledge of this.

There are clearly many other areas of law and business generally, which the valuer may have to take into account. In practice, the practitioner cannot have all the relevant skills to make a valuation. In a real purchase situation, where the amounts are sufficiently large, the purchaser would have access to various advisers, especially in more esoteric areas. Any practitioner must consider carefully whether he has access to the relevant knowledge of the industry to undertake any fiscal valuation. The valuer must have, at least, a broad awareness of the factors that could affect a company's fortunes, often gained by simply asking the right questions. The valuer should go through a similar exercise to that undertaken for a due diligence report. In this, he is likely at least to raise the pertinent points even if he cannot answer them himself.

1.3 The industry and the economy

No company operates in isolation. The state of the economy of the country in which it operates will have a direct bearing on the projections of a company's performance. The industry in which the company has its trade has, if anything, an even more immediate impact. For a property investment company, one needs to consider interest rates in the economy and, perhaps, the particular industry in which its tenants operate. An investment company will look directly at the national and international economy and the industries in which it has invested.

The way in which a consideration of the national economy and the state of the particular industry is brought into a share valuation is well illustrated in *Caton's*

Administrators v Couch [1995] STC (SCD) 34 **case 38**. In this Special
Commissioners' decision, the company's trade and its standing in the industry
is outlined (at 39(e)–(j)). The reaction to the company position is the basis on
which trading results are considered (at 30(j)).

Another example of a valuation being related to the fortunes of the industry
in which it operates is given in the Special Commissioners' elegant description
of the state of the sherry trade and the position of Gonzalez Byass in that trade
in *Hawkings-Byass v Sassen* [1996] STC (SCD) 319 **case 40**. In considering the
values to be placed on shareholdings in Gonzalez Byass Ltd, the Special
Commissioners said:

> 'There had been a gentle decline partly owing to a change in United
> Kingdom taxation in about 1984 which made sherry more expensive.
> (Geoffrey attributed the decline to changing habits in the United Kingdom,
> people eating lighter food and drinking less heavy wine.) Sales had peaked
> in 1979 but this was an artificial peak created by certain houses in Spain
> which exported a large amount of sherry of no great quality to qualify for
> a tax rebate. (Geoffrey gave evidence to the same effect). He did not think
> that the industry in Spain was, as was stated by Mr Baker in his report "in
> the doldrums" in March 1982. Gonzalez Byass certainly was not. It was in a
> very strong position; it was at its height in 1982 (an opinion held also by
> Nicholas and by Geoffrey who distinguished between increasing branded
> sales and bulk unbranded sherry which was in the doldrums). There was
> overproduction in 1980 following the planting up of new vineyards in the
> 1970s. But, as Mr Hines put it, Gonzalez Byass did not subscribe to the South
> Sea Bubble; it had not overplanted. It was well run and financially sound;
> it was not overextended like Domecq which was ripe for a bid (from a
> reputable suitor) (see the *Financial Times* 27 March 1982).'
>
> ([1996] STC (SCD) 319 at 327b **case 40 para 4**)

1.4 The rights of a shareholder

In *Short v Treasury Commrs* [1948] 1 KB 116, CA, Evershed LJ said:

> 'Shareholders are not, in the eyes of the law, part owners of the undertaking.
> The undertaking is something different from the totality of the
> shareholdings.'
>
> (at 122)

A share can usefully be regarded as a bundle of rights in relation to a company.
The specification of the rights is given in the articles. It is frequently the case
that shareholders in a company have entered into an agreement amongst
themselves which may, for example, provide an agreement to limit dividends,
or to offer shares for sale to other shareholders first or to act in concert. All

these rights may be enforceable against the other individuals who are shareholders by proceedings in the courts. However, they are not rights in the company unless they have as their origin the articles of association of the company. (See section **1.2(b)** above.)

A most important difference between a fiscal valuation and many commercial valuations is that in the former it is prices that would be offered by a hypothetical purchaser that are considered. As the purchaser is hypothetical, nothing can be said about the rights that the purchasers would acquire by looking at an agreement between individuals who have chosen to sign a shareholders' agreement. A hypothetical purchaser will take the shares subject to the articles and not subject to anything else.

It is the rights in the articles that form the basis of the valuation. The rights attaching to a share can be put into three categories:

● the right to vote;
● the right to income; and
● rights in a winding-up.

These translate into the exercise of valuing a shareholding as:

(a) *the extent to which ownership of the shareholding can determine the actions of the company.* The larger the percentage of the total votes available that attaches to the shareholding the greater the intrinsic value of that shareholding. However, the increase in value is not even; instead it is a series of steps that reflect the rights given to a shareholder in the Companies Acts. These can be summarised as:

100% shareholding	Action can be taken without reference to any other shareholder.
90% shareholding	Companies Act 1985, ss 428 and 429 give a procedure whereby the 90% shareholder can require the minority shareholders to sell to him their holdings.
75% shareholding	The shareholder can pass a special resolution to put the company into liquidation or sell the business as a going concern.
50% plus shareholding	The shareholder appoints the directors and, hence, can take over day-to-day control of the company.
50% shareholding	If the shareholder has exactly 50% of the votes, he does not have control but, nevertheless, stops control by any other shareholder.
25% plus shareholding	The shareholder can block a special resolution for the liquidation or sale of the business as a going concern.

| 10% plus shareholding | The shareholder is vulnerable to actions taken by other shareholders acting in concert. |
| 10% minus shareholding | The holding can be subject to compulsory acquisition. |

(b) *the right to income.* There are two types of income to be considered. The right of the shareholder, per se, is to receive the same dividend per share as all other shareholders of the same class. The right to declare a dividend rests with the directors, not the shareholders. Directors can, moreover, declare an interim dividend without reference to the shareholders. For a final dividend, the power of the shareholders is negative not positive in that the shareholders in general meeting can vote against a dividend but cannot increase the dividend above the figure proposed by the directors. The commercial reality of dividends in an unquoted company is, thus, a direct consequence of the size of the shareholding held. If more than 50 per cent of the voting shares are held, the shareholder has the power to appoint directors who will declare dividends in accordance with the shareholder's wishes, subject only to the requirement that dividends must be financed out of realised profits. It follows that the past history of dividends paid by a company is, in the author's view, irrelevant when valuing a majority shareholding. The purchaser of the shareholding controls the board of directors; he can choose to increase dividends in the future, decrease them or simply fail to declare a dividend.

The other aspect of income is the income of the company; that is, the profits generated by the company's activities. Even if profits are not distributed as dividends which are received in the short term, they benefit the shareholder in the long term. Undistributed profits can finance the company's continuing activities, or reduce bank borrowings or provide funds for an investment that, itself, produces further profits. The profits generated by a company are, thus, in every case, a material consideration in estimating the value of a shareholding. It will often be the case that the company's profitability is the single most important determinate of share price.

There is a temptation to treat a share valuation as an arithmetical exercise, whereby simple arithmetic applied to profits of preceding years is taken to specify the value of shares today. This temptation must be resisted. In principle, the share valuation exercise is an attempt to estimate the sum that an investor would pay for a shareholding. An investor is interested in the future, not the past. The view may be formed that the only guide available to the future is the past. However, in principle, earnings in the past have either been distributed as dividend or have been converted to assets of the company. What the investor is paying for is earnings in the future.

(c) *winding-up.* The importance of assets in estimating the value of a particular shareholding varies widely. It is, however, a bold valuer that will claim that assets (or the lack of assets) have no relevance to the valuation he is undertaking. A shareholding brings with it an entitlement to receive a distribution in a winding-up. The extent of that entitlement varies widely, both as a consequence of the variety of provisions in the company articles and as a consequence of the financial position of the particular company.

An asset valuation is, in one respect, a consideration of the funds that would be distributed by virtue of the particular shareholding to be valued. This can be viewed in its pure form as the break up value or in a modified form as the value of the company's assets that are currently in use in the business. Occasionally, it is necessary to look at the break up value. If so, allowance needs to be taken, as appropriate, for costs such as redundancy payments that are incurred on a liquidation or disposal of a particular trade. More frequently, the asset value that is considered is the nature of asset backing supporting the price that is suggested as appropriate for the shareholding in the light of the profitability of the company.

For an investment company (including a property investment company) the assets available in a winding-up may have a greater effect on the share valuation than the earnings of the company as, typically, in such a company the costs of a winding-up are relatively low.

2 The meaning of market value

2.1 Statutory provision

For capital gains tax TCGA 1992, s 272(1) states:

> 'In this act market value in relation to any assets means the price at which those assets might reasonably be expected to fetch on a sale in the open market.'

The section continues by providing that no reduction shall be made in the market value by virtue of the fact that the market is changed by the deemed sale.

For inheritance tax the basic rule for valuation is given in IHTA 1984, s 160 which states:

> '... the value at any time of any property shall for the purposes of this Act be the price which the property might reasonably be expected to fetch if sold in the open market at that time; but that price shall not be assumed to be reduced on the ground that the whole property is to be placed on the market at one and the same time.'

2.2 Date of valuation

Inheritance tax statute specifies that all assets in an estate are to be valued at the time of death. In the statutory provisions for capital gains tax, the time at which the valuation is to apply is implicit rather than explicit. By referring to the valuation on disposal being that which the shares might 'be expected to fetch on a sale in the open market', it is clear that the valuation must be at the exact time of the disposal; there is no scope for any argument that the time was not appropriate for making a sale. Whereas in the real world, a vendor will ask for offers for his shareholding and be prepared to wait until he receives an acceptable offer, the statutory fiction is that the sale is made at the specified date.

In *Duke of Buccleuch v IRC* Lord Reid said:

> 'But here what must be envisaged is sale in the open market on a particular day. So there is no room for supposing that the owner would do as many prudent owners do – withdraw the property if he does not get a sufficient offer and wait until a time when he can get a better offer. The commissioners

must estimate what the property would probably have fetched on that particular day if it had then been exposed for sale, no doubt after such advance publicity as would have been reasonable.'

(1 AC 506, HL at 525 **case 28 para 8**)

The statutory fiction is that a sale is always possible. This is demonstrated most dramatically in *Re Aschrott* [1927] 1 Ch 313 **case 13**. That case concerns estate duty payable on the estate of a German subject who died on 5 May 1915, in Berlin, leaving shares in English, South African and American companies, the share certificates being physically located in London at the time of his death. At the start of the First World War, Parliament had passed the Trading with the Enemy Amendment Act 1914 which made it illegal for an enemy alien to sell shares during the course of the war. The High Court held that this in no way inhibited the operation of the statutory fiction that a sale was postulated as taking place.

The valuation is a reflection of the return an investor expects to make in the future. However, the facts on which the investor estimates his future return are limited to those facts which are known on the valuation date. The valuation is undertaken without reference to events after that date. However, the purchaser is deemed to have all information available to him that would reasonably be expected to be ascertained by an investor. Thus, in *Marks v Sherred* [2004] STC (SCD) 362 **case 46** the argument that the results of the accounting period ended 31 March 1982 (the valuation date) would not be known on that date as the accounts would not then have been drawn up was rejected. Colin Bishopp, Special Commissioner said:

'Mr Ruse's point, with which I entirely agree, was that the actual figures for 1982 were the best available guide to what the hypothetical purchaser, making proper enquiries, would have been able to discover from the available information. I accept the validity of the argument advanced by Michael Gibbon, counsel for the respondent, that Miss Mullen's approach of largely ignoring what actually happened during the course of the year to 31 March 1982 cannot be right.'

([2004] STC (SCD) 362 at 368h/j **case 46 para 23**)

Moreover, the rule that events after the valuation date are to be ignored does not exclude taking account of the opinion held by prospective purchasers on the date of valuation as to likely future occurrences.

More often than not, the valuation date is during the course of an accounting period that has not been completed. This situation was addressed by Mr Justice Danckwerts in *Re Holt* who said:

'When the deceased died on 11 March 1948, the accounts for his last year were not finally completed, but it is fair to assume that information as to the approximate results of the year's trading would have been ascertained by a prospective purchaser.'

((1953) 32 ATC 402 at 404 **case 25 para 10**)

A similar approach was taken by Lord Fleming in *Salvesen's Trustees v IRC*, who said :

> 'I quite recognise that the problem I have to deal with must be solved in the light of the information available at or about the time of the testator's death, but I think that, however, does not debar me completely from making any reference to the balance sheet at 31 July 1927, which includes a period of nearly three months prior to the testator's death.'
>
> ((1930) 9 ATC 43 at 51 **case 15 para 7**)

In *IRC v Marr's Trustees*, Lord Johnston rejected an application by the Revenue to have a farm valuation revised to reflect the actual sums raised at cattle sales subsequent to the valuation date. The sales having raised nearly twice the sum recognised in the valuations:

> 'I should have no hesitation in saying that the herd must be valued at the date of the death, though it might have been imprudent to bring it to the hammer till three or four months later, and that the Commissioners of Inland Revenue were not entitled to have a valuation as in October, when the best market may be anticipated, or a valuation based on the result of actual sale at that period.'
>
> ((1906) 44 SLR 647 at 648 **case 7 para 11**)

2.3 A hypothetical sale

Lord Ashbourne described the approach he was required to take to the valuation of unquoted shares in these terms:

> 'How can such shares in such a Company with such articles have their value estimated at the price which, in the opinion of the Commissioners, such property would fetch if sold in the open market? An actual sale in open market is out of the question. A feat of imagination has to be performed. Two suggestions have been put forward in argument. The Attorney-General says that the Commissioners should assume an unfettered sale in the open market to the highest bidder, who would be free from the clogs on alienation contained in the articles. The defendants, on the other hand, contend that the Finance Act is satisfied by taking the par or "fair value" of £100 per share as the capital value which the Commissioners should estimate as the price which the shares would fetch if sold in the open market. Each side rushes into an indefensible extreme. The argument of the Attorney-General, which seeks to brush aside the articles and to vest in the executors a property which Henry Jameson never possessed, would ascribe to the Finance Act the power of making a new subject-matter. The argument of the defendants clings desperately to the articles, and gives really no adequate significance to the words of the Act requiring the Commissioners to estimate the price

which the shares would fetch in the open market. The solution lies between the two. The Attorney-General must give more weight to the articles, and the defendants to the statute. It requires no tremendous imagination to conceive what a purchaser would give in the open market for Henry Jameson's shares as Henry Jameson himself held them at his death – for the right to stand in his shoes.'

(*Attorney-General v Jameson* [1905] 2 IR 218 at 227 **case 6 para 21**)

The process was put into often quoted, and colourful, language by Danckwerts J:

'The result is that I must enter into a dim world peopled by the indeterminate spirits of fictitious or unborn sales. It is necessary to assume the prophetic vision of a prospective purchaser at the moment of the death of the deceased, and firmly to reject the wisdom which might be provided by the knowledge of subsequent events.'

(*Re Holt* (1953) 32 ATC 402 at 403 **case 25 para 5**)

A modern description of the way in which this hypothetical transfer takes place is:

'Once it is established that the method of valuation is on the basis of a sale in the open market what is contemplated is a notional sale between a notional vendor and a notional purchaser: one does not postulate a particular vendor or a particular purchaser. One cannot assume that the hypothetical vendor of a minority holding of shares in a company would only sell his holding in conjunction with the other holders so that its value should be assessed on the basis of a sale of all the shares. However, it was ... counsel's ... main submission that the 49 shares should not be valued on the basis of a sale of such a holding in the open market but rather that they should be valued on the basis of what could be realised for them by means of a share exchange scheme, whereby the whole of the share capital of Potterhanworth might have been exchanged for shares in turn converted into cash. For reasons already given, I reject that submission.'

(Balcombe J in *Battle v IRC* ([1980] STC 86 at 91 **case 32 paras 12–13**)

The thought process of our hypothetical purchaser was explained by Lord Fleming as:

'It is to be presumed that the hypothetical purchaser having obtained all the relevant information would consider in the first place the risks which are involved in carrying on the business, and would fix the return which he considered he ought to receive on the purchase price at a rate per cent. The only other factor which he would then require to determine would be the annual profits which he would derive from the carrying on of the business. The determination of these two factors would enable him to fix the capital value of the business. A seller looking at the matter from the opposite point of view would deal with it on similar lines.'

(*Findlay's Trustees v IRC* (1938) 22 ATC 437 at 440 **case 18 para 5**)

In another case, Lord Fleming explored further the approach taken by a hypothetical purchaser:

> 'Apart from any conclusion which an intending investor might draw from the break-up of the undertaking, he would, I feel sure, especially when he was informed that it was intended to continue the company's trading operations, examine the most recent balance sheet carefully with a view to obtaining some indication of the value of the concern as a going undertaking. A person who was being invited to acquire a third of the shares of a private company which imposed stringent conditions on the right of transfer would certainly wish to ascertain the value at which the assets had been entered in the last balance sheet. As a prudent person he would, of course, keep in view that he was purchasing the shares in October 1926 and that the balance sheet shows the affairs of the company as at July 1926 and he would make inquiry as to the alterations in its financial position which had taken place between these two dates. But he would first examine the balance sheet and I think that he would be very favourably impressed by the fact that the assets showed a surplus of upwards of £900,000 over its capital.'
> (*Salvesen's Trustees v IRC* (1930) 9 ATC 43 at 50 **case 15 para 7**)

In this hypothetical sale, the vendor is deemed to have acted in a way which one would expect of a real owner preparing for a real sale of unquoted shares. That is, whatever steps that would normally be taken by a vendor are deemed to have taken place. Thus, in *Duke of Buccleuch v IRC* [1967] 1 AC 506, HL **case 28**, value was determined on the assumption that the land owned by the Duke of Devonshire at his death, which extended to some 186 square miles, would have been advertised in appropriate sized lots and all the preparation that normally occurs before a substantial auction would have been dealt with.

2.4 On the open market

The concept of 'the open market' that is specified in the statutory provision was described by Swinfen Eady LJ as:

> 'A value, ascertained by reference to the amount obtainable in an open market, shows an intention to include every possible purchaser. The market is to be the open market, as distinguished from an offer to a limited class only, such as the members of the family. The market is not necessarily an auction sale. The section means such amount as the land might be expected to realise if offered under conditions enabling every person desirous of purchasing to come in and make an offer, and if proper steps were taken to advertise the property and let all likely purchasers know that the land is in the market for sale. It scarcely needed evidence to inform us – it is common knowledge – that when the fact becomes known that one probable buyer desires to obtain any property, that raises the general price or value

of the thing in the market. Not only is the probable buyer a competitor in the market, but other persons, such as property brokers, compete in the market for what they know another person wants, with a view to a resale to him at an enhanced price, so as to realise a profit. A vendor desiring to realise any land would ordinarily give full publicity to all facts within his knowledge likely to enhance the price. The local conditions and requirements, the advantages of the situation of the property for any particular purpose, and the names of the persons who are probably buyers, would ordinarily be matters of local knowledge to the property brokers and agents and speculators.'

   (*IRC v Clay, IRC v Buchanan* [1914] 3 KB 466 at 475 **case 8 para 13**)

Thus, 'the open market' for unquoted shares includes all manner of people. It is a matter of fact in any particular case as to who may be in that market. It will often be the case that members of the family, some of whom may already have shares, are included in the market, as well as strangers and outside investors. An important bidder in such an open market will be the individual unconnected with the company who considers that if he acquires a block of shares he could later sell them to another shareholder, to whom the particular shareholding may have a special value. It follows that, as a preliminary in considering the market value of unquoted shares, it is always necessary to ascertain who owns the other shareholdings in the company. The value of a 2 per cent holding is likely to be very much higher if there are only two other shareholders, each of whom owns 49 per cent than if there is a single shareholder owning the remaining 98 per cent of the issued share capital.

2.5 Restrictions on transfer

TCGA 1992, s 272(1) gives the basic valuation principle as:

   'in this act "the market value" in relation to any assets means the price which those assets might reasonably be expected to fetch on a sale in the open market.'

In *Attorney-General v Jameson* [1904] 2 IR 644 and [1905] 2 IR 218 **case 6** the equivalent statutory provision (for estate duty) was FA 1894, s 7(5) which states:

   'the "principal value of any property shall be the price which, in the opinion of the Commissioners, such property would fetch if sold in the open market at any time of the death of the deceased".'

In this case, in the hearing before the Court of Appeal the personal representative claimed that shares had no value (or negligible value) because the articles of the company gave the right to the directors to refuse to register a transfer of shares and such a refusal would have been given to a request to register a shareholder who was not a member of the family (see [1905] 2 IR 218 at 227 **case 6 para 21**).

Palles CB ruled that the statutory provision requires a value to be placed on the shares on the assumption that the shares were placed on the open market and the purchaser would be registered as a member of the company:

> 'for the purpose of ascertaining the value, the question is not whether it is capable of being sold in the open market. If the Articles of Association are valid, these shares are not saleable in the open market; but under sub-sect 5 we are bound to assume that they are capable of being so sold, because the valuation is to be based, not upon an actual, but upon a supposed sale, and that supposed sale is one in the open market. The question is, assuming that they were capable of being sold in the open market, what would they fetch on such sale? And upon this supposition, which is the supposition the state directs us to make, we must exclude the consideration of such provisions in the Articles of Association as would prevent a purchaser at the sale from becoming a member of the company, registered as such in respect of the shares purchased by him at such supposed sale. If we do not, we do not give effect to the assumption the statute coerces us to make.'
>
> ([1904] 2 IR 218 at 276 **case 6 para 61**)

This decision was discussed at length by the House of Lords in *IRC v Crossman* (1936) 15 ATC 94 **case 17**. In that case, it was held that the statutory hypothesis of a hypothetical sale required a sale to be fully effected, including the purchaser being placed on the register of members, but the rights attaching to the shares were not changed. Hence, where shares have a pre-emption right or restriction on transfer, the hypothetical purchaser takes those shares subject to those restrictions. It must follow that the price the hypothetical purchaser is prepared to pay is likely to be reduced by his inability (or reduced ability) to, in turn, make a sale of the shares he has acquired.

In *Re Lynall deceased* confirming the majority decision in *IRC v Crossman*, Viscount Dilhorne said:

> 'In my view the decision in that case was right. Parliament has enacted that the price the shares would fetch if sold in the open market has to be assessed. There could be no sale on the open market on 21 May 1962 unless the directors agreed to the registration of the transfer of the shares and Mr Lynall refused to purchase the shares at £1 a share. Therefore, for the price the shares would fetch if sold in the open market to be assessed, it must be assumed that the directors had so agreed and Mr Lynall had refused to buy. As Mr Harman said in the course of his argument for the Crown, if property is only saleable in the open market in certain circumstances, then when the Act requires the property to be valued at the price which it would fetch if sold in the open market, one must proceed on the basis that those circumstances exist. This does not mean that the shares change their

character. The shares bought by the hypothetical purchaser will be subject
to the restrictions imposed by article 8.'

((1971) 47 TC 375 at 412 **case 29 para 95**)

2.6 What information?

In *Re Lynall deceased* (1971) 47 TC 375 **case 29** the court considered in some
detail the evidence given as to what information was actually available to a
purchaser at the valuation date. Following that case, in Finance Act 1973, s 51,
Parliament put a deeming provision into statute by inserting identical
provisions into a statutory code for valuation for capital gains tax and for
inheritance tax, TCGA 1992, s 273(3) and IHTA 1984, s 168(1). Both Acts state:

> '… it shall be assumed that, in the open market which is postulated for the
> purposes of that determination, there is available to any prospective
> purchaser of the asset in question all the information which a prudent
> prospective purchaser of the asset might reasonably require if he were
> proposing to purchase it from a willing vendor by private treaty and at arm's
> length.'

It is important to note that statute does not specify that all information is
available to the hypothetical purchaser. In *Percival v Wright* [1902] 2 Ch 421 the
court considered the situation where, at the valuation date, the directors of the
company were in the course of negotiating a sale of the undertaking at a price
considerably higher than that which would be regarded as the market price if
there was no knowledge of these negotiations. The court rejected the
suggestion that a director has a fiduciary duty to shareholders to disclose
information that is directly relevant to the value of shares. This was information
that was not actually available to shareholders and, moreover, would not be
made available to a prospective purchaser of shares in the company. Hence,
this information is to be ignored in undertaking a valuation.

An interesting analysis of the effects of the statutory information provision
when determining value for capital gains tax purposes of a minority
shareholding was undertaken by Dr AN Brice sitting as a Special Commissioner
in *Caton's Administrators v Couch* [1995] STC (SCD) 34 **case 38 paras 70–74**. The
Special Commissioner noted there was no legal obligation on the directors to
disclose unpublished confidential information and that some of this
information might prejudice the interests of the company. However, in the
Commissioner's judgement, she accepted the evidence of one of the expert
witnesses that, where the outlay on purchasing the shares was substantial, then,
irrespective of the small percentage holding that is being acquired, the
purchaser would always enquire about approaches for sale because restrictions
on transfer would lock him into his investment and he would only have an exit
if the company were sold. Further, such a purchaser would have made enquiries

about up-to-date management accounts and budget forecasts and such information would have been supplied to such a purchaser (at 50f and 51c).

In *Caton's Administrators v Couch* [1995] STC (SCD) 34 **case 38**, the evidence of the expert witness was accepted that the information would have been made available to the prospective purchaser investing a large sum.

A difficult situation arises where a purchaser of the shareholding to be valued would require certain information but it is accepted that this information would be withheld by directors as its release on that particular date would damage the interests of the company. Such a case has not been considered by the courts and the judicial approach must be a matter of conjecture. In the author's view, the true interpretation of the statutory requirement in FA 1973, s 51 is that one must consider the information that would, in fact, be provided to an actual purchaser of that number of shares on that particular date. If, as a matter of fact, the release of certain information was so prejudicial to the interests of the company that no reasonable board of directors would release such information, it is suggested that the correct valuation approach is to assume that information is not available.

2.7 Hypothetical costs of a hypothetical sale

In an actual sale of unquoted shares, the vendor may expect to pay substantial fees to his professional advisers and, perhaps, suffer other expenses of selling. In ascertaining the market value of shares at the valuation date, a hypothetical sale is envisaged and there is no scope for reducing the value by costs that would arise if the shares were sold in the real world. Statute specifies that the value is the price which the shares 'might reasonably be expected to fetch' (TCGA 1992, s 272(1)) not the price which the vendor would have received.

In *Duke of Buccleuch v IRC* Lord Guest commented:

'The words "price the property would fetch" in section 7(5) mean that it is not the price which the vendor would have received but what the purchaser would have paid to be put into the shoes of the deceased.'

([1967] 1 AC 506, HL at 541 **case 28 para 56**)

2.8 An arithmetic exercise or an exercise in judgement?

In the Privy Council case of *Attorney-General of Ceylon v Mackie* Lord Reid said:

'Where the past history of a business shows consistent results or a steady trend and where there has been no disruption of general business conditions it may well be possible to reach a fair valuation by a theoretical calculation. But in this case neither condition was satisfied. The profits and losses of the company had fluctuated so violently in the past that, as the second witness for the appellant admitted, it is impossible to choose any five consecutive years in the company's history the result of which would be reflected in the next year's profits. It is, therefore, in their Lordships' judgement, not possible in this case to derive by an arithmetical calculation from past results anything which could properly have been regarded in 1940 as an average maintainable profit, and in addition there were extremely uncertain conditions in 1940. The appellant's witnesses made no allowance for these facts, and were not able to give informed evidence on the question whether a purchaser could have been found in 1940 willing to lay out the large sum required.'

([1952] 2 All ER 775 at 779 **case 24 para 7**)

Share valuation is sometimes dubbed as 'an art not a science'. Although this is a well-known aphorism, it may be that it does not add very much to the understanding of what is required and could be regarded as misleading. What is clear is that there is no arithmetic that leads directly to a value: judgement is always required. However, share valuation can be seen to be a science in the same way that economics is a science. It is not a natural science but does lend itself to a scientific approach, as economics does. A share valuation can only be discerned by a logical process, tested empirically against the surrounding business world. It also no doubt succumbs to human behaviour and in particular the hopes and fears of individuals or, rather, their degree of optimism or pessimism at a given time. There is usually a wide range of valuations suggested by experts, each of which has been determined by largely objective criteria. The ultimate resolution of the value, such as by a court or the commissioners, becomes, perhaps, one of impression, guided by the expert valuations and ultimately subject to the challenge of common sense. In *Re Holt*, Danckwerts J said:

'In my task I have had the assistance of a number of experts on each side, who differ in their opinions in the manner in which experts normally do, and the frankest of them admitted that certain of his calculations were simply guesswork. It seems to me that their opinions are indeed properly described as guesswork, though of course it is intelligent guesswork ... Their methods of calculation appear to me to be inevitably uncertain and controversial ...

Having carefully considered the evidence ... and making the most intelligent guess that I can, I have come to the conclusion that these shares of John Holt & Co (Liverpool) Ltd, if sold on the hypothetical open market which the authorities and the section in the Act require me to assume, would fetch a price of 19s a share.'

((1953) 32 ATC 402 at 403 and 410 **case 25 paras 6 and 36**)

2.9 Value of quoted securities

2.9.1 Capital gains tax

TCGA 1992, s 272(3) provides, in the absence of special circumstances, that the value to be taken for quoted shares and securities is taken from the Stock Exchange Official List. There are two alternative methods of calculation using the prices quoted in the list. The first method is to take the range of prices shown in the list, which is the buying and selling prices at 3.30pm on the day. The price taken for the market value is then one quarter up from the lower of these two prices. The second method is to look at the highest and lowest prices of 'marked bargains' executed on the day and to take the value half way between the two prices. 'Marked bargains' are less frequently found than formerly and it is often the case that only the first method of valuation is possible. Where, however, both methods are possible, the value taken as the market value is the lower of the two different prices calculated by following the two different methods.

Where there is a more active market for the particular shares at another stock exchange, the value used is that which applies in the more active market. Where valuation is required for a non-business day, the value is taken from the daily official list for the business day immediately preceding the date of valuation and for the business day immediately following that date; the lower of these two values is then used (TCGA 1992, s 272(4)).

Where the value is on a date prior to 13 December 1979, and there was a restriction imposed under Exchange Control Act 1947, an adjustment is made so that the value taken is that which would have actually been received (on a sale) or paid (on a purchase) (TCGA 1992, Sch 11, para 7(5A)).

TCGA 1992, s 272(3) contains the interesting proviso that the price on the Stock Exchange Daily Official List shall be taken 'where in consequence of special circumstances prices quoted in that List are by themselves not a proper measure of market value'. In *Hinchcliffe v Crabtree* (1971) 47 TC 419 **case 30**, the House of Lords rejected the argument that a takeover bid that was not known to the market on that date was a 'special circumstance' that should lead to another price being substituted for the price on the London Stock Market.

2.9.2 Inheritance tax

Unlike capital gains tax, there are no statutory provisions specifying the way in which the price of a quoted security is to be ascertained. However, in practice, the rules specified for capital gains tax are applied.

Following the opening of the Unlisted Securities Market on 10 November 1980, the Revenue issued a Statement of Practice (SP 18/80) in which it is stated that the Revenue consider that shares on the USM are not 'listed' within the meaning of the Taxes Acts, but are treated as being 'dealt in (regularly or from time to time) on a recognised stock exchange'. Revenue practice is to take the details of bargains done on the USM as initial evidence of the value of the shares. However, HMRC Share Valuation is instructed to consider whether a value offered on the basis of those bargains can be accepted as an adequate reflection of the open market value. It would appear that the same approach is taken by the Revenue in respect to prices on the Alternative Investment Market (AIM) which opened on 19 June 1995. In the author's experience, HMRC Share Valuation treat prices on the Nouveau Marché in Paris in the same way as on the London AIM.

3 Valuation for capital gains tax

In this section the occasions for market value to be determined are identified and discussed. The valuation rule given in statute is then discussed as illuminated by decided cases.

The provisions relating to capital gains tax are taken first, as numerically the largest number of valuations is undertaken for the purpose of capital gains tax. Matters that are common to all taxes are, thus, considered in the capital gains tax section.

3.1 When market value is required

Market value is required for use in a capital gains tax computation on the following occasions:

- unquoted shares held at 31 March 1992 (TCGA 1992, s 35(2));
- unquoted shares held at 6 April 1965 where election has been made for time apportionment not to apply (TCGA 1992, Sch 2, para 17(2));
- disposals of unquoted shares between connected persons (TCGA 1992, s 18(2));
- gifts or other disposals of unquoted shares at under value (TCGA 1992, s 17(1)(a));
- a disposal for a consideration that cannot be valued (TCGA 1992, s 17(1)(b));
- other transfers of unquoted shares that are made otherwise than by way of a bargain at arm's length (TCGA 1992, s 17);
- transfer of unquoted shares at death (TCGA 1992, s 62);
- unquoted shares held in an interest in possession settlement on the occasion of the death of the life tenant (TCGA 1992, s 72);
- beneficiary of a settlement becoming absolutely entitled to unquoted shares (TCGA 1992, s 71);
- part disposals (TCGA 1992, s 42); or
- shares given as Sch E emoluments (TCGA 1992, s 17(1)(b)).

In addition, various occasions of charge require a determination of value that passes, which may be measured by a change in the value of unquoted shares. This is found, for example, in the value-shifting provisions of TCGA 1992, s 29, the effect of which is to deem a disposal for capital gains tax purposes where a person controlling a company exercises control so that value passes out of shares in the company that he owns, or which are owned by a connected person.

There is, perhaps, a temptation to assume too rapidly that a transaction takes place 'otherwise than by way of a bargain at arm's length'. In *Bullivant Holdings Ltd v IRC* [1998] STC 905, two shareholders received £12,500 each for a 25 per cent holding of HBH Publishing Ltd ords. It was agreed that the value of a 50 per cent holding in that company was £350,000. The court upheld the finding of fact by the Special Commissioner that the two shareholders were content to sell their shares in this company for a very low price because they wanted the £500,000 which had been offered for their shares in another company, Bullivant Holdings Ltd, and saw no way of getting a better price for the shares in question. Hence, it was held, the transaction was by way of a bargain at arm's length and, thus, the market value of the shares could not be substituted for the consideration actually paid.

Where the Revenue seek to substitute market value for consideration paid, the onus of proof is on the Revenue to show that there was an element of bounty (*Re Thornley* (1928) 7 ATC 178), unless statute directs market value (notably, when the transfer is between connected persons).

3.2 Self-assessment and share valuation

For an individual, there is a requirement imposed on the taxpayer to compute the capital gain arising on any disposal (TMA 1970, s 8(1) and (1AA)). It follows that where statute requires market value to be used in a computation, the onus is on the taxpayer to determine that market value and incorporate it in his computation. Equivalent provisions apply to trustees (TMA 1970, s 8A(1) and (1AA)), partnerships (TMA 1970, s 12AA(7)(a)), personal representatives (TMA 1970, ss 74, 7(1) and 8(1)) and a company subject to corporation tax on its capital gains (TMA 1970, s 11AA(1)).

The requirement is that the taxpayer, or his agent, is to compute the chargeable gain arising in respect of each disposal during the fiscal year. This chargeable gain is computed after allowing for indexation allowance and any reliefs, such as taper relief and retirement relief. The tax return form requires the statement of the chargeable gain, hence the taxpayers' statutory obligation under TMA 1970, s 8(1) has not been fulfilled if he merely declares sale proceeds and cost, expecting HMRC to compute the gain. Even if the taxpayer requests HMRC to compute his liability, it is for the taxpayer, not HMRC, to calculate taper relief, indexation allowance and any retirement relief, or other reduction in the gain.

3.3 Enquiring into a valuation in a tax return

Unless the circumstances are such as to constitute negligence or wilful default, HM Inspector of Taxes must accept the gain computed by reference to the taxpayer's estimated market value, unless HM Inspector of Taxes issues a formal notice in writing to the taxpayer stating that he is enquiring into the tax return. Where the return was submitted by 31 January after the fiscal year, the formal notice of enquiry must be issued by 31 January one year later (TMA 1970, s 9A). Once the notice has been issued, HMRC are empowered under TMA 1970, s 19A to call for documents in relation to, *inter alia*, the estimate of the market value. It is, thus, necessary for a s 9A notice to be issued each time the local district wishes to refer a valuation to HMRC Share Valuation.

There is no distinction made in statute between, on the one hand, a notice issued as a result of the Inspector wishing to test the entries made on the tax return form in relation to capital gains, and, on the other hand, an enquiry into tax return entries in relation to income. TMA 1970, s 9A(3) prohibits a second enquiry on a tax return once the first enquiry has been completed. This means that, in the absence of fraud, neglect or incomplete disclosure, once a Revenue officer has issued a notice under TMA 1970, s 28A(5), stating that he has completed his enquiries into a tax return, he is estopped from making further enquiries on any aspect of that return. Thus, enquiries on income cannot be followed by enquiries on capital gains, if the notice of completion has already been given.

It is the common experience of taxation practitioners that there is frequently a very considerable delay between the returning of a capital gains tax computation and the ultimate agreeing of a valuation incorporated in that computation. Where this agreement gives rise to additional payment or repayment of tax, interest runs on that payment or repayment from the due date, normally 31 January following the fiscal year.

At the Press Conference on 12 January 1994, a question was put as to the liability of the taxpayer to a surcharge where the value that is ultimately agreed is substantially different from that which was put into the capital gains tax computation submitted by, or on behalf of, the taxpayer. A senior Revenue spokesman stated:

> 'Provided a reasonable estimate was made and provided a professional valuer can show it was a reasonable estimate, there would be no question of Inland Revenue raising a surcharge in these circumstances.'

TMA 1970, s 8 requires that a tax return be submitted by the due date (normally 31 January following the fiscal year).

In order to satisfy this requirement, it is sometimes necessary for the taxpayer to use a judgemental figure.

Such a judgemental figure will arise in two types of situation. First, when records are not available and a figure is inserted which could have been accurately determined from records, had they been available, secondly, where a figure is inherently judgemental, such as a valuation.

Where a taxpayer uses a judgemental figure, which he has identified as such, HMRC practice is to regard his tax return as complete and correct as long as the taxpayer has done his best to provide an accurate figure, using all the proper sources of knowledge available to him at the time the return is made. If it is subsequently found that the estimate has not made proper use of available sources of knowledge – if, for example, the estimate was unreasonable in the light of the facts available to the taxpayer – the return would be regarded as incomplete or incorrect and, if made negligently, could attract a penalty. This practice is in accordance with the judgement in *Dunk v General Commissioners for Havant* [1976] STC 460, where Goulding J said:

> 'If he has done his best and, of course, he is under a duty to use all proper courses of knowledge – he will not, in my view, be guilty of making a false statement, providing, as I say, he puts in a genuine estimate and, if necessary explains that it is not reliable.'

Where market value is required for unquoted shares, The Revenue consider that a taxpayer has not fulfilled his duty to provide an accurate figure unless he has engaged the services of a person with the appropriate expertise to undertake a valuation of unquoted shares. The Revenue accept that an accountant in practice is such a person. Exceptionally, where the taxpayer himself has the relevant expertise and can demonstrate that he undertook a valuation in the same manner as would be adopted by an independent valuer, the Revenue will accept that the tax return is complete and correct. As long as the taxpayer obtained advice from an appropriate expert, a penalty will not be sought where the value ultimately negotiated with HMRC Share Valuation is different from the value used by the taxpayer.

HMRC practice is for the notice of commencement of an enquiry to be sent out by the local tax office and for the local tax office to be responsible for notifying the taxpayer of completion of the enquiry. The local tax office instructs Share Valuation to negotiate a value. Correspondence on the valuation during the course of the enquiry is normally directly between the agent and the specialist office. It is to be expected that in very many cases correspondence on a valuation and the subsequent negotiation of an agreed figure will extend over a considerably longer period than is required for the general tax office to consider any other entries on the tax return into which they wish to enquire. As only one enquiry per tax return is possible, the enquiry remains open until the valuation is agreed (or an HMRC officer amends the self-assessment to reflect a valuation proposed by Share Valuation, there having been no agreement). In law, it is possible for HMRC to consider other items on the tax return at any time up to the issue of notice of completion of enquiry that will be required after the valuation has been disposed of. In practice, HMRC state that a local district will inform a taxpayer that its investigation of the tax return is complete, other than the determination of a valuation. After such notification, HMRC will not raise any questions on the tax return other than directly in relation to the valuation concerned (Inland Revenue press release, 28 January 1999 [1999] STI 219).

3.4 Agreeing a valuation before making a return

After making a disposal of an asset, it is possible for an individual or trustee to notify HMRC of the valuation that it is proposed to incorporate in the capital gains tax computation on that disposal and invite HMRC agreement to this valuation. This request is made on HMRC Form CG 34, which is reproduced in Appendix 5. The request can be made at any time after the disposal that triggers the gain. A request cannot, however, be made before there is a capital gains tax disposal. The effect of this arrangement is that it is possible for correspondence aimed at agreeing a valuation to take place over a period of up to 22 months prior to the due date for submission of the tax return reporting the gain that has been crystallised.

The application is made to the local tax office to which the self-assessment tax return will be sent. Where the valuation is of unquoted shares, the local tax office will refer the request to HMRC Share Valuation, which will then correspond with the taxpayer, or his agent, as appropriate. Once HMRC agreement has been obtained to a valuation, HMRC undertake not to challenge the use of that valuation in the tax return 'unless there are any important facts affecting the valuation that you have not told us about' (Inland Revenue press release, 4 February 1997).

3.5 Market value at 31 March 1982

TCGA 1992, s 35(2) states:

> '... in computing for the purpose of this Act a gain or loss accruing on the disposal it shall be assumed that the asset was on 31 March 1982 sold by the person making the disposal, and immediately reacquired by him, at its market value on that date.'

Of crucial importance in determining the market value of a holding of unquoted shares is the size of the holding in relation to the issued shared capital at valuation date.

Statute postulates a sale and reacquisition of 'the asset'. TCGA 1992, s 104(1) has the effect that all shares of the same class acquired by the same person in the same capacity are pooled together and become indistinguishable parts of a single asset. (FA 1998, s 23(1) changes this treatment for shares acquired on or after 6 April 1998 but does not affect the shares held at 31 March 1982.)

The statutory provision has the effect that any disposal of shares acquired prior to 6 April 1998 is a part disposal, if the taxpayer retains further shares of the same class in the company. Hence, under statute, it is necessary to value the shareholding that remains. However, HMRC practice is to apportion the base cost between the shares that have been sold and the shares that remain. HMRC *Capital Gains Manual* para 50728 instructs the local district to use this non-statutory method of computation unless the taxpayer objects. HMRC clearly accept that the practice given in its manual at para 50728 is not the statutory treatment. It is not clear what HMRC consider would be the calculation if the statutory provisions are followed. At one time, the Revenue published its view in *Capital Gains Manual* paras 50874 and 50902 as:

'Although a 1982 holding represents a share pool which was frozen in 1982, it was not created until 1985. Any disposal of shares held in 1982 made between 1982 and 1985 would not be included in the 1982 holding and should not be included in the valuation.'

And the 1982 holding that requires to be valued in a capital gains tax computation is:

'The share pool that was frozen when FA 1982 came into force, less any disposals between 1982 and 1985.'

However, these pages have now been removed from the HMRC Manual. It would appear, therefore, that HMRC have reconsidered their view and are likely to have concluded that the author's interpretation given above is correct.

This can best be demonstrated by means of an example:

A private company has 100 shares in issue. In April 1990, Jeremy purchased 51 ords, paying £51,000. In October 1999, he sells two ords, receiving £20,000. The value of ords in October 1999 is:

51% holding	£10,000 per ord
49% holding	£4,000 per ord
2% holding	£1,000 per ord

The statutory method

Applying TCGA 1992, ss 42(1), 104(1) and (6) there is a part disposal, the value B in the normal part disposal formula being £4,000 per ord. On this basis the calculation is:

		£
Sale proceeds, Oct 99		20,000
Attributable cost, April 90		
	$£51,000 \times \dfrac{20,000}{20,000 + 196,000}$	=(4,722)
Gain before indexation allowance and taper relief		£15,278
Cost c/f		£46,278

The practical method

The following calculation is acceptable to HMRC:

	£
Sale proceeds, Oct 99	20,000
Cost 2/51 × £51,000	(2,000)
Gain before indexation allowance and taper relief	£18,000
Cost c/f	£49,000

When it is necessary to determine the 1982 value, the value to be taken is calculated by considering the value of the total number of shares in the company that were held at that date. The effect of this can be illustrated as follows:

Albatross Ltd has 100 shares in issue

At 31 March 1982 Adam holds 60 shares

Adam makes the following disposals: 1992, 51 shares; 2000, 9 shares.

If the value of the 60 shares held at 31 March 1982 was £600,000, the capital gain arising on each of the disposals (using the HMRC approved 'practical method') is calculated by using the base cost of the shares disposed as £10,000 per ord.

There is, thus, no difference between the base cost per share used in 1992 when the taxpayer sold a controlling interest and the value used in 2000 when the taxpayer sold a small (and probably non-influential) minority holding.

The above analysis does not hold true where there has been a disposal of shares between 31 March 1982 and 6 April 1985. TCGA 1992, s 109 defines a '1982 holding' as a holding which falls within that description 'for the purposes of FA 1985, Sch 19 Part II'. The purposes of that schedule of FA 1985 are, not surprisingly, for shares held in 1985. If there has been a disposal of shares between 1982 and 1985 the shares that have been sold are not part of the holding at 6 April 1985 and, hence, not within the remit of FA 1985, Sch 19. It would seem to follow, therefore, that the number of shares in the '1982 holding' is the number of shares held at 31 March 1982 less shares sold during the next three years. (Exceptionally shares sold will not reduce the size of the pool if they are matched with shares acquired after 31 March 1982.) The basic principle of valuing the entire holding at 31 March 1982 is given by s 104. The effect of s 109 is to treat acquisitions on or after 6 April 1985 as separate from that single asset. The definition of a '1982 holding' as being shares held at 1985 is specified in s 109(1) as applying solely to that section. On this argument, it does not affect the identification of the number of shares as at 31 March 1982 for the purpose of s 104 and, in particular, does not impinge on the valuation provision in TCGA 1992, s 272

3.6 Connected persons

TCGA 1992, s 18(2) provides that whenever there is a transaction between connected persons, the transaction is treated as 'otherwise by way of a bargain made at arm's length'. This brings into operation the provision of TCGA 1992, s 17(1)(a) whereby the actual consideration that passes is ignored and market value is taken as the sale proceeds and acquisition costs respectively.

For the purpose of capital gains tax (and corporation tax on capital gains), there are five categories of connected person:

(a) A taxpayer is connected with his/her spouse, brother, sister, ancestor or lineal descendant and also with the spouse of any individual in this list (TCGA 1992, s 286(2)). Moreover, an individual is connected with any relation (within any of the previous categories) of his spouse. For capital gains tax purposes, an individual's uncle, aunt, nephew or niece is not a connected person. (By contrast, these categories are, within the definition of 'connected persons' for inheritance tax purposes.)

   The provisions for inter-spouse transfer cease at the end of the fiscal year of separation (TCGA 1992, s 58(1)). However, spouses continue to be connected persons, even after separation. They remain as connected persons until a decree absolute has been granted on a divorce.

(b) A settlor is connected with the trustees of the settlement that he has created and the trustees are connected with any person who is connected with the settlor (TCGA 1992, s 286(3)).

   In this definition, a 'settlor' is not solely the individual named on the settlement deed but is any person who has provided funds for the purpose of the settlement or made a reciprocal arrangement with another person to enter into the settlement (ITTOIA 2005, s 620(3)(c) imported for capital gains tax by TCGA 1992, s 286(3ZA)).

   A trustee is connected with any close company of which the trustees of the settlement are participators, any company controlled by such a company and any company that would be a close company if it were resident in the UK (TCGA 1992, s 286(3A)).

   When considering those individuals with whom the trustee is connected, two rules are important:

   The first rule is when there is a transaction in trust property; the relationship is solely in respect of the trusteeship. The personal characteristics of the trustee are ignored. Thus, if a trustee were to sell trust property to his own wife that is not a transaction between connected persons if the wife is not connected with the settlor of the trust.

   The second rule is that no connection can be made through a deceased individual. Thus, after the death of the settlor of a trust, the trustees are not connected with any individual (although they would be connected with a company that they control).

(c) A person is connected with any person with whom he is in partnership. In addition, he is connected with the spouse of any partner and with the brother, sister, ancestor or lineal descendant of any partner. However, this connection does not apply 'in relation to acquisitions or disposals of partnership assets pursuant to bona fide commercial arrangements' (TCGA 1992, s 286(4)).

The interpretation of the proviso to TCGA 1992, s 286(4) is difficult. Where the partnership contracts with an individual partner to sell to that partner, for a commercial consideration, an asset which has previously been on the partnership balance sheet, it is clear that the subsection operates so that the transaction is not treated as being made between connected persons. However, it is less clear where the asset in question has not been on the partnership balance sheet. This is commonly the case in partnerships where goodwill is transferred between partners and neither the goodwill nor its transfer is shown in the accounts of the partnership. Probably the better view of such a transaction is that a distinction has to be drawn between:

(i) an asset owned by the partnership, which is a 'partnership asset' within the meaning of TCGA 1992, s 286(4) and;

(ii) an individual's interest in the partnership, which is not a 'partnership asset' within the meaning of TCGA 1992, s 286(4).

However, this analysis seems to presuppose that one can recognise the partnership as an entity. In English law a partnership is not a legal entity and, furthermore, TCGA 1992, s 59(b) specifies that partnership dealings shall be treated as dealings by the partners and not by the firm as such.

HMRC practice is to treat any transaction between an incoming partner and the existing partners that is a bona fide commercial arrangement as being made otherwise than between connected persons (HMRC Statement of Practice D12 para 7).

(d) TCGA 1992, s 286(5) provides a company is connected with another company:

(i) if the same person has control of both, or a person has control of one and persons connected with him, or he and persons connected with him, have control of the other; or

(ii) if a group of two or more persons ('Group 1') has control of Company 1, and a group of two or more persons ('Group 2') has control of Company 2. And the same persons comprise Group 1 and Group 2, or could be regarded as consisting of the same persons by treating (in one or more cases) a member of either group as replaced by a person with whom he is connected.

(e) A company is connected with an individual if that individual has control of it or where a group of individuals who are connected persons have control of the company (TCGA 1992, s 286(6)). Further, any two or more persons acting together to secure and exercise control of a company are treated in relation to that company as connected with each other (TCGA 1992, s 286(7)). For a discussion on this in relation to Business Expansion Scheme relief, see *Cook v Billings* [1999] STC 661.

Even though the parties have negotiated on an arm's length basis, if they are in fact connected the market value must be applied. The actual proceeds might well equate to the market value in that case but not necessarily and particularly so if, for some reason, one of the parties got his sums wrong.

If there is a transaction between connected persons but with consideration passing on the basis of a negotiated sale, perhaps the seller could agree with the purchaser to enter into a holdover election if the open market value should prove to be greater, so that at least in practice the actual consideration is used as the basis of taxing the seller.

There could be an inheritance tax implication. However, IHTA 1984, s 10 might come to the aid of the parties, but only if the price reflected that applying in free negotiations.

3.7 Series of transactions

When statute requires that the capital gains tax computation is drawn up on the basis that the sale proceeds on a disposal are deemed to be the market value of the shareholding which is the subject of the disposal, the basic rule is that the value is the value of the size of shareholding disposed of by the transaction, not the value of the number of shares owned. Hence, a taxpayer who owns 90 per cent of the shares and makes a gift of 4 per cent is deemed to have received the value of a 4 per cent holding, valued in isolation. This follows from the wording of TCGA 1992, s 17(1), which requires that:

'a person's ... disposal of an asset shall ... be deemed to be for a consideration equal to the market value of the asset.'

This basic rule is overridden in two circumstances.

First, by way of two or more transactions, shares are disposed of to one or more connected persons, the number of shares thus transferred within any six-year period is aggregated and the consideration for each disposal is computed pro rata to the value of the total number of shares transferred in the six-year period (TCGA 1992, s 19).

Applying this rule, it is possible for the market value on a disposal to be determined but then to be displaced by a subsequent disposal. On the other hand, if the acquirer of the shares has in turn sold them, there could be a recalculation of his gain. It would be very easy to lose sight of the effect on the purchaser.

TCGA 1992, s 19 is essentially an anti-avoidance provision to prevent the fragmentation of value by a series of transactions. Having said that, in some instances the application of s 19 could be advantageous. For example, a gift of a minority holding might produce a loss (restricted in its use) or a loss of indexation allowance. A subsequent transaction with a connected person might then be made but with the benefit of, say, retirement relief. The effect of this, on the facts, might be such as to not give rise to any tax liability on the first disposal but give a higher base cost to the connected party acquiring the shares on the second transaction.

The provisions of s 19 come into effect whenever the two parties are connected persons, even if there is a particular treatment specified by statute for the particular transaction. Thus, s 19 would seem to apply in the following instance. Horace makes a gift of a 10 per cent shareholding to his son and then, five years later, transfers a 45 per cent shareholding to his wife. Although s 19(2) does not affect the inter-spouse provisions of s 58, it does not seem to prevent a recalculation on the first disposal to the son. This does make sense, otherwise it would be very easy to circumvent s 19 by the simple expedient of an inter-spouse gift and then a subsequent transfer to a connected party.

This can be illustrated as follows:

Wilkins Ltd has 100 ords in issue.

At all material times, the value of shares in Wilkins Ltd is:

100% holding	£20,000 per ord
55% holding	£15,000 per ord
40% holding	£9,000 per ord
30% holding	£8,000 per ord
20% holding	£3,000 per ord

Bill makes the following gifts of Wilkins Ltd ords:

on 1 April 1990	30 ords to his son
on 1 May 1991	10 ords to his son
on 1 June 1992	20 ords to his nephew
on 1 August 1993	15 ords to his daughter
on 1 May 1997	25 ords to his daughter

The deemed sale of these gifts is:

(i)	1 April 1990:	30 @ £8,000 = £240,000
(ii)	1 May 1991:	10 @ £9,000 = £90,000
		disposal on 1 April 1990 revised to
		30 @ £9,000 = £270,000
(iii)	1 June 1992:	20 @ £3,000 = £60,000

(a nephew is not a connected person)

(iv)	1 August 1993:	15 @ £15,000 = £225,000
		disposal on 1 May 1991 revised to
		10 @ £15,000 = £150,000
		disposal on 1 April 1990 revised to
		30 @ £15,000 = £450,000
(v)	1 May 1997 :	25 @ £9,000 = £225,000

> (The disposals on 1 April 1990 and 1 May 1991 are not linked transactions as they were over six years prior to the date of this disposal.)
> (The disposal on 1 August 1993 is not revised as linking with that date does not increase the deemed sale consideration.)

Although the general scheme of self-assessment is that the effect of any amendment on tax payable is brought into the self-assessment for the year in which the amendment arises, there is no such provision for amendments caused by the operation of this particular rule. Instead, s 19(4) provides that 'all such assessments and adjustments of assessments shall be made as may be necessary ... on each such occasion'. The effect of this is that a gift can cause an additional tax liability to arise in a fiscal year up to five years previously. The due date for payment of this additional tax liability is 31 January following the older fiscal year, with interest charged from that date.

When shares are to be passed to the next generation, it is important to consider the effect of TCGA 1992, s 19 on the valuation to be used. For example:

A company has 1,000 shares in issue: 500 are held by husband
                                              500 are held by wife

Your clients wish to make a gift of 500 shares to their two children.

Alternative A:
Husband makes gift to child 1 and child 2
Valuation required: 500 ords (50% shareholding)

Alternative B:
Husband gives 250 shares to child 1
Wife gives 250 shares to child 2
Valuation required: 250 ords (two 25% shareholdings)

3.8 Inheritance tax valuation used for capital gains tax

TCGA 1992, s 274 provides that where 'on the death of any person inheritance tax is chargeable on his estate ... and the value of an asset forming part of that estate has been ascertained ... for the purpose of that tax, the value so ascertained should be taken for [capital gains tax purposes] to be the market value of that asset at the date of the death'.

When valuing for inheritance tax purposes, the value of related property must be taken into account. Where value is for capital gains tax purposes, related property is not in point. However, the effect of TCGA 1992, s 274 is that a valuation that has been undertaken under inheritance tax principles automatically applies to determine a valuation of capital gains tax, even though the valuation may be determined by reference to related property.

This can have a very significant effect on the computation of the gain. Consider, for example, a company with an issue shared capital of 100 ords. Ten shares are owned by the deceased; a further 80 shares are owned by his spouse. After his death, the personal representatives sell the shareholding. If the value of the deceased's shareholding is not 'ascertained' for the purposes of inheritance tax, the acquisition cost on the capital gains tax disposal is taken as the value of a 10 per cent shareholding in the company. If, however, the value of that shareholding is 'ascertained' for inheritance tax purposes, the effect of TCGA 1992, s 274 is that the 'acquisition cost' brought into the capital gains tax computation for the executors is one ninth of the value of a 90 per cent holding, which is likely to be very substantially higher.

The Revenue view is that acceptance of a taxpayer's valuation, where no inheritance tax is payable, does not constitute the value being 'ascertained'.

3.9 Costs of valuation

TCGA 1992, s 38(2) allows as a deduction in computing the gain:

'The incidental costs to the person making the disposal of the acquisition of the asset or of its disposal shall consist of expenditure wholly and exclusively incurred by him for the purposes of the acquisition or, as the case may be, the disposal, being fees, commission or remuneration paid for the professional services of any surveyor or valuer, or auctioneer, or accountant, or agent or legal adviser ... and costs reasonably incurred in making any valuation ... including in particular expenses reasonably incurred in ascertaining market value where required by this Act.'

The Revenue interpret this provision as follows:

'In computing the gain arising on the disposal of an asset, the incidental costs of disposal are allowable. These costs are defined in the legislation ... They include the reasonable costs incurred in ascertaining the market value of the asset for capital gains purposes (for example, a 31 March 1982 valuation for rebasing purposes) ...

We have been asked in particular whether the costs of agreeing a valuation with the Inland Revenue would be allowable ...

In our view, the relevant legislation ... allows the reasonable costs incurred in making the valuation, so that the gain can be calculated and returned, to be deducted. Any costs subsequently incurred, for example in negotiating with the District Valuer or with the Shares Valuation Division, or in litigating the matter before any tribunal or the Courts, are not allowable.'

(Inland Revenue Interpretation RI 63)

The statutory provision was considered in *Caton's Administrators v Couch*, where the administrators sought to deduct the costs of the appeal before the Special Commissioner. In reversing the decision of the Special Commissioner on this point, Morritt LJ in the Court of Appeal said:

> 'To construe the paragraph as the Administrators suggest would be a positive deterrent to reaching a sensible agreement with the Revenue as to the quantum of liability. It would give rise to the absurd position that on an appeal against an assessment which had failed the assessment would nevertheless require reduction to take account of such costs of the unsuccessful appeal as had been reasonably incurred ... So absurd a result may be avoided by adopted the construction advanced by the Revenue.
>
> ... I conclude that the costs and expenses which a taxpayer may deduct pursuant to [TCGA 1992, s 38(2)(b)] ... in respect of any particular disposal are limited to those which he incurs in complying with his obligations under TMA 1970 s 12 [the obligation to submit a tax return] and do not extend to costs incurred in negotiating over or contesting has liability to capital gains tax arising out of that disposal. The effect, but not the reason for, that conclusion is to preclude the deduction of costs by a taxpayer in conducting a tax controversy with the Revenue.'
>
> ([1997] STC (SCD) 970 at 980a **case 41 paras 32 and 33**)

4 Valuation for inheritance tax

4.1 Statutory provision

The basic rule for valuation is given in IHTA 1984, s 160 which states:

> '... the value at any time of any property shall for the purposes of this Act be the price which the property might reasonably be expected to fetch if sold in the open market at that time; but that price shall not be assumed to be reduced on the ground that the whole property is to be placed on the market at one and the same time.'

The basic provision, as stated, is identical to that which applies for capital gains tax (see section **3.1**). However, what is actually valued is not the shareholding that is transferred but the difference between the value of the shareholding before the transfer and the value after the transfer (IHTA 1984, s 3(1)). This can be illustrated as shown:

Cyril Ltd, a family property company has 100 ords in issue.

Cyril owns 60 ords.

Cyril gives his daughter 17 ords.

Valuation required for Capital Gains Tax:
Value of 17 ords

Valuation required for Inheritance Tax

The transfer of value is the difference between:
Value of 60 ords and
Value of 43 ords

4.2 Death

For inheritance tax, the measurement of the value of the estate at death is the most frequent reason for requiring a valuation of unquoted shares.

IHTA 1984, s 4(1) provides that inheritance tax is charged as if, immediately before the death, there is a transfer of value of a sum equal to the value of the holding at that time. Where the shareholdings of a personal company or of a company whose operations have been dominated by the deceased, the death may, itself, substantially depress the value of the shares. IHTA 1984, s 171 has the effect that the share valuation is undertaken as if the death has incurred. This means that shares are valued taking account of the fact that the company no longer has the benefit of the services of the deceased. This can significantly depress the value of the shares if the deceased was the driving force behind the company. Conversely, where the company has taken out key-man insurance, an effect of death is likely to be that the company is due to receive a sum of money arising under the insurance policy. (Any corporation tax due on the receipt will need to be taken into account.) The effect of s 171 is that the cash due to be received by the company is brought into consideration in valuing the shares.

When the deceased was a beneficiary of a trust in which he had an interest in possession, IHTA 1984, s 49(1) has the effect that the deceased is treated as if he was beneficially entitled to shares held in that trust. It is frequently the case that the deceased will have had shares registered in his own name and other shares in the same company have been held in trust, with the deceased having a right to income arising from the trust. The first shareholding is part of the estate at death and is subjected to a charge to inheritance tax by the operation of IHTA 1984, s 4. The second shareholding is brought into charge, with inheritance tax payable by the trustees, by the operation of IHTA 1984, s 49. IHTA 1984, s 4 specifies that death is to be treated as the transfer of value of the deceased's estate. IHTA 1984, s 5 defines 'estate' as the property to which the deceased is beneficially entitled. IHTA 1984, s 49 specifies that interest in possession is to be treated as a beneficial entitlement. Hence, it would appear one adds the shares in the settled estate to those in the free estate and values the aggregate.

However, when an interest in possession terminates, s 52(1) specifies that this is a transfer of value 'of property in which his interest subsisted'. That is, one values the shares in the settled estate without reference to shares in the free estate.

The wording of s 105, for the purpose of business property relief, requires one to look at shares and securities 'owned by the transferor'. As s 39 deems the deceased to be beneficially entitled to shares held in an interest in possession settlement, business property relief is granted where the conditions are satisfied by aggregating the holding in the free estate and the holding in trust. This was of considerable practical importance prior to 6 April 1996 when it was necessary for unquoted shares to be 25 per cent or more of the issued share capital in order for 100 per cent business property relief to apply. The provision continues to be of importance where securities, other than shares, are held. Debentures, for example, issued by a company only attract business property relief if the deceased owned (or was deemed to own) unquoted shares in the company which numerically have given the deceased control of the company immediately prior to the death (IHTA 1984, s 105(1)(b)).

The valuation provisions illustrated by the cases discussed in Chapter 2 (capital gains tax) apply also to valuations for inheritance tax. As a valuation at death is a valuation of an entire estate, case law on the aggregation of the holdings is considered in this section, rather than above, together with the statutory provision for related property. Also discussed in the section are the cases where the circumstances of individual shareholders were held to be relevant, either because of the ratio in which shares were held, or because of a special purchaser in the market.

4.3 Related property

Where there is related property, the value per share is computed by reference to the size of the holding represented by the holding in the estate plus related property (IHTA 1984, s 161).

The contrast between the provisions for related property and the treatment of shares held in trust (see section **2.2**) can be illustrated:

Davina Ltd has 100 ords in issue.

Donald dies.   10 ords are in his estate.   35 ords are in his widow's estate.

At the time of death, a further 42 ords are in a trust and he was entitled to receive the income of the trust.

The valuations required are:
 (i) under the related property rule:
      10 ords, valued at the price per ord of a 45% holding (10% in his estate plus 35% in his wife's estate)
(ii) Under the interest in possession rule:
      42 ords, valued alone.

Unquoted shares and other property is related property if either:
 (i) it is in the estate of his/her spouse; or
(ii) the taxpayer or the spouse has made an exempt transfer of the shares or other property to a charity after 15 April 1976 and the shares or other property had been the property of the charity at any time during the previous five years.

In applying these tests, excluded property is treated as if it was not excluded. The effect of this can be illustrated:

Ermintrude is domiciled abroad but has lived in the UK for 16 years. She owns 50.5% of the issued share capital of a foreign company. Acting on advice in her 16th year of residence she gifts a 1% shareholding to a charity. She continues to live in the UK and dies 20 years later having retained the 49.5% holding herself. If the charity still owns the 1% holding it has been given the value placed on the shares in her estate at death is the value per share of a controlling interest in the company.

The related property rule has the result that an advisor should consider carefully the order in which shares are gifted if more than one person is to make gifts. This can be illustrated:

A company has 1,000 shares in issue. Husband owns 70 shares, wife owns 480 shares, the three children own 150 shares each. The parents wish to give their children all the shares they hold.

Share values are:	55% holding	£1,000 per ord
	48% holding	£550 per ord
	7% holding	£300 per ord

Arrangement 1: Wife gives 48 ords, then husband gives 7 ords:

	£	£
Wife's transfer:		
480 ords @ £1,000 per ord	480,000	
0 ords	nil	
Diminution in estate:	480,000	
Husband's transfer:		
70 ords @ £300 per ord	21,000	
0 ords	nil	
Diminution in estate	21,000	
Aggregate of transfers		501,000

Arrangement 2: Husband gives 70 ords, then wife gives 480 ords

Husband's transfer:		
70 ords @ £1,000 per ord	70,000	
0 ords	nil	
	70,000	
Wife's transfer:		
480 ords @ £550 per ord	264,000	
0 ords	nil	
	264,000	
Aggregate of transfers		334,000

Statute imposes this valuation provision wherever there is an asset in the related property, the existence of which increases the value of the unquoted shares in the estate under consideration. Thus, if the deceased owned shares in a farming company, and the widow owns the land that is farmed, it is necessary when valuing the farming company shares to take account of the land holding held by the spouse. This is more particularly the case if there are arrangements in place so that the farming company does not pay a full market rent for the land it farms. Similarly, in principle, a debenture in the estate of the spouse of the deceased could be relevant in estimating the value of shares in the same company that were held in the deceased's estate.

4.4 Aggregate holdings

In *IRC v Gray*, the court considered the valuation to be placed on 3,000 acres of farmland held by Lady Fox at the time of her death and also her 92.5 per cent interest in the farming partnership that farmed the land in question. Hoffman LJ said:

> 'The principle is that the hypothetical vendor must be supposed to have "taken the course which would get the largest price" provided that this does not entail "undue expenditure of time and effort". In some cases this may involve the sale of an aggregate which could not reasonably be described as a "natural unit". Suppose, for example, there is evidence that at the relevant time a prudent seller would have discovered that a higher price could be obtained by the combined sale of two items which might otherwise have been thought entirely unrelated to each other. Such circumstances might arise from the peculiar demands of a small number of potential buyers or even those of a single one. In my view the hypothetical seller would in those circumstances have been, subject to the caveat I have mentioned, willing to sell the items together. The fact that no one would have described them as a "natural unit" is irrelevant.'
>
> ([1994] STC 360 at 377j **case 37 para 31**)

The principle enunciated in *IRC v Gray* follows the decision in *Attorney-General of Ceylon v Mackie & Anor*. In that case, the deceased held 'management shares' and preference shares. Lord Reid said:

> 'It was admitted for the appellant that no purchaser would have paid anything like Rs250 per share for the management shares in face of the company's articles unless he could buy at the same time a large block of the preference shares and so have a majority of votes. But the appellant contends that the respondents must be supposed to have taken the course which would get the largest price for the combined holding of management and preference shares and to have offered for sale together with the management shares the whole or at least the greater part of the preference shares owned by the deceased. In their Lordships' judgement this contention is correct.'
>
> ([1952] 2 All ER 755 at 778 **case 24 para 3**)

The principle of aggregation to maximise the value, does not require aggregating shareholdings held by different shareholders, unless this is provided by statute under related property rules. In *Battle v IRC* [1980] STC 86 **case 32**, two brothers, Anthony and Robin, each received 49 out of the 100 issued shares in an investment company. The court refused to accept the approach that the value of a holding of 49 shares was one half of the value of a 98 per cent shareholding.

The principle is that shares are to be offered for sale in a manner that achieves the best price. This could mean that the holding should be valued as if it were offered for sale split into readily marketable units. This is illustrated in *Ellesmere v IRC* [1918] 2 KB 735 **case 11** and in *Duke of Buccleuch v IRC* [1967] 1 AC 506, HL **case 28**. Both cases concern land holdings. In the latter case, the estate was of 119,000 acres. The court upheld the Revenue's approach that it should be valued as if it were sold in 532 separate units. This approach may be relevant, on occasion, in the valuation of unquoted shares. Where a company carries on a number of disparate and separately organised trades, greater value could be obtained by a split of the company. When valuing a majority shareholding in such a company, it is considered that some regard should be had to the possibility of achieving higher proceeds by such a split, especially if the circumstances of the company are such that a split is likely.

4.5 Identity of potential purchaser

The general principle is that a fiscal valuation of a shareholding is made on the basis of a hypothetical vendor and a hypothetical purchaser (see section **2.3**). However, it is a useful corrective to over-theorising to note the words of Lawton LJ in *Trocette Property Co Ltd v Greater London Council*:

> 'It is important that this statutory world of make-believe should be kept as near as possible to reality. No assumption of any kind should be made unless provided for by statute or decided cases.'
>
> ((1974) 28 P&CR 408 at 420)

This approach was followed in *Walton v IRC*, which concerned a valuation of £6,500 being put on a one-third interest in the tenancy of a Northumbrian hill farm that extended to 459 acres. The Revenue submitted that account should be taken of the sum of £200,000 which it was estimated could be realised if the marriage value of the freehold and the tenancy was unlocked. Peter Gibson LJ said:

> 'It is not necessary for the operation of the statutory hypothesis of a sale in the open market of an interest in a tenancy that the landlord should treated as a hypothetical person, and it is a question of fact to be established by the evidence before the tribunal of fact whether the attributes of the actual landlord would be taken into account in the market. I would add that the same logic requires that in the case of a deceased partner owning an interest in a tenancy which is a partnership asset, regard should be had to the actual intention of the actual surviving partner and not to a hypothetical partner.'
>
> ([1996] STC 68, CA at 88b)

The position was stated succinctly by Evans LJ:

'... the sale has to take place "in the real world" and that account must be taken of the actual persons as well as of the actual property involved. The Lands Tribunal's figure is not artificial or unreal, but rather the reverse. It reflects the realities of the situation.'

([1996] STC 68, CA at 90a)

4.6 Special purchaser

The considerations outlined above in section **3.5**, led inevitably to the much-debated concept of a 'special purchaser'. In *IRC v Clay, IRC v Buchanan* the concept of a special purchaser was formulated by Cozens-Hardy MR in the following terms:

'An "open market" sale of property "in its then condition" presupposes a knowledge of its situation with all surrounding circumstances. To say that a small farm in the middle of a wealthy landowner's estate is to be valued without reference to the fact that he will probably be willing to pay a large price, but solely with reference to its ordinary agricultural value, seems to me absurd. If the landowner does not at the moment buy, land brokers or speculators will give more than its purely agricultural value with a view to reselling it at a profit to the landowner.'

([1914] 3 KB 466 at 472 **case 8 para 3**)

In *IRC v Clay*, the valuation concept was applied to a house next to a nurses' home. In *IRC v Crossman* (1936) 15 ATC 94 **case 17**, the concept was applied to a shareholding, as it was in *Re Lynall deceased* in which Harman LJ said:

'It was the taxpayer's argument that directors must be excluded from amongst possible purchasers because they would be "special" purchasers. I do not accept this, and am of opinion that this is not an ingredient in the *Crossman* decision. In *Crossman's* case it was decided that the fact that a "special" purchaser, namely a trust company, would have offered a special price must be ignored, but this was because that particular purchaser had a reason special to him for so doing. So, here, a director who would give an enhanced price because he would thus obtain control of the company would be left out of account. But that is not to say that directors as such are to be ignored. All likely purchasers are deemed to be in the market. What the Act says is that the sale is to be treated as an open market sale, that is to say, the restrictions on transfer are to be ignored for the purpose of the hypothetical sale which is to fix the price, but I cannot see why the hypothetical sellers are not to be treated as being what they are, namely, directors in possession of the information which a purchaser would reasonably require and which on the evidence he would have obtained if he were to be a willing purchaser.'

((1971) 47 TC 375 at 396 **case 29 para 48**)

This is a difficult area. There is a distinction between a special purchaser and a special price. If, though, a particular individual would have been in the market at the relevant date and would be prepared to pay a higher price because of the particular benefit to him, then that is the open market value. In the earlier example of two 49 per cent holdings and a 2 per cent balance of power holding, in a sense either of those 49 per cent shareholders is a special purchaser who is prepared to pay more than a 2 per cent holding valued on its own.

4.7 Associated operations

IHTA 1984, s 268(3) provides statutory treatment for the situation where a single shareholding, for example, is transferred by a series of transactions, or where one operation takes place that paves the way for another. In such a situation, s 268 operates to treat the transfer of value as taking place at the time of the last of the operations and the value of the transfer is the diminution in the estate occasioned by considering all the associated operations as a single transfer.

Where this applies to a holding of unquoted shares, the valuation is performed as at the date of the last of the operations. The diminution in the estate is measured by the difference between the value of the total holding (considered with any related property) before the start of the associated operations, less the value that remains in the estate (including any related property) at the end of the associated operations.

4.8 Cost of valuation

There is no provision for deducting the cost of a valuation undertaken to determine the liability to inheritance tax.

5 Valuation for income tax and other taxes

5.1 Income tax

5.1.1 Overview

The market value of an unquoted shareholding is required for income tax purposes on the following occasions.

- Shares obtained as a benefit of employment subject to Sch E (ITEPA 2003, s 62(3), see *Weight v Salmon* (1935) 19 TC 174).
- Shares issued in a share option scheme (ITEPA 2003, ss 471–479).
- Shares received as payment for sale of stock (see *Gold Coast Selection Trust Ltd v Humphrey* (1948) 30 TC 209 **case 20**).
- Transactions in land charged under Sch D, Case VI (ITA 2007, ss 752–772 include a charge arising on gains made in shares where these are part of transaction within the scope of the anti-avoidance provisions of those sections).

For a charge arising on an employee given shares, or an option over shares, by his employer, ITEPA 2003, s 421(1) imports the capital gains tax rules for determining the market value. However, the valuation provision applies only to a charge arising under ITEPA 2003, ss 417–484. Where the tax charge arises under some other provision, income tax does not have statutory rules for the approach to be taken in estimating the value of unquoted shares. Basic principles derived from case law discussed in Chapters 2 and 3 can be taken to be relevant, apart from the provisions discussed on deeming information to be available to the hypothetical prospective purchaser. Where the capital gains tax and inheritance tax deeming provisions do not apply (TCGA 1992, s 273 and IHTA 1984, s 168) the information to be taken into account in measuring value for income tax purposes is the information that is actually available to purchasers in the hypothetical market at the valuation date and any information not actually available is to be ignored (*Re Lynall deceased* (1971) 47 TC 375 **case 29**). In addition, the provision that the value is not to be taken as depressed by the fact that the market is swamped by the number of shares issued is a statutory provision for capital gains tax and inheritance tax (TCGA 1992, s 272 and IHTA 1984, s 160); hence, it has no application for income tax. Further, there is no statutory provision for income tax requiring the valuer to ignore restrictions placed on shares, other than the necessary hypothesis that the transfer can occur to a hypothetical purchaser. In *Ede v Wilson & Cornwall* (1945) 26 TC 38 it was accepted that the value of shares granted in Ansells Brewery Ltd was reduced by the restrictions placed on the shares, when these were held by the employees.

5.1.2 Income tax on share options

FA 2003 made some very substantial amendments to the taxation of employee shares and securities generally, by substituting various provisions in ITEPA 2003, Part 7. There are some complex formulae in ITEPA 2003, s 428 dealing with restricted securities. This introduces, in particular, the following concepts.

'UMV' which is the market value of the securities immediately after the chargeable event but for any restrictions.

'IUMV' which is what would have been the market value of the securities at the time of the acquisition but for any restrictions.

'IUP' which is represented by the formulae:

$$\frac{IUMV - DA}{IUMV}$$

These rules are very complex and can produce some odd effects. In some cases the taxation consequence can be mitigated by making an election under ITEPA 2003, s 431 so as to value shares at the time of acquisition on the basis that they are not restricted securities. A restricted security is defined by ITEPA 2003, s 423 and there are important differences between the type of restriction where, if certain circumstances arise or do not arise, there will be a transfer, reversion or forfeiture of the shares and the person will receive less than market value, compared to other restrictions. By making the election, market value is then determined as if there were no provision for transfer, etc. The other block of restrictions is simply any restriction on the freedom of the person to dispose of the shares or proceeds of their sale, such as the standard pre-emption provisions in the articles of association or possibly a shareholders' agreement. The broad effect of these provisions is that where there is a difference between the restricted value of the shares and the unrestricted value, this could result in part of the proceeds on a sale being subject to tax as employment income (with PAYE and NIC implications in most cases) instead of capital gains tax.

5.1.3 Income tax on share options – no restriction on securities issued

Assume that a company wishes to issue shares to employees. If there is only one class of shares and there are no separate restrictions applying to those shares whether in the articles of association or an agreement external to the company, there should not be an income tax charge at any point as all the shares are subject to the same restrictions, provided market value is paid. There would usually be a pre-emption provision but all shares would be subject to that. However, supposing the articles distinguish between shares issued to employees and other shares so that on an employee leaving the company a transfer notice is deemed to have been given by that employee, such that the other shareholders have the right to acquire those shares, those other shareholders do not have to acquire those shares but have the ability to do so. Assume further that the transfer notice is given on the basis of fair market value which implicitly assumes the appropriate discount for a minority shareholding. This is a restriction that applies to only some of the shares effectively and so there can potentially be an income tax charge at a future date. The other shareholders are not deemed to have given a transfer notice in any circumstances but if they wish to sell those shares they must go through the same procedure and on the same basis of valuation. As with the employees' shares, this cannot force anyone to purchase the shares. The question arises: is there a difference in value between shares issued to employees in that situation and other shares where the only difference is the deemed transfer notice that an employee gives on leaving employment? Suppose, based on the principles set out above, that the shareholding in question will be valued at £3 per share for a non-employee. That share is not restricted as such although strictly if a board of directors can refuse to register a transfer, that could be said to be a restriction. Given the nature of an unquoted company, though, that itself would not be expected to provide any difference in valuation and so for practical purposes £3 could be argued as the unrestricted value. It could be further argued then that the corresponding holding of an employee would be worth slightly less, simply because they can be forced to share their shares rather than hang on to them in the hope of, perhaps, receiving a higher price if the company is ever sold to a third party. An employee would receive market value at the time if the other shareholders take up their right to acquire those shares and so in that sense the employee is not losing any value. The position of a purchaser of those shares would depend in turn on whether they are an employee and so it is not so much the status of the present holder that affects this but that of a future holder. On this basis, it could be argued that there is no difference in value and if in fact the shares are issued at the same value there ought not to be any employment income charge, applying ITEPA 2003, s 428. However, HMRC appear to accept that there is some small difference in this situation which could, be, say, 5 per cent, in which case if the shares are issued at £2.85 instead of £3, there is no employment income charge at the time but the corresponding percentage of the proceeds on a sale would then be subject to income tax and with a PAYE, etc obligation on the company. By making a ITEPA 2003, s 431 election, though, the employee would accept that at that point there is a gain of 15 pence per share and would pay tax on that but without any risk later on of any part of the proceeds being subject to income tax. In that sense, an employee is paying tax now for a future benefit, but if that benefit does not arise a tax charge would have been created without any benefit. That, though, is a matter of hindsight because the s 431 election, to be valid, must be made within 14 days of the issue of shares.

5.1.4 Income tax on share options – restricted securities

Assume further, though, that instead of there simply being a deemed transfer notice on an employee leaving, a separate class of shares is created for employees who leave. A common formulation is that shares of this class are repurchased at the sum paid for subscription, if the employee leaves the company within three years of issue. Supposing, therefore, to allow for that restriction, the shares are valued at £1.50 instead of £3 per share, the lower value recognising the risk to any purchaser that, in the first three years of ownership, the purchaser would receive no more than £1.50 per share. In that situation, the amount of the employment income charge on a sale could be quite considerable as it could effectively be 50 per cent of the proceeds. That is the situation where in particular a s 431 election could be beneficial, but, as a consequence, an employment income charge arises at the time of issue based on £3 per share. If the shares are issued in a start up situation and everyone subscribes at the same figure (and especially so if this is par as shares cannot be issued at a discount) there should be no concern because the market value with the restrictions is less than the amount actually being paid by the employee.

If the shares are issued under the Enterprise Management Incentives (EMI) rules, different considerations apply because there is only a charge to income tax on exercise if the market value of the shares at the date of grant is greater than the exercise price. There are no special rules in arriving at market value for this particular purpose and on acquisition following exercise of an option, ITEPA 2003, s 431A deems a s 431 election to have been made by the employee so that there is no charge on a subsequent sale of the shares, for example. The restrictions are taking into account, though, in determining the limits that are imposed on shares issued to employees under EMI, such as the £100,000 per employee limit. For the purposes of that provision, therefore, shares are valued without restrictions but only for that purpose.

5.2 Other taxes

5.2.1 Stamp duty

Prior to 1985, many valuations were required to determine stamp duty. However, FA 1985, s 82(1) abolished the charge to duty calculated by reference to the value of shares transferred, for any transfer made on or after 26 March 1985.

5.2.2 Value added tax

Although there are provisions for market value in VAT legislation, it must be extremely rare for these to apply to unquoted shares. If this were the case, reference should be made to the valuation provisions of VATA 1994, s 19(5) and Sch 6, para 6.

6 Valuation techniques

'A share in a joint stock is an entirely conventional creation; the congeries of rights and liabilities of which it consists is the creature of the Companies Acts and the memorandum of the particular company. Within the law the rights and liabilities appurtenant to a share may vary widely. But it cannot exist independently of the inherent attributes with which it has been created.'

(per Lord MacMillan in *IRC v Crossman* (1936) 15 ATC 94 at 118
case 17 para 82)

This chapter addresses the techniques that can be used to put a value on this conventional creation, a share. The appropriateness of different techniques varies according to different classes of shares, different shareholdings and different types and situations of a company. When concerning oneself with arithmetic calculations following one or another technique, it is important to keep in mind that what we are valuing is a congerie of particular rights specified in the articles of a particular company.

6.1 Earnings basis

If we pose the question: 'Why will someone pay money for this share?' the answer is, clearly, to obtain benefit in the future. The only benefit that arises is the benefit of profits generated by the company. Where the investment is in a property investment company, the major profit anticipated may well be the profit generated on the ultimate disposal of the company's investments. A property investment company is required by Accounting Standards to value property it owns at its current market value in each annual set of accounts. Hence, the published balance sheet anticipates a portion of the profit that is anticipated ultimately to arise on disposal of investment properties. For a trading company, the link is more direct. What the prospective purchaser is prepared to pay for the shares is a reflection of the profits he anticipates the trading company will make in the future. His enjoyment of those profits will rarely be immediate, as few companies have a policy of distributing 100 per cent of earnings but, as discussed in section **5.1**, earnings, even when not distributed, benefit the shareholder in the long term. Viewed in this manner, the price that will be paid for a share is a direct reflection of the value it is perceived will flow from ownership of that share. As the values that will flow are a direct consequence of the profits that will be generated by the company, a central part in share valuation must be the measurement of earnings.

Central to the argument given above is that an investor looks to the future. Arithmetic measure of profits will nearly always be on profits generated in the past. However, it is essential for the valuer to recognise that he is looking to the future and the only relevance of the past is the extent to which he believes the results of the past will be replicated in the future.

In *Caton's Administrators v Couch* [1995] STC (SCD) 34 **case 38**, a simple approach to earnings information is adopted by the Commissioner (at 52h–53a **case 38 para 82**). In order to prepare a value on 7 September 1987, he looks at profits for the years ended 30 August 1984, 1985, 1986 and the information available for 1987. He then considers the evidence that has been presented to explain why exceptionally large profits were anticipated for 1987. The object of this analysis is to suggest a level of profit that is reasonable to assume will be sustainable in future years.

Earnings basis is certainly relevant to a controlling interest, as the investor effectively has direct access to earnings and, by controlling the composition of the board, has a large degree of control over directors' emoluments and dividend policy. There is also more scope to dictate when the entire shareholding is ready for sale. An influential minority holding can at best thwart a sale, although this also might be true of someone holding more than 10 per cent, unless a purchaser is happy to be involved with a minority shareholder. That minority shareholder might, though, be in a worse position and so in practice is likely to go along with an offer for the entire company, provided it is generally fair.

Unless shareholdings are fragmented, even an influential minority shareholder would find that his influence is largely negative. There is no logical reason why a large minority shareholder should be entitled to a seat on the board and particularly so in the case of a family company that is closely knit. He can have no say, therefore, in dividend policy and so if there are no dividends, the only cash flow from his holding is likely to be on either the disposal of the entire company (the likely best outcome) or simply being able to sell his shares to another party, including an existing shareholder.

What the earnings can do, perhaps, to the minority shareholder, is suggest what value the company might realise on a total sale and so the maximum sale proceeds are likely to be the appropriate percentage of that figure. It then has to be judged when a sale is likely, if at all, and discount that for the time factor, risk and general uncertainty. Much would depend upon the overall size of the company as the larger it is the more likely that, with earnings growth in particular, it would become more attractive to the outside world as a target and the shareholdings might become more fragmented. This is often the case in large private companies as they move through the generations and the shares are inherited by a large number of individuals, in a pyramid fashion. There is likely to be pressure for an improved dividend policy, given profitability, and perhaps even a market of some sort for shares, as some family members are interested in converting their holdings into cash and other family members become interested in topping up their holdings.

A minority shareholder could well be locked in for years. Unless dividends are declared, no income is received from his holding. At best, he has a nuisance value, which may lead another shareholder to buy him out. When valuing such a shareholding, it is relevant to consider what funds are available to the other shareholders as they are likely to be those who would offer the best price, provided they have the resources. It should be borne in mind that the company is a potential purchaser on a buy back of its own shares, again subject to having sufficient funds to meet a purchase. Even so, the other shareholders must agree to this, which simply becomes a convenient means of financing the acquisition rather than finding monies personally.

Non-dividend paying companies are more problematical, as recognised by HMRC Share Valuation. HMRC Share Valuation manual states:

> 'Ascertaining the necessary details of the properties in the portfolio and estimating their value is fraught with difficulties.'
>
> (SVM1870)

The manual advises use of the P/E ratio, but then goes on to state:

> 'The valuation approaches described above can make the valuation of minority holdings in non-dividend paying companies appear a somewhat mechanical arithmetical exercise. That is far from the truth. A good share valuer is not an automaton: [a good share valuer] thinks both imaginatively and realistically about every valuation.
>
> The valuer should always stand back and cross-check with common sense to ensure that the valuation does in fact reflect realism. Merely to value all shareholdings on the same basis by simply applying arithmetical formulae, irrespective of the particular circumstances, serves no useful purpose. In every case it is necessary to use judgement even though in some cases such judgement will be more informed than others: but in all cases it means thinking about the company.'
>
> (SVM17040)

If a majority shareholding is being valued, there is, in the author's view no difference in valuing the shares of a company that pays a dividend and a company that has reserves but chooses not to pay a dividend. The payment of a dividend is entirely in the hands of the directors and the holder of a majority holding can appoint directors to pay, or not to pay, a dividend as he wishes.

When valuing a minority holding in a family company, it is necessary to consider why the company has its dividend policy. Several family companies are known to the author that pay a dividend of a regular sum each year, irrespective of profits generated. The payment of the dividend is made simply because the family members who hold the shares expect a constant income. The directors feel that it is their duty, as family members, to pay a constant dividend. When valuing a shareholding for a fiscal purpose, the valuation is based on the amount that a hypothetical unconnected purchaser would pay. That is different from a family member. If an unconnected person were to hold a significant number of shares, it is perfectly possible that the directors of the family company would simply stop paying dividends.

Conversely, a company that has no history of paying dividends may be encouraged to pay dividends in the future if the majority of shares are held by directors who can receive a quasi remuneration from a dividend without the necessity of paying NICs. Such a change will clearly benefit the shareholder who is not a director.

In the author's view, the presence or absence of a dividend should rarely influence the valuation of the shareholding, unless there are cogent reasons for believing that the dividend will continue either as a fixed amount each year or as a fixed percentage of the company's earnings each year.

6.1.1 Earnings per share

SSAP 3, as amended by FRS 3, defines 'earnings per share' as:

> 'The profit in pence attributable to each equity share, based on the profit (or in the case of a group, the consolidated profit) of the period after tax, minority interests and extraordinary items and after deducting preference dividends and other appropriations in respect of preference shares, divided by the number of equity shares in issue and ranking for dividend in respect of the period.'

Since 1992, earnings per share has been calculated on profit after extraordinary items. Before 1992, earnings per share was calculated on profit before extraordinary items. This creates a problem where it is appropriate to look at profit generated in accounting periods, some of which fall before the 1992 amendment to SSAP 3 (carried forward into FRS 3) and some of which fall after the 1992 amendment. This was illustrated most graphically by the directors of Grand Metropolitan plc, who chose to restate their accounts for the year ended 30 September 1992 on the basis of adopting the amendment for that year. The results were as follows:

Old Method		New Method	
	£m		*£m*
Operating profit	1,073	Continuing business	905*
		Discontinued business	132
		Operating profit	1,037
		Continuing business	28
		Discontinued business	(446)
Exceptional items	48	Exceptional items	(418)
Interest	(171)	Interest	(171)
Profit before tax	950	Profit before tax	448
Tax and minorities	(350)	Tax and minorities	(230)
Profit after tax	645	Profit after tax	218
Extraordinary items	(427)	Profit for the year	218
Profit for the year	218		
Earnings per share	32.4p	Earnings per share	11.0p
		* £1,073m less £36m reorganisation costs	

6.1.2 Adjusted earnings

The value of a shareholding is the value that shareholding would have for the person acquiring the holding. In a fiscal valuation, this is a hypothetical purchaser. Depending upon the particular circumstances of the company, its other shareholders and the position of the company in the industry, this may be one of an indeterminate number of potential hypothetical purchasers bidding to acquire the holding for its inherent qualities. Alternatively, the hypothetical purchaser may be in the market where there is a special purchaser who wishes to acquire the shares for his own specific purpose.

A special purchaser may be another company in the same industry, which would be interested in acquiring a controlling shareholder with a view to absorbing the administration of the target company into its own established management team, thereby taking advantage of economies of scale. The basis of a share valuation is the benefit to be obtained from the share ownership in the future. It follows that, in this scenario, the earnings that could be enjoyed by the company purchasing the shares would be enhanced by saving on administration cost.

An alternative scenario is presented in the situation that is common in family companies where the same individuals are the directors and the shareholders and the profits generated are passed to those individuals by means of enhanced directors' remuneration, perhaps in order to permit increased pension provisions. The hypothetical purchaser with which we are concerned would, in this situation, first need to consider whether, as a shareholder of the size of shareholding on offer he could stop – or, at least, limit – excessive directors' remuneration. If he formed the view that he could do so, he would wish to calculate the earnings of the company ignoring the payroll cost of payments to directors in excess of the market salary for performing the particular task and, also, ignoring payments to directors who were not necessary for the actual operation of the company's business. There are many further reasons for adjusting the company's published results before undertaking calculations that lead to a valuation.

It is considerably easier to undertake adjustments on pre-tax profits. For this reason, and also for the reason discussed in section **6.1.3**, it is suggested that all earnings calculations be undertaken on the basis of pre-tax profits, the tax charge being deducted as a final step.

A possible adjustment of the profits is illustrated in the following example:

A value at 31 March 1982 is to be determined of a 55 per cent shareholding in a trading company with the following published results:

	Pre-tax profits	£
	y.e. 31 December 1981	600,000
	y.e. 31 December 1980	400,000
	y.e. 31 December 1979	700,000
	y.e. 31 December 1978	20,000
	y.e. 31 December 1977	100,000

	Directors' remuneration £	Pension contribution £
y.e. 31 December 1981	200,000	100,000
y.e. 31 December 1980	300,000	100,000
y.e. 31 December 1979	50,000	50,000
y.e. 31 December 1978	500,000	300,000
y.e. 31 December 1977	100,000	100,000

For the accounts year ending (y.e.) 31 December 1981 a new accounting basis was adopted for stock.

Restatement of stock on the new basis prices:

	As reported £	Restated £
31 Dec 81	1,000,000	1,000,000
31 Dec 80	1,200,000	1,100,000
31 Dec 79	800,000	600,000
31 Dec 78	1,100,000	800,000
31 Dec 77	500,000	450,000

It is considered that reasonable remuneration for the directors would be £100,000 plus pension contributions of £20,000, at 31 December 1981 prices.

An appropriate index for directors' remuneration is chosen, which gives the following index numbers:

1981	149.6
1982	133.8
1983	113.4
1984	99.8
1985	92.4

On the basis of the above figures, the following calculation of adjusted earnings is undertaken:

	Reported Profits	Add back directors' remuneration and pension	Reasonable remuneration and pension	Adjustment for opening stock	Adjustment for closing stock	Adjusted pre-tax profits
	£	£	£	£	£	£
y.e. 31 Dec 81	600,000	300,000	(100,000)	100,000	–	900,000
y.e. 31 Dec 80	400,000	400,000	(89,000)	200,000	(100,000)	811,000
y.e. 31 Dec 79	700,000	100,000	(76,000)	300,000	(200,000)	824,000
y.e. 31 Dec 78	20,000	800,000	(67,000)	100,000	(300,000)	553,000
y.e. 31 Dec 77	100,000	200,000	(62,000)	150,000	(100,000)	288,000

It is important that a valuer should be aware of the level of inflation that has existed in the economy during the period under inspection and consider whether the characteristics of the particular business being analysed are such that inflationary pressures on either costs or selling prices can affect reported profits. It is instructive to note that the retail prices index rose by 78 per cent over the five years up to 31 March 1982. It is important to bear this in mind when inspecting accounts over that five-year period. Some share valuers perform calculations based on profits adjusted by the change in retail prices index. It is suggested that this is not an appropriate approach as profitability of an enterprise is not linked to costs in the economy in such a direct fashion. In many cases the use of weighted average, which gives greater importance to the results of years closer to the valuation date, is sufficient.

6.1.3 Taxation

Rates of tax applied on company profits have been:

Year beginning 1 April	Full rate	Small companies' rate	Rate on capital gains See note
2006	30%	19%	
2005	30%	19%/0%	
2004	30%	19%/0%	
2003	30%	19%/0%	
2002	30%	19%/0%	
2001	30%	20%/10%	
2000	30%	20%/10%	
1999	30%	20%	
1998	31%	21%	
1997	33%	23%	
1996	33%	24%	
1995	33%	25%	
1994	33%	25%	
1993	33%	25%	
1992	33%	25%	
1991	33%	25%	
1990	34%	25%	
1989	35%	25%	
1988	35%	25%	
1987	35%	27%	
1986	35%	29%	30%
1985	40%	30%	30%
1984	45%	30%	30%
1983	50%	30%	30%
1982	52%	38%	30%
1981	52%	40%	30%
1980	52%	40%	30%
1979	52%	40%	30%
1978	52%	42%	30%
1977	52%	42%	30%
1976	52%	42%	30%

Note: *Since 1986, capital gains have been taxed at the corporation tax rate applicable to the total profits of a company*

This table demonstrates that there has been a very significant change in the rates of tax suffered by a company on its profits. Arithmetic calculations for an earnings basis valuation are very frequently performed on five years' profits. As is clear from the table above, there have been periods when the rate of corporation tax has remained constant for a significant number of years. There have been other periods of rapid change. In the four years from 1982 to 1986, the rate dropped from 52 per cent to 35 per cent. The golden rule in share valuation is to estimate the price that would be paid for benefit received in the future. If you are valuing a shareholding in 1986, it is the rate of 35 per cent that you build into your calculation, as this is the rate you expect to pay in the future; the higher rates are history and irrelevant. (If the company makes profits that are always likely to be within the band for small companies rate, the rate of 29 per cent is the relevant rate.) A hypothetical purchaser in 1986 would not be interested in the rate of corporation tax for 1981. Calculations should, thus, be performed on the basis of the rates of tax that will apply in the future, insofar as these are known at the valuation date.

For a 31 March 1982 valuation, the information on tax rates available on that date was an announcement made by Geoffrey Howe, the Chancellor of the Exchequer, in his Budget on 9 March 1982. The Chancellor announced that the full rate of corporation tax from 1 April 1981 was to be 52 per cent and was to be applied to profits over £225,000, with a small companies' rate of 40 per cent applied to profits under £90,000. This gave a marginal rate of 60 per cent. (It was then the practice to announce rates of corporation tax at the end of the financial year.) In the author's view, the appropriate way of calculating company earnings in relation to a share valuation as at 31 March 1982 is to apply to an anticipated maintainable pre-tax earnings the rate of corporation tax that was announced on 9 March 1982.

In published statistics, there are two approaches to the calculation of earnings per share. The *Financial Times* (see Appendices 4 and 8) uses 'actual basis' earnings per share in its statistics; on this basis, earnings per share. is calculated using the tax actually paid by the company. The *Investors Chronicle* uses 'full basis' earnings per share in its statistics; on this basis, earnings per share is calculated using the full charge to tax, being the tax paid plus the charge to deferred tax plus deferred tax not provided. Whilst an understanding of this is necessary to interpret published statistics, it is suggested that when calculating the adjusted earnings of a target company, the logic of focusing on the future rather than the past requires a notional tax charge to be computed at the rate of tax that it is known will be applied in the future. It is suggested that this rate of tax should be applied to the adjusted profits, as computed. In that way, account is made of the tax charge that will ultimately be borne, without having to take account of the timing differences that still apply, although less than previously, between the measurement of accounting profit and the measurement of profit for tax purposes.

For many companies the size of profits is such that it is clear that the notional tax charge should be calculated at the full rate of corporation tax. Other companies have profits at a level such that it is equally clear that the small company rate is the rate that is applicable. More difficult judgement is required where profits suffer the marginal rate between the full rate and the small company rate, or for companies whose profits oscillate between rate bands. Again, it is suggested that the logic of the principle of valuation as looking to the future requires a view to be taken of the rate that is expected in the future. It is considered that it is not valid to apply different rates to the profits of different years, even where the oscillation in the profit is such that some years would attract only the small company rate whereas others would attract the full rate.

From 1 April 2000 to 31 March 2002, the first £10,000 of profit attracted corporation tax at 10 per cent only (FA 1999, s 26) and from 1 April 2002 to 31 March 2006 no corporation tax was charged on the first £10,000 of profit (ICTA 1988, s 13AA). However, there was a marginal rate of 22.5 per cent applied to profits between £10,000 and £50,000, which had the effect that a company generating profit above £50,000 received no benefit from the new corporation tax starting rate of 10 per cent/0 per cent. For the majority of share valuations, therefore, this starting rate can be ignored.

6.1.4 P/E Ratio

The price/earnings (P/E) ratio and earnings per share have an inverse link:

$$P/E \text{ ratio} = \frac{\text{price} \times \text{no of shares}}{\text{earnings}}$$

$$\text{earnings per share} = \frac{\text{earnings}}{\text{no of shares}}$$

$$\text{therefore, } P/E = \frac{\text{price}}{\text{earnings per share}}$$

HMRC Share Valuation rely heavily on use of P/E ratios. The HMRC Share Valuation Manual states, even for non dividend paying companies:

'The P/E ratio method is to be preferred for the following reasons:

- it is less unwieldy than using percentages
- the relationship between the earnings per share and the price can be seen more readily
- the grossing-up stage can be omitted
- the press and accountants refer to it rather than to earnings yields.

The disadvantages of the method referred [in the manual] have become less significant as companies' actual tax charges have become closer to "full" tax charges.'

(SVM17040)

The instruction given to HMRC valuers is:

'Comparisons with the stock market
The first action to be taken when comparing an unquoted company with the stock market is to find a direct quoted comparable. Depending on the nature

of the business and the size of the unquoted company concerned, a search for suitable comparables should be made in all the quoted markets. Although companies quoted on the main market are usually far too big and diversified to be compared directly with the general run of unquoted companies which pass through the Shares Valuation Division, it may be possible to find a more suitable quoted comparable in the Alternative Investment Market (AIM), formerly the Unlisted Securities Market (USM) and Rule 4.2. In this search it is not likely that an exactly identifiable company can be found, but where a company is engaged in a broadly comparable trade it is possible to make adjustments for the differences, e.g., higher dividends.

Failing such a comparable it might be possible to use a particular sector. In such an exercise care should be taken to consider whether industry constituents which are for one reason or another way out of line with the average should be included or whether a comparison with only certain of the constituents is appropriate.

Occasionally it may be necessary to have regard to quoted P/E ratios found in the Financial Times Actuaries Share Indices [FTASI]. However, there are drawbacks due to the fact that the companies which make up the constituents of Financial Times Actuaries Share Indices are:

- very large organisations "blue chip" status
- invariably dividend paying, so a straight comparison between the P/E ratio from FTASI and a non-dividend paying unquoted company is not usually possible.

It would be logical to assume however that since an important factor determining price will be dividend return, a quoted company which does not pay a dividend for any length of time would have a much lower P/E ratio than a similar quoted company which was paying a dividend.

Adjustments to make

It is reasonable to assume that the required P/E ratio for unquoted companies which are not paying a dividend will be some fraction of the P/E ratio obtainable in the quoted market.

In determining what fraction (or multiple) to take the valuer should consider amongst other things:

- what level of dividend the company could afford; and
- when the company could/might pay a dividend.

There are no hard and fast rules and valuers should treat each case on its own merits.

As a guideline in the case of small non-influential minority holdings in small trading companies it might be reasonable to start from a required P/E ratio of between 1/4 and 1/5 of the quoted ratio (or 4 to 5 times the Financial Times Actuaries Share Indices earnings yield).

NB Higher or lower figures may be dictated by the quality of the unquoted company.'

(HMRC Share Valuation Manual, SVM17040)

There are very real difficulties in using published P/E ratios as a guide for the valuation of shares in a private company. A P/E ratio published in the *Financial Times* is calculated on prices being paid for very small percentages of the company's issued share capital. The purchase is being made, whether by an individual or by an institution, in the expectation of receiving a regular dividend or, sometimes, taking advantage of an increase in the share value in a relatively short period of time. A person purchasing a holding in a small private company is probably purchasing a significant percentage of the total issued share capital and is likely to expect to retain that shareholding for a significant length of time. A professional investor in a quoted company is likely to know a great deal about the performance of the individuals who manage the company but very little of the personal qualities of those individuals, their aspirations and who is likely to follow in the direction of the company. The situation for a small family company is typically the reverse of this.

A further very substantial problem is that quoted companies do not adequately reflect the range of industries in the economy. There are no quoted farming companies and there are no quoted companies investing in residential property. Hence, the appropriate P/E ratio to be applied in valuing a company of either of these two types is a matter of conjecture. Even when there are several quoted companies in the industrial sector in which the target company operates, the comparison may be flawed. Many quoted companies are conglomerates whereas most unquoted companies concentrate their activities in one industrial sector, often in a very narrowly defined part of that sector. It is not unusual to find an unquoted company relying for a very substantial percentage of its profit on one particular product.

An alternative approach is to estimate a P/E ratio by virtue of the required yield. Any investor can purchase Government Stock and be certain that investment is returned by redemption at par on the stated date (or, in the case of index linked stock, the certainty is that redemption is a return of the 'true' value of the sum invested). For an investor to purchase shares in a quoted company, he accepts a risk and, therefore, requires an anticipated return significantly higher than that available from gilts. For an investor to purchase shares in an unquoted company, not only does he accept the commercial risk but he accepts the very real risk (or, perhaps, certainty) that it will be difficult to sell his shareholding. Hence, the price paid for shares in an unquoted company should reflect a very high anticipated yield. A yield two to three times that available on gilts is not uncommonly used in calculations.

This approach can, however, be criticised as it does not readily allow for the differences in P/E ratios that are experienced between different industries.

6.1.5 P/E ratios in practice

It would no doubt be helpful to give some idea of the range of appropriate P/E ratios. This is, though, a very difficult exercise and could end up with too rigid an approach. Nevertheless, the practitioner will probably look for some guidance, otherwise he will be completely in the dark. The HMRC Share Valuation Manual does not now give a table of pre-tax profit multiples. A previous edition of the manual gave pre-tax profit multiples for the period 1979 to 1986. If the later years in that table are taken, the pre-tax multiples are somewhere between 5 and 9. If converted to post tax multiples, taking a 20 per cent tax rate, the ratios would become somewhere between 6.5 and 11.5.

For a company with a solid performance and a wide customer base, etc so that earnings are likely to be maintained, a ratio higher on the scale could be applied. On the other hand, a one product or one customer company, with considerable risk if that product should be overtaken by technology, for example, or the main customer lost, suggests higher risk and therefore at the other end of the multiple scale. A company dealing in luxury goods or services must be of higher risk if a recession is expected, whereas in boom conditions its profits might be expected to jump. The profitability is likely, though, to be volatile, so simply taking current maintainable profits and applying a multiple to that would not seem to be sensible, without reflecting the volatility factor to some degree. If the country is in recession and this affects the profitability, the valuer needs to take a balanced view as to what the future is likely to hold and perhaps discount to a large degree the current poor results. This is certainly very subjective but is all a potential investor could do. This comes back to the point, though, that the fiscal valuer cannot pick his time as in reality a company is not likely to be put on the market in poor trading conditions, unless it is not likely to trade out of those conditions and a sale is the only realistic step to take.

6.2 Assets basis

6.2.1 Value to the business

It is necessary to approach an asset basis calculation with caution. The following illustration shows the type of calculation often produced:

A trading company has 100 shares in issue. Its balance sheet can be summarised as follows:

	£	£
Factory (freehold)		2,800,000
Other assets		1,000,000
Taxation	(200,000)	
Other liabilities	(500,000)	
		3,100,000

The current market value of the freehold is £5,000,000.

The full asset value could be calculated as:

	£	£
Factory	5,000,000	
Other assets		1,000,000
Deferred tax charge on revaluation £5,000,000 − £2,800,000 @ 30% =		(660,000)
Other liabilities, as stated £200,000 + £500,000	(700,000)	
		4,640,000
Full asset value per ord	£464,000	

This calculation can be criticised on at least three grounds:

(a) No liability for anticipated costs of breaking up the business has been put into the calculation and, hence, the calculation must be on the basis of the use for the assets in the continuing trade of the company. Why, then, is a deduction made for the tax that would be payable if a capital gain were triggered by the sale of the factory? Even if it were sold, presumably the continuing needs of the business would require purchase of new premises with rollover relief being claimed.

(b) If this is a calculation of full asset value of the company, the most important asset is omitted. The most attractive feature of a trading company with a successful history is the goodwill it has generated. Should not goodwill be in the calculation of full asset value?

(c) The value of assets to a continuing business is the value those assets have in the business itself. There is no indication from this calculation that this has been considered. It could be argued that the price that could be fetched for selling the factory is irrelevant in the context of the company's trade continuing to be housed in that factory. A better measure could be the capitalised value of rent that would be paid if the company were a tenant.

When valuing shares of an investment company the asset basis is appropriate.

It can be argued that if a company has substantial assets, the investor takes a lower risk in purchasing the shares than if the company has a low net asset figure. This is, however, not always the case and it is difficult to directly judge the effect an asset base should have on a share value that is computed primarily on the earnings basis. (One way of attempting to solve this dilemma is to use a hybrid basis – see section **6.6** for a description of this basis and the criticism of it that leads to its rejection by HMRC Share Valuation.)

An asset basis is, however, relevant for a trading company in the following situations:

(a) The company is about to go into liquidation.
(b) The assets of the company are under-utilised and the company is loss making. (Here, a valuation of the majority shareholding could be on the basis that a purchaser would acquire the shares in order to liquidate the company and realise the assets. However, it is suggested that a substantial discount should then be put against the asset value to reflect the profit that a sophisticated investor of this nature would require.)
(c) Where there is an easily assessable market for significant sized assets in the company and the disposal of those assets would not adversely affect the trade of the company.

6.2.2 Break up value

In *Denekamp v Pearce*, a valuation for capital gains tax purposes at 31 March 1982 was required of a 24 per cent shareholding in a cash and carry business. This business had shown decline in profit and had moved into loss in the year immediately prior to the valuation date. In his judgement, THK Everett, the Special Commissioner said:

'Three possible scenarios concerning the future of the company post-1982 would be considered by the hypothetical purchaser. First the company might continue to trade for some time in the future. That would be unattractive to a purchaser to say the least. He would receive no dividend, could not compel the Board to accept him as a director nor could he enforce a liquidation. Secondly, the Board might decide to liquidate the company (as in fact happened in 1987). Although as things happened the 1987 liquidation proved a success, owing to the efforts of the taxpayer and his colleague, I believe that the prospect of an early liquidation of the company would not be attractive to a potential purchaser of the taxpayer's shares. He would be thinking in terms of a forced sale and its likely poor outcome.

Finally, there was the prospect of a sale of the company. The purchaser would know that the company had been on the market since 1981 with little interest shown but it is possible that he might be made aware of the interest of the businessman. The aborted meeting between the taxpayer and his father and the businessman took place in April 1982 and arrangements for such an appointment may well have been in place by 31 March 1982.

Like Mr Vassie, I take the view that a potential purchaser, being prudent and weighing everything in the balance, would have come to the conclusion that a sale of the company sometime in the future was the most likely outcome … '

([1998] STC 1120 at 1126h case 42 paras 39–41)

In that case, the Commissioner favoured a discount of 55 per cent.

In *M'Connel's Trustees v IRC* 1927 SLT 14 **case 12**, the court considered the valuation of a company that had made a loss in every year since its incorporation. The valuation approved by the court was on the basis of the realisable value of the assets in the company, less a reasonable sum to pay for the expenses of liquidating the company. It would be noted that the valuation was of a 99.8 per cent shareholding.

A similar approach was taken in *Re WF Courthope deceased* (1928) 7 ATC 538 **case 14**, where a brewing company had sold its brewing business. In that case, Rowlatt J approved a valuation based on the assumption that the assets stripper would be looking for a profit of 50 per cent.

6.2.3 Goodwill

Central to the consideration of an asset basis is goodwill. Where goodwill is purchased, it will appear in the balance sheet. However, for accounting periods ending after 22 September 1998, FRS 10 requires that purchased goodwill be amortised on a straight line basis. The effect of this is that, for a valuer, the figure shown for goodwill in a balance sheet is unlikely to be of significant relevance. Most goodwill is generated and, hence, there is no entry made for it in a company's published financial statements.

The valuation of goodwill was considered in *Buckingham v Francis*. Staughton J said:

> 'There is respectable authority for the method adopted by Mr Humpage for some companies in some circumstances. See the Accountants Digest No 132, para 11.2:
>
> "*Super profits approach.* The super profits approach has a long and ancient pedigree and appears in one form or another in most texts. The idea behind it is that there is a normal rate of return that can be earned on assets of a certain type but over a number of years it may be possible to earn profits in excess of this normal level. This method assumes that the purchaser will buy, in addition to the normalised value of the assets, a number of years super profits."'

([1986] 2 All ER 738 at 741)

The calculation method is stated expressly in the judgement of Lord Fleming in *Findlay's Trustees v IRC*:

'The only factor still in dispute is the figure of net profit which the purchaser may reasonably expect to earn from the business. Mr Geoghegan and Mr Robson are agreed with regard to the methods by which the net profits should be ascertained. They both take the view that for this purpose the net profits must include income tax and also the interest payable on debentures. They are also agreed that, when the figure of profits which the purchaser may expect to earn from the business is fixed, it should be multiplied by eight in order to ascertain the *cumulo* value of the whole business. The difference between them is that Mr Robson takes as his figure of expected profits the average of the three years prior to the deceased's death, whereas Mr Geoghegan takes the actual profits for the last of these years. Mr Robson takes the average for three years at £147,510, and multiplies it by eight, which gives him £1,180,080. From that he deducts the value of the tangible assets, £707,680, leaving a balance of £472,400, which he takes to be the goodwill of the whole business. Mr Geoghegan takes the profits for the year ended 1930 as £124,721, and multiplies it by eight, which brings out a figure of £997,768. From this he deducts the value of the tangible assets as before, £707,680, leaving £290,088 as the value of the goodwill.'

((1938) 22 ATC 437 at 441 **case 18 para 6**)

This case neatly demonstrates the difficulty faced by a valuer in choosing to use the assets basis of valuation as giving a more reliable result than the earnings basis. In using the assets basis, a significant figure is put to the value of goodwill, being an asset of the business. However, the way in which that asset value is calculated is by reference to the earnings of the business. When, then, is the asset basis used if the largest asset is calculated on earnings?

Goodwill can be distinguished from trademarks and other intangible rights, which are considered in Chapter 13.

6.3 Discount for non-marketability

In the 1980s it was routine with many accountants to produce an arithmetic calculation of the value of an unquoted shareholding and then to add, as a final line, a percentage discount for non-marketability of the shares. The Inland Revenue Shares Valuation Division (as it then was) routinely rejected the discount for non-marketability, on the basis that the P/E ratio used in the calculation already reflected the difficulty of marketing the holding being valued. Since the enactment of FA 1988, the largest number of share valuations that has been required by the majority of practitioners relate to the 31 March 1982 value of shares, being the base cost in a capital gains tax computation. It was interesting to see how often the final line in the computation sent to Shares Valuation Division no longer appears; no discount for non-marketability is offered.

The rationale of a discount for non-marketability arises from the principle that has its clearest expression in the judgement of Plowman J in *In re Lynall deceased*:

> 'It is common ground that the shares must be valued on the basis of a hypothetical sale on 21 May 1962 ... on the hypothesis that no one is excluded from buying and that the purchaser would be registered as the holder of his shares but would then hold them subject to the articles of association of the company, including the restrictions on transfer.'
>
> ([1971] 3 All ER 914, HL at 377 **case 29 para 4**)

Thus, the discount that is applied is not for marketability on the hypothetical sale being considered; it is for the lack of marketability of the shares that the hypothetical purchaser acquires. Viewed in this manner, the use of a specific discount figure in all valuations is clearly incorrect. If the valuation is of a minority interest in a company that has a regular pattern of dividends, the valuation may be based on the dividend flow that is expected. In this case, the difficulty in selling the shareholding in the future is likely to have a less depreciatory effect than a holding in a non-dividend paying company where the benefit expected from the shareholding is the increase in value that can be realised on a subsequent sale. It is suggested that it is also necessary to consider the likelihood of an offer being made for the entire share capital of the company. Here, it is necessary to look at the ownership of the other shares in the company. If the view is taken that other shareholders would wish to block such a sale and their shareholding were such that this is possible, a discount for non-marketability would still be appropriate. If, however, the personal circumstances of the other shareholders and the pattern of share ownership in the company is such that a sale by all shareholders, including the hypothetical purchaser, is a likely outcome, there would seem to be no justification for discount for the non-marketability.

There are, perhaps, two separate lessons to be learnt from the above judicial comment. First, the valuer should be clear as to whether or not the P/E ratio he suggests reflects the difficulty that may be faced by the hypothetical purchaser in selling his holding. If the P/E ratio already takes account of this, no further deduction would appear to be appropriate. Secondly, if a discount for non-marketability is specified separately, the actual percentage is far from a constant number applied in each and every valuation; as much thought needs to be put into the determination of the percentage discount as is required in all other aspects of the valuation.

A useful illustration of the application of a discount for non-marketability is given by the judgement of Danckwerts J in *Re Holt*. In that case, the valuation is of a sizeable minority holding of both ords and prefs in a trading company:

> 'Mr Benson thought that having regard to the steady dividend policy of the company a purchaser would count on a dividend at the rate of 5 per cent not being reduced, but on the other hand he would not expect it to be

increased. Mr Benson thought that the absence of any quotation of the shares on the Stock Exchange and the restrictions on transfer to which the purchaser would be subject when he got on the register, were factors which would make a purchaser require a further 1½s per cent of income yield in reaching the appropriate price for the shares.

Mr Benson supported his evidence with various tables containing the figures relating to various companies whose shares had a quotation on the Stock Exchange, and other figures obtained from the Actuaries' Investment Index. Such tables are not without a value, as they provide some possible basis of comparison for the purpose of checking the calculations of a witness, but it is easy to attack them on the ground that the varying circumstances of the companies, and the company not quoted on the Stock Exchange, may render the comparison of little value. On this basis Mr Benson reached a figure of 15s 2d per share, and to this he added the sum of 1s 6d, making a figure of 16s 8d. The addition of 1s 6d represented Mr Benson's estimate of the allowance which a purchaser might make in his offer for the possibility sooner or later of the company's shares being offered to the public, with a resulting capital accretion in some way to the shares held by a previous purchaser. Mr Benson considered that the time for this event would be later rather than sooner, and this was one of the points on which his evidence differed considerably from that of the witnesses for the Commissioners of Inland Revenue, who considered that the issue of shares to the public would be sooner rather than later, and attributed a much greater value to this factor. Finally, Mr Benson added a further sixpence to his estimated price as representing the amount of the net dividend likely to be declared in respect of the year 1947. Thus the value which he placed upon the shares was 17s 2d a share.'

((1953) 32 ATC 402 at 405 **case 25 paras 14–15**)

As can be seen, the discount suggested by the expert in this case was 30 per cent. Another witness, Frank Samuel, suggested a discount of 33 per cent (at 406/407) and his calculations resulted in a value of 12s 8d. A further witness, Roger Hornby, a stockbroker, declared that the practice of his firm was to deduct 20 per cent as a discount of a non-marketability and suggested a price of 16s (at 407). The witness called by the Revenue, Sir Harold Barton, did not suggest a discount for non-marketability and suggested a price of 25s, having previously, in correspondence, suggested a value of 34s (at 407). The court determined the value at 19s (at 410). In his judgement, Danckwerts J criticises the Revenue witness for ignoring or minimising the importance of the history of the company's trading, the possibility of losses and the effects of inflation. He does not, however, specifically criticise the lack of a discount for non-marketability in the evidence on behalf of the Revenue. As expected, the judgement does not give an arithmetical calculation to arrive at the value of 19s per share.

An interesting comment is made by Christopher Glover in ICAEW Accountants Digest 299: *The Valuation Of Unquoted Shares*:

'An informal survey of investment practice carried out by the author in 1981 indicated no pattern at all in these discounts. Indeed, there was considerable irrationality. Some investors did not even apply discounts for lack of marketability; others applied them selectively, and none agreed on a common level of discount. The most popular discount level amongst those who felt strongly on this matter seemed to be 25 per cent, although for some institutions it was as high as 50 per cent. The position was further clouded by the practice among some professionals of including in this discount an allowance for other factors such as risk.

In the United States various research studies have been carried out on the discount for lack of marketability. The SEC Institutional Investor Study Report of 1971 compared the price of quoted US stocks with that of their counterpart letter stocks. For the category which has most in common with the typical private company in the United Kingdom – most of the discounts fell in the 30 to 40 per cent range. Other US studies indicate an average discount for lack of marketability of 35 per cent.'

The informal survey undertaken by Christopher Glover was before the advent of the critical 1982 capital gains tax Base Cost Valuations. Writing in 1993, he says that he, personally, favours applying a discount for non-marketability when valuing the shares in the larger unquoted company, where comparison with quoted companies is appropriate but he does not, personally, apply a discount for the smaller private company as then his approach is to use a rate of return that allows for the lack of marketability.

6.4 Dividend basis

6.4.1 Calculation

Dividend yield for an individual company share is reported in figures published in the *Financial Times* and elsewhere as the net yield. That is, the calculation is on the cash dividend actually received. However, in the FT Actuaries table, the yield is the gross yield; that is, the calculation is on the cash dividend plus its accompanying tax credit. From 6 April 1999, the yield reported in the tables is, thus, higher than is actually available to a taxpayer who can neither use nor reclaim the tax credit, such as a pension fund.

When calculating the dividend yield, it is important to take account of the different sizes of tax credit that have applied to dividends. Prior to 6 April 1973, dividends were declared gross. From 6 April 1973 to 5 April 1993, the tax credit was at the basic rate of tax. From 6 April 1993 to 5 April 1999, the tax credit was 20 per cent. From 6 April 1999, the tax credit is 10 per cent. In all cases, the percentage applied is to the gross dividend (that is, the net dividend plus the tax credit).

In order to convert a net dividend to a gross dividend the calculation is:

$$\text{Gross dividend} = \frac{100 \times \text{net dividend}}{100 - \text{tax credit}}$$

Rates of tax credit applied to the gross dividend equivalent are:

2006/07	10%
2005/06	10%
2004/05	10%
2003/04	10%
2002/03	10%
2001/02	10%
2000/01	10%
1999/00	10%
1998/99	20%
1997/98	20%
1996/97	20%
1995/96	20%
1994/95	20%
1993/94	20%
1992/93	25%
1991/92	25%
1990/91	25%
1989/90	25%
1988/89	25%
1987/88	27%
1986/87	29%
1985/86	30%
1984/85	30%
1983/84	30%
1982/83	30%
1981/82	30%
1980/81	30%
1979/80	30%
1978/79	33%
1977/78	34%
1976/77	35%
1975/76	35%
1974/75	33%
1973/74	30%

If it is assumed that the dividend will stay at a constant amount each year, the calculation of share value on a dividend basis is:

$$\text{Share value} = \frac{\text{Dividend}}{\text{Required yield}}$$

Example:

A company is expected to declare a dividend of 5 pence (gross) every year.

The required yield is 15%

$$\text{Share value} = \frac{5p}{15\%} = 33.3p$$

If a company is expected to increase its dividend by a constant percentage each year, the constant growth formula can be used:

$$\text{Share value} = \frac{\text{Current dividend}}{\text{Required yield} - \text{Rate of dividend growth}}$$

Example:

As above, with the dividend expected to increase by 3 per cent per annum each year:

$$\text{Share value} = \frac{5p}{15\% - 3\%} = 41.7p$$

The constant growth formula above assumes that the share will be held in perpetuity. A more sophisticated calculation can be undertaken to amalgamate the two dividend flow with the proceeds of a sale after a specified number of years. Such a calculation is undertaken by using discounted cash flow (see section **6.8**).

6.4.2 Use of dividend basis

It is important to note that the above calculations take account of the dividend only. This is rarely the sole factor to be used in valuing an unquoted shareholding.

A severe criticism of any dividend basis of valuation, even when used as one of several tools in a valuation, is that the valuer must first form a view as to the dividends that will be applied in the future. In this context, 'the future' is the entire period for which it is anticipated that the hypothetical purchaser will retain the share. Many listed companies seek to maintain a constant level of dividend, often a dividend with a constant annual growth. Many listed companies fail to fulfil such hopes. Very few unlisted companies have such a stated objective and the difficulty of maintaining a constant rate of dividend growth for a company in a small part of an industry is readily apparent. Unless the dividend is a very small percentage of profits, an expectation of constant dividend growth is an expectation of constantly increasing profits. Given that the economy is, to a large extent, subject to a cyclical movement between expansion and retrenchment and an individual company's products will be, moreover, subject to changes in fashion and technological advance, it can readily be appreciated that a small company cannot realistically expect to have constantly increasing profits out of which constantly increasing dividends can be paid. A use of a dividend growth model can be criticised as imposing an inappropriate theory of company behaviour.

In the small percentage of cases where an unlisted company pursues a defined dividend policy, experience shows that the dividend is a very small percentage of earnings. In such a case, the criticism can be levied that it is the earnings that are of primary importance and the valuation should take account of this. In practice, the dividend basis is likely to be of use only as an element in a hybrid valuation (see section **6.6**).

In practice, only a minority of unquoted companies declare a dividend each year. For many unquoted companies, particularly those where the shareholders are all members of a closely knit family, the size of the dividend is directly linked to the personal circumstances of the shareholders, their need for cash and their particular taxation situations. Since the abolition of investment income surcharge in 1984, the net receipt from a dividend has been higher than the net receipt from a salary paid by the company, NICs being levied on salaries and not on dividends. With the abolition of ACT with effect from 6 April 1999, the attraction for a company of declaring a dividend is again increased as the payment of a dividend does not require any early payment of funds to HMRC. If, however, a minority shareholding that is the subject of the valuation were to be purchased by the hypothetical purchaser who is not a member of the family, he should expect that the directors will thenceforth avoid declaring a dividend and seek to cast remuneration to family members by taking them into the employment of the company. It follows that the history of dividends is frequently an irrelevance in valuing an unquoted shareholding.

6.4.3 Notional dividend

The dividend basis is undoubtedly attractive to a valuer as it provides an easy arithmetic calculation. Some valuers answer the criticisms levied above in section **6.4.2** by applying dividend yield calculations to a 'notional dividend'. Such a notional dividend is typically measured as one half of the company's post-tax profits. In the author's view, this merely adds a further unwarranted assumption to the criticisms discussed above in using dividends as a basis for valuation. The author sees nothing in the concept of a notional dividend that attracts him to use this approach.

6.5 Actual sales

At first sight, the clearest, simplest and most reliable way of determining the value of a share is to discover the price at which shareholdings in that company have actually been bought and sold. The price paid in actual sales does not, however, determine the market value at the valuation date. In *McNamee v IRC* [1954] IR 214 **case 26** the valuation was required of a holding of 175 shares as at the death of the shareholder on 17 October 1950. The company secretary negotiated the sale of that shareholding of the deceased in January 1951 and obtained a price of £1 10s per share. Previous sales had taken place at £1 and £1 5s ([1954] IR 214 at 224 **case 26 para 13**). That did not stop the judgement of the court being that the value for estate duties purposes was £1 12s 6d, a price higher than had ever been achieved in an actual sale. This does not mean that prices achieved at actual sales are to be ignored, or are inadmissible. Actual prices achieved on actual sales are part of the evidence to be considered in valuing a shareholding, as are values agreed with HMRC at other times and for other purposes (*IRC v Stenhouse's Trustees* [1992] STC 103 **case 36 para 13**).

In his judgement in *McNamee v IRC*, Maguire J said:

> 'The Finance Act 1894, s 1, enacts that estate duty shall be levied ... [on] the price which ... such property would fetch if sold in the open market at the time of the death of the deceased ...
>
> Accepting Mr McNulty's evidence as to the bona fides of the sale of these shares to Mr Kilpatrick, and granting that this price of £1 10s 0d is the highest ever paid for these shares in the history of the Company, I still must bear in mind that this was not a sale in any real or imaginary open market. I must make allowance for a sale in an imaginary open market ... I have given anxious thought and consideration to this, perhaps, in some ways, the most difficult part of task. I am satisfied that not more than £1 12s 6d – certainly not more than that – might have been obtained in the open market, an imaginary open market, for this lot of 175 shares. Accordingly I fix and determine the value of these shares at £1 12s 6d each.'
>
> ([1954] IR 214 at 216/220 **case 26 paras 2 and 21**)

An alternative approach is to look at the prices for dealings in shareholdings in a comparable company.

As a practical point, an actual sale of the shareholding being valued if it takes place shortly after the valuation date and is to an unconnected third party, is likely to have a significant influence on the negotiations between the valuer and HMRC Share Valuation, if such negotiations are continuing at the date of the sale. Such a situation is not uncommon when the valuation is for the purpose of determining a charge to inheritance tax arising at a death. A valuation at death must take into account the effect of the death (IHTA 1984, s 171). The actual effect of the death, in these circumstances, appears to be that the shares passed to the personal representatives who then quickly sold them to a third party. Of course, it may not be clear at the date of death that this will actually happen, but regard should be taken of the fact that such a sale is possible. For a sale of private company shares in the real world, it is often necessary for other shareholders to sell their shares at the same time if the best price is to be achieved. The co-operation of other shareholders may not have been reasonably foreseeable at the date of death. These are all factors that can be enquired into by the valuer. If shares to be valued are actually sold shortly after the valuation date, and this was readily anticipated at the valuation date, the valuation approach in such a circumstance could be to take the actual sale price and deduct an appropriate discount. The size of the discount would reflect the degree to which, given the death of the shareholder, a hypothetical holder of the shares at the date of death could have reasonably expected the course of events that actually occurred leading to the actual sale that was made.

In the Irish case of *McNamee v IRC* [1954] IR 214 **case 26**, a valuation was required of a small minority shareholding in the estate of Thomas McNamee deceased who died on 17 October 1950. The actual shareholding was sold by the executor to a Mr Kilpatrick. The negotiations for the sale took place in January 1951 and registration was on 19 September 1951 (at 224). Between these two dates, Mr Kilpatrick was appointed a director of the company (at 216). Evidence was given of other actual sales. 150 ords were sold in 1946 at £1 per ord and 777 ords were sold in May 1949 for £1 5s (at 224). The judge said:

> 'I am satisfied that the sale by him of these shares to Mr Kilpatrick was a bona fide business transaction at the best price obtainable by him at the time and in the circumstances.'
>
> ([1954] IR 214 at 229 **case 26 para 21**)

In the commercial world, the sale of the entire share capital of an unlisted company is often between unconnected parties and after considerable negotiation. The price paid can usually, thus, be regarded as an arm's length price. It must, however, always be borne in mind that this is a sale that is of 100 per cent of the share capital and is made when the vendor(s) has/have decided to accept the price offer, rather than retain the shares. Even where the sale is by a large number of shareholders, most if not all of whom are, thereby, selling minority holdings, the circumstance is an acquisition by the purchaser of the entire share capital. The hypothetical sale that is postulated in a fiscal valuation is a sale of the shareholding that is to be valued, not of the whole company, and there is no scope for the hypothetical vendor deciding to retain the shares until a better price is bid. It follows that whenever the actual price paid in actual sales is brought into a valuation, careful consideration should be given as to how these facts reflect on the value in the hypothetical sale that is required by statute.

The larger number of actual sales of unquoted shares takes place within a family group or between individuals who already have a connection through the company. The price paid on a transaction where there is such a family or business connection is often not a good indication of the value that must be placed under the statutory hypothesis.

6.5.1 Offer on the table at the time of valuation

There could well be negotiations in place for the sale of, say, the entire share capital of the company at the relevant date for the fiscal valuation. Thus, a minority holder could be in the position of the windfall gain based on his share of the overall value without discounts. The expression 'there's many a slip 'twixt cup and lip' comes to mind in these circumstances. If there are problems in due diligence or for some other reason the purchaser withdraws, the minority shareholder in particular is back to where he started. Anyone paying a price close to full value on a sale could be prejudiced seriously and so is likely to discount that price to protect this. This is perhaps another example where in practice a sale would not take place as the existing shareholder would almost certainly sit tight in the hope that the sale does go through.

Some years ago a client with an influential minority holding was considering the possibility of transferring shares to an overseas trust. By the time the client got round to doing something, there was an offer on the table. The transfer of slightly less than 25 per cent of the company was made to overseas trusts and about five months later the purchase did complete. However, in between, there were times when both parties walked away from the negotiating table and so there was a possibility of nothing happening. The shares were sold on the basis of an earnout as a top-up payment. After much argument with HMRC Share Valuation, the value for the holding transferred to the trusts was 45 per cent of the eventual base sale proceeds, ignoring the potential for additional consideration under the earnout.

6.6 Hybrid technique

The hybrid technique is an attempt to bring together different valuation approaches to give weight to various elements. In the UK, the strongest advocacy of the hybrid valuation approach is by Eastaway, Booth and Eamer. In their book is a graph that suggests the relative size of weighting to be applied to each element in the valuation, the ratio between the elements being determined by the size of the shareholding. Separate graphs are produced for a trading company and investment company.

The arithmetic form of a valuation prepared under the hybrid technique is illustrated by the following, which is taken from Eastaway, Booth and Eamer, *Practical Share Valuation*:

Value Element	Amount £	Weighting	Value £
Assets	3,000,000	12%	360,000
Earnings	4,000,000	18%	720,000
Dividends	2,000,000	60%	1,200,000
Prior sales	1,000,000	10%	100,000
			2,380,000
Less discount for non-marketability (say)		35%	(833,000)
			1,547,000

Elsewhere, it has been suggested that weighting of three elements can be applied as follows:

Valuation of shares in a trading company

	Asset basis	Weighting Earnings basis	Dividend basis
75–100% holding	80%	10%	10%
51–74% holding	20%	75%	5%
26–50% holding = largest holding	20%	65%	15%
= another holding is larger	10%	40%	50%
1–25% holding	10%	25%	65%

Valuation of shares in an investment company

	Asset basis	Weighting Earnings basis	Dividend basis
75–100% holding	90%	10%	0%
51–74% holding	50%	50%	0%
26–50% holding = largest holding	40%	20%	40%
= another holding is larger	20%	30%	50%
1–25% holding	20%	10%	70%

Judicial recognition of the hybrid technique is given by the judgement in *Central Trust Co v United States* (1962) 10 AFTR 2d 6203m (305 F 2d 393), where Saul Richard Gamer, the trial commissioner, in his judgement, said:

'The proper use of the comparative appraisal method, applying the principles already indicated, should provide a reasonably satisfactory valuation guide in these cases. In its application, it would under all the circumstances herein involved appear appropriate to select the three factors of (1) earnings, (2) dividends and dividend-paying capacity, and (3) book value, as being the important and significant ones to apply.'

(at 6216)

It is essential to note that this is a US case and, hence, not a precedent in any of the UK legal jurisdictions. Although, in principle, as the USA has a system of common law and US cases can be cited as persuasive authority in English courts, the decision is, arguably, a decision of fact and not of law and is given by a trial commissioner of a court of first instance. The decision is, thus, unlikely to carry the same weight as if it had been the decision of the higher US court, particularly as the English courts have not followed this line of valuation.

For the author, the hybrid technique has a certain attraction in that it gives an arithmetic solution to the problem of balancing a number of elements that need to be brought into a valuation. However, the author is not comfortable with the highly prescriptive application of the technique that is followed by many practitioners. In this connection, it must be noted that Eastaway and Booth, themselves, warn against unthinking acceptance of the percentage ratings suggested. For the author, a particular difficulty with the hybrid technique, as illustrated in the table above, is the strong influence that it gives to the dividend basis. As is clear from the comments in section **6.4**, the author considers the dividend basis is rarely appropriate in valuing unquoted shares and the concept of a notional dividend is, in his view, flawed.

6.7 Comparison with published prices

The stock market is an open market with prices on bargains being readily obtainable. An approach to valuing an unquoted shareholding could, thus, be by identifying prices actually paid in stock market bargains for quoted shares in a comparable company. These prices are readily obtainable in the Stock Market Official Daily List and are reported in the *Financial Times* and other newspapers. *The Stock Exchange Official Yearbook* provides a classification of quoted companies by sub-sector of the FT Actuaries All Share Index and this is a convenient starting point in a search for comparable companies. An alternative is the *Investors Chronicle* which analyses prices and yields of quoted companies by the sector in which they are clarified. An Extel card is available for each company and can be consulted to provide price information linked with the company's published accounts and factual information on acquisitions by the company, any reorganisations and analysts reports.

If the valuation of an unquoted shareholding is to be undertaken by comparison with reported figures, it is not appropriate to make the comparison with a single quoted company. Such a comparison, therefore, requires the valuer to glean information on a reasonable number of companies and to analyse that information to ascertain the degree to which each company selected can be regarded as comparable to a company whose shareholding is to be valued. A warning as to the possible inappropriateness of a comparison of this type is given by Plowman J in *Re Lynall deceased*, who said:

> 'Two approaches to the problem of an appropriate yield have emerged during the course of this case. The first is to take a purely arbitrary figure based on experience and expertise and work from that. The other is to ascertain the yield which can be obtained on investments in companies in the same general field of industry in the public sector, and then to apply an arbitrary figure of discount for the fact that one is dealing not with a public company but with a private company. The latter method has the advantage over the former that it at least starts on a factual basis, but it is open to criticism on a number of counts. For example, dividend policy in a private company is likely to be entirely different from dividend policy in a public company; and the regulations affecting the transfer of shares are likely to be entirely different in the two cases. Moreover, it is in the company, Linread Ltd, and its management and not in the industry that the hypothetical purchaser is likely to be interested. These are only examples, and there are no doubt numerous other factors which influence the stock market but are irrelevant in considering the value of shares in a private company, and in particular this company. It can, however, I think, safely be said that any method of calculation involves the introduction of at least one arbitrary figure somewhere along the line.'
>
> ([1971] 47 TC 375 at 387 **case 29 para 24(1)**)

Despite the generally adverse judicial criticism of the comparative approach, this is much used by HMRC Share Valuation. The approach favoured by HMRC Share Valuation is well illustrated in the following long extracts from the HMRC Share Valuation Manual when dealing with dividend paying companies:

'Comparisons with the "public sector"

By the "public sector" Mr Justice Plowman had in mind the only available market in equities that exists – The Stock Exchange. Despite the criticisms levelled against such comparisons the yields available in respect of companies operating broadly in the same industry illustrate:

> the state of the market at any given time from a potential investor's point of view which has to be postulated in the open market conditions

> the effects of relevant external factors on companies operating in more or less similar commercial fields; e.g. the economic climate, the political situation, and the movement of interest rates or sterling

the kind of yields that are required of equities (growth stocks) as opposed to fixed interest (safe income producing) stocks.

So, yields based on quoted prices are relevant, not because the company to be valued is quotable; but because they provide a **starting point** to which adjustments can be made for the points of difference.

As Sir Henry Benson stated in reply to a question concerning the determination of the dividend yield when giving his testimony to the House of Lords in *Lynall.*

"I first looked – and this so far as I am aware, indeed is the traditional method, the one which is applied in practice in my experience – at the dividend yields which were in fact being earned on quoted companies at about that time in this class of industry."

...

Adjustments to the quoted yield

If quoted yields are a starting point how then is the valuer to set about the task of applying "an arbitrary figure of discount" to arrive at the hypothetical purchaser's required yield?

As Justice Plowman said in the *Lynall* case, the discount is made:

"for the fact that one is not dealing with a public company ."

The valuer must decide what the differences are between the quoted sector and the company which is being valued. Then having appraised these points of difference, adjustments to the quoted yield are necessary. This will involve the valuer considering all or some of the following:

absence of quotation,
restriction on transferability;
control (are the shares tightly controlled?);
unusually high/low dividend cover;
liquidity and gearing;
size and diversification; and

any other exceptionally good or bad features.

The level of adjustment

For the absence of quotation and normal restrictions on transfer it is suggested that an uplift to the quoted yield of between 20 and 30% is appropriate along the lines recommended in the decided cases (e.g. *re Holt, re Crossman, re Lynall*).

For the other differences between the company and the quoted comparables, the adjustments will vary from company to company since no two companies are alike.

It will perhaps be the case that if the valuer is making comparisons with a number of quoted companies operating in the same sector which are broadly of the same size, then the adjustments will not be as great as if comparisons are being made with the Financial Times Actuaries Share Indices or one or more of its sectors.

Debit points such as:

>   poor liquidity
>   size in the case of a small company
>   poor dividend cover

will increase the required yield.

Plus points such as:

>   good dividend cover
>   good liquidity
>   low gearing

will reduce the required yield.

One method of making these adjustments is to add or deduct percentage points from the quoted yield.

Example

Starting – point	comparable quoted yield	4.80%
Plus	– 20%–30% uplift for absence of quote/restrictions on transfer;	0.96–1.44%
Say therefore		5.76–6.24%

>   Further adjustments should then be made to account for the differences in size and diversity and, possibly, liquidity, between the unquoted company and those in the quoted sector. A required dividend yield would then be around 8.5–9.5%.

>   An alternative method would be to look for a required yield of around double the quoted yield as a starting point. In the above example this would give 9.6%. This could then be fine tuned to reflect the precise situation of the particular company.

The above example is a broad illustration only; it must be stressed that each situation should be considered on its own merits.

The position might be e.g. that the **only** difference between a particular company and the quoted sector is the normal restrictions on transfer. In such a case a yield fairly close to the quoted yield might be appropriate.

The other extreme might be a small company with poor dividend cover where a multiple of 3 or 4 times the quoted yield might be reasonable.'

(HMRC Share Valuation Manual, SVM14040 and SVM14050)

The Manual then continues to give the Share Valuation examiner instructions as to the manner of selecting quoted companies which are potentially comparable (SVM14060). This is followed by instructions as to how to compare unquoted companies where there are no direct comparables (SVM14070). This latter incorporates the instruction:

'Valuers may ask themselves why bother undertaking a detailed comparability exercise which is so often time consuming. The answer here is that where the size etc. of the unquoted company makes a comparability exercise feasible it will normally give a much more accurate guide.'

The quoted P/E ratio has the following defects, when used in estimating the value of unquoted shares:

- P/E ratios vary considerably from industry to industry and even within an industry. An average can be deduced such as from the FT actuaries index but an average is simply that. The valuer of an unquoted company is considering that particular company.
- Following on, it is very difficult to find a comparable clearly and why choose something that is the closest, even though in reality it has no similarities whatsoever.
- A quoted P/E ratio fluctuates from day to day, depending upon the share price. It also reflects the more robust conditions in the market generally, whereas unquoted companies could well buck the trend and especially if the company is in a niche market.

At the time of writing this third edition, P/E ratios reported in today's *Financial Times* for main market trading companies range from 5.2 to 108.8, both extremes being found in the single category 'Food and Beverages'. (An even larger range can be found for investment companies.) The reason for the great variation is that the market price is that paid by the investor looking to the future whereas the reported P/E ratio is past performance. In 1936 John Maynard Keynes compared the behaviour of investors to a beauty contest where the judges are the readers of a newspaper. The task is not to decide which contestant is the prettiest but to have a choice that is the closest to the average choice of all readers. You must choose the faces that will please others most.

No one really knows what is going to influence future earnings and dividends and so investors spend their time trying to anticipate how the view held by all other investors will change. This is an approach that rarely translates into a valuation exercise for the shares of an unquoted company.

If profits are expected to increase then dividends should increase likewise, which has a further effect in increasing the desirability of a share. The valuer of an unquoted company, though, is looking to current and future maintainable earnings and so it cannot be appropriate to apply a quoted P/E ratio, based on historical data, to current earnings. Admittedly, an adjustment could be made for this, but if the valuer is not careful it simply becomes an arbitrary exercise with no grounding in reality or common sense. Why start with a P/E ratio at all? The author's criticism applies to one aspect of the evidence in *Caton's Administrators v Couch* [1995] STC (SCD) 34 **case 38**. The Revenue's valuer looked at quoted companies that he considered comparable and found that the reported P/E ratio was in the region of 18. He thought that too high so adjusted it to 12 to 14. It is difficult to see the value of looking at the quoted P/E ratio in the first place if he simply came to the conclusion that it was too high and knock a third off. No doubt this made sense in the context of the historical versus current comparison, but it does demonstrate the impossibility of making a real comparison. The taxpayer's expert witness, Bruce Sutherland, did not look at earnings at all in his valuation, but looked more to earnings as a source of dividends in the future.

The quoted P/E ratio is simply the result of taking the price found by the market divided by the historical earnings per share. This is simply an arithmetical result of those two figures. The P/E ratio is not used to determine the value of the share, whereas in unquoted companies the P/E ratio is the factor applied to earnings to arrive at the price. Thus, the quoted sector and the unquoted sector start from different ends.

The quoted share price is usually based on actual transactions involving a very small percentage of a company's issued share capital. Thus, it is quite often less than one per cent of the total and is simply representative of that and not of the value of the company as a whole. Indeed, as has been observed, on a takeover bid for a company the price usually increases, reflecting a premium for the value of even a quoted company as a whole.

It almost seems to come back to this, that a quoted P/E ratio can be used only if it seems a sensible figure and if it is not, it should be adjusted to arrive at such a figure. Why not start with a sensible figure in the first place based on expected returns from an unquoted company in terms of earnings and overall price? Thus, the quoted P/E ratio seems to have no influence whatsoever in reality given that it is ignored if it produces the wrong figure.

6.8 Discounted cashflow

Discounted cashflow is a method that is widely used to evaluate a capital project and is also frequently used to value a brand. In the UK, it is rarely used to value a shareholding.

The method requires the valuer to estimate what receipts will arise from the shareholding, both dividends and a capital receipt on the ultimate sale. These receipts are then discounted to the present by application of an appropriate discount rate. The aggregate of the receipts thus discounted is then the maximum price that would be justified for the investor to pay for the shareholding.

The basic formula for determining net present value is:

$$\frac{C_1}{1+K} + \frac{C_2}{(1+K)^2} \quad \frac{C_n}{(1+K)^n} + \frac{R}{(1+K)^n}$$

Where:

C = the cashflow forecast for each of the years 1 to n.

K = the discount rate (otherwise known as the cost of capital, or interest rate for the year, or required rate of return) expressed as a decimal.

R = the residual value of the business at the end of year n, less any remaining debt.

Each of the three elements required to perform the calculation presents problems to the valuer when the calculation is of the value of a shareholding.

In its pure form, C is the expected dividend. As discussed in section **6.4**, this is likely to be uncertain in all but the most rare situations. More usually C is taken to be the earnings of the company. The comments in section **6.1** on the use of the earnings basis, thus, apply equally here.

R is, of course, the price at which the shareholding will be sold at some date in the future. Although this is not the same as a share value under the statutory hypothesis, much of what is said about share value today applies equally to this value in the future. Hence, a real criticism of the discounted cash flow method is that it is essentially circular in that in order to compute a share value today it is necessary to compute a share value in the future. This difficulty disappears if it is assumed that the shareholding will be retained into infinity as the formula then operates to make the final factor 0.

The actual arithmetic value that is computed using discounted cash flow is heavily dependent on the value for K. When discounted cash flow is used to evaluate a capital project, it is likely that it is within the context of investment within a particular company, where the company has a policy of requiring a specified rate of return. To use discounted cash flow to estimate a share value for fiscal purposes, it is necessary, in principle, to consider all the different rates of return that will be required by all the hypothetical purchases in the hypothetical open market.

Discounted cash flow is recognised as a valid method of valuation in HMRC Share Valuation Manual (see SVM12050)

6.9 Risk analysis

The somewhat dismissive comments made on discounted cash flow as a valuation technique in section **6.8** may hide a potentially valuable use of discounted cash flow. Because it is a mathematical technique, once all the information has been input into a computer program, it is a work of a few minutes to obtain a variety of calculations based on a variety of values of the two determinates R and K. Depending on the nature of the information input, it may or may not be as easy to calculate by varying the value of C.

Varying the determinates in this way gives an indication of how sensitive the NPV is to changes. This is, in essence, risk analysis. Risk analysis is not greatly used in fiscal share valuations but has the potential to be a powerful weapon with which to argue against values suggested in negotiation that the valuer finds unacceptable. This will, perhaps, be most particularly the case where an HMRC officer argues a value based on comparability with quoted companies. Here, the valuer may accept various aspects of comparability but feel that inadequate notice has been taken of the fact that the investor in unquoted shares is accepting a much higher risk than an investment in the quoted comparables.

The principles of risk analysis can be illustrated as follows:

Company A (Food retailer)

Assumed state of the economy	*Probability*	*Rate of return*	*Probability-weighted outcome*
(1)	(2)	(3)	((2) × (3))
		%	%
Boom	0.3	35	10.5
Normal	0.4	27.5	11.0
Recession	0.3	20	6.0
	1.0		27.5
'Expected' rate of return = 27.5%			

Company B (Civil engineering)

Assumed state of the economy	Probability	Rate of return	Probability-weighted outcome
(1)	(2)	(3) %	((2) × (3)) %
Boom	0.3	95	28.5
Normal	0.4	35	14.0
Recession	<u>0.3</u>	(50)	<u>(15.0)</u>
	1.0		27.5
'Expected' rate of return = 27.5%			

Clearly, an investment in Company B carries more risk than one in Company A. With Company B there is a 30 per cent probability of losing money; with Company A the worst that can happen is that the rate of return falls to 20 per cent instead of the 'expected' 27.5 per cent. The standard deviation of Company A's rate of return is 5.8 per cent and that of Company B, 56.5 per cent.

If the probability distribution is normal (ie bell-shaped when graphed) there is a 68 per cent chance that the actual rate of return on Company A's shares will fall within one standard deviation of the 'expected' rate of return. In other words there is a two out of three chance that Company A's realised rate of return will be between 21.7 per cent and 33.3 per cent (ie 27.5 per cent plus or minus 5.8 per cent). For Company B the range is much wider, minus 29 per cent and 84 per cent (ie 27.5 per cent plus or minus 56.5 per cent), and this indicates the extent to which Company B is a riskier investment than Company A.

For further discussion of risk in assessment see Accountants' Digest 299: *The Valuation of Unquoted Shares* by Christopher Glover.

6.10 Use to purchaser

Implicit in much of the foregoing discussion is the notion that the purchaser will evaluate the shareholding by looking at it in isolation from any activity he undertakes himself or any other investments he has. This may not, necessarily, be the case. Depending on the particular characteristics of the company and the shareholding, there could be other companies who are in the market for the purchase of the shares and whose intention on purchase would be to merge the commercial activities of the target company with their own activities. This could be attractive in order to reduce administration costs, or to capture a larger percentage of the market for a similar product or to gain the benefits from wider geographical operation or vertical integration. Much of the discussion of the case law on a special purchaser (see section **4.6**) is relevant in this context. When valuing a controlling interest in a trading company, regard should always be taken of the possibility of a sale to another company. This possibility may also be relevant for a minority interest, where some or all of the other shareholdings in the company are held by individuals (or companies) who could be reasonably expected to link in with such an onward sale.

6.11 Different classes of shares

Where a company has more than one class of share in issue, the valuer has to deal with the additional problem as to how the value of the company is apportioned amongst the different classes of share.

The golden rule in such a situation is always for the valuer to read the company's articles and ensure that he fully understands exactly what rights are enjoyed by the holders of the different classes of share.

It is not uncommon for a company's issued share capital to consist of one class of ordinary shares and one or more classes of preference shares. In such a situation, the valuation of the preference shares can follow the procedure outlined in section **7.1** and the ordinary shares can be valued by treating the dividend on the prefs as a deduction from the earnings of the company.

Where there is a class of ordinary shares with a dividend entitlement but no voting power, it is probably relevant to apply the discount that can be observed in the holdings of companies with the similar share structure when both classes of shares are quoted on the stock market. Experience from the stock market, would seem to suggest that a discount of some 15 per cent is appropriate when valuing the non-voting ords.

A particular difficulty sometimes arises as a result of share issues made in the course of a tax mitigation exercise. In around 1983, a scheme was advocated whereby a company declared a bonus issue of shares. The bonus shares issued had special rights. During the period of ten years following issue, if any dividend was declared the entitlement for the dividend on each new share was one-hundredth of that on each original share. Similarly, in a winding-up during this period, the entitlement to the holder of a new share was only one-hundredth of the holder of each original share. On the tenth anniversary of the issue, the positions reversed so that the new share thereafter carried the right to 100 times the dividend paid on each original share and in the event of a winding-up received 100 times the sum received by the holder of an original share.

The writer was required to value, for capital gains tax purposes, a holding of the new shares which passed into a trust by the controlling shareholder of the company disclaiming his entitlement to the bonus. There were also certain capital transfer tax valuations required. In order to attribute a value to these newly issued bonus shares, the author valued the company as a whole, then used a discounted cash flow calculation to divide that value between the original shares and the new 'funny' shares before, finally, applying an appropriate discount. Agreement with the (then) Inland Revenue Shares Valuation Division was obtained 13 years after the completion of the transaction, the taxpayer having died in unfortunate circumstances in the intervening period.

The approach taken by the Shares Valuation Division in this particular case was conceptual rather than arithmetical. In essence, the argument of the Shares Valuation Division was that the 'funny' shares had a high value as the hypothetical purchaser of these shares would know that by sitting tight for ten years the larger part of the value of the company would accrue to his shareholding. The counter argument was, of course, that the hypothetical purchaser would be a detested outsider in a company whose other shareholders would do whatever they felt necessary to ensure that value did not pass to him. The manner of the agreement in which the shares had been issued illustrated to the hypothetical purchaser that the shareholders were prepared to engaged in complex arrangements to achieve their desired objectives.

7 Valuing preference, fixed interest, deferred shares and debentures

7.1 Preference shares

It is suggested that an appropriate approach to the valuation of a traditional preference share is to take the average yield for quoted preference shares in a broadly comparable industry and raise this by 20 per cent to allow for non-marketability.

Care should, however, be taken to ensure that what is being valued is actually a preference share, as is normally understood. That is:

(a) the right is to a fixed dividend;
(b) there is no entitlement to vote unless the dividend is not paid;
(c) there is no right to participate in any surplus; and
(d) in a winding-up the shareholder receives par (if there are sufficient funds), and no more.

If the articles of association specify other characteristics for the 'preference share', it may be more appropriate to treat the share as a special class of ordinary share.

Dividends are now expressed as net plus the tax credit for the time being (since 6 April 1999, 10 per cent). If the valuation is for a date prior to 6 April 1973, the dividend will be expressed as a gross dividend.

7.2 Fixed interest shares

These are normally valued by reference to the formula:

$$P = {}^r/_{y} + \frac{I - {}^r/_{y}}{(I + {}^y/_2)^{2t}}$$

Where:

$r\%$ = the rate of interest on the security;
t = the number of years to redemption;
$y\%$ = the required yield; and
I = the nominal rate of interest.

An unquoted company is likely to require a small premium (perhaps 5 per cent) above the yield available from quoted corporate stocks. Thus, if the current average yield of corporate stocks is 10 per cent, a return of 12 per cent would be appropriate for a fixed interest security in a large unquoted company. It is rare for small unquoted companies to issue fixed interest securities; if this were the case, individual attention would need to be paid to the circumstances and, hence, attractiveness to a hypothetical purchaser of such a security.

Since 1999, the *Financial Times* has not published an index of yields on corporate stocks. However, these can be obtained from many firms of stockbrokers.

7.3 Deferred shares

The author's experience of valuing deferred shares is referred to in section **6.11**. If it is necessary to value the deferred shares on their own, calculations are required as to net present values. This requires a discount rate to be determined. It is suggested that a high discount is required (perhaps 15–20 per cent per annum) to reflect the risk accepted that events during the deferral period will rob the shares of their potential value.

It should be noted that, for inheritance tax purposes, the value of deferred shares alone is rarely required. The essence of the charge to inheritance tax is the diminution in the estate. Where a company issues deferred shares and the deferred shares received by one shareholder are passed to other shareholders or into trust, the valuations required are as follows.

1. The value of the ordinary shares before the bonus issue – a traditional valuation.
2. The value of the ordinary shares without the deferred shares, after the bonus issue.

The Revenue view is that value 2 is very low as by waiving the entitlement to the deferred shares, the shareholder has taken out of his estate the value of the ordinaries at the end of the period of deferral.

7.4 Debentures

Debentures are valued by reference to the yield. As with fixed interest securities, it is suggested that a debenture in a large unquoted company should be valued on the basis of the return available on a debenture issued by a quoted company, plus a premium, perhaps, 5 per cent on the interest rate charged. (That is, where a quoted company would issue a debenture with a yield to maturity of 10 per cent, an equivalent debenture issued by an unquoted company could be valued on the basis that the yield to maturity is required to be 12 per cent.)

8   Illustrations of valuations

Example 1 – Valuing the company as a whole

ABC Limited has the following results according to its accounts for the following accounting periods to 31 December:

Year	Pre-Tax Profits £	Post-Tax Profits £
2006	125,000	105,000
2005	110,000	85,000
2004	80,000	55,000

A simple, but arithmetical, approach to value the company as a whole could be as follows.

First, arrive at estimated maintainable profits, which could be by weighted average of the pre-tax profits. It is better to use pre-tax profits as tax rates vary. It is the latest known tax regime that is relevant in determining post-tax profits.

	£		£
2006	125,000	x 3	375,000
2005	110,000	x 2	220,000
2004	80,000	x 1	80,000
		x 6	675,000

Weighted average: £675,000 ÷ 6 = £112,500

If a P/E ratio is determined on the basis of post-tax profits it is necessary to deduct corporation tax from the average. Given that this is a small company the rate would be 19 per cent, and assuming also that a purchaser would not be in a position of paying at the main corporation tax rate. There would probably be disallowable expenses so allowing for this the post-tax profits using a rate of 19 per cent could be, say, £90,000.

Determining the suitable P/E ratio is more difficult. The HMRC Share Valuation approach is to look at quoted sector comparables, although for reasons given in the text this is not an easy task. Indeed, if it does not produce anything that appears sensible it could be disregarded. However, if for the purpose of this illustration it is assumed that a suitable company on the quoted market has a P/E ratio of 15, it might be concluded that for this particular company a P/E ratio of 8 is appropriate. This could allow for modest asset backing, lack of a market in the same way as quoted shares and the fact that the quoted P/E ratio takes in account others factors such as anticipating future dividends and profits.

Applying the P/E ratio of 8 produces a value, therefore, of £90,000 $\times$ 8 = £720,000.

This example assumes that the profits do not require adjustment. If, by way of contrast, directors' salaries are unreasonably high, or premises are occupied rent-free, an adjustment to reported profits should be made to reflect the cost that would be suffered if all transactions were at arm's length. For example, if the directors' salaries charged in arriving at the above figures were £200,000 whereas a reasonable figure would have been £125,000, the maintainable profit should be increased by £75,000 for this. If the business premises are occupied rent-free, whereas the market rent is £25,000 per annum, the profits should be reduced by that figure. Thus, the future maintainable profits before tax would be increased by a net figure of £50,000, so that the weighted average is £162,500, instead of £112,500. If an adjustment of this nature is made, it is important to consider whether the adjustment should vary from year to year, to reflect market figures, such as directors' salary inflation in the marketplace. The difficulty with any adjustment is, however, that there is frequently insufficient published data available on market rates. The valuer will usually have to make an informed guess of the salary that would be paid to an unconnected third party to perform the duties actually performed by family members.

Example 2 – A more sophisticated approach to maintainable earnings

Suppose that the company in Example 1 has been going through a period of substantial investment, developing a product range. The profits from 2004 to 2006 have been subject to substantial expenditure on research and development and marketing. The product range is now complete and as a result it is forecast that the company is likely to make pre-tax profits of £300,000 in the year 2007 rising to £500,000 in the fifth year of the projections. These profits are also after providing the research and development cost to maintain and improve the product range.

In these circumstances it would clearly be inappropriate to take the simple approach in Example 1 by applying historical profits even on a weighted basis. The company has moved up a gear and it can be seen with reasonable certainty, as far as can be, that the higher level of profits would be earned, at least in the first year or two of the new cycle.

It might be concluded as a result of this that the maintainable profits are, say, £350,000 before tax and £250,000 after tax (allowing for the main corporation tax rate of 30 per cent on these profits). However, it might be argued that the company is higher risk in that the greater level of business could require more investment in working capital such as stock and debtors. There is also the fact that the profits are still to be earned and cannot be assumed simply based on projections. A slightly lower P/E ratio than that used in Example 1 might be appropriate, so is reduced to, say, 6.

This, therefore, produces a value for the whole company of £250,000 × 6 = £1,500,000.

This continued example refers to the company incurring expenditure on research and development. Research and development can attract a special tax relief, computed by adding 50 per cent to certain costs (mainly salaries and consumable expenditure on research, etc) in arriving at taxable profits. In some cases this relief eliminates the tax charge that would otherwise arise. (The relief given is by FA 2000, Sch 20, for small and medium-sized enterprises and by FA 2002, Sch 12 for large enterprises.) However, this is very much a one-off type of relief although for certain companies research and development is a continuing process and in those cases it could be expected that the effective corporation tax rate for the foreseeable future would be lower. If pre-tax profits are used as the basis for applying a suitable multiple then again this particular issue does not raise its head except insofar as such a business may attract a higher multiple because of its tax-favoured status. Even so, it is thought that in most instances the impact should be relatively slight as there can be no certainty that this relief will continue and a purchaser must be prepared to finance the expenditure going forwards. For the same reason, if a P/E ratio is used, there is still a case for applying the corporation tax rate to the profits without the R&D tax credit relief, at the very best rounding the tax charge down slightly to reflect the possibility of the relief continuing. For a company, though, that has developed a particular project and that is the very business that the purchaser is really acquiring, the past tax charge, benefiting from R&D tax credit relief, is unrepresentative for the future and should be ignored.

Example 3 – A company with surplus assets

If the profits and general facts in Example 1 are again assumed, it might be the case that the company has assets not required for trading purposes.

For example, it has been profitable but has reinvested a large part of each year's surplus in quoted investments. Simply multiplying the profits by a P/E ratio would not be appropriate. The surplus investments should be valued separately. As an aside, in advising on the capital gains tax liability the effect of the surplus investments for business asset taper relief should be borne in mind, given the relatively narrow definition of a trading company/group in TCGA 1992, Sch A1, paras 22A and 22B.

Assume that the post-tax profits average of £112,500 includes £7,500 from the surplus investments, which are valued at £200,000.

Adjusting for the investment income, the maintainable profits become £105,000.

The company could therefore be valued as follows:

	£
£105,000 × 8	840,000
Value of investments surplus to trading requirements	200,000
Value of company	1,040,000

If the company simply had bank deposit interest from money that was surplus from time to time an adjustment would not normally be required, as the cash is used in the trade.

Example 4 – Valuing a less than 100 per cent holding

(a) A 75 per cent holding and above

Assuming this also gives the same percentage of voting rights, this enables the holder of those shares to wind up the company and change the articles of association by special resolution. It is almost absolute control, subject as always to acting fairly. A discount is required to reflect the minority interest. An appropriate discount could be (say) 5 per cent.

If the company in Example 1 is used this means that a 75 per cent holding will be valued as follows:

	£
75% × £720,000	540,000
Less: discount in the region of 5% (say)	(27,000)
Value of 75% holding	513,000

(b) 75 per cent holding with dissident minority holders

This all depends upon the particular facts but it might be the case that there is a litigious minority shareholder, who is particularly difficult. The only way to resolve this might be to pay a much higher price than the minority holding is in fact worth. A purchaser of a 75 per cent holding is taking an adverse factor on board, in acquiring the shares and so could well seek a higher discount for this. Instead of 5 per cent this might increase this to, say, 7.5 per cent so the value could be adjusted accordingly. There is, though, no hard and fast rule.

(c) A holding of 55 per cent

A holding of over 50 per cent gives day-to-day control including the ability to pass ordinary resolutions, particularly in the appointment of directors. This is, though, subject to the particular articles of association and possibly a shareholders' agreement. A holder of 55 per cent could, therefore, determine the constitution of the board of directors and level of remuneration, provided that power is not abused.

A discount of 15 per cent is likely to be appropriate in this example, in which case the same company in Example 1 would produce the following valuation for a 55 per cent holding.

	£
55% × £720,000	396,000
Less: discount of approximately 15% (say)	(59,000)
Value of 55% holding	337,000

(d) A 50 per cent holding

On its own this does not give the ability to pass ordinary resolutions or give absolute control over the constitution of the board of directors. However, the remaining holding might be so fragmented that it is almost as good as a 50.1 per cent interest. Much again depends upon the facts. If there is a reasonable chance of being able to have effective control of the company because of the distribution of the other 50 per cent, a discount, of say, 25 per cent might be appropriate. Thus, the same company would be valued as follows for a 50 per cent holding:

	£
50% × £720,000	360,000
Less: discount of 25%	(90,000)
Value of 50% holding	270,000

Example 5 – Liquidation basis

XYZ Limited has been trading unprofitably for several years and has reached the point where the only sensible option is to place it in a members' voluntary winding-up before assets are dissipated forever.

Assume that the valuation in question is that of a 60 per cent holding, arising by virtue of a death on 31 March 2007. There is only one class of shares in issue and the latest management accounts of the company at around the time of the death can be summarised as follows:

	£	£
Freehold property	250,000	
Plant and machinery	75,000	325,000
Net current assets		
Stock and work in progress	120,000	
Debtors	220,000	
	340,000	
Less: liabilities	(145,000)	195,000
Net assets		520,000

This is represented wholly by ordinary share capital and reserves. The question is, what would someone pay on the open market for a 60 per cent holding in the above company, in the knowledge that if it continues to trade it would continue to either make losses or minimal profits? Either way, the balance sheet is not likely to be improved and as indicated the likely option is a members' voluntary winding-up. However, there is no certainty and a 60 per cent shareholder could not dictate this without the acquiescence of other shareholders representing at least 15 per cent of the issued shares.

The starting point is to value the company as a whole and to do this it will be necessary to discount the plant and machinery and stock and debtors on the grounds that these are not likely to realise their book value. However, the freehold property is estimated to be worth £400,000 (net of costs of sale) and on which the corporation tax would be £50,000.

Thus, the value of the company in liquidation could be as follows:

	£	£
Freehold property	400,000	
Less: estimated corporation tax on disposal	(50,000)	350,000
Plant and machinery at second-hand value (say)		20,000
Stock and work in progress at 50%		60,000
Debtors at (say) 75% of book value		165,000
		595,000
Less: creditors	(145,000)	
Redundancy and related costs	(40,000)	
Cost of liquidation (say)	(20,000)	(205,000)
Net assets		390,000

A straight 60 per cent of that figure would produce a value of £234,000. However, it is necessary to discount this figure for the following factors in particular.

- A liquidation might not ensue if 75 per cent do not vote in favour.
- There is likely to be a time delay so there is no certainty that the above

figures will in fact be produced and could be worse (it might even be better but a purchaser is likely to ignore that).

- A purchaser of a 50 per cent shareholding would expect to make a profit not only for the time cost of money but the risk factor as well.

Thus, a purchaser of a 60 per cent holding might discount the net asset value of that holding by, say, one third, producing a value, therefore, of £156,000.

If the individual in question held 75 per cent, a lower discount would be expected because of the ability to place the company in a winding-up without the agreement of the other shareholders. Nevertheless, some discount would be required because a purchaser would not pay £1 to receive back £1 on the finalisation of liquidation. A profit of some sort should be assumed, but this is likely to be much lower than one-third as in the above illustration. In that case, a discount of, say, 20 per cent might be appropriate, producing a value, therefore, for a 75 per cent holding of £235,000.

Example 6 – Valuation of non-influential minority holding

Assume an individual holds 10 per cent of the issued ordinary shares in an unquoted trading company that has a history of paying dividends. The dividends per share have been as follows, there having been no changes in the issued share capital in that time:

Calendar year	pence per share (net)
2006	10
2005	8
2004	7
2003	6.5

In each of those years the dividend has been covered at least twice. In the latest annual report the directors have indicated that the trading outlook is good and profits are expected to rise. The directors also indicate the continuation of their dividend policy, with suitable increases depending upon profitability.

The company's business is relatively low risk and is a reasonably sized family company that has been in existence for many years. Profits are expected to increase by no more than 2 or 3 per cent per annum over inflation.

The starting point is to determine what might be an appropriate yield for such an unquoted company. Suppose that the quoted sector closest to the company indicates a current dividend yield (net) of 2.5 per cent per annum, although just over a year ago it was 3.5 per cent per annum. The quoted market has improved because of the expectation of improved profits and trading conditions generally. The quoted yield might, therefore, be adjusted to, say, 3 per cent and then needs to be further adjusted to allow for the added risk of an unquoted company and the absence of a market. To allow for this the required yield is determined at 2.5 times the quoted yield, producing, therefore, 7.5 per cent net. Thus the value would be as follows based on a dividend per share of 10 pence:

$$10p \times \frac{100}{7.5} = £1.33$$

This is really the lowest value of the shares. Supposing there is a chance of an offer being made for the entire share capital. For example, there may be a competitor known to be looking for a similar company to expand its base. It is unlikely that a 10 per cent shareholder would be privy to information on approaches made to the company and neither would it be information that a prudent purchaser with a 10 per cent holding could reasonably require (for open market purposes in determining capital gains tax and inheritance tax valuations).

If current earnings are capitalised this might produce, say, a value per share of £5 if there is a takeover. However, any purchaser of a 10 per cent shareholding would discount heavily the prospect of a takeover as nothing may happen. He could be left holding an unquoted shareholding with the prospect of a dividend but no guarantee. To allow for the possibility of a takeover, though, he might be prepared to pay a premium on the dividend basis of £1.33. If the maximum price he is likely to realise is £5, he might, for example, be prepared to pay £1.75 per share.

A more optimistic purchaser could take a different view and pay a higher amount than £1.75 per share. However, if they were to pay, say, £2.50 per share and the takeover did not occur then the net dividend is reduced to 4 per cent, which is not much different than that which can be received after tax on a government stock. Unlike a government stock, an investment in unquoted shares is relatively illiquid as well as being inherently riskier and so a purchase at £2.50 per share will be at the outer range of acceptable figures, containing a much higher element of speculation. This does illustrate, though, that there is no precise figure and in the real world much depends upon various factors including those not directly related to the company, such as the economy generally and character traits of the seller and purchaser.

Example 7 – Dividends expected to increase substantially

If the previous example is continued, there could be particular reasons why the dividend in the future is likely to be substantially in excess of that in, say, 2008. The company may have been undergoing a programme of expansion by establishing new outlets that are now achieving their sales targets. The overheads are likely to be fixed and are not expected to increase substantially, whereas gross profits will increase. On this basis, and assuming the same dividend cover, the directors could declare dividends of 20 pence per share in future and reasonable increases thereafter.

In this situation, it would be unrealistic to base the value simply on a historical dividend of 10 pence per share, but equally to value it on 20 pence per share would not be attractive to a purchaser. There can be no certainty that increased profits will be achieved and even if they are it is up to the directors to declare the increased dividend. They might decide to maintain the dividends at a more modest level and retain the profits in the business to expand further. That might in turn produce higher dividends in later years but clearly with a higher risk on earnings if not successful. On a comparable 20 pence per share basis the valuation would be £2.66. That value should, therefore, be discounted to reflect the uncertainties. A 25 per cent discount would produce a value of roughly £2 per share, which would not seem unreasonable.

If in fact dividends are expected to grow at a very high rate, some allowance should be made for this. Nevertheless, there are even greater risks as nothing can be predicted with that amount of certainty, particularly so for circumstances that are further in the future. Mathematical models could be created assuming rates of growth in dividend and discounting back factors. At the end of the day it must be a common-sense approach as all mathematical calculations are dependent upon the fundamental assumptions.

To allow for the prospect of dividends increasing at a higher rate than the norm could be achieved either by reducing the required yield or applying a premium to the value produced on the existing required yield basis. Either basis ought to produce a not too dissimilar figure, which again must be tested by common sense.

Example 8 – An influential minority holding

An individual holds 40 per cent of the issued ordinary capital of a trading company. On an earnings basis the shares are valued at £8 per share. Relatively small dividends are paid, which are covered five or six times. On the actual dividend basis the value is only £1 per share.

A holding of this size has influence in that it can prevent the winding-up of the company or the passing of special resolutions. It may also be sufficient with other shareholders to have effective day-to-day control. It could also have some influence if there is an offer for the entire company; as such a shareholder is likely to be privy to such information that would reasonably be required by a purchaser. The holding, in conjunction with other shareholders, could give a board appointment and the ability to obtain directors remuneration and determine dividend policy. A valuation by reference to earnings could, therefore, be appropriate, much again depending upon the facts and the distribution of the remaining shareholdings. It would not be unreasonable to apply a discount of 60 per cent to the earnings basis, which would produce a value per share of £3.20. This does not seem unreasonable given the minimum value based on the dividend yield, where that is based on a modest dividend policy.

Example 9 – A property investment company

The assets of CP Holdings Limited at 31 March 2007 are as follows:

	£
Commercial properties – at valuation	800,000
Net current assets	150,000
Net assets	950,000
This is represented by the following:	
Preference shares of £1 each	100,000
Ordinary share capital	75,000
Profit/Loss account	775,000
	950,000

If the properties were sold at current market value, corporation tax on a capital gain of £150,000 would be payable. The preference dividends carry a cumulative dividend of 5 per cent net. The preference shares are only payable at par on a winding-up. Assume that an individual dies on 31 March 2007 holding the following:

10,000 £1 preference shares
45,000 £1 ordinary shares (representing 60 per cent)

The valuation of the shareholdings could be as follows:

Preference shares

The only return on these shares is the dividend with no redemption right whatsoever unless the company is liquidated. Assuming that the dividend is covered adequately, the dividend is relatively secure. There is, though, a risk of some sort and lack of marketability. If a medium-dated government stock redemption yield is, say, 6 per cent gross per annum then to allow for these factors a comparable yield of 10 per cent might be required. Allowing for income tax at 40 per cent would require a net dividend on the preference shares of 8 per cent. The actual net dividend is 5 per cent so the value of the preference shares would be as follows:

£1 nominal value $\times \frac{5}{8} = 62\frac{1}{2}$p

Ordinary shares

The valuation of 100 per cent could be as follows:

	£	£
Net assets as above		950,000
Less: allowance for part of corporation tax		
if property is sold (say)	50,000	
Preference shares	100,000	(150,000)
Value of ordinary shares		800,000
The 60% holding could then be valued as follows:		
60% × £800,000		480,000
Less: discount for lack of total control, etc		
10% (say)		(50,000)
Value of 60% holding		430,000

The preference shares have been deducted at full nominal value as that is the figure that will be repaid eventually. Moreover, the dividend payable is not too different from the non-bank borrowings. However, if the dividend yield were substantially more or less than an equivalent interest rate some adjustment could be made to the deduction for the preference shares to reflect this.

9 Shares in a trading company

9.1 Controlling interest

9.1.1 Introduction

The test as to whether a shareholding gives a controlling interest is to ask whether the shareholder has the ability, de facto, to determine the composition of the board of directors. Clearly, a person who owns 51 per cent or more of the shares of a company can exercise his shareholder's rights in a general meeting to bring to an end the service contracts held by individual directors or can vote other individuals onto the board so as to 'swamp' any existing directors who would not act in accordance with his wishes. In the UK (although, not apparently, in the USA) if exactly 50 per cent of the shares is held, the shareholder who has a chairman's casting vote is held to control the company (*IRC v BW Noble Ltd*, KBD 26 November 1926, not reported). In many companies, de facto control is exercised by an individual shareholder who holds less than 50 per cent of the total votes, the remaining shareholdings being widely dispersed amongst unconnected persons. In this situation, also, the considerations outlined below for valuing a controlling holding are considered to be applicable.

The value of an unincorporated business to its owner is the profits that are generated by that business. The controlling shareholder of a trading company is in a similar position commercially. It follows that the appropriate approach is to prepare a valuation on the earnings basis. It could be that the company has assets that are not used in the trade. In this case, it is suggested that an estimate be made of the proceeds that could be obtained on the disposal of those assets. The earnings basis value for the company then has added to it these expected sale proceeds, less any tax arising on the disposal. This approach can also be followed in the situation where a company carries on a number of disparate trades and there is a proposal to sell one of the trades outside the company.

When undertaking an earnings basis valuation, it is essential first to adjust reported profits, as discussed in section **6.1.2** in order to obtain a figure of profit that would be available if the company were controlled by the hypothetical prospective purchaser. Thus, excessive directors remuneration is removed. If the likely purchaser is another company which would undertake the administration of the target company without additional expenditure, the administrative costs suffered historically by the target company can, in whole or in part, be added back.

The earnings basis provides two alternative approaches to the valuation of a controlling interest. First, comparison can be made with comparable companies (see section **6.7**). Secondly, the earnings basis with an appropriate P/E ratio can be applied to suggest a valuation (see section **6.1**). This latter method is sometimes referred to as 'the investment approach' and is likely to be the approach that should be favoured.

On obtaining information on the trading performance that has been achieved, the valuer will need to restate the profits by substituting costs at the level that will be suffered by the hypothetical purchaser, insofar as these are different from costs actually suffered historically. It is at this point that the valuation of a controlling interest shows the greatest difference from that of a minority interest. The person who controls a company controls its expenditure and the manner in which it generates profit. Although much of the calculation will be based on historic results, the valuer should never lose sight of the fact that what he is valuing is the benefit that would accrue to the purchaser in the future. The reason for looking at the past is merely that this may be an indicator for the future.

It is a common experience of a valuer that a client who understands this basic principle will supply the valuer with management information giving a profit forecast for the year and, sometimes, for future years. It is suggested that such forecasts be received with a considerable degree of scepticism. In most businesses, the reliability of forecast is not high. Further, the forecast will have been prepared on the basis of the operation as carried out under the current ownership. The ownership of a controlling interest by a hypothetical purchaser may be exercised in a very different manner with very different financial results.

The basic principle in valuing any shareholding is to ascertain the highest price that would be offered by the various hypothetical purchasers. If the value of a company with several divisions could be maximised by the sale of one of those divisions, then the share value when considering a controlling interest could be calculated on the assumption that a purchaser would make an offer for the shares with the intention of maximising the value of the company by splitting off and selling the particular division.

Different arguments are advanced in favour of the two alternative approaches to valuation of a controlling shareholder.

In favour of the comparable company approach is the argument that this is more objective in that it is based on prices at which shares of comparable companies change hands. However, we are here considering the value to be placed on a controlling interest. Stock market reports record, in the main, prices at which small minority holdings are bought and sold. To be comparable, it is necessary to look at the price paid for shares where there is a takeover. This is, however, a dangerous comparison to make. It will be very rare indeed that a quoted company that has been taken over close to the valuation date is directly comparable with the company whose shares are to be valued. Further, takeovers in the stock market and, in particular, the large takeovers that attract the greatest press coverage, take place in the context of a substantial number of shareholders being persuaded to dispose of shares on which, typically, they have had a regular stream of dividends in exchange for cash or, very frequently, in exchange for shares in an even larger company, again with a track record of six-monthly dividends. Despite the Revenue's enthusiasm for the comparable company approach, the search for a truly comparable company in a truly comparable situation is likely to be fruitless. HMRC Share Valuation Manual suggests (at SVM14040–SVM14050) that the valuer can usefully compare the holding in the unquoted company with published material on quoted companies in the particular industrial sector in which it operates. As the author sees it, if the target company cannot be compared with any individual company, a valid comparison cannot be made between the target company and a list of quoted companies, none of which is comparable.

The investment approach of computation on the earnings basis, after careful adjustment of the earnings to reflect the position of the hypothetical purchaser, may seem less objective but is the approach that would actually be adopted by a prospective commercial purchaser for the business.

In valuing a controlling interest, the most important figure for the valuer to arrive at is his estimate of future maintainable earnings. The past is simply that and at best it is a guide to the future. A valuer ought, however, to look at budgets around the date of valuation and longer term forecasts generally if available, discounting the latter heavily if, in his view the forecasts are based on little more than hope. In the author's opinion, it is frequently valid to look at the accounts that span the valuation date. A valuation cannot use the benefit of hindsight; however, the period of trading up to the valuation date (that is, part of the period covered by the accounts) is likely to have a great influence on the price that was paid for the shares at the valuation date. Whether or not the information for that period is available to the valuer in a fiscal valuation is largely dependent on the size of the investment that would be involved in purchasing the shares to be valued. In *Marks v Sherred* [2004] STC (SCD) 362 **case 46**, Ross Marks Ltd made up its accounts to 31 March each year and a value was required at 31 March 1982. The value of the taxpayer's shareholding was £633,006. The Special Commissioner, Colin Bishopp, ruled that for an investment of this size the hypothetical purchaser would obtain information (and require information to be collated, if it was not routinely recorded) which would give the trading results for the year (or, at a minimum the 11 months) leading up to the valuation date (see [2004] STC (SCD) 362 at 368h **case 46 para 23**).

Looking at past earnings, the valuer must look at these very critically, not only adjusting for excessive directors' emoluments (or even increasing the level if they are below the market rate for the job) but also looking for:

- exceptional amounts, such as a one-off contract that might not be repeated;
- reorganisation costs;

- discontinued activities;
- leases with low rents which are about to be reviewed where significant;
- the need to replace plant and machinery with an increased annual cost thereafter perhaps;
- increase in raw materials for the future where not linked to a corresponding increase in the output price; and
- many other factors.

If budgets are prepared, many of these factors should be apparent from that but they will still need adjustment for costs that have not yet hit the profit and loss account.

9.1.2 Interest paid

The finance for a company's trade is provided in a variety of forms, notably:

- funds raised on share issues;
- retained profits;
- debentures;
- long-term bank loans; and
- short-term borrowing (notably on overdraft).

When considering the value of a controlling interest, it is necessary to consider whether the manner in which the trade has been financed in the past will continue under the new ownership. If funding is likely to be made in a different manner from that historically, it will be necessary to adjust the reported results for past periods to reflect the funding that will be required under the new ownership. A clear instance of this is where the valuation is on the basis that the surplus assets, or a trading division, will be sold. In such a case, the company will have sale proceeds that may drastically reduce the bank borrowing requirement.

It is suggested by some valuers, particularly in the commercial field, that an earnings basis calculation should be undertaken by considering earnings before payment of interest and then the 'core debt' of the business should be deducted from the capitalised value of earnings. There are at least three arguments to be advanced against this approach.

First, it can be very difficult to identify an amount that should be considered as 'core debt'. In a recent valuation, the author has considered a company where the bank balance during the course of 12 months ranged from £40,000 credit to £1,500,000 overdrawn. The oscillation in the bank balance was in part a result of the timing of sale receipts but, of even greater effect was variation through the year in the speed with which trade creditors were satisfied.

Secondly, the approach seems akin to an addition of an asset value for a surplus asset of the company that is to be sold. Unless there is a real intention of a purchaser to fund the 'core debt', it is difficult to see why that liability should be different from any other liability of the company. As in the fiscal valuation we are looking at a hypothetical purchaser, any approach that requires consideration of a purchasers 'real intentions' appears almost theological.

Thirdly, what is being purchased is, as previously discussed, a profit flow. Interest is, commercially, an expense of obtaining the profit flow in the same manner as all other expenses. It may be appropriate to adjust prior years' profits to reflect a substantial change in interest rates that has arisen since that time but it is difficult to see why it is appropriate for this expense to be removed and a capital sum deducted.

9.2 Minority interest

9.2.1 Dividend paying company

The first, and primary, question to be answered when considering the valuation of the minority holding in a trading company that has paid a dividend is whether the hypothetical purchaser has a reasonable expectation of a regular dividend being received on the shares that he buys. As is clear from the comments in section **6.4**, the author considers that in more cases than not the answer to this question is 'no'.

If dividends have been paid in the past simply because this is a tax efficient way of remunerating members of the family for their work in the business, it will be most surprising if a new shareholder from outside the family were to be given the opportunity of enjoying a dividend income in the future.

Where the dividend paid is a tiny proportion of profits generated the dividend basis for a valuation will prove inadequate.

It follows, in the author's view, therefore, that use of the dividend basis for valuing an unquoted holding is relevant only for large unquoted companies, where there are many different (and probably unconnected) shareholders who, typically, have small percentage shareholdings each.

The dividend basis of valuation is, however, favoured by HMRC Share Valuation. Instructions given to examiners in HMRC Share Valuation are as follows:

'The valuation process

...

This chapter will be concerned with the method employed in the valuation of minority holdings in trading companies which pay regular dividends on their ordinary share capital. In these cases the usual method of valuation is by reference to the dividend yield ...

The Maintainable Dividend

As the purchaser of a minority holding is primarily concerned with the return on the investment, the level of future dividends is very relevant to the valuation of such holdings.

The imponderable – dividend % – in the equation is actually the valuer's assessment of future maintainable dividends.

The valuer will be concerned with each of the following factors in order to decide what the level of future dividends is likely to be:

● The past record
● The company's earnings
● The prospects for the future.

The past record

The company's dividend paying record must be examined for fluctuations and trends, looking particularly for any indications for the future. The past performance (i.e. the track record) of the company is certainly one method of gauging future dividend policy.

The company's earnings

...

In order to determine the level of future dividends there is undoubtedly a need to establish the level of maintainable profits which means considering the company's past profit record (making adjustments where necessary) and having regard to any indications there might be for the future.

It may be necessary to ask for more information about the current year's results and for any forecasts of future profits that might be available.

The key word is maintainable profits. If there is a clear trend, the use of any kind of average will not result in a figure which is representative of maintainable earnings ...

Nevertheless an average may sometimes be useful when no forecasts are available and a company has experienced fluctuating profitability. It might be appropriate to use a weighted average in these circumstances so that greater emphasis can be placed on the latest results.

Examples

		1982 £	1983 £	1984 £
Profits before tax	a	75,000	100,000	80,000
	b	75,000	115,000	180,000

In example **a** unless information is available to indicate the trend of future profits, it is likely that an average of the last three years results would provide the valuer with a reasonable estimate of maintainable profits. A straight average would in the circumstance be appropriate simply because there is very little difference in the figures for 1982 and 1984:

$$\frac{(75,000 + 100,000 + 80,000)}{3} = £85,000$$

The matter is more problematical in example **b** because there is a distinct upward trend in profits. In this situation the valuer must consider the accounts very carefully to see if there is any indication either that the profits are likely to:

1. level out at £180,000;
2. continue to rise (in which case the valuer should follow the trend and perhaps suggest maintainable profits of, say, £240,000);
3. fall.

If the latter, then it might be appropriate to adopt a weighted average, viz:

$$\frac{(75,000 \times 1) + (115,000 \times 2) + (180,000 \times 3)}{6} = \text{Say, } £141,000.$$

At all times the valuer must have regard to the reasons behind substantial changes in the profits and consider whether any one year's figures are, for any reason, exceptional.

Because of the effect of:
    deferred taxation/capital allowances
    exceptional/extraordinary items in the accounts.'
        (HMRC Share Valuation Manual, SVM14010 and SVM14020)

9.2.2 Minority interest – non-dividend trading company

For the reasons given in section **9.2.1**, the author considers that most trading companies, whether or not they have paid dividends in the past, should be valued by reference to earnings and not by reference to dividends.

When a shareholding in an unquoted trading company is purchased, the purchaser is looking to obtain the benefit of the company's earnings. In this respect, the holder of a minority interest is in the same position as the holder of a majority interest. The same basic approach to valuation should be taken; that is, the valuation is an earnings basis.

When valuing a minority interest in an unquoted trading company, the following differences arise in the approach from that which is adopted in a majority interest:
(a) The minority shareholder does not control the board and, hence, no adjustment can be made to actual earnings achieved by virtue of excess directors remuneration, unless there is evidence that this remuneration will be limited in the future.
(b) A second consequence of the lack of control is that the shareholder has no individual influence on the sale of any excess assets in the company, or the disposal of a trading division, for example. Hence, there is no basis for adding the expected sale proceeds of an asset, etc, as was suggested in the case of a valuation of majority holding, unless, again, there is clear evidence that such a sale is contemplated.
(c) In capitalising earnings, the P/E ratio used will be significantly below that which would be applied to a majority shareholding. It is suggested that, typically, the P/E is likely to be one half of that which applies for a majority holding.

For reasons stated in section **6.7**, it is suggested that it will rarely be productive to search for comparable quoted companies. However, HMRC Share Valuation advocates such a process even for a minority holding in an unquoted trading company that does not pay dividends. The HMRC Share Valuation Manual states:

'It is reasonable to assume that the required P/E ratio for unquoted companies which are not paying a dividend will be some fraction of the P/E ratio obtainable in the quoted market.

In determining what fraction (or multiple) to take the valuer should consider amongst other things:

- what level of dividend the company could afford; and
- when the company could/might pay a dividend.

There are no hard and fast rules and valuers should treat each case on its own merits.

As a guideline in the case of small uninfluential minority holdings in small trading companies it might be reasonable to start from a required P/E ratio of between 1/4 and 1/5 of the quoted ratio (or 4 to 5 times the FTASI earnings yield).

NB Higher or lower figures may be dictated by the quality of the unquoted company.

Review the values in the light of common sense'
(HMRC Share Valuation Manual, SVM17040)

9.2.3 Influential minority holdings

The author regards an influential minority holding as one where the shareholder's votes are between 25 per cent and 50 per cent of the total votes on the issued share capital. Such a shareholder is able to block a winding-up or a reorganisation. This is a negative power, but an important one. The majority cannot change the fundamental structure without the consent of the influential minority holding. If the remainder of the shareholdings are fragmented a large minority holding could wield considerable positive influence.

It has been put to the author by HMRC Share Valuation that a shareholder with a holding of this size can expect to be given a seat on the board of directors. In the experience of the author, this is an incorrect assumption for an unlisted company. In the author's experience, the board of an unlisted company is made up of the majority shareholder plus those he has chosen to serve with him, either because of their personal qualities or because of a family connection. It is not the author's experience that the size of shareholding is of particular relevance. As a valuation is looking at the price that would be offered by the hypothetically unconnected shareholder, the most valid assumption is, the author suggests, that the purchaser would be not so much an influential minority shareholder but a detested outsider. This is not to say that the percentage discount on value should be as great as for a smaller size shareholding, but it is to stress the crucial distinction between a majority shareholder and a minority shareholder. This is illustrated in *Irvine and another v Irvine and another* [2006] 4 All ER 102 **case 50** where a valuation of a 49.96 per cent shareholding for the purpose of a buy-out order under oppression of a minority case was held to require the discount appropriate to a minority shareholding.

In valuing an influential minority holding, there is no doubt that some reference to earnings is relevant but with a much higher discount compared to that applied to a controlling interest. The level of dividends may be a relevant factor, although this would depend on (1) the identity of the other shareholders; (2) the size of the company; and (3) the company's overall profitability. If a purchaser can see that there is a prospect of increasing earnings with a view to selling the company (possibly a flotation, if the company is large enough) then he will have an eye to his exit. An investor might then consider what he could expect to receive in the foreseeable future on a sale and then discount this heavily for the time, risk and uncertainty of a sale. This could then be compared with a straight dividend capitalisation basis to get a feel for a fair value.

In many ways, this type of holding is the most difficult type to value.

9.2.4 Non-influential minority holdings

This would be any holding with less than 25 per cent of the voting rights, although even in this overall band there are differences.

A very small holding in a dividend paying company would normally be valued simply by reference to the likely future dividend. The larger the company the greater the certainty that the dividend will continue to be paid, particularly if it is run on similar lines to a quoted company. Dividend cover is also a factor to take into account. In the case of the very small company where the family is very much in control, the actual dividend may be less certain and at greater risk of the directors simply not declaring it in later years.

Where the sum to be invested is large, the approach to be adopted is very different from that when only a small sum of cash is to be put at risk by making the purchase. In *Caton's administrators v Couch* [1995] STC (SCD) 34 **case 38** the 14 per cent holding to be valued was potentially worth a considerable amount of money. The company in question was clearly large and it was held that a purchaser would require a good deal of information, much of which would ordinarily be confidential. It is perhaps interesting to note the different approach that Bruce Sutherland took compared to the valuation of the Revenue's expert in the *Caton* case, particularly on the valuation without the prospect of a sale. Bruce Sutherland looked at maintainable future earnings, only to assess the likely dividend that the 14 per cent shareholder could expect, whereas the Revenue's expert worked on a multiple of earnings basis, heavily discounted because of the size of the holding. In fact, it seems that if either valuer had taken a slightly different view on dividend yield or multiple adopted, they could have arrived at exactly the same figure!

9.3 Loss making companies

The valuation of shareholdings in a loss making trading company is difficult, in particular where a company enjoys profits some years and suffers losses other years.

For an unquoted company, there must be a preliminary question in any situation as to whether the reported result is, in commercial terms, a loss or whether it is a profit that has been turned into a deficit by the payment of excessive directors remuneration (or occasionally, other payments made to benefit shareholders or their families). If the loss arises from excess directors remuneration, the principle for valuing a majority shareholding is straightforward. Historic profits are adjusted, as discussed in section **6.1.2**. As this then produces a set of profit figures, the normal earnings basis valuation outlined in section **6.1** is appropriate.

Where, however, the holding to be valued is a minority holding, it has to be recognised that the hypothetical purchaser will not be in a position to insist on directors remuneration, etc being reduced so that a profit is enjoyed in the future. Ultimately, of course, a company must either make a profit or be wound up but this is of little comfort to the minority shareholder. If after careful examination, it is clear to the valuer that the company is unlikely to make profits in the future and the proceeds to be enjoyed by the minority shareholder on a winding-up are small, then only a nominal value can be ascribed to the shares.

Having dealt with the preliminary question of whether the loss figures need adjusting, the primary question to be addressed when considering the valuation of a holding in a loss making company is whether or not the company is likely to go back into profit in the foreseeable future. If the valuer considers that the answer to this is 'yes', then a conventional earnings basis valuation can be made using profits that are anticipated on a conservative forecast. Even with a conservative forecast of profits, it will be appropriate to provide an additional discount for the discouraging effect on hypothetical potential purchasers of losses that are currently being suffered.

If the view is taken that the company will not be likely to move back into profit in the foreseeable future, the commercial approach must be that the company sells its business or goes into voluntary liquidation. In the latter scenario, an asset basis valuation is appropriate. If the business is readily saleable, the price that would be expected to be received for the business is brought into the asset valuation, with provision being made for the tax charge that arises on the capital gain (if any) made on the sale of the business. If the likely route is a voluntary liquidation, the costs of winding up the business must be recognised in the asset base valuation. This is likely to include redundancy payments for workers.

10 Valuing shares in property and other investment companies

10.1 Investment company

The value of an investment company is the value of the investments held. However, a hypothetical purchaser of shares of the company would require a discount from the value of the underlying investment to make it worth his while purchasing the shares as opposed to purchasing the investment itself. This is illustrated in *Battle v IRC* [1980] STC 86 **case 32**. In that case, the only asset of the company was a holding in 4.5 per cent British Gas Stock 1969–72 which, at the valuation date, had a value of about £102,000. A 49 per cent shareholding was held by each of two brothers. The court upheld a valuation where the value of each brother's shareholding was taken to be the value of the underlying gas stock less a discount of 2.5 per cent. This discount is much lower than would normally be expected from a 49 per cent shareholding. However, it is most unusual for a company to be created for the sole purpose of holding a government stock. In this particular case, the motive was an attempted estate duty mitigation scheme.

Since the first edition of this book HMRC Share Valuation has increased the size of discount to be regarded as the norm. HMRC Share Valuation Manual now states:

'As soon as the valuer has obtained a schedule of the investments held by the company and ascertained the market value thereof, where appropriate a discount (which tends to be lower than those which apply for property companies because securities are more readily and cheaply disposed of than properties) should be applied. Details of comparable discounts for quoted investment trusts can be found in the Pinchin and Denny lists retained in the Information Library.

As a **rough** guide the levels of discount shown at SVM 18060 [see below] are also suggested for investment companies ...

The following levels of discount are suggested **after deducting the allowance for contingent tax.**

Size of holding	Discount
75% – 100%	NIL – 5%
50% + to 74.9%	10% – 15%

50% Holding

For a holding of this size full information would be available on the company properties but a discount of around 20% would be appropriate.

Influential Minority Holdings

Similar considerations would apply as above although the level of available information would need to be borne in mind. The discount should be adjusted to reflect the lack of management control.

A suggested range of discounts is 25% to 40% **but it is emphasised that valuers must rely on the facts of the particular case and their own experience when deciding upon a reasonable level of discount.**

Uninfluential Minority Holdings

These are the most difficult to value because of:-

● the difficulty in identifying, and establishing the market value of the portfolio
● uncertainties as to the appropriate level of discount, particularly in cases where the quality of the properties is poor and no return is anticipated in the short to medium term.'

(HMRC Share Valuation Manual, SVM18110 and SVM18060)

10.2 Property company

There are, broadly, three types of property company, namely:

(a) Property dealing companies.
   In the case of the dealing companies, property is bought with the expressed intention of disposing of it and hopefully making a profit on the resale.
(b) Property development companies.
   A development company is one which buys land or property for the purpose of development and either undertakes such development itself so that it can be likened to a building or construction company or may contract out the actual building work.
(c) Property investment companies.
   The most obvious example of a property-type company must be the investment or holding company which derives its profits as rents from shops, offices, industrial or residential property.

Property dealing is a trade and shares in a property dealing company should be valued using the same approach as is relevant for a trade. This view is shared by HMRC Share Valuation (see HMRC Share Valuation Manual, SVM18010).

A property development company may be a building property for sale or may be a building to create an investment. In the first case, the same consideration applies as with a property dealing company, although, typically, the trade consists of a single development. If this is the case, then annual figures of profit are likely to be largely irrelevant. What is necessary is to ascertain the likely profit arising on the single project, as the shareholder is acquiring an interest in that property. On the other hand, a property development company that is developing with a view to letting the property in the long term is akin to a property investment company and the valuation of its shares should be undertaken on that basis.

Shares in a property company have traditionally been valued on the basis of the net asset value of the company, with a discount being applied. The valuer should expect that HMRC Share Valuation will refer the question of property valuation to the District Valuer. It is, therefore, appropriate to obtain a valuation of the property from a competent valuer who is able to negotiate with the District Valuer. HMRC instructions to HMRC valuation staff stress the importance of considering the value of a property to a company, which may not be simply a reflection of current rentals but may need to take into account the potential for growth in rental returns (see HMRC Share Valuation Manual, SVM18040).

The HMRC view as to the approach to be taken to the valuation of various sizes of shareholdings is given above in section **10.1**; HMRC not distinguishing between a company created to invest in property and a company created to invest in any other type of investment.

The approach of the courts is illustrated in *Shinebond v Carrol* where a valuation was required as at 31 March 1982 of the entire issued share capital of the company. The Special Commissioner stated:

'... a hypothetical prospective purchaser would have valued the company by adding the value of the property to its other assets and deducting its liabilities.'

([2006] STC (SCD) 147 at 150g **case 48 para 12**)

The Special Commissioner then valued the shares as market value of the property as determined by the Lands Tribunal plus other net assets, without discount. (See the author's commentary on **case 48** for his criticism of the lack of a reduction for the contingent tax liability and for the author's view that a discount recognising the contingent tax liability is appropriate, the size of the discount being determined by the likelihood of the tax liability being triggered in the foreseeable future.)Regard should also be taken of the gearing of the company; that is the extent to which the assets are financed by external borrowings. If gearing is low, the company is in a better position to finance the void periods that inevitably arise in any letting, to deal with any temporary reduction of income, such as through the failure of a tenant to pay the rent, and is also in a good position to develop its activities by further acquisition. In this situation, the discount is likely to be at the lower end of the suggested range. Conversely, where gearing is high, a discount at the higher end of the range is appropriate. In some circumstances, the gearing is such that when there is an indication of an adverse movement in the property market a very substantial increase in the discount is appropriate.

In practice, a potential purchaser would take a view on each property forming part of the portfolio. He would be looking at the nature of the leases and in particular their rent review provisions and whether or not repairs are the responsibility of the landlord or tenant. If leases are about to come to an end it needs to be considered whether or not the lessee will renew and generally whether there is a market, and at what rent, etc for a particular property.

A company may be sitting on sites that have valuable redevelopment potential and certainly the valuer ought to have an eye to this. This could also be relevant particularly to farmers where, certainly in this area, land with an agricultural value of say, £3,000 per acre can be turned into £750,000 per acre with the magical stamp of approval of the local planning authority.

If the property company has significant investment in residential property, any suggestion that the shares should be valued by reference to a comparable quoted company should be resisted. There is no quoted UK company that has as its main activity investment in residential property.

11   Valuing shares in a farming company

The characteristic that is particular to farming companies is that even a very well run operation produces a very low return on capital employed. At the time of writing, farmland in Eastern England is fetching around £3,150 per acre on sale. In this year's harvest, the sale price of wheat is around £275 per acre's yield. Sprays and fertilisers cost the farmer around £100 per acre, operational costs a further £100 and rent £50–£60 per acre. Hence, the profit margin is £15–£25 per acre, a return on capital of between 0.5 per cent and 0.8 per cent *before* overheads. Much of the profit from farming comes from the single farm subsidy, which has now replaced the large number of individual subsidies for specified crops and animals.

The valuation of shares in a farming company is particularly difficult for four reasons:

(a) shares in farming companies are rarely bought and sold in the real world;
(b) farming is a manufacturing operation where the manufacturer does not have the ability to determine the price of his product, but is forced to accept the price in the marketplace;
(c) future results of every farming company are substantially dependent on government (including EU) payments;
(d) the capital employed in a farming operation is a much greater multiple of turnover than would be expected in the case of any industrial manufacturing company.

Until the mid 1980s, the Revenue appeared to approach the valuation of shares in a farming company on the same basis as for any other trading company. This led to the acceptance of modest values for shares in farming companies. In the late 1980s, the attitude of the (then) Inland Revenue Share Valuation examiners appeared to change and this is borne out by the Inland Revenue Share Valuation Manual, which was first made publicly available on 6 May 1998. The edition of HMRC Share Valuation Manual which is current at the time of writing directs HMRC Share Valuation examiners to consider the valuation of shareholdings in farming companies using the criteria that are also adopted for property and investment companies (see SVM18030–SVM18120), stating:

> 'Farming companies present the share valuer with special problems because of their unique nature. While they are largely, if not wholly, dependent upon the land they farm, they are nevertheless trading companies whose production can be regarded as manufacturing. They are, of course, reliant to a substantial extent on the weather.'

In valuing a shareholding in a farming company, it is necessary to recognise two distinct categories of company:

- a company that owns the land it farms; and
- a company that rents the land it farms.

With companies in the first category, the approach taken by HMRC Share Valuation is to treat the company as if it were a property investment company. Hence, a value of the land is taken, perhaps by reference to the District Valuer, and a discount applied by reference to the size of the shareholding. Although there is undoubtedly some merit in this approach, it is suggested that valuers should be prepared to argue with HMRC that discounts for a farming company should be significantly greater than would be applied to a property company.

Where the farming company is a tenant, the terms of the tenancy should be ascertained. If the company is the tenant on a tenancy created before 1 September 1995, the tenancy is almost certainly subject to the Agricultural Holdings Act 1968, which has the effect that the company is a tenant in perpetuity, subject only to the company paying the rent when due and being able to satisfy any covenants in relation to the proper management of the land. In order to avoid the tenancy and perpetuity, it was common practice for the tenant on the lease to be named as an individual, who acted as nominee of the company. The effect of this arrangement is that the tenancy ceases at the death of that individual. However, under the Agricultural Holdings Act 1968, the individual heir is entitled to take over the tenancy at the death, subject to certain conditions, notably that the heir does not have another agricultural holding in the vicinity. In this way, whilst not guaranteeing a tenancy in perpetuity, the company has a large measure of security of its tenancy. Where agricultural land is sold by the landlord, the tenant has a statutory right to receive compensation equal to three years' rent. The practice in the farming community has been that when tenanted land is sold, the tenant has been paid a sum equal to 50 per cent of the difference between the freehold value of the land with vacant possession and the value of the freehold encumbered by the agricultural tenancy. At the time of writing, in the East of England, these values are of the order of £3,150 and £2,100, respectively. Hence, a payment to a tenant of some £525 per acre would be expected. It is common practice for the District Valuer to advise that a tenancy held by a company (or by an individual acting as nominee of a company) should be valued in this manner.

Where a tenancy was created on or after 1 September 1995, Agricultural Holdings Act 1968 provisions do not apply. Instead, the landlord and the tenant are at liberty to specify whatever terms they choose. If the company has been well advised, one would expect to find that the terms are such that no tenancy value is imputed on the company. In such a case, it is suggested that the correct approach to valuation of the company shares is that which would be applied to any other trading company.

Frequently, the company will be the tenant of land that is owned by an individual who is a shareholder in the company. Where the valuation is for inheritance tax purposes, the question arises as to whether the value in the estate should be ascertained by aggregating the shareholding in the company with the freehold, subject to the company's tenancy. This question has not been addressed by the courts. However, in *IRC v Gray* [1994] STC 360 **case 37**, the Court of Appeal considered the situation where an individual owned the freehold of agricultural land which was let to a partnership, in which the individual held a 92.5 per cent share. The parties agreed that the land in question was worth £2,751,000 tenanted and £6,125,000 with vacant possession. The Court of Appeal upheld the finding of the Lands Tribunal that the way in which the hypothetical sale that is required under the statutory hypothesis would have been conducted was to sell the land subject to the tenancy and the 92.5 per cent partnership interest in a single sale. Evidence that HMRC Share Valuation is cognisant of the value of the freehold plus the tenancy being, together, higher than the sum of the two separate values is given in HMRC Share Valuation Manual:

> 'Where the valuation is of a control holding for CTT or IHT purposes and there is evidence that the transferor's estate includes land, or an interest in land, let or leased to the company, immediate reference should be made to the C1 in SV HQ to consider a package argument.'

(SVM18120)

HMRC instructions to Share Valuation examiners state:

'Farming companies present the share valuer with special problems . . .

It is important to ascertain whether or not the company owns the land it farms. This is a fundamental importance in deciding how to approach the valuation of its shares.

Often the company may hold an agricultural tenancy which can offer a high degree of statutory protection to the tenant of agricultural property. Whilst such a tenancy is not assignable, it may be passed on through a disposal of the shares of the company. As such this should be reflected in the market value of the shares since an agricultural tenancy may be a valuable asset.

Whether or not the company's accounts show deduction of rent, early enquiry should be made as to whether there is land tenanted by the company and once the existence of an agricultural tenancy has been established the case should be sent to the C1 in SV HQ to note.

Similarly if there are any doubts as to the existence of a valid tenancy the matter should again be referred to SV HQ for advice on how to proceed.

If the farming company's assets do not include agricultural land, either freehold, leasehold or by virtue of an agricultural tenancy, it would be normal to treat it in the same way as a trading company. Although a break-up valuation might be one approach in these circumstances, it should be borne in mind that farming companies are particularly stable and a company could continue to farm land in which it has no legal interest for a considerable time. As there are no quoted farming companies, a comparability exercise would not be possible.

In cases where farming companies own their agricultural land or have an agricultural tenancy it is generally considered appropriate to proceed with the share valuation on an assets basis. In general the valuation of straightforward control holdings may proceed on this basis, although it is likely that any freehold property shown in the company accounts will be included at a fraction of its true open market value.

The way in which the other shares are held is of particular importance in the valuation of farming companies. The valuation of minority interests can present particular problems. Very often the company is closely controlled within a particular family and an outside purchaser of even a significant minority shareholding cannot guarantee that he will be allowed to play a part in the running of the company. Given the close family ties and the fact that the family is usually being provided with a family home as well as a way of life, together with an income, the prospects of realising any return may be more remote than investments in trading companies...

Any company showing regular and significant losses cannot carry on indefinitely and those companies owning freehold property, especially on the urban fringe, do have a certain amount of hope value. Indeed towards the end of the 1980s the number of farmers leaving the land due to shrinking incomes and soaring debt rose steadily.

The underlying assets of a farming company can therefore play a very relevant part in the valuation of minority holdings, but it must be recognised that more substantial discounts are appropriate than those which one would expect to find offered for, say, a property investment company.

Other assets which may require revaluing are livestock, (especially those included in the accounts on the herd basis which reflects historical cost) milk quotas after 1984, potato quotas, beef and sheep quotas.'

(HMRC Share Valuation Manual, SVM18120)

12 Commercial valuation on the sale of a company

12.1 The nature of a commercial valuation

It is common to hear it stated that a commercial valuation and a fiscal valuation are two totally different valuations, with no connection between them. This is wrong. As we explored in Chapter 1 of this book, the principle of a fiscal valuation is the price that would be paid on the open market that is postulated. All the techniques that are available to the valuer of a company that is about to be put on the market for sale are equally available to the practitioner who undertakes a fiscal valuation. The actual price put on the shareholding is, nevertheless, frequently very different. There are two reasons for this.

First, when valuing at the time of sale you know the identity of the purchaser. When a valuation is required to put a price tag on a small unquoted company that is to be offered for sale, you may not know which individual person or company will make the purchase but you will usually be clear as to the type of person who would be interested in making such a purchase. The characteristics, if not the actual identities, of those purchasers can be ascertained. The valuer can, thus, assess the value of the shares to a purchaser of the type that has been identified. From this a reasonable estimate can be usefully made of the price that would be offered by the potential purchasers.

Secondly, it is very rare that a commercial valuation is of less than 100 per cent of the issued share capital. Even where the valuation is required for a proportion of the shares, such as when a business partner is bought out by his co-owners, the circumstances of the agreement (if not the company's articles) frequently require that the value of that shareholding is the proportionate part of the value of the entire issued share capital of the company.

Although, in practice, a commercial valuation is most likely seen as a prelude to a sale, in the end the valuation becomes irrelevant. It is simply a guide figure and the price actually paid is whatever can be agreed by negotiation between a seller and purchaser. Indeed, perhaps one of the main differences between a fiscal valuation and a commercial valuation is that in the latter there are negotiations that can, in practice, push the sale figure way beyond that which would be envisaged in the valuation for tax purposes. Timing is everything in practice. If a purchaser is desperate for a new business he may well pay well over the odds and surprise everyone.

12.2 A known purchaser

Having gathered together all available relevant information and understood the nature of the business of the company, the starting point for a valuation must always be a calculation of maintainable earnings. Unless dealing with an investment company, the company's assets are rarely of significant value in their own right. Rather, their value is in generating earnings which create wealth for the shareholder. It is always worthwhile when undertaking a fiscal valuation to consider whether a change in the *modus operandi* of a company would lead to enhanced earnings. When dealing with a commercial valuation, where the identity of the prospective purchaser is known, a major uncertainty is taken out of the valuation. The calculation that then needs to be undertaken of earnings is the earnings that would be generated when the business of the company is carried out by the potential purchaser. Often a potential purchaser will have an existing trade in the same industry. Sometimes, the motive in making the purchase is vertical integration, or, perhaps, horizontal integration. Whatever the motive for purchase, the likelihood is that the purchaser will be expecting to generate a higher profit than that from the trade under the previous ownership.

The earnings generated when the trade of a company is carried on in a commercial group are generally higher than those generated when the trade is carried on in isolation for any one (or more) of the following reasons.

- Administration costs are shared.
- There are savings in production costs.
- Joint marketing is less costly per unit sold.
- The products can be sold to a wider market.
- The expertise in the potential purchaser can be utilised.
- There is spare capacity in the potential purchaser.
- There is vertical integration, with one company producing for the other.
- There could be a better pooling of ideas and use of research departments, etc.
- A market perception which helps and the overall strength of the combined organisation.

Care needs to be taken in evaluating the advantage of a commercial grouping. Economists analyse the effects of an increase in the size of a commercial operation as providing economies of scale until the optimum size is reached, after which an increase in size gives reduced profitability, the diseconomies of scale. The financial savings that can be achieved by a single sales force promoting the production of both companies may be outweighed, wholly or in part, by the additional cost of the extra administration required. The advantages of selling in a wider geographical market can be counteracted by the extra cost of delivering to many extra locations. The enthusiasm that is evidenced by the entrepreneur contemplating a purchase can wane in the cold light of experience.

Nevertheless, the expectation must be that the purchase of a company and its business by another company in the same industry is likely to result in higher earnings than would be achieved if the companies remained separate.

When preparing a valuation, it is important to remember that the earnings that are relevant to the potential purchaser are not past earnings but, rather, the future earnings that can be anticipated if the purchase is made. This can mean that past earnings seem to be irrelevant. A prime example is the high prices achieved for internet businesses in 1999. They had yet to make a profit but were valued at stratospheric figures. As has been said, a business of this nature achieves its highest valuation when it is travelling. As soon as it has arrived, and the reality is known, its value may well have peaked (at least, until actual profits are generated).

12.3 Unknown purchasers

A fiscal valuation is frequently performed without consideration of the characteristics of the potential purchasers. Case law abounds with reference to 'the hypothetical unconnected purchaser'. Calculations are often performed on an inward-looking basis. There is careful analysis of the company's historic performance but insufficient regard is taken of characteristics of potential purchasers. This is often simply a consequence of intellectual laziness. If there is a sale, whether a real sale or a hypothetical sale, there is a purchaser – whether potential or real. That purchaser has characteristics. It is essential when considering a commercial sale to identify those characteristics. It may not be possible to be clear as to the actual identity of particular potential purchasers. However, it must be rare for it not to be possible to identify the characteristics of specified categories of likely purchasers.

Let us take as an illustration a family printing business that is put up for sale. Other printing businesses in the geographical area may be interested in a purchase to reduce production costs. These can be evaluated. A publisher or a designer may be interested in purchasing a printing business in order to produce his product. Again, the increased earnings by virtue of vertical integration can be computed. Another printing business may be interested in marketing the aggregate production capacity using just its own sales force. The effect of this can be evaluated.

It is not necessary to name the purchaser in order to compute the potential saving from aggregation.

12.4 Individuals

The world is made of individuals, each with his hopes, his fears, his wealth and his poverty. The shareholders of a company are individuals (even if it is a corporate shareholder, there are, ultimately, individuals that own the corporation). The actual circumstances, both financial and otherwise, of the individual shareholders of a company can have a very significant effect on the price to be paid for shares.

Consider the following shareholdings:

Father	(age 64)	30% shareholding
1st son	(age 35)	30% shareholding
2nd son	(age 32)	30% shareholding
Mother	(age 63)	10% shareholding

What is the value in the commercial marketplace for the father's 30 per cent holding? The value of his shareholding is heavily influenced by the personal characteristics of the two sons. Let us say that one son is highly capable and of great benefit to the business. In practice, it is sometimes the case that one of the sons is key to the business and any purchaser would require that son to be tied in for a period of time, with the hope even that that son would become integrated in the new organisation, becoming a long-term member of management. That is certainly relevant in a commercial valuation or sale of a company and as a result the other shareholders are likely to benefit from the involvement of that son, as it will first help to sell the company and secondly perhaps obtain a better price. It is difficult to see how that can be introduced into a tax valuation, because if the son in question were not to be become involved he cannot be made to (even though his own interest might be prejudiced). Another company in the same industry could find the purchase of the father's shares highly attractive if it was made in conjunction with the granting of a beneficial employment contract to the capable son, so that the business then prospers under the son's management, assisted by the skill and experience of the acquiring companies executives. This conclusion may, however, presuppose a measure of co-operation between the two brothers.

If, on the other hand, good work undertaken by one brother is constantly undone by the other, the attraction of acquiring the father's shareholding is greatly diminished.

13 The valuation of intangibles

13.1 What is an intangible?

In a sense, any share valuation is a valuation of an intangible as a share has no intrinsic value; rather it is merely a bundle of rights that may give economic benefit to its holder. More usually, however, the word, intangible, is used to denote the following:

- goodwill;
- patent rights;
- copyright;
- brand name or trademark; and
- know-how.

Other intangibles include:

- designs and service marks;
- confidential information which is perhaps linked to know-how;
- the value of sports stars such as footballers; and
- a *Marren v Ingles* right.

13.2 Goodwill

There is a specialised meaning of the word 'goodwill' – that is, goodwill arising on consolidation. This is an arithmetic difference that is displayed on the balance sheet of a group of companies, when the accounts of subsidiaries are consolidated with those of the holding company. It is the difference between an amount paid and the physical assets received.

This aside, the essence of the concept 'goodwill' can probably be best explained for a retail company or a wholesale company by an illustration.

If I go home tonight and see that I need to buy groceries, I am likely to get into my car and drive to my local grocer Snelly. I do that without debating the merits of different shops. I am used to buying eggs, milk and ham at Snelly, and so that is where I go. The goodwill of Snelly Ltd is, in essence, precisely that almost unthinking action by not only me but by most of the people in my town. This is the inherent goodwill of Snelly Ltd. If Snelly were to make losses, the inherent goodwill would remain. Losses do not eliminate the inherent goodwill of a company, although losses may make it more difficult to fend off predators. It may be that competitors may not be prepared to purchase Snelly's goodwill, were it to be offered for sale, as they may make the commercial decision that by doing nothing Snelly will disappear. However, this does not mean that while

Snelly continues to trade there is less goodwill. Even if Snelly produces losses for several years, as long as retailing is a worthwhile financial operation, it is not unreasonable for someone with the relevant retail knowledge and proper business skills to pay to acquire the inherent goodwill of Snelly.

Goodwill is a difficult right to define. Although the courts have identified goodwill as a separate asset (see *IRC v Muller & Co Margarine Ltd* [1901] AC 217 per Lord MacNaghten at 223–224 **case 4 para 5** and its predecessor *Cruttwell v Lye* (1810) 17 Ves 335) economists question as to whether goodwill is a separate property right at all. It is often made up of an amalgamation of several types of intellectual property, such as business contracts (including employees) and other specific intellectual property rights. This would also include the value of a particular brand name. Moreover, in some cases it is linked very closely to location and is therefore part of the property value, arguably. For example, a health and fitness centre can be valued at several times the value normally attributed to bricks and mortar as a consequence of proven ability to generate high profits at its particular site. The site is critical. Customers expect to go to that site; they do not search for the name under which the health and fitness centre trades. The Revenue refer to a distinction between inherent goodwill of this nature and free-standing goodwill. In the case of inherent goodwill, it is not really possible to transfer the goodwill independently of the property to which it attaches.

How then to value this goodwill? A simplistic approach is to say that value of goodwill is the difference between the capitalised value of earnings and the physical assets utilised in the business.

Whilst this may appear to be a neat formulation, its practical use in providing a measurement is limited. If the reason for valuing goodwill is the calculation of a value to be placed on the share capital of a company, then it is likely to be more appropriate to value the company by reference to earnings than to try and isolate a value for goodwill. Exceptionally, the value placed on the shareholding needs to be increased to reflect goodwill that has recently been generated or purchased and has not been reflected in historic earnings.

Where a value is required for goodwill without it being linked to a share value, it is suggested that the most useful approach is to calculate the increase in profit that would accrue to an acquiring company on acquisition of the goodwill. The increased profit is then capitalised by applying a P/E ratio.

An example of an instance where this may be of relevance is the goodwill that is represented by a list of customers. It is possible, at least in principle, to compute the profit that arises on sales to the defined list of customers and a multiple of that profit can be taken to be the value of goodwill in that list. In a commercial deal, it is not uncommon for a value to be placed on a list of customers. This is certainly relevant to mail order businesses who frequently buy lists of customers from another business. These lists have a limited life, particularly, if the list is purchased without an arrangement that address changes will be notified to the purchaser of the list and the value of a list must be assessed by reference to its age and continuing usefulness to the business that has purchased it. Arguably, this is a separate type of asset, although part of the overall commercial goodwill of the company that holds the list.

13.3 Patents

A patent is the right of an inventor that has been registered. A patent can be bought or sold. A patent has no intrinsic use. Rather, it has a use to the business that exploits the invention. This means that a patent only has a value to its owner in two circumstances. First, it is expected to be of use to its owner for its owner's business. Secondly, it is expected to be of use to someone else who is prepared to purchase it or pay royalties for the right to access the patented invention. Most patents registered at the Patent Office at any one time have no value; a few have an extremely high value. Technological change will mean that the majority of patents that are perceived today to have a high value will be of no value in 20 years time.

Where a patent is owned by one person and the patented process used by another, the most usual financial arrangement is for there to be a percentage royalty payable by the user to the patent owner. The royalty is most commonly computed by reference to sales of the product manufactured using the patented process. Less commonly, the royalty is a percentage of profits generated from the use of the patented process.

To value a patent, three alternative methods are commonly used:

- premium profits;
- residual value; and
- royalties foregone.

The premium profits route seeks to isolate the profits accruing to the owner of the patent over and above the profits that would have been generated if the patent was not held.

In the residual value approach, the business is valued twice – once with the patent and once without it.

In the third approach, an estimate is made if the royalties that would have been payable if the patent had been owned by a third party. The royalty flow is then capitalised.

This can be illustrated thus:

- Patent expires in 17 years from valuation date.
- Market royalty rate: 5 per cent.
- Corporation tax: 30 per cent.
- Discount rate (calculated by the comparable companies, increased to reflect the risk of the patented invention being rendered worthless by technological change): 12 per cent.

The sales and consequent patent royalties are estimated as:

Year	Sales £m	Post-tax patent royalties £m
1	4.9	0.17
2	8.3	0.29
3	11.7	0.41
4	15.7	0.55
5	19.4	0.68
6	22.9	0.80
7	24.9	0.87
8	29.7	1.04
9	25.7	0.90
10	22.0	0.77
11	17.1	0.60
12	13.4	0.47
13	8.5	0.30
14	5.1	0.18
15	3.4	0.12
16	2.0	0.07
17	0.6	0.02

Year	£m	NPV factor	NPV £m
1	0.17	0.89	0.15
2	0.29	0.80	0.23
3	0.41	0.71	0.29
4	0.55	0.64	0.35
5	0.68	0.57	0.39
6	0.80	0.51	0.41
7	0.87	0.45	0.39
8	1.04	0.40	0.42
9	0.90	0.36	0.32
10	0.77	0.32	0.25
11	0.60	0.29	0.17
12	0.47	0.26	0.12
13	0.30	0.23	0.07
14	0.18	0.20	0.04

Year	£m	NPV factor	NPV £m
15	0.12	0.18	0.02
16	0.07	0.16	0.01
17	0.02	0.15	0.00
			3.64

NPV of patent £3.64m

In valuing a patent it is necessary to understand the customary practice in the particular industry to which the patent applies. Different industries have different customs as to the way in which patent royalties are commonly measured and, also, have differences in the percentage of sales that is customarily paid as royalty to the patent holder.

In the above example, the valuation is based on the duration of the patent right. That is, the period for which it can be enforced at law. Although a patent may last for 17 years, that is probably several years too long for most modern inventions. In practice, therefore, could a valuation be based on the 17th year, right? Moreover, even having arrived at a discounted value, is that the figure someone would pay? Although, in this illustration the discount rate has been increased to allow for risk, would a purchaser wish to put in something further for a profit? If everything is in the discount rate, then no further adjustment may be required; everything depends, therefore, upon the rate chosen. It could be that sales revenue towards the end of the period chosen should be discounted at a higher rate than that used in the early years to reflect the fact that there is greater uncertainty the further into the future.

The reason for registering a patent is to prevent others from exploiting the invention. In that sense, it becomes a legal bar even if someone comes up with the same idea independently but at a later date (or fails to register their idea). Its value is then dependent on the ability of the inventor (or an assignee) to exploit the invention profitably. An inventor often does not have the resources to do this, given the likely requirement of capital investment and the creation of an organisation, including marketing expertise. It is commonplace that the value of an invention cannot be exploited by its inventor as he does not have access to the technology or the investment capital required to exploit it and the companies with the necessary funds choose to use a product or process of their own invention that is similar but which can be distinguished sufficiently to allow a separate patent registration.

An employee who invents something in that capacity will usually find that his invention belongs to his employer.

13.4 Copyright

Copyright exists in written work, drawings and also designs. Where the work was created on or after 1 January 1996, the normal term of copyright is the lifetime of the author plus a further 70 years. This new period applies to:

- works created on or after 1 January 1996;
- works already in copyright on 31 December 1995, which will benefit from 'extended copyright'; and
- works in which copyright had expired, but the author died less than 70 years ago (ie the author died in the years 1926–95 inclusive).

As with patents, the capital value of a copyright is best calculated by reference to the expected royalty flow. In a commercial context, it is frequently the value of a copyright in an industrial design that is at issue. In most instances a design has a restricted useful life although, commonly, the length of that life is not certain at the time of valuation. It is, thus, rarely appropriate to apply a 'quasi P/E ratio' based on a past flow of royalties. A better result is probably to be achieved by a discounted cash flow exercise on expected future royalty income.

Where the valuer is faced with the question of valuation of a copyright of an artistic work, the fickle nature of the public's appreciation of art must indicate caution in applying too high a multiple of annual royalties. The volume of sales of *Pride and Prejudice* is high, 183 years after Jane Austen's death; most written work suffers a less happy fate.

13.5 Brand names

We go to a pub and order a Guinness. To clean the house we use a Hoover. Brand names have a very powerful place in society and in industry. A brand name can be registered as a trademark. A brand name, whether or not registered, can be bought and sold. Much work has been undertaken on the calculation of value in the best known brand names. This led in the 1980s to values for brand names appearing on balance sheets of listed companies such as Xerox and Hovis MacDougall; the value being the company's own estimate of the value that it had built up through successful marketing. Against the scepticism that has sometimes been shown can be put the fact that brand names are actually bought and sold commercially, sometimes for very significant sums. It could be that the putting of value on the balance sheet in the first place has helped the market in selling brand names.

In principle, the same valuation method can be used to value a brand name as for valuing a patent. In practice, companies with strong brands usually also have strong distribution networks, as well as a high level of expertise in the management of the company and marketing of the product. It is, then, not possible to be certain that the high level of profit on sales of the brand is due to the brand name, or whether it derives from good marketing and good management of distribution.

The method used to value a brand name is frequently the premium profit approach (see section **13.3**). This can be undertaken in at least three different ways:

- *Margin differential.* The premium profit is computed by comparing the actual operating margin of the business owning the brand name to the 'normal' operating margin achieved by businesses that do not own a significant brand name.
- *Return on assets differential.* The premium profit is assessed by comparing the return on capital employed related to the brand name against the normal return on capital employed in businesses that do not benefit from the brand name.
- *Pricing differential.* The price per unit of the branded product after deducting brand development costs is compared to the price of the generic equivalent.

The approach in the first of these three options can be illustrated as follows.

Example

Five years branded business' sales forecast:		
		£m
Year 1		19.3
Year 2		21.1
Year 3		23.2
Year 4		25.4
Year 5		27.9
Operating margin branded business	10%	
Operating margin of equivalent unbranded business	6%	
Hence, premium profit margin	4%	

Assumptions:
Corporation tax 30%
Terminal value is expected cash flow in year 5 × earnings multiple of 10
Appropriate discount rate for branded business cash flows is 12%

Calculation

	Premium cash flows £m	Terminal value £m	Total £m
Year 1	0.54	0.00	0.54
Year 2	0.59	0.00	0.59
Year 3	0.65	0.00	0.65
Year 4	0.71	0.00	0.71
Year 5	0.78	7.85	8.63

Year	£m	NPV factor	NPV £m
1	0.54	0.89	0.48
2	0.59	0.80	0.47
3	0.65	0.71	0.46
4	0.71	0.64	0.45
5	8.63	0.57	4.90
			6.76

Value of brand: £6.76m

A criticism of this calculation is that the greatest part of the value is derived from the terminal value in year 5. This seems to beg the very question itself, which is how to value a brand name. The terminal value of the brand cannot really be known without the proverbial crystal ball and so how is that figure arrived at? In arriving at the profitability of a brand name, it is really the gearing effect that is relevant. The production costs for a particular item might be very similar to other products in the market. The value is being able to charge an extra penny or two on a bar of chocolate or a pint of beer; this is a straight increase in pre-taxed profits. Thus, the brand name can be seen as having some sort of gearing effect. What we have is, in effect, an additional value added to the product, which on a capitalised basis produces a value for the brand name, that value being in addition to the goodwill value of the business generally.

Using the same data, an alternative calculation can be performed, based on the (perhaps) more reliable estimate of revenue in year 1, rather than in later years.

Alternative Calculation

Branded business:	£m
Fully taxed profit year 1 (calculated on operation margin of 10%)	1.35
Earnings multiple	x10
Branded business value	13.5

Unbranded business:	£m
Fully taxed profit year 1 (calculated on operating margin of 6%)	0.81
Earnings multiple	x10
Unbranded business value	8.1
Value of brand: (calculated as branded business value less unbranded business value)	£5.4m

13.6 Know-how

Know-how is typically the contribution to a manufacturing business of a systems engineer. Of vital importance to manufacturing industry generally, know-how relates to a method of organising production, rather than to the techniques employed. In contrast to patents, whilst know-how has undoubtedly a value, know-how is rarely bought and sold.

APPENDICES

Appendix 1
Checklist for a valuation report

The following is a checklist of items of information that can usefully be brought together when preparing to undertake a valuation of shares in an unlisted trading company. Appropriate alterations are required when the company is a property company or other investment company.

1 The company

1.1 Full accounts of the company for the five years prior to valuation date.
1.2 Management accounts of the company for the period from the last accounting date to the valuation date.
1.3 Management forecasts produced prior to the valuation date.
1.4 The proposed use of any cash balances in the balance sheet.
1.5 Any significant additional bank borrowings anticipated.
1.6 Capital commitments.
1.7 Anticipated capital expenditure, not committed.
1.8 Memorandum and articles of association.
1.9 Shareholders' Agreement.
1.10 Estimates of property valuation.
1.11 Details of leases, particularly to estimate liabilities, such as dilapidations.
1.12 Details of any assets not shown on the balance sheet, such as intellectual property rights.
1.13 Details of key employees (inspect service contracts).
1.14 An estimate of the market salary for the work actually undertaken by each director.
1.15 Tax computations for same periods as accounts.
1.16 Have the accounts been affected by any non-recurring items not disclosed when material?
1.17 Copies of board minutes (depending upon the size of the holding, ie whether or not a purchaser could reasonably expect these).
1.18 A note of any pending litigation matters, where material.
1.19 Details of any surplus assets, including poorly utilised factory space.
1.20 Confirmation that plant and machinery, etc is adequate for future requirements. (Consider the affect of technological change.)
1.21 Is the company affected by environmental matters that could give rise to liabilities in the future?

2 The company's trade

2.1   Data on sales prior to valuation date.

2.2   Sales forecasts prepared prior to valuation date.

2.3   Major customers.

2.4   Major contracts being performed.

2.5   Major future contracts anticipated at the valuation date.

2.6   Production records prior to the valuation date.

2.7   Production forecasts made prior to the valuation date.

2.8   Changes in production methods anticipated at the valuation date.

2.9   Capital expenditure either incurred or anticipated that would have an effect on production.

2.10 Sales brochures, giving an understanding of the product.

2.11 Details of any new products or services likely to come on stream in the near future.

2.12 Spending on technology, etc for, say, the previous three years.

2.13 Details of any changes to the business in recent years, such as the closure of a division.

2.14 Is there any new legislation or expected legislation likely to affect the business?

2.15 Are there any international aspects likely to affect the business such as difficulties in obtaining supplies purchased in particular overseas territories or sales in particular overseas markets?

2.16 To what extent is the business susceptible to changes in technology?

3 The industry

3.1   Collate newspaper and magazine reports on performance of the industry around the valuation date.

3.2   Collate information on the size and geographical spread of the industry.

3.3   Consider the volatility of financial performance in the industry.

4 The national economy

4.1   Bank base rate.

4.2   Financial Times indices.

4.3   The economic cycle.

4.4   Consider how the industry performs in relation to the economic cycle.

5 Potential purchasers

5.1   Other shareholders.
5.2   Potential outside purchasers.
5.3   Inherent attraction (or otherwise) of shareholding.

6 Actual sales

6.1   Dates.
6.2   Prices paid.
6.3   Relationship between vendor and purchaser.
6.4   Obtain details of any offers made for the shares or business (or a part of it) before or after the valuation date.

7 Comparables

7.1   Identify comparable companies.
7.2   Identify any actual sales of shares in comparable companies. If possible, obtain full details of the circumstances surrounded such sales:

- Was the sale at arm's length?
- Was the sale linked to continuing employment?
- Was the share sale part of the sale of the whole company?

7.3   Determine the discount/premium that could be applied in relation to comparable share sales.

Appendix 2
Organisation of HMRC Share Valuation

Share Valuation is the specialist division of HMRC that is based within Capital Taxes Office and under the administration of the controller of Capital Taxes, but which is responsible for advising all departments of HMRC on share valuations. Share Valuation addresses are:

England, Wales & Northern Ireland   Scotland
Fitz Roy House Mulberry House   Meldrum House
PO Box 46   15 Drumsheugh Gardens
Castle Meadow Road   EDINBURGH, EH3 7UH
NOTTINGHAM, NG2 1BD   DX: 542002 Edinburgh 14
DX: 70103 Nottingham 4   Tel: 0131 777 4180
Tel (customer service): 0115 974 2374   Tel (customer service):
Tel (general valuation enquiries):   0115 974 2374
0115 974 2222
Fax: 0131 777 4170
Tel (foreign enquiries): 0115 974 2300
Tel (share option enquiries): 0115 974 2355
Fax: 0115 974 2197

Valuations are referred to HMRC Share Valuation from local districts (for capital gains tax), from Capital Taxes Office (for inheritance tax) from Employee Share Schemes (for the value of shares for an approved option scheme) and from other specialist divisions, including enquiry branch. Where the market value to be tested has been returned on a taxpayer's self-assessment, it is the responsibility of the local district that receives the assessment to send the taxpayer a notice of commencement of an enquiry and to close the enquiry at the end of negotiations. Neither action is taken by HMRC Share Valuation itself. Once reference is made to HMRC Share Valuation, however, correspondence is normally between the taxpayer or his agent and HMRC Share Valuation direct.

In addition to valuing shares, HMRC Share Valuation has responsibility for most other valuations required for fiscal purposes, including:

- Loans to companies at less than face value.
- Goodwill of sole traders and partnerships.
- Brand names.
- Foreign land.
- Lloyds underwriting interests.
- Livestock and bloodstock.
- Suspended and cancelled quotes on the Stock Exchange.

- Bullion.
- Wine and spirits.
- Yachts, ships, aircraft and mobile homes.
- Royalties, patents and copyrights.
- Chattels.

HMRC Share Valuation is organised into four valuation groups, each headed by an assistant director reporting to the deputy director of Share Valuation. Each valuation group is divided into between two and five teams. The specialisms of the teams are, at the time of writing:

Aircraft/Boats/Ships	Team 1A
Banks Team	Team 1B
Bloodstock	Team 4A
Brand Valuations	Team 1B
Broadcasting	Team 3A
Bullion	Team 2B
Chattels	Team 4A
Copyrights/Publishing	Team 3A
Football Clubs	Team 2E and 1C
Goodwill	Team 1A, 1B and 1C
Insurance Companies	Team 3B
Intellectual Property	Team 1B
Livestock	Team 4A
Lloyds Brokers	Team 1C
Lloyds Underwriting	Team 1C
Media	Team 3A
Mineral Valuations	Team 1B and 2C
Mobile Homes	Team 1A
Oil extraction, petrochemicals, fishing	Team 4C
Pension Schemes	Team 4B
Royal Albert Hall valuations	Team 2B
Royalties	Team 3A
Shareholders' Agreements	Valuation Group 2 Assistant Director
Special Circumstances	VG4 (Information Support)
Underwriting companies	Team 1C
Wines and Spirits	Team 2C
Yachts, Boats, Ships	Team 1A

HMRC Share Valuation is organised so that each individual examiner has a range of company reference numbers. These are the same numbers as are used by the Registrar of Companies. This means that valuation of a particular company's shares will normally always be inspected by the same examiner.

The practitioner should be aware of the significant quantity of information available to HMRC Share Valuation. The library of Share Valuation contains all editions of the following:

Accountancy	Exchange & Mart
Acquisitions Monthly	Extel Capital Gains (Monthly Supp)
All England Law Reports	Farmers Weekly
Ascot Bloodstock Sales Catalogues	Farm Tax Brief
The Author	Financial Dagblad
Basler	The Financial Post
Barons	Financial Times
Bloodstock Sales Review	The Financial Times Monthly Index
The Bookseller	FT Music & Copyright
Borsen Zeitung (Newspaper)	General Insurance Magazine
British Tax Review	The Grocer
Broadcast	The Guardian (Newspaper)
Capital Taxes – Planning	Halsbury's Laws of England
Chaseform	HMSO Daily List
Chasers & Hurdlers	Horse and Hound
Chatset Guide to Syndicate Run Offs	Horses in Training
Colombo Stock List	Insurance Directory
(LA) Cote des Fosses (Newspaper)	Investors Chronicle
Counsel (circ with New Law Journal)	Kenya Standard
Country Life	Law Reports
Daltons Weekly	Law Society Gazette
Decanter	Lloyds League Tables
Digest of Lloyd's News	Luxembourg Stock Exchange
Doncaster Bloodstock Sales	Madras Stock Exchange
Dymond's Capital Taxes	Marketing Magazine
Earnings Guide Monthly	Mathieson's Stock Exchange Investment List
Economist	Money Management
Engineering	Moody's Bank & Finance
Estates Gazette	Moody's International
Extel	News Cards
Moody's Industrial	Straits Times
Moody's OTC Unlisted	Sunday Times
Moody's OTC Industrial	Tattersalls
Morgan Grenfell Investment Trust Companies	Taxation
Morning Post	Taxation Practitioner
Neur Zutchet Zeitung (Newspaper)	Tax Bulletin
New Law Journal	Tax Information Bulletin
Pacemaker & Thoroughbred Breeder	Tax Journal
Palmers Company Law	Times (Newspaper)
Publishing News	Turf Directory
Race Form	Toronto Stock Exchange
Racehorses	Unlisted Securities Market -Market Data (Hoare Govett Ltd)
Racing Post	Weekly Law Report
Solicitors Journal	Yachting World
Statistical Record	

Appendix 3
Inland Revenue Help Sheet IR 295

Claim for hold-over relief - Sections 165 and 260 TCGA 1992

	Transferor		Transferee
Name		Name	
Address		Address	
	Postcode		Postcode
HMRC office		HMRC office	
Tax reference		Tax reference	

Except in case of a gift in settlement, the claim must be made by both transferor and transferee. If the transferor or transferee has no HM Revenue & Customs office or tax reference please explain why.

I/We hereby claim relief under Section 165/Section 260 TCGA 1992 in respect of the transfer of the asset specified below. The particulars given in this claim are correctly stated to the best of my/our information and belief.

Description of asset and date of disposal

√ one box

The gain held over is £ _____ A calculation is attached ☐

I/We apply for deferment of valuations and have completed the second page of the claim form. ☐

I/We qualify for relief because √

- the asset is used for the business of *Please insert name of person* _____ ☐

- the asset consists of unlisted shares or securities of a trading company or holding company of a trading group ☐

- the asset is agricultural land ☐

- the asset consists of listed shares or securities of the transferor's personal company or, where trustees are the transferors, a company in which they had 25% of the voting rights ☐

- the disposal was a chargeable transfer, but not a Potentially Exempt Transfer, for Inheritance Tax purposes ☐

- Capital Taxes Office reference number _____

- the disposal was exempt from Inheritance Tax under IHTA Section *Please insert Section number* _____ ☐

Signed		Signed	
Date	/ /	Date	/ /

Appendix 3 Inland Revenue Help Sheet IR 295

Help Sheet IR295

For the Capital Gains Pages

Request for valuations to be deferred

The disposal meets the conditions of Statement of Practice SP8/92. We jointly request that SP8/92 be applied, so that formal agreement of values can be deferred. We accept the terms upon which SP8/92 applies. We are satisfied that the value of the asset at the date of transfer is such that there would be a chargeable gain but for the claim.

Transferor

Signed _____

Date ___ / ___ / ___

Transferee

Signed _____

Date ___ / ___ / ___

The details required are as follows; where estimated figures are used please use the codes at the bottom of the form. Acceptance of the claim does not bind us to accepting the values shown. The claimants are not bound by the values shown.

If there is insufficient space or you find it more convenient, please give the details on a separate sheet. You can give the information in the form of a calculation if you prefer.

1	Date of acquisition and cost	___ / ___ / ___	£
2	Date and cost of additional allowable expenditure	___ / ___ / ___	£
3	Value at 31 March 1982, if relevant		£
4	Value of asset at date of transfer		£
5	If asset consists of shares or securities details of any relevant bonus issues or reorganisations		
6	If the disposal is a part disposal, details of and value of part retained		

Notes

- The disposal of part of a shareholding may be a part disposal. If there is an entry in box 6, the figures at boxes 1 to 3 are those for the whole asset, not just the part disposed of.

- Where the figures given are values and not actual costs, please write whichever of the following letters is appropriate in the box, after the figures:

  A   value agreed by us

  V   valuation by professional valuer but not agreed by us

  E   our estimate of the value.

[Source: HM Revenue & Customs (see www.hmrc.gov.uk)]

Appendix 4
FT Actuaries Table for 31 March 1982

| EQUITY GROUPS & SUB-SECTIONS | Wed March 31 1983 | | | | | Tue Mar 30 | Mon Mar 29 | Fri Mar 26 | Thurs Mar 25 | Year ago (approx.) |
Figures in parentheses show number of stocks per section	Index No.	Day's Change %	Est. Earnings Yield % (Max.)	Gross Div. Yield % (ACT at 30%)	Est. P/E Ratio (Net)	Index No.	Index No.	Index No.	Index No.	Index No.
1 CAPITAL GOODS (208)	370.64	+1.1	9.82	4.29	12.61	366.73	363.94	366.12	368.45	342.27
2 Building Materials (23)	327.18	-0.7	13.54	5.25	8.86	329.64	329.40	330.66	332.75	307.60
3 Contracting, Construction (28)	607.03	+0.2	14.43	4.75	8.20	605.88	607.31	610.06	614.54	575.46
4 Electricals (31)	1288.40	+1.3	7.25	2.30	17.63	1271.26	1258.90	1265.09	1273.00	1088.97
5 Engineering Contractors (9)	496.11	+0.7	13.01	5.92	8.95	492.51	493.41	498.57	501.63	444.65
6 Mechanical Engineering (67)	196.40	+2.4	11.79	5.75	10.34	191.88	188.79	189.39	190.61	208.35
8 Metals and Metal Forming (11)	163.20	+2.0	9.76	7.26	13.20	159.95	158.21	161.08	162.57	156.13
9 Motors (21)	96.58	+0.6	2.60	6.88	-	95.98	95.70	96.24	96.11	98.30
10 Other Industrial Materials (18)	374.03	+0.8	9.75	5.66	12.41	371.23	369.21	373.54	376.15	355.29
21 CONSUMER GROUP (201)	303.72	+1.5	12.16	5.50	10.08	299.37	296.55	296.40	297.95	266.21
22 Brewers and Distillers (21)	308.27	+1.4	15.34	6.33	7.86	303.89	299.88	299.23	298.80	285.46
25 Food Manufacturing (22)	277.60	+1.3	15.32	6.53	7.85	247.10	271.51	271.72	273.60	251.35
26 Food Retailing (14)	607.35	+0.3	8.86	3.30	13.77	605.79	602.11	603.70	607.20	524.08
27 Health and Household Products (8)	395.52	+1.8	8.34	4.03	14.01	388.65	382.50	383.70	387.01	285.87
29 Leisure (24)	454.55	+2.6	9.90	4.99	12.49	442.87	438.52	440.85	444.61	402.27
32 Newspapers, Publishing (12)	526.71	+0.7	10.78	5.94	12.41	523.16	521.37	525.77	527.10	489.01
33 Packaging and Paper (14)	147.95	+1.5	13.29	7.16	9.00	145.79	146.01	147.37	148.32	138.48
34 Stores (45)	283.07	+1.3	10.05	4.74	13.33	279.36	277.12	275.59	276.63	266.70
35 Textiles (23)	176.18	+0.5	9.61	5.68	13.42	175.32	172.83	172.72	173.64	150.02
36 Tobaccos (3)	313.05	+2.3	19.57	8.33	5.82	305.93	304.65	303.16	306.32	219.38

39	Other Consumer (15)	296.35	+0.5	1.52	5.33	-	294.90	291.83	294.06	293.39	273.87
41	OTHER GROUPS (78)	257.45	+1.0	13.09	6.04	9.21	254.88	253.32	253.91	256.31	221.68
42	Chemicals (16)	335.63	+1.6	13.29	6.88	8.99	330.42	328.80	329.33	334.47	259.25
44	Office Equipment (4)	126.85	-0.3	12.69	6.78	9.59	127.24	126.15	125.24	127.28	118.81
45	Shipping and Transport (13)	583.96	+1.0	18.79	6.33	6.31	578.02	575.08	578.08	580.08	611.63
46	Miscellaneous (45)	327.44	+0.7	11.31	5.00	10.82	325.27	322.93	324.16	325.45	288.91
49	INDUSTRIAL GROUP (487)	320.67	+1.2	11.43	5.13	10.73	316.71	314.08	314.79	316.75	285.88
51	Oils (13)	681.00	+0.7	18.34	8.50	6.36	676.22	662.22	692.64	682.47	782.54
59	500 SHARE INDEX	350.07	+1.2	12.50	5.65	9.70	346.04	342.49	345.58	346.57	325.56
61	FINANCIAL GROUP (117)	259.41	+0.6	-	6.20	-	257.78	256.31	257.98	258.99	256.44
62	Banks (6)	271.62	-1.1	38.82	7.87	2.82	274.76	272.62	274.23	275.89	234.21
63	Discount Houses (9)	232.06	-	-	9.34	-	232.06	236.90	236.90	236.33	306.68
65	Insurance (Life) (9)	268.94	+3.2	-	6.26	-	260.69	258.47	259.55	259.20	270.95
66	Insurance (Composite) (10)	164.31	+0.8	-	8.29	-	163.06	163.34	166.81	167.33	168.51
67	Insurance Brokers (7)	484.75	+1.7	10.88	5.14	12.55	476.51	470.35	468.85	469.14	353.66
68	Merchant Banks (12)	153.61	+2.9	-	5.46	-	149.28	148.04	145.63	145.83	158.67
69	Property (49)	460.26	+0.7	4.70	3.24	28.40	457.00	453.86	455.92	459.00	511.09
70	Other Financial (15)	179.90	-0.4	18.25	6.36	6.56	180.69	179.34	179.26	179.64	172.45
71	Investment Trusts (112)	298.53	+0.7	-	5.40	-	296.47	295.53	295.84	295.60	301.11
81	Mining Finance (4)	204.98	+0.3	16.53	6.93	7.35	204.30	203.33	204.68	207.85	240.32
91	Overseas Traders (17)	383.44	+0.4	13.65	8.30	8.94	381.88	380.61	381.64	383.51	448.04
99	ALL SHARE INDEX (750)	326.59	+1.0	-	5.80	-	323.31	320.46	323.00	324.02	311.45

FT Actuaries Table for 31 March 1982

FIXED INTEREST — PRICE INDICES

	Wed Mar 31	Day's change %	Tue Mar 30	xd adj. today	xd adj. 1982 to date
British Government					
1 5 years	111.06	+0.32	110.71	–	2.89
2 5-15 years	110.94	+0.94	109.92	–	3.43
3 Over 15 years	115.38	+0.98	114.26	–	3.04
4 Irredeemables	122.45	+1.35	120.81	–	1.62
5 All Stocks	112.15	+0.77	111.30	–	3.11
6 Debentures and Loans	87.83		87.44	–	3.51
7 Preference	64.72		64.72	–	2.52

AVERAGE GROSS REDEMPTION YIELDS

		Wed Mar 31	Tue Mar 30	Year ago (approx.)
British Government				
Low Coupons				
1	5 years	11.69	11.91	11.40
2	15 years	12.73	12.86	11.95
3	25 years	12.59	12.69	12.03
Medium Coupons				
4	5 years	13.90	14.05	13.02
5	15 years	13.73	13.88	13.43
6	25 years	13.27	13.41	13.11
High Coupons				
7	5 years	13.87	14.02	13.02
8	15 years	13.90	14.08	13.63
9	25 years	13.32	13.58	13.23
10	Irredeemables †	12.38	11.43	12.21
Debs & Loans				
11	5 years	14.72	14.82	14.12
12	15 years	14.64	14.71	14.30
13	25 years	14.60	14.65	14.31
14	Preference†	15.19	14.37	15.19

† Flat yield. Highs and lows record, base dates, values and constituent changes are published in Saturday issues. A new list of constituents is available from the Publishers, The Financial Times, Bracken House, Cannon Street, London, EC4P 4BY, price 15p, by post 28p.

Appendix 5
Application for post-transaction valuation check

Application for post transaction valuation check

Please complete all relevant items and send the application to your HMRC Office (**not** to any of the Valuation Offices)

Taxpayer details

Name _____

Address _____

_____ Postcode _____

Reference   National Insurance number *(where appropriate)*

[   ]   [| | | | |]

Agent's name _____ Reference _____

Address _____

_____ Postcode _____

Details of disposal

Date of disposal   [/   /   ]

Name and address of purchaser

Name _____

Address _____

_____ Postcode _____

Reason for valuation

√ *as appropriate*

[ ] Rebasing to 31 March 1982

[ ] Market value disposal (disposal to a connected person or a bargain not at arm's length)

[ ] Negligible value claim

[ ] Other - *please specify* _____

Valuation required

Description of asset to be valued	Valuation date	Valuation offered

Shares   - The description should include the name of the company, the registration number (if known), the class and the number of shares to be valued. Enter in the table your valuation **per share** and not the total value of your holding.

Goodwill - The description should provide sufficient information to identify the asset. If an incorporation is involved the details provided should identify the name and nature of the business from which the transfer has been made and also, the name and company registration number of the recipient company together with the registered office address.

Land   - The description should provide sufficient information to identify the property, with details of your interest in the property and details of any tenancies existing at the valuation date. The term 'land' includes both land and buildings.

Other   - The description should provide sufficient information to identify the asset.

CG34

You should also provide

√ to show items enclosed

☐   A capital gains computation for the disposal with an estimate of your capital gains tax liability for the tax year in which you made the disposal, or for companies the corporation tax liability on chargeable gains, or for partnership disposals, estimates of the liabilities of the individual partners

☐   Details of any reliefs due or to be claimed in respect of the disposal

☐   A copy of any valuation report obtained

☐   If available, the cost and date of acquisition of the asset and details of any improvements made

☐   For **share** valuations - full accounts for the three years up to the valuation date

☐   For **goodwill** valuations - full accounts for the three years up to the valuation date

☐   For **land** valuations -

     • if you held a leasehold interest, a copy of the lease applying at the valuation date

     • if the land was let at the valuation date, a copy of any tenancy agreement applying at that date

     • a plan showing the location of the land if the valuation is of undeveloped land

☐   Any other papers you feel may be relevant

Use this space to provide any other information that you consider is relevant to your valuation

---

2

[Source: HM Revenue & Customs (see www.hmrc.gov.uk)]

Appendix 6
Retail Prices Index

Year	Jan	Feb	Mar	Apr	May	Jun	Jul	Aug	Sep	Oct	Nov	Dec	Avg
1925	6.5	6.5	6.5	6.3	6.3	6.2	6.3	6.4	6.3	6.4	6.4	6.4	6.4
1926	6.3	6.3	6.2	6.1	6.0	6.1	6.2	6.2	6.2	6.3	6.5	6.5	6.2
1927	6.3	6.2	6.2	6.0	5.9	5.9	6.0	5.9	6.0	6.0	6.1	6.1	6.1
1928	6.1	6.0	5.9	5.9	5.9	6.0	6.0	6.0	6.0	6.0	6.0	6.1	6.0
1929	6.0	6.0	6.0	5.9	5.8	5.8	5.8	5.9	5.9	6.0	6.0	6.0	5.9
1930	6.0	5.9	5.8	5.7	5.6	5.6	5.6	5.7	5.7	5.7	5.7	5.6	5.7
1931	5.5	5.5	5.4	5.3	5.3	5.3	5.3	5.3	5.3	5.3	5.3	5.4	5.4
1932	5.3	5.3	5.3	5.2	5.2	5.1	5.2	5.1	5.1	5.2	5.2	5.2	5.2
1933	5.1	5.1	5.0	5.0	4.9	4.9	5.0	5.0	5.1	5.1	5.2	5.2	5.1
1934	5.1	5.1	5.1	5.0	5.0	5.0	5.1	5.1	5.2	5.2	5.2	5.2	5.1
1935	5.2	5.1	5.1	5.0	5.0	5.1	5.2	5.2	5.2	5.3	5.3	5.3	5.2
1936	5.3	5.3	5.3	5.2	5.2	5.2	5.3	5.3	5.3	5.4	5.5	5.5	5.3
1937	5.5	5.5	5.5	5.5	5.5	5.5	5.6	5.6	5.6	5.7	5.8	5.8	5.6
1938	5.8	5.7	5.7	5.6	5.6	5.6	5.8	5.6	5.6	5.6	5.6	5.6	5.7
1939	5.6	5.6	5.5	5.5	5.5	5.5	5.6	5.6	5.6	6.0	6.1	6.3	5.7
1940	6.3	6.4	6.5	6.4	6.5	6.6	6.8	6.7	6.8	6.8	7.0	7.1	6.7
1941	7.1	7.1	7.1	7.2	7.2	7.2	7.2	7.2	7.2	7.2	7.2	7.3	7.2
1942	7.2	7.2	7.2	7.2	7.2	7.2	7.2	7.3	7.2	7.2	7.2	7.2	7.2
1943	7.2	7.2	7.2	7.2	7.2	7.2	7.2	7.2	7.2	7.2	7.2	7.2	7.2
1944	7.2	7.2	7.2	7.2	7.2	7.2	7.3	7.3	7.3	7.3	7.3	7.3	7.3
1945	7.3	7.3	7.3	7.3	7.4	7.4	7.5	7.4	7.4	7.4	7.4	7.4	7.4
1946	7.4	7.4	7.4	7.4	7.4	7.4	7.4	7.4	7.4	7.4	7.4	7.4	7.4
1947	7.4	7.4	7.4	7.4	7.4	7.4	7.4	7.4	7.4	7.4	7.6	7.6	7.4
1948	7.6	7.8	7.8	7.9	7.9	8.1	7.9	7.9	7.9	7.9	8.0	8.0	7.9
1949	8.0	8.0	8.0	8.0	8.2	8.2	8.2	8.2	8.2	8.3	8.3	8.3	8.2
1950	8.3	8.3	8.3	8.4	8.4	8.4	8.4	8.3	8.4	8.5	8.5	8.5	8.4
1951	8.6	8.7	8.7	8.9	9.1	9.2	9.3	9.3	9.4	9.5	9.5	9.6	9.2
1952	9.7	9.8	9.8	9.9	9.9	10.1	10.1	10.1	10.0	10.1	10.1	10.2	10.0
1953	10.1	10.2	10.3	10.4	10.3	10.4	10.4	10.3	10.3	10.3	10.3	10.3	10.3
1954	10.3	10.3	10.4	10.4	10.4	10.4	10.7	10.6	10.5	10.6	10.7	10.7	10.5
1955	10.7	10.7	10.7	10.8	10.8	11.0	11.0	11.0	11.0	11.2	11.3	11.3	11.0
1956	11.2	11.2	11.4	11.6	11.5	11.5	11.5	11.5	11.5	11.6	11.6	11.6	11.5
1957	11.7	11.7	11.7	11.8	11.8	11.9	12.0	12.0	11.9	12.0	12.1	12.2	11.9
1958	12.2	12.1	12.2	12.3	12.3	12.4	12.2	12.2	12.2	12.3	12.4	12.4	12.3
1959	12.4	12.4	12.4	12.3	12.3	12.3	12.3	12.3	12.2	12.3	12.4	12.4	12.3
1960	12.4	12.4	12.3	12.4	12.4	12.5	12.5	12.4	12.4	12.5	12.6	12.6	12.5
1961	12.6	12.6	12.7	12.7	12.8	12.9	12.9	13.0	13.0	13.0	13.1	13.2	12.9
1962	13.2	13.2	13.3	13.5	13.5	13.6	13.6	13.4	13.4	13.4	13.5	13.5	13.4
1963	13.6	13.7	13.7	13.8	13.7	13.7	13.7	13.6	13.7	13.7	13.8	13.8	13.7
1964	13.8	13.9	13.9	14.0	14.2	14.2	14.2	14.3	14.3	14.3	14.4	14.4	14.2
1965	14.5	14.5	14.5	14.8	14.9	14.9	14.9	14.9	14.9	15.0	15.0	15.1	14.8
1966	15.1	15.1	15.2	15.3	15.5	15.5	15.4	15.5	15.5	15.5	15.6	15.6	15.4
1967	15.7	15.7	15.7	15.8	15.8	15.9	15.8	15.7	15.7	15.8	15.9	16.0	15.8
1968	16.1	16.2	16.2	16.5	16.5	16.6	16.6	16.6	16.6	16.7	16.8	17.0	16.5

1969	17.1	17.2	17.2	17.4	17.4	17.5	17.5	17.4	17.5	17.6	17.7	17.8	17.4
1970	17.9	18.0	18.1	18.4	18.5	18.5	18.6	18.6	18.7	18.9	19.0	19.2	18.5
1971	19.4	19.6	19.7	20.1	20.3	20.4	20.5	20.5	20.6	20.7	20.8	20.9	20.3
1972	21.0	21.1	21.2	21.4	21.5	21.7	21.7	21.9	22.0	22.3	22.4	22.5	21.7
1973	22.7	22.8	22.9	23.4	23.5	23.7	23.8	23.8	24.0	24.5	24.7	24.9	23.7
1974	25.4	25.8	26.0	26.9	27.3	27.6	27.8	27.8	28.1	28.7	29.2	29.6	27.5
1975	30.4	30.9	31.5	32.7	34.1	34.8	35.1	35.3	35.6	36.1	36.6	37.0	34.2
1976	37.5	38.0	38.2	38.9	39.3	39.5	39.6	40.2	40.7	41.4	42.0	42.6	39.8
1977	43.7	44.1	44.6	45.7	46.1	46.5	46.6	46.8	47.1	47.3	47.5	47.8	46.2
1978	48.0	48.3	48.6	49.3	49.6	50.0	50.2	50.5	50.7	51.0	51.3	51.8	49.9
1979	52.5	53.0	53.4	54.3	54.7	55.7	58.1	58.5	59.1	59.7	60.3	60.7	56.7
1980	62.2	63.1	63.9	66.1	66.7	67.4	67.9	68.1	68.5	68.9	69.5	69.9	66.9
1981	70.3	70.9	72.0	74.1	74.6	75.0	75.3	75.9	76.3	77.0	77.8	78.3	74.8
1982	78.7	78.8	79.4	81.0	81.6	81.9	81.9	81.9	81.9	82.3	82.7	82.5	81.2
1983	82.6	83.0	83.1	84.3	84.6	84.8	85.3	85.7	86.1	86.4	86.7	86.9	85.0
1984	86.8	87.2	87.5	88.6	89.0	89.2	89.1	89.9	90.1	90.7	91.0	90.9	89.2
1985	91.2	91.9	92.8	94.8	95.2	95.4	95.2	95.5	95.4	95.6	95.9	96.0	94.6
1986	96.2	96.6	96.7	97.7	97.8	97.8	97.5	97.8	98.3	98.5	99.3	99.6	97.8
1987	100.0	100.4	100.6	101.8	101.9	101.9	101.8	102.1	102.4	102.9	103.4	103.3	101.9
1988	103.3	103.7	104.1	105.8	106.2	106.6	106.7	107.9	108.4	109.5	110.0	110.3	106.9
1989	111.0	111.8	112.3	114.3	115.0	115.4	115.5	115.8	116.6	117.5	118.5	118.8	115.2
1990	119.5	120.2	121.4	125.1	126.2	126.7	126.8	128.1	129.3	130.3	130.0	129.9	126.1
1991	130.2	130.9	131.4	133.1	133.5	134.1	133.8	134.1	134.6	135.1	135.6	135.7	133.5
1992	135.6	136.3	136.7	138.8	139.3	139.3	138.8	138.9	139.4	139.9	139.7	139.2	138.4
1993	137.9	138.8	139.3	140.6	141.1	141.0	140.7	141.3	141.9	141.8	141.6	141.9	140.6
1994	141.3	142.1	142.5	144.2	144.7	144.7	144.0	144.7	145.0	145.2	145.3	146.0	144.1
1995	146.0	146.9	147.5	149.0	149.6	149.8	149.1	149.9	150.6	149.8	149.8	150.7	149.0
1996	150.2	150.9	151.5	152.6	152.9	153.0	152.4	153.1	153.8	153.8	153.9	154.4	152.7
1997	154.4	155.0	155.4	156.3	156.9	157.5	157.5	158.5	159.3	159.5	159.6	160.0	157.5
1998	159.5	160.3	160.8	162.6	163.5	163.4	163.0	163.7	164.4	164.5	164.4	164.4	162.9
1999	163.4	163.7	164.1	165.2	165.6	165.6	165.1	165.5	166.2	166.5	166.7	167.3	165.4
2000	166.6	167.5	168.4	170.1	170.7	171.1	170.5	170.5	171.7	171.6	172.1	172.2	170.3
2001	171.1	172.0	172.2	173.1	174.2	174.4	173.3	174.0	174.6	174.3	173.6	173.4	173.4
2002	173.3	173.8	174.5	175.7	176.2	176.2	175.9	176.4	177.6	177.9	178.2	178.5	176.2
2003	178.4	179.3	179.9	181.2	181.5	181.3	181.3	181.6	182.5	182.6	182.7	183.5	181.3
2004	183.1	183.8	184.6	185.7	186.5	186.8	186.8	187.4	188.1	188.6	189.0	189.9	186.7
2005	188.9	189.6	190.5	191.6	192.0	192.2	192.2	192.6	193.1	193.3	193.6	194.1	192.0
2006	193.4	194.2	195.0	196.5	197.7	198.5	198.5	199.2	200.1	200.4	201.1	202.7	198.1
2007	201.6												

Appendix 7
NPV tables

Present value factors

Present value of £S at the end of n Years: $\dfrac{S}{(1 + r)^n}$

Appendix 7 NPV Tables

N	1%	2%	3%	4%	5%	6%	7%	8%	9%	10%	N
01	0.99010	0.98039	0.97007	0.96154	0.95238	0.94340	0.93458	0.92593	0.91743	0.90909	01
02	0.98030	0.96117	0.94260	0.92456	0.90703	0.89000	0.87344	0.85734	0.84168	0.82645	02
03	00.97059	0.94232	0.91514	0.88900	0.86384	0.83962	0.81630	0.79383	0.77218	0.75131	03
04	00.96098	0.92385	0.88849	0.85480	0.82270	0.79209	0.76290	0.73503	0.70843	0.68301	04
05	00.95147	0.90573	0.86261	0.82193	0.78353	0.74726	0.71299	0.68058	0.64993	0.62092	05
06	00.94204	0.88797	0.83748	0.79031	0.74622	0.70496	0.66634	0.63017	0.59627	0.56447	06
07	00.93272	0.87056	0.81309	0.75992	0.71068	0.66506	0.62275	0.58349	0.54703	0.51316	07
08	00.92348	0.85349	0.78941	0.73069	0.67684	0.62741	0.58201	0.54027	0.50187	0.46651	08
09	00.91434	0.83675	0.76642	0.70259	0.64461	0.59190	0.54393	0.50025	0.46043	0.42410	09
10	00.90529	0.82035	0.74409	0.67556	0.61391	0.55839	0.50835	0.46316	0.42241	0.38554	10
11	0.89632	0.80426	0.72242	0.64958	0.58468	0.52679	0.47509	0.42888	0.38753	0.35049	11
12	0.88745	0.78849	0.70138	0.62460	0.55684	0.49697	0.44401	0.39711	0.35553	0.31863	12
13	0.87866	0.77303	0.68095	0.60057	0.53032	0.46884	0.41496	0.36770	0.32618	0.28966	13
14	0.86996	0.75787	0.66112	0.57747	0.50507	0.44230	0.38782	0.34046	0.29925	0.26333	14
15	0.86135	0.74301	0.64186	0.55526	0.48102	0.41726	0.36245	0.31524	0.27454	0.23939	15
16	0.85282	0.72845	0.62317	0.53391	0.45811	0.39365	0.33873	0.29189	0.25187	0.21763	16
17	0.84438	0.71416	0.60502	0.51337	0.43630	0.37136	0.31657	0.27027	0.23107	0.19784	17
18	0.83602	0.70016	0.58739	0.49363	0.41552	0.35034	0.29586	0.25025	0.21199	0.17986	18
19	0.82774	0.68643	0.57029	0.47464	0.39573	0.33051	0.27651	0.23171	0.19449	0.16351	19
20	0.81954	0.67297	0.55367	0.45639	0.37689	0.31180	0.25842	0.21455	0.17843	0.14864	20
21	0.81143	0.65978	0.53755	0.43883	0.35894	0.29415	0.24151	0.19866	0.16370	0.13513	21
22	0.80340	0.64684	0.52189	0.42195	0.34185	0.27750	0.22571	0.18394	0.15018	0.12285	22
23	0.79544	0.63416	0.50669	0.40573	0.32557	0.26180	0.21095	0.17031	0.13778	0.11168	23
24	0.78757	0.62172	0.49193	0.39012	0.31007	0.24698	0.19715	0.15770	0.12640	0.10153	24
25	0.77977	0.60953	0.47760	0.37512	0.29530	0.23300	0.18425	0.14602	0.11597	0.09230	25

Annuity table

Sum required to purchase an annuity paying £S at the end of each year for n years, with the sum invested at interest rate r:

$$S\left(\frac{\left(1-\left(1+r\right)^{-n}\right)}{r}\right)$$

Year	1%	2%	3%	4%	5%	6%	7%	8%	9%	10%	Year
1	0.9901	0.9804	0.9709	0.9615	0.9524	0.9434	0.9346	0.9259	0.9174	0.9091	1
2	1.9704	1.9416	1.9135	1.8861	1.8594	1.8334	1.8080	1.7833	1.7591	1.7355	2
3	2.9410	2.8839	2.8256	2.7751	2.7232	2.6730	2.6243	2.5771	2.5313	2.4868	3
4	3.9020	3.8077	3.7171	3.6299	3.5459	3.4651	3.3872	3.3121	3.2397	3.1699	4
5	4.8335	4.7134	4.5797	4.4518	4.3295	4.2123	4.1002	3.9927	3.8896	3.7908	5
6	5.7955	5.6014	5.4172	5.2421	5.0757	4.9173	4.7665	4.6229	4.4859	4.3553	6
7	6.7282	6.4720	6.2302	6.0020	5.7863	5.5824	5.3893	5.2064	5.0329	4.8684	7
8	7.6517	7.3254	7.0196	6.7327	6.4632	6.2098	5.9713	5.7466	5.5348	5.3349	8
9	8.5661	8.1622	7.7361	7.4353	7.1078	6.8017	6.5152	6.2469	5.9852	5.7590	9
10	9.4714	8.9825	8.5302	8.1109	7.7217	7.3601	7.0236	6.7101	6.4176	6.1446	10
11	10.3677	9.7868	9.2526	8.7604	8.3064	7.8868	7.4987	7.1389	6.8052	6.4951	11
12	11.2552	10.5753	9.9539	9.3850	8.8632	8.3838	7.9427	7.5361	7.1607	6.8137	12
13	12.1338	11.3483	10.6349	9.9856	9.3935	8.8527	8.3576	7.9038	7.4869	7.1034	13
14	13.0038	12.1062	11.2960	10.5631	9.8986	9.2950	8.7454	8.2442	7.7861	7.3667	14
15	13.8651	12.8492	11.9379	11.1183	10.3796	9.7122	9.1079	8.5595	8.0607	7.6061	15
16	14.7180	13.5777	12.5610	11.6522	10.8377	10.1059	9.4466	8.8514	8.3125	7.8237	16
17	15.5624	14.2918	13.1660	12.1656	11.2740	10.4772	9.7632	9.1216	8.5436	8.0215	17
18	16.3984	14.9920	13.7534	12.6592	11.6896	10.8276	10.0591	9.3719	8.7556	8.2014	18
19	17.2261	15.6784	14.3237	13.1339	12.0853	11.1581	10.3356	9.6036	8.9501	8.3649	19
20	18.0457	16.3514	14.8774	13.5903	12.4622	11.4699	10.5940	9.8181	9.1203	8.5136	20
21	18.8571	17.0111	15.3149	14.0291	12.8211	11.7640	10.8355	10.0168	9.2922	8.6487	21
22	19.6605	17.6580	15.9368	14.4511	13.1630	12.0416	11.0612	10.2007	9.4424	8.7715	22
23	20.4559	18.2921	16.4435	14.8568	13.4885	12.3033	11.2722	10.3710	9.5802	8.8832	23
24	21.2435	18.9139	16.9355	15.2469	13.7986	12.5503	11.4693	10.5287	9.7066	8.9847	24
25	22.0283	19.5234	17.4131	15.6220	14.0939	12.7833	11.6536	10.6748	9.8226	9.0770	25

Appendix 8
Formulae, etc

Dividend yield

$$= \frac{\text{Nominal value}}{\text{Price}} \times \text{Dividend}$$

Example:

Nominal value	£1
Dividend	24.5p
Price	£1.75
Yield	$\frac{100 \times 24.5}{175} = 14\%$

Price Earnings Ratio

$$= \frac{\text{Price per share}}{\text{Earnings per share}}$$

Example:

Insured share capital	100,000 £1 ords
Post-tax profits	£50,000
Share price	£4

$$\text{Price per share} = 400\text{p}$$
$$\text{Earnings per share} = £50,000 \div 100,000 = 50\text{p}$$
$$\text{In P/E} = \frac{400}{50} = 8$$

Dividend cover

$$= \frac{\text{Earnings}}{\text{Dividend}}$$

Example:

Insured share capital	100,000 £1 ords
Post-tax profits	£50,000
Dividend	24.5p

Therefore dividend cover $= \dfrac{50p}{24.5p} = 2.04$

Net present value

(1) A single receipt/payment of £S made n years in the future, discounted at r per annum.

$$\frac{S}{(1 + r)^n}$$

(2) Capital sum required to purchase an annuity paying £S at the end of each year for n years, invested at interest rate r

$$\frac{S\,(1 - (1 + r)^{-n})}{r}$$

Discounted cash flow

The basis formula for determining present value is

$$\frac{C_1}{1 + K} + \frac{C_2}{(1 + K)^n} \quad \frac{C_n}{(1 + K)^n} + \frac{R}{(1 + K)^2}$$

Where:

C = the cash flow forecast for each of the years 1 to n.

K = the discount rate (otherwise known as the cost of capital, or interest rate for the year, or required rate of return) expressed as a decimal.

R = the residual value of the business at the end of year n, less any remaining debt.

Earnings per share

$$= \frac{\text{Post-tax profits}}{\text{Number of shares in issue}}$$

Example:

Pre-tax profits	£1,000,000
Tax payable	£500,000
Tax charge in accounts	£200,000
Deferred tax not provided	£150,000
Ordinary shares	300,000
5% preference shares	400,000

It is suggested that e.p.s calculated on tax payable is not of particular relevance as this requires the liability to taxation in a future period that arises from activities in the current accounting period two alternative calculations are:

'Actual' basis, which is the technique used for reporting company results in the *Financial Times*.
'Fully taxed' basis, which is the technique used for reporting company results in the *Investors Chronicle*.

In either case, in order to calculate the e.p.s on ordinary shares, profits attributed to the preference shareholders must first be deducted.

Calculation of e.p.s on 'actual' basis:

	£
Pre-tax profits	1,000,000
Less: tax charged in accounts	(200,000)
Less: due on prefs	(20,000)
	780,000 ÷ 300,000 = 260p

Calculation of e.p.s on 'full' basis:

	£
Pre-tax profits	1,000,000
Less: full tax charge	(350,000)
Less: due on prefs	(20,000)
	630,000 ÷ 300,000 = 210p

PART 2
Cases

CASES

Case 1
Birch v Cropper

[1889] 14 AC 525, HL

House of Lords

9 August 1889

This case can be regarded as the first case to reach the courts where the dispute is a valuation for a tax purpose.

It is sometimes appropriate to value a shareholding by reference to the breakup value of a company (see Part 1, section **6.2.3**). When applying this method of valuation, it is the rights of the shareholder in a winding-up that is to be considered; the rights to distributions of profit, or entitlement to dividend, have no necessary relevance in a winding-up.

The articles of The Bridgewater Navigation Company Limited are silent on the rights in a winding-up. The House of Lords held that, where articles are silent, and a company has two or more different classes of shares, the rights of the different classes to a distribution in a winding-up are equal. Any share valuation should recognise this fundamental equality amongst the different classes.

It was not until the passing of Companies Act 1862 that a trader could choose to trade as a company. The concept of a company had been known in English law for many years before then but, until that time, a private Act of Parliament or a Royal Charter was required to form a company; neither alternative being a viable option for the normal entrepreneur. The East India Company was founded by Royal Charter on 31 December 1599 with 218 shareholders. Under the Companies Act 1862, any seven men could create a company by the simple process of subscribing to a memorandum of association and thereby, for the first time, acquire the advantage of limited liability for the shareholders. The Bridgewater Navigation Company Limited was created in 1872. It was then one of, perhaps, only 8,000 companies incorporated in England and Wales. For the court, and the parties in this case, the concept of a share with limited liability in a trading company of this nature was relatively new; the relationship between the nominal value of a share and its open market value had not been explored in the courts. It should, therefore, be of no surprise that the approach taken in the court considered not merely the provisions of company law given by the new statute, but also concepts of equity developed by the courts over preceding centuries. The judgement is informed by provisions that had long been applied to regulate the relationship between partners in a partnership.

In 1887, the Manchester Ship Canal Company purchased the Bridgewater Canal Navigation Company for £1,710,000. The debts and liabilities of The Bridgewater Canal Navigation Company were discharged and all shareholders repaid the capital they had paid up on their shares. The question then to be answered by the court, ultimately by the House of Lords, was how the remaining surplus of about £500,000 was to be distributed amongst the two different classes of issued share. What value was to be attributed to the ordinary shares and what value to the preference shares? (See [1889] 14 AC 525 at 530 **case 1 para 3**.)

The company's articles of association specified the way in which a dividend declared out of net profits of the year was to be apportioned between the ordinary shareholders and the preference shareholders. No provision in the articles of association specified the way in which the value received by a company on the sale of its business should be divided between these two classes of shareholder on the occasion the company's winding-up.

Lord Herschell approached the question by making a contrast between the rights of the different shareholders during the life of the company and the rights of shareholders, together, at the end of the company's life:

> 'all question of preference is now at an end, and the shareholders are to be dealt with as having equal rights, because the provision of the articles creating the preference shares as regards dividend to arising on the working on the capital is at an end. We must deal with them all as shareholders having equal rights.'
>
> ([1889] 14 AC 525 at 532 **case 1 para 8**)

The subscription price for preference shares had been higher than the subscription price payable for ordinary shares. However, as Lord Herschell noted:

> 'the payment of £3 10s per share was not the only contribution made by the ordinary shareholders to the assets of the company. They had each come under liability to pay the balance due on the shares held by them. Such a contribution might in many cases be just as valuable and tend just as effective to the prosperity of the company as if they had actually paid the amount.'
>
> ([1889] 14 AC 525 at 533/534 **case 1 para 8**)

For Lord Herschell, in the absence of a contrary statement in the company's articles of association, every share in the company ranks *pari passu* on a liquidation.

In giving the second speech Lord Fitzgerald takes as his starting point that there is no contract as to the mode of division of the surplus and, hence, it must be divided on equitable principles (see [1889] 14 AC 525 at 541 **case 1 para 18**). Lord Fitzgerald concluded:

> 'I am clearly of opinion that the only equitable principle to be acted in this case is that of equality ... [E]ach and every shareholder should receive in respect of his share an equal proportion of this surplus.'
>
> ([1889] 14 AC 525 at 542 **case 1 para 23**)

Lord Macnaghten comes to the same conclusion but by a third route. Unlike his fellow judges, he recognised the fundamental distinction between rights in a partnership and rights in a company. Partnership rights are based on principles of equity (which were subsequently codified, but not created, the following year, by Partnership Act 1890); a company is a treated of statute and the rights in a company are those specified in statute:

> 'It is, perhaps, rather beside the mark to discuss the general doctrines of partnership and to examine particular cases of partnership contracts. The schedule of the Act and the directions to be found there are, I think, a safer guide than any analogies can be.'
>
> ([1889] 14 AC 525 at 543 **case 1 para 26**)

Lord MacNaghten drew attention to the fact that the different classes of shares had different paid up amounts, some being fully paid up, others being only partly paid up and the entitlement to dividend varied according to whether or not a share had been fully paid (see [1889] 14 AC 525 at 543 **case 1 para 26**). The return of capital that had already been made to the shareholders took account of the differing extent to which different classes of shareholders had contributed. After an analysis of provisions of Companies Act 1862 relating to a winding-up (see [1889] 14 AC 525 at 544 **case 1 paras 30 and 31**), Lord Macnaghten concluded that once the capital subscribed had been repaid, the preference shareholders and the ordinary shareholders were placed on exactly the same footing:

> '[preference shareholders] must have the rights of shareholders, but I cannot see why they should claim more.'
>
> ([1889] 14 AC 525 at 548 **case 1 para 37**)

This case is, thus, authority for the proposition that in valuing a share-holding, any consideration of the value accruing on a winding-up should assume a repayment of capital subscribed and then an equal division of the surplus.

Judgement

References, example '(pg529)', are to [1889] 14 AC 525, HL.

In all cases in this volume, the page reference is given at the end of the page as originally published in the source to which reference is made. Thus, the opening words of Lord Hershell in this case are referenced [1889] 14 AC 525 at 529.

1 LORD HERSCHELL: (Aug 9.) My Lords, the only question for determination in this case is upon what principle the balance of the proceeds of the realisation of the assets of the Bridgewater Navigation Company remaining after satisfying all the liabilities of the company and returning to the shareholders the paid-up capital, is to be distributed as between the holders of the ordinary and preference shares of the company. The company was formed in 1872 for the purpose of acquiring the Bridgewater and other canals, with a capital of £500,000 divided into 500 shares of £1000 each. By resolution duly passed in September of that year, it was provided that the capital instead of being divided into shares of £1000 should be divided into 50,000 shares of £10 each, and should be increased to £1,300,000 consisting of 130,000 shares of that amount.

2 Prior to April 1880, 100,000 shares out of the capital of £1,300,000 had been issued as ordinary shares, upon which £2 10s per share had then been paid; and on the 27th of that month it was resolved at an extraordinary meeting that the balance of the uncreated capital, viz £300,000, should be created, and that the 30,000 new shares should be issued as preference shares entitling the holder to a preferential dividend of 5 per cent. In pursuance of this resolution the shares were issued accordingly, and the additional capital of £300,000 was paid up. At the same time a call of £1 was made on the ordinary shares, raising the amount paid up on them to £3 10s per share.

3 In 1887 the Manchester Ship Canal Company purchased the undertaking and assets of the Bridgewater Canal Navigation Company for the sum of £1,710,000, and it was thereupon *(pg529)* resolved that the latter company should be wound up voluntarily. In the September following the liquidators repaid to the preference and ordinary shareholders the amount of capital paid up on their shares. After making this return to the shareholders, and after discharging all the debts and liabilities of the company there remained in the hands of the liquidators a surplus of about £500,000. The question is how this surplus ought to be distributed amongst the ordinary and preference shareholders respectively?

4 The Court below has determined that the distribution ought to be made in proportion to the amounts respectively paid up on their shares, and your Lordships have to determine whether this is the correct principle to apply. It is contended on behalf of the appellant, who represents the ordinary shareholders, that they are entitled to the whole of the surplus; but failing this contention, it is insisted that the division ought to be made according to the capital subscribed and not to the amount paid up on the shares.

5 The Companies Act affords very little assistance in terms towards a decision of the question. It provides that in the case of a voluntary winding-up the property of the company shall be applied in satisfaction of its liabilities, and subject thereto shall, unless it be otherwise provided by the regulations of the company, be distributed amongst the members according to their rights and interests in the company. But this leaves undetermined what those rights and interests are.

6 The learned counsel for the appellant argue that except in so far as the provisions of the Companies Acts necessarily create a distinction between the rights of its members and those of partners, the principles of the law of partnership are applicable and ought to be applied: and they urge that in the case of a partnership, unless the terms upon which it is entered into provide otherwise, surplus assets are distributable amongst the partners in the proportions in which they are entitled to share the profits. Even assuming that the doctrine laid down with regard to the division of surplus assets, in the case of a partnership, be correct (upon which I pronounce no opinion), I am unable to see how it establishes the appellant's claim, that the ordinary *(pg530)* shareholders should receive the whole of the assets. The appellant's argument appears to assume that the preference shareholders are not entitled to any share of the profits of the company. I do not think this is the case. What they are to receive is indeed limited in its amount, but it is none the less a share in the profits. To treat them as partners receiving only interest on their capital and not entitled to participate in the profits of the concern, or to regard them as mere creditors whose only claim is discharged when they have received back their loan, appears to me out of the question. They are members of the company, and as much shareholders in it as the ordinary shareholders are; and it is in respect of their thus holding shares that they receive a part of the profits. I think therefore that the first contention of the appellant wholly fails.

7 The other point raised by the appeal is to my mind one of considerable difficulty. There is no decision bearing directly upon the point, and it must therefore be determined upon general principles of equity. Some stress was laid in the Court below upon the decision in the case of *Sheppard v Scinde, Punjaub and Delhi Railway Company*; but I do not think that case can be relied on as an authority except where the circumstances are precisely similar. All the noble and learned Lords who took part in the consideration of that case in this House rested their opinions upon the very special facts of the case, and intimated that they were not laying down any general principle.

8 The view taken by the Court below has presented to my mind from the outset some formidable difficulties. I cannot but feel that it would in some cases be most inequitable to take into consideration in distributing the surplus assets only the amount of capital paid up by the several classes of shareholders, and to make the distribution accordingly. In the Court of Appeal Cotton and Fry LJJ were guided to their conclusions by the provisions contained in the articles of association of this particular company. With all deference I do not think that they really afford the assistance that was supposed. The 85th article of association prescribes that the net profits of each year shall be divided pro rata upon the whole paid-up capital of the *(pg531)* company and that the directors may declare a dividend to be payable thereout on the shares in proportion to the amounts paid up thereon. But this article is clearly inapplicable to the preference shareholders who do not share pro rata in the profits of the year. Their rights are determined by the resolution creating the new capital which provided that the new shares were to entitle the holders thereof to a dividend of 5 per cent per annum 'upon the amount for the time being called up thereon,' and taking precedence over all dividends on the ordinary shares. This clearly, by implication, excludes in the case of these shares the operation of article 85. Cotton LJ, after pointing out, I think correctly, that under the articles, both as regards the ordinary shareholders and the preference shareholders respectively, *inter se*, the right to the dividend was to be on the footing of its being in proportion to the sum paid up on the shares, proceeds to say: 'That is the footing on which to decide it. All question of preference is now at an end, and the shareholders are to be dealt with as having equal rights, because the provision of the articles creating the preference shares as regards dividend to arise on the working of the capital is at an end. We must deal with them all as shareholders having equal rights without reference to profits, and, in my opinion, when that is so, and when there is the indication in the articles of association which form the contract of partnership that profit is to be divided when it is a going concern and arising from the working of the business in accordance with the sums paid upon each share, than in this particular case, and having regard to that provision, the true equitable mode of dividing this sum is to divide it among all the shareholders in accordance with and in proportion to the amount paid up by them on their shares.' I have a difficulty in seeing how the provisions of the articles alluded to show that the equitable mode of distribution is that suggested. It is conceded that they cease to be applicable when the company comes to be wound up, but if they are to be regarded at all, I think that their full effect must be borne in mind. It is not the case that when the company was a going concern the profits earned were to be divided in accordance with the sums paid on each share. The share of the profits to which the *(pg532)* preference shareholders were entitled was limited in amount. It did not depend upon the proportion which the profits bore to the total paid-up capital. And the ordinary shareholders were in fact receiving a proportion of the profits exceeding that to which they would have been entitled had such profits been divided to each shareholder in proportion to the capital paid up. I do not say that this indicates the mode in which the surplus assets should be distributed, but it does appear to me to shew that it does not follow from the method in which profits were divided that the equitable mode of dividing surplus is to let all the members share alike in proportion to the amount paid up on their shares. In the present case, too, it cannot be doubted that in estimating the price to be paid by the canal company the future prospects of the Bridgewater Company, the probable development of its property and the increase in its value were taken into account. In these future prospects the preference shareholders had no concern save in so far as they improved the security for the payment of their interest. If that security was already ample the benefit arising from the increased value of the company's undertaking would, down to the time of its being wound up, enure entirely to the ordinary shareholders. And yet in so far as the price represented this increased future value the result of the decision is to give to the preference shareholders approximately one-half of it. Now, I do not mean to say that any principle can be laid down which will ensure perfect equality in this respect, but that which has been adopted appears to me to tend to raise the inequality to a maximum. The articles of association do not appear to me to afford the means of deciding this case upon any special grounds peculiar to this company. Their provisions are such as are commonly to be found regulating the distribution of profits in the case of joint stock companies. I think the determination of the question at issue must be arrived at upon principles wider and of more general application. In my opinion one consideration of essential importance, if an equitable distribution of the assets is to be attained, has been altogether lost sight of. The payment of £3 10s per share was not the only contribution made by the ordinary shareholders to the assets of the company. They had each come under liability *(pg533)* to pay the balance due on the shares held by them. Such a contribution might in many cases be just as valuable and tend just as effectually to the prosperity of the company as if they had actually paid the amount. I cannot think that this ought to be disregarded in estimating the respective rights and interests of members in the company and its property.

9 In the case of *Sheppard v Scinde, Punjaub and Delhi Railway Company* Bowen LJ said: 'Was the sum produced in any way by the liability to pay calls? That is a question of fact, and I am satisfied that the liability to pay calls was not in any way an element in the production of this purchase-money.' I am not by any means prepared to say the same of this company. On the contrary I think it most probable, looking to the large sums of money raised on loan at a moderate rate of interest, that the liability of the shareholders did add very materially to the ease with which these loans were obtained, and to the consequent development and prosperity of the undertaking. In the same case Fry LJ said: 'It seems to me that in this case distribution must be proportionate to contribution. But it is said, suppose the property to have been produced not by unequal contributions but by unequal liabilities to pay, the proceeds must be distributed according to the unequal liabilities. I agree that in that case the distribution must be guided by the amount of the liabilities. I conclude that in this case the assumption of liability by the shareholders has not in any way produced the property, and that it cannot be said that the capital has been in the least increased by the liability.' In the present case that learned judge appears to have discarded altogether these considerations, apparently because he thought the matter settled by the terms of the articles of association; but for the reasons I have given I cannot concur in this view. I am fortified by the observations of the two learned judges I have quoted in the view that a scheme of distribution which overlooks an important part of the contribution can scarcely be regarded as equitable. It would be impossible to my mind to enter upon an inquiry in each individual case how much the liability incurred and the money provided had respectively contributed to the prosperity of the company or the *(pg534)* value of its property. Some general rule must be laid down. I quite admit that it may be urged with force that if the distribution is to follow, not the paid-up but the subscribed capital, the liability would always be treated as of as much value as actual money. But if there must be a general rule and I have to choose between so regarding it or treating it as valueless, I believe the former would on the whole be the more equitable course. I of course exclude such a case as that of the *Scinde Railway*, where the constitution of the company determined the amount of purchase money to be given for the undertaking, and by the mode in which it was to be ascertained indicated what was the equitable mode of distributing it. In making these observations with reference to the unpaid liability upon shares I do not desire to be understood as indicating that they are decisive of the question how surplus assets are to be divided, but only as explaining why I cannot feel satisfied that the principle which has been adopted in the Court below is the correct one. Let me put an illustration which occurred to me whilst the appeal was under argument. Take the case of a company whose entire paid-up capital was obtained by the issue of preference shares bearing a limited rate of interest, nothing being paid upon the ordinary shares. The prosperity of such a company might be very largely due to the liability of the ordinary shareholders which might be just as valuable to the company as if they had paid a large sum on their shares, yet in such a case if the undertaking were sold, the whole of the surplus after discharging the liabilities of the company and returning their capital to the preference shareholders, would on the principle adopted by the Court 'below have been the property of such shareholders, and it must have, been declared that the ordinary shareholders had no title to it, or to share in its distribution, that though members they had no 'rights or interest' in the company. I admit that the case I have put is an extreme though it is not an impossible one, but I think it may well be put to test the equity of the principle laid down. It may be said that in the case I have put the profits could not be payable according to the amount paid up on the shares, and that in that case some other principle must be applied, and the amount subscribed or some other test must be taken. But if *(pg535)* this be so the principle on which assets were to be distributed would be altered, it may be in a manner most detrimental to the ordinary shareholders, as soon as any call, however small, was made on the shares.

10 I turn now to the considerations which have led me to the conclusion that the surplus ought to be divided amongst the shareholders according to the shares which they hold in the company.

11 The present company has been prosperous, and the result of the winding-up is to leave a considerable surplus of assets over liabilities after returning all the capital. But I think we are naturally led to inquire how the different classes of shareholders would have been dealt with if the reverse had been the case, and a loss had resulted. This has been the subject of decision. It has been held, and I think rightly, that in such a case where there is no provision to the contrary in the articles of the company the loss is not to be borne in the proportion in which it has been declared in the present case that the surplus is to be distributed. In the case of the *Anglesea Colliery Company* it was held by Lord Hatherley when Vice-Chancellor, and his judgment was affirmed on appeal, that the liquidators were entitled to make a call for the purpose of adjusting the rights of the members so that the losses should fall equally on all, without regard to the amount which they had paid up on their shares. And in the case of *Ex parte Maude* where some of the shareholders had paid £20 and others £25 a share, and a surplus was left after discharging the liabilities of the company, the liquidators were held to be bound to pay out of these assets £5 to each shareholder who had paid £25 before distributing the surplus rateably. One of the articles of that company provided that the directors might declare a dividend to be paid to the shareholders in proportion to the number of their respective shares 'and the amount paid up thereon respectively,' and this was relied on as shewing that the loss ought to be proportioned to the amount paid up. Mellish LJ however said: 'In my opinion we cannot draw any inference from article 114 beyond that which it states, and we cannot infer that the shareholders meant to make such an important alteration as that in case of the company *(pg536)* being wound up the losses should be divided in proportion to the amount paid up and not to the amount subscribed.' And he held that the true view of the Companies Act was that the losses were to be borne, not in proportion to the amount paid up, but to the subscribed capital. Where the articles are silent on the subject, why should a different rule prevail as regards surplus assets? Where there is no agreement as to either it would seem only natural and equitable, that loss should be borne and benefits shared in the same proportion. And, in my opinion, this is the true principle to apply. In the course of the argument, I put the case of a company being wound up, having a large asset of doubtful value, and not capable of immediate realisation. In such a case it might be necessary or prudent to call up the unpaid capital in order to discharge the liabilities of the concern, even though it turned out that this asset was more than sufficient to meet them. If the capital were thus called up the surplus would be distributed rateably amongst all the shareholders, whereas supposing the judgment under appeal to be correct, if the asset had been first realised, the distribution amongst the two classes of shareholders would have been very different. The rights and interests of the shareholders in the company would thus be made to depend on the urgency of the creditors or the timidity of the liquidators, a result neither satisfactory nor equitable. I observe that the same consideration occurred to Mellish LJ in the case I have just referred to. He said, 'If any other construction were adopted it would make the way in which the losses are borne depend upon the accident whether the assets could be immediately realised, or whether it was necessary to make a call to pay the debts. If the £5 per share had been called up to pay pressing debts, it could not be denied that the assets when got in would be divided pro rata; that is to say, the losses would be borne by the shareholders in proportion to their subscribed capital. Here it happened that the assets were immediately realised or that the creditors did not press for payment, so that a call was not necessary before the assets were divided, but that accident ought not to alter the way in which the assets are to be divided.' Surely all this applies with equal force to the profit resulting on the winding up of the undertaking. The *(pg537)* truth is that each member who has subscribed for a £10 share owns the same share in the company whether it be or be not paid up, and if he is so regarded for the purpose of meeting losses, I cannot see that it is equitable that he should be otherwise dealt with when we are considering to what share of the profit he is entitled. When the whole of the capital has been returned both classes of shareholders are on the same footing, equally members and holding equal shares in the company, and it appears to me that they ought to be treated as equally entitled to its property. It may be that the principle which I recommend your Lordships to adopt will not secure absolutely equal or equitable treatment in all cases, but I think that it will in general attain that end more nearly than any other which has been proposed.

12 I am therefore of opinion that the judgment appealed from should be reversed; and that it should be declared that the balance of the proceeds of sale ought to be divided amongst the holders of all the shares in the Bridgewater Navigation Company Limited, in proportion to the shares held by them respectively.

13 I accordingly move your Lordships that the judgment appealed from be reversed, and that the declaration I have just read be made, and that (as agreed between the parties) it be further declared that the costs of the liquidators and of the appellant and the respondents, both in the court below and in your Lordships' House, as between solicitor and client upon the higher scale, may properly be retained and paid by the liquidators out of the assets of the Bridgewater Navigation Company.

14 LORD FITZGERALD: My Lords, my noble and learned friend who has just spoken has in his exhaustive judgment not only carefully given all the facts and criticised and disposed of the various contentions, but he has also examined the case in all its bearings and fully and clearly indicated his reasons for not adopting the decision of the Court of Appeal. I concur in the conclusions at which he has arrived, though I do not find it necessary to say that I accept all the reasons of my noble and learned friend. I am to be followed by a second elaborate speech from my noble and learned friend (Lord Macnaghten), the notes of which I have read, and as he *(pg538)* arrives at the same result I need not express my concurrence a second time. Coming between such weighty authorities I confidently anticipate your Lordships' sanction to my being concise.

15 The Bridgewater Canal Company Limited, formed in 1872, had become the proprietors of an extensive and valuable undertaking which appears, as far as we can judge, to have been worked ably and profitably with an increasing business down to 1880 when the company deemed it expedient to raise £600,000 for the purpose of paying off a mortgage of the like amount, and their financial plan appeared to be as follows – the company had already called up £250,000 of their subscribed capital – they made a further call of £1 a share, amounting to £100,000, and, in the exercise of the powers which they undoubtedly had, they passed a resolution calling into existence their uncreated capital by the creation of 30,000 further shares of £10 each, to be paid up in full within the two years succeeding. The terms and conditions on which the new shares were to be issued and the new shareholders to be received in respect of those shares as members of the company are fully stated in the letters of allotment. 'Allotment letter, dated 27th April 1880. The Bridgewater Navigation Company Limited, 5 per cent preference shares. Sir, I beg to inform you that at an extraordinary general meeting of the members of the Bridgewater Navigation Company, Limited, held on the 27th April 1880 the following resolution was passed: – That the balance of the uncreated capital of the company, namely, £300,000, be now created, and that there be issued 30,000 new shares of £10 each on the following terms and conditions, namely – (1). The new shares to entitle the holders thereof to a dividend after the rate of 5 per cent per annum upon the amount for the time being called up thereon, and taking precedence of and priority over all dividends and claims of the holders of the ordinary shares of the company. (2). The calls upon the new shares to be payable as follows: – £1 per share on the 30th June 1880; £1 10s per share on the 31st December 1880; £2 10s per share on the 30th June 1881; £2 10s per share on the 31st December 1881; £2 10s per share on the 30th June 1882. (3). Interest at the rate of 5 per cent per annum to commence from the date when each call becomes due. *(pg539)* (4). Any moneys paid and received with the consent of the directors in advance of calls to bear interest at the rate of 4 per cent per annum. That in the first instance the new shares shall be allotted to the holders of ordinary shares registered in the books of the company at this date as near as may be in the proportion of three new shares for every ten ordinary shares. That any new shares not accepted by the members to whom they are allotted remain at the disposal of the directors, to be issued at such times, on such terms, and in such manner as they may think fit for the benefit of the company. An allotment of your proportion of the new shares is annexed hereto.'

16 The subsequent practice of the company seems to have been to pay out of profits to the preference shareholders the preference dividend of £5 per cent, and the nett residue of the annual profits after deducting all outgoings and providing for a reserve was distributed equally amongst the holders of the original £10 shares on which £3 10s only had been paid up.

17 The next step was the statute sale of the whole undertaking to the Manchester Ship Canal Company. It seems to have been a successful stroke of business for the Bridgewater Company, and probably was not a losing one to the Manchester Company, as they got a property necessary for the purposes of their great undertaking, and got it as a going and profitable concern, with fair prospects of increasing annual profits. The Bridgewater Company as a working company having thus come to an end, a voluntary winding-up was resorted to. The liquidators paid off every liability, and they further paid to the preference shareholders their whole capital with interest at 5 per cent, and to the ordinary shareholders their capital with their share of profits. The Bridgewater Company thus became clear of every liability, and. the liquidators found that there remained the clear surplus of £550,000 to be distributed amongst those who had been the shareholders, whether ordinary or preference. The question is, on what principle is that surplus to be divided?

18 The case came first before North J and the Court of Appeal adopted his decision. North J says, at page 113: 'I find, therefore, that the parties have not entered into any contract as to the mode of division of this surplus, and that it is to be *(pg540)* divided on equitable principles. There is little direct authority to assist me in the matter.' I quite concur so far with the learned judge. At page 114 he adds: 'But the question I have to decide is not what is a reasonable mode, but what is the equitable mode of distributing the increment in question. In my opinion the recent case before the Court of Appeal of *Sheppard v Scinde, Punjaub, and Delhi Ry Co* is so like the present as not only to assist me, but to furnish an authority I ought to follow.' That case as an authority on the present appeal has already been disposed of by my noble and learned friend. North J then quotes a passage from the judgment of Cotton LJ, in the *Scinde case.* – 'I think the general law is, that after providing for the capital at the credit of each partner, the surplus assets should be distributed in the proportions in which the capital has been contributed by the partners.' There is the principle on which North J acted as the equitable mode of distributing the surplus. The Court of Appeal adopted it.

19 My Lords, I have felt myself unable to act on this supposed rule as applicable to such an undertaking as the Bridgewater Canal Company Limited, and there is no authority for doing so. It may fit an ordinary common law partnership, but when applied to an association such as is now before us, it works out inequality and injustice and not equity. The error seems to me in supposing that there is an exact analogy between an ordinary commercial partnership and a statutable undertaking called into existence under the Joint Stock Companies Acts and regulated by the statute and its own memorandum of association and articles. There may be likeness in some particulars, but there is no real analogy.

20 Then what rule is to guide this distribution? There is in my opinion no contract to guide us in the circumstances which have arisen, and there is nothing to be found in the memorandum of association, or in the articles, or in the statutes, to give us any real help. The resolutions calling into existence the preference shares are equally a blank on the subject, but I have no doubt that the able men who then directed the affairs of the company, if they had foreseen the probability of a surplus on winding-up, *(pg541)* would have been the last to agree to give up the lion's share to the preference shareholders.

21 Then, on what rule or principle are we to proceed? I concur in what my noble and learned friend has adopted as the equitable principle: to be acted on. There is a clear stage to act on. The shareholders have been reduced to one common level. Each shareholder of a share represents a former share in the company, and we have some authority that between the several classes of shareholders each represents £10 in the subscribed capital of the company, and that for the present purpose, and in this particular case, it matters not whether the £10 had been actually paid up in full, or subscribed for and partially paid.

22 We have some authority for this in *Oakbank Oil Company v Crum*, which, though not an authority in point, at least imports that the proper interpretation of 'share' is the shareholder's proportion in the subscribed capital of the company which appears in his name on the register of shareholders.

23 My Lords, I am clearly of opinion that the only equitable principle to be acted on in this case is that of equality. That is an equitable principle, and, in giving effect to that rule, each and every shareholder should receive in respect of his share an equal proportion of this surplus.

24 LORD MACNAGHTEN: My Lords, the question involved in this appeal is said to be novel. No direct authority on the point was cited. Nor am I aware of any, except a decision of Stirling J, *In re London and Brighton Stock Exchange Co Limited*, on the 12th of August 1887, which is only to be found in the *Times' Reports*. The case of *Sheppard v Scinde, Punjaub and Delhi Ry Co*, which was treated as an authority in the courts below, has since been reviewed in this House, and, in affirming the decision of the Court of Appeal, every one of the noble and learned Lords who addressed the House relied simply and solely on the special circumstances of the case.

25 The question before your Lordships is this: In the liquidation *(pg542)* of a company limited by shares, what is the proper mode of distributing assets not required for payment of debts and liabilities, or for the costs of the winding-up, or for the adjustment of the rights of the contributories amongst themselves? As incidental to that question, your Lordships have to consider whether the mode of distribution can be affected by one or more of the following circumstances: – (1.) That the shares of the company were paid up unequally, some being fully paid up, others being paid up only in part. (2.) That the fully-paid-up shares were issued separately as preference shares, carrying a preferential dividend of 5 per cent, without any further right to participate in the profits of the business. (3.) That by the regulations of the company dividends on the company's shares were payable in proportion to the amounts paid up thereon.

26 The answer, as it seems to me, must depend on the principles applicable to companies limited by shares, and on the provisions contained in the Companies

Act 1862. It is, perhaps, rather beside the mark to discuss the general doctrines of partnerships and to examine particular cases of partnership contracts. The scheme of the Act and the directions to be found there are, I think, a safer guide than any analogies can be.

27 Every person who becomes a member of a company limited by shares of equal amount becomes entitled to a proportionate part in the capital of the company, and, unless it be otherwise provided by the regulations of the company, entitled, as a necessary consequence, to the same proportionate part in all the property of the company, including its uncalled capital. He is liable in respect of all moneys unpaid on his shares to pay up every call that is duly made upon him. But he does not by such payment acquire any further or other interest in the capital of the company. His share in the capital is just what it was before. His liability to the company is diminished by the amount paid. His contribution is merged in the common fund. And that is all.

28 When the company is wound up, new rights and liabilities arise. The power of the directors to make calls is at an end; but every present member, so far as his shares are unpaid, is liable to contribute to the assets of the company to an amount *(pg543)* sufficient for the payment of its debts and liabilities, the costs of winding-up, and such sums as may be required for the adjustment of the rights of the contributories amongst themselves.

29 In the case of compulsory winding up, the Act says, in sect 109, that 'the Court shall adjust the rights of the contributories amongst themselves, and distribute any surplus that remains amongst the parties entitled thereto.'

30 In the case of voluntary winding up, the language is not quite the same, and the directions are rather more explicit; not that there can be any differences as to the proper mode of distributing assets in the two cases; no one has suggested that. A sufficient reason for the differences of language is, I think, to be found in the circumstances that while the privilege of voluntary liquidation is confined to companies under the Act, any partnership or association consisting of more than seven members may be wound up compulsorily. To meet every case of compulsory liquidation it was necessary to use the most general language. Besides it is obvious that specific directions, useful and proper for the guidance of voluntary liquidators, are not so requisite when the liquidation is under the Court. As Lord Cairns points out in *Webb v Whiffin*, 'it was naturally thought important in the case of voluntary windings up to make specific provisions and to give specific directions as to matters which were supposed to be so plain and so necessarily consequential upon the general scheme of the Act, that in a winding-up under an order of the Court, it was not thought necessary to give express directions upon these matters of detail.' I cannot therefore agree with Cotton LJ that sects 109 and 133 are to be read together, with the result that the more general language of sect 109 is to neutralise or obscure the prima facie meaning of the more specific directions given in the case of a voluntary winding-up.

31 The consequences that are to ensue upon the voluntary winding-up of the company are to be found in sect 133. It is there provided that 'the property of the company shall be applied in satisfaction of its liabilities, *pari passu,* and subject thereto, shall, unless it be otherwise provided by the regulations of the company, be distributed amongst the members according to their *(pg544)* rights and interests in the company.' Then the section goes into details as to the powers of the liquidators, and ends by saying that 'the liquidators shall pay the debts of the company, and adjust the rights of the contributories amongst themselves.'

32 Now in the case of members of a company limited by shares, what are 'their rights and interests in the company,' in the absence of any special regulation, and what are the rights of the contributories amongst themselves which have to be adjusted in the winding-up?

33 Amongst the rights to be adjusted, the most important are those which arise when there is a difference between shareholders in the amount of calls paid in respect of their shares. Before winding-up no such rights exist; whatever has been paid by the shareholders of one issue in excess of the contributions of their fellow shareholders of a different issue, must have been paid in pursuance of calls duly made or in accordance with the conditions under which the shares were held. While the company is a going concern no capital can be returned to the shareholders, except under the statutory provisions in that behalf. There is therefore during that period no ground for complaint; no room for equities arising out of unequal contributions. In the case of winding-up everything is changed. The assets have to be distributed. The rights arising from unequal contributions on shares of equal amounts must be adjusted, and the property of the company, including its uncalled capital not required to satisfy prior claims, must be applied for that purpose. But when those rights are adjusted, when the capital is equalised, what equity founded on inequality of contribution can possibly remain? The rights and interests of the contributories in the company must then be simply in proportion to their shares. This was the view of Stirling J in the case I have referred to. Your Lordships, however, were reminded more than once that 'the Act does not say so.' You were told that if that had been the meaning of the legislature, nothing would have been more easy than to have said in so many words that the distribution amongst the members should be 'in proportion to their shares.' This argument would have had much weight but for one circumstance. It overlooks the fact that the provisions for voluntary *(pg545)* liquidation apply to some companies which have not a capital divided into shares.

34 It now only remains to deal with the various claims put forward in the course of the argument.

35 The ordinary shareholders say that the preference shareholders are entitled to a return of their capital, with 5 per cent interest up to the day of payment, and to nothing more. That is treating them as if they were debenture-holders, liable to be paid off at a moment's notice. Then they say that at the utmost the preference shareholders are only entitled to the capital value of a perpetual annuity of 5 per cent upon the amounts paid up by them. That is treating them as if they were holders of irredeemable debentures. But they are not debenture-holders at all. For some reason or other the company invited them to come in as shareholders, and they must be treated as having all the rights of shareholders, except so far as they renounced those rights on their admission to the company. There was an express bargain made as to their rights in respect of profits arising from the business of the company. But there was no bargain – no provision of any sort – affecting their rights as shareholders in the capital of the company.

36 Then the preference shareholders say to the ordinary shareholders, 'We have paid up the whole of the amount due on our shares; you have paid but a fraction on yours. The prosperity of a company results from its paid-up capital; distribution must be in proportion to contribution. The surplus assets must be divided in proportion to the amounts paid up on the shares.' That seems to me to be ignoring altogether the elementary principles applicable to joint-stock companies of-this description. I think it rather leads to confusion to speak of the assets which are the subject of this application as 'surplus assets' as if they were an accretion or addition to the capital of the company capable of being distinguished from it and open to different considerations. They are part and parcel of the property of the company – part and parcel of the joint stock or common fund – which at the date of the winding-up represented the capital of the company. It is through their shares in the capital, and through their shares alone, that members of a company limited *(pg546)* by shares become entitled to participate in the property of the company. The shares in this company were all of the same amount. Every contributory who held a preference share at the date of the winding-up must have taken that share and must have held it on the terms of paying up all calls duly made upon him in respect thereof. In paying up his share in full he has done no more than he contracted to do; why should he have more than he bargained for? Every contributory who was the holder of an ordinary share at the date of the winding-up took his share and held it on similar terms. He has done all he contracted to do; why should he have less than his bargain? When the preference shareholders and the ordinary shareholders are once placed on exactly the same footing in regard to the amounts paid up upon their shares, what is there to alter rights which were the subject of express contract?

37 Observe how unreasonable this contention on the part of the preference shareholders is. They do not propose to unravel the accounts of the company or to inquire how long the company had the benefit of the contributions from each of the two classes of shareholders, or what was the position of the company when those contributions were made. It may be that the founders of the company made a lucky hit at the outset. Good management may have had something to do with the success of the company. And after all, something may perhaps be put down to the fact that the ship canal company was forced to buy a property which lay directly in the track of its undertaking. The preference shareholders discard all these considerations. They take the date of the winding-up as the date which governs the rights of the shareholders in the distribution of what they call surplus assets. They say, 'Our payments then were in excess of the payments of the ordinary shareholders.' But that is a mere accident. There was a time not very long ago when the contributions of the ordinary shareholders were in advance of those of the preference shareholders. If the company had gone on they might soon have been on a level again. The prosperity of this company was certainly not due to the contributions of the preference shareholders. They did not come on the scene till just before the last act. It so happens that the very same directors' report which records their *(pg547)* final payment, calls attention to the ship canal as a practical project. When the preference shareholders were invited to come in the prosperity of the company was assured. The business was flourishing; the shareholders were receiving dividends of 8 per cent with occasional bonuses, and the directors were in a position to borrow at 4 per cent. Instead of borrowing, the company resolved to issue these preference shares, on the condition that they should be fully paid up within a limited time. As the company chose to admit Mr Rigby's clients as shareholders they must have the rights of shareholders, but I cannot see why they should claim more.

38 Then it is said on behalf of the preference shareholders that the provision for payment of dividends in proportion to the amounts paid up on the shares leads to an inference that the distribution of surplus assets was to be made in the same proportion. I do not think it leads to any inference of the kind. It is a very common provision nowadays, though it is not what you find in Table A. And it is a very reasonable provision, because during the continuance of the company, and while it is a going concern, it prevents any sense of dissatisfaction on the part of those who have paid more on their shares than their fellow shareholders of a different issue. But when it has come to an end I cannot see how it can be used to regulate or disturb rights with which it had nothing to do even while it was in force.

39 I am therefore of opinion that the judgment of the Court of Appeal must be varied, and that it should be declared that subject to the payment of the costs, charges and expenses of the winding-up, including the costs of all parties in this application here and in the courts below, the assets of the company remaining undistributed other than the reserve fund, which is not the subject of this application, ought to be distributed among all the shareholders in proportion to their shares.

Case 2
McIlquham v Taylor

[1895] 1 Ch 53

[1894 M 80]

High Court

13 July, 7 August, 13 November 1894

Court of Appeal

13 November 1894

A reference to value in relation to shares is the price that would be fetched by the sale of the shares; it is not the nominal value of those shares.

In our second share valuation case from the 19th century, the Court of Appeal was required to consider the relationship between value as expressed in a contract and the par value of shares in a limited liability company.

A covenant had been made under a deed dated 2 December 1892. This covenant stated that Henry Taylor would, as additional consideration for a lease he purchased, pay £1,000 'in fully paid-up shares in a company to be formed ... for working a mine'.

HE Taylor Limited was formed on 20 May 1893. The company was not a success. By the time the payment required under the deed of 2 December 1892 was required under the covenant; the shares in the company were worthless.

Henry Taylor sought to perform his duty under the covenant by passing shares having a nominal value of £1,000. James McIlquham sought an order that the covenant could only be discharged by the payment of £1,000 in cash, as the shares were worthless.

For Lord Halsbury in the Court of Appeal, there was no ambiguity in the covenant and he had no doubt of its construction given these circumstances. The shares were not worth £1,000 and, hence, Henry Taylor could not discharge his liability by transferring shares with a nominal value of £1,000.

Lindley LJ and Rigby LJ agreed. Shares are to be valued by reference to their market value judged in relation to the affairs of the company. The nominal value of shares is no guide to their market value and, specifically, does not provide a 'floor value'. As Rigby LJ put it succinctly:

> 'What does "worth" mean? It means worth in the sense of the real value to be ascertained in some manner. There can be no difficulty in ascertaining it; it does not mean nominal value. A thing may be of the nominal value of £100,000, or, as in this case, £1,000, and yet not be worth a farthing.'
>
> ([1895] 1 Ch 53 at 64 **case 2 para 6**)

As £1,000 of value could not be paid by transferring shares (because they were all worthless), the court ordered James McIlquham and William Mitchell (the second plaintiff) to pay £1,000 in cash to Henry Taylor.

High Court Judgement

References, example '(pg57)', are to [1895] 1 Ch 53.

1 **STIRLING J** (after stating the facts, and observing that there had been a breach of the covenant to transfer £1,000 worth of fully paid shares within twelve calendar months of the date of the deed, continued): – Under these circumstances it was contended that the contract was to hand over or transfer to the Plaintiffs the shares described in the covenant, or in default to pay £1,000, and it was said that, in consequence of default made by the Defendant, the £1,000 is now payable. In support of that contention the case of *Deverill v Burnell* was cited. For the Defendant it was argued that the covenant is to perform one of two alternatives – either within twelve months to pay £1,000 or to transfer the shares; that the result of the breach is that the Defendant has become liable to pay damages, but that such damages are to be assessed on the footing that the Defendant is entitled to select for performance that alternative which is the least burdensome to him. In support of that contention two cases were cited: *Cockburn v (pg57) Alexander* and *Robinson v Robinson*, and it was said that, the shares being worthless, the Plaintiffs are entitled to nominal damages only. To this it was answered, that the Defendant has put it out of his power to perform the one branch of the covenant by forming the company with its capital divided into preference and ordinary shares, and that, even if the covenant be alternative, he must, under the circumstances, perform that branch of it which provides for payment in cash. I have come to the conclusion that the Plaintiffs are right in that contention, and it is consequently unnecessary to say what, in my view, is the strict construction of the covenant. I think that the shares which the Defendant undertook to transfer were to be shares in a company in which the shareholders all stood on a footing of equality. If the case were one of

partnership, it would come within the *Partnership Act* 1890, which provides, in sect 2, sub-sect 1, in accordance with the law as it was before the Act, that, subject to any agreement express or implied between the partners, all the partners are entitled to share equally in the capital and profits of the business, and must contribute equally towards the losses, whether of capital or otherwise, sustained by the firm. Therefore partners, in the absence of express stipulation, stand on an equal footing. In the same way, upon an agreement for a partnership, if the shares are not defined, the partners must come in on equal terms. As regards the position of shareholders in a company, as to whom nothing is said as to their rights inter se, the law may not be in a very settled state. The point was referred to in the House of Lords in *British and American Trustee and Finance Corporation v Couper*. Lord Macnaghten there says: 'In the case of *Hutton v Scarborough Cliff Hotel Company*, the company's memorandum of association declared that the capital was divided into a certain number of shares. There was nothing in the memorandum or in the articles to indicate that the shares might be of different classes. The directors found that they could not issue the whole as ordinary shares. A special resolution was passed authorising the directors to issue a certain number as preference shares. The proposed issue was *(pg58)* restrained at the suit of an ordinary shareholder, on the ground mainly that, although the company had passed a special resolution authorising the issue of preference shares, they had not in terms altered one of the original articles which provided for equality among shareholders in respect of dividends. The company then passed a special resolution altering the obnoxious article. They were again met by an application for an injunction, and the injunction was granted by Vice-Chancellor Kindersley on the ground that there was an implied stipulation in the memorandum of association that all the shareholders should stand on an equal footing as to the receipt of dividends, and that what was proposed to be done was 'contrary to the very nature of a joint stock company,' and was 'an alteration in the constitution of the company.' It is difficult to understand what the learned Vice-Chancellor meant by the expression 'constitution of the company,' and it is difficult to deal with an argument resting on a phrase so vague. Nor is it easy to understand the Vice-Chancellor's view, that equality among shareholders in respect of dividends was an 'implied stipulation in the memorandum.' There is nothing in the Act of 1862, or in any other Act, requiring the memorandum to contain any reference to the rights of shareholders inter se. The division of the capital into shares of a certain fixed amount which must appear in the memorandum would not be altered or affected by issuing some of the shares as preference shares. The practical result of the decision has been that, except in cases coming within the rule laid down in *Harrison v Mexican Railway Company* – a decision which has not met with universal acceptance – no company limited by shares that has not taken power by its memorandum to issue preference shares has been able to raise additional capital in the manner most advantageous to its shareholders and its creditors. It seems to me that the decision in *Hutton v Scarborough Cliff Hotel Company* was not founded upon a sound view of the Companies Act 1862 and I respectfully dissent from it. I have the less hesitation in expressing this view because I find that Lord Justice Cotton has disapproved of the chief ground on which the decision was based. 'In reality,' he says, in *Guinness v Land **(pg59)** Corporation of Ireland*, 'it is not by implication from the construction of the memorandum that the equality of the shareholders as regards dividends arises, but by the implication which the law raises as between partners, unless their contract has provided the contrary.' Lord Justice *Lindley*, in a later case, takes the same view. I agree that the equality of shareholders as regards dividends is not an implied condition of the memorandum. But I doubt whether it is necessary to have recourse to the doctrines of partnership. It seems to me that if the sum of the interests of persons concerned in a joint adventure is divided into shares of equal amount distinguished by numbers for the purpose of identification, but with no other distinction between them, express or implied, it follows as a self-evident proposition that the interests of the shareholders in respect of their shares as regards dividend and everything else must be equal.'

2 The law, then, is that under an ordinary memorandum of association, according to which the capital of a company is divided into shares of equal amount, the interests of the shareholders must be equal in all respects. Whether in a company so constituted preference shares can be issued is a question the final decision of which has not yet been given, although, perhaps, in the present state of the authorities, it may be concluded in the Courts of first instance by *Hutton v Scarborough Cliff Hotel Company*. However this may be, if preference shares were to be issued, a resolution of the company would be necessary to sanction the issue, and every shareholder would have an opportunity of voting on the question. In the present case the shares to be transferred under the agreement were to be shares in a company to be formed by the Defendant, the capital of which was not to exceed £12,000. In the absence of any stipulation to the contrary that means, in my judgment, a company having its capital divided into shares, all of which were to stand on an equal footing. If a company with preference or priority as regards part of its capital had been contemplated, I can hardly doubt that the agreement would have contained a stipulation as to the proportion of the preference capital and the ordinary capital, and **(pg60)** as to whether the shares that were to be taken in payment were to be of one class or the other, or, if both, in what proportions. It seems to me that it could not have been intended to leave it to the Defendant to say whether all the shares except 100 should be issued as preference shares, carrying interest at any rate which he might think fit to determine. In my judgment, therefore, the company which was formed by the Defendant was not one in which the Plaintiffs could be compelled to accept shares, and, that being so, 'I think that the Defendant is bound to perform the other alternative of the covenant. As to that I may refer to the case of *Studholme v Mandell*. There an action of covenant was brought by the plaintiffs upon covenants in an indenture by which the plaintiffs demised a mill to the defendant, and in which the defendant covenanted to leave the mill-stones in as good condition as he found them, or to pay to the plaintiffs so much as they should be damnified; the damage to be estimated by *A* and *B*, who viewed them when the defendant entered upon the premises. The plaintiffs assigned for breach, that the defendant had left the mill-stones damnified, and had not made satisfaction. The defendant pleaded that *A* and

B had not estimated the damage. The plaintiffs demurred. It was argued for the defendant, that this was a condition disjunctive, and therefore the leaving of the mill-stones damnified would not be a breach, because at the time of the covenant he had elected to perform the one or the other part; therefore (according to *Laughter's Case*), without estimation by *A* and *B* of the damage of the mill-stones, the defendant was excused from the performance, because it was impossible for him to make the adjudication, or to compel *A* and *B* to do it; and till that be done, the defendant could not be liable, no more than if *A*, entering into bond to perform the award of *B* and *C*, and *B* and *C* would not make any award. Against that it was said in effect, 'These covenants are part of the condition of the bond. And since the latter part of this disjunctive covenant is for the safety of the defendant, it belongs to him to procure this estimation, or otherwise he shall be liable. If the estimation *(pg61)* ought to be made by such persons as the obligee should appoint, and the obligee had refused to appoint, this would have excused the defendant; because the performance of the covenant is rendered impossible by the act of the obligee. But in this case the fact is contrary.' And of that opinion was the whole Court, and Treby CJ, put this case, A in consideration of £100 bound himself in a bond, with condition either to make a lease for the life of the obligee before such a day, or to pay him £100. The obligee died before the day, yet it was adjudged that the obligor should pay the £100, and not the damages which had been suffered if he had got a lease for his life, and accordingly there was judgment for the plaintiff.

3 It seems to me that that is an authority that in such a case as the present, the default in the performance of the one alternative being due to the act of the Defendant, who might have formed his company in another way, he is bound to perform the other alternative. Consequently, there must be judgment for the Plaintiffs for £1,000 with costs.

Judgement in the Court of Appeal

4 LORD HALSBURY: I confess that in this case I have not been able to entertain any doubt from the first time when the covenant was read to me. I should construe it as I should construe the language of any ordinary document. I think if the covenant itself is not ambiguous I have no right to refer either to the recitals or to the statement of the consideration; and it seems to me, without at all going into the reasons of the learned Judge below for his judgment, that it would not be proper to hold that those words are not to be taken in their ordinary natural meaning – that the Plaintiffs were to have £1,000 worth of shares. It is vain to contend that if you take any other construction of the language you do not have to strike out the word 'worth' altogether. Therefore, upon the ordinary principle of construction, if there is nothing cutting down the natural meaning of the word I must construe it to be the natural meaning of the word. You cannot construe an instrument of this sort by striking out a word, and asking us to read the document in such a way as to make that word inoperative. I am of opinion that the Court below was right – that the true construction of the language is that there were to be £1,000 worth of shares; and it is admitted that these shares were not worth £1,000. The appeal must be dismissed with costs.

5   LINDLEY LJ: I am of the same opinion. The covenant is by Taylor that he will within twelve calendar months of the date of the document pay £1,000, or hand over to, or otherwise transfer into the names of, the Plaintiffs £1,000 worth of fully paid-up shares in a company to be formed by Taylor, the capital of which is not to exceed £12,000. Now, what does that mean? Mr Graham Hastings has invited us to construe it that he will pay £1,000 in *(pg63)* cash or in shares, meaning that he will transfer shares to the nominal value of £1,000. I do not think that that is the fair meaning of the language used. I put to Mr Graham Hastings another aspect of the case: supposing these shares had gone up, and Taylor had offered and tendered a smaller number than £1,000 in nominal value, but £1,000 worth in the market, what would have been the answer? The shares would be taken at their value according to the market. It is the same question from another point of view; but it strikes me that the answer to it is clear. No one in the case supposed could have accused Taylor of breaking his contract; he would have done exactly what he said he would do – paid £1,000 worth of shares. Reliance has been placed on the recitals, and the recitals, no doubt, express the intention of the parties in language somewhat different; but I do not think it is right to construe the plain words of this covenant with reference to the language of the recitals, more especially as the draftsman has departed from the view which he entertained when he drew the recital. There is no covenant here to form a particular company with a defined capital. The covenant is to pay the money or £1,000 worth of shares in a company to be formed; and although, of course, the recitals from one point of view help Mr Graham Hastings, the covenant that he is to pay £1,000 worth is against him. I think the only safe way is to adhere to the language of the covenant, which, to my mind, is perfectly plain.

6   RIGBY LJ: I am of the same opinion. The word 'worth' is not only an important word, but it appears to me to be the important word in that covenant. What does 'worth' mean? It means worth in the sense of the real value to be ascertained in some manner. There can be no difficulty in ascertaining it; it does not mean nominal value. A thing may be of the nominal value of £100,000, or, as in this case, £1,000, and yet not be worth a farthing. I do not consider that the covenant is in any way ambiguous. If it had been, I do not see that we should have got any light from the recitals, or from the consideration, because I consider they are very ambiguous, and that they do not exclude the meaning *(pg64)* which is given in the covenant. The better way, however, to put it, undoubtedly is that unless we see that there is something ambiguous in the covenant itself, we ought not to care about the consideration. *(pg65)*

Case 3
Borland's Trustee v Steel Brothers & Co Ltd

[1901] 1 Ch 279

[1900] B 1253

High Court

13, 14 November 1900

When valuing a shareholding in a company, one is valuing a bundle of rights and obligations that are held by virtue of owning the share.

The basic principle applied is that the hypothetical unconnected purchaser steps into the shoes of the vendor. This means that not only is he the owner of the shares being valued (and has his ownership registered by the company) but, also, he is bound by the company's articles. Farwell J views the articles as constituting a binding contract:

> 'I have said that these articles are nothing more or less than a personal contract between Mr Borland and the other shareholders in the company under the 16th section of the Companies Act 1862.'

It is important to note the distinction between the facts in *In re The Isle of Thanet Electricity Supply Co Ltd* and those in *Borland's Trustee v Steel Brothers & Co Ltd* [1901] 1 Ch 279 **case 3**. In the *Borland's* case, the agreement between the shareholders is contained within the articles; in the *Isle of Thanet* case, it is not.

The value of the shareholding is, thus, the value of the rights and obligations the shareholder has to the company and the rights and obligations the shareholder has to other shareholders; the obligations can include restrictions on the shareholder's future actions. A mistake that is commonly made by practitioners in commencing a valuation of a shareholding is to assume that the only rights and obligations to be considered are those arising from a standard shareholding in a standard company. *Borland's Trustee v Steel Brothers & Co Ltd* is the useful corrective to this lazy approach. It is essential to consider the specific rights given by the particular articles of association adopted by that company and to enquire whether there is any shareholders agreement that has continuing effect after the change of identity of the shareholder. This case discusses the nature of that bundle of interest that we call a shareholding; it provides the bedrock of any valuation exercise.

The case needs to be considered in its historical context. The articles of association in dispute were drawn up in 1890. Although limited liability companies had then been available for 35 years, the number of companies was relatively small; even substantial businesses were more typically carried in partnership. Partnerships and trusts had been known to English law for many centuries; articles of association were a new statutory creation. It should, thus, be of no surprise that the submissions made to the court were framed in terms of the developed law of partnerships and the law of trusts and how this body of case law should influence the interpretation of the new statutory creature, the articles of association of a company.

Steel Brothers & Co Limited was incorporated in 1890. The capital of the company was reorganised by an extra-ordinary general meeting (EGM) on 11 June 1897, when new articles of association were adopted and the company's share capital was divided into 1,600 £1 preference shares (fully paid) and 1,600 £100 ordinary shares (£80 paid).

JE Borland held 160 £1 preference shares and 80 £100 ordinary shares.

On 22 February 1900, JE Borland was adjudicated bankrupt. By that date, he had disposed of his holding of preference shares and reduced his holding to 73 £100 ordinary shares (partly paid).

The company's articles of association, following the 1897 EGM, provided that a shareholding be surrendered if the shareholder became bankrupt. The articles gave pre-emptive rights to existing shareholders to purchase any shares in the company for a sum described by article 50 as 'the fair value'. Article 53 stated:

'the sum fixed by a transfer notice as the fair price for a share should in no case exceed the par value of the share; and that the par value of a share should, for the purpose of the article, be deemed to be the amount paid up, or properly credited as paid up, on such share, plus, in the case of an ordinary share, (a) a sum bearing the same ratio to the market value of the investments of the reserve fund account of the company as the capital paid up on the share sold should bear to the total paid-up ordinary capital; (b) a sum equal to one quarter of a sum bearing the same ratio to the company's "plant depreciation account" as the capital paid up on the share sold should bear to the total paid-up ordinary capital; and (c) interest at 5 per cent per annum on the total sum arrived at after making such additions as aforesaid, computed from such times and in such manner as were therein more particularly specified. And it was further provided by the same article that a certificate of the auditor of the company should be final and conclusive on all parties as to the par value of any share.'

The par value of JE Borland's 73 shares, calculated according to article 53, was about £8,650, whereas the real value of them, Mr Borland's trustee in bankruptcy alleged, having regard to the amount of the dividend paid upon them between the years 1892 and 1899, and to the general financial position of the company, was about £34,000.

The company had paid large dividends in some years, but the dividends had fluctuated from £51 per share in 1893 to £2 12s 6d per share in 1896; the average dividend for the years 1892–99 was about £45 per share.

Counsel for the trustee in bankruptcy submitted that the valuation provisions of the articles of association should be set aside on one of two alternate grounds.

1. There is a long standing rule of trust law that any provision is void if it operates to hold property in trust in perpetuity. (This is recognised in modern trust deeds by normally restricting the life of the trust to 80 years, 100 years in the case of a trust under the law of Jersey.) The restriction in the Articles, submitted Counsel, is a restriction of absolute ownership and, thus, creates (or is akin to) a trust which is void as it offends the law of perpetuities.

2. The effect of the valuation provision in the articles is to limit the sum receivable by the trustee in bankruptcy and, thus, restrict the amounts he can distribute to the bankrupt's creditors. The provision in the article, thus, Counsel argued, was void as a fraud on the bankruptcy law.

Farwell J, in a robust judgement, upheld the freedom of the members of a company to establish articles of association in accordance with their wishes and supported the proposition that the Articles, once established, were binding on the shareholders subsequently.

In respect of the first submission, Farwell J identified the nature of articles of association as personal contracts and said:

> 'In my opinion the rule against perpetuity has no application whatever to personal contracts.'
>
> ([1901] 1 Ch 279 at 289 **case 3 para 2**)

> '[Counsel for the trustee in bankruptcy] is applying to company law a principle which is wholly inapplicable thereto. It rests, I think, on a misconception of what a share in a company really is. A share is the interest of a shareholder in the company measured by a sum of money, for the purpose of liability in the first place, and of interest in the second, but also consisting of a series of mutual covenants entered into by all the shareholders *inter se* in accordance with s16 of the Companies Act 1862.'
>
> ([1901] 1 Ch 279 at 288 **case 3 para 1**)

'Mr Borland was one of the original shareholders, and he and his trustee in bankruptcy are bound by his own contract. I do not know that I am concerned to consider the case of other shareholders who come in afterwards; but if I am, the answer so far as they are concerned is that each of them on coming in executes a deed of transfer which, in the terms in which it is executed, makes him liable to all the provisions of the original articles.'

([1901] 1 Ch 279 at 290 **case 3 para 3**)

Farwell J then dismissed the argument that the articles contravened bankruptcy law by noting that all shares in the company are subjected to the same valuation provision. He pointed out that there is no provision that applies to any one person in a way that is different to another, other than by reference to the class of shares that is held:

'I find the price is a fixed sum for all persons alike'

([1901] 1 Ch 279 at 291 **case 3 para 4**)

This case is, thus, the basis for the valuation principle that one must always look first at the articles of association and treat those articles as applying to the shares being valued. If, as will nearly always be the case, the articles provide rights and liabilities expressed in terms of a class of shares, there is then no scope for arguing that the identity of an individual shareholder gives that shareholder greater or lesser rights or greater or lesser liabilities than any other person who may hold those shares. In a fiscal valuation, we consider the price that would reasonably be expected to be offered by a hypothetical unconnected purchaser of the shares. Our valuation must be undertaken on the basis that this notional person acquires the shares subject to any valuation formula in the articles.

It is important to note that the decision in *Borland's Trustee v Steel Brothers & Co Ltd* does not mean that a share valuation is the adoption of a simple arithmetic valuation formula in the articles. The valuation must always reflect the statutory hypothesis for fiscal purposes, which is that the value is the amount that would be offered by a hypothetical unconnected purchaser who has full knowledge of all relevant rights and obligations arising from the articles and from any shareholder's agreement, including any formula for valuation given in either the articles or the agreement. It is perfectly possible for the hypothetical unconnected purchaser to offer more than the value given by a formula in the articles; this will be the case where the dividend flow (for example) gives a return on the investment to justify a payment greater than the formula in the articles.

Judgement

References, example '(pg287)', are to [1901] 1 Ch 279.

1 **FARWELL J** (after stating the facts and referring to the articles of association): It is said that the provisions of these articles compel a man at any time during the continuance of *(pg287)* this company to sell his shares to particular persons at a particular price to be ascertained in the manner prescribed in the articles. Two arguments have been founded on that. It is said, first of all, that such provisions are repugnant to absolute ownership. It is said, further, that they tend to perpetuity. They are likened to the case of a settlor or testator who settles or gives a sum of money subject to executory limitations which are to arise in the future, interpreting the articles as if they provided that if at any time hereafter, during centuries to come, the company should desire the shares of a particular person, not being a manager or assistant, he must sell them. To my mind that is applying to company law a principle which is wholly inapplicable thereto. It is the first time that any such suggestion has been made, and it rests, I think, on a misconception of what a share in a company really is. A share, according to the plaintiff's argument, is a sum of money which is dealt with in a particular manner by what are called for the purpose of argument executory limitations. To my mind it is nothing of the sort. A share is the interest of a shareholder in the company measured by a sum of money, for the purpose of liability in the first place, and of interest in the second, but also consisting of a series of mutual covenants entered into by all the shareholders *inter se* in accordance with s16 of the Companies Act 1862. The contract contained in the articles of association is one of the original incidents of the share. A share is not a sum of money settled in the way suggested, but is an interest measured by a sum of money and made up of various rights contained in the contract, including the right to a sum of money of a more or less amount. That view seems to me to be supported by the authority of *New London and Brazilian Bank v Brocklebank.* That was a case in which trustees bought shares in a company whose articles provided 'that the company should have a first and paramount charge on the shares of any shareholder for all moneys owing to the company from him alone or jointly with any other person, and that when a share was held by more persons than one the company should have a like lien *(pg288)* and charge thereon in respect of all moneys so owing to them from all or any of the holders thereof alone or jointly with any other person.' One of the trustees was a partner in a firm which afterwards went into liquidation, at a time at which it owed the company a debt which had arisen long after the registration of the shares in the names of the trustees. It was held that the shares were subject to the lien mentioned for the benefit of the company, notwithstanding the interest of the *cestuis que trust* which was said to be paramount. If there had been any substance in the suggestion now made, namely, that the right to the lien was the right to an executory lien arising from time to time as the necessity for it arose, it might have been put forward in that case; but the decision was based on a ground inconsistent with any such contention, namely, that the shares were subjected to this particular lien in their inception and as one of their incidents. Jessel MR likened it to the case of a lease.

Holker LJ said: 'It seems to me that the shares having been purchased on those terms and conditions, it is impossible for the *cestuis que trust* to say that those terms and conditions are not to be observed.'

2 Then it is said that this is contrary to the rule against perpetuity. Now, in my opinion the rule against perpetuity has no application whatever to personal contracts. If authority is necessary for that, the case of *Witham v Vane* is a direct authority of the House of Lords; and to my mind an even stronger case is that of *Walsh v Secretary of State for India*. A stronger instance of the unlimited extent of personal liability could hardly be cited; the Old East India Company in 1760, or thereabouts, entered into a covenant with the first Lord Clive, that in the event of the company ceasing to be the possessors of the Bengal territories they would repay to Lord Clive, his executors or administrators, a sum of about eight lacs of rupees, which had been transferred to them for certain particular purposes. The actual event did not happen till nearly a century later; and, as Lord Selborne pointed out in *Witham v Vane*, the question of perpetuity was put *(pg289)* forward tentatively in argument in the House of Lords; but Lord Cairns with his usual discretion did not press it.

3 I have said that these articles are nothing more or less than a personal contract between Mr Borland and the other shareholders in the company under the 16th section of the Companies Act 1862. Mr Borland was one of the original shareholders, and he and his trustee in bankruptcy are bound by his own contract. I do not know that I am concerned to consider the case of other shareholders who come in afterwards; but if I am, the answer so far as they are concerned is that each of them on coming in executes a deed of transfer which, in the terms in which it is executed, makes him liable to all the provisions of the original articles. Mr Borland cannot be heard to say there is any repugnancy or perpetuity in the covenant he has entered into, and his trustee in bankruptcy stands in no better position. Counsel for the plaintiff attempted to apply the reasoning in *Gomm's Case* to the present case, and to argue that if the contract was merely personal it did not affect the trustee in bankruptcy, and that if it was an executory limitation it was void. But that is in my opinion unsound; the trustee is as much bound by these personal obligations of the bankrupt as the bankrupt himself, if he were not bankrupt, would be.

4 Then comes the question whether or not these provisions constitute a fraud on the bankruptcy law. I will take the principle as stated by James LJ in *Ex parte Jay*. The principle is 'that a simple stipulation that upon a man's becoming bankrupt that which was his property up to the date of the bankruptcy should go over to some one else and be taken away from his creditors, is void as being a violation of the policy of the bankrupt law.' In this particular case I find that all the shares are subjected to art 58. There is no idea of preferring any one person to another, except so far as is pointed out by art 47, under which by contract the original shareholders, at the time of the passing of the special resolution for the new articles, retained for themselves the right to refuse the compulsory sale of their shares until they should die, or *(pg290)* voluntarily transfer the same, or should become bankrupt. It is said that these last words constitute a fraud on the bankruptcy law, and are void. In my opinion that is not so. If I once arrive at the conclusion that these provisions were inserted bona fide – and that is not contested – and if I also come to the conclusion that they constitute a fair agreement for the purpose of the business of the company, and are binding equally upon all persons who come in, so that there is no suggestion of fraudulent preference of one over another, there is nothing obnoxious to the bankruptcy law in a clause which provides that if a man becomes bankrupt he shall sell his shares. That is the first step. I am not sure that counsel would have contested that alone. But then the question of price arises. Now I find the price is a fixed sum for all persons alike. No difference in price arises in case of bankruptcy: the effect of bankruptcy is merely to except the bankrupt from the privileges of art 47. The particular benefit reserved to the holders of the shares therein specified is by contract abrogated in the case of their becoming bankrupt, for the purpose of giving effect to the general scope of the articles, which was that there should be in the company, if it were so desired, none but managers and workers in Burma. There is nothing repugnant to any bankruptcy law in such a provision as that. Is there anything repugnant in the way in which the value of shares is to be ascertained? If I came to the conclusion that there was no provision in these articles compelling persons to sell their shares in the event of bankruptcy at something less than the price that they would otherwise obtain, such a provision would be repugnant to the bankruptcy law; but it is not so. They all stand on the same footing, and the proper value is to be ascertainable for all alike. These shares can have no value ascertainable by any ordinary rules, because having held, as I do, that the restrictive clauses are good, it is impossible to find a market value. There is no quotation. It is impossible, therefore, for any one to arrive at any actual figure, as to which it may be said it is clear that that is the value, or something within a few pounds of the value. Having regard to the fluctuation in profits that has occurred, it is *(pg291)* impossible to say the value can be ascertained upon a 10 or 20 per cent basis – that must be illusory. If it were necessary – I do not think it is – I should be prepared to hold upon the evidence that the price offered by the company in this particular case represents the fair value. I think that by no means an unfair test is afforded by the fact that Mr Borland himself in January 1899 sold some of his shares at about the same price. It is not immaterial to consider that two other persons under the compulsory power have been compelled to sell and have not objected. So far as I can see, the terms are reasonably fair, and, assuming that it is a fair mode of arriving at the value – and I think it is – I do not see that it differs from the ordinary provision for valuation such as I find in *Whitmore v Mason* applicable to those cases where assets are capable of valuation. I have to bear in mind that I am dealing with a company whose assets are really in a sense incapable of valuation, but in which the parties have agreed on a basis of valuation which seems to me to be fair. I think I should be straining the principle of the cases on fraud in bankruptcy if I came to the conclusion that an agreement like this, which was come to between the parties after discussion and discontent on the part of some of them, ought to be set aside on the suggestion that it might result in an unfair price. The particular passage to which counsel for the defendant referred in the case of

Whitmore v Mason was at the end of the judgment. In that case Page Wood V-C had before him a partnership deed which contained an article under which, in case of bankruptcy, the partners were to forfeit the whole value of a certain lease. That was held to be bad, and if there had been anything of the sort here I should, of course, have held it bad too. But there was also a provision, which was held to be good, that there was to be a valuation of the share of the bankrupt partner, and the Vice-Chancellor says at the end of his judgment: 'Where there is a bona fide intention to secure the going on of the concern, by the other parties handing over to the creditors all that the creditors ought to take, I cannot conceive there is any fraud on the bankruptcy laws.' In my opinion that *(pg292)* exactly expresses the facts of the present case as proved to me, and I think I am following that case when I hold that there is no fraud on the bankruptcy law here.

5 Then there are one or two other somewhat minor points made by counsel for the plaintiff. First, he says that these provisions are *ultra vires*. That point turns upon the provisions of the articles which constitute the machinery by which the compulsory sale is to be carried out. The company is constituted an agent for receiving purchase-money: I do not think it comes to more than that; and the company is constituted the agent for sale of the shareholder who is asked to sell. Counsel for the plaintiff says, first of all, that that is not within the memorandum of association. In my opinion it is within the words of sub-s (*d*) of clause 3 of the memorandum – 'To transact and carry on all kinds of agency business.' Then it is said that it is contrary to the Companies Act 1862, and is ultra vires in that sense. I cannot see for myself that there is any trafficking in shares in any way, or that the company is in any way mixed up in anything contrary to the Act. In my opinion that objection fails.

6 The last point is a technical one and turns on art 58a. [His Lordship read the article, and continued: –] The notice was given on March 7. The general meeting at which the dividend was declared was held on February 16. It is said that that was not a general meeting properly so called for this purpose, because of art 72, which provides that 'General meetings shall be held once in every year, at such time and place as may be prescribed by the company in general meeting, and, if no time and place is prescribed, in the month of April in every such year at such time and place as may be prescribed by the directors.' I am told, however, that a general meeting has never been called in April at all. It was held in February and in March in preceding years. Under those circumstances I consider that the company has waived art 72, and on the question whether the terms of art 58a have been complied with, and whether the notice has been given during the first month next after a general meeting of the company at which an annual dividend on the ordinary shares has either been *(pg293)* declared or, profits permitting, would have been declared, it is clear that the only dividend was in this instance declared at the meeting on February 16, and that the plaintiff has either accepted or applied for it.

7 That, I think, disposes of all the points that have been raised; and the necessary result is that I dismiss the action with costs. *(pg294)*

Case 4
IRC v Muller & Co Margarine Ltd

[1901] AC 217

House of Lords

20 May 1901

A valuation of a shareholding in a trading company will always consider, either explicitly or by default, the value of the goodwill of the trade. This case is an early judicial analysis of the nature of the goodwill of a trading company.

The specific point at issue is a statutory charge that was repealed by FA 1999, Sch 20. Prior to its repeal, Stamp Act 1891, s 59 charged stamp duty on a document selling an interest in property located in the United Kingdom. Two issues fell to be determined by the House of Lords:

(i)   whether goodwill is 'property'; and
(ii)   what is the location of the goodwill of a UK based trade that is the subject of a contract for a sale made in Germany.

It is the judgement on the first issue that is of continuing relevance, in particular the careful analysis by the House of Lords of the nature of goodwill.

For many years an unincorporated business, Muller & Co, had carried on a wholesale business as manufacturer of margarine and other butter substitutes at Gildehaus in Germany. In October 1897, a document was executed under seal transferring the business to the newly created company Muller & Co Margarine Limited. The deed was executed in Amsterdam and also in England. The value of the property transferred was £71,418. Stamp duty of £387 5s was levied on the goodwill transferred. The company appealed against the assessment to stamp duty on the transfer of goodwill.

In his leading judgement, Lord Macnaghten analysed the nature of goodwill as follows:

'It is very difficult, as it seems to me, to say that goodwill is not property. Goodwill is bought and sold every day. It may be acquired, I think, in any of the different ways in which property is usually acquired. When a man has got it he may keep it as his own. He may vindicate his exclusive right to it if necessary by process of law. He may dispose of it if he will – of course under the conditions attaching to property of that nature.'

([1901] AC 217 at 223 **case 4 para 4**)

'What is goodwill? It is a thing very easy to describe, very difficult to define. It is the benefit and advantage of the good name, reputation and connection of a business. It is the attractive force which brings in custom. It is the one thing which distinguishes an old-established business from a new business at its first start. The goodwill of a business must emanate from a particular centre or source. However widely extended or diffused its influence may be, goodwill is worth nothing unless it has power of attraction sufficient to bring customers home to the source from which it emanates. Goodwill is composed of a variety of elements. It differs in its composition in different trades and in different businesses in the same trade. One element may preponderate here and another element there. To analyse goodwill and split it up into its component parts, to pare it down as the Commissioners desire to do until nothing is left but a dry residuum ingrained in the actual place where the business is carried on while everything else is in the air, seems to me to be as useful for practical purposes as it would be to resolve the human body into the various substances of which it is said to be composed. The goodwill of a business is one whole, and in a case like this it must be dealt with as such.'

([1901] AC 217 at 223/224 **case 4 para 5**)

Lord Linley considered that goodwill is more restricted in its meaning and is more strongly tied to location:

'Goodwill regarded as property has no meaning except in connection with some trade, business, or calling. In that connection I understand the word to include whatever adds value to a business by reason of situation, name and reputation, connection, introduction to old customers, and agreed absence from competition, or any of these things, and there may be others which do not occur to me. In this wide sense, goodwill is inseparable from the business to which its adds value, and, in my opinion, exists where the business is carried on. Such business may be carried on in one place or country or in several, and if in several there may be several businesses, each having a goodwill of its own.

That in some cases and to some extent goodwill can and must be considered as having a distinct locality, is obvious, and was not in fact disputed. The goodwill of a public house or of a retail shop is an instance. The goodwill of a business usually adds value to the land or house in which it is carried on if sold with the business; and so far as the goodwill adds value to land or buildings, the goodwill can only be regarded as situate where they are. In such a case the goodwill is said to be annexed to them.'

([1901] AC 217 at 235 **case 4 paras 40 and 41**)

In undertaking a share valuation, any goodwill owned by the company is property of the company and has a value in just the same way as real estate has a value for the company. In an earnings valuation, the value of a company's shareholding is measured by applying a multiple to the profits generated by the company's activities. This is, inherently, giving a capital value to the profits generated by the utilisation of the goodwill employed by the company in its trade.

In just the same way as ownership of a share is the holding of a bundle of rights by the shareholder, so a company's ownership of goodwill is a bundle of rights relating to trading activities. In the case of an incorporated trade, those rights are owned by the company. In his judgement, Lord Davey reminds us that we have to identify the rights that constitute the property known as goodwill by reference to the law that applies to those rights:

'The subject of the contract is the sale as a going concern of a German manufacturing and commercial business carried on by a German in Germany. What rights pass to the purchaser of the goodwill, in my opinion, depends prima facie on the German law. It is said that the purchaser might remove the business (say) to England. Whether he could do so and still retain the rights conferred by the contract is, in my opinion a question of German law.'

([1901] AC 217 at 226 **case 4 para 11**)

Judgement

References, example '(pg222)', are to [1901] AC 217.

1 **LORD MACNAGHTEN:** May 20. My Lords, in this case your Lordships have listened to an interesting disquisition on the subject of that which is commonly called goodwill. Most, if not all, of the many cases touching upon that subject have *(pg222)* been cited at the bar with the view of satisfying your Lordships that the goodwill of a foreign business, which was confined within certain known and narrow limits on the Continent, and which apparently never had a single customer in this country, cannot be described as "property locally situate out of the United Kingdom".

2 There are two questions in the case – (1) Was this agreement made in England? and (2) Was the goodwill of this business property 'locally situate out of the United Kingdom'?

3 As to the first question I do not think there can be any difficulty. It seems to me that, according to the true construction of the Stamp Act of 1891, an agreement is made in England if it is executed in England by a party to the agreement whose execution is required to make the instrument on the face of it complete and perfect. The argument that, because s59 of the Act speaks of an agreement for sale and not of an agreement for sale and purchase, regard is only to be had to the execution by the vendor, is, in my opinion, too refined to be substantial. I think the agreement was made in England, and not the less so because it may also be described with equal propriety as made abroad.

4 I now come to the second point. It was argued that if goodwill be property, it is property having no local situation. It is very difficult, as it seems to me, to say that goodwill is not property. Goodwill is bought and sold every day. It may be acquired, I think, in any of the different ways in which property is usually acquired. When a man has got it he may keep it as his own. He may vindicate his exclusive right to it if necessary by process of law. He may dispose of it if he will – of course under the conditions attaching to property of that nature.

5 Then comes the question, Can it be said that goodwill has a local situation within the meaning of the Act? I am disposed to agree with an observation thrown out in the course of the argument, that it is not easy to form a conception of property having no local situation. What is goodwill? It is a thing very easy to describe, very difficult to define. It is the benefit and advantage of the good name, reputation, and connection *(pg223)* of a business. It is the attractive force which brings in custom. It is the one thing which distinguishes an old-established business from a new business at its first start. The goodwill of a business must emanate from a particular centre or source. However widely extended or diffused its influence may be, goodwill is worth nothing unless it has power of attraction sufficient to bring customers home to the source from which it emanates. Goodwill is composed of a variety of elements. It differs in its composition in different trades and in different businesses in the same trade. One element may preponderate here and another element there. To analyse goodwill and split it up into its component parts, to pare it down as the Commissioners desire to do until nothing is left but a dry residuum ingrained in the actual place where the business is carried on while everything else is in the air, seems to me to be as useful for practical purposes as it would be to resolve the human body into the various substances of which it is said to be composed. The goodwill of a business is one whole, and in a case like this it must be dealt with as such.

6 For my part, I think that if there is one attribute common to all cases of goodwill it is the attribute of locality. For goodwill has no independent existence. It cannot subsist by itself. It must be attached to a business. Destroy the business, and the goodwill perishes with it, though elements remain which may perhaps be gathered up and be revived again. No doubt, where the reputation of a business is very widely spread or where it is the article produced rather than the producer of the article that has won popular favour, it may be difficult to localise goodwill. But here, I think, there is no difficulty. We have it in evidence that the firm of Muller & Co had no customers out of Germany, and it is a significant fact that the protected area – the limit within which the vendor is prohibited from setting up in business – is the limit of fifty miles from Gildehaus. Moreover, under the Stamp Act of 1891 we are not required to define the local situation of the goodwill. We have only to determine whether it is or is not situate out of the United Kingdom. Surely, if there were an agreement made in England for the sale of a local German newspaper, the *(pg224)* circulation of which did not extend beyond a limited district in Germany, no one would doubt that the goodwill of that business was locally situate out of the United Kingdom; and so it must be, I think, in the present case.

7 I am therefore of opinion that the judgment of the Court of Appeal is right and ought to be affirmed, and I move your Lordships accordingly.

8 LORD DAVEY: My Lords, the questions on this appeal arise on the construction of a few words in s59, sub-s 1, of the Stamp Act, 1891. By an agreement under seal the goodwill of a business carried on in Germany, together with the factory and buildings in which the business was carried on, and all the plant, machinery, apparatus, rolling stock, and chattels employed in the business except stock-in-trade and all pending contracts and orders in connection with the business, books of account, documents and papers, was agreed to be sold for a lump sum to the respondents, who are an English company. The principal question is, whether the goodwill so agreed to be sold was either wholly or partially 'property situate out of the United Kingdom' within the meaning of the exception in the section referred to. But other subsidiary points have been argued to which I will first address a few remarks.

9 First, it was said that the agreement was not made in England because the vendors executed it in Amsterdam. It was not, however, a completed agreement for purchase and sale till it was executed by the purchasers, and that was done in England. It was argued that the acceptance by the purchasers might have been proved by oral evidence, which is true. But what we have to deal with is the document in which the acceptance by the purchasers was expressed by the execution of it in this country.

10 Another point made was on the construction of the section. It was suggested that the word 'property' ought to be read as *ejusdem generis* with the words which immediately precede it, namely, 'lands, tenements, hereditaments or heritages,' and to be confined to real property. The first observation which occurs to one is that if such had been the intention it *(pg225)* would have been so easy to have expressed it – to have said 'real property.' But the word 'property' occurs in two places in the earlier part of the section. It is there used in its widest sense as meaning property of every description, and I can find no sufficient reason in the context for thinking that it is used in a more restricted sense in the passage in question. The clause is drawn in rather a confused manner. The material words are, 'any contract or agreement . ... for the sale of any estate or interest in any property except lands, etc, or property locally situate out of the United Kingdom or goods, etc.' Whatever the word 'property' means in the words imposing the duty, I think it must have the same meaning in the words of exception. It is not disputed that property in its wider sense may include whatever rights or benefits pass under the term 'goodwill.'

11 I pass now to the principal question which has been argued, namely, whether goodwill can be said to be situate outside the United Kingdom or to have any local situation. A more accurate way of stating the question would, in my opinion, be whether the goodwill which is comprised in this contract has a locality for the purpose of the Stamp Act. Now, the subject of the contract is the sale as a going concern of a German manufacturing and commercial business carried on by a German in Germany with the buildings in which the business is carried on, and all the plant, etc, necessary for carrying it on. It does not appear to me that the mention of goodwill adds anything to that which would be included in a sale of the business. What rights pass to the purchaser of the goodwill, in my opinion, depends prima facie on the German law; but the parties have to a certain extent defined them for themselves, as 'the exclusive right to use the name of Muller & Co as part of the name of the company, and to represent the company as carrying on the said business in continuation of the vendors and in succession to them,' and they have protected the purchaser by the vendor's covenant not to carry on the business of manufacturers of margarine at any time thereafter within fifty miles of the business premises. It is said that the purchaser might remove the business (say) to England. Whether he *(pg226)* could do so and still retain the rights conferred by the contract is, in my opinion a question of German law. It seems to me, however, immaterial whether they can do so or not, because (I repeat) this business was at the date of the contract in Germany. What we have to look at is the state of things at the date of the contract; and the possibility of its removal no more affects the question than if it were a valuable chattel such as a picture or a statue.

12 The position taken up by the Attorney-General was a singular one, and somewhat embarrassing to persons who have to stamp their contracts. He admitted that, so far as the goodwill was attached to the business premises and thereby enhanced their value, he did not claim that an *ad valorem* stamp should be affixed in respect of that value. But I am not aware that you can split up goodwill into its elements in that way, and I see great difficulty in doing so. The term goodwill is nothing more than a summary of the rights accruing to the respondents from their purchase of the business and property employed in it. As that business and property undoubtedly had their local habitation in Germany at the date of the contract, I have no difficulty in the conclusion that the Court of Appeal were right, and this appeal ought to be dismissed.

13 I do not find it necessary to say anything about the numerous cases which were referred to in the course of the argument, because, in my opinion, they have no direct bearing on the case, nor do I express any opinion on the abstract question whether an incorporeal right can have a local situation, beyond saying that I am not impressed with the difficulty of holding that it may have one for revenue purposes in analogy to the decisions in the probate cases.

14 LORD JAMES OF HEREFORD: My Lords, I share the view that the judgment of the Court of Appeal is correct, and that this appeal should be dismissed. For the reasons already given I think the contention of the Crown, that this contract was made in England, is correct. The principal question for decision by your Lordships no doubt afforded great opportunity for ingenious argument; but that question can, I *(pg227)* think, easily enough be solved by the application of mere common sense.

15 The question whether the agreement for the sale of the goodwill of a manufacturing business should be charged with an *ad valorem* stamp under the Stamp Act of 1891; depends upon the application of certain facts existing in this case to the words of that Act. The business sold was a wholesale manufacturing business carried on in premises situated at Gildehaus in Germany. All the stock and plant of the company were on those premises. All the customers of the company were resident in Germany.

16 Now, as the Stamp Act imposes no duty on agreements referring to property locally situate out of the United Kingdom, the question arises, Where is the goodwill of this business to be found? I would premise that in my view no substantial difference can be established between the words 'locally situate' and the word 'situate.' It is admitted that goodwill is property within the Act – and the Act assumes that the property, prima facie all the property mentioned in the Act, may be situate out of the United Kingdom. Now, in this case we have a business in respect of which a goodwill exists. This business without doubt lies abroad. It cannot be otherwise, for premises, plant, manufacture, trade residence of customers, are all in Germany. And this business, locally situate out of the United Kingdom, has a goodwill attached to it. It is difficult to separate them – certainly out of the business the goodwill springs, and its value depends entirely upon the local existence of the premises and the manufactory, and the existence and action of more or less local customers. The parties to the agreement certainly attached value to the continuance of the business in the locality; for the vendor contracted not to carry his business on within fifty miles of the existing premises.

17 I entirely dissent from the view that the goodwill of a business, either wholesale or retail, cannot be locally situated. On the contrary, I should say that the goodwill of most businesses is locally situated. There may be exceptions, but this case is not one of them, and I therefore think that no *(pg228)* stamp duty is chargeable upon that part of the agreement which refers to the goodwill of the business sold, and that therefore the judgment of the Court of Appeal should be affirmed.

18 LORD BRAMPTON (after stating the facts given above): Upon this state of things, the first question raised is whether this instrument of agreement was made in England; for upon it, and it alone, if at all, can the stamp duty now sought to be imposed be charged.

19 If the question were, in which country was the instrument executed? the only possible truthful answer would be, partly in Holland and partly in England. But when the question is, where was the *contract* made?, one is driven to say, it was not in Holland, for while in that country, though it was then signed and sealed by the vendor and two of the intermediates, it lacked the execution of the syndicate and of the vendee, which was essential to its validity as a contract. It only became a perfect contract when the purchasing company and the syndicate affixed their respective common seals to it. It was suggested, however, that there must have been an oral contract made in Germany before the written instrument was prepared; that, however, would not assist the respondent company, for it is only the written instrument which requires to be, or is capable of being, stamped. I may add that by the Stamp Act the duty is to be paid by the purchaser, and the written instrument could not bind the purchasing company until it was executed by that company's common seal. So far as the contract by the purchasers was concerned, it was entirely made in England. For these reasons I have no hesitation in answering the first question in the affirmative in favour of the Crown.

20 As to the second question, I think it is very clear that no equitable estate or interest in the property was ever vested in either Newman, Wigley, or the syndicate. The whole interest, both legal and equitable, remained in the vendor until the rights of option to purchase were exercised by the intermediate parties in the manner hereinbefore described, and carried out *(pg229)* by the written contract. This question, therefore, must be answered in the negative against the Crown.

21 The remaining question is, whether the goodwill of the business, sold as it undoubtedly was in one contract, and as part of one subject-matter of sale, with the buildings, houses, and land in and upon which the business was carried on by the vendor, was property locally situate out of the United Kingdom. I think it was. Whether the goodwill and the land and the factory are rightly to treated as combined and inseparable, or as separated from each other, each is undoubtedly property within the meaning of the Stamp Act, and has been decided so to be by a long string of cases, of which I will only mention that of *Potter v Commissioners of Inland Revenue.*

22 Granting that a goodwill is property, the question still remains, Was the goodwill in this case, when it was purchased by the company, 'property locally situate out of the United Kingdom'? The answer to this depends, in my judgment, upon whether at the time of the making of the written contract the goodwill was attached to and incorporated with the business premises, and formed in the hands of the then vendor an inseparable property, very valuable in its combination as giving to the premises a character and an increase of value which, stripped of the goodwill, they would not have possessed, and which represents the value of the profit-earning quality of those premises, when and so long as they are used by the then occupier, for carrying on in them the business he had created within them, by reason of the attraction of customers from any of those causes which tend to make a prosperous business; for that is what the vendor had to sell, and sold; and the question must be determined having regard to the time when the contract of sale was made, and not regarding anything the vendee might think fit to do with the premises in the future.

23 This word 'goodwill,' when used in connection with the sale and purchase of a trade, must, I think, be interpreted according to its popular acceptation. Taken its strictest sense, 'goodwill' would hardly be a saleable commodity at all.

24 I do not say there may not be such a thing as a goodwill of *(pg230)* a business utterly unconnected with the premises in which the business has been previously carried on, for it is quite possible that a man retiring from business might wish to retain the premises for his own private use, and sell merely the goodwill; but, as was pointed out by Pollock CB in *Potter's Case*, there is a wide difference between the sale of a goodwill together with the premises in which the trade is then carried on, whereby the value of the premises is enhanced, and the sale of a goodwill without any interest in land or buildings connected with it, and which is merely the advantage of the recommendation of the vendor to his connections and customers, and his covenant to allow the vendee to use his trade name, and to abstain from competition with him.

25 In the first of these cases the trade and the premises are inseparable so long as the trade is therein carried on. The advantages and facilities constituting the goodwill are all more or less derived from them, or the profitable results of such goodwill are therein realized. The goodwill of a trade carried on in a shop is as essential to the tradesman as the shop itself, which is benefited by it. What is the trade of a shop but the business done in it, and how is that custom brought to the shop but by the goodwill attached to it? The combination of a suitable shop with the trade done in it, and the goodwill inducing that trade, seem to me to be inseverable. In my judgment, it matters not whether the business be a manufacturing one, or that of a shopkeeper, or a publican, or a brewer; in each case the seller of his business premises with his goodwill sells, and the purchaser buys, the outgoing man's premises, with, so far as in him lies, the whole business carried on therein as a going concern, with the same prospects the vendor himself would have had, had he continued it; and I think it immaterial whether the business has been built up by reason of the personal good qualities of the outgoer, the goodness of his wares or merchandise, the good situation of the premises, or the absence of competition; in each case the business and custom, in fact, have been attracted to the house or premises, and when the incomer takes possession, he takes all the chances *(pg231)* offered and conveyed to him by his purchase, of standing, so far as the business ,s concerned, in the shoes of the outgoer, and he must rely upon his own good qualities and aptitude for his undertaking to continue the prosperity of the business and profit by his bargain.

26 Dealing with an argument touching an injury to the custom of a public-house, Lord Westbury in *Ricket v Metropolitan Ry Co* says: 'It is a fallacy, almost a mockery, to answer, the custom is one thing and the house another; and the injury is to the custom, not to the house. You cannot sever the custom from the house itself, or from the interest of the occupier, for the custom is the thing appertaining to the house which gives it its special character, and constitutes its value to the occupier.' In short, as was observed by the Court of Exchequer, 'the goodwill is part of the value of the property.' The judgment of Lord Esher MR in *Commissioners of Inland Revenue v Angus* is to the same effect.

27 It must not for a moment be imagined that these observations are intended to affect in the least degree the present mode of assessing, for sale or compensation purposes, the value of premises to which a goodwill is attached.

28 In this case the business sold was commenced and its reputation was made and established, on these premises, and nowhere else. The margarine and butter substances have all been there manufactured, at this factory; all the orders of customers, for the most part resident in Germany, have been received at it, and from it the manufactured commodities have been delivered. I care not to inquire into the reasons for its success, for there is the business, consisting of goodwill and premises combined, for which, in their combination as vendors, the vendees voluntarily consented to pay the large sum of money mentioned in the contract.

29 The vendees may, of course, deal as they please with the future of that which they have bought. We have only to deal with it as it stood at the time of the sale. I cannot understand how that business goodwill, so attached, can be treated, or spoken of, as being otherwise than locally situate in Germany. *(pg232)*

30 The cases referred to in the Divisional Court and in the Court of Appeal have been so completely disposed of by each of the Lord Justices, that I do not feel it necessary to say more about them; both are distinguishable from the present, even if rightly decided.

31 I think the judgment of the Divisional Court was rightly reversed by the Court of Appeal, and that this appeal should be dismissed with costs.

32 LORD ROBERTSON: My Lords, I am bound to say that on the main question argued my judgment, which is against the appellants, is dependent on a fact which does not appear in the stated case; but the learned Attorney-General argued upon the assumption that it is true as stated by the respondents' solicitors in their letter of December 14, 1897 (in answer to a categorical question of the Board of Inland Revenue) that 'the whole of the regular customers' [of Muller] 'are resident within the country in which Gildehaus is situate, namely, Germany, and that there is no trade whatever transacted outside the latter country.' Now, when this is taken along with the fact that the manufactory and, so far as appears, the office were at Gildehaus, the case is, so far as facts are concerned, as compact and free from complication as any case could be which gives rise to the present question. So far as the seat of trade and so far as the trade itself are concerned, everything is out of the United Kingdom, and of nothing connected with the trade can it be predicated in any sense whatever that it was not out of the United Kingdom.

33 This consideration seems to me to lift the case clean over such questions and phrases as whether the goodwill is attached or affixed to the manufactory. I do not accede to the view that the goodwill is affixed or attached to the manufactory. Supposing that the products of the manufactory were all exported to England and sold to English customers, I should find it difficult to hold that the goodwill was out of England merely because the manufactory was. The application of the words 'locally situate' would then present a different question, requiring, I should think, a different answer. Again, if the *(pg233)* facts as to the distribution of the products were more complicated, as, for example, if the trade were diffused over England and other countries, then the location of the goodwill would be a more complex, although I do not by any means think an insoluble, problem.

34 I confess I find no repugnancy in affirming of the goodwill of a business that it is locally situate somewhere. It is, I should say, locally situate within the geographical limits which comprehend the seat of the trade, and the trade. That sounds like a very cautious statement, and fortunately it is enough for the present question. It seems to me that in the statute the distinction drawn is between what from a British point of view we should call British property and foreign property; and the goodwill of a business which begins and ends abroad is, I think, property locally situate outside the United Kingdom.

35 On the point as to the place of the execution of the agreement, I have nothing to add.

36 LORD LINDLEY: My Lords, before addressing myself to the main controversy in this case, I will say a few words on one or two minor points arising on the construction of s59 of the Stamp Act 1891.

37 It was said that the agreement for sale in this case was not made in England, because the selling company signed it abroad and the purchasing company signed I it in this country. Until the purchasing company signed it there was no written agreement, but only an offer to sell. The document was made complete as a contract for sale by what was done in this country, and I have no doubt, therefore, that s59 applied to it.

38 Then comes the question whether the word 'property' in the exception is confined to real property or extends also to personal property. In my opinion, it includes personal property. Property is used in the widest possible sense in the earlier part of the section, and it appears to me to be used in the same sense when repeated in the exception. The words 'lands, tenements, and hereditaments' themselves exhaust real property, *(pg234)* and the introduction after them of the word 'property' shews that something more is to be excepted. Nothing more can be suggested which is ejusdem generis, and nothing but personal property remains. Upon this point my own opinion coincides with that of Rigby LJ in the case of the *Smelting Company of Australia.*

39 But even if the word 'property' in the exception extends to corporeal personal property which can have a local situation, it is contended that incorporal property, such as goodwill, cannot be said to be locally situate anywhere, and cannot, therefore, fall within the exception. This is the main contention of the appellants. It is necessary to deal with it, as it has not been contended that goods, wares, and merchandise cover goodwill, and if goodwill is to be excepted it must be because it is property locally situate abroad.

40 Goodwill regarded as property has no meaning except in connection with some trade, business, or calling. In that connection I understand the word to include whatever adds value to a business by reason of situation, name and reputation, connection, introduction to old customers, and agreed absence from competition, or any of these things, and there may be others which do not occur to me. In this wide sense, goodwill is inseparable from the business to which its adds value, and, in my opinion, exists where the business is carried on. Such business may be carried on in one place or country or in several, and if in several there may be several businesses, each having a goodwill of its own.

41 That in some cases and to some extent goodwill can and must be considered as having a distinct locality, is obvious, and was not in fact disputed. The goodwill of a public-house or of a retail shop is an instance. The goodwill of a business usually adds value to the land or house in which it is carried on if sold with the business; and so far as the goodwill adds value to land or buildings, the goodwill can only be regarded as situate where they are. In such a case the goodwill is said to be annexed to them.

42 This consideration alone would, in my opinion, suffice for the *(pg235)* determination of this case; for the factory, business, and goodwill were all sold together for a lump sum, and I do not myself see why the goodwill should be dealt with as having value apart from the factory. But even if the goodwill in the case before us can be properly regarded as to some extent separable from the factory, I still think it must be treated as locally situate abroad.

43 The goodwill sought to be taxed is that of a manufacturer of margarine. His business was to manufacture and sell. His factory was in Germany; the owner was a German living in Germany; he had no agency or place of business abroad; his customers were all in Germany, and his business, so far as selling was concerned, was a wholesale and not a retail business. He convenanted not to carry on business within fifty miles of the old place. If, therefore, the goodwill of a wholesale manufacturer can be regarded as situate anywhere, the goodwill in this case can only be regarded as situate in Germany. Not one of its elements is, or can possibly be, regarded as situate anywhere else. The contention for the Crown was that some part of the goodwill, namely, such part of it as did not simply enhance the value of the land and buildings of the factory, could not be regarded as situate anywhere, and was, therefore, liable to stamp duty. This view, if sound, would be very embarrassing to buyers and sellers, who have to see that they stamp their agreements properly. But the view contended for is, in my opinion, quite untenable.

44 Goodwill is only taxable as property; and the legal conception of property appears to me to involve the legal conception of existence somewhere. Incorporeal property has no existence in nature and has, physically speaking, no locality at all. We, however, are dealing not with anything which in fact fills a portion of space, but with a legal conception, or, in other words, with rights regarded as property. But to talk of property as existing nowhere is to use language which to me is unintelligible.

45 The authorities which bear upon the locality of incorporeal personal property for purposes of probate appear to me to afford the best guides for the solution of the case before us. *(pg236)* Those cases tend strongly to shew that, for purposes of probate, goodwill, except so far as it merely enhances the value of lands and hereditaments, must be regarded as personal property situate somewhere; and if this were a probate case I do not suppose that any one would say that the goodwill with which we have to deal would be regarded as in any sense situate in this country. The *Commissioners of Stamps v Hope*, in which the locality of debts for probate purposes is considered, contains some valuable general remarks on the subject; but there is nothing in that case which conflicts with the view I take of this goodwill.

46 It may perhaps be true that property which has no physical existence may, if necessary, be treated for some purposes in one locality, and for other purposes in some other locality. But, until the necessity for so treating it is apparent, I see no justification for introducing confusion by judicially holding the same property to be legally situate in two different places at one and the same time. But this confusion would be introduced if your Lordships were to decide that the analogy of probate cases was to be no guide in dealing with liability to stamp duty.

47 I am not aware of any case in which goodwill, as property, has been treated as having no locality for legal purposes. The *Smelting Company of Australia, Limited v Commissioners of Inland Revenue*, so much relied upon by counsel for the Crown, was not a case of goodwill at all. The property then in question was not the goodwill of a business, but a share in an Australian patent, and a licence to use the same in Australia. This share and licence belonged to an English registered company, which agreed to sell it to another English company, and

the question was whether the instrument of agreement required a stamp. The Court decided that the share and licence were property, and came within the first part of s59, clause 1, of the Stamp Act, 1891. But they held that such property could not be regarded as locally situate abroad. Lord Esher and Lopes LJ considered that incorporeal personal property could not be said to be situate anywhere. This is, *(pg237)* of course, true, physically speaking, but not, I think, in contemplation of law. Rigby LJ did not adopt the reasoning of the other members of the Court. He referred to the probate decisions; but he considered that, as the property was saleable and sold in this country, it could not be regarded as locally situate out of it. I am not myself able to adopt this conclusion arrived at by Rigby LJ. Any property situate anywhere can be agreed to be sold or purport to be sold in any other country, and the test of locality relied upon by the Lord Justice was not, I think, the true one. The patent was not assignable without registration in Australia, and the view of the Lord Justice is, I think, opposed to *Attorney-General v Dimond*, the case of French Rentes. Be this as it may, in the Australian patent case the Court was not dealing with the goodwill of a foreign manufacturing business, and it would be wrong, I think, to treat the decision as governing the case before us.

48 In my opinion, the decision appealed from ought to be affirmed, and the appeal dismissed with costs.

49 EARL OF HALSBURY LC: My Lords, I regret to say I am unable to concur in the view which has found favour with your Lordships in this case.

50 The goodwill of a business is what the word itself expresses, although the concurrence of so many of your Lordships leads me to doubt what I should otherwise have had no doubt upon. The advantages which may be conferred upon a business, either by its local situation or by its attractive appearance, have nothing to do with the goodwill, although they may have originally contributed to produce it, and may, to some extent, be connected with the nature of the business, which itself, however, is a different thing. 'The goodwill thereof' is a right which has to be assumed to exist separately. Like every other thing which suggests one simple idea, it is difficult, if not impossible, to define it. The right to trade under the name of a firm which has acquired a reputation is not confined to a particular locality or to any particular premises. The right would remain if the business were transferred to another site *(pg238)* elsewhere, or if the premises were entirely altered. In the case of a public-house, owing to the convenience of its situation and its being known as a favourite place of resort, the advantages of its situation are so mixed up with the goodwill of the business that, as a matter of fact, it may well be that it is very difficult to sever them, and to say how much is goodwill and how much is local situation. But those difficulties of fact will not necessarily make their separate existence impossible. In compensation cases, for instance, where a man is being turned out of his holding and has to be put into the same position, so far as compensation can do it, by money which is to be awarded to him, it is unnecessary to regard any such severance into the different elements which make up the advantages of his holding. He is to be compensated for the loss which he has sustained by the alteration of his premises, or the removal of his trade from those premises, and for the extent to which his business may be injured under the circumstances, and it would be quite unnecessary to consider how much he is to be allowed for each element because he is, so far as the tribunal can do it, to be placed in the same position as he was in before. The illustrations which are given of businesses, for instance, the business of a local newspaper, seem to me not to touch the question. It may be very probable that in such a case there would be no goodwill of the business, or very little, but the mere fact that the business was practically, or altogether, local would not make the goodwill of the business simply local, unless by the contract of sale it was confined to a particular spot. In the particular case now under review, the vendors would not be entitled to come to this country and set up a business here under that name and claim the goodwill of customers who might have been brought together in Germany. The right to the goodwill was absolutely transferred to the vendees here. I think if, in order to ascertain what would be the rights of the parties, one looked at the contract apart from any question arising as to the limit of fifty miles, one would see that the thing transferred was the goodwill of that business, whatever it consists of: that would be in every part of the world. The question whether it would *(pg239)* be worth the while of the parties to transfer it is a question quite beside that which in point of law constitutes goodwill. I am wholly unable to see that goodwill itself is susceptible of having any local situation.

51 In my opinion, therefore, the judgment of the Court of Appeal ought to be reversed; but as the majority of your Lordships take a different view, of course the appeal will be dismissed, and the judgment of the Court of Appeal affirmed. *(pg240)*

Case 5
Re Gough & Aspatria, Silloth & District Joint Water Board

[1904] 1 KB 417

Court of Appeal

22 January 1904

This case is the first decision by a court on the approach to be taken where there is a special purchaser (see section **4.6**). This is a difficult concept. In an important sense, every person who would offer a price for shares is a 'special purchaser'. That is, the price that will be offered commercially is the value that that shareholding would have when added to the other interests of the offerer. Different potential purchasers will find a shareholding at different values. This can be illustrated, perhaps, by considering a majority shareholding in a retail trade in a particular part of the country. A company that carries on a complementary trade in the same geographical area would probably be able to reduce administration costs if it were to acquire that shareholding; this reduction in costs is not available to a company whose trade is neither complementary nor geographically close. In valuing a shareholding, the value that would be offered by the former company would, clearly, be taken into account. Sometimes, there is a value in a shareholding that is available only to one potential purchaser. It is such a situation that is addressed in Re Gough & Aspatria, Silloth & District Joint Water Board. In this case, it was only the company exercising its compulsory purchase rights that was able to use the land holding for making a reservoir. The value of the land for use as a reservoir was substantially greater than the value of that land for any other use. This case holds that the value to such a 'special purchaser' is to be taken as the value determined under the statutory conditions that are applied for determining compensation to be paid on a compulsory purchase. In the author's view, this principle applies whether the valuation is of land compulsorily purchased or the valuation is of a shareholding that is the subject of a fiscal valuation. Thus, the effect of this decision of the Court of Appeal is that the higher price that would be paid by a potential purchaser of shares who has a particular interest in acquiring the shares must be taken into account in a share valuation.

The decision in *Re Gough & Aspatria, Silloth & District Joint Water Board* was followed by the Court of Appeal ten years later in *IRC v Clay, IRC v Buchanan* [1914] 3 KB 466 **case 8**.

A special purchaser may be prepared to pay a higher price for the shares than other potential purchasers. The purchaser for whom the shareholding is of particular value may not, of course, in a commercial bidding process offer the full value to him of the shares; he will hope to acquire the shares for less. However, in valuing shares under the statutory provisions that apply to a fiscal valuation, we must assume that all potential bidders have full knowledge of all facts that are in the public arena (and, for capital gains tax and inheritance tax, knowledge of many facts that are not public – see section **2.6**). The knowledge that there is a potential special purchaser may cause speculators to offer a price above that offered by the generality of purchasers, a speculator investing his funds with a view to making an onward sale to the special purchaser. It follows that the higher price that would be offered by a special purchaser must be reflected in a share valuation and will, frequently, determine the level of price of a shareholding.

The Aspatria, Silloth and District Joint Water Board exercised its statutory powers of compulsory purchase to acquire land on which it proposed to make a reservoir. The parties could not agree on the compensation to be paid to the landowner, Miss Gough. The matter went to arbitration. The compensation awarded in the arbitration took account of the particular attraction of this specific site for the construction of a reservoir and, hence, the higher price that a water company would have been prepared to pay on the open market for the site in question.

All three judges in the Court of Appeal upheld the approach taken at the arbitration whereby the market value of the land was the higher price that would have been offered by this special purchaser.

Lord Alvisdon CJ quoted, with approval, the judgement of Wright J in *Countess Ossalinsky v Corporation of Manchester* (unreported):

> 'If there is a site which has peculiar advantages for the supply of water to areas within a certain distance, if those valleys are what might be called natural customers for water by reason of their populousness and of their situation – if the site has peculiar advantages for supplying in that sense. I think it may be taken that there is a natural value in the site for the purposes of water supply, and that it should be taken into consideration.'

Judgement

References, example '(pg421)', are to [1904] 1 KB 417.

1 LORD ALVERSTONE CJ: The point that has been raised in this case is of importance; but, as I said in the course of the argument, it is covered by authority, and if it is to be decided in the way suggested by the learned counsel for the Water Board it must be left to the House of Lords to do so. I have often regretted that the case of *Riddell v Newcastle and Gateshead Waterworks* did not find its way into any of the reports, and I am glad that it should now be brought to notice. In this case the umpire has found in his award that owing to the natural configuration of the lands with which he was dealing they are peculiarly adaptable for the construction of a reservoir, and he has estimated the compensation to be paid if this element is one that can properly be taken into consideration, in arriving at the compensation to be paid, at the sum of £1,636. It is contended on behalf of the purchasers that the value so arrived at is not a proper subject for compensation. Two grounds are put forward in support of this view – first, that, in the absence of evidence of competition for the site, the purpose of the purchase under statutory powers must be absolutely excluded in arriving at the amount of compensation; and, second, that the umpire has arrived at the sum of £1,636 on the supposition that there is or may be some other possible purchaser, and that no evidence was given to that effect. I think that both these points were decided in the case of *Riddell v Newcastle and Gateshead Waterworks*, to which I have already referred. In that case, as in this, a question had been raised *(pg420)* as to the right to sell water. I was counsel in that case, and when it came before the Court of Appeal I found myself in difficulties as to the question of the sale of water, and I then argued that the arbitrator had excluded from his assessment of compensation the element of the natural adaptability of the site for the purpose of a reservoir. A summary of the judgment of Bramwell LJ is given in Mr F Balfour Browne's *Law of Compensation*, p.16. It is as follows: 'The arbitrator had awarded the £17,000 as compensation in respect of the lands, tenements, rights, easements, and premises required to be purchased, and it was clear that he included in that all rights in respect of water which might accumulate on the land. The arbitrator then stated that a claim had been made in respect of the water which the company could collect, or divert, and impound by the works. That referred, without doubt, to damage which might happen to other lands of Mr Riddell by the company intercepting the water that would have flowed to them. If that was the proper construction of the award, it could not be impeached. The counsel for the appellant had attempted to place a different construction on it, but their construction could not be maintained. It was impossible to suppose that an arbitrator, especially one who had so much experience in such matters as Mr Clutton, could have made the double mistake, first of omitting to consider any additional value which might attach to the land in consequence of its being a suitable site for a reservoir, and then of concealing his mistake by the language of his award.' From the shorthand note of the judgment of the Court of Appeal I find that the other members of the Court express the same view. Thus Brett

LJ at the beginning of his judgment said that it was clear that the arbitrator had given compensation for the damage sustained by reason of the execution of the works, and added: 'It seems to me clear that that would give the value of the land taking into account its, position and all its capabilities for any particular purpose'; and Cotton LJ said that he could not come to the conclusion that the arbitrator had not taken into consideration *(pg421)* all the capabilities of the land, 'including any value arising from the fact of its being well watered land, or land available for the purpose of making a reservoir or anything else connected with traffic in water.' Throughout the judgments there is not a word about its being necessary to find present customers other than the purchaser under statutory powers. The Court of Appeal refused to send the case back to the arbitrator, and I am satisfied that they meant to decide that the element of value for special adaptability had been, and had rightly been, taken into consideration by the arbitrator. I think I may add that in consequence of that case I consulted Thesiger LJ, who had great experience in arbitration cases, and he told me that the judgment of the Court of Appeal on this point was in accordance with the practice in compensation cases. I also discussed the matter with three of the most experienced surveyors, who confirmed the view as to the practice of the profession. The case of *Countess Ossalinsky v Corporation of Manchester*, which also is unreported, was an instance of the same rule. There the Queen's Bench Division held that the suitability of the site for the purpose of a reservoir was an element that ought not to be omitted in assessing compensation: as I pointed out in the course of the argument, the question in the present case is one rather of fact than of law. My brother Wright did not add, as has been suggested, anything to the findings of the umpire. He said in giving judgment: 'If there is a site which has peculiar advantages for the supply of water to a particular valley or a particular area of any other kind, or to all valleys or areas within a certain distance, if those valleys are what might be called natural customers for water by reason of their populousness and of their situation – if the site has peculiar advantages for supplying in that sense – apart from value created or enhanced by any Act of Parliament or scheme for appropriating the water to a particular local authority, I think it may be taken that there is a natural value in the site for the purposes of water supply, and that it should be taken into consideration'; and he added: 'It would be otherwise, no doubt, if there was no natural value in the place as a water site apart from the *(pg422)* particular scheme or Act of Parliament, or, in other words, there is no value for which compensation ought to be given on this head if the value is created or enhanced simply by the Act or by the scheme of the promoters.' In my opinion that clearly expresses what is the law on the matter.

2   The appeal from the judgment of my brother Wright must be dismissed.

3   **COLLINS MR:** I am of the same opinion. It is alleged on behalf of the Water Board that, taking the facts as found by the umpire in his award, it follows as a matter of law that the element of the adaptability of this site for the purposes of a reservoir ought not to be included in assessing compensation. The umpire has included it, and it seems to me that in so doing he has followed the prima

facie presumption that this element of adaptability ought to find a place in the estimate of the amount of compensation. That view is supported by authority and by long practice; but underlying it is the question, which is one of fact for the arbitrator, whether there is a possible market for the site, and in determining that the statutory purchase is not to be considered. To exclude the element of adaptability it would be necessary, as it seems to me, to shew that there is no reasonable possibility of the site coming into the market. The value of the possibility if it exists is a question entirely for the arbitrator.

4 ROMER LJ: I entirely agree. *(pg423)*

Case 6
Attorney-General v Jameson

[1904] 2 IR 644

High Court (Ireland)

26–28 November 1903, 13 February 1904

[1905] 2 IR 218

Court of Appeal

21–23 November, 19 December 1904

A-G v Jameson is the first case, chronologically, where the court gives a full description of the process required to place a valuation on a shareholding for a tax purpose. In the years since this ruling by the Court of Appeal, the principles of the valuation process have been elaborated in subsequent cases but not overturned. The description of the process in this case is as valid today as when it was given in 1905.

The case is an Irish case. In 1904 Ireland was a part of the United Kingdom and Finance Act 1894, the statutory provisions of which were the subject of this court decision, was a statute of the entire United Kingdom. Hence, this case is a precedent, which binds the Court of Appeal and lower courts.

Henry Jameson died on 15 September 1901. In his estate was a holding of 750 John Jameson & Son Limited ordinary shares. The company was, and continues to be, Whiskey Distillers of Dublin. John Jameson, George Jameson and William Robertson were appointed executors of the will of Henry Jameson. Estate duty at 6 per cent was payable on the value of the shareholding.

The articles of association of John Jameson & Son Limited gave pre-emptive rights to other shareholders and empowered the directors to refuse to register a transfer to a non-member of whom they did not approve. The articles contained a provision for the price to be paid by a shareholder purchasing another's shares as the 'fair value thereof'. Article 9 of the articles defines the 'fair value' of shares, for the purpose of the articles, being defined as a sum of £100, or such other sum as should from time to time be fixed as the 'fair value' by resolution of the company in general meeting.

The executors argued that the value of the 750 shares was £75,000, as this sum is calculated by £100 × 750 shares, in accordance with the formula in the articles, there never having been any resolution of company in general meeting to the contrary.

For several years prior to Henry Jameson's death, the 750 shares had yielded a dividend of at least £50 per annum (ie 20 per cent of the value calculated in accordance with the articles).

The articles were described in the High Court by Kenny J as being in a great measure identical to, or similar to, those in common use where it is desired by the promoters of a company to keep its shares in the hands of a limited class of persons, and to prevent the intrusion, so far as possible, of members of the general public in the management of its affairs. The scheme of the articles, as given by Kenny J was:

- Article 6 – a transfer to a non-member is prohibited, if any member is willing to purchase the shareholding at a 'fair value'.
- Article 20 – the directors are empowered to refuse to register a transfer to anyone who is not a member.
- Article 23 – if the directors refuse to register a transfer, the transfer is void.
- Article 7 – the company is appointed agent for any shareholder proposing to make a transfer.
- Article 8 – the company gives notice to existing shareholders of the availability of shares, shareholders having 28 days in which to offer to pay the 'fair value'.
- Article 11 – if no existing shareholder offers to purchase the holding, the shares can be sold to a non-member at any price.
- Article 9 – the fair value is stated to be £100 per share, with a provision for a resolution for this to be altered by a resolution of the shareholders. (No resolution had been made and, hence, the 'fair value' under Article 9 was at £100 per share at the date of death.)

The first argument put by the Crown was that some of these articles are invalid and void.

This argument was quickly dismissed by the Court of Appeal, Lord Ashbourne saying:

'There is no repugnancy in the articles. The owners are given a regulated and controlled freedom of disposition.

I see nothing to induce me to set aside or disparage any of the articles in the Jameson Company on any of the grounds put forward by the Crown. Therefore, I take the case to be that the executor took on his death the same subject-matter which Henry Jameson owned in his lifetime, and was at his death competent to dispose of, ie the 750 shares in the Jameson Company, subject to and controlled by its Articles of Association. To hold otherwise would be to say that the shares were more valued to the hands of his executors than in the hands of Henry Jameson, that he was fettered while they were free – that the articles bound him and he could not control them. He deliberately became a shareholder in this family company with its articles and its contracts, and his shares cannot be considered apart from this contractual position. The share cannot be split up and considered apart from its contractual incidents. The articles are part and parcel of the share, and not collateral and separable. He must be assumed to have absolutely bound himself to obey and conform to the articles.'

([1904] 2 IRC 644 at 675 **case 7 para 18**)

As well as disposing of any argument that such articles are not effective, this quotation expresses an important principle of share valuation. When assessing the price that a willing buyer would offer, it must be assumed that he will take the shares subject to the articles, as they stand. This is in contrast to the statutory fiction that the transfer to him is unfettered by any provision of the Articles that would, in the real world, prohibit any transfer to which the directors would not give approval. This point was also addressed by Lord Ashbourne:

'How can such shares in such a company with such articles have their value estimated at the price which, in the opinion of the Commissioners, such property would fetch if sold in the open market? An actual sale in open market is out of the question. A feat of imagination has to be performed. Two suggestions have been put forward in argument. The Attorney-General says that Commissioners should assume unfettered sale in the open market to the highest bidder, who would be free from the clogs on alienation contained in the articles. The defendants, on the other hand, contend that the Finance Act is satisfied by taking the par of "fair value" of £100 per share as the capital value which the Commissioners should estimate as the price which the shares would fetch if sold in the open market. Each side rushes into an indefensible extreme. The argument of the Attorney-General, which seeks to brush aside the articles and to vest in the executors a property which Henry Jameson never possessed, would ascribe to the Finance Act the power of making a new subject matter. The argument of the defendants clings desperately to the articles, and gives really no adequate significance to the words of the act requiring the Commissioners to estimate the price which the shares would fetch in the open market. The solution lies between the two. The Attorney-General must give more weight to the articles, and the defendants to the statute. It requires no tremendous imagination to conceive what a purchaser would give in the open market for Henry Jameson's shares as Henry Jameson himself held them at his death – for the right to stand in his shoes.'

([1904] 2 IRC 644 at 226/227 **case 7 para 21**)

The value of a shareholding is a question of fact and, thus, is entirely within the jurisdiction of the Commissioners. A finding of fact cannot be made by the court on appeal. The role of the court is to make a decision as to the law underlying the manner in which the Commissioners judge value. This is clearly borne out by the subsequent words of Lord Ashbourne:

'That is, he held shares earning 20 per cent interest with power of disposition to sons and brothers subject to, but himself possessed of the power of pre-emption; and if that power of pre-emption was not used against him – a most improbable event indeed – he might sell as he best could at any price, and to any person he could. This, although not valuable as owning shares absolutely free and unfettered in power of disposition, was obviously much more valuable than the "fair value" of the articles. I am not a valuer or a Commissioner, but I do not see any overwhelming difficulty in estimating the price which such valuable shares would fetch if sold in the open market.'

([1904] 2 IRC 644 at 227 **case 7 para 21**)

This case also contains an important judicial statement as to the nature of a company share. The interest of a shareholder is in the shares he holds; a shareholder does not have an interest in a portion of the assets of the company. As stated by Kenny J in the High Court hearing of the case:

'No shareholder has a right to any specific portion of the company's property, and save by, and to the extent of, his voting power at a general meeting of the company, cannot curtail the free and proper disposition of it. He is entitled to a share of the company's capital and profits, the former, in the words of Farwell J, being measured by a sum of money which is taken as the standard for the ascertainment of his share of the profits. If the company disposes of its assets, or if the latter be realised in a liquidation, he has a right to a proportion of the amount received after the discharge of the company's debts and liabilities. In acquiring these rights – that is, in becoming a member of the company – he is deemed to have simultaneously entered into a contract under seal to conform to the regulations contained in articles of association (Companies Act 1862, s16). Whatever obligations are contained in these articles, he accepts the ownership of the shares and the position of a member of the company, bound and controlled by them. He cannot divorce his money interest, whatever it may amount to, from these obligations. They are inseparable incidents attached to his rights, and the idea of a share cannot, in my judgment, be complete without their inclusion.'

([1904] 2 IRC 644 at 669/670 **case 7 para 13**)

Fitz Gibbon LJ, in his judgement, placed great stress on the shareholding as being a bundle of indivisible rights and obligations:

'In my opinion each of these shares, with all rights and liabilities, and all advantages and disadvantages, incident to its ownership, passed on Henry Jameson's death to his executors as one indivisible piece of property ... The basis of my construction of the Act is the unity and indivisibility of Henry Jameson's property in the shares. I cannot adopt any procedure, or accept any solution of the question in dispute, which splits up that interest for any purpose.'

([1904] 2 IRC 644 at 228 and 230 **case 7 paras 23 and 28**)

Fitz Gibbon LJ also expressly made the point that the pre-emption rights over the other shareholdings in the company have the effect of increasing the value of the shareholding in question:

'The right of pre-emption against Henry Jameson's shares in certain events, if legal, is a depreciating incident; but the right of Henry Jameson, or of any person "standing in his shoes", to exercise the corresponding right of pre-emption against the other shares of the company in the like events, is an appreciating incident, of Henry Jameson's property, which, in my opinion, is to be valued as a whole.'

([1904] 2 IRC 644 at 231 **case 7 para 31**)

Fitz Gibbon LJ expressed his dissatisfaction at the procedure followed in this case (see [1904] 2 IRC 644 at 228/229 **case 7 para 25**). Whilst a determination of value by the Commissioners could be the subject of an appeal under the provisions that then applied to a estate duty, this procedure was not followed and, instead, the Kings Bench Division, on which three judges sat together, was called upon to make an interlocutory declaration, the five judges in the Court of Appeal then hearing an appeal against this interlocutory declaration. The consequence of following this procedure was that the Court of Appeal, in the words of Fitz Gibbon LJ gave 'nothing more than a judicial paraphrase of the simple words of the Finance Act, leaving the Commissioners to do their duty under section 7(6), with any help they can get from that paraphrase'.

Hence, the value that was finally determined for the shareholder is not reported in the published notes of this case.

Judgement

References, example '(pg529)', are to [1904] 2 IR 644.

1 **KENNY J:** Whether we regard the large questions of principle that have been argued, or the amount of Crown duty alleged to be involved, this case is one of the first importance. If the Crown's contention be correct *in omnibus*, one result at least must follow – that company promoters and their legal advisers will have to revise the views they have hitherto held, and which the public have accepted, as to the form that articles of association can legally assume in cases where it is desired to form what is known as a private limited liability company. A further consequence of our holding with the Crown may be that many private companies now in existence may find that the contract which unites their members is, in its vital part, essentially illegal and incapable of enforcement. Apart from these somewhat grave matters, the amount of duty in controversy in this case is a very considerable one, exceeding, so far as I can see, the sum £16,000.

2 The object of the suit is to establish liability on the part of the personal estate of the late Mr Henry Jameson for estate duty payable on certain shares held by him in the firm of John Jameson & Son Limited. The defendants are Mr Jameson's executors, and the information asks for a declaration that upon his death estate duty became payable under the provisions of the Finance Act 1894, on the 'principal value,' – estimated as provided by section 7, sub-sect 5, of the Act – of 750 shares in the firm of John Jameson & Son Limited, and that such value is not limited to the par or 'fair value' of £100 a share, notwithstanding the special provisions as to the 'fair value' and as to the alienation of the shares of the Company contained in the articles of association of the latter. There is an alternative prayer, namely, that the Court may determine in what manner the 'principal value' of the shares is to be ascertained, and what is the 'principal value' for the purpose of the Act. Finally, it asks that the defendants *(pg662)* – the executors – may be ordered to pay the amount of the duty, when so ascertained, to the Commissioners of Inland Revenue.

3 The phrase 'principal value' occurs in the 1st and 7th sections of the Act. The former section provides for the levying and payment of estate duty, and is as follows:

> 'In the case of every person dying after the commencement of this part of this Act, there shall, save as hereinafter expressly provided, be levied and paid upon the principal value, ascertained as hereinafter provided, of all property, real or personal, settled or not settled, which passes on the death of such person, a duty, called 'estate duty,' at the graduated rates hereinafter mentioned, and the existing duties mentioned in the First Schedule to this Act shall not be levied in respect of property chargeable with such estate duty.'

4 Section 7, which deals with the ascertainment of the value of property, by its 5th sub-section enacts that -

'The principal value of any property shall be estimated to be the price which, in the opinion of the Commissioners, such property would fetch if sold in the open market at the time of the death of the deceased.'

5 It is on the language of this sub-section, in relation to the special circumstances of the present case, that the Crown asks for a determination from this Court.

6 The answer of the defendants submits that the 'principal value' of the 750 shares is for the purpose of estate duty necessarily the same as the aggregate of the 'fair value' of each share, viz, £100, as fixed by the articles of association of the Company, inasmuch as if there was a market for the shares they could not, having regard to the articles, have realised more than £100 each, and would not perhaps realise even that sum. This submission is in effect an argumentative denial of the allegation in the 12th paragraph of the information, that the principal value of the shares is much greater than the par or 'fair value.' It seems to me that this Court is not competent to give an opinion as to the value of these shares. The matter is one for the Commissioners of Inland Revenue themselves, with or without the aid of an expert whose business it is to make such valuations and to calculate the chances in any given state of circumstances. We could not *(pg663)* possibly say, with the Attorney-General, that these shares, if sold in the open market, would fetch more than £100 each; nor could we say, with the defendants, that they are worth only £100, if they are worth anything at all. All we can do, in my opinion, is to decide the legal points that lie at the threshold of any inquiry as to value, so as to make clear the way for the Commissioners or their expert. As these points have been developed in argument, they raise two questions, namely – (1) the validity of certain non-alienation clauses contained in the articles of association; and (2) the effect of the articles, assuming that they are legal, having regard to the Finance Act 1894. As to the suggestion of invalidity, one looks in vain to find a trace of it in the information. Indeed, the latter is framed from the point of view of the articles being accepted as valid and binding; and so little weight was attached to the argument based on invalidity, that, in his opening statement, the Attorney-General challenged only the 11th article, which is one of the least offending. In my opinion it is not open to the Crown to raise this point of invalidity; but as it had been so fully discussed, I propose to give my opinion on it. On the second question, the alleged modifying effect of the Finance Act is put forward in the information only inferentially. The submission of the Crown is that the 'principal value' of the shares is not *merely* the amount actually paid upon them. In others words, that the value of each share exceeds £100.

7 The information does not state any specific ground for this contention, save by a general reference to the words of the Finance Act; but the argument at the bar has been, not that the suppositious sale under the 7th section is to be regarded as one in which the thing sold is free from all restrictions on alienation, present and future, as claimed in the letter of the Commissioners dated the 21st April, 1902, but as one in which the executors were to be assumed as now selling to any person they chose, and at any price they could obtain, but subject to the restricting effect of the articles on all subsequent dealings by the purchaser and his successors in title with the shares so sold. If the argument founded on invalidity were to succeed, then the supposititious sale contemplated by the section would be of shares assumed to be absolutely free and unfettered, not alone now, but in all future dealings with them. *(pg664)*

8 The facts of the case are extremely short and simple. The firm of John Jameson & Son Limited was incorporated as a company limited by shares, in the month of October, 1891. Its capital was £450,000, divided into 4,500 shares of £100 each. The original shareholders to whom this capital was allotted numbered eleven – all of the family and name of Jameson – amongst them being the late Mr Henry Jameson, to whom was allotted 750 shares, and who retained them up to the time of his death. The dividends on its capital, payable by the Company for some years previously to Mr Jameson's death, were at the rate of £20 per cent per annum. Mr Henry Jameson made his will, dated the 26th July, 1901, whereby he bequeathed his 750 shares (with other property) to his executors on certain trusts, and appointed the defendants executors of his will. Two of these gentlemen are shareholders in the Company, namely, John Jameson and George Jameson. The testator died on the 15th September, 1901, and probate was granted to the three executors, whereupon, without prejudice to any greater liability, they paid estate duty on the basis of the 750 shares, being value for £75,000, and no more. The Company registered in their books as shareholders in respect of the 750 shares only the defendants John Jameson and George Jameson, and the shares are now standing in their names.

9 The articles of association of the Company are in a great measure identical with, or similar to, those in common use where it is desired by the promoters of a company to keep its shares in the hands of a limited class of persons, and to prevent the intrusion, so far as possible, of members of the general public in the management of its affairs. The provisions of the articles by which it is sought to effect this purpose are set forth in the information. Briefly stated, the scheme is this. With certain exceptions, which it is important to call attention to, no share is to be transferred to a person who is not a member, so long as any member is willing to purchase it at the 'fair value' (article 6); and the directors may refuse to register any transfer to a transferee not being already a member, of whom they do not approve (article 20); and any such transfer is to be void (article 23). A shareholder proposing to transfer – and in my opinion this contemplates only the case of a proposed transfer to a non-member who is not a son or brother *(pg665)* of the proposed transferor, or a son or brother of some other existing member (article 18) – must give the Company notice of his intention, whereupon the Company is deemed to be his agent for the sale of the share to any member of the Company at the 'fair value' (article 7); and if within twenty-eight days a member willing to purchase be found, the selling shareholder, on receiving notice, is to be bound to transfer to such member on payment of the 'fair value' (article 8); and if he makes default in transferring, the Company may cause the name of the purchasing member to be entered on the register as the holder of the share (article 10). If a purchasing member be not found within twenty-eight days, the selling shareholder may, within three months, sell and transfer the share to any person (subject to the approval of the directors), and at any price (article 11). In article 16, personal representatives of a deceased member are specially dealt with. They are to be the only persons recognised by the Company as having any title to the shares registered in the name of the deceased member, and, by article 17, a person becoming entitled to a share in consequence of the death of any member may, subject to the approval of the directors, and 'subject to the regulations herein contained' transfer same to himself or any other person. At first sight the last-mentioned article would seem to contemplate the right of a personal representative to sell to any member of the public; but the qualifying words, 'subject to the regulations herein contained,' and a reference to articles 18 and 22, satisfy me that no such unrestricted right was intended to be given. If it were, the power expressly conferred by the 18th article on personal representatives to transfer to the son or brother of the deceased member, or of any existing member, would be surplusage. Furthermore, the 22nd article has a special reference to the power conferred by the 17th of transfer to the person entitled on death, or to any other person, for it confers express authority on the directors, in a case where the person entitled is not already a member, to give him notice that they decline to admit him as a member, whereupon a notice of transfer, such as is provided for in article 7, is to be deemed to have been served.

10 In the case of bankruptcy the provision against unrestricted sale is still more drastic, for the notice of transfer by the assignees *(pg666)* is to be deemed to have been served as of the date of the bankruptcy. The only remaining article that I need notice is one of the greatest importance – the existence of which has largely contributed, if not indeed given rise, to the present controversy. It deals with the matter of the 'fair value' of a share. It will be found on reference to the notes to Mr Palmer's excellent collection of precedents in Company conveying that in the case of private Companies different modes are suggested for the ascertainment of the 'fair value' on payment of which shares may be transferred. It might be ascertained by arbitration, or it might be a sum to be fixed by the Company in general meeting in each year, or a sum to be fixed by the auditor, or a sum equal to the amount paid up on the share. This last suggestion is not unlike that put forward in *Lindley on Partnership*, 6th ed, 430, for the purpose of avoiding a sale on dissolution of an ordinary firm, namely, to specify in the partnership deed a sum at which the share of an outgoing or deceased partner may be taken by his co-partners. In the present case the 9th article provides that the fair value of a share is to be £100, or such other sum as shall from time to time be fixed as the 'fair value' by resolution of the Company in general meeting. It does not appear that the fair value was ever altered from the original sum so fixed – the late Mr Jameson, with his great voting power derived from 750 shares, and his co-members, being apparently satisfied that, notwithstanding the high dividend so stated to have been paid of late years, there was no occasion for an increase in the selling or 'fair value'. It may be that with trade fluctuations, known only to themselves, they regarded the par value as the 'fair value'. However that may be, all we know is that the concern was paying £20 per cent dividend, and that the 'fair value' was left at the sum that was fixed in the year 1891.

11 Before approaching the questions of invalidity and the Finance Act, it will be well to arrive at a conclusion as to what, upon the true construction of the articles of association, and on the assumption that the latter are binding on all members of the Company, is the nature of the restrictions imposed on the right of free alienation of the shares. It is plain from article 6 that a member *(pg667)* cannot sell and transfer to any member of the public whom he may select, and that the class with whom he may deal is a very restricted one. The prohibition contained in the article is itself limited inasmuch as it applies only 'save as hereinafter provided.' It seems to me after a very careful reading of the articles that these words refer to (*inter alia*) the sanction given by the 18th article to a transfer by a member or his personal representatives to any son or brother of the former, or of any other member. Such a transfer, though expressly permitted, would be subject to the general approval of the directors. In the view I take it is open to any member and to the personal representatives of any member to sell and transfer without reference to the 'fair value' clauses and at a price outside the £100 per share – if vendor and purchaser so agree – to (1) any other existing member; (2) any son or brother of the selling or deceased member; or (3) any son or brother of any other existing member. I think that the procedure for ascertaining whether a member is willing to purchase a share, and for compulsory transfer at the 'fair value' to the member when so ascertained, is not applicable to cases of proposed sales to any of the persons I have just indicated. Therefore, within these classes a share can, in my opinion, be sold and transferred at the best price the seller can obtain by agreement. But with the exception of the sons and brothers mentioned in article 18, it is clear to me that no member of the Company can by a voluntary act *inter vivos* force an outsider on the Company so long as any existing member is willing to buy him out at the 'fair value.' No doubt, he could declare a trust of his shares for an outsider; but if he does so, he remains the registered member, and the purchaser from him has mere equitable rights enforceable against him alone. Such a purchaser in equity could not insist on being registered in the Company's books. Indeed, a question might arise on which it is unnecessary I should give an opinion – whether if the mode of completion of the sale took the form of an actual transfer and not a mere declaration of trust, it would not under article 23 be absolutely void as between the vendor and purchaser. If a member cannot substitute an outsider as a new member in his place by act *inter vivos* against the will of his brother shareholders, I think it is equally clear that on his death his personal representatives *(pg668)* cannot do so. Articles 6, 17, 18, 22, and 23 appear to be decisive on the point.

12 Now, are these articles of association, so far as they are restrictive of the free right of alienation, invalid and void, and if so, on what ground? The Crown contend that they are so from two points of view; first, that they infringe the rule against perpetuities, and secondly, that they are repugnant to absolute ownership. Both points are covered by authority, which, though but the decision of a Court of first instance, is entitled to the greatest respect. The judgment is that of Farwell J in *Borland's Trustee v Steel, Bros & Co Limited*, and it is a very lucid and able statement of the law in which I venture to express my concurrence. There, as here, there was a private company with articles of association not unlike those in the present case, so far as restrictions on the free disposition of the shares were concerned. There was a limited class who alone could take transfers, and a 'fair value' price, which amounted in the aggregate to £8,650 while the plaintiffs alleged that the real value was £24,000. The average dividend for seven years had been about 45 per cent, and the general financial position of the Company was sound. Three substantial points were argued – perpetuity, repugnancy, and public policy. The shareholder Borland had become a bankrupt, and it was contended for his trustee that the particular articles were obnoxious to the Bankruptcy Law. On all three points Farwell J held with the Company.

13 In considering whether that case was rightly decided, it is important to bear in mind the character of the property in question. It is not the property of the Company that is subjected to restrictions on alienation. The assets of the Company, its premises, stock in trade, etc, are all capable of being disposed of without limitation or fetter of any sort. No shareholder has a right to any specific portion of the Company's property, and save by, and to the extent of, his voting power at a general meeting of the Company, cannot curtail the free and proper disposition of it. He is entitled to a share of the Company's capital and profits, the former, in the words of Farwell J, being measured by a sum of *(pg669)* money which is taken as the standard for the ascertainment of his share of the profits. If the Company disposes of its assets, or if the latter be realised in a liquidation, he has a right to a proportion of the amount received after the discharge of the Company's debts and liabilities. In acquiring these rights – that is, in becoming a member of the Company – he is deemed to have simultaneously entered into a contract under seal to conform to the regulations contained in the articles of association (Companies Act 1862, sect 16). Whatever obligations are contained in these articles, he accepts the ownership of the shares and the position of a member of the Company, bound and controlled by them. He cannot divorce his money interest, whatever it may amount to, from these obligations. They are inseparable incidents attached to his rights, and the idea of a share cannot, in my judgment, be complete without their inclusion. This was the view taken by Farwell J, whose language was adopted by FitzGibbon LJ, in *Casey v Bentley*. He could not, nor could his personal representatives, retain the mere money interest and repudiate the contracts entered into in connexion with it. The money interest and the contractual obligations form one whole, and no member could be heard to say that he had a right to retain the former and disclaim the latter. But even if the Crown, for the purpose of the supposititious sale under the Finance Act, could be so heard, I am of opinion, with Farwell J, that there is no remoteness and no repugnancy. There is no interest in land, legal or equitable, vested in the defendants by reason of their testator's membership in their company. His property in the Company was represented by contractual rights that created no such interest, and if so, the restrictive clauses are not obnoxious to the rule against perpetuities: *London & South-Western Railway Co v Gomm*. As to repugnancy, the invalidity must arise either from the creation of a limited class of permissible transferees, or from the nature of the pre-emption price or 'fair value.' There is no suggestion that the articles were framed with any indirect purpose, or that the promoters had any object unless the perfectly *bona fide* one of retaining, as far as possible, the management of the concern in *(pg670)* the family of Jameson. Suppose it was provided that the 'fair value' was to be such a sum as might be settled by two arbitrators to be appointed by the Company and a selling member, with liberty to them to call in an umpire – or that it was to be taken as a capital sum to be arrived at on the basis of £100 for every 5 per cent of dividend paid for the preceding three years, would the fact that only a limited class could purchase, be any objection? I think we must consider the question of limited class by itself, and on the assumption that the 'fair value' means a price to which no objection could be urged. If so, how is the selling shareholder prejudiced? How is the restriction opposed to his just rights? Unless it could be successfully contended that all pre-emption powers are nugatory, I can see no difference between giving the right to one individual and giving it to several. There is nothing to prevent a man from agreeing for a purchase of property, and giving a right of pre-emption as part of his contract. How does such a case differ from the present, unless that here the right is given to several? The circumstances are wholly different from those in which there is a grant or devise of property in terms conferring absolute ownership followed by a defeasance in derogation of the natural incidents of the estate which had been already conferred. In the present case there is no absolute estate, right, or interest, conferred, the natural incidents of which are subsequently fettered. The thing acquired by membership in the Company is, from its initial stage, a restricted and fettered thing. It never had attached to it any rights of free alienation which were sought to be affected. I cannot but think that such cases as those of *Attwater v Attwater*, *In re Rosher*, and *Dugdale v Dugdale*, where a condition was held to be repugnant, resulted in a complete defeat of the plain intention of the testator in each case; where if he had used slightly different language, he would have effectually carried out his wishes. I think that this class of case cannot be applied to the present, where the share is the creature of a special contract, and no natural or inherent right is derogated from.

14 Coming now to the other alleged ground for the contention of *(pg671)* repugnancy, namely, the amount of the pre-emption price, or 'fair value,' I shall assume, for the sake of argument, that each share was worth much more than £100 at the time of Henry Jameson's death. There is no absolute prohibition against alienation. If I am right in my construction of the articles of association, the share may be sold in one state of circumstances for as much as the parties may agree upon. In another state of circumstances the 'fair value' may have to be accepted. It seems to me that the reason I have given for holding there is no

repugnancy in the restriction of alienation to a class, apply equally to the contention based on the 'fair value' price. Was the creation of a price other than an open market price invalid? In the case of an ordinary partnership a provision to that effect is valid: *Lindley on Partnerships*, citing *Essex v Essex*, a case that met with the approval of Fry J, in *Cox v Willoughby*. If so, I would think that the case is an *a fortiori* one, when it assumes the form of a clause in articles of association. But then, if there is no absolute legal prohibition against a 'fair value' price, where are we to draw the line when the question is only one of amount? I confess I am wholly unable to say whether in the circumstances £100 per share is an unfair price. There was power in the articles to alter it by resolution in general meeting: no such resolution was ever passed. For aught I know, there may have been low dividends in the years before the £20 per cent was paid, or there may have been circumstances connected with the Company's trading that may have led this body of business men to the conclusion that the time had not come for a revision of article 9. What is admitted is, that the testator had an immense interest in the share capital of the Company, with a proportionate voting power; that John Jameson, one of the directors, had at least in 1891 a corresponding interest, and that both of them – to say nothing of the other members with small interests – appear to have rested satisfied with the par value as the 'fair value'.

15 I therefore think that the contention of the Crown wholly fails so far as it attacks the validity of the articles of association.

16 The remaining question is with reference to the effect of the *(pg672)* Finance Act of 1894. Estate duty is to be paid upon the 'principal value' of all property which passes on death (section 1), and that 'principal value' is to be ascertained as thereinafter provided, namely, by the price which in the opinion of the Commissioners such property would fetch if sold in the open market at the time of the death of the deceased (section 7, sub-sect 5). Before considering the true meaning of this sub-section, it is very important to keep before one's mind that we are not in this case dealing with all property that 'passed' on the death of the deceased. The information is conversant only with the personal property which the deceased was competent to dispose of at his death, on which alone the defendants as his executors are compellable to pay estate duty pursuant to the Act (sect 6, sect 8 (3)). Other property may have passed on his death; but unless the deceased was competent to dispose of it, the executors are under no liability to pay duty on it, though it is permissible to them to do so if they so desired (section 6 (2)). In dealing with those shares, it therefore becomes necessary to inquire what is the nature – firstly, of the subject-matter that passed on the death and of which the deceased was competent to dispose; and secondly, of the supposititious sale under the 5th sub-section of the 7th section of the Act. I do not propose on this branch of the case to repeat the considerations that influenced me on the question of repugnancy in arriving at the conclusion that the interest of the deceased in the Company was one in which, from its very creation, the elements of free and uncontrolled disposition were absent. Compared with the absolute right to go into the open market and sell to any outsider and for the best price property that was subject to no restrictions on alienation present or future – this interest was what I may venture to call a dwarfed and stunted thing. But it and it alone, was what the deceased had power to dispose of in his lifetime, and which his executors were competent to sell and transfer after his death. How, then, does the Finance Act operate on such a subject-matter? I cannot help expressing my surprise that this question of the value of shares in a private company never presented itself before 1894. For probate and residuary account purposes the ascertainment of the market value would seem to have been just as necessary before as after the Act. Are we now to say that for the purposes *(pg673)* of levying estate duty the executors are to be supposed to have in their possession a marketable commodity affected by less restrictions than it was subject to in the hands of their testator? The Crown argument goes to this, that there cannot be such a supposititious sale as is contemplated by the 5th sub-section unless we proceed on the basis of a sale to any member of the public, and thus permit, by assumption, an evasion of the 18th article of association which would be forbidden in the actual working of the Company; and, in the administration of the estate of the testator, could not be effected. I cannot think that the Legislature contemplated such a metamorphosis of the incidents of the particular property by the use of the words 'if sold in the open market.' Suppose the property was a leasehold with a condition against alienation unless to certain persons, or subject to a pre-emption right in a third person which was to come into existence on the death of the party whose estate was under consideration, could it be said in the first case, that a valuation was to be made on the assumption that the property might be sold to anyone; and, in the second case, on the assumption that the pre-emption price was to be disregarded? If so, it might turn out in both cases that the actual benefit to the estate of the deceased would be much less than the amount of the valuation placed on the estate by the Commissioners. Surely such a state of things was never contemplated. It may be that a case like the present was not present to the minds of the framers of the Act, and is unprovided for. However that may be, we are bound, in the case of a statute imposing a tax, to adopt a construction favourable to the subject, unless it is clear that he comes within the letter of the law. This rule is forcibly expressed by Lord Cairns in *Partington v The Attorney-General,* and by Lord Blackburn in *The Oriental Bank Corporation v Wright,* where he says that 'The intention to charge the subject must be shown by clear and unambiguous language'.

17 Applying the principle, I am of opinion that, putting it at the lowest, there is no sufficient language in the section to support the Crown contention, which, in the words of Mr Ronan, suggests a suppositious sale of a class of property different from that which *(pg674)* Mr Jameson possessed. I am consequently of opinion that the assumed sale in the section must be regarded as one not capable of being made to any member of the public unrestrictedly, but, on the contrary, a sale subject to the provisions in articles Nos 18, 6, 7, 8, 9, 10, and 11 of the articles of association.

18 I wish to add that I quite appreciated the force of the Attorney-General's argument that if the defendants' contention be right the Crown might, in every case like the present, be deprived of the duty on so much of the property passing on the death as would not benefit the estate of the deceased, inasmuch as in a case like the present the duty on the difference between the valuations on a free and on a restricted sale does not appear to be capable of being levied from anyone. The case is, I think, analogous to that which I have already put of a leasehold with a condition against alienation or subject to a right of pre-emption. The leasehold without any restriction on alienation may be worth a considerable sum. Supposing that a sale by executors be not prohibited, but the fetter is to re-attach in the hands of the purchaser from them, it is obvious that the premises will not be worth as much as in the former case. The right of free sale must have a money value. To whom in these circumstances does the difference between the two values pass, and how can duty be levied on it at all? In the case of a pre-emption right, is duty to be payable on the difference between the pre-emption price and the actual unrestricted selling value, and if so, by whom? I do not think we are called on to answer this question, as the subject-matter of the present information is merely the amount of the estate duty payable on what the deceased was competent to dispose of.

19 The result of the conclusions I have arrived at is, that while the principal value ought to be ascertained having regard to the articles of association, it does not at all follow that such principal value might not, in the opinion of an expert, exceed the par or 'fair value' of £100. The possibility of a sale by private agreement at a higher price to a member of the limited class of permissible transferees; the payment of the large dividend; the position, stability, and character of the Company; the special pre-emption rights attaching to the ownership of the shares, would all be, in my opinion, elements in the estimation of a price, before the obligation *(pg675)* to accept par value came into operation. I therefore think that the Attorney-General is entitled to a declaration as to the manner in which the principal value is to be ascertained, having regard to the articles of association, and the 7th section of the Act, and that the form of our judgment should be as follows:

> 'The Court doth declare that the principal value of the shares in John Jameson & Son, Limited, to which Henry Jameson was entitled at the time of his death, is to be estimated at the price which the same would, in the opinion of the Commissioners, fetch if sold in the open market at the time of such death; and that, in estimating such "principal value," regard is to be had to the special provisions in the articles of association with reference to alienation and transfer of the shares of the Company, and as to "fair value"; but that the amount of such principal value is not necessarily limited to the par or "fair value" of £100 a share.'

20 The Crown has failed, in my opinion, on the main and substantial contentions before us, viz, the validity and construction of the articles of association, and the interpretation of the Finance Act; and I think they should pay the defendants' costs.

21 BOYD, J: The firm of John Jameson & Son has been in existence for a great many years, and was conducted as a private concern until the year 1891. In that year it was converted into what is popularly known as a Family Company, under the Companies Acts, in pursuance of an agreement dated the 15th September, 1891. This agreement was the basis of the arrangement embodied in the articles of association, and all the members of the firm were parties thereto and bound thereby. The articles of association, prepared in accordance with the said agreement, set forth in detail the terms on which the Company was formed, and each member of the old firm, which had consisted of eleven gentlemen named Jameson, signed same and agreed to conform thereto. Article 4 provides for the appropriation of the shares amongst the several members of the firm. Article 6 provides for the transfer and transmission of such shares, and expressly states that 'no share shall, save as hereinafter provided, be transferred to a person who is not a member so long as any member is willing to purchase the *(pg676)* same at the fair value'; and article 8 provides that any retiring member 'shall *be bound* to transfer the share to the purchasing member.' The *fair* value of a share is fixed by the 9th article at '£100 or such other sum as shall from time to time be fixed as the fair value by resolution of the Company in general meeting.'

22 There has been no resolution of the Company altering the fair value, so we must assume that all the members were willing to continue to be bound by the fair value originally fixed.

23 At the time it was arranged to convert the partnership of John Jameson & Son, then existing, into a joint stock company, every member of the firm had complete dominion and control over all the rights he possessed in the partnership, and it was competent for him to enter into any agreement he thought fit with the other members. All the members apparently agreed that it was desirable that the fair value of the shares allotted to each of the old members should be fixed by the articles, and that such restrictions should be imposed by the articles as would, so far as possible, prevent outsiders being enabled to become members of the Company, and accordingly such restrictions are imposed by articles 6 to 28. The entire capital of the Company was £450,000, and the par value was fixed as the fair value of each share, and it is not alleged there was any fraud or sinister purpose in so fixing it.

24 Henry Jameson, one of the parties who signed the said articles of association, was allotted, by the said articles, 750 of the 4500 shares into which the capital of the Company was divided. He died on 15th September, 1901, and the question raised by the information in this case is as to the amount at which the said shares should be valued for the purposes of estate duty. The Attorney-General has contended that under the Finance Act 1894 the principal value of the shares so held by Henry Jameson is 'to be estimated to be the price which such property would fetch 'if sold in the open market at the time of the death of the deceased,' and that if these shares were sold in the open market, they would sell for very much more than the sum fixed as the fair value. He also contended that the articles of association of the Company as to the transmission and transfer of the shares are void as being repugnant to absolute ownership, or as tending to perpetuity, and that the fair value of a share as fixed by the articles is not the principal *(pg677)* value as defined by the Finance Act. He relied on the fact which is admitted by the defendants, that for some years prior to the death of Mr Jameson, and at the time of his death, 20 per cent dividends were paid on said shares.

25 There is no evidence as to the rate of interest received by the members prior to the incorporation.

26 Sect 1 of the Finance Act 1894 enacts that estate duty shall be levied and paid upon the principal value of all property *which passes* upon the death of a person. Sect 2 (*a*) provides that property passing on the death of the deceased shall be deemed to include property of which the deceased was at the time of his death *competent* to dispose. Sect 6, sub-sect 2, provides that 'the executor of the deceased shall pay the estate duty in respect of all personal property of which the deceased was competent to dispose at his death on delivering the Inland Revenue affidavit, and may pay in like manner the estate duty in respect of any other property passing on such death which by virtue of any testamentary disposition of the deceased is under the control of the executor, or in the case of property not under his control, if the persons accountable for the duty in respect thereof request him to make such payment.' Sect 7, sub-sect 5, provides that 'the principal value of any property shall be estimated to be the price which, in the opinion of the Commissioners, such property would fetch if sold in the open market at the time of the death of the deceased.'

27 It is manifest from these provisions that the property in the shares held by Mr Henry Jameson, of which he was at the time of his death competent to dispose, or which was under the control of his executors, was merely the property he had in the shares subject to the restrictions and conditions imposed thereon by the articles of association, and that his executors, under sect 6, are only liable to pay duty on such property subject to such restrictions and conditions. The question, then, in this case is, what is the principal value of such property if sold in the open market fettered with these restrictions and conditions.

28 In my opinion, sect 7, sub-sect 5, merely provides for ascertaining the principal value of the property which passed to the executors, as it is not alleged that any other persons accountable *(pg678)* for the duty, if there be such, have requested the executors to pay anything for them.

29 In the case of *Borland's Trustee v Steel, Bros & Co*, which was a case in many respects similar to the present, Mr Justice Farwell decided against the views contended for by the Attorney-General in this case. That was a case in which the transmission of the shares arose upon the bankruptcy of the shareholder. Upon an adjudication in bankruptcy, all the estate of the debtor vests in his

PART 2 Cases

trustee or assignees. The articles of association contained restrictive clauses practically similar to those in the present case, and also contained a clause (article 53) fixing the fair price of a share at the par value thereof, as in this case, which was £100. The interest for a period of seven years paid on the shares averaged about 45 per cent. It was argued in that case that shares which were receiving such dividends were of far greater value than the par value. In his judgment, at page 291, Mr Justice Farwell states his opinion on this point as follows: – These shares can have no value ascertainable by any ordinary rules, because, having held as I do that the restrictive clauses are good, it is impossible to find a market value. There is no quotation. It is impossible, therefore, for anyone to arrive at any actual figure as to which it may be said to be clear that that is the value, or something within a few pounds of the value.' This case was quoted in the arguments in the case of *Casey v Bentley*, and referred to with approval by FitzGibbon LJ, in his judgment at p.393. I entirely agree with the judgment of Mr Justice Farwell, which I am of opinion governs and decides all the points in this case. By the death of Mr Jameson, nothing passed to his executors, except what he himself possessed. Had Mr Jameson desired during his lifetime to sell his shares, he could not have claimed the right to sell them at a greater price than the fair value fixed by the articles of association. This price and the restrictive clauses were as much terms of his contract as his title to the shares. His title was clogged with these clauses, and he accepted the shares which were *allotted* to him (see article 4) on the terms and conditions agreed to by him and the other shareholders. On his death nothing more *(pg679)* *passed* to his executors than he had. With the restrictive conditions in the articles by which a purchaser of his shares would be bound if sold in the open market, it would be folly on the part of such purchaser to give even the par value, as he could not have the shares transferred to him in the books of the Company, or registered in his name, or receive dividends thereon.

30 We know, from our experience of what has befallen several well-known distillers in this city, which for long years produced large profits for their proprietors, how uncertain and fluctuating are the profits of this business; and I do not think much stress can be laid on the fact of the dividends which have for some years been paid by the company in this case as being any test of the value of the shares. No doubt the members knew and considered this fact when they fixed the fair value of a share at £100.

31 Family and private joint stock companies, with restrictive clauses similar to those in this case, have been in existence long prior to the Finance Act of 1894, and the Company of John Jameson & Son Limited was itself incorporated in 1891, three years before the passing of the Act. These companies are most useful and beneficial to traders; and if it were intended that the provisions in their articles of association as to fair value should be controlled and subject to the construction sought to be placed on the 'principal value' as defined in the Finance Act 1894, I think it should have been done in clear and unambiguous language. In the case of *Partington v The Attorney-General*, Lord Cairns, in his judgment (page 122), states: – 'I am not at all sure that, in a case of this kind –

a fiscal case – form is not amply sufficient; because, as I understand the principle of all fiscal legislation, it is this: If the person sought to be taxed comes within the letter of the law, he must be taxed, however great the hardship may appear to the judicial mind to be. On the other hand, if the Crown, seeking to recover the tax, cannot bring the subject within the letter of the law, the subject is free, however apparently within the spirit of the law the case might otherwise appear to be. In other words, if there be admissible, in any statute, what is called an equitable construction, certainly such a construction is not admissible in a *(pg680)* taxing statute, where you can simply adhere to the words of the statute.'

32 In *The Oriental Bank Corporation v Wright*, the same principle is laid down and acted on. In his judgment, at page 856, Lord Blackburn states: – 'Their Lordships, therefore, having regard to the rule that the intention to impose a charge on the subject must be shown by clear and unambiguous language, are unable to say that the obligation of the Bank to make the return applied for, and its consequent liability to pay duty on the notes put into circulation by its Kimberley Branch, are so clearly and explicitly imposed by the present Act as to satisfy this rule.' In that case the language of the Act was stronger against the Bank than the language of the Finance Act is against the defendants in the present case.

33 Since the passing of the Finance Act in 1894, the Crown has never, so far as I know, or as appears from the Law Reports, taken any proceedings to establish the rights claimed in the present case. We have been strongly pressed in the arguments for the Crown in this case with the results which may ensue if we decide against the contention of the Crown. I shall only refer to another portion of Lord Blackburn's judgment in the *Oriental Bank* case, in which he says, in reference to a similar argument in that case: 'But if the Legislature, from want of foresight, or for any other reason, has omitted to provide for such a case, it is the province of the Legislature itself, and not of the Courts, to supply the omission'.

34 The Crown, in effect, asks us to add to section 7, sub-section 5, some such words as the following, 'freed from any agreement or restrictive conditions affecting such property or the sale or transmission thereof.' This we cannot do. It is the province of the Legislature.

35 I have had the advantage of reading the judgment of my brother Kenny; and as I entirely agree with him in the conclusions at which he has arrived, I do not consider it necessary for me to go further into the facts or arguments than I have done.

36 We are not in a position to say what is the principal value of the late Mr Jameson's shares, as we are asked to do by the information: *(pg681)* the duty to do so is imposed upon the Commissioners, and they have not discharged that duty.

37 I am of opinion that the defendants are entitled to our judgment in their favour.

38 PALLES CB: I am unable to agree in the view which my learned colleagues take of the question involved here.

39 I am of opinion that the Attorney-General is entitled to judgment in the terms of the first alternative of the prayer of the information, viz, that the 'principal value' of the shares is the price which they would have fetched if sold in the open market at the time of the death, and that such value is not limited to the par value of £100 a share, notwithstanding the special provisions contained in the articles of association. I am further of opinion that he is entitled to a declaration that the price should be that which, in the opinion of the Commissioners, would have been fetched if the sale in the open market were upon the terms that the purchaser thereat should be entitled to be, and should be, registered as a member of the Company in respect of the purchased shares.

40 The substance of the argument for the defendant was that the executors were, on the death of the deceased, under an enforceable obligation to sell the shares at £100 each, and that this obligation ascertained and fixed their *maximum* value for the purpose of the Finance Act. During the argument I asked Mr Ronan whether he contended that the provisions in the articles amounted to, or contained, 'a *bona fide* contract of purchase of the shares from the deceased for full consideration in money or money's worth, paid to him for his own use or benefit,' within sect 3 of the Finance Act; or that the case was otherwise within that section. He replied that he did not; and, consequently, I have this 3rd section out of consideration altogether.

41 This being so, were it not for the elaborate and lengthened arguments that have been addressed to us (some of which have found acceptance with my learned brethren), I should have thought the question capable of an easy and simple solution. I should have thought that as the entire property, legal and equitable, *(pg682)* in the shares, which produced £15,000 a year, was vested in the deceased as a member of the Company, those shares were part of the property which 'passed' on his death; and having regard to the exclusion of the 3rd section, I should have deemed it immaterial, for the purposes of the Finance Act, to inquire to whom they had so 'passed.' Assuming the provisions in the articles to have been valid and enforceable, I should have held that the value of such shares, subject to the right of pre-emption, was properly within sect 1 of the Act, and that the residue of the shares – in other words, so much of them as was of a value equivalent to that of the right of pre-emption – was properly within sect 2, sub-sect (*b*), being property in which the deceased had an interest ceasing on his death, 'in respect of which a benefit accrued or arose by the cesser of such interest,' and which therefore was to be 'deemed to pass.' The question then would have seemed to me to have reduced itself to one of valuation.

42 Now, the value, we know, by sect 7, sub-sect 5, is 'the price which, in the opinion of the Commissioners,' the shares 'would fetch *if* sold in the open market at the time of the death.' The sale here supposed should, I would have thought, be a sale of the *property* which the deceased had in the shares at the time of his death – that is, of the entire legal and equitable interest therein, of that interest by virtue of which the deceased had been, and had been entitled to be, 'a member' of the Company in respect of such shares; a sale by virtue of which the purchaser thereat would have been entitled to have had that which he had bought vested in him in the same manner as it had been vested in the deceased, and consequently under which he would be entitled to be registered as a member of the Company in respect of those shares. If this view be right, the case of the defendants would, admittedly, fail.

43 Having regard, however, to the difference of opinion amongst us, I would not deem it courteous to express my opinion so summarily, and I accordingly proceed to give, in some greater detail, my views upon the principal points of difference between me and my learned brethren, although I doubt whether by so doing I add any force to what I have already said.

44 The vital differences between us appears to be the subject-matter *(pg683)* upon which the Crown are, upon this information, entitled to recover duty. My learned brethren hold that the subject-matter is not *all* the property in the shares which passed upon the death, but is limited to the portion of that property 'of which the deceased was competent to dispose at his death,' being the portion in respect of which the executors are the persons who, under sect 6, sub-sect 2, are primarily liable to duty. I, on the other hand, hold that the subject-matter is the entire property in such shares, including therein as well that portion thereof which might have passed under the articles to 'purchasing members,' as the residue which passed by his will.

45 There are, I think, two answers to the views of my colleagues upon this point. First, inasmuch as the shares have since the death been actually transferred to, and are now vested in, *two* of the executors who are also two of the defendants, those two defendants are liable to the duty on the entire value of them, under sect 8, sub-sect 4. The information, in paragraph 10, states facts sufficient to raise this ground of liability, and the difference between the liability of two of the defendants as distinguished from that of the three, especially when not raised by the answer, is too fine in a suit such as the present, which has been brought and has been argued upon broad questions of liability, and which ought not to be disposed of on questions of pleading or parties, if indeed the mere fact of the shares having become so vested is not sufficient to show that the right of pre-emption, if it ever existed, was not exercised, so that the entire interest in the shares passed by the will.

46 But, secondly, the sum at which the principal value is to be estimated is the price which, '*in the opinion of the Commissioners,*' would be fetched at a sale supposed to have been effected under particular circumstances; and, surely, if there be a difficulty, as there is, as to the nature of that supposed sale, the Crown is entitled to come into this Court and ask us to make such declaration as to the true nature of the sale, to be supposed under the circumstances of this case, as will enable the Commissioners to perform their statutory duty to the Crown. The personal non-liability of one or more of the defendants cannot affect the declarations asked for in the first paragraph of the prayer. *(pg684)*

47 This difference between us appears to pervade the application to the circumstances of the case of the expression 'such property' in the first sentence of sect 7, sub-sect 5:

> 'The principal value of any property shall be estimated to be the price which, in the opinion of the Commissioners, *such property* would fetch if sold in the open market at the time of the death of the deceased.'

48 'Such property' plainly means the property which 'passed,' or is to be 'deemed to have passed,' on the death; and in the present case, as the deceased had the entire interest, legal and equitable, in the shares, that interest is the property which answers the description of *such property* in sub-sect 5, and which is to be the subject-matter of the supposed sale.

49 The judgment of my learned brothers is based on the assumption that this property is identical with that which, under the articles of association, the so-called 'purchasing member' would have acquired by a compulsory transfer on payment of £100 a share, had that compulsory transfer in fact taken place. If this assumption is erroneous, the entire basis of their reasoning fails; because, if that which is the subject-matter of the compulsory sale for £100 is not identical with that which passed at the death, you cannot measure, as they have done, the value of the latter by the price of the former. Now, in my opinion, this assumption is erroneous. Nothing could have passed under such a compulsory transfer which was not in the executors, as such, at the time of the transfer; and assuming, as I do in this part of my judgment, that the articles are valid, it is clear that, on their true construction, something less than the entire legal and equitable property in a share is vested in the executors of a member, until the persons entitled decline to avail themselves of their right to insist on a compulsory transfer.

50 In the first place, admittedly the legal estate in a share cannot be vested in an executor until such executor is registered as a member; and such registration, if it at all takes place, must necessarily be subsequent to the election not to insist on a compulsory transfer. This is the first broad ground of distinction between two entities which have been treated as identical.

51 But, further, the equitable interests are not identical. The *(pg685)* deceased had, as I have said, on his death, the entire of the interest. What equitable interest do the articles of association contemplate the executors of a deceased member as having prior to a compulsory transfer? This very clearly appears from such of the articles as have been referred to by Kenny J; but as I desire this judgment to be self-contained, I shall myself refer to such of them as I deem material.

52 The rights of the executors of a deceased member are declared by clauses 16 and 17. By clause 16:

'The executors or administrators of a deceased member shall be the only persons recognised by the Company as having title to the shares registered in the name of such member.'

By clause 17:

'Any person becoming entitled to a share in consequence of the death of any member, upon producing such evidence that he sustains the character in which he proposes to act under this clause, or of his title, as the directors think sufficient, may, *subject to the regulations herein contained*, transfer such share to himself or to any other person.'

53 Thus the right of the executors to transfer the shares to themselves, or to any other person, is subject to the regulations in the articles. But one of those regulations is contained in clause 6, which provides that, save as thereinafter mentioned (a qualification which, for the purpose of this judgment, is immaterial, as it excepts only transfers to a son or brother of a deceased member):

'No share . shall be transferred to a person who is not a member, as long as any member is willing to purchase the same at the fair value.'

To give effect to this provision, clause 7 provides that -

'The person, whether a member of the Company or not, proposing to transfer the same, shall give a notice to the Company called a transfer notice.'

54 This notice, it is contended – and, for the present, I assume – places the person who gives it under an obligation to sell the share to a member at what is euphemistically called 'the fair value' – a value which, by clause 9, was, at the death of the deceased, £100. *(pg686)*

55 Clause 20 empowers the directors to -

'Refuse to register the transfer of a share . to a transferee, not being already a member, of whom they do not approve.'

Then, clause 22 provides for the case of -

'Any person, not being already a member, becoming *entitled*, either on producing evidence that he sustains any particular character, or without producing such evidence, to transfer a share to himself, either alone or in conjunction with another person, whether already a member or not.'

56 That is, it provides for a class of cases which includes that of the executors of a member satisfying the directors that they are executors, and consequently includes this case. What is the provision for such a case?

'The directors may give notice to such person that they decline to admit him as a member, and thereupon the Company shall be deemed to have been served with a transfer notice in respect of such share.'

In other words, the executors shall be bound to sell at what is called the 'fair value.'

57 Ultimately, clause 23 declares void a transfer made to any person, not being already a member, of whom the directors shall not approve.

58 Thus, the right of an executor under clause 17 to transfer his testator's shares to himself or any other person is, by the operation of the other clauses I have referred to, subjected to an obligation of compulsory sale to some existing member at £100 a share, at least if there is no existing member, or any son or brother of a member, willing to purchase otherwise than under the provisions of the articles. The right of the executors to transfer, subject to this obligation of compulsory sale, is the only right or interest to or in the shares of their testator which, under the articles, remains in them; and this right or interest is plainly not the entire equitable interest in the shares – indeed, under the existing circumstances of the Company, probably it is not more than one-third, and possibly is not more than one-fifth, of the entire equitable interest. To me, however, the amount of the difference in value between the whole and the part is immaterial. *(pg687)* It is sufficient that it is part only, and not the entire, of the equitable interest.

59 This argument may be stated more tersely thus. That which passed, or is to be deemed to have passed, at the death, is the entire estate in the shares; that which is the subject of the compulsory sale is the equitable interest therein, subject to the right of pre-emption. The difference in value between the two subject-matters is the value of the right of pre-emption.

60 Mr Ronan treated these two properties – the entire and the part only of the equitable interest – as the same thing, but attributed to that one thing different values at different times, calling the value of the former 'the holding value,' and that of the other 'the selling value.' I deem the distinction to be a very different one. I deem it to be a distinction, not between the value in two different aspects, or at two different times, of the same one thing, but between two different properties – a whole and a part – each having necessarily a different value. But however this may be, the deceased had at the time of his death the entire legal and equitable interest in the shares; and as it is admitted that the case is not within sect 3; and treating, as I must do, that which the Legislature has said shall be 'deemed to have passed' as having in fact passed, I cannot see any answer to the argument of the Crown that the entire equitable interest passed at the death within the meaning of the Act. Nor, having regard to that admission, can I see the materiality, for the purposes of the Act, of the fact that the equitable interest which so passed consisted in part of a right of pre-emption, so that, in the event of that right being exercised, part of that equitable interest would have passed under the will to the executors, and the other part under the articles to purchasing members. That right of pre-emption either was or was not a valuable thing. Had it been of no value, then, in substance, the entire of the equitable interest would have passed by the will, and the rights of the parties and of the Crown would have been the same as if such right of pre-emption had not existed. Upon the other hand, if the right of pre-emption were a thing of value, then so much of the equitable interest in the shares as consisted of that right of pre-emption passed to the member who, under the articles, would be entitled to purchase, and that *(pg688)* interest is within sect 2, and to be deemed to have 'passed at the death,' the residue only of the equitable interest passing by the will, and being within sect 1. But, in respect of the Finance Act, in a case such as the present, which is outside sect 3, the question is, not *to whom* the property passed, but whether it *passed at all.* It is immaterial whether it passed by act *inter vivos* or by will, whether it passed under the articles of association to other members of the Company, to legatees, or to strangers. The question is, What passed, or is to be deemed to have passed? And on everything within that description duty is payable. At the moment of his death the testator had in him property producing £15,000 a year. Upon his death that property necessarily ceased to be in him, and passed to some person or persons. By what machinery it passed I care not. What value the parties put upon it in their dealings *inter se* I care not. I hold that duty must be paid on the entire of it, irrespective of these accidental circumstances, and must be paid upon its value, as ascertained in accordance with the Act.

61 This brings me again to the valuation provision. By sect 7, sub-sect 5, the 'principal value of any property shall be the price which, in the opinion of the Commissioners, such property would fetch if sold in the open market at the time of the death of the deceased.' I hold, as I have already said, that 'such property' there includes the entire property in the shares which were vested in the deceased at the moment of his death; and that, for the purpose of ascertaining the value, the question is not whether it is capable of being sold in the open market. If the articles of association are valid, these shares are not saleable in the open market; but under sub-sect 5 we are bound to assume that they are capable of being so sold, because the valuation is to be based, not upon an actual, but upon a *supposed* sale, and that supposed sale one in the open market. The question is, assuming that they were capable of being sold in the open market, what would they fetch on such sale? And upon this supposition, which is the supposition the statute directs us to make, we must exclude the consideration of such provisions in the articles of association as would prevent a purchaser at the sale from becoming a member of the Company, registered as such in respect of the shares purchased by him at such *(pg689)* supposed sale. If we do not, we do not give effect to the assumption the statute coerces us to make.

62 I trust that this detailed statement of my views has made clear that which I stated in a few sentences at the commencement of my judgment. It is a vital difference between my view and that of my brethren.

63 There is, however, another difference between us; and although, in my opinion, it does not affect the result, I prefer not to allow it to pass unnoticed. I understand my learned brothers to consider the provisions affecting the transferability of a share to be *inherent* in the nature of a share in this Company, as now constituted, in the same manner as would be conditions in a lease entitling the landlord to re-enter in specified events upon payment to the tenant of a stipulated sum as compensation. I confess I cannot so regard them. I am of opinion that these provisions are collateral to the shares, and that the character and nature of a share in this Company is identical with that which it would have been had the articles not contained those clauses. The essential nature of a share in this Company is regulated by its memorandum of association. The Companies Act 1862, section 8, requires the memorandum to contain – (*a*) the amount of the capital with which the Company proposes to be registered, divided into shares of a certain fixed amount. Thus, it is of the essence of a share that it is the *entire property* in an *aliquot* part of the capital. No doubt a member may, by agreement, deal with his share in such a manner as to reduce *his equitable* interest in the share to something less than the entire, eg to a life estate; or he may so bind himself that, on a particular event, or on a concurrence of events, he will divest himself of the entire of his equitable interest therein, either with or without his legal interest. But notwithstanding all this, a share in this Company will continue – must continue – to be the entire property in an aliquot part of the capital.

64 Again, under the statute a share must be a *fixed* amount of the capital; and this provision admits of no qualification. If you frame a memorandum in such a way as to violate that provision of the Act, it is an illegal memorandum, and insufficient to constitute a Company. For example, suppose a memorandum of association provided that a share should be a fixed amount of the capital, say *(pg690)* £100 (the one-thousandth part of an entire capital of £100,000), subject to this, that if the member in whom it was vested died or assigned the share, such share should shrink to and become (say) the one two-thousandth part of the capital of the Company, and that the other two-thousandth part of the capital thus taken from the share in question should be added in designated portions to, and become parts of, other shares, such a memorandum would, in my opinion, be void and illegal, and inoperative in law to constitute a Company. Thus I hold that it is impossible to contend that these shares are such that, *proprio vigore* and automatically, they shrink to one-third or one-fifth of their former value on the death of the holder, or upon his assignment, and resume their former value upon a new member being registered in respect of them. This result, if it takes place at all, does so, not by reason of the nature of the share, but by reason of the collateral agreement affecting it contained in the articles – articles, it is to be remembered, which are capable of variation – and articles the provisions of which, *quoad* the matter here in controversy, I hold to have no greater effect than would an agreement to the same effect between the same parties, not contained in the articles. I am of opinion that all matters resting upon collateral agreement, as distinct from those arising from the nature of the property itself, are immaterial in questions arising on the Finance Act, where sect 3 does not come into operation.

65 So far I have assumed the provisions affecting the transferability of these shares contained in the articles of association to be valid, and enforceable at the suit of the member designated by the articles as 'the purchasing member'; and as I am of opinion that even on this assumption the Crown is entitled to the judgment for which it asks, it is immaterial for me to consider whether these provisions are so enforceable. Upon this question, which, in my opinion, involves grave and difficult questions (and which, possibly, as my brothers suggest, is not open for consideration upon the information), I shall not enter. I desire, therefore, to be understood as not offering any opinion upon the decision of Mr Justice Farwell in *Borland's Trustee v Steel, Bros & Co Ltd*, *(pg691)* which has been so much relied upon, or upon its bearing upon the question for *(pg692)* decision here.

Judgement of the Court of Appeal

1 LORD ASHBOURNE C: This is an appeal from the King's Bench Division on an information by the Attorney-General, and raises important questions on the construction of the Finance Act 1894.

2 The object of the suit is to obtain declarations as to the amount of the liability of the personal estate of the late Henry Jameson for estate duty in respect of 750 shares held by him in the well-known firm of John Jameson & Son Limited.

3 The Finance Act provides (sect 7) that the Commissioners shall themselves estimate the price which, in their opinion, the property would fetch if sold in the open market; and that, subject to the provisions of the Act, the value of any property for the purpose of estate duty shall be ascertained by the Commissioners in such manner and by such means as they think fit; and they may employ a valuer for the purpose. An appeal to the High Court is also given by sect 10 to any person aggrieved by the decision of the Commissioners.

4 I mention these provisions at the outset to draw attention to the fact that the Commissioners have never yet estimated the value or employed a valuer, and this case is not an appeal by a person aggrieved by their estimate, none having been made. It comes before us on an information by the Attorney-General seeking for a declaration – not fixing the price or value – but which may guide or assist the Commissioners in the performance of their clear statutable duties.

5 I cannot but think the method adopted somewhat inconvenient; but as the case is now before us, I will give my opinion on the various matters dealt with in the judgment now under review, and in the arguments addressed to us.

6 The facts of the case are sufficiently clear. Henry Jameson by his will, dated 26th July 1901, appointed his two nephews, the defendants John Jameson and George Jameson (both then and *(pg220)* now members of the Company), and his son-in-law, William Robertson, to be his executors, leaving to them all his property upon trust for his children.

7 Henry Jameson died on the 15th September, 1901, and his said will was duly proved by his aforesaid executors on 19th November, 1901. The defendants paid to the Commissioners of Inland Revenue £7243 6s 4d for estate duty in respect of personal property. Part of the testator's personal estate at his death consisted of the aforesaid 750 shares, portion of the sum of 4500 shares of £100 each which represented the capital of the Company.

8 The articles of association of the Company contained (*inter alia*) the following provisions relating to the registration of the holders, and to the alienation of shares in the Company: -

> **5** The Company shall be entitled to treat the registered holder of any share as the absolute owner thereof, and shall not be bound to recognise any equitable or other claim to or interest in such share on the part of any other person save as herein provided.

> **6** A share may be transferred or bequeathed to any person who is already a member, but no share shall, save as hereafter provided, be transferred to a person who is not a member so long as any member is willing to purchase the same at the fair value.

> **7** In order to ascertain whether any member is willing to purchase a share, the person, whether a member of the Company or not, proposing to transfer the same (hereinafter called the retiring member) shall give notice in writing (hereinafter called the transfer notice) to the Company that he desires to transfer the same. Such notice shall constitute the Company his agent for the sale of the share to any member of the Company at the fair value. The transfer notice may include several shares, and in such case shall operate as if it were a separate notice in respect of each. The transfer notice shall not be revocable, except with the sanction of the directors.

> **8** If the Company shall within twenty-eight days after being served with notice shall be bound upon payment of the fair value to transfer the share to the purchasing member.

9 The fair value of a share shall be £100, or such other sum as shall from time to time be fixed as the fair value by resolution of the Company in general meeting.

...

11 If the Company shall not, within twenty eight days after being served *(pg221)* with the transfer notice, find a member willing to purchase the share, and give notice in manner aforesaid, the retiring member shall, at any time within three months afterwards, be at liberty, subject to clause 31 hereof, to sell and transfer the shares (or those not placed) to any person (subject to the approval of the directors), and at any price.

...

16 The executors or administrators of a deceased member (not being one of several joint-holders), shall be the only persons recognised by the Company as having any title to the shares registered in the name of such member; and in case of the death of any one or more of the joint-holders of any share the survivors shall be the only persons recognised by the Company as having any title to or interest in such share.

17 Subject to the approval of the directors, any committee of a lunatic member, and any person becoming entitled to a share in consequence of the death of any member, upon producing such evidence that he sustains the character in respect of which he proposes to act under this clause, or of his title, as the directors think sufficient, may, subject to the regulations herein contained, transfer such shares to himself or to any other person.

18 Subject to the approval of the directors, any share may be transferred by a member to any son or brother of any existing member, and any share of a deceased member may be transferred by his executors or administrators to any son or brother of such deceased member, or to any son or brother of any existing member.

...

20 The directors may refuse to register any transfer of a share where the Company has a lien on the share, or to a transferee not being already a member of whom they do not approve.

...

22 If any person not being already a member shall have become entitled (either on producing evidence that he sustains any particular character, or without producing such evidence) to transfer a share to himself either alone or in conjunction with any other person, whether already a member or not, the directors may give notice to such person that they decline to admit him as a member, and thereupon the Company shall be deemed to have been served with a transfer notice in respect of such share.

23 A transfer made to any person not being already a member, of whom the directors shall not approve, shall be void.

9 The dividends paid by the Company on these shares for several years previous to the testator's death were at the rate of 20 per cent per annum.

10 The defendants John Jameson and George Jameson (who were already shareholders in their own right) were registered as *(pg222)* shareholders in the books of the Company in respect of the said 750 shares.

11 Under these circumstances the Attorney-General, on behalf of His Majesty, filed an information praying: – That it may be declared that upon the death of the said Henry Jameson, estate duty became payable under the provisions of the Finance Act 1894, upon the principal value of the said 750 shares in the said Company, being the price which same would fetch if sold in the open market at the time of the death of the deceased, and that such value is not limited to the 'fair value' of £100 a share, notwithstanding the special provisions as to the 'fair value,' and as to the alienation of the shares of the said Company contained in the said articles of association, or that it may be determined in what manner such value is to be ascertained, and what is the principal value of such shares for the purposes of the said Act. An account was also prayed for.

12 The defendants, in the defence, urged that the value of the 750 shares was for the purposes of estate duty necessarily the same as the 'fair value' fixed by the articles of association; that the right of pre-emption and restrictions on transfer and sale in the case of such shares cannot be treated as non-existent in arriving at the value of the shares for the purpose of estate duty, and, having regard to all these considerations, the defendants say that the principal value of the shares, being the price which same would fetch in the open market, was not greater than the 'fair value,' as fixed by the articles of association. The defendants also submitted that the Commissioners should have properly assessed what in their opinion would be the price which the shares would fetch if sold in the open market at the time of the death of the deceased, and should have demanded from the defendants the estate duty payable in respect thereof, and then the defendants, if dissatisfied, would have had the right of appeal to the High Court under section 10 of the Finance Act 1894.

13 When the case came before the King's Bench Division, Mr Justice Kenny and Mr Justice Boyd gave judgment for the defendants, while the Lord Chief Baron was more in favour of the Crown contention, and the Attorney-General has appealed.

14 The case is of the highest importance, and is not free from *(pg223)* difficulty. It would appear that no similar case under the Finance Act has as yet come before the Courts, and we have been pressed by the defendants' counsel that if the words of the Act are doubtful, or uncertain, or incomplete, we should steadily bear in mind that in the case of a statute imposing a tax, we should adopt a construction favourable to the subject unless it is clear that he comes within the letter of the law. This rule is clearly enunciated in the cases of *Partington v The Attorney-General*, and the *Oriental Banking Company v Wright*.

15 The Finance Act of 1894 enacts that estate duty shall be levied and paid upon the principal value of all property which passes on the death of any person dying after 1894 (section 1), of which the deceased was competent to dispose (sections 2 and 6), and that the principal value is to be estimated to be the price which, in the opinion of the Commissioners, such property would fetch if sold in the open market at the time of the death of the deceased (section 7, (5)).

16 What is the meaning of this enactment as sought to be applied to Henry Jameson's 750 shares? The Court has no power to ascertain the principal value. The Commissioners have formed no estimate, and expressed no opinion. The Attorney-General has filed the information practically to obtain a declaration that the estimate of the defendants is wrong, that the payment already made is insufficient, and that the 'fair value' is to be disregarded, and this for the guidance of the Commissioners who have not as yet performed their statutory duty. The course taken by the Crown compels us to consider with care in reference to these 750 shares what passed on the death of Henry Jameson. The only possible answer that can, in my opinion, be given is – the entire property in the shares, so far as he was competent to dispose of them at the time of his death. He was only competent under and pursuant to the articles of association. These articles defined and circumscribed his powers. At the time of his death he was not competent to dispose of the shares without complying with those articles. The articles also prescribed the position of his executors in reference to his shares. Can it for a moment be *(pg224)* suggested that the shares were one thing in the hands of Henry Jameson, and something else in the hands of his executors? Surely there must be the same subject-matter before and after death.

17 This was a private Company framed with all the pride of success by the Jameson family. Their absolute *bona fides* is admitted. The idea of *doing* the Revenue or creditors never crossed the minds of the founders. If there was any idea of fraud, the Court would be strong enough to refuse to be bound by the articles, as in the cases of *Wilson v Greenwood* and *Collins v Barker*. The general scope of the articles was that there should be in the Company, if it were so desired, none but members of the Jameson family. The articles were frankly directed to this end.

18 The answer to this claimed obligation made by the Crown is that some of the articles are invalid and void. But which of the articles are invalid, and why? The Crown does not come to close quarters on the question. The case was not made in the information. There is no repugnancy in the articles. The owners

are given a regulated and controlled freedom of disposition. The suggestion of perpetuity was only faintly hinted at. The bankruptcy contention was indeed suggested by the Attorney-General, but was met by a convincing argument on the articles of association, and the facts of the case. The defendants also relied on *Borland's Case*, which, however, was far stronger than the present, and I do not deem it necessary to discuss this bankruptcy point. I see nothing to induce me to set aside or disparage any of the articles in the Jameson Company on any of the grounds put forward by the Crown. Therefore, I take the case to be that the executor took on his death the same subject-matter which Henry Jameson owned in his lifetime, and was at his death competent to dispose of, ie the 750 shares in the Jameson Company, subject to and controlled by its articles of association. To hold otherwise would be to say that the shares were more valuable in the hands of his executors than in the hands of Henry Jameson, that he was fettered while they were free – that the articles bound him and he could not control them. He *(pg225)* deliberately became a shareholder in this family Company with its articles and its contracts, and his shares cannot be considered apart from this contractual position. The share cannot be split up and considered apart from its contractual incidents. The articles are part and parcel of the share, and not collateral and separable. He must be assumed to have absolutely bound himself to obey and conform to the articles.

19 I am unable to see that the provisions as to pre-emption and 'fair value' can be ignored and put aside as separate. They must be faced and dealt with as reasonable methods honestly adopted by this Company for the safeguarding of the continuance of the Jameson interest in this Jameson Company.

20 The 9th article gave power to vary the 'fair price' from time to time, and that it has not been varied may have been the considered action of the shareholders having regard to the uncertainties of commerce, and the common interest of the shareholders. The defendants resolutely contend, having regard to the circumstances and the facts, and the articles, that the 'fair value' is really the soundest way to gauge the price as if the share was sold in the open market.

21 But these observations are really preliminary to considering the effect of the Finance Act 1894. How can such shares in such a Company with such articles have their value estimated at the price which, in the opinion of the Commissioners, such property would fetch if sold in the open market? An actual sale in open market is out of the question. A feat of imagination has to be performed. Two suggestions have been put forward in argument. The Attorney-General says that the Commissioners should assume an unfettered sale in the open market to the highest bidder, who would be free from the clogs on alienation contained in the articles. The defendants, on the other hand, contend that the Finance Act is satisfied by taking the par or 'fair value' of £100 per share as the capital value which the Commissioners should estimate as the price which the shares would fetch if sold in the open market. Each side rushes into an indefensible extreme. The argument of the Attorney-General, which seeks to brush aside the articles and to vest in the executors a property which

Henry Jameson never possessed, would ascribe to the Finance Act the *(pg226)* power of making a new subject-matter. The argument of the defendants clings desperately to the articles, and gives really no adequate significance to the words of the Act requiring the Commissioners to estimate the price which the shares would fetch in the open market. The solution lies between the two. The Attorney-General must give more weight to the articles, and the defendants to the statute. It requires no tremendous imagination to conceive what a purchaser would give in the open market for Henry Jameson's shares as Henry Jameson himself held them at his death – for the right to stand in his shoes. That is, he held shares earning 20 per cent interest with power of disposition to sons and brothers subject to, but himself possessed of the power of pre-emption; and if that power of pre-emption was not used against him – a most improbable event indeed – he might sell as he best could at any price, and to any person he could. This, although not so valuable as owning shares absolutely free and unfettered in power of disposition, was obviously much more valuable than the 'fair value' of the articles. I am not a valuer or a Commissioner, but I do not see any overwhelming difficulty in estimating the price which such valuable shares would fetch if sold in the open market.

22 The order framed by Mr Justice Kenny is not inconsistent with anything that I have said, although I think that my reasoning would go to suggest a higher price, and I cannot regard the order framed as giving sufficient guidance. It appears to take too narrow a view of the rights of the Crown. The Commissioners should estimate the principal value at the price which same would fetch if sold in the open market on the terms that the purchaser should take and hold them subject to the articles of association. In the result I cannot adopt the contention of either the Attorney-General or of the defendants, and I think that the order should be modified in the direction indicated; and giving no costs of the appeal to either side, we do not interfere with the costs before King's Bench Division. *(pg227)*

23 FITZ GIBBON LJ: The Finance Act 1894, section 1, directs that estate duty shall be levied and paid upon '*the principal value*,' ascertained as thereinafter provided, of all property which passed on the death of Henry Jameson. That property included his 750 ordinary shares of £100 each in John Jameson & Son Limited. In my opinion each of these shares, with all rights and liabilities, and all advantages and disadvantages, incident to its ownership, passed on Henry Jameson's death to his executors as one indivisible piece of property. In conveyancing phraseology, the executors took each share 'to hold in as full and ample a manner as the same was held by Henry Jameson at his death.' The Finance Act, section 2 (1) (a), *includes* in property passing, 'property of which the deceased was at the time of his death competent to dispose.' In my opinion Henry Jameson was competent to dispose of his shares and of all his interest therein, within the meaning of that sub-section. In my opinion, on his death, there was no cesser of any interest in them, and no benefit in respect of them accrued or arose to any person, by any title or from any source other than the passing of the property to his executors.

24 Section 7 enacts the manner of 'determining the value of any estate for the purpose of estate duty.' Sub-section (5) converts *value* into *price*, and enacts that 'the principal value of any property shall be estimated to be the price which, in the opinion of the Commissioners, such property would fetch if sold in the open market at the time of the death of the deceased,' that is to say, the price estimated to be obtainable on an assumed sale. The Commissioners have exclusive jurisdiction to estimate that price in the first instance. Section 10 (1) provides that 'any person aggrieved by the amount of duty claimed by the Commissioners, on the ground of the value of any property, may appeal to the High Court, and the amount of duty shall be determined by the High Court'; with a further appeal by leave under sub-section (2).

25 It seems to me to be regrettable that the procedure thus provided was not followed, and that the King's Bench Division was called upon to make an interlocutory declaration, which has been *(pg228)* brought here upon appeal, and which, whenever or however varied here, or elsewhere, can be nothing more than a judicial paraphrase of the simple words of the Finance Act, leaving the Commissioners to do their duty under section 7 (6), with any help they can get from that paraphrase, but leaving any assessment which they might make liable to appeal; not to an interlocutory appeal raising abstract questions of interpretation and logomachy, but to a final appeal, upon which not only those questions, but the result of the correct application of right principles to the facts of the case, would be cognisable, and the only question of human interest in the whole business, namely – 'How much are Henry Jameson's executors to pay for estate duty?' – could be settled.

26 If we are to interpret the Finance Act in advance, I cannot improve on the terms of the declaration which will be read by Holmes LJ. But the difficulty of framing any paraphrase of which the meaning or effect will be certain, appears already from the fact that Kenny J, and Boyd J, agreed upon an order of which, though it directs regard to be had to the articles of association, Kenny J says that the result of his conclusion is that 'it does not at all follow that the principal value of the shares in question might not exceed the gross or fair value of £100'; and, though it declares that the value is to be ascertained as on a sale in the open market, Boyd J says: – 'With the restrictive conditions in the articles by which a purchaser of the shares would be bound, if sold in the open market, it would be folly on the part of such purchaser to give even the fair value'.

27 In this Court the Lord Chancellor has said that he is not certain that there is anything inconsistent with our Order in the Order of the King's Bench, though none of us, I believe, accepts all that is said in either of the judgments that expounded that Order. I am far from certain that my idea of the effect of our Order is the same as that of my colleagues; and if the judgment of the Lord Chief Baron had ended with its first paragraph, or if that paragraph could now be taken as fully expressing his interpretation of the Act, I should have concurred with him. He said that 'the Attorney-General was entitled to a declaration that the price should be that which, in the opinion of the

Commissioners, would have been fetched if the sale in the open market were upon *(pg229)* the terms that the purchaser thereat should be entitled to be, and should be registered as, a member of the Company in respect of the purchased shares.' But he said further on, that it was 'on the value of the right of pre-emption' that the defendants were trying to escape the liability of paying death duty, and this has been read as implying an opinion that the liability to pre-emption is to be left out of account in valuing the shares for estate duty.

28 The basis of my construction of the Act is the unity and indivisibility of Henry Jameson's property in the shares. I cannot adopt any procedure, or accept any solution of the question in dispute, which splits up that interest for any purpose.

29 In my opinion sect 7 (5) turns 'value' into 'price' for the purpose of estimating its amount; that price is to be ascertained upon a sale assumed to take place 'in the open market,' and that means the price which would be obtainable upon a sale where it was open to everyone, who had the will and the money, to offer the price which the property of Henry Jameson in the shares was worth as he held them. The price was to be that which a purchaser would pay for the right 'to stand in Henry Jameson's shoes,' with good title to get into them and to remain in them, and to receive all the profits, subject to all the liabilities, of the position. The price was what the shares were worth to Henry Jameson at his death – in other words, it was what a man of means would be willing to pay for the transmigration into himself of the property which passed from H Jameson when he died.

30 But that property, like all property that I know of (except, perhaps, the gold coin of the realm), has its incidents, advantageous and disadvantageous. These include the operation of the articles of association, so far as they are legal. Since the first 'Companies Act,' property of countless value has been created under articles of association, and has passed by transfer and on death. Since the Finance Act, it has been valued and assessed for 'estate duty'; until this case, I am not aware of any attempt made by the Crown to enhance the value for the purpose of assessment above the value to the holder; but this would be the effect of estimating the value under sect 7 (5), upon the assumption that any depreciating incidents affecting the property in the hands of *(pg230)* the holder while he lived were to be left out of account in determining the price which an imaginary purchaser would give for it in a supposed 'open market.'

31 The right of pre-emption against Henry Jameson's shares in certain events, if legal, is a depreciating incident; but the right of Henry Jameson, or of any person 'standing in his shoes,' to exercise the corresponding right of pre-emption against the other shares of the Company in the like events, is an appreciating incident, of Henry Jameson's property, which, in my opinion, is to be valued as a whole.

32 Restrictions upon alienation exist in many forms, and widely vary in degree. The transfer fee of half-a-crown on shares is one; a condition against alienation, making assignment of land illegal and void under the Sub-letting Acts is another. The decision of the majority of this Court in *Casey v Bentley* is an instance of the serious consequences which may be held to flow from an article of association which limits the transfer of shares to purchasers approved by directors. But all these things are, in their nature, only so many incidents of property, affecting it alike in the hands of any one, and affecting both its value and its price.

33 Decisions in bankruptcy, based on public policy, and on the statutory provisions against placing property beyond the reach of creditors, are not applicable to a statute for ascertaining the value of property for the purpose of taxation.

34 It is impossible, at this day, to hold that the articles of J Jameson & Son Ltd are illegal and void under the Finance Act, or that estate duty is to be assessed and levied upon the shares of the Company, or on any like shares, upon a principle, or an assumption, which would enhance their value for taxation when passing on death, beyond their actual value to a living owner, when depreciated by lawful restrictions upon transfer, imposed by the articles of association.

35 The Commissioners, when fixing the value of the property for taxation at the price which, in their opinion, it would fetch in the open market, cannot estimate that price on an assumption that the purchaser was to get, and consequently would be willing to pay *(pg231)* for what neither Henry Jameson nor any other shareholder, past present or future, in this Company ever had or can have, viz shares in John Jameson & Co Ltd, freely transferable to any person whomsoever, as distinguished from shares freely transferable only to existing members. of the Company, or to their sons or brothers, and liable to serious restrictions and conditions upon transfer to others.

36 Regretting that we cannot now hear, decide, and end the whole case, I concur in the definition of the meaning of the Finance Act which my colleagues have prepared.

37 I wish we could have acted upon the defendants' answer, paragraph 5 -

'The defendants will submit that the Commissioners of Inland Revenue should have properly assessed what, in their opinion would be the price which the said shares would fetch if sold in the open market at the time of the death of the deceased, and should have demanded from the defendants the estate duty payable in respect thereof, and then the defendants, if dissatisfied with the amount of such assessment, would have had the right of appeal to the High Court of Justice in Ireland, under sect 10 of the Finance Act 1894, and could have had the amount of duty payable by them determined by this Court on a petition, and they will submit that these proceedings are unnecessary and oppressive.'

38 But the defendants have not relied on this submission as a defence; on the contrary, they have set up and persisted in the defence that estate duty is not assessable upon any sum greater than the value fixed by the articles of association, and that defence is, in my opinion, unsustainable.

39 WALKER LJ: The question raised by the information in this case is what is the estate duty payable by the executors of Henry Jameson in respect of 750 shares in the Company of John Jameson & Son, held by him at the time of his death on the 15th September 1901?

40 The firm of John Jameson & Son was turned into a Limited Company in October 1891. The capital consisted of 4500 shares having a nominal value of £100 each. Thus the *(pg232)* nominal capital was £450,000, and Henry Jameson held one-sixth of it at the time of his death. For a considerable time, and at the date of his death, 20 per cent was being paid on the shares. It is obvious, therefore, apart from special circumstances connected with the shares, that they far exceeded in intrinsic value the nominal value.

41 But the Company, which was regulated by articles of association of October 1891, was intended to be a private one and restricted as far as possible to members of the Jameson family, and for that purpose the articles contain elaborate provisions applicable both to existing members and executors of deceased members. A pre-emption price at which is called the 'fair value' fixed (subject to revision) at £100 was named. Under the 18th clause any share may be transferred by a member, subject to the approval of the directors, to any son or brother of said member or son or brother of any existing member, and any share of a deceased member may be transferred by his executor to the same limited class; but subject to clause 18 the provision in clause 6 operates, which is 'a share may be transferred or bequeathed to any person who is already a member, but no share shall be transferred to a person who is not a member so long as any member is willing to purchase the same at the fair value,' and notice of transfer is required. Clause 11 of the articles provides for a case in which no member willing to purchase the share can be found. In that event 'the retiring member shall' (within the time limited) 'be at liberty, subject to clause 31 hereof, to sell and transfer the shares (or those not placed) to any person, subject to the approval of the directors, and at any price.' This was the character of the property the subject of the information. There is also a provision limiting the general rights of assignees in bankruptcy, the validity of which I do not think it necessary to consider at all. Henry Jameson appointed as his executors John Jameson and George Jameson, both already members of the Company, and also William Robertson; and after the death of Henry Jameson, the Company registered John Jameson and George Jameson as members in respect of the 750 shares.

42 The Crown claimed estate duty from the executors in respect of the 750 shares. The executors contended that they *(pg233)* were only liable to pay duty at the fair value rate, viz £100 per share. The contention of the Crown on the other hand is stated in the first paragraph of the prayer of the information, viz, 'That it may be declared that upon the death of the said Henry Jameson estate duty became payable under the provisions of the Finance Act 1894, upon the principal value of the said 750 shares in the said John Jameson & Son Limited Company, being the price which same would *(pg234)* fetch if sold in the open market at the time of the death of the deceased testator, and that such value is not limited to the par or fair value of £100 a share, notwithstanding the special provisions as to the "fair value," and as to the alienation of the shares of the said Company contained in the said articles of association of the said Company, or that it may be determined in what manner such value is to be ascertained, and what is the principal value of such shares for the purposes of the said Act,' and the information asks for an account of the amount due and payment by the defendants, the executors.

43 The Finance Act of 1894 makes estate duty leviable upon the principal value (ascertained as provided) of all property, real or personal, settled or not settled, which passes, i.e., changes hands, on the death of such person.

44 Different views have been expressed as to the effect of the 1st and 2nd sections of the Act *inter se*, but I do not think it is material for the purposes of this case to consider them.

45 It is clear that on the death of Henry Jameson all the interest of every kind which he had in the 750 shares became subject to the liability to estate duty. The Act, however, makes the executors liable for it directly in respect only of the property of which the testator was competent to dispose. At the time of the filing of the information the 750 shares had been registered in the names of John Jameson and George Jameson, and it seems to me therefore they are precluded from saying that all the interest of every kind which Henry Jameson had was not vested in them, and the question becomes one, I think, of valuation for the purposes of duty. That we find in section 7, sub-section 5: 'The principal value of any property shall be estimated to be the price which, in the opinion of the Commissioners, such property would fetch if sold in the open market at the time of the death of the deceased'.

46 The decree pronounced by the majority of the Judges of the King's Bench Division follows in its first part the words of section 7, sub-sect 5, and then proceeds, 'and that in estimating such principal value regard is to be had to the special provisions in the said articles of association dated the 9th October 1891, with reference to alienation and transfer of the shares of the said Company and as to fair value, but that the amount of such principal value is not necessarily limited to the par or "fair value" of £100 a share'. That word 'necessarily' plays an important part in the declaration, coupled with the glossary in the judgments.

47 There is, I think, some ambiguity in the language of that decree standing by itself, but its real meaning appears from the passage in the judgment of

Mr Justice Kenny, at p675 of the report, in which he sums up the result of his conclusion as leading up to the declaration. In my opinion the declaration as interpreted by his judgment stops short of what the rights of the Crown are under the 7th section, to which we must give full effect. I think the test of value, under section 7, is what the shares would fetch if sold in 'open market' – an hypothetical 'open market,' upon the terms that the purchaser would be entitled to be registered in respect of the shares, but would himself thereafter hold them subject to the provisions of the articles of association, including those relating to the alienation and transfer of them, and this price is not limited to the 'fair value.' This would be much what would exist if clause 11 of the articles were applied. I am not aware that this view conflicts with the general conclusions of the Lord Chief Baron, stated at p.682 of the report. It is not necessary for me to consider the validity of the clauses in the articles. The information does not challenge their legality, but I am not to be taken as accepting the argument of the Attorney-General as to their being invalid on the ground of repugnancy, or as offending against the law of perpetuity, or against public policy. I do not understand that last contention as regards a taxing statute, though I could the evasion of it, which, in the present case, could not arise having regard to the dates. While thinking that the decision appealed from falls *(pg235)* short of the real rights of the Crown, I also think that the argument for the Crown cannot, as to the position of the purchaser buying in the hypothetical 'open market,' be accepted. I do not suggest that the award of costs against the Crown in the Court below should be interfered with, but I think there should be no costs of the appeal.

48 It is for the Commissioners, and not for us, to estimate the price under the 7th section; and they are enabled to obtain expert evidence to guide them in applying the principle which we lay down, and that estimate called 'the amount of duty' can be appealed against.

49 HOLMES LJ: The questions involved in this appeal have been so fully considered by the Divisional Court as well as by my colleagues that I can state the grounds of my conclusion with comparative brevity.

50 The late Henry Jameson at the time of his death was possessed of 750 fully paid up shares, portion of the 4500 shares of £100 each which formed the capital of a joint stock Company known as John Jameson & Son Limited, which was registered on the 9th October 1891. This Company was one of the class sometimes described by Judges and text-writers as 'private,' of which the distinguishing feature is that their shares are not intended to be sold to the public in open market, but are to be retained as far as possible in the hands of the original shareholders and of members of their families. The articles of association imposing restrictions on the free disposition of the shares in John Jameson & Son Limited are fully set out in the report of this case in the King's Bench Division. It is enough to say, that while a share may be transferred or bequeathed to any person who is already a member, or may, subject to the approval of the directors, be transferred by a member, his executors, or administrators, to a son or brother of such member, or to the son or brother of another member, there cannot be a transfer to anyone else so long as a member is *(pg236)* willing to purchase at what is called the 'fair value,' stated in the articles to be £100, or such other sum as shall from time to time be fixed by a resolution of the Company in general meeting. Means are prescribed for ascertaining whether any member is willing to purchase at the 'fair value' a share thus offered for sale; and it is only in the event of no such purchaser being found that the seller may sell to any person and at any price.

51 It was argued in the Divisional Court that these restrictions were void on three grounds – (1) as infringing the rule against perpetuity; (2) as being repugnant to the absolute dominion over property which its owner ought to possess; and (3) as being contrary to public policy. I am relieved from considering these propositions. The Attorney-General has admitted without reserve that the articles of which I have given an abstract are legal, and bind the Company and its members as well as any outsider who is permitted to purchase a share.

52 The appeal has proceeded on this basis, and, while I have no reason to doubt the correctness of this view of the law, I am not called on to express an independent opinion upon it. The Attorney-General, however, while making the foregoing admission, has argued that the articles are invalid against assignees or trustees in bankruptcy. This may or may not be so. I think that it would depend largely, if not altogether, on the history of the particular Company, and on the circumstances that led to the membership of the bankrupt shareholder. But however this may be, I do not see the analogy or relevancy of cases under bankruptcy law to the matter now to be decided. We are not dealing with a device to avoid liability under the Finance Act. The Company was registered some years before that statute passed, and the articles of association followed precedents that had been in use for a quarter of a century. The shares were from the first subject to provisions which affected their value in the hands of the shareholders; and the Legislature having imposed a tax, which is to be measured by the value of the property, we are to determine how such value is to be ascertained. The case is thus reduced to what is not only a narrow but also a simple issue, which becomes still simpler when it is freed from an element of confusion to which considerable prominence was given during the argument. By the first section of the Finance Act estate duty is to be levied and paid upon the principal value of all property settled or not settled, which passes on the death of the deceased. Now, many persons are entitled during their lives to interests in property, real and *(pg237)* personal, which they have no power to dispose of, and which pass to other persons on their deaths. Estate duty is by the terms of the Act to be levied and paid upon such property, not indeed out of the assets of the deceased, but by the persons to whom the property passes. The Solicitor-General endeavoured to show that the property in the shares to which Henry Jameson was entitled was of a two-fold character – one part of which he was entitled to dispose of at his death, the other passing, as I understand the argument, to the other members of the Company.

53 If this is correct, there is, I think, no answer to the comment of Kenny J that 'the information is conversant with the personal property which the deceased was competent to dispose of at his death, on which alone the defendants as his executors are compellable to pay estate duty.' But there is really no ground for the contention of the Solicitor-General. Henry Jameson, during his life, by virtue of his ownership of the shares, was entitled to receive the dividends payable thereon, and to have such right of pre-emption over the other shares of the Company as is conferred by the articles of association, his own shares being at the same time subject to a similar right of pre-emption by the other members of the Company. Such right, however, did not apply to a transfer or bequest to a son or brother, and he appointed as executors his two brothers, the defendants, John Jameson and George Jameson, who are now the registered owners, and have the same interest in the shares as their testator. They, like him, are entitled to receive the dividends, and to have such right of pre-emption as he had, while no greater right of pre-emption over his shares passed on his death to the other members, than what they were entitled to in his lifetime. It is, therefore, unnecessary for me to consider what would have been the result if the executors had been strangers, as in the events that have happened the defendants are liable to pay estate duty on the principal value of the shares as they stood in Henry Jameson's name immediately before his death. If I were obliged to ascertain this value from the first section of the Act alone without reference to section 7, I would hold that it was the sum that Henry Jameson would have obtained if he could have sold and transferred the shares, in the words of clause 11 of the articles of association, to any person and *(pg238)* at any price, the purchaser to have the same rights therein, and to be subject to the same liabilities, as himself. I need hardly say that this sum would be different from the £100 per share at which the 'fair value' is now fixed. The dividend of 20 per cent per annum paid for years, and likely to continue, would attract men who buy securities to hold as an investment and not to resell, especially as the purchaser would always be at liberty to transfer to a son or brother. On the other hand, the price would not be as high as that of a security, equally good in other respects, that could be disposed of at any time in the open market. Turning to the 7th section of the Act, I find therein the very test of value which I should have applied in its absence. 'The principal value shall be estimated to be the price which, in the opinion of the Commissioners, such property would fetch if sold in the open market at the time of the death of the deceased.' The Attorney-General and the defendants agree in saying that in this case there cannot be an actual sale in open market. Therefore, argues the former, we must assume that there is no restriction of any kind on the disposition of the shares and estimate that would be given therefor by a purchaser, who upon registration would have complete control over them. My objection to this mode of ascertaining the value is that the property bought in the imaginary sale would be a different property from that which Henry Jameson held at the time of his death. The defendants, on the other hand, contend that the only sale possible is a sale at which the highest price would be £100 per share, and that this ought to be the estimated value. My objection is that this estimate is not based on a sale in open market as required by the Act. Being unable to accept either solution. I go back to my own, which is in strict accordance with the language of the section. I assume that there is such a sale of the shares as is contemplated by article 11, the effect of which would be to place the purchaser in the same position as that occupied by Henry Jameson. An expert would have no difficulty in estimating their value on this basis. It would be less than the Crown claims, and more than the defendants offer; but I believe that it would be arrived at in accordance not only with the language of the Act, but with the methods usually employed in valuing property. *(pg239)*

54 While I concur in much of the judgment of Kenny J and while, like him, I am unable wholly to accept the arguments of either side, I fear that we have not come to the same conclusion.

55 There is, I think, a want of precision in the language in which he has formulated his principle of valuation, and the order of the Divisional Court is vague and uncertain. I would prefer a declaration that the principal value of the shares is to be estimated at the price which, in the opinion of the Commissioners, they would fetch if sold in the open market, on the terms that the purchaser should be entitled to be registered as holder of the shares, and should take and hold them subject to the provisions of the articles of association, including the articles relating to alienation and transfer of the shares of the Company. *(pg240)*

Case 7
IRC v Marr's Trustees

(1906) 44 SLR 647

High Court

21 December 1906

The value to be placed on a shareholding for a tax purpose is the amount considered to be the highest sum a willing purchaser would have been prepared to offer on the date of valuation. Following the valuation date, there may be sales of shares, in the open market or otherwise; the price achieved on those sales does not determine the value on the valuation date, which is the only value required.

This case enunciates the basic principle that one looks at the specific date of disposal (for capital gains tax) or the specific date of transfer (for inheritance tax).

In this case, William Smith Marr died on 7 June 1904 and in his estate was a herd of prize shorthorn cattle. This herd was valued at £9,031. Four months later on 11 October 1904, the herd was sold for £17,722 17s.

The Revenue attempted to assess estate duty on the basis of the sale price achieved four months after the death. As this was resisted by the executors, the Commissioners of Inland Revenue raised an action to compel Mr Marr's trustees to lodge 'a full and true corrective inventory, duly stamped, of all the personal or moveable estate and effects of the said deceased William Smith Marr, including therein the full and true value of the herd of shorthorn cattle which belonged to him, based on the proceeds actually realised through sale' (per Lord Johnston [1906] 44 SLR at 647 **case 7 para 2**).

Estate duty operated on the basis that tax was applied to what was specified in statute as 'the principal valuation'. The statute considered in *IRC v Marr's Trustees* stated:

'The principal value of any property shall be estimated to be the price which, in the opinion of the Commissioners, such property would fetch if sold in the open market at the time of the death of the deceased.'
(FA 1894, s 7(5))

The statutory provision currently applicable for capital gains tax states:

> 'In this Act "market value" in relation to any assets means the price which those assets might reasonably by expected to fetch on a sale in the open market'
>
> (TCGA 1992, s 272(1))

For inheritance tax, the statutory rule is:

> 'the value ... of any property sold for the purpose of this act be the price of which the property might reasonably be expected to fetch if sold on the open market at that time.'
>
> (IHTA 1984, s 160).

All three formulations require a price to be determined by reference to a single valuation date.

Lord Johnston rejected the application by the Commissioners of Inland Revenue by saying:

> 'I am of opinion that the position taken by the Commissioners of Inland Revenue is not well founded ... Now, property regarded in view of this provision may be of different descriptions. It may be perishable in its nature. It may be by nature fluctuating in value, not so much with reference to the market as with reference to natural increment in value, and it may be by nature of a fixed and, as regards the question at issue, practically unchanging value.
>
> Notwithstanding these differences the value for estate duty is to be taken at the price which the property would fetch in open market at the time of the deceased's death.'
>
> ([1906] 44 SLR at 647 **case 7 paras 4–6**)

> 'I think that the sale which actually did take place in October was accompanied by certain adventitious circumstances which, though they redounded very much to the advantage of the estate, render the sale price obtained a misleading criterion of the true market value of the herd at the date of the death, or indeed at any other date.'
>
> ([1906] 44 SLR at 648 **case 7 para 13**)

This case is a useful corrective to a practice that seems to have developed in HMRC Share Valuation when that division is asked to consider the valuation of chattels at death. The author has experienced correspondence from the division suggesting that the best measure of value at the date of death is obtained by the price chattels fetched when auctioned subsequently. That is not the best evidence. As is clear from the judgement in *IRC v Marr's Trustees* the best evidence is the valuation of an expert as at the date of death.

The case is of interest, also, for the comment made by Lord Johnston on the nature of the evidence from the expert witness. Those who supply evidence in court may find the judge's words instructive:

> 'Great exception was taken by counsel for the Commissioners to the manner of Mr Ritchie's valuation, in respect that he had valued this herd of prize cattle more or less in the slump and not as individual animals. But I think it right to state that I was much impressed by Mr Ritchie's appearance in the witness-box. He was not a voluble witness, and did not always find it easy to put in words a reason for the faith that was in him but he had lived for years with the herd under his eye ... I would infinitely rather trust his trained and practical intuition, though it may appear on paper to produce somewhat of a rule of thumb result, than many a more apparently scientific valuation by classification. And I am persuaded that Mr Ritchie's valuation of June is a fair valuation, against which the Commissioners of Inland Revenue have no just cause of complaint.'
>
> ([1906] 44 SLR at 648 **case 7 para 12**)

> 'I shall therefore assoilzie the defenders with expenses.'
>
> ([1906] 44 SLR at 648 **case 7 para 14**)

The decision in this case gives clear authority for the valuer to reject any suggestion that the price achieved at an actual sale necessarily determines the market value to be taken for a tax purpose.

Judgement

References, example '(pg647)', are to (1906) 44 SLR 647.

1 **LORD JOHNSTON:** The late William Smith Marr, farmer, Uppermill, in the parish of Tarves, Aberdeenshire, who died on 7 June 1904, was the owner and breeder of one of the most famed herds of prize shorthorn cattle in Scotland. An inventory of his personal estate was lodged by his executors, in which his stock of cattle, including the shorthorn herd, was entered at the valuation put upon them by Mr William H Ritchie, Old Meldrum, viz – £9,031. This valuation was made on 20 June 1904, just about a fortnight after Mr Marr's death. And estate duty has been paid on that amount. The herd was not disposed of until 11 October 1904, when it realised the sum of £17,722, 17s, being greatly in excess of the value put upon it in the inventory.

2 The Commissioners of Inland Revenue being dissatisfied with the value put on the herd in the inventory for the purpose of estate duty, as largely an underestimate, have raised the present action to compel Mr Marr's trustees to lodge 'a full and true corrective inventory, duly stamped, of all the personal or moveable estate and effects of the said deceased William Smith Marr, including therein the full and true value of the herd of shorthorn cattle which belonged to him, based on the proceeds actually realised through sale.' The Commissioners therefore confine their demand to an account stated on the basis of the sale prices, and in support of their summons they state – Condescendence 5 – 'The price fetched in the open market, when the herd was exposed for sale within four months after the deceased's death, affords a reasonable and proper criterion of the value of this portion of the deceased's estate. The amount actually realised formed and falls to be treated as an important asset of the estate, allowance being made for such outlay as was incurred by the defenders, as executors, in the keep and care of the herd. The balance after making this allowance represents truly the value of the herd at the deceased's death.'

3 They plead (1) the Commissioners of Inland Revenue are entitled to recover the full amount of estate duty based on the actual proceeds of the cattle sold in open market.

4 I am of opinion that the position taken by the Commissioners of Inland Revenue is not well founded. The question depends upon the statutory provision – Finance Act 1894, section 7(5) – which states: "The principal value of any property shall be estimated to be the price which, in the opinion of the Commissioners, such property would fetch if sold in the open market at the time of the death of the deceased."

5 Now, property regarded in view of this provision may be of different descriptions. It may be perishable in its nature. It may be by nature fluctuating in value, not so much with reference to the market as with reference to natural increment in value, and it may be by nature of a fixed and, as regards the question at issue, practically unchanging value.

6 Notwithstanding these differences the value for estate duty is to be taken at the price which the property would fetch in open market at the time of the deceased's death.

7 Where property is of a perishable nature, as for instance a cargo of fruit or other perishable article, no question can arise.

8 Where property is by nature of a practically fixed value, as for instance lands or houses, there may be a little more difficulty. In the case of house property, at any rate, there is a natural time of the year which is regarded as the proper property market, and unless a house has some special attractions it can hardly be said that there is an open market, say in the month of August, should that be the time of the deceased's death. Though the house may not be actually saleable then, yet values change so gradually that there is no difficulty in a skilled valuator putting a proper value upon the house even in August with *(pg647)* his knowledge of past markets and present prospects. There will be no substantial change in the intrinsic value of the house between August, when it may have to be valued, and the following February, when it may have to be sold for entry at the ensuing May.

9 But when one comes to deal with a subject of a fluctuating value, the fluctuation depending upon natural increment or rather on the excess or otherwise of natural increment over natural decrement, a different question arises. Such a subject is a herd of cattle. It is in a definite ascertainable condition at the date of the deceased's death. But in the lapse of months important changes take place. At the date of the death a cow may be two or three weeks from calving. In the course of three or four months the risks of calving and the risks to the life of a young calf are over. The cow in calf is one thing, the cow and her calf on its feet and three or four months old is a totally different thing. Again a calf a few weeks old at the date of the death and a calf some months old at a date posterior to the death are also very different things. The calf is over the troubles of its early weeks and every month is developing more of its quality. Similarly a cow may have been put to the bull shortly before the death and in the course of three or four months may prove either to be barren or to be in calf. Again losses by deaths occur from time to time, and cattle which may be perfectly healthy at the date of the death of the owner may either singly or as a herd be afflicted with disease rendering them valueless at the end of three or four months. It is, I think, therefore obvious that to call for a valuation (and no valuation can be better than actual exposure to sale by auction) at a date three or four months posterior to the date of the death would not give the true value of the herd at the date which the statute itself fixes, viz, the date of the death.

10 Now, if what I have already said would be true of an ordinary herd of cattle, it is true to a greatly enhanced degree in the case of a herd of prize cattle, whose risks and whose variations in individual value are extreme in degree when compared with those of an ordinary herd. Moreover, if what I have said above is true generally there could not be two periods in the year better suited to display the difference in values than the dates with which we are concerned, viz, 7 June and 11 October. In June the herd is in a transition state, the majority of the calves have been recently dropped, some of the cows are uncalved, and the herd has had none of the benefit of a summer's grass. By October the condition of the herd is set for the season, the cattle have, in agricultural phrase, got the bloom on them, and there can be no question that in the interest of the estate the trustees acted prudently in taking the risk of carrying the herd through the summer and selling it in October rather than selling it at once, and they also acted prudently in not taking the risks of carrying it through the winter and selling it in February, which is the other chief market month for prize cattle, and when if everything had gone well the herd would have been of still greater intrinsic value, though I doubt whether it would have met with as good a market.

11 Even if I had not to consider the special circumstances to be immediately adverted to, I should have no hesitation in saying that the herd must be valued at the date of the death, though it might have been imprudent to bring it to the hammer till three or four months later, and that the Commissioners of Inland Revenue were not entitled to have a valuation as in October, when the best market may be anticipated, or a valuation based on the result of actual sale at that period.

12 Great exception was taken by counsel for the Commissioners to the manner of Mr Ritchie's valuation, in respect that he had valued this herd of prize cattle more or less in the slump and not as individual animals. But I think it right to state that I was much impressed by Mr Ritchie's appearance in the witness-box. He was not a voluble witness, and did not always find it easy to put in words a reason for the faith that was in him but he had lived for years with the herd under his eye, with the markets for Aberdeen prize cattle under his close observation, and with every opportunity of becoming conversant with the ups and downs of the business. I would infinitely rather trust his trained and practical intuition, though it may appear on paper to produce somewhat of a rule of thumb result, than many a more apparently scientific valuation by classification. And I am persuaded that Mr Ritchie's valuation of June is a fair valuation, against which the Commissioners of Inland Revenue have no just cause of complaint. I am none the less convinced of this, that the trustees knew, and that Mr Ritchie knew, that the interest of the estate was to have a fair if not a full valuation, having regard to the credit of the herd, the collection of which had been the work of Mr Marr's life, and which was the one real asset of his estate after his death.

13 But I think that the sale which actually did take place in October was accompanied by certain adventitious circumstances which, though they redounded very much to the advantage of the estate, render the sale price obtained a misleading criterion of the true market value of the herd at the date of the death, or indeed at any other date. These circumstances were, shortly, that a sudden and unexpected demand had arisen from the great Argentine breeders, which sent their agent Mr Rodger into the field for the first time with an almost free hand, and that not merely for high grade and mature bulls, to which the Argentine stock growers had chiefly confined themselves, but also for young stock and breeding cows. But even this was not the real cause of the great success of the sale. The real cause of its success with this. Tuberculosis is the great enemy of prize stock. The Argentine Government will not admit it, or indeed *(pg648)* any stock, without a careful veterinary examination at their own ports. Consequently their buyers in this country cannot buy without insuring against the risk of the stock being rejected on its arrival at the Argentine ports. Underwriters are accustomed to insure against this risk, provided they have a reliable veterinary certificate before delivery. This they can rarely get when the sale is in public market, consequently they buy by private bargain, and their buyers do not appear as bidders at auction unless in exceptional cases. But Mr Rodger had accidentally found an underwriter who, I assume in ignorance of what he was doing, undertook the risk of rejection on landing in the Argentine without stipulating for the necessary tuberculosis certificate. Hence Mr Rodger was able to intervene at the sale not only with a free hand as to price, but untrammelled by the necessity of obtaining the tuberculosis certificate, and I think that it is not too much to say, as many of the witnesses did, that his advent made the sale. As an illustration of the consequence, the highest priced animal, which he bought at a price of 1,200 guineas, was rejected on examination, and afterwards sold for £100 on account of the underwriters, for show purposes merely. Such adventitious circumstances could not possibly enter into the valuation of the herd as a marketable commodity, either at the date of the death or at the date of the sale.

14 I shall therefore assoilzie the defenders with expenses.

15 The Lord Ordinary assoilzied the defenders. *(pg649)*

Case 8
IRC v Clay, IRC v Buchanan

[1914] 3 KB 466

Court of Appeal

28 May 1914

This is the second reported case to consider the effect on a fiscal valuation of a special purchaser. The first case was *Re Gough & Aspatria, Silloth & District Joint Water Board* [1904] 1 KB 417 **case 5**, which was determined by the Court of Appeal ten years earlier.

All potential purchasers must be considered in estimating the value of a shareholding. This includes the potential purchaser for whom the shares have a particular value, perhaps because by adding these to his existing holding, a majority shareholding is acquired.

This case concerns a valuation required for the purpose of computing a liability to increment value duty under FA 1910, s 25.

Mrs Buchanan purchased 83 Durnford Street, East Stonehouse in 1902 for £700. House number 84 was used as a nurses' home and the owners of that property wished to purchase the adjoining house to extend the nurses' home. After negotiation, Mrs Buchanan agreed to sell number 83 to Clay and others, trustees of the nurses' home, for £1,000.

The tribunal valued the property, for the purpose of increment value duty, as £1,000; that is, the sum for which it was sold. The Crown applied to the Court of Appeal stating that the tribunal had misdirected itself in law and the value to be taken was the value of the property for private occupation, ignoring other factors, which was agreed to be £750.

FA 1910, s 25(1) declared that the value required for the purpose of computing increment value duty is the amount 'which the fee simple of the land, if sold at the time in the open market by a willing seller ... might be expected to realise'.

In dismissing the Revenue's appeal, Cozens-Hardy MR enunciated the principle that, in valuing an asset, the price that would be offered by a special purchaser must be brought into consideration:

'"Open market" includes a sale by auction, but it is not confined to that. It would include property publicly announced in the usual way by insertion in the lists of house agents. But it does not necessarily involve the idea of a sale without reserve. I can see no ground for excluding from consideration the fact that the property is so situate that to one or more persons it presents greater attractions than to anybody else. The house or the land may immediately adjoin one or more landowners likely to offer more than the property would be worth to anybody else. This is a fact which cannot be disregarded …

… An "open market" sale of property "in its then condition" presupposes a knowledge of its situation with all surrounding circumstances. To say that a small farm in the middle of a wealthy landowner's estate is to be valued without reference to the fact that he will probably be willing to pay a large price, but solely with reference to its ordinary agricultural value, seems to me absurd. If the landowner does not at the moment buy, land brokers or speculators will give more than its purely agricultural value with a view to reselling it at a profit to the landowner.'

([1914] 3 KB 466 at 472 **case 8 paras 2 and 3**)

Pickford LJ specifically rejected the concept that the valuation exercised postulates how a property would be sold at auction:

'It is not uncommon that where a person or public body is known to be very anxious to purchase a price of property, speculators will run the price up on the chance of buying it at a price which the person or body is not prepared at that moment to go, hoping that their needs will eventually oblige them to buy from the speculator at a profit. I do not think that the effect of the needs of a probable purchaser can be confined to the amount of the one bid which will take the offer above the bare dwelling-house value. The valuer has come to the conclusion that under all the circumstances the amount this house might be expected to realise in the open market would be £1,000, an amount, it is to be noticed, less than the trustees were in fact willing to give. I do not see that he has applied any wrong principle, and I do not see my way to say that he and Scrutton J, who also had evidence before him and came to the same conclusion, were wrong. He would have applied a wrong principle if he had said that he was limited to the dwelling-house price, plus one bid of a small sum by the trustees.'

([1914] 3 KB 466 at 480 **case 8 para 28**)

The decision in this case also gives judicial guidance on the approach to be taken in valuation to the concept of 'a willing seller'. This is a formulation used in the definition of market value for increment value duty.

It is also a formulation used in US tax legislation. The words 'a willing seller' do not appear in the current statutory provisions for valuation for the purposes of capital gains tax, inheritance tax, stamp duty or income tax. The view taken by some writers, including the present writer, is that this concept is not part of the principle of valuation that is to be applied in determining a value for the purposes of the taxes that are currently imposed. This is in contrast to the view expressed by HMRC Share Valuation, being most clearly expressed by Harry Booth, former controller of Inland Revenue Share Valuation in his book *Practical Share Valuation*. For Harry Booth, the concept of 'a willing seller' is inherent in the concept of valuation.

The approach taken by Cozens-Hardy MR to the concept in relation to FA 1910 increment land duty is:

> 'The other point is as to the meaning of "willing seller". It is urged that Mrs Buchanan never was a willing seller; that she never wished to vacate the house in which she was living, and that it was only after pressure from the trustees that she agreed to sell for £1,000. I am disposed to think that a willing seller is a person who is a free agent and cannot be required by virtue of compulsory powers to sell, and that Mrs Buchanan was a willing seller when, in 1910, she voluntarily agreed to accept £1,000. If, however, contrary to my view, she was not a willing seller, the problem still remains, for the existence of a willing seller, whether Mrs Buchanan or not, must be assumed for the purpose of the section.'
>
> ([1914] 3 KB 466 at 472 **case 8 para 4**)

Swinfen Eady LJ saw it in these terms:

> 'A sale by a willing seller is distinguished from a sale which is made by reason of compulsory powers, where the vendor frequently obtains an addition to the price by reason of being under compulsion to sell. It does not mean a sale by a person willing to sell his property without reserve for any price he can obtain. Mrs Buchanan was a willing seller when she accepted £1,000. The fact that she was persuaded or induced to agree voluntarily to sell at that price did not make her any the less a willing seller. There was no evidence of any compulsion; there was friendly bargaining, some discussion, some haggling about price, and then an agreement come to. This is the normal course of most private contract sales. She was none the less a willing seller because she had not previously put the property into the hands of an agent for sale. She was willing to sell at a price, she was offered a price, less than the maximum which the intending purchasers were willing to give, and she took it.'
>
> ([1914] 3 KB 466 at 476 **case 8 para 15**)

Judgement

References, example '(pg472)', are to [1914] 3 KB 466.

1 **COZENS-HARDY MR** (28 May): This appeal – for I take the two as really one appeal – raises an important question under s25 of the Finance Act of 1910. That section provides that the 'gross value' of land means the amount which the fee simple of the land if sold at the time in the 'open market' by a 'willing seller' in its then condition (subject to certain deductions) might be expected to realise. The facts are not in dispute. Mrs Buchanan was owner and occupier of No 83, Durnford Street, East Stonehouse, having purchased it in 1902 for £700. In September 1910 she sold it to Clay and others for £1000. The purchasers were the trustees of a nurses' home, No 84, who wanted the house for the purpose of extending their home. In 1908 they had offered Mrs Buchanan £850, which she declined. Negotiations were resumed in 1910, and after some bargaining she agreed to sell for £1000. The trustees would have been prepared to give £1100. Regarding No 83 solely as a residence for private occupation, its value was not more than £750. The referee found the gross value as on 30 April 1909 to be £1000, and Scrutton J has upheld that view. The contention on the part of the Crown is that the gross value is £750 only.

2 The contest before us has turned mainly upon the words 'open market' and 'willing seller.' I think the view ultimately taken by counsel for the appellants, and also for the respondents, as to the meaning of 'open market' is correct. 'Open market' includes a sale by auction, but it is not confined to that. It would include property publicly announced in the usual way by insertion in the lists of house agents. But it does not necessarily involve the idea of a sale without reserve. I can see no ground for excluding from consideration the fact that the property is so situate that to one or more persons it presents greater attractions than to anybody else. The house or the land may immediately adjoin one or more landowners likely to offer more than the property would be worth to anybody else. This is a fact which cannot be disregarded. The Solicitor-General ultimately admitted that some regard must be had to the fact. But he urged that we ought only to consider first what an outside purchaser would give, say £750, and then allow the adjoining owner one more bid – in other words, something very small beyond the £750. We had our attention called to the valuable judgments of Lords Johnston and Salvesen in the recent Scotch case of *Glass v Commissioners of Inland Revenue*, and I accept their view of the meaning of the words 'open market.' The price at which the property was sold in 1910 is not the test of the gross value in April 1909, but it cannot be disregarded.

3 I adopt the language of Scrutton J: 'He' (the referee) 'was right in this, not because of the sale for £1000, but because of the reasonable expectation that a willing seller could get £1000 or more from the nurses' home.' An 'open market' sale of property 'in its then condition' presupposes a knowledge of its situation with all surrounding circumstances. To say that a small farm in the middle of a wealthy landowner's estate is to be valued without reference to the fact that he will

probably be willing to pay a large price, but solely with reference to its ordinary agricultural value, seems to me absurd. If the landowner does not at the moment buy, land brokers or speculators will give more than its purely agricultural value with a view to reselling it at a profit to the landowner. It is for the referee, whose competence is not challenged, to arrive at a figure. The Court ought not, as a rule, to review his decision on what is in truth a question of fact. I see no ground for supposing that there has been any misdirection in point of law. *(pg472)*

4 The other point is as to the meaning of 'willing seller.' It is urged that Mrs Buchanan never was a willing seller; that she never wished to vacate the house in which she was living, and that it was only after pressure from the trustees that she agreed to sell for £1000. I am disposed to think that a willing seller is a person who is a free agent and cannot be required by virtue of compulsory powers to sell, and that Mrs Buchanan was a willing seller when, in 1910, she voluntarily agreed to accept £1000. If, however, contrary to my view, she was not a willing seller, the problem still remains, for the existence of a willing seller, whether Mrs Buchanan or not, must be assumed for the purpose of the section.

5 In my opinion, the judgment of Scrutton J, affirming the decision of the referee, was correct, and this appeal must be dismissed with costs.

6 SWINFEN EADY LJ: This is an appeal from the decision of Scrutton J reported in [1914] 1 KB 339, where the facts are fully stated.

7 The Solicitor-General has contended that in arriving at 'the gross value of land,' pursuant to the provisions of s25, sub-s 1, of the Finance (1909–10) Act 1910, and in ascertaining the amount 'which the fee simple of the land, if sold at the time in the open market by a willing seller . … might be expected to realise,' we must disregard the fact that the property has a special value to one particular person, who would be willing to give substantially more than any other person, and also disregard the influence upon the market which the knowledge of this fact would create.

8 He further urged that at most there could only be allowed some slight increase on what he contended would otherwise be the market value of the land, so as to represent the amount of one bid at an auction which the particular person would probably make over all other persons to secure the property – say £50 extra, or the like.

9 The house in question, 83 Durnford Street, East Stonehouse, Plymouth, has been valued in the provisional valuation as on 30 April 1909 as altered and settled by the referee, at £1000 *(pg473)* and, deducting £800, the assessable site value is fixed at £200. On the occasion of the sale, the amounts as altered and settled by the referee are the same, so that no increment duty is payable.

10 The appellants claim that the original amount in the provisional valuation, namely, £750, should be restored, as that figure represented the market value of the house irrespective of the wants of the nurses' home next door. On 18 September 1908 Mrs Buchanan refused an offer of £850 made by the nurses' home for the house. On 2 March 1910 it was reported to the nurses' home that Mrs Buchanan would not take less for the house than £1100, and in August 1910 they determined to offer £1100, if it could not be obtained for less; but on 29 September 1910, it was agreed to be sold by Mrs Buchanan to Dr Clay and others on behalf of the nurses' home for £1000.

11 The referee found that the value, both on 30 April 1909 and on 29 September 1910, was £1000. This was less than the nurses' home had determined to give, and was prepared to offer, if they could not obtain the property cheaper. The house could not be rebuilt so as to give the same accommodation as at present for less than £1200. The learned judge below found as a fact that 'as a private residence, and having regard to the other houses offering, No 83 was not worth more than £750 which was the utmost such people could be expected to give,' but that 'to the nurses' home, which owned the neighbouring house, and needed further accommodation near, No 83 was so adjacent, and offered such suitable accommodation, that it would be advantageous to them to pay at least £1000, probably more, for it, and the £1000 actually paid was a profitable business transaction to the nurses' home and not a fancy price. It was not worth any one else's while to pay a sum substantially larger than £750, except in the hope of reselling to the nurses' home, to which the house was obviously of considerable value and a likely subject of purchase.' This is prefaced by this line: 'After listening to the evidence I find the following facts,' and then he states what I have read.

12 The Solicitor-General contended that as the section said 'if *(pg474)* sold at the time in the open market,' the price which only one particular buyer was prepared to pay must be excluded from all consideration; it might possibly be a fancy price which had no relation to market price; that a reference to open market shewed that the statute referred to a current market price of land, a price which one or more valuers might determine to be the market value of the land.

13 In my opinion this contention is unsound. A value, ascertained by reference to the amount obtainable in an open market, shews an intention to include every possible purchaser. The market is to be the open market, as distinguished from an offer to a limited class only, such as the members of the family. The market is not necessarily an auction sale. The section means such amount as the land might be expected to realise if offered under conditions enabling every person desirous of purchasing to come in and make an offer, and if proper steps were taken to advertise the property and let all likely purchasers know that the land is in the market for sale. It scarcely needed evidence to inform us – it is common knowledge – that when the fact becomes known that one probable buyer desires to obtain any property that raises the general price or value of the thing in the market. Not only is the probable buyer a competitor in the market, but other persons, such as property brokers, compete in the market for what they know another person wants, with a view to a resale to him at an enhanced price, so as to realise a profit. A vendor desiring to realise any land would ordinarily give full publicity to all facts within his knowledge likely to enhance the price. The local conditions and requirements, the advantages of the situation of the property for any particular purpose, and the names of the persons who are probable buyers, would ordinarily be matters of local knowledge to the property brokers and agents and speculators. In order to arrive at the amount which land might be 'expected to realise,' all these matters ought to be taken into consideration. 'Expected' refers to the expectations of properly qualified persons who have taken pains to inform themselves of all the particulars ascertainable about the property, and its capabilities, the demand for it, and the likely buyers. The price actually realised by a sale *(pg475)* is not necessarily the price which it might have been expected to realise, but if the valuer be competent, and has taken proper pains in the matter, there ought to be little difference between the two figures. The fact that No 83 had a potential value, by reason of its proximity to the nurses' home, and the very rapid increase of the work of that institution, pointing to a necessary extension at an early date, ought properly to be taken into consideration in arriving at the value it might be expected to realise. The Solicitor-General urged that after the addition of the new wing to the old building, which followed upon the refusal by Mrs Buchanan of the offer of £850 on 18 September 1908, this element of value disappeared. This is not the case in fact. The report of the institution for 1908–9 shows the leaps and bounds by which the work was increasing, and points to a further extension of premises being necessary in the near future, and this extension indeed became extremely urgent in the following year.

14 It was then urged by the Solicitor-General that if the probability of this special buyer purchasing, above the price, which but for his needs would have been the market price, could be taken into consideration at all, then only one further point or bid could be allowed, and it must be assumed that this special buyer would have become the purchaser upon making this one extra bid. Such an assumption would ordinarily be quite erroneous. The knowledge of the special need would affect the market price, and others would join in competing for the property with a view of obtaining it at a price less than that at which the opinion would be formed that it would be worth the while of the special buyer to purchase.

15 It was then urged that the vendor in the present case was not a willing seller, as she had to be persuaded to sell at the sum of £1000. It appeared, however, that her son-in-law was consumptive, and that his wife did not think Durnford Street quite the right place for him to live in, and that was one motive for her yielding to the solicitations of Dr Clay on behalf of the home. She was a willing seller at £1000. A sale by a willing seller is distinguished from a sale which is made by reason of compulsory powers, where the vendor frequently obtains an addition *(pg476)* to the price by reason of being under compulsion to sell. It does not mean a sale by a person willing to sell his property without reserve for any price he can obtain. Mrs Buchanan was a willing seller when she accepted £1000. The fact that she was persuaded or induced to agree voluntarily to sell at that price did not make her any the less a willing seller. There was no evidence of any compulsion; there was friendly bargaining, some discussion, some higgling about price, and then an agreement come to. This is the normal course of most private contract sales. She was none the less a willing seller because she had not previously put the property into the hands of an agent for sale. She was willing to sell at a price, she was offered a price, less than the maximum which the intending purchasers were willing to give, and she took it.

16   There was a considerable body of evidence reheard before Scrutton J, and the sum of £1000 was arrived at because that was the sum which the land if sold at the time in the open market in its then condition might have been expected to realise. It happens also to be the price actually realised, but the figure was not arrived at on the latter ground.

17   I agree with the judgment of Scrutton J, and also with the reasons given in the judgments of Lord Johnston and Lord Salvesen in the Court of Session in the case of *Glass v Commissioners of Inland Revenue*, of which shorthand notes have been furnished to us.

18   I think this appeal should be dismissed.

19   **PICKFORD LJ:** This was an appeal from Scrutton J relating to the gross value of premises in Stonehouse, under the Finance (1909–10) Act 1910. The facts are fully stated in the judgment of the learned judge, and it is only necessary here to state them shortly.

20   The premises were known as No 83, Durnford Street, and were next to premises used as a nurses' home at No 84 in the same street. The house was bought by the respondent in 1902 for £700, and its value as a private dwelling-house only was £750. The trustees of the nurses' home, however, had been for *(pg477)* some years anxious to buy No 83 for the purpose of extending their home, and in 1908 had offered £850. for it, which the respondent refused. They then built a new wing to the home on other land adjoining No 83, but they still wished to buy that house, and negotiations were renewed between them and the respondent. She was not anxious to leave the house, but after some persuasion from the trustees was induced to sell it to them at £1000. The trustees were willing at that time to have given £1100 if necessary. Whether they would have given still more does not appear. Upon this state of facts, the referee and Scrutton J fixed the gross value at £1000. The appellants contended that the gross value should be £750, and a small sum which I will mention later.

21   The case turns upon the application to the facts of s25, sub-s 1, of the Finance Act 1910, by which the gross value is defined as 'the amount which the fee simple of the land, if sold at the time in the open market by a willing seller … might be expected to realise.'

22 It was argued for the appellants that the respondent was not a willing seller as she was only tempted by an exceptionally high offer, and that the market value to a willing seller was not to be measured by the price given by the trustees of the nurses' home in consequence of their special wants.

23 I think that 'sold in the open market' means sold in such a way that any one wishing to purchase was able to do so, eg by auction or by putting the house into the hands of an agent to sell, and I think a willing seller means one who is prepared to sell, provided a fair price is obtained under all the circumstances of the case. I do not think it means only a seller who is prepared to sell at any price and on any terms, and who is actually at the time wishing to sell. In other words, I do not think it means an anxious seller.

24 In this case the house was only worth £750 if it were sold as a dwelling-house, and, unless there were some other elements to be considered, that would be its value. But there was another element here, ie the fact that the trustees of the nurses' home wished to buy the house, and were willing to give more than its value as a dwelling-house for it, although it was *(pg478)* not known to what price they would go, and the exact amount of knowledge of their intentions amongst those persons who were likely to buy houses was not clearly shown.

25 It is, however, impossible to suppose that the wish of the trustees to buy the house was entirely unknown to those interested in property sales, and if the sale took place, either by auction or through an agent, the willing seller would be careful to see that that fact was made known.

26 I assume that the gross value is not to be measured necessarily by the price given by a buyer who is peculiarly in need of the particular piece of property, but it seems to me clear that the fact of there being such a person in the market must have an influence on the value in the open market. I think the position is well expressed by Lord Johnston in the Scotch case of *Glass v Commissioners of Inland Revenue* to which we were referred. The learned judge says: 'Where a public body is expected in the near future to require certain property, there are generally found, and must be assumed to be, people who are prepared to trade on that fact, and prepared to bid up to a point to which they think they may safely go and leave themselves a chance of profit in turning over the property to the Commissioners. That point will doubtless be below the value to the public body, but where, as here, the public body has no compulsory powers, all depends upon how near a certainty it is that the Commissioners must acquire, if indeed the acquisition by the public body of compulsory powers or the adoption of some other course of obtaining their end is feasible. The phrase 'willing seller' is not to receive a restricted meaning. He is only hypothetically willing if he gets the advantage of all surrounding circumstances, and this is implied in the further expression 'in its then condition'. Substituting the trustees of the nurses' home for Commissioners, I think this applies to this case.

27 It is not denied by the appellants that the wish of the trustees to buy the house is a fact to be considered, but it is said that the only effect to be given to it is that a small sum is to be added to the value of £750 to represent a final bid *(pg479)* made by the trustees in order to acquire the property. This seems to me to be a fallacy, and to ignore what is common experience. It assumes that the dwelling-house value, £750, having been reached, everybody except the trustees will decline to make any further offer, and allow the trustees to become the purchasers by a single offer, which exceeds that amount in however small a degree.

28 It is not uncommon that where a person or public body is known to be very anxious to purchase a piece of property, speculators will run the price up on the chance of buying it at a price to which the person or body is not prepared at that moment to go, hoping that their needs will eventually oblige them to buy from the speculator at a profit. I do not think that the effect of the needs of a probable purchaser can be confined to the amount of the one bid which will take the offer above the bare dwelling-house value. The effect on the market of such a probable purchaser is a matter to be estimated by the referee. I agree with Scrutton J that the referee is not bound to take the actual figure given, and should not do so arbitrarily, but should consider all the circumstances and estimate what he considers the value in the open market. Here he has done so, and has come to the conclusion that under all the circumstances the amount this house might be expected to realise in the open market would be £1000, an amount, it is to be noticed, less than the trustees were in fact willing to give if compelled. I do not see that he has applied any wrong principle, and I do not see my way to say that he and Scrutton J, who also had evidence before him and came to the same conclusion, were wrong. He would have applied a wrong principle if he had said that he was limited to the dwelling-house price, plus one bid of a small sum by the trustees.

29 The appeal should be dismissed. *(pg480)*

Case 9
Glass v IRC

[1915] CS 449

High Court

20 March 1914, 6 February 1915

The valuer must consider alternative uses.

Land value duty (under FA 1910, s 25) fell to be charged on the value of two farms, Easter and Wester Feal.

The relevant tribunal declared the total value as at 30 April 1909 to be:

Total value	£3,379.00
From which deducting for value of buildings, etc	675.00
Giving an original assessable site value of	£2,704.00

Robert Glass valued the two farms as:

Total value	£5,000.00
From which deducting for value of buildings, etc	675.00
Giving an original assessable site value of	£4,325.00

FA 1910, s 25(1) required the value to be that which the property might have been expected to realise at 30 April 1909, if sold (1) 'in the open market'; (2) 'by a willing seller'; and (3) 'in its then condition'.

Lord Johnston directed the tribunal to reconsider the valuation, explaining the effect of the statutory provision in the following words:

'... I think that the referee must assume a little of the hypothetical spirit of the Act, and if he postulates an open market and a willing seller where there are none, must also allow for the competing buyer where the circumstances reasonably admit of the hypothesis ... I think the referee is mistaken in assuming that open market necessarily means sale by auction. A sale takes place in open market if the subject is put on the market and the best offer taken, however made. But he is further mistaken, I think, in that he has forgotten that, where a public body is expected in the near future to require certain property, there are generally found, and must be assumed to be, people who are prepared to trade on that fact, and prepared to bid up to a point to which they think they may safely go and leave themselves a chance of profit in turning over the property to the public body ...

I am clear, therefore, that the referee, instead of assuming that the Kirkcaldy Commissioners would be the sole offerers for the property if placed on the market, or the sole bidders at the hypothetical auction, has got to assume that there will be competition, the weight of which will depend on the prospect of the Commissioners actually requiring the lands. For if they do require them they must take care that they prevail in that competition. The problem for a valuator is therefore not an easy one ... I have no doubt the referee here will apply himself to the question, as it is now explained to him, with the conspicuous fairness which is manifest in his explanation of the course which he himself formerly took, and with the ability he always displays.'

([1915] CS 449 at 456/457 **case 9 paras 8 and 9**)

In the following judgement, Lord Salvesen identifies the information which was available at the valuation date as to the intention of a water company to purchase the land some two years later ([1915] CS 449 at 458 (**case 9, para 12**)). He said:

'These being the facts, I am clearly of opinion that the contingency, and by no means remote contingency, of the Commissioners desiring to purchase the lands, gave them an element of value in excess of what they possessed for merely agricultural purposes.'

(at 458 **case 9 para 13**)

In the context of a share valuation, it is necessary to consider whether the value would be increased by another use. This is most likely to be of relevance in valuing a majority shareholding, as the shareholder alone could decide to conduct the company's business in a different way, perhaps using the company's property for another purpose.

Judgement

References, example '(pg453)', are to [1915] CS 449.

1 **LORD JOHNSTON:** The referee has had to value the farms of Easter and Wester Feal, in the county of Kinross, as at the passing of the Finance (1909–10) Act 1910 (30 April 1909), in order to fix their original assessable site value.

He has found the original total value to be	£3379.00
from which deducting for value of buildings, &c	675.00
gives an original assessable site value of	£2704.00
The appellant, who is the owner of Easter and Wester Feal, maintains that the original total value was	£5000.00
which would have given, deducting value of buildings, &c, amounting to	675.00
an original assessable site value of	£4325.00

He supports this contention by the fact that in October 1911 the lands actually sold for £5000, and by the allegation that nothing had occurred between 30 April 1909 and October 1911 to affect the value of the lands.

2 The facts are that in December 1908 the Kirkcaldy and Dysart Water Commissioners, finding it necessary in order to protect the purity of their water supply drawn from the south side of the Lomond Hills, in the county of Kinross, sought to obtain power to acquire lands within the catchment area of their reservoirs. They did not seek to obtain compulsory powers. They contented themselves with obtaining power to acquire by agreement and to hold lands for the above purpose, and to raise the necessary capital. I think that it is desirable to note the precise position in which they were placed by their Provisional Order of 1908. This proceeds on the preamble, *inter alia*; – – 'And whereas it is expedient that the Commissioners should be authorised by agreement to acquire and hold any lands within the drainage area of the waterworks of the Commissioners for the purpose of securing the purity of the water in such drainage area, and of protecting such water against pollution, nuisance, encroachment, or injury'; and enacts, section 4, – 'The Commissioners may hold any lands acquired by them for the purposes of their waterworks, and may also by agreement acquire by purchase, feu, lease, or otherwise, and hold the lands and estates of Drumain and Holl, in the parish of Leslie and county of Fife, so far as lying within the drainage area, and any other lands within the drainage area, or take servitudes or restrictions in or over any such lands which may in their opinion be necessary or desirable for the purpose of securing the purity of the water in the *(pg453)* drainage area, and of protecting their water supply against pollution, nuisance, encroachment, or injury.' Easter and Wester Feal are admittedly within the Commissioners' catchment area.

3 The referee was of opinion that the appellant's contention was not well founded, inasmuch as he himself held 'that the total value of the property at the former date is as stated above, viz, £3379, and that the consideration on the subsequent sale cannot be taken as a true standard of value, and, under section 25(1) and (3) of the Act, is in excess of the value that the property might be expected to realise "if sold at the time in the open market by a willing seller in its then condition."'

4 Had the appellant continued to maintain his contention that the original total value must be ascertained on the basis of the sale for £5000 in October

1911, I could not have sustained that contention. But at the discussion before this Court the appellant took lower ground and contented himself with maintaining that the subjects in question had in 1908–9, and particularly at 30 April 1909, an element of value which the referee had refused to take into consideration. When this was made clear, the learned Solicitor-General practically admitted that he could not support the referee's determination. The case is a very exceptional one, and quite novel, and I am not surprised that the referee has fallen somewhat into error. But in justice to the appellant, I am satisfied that the case must be sent back to the referee to inform himself of certain matters which he has considered unnecessary or irrelevant, and to re-value the subjects in the light of these facts.

5 The appellant, when the case was first before us, asked that he might be allowed certain proof which he thought necessary in order to inform us of the facts which the referee ought to have had before him, and which whoever is to value the subjects in question in terms of the Act must have before him – whether this Court, the referee, or someone else. We thought that, before we could dispose of the question thus disclosed, we should know rather more of what was in the mind of the referee, and accordingly certain questions were addressed to him to be answered for the information of the Court. We have been much advantaged by the referee's clear and concise answers to our questions. I shall only refer to three of these questions and the answers. – [His Lordship then narrated the questions and answers, quoted supra, p 452]. From these answers it appears, I think, that the referee has misconceived the situation presented to him. He is to value the property at the value it might have been expected to realise at 30 April 1909, if sold (1) 'in the open market'; (2) 'by a willing seller'; and (3) 'in its then condition' – (Finance Act, section 25 (1)). The first half of answer 6 is quite sound. It is in the second part of that answer that I think the referee has misled himself. The word 'normal' was used in question 4 with a definite intention, viz: – to indicate the value of the land, assuming that there were no exceptional surrounding circumstances; in point of fact in this case such value would have been confined to pure agricultural or more properly pastoral value. But the term 'normal' was used as in contradistinction to 'market value in its then condition.'

6 The present question must, I think, be distinguished from cases of *(pg454)* compensation where land is taken under compulsory powers. In the latter case it is recognised as a guiding rule that the value to the buyer is not the **de quo**, but the value to the seller, and that therefore the seller does not get a fortuitous advantage from the passing of the Act conferring the powers. But, though the seller cannot say 'your Act ties you, the buyer, to take my lands or to abandon your scheme, and therefore the value is its value to you, the buyer, and your necessity is my opportunity,' it is at the same time recognised as a further rule, that the passing of the Act conferring the powers is not to deprive the seller of any adventitious advantages which its position, its configuration, existing surroundings, and similar considerations give to his property. Two instructive cases on this subject in England were quoted to us, *Gough's* case, and *Lucas's* case. These illustrate the distinction between the possibility which attaches to certain lands prior to and independently of their being scheduled to be taken under compulsory powers and the realised possibility, as I think it has been called, which attaches to the same lands after the empowering Act is passed.

7 Now the present case is, for two reasons, not *in pari casu* with one where lands are taken under compulsory powers. In the first place the Water Commissioners have not got compulsory powers. They have avoided the expense and the difficulties which they must have encountered had they gone to Parliament for compulsory powers, and they have, as a counter to this advantage, placed themselves in the position of having to bargain for what lands they require with those who are able fairly to gauge the Commissioners' necessity and are entitled to make use of their knowledge. And, in the second place, the problem for the referee under the statute of 1910 is a totally different one from that presented to the arbiter under a compulsory taking. What the former has to do is to estimate and fix the value in the open market of the lands in question at a specified date, viz, 30 April 1909, in order that this value may become the datum for ascertaining for the purpose of taxation the increase, if any, in value on subsequent transactions. If there is a cause which operates on the value at the date of the original valuation, and which continues to operate in an increased degree at the date of the first subsequent transaction, it would be manifestly unfair to take it into consideration in the latter case and not in the former. So it seems to me that if the potentiality at the date of the original valuation has become not merely an increased potentiality, but has ripened into an actuality at the date of the subsequent transaction, it would be manifestly unfair to exclude it from consideration in the original valuation, when automatically it enters into and even dominates the actual value on the subsequent transaction. Let me take the case in question. Apart from the Provisional Order, it had by 1908 – and *a fortiori* after the Commissioners had obtained their Provisional Order – become common knowledge of the district that the Commissioners might sooner or later require to obtain possession of the lands of Feal by agreement, or else would have to obtain compulsory powers, or hit upon *(pg455)* some scheme costing money to obviate the necessity of acquiring Feal. Suppose that they had made no move, but that after the lapse of five years it came to be understood that they must immediately acquire the lands, I cannot doubt that in that case, had they then been revaluing on the death of the proprietor, the Inland Revenue authorities would have been astute to find an increment of value in the increased potentiality attaching to the lands. Why, then, should the original though lesser potentiality not be valued at the earlier date of 1909. I can see no reason whatever. And no difference is occasioned by the fact that original potentiality is in the case in question brought into comparison not merely with an enhanced potentiality, but with a realised possibility.

8 The referee has in theory regarded the possibility attaching to the lands in 1909 as something affecting the value. In practice he has given to it no effect, but has admittedly stuck to agricultural value, because apparently he thinks that, if the subjects had been sold in open market, the Commissioners would have had it all their own way, and would have had no competitor, except, possibly, at agricultural value. I am unable to agree with him. The same might have been said with equal force in all cases of statutory valuation for rating or otherwise. They all perforce involve something of the hypothetical and unreal – and none more than valuations under the Finance Act 1910. In order to do justice to the appellant, I think that the referee must assume a little of the hypothetical spirit of the Act, and if he postulates an open market and a willing seller where there are none, must also allow for the competing buyer where the circumstances reasonably admit of the hypothesis. He would do so fast enough if the subject had any potential feuing value, though no hypothetical feuar was in sight. I think the referee is mistaken in assuming that open market necessarily means sale by auction. A sale takes place in open market if the subject is put on the market and the best offer taken, however made. But he is further mistaken, I think, in that he has forgotten that, where a public body is expected in the near future to require certain property, there are generally found, and must be assumed to be, people who are prepared to trade on that fact, and prepared to bid up to a point to which they think they may safely go and leave themselves a chance of profit in turning over the property to the public body. That point will doubtless be below the value to the public body, but where, as here, the public body has no compulsory powers, all depends upon how near a certainty it is that the Commissioners must acquire. In fact if the acquisition by the public body has become a practical certainty, the margin depends upon what it would cost the public body to obtain compulsory powers, or to adopt some other course of attaining their end, if such is feasible. The phrase 'willing seller' is not to receive a restricted meaning. He is only hypothetically willing if he gets the advantage of all surrounding circumstances, and this is implied in the further expression 'in its then condition.'

9 I am clear, therefore, that the referee, instead of assuming that the Kirkcaldy Commissioners would be the sole offerers for the property if placed on the market, or the sole bidders at the hypothetical auction, has got to assume that there will be competition, the weight of which will *(pg456)* depend on the prospect of the Commissioners actually requiring the lands. For if they do require them they must take care that they prevail in that competition. The problem for a valuator is therefore not an easy one, but it is one of a class with which valuators are constantly being faced. In many respects it is much akin to a case of land adjoining a large work or to a case of prospective feuing value, as to which I have never found valuators make any difficulty, though I have often found them arrive at very different results. I have no doubt the referee here will apply himself to the question, as it is now explained to him, with the conspicuous fairness which is manifest in his explanation of the course which he himself formerly took, and with the ability he always displays.

10 But there is still another point which requires consideration. Before the referee the appellant asked a proof of a number of matters which he considered had an important bearing on the question which had to be determined. Acting on instructions, the referee refused to allow proof. These instructions interfere with the independence of the referee, and I think your Lordships agree with me, have had in this case a most unfortunate result. If they are to be complied with, they prevent the referee from informing himself of facts which it may be necessary for him and for us to know. Fortunately they are not binding on this Court. The appellant was entitled to bring these facts before the referee, and a great deal of the time of the Court has been wasted and expense to the parties has been caused in consequence of their not being brought before him, and through him before the Court. When the case first came before the Court the appellant craved leave to lead evidence on four points as follows: – [His Lordship narrated the four points quoted *supra*, p 451]. After the referee had been communicated with by the Court, the appellant tabled a minute (No 14 of process) in which he specifically condescended on the circumstances which he was prepared to prove in support of the first of these heads, and the respondents found it expedient to tender an unqualified admission of the whole of these facts. Proof, therefore, on head 1 above is no longer necessary. The other three heads remain to be considered. I do not think that we can exclude proof on any of them. I think that such proof is necessary to ensure that the individual appellant will get justice in this revenue proceeding. These matters bear materially upon the valuation which the referee has got to make, but they are not that valuation itself. I therefore think that we must authorise and instruct the referee to take further proof. I should have been inclined to limit a proof to these heads. But I understand that your Lordships think that the allowance had better be general, relying on the parties to use the opportunity with discretion, and in this I readily acquiesce. The referee will take the proof under no restriction. He takes it under the authority of this Court. But it must be understood that the case is an exceptional case.

11 LORD SALVESEN: The question in this case is whether the referee, in fixing the market value of the appellant's farm Easter and Wester Feal, under section 25(1) of the Finance Act 1910 was entitled to leave out of view the circumstance that these lands might have a special value as *(pg457)* at 30 April 1909, at which the valuation fell to be fixed, by reason of their special suitability for the purposes of the Kirkcaldy Water Commissioners, who have in fact since acquired them. That the referee did in fact value the farm as an agricultural subject only, and not as possessing any special value, is, I think, apparent from his answers to the queries framed by this Court. In answer to the sixth query he points out that the Commissioners did not purchase in the open market but by private bargain; and adds, 'Had they purchased in the open market, by auction for instance, they would have been in the position of purchasing these lands at an enhanced bid of a few pounds over another bidder.' He has apparently assumed that no other bidder would have offered more than the fair agricultural value of the subjects, and that the Commissioners by making a slightly higher bid would have been able to secure the lands for their own purposes.

12 In my opinion this assumption and the conclusion in law at which the referee arrived are alike unwarranted. It is true that the valuation is to proceed as if it were made at the statutory date, which was more than two years before the actual sale to the Commissioners; but the probability of the Commissioners requiring the land for the purposes of their undertaking was known long before then. In December 1908 they had actually obtained a provisional order under which they were authorised to acquire any lands within their drainage area for the purpose of securing the purity of the water and of protecting it against pollution. They had already acquired the adjoining estate of Drumain and Holl by purchase for that purpose, and the appellant's farm, being contiguous, formed the next most desirable area to acquire. It was reasonably certain that within no very long space of time the Commissioners would be forced to acquire it in order to preserve the purity of the water in their reservoirs. The Local Government Board had, so far back as 1904, called attention to the pollution caused by agricultural operations, and particularly by the pasturing of horses and cattle in the catchment areas. The Commissioners had been advised at that time that the only way to secure the purity of the water was to discontinue the grazing of cattle altogether, and this they could only effect by getting the land into their own hands, as the proprietor could not be restrained by any legal action from putting his land to an ordinary agricultural use. The fact that the Commissioners only obtained powers of private purchase and not compulsory powers was far from being a disadvantage to the proprietor. Indeed, it put him in a stronger position, because it enabled him to dictate his own terms should the Commissioners find it necessary, in order to secure the purity of the water they supplied, to discontinue the grazing of cattle and horses. Under such circumstances the Commissioners would be in the dilemma of having either to concede the owner's terms, or to construct purification works, or to apply for compulsory powers. Either of the last two alternatives would, of course, involve considerable cost.

13 These being the facts, I am clearly of opinion that the contingency, and by no means remote contingency, of the Commissioners desiring to purchase the lands, gave them an element of value in excess of what they possessed for merely agricultural purposes. Such an element of value is *(pg458)* strictly analogous to the value which an estate possesses because of its possessing natural advantages for supplying a district or area with water; and in two reported cases in England (*Gough* and *Lucas*, it has been decided that the adaptability of a site for the purposes of a reservoir or for the supply of water to a populous area ought to be taken into account in assessing compensation, and that although it is not shown that the land could be similarly used by any other local authority than the one which had obtained compulsory powers. I think the case here is *a fortiori*. If this farm had been advertised for sale as at 30 April 1909, I cannot doubt that a special point would have been made of the probability of its being required by the Kirkcaldy Water Commissioners at no distant date, and of the fact that they possessed only powers of purchase by private agreement. I think it highly probable that in these circumstances more than one speculator would have come forward with offers substantially in excess of the agricultural value, in the reasonable expectation that they would sooner or later find a purchaser in the Water Commissioners at a figure that would yield them a profit on the transaction. The case appears to me to be exactly in the same position as that figured by Mr Justice Bray in the case of *Lucas*, of land lying in the neighbourhood of existing public works which there was reason to anticipate would soon require additional land for extension; or, indeed, of any land lying in the neighbourhood of a populous place which it might be expected would be taken up by builders for feuing purposes. Mr Constable, in his argument for the appellant, did not contend that the referee was bound to value the lands at the figure at which they were afterwards sold; and the Solicitor-General in the end appeared to me to concede that the contingency I have referred to did form an element of value which the referee was bound to take into account. As he has not done so I think we must remit back to him to ascertain the amount of this enhanced value, and to add it to the agricultural value which he has already fixed. I have no doubt that he is very competent to do this, and will act with discretion and fairness in carrying out his valuation.

14 LORD CULLEN: The questions raised in this appeal are whether the referee has erred in law or in fact in fixing the total value of the lands of Feal, as at 30 April 1909, in terms of section 25 of the Finance (1909–10) Act 1910 at £3379. The definition of the statutory total value falling to be fixed is contained in subsection 3 of section 25. It hinges on the value of the lands as on a sale in open market by a willing seller at 30 April 1909.

15 The lands are agricultural lands of an ordinary character; and it is not contended by the appellant that the sum of £3379 fixed by the referee is below what may be called their normal value. It happens, however, that the lands adjoin reservoirs belonging to the Kirkcaldy and Dysart Waterworks Commissioners. Drainage pollution from them had been injurious to the water in the reservoirs, and in 1908 the Water *(pg459)* Commissioners obtained powers enabling them to acquire the lands by private agreement. The outcome of this was that in October 1911 the Commissioners bought the lands at the price of £5000, which was largely in excess of the amount at which the referee has fixed the total value thereof, as at 30 April 1909.

16 The need of the Water Commissioners to buy the lands for the protection of their reservoirs created a peculiar market in which the owner, being free to sell or not, was enabled to extract from the Commissioners an adventitious or exceptional price, reflecting the special value to them of the lands for the purposes of their undertaking. It is not now maintained by the appellant that this adventitious price of £5000 falls to be taken as ruling the statutory total value as at 30th April 1909, which value, as I have said, hinges on the open market value of the lands at that date as on a sale by a willing seller. The appellant maintained, however, that the known need of the Commissioners to buy the lands for the protection of their undertaking must be presumed to have enhanced, to some extent not stated by him, the price which could have been got for them on a sale in open market. *Esto* the normal market value was £3379 or thereby, it is possible, the appellant maintains, that some speculator might have paid more than that figure, with the object of making a profit through a subsequent re-sale to the Commissioners. This view seems to assume that if, on 30 April 1909, there had been an actual sale in open market by the owner as a willing seller, the Commissioners would not have taken advantage of the sale in order to buy, but would have stood aside and have allowed the lands to be bought by someone else, who would in consequence have been enabled to exploit the special market created by the need of the Commissioners, and so to extract from them an enhanced and exceptional price. The Commissioners might have taken this prejudicial course. But it does not seem to me legitimate to assume that they would have done so. An estimate of the price obtainable for lands in the open market must proceed on the footing of people acting in the way which is in accordance with their interests. Now, on the facts before us, I do not think it can be said that the need of the Commissioners to buy the lands was a matter related to an indefinite future. It was a present realised need. They had obtained power to acquire the lands, and they did acquire them after bargaining with the owner, in October 1911. I think one must presume that if there had been an actual sale in open market on 30 April 1909 the Commissioners would, in accordance with their interests, have bought at such sale. If so, what would they presumably have had to pay in order to acquire the lands? In the special market represented by their need to buy the lands for the purposes of their undertaking there was no competition. The value of the lands for the purpose of protecting their reservoirs from pollution was peculiar to themselves. No one else was interested in that purpose. A speculator would have had no interest to compete with them. Hence the Commissioners, as presumable buyers at the supposed open market sale, would not, it seems to me, have needed to offer more than a price which was one point higher in the bidding than the amount representing the normal or general value of the lands to the general public. The *(pg460)* referee has proceeded on this footing in fixing the total value. I think his ratio is sound; but he ought to have added to the £3379 an amount representing the Commissioners' 'enhanced bid,' bringing up the total value to, say, £3400. The court pronounced the following interlocutor: -

> '... We recall *in hoc statu* the decision of the referee, and remit to him, in view of our opinions this day pronounced (a copy of which will be furnished to him), to allow the appellant to lead evidence on the subjects set forth in the first head of the minute for the appellant, No 12 of process, and also in the minute for the appellant, No 14 of process, so far as not admitted, and to the respondents a conjunct probation; for that purpose grants to each of the parties diligence for citing witnesses; and to re-value the property in the light of the evidence adduced, and to report to the Court said valuation.'

Case 10
Re Yenidje Tobacco Co Ltd

[1916–17] All ER Rep 1050

Court of Appeal

27, 28 July 1916

This case is one of a series of cases on a type of company that is referred to as a 'quasi-partnership'. This is the first valuation case to be considered by the courts on this basis. The concept of 'quasi-partnership' is used, and developed, in *Ebrahimi v Westbourne Galleries Ltd* [1972] 2 All ER 492 **case 31**, *Re Bird Precision Bellows Ltd* [1985] 3 All ER 523, CA **case 35**, *CVC v Demarco Almeida* [2002] UKPC 16, PC **case 45** and *Strahan v Wilcock* [2006] EWCA Civ 13, CA **case 49**. The last of these cases is particularly important in that the Court of Appeal gives a definition of a 'quasi-partnership' company.

In certain circumstances, the relationship between two or more individuals who are the directors and shareholders of the company is akin to the relationship between partners in a partnership. Where this is the case, the principle of a court order being made where it is 'just and equitable' applies equally to such a company as to a partnership. Where there is a quasi-partnership, the expectation is that a shareholding, and even a small minority shareholding, is valued as the appropriate fraction of the value of the entire company.

Marcus Weinberg and Louis Rothman established a trade as tobacco manufacturers, trading as a limited company, Yenidje Tobacco Co Ltd. From the incorporation of the company onwards, each held the same number of voting shares in the company.

There was a provision in the articles of association of the company that there shall be no casting vote, and that one director alone forms a quorum.

Mr Litiger was employed by the company as its factory manager. Louis Rothman considered he should be dismissed. Marcus Weinberg considered he should be retained. The matter was referred to an arbitrator. Counsel for Louis Rothman presented to the arbitrator the case for the dismissal of Mr Litiger. Counsel for Marcus Weinberg presented to the arbitrator the case for the retention of Mr Litiger. The presentation on this single point took 18 days. The arbitrator ruled that Litiger ought to be continued in employment. Louis Rothman refused to accept this decision.

Louis Rothman commenced court proceedings charging Marcus Weinberg with fraud in obtaining the agreement under which he, Rothman, sold his business to the company.

Marcus Weinberg brought a petition for the court to order that the company be wound up. The petition was opposed by Louis Rothman. Companies Act 1908, s 129 provided that the court has discretion to make an order winding up a company where it is 'just and equitable' so to do. (The provision is now found in Insolvency Act 1986, s 122(1)(g).)

In his leading judgement in the Court of Appeal, Lord Cozens-Hardy said:

> 'I have treated this matter as a partnership. Under the Partnership Act, of course, the application for a dissolution would take the form of an action. This is not a partnership strictly, it is not a case in which it can be dissolved by action. But ought not the same principles precisely to apply to a case like this, where, in substance, it is a partnership. It is a partnership taking the form or the guise of a private company ... I think that in a case like the present we are bound to say that circumstances which would justify the winding-up of a partnership by action are circumstances which should induce the court to exercise its jurisdiction under the "just and equitable" clause and to windup the company.'
>
> ([1916–17] All ER REP 1050 at 1052 **case 10 para 5**)

The finding of the Court of Appeal in *Re Yenidje Tobacco Co Ltd* was specifically approved by the House of Lords in a *Ebrahimi v Westbourne Galleries Ltd*. In his leading judgement, which was specifically approved by each of the other four judges, Lord Wilberforce stressed that the judgement in *Re Yenidje Tobacco Ltd* is to be applied wherever a company is correctly identified as 'quasi-partnership'. Lord Wilberforce said:

> 'In England, the leading authority is the Court of Appeal's decision in *re Yenidje Tobacco Co Ltd*. This was a case of two equal director shareholders with an arbitration provision in the articles between whom a state of deadlock came into existence. It has often been argued, and was so in this House, that its authority is limited to true deadlock cases. I could, in any case, not be persuaded that the words "just and equitable" need or can be confined to such situations. Lord Cozens-Hardy MR clearly puts his judgement on wider grounds.'
>
> ([1972] All ER 492 at 497 **case 31 para 8**)

Where the company whose shares are to be valued is correctly identified as a 'quasi-partnership', the effect of this judgement on the share valuation is, in the author's view, twofold.

1.   Where the purpose of the valuation is to identify a fair price to be paid for a shareholding surrendered by a retiring director/ shareholder, the price is computed by a valuation of the whole company (or, more precisely, of a 100 per cent shareholding in the company). The value of the proportionate part is then calculated without any discount.

2.   Where a valuation is required for a capital gains tax purpose or an inheritance tax purpose, one or more of the other shareholders in the company may constitute a 'special purchaser' who would be expected to be prepared to pay a proportionate part of the company's full value. The extent to which this consideration bears on the resultant valuation will depend on the particular circumstances of the company at that time and the particular characteristics of the remaining shareholders.

Judgement

References, example '(pg1050)', are to [1916–17] All ER Rep 1050.

1 LORD COZENS-HARDY MR: This is an appeal from a decision of Astbury J who ordered a private company to be compulsorily wound-up. *(pg1050)* I think it right to consider what is the precise position of a private company such as this, and in what respects it can fairly be called a partnership in the clothes or under the guise of a private company.

2 In the present case two tobacco manufacturers, one Rothman and the other Weinberg, were minded to amalgamate their businesses. They formed a private limited company, under the constitution of which they are the sole shareholders. Although the holdings of the two members in 'B' shares and preference shares are unequal – one having a larger holding than the other – the only shares which give the power of voting – that is, the 'A' shares – carry precisely equal voting rights, because each of the two shareholders hold an equal number of shares of that class. There is a provision in the articles of association of the company that there shall be no casting vote, and that one director is to form a quorum. There is a provision that in the event of a dispute between the directors the matter in dispute shall be referred to arbitration, but there is no provision whatever in the articles, and I cannot imagine such a provision, that in the general management of the company all disputes between the directors shall go to arbitration. Certainly, having regard to the result of the one arbitration which has been held, it would be absurd to suggest that the working out of that provision costs little. The one dispute to which I have just referred was about a Mr Litiger who was in the employment of the company as its factory manager. That dispute was referred to two arbitrators who could not agree. An umpire was appointed, and the result was that the parties were some eighteen days before the arbitrators and umpire, the costs of the arbitrators and umpire alone amounting to upwards of £1,000, to say nothing of the costs of the two parties each of whom had to pay his own costs. In those circumstances, supposing this had been an ordinary partnership between two people having equal shares, there being no provision to terminate it, what would have been the position? I think that it is quite clear that under the law of partnership, as has been asserted in this court for many years and is now laid down by the Partnership Act 1890 that state of things might be a ground for a dissolution of the partnership, for the reasons which are stated by Lord Lindley in his book on *Partnership* (6th Edn 657) in the passage which I will read, and which I think it is quite unnecessary to state is justified by the authorities to which he refers:

'Refusal to meet on matters of business, continued quarrelling, and such a state of animosity as precludes all reasonable hope of reconciliation and friendly co-operation, have been held sufficient to justify a dissolution. It is not necessary, in order to induce the court to interfere, to show personal rudeness on the part of one partner to the other, or even gross misconduct as a partner. All that is necessary is to satisfy the court that it is impossible for the partners to place that confidence in each other which each has a right to expect, and that such impossibility has not been caused by the person seeking to take advantage of it.'

3 Here we have this fact. Rothman has commenced an action charging Weinberg with fraud in obtaining the agreement under which he, Rothman, sold his business to the company. I ask myself the question: When one of the two partners has commenced and has not discontinued an action charging his co-partner with fraud in the inception of the partnership, is it likely, is it reasonable, is it common sense, to suppose those two partners can work together in the manner in which they ought to work in the conduct of the partnership business? Can they do so when things have reached such a pass that after the eighteen days' arbitration which terminated in favour of Weinberg on the only point that was referred, Rothman declines to give effect to it, in the sense that, although the award decided that Litiger had not been dismissed and ought to be continued as a servant of the firm until removed, Rothman will not allow him to come and do his work, so that he, Litiger, is in the happy position now of receiving his wage of £5 a week without being allowed to do any work for the company in respect of which he is a *(pg1051)* servant. The matter does not stop there. It is sworn to that these two directors are not on speaking terms, and the so-called meetings of the board of directors have been almost a farce. They will not speak to each other on the board. Some third person has to convey communications which ought to go directly from one to the other.

4 Is it possible that it is not 'just and equitable' [within now s222(f) of the Companies Act 1948] that that state of things should not be allowed to continue, but that the court should intervene and say: 'This is not what the parties contemplated by the arrangement which they entered into?' They assumed, and it is the foundation of the whole of the agreement which was, made, that the two would act as reasonable men with reasonable men with reasonable courtesy and reasonable conduct in every way towards each other, and that arbitration was only to deal with some particular dispute between the board which might be wanted to go to arbitration. Certainly the state of things that the only two directors will not speak to each other and no business can be conducted which deserves the name of business in the affairs of the company should not be allowed to continue.

5 I have treated this matter as a partnership. Under the Partnership Act, of course, the application for a dissolution would take the form of an action. This is not a partnership strictly, it is not a case in which it can be dissolved by action. But ought not the same principles precisely to apply to a case like this, where, in substance, it is a partnership. It is a partnership taking the form or the guise of a private company, and it is a private company as to which there is no way to be found out of the state of things which now exists except by means of a compulsory order. It has been urged upon us that, although it is admitted that the 'just and equitable' clause in s129 of the Companies (Consolidation) Act 1908 (s129 (vi)) which provides that a company may be wound-up by the court 'if the court is of opinion that it is just and equitable that the company should be wound-up' is not to be read as being *ejusdem generis* with the preceding provisions of the section which afford certain specific grounds for winding-up [now s222(f) of the Act of 1948], it has been held not to apply except where the substratum of the company has gone and there is a complete deadlock. Those are the two instances which are given. But I should be very sorry to suppose that they are strictly the limits of the 'just and equitable' clause as found in the Companies (Consolidation) Act 1908. I think that in a case like the present we are bound to say that circumstances which would justify the winding-up of a partnership by action are circumstances which should induce the court to exercise its jurisdiction under the 'just and equitable' clause and to wind-up the company. Astbury J dealt with this case, as it seems to me, in a most satisfactory way. At the end of his judgment he said that he tried to suggest a solution. He suggested that the two shareholders should 'continue for six months to see if they can get on better, or that they should appoint one or more additional directors to assist them in the business.' But this neither would do. If ever there was a case of deadlock I think that it exists here. But, whether it exists or not, I think that the circumstances are such that we ought to apply, if necessary, the analogy of the partnership law, and to say that this company is now in a state which could not have been contemplated by the parties when the company was formed and ought to be terminated as soon as possible. We are told that the court ought not to interfere because the company is prosperous making large profits, rather larger profits than before the dispute became so acute. I think one's knowledge from what one sees in the streets can quite account for that. The number of cigarettes that are sold is enormous, and we can take judicial notice of that in judging whether the business is much larger than it was before. Whether there would be such profits made in circumstances like this or not, it does not seem to me to remove the difficulty which exists, which is contrary to the good faith and essence of this, that the parties formed the scheme of a company managed by these two directors which should be worked *(pg1052)* amicably, and it would not justify the continuance of the state of things which we find here. In my opinion, the appeal fails and ought to be dismissed with costs.

6 PICKFORD LJ: I agree.

7 WARRINGTON LJ stated the facts and continued: If this had been an ordinary partnership, with an action for dissolution, it seems to me quite clear that the plaintiff – the petitioner in this case is equivalent to the plaintiff – would have had sufficient ground for a dissolution of partnership according to the ordinary principle by which the court is guided in such matters. Section 129 of the Companies (Consolidation) Act 1908, which defines the grounds upon which the court can make an order for winding up a company, includes the provision that such an order may be made if the court is of opinion that it is 'just and equitable that the company should be wound up.' At one time it was thought and there was judicial opinion in support of it, that in order to bring the case within that statutory provision it must be shown to be *ejusdem generis* with a number of other grounds which had been specified in a previous part of the section. But that opinion has long been abandoned, and the court has in more cases than one expressed the view that a company may be wound up if, for example, the state of things is such that what may be called a deadlock has been arrived at in the management of the business of the company. I am prepared to say that in a case like the present, where there are only two persons interested, where there are no shareholders other than those two, where there are no means of overruling by the action of a general meeting of shareholders the trouble which is occasioned by the quarrels of the two directors and shareholders, the company ought to be wound-up if there exists such a ground as would be sufficient for the dissolution of a private partnership at the suit of one of the partners against the other of the partners. Such ground exists in the present case. I think, therefore, that it is 'just and equitable that the company should be wound up'.

8 There is one other point to which I ought to refer. It is said that according to the constitution of the company there is provided a means by which the quarrels of these directors can be overridden for the benefit and advantage of the company and the deadlock can be got rid of. The means suggested is the provision in s106 for reference to arbitration. But, in my judgment, that article does not contemplate a case such as the present, where in the daily intercourse between the two directors they are unwilling to speak to each other and discuss the affairs of the company. It relates, I think, to specific cases where a particular resolution important to the company cannot be passed because of a difference of opinion between the two directors, and it is, therefore, necessary to obtain the authority of some third person who will say what is to be done. It seems to me that that has no reference to the ordinary everyday business of the company and its conduct, and that it really does not provide the means of getting rid of the difficulties which are encountered in the present case. For these reasons I think that the order made by Astbury J was quite right and that the company must be wound up. *(pg1053)*

Case 11
Ellesmere v IRC

[1918] 2 KB 735

High Court

5 July 1918

When postulating the hypothetical sale required to determine the market value, it is assumed that the property is sold in whatever manner would be adopted by a vendor wishing to maximise the sale receipt. Hence, if the higher price were to be obtainable by dividing the holding into several lots, it is that higher aggregate price that is to be taken as the market value. This basic principle was established decision of the High Court in 1918.

The corollary to this principle was declared in 1994 by the judgement of the Court of Appeal in *IRC v Gray* [1994] STC 360 **case 37** where the court approved the approach taken by the Revenue valuer where two separate assets in the estate of the deceased were valued by aggregating them. In *IRC v Gray*, the court declared that the assets to be valued together were: (1) 3,000 acres of farmland subject to an agricultural lease; and (2) a 92.5 per cent interest in the farming partnership that was a tenant under the lease.

The third Earl of Ellesmere died on 13 July 1914. Estate duty required to be assessed on a landed estate of 2,757 acres around the town of Brackley. The estate included farmland, houses, shops, business premises and woodland.

After the death of the Earl of Ellesmere, his executors sold the landed estate as a single lot, receiving £68,000. The purchaser then subdivided the estate and sold it in several lots, obtaining a total of £81,000, including the value of the lots he retained unsold. Estate duty was levied on the basis of a value at the date of death as £77,000, the Revenue valuer contending that this was the sum that would have been obtainable by a sale on that day if the estate had been divided into lots and each lot sold separately. The tribunal at first instance upheld the approach taken by the Revenue valuer.

The approach of determining a value by postulating a subdivision into lots was upheld in his judgement by Sankey J:

'Now the Act of 1894 says that the value of the property shall be estimated to be the price which it would fetch if sold in the open market. That, in my opinion, does not necessarily mean the price which it would fetch if sold to a single purchaser. There may be many cases where a sale to a single purchaser cannot realise "the price which it would fetch if sold in the open market". Take the case of an owner having property including a colliery and a draper's shop. It is conceivable that if the colliery and the draper's shop were sold separately the best possible price might be obtained for each. On the other hand a purchaser who was anxious to buy the draper's shop might not wish to be encumbered with a colliery, and vice versa, and consequently if the owner insisted upon selling the whole property to one purchaser he would not obtain the market price which the Act contemplates. So, too, with regard to property of the same character situate in different areas. It may well be that if in such case the vendor insists upon the different parts being all sold to the same person he will not get as good a price as if he allowed different persons to buy the portions situate in the different districts.

Here the referee held that because the property was of a miscellaneous character and not lying in a ring fence the price paid by the single purchaser was not the true value. I think he was entitled so to hold, and that the contention as to misdirection fails.'

([1918] 2 KB 735 at 739/740 **case 11 para 2**)

When valuing a shareholding, the value required is the maximum that can reasonably be expected to be offered for the holding. In considering this, on the authority of *Ellesmere v IRC* [1918] 2 KB 735 **case 11** the valuer must consider not only all possible potential purchasers, but also a combination of purchasers, or, on the authority of *IRC v Gray* [1994] STC 360 CA **case 37** the combination of the shareholding with another asset in the estate.

Judgement

References, example '(pg738)', are to [1918] 2 KB 735.

1 SANKEY J: This is a petition by way of appeal by the Earl of Ellesmere against the decision of a referee appointed under the Finance (1909–10) Act, 1910, upon an appeal against the decision of the Commissioners of Inland Revenue determining the principal value of an estate in Northants called the Brackley estate for the purpose of estate duty upon the death of the late Earl. By s7, sub-s 5, of the Finance Act 1894, 'The principal value of any property shall be estimated to be the price which in the opinion of the Commissioners, such property would fetch if sold in the open market at the time of the death of the deceased'; and by s60, sub-s 2, of the Finance (1909–10) Act 1910, 'In estimating the *(pg738)* principal value of any property under s7, sub-s 5, of the principal Act . the Commissioners shall fix the price of the property according to the market price at the time of the death of the deceased, and shall not make any reduction in the estimate on account of the estimate being made on the assumption that the whole property is placed on the market at one and the same time.' Upon the death of the late Earl his successor resolved to sell the estate and for that purpose consulted an eminent firm of auctioneers, with the result that he determined to sell it in one lot. It was well advertised, and various offers for its purchase were received. Eventually an offer was made to buy the whole estate for £68,000, which offer, on the advice of the auctioneers, was accepted. Subsequently the purchaser resold the farms to the tenants, and put up the other portions of the estate for sale by auction in lots. The bulk of the lots was re-sold for about £65,000, the residue being still in the purchaser's hands at the time of the appeal to the referee. The Commissioners of Inland Revenue fixed the market price of the estate at £77,000, and the Earl appealed to a referee, contending that the market price was the sum for which it had actually been sold. The Commissioners on the other hand contended that, having regard to the varied character of the property and the fact that it did not all lie together, the price realised by a sale in one lot could not represent the true value. The referee upheld the contention of the Commissioners, though he reduced their figure to £75,618, and he ordered the appellant to pay the Commissioners' costs of the appeal. From that decision the present appeal is brought. It is said that the referee misdirected himself upon the question of the value, and also that he had no jurisdiction to make a successful appellant pay costs.

2 Now the Act of 1894 says that the value of the property shall be estimated to be the price which it would fetch if sold in the open market. That, in my opinion, does not necessarily mean the price which it would fetch if sold to a single purchaser. There may be many cases where a sale to a single purchaser cannot realise 'the price which it would fetch if sold in the open market'. Take the case of an owner having property including a colliery and a draper's shop. It is conceivable that if the colliery and the draper's shop were sold separately the best possible price might be obtained for *(pg739)* each. On the other hand a purchaser who was anxious to buy the draper's shop might not wish to be encumbered with a colliery, and vice versa, and consequently if the owner insisted upon selling the whole property to one purchaser he would not obtain the market price which the Act contemplates. So, too, with regard to property of the same character situate in different areas. It may well be that if in such case the vendor insists upon the different parts being all sold to the same person he will not get as good a price as if he allowed different persons to buy the portions situate in the different districts. No doubt a sale in one lot of a varied property such as that in the present case may be highly convenient to the vendor. He may want to get the money quickly; he may not care to risk an auction. He may be going abroad, or may be called up to serve in the Army, and it may be of great importance to him to sell at once. But it does not at all follow that the price which he obtains under such circumstances is 'the price which it would fetch if sold in the open market'. What is meant by those words is the best possible price that is obtainable, and what that is is largely, if not entirely, a question of fact. I can readily conceive cases in which a sale of the whole property in one lot would realise the true market price, but I can equally imagine cases in which it would not. Here the referee held that because the property was of a miscellaneous character and not lying in a ring fence the price paid by the single purchaser was not the true value. I think he was entitled so to hold, and that the contention as to misdirection fails.

3 I now come to the second ground of the appeal, relating to the question of costs. Sect 33, sub-s 3, of the Act of 1910 says that the referee 'may, if he thinks fit, order that any expenses … incurred by the Commissioners be paid by the appellant.' It clearly gives him a discretion, but it was contended that in awarding costs against the appellant the referee was not exercising that discretion judicially, for, it was said, the appellant was in the position of a defendant before the referee and was successful to a substantial amount, he having secured a reduction of £1382 in the assessment. I think that contention cannot be supported. In my opinion the appellant before the referee was in the position of a plaintiff. The Commissioners had fixed the value at £77,000, and the onus lay *(pg740)* upon the appellant to show that that figure ought to be reduced. It was for him to begin.

4 There is, I think, no authority for the proposition that a plaintiff who is to some extent successful may not be made to pay the costs of the defendant. Moreover, here the appellant was unsuccessful upon the real question that the parties went before the referee to fight, the question of principle. No doubt there was a reduction in the assessment to a substantial amount, but that was not the main point of the dispute between them. I think that the referee had a discretion under the circumstances to order the appellant to pay the whole of the costs. I am of opinion that the true rule in such case (and I must not be understood as laying down a rule applicable to other Acts of Parliament in which different words may be used) is that there is jurisdiction in the referee to make the party who invokes the assistance of the Court pay the costs notwithstanding that he is partially successful. I cannot interfere with the referee's exercise of his discretion. *(pg741)*

Case 12
M'Connel's Trustees v IRC

1927 SLT 14

High Court

19 June 1926

This is the first reported case where the court is asked to determine the method of valuation to be used. The case centres on a dispute between the earnings basis advocated by the taxpayer and the asset basis advocated by the Revenue.

John Wanklyn M'Connel died on 28 May 1922. His estate, which attracted estate duty at the rate of 15 per cent, included a holding of 998 ordinary shares in Knockdolian Estates Limited. The executors filed a Revenue account stating that the value of this shareholding was £998, their valuation being based on the history of losses of the company and the absence of dividend. The Revenue contended that as the shareholding in the estate constituted 99.8 per cent of the company's issued share capital, the valuation of the shares should be computed by reference to the value of the company's assets. The Revenue contended that the value of the shareholding was £45,908.

The case appears to have had its origins in a tax mitigation scheme. Knockdolian Estates Limited was incorporated on 2 March 1920 with a share capital of 1,000 £1 ordinary shares, of which 998 ords were issued to John M'Connel. One share was issued to his wife and one share issued to a solicitor. On 1 May 1920, John M'Connel transferred his landed estate at Knockdolian into the company in exchange for a cash payment of £1,000 and the issue to him of preference and debenture stock with a nominal value of £15,750. In June 1920, the company purchased an adjoining estate, using cash lent to the company by John M'Connel.

At the date of John M'Connel's death, two years after the incorporation of the company, the assets in the company consisted of:

	Value at 28 May 1922
Estates of Knockdolian and Glentig	£46,370
Quoted stocks and shares	£10,018
	£56,388

Since this incorporation the trading results of the company had consistently shown a loss:

Year ended 31 March 1921	£(530)
Year ended 31 March 1922	£(1,738)
Year ended 31 March 1923	£(785)

The Revenue considered that a small discount applied to the full asset value was appropriate. This, in their calculations, gave, for a holding of 998 shares, a market value of £45,908.

The executors maintained that the shares must be valued on the footing that the company was a going concern, with reference to the provisions of the memorandum and articles of association, to the past history of dividends and to future prospects for dividends from the company.

Lord Fleming agreed that the points made by the executors were all circumstances to be taken into account in valuing the shares and observed that the Revenue valuation did, indeed, provide for a discount for a full asset value. In supporting the approach to the valuation of this large majority on the basis of full asset value, Lord Fleming said:

'A share in a limited company gives the holder a right, not only to participate in a division of the profits, but also to participate in the division of the capital. A share in a company represents a share in the assets or capital belonging to that company. For reasons which are not difficult to understand, this company took over valuable assets in circumstances which rendered it unlikely that the company would ever become a profit-earning concern. But the transfer of these assets to the company did not destroy their value. The Commissioners have based their valuation upon the price which they estimate the shares would have fetched in the open market at the date of Mr M'Connel's death, and in making this estimate they have taken into account the capital value of the assets belonging to the company. In my opinion, in doing so they acted on a proper principle, and they would have fallen into error if they had neglected to take account of this factor. A purchaser of the shares, buying them as ordinary investment and considering what they were worth, would certainly have been influenced by the fact that the holder of these shares would be in a position to put the company into voluntary liquidation and to realise the whole assets and divide the value thereof amongst the shareholders ... I am of opinion that the decision of the Com- missioners of Inland Revenue was right and should be affirmed.'

([1927] SLT 14 at 15 **case 12 para 1**)

It is to be noted that the company was, in essence, a property investment company. The modern share valuation approach would, in such a case, clearly follow the approach suggested by the Revenue and supported by the judge in this case, rather than the executors' approach.

Although it was not necessary, in this particular case, to consider the subdivision of the shareholding in order to determine the value of the shareholding, Lord Fleming made an interesting comment in *obiter*:

> 'Even if the shares had been sold in a number of different lots, I feel satisfied that the purchasers would all have given a price which was related to the capital value of the undertaking on realisation. A purchaser of a small lot of the shares would naturally have assumed that purchasers of the remaining shares would wish to make the most they could out of their shares, and would concur with him in taking the necessary steps to have the assets of the company realised to the best advantage.'
>
> ([1927] SLT 14 at 16 **case 12 para 1**)

This additional comment by Lord Fleming may give support to an argument that a discount from full asset value should be taken as the market value of a smaller shareholding in a company of this nature, if other similar size shareholdings are held by persons with whom the hypothetical unconnected purchaser could reasonably expected to co-operate to maximise the return on the investment by winding up the company.

Judgement

References, example '(pg15)', are to 1927 SLT 14.

1 LORD FLEMING: This is an appeal by the trustees and executors of the late John Wanklyn M'Connel, Knockdolian, Colmonell, against an amended claim by the Commissioners of Inland Revenue for estate duty under the Finance Act 1894. The claim was made upon the basis that the value of 998 shares held by the deceased in a company known as 'Knockdolian Estates Ltd' was £45,908. The appellants ask me to find that the sum of £998 represented the true value for estate-duty purposes of the shares and that the assessment should be altered accordingly. The company was registered under the Companies Acts on 2 March 1920 to carry on the business of owners, etc, of landed estates and other properties, heritable or moveable, in any part of Great Britain, and in particular the lands and estate of Knockdolian, and to carry on the business or businesses of farming, and for the purposes set forth in the memorandum and articles of association. On 1 March 1920 Mr M'Connel entered into an agreement to sell to the company the lands and estate of Knockdolian and certain preference and debenture stock of the face value of £15,750, and that for the sum of £1,000 sterling. Thereafter a disposition of Knockdolian was granted by Mr M'Connel in favour of the company, and the said stocks were also duly transferred by him to the company. The capital of the company was £1,000 divided into 1,000 shares of £1 each, fully paid, whereof 998 shares were held by Mr M'Connel at the date of his death, one share by his widow, and one share by Mr James Edward Shaw, solicitor, Ayr. At Whitsunday 1920 the company acquired the adjoining property of Glentig at the price of £6,250, the money being supplied by Mr M'Connel. Mr M'Connel died on 28 May 1922, and in the inventory of his estate the value of the deceased's shareholding in the company was given up at £998. At the debate the only question which was argued was whether the Commissioners had adopted the proper principle in valuing these shares. The petitioners stated that they did not wish to raise any question with regard to the actual figures, and that, if the principle of valuation adopted by the Commissioners was sustained, they had no complaint to make with regard to the amount of the valuation. They maintained that the proper method of valuing the 998 shares is to estimate the price at which they would have sold in open market at the date of Mr M'Connel's death. This is the method prescribed by the statute (Finance Act 1894, section 7(5)), but the real controversy between the parties is as to how the method ought to be applied. The petitioners found upon the fact that for each of the three years after its formation the company made a loss, and they say that there was never any prospect of the company earning profits or being in a position to pay a dividend. They maintained that the shares must be valued on the footing that the company is a going concern, and with reference to the provisions of the memorandum and articles of association and also to the past history and future prospects of the company, from a dividend-earning point *(pg15)* of view. These are all circumstances which fall to be taken into account, but in my opinion they are by no means the only factors in the calculation. A share in a limited company gives the holder a right, not only to participate in a division of the profits, but also to participate in the division of the capital. A share in a company represents a share in the assets or capital belonging to that company. For reasons which are not difficult to understand, this company took over valuable assets in circumstances which rendered it unlikely that the company would ever become a profit-earning concern. But the transfer of these assets to the company did not destroy their value. The Commissioners have based their valuation upon the price which they estimate the shares would have fetched in the open market at the date of Mr M'Connel's death, and in making this estimate they have taken into account the capital value of the assets belonging to the company. In my opinion, in doing so they acted on a proper principle, and they would have fallen into error if they had neglected to take account of this factor. A purchaser of the shares, buying them as an ordinary investment and considering what they were worth, would certainly have been influenced by the fact that the holder of these shares would be in a position to put the company into voluntary liquidation and to realise the whole assets and divide the value thereof amongst the shareholders. Even if the shares had been sold in a number of different lots, I feel satisfied that the purchasers would all have given a price which was related to the capital value of the undertaking on realisation. A purchaser of a small lot of the shares would naturally have assumed that purchasers of the remaining shares would wish to make the most they could out of their shares, and would concur with him in taking the necessary steps to have the assets of the company realised to the best advantage. It may be noted that the company had, under its memorandum and articles of association, power to sell its whole assets. In my opinion, it is a mistake to suppose that the value of a share in a company is to be ascertained with reference merely to the income which it yields, and without any regard to its capital value. I am of opinion that the decision of the Commissioners of Inland Revenue was right and should be affirmed. I shall accordingly affirm the decision complained of. *(pg16)*

Case 13
In re Aschrott

[1927] 1 Ch 313

[1926] A 260

High Court

28 October 1926

The statutory valuation provision for inheritance tax states the value is the price 'which the property might be reasonably be expected to fetch if sold in the open market' (IHTA 1984, s 160). As this case demonstrates, this requires the statutory hypothesis that a sale is permitted and actually possible. If, in the real world, there is a legal bar to a sale of the shares in question, that legal bar is to be disregarded for the purpose of valuation.

The valuation provisions for taxes other than inheritance tax use a slightly different formulation of words. However, the effect would appear to be identical, in that when valuing a shareholding for any current tax charge, any legal barrier to the transfer must be ignored. The equivalent provision for capital gains tax is 'the price which those assets might reasonably be expected to fetch on a sale in the open market' (TCGA 1992, s 272(1)). Where there is a charge to income tax on an employee or director receiving a share or a share option, ITEPA 2003, s 421(1) states: '"Market value" has the same meaning as it has for the purposes of TCGA 1992 by virtue of part 8 of that Act.' The only possible exception to this rule is when valuing a shareholding for an income tax charge that is not connected with an employee's share option. There are then no statutory rules for the method of valuation. It is, however, difficult to imagine a court accepting the proposition that a valuation should then be performed on the assumption that there is a legal barrier on a sale.

On 5 May 1915 the testator died. He was a German citizen. He died in Berlin, being domiciled in Germany. His will provided for an undivided 3/5th share of his estate to pass to named beneficiaries in Germany and Austria and an undivided 2/5th share of his estate to pass to British and Polish beneficiaries. Strauss was one of the British beneficiaries, resident in Britain.

The testator's will was proved in Germany in 1915. The estate in Britain had to wait for the end of the First World War before any action could be taken in respect of the inheritance of those resident in the UK. On 24 November 1922, Strauss was given a grant of administration empowering him to deal with the testator's property in England, subject to an undertaking to account the Public Trustee for any entitlement accruing to enemy beneficiaries. UK estate duty at 5 per cent was paid prior to the grant of administration.

The estate included stocks, shares and other securities in English, South African and American companies. The share certificates for all these holdings were held in London. At the commencement of the First World War, the UK Parliament had enacted the Trading with the Enemy Amendment Act 1914. Section 5 of the Act provides that, while the Act is in effect, no recognition is given in English law to any legal or beneficial title that would be held by an enemy alien. Hence, at the date of death, during the First World War, the deceased was not recognised as having title to the shareholdings shown by the certificates in London.

Strauss, as administrator, advanced three propositions.

1.   The effect of the wartime legislation was to cause the shareholdings to be property situated outside the UK and, thus, not subject to UK estate duty.
2.   The wartime legislation had the effect that the shares were not part of the estate as the deceased was an enemy alien.
3.   The value of the shares was £nil as the wartime legislation did not permit a sale of shares by an enemy alien.

Eve J ruled that the shares continued to be correctly regarded as assets situated in the UK and the testator's disability did not prevent his disposition becoming effective. Thus submissions 1 and 2 were defeated.

As regards the effect of the legal prohibition on the valuation of the shares, Eve J said:

> 'By s7, sub-s 5, of [Finance Act 1894], it is provided that "The principal value of any property shall be estimated to be the price which, in the opinion of the Commissioners, such property would fetch if sold in the open market at the time of the death of the deceased". At the testator's death, part of the property passing under his will consisted of shares saleable in the open market. It is true that, by reason of the subsisting war, he was disqualified, and his executors after his death were disqualified, from transferring the shares, but these shares were only part of the share capital of the several companies in which he was interested, and, in order to ascertain the market price of the shares which were disposed of by his will the broker was bound, I think, to find out at what price similar shares were being sold and dealt with on

the market, and to return that as being the correct valuation; it was not open to the valuer to say: "The market price of shares in this particular company is so much, but, in view of the fact that the transferor of these shares is an alien enemy, the market for some of the shares (those which he would be purporting to transfer) would be nil". That, it seems to me, would not have been applying the test which he was, under the statute, bound to apply. He was to certify the value of shares of these particular companies, and not what was the value of shares held by somebody at the moment incompetent to transfer.'

([1927 1 Ch 313 at 322 **case 13 para 4**)

Thus, this case is authority for the proposition that any legal bar to transfer must be ignored in valuing a shareholding. It is also authority for the proposition that in valuing a shareholding, the identity of the shareholder is ignored. Different owners do not have different prices.

Judgement

References, example '(pg320)', are to [1927] 1 Ch 313.

1 **EVE J:** The question whether estate duty is payable on all or any of the shares referred to under the headings A, B, and C in the first question of the summons depends upon the answer to the inquiry whether they can be brought within any of the exceptions in the Finance Act 1894. It has been argued in the first place that they are excepted under s2, sub-s 2, as being property passing on the death of the deceased situate out of the United Kingdom in respect of which under the law in force before the passing of the Act legacy or succession duty would not have been payable. Were these shares in companies registered in South Africa and America, but having offices in England where certificates could be produced, transfers passed, and the names of transferees entered on the register, property situate out of the United Kingdom? *Prima facie* their locality, and in particular in those cases where the certificates were within the jurisdiction, was in this country. The evidence of title is the register, and according to the case of *Attorney-General v Higgins*, that determines the locality of the shares. But it is urged on behalf of the beneficiaries that in this case the property ought to be held to have been out of the United Kingdom, because at the date of the testator's death the registration office in this country had ceased to be available to the testator and those claiming under him, in that they were restrained by the emergency legislation from disposing *(pg320)* of or dealing with these shares by way of transfer or otherwise. In the condition of things subsisting at the testator's death and for a long time after that event, it is argued that the shares had lost their locality in this country, and that during this suspensory period their locality ought to be determined by the rule frequently adopted for income tax purposes – namely, that shares in a company

are regarded as locally situate at the place where the company carries on its administrative business and is domiciled. Applying this rule it is contended that these shares ought to be regarded as locally situate where these mining and other companies were respectively resident and carrying on business, that is to say, in South Africa and the United States. I cannot agree. In my opinion the fact that the testator's power of disposing of the shares and effecting any transfer of them had been temporarily suspended could not operate to change the location of the particular shares held by alien enemies, leaving unchanged the locality of shares held by those shareholders whose power of disposition was not affected by the legislation I have referred to. The shares remained throughout locally situate in this country.

2 But then it is said the Finance Act contains no provision under which the executor in the circumstances subsisting at the testator's death could properly include these shares in the accounts annexed to the affidavit leading to probate under s8, sub-s 3, because they did not constitute property of which the deceased was competent to dispose at his death. But this argument not only overlooks s22, sub-s 2 *(pg321)* (*a*), of the Act, but ignores the fact that the testator's disability did not prevent his dispositions becoming effective, although it is true that under the Treaty they have been diverted in the case of the alien enemy beneficiaries.

3 I think both points advanced by Mr Radcliffe fail; the shares were locally situate in England and the administrator was bound to include them as property of which the deceased was competent to dispose, and is accountable to the extent of the assets he has received for the estate duty in respect thereof under s6, sub-s 2.

4 The second question in the summons relates to the value to be placed on the shares. By s7, sub-s 5, of the Act, it is provided that 'The principal value of any property shall be estimated to be the price which, in the opinion of the Commissioners, such property would fetch if sold in the open market at the time of the death of the deceased.' At the testator's death, part of the property passing under his will consisted of shares saleable in the open market. It is true that, by reason of the subsisting war, he was disqualified, and his executors after his death were disqualified, from transferring the shares, but these shares were only part of the share capital of the several companies in which he was interested, and, in order to ascertain the market price of the shares which were disposed of by his will the broker was bound, I think, to find out at what price similar shares were being sold and dealt with on the market, and to return that as being the correct valuation; it was not open to the valuer to say: 'The market price of shares in this particular company is so much, but, in view of the fact that the transferor of these shares is an alien enemy, the market for some of the shares (those which he would be purporting to transfer) would be nil.' That, it seems to me, would not have been applying the test which he was, under the statute, bound to apply. He was to certify the value of shares of these particular companies, and not what was the value of shares held by somebody at the

moment incompetent to transfer. I think therefore the valuation proceeded upon the strict lines laid down by the statute.

5 The Inland Revenue authorities by way of concession are willing to allow a sum to be deducted from this valuation equivalent to the estate duty already paid in South Africa, and the value put upon the South African shares will be reduced accordingly. *(pg322)*

Case 14
In re W F Courthope deceased

(1928) 7 ATC 538

High Court

26 June 1928

This case looks at the valuation computed on a break-up basis. The valuation is not the value of the aggregate of assets that would be taken from the company. The valuation is of the shares of the company and, hence, is the highest sum that could reasonably be expected to be paid by a purchaser who would make the purchase in order to break up the company.

In the particular circumstances of this particular case, the decision of the court was that a purchaser with such an intention would look to receive a profit of 50 per cent of the sum he paid for the shares; that is a discount from break-up value of $33\frac{1}{3}$ per cent.

William Francis Courthope died on 30 March 1924. He had been a director of a private company. In his estate were 1,500 prefs and 2,000 ords in the company, being $47\frac{1}{2}$ per cent and 50 per cent of the total number of shares in the respective classes. His shareholding was the largest shareholding in the company.

The company had carried on a brewery business for a number of years but by the time of Courthope's death, the trade had ceased. The company's property had been sold. The company had paid all its creditors, other than interest free loan it had received from its directors. The company was solvent and, in principle, could be regarded as a going concern in that there was no legal bar to it continuing as an active company. It could have recommenced a brewery business, if that had been the wish of the directors; alternatively, the directors were free to decide to carry on another business. In fact, it appears that the company was subsequently wound up and its assets distributed to its shareholders at some date after the death of William Courthope.

It should be noted that the shareholding to be valued was not a majority shareholding and the shareholder did not have the ability to appoint a board of directors of his choosing.

Rowlatt J approved the valuation approach based on the amount that a shareholder would reasonably be expected to received on a winding-up. This break-up value, in the judgement of Rowlatt J, then requires to be discounted in order to recognise the profit that any prospective purchaser would expect to make if he purchased a large majority shareholding of this nature with a view to receiving his proportionate part of the break-up value on a subsequent liquidation.

Rowlatt J put it in these terms:

> 'If you tried to find a purchaser for these shares in my view he would probably say to himself, "Well this is a thing to buy to wind up," as Mr Stamp suggested, but I cannot help thinking that he would discount the value rather heavily because he would say: "Well, I may be met with difficulties; I shall not buy a controlling interest. Lawyers tell me that I possibly might be able to compel a winding up. There are cases upon it and all the rest of it, but I do not know how that may be," and so on and so on, and I think myself that he would only from that point of view go in for this purchase on the footing that if he succeeded in getting the company wound up he would make a profit in a few years of something like 50 per cent. On that sort of footing, allowing everything, I will not go through it all, I think the value of these shares may fairly be put at £13. Treating it as something about £19 or £20, and allowing for a possible profit of 50 per cent if the winding up were carried through without a hitch, I think that is a fair price. Therefore I shall say that they are worth £13.'
>
> ((1928) 7 ATC 538 at 540 case 14 para 1)

This case is clear authority for the approach that in valuing on the basis of break-up value, a discount must be applied. In the author's view, a discount of $33\frac{1}{3}$ per cent is higher than he would normally expect. However, the percentage discount must be judged in each case on the basis of the facts, as at the valuation date, that apply to that particular case. The discount applied to a majority shareholding, where the shareholding gives the right to appoint a board of the shareholder's choosing, would clearly be a much smaller discount percentage. Where a company has disposed of its property and has commenced on the path leading to a winding-up over a predetermined timetable, the author considers that a low discount would be appropriate in valuing a minority shareholding. Depending on the circumstances of the particular case, the discount could be as low as 20 per cent or even 10 per cent.

Judgement

References, example '(pg540)', are to (1928) 7 ATC 538.

1 MR JUSTICE ROWLATT: In this case I have rather a troublesome question to decide, and a question which in a way requires one to deal with knowledge which one has as to what influences people in the business world. These shares according to the Act of Parliament fall to be valued at the price they would have fetched if sold in the open market at the date of the death. At the death it seems to be quite clear that the market element must come in, the attractiveness or unattractiveness of the thing in the market must come in. The fluctuation of the market at the time obviously comes in because it says 'at the date of the death'. I am not entitled and I ought not to take the thing and simply pull it to pieces and find out what the assets are and treat them as liquidated and find what the balance is and arrive at that sum and say what it is. I have, of course, to consider those questions, but I have to consider them through the supposed purchaser in the market. I have to look for a man who after he has considered those things and has considered everything else and what else he could do with his money and all the rest of it finally makes up his mind to give a certain price. That is the sort of way in which I have to look at it. The position of these shares in this company was very odd, practically half the share capital of the company but not quite. I need not go through the facts again, but I think I may take it, in fact both sides agree as to this, I think, that it is a better proposition to look at it from the point of view of what it would be worth wound up than from the point of view of what it would make carrying on. If you tried to find a purchaser for these shares in my view he would probably say to himself, 'Well this is a thing to buy to wind up,' as Mr Stamp suggested, but I cannot help thinking that he would discount the value rather heavily because he would say: 'Well, I may be met with difficulties; I shall not buy a controlling interest. Lawyers tell me that I possibly might be able to compel a winding up. There are cases upon it and all the rest of it, but I do not know how that may be,' and so on and so on, and I think myself that he would only from that point of view go in for this purchase on the footing that if he succeeded in getting the company wound up he would make a profit in a few years of something like 50 per cent. On that sort of footing, allowing for everything, I will not go through it all, I think the value of these shares may fairly be put at £13. Treating it as something about £19 or £20, and allowing for a possible profit of 50 per cent if the winding up were carried through without a hitch, I think that is a fair price. Therefore I shall say that they are worth £13. *(pg540)*

Case 15
Salvesen's Trustees v IRC

PART 2 Cases

(1930) 9 ATC 43

High Court

18 January 1930

The importance of this case is that the judgement of Lord Fleming gives a full account of the way in which the process of valuing a shareholding is a matter of balancing the many different elements. Lord Fleming's judgement is a model for a share valuation report.

In the course of the comprehensive judgement, the effect on value of the type of pre-emptive provisions commonly found in private companies is explored. The rule is restated that a hypothetical unconnected purchaser will be registered as shareholder, irrespective of any contrary provisions in the company's articles, but will then hold the shares subject to those provisions. Importantly, Lord Fleming then gives a useful and practical illustration of the principle by stating the actual numerical effect this has on the value of the shareholding.

Lord Fleming approves the opinion of an expert witness that the depreciating effect, in the circumstances of this case, might be 8s 4d. This is 7.5 per cent of what appears to be the full asset value per share but 50 per cent of the value suggested by that expert witness, before taking into account the depreciatory effect of the pre-emption provisions that would apply to the shares once they had been acquired by the prospective purchaser ((1930) 9 ATC 43 at 53 **case 15 para 9**).

Johan Thomas Salvesen died on 24 October 1926. In the estate were 33,333 South Georgia Co Ltd £1 ordinary shares (33⅓ per cent of the issued share capital). The company's business consisted chiefly of whaling in the South Atlantic and Antarctic Ocean. The company produced high profits up to the end of the First World War but then suffered heavy losses in the years 1918 to 1921. In the four years from 1922 to the date of death in 1926, the company returned to the profitability, having a profit of £280,189 for the accounting period immediately prior to the date of death.

Dividend payments had been small, the directors having throughout the course of the company's history adopted a very conservative policy in

321

regard to distributions. By the time of Johan Salvesen's death, revenue reserves of £900,000 had accumulated in the company.

The articles of association restricted the transfer of shares and gave pre-emptive rights to other shareholders. In addition to the customary pre-emptive provisions, Article 12 provided that no single shareholder could have a holding of less than 10 per cent:

> **'Compulsory Retirement**
> 12. The company may, at any time, by extraordinary resolution, resolve that any shareholder, other than a director or a person holding more than 10 per cent of the shares of the company, do transfer his shares. Such member shall thereupon be deemed to have served the company with a sale notice in respect of his shares in accordance with Clause 6 hereof, and all the ancillary and consequential provisions of these articles shall apply with respect to the completion of the sale of the said shares.'

The Revenue valued the shareholding at £5 10s per share. The executors initially valued the shareholding at £2 per share but then subsequently claimed that the value was no more than the par value of £1 per share as a consequence of the combined depreciatory effects of the articles and the conservative dividend policy followed by the directors. (Averaging 24d per annum for each £1 ord.)

In his judgement, Lord Fleming deals with no fewer than ten points of principle relating to this share valuation, all of which are as valid today as when the judgement was given in 1930.

1. The depreciatory effect of an article prohibiting a shareholding of less than 10 per cent.
2. The influence of the company's profit record.
3. The influence of the company's dividend record.
4. The adequacy of the company's resources.
5. The effect of the asset value on a minority interest.
6. The nature of a willing buyer.
7. The extent to which post-valuation documents may be considered.
8. The influence of the state of the industry.
9. The effect of restrictions on transfer.
10. The ability of the directors.

The depreciatory effect of an article prohibiting a shareholding of less than 10 per cent

Lord Fleming said:

> 'The terms of that article [Article 12] are very drastic and unusual. It provides for the compulsory retiral from the company of a person holding not more than 10% of the shares of the company and would not therefore apply directly if the whole of the testator's shares were transferred to one individual. Nevertheless, I am of opinion that this article would have considerable effect in depreciating the value of the shares. Its effect would be to prevent them being sold in lots of less than 10,000 shares. Furthermore, a person who was considering what price he ought to offer for the whole of the testator's shareholding would certainly take into account that he could not transfer less than one-third of the holding even to one of his own relatives without the transferee being under liability to have his shares transferred compulsorily to the other members of the company at not more than their par value.'
>
> ((1930) 9 ATC 43 at 45 **case 15 para 1**)

The influence of the company's profit record

Eight hundred words of Lord Fleming's judgement at para 4 are devoted to a commentary on the profits of the company made over a 17-year period, starting with 1909 and ending in 1926, the valuation date.

The profits are not described in isolation; each year's profit is related to the circumstances of the whaling industry at that time. The approach of the court is, thus, not to consider any one element in isolation but to look at the interrelation between the different elements of profitability, dividends, the state of the industry and the directors' abilities. The share value is then determined following this consideration of these factors taken together and looked at in the round.

The influence of the company's dividend record

Dividends are considered by contrasting those paid by South Georgia Company Ltd with those paid by its competitors:

> 'Notwithstanding the very large profits earned in these years the sums distributed in dividends were moderate in the extreme. For 1922/23 there were distributed in dividend £10,000, representing a dividend of

10 per cent; for 1923/24 there was distributed £11,625, presenting a dividend of 15%; for 1924/25 there was distributed £16,000, presenting a dividend of 20%; and for 1925/26 there was distributed £16,000, presenting a dividend of 20%. I think it must be admitted that since 1922 the directors of this company have adopted a very conservative policy as regards the declaration of dividends. Sir Wm M'Lintock, in giving evidence for the Crown, contrasted the proportion of earnings distributed as dividend in this company and in certain Norwegian companies, and I think that he was successful in showing that this proportion was much higher in the Norwegian companies.'

((1930) 9 ATC 43 at 47 **case 15 para 4**)

The adequacy of the company's resources

Lord Fleming described at length the manner in which a prospective shareholder would decide the price he might offer for the shares. The following short summary illustrates the process he postulated:

'A person who was being invited to acquire a third of the shares of a private company which imposed stringent conditions on the right of transfer would certainly wish to ascertain the value at which the assets had been entered in the last balance sheet. As a prudent person he would, of course, keep in view that he was purchasing the shares in October 1926 and that the balance sheet shows the affairs of the company as at July 1926 and he would make inquiry as to the alterations in its financial position which had taken place between these two dates. But he would first examine the balance sheet and I think that he would be very favourably impressed by the fact that the assets showed a surplus of upwards of £900,000 over its capital.'

((1930) 9 ATC 43 at 50 **case 15 para 7**)

He then highlighted the fact that his reading of the accounts raised unexplained questions as to the values given in the accounts of whaling vessels and continued:

'A prudent investor, who investigated this matter, might come to the conclusion that the allowance for depreciation did not represent replacement costs, and that a larger allowance ought to be made for this circumstance ... While I think this circumstance would weigh with the intending investor, I do not mean to say that he would assume that there was any likelihood of the assets of the company being realised – say by sale to another company – and of his being paid out the capital value of his share. On the contrary he would, I assume, be informed that if he became a shareholder, the only means open to him of realising his capital would be to avail himself of the very restricted right of transfer given by the articles. He would, of course, also know, when he came to make his purchase, that by that time an important change had taken place in the financial position of the company and that the directors had decided to continue trading for another year and had committed themselves to the extent of about £300,000. He might, as I have already said, regard this as evidence of the confidence which the directors had in the future of the company, and in any event I do not think that he would suppose that there was any risk of the whole of that £300,000 being lost ... The investor would, of course, also recognise that, owing to the restrictions of the right of transfer, a very important matter from his point of view was whether the rate of profit earned and dividends declared would be maintained in the future.'

((1930) 9 ATC 43 at 50 **case 15 para 7**)

At several places in his judgement, Lord Fleming draws attention to the very significant revenue reserves of £900,000 that had been built up from the company's undistributed profit. Although the valuation was made on the basis of a shareholder assuming the continuing of the whaling trade, Lord Fleming also looked at the break-up value that would pass to a shareholder if the company were to be wound up:

'I think it would be safe to assume that the break-up value of this concern was well over £400,000 and might even be as much as £500,000. This means that, on a break-up basis, the £1 shares were worth £4 or £5. It does not, however, at all follow that the shares have the same value on the footing that the company is a going concern, but the fact that this figure might have been realised on a break-up basis suggests to me that the shareholders were so confident of the future of the concern that they preferred to continue trading rather than realise this large appreciation in the capital value of the shares.'

((1930) 9 ATC 43 at 49 **case 15 para 6**)

The effect of the asset value on a minority interest

The valuation is of a large minority. Nevertheless Lord Fleming recognised that the asset value would be an element in the decision of a prospective purchaser as to the price he would offer. In his valuation, Lord Fleming does not give a numerical weighting to the asset value but notes:

'I do not think it is possible upon the material available to estimate any specific figure. But even if a large allowance were made, it seems clear that the balance sheet shows the capital value of each share at a sum in excess of the £5 10s claimed by the Crown.'

((1930) 9 ATC 43 at 50 **case 15 para 7**)

The nature of a willing buyer

Lord Fleming said

> 'The hypothetical buyer in the open market is presumed to be able to obtain registration of the transfer in his favour, but thereafter he is deemed to hold his shares subject to the provisions of the Articles of Association. I think that this means that he is deemed to hold them subject not only to the disabilities imposed by the articles but also to the privileges conferred by the articles ...'
>
> ((1930) 9 ATC 43 at 45 **case 15 para 1**)

The extent to which post-valuation documents may be considered

It appears that around the valuation date, 24 October 1926, there was very real uncertainty of the prospects for the profitability of the whaling trade. In the event, the accounting period that started on 1 August 1926, three months before the date of death, and ended nine months after the date of death, was a profitable period. Lord Fleming then considered whether he was entitled to look at the accounts drawn up to a date after the valuation date and, if so, what of the nature of the guidance he could obtain from them as to the information available at the valuation date:

> 'I quite recognise that the problem I have to deal with must be solved in the light of the information available at or about the time of the testator's death, but I think that, however, does not debar me completely from making any reference to the balance sheet at 31 July 1927, which includes a period of nearly three months prior to the testator's death. The profit made in that year was £171,122 and the directors set aside £400,000 as a dividend reserve. This seems to indicate that the directors must have considered that the undistributed profits that they had in hand at the end of the previous year were far more than was necessary for trading purposes and might have been used by them to maintain the rate of dividend in bad years ... The general conclusion which I draw from an examination of this balance sheet is that the intending investor would be very favourably impressed with the position and prospects of this company and that it would incline him to regard the shares as being much in excess of their nominal value.'
>
> ((1930) 9 ATC 43 at 51 **case 15 para 7**)

> 'I feel bound to say that these figures suggest to me very strongly that it would be quite fallacious to value these shares merely on the basis

of the dividends paid and without regard to the amount of the profits which were earned but not distributed.'

((1930) 9 ATC 43 at 48 **case 15 para 5**)

The influence of the state of the industry

Lord Fleming's judgement contains a 1,100 word analysis at para 8 of the future prospects of the whaling industry and their effect on the South Georgian Company Limited ((1930) 9 ATC 43 at 51–53 **case 15 para 8**).

The approach taken by the judge in this case should be a useful corrective to the all too common tendency of a valuer suggesting a value for shares without adequate understanding of the industry in which the particular company operates. No matter how effective a particular board of directors may be in controlling a particular company, the price of that company's shares is fundamentally affected by the prospects for the industry in which the company has its business.

The effect of restrictions on transfer

'... I have to consider the effect which the restrictive conditions in the articles would have on the value of the shares. I may say at once that I regard these restrictions as depreciating their value very considerably. Nobody, except a person who was prepared to have his capital locked up for many years, could afford to buy them at more than par value. I imagine that there are a very limited number of persons who would be prepared to pay £5 10s for a £1 share which might only be realisable at par or less. The prospective buyer at the price fixed by the Commissioners would have to be able to find over £152,000 and, in order to avoid a loss on his capital, he would have to be prepared to hold the shares himself for an indefinite period or transfer them to one or more of the persons mentioned in the articles, subject, however, to the condition that no transferee held less than 10,000 shares. All the witnesses were agreed that the restrictions would depreciate the value of the shares, but the only witness who put any money value on this restriction was Mr Robertson-Durham, who said that, in his opinion, it might make a difference of as much as 8s 4d on his value of £1 6s 8d and, in my opinion, this figure is not by any means excessive.'

((1930) 9 ATC 43 at 54/55 **case 15 para 10**)

The actions of the directors

Although Lord Fleming does not look at the specific individuals who are the directors, he considers in his thoroughgoing review of the valuation exercise, the role played by the directors in the decisions they have to make.

After commenting on the low level of dividends, he said:

> 'This was quite a rational and intelligible policy in a private company, though it may not have been a course which the directors of a large public company would or could have taken ... The directors of this company may have adopted a policy of only distributing a small part of the profits as dividend, but it was impossible for them to pursue such a policy indefinitely. I cannot doubt that when they were satisfied that they had reached the stage at which the profits could no longer be usefully employed in the business they would have distributed them to the shareholders. The hypothetical person, who I am to assume is the purchaser of these shares, might be apprehensive that he would find himself in an uncomfortable position as an intruder into a family concern, but I feel confident that in their own interest, if for no other reason, the directors of the company would continue to manage it as successfully in the future as they had done in the past.'
>
> ((1930) 9 ATC 43 at 54 **case 15 para 9**)

> 'The hypothetical purchaser of shares would no doubt be influenced by the opinion of the company held by the directors and shareholders as shown by their own actings and also attach weight to their knowledge and experience of the industry. It appears from the evidence of the chairman of the company that he has had a long and intimate knowledge and experience of the industry. The hypothetical buyer would see from the accounts that he and the other directors were quite willing year after year to embark the large profits, which they had already made from the industry, in another year's trading and would draw his own conclusions from that circumstance.'
>
> ((1930) 9 ATC 43 at 49 **case 15 para 6**)

Judgement

References, example '(pg45)', are to (1930) 9 ATC 43.

1 **LORD FLEMING:** I refer to my previous opinion issued with reference to the interlocutor of 2 April 1929. Following the case of *The Attorney-General v Jameson*

(1904 2 IR 644) and (1905 2 IR 218), I held that the principal value of the shares belonging to the late Mr JT Salvesen fell to be estimated at the price which, in the opinion of the Commissioners, they would fetch if sold in the open market on the terms that the purchaser should be entitled to be registered as holder of the shares and should take and hold them subject to the provisions of the articles of association, including the articles relating to the alienation and transfer of shares. I need not refer in detail to the restrictions which are imposed by the articles on the right of a shareholder to transfer his shares, as I dealt fully with that matter in my former opinion. There are, however, two points upon which it is necessary to make some addition to what I then said. The hypothetical buyer in the open market is presumed to be able to obtain registration of the transfer in his favour, but thereafter he is deemed to hold his shares subject to the provisions of the articles of association. I think that this means that he is deemed to hold them subject not only to the disabilities imposed by the articles but also to the privileges conferred by the articles, and that he has accordingly the same rights as the original shareholders had to transfer his shares to his relatives or to his executors in terms of the articles of association. Similarly, in the event of any other member desiring to sell his shares, he would have the same rights as the original shareholders to acquire a proportion of them in terms of the articles. The fact that the hypothetical buyer is deemed to have the right not only to hold the shares himself but to transfer them in terms of the articles to relatives and other persons, is a circumstance which has got to be taken into account in considering the effect of the restrictive conditions on the value of the shares. In the course of the proof and also at the hearing, attention was directed to Article 12. The terms of that article are very drastic and unusual. It provides for the compulsory retiral from the company of a person holding not more than 10 per cent of the shares of the company and would not therefore apply directly if the whole of the testator's shares were transferred to one individual. Nevertheless, I am of opinion that this article would have considerable effect in depreciating the value of the shares. Its effect would be to prevent them being sold in lots of less than 10,000 shares. Furthermore, a person who was considering what price he ought to offer for the whole of the testator's shareholding would certainly take into account that he could not transfer less than one-third of the holding even to one of his own relatives without the transferee being under liability to have his shares transferred compulsorily to the other members of the company at not more than their par value.

2   The estimation of the value of a share in a company, whose shares cannot be bought and sold in the open market, and with regard to which there have not been any sales on ordinary terms, is obviously one of difficulty. There has been *(pg45)* one transfer by Mr Theodore Salvesen of 5,000 shares to his son at their par value, but the petitioners did not found upon this transaction as being any real guide to the value of the shares. The problem can only be dealt with by considering all the relevant facts so far as known at the date of the testator's death and by determining what a prudent investor, who knew these facts, might be expected to be willing to pay for the shares. Counsel for both the petitioners and respondents accordingly assumed that the prospective buyer would inform himself of all the relevant facts and, in particular, would have made available to him the accounts of the company. The relevant facts may, I think, be classified under the following heads: (1) The history of the whaling industry; (2) the history of the company from its inception to the date of the testator's death and particularly its position at that date; (3) the prospects of the whaling industry generally at that date and of this company in particular; and (4) to what extent the restrictions in the articles might be expected to depreciate the value of the shares. I shall consider these different matters in their order.

(1) The History of the Whaling Industry

3 Without going into this matter in detail, it is sufficient to say that at one time or another the whaling industry has been prosecuted in different parts of the world, and that in course of time the industry has either completely collapsed or been reduced to unremunerative dimensions in all these places owing to the depletion of the stocks. The whale is a migratory animal, and may desert the waters which it has been accustomed to frequent, owing either to natural causes or to intense persecution by man. All the witnesses accordingly assumed that whaling must be regarded as a highly speculative industry. But no instance was mentioned in the evidence of whales suddenly and completely deserting a locality which they had previously frequented, without any indication being given either by reduced catches or otherwise of the probability of the happening of such an event. I understand that whaling first began in the waters around South Georgia at or about the time this company was formed, and while the accounts show that there have been in some seasons poor catches, which resulted in some instances in heavy losses, there has been no season in which the whales have failed completely and in which the value of the products obtained from them was either nil or negligible.

(2) The History of the Company and its Position at the date of the Testator's Death

4 The company was formed in the year 1909. The powers conferred upon it by its memorandum are very wide, but I gather that the principal object of the company was to prosecute whaling in the waters around South Georgia. The original capital of the company was only £20,000, which seems a small capital for an enterprise of this kind, but the shareholders of the company (apart from those who held only one share) were the partners of Christian Salvesen & Co, and throughout its existence, and especially until the capital was increased to £100,000 in 1922, it was financed by large advances made by that firm, who acted as its bankers and managers. The history of the company may be gathered from its balance sheets. In the year 1909–10 it made a profit of £3,342 after writing off 10 per cent on the value of the station in South Georgia. The practice of the company throughout has been to write off depreciation at the rate of 10 per cent on its buildings and also on its ships, which are the only fixed assets that it has ever owned. In the year 1910–11 it made a profit of £35,142 and declared a dividend of 100 per cent, so that, as the result of the second year of the company's trading, the shareholders received back the amount of their subscribed capital. In the years 1911–12 and 1912–13 the company made losses of £444 and £3,141 respectively, but in the latter of these years it put *(pg46)* £10,000 to reserve account. In 1913–14 the company made a profit of £12,205 and declared a dividend of 50 per cent. In 1914–15, being the first war year, the company made a profit of £46,388 and paid a dividend of 60 per cent. There was some difference of opinion among the witnesses as to whether any account should be taken of the war years, including in that expression not only the period of hostilities but also the period of economic disturbance which followed upon the war, and particularly the 'slump' year of 1920–21. I think, however, that as this company has been in existence for over 20 years it is not unfair to take account of its profits and losses during the whole period it has been trading, though, of course, the special conditions prevailing during the war years and, in particular, the relaxation of all restrictions on whaling, must be kept in view. The profits were enormously inflated during some of the boom years of the war, but, as will appear later on, they were just as much deflated when the fall in prices took place after the way. In 1915–16 the company made a profit of £41,230 and paid a dividend of 100 per cent. In 1916–17 the company made a profit of £87,132, but no dividend was declared. £20,000 was, however, transferred to reserve, and this brought the reserve up to £30,000. Notwithstanding the fact that the turnover in this year amounted to over £600,000, the company made a profit of only £12,115. The next three years were the worst in the company's history. The losses were due partly to transport difficulties and partly to the great reduction of prices which took place during the year 1920–21. In 1919–20 the price per ton of whale oil was £87, but when it was decontrolled in the following year the price fell to £31 5s. It appears that there is a buying syndicate in the whale oil trade which practically eliminates competitive buying. The price of oil has fallen since 1926, but I do not think that anything was proved to suggest that a prospective buyer in October 1926 would have been warned of the probability of that happening. In 1918–19 the amount of the loss made by the company was £79,183. In 1919–20 there was a credit balance of £659, and in 1920–21 there was a debit balance of £79,767. I think the petitioners' counsel was right in his contention that on the balance sheet of 1919–20 the company was insolvent, and, indeed, if it had been wound up at this date the loss might possibly have been greater than would appear from the balance sheet. As I have already stated, however, the company was throughout financed by the firm of Christian Salvesen & Co, and this firm in the following year provided the company with the capital necessary to enable it to carry on. The whaling season extends from September to May, but the principal product of whaling, namely, whale oil, is delivered about the end of the season and no part of the price is received until at or about that time. On the other hand, at the beginning of and during each season, very large sums require to be disbursed for stores, coals, etc, and the company had to lie out of these expenses for a long period. It is quite obvious that it would have been difficult for this company to carry on with its comparatively small capital of £20,000 had it not been for the fact that the individual shareholders, through their firm, were willing to provide it with the necessary financial accommodation. Accordingly, notwithstanding its financial position at the end of the year 1920–21, the company was able to continue trading in the following season and made a profit of £78,540, which was applied almost entirely in wiping off the sum at the debit of profit and loss, namely, £61,966. The next four years of the company were exceedingly profitable, the balances at the credit of profit and loss being respectively £175,365, £156,775, £329,832, and £280,189. I should, however, qualify these figures by stating that, as regards the year 1923–24, the company had a windfall from a PPI insurance of about £50,000, and I understood all *(pg47)* the witnesses to be agreed that this windfall should not properly enter the profit and loss account at all. Notwithstanding the very large profits earned in these years the sums distributed in dividends were moderate in the extreme. For 1922–23 there was distributed in dividend £10,000, representing a dividend of 10 per cent; for 1923–24 there was distributed £11,625, representing a dividend of 15 per cent; for 1924–25 there was distributed £16,000, representing a dividend of 20 per cent; and for 1925–26 there was distributed £16,000, representing a dividend of 20 per cent. I think it must be admitted that since 1922 the directors of this company have adopted a very conservative policy as regards the declaration of dividends. Sir Wm M'Lintock, in giving evidence for the Crown, contrasted the proportion of earnings distributed as dividend in this company and in certain Norwegian companies, and I think that he was successful in showing that this proportion was much higher in the Norwegian companies. The figures shown for the years 1923–24, 1924–25, and 1925–26 in No 27 of process are very remarkable. The company distributed 17 per cent of its earnings as dividend in the years 1923–24, 4.78 per cent in the years 1924–25, and 5.67 per cent in the years 1925–26, whereas the smallest proportion of similar distributions in the Norwegian companies during these years were 57 per cent, 32 per cent, and 35 per cent. I should add that the shares of the Tonsberg Company and Vestfold Company – both Norwegian companies – were quoted in the open market about the date of the testator's death at prices of 272 and 177 per cent respectively. I do not think, however, I have sufficient information with regard to these companies, their histories and balance sheets, to make the figures with regard to the prices of their shares of much value.

5 There are several conclusions of a general character which were drawn by the accountants from the companies' accounts which have considerable bearing on the question I have to determine. The average dividend paid over the whole period was 24 per cent on the subscribed capital of the company. With regard to this figure, however, the fact to which I have already referred must be kept in mind, namely, that at all events until 1922, when the capital was increased, the business of the company was to a large extent carried on not with its own capital but with the capital borrowed from Christian Salvesen & Co. Another general figure of some importance is this, that during the whole period, and after writing off depreciation on the fixed assets at 10 per cent, the

average annual profits earned amounted to 164 per cent on its capital. The net profits which were earned during the same period amounted to considerably over £1,000,000, whereas I was informed there was distributed amongst the shareholders in dividends about £115,000, the remainder being retained in the business. I feel bound to say that these figures suggest to me very strongly that it would be quite fallacious to value these shares merely on the basis of the dividends paid and without regard to the amount of the profits which were earned but not distributed.

6 Such having been the history of the company up to the date of the testator's death, I now turn to examine more closely its financial position at that date. The last balance sheet made up prior to the testator's death contains some very striking figures. The assets of this concern, which had commenced its trading operations 17 years before with a capital of £20,000, are now valued at £1,012,846, the amount standing at the credit of profit and loss is £903,564, of which only £16,000 was distributed in dividend. The nominal reserves stand at the sum of £170,000. The important matter is, however, the assets side of the balance sheet. There was some discussion with regard to the basis on which the shares fell to be valued, namely, as to whether they should be valued on the *(pg48)* footing that the company was a going concern or on the footing that it went into liquidation at the date of the testator's death. The shares were originally valued by the secretary with the approval of the auditors on the basis of an immediate liquidation at £2 each and without taking any account of the restrictive conditions. It was ultimately common ground, however, that the shares fall to be valued on the footing that the company was a going concern. But it is not immaterial to have regard to the value of this concern on a break-up basis on the figures contained in the last balance prior to the testator's death. It is of importance for this, if for no other reason, that presumably the shareholders believed that it would be more advantageous for them to continue trading than it would have been to wind up the concern at the end of the season 1925–26. I do not propose to go into the question of whether there was any break-up value in the fixed assets of this concern, namely, the station and the ships. The point which the Crown witnesses desired to make on this matter can be made even on the assumption that these assets had no break-up value at all. The other assets of the company shown in the balance sheet included a sum of £479,654 due to company by the firm of Christian Salvesen & Co. The company had also investments of the value of £27,853, which it was taken would realise that sum. Stocks are entered in the balance sheet at £50,621. I confess I do not altogether understand why they should realise much less than this sum on a break-up basis as was suggested by the auditors, but, in any view of the matter, I think it may be taken that the liquid assets of the company, that is to say assets that could be turned into cash at short notice, amounted to over £500,000. Now I recognise that to wind up a concern like this would be a complicated matter and might cost a large sum of money, but I think it would be safe to assume that the break-up value of this concern was well over £400,000 and might even be as much as £500,000. This means that, on a break-up basis, the £1 shares were worth £4 or £5. It does not, however, at all follow that the shares have the same value on the footing that the company is a going concern, but the fact that this figure might have been realised on a break-up basis suggests to me that the shareholders were so confident of the future of the concern that they preferred to continue trading rather than realise this large appreciation in the capital value of the shares. The hypothetical purchaser of shares would no doubt be influenced by the opinion of the company held by the directors and shareholders as shown by their own actings and also attach weight to their knowledge and experience of the industry. It appears from the evidence of the chairman of the company that he has had a long and intimate knowledge and experience of the industry. The hypothetical buyer would see from the accounts that he and the other directors were quite willing year after year to embark the large profits, which they had already made from the industry, in another year's trading and would draw his own conclusions from that circumstance. Prior to the testator's death, the company had made arrangements for trading in the ensuing season and had either expended or committed itself to an amount of about £300,000, and intending shareholders might regard this circumstance also as cogent evidence of the confidence which the directors had in the immediate future of the company. I must, however, qualify this by adding that, though it may show that, it does not by any means necessarily show that the directors were confident that the rate of profit which had been earned for the four previous years would be maintained in the future and it must be borne in mind that the point of view of a shareholder who acquired his shares at par would be quite different from that of a prospective shareholder who is being asked to pay £5 10s for the shares offered to him. *(pg49)*

7 Apart from any conclusion which an intending investor might draw from the break-up value of the undertaking, he would, I feel sure, especially when he was informed that it was intended to continue the company's trading operations, examine the most recent balance sheet carefully with a view to obtaining some indication of the value of the concern as a going undertaking. A person who was being invited to acquire a third of the shares of a private company which imposed stringent conditions on the right of transfer would certainly wish to ascertain the value at which the assets had been entered in the last balance sheet. As a prudent person he would, of course, keep in view that he was purchasing the shares in October 1926 and that the balance sheet shows the affairs of the company as at July 1926 and he would make inquiry as to the alterations in its financial position which had taken place between these two dates. But he would first examine the balance sheet and I think that he would be very favourably impressed by the fact that the assets showed a surplus of upwards of £900,000 over its capital. On this basis the capital value of the share would be in excess of the sum of £5 10s which the Crown say he would be willing to pay. Some challenge was, however, made of the value of the assets shown in this balance sheet, and particularly of the value of the steamers. I quite understand the view that on a break-up basis the value of the ships, which were entered in the balance sheet at £452,122, might amount to a very small sum. A large number of the vessels were specially fitted out for whaling and it might well happen at any particular time that there was no demand for such vessels and that therefore they would have merely scrap value. But when one comes to regard the matter of the value of the vessels as a going concern, the position seems to me different. A number of the vessels were built and acquired in the years 1925 and 1926, and I do not quite follow why, assuming 10 per cent is a fair rate of depreciation on them – as I think it is – the vessels should be less valuable than the amount to which they have been written down. Having been built quite recently they were presumably up to date vessels and there is nothing in the evidence to suggest that, if the company wished to replace them at the end of ten years, the cost would be any greater than it was at the time they were built. It must be admitted, however, that a number of the other vessels are in a different position. They were much older – I may observe parenthetically that the ages of some of them indicate that 10 per cent is a generous rate of depreciation – and, as they were quite recently acquired, I find it difficult to understand why their depreciated value should not fairly represent their value to a going concern. But, on the other hand, as they were old vessels it may be presumed that they would not last at the longest more than 10 years. If and when they came to be replaced by new vessels, the cost of such new vessels would presumably be much greater than the original cost of the old vessels. A prudent investor, who investigated this matter, might come to the conclusion that the allowance for depreciation did not represent replacement costs, and that a larger allowance ought to be made for this circumstance. I do not think it is possible upon the material available to estimate this at any specific figure. But even if a large allowance were made on this head, it seems clear that the balance sheet shows the capital value of each share at a sum in excess of the £5 10s claimed by the Crown. While I think this circumstance would weigh with the intending investor, I do not mean to say that he would assume that there was any likelihood of the assets of the company being realised – say by sale to another company – and of his being paid out the capital value of his share. On the contrary he would, I assume, be informed that if he became a shareholder, the only means open to him of realising his capital would be to avail himself of the very restricted *(pg50)* right of transfer given by the articles. He would, of course, also know, when he came to make his purchase, that by that time an important change had taken place in the financial position of the company and that the directors had decided to continue trading for another year and had committed themselves to the extent of about £300,000. He might, as I have already said, regard this as evidence of the confidence which the directors had in the future of the company, and in any event I do not think that he would suppose that there was any risk of the whole of that £300,000 being lost. In the worst years which the company had there were always large credits from the sale of oils and in no case was the total amount laid out in expenses, &c, lost. The largest figure the loss in any year ever reached was less than £80,000. The investor would, of course, also recognise that, owing to the restrictions on the right of transfer, a very important matter from his point of view was whether the rate of profit earned and dividends declared would be maintained in the future. Apart from the prospects of the whaling, which I will deal with later, I think he would take the view that, even if the trading were not very successful in the immediate future, the reserves of this company were so large that it would have no difficulty in maintaining the rate of dividend which it had then been paying for some years. Twenty per cent on a capital of £100,000 means £20,000, and accordingly £100,000 would have provided a reserve to pay dividend at this rate for five years. In any view of the value of the assets of this concern, it had reserves of more than £500,000 and it could accordingly easily have maintained this dividend for five years, even if no net profits had been earned during that period, and left the company with a pretty ample margin for working capital. I think that in addition it would have been able to meet losses at least as large as any that it had experienced, in its past history. I quite recognise that the problem I have to deal with must be solved in the light of the information available at or about the time of the testator's death, but I think that, however, does not debar me completely from making any reference to the balance sheet at 31 July 1927, which includes a period of nearly three months prior to the testator's death. The profit made in that year was £171,122 and the directors set aside £400,000 as a dividend reserve. This seems to indicate that the directors must have considered that the undistributed profits that they had in hand at the end of the previous year were far more than was necessary for trading purposes and might have been used by them to maintain the rate of dividend in bad years. It was admitted by the accountants examined by the petitioners that the value of the assets shown in the balance sheet was important as showing that an intending purchaser would have ample security for his capital. I go further, however, and think that these assets indicate, to some extent at all events, the capital value of the share in this concern which he was acquiring and also furnished ample security for payment of dividends in lean years. It may here be observed that the longest period of depression which this company experienced was the three years 1918–19, 1919–20 and 1920–21 and the net amount of the loss during those years was less than £160,000. The general conclusion which I draw from an examination of this balance sheet is that the intending investor would be very favourably impressed with the position and prospects of this company and that it would incline him to regard the shares as being much in excess of their nominal value. But the investor would have also to consider:

(3) The future prospects of the industry and of this company

8 As I have already said, whaling is admittedly a speculative industry. The raw material of the industry is the whale and if no whales are available the industry must collapse. The intending investor would realise this obvious fact *(pg51)* and it may be presumed that he would make some inquiry into the matter. He would find that it was engaging some attention at this time. The research ship 'Discovery' had been sent out by the British Government to the South Atlantic and Antarctic Seas in the year 1925 to make scientific observations which might serve as a basis for the regulation of the whaling industry, but I gather that no report had been made by the Committee prior to the material date. The whaling industry in the South Georgia waters has all along been under

Government control. The shore stations are leased from the Government and licences are required from the Government for the prosecution of whaling within territorial waters. There are restrictions on the number of whale catchers that may be employed, but no restriction on the number of whales that may be caught. The licences are liable to recall by the Government in the event of the regulations being contravened, but, apart from what might result from the 'Discovery' investigations, it does not appear that there was much risk in 1926 of the company's operations being interfered with by the Government. I gather that pending a definite recommendation from the 'Discovery' Committee the policy of the Government is to maintain the status quo and not to issue any other licences and this policy is not to the disadvantage of the company. The possibility of further Government control and restriction was, however, being spoken about at this time and the prospective investor would no doubt hear of this. An extension of Government control has two aspects. It would presumably prevent the indiscriminate slaughter of whales with a view to maintaining an adequate stock, and this would no doubt in the long run be in the interests of the industry and of the companies engaged in it. But, on the other hand, it might be found necessary to impose severe restriction for some years on the number of whales which the licence holders were permitted to kill and the prosecution of the industry might become less remunerative or even unremunerative during this period. As I have already indicated, I think the intending investor, looking at the matter from a practical point of view, would probably be influenced by the fact that the shareholders of this company, who probably knew as much about the matter as anyone, were so confident that there was no immediate prospect either of the disappearance of the whales or of the industry being prejudicially affected by Government interference that they had spent large sums of money in recent years in purchasing whaling vessels, though their previous policy had been to hire them, and had also committed themselves to the extent of £300,000 for that season's trading. The evidence of Mr Borley, a naturalist in the employment of the Colonial Office, indicates that, though the matter was engaging attention at this time, there was no evidence to suggest that there was any likelihood of the disappearance or even serious diminution in the number of the blue whales and the fin whales, which constitute the major portion of the catch. He expressed the view that there was not likely to be any decline or collapse of the industry for a very considerable number of years after 1926, and in point of fact it appears from his evidence, and from the report of the 'Discovery' investigations, that the seasons 1926–27 and 1927–28 were very successful. While I think the intending investor would have no reason to suppose that whales were likely to disappear, on the other hand I think he must be presumed to know that there might be in the future, as there had been in prior years, such a falling off in their number in a particular season as to render the trading for that season unremunerative and even to result in a large loss. The possibility of further Government control and restriction of the industry was a thing, however, which an investor might also regard as introducing an element of doubt and which might depreciate the amount he would be willing to offer for the shares. Another *(pg52)* disturbing factor in the situation at this time was the commencement of Pelagic fishing. Pelagic fishing is fishing for whales on the high seas, and its characteristic feature is that, instead of the whale catchers being based on a shore station, they are based on a factory ship which operates on the high seas and performs all the functions of the shore stations and in particular the boiling of the whale for the purpose of obtaining oil from it. Pelagic fishing has turned out to be very successful, but it was in its initial stages in 1926, and the only vessel which operated in that year was not very successful. What I am concerned with is not the development of Pelagic fishing since 1926, but the knowledge that an intending investor would probably have of it in that year and whether it would influence his views as to the value of the shares. Mr Borley indicates in his evidence that he thought it was not occasioning much serious concern to those in the industry at that time, and I agree with this view. In 1926 no licences were required for Pelagic fishing and, if it turned out to be successful, it would probably mean more competition in the whaling industry. Companies which had licences from the Government, as the South Georgia had, could engage in Pelagic fishing as well as in fishing in territorial waters, but it is in evidence that a very large expenditure would be required to enable them to do so. On this matter I take the view that a prudent investor would regard the past history of the company as a fairly reliable guide as to what its future might be expected to be, but he would, I think, also have in mind that two disturbing elements had made their appearance in 1926 and might reasonably enough form the opinion they would cause serious difficulties in the industry in the years to come. But the past history of the company would no doubt lead him to take the view that if the conditions in the industry were favourable, this company would, as it had done in the past, take full advantage of them.

9 Having dealt with the different matters, which I think the hypothetical buyer would investigate, I must now direct my attention to the views of the experts for the petitioners and for the Crown. Mr Robertson-Durham and Mr Macfarlan, who gave evidence on behalf of the petitioners, took the view that the prospective purchaser would look for a return of 15 per cent on his investment and on this basis they valued the shares at £1 6s 8d. I do not think any exception whatever can be taken to the yield which they thought that the investor was entitled to look for. Sir William M'Lintock and Professor Annan, who gave evidence for the Crown, were prepared to concede to the prospective investor a return of 40 per cent. The difference between Mr Robertson-Durham and Sir William M'Lintock is, however, this. Mr Robertson-Durham's figure of 15 per cent is based upon the dividend actually paid to the shareholder and does not take account directly, at all events, of profits actually earned, but not distributed as dividend. As I have already pointed out, there was, as I think, little risk of the dividend, which the company had been paying, not being maintained in the immediate future. But I cannot think it is right to ignore the very large sums which this company had actually earned but had not distributed as dividend. I accept the evidence which was given by Sir William M'Lintock as regards this matter with this exception, that I do not subscribe to his view that the shareholders acted irrationally in not distributing the profits which they had earned. Whaling is a speculative industry and I think the shareholders of

this company in the four years prior to the date of the testator's death had been earning the prizes which their courage and prudence deserved, but their confidence in the industry had been all along such that they were not content merely to reap their harvest and invest it, say, in less speculative securities, but reinvested it in the industry in the expectation, I cannot doubt, that they would *(pg53)* earn still greater prizes. This was quite a rational and intelligible policy in a private company, though it may not have been a course which the directors of a large public company would or could have taken. Assuming that in the future the company has its ups and downs as it has had in the past, its reserves must ultimately, according to all reasonable probabilities, enure to the benefit of the shareholders. Indeed the evidence for the petitioners seems to suggest that the company had reached a point at which no further development was possible. If this be so, it could not go on indefinitely piling up its reserves and the shareholders must have got the benefit either in increased distributions of profits or in bonus shares. If a company retains reserves beyond what can be utilised in the business, the only other thing that can be done with the money is to invest it outside the business, in which case the shareholders get the benefit of the interest and dividends therefrom. The directors of this company may have adopted a policy of only distributing a small part of the profits as dividend, but it was impossible for them to pursue such a policy indefinitely. I cannot doubt that when they were satisfied that they had reached the stage at which the profits could no longer be usefully employed in the business they would have distributed them to the shareholders. The hypothetical person, who I am to assume is the purchaser of these shares, might be apprehensive that he would find himself in an uncomfortable position as an intruder into a family concern, but I feel confident that in their own interest, if for no other reason, the directors of the company would continue to manage it as successfully in the future as they had done in the past. While I accept Sir William M'Lintock's view with regard to the reserves in this company, I am unable to agree with him in thinking that the prospective purchaser would base his offer on the footing that the company would be able to give him a return in profits distributed or undistributed of 40 per cent. Sir William, as he explained in his evidence, disregarding altogether the sum obtained in respect of the cargo of the 'Niko,' took the average amount of profits for the last three years at £220,000. If this profit were maintained in the future, it would warrant a price of £5 10s per share on the basis of a 40 per cent yield. Apparently at the time Sir William fixed this figure as the value of the shares he had only seen the accounts of the company for four years. These four years were the most favourable in the company's existence. Sir William did not see the accounts for the earlier years until the morning of the day he gave his evidence, and I am inclined to think that, if he had seen them earlier, he might have modified his valuation of £5 10s per share. While I think that the intending investor would take a favourable view of the prospects of this company I do not think that there is anything in the evidence which would justify him in forming a confident opinion that the exceptional prosperity which prevailed during the four years prior to the testator's death would be an absolutely safe guide for the future. I referred to the 1927 balance sheet for a point in favour of the Crown. I now refer to it for the purpose of pointing out that the balance at the credit of the profit and loss account in that year does not yield a return of 40 per cent on a value of £5 10s per share and rather disproves the hypothesis on which the case for the Crown is based.

10 (4) The last matter which I have to consider is the effect which the restrictive conditions in the articles would have on the value of the shares. I may say at once that I regard these restrictions as depreciating their value very considerably. Nobody, except a person who was prepared to have his capital locked up for many years, could afford to buy them at more than par value. I imagine that there are a very limited number of persons who would be prepared to pay £5 10s for a £1 share which might only be realisable at par or less. The prospective *(pg54)* buyer at the price fixed by the Commissioners would have to be able to find over £152,000 and, in order to avoid a loss on his capital, he would have to be prepared to hold the shares himself for an indefinite period or transfer them to one or more of the persons mentioned in the articles, subject, however, to the condition that no transferee held less than 10,000 shares. All the witnesses were agreed that the restrictions would depreciate the value of the shares, but the only witness who put any money value on this restriction was Mr Robertson-Durham, who said that, in his opinion, it might make a difference of as much as 8s 4d on his value of £1 6s 8d and, in my opinion, this figure is not by any means excessive. Sir William M'Lintock did not put a definite sum on the depreciating value of these restrictions, but I cannot doubt that he took them into account when he allowed the intending investor the large yield of 40 per cent on the price paid by him.

11 The estimation of the value of shares by a highly artificial standard which is never applied in the ordinary share market must be a matter of opinion and does not admit of precise scientific or mathematical calculation. For the reasons I have indicated I find myself unable to accept the value that is put forward either by the petitioner or the Crown. Giving the best consideration I can to all the different matters to which I have referred, I estimate the value of a £1 share in this company on 24 October 1926 at £3. *(pg55)*

Case 16
Smyth v IRC

(1931) IR 643

High Court

10, 11, 12, 23 March 1931

This case considers the adjustment required to publish earnings figures in order to reflect the fact that the directors extracted profit by increasing their remuneration.

Edward Weber Smyth died on 23 May 1928. In his estate was a holding of 18,501 ordinary shares in Robert Smyth & Sons Ltd, tea and wine merchants, a company that carried on a retail business in Dublin.

The shareholding in the estate comprised 80.4 per cent of the issued share capital of the company, with a further 18.5 per cent being held by the deceased's son.

During the five years prior to the date of death directors' remuneration totalling £14,094 had been taken, which amounted to 73 per cent of the company's profits prior to the deduction.

The executors valued the shareholding at £13,876. The Revenue considered that, in making the valuation, directors' remuneration in excess of that which would be paid to an unconnected third party should be added back. The Revenue valued the shareholding at £20,814.

In his judgement Hanna J does not specifically state that it is necessary to add back the excess to directors' remuneration in order to calculate the market value of the share but this is inherent in his judgement:

'The principal item in dispute is the method and amount of remuneration of the two directors. The witnesses for the Revenue submitted that the directors' remuneration, at a figure of £3,000 per annum, for such a business was out of all proportion to the value of their services or the nature of the business, and was such as no public company would pay, running the business on a commercial basis. In this I agree.'

((1931) IR 643 at 654 **case 16 para 9**)

The judgement is also of interest as a good illustration of the approach that must always be taken in judging market value. No valuation should be based on one measure alone, all relevant measures should be considered, then the valuer stands back and looks at the matter in the round, before suggesting a value of the shareholding. In his judgement, Hanna J brought into his consideration of the share value:

1.   the history of the company ((1931) IR 643 at 652 **case 16 para 6**);
2.   the structure of shareholdings in the company (at 652 **case 16 para 6**);
3.   the premises occupied by the company (at 652 **case 16 para 6**);
4.   the value of the company assets (at 653 **case 16 para 7**);
5.   the financial health of the company (at 653 **case 16 para 7**);
6.   the directors' remuneration and their duties (at 653 **case 16 para 8**);
7.   the dividends paid (at 653 **case 16 para 8**);
8.   the potential purchasers of the shareholding (at 654/655 **case 16 paras 10–12**); and
9.   the effect of the restrictions on transfer (at 655 **case 16 para 13**).

He concludes:

> 'From the point of view of their pleadings each party has taken up an extreme view, and elects to stand upon one point: the petitioners, on the actual profit earning capacity based on the past balance sheets; and the Revenue, on the value of the shares in relation to the capital, disregarding the figures in the balance sheets. In this I think both are wrong. In my opinion, in estimating the price, every advantage and disadvantage to the company, and every benefit and clog attaching to the share, as well as the nature of the particular company, must be considered. According as the facts differ more weight will be given to one element than to another. You must consider the profit-earning capacity, the return for the purchaser's investment, the general solvency of the company, the extent of the security in the shape of assets, the nature of the management, the objects of the company, its methods of business, the capital value of the assets of the company, the restrictions upon the transfer of the shares, and the amount of liabilities. On some of these elements persons accustomed to value can place a relevant figure, but the test for some of the others is merely general business experience.'
>
> ((1931) IR 643 at 656 **case 16 para 14**)

The judgement also considers the nature of the potential purchaser of shares, under the statutory provision. The valuation provisions for both inheritance tax and capital gains tax postulate a sale in the open market to a purchaser who is often referred to as 'a hypothetical unconnected purchaser'. In this case, the Revenue stated in evidence that in valuing the shareholding they made the assumption that the purchase would be made by someone purchasing the shareholding *en bloc* for the purpose either of obtaining control of the firm, so as to extinguish it, or to amalgamate it with some other firm, or for the purpose of pure speculation, to wind up and take his profit on the excess of the realisable assets over liabilities.

This was rejected by Hanna J:

> 'I think that the weakness underlying the submission of the Revenue Commissioners is the assumption that the shares in this case would be necessarily, or even likely to be, sold *en bloc* to one purchaser. I do not think that the section of the Act contemplates in the term "open market", not only a market which is hypothetical, but also only hypothetical purchasers wanting a block of shares. In my judgement, you must take into consideration the possibility of the shares being divided up among several purchasers, either members of the family or of the public. In visualising the hypothetical open market I consider that it may contain some persons looking merely for a return for their money in a going concern, or some members of the family anxious to buy, and perhaps willing to give more than the ordinary buyer, in order to keep the business in the family, as well as the block purchaser, who wants to wind up the company for some reason, or to have a profit on his speculation.'
>
> ((1931) IR 643 at 655 **case 16 para 12**)

Thus, the case provides judicial authority for the principle that all possible purchasers must be considered when valuing a shareholding for fiscal purposes.

Judgement

References, example '(pg651)', are to (1931) IR 643.

1 HANNA J (23 March): The questions arising before me in this case are of some importance and difficulty, affecting (1) the principles upon which, for the purposes of estate duty, the Court should assess the value of shares held by the deceased in a private trading company; and (2) what matters can, in the circumstances of the case, be properly taken into consideration in the application of these principles to the actual shares under consideration.

2 The case comes before the Court by way of appeal from the Revenue Commissioners on a petition by Elizabeth Anna Smyth and Weber Smyth, the executors of Edward Weber Smyth, deceased, under sect 10 of the Finance Act

1894, to determine the amount of the estate duty payable upon 18,501 shares held by the deceased in Robert Smyth & Sons Limited, carrying on business at Stephen's Green, Dublin. The company is a private (not a public) company, whose business has been carried on by the Smyth family, from father to son, for over a century; and under article 25 of the articles of association the transfer of the shares is restricted, inasmuch as the directors have power to refuse to register a transfer to a transferee of whom they do not approve.

3 Sect 7 of the Finance Act 1894 enacts the manner of determining the value of any estate for the purpose of estate duty; and sub-sect 5 enacts that the principal value of any property shall be estimated to be the price which, in the opinion of the Commissioners, such property would fetch if sold in the open market at the time of the death of the deceased. There is no open market for such shares, and the Court has to construct a hypothetical market in which to obtain a price for the shares. That is one of the difficulties of assessment in the case, and the other main difficulty is that the shares are subject to a restriction upon transfer.

4 Though some questions raised in this case have not been the subject of legal authority that might assist the Court, much of the difficulty is removed by the decision of the Irish Court of Appeal in the case of *Attorney-General v Jameson,* where *(pg651)* it was distinctly laid down, in the case of shares subject to restriction, that the principal value of the shares is to be estimated at the price which the shares would fetch if sold in the open market, on the terms that the purchaser should be entitled to be registered as holder of the shares, but should take and hold them subject to the provisions of the articles of association, including the article relating to restriction of transfer: see the judgment of Holmes LJ, p 240. We have to assume an unobjectionable purchaser, and try to determine what would be the price that he would be prepared to pay in the open market, holding the shares subject to any disabilities or restrictions. In other words: What is the value of the shares that the hypothetical buyer acquires at an assumed sale?

5 The next question that arises, upon which much evidence and argument have been given, is as to what matters can be properly regarded by the Court in applying the principle referred to. Here the parties come into acute conflict upon their contentions, which were: on the part of the appellants and petitioners, that the Court should consider mainly, if not altogether, the low average rate of net profit in fact paid by the company during the past six years; and, on the part of the Revenue Commissioners, that in this case the true guide was the excess of the assets over liabilities in a voluntary winding up, the company being in an extremely solvent condition. The appellants valued the shares at 15s each, and the Commissioners at 22s 6d.

6 It is necessary before approaching these topics to state briefly the history and position of the company in so far as they are relevant to the question the Court has to decide. The business was originally founded in 1807, and has been continuously, since 1839, carried on in the same place in Stephen's Green, Dublin, from father to son. The business during all that time has been confined to tea, wine, and whisky, and, on the evidence, is of a unique and very high-class character. The business was turned into a limited company in 1898, with a share capital of £30,000, divided into 30,000 shares of £1 each, of which 23,007 had been issued, and it was turned into a private company, by special resolution, on 10 July 1908. The shares were always held by the family, and at the date of the death of the deceased he held 18,501, and 4,251 were held by the petitioner, Weber Smyth, who is a son of the deceased, and assistant managing director of the company. The shares, being shares in a private company, and subject to restriction on transfer, were never dealt in on the Stock Exchange, nor was there at any time any market quotation. The business premises are held by the company on a yearly tenancy at a rent of £200. The shop front in Stephen's Green is about 48 feet, with 150 feet depth, and there is a back entrance in Anne's Lane. The poor law valuation is £310 per annum. The premises in Stephen's Green were owned by the deceased, and the rent of £200 was an agreed sum, to be charged against the company in the accounts. I find that the ordinary letting value of the premises would be £650 a year. *(pg652)*

7 As to the business itself, I find that it was in an extremely prosperous condition. The value of the stock in hands was disputed, but I find that it was approximately of a value of £25,000 at market price on the date of the death, and outstanding debts were valued at £8,500, against which a reserve of only £750 was kept. The proportion of bad or doubtful debts was extremely small. The whole assets of the company probably amounted in value to £40,000. While it is not necessary for my purpose to ascertain the exact figure, it is necessary to form an opinion of the general stability of the firm. The turnover per annum was between £39,000 and £40,000. Against all this the sundry and cash creditors of the company amounted to only £2,543, a very satisfactory position. I estimate that the average gross profits, before deducting directors' remuneration or depreciation, were over £4,000 a year for the past six years.

8 The nature of the management and the remuneration of the directors were much discussed. The testator, until a short time before his death, at the age of 85, actively controlled, and attended daily to, the business. His son, Weber Smyth, who had been in the business from boyhood, was assistant managing director. Both these gentlemen came into daily personal contact with their customers, and this personal element was much relied upon by the petitioners. The testator was an expert in teas and wines. Now, as to the remuneraton: until 1907 they were getting dividends on whatever shares they held, and Mr Weber Smyth had a comparatively small salary. In that year a difference was made in the income tax on earned and unearned income and it was arranged that the benefit of the reduction in tax on earned income could be obtained by giving a salary, which, in the first instance, varied in proportion to the number of shares held. In 1918 this variation was abandoned, and fixed salaries were given of £1,500 to the deceased and £750 to Mr Weber Smyth. In 1920 these were raised to £2,000 and £1,000, and, save for a short period when they were slightly reduced, these salaries continued until the death of Mr Weber Smyth, senior. Being a family company, in which no one was really interested except the two directors, the profits could be divided up either as salaries or dividends as they liked, and they preferred to give them as salary. The result of this was that for the last six years the actual dividend paid averaged 5.3 per cent, a rate of dividend which the Revenue Commissioners submitted was illusory as a test of the profit-earning capacity of the company. In this I think the Commissioners are right.

9 The first question presented for consideration on the petition is whether the dividend-earning capacity of the company is the sole or the proper test of the value of the shares in the hypothetical open market. The Revenue Commissioners submit that not only is it not a test, but, even if it is to be considered at all, the figures presented by the petitioners must be severely criticised. The contention of the Revenue Commissioners is that *(pg653)* the earning capacity of the company is not represented by the average of 5.3 per cent for the last six years' trading, but by a figure of 12 per cent. On this subject the principal item in dispute is the method and amount of remuneration of the two directors. The witnesses for the Revenue submitted that the directors' remuneration, at a figure of £3,000 per annum, for such a business was out of all proportion to the value of their services or the nature of the business, and was such as no public company would pay, running the business on a commercial basis. In this I agree; but, on the other hand, considerable weight must be given to the view put forward by the petitioners that it was a family company, where greater latitude would be given in the remuneration of the directors, who were the principal owners; and that it was a unique business, in which both the directors had special knowledge, and to which they gave constant daily attention, and had a special personal relationship with the majority of the customers. A purchaser in a hypothetical market of any of these shares would recognise the value of these factors, and make due allowance for much more than the ordinary remuneration. The evidence on either side went into great detail, and after the consideration of it I think that this company can be fairly regarded as one capable of earning on a commercial basis 10 per cent on its capital, and I so find. But, if this is to be taken as the principal test, it must be subject to the consideration, on the one hand, of the restriction upon the transfer of the shares, and, on the other, of the added value by reason of the splendid security of the company's position.

10 There is only one measure of value in this case that is almost agreed upon. It is clear from the evidence of the stockbrokers and accountants who were called as witnesses that in the case of a private trading company, with a restriction such as this on the transfer of the shares, a 10 per cent dividend is generally regarded as giving par value to the shares. Being of opinion that the contention of the petitioners, namely, that the dividend-earning capacity is the only test, cannot be sustained, and that these other matters I have mentioned must be taken into consideration, I am also of opinion on the evidence that the principal matter that influence a purchaser in such a case is the return upon the money invested by him in the purchase of the shares.

11 The Revenue Commissioners have presented a contrary view, substantially in the following form: – They say that the most likely purchaser of the shares in this case would be someone desiring a block of shares, buying them *en bloc* for the purpose either of obtaining control of the firm, so as to extinguish it, or to amalgamate it with some other firm, or for the purpose of pure speculation, to wind up and take his profit on the excess of the realisable assets over liabilities. On this assumption there is undoubtedly much in the view they submitted, as such a purchaser would not pay much attention to the dividend-earning capacity of the company. If such a purchaser were in existence, *(pg654)* the Revenue contend, on the figures which have been submitted to me, that he could safely give 27s or 30s per share. Their submission (and there is some evidence to support it) is that where 80 per cent of the shares of the company are put up for sale, the most likely purchaser would be one of this character. They rely on the Scottish case of *M'Connell's Trustees v Commissioners of Inland Revenue*, but I think they pressed it further than was justifiable. I agree with Lord Fleming's view: 'That it is a mistake to suppose that the value of the share in a company is to be ascertained with reference merely to the income which it yields, without any regard to its capital value.' It is not necessary to go into the facts of that case, which were rather unusual by reason of the discrepancy between the assessment of the £45,908 made by the Commissioners on the shares in the Knockdolian Company and the claim by the trustees that they should be valued only at £998. Undoubtedly, a share in a limited company gives the holder a right not only to participate in the division of profits, but also to participate in the division of the capital.

12 I think that the weakness underlying the submission of the Revenue Commissioners is the assumption that the shares in this case would be necessarily, or even likely to be, sold *en bloc* to one purchaser. I do not think that the section of the Act contemplates in the term 'open market,' not only a market which is hypothetical, but also only hypothetical purchasers wanting a block of shares. In my judgment, you must take into consideration the possibility of the shares being divided up among several purchasers, either members of the family or of the public. In visualising the hypothetical open market I consider that it may contain some persons looking merely for a return for their money in a going concern, or some members of the family anxious to buy, and perhaps willing to give more than the ordinary buyer, in order to keep the business in the family, as well as the block purchaser, who wants to wind up the company for some reason, or to have a profit on his speculation. When you have all these assembled – and you must contemplate such a possibility – it is not easy to determine with arithmetical accuracy what price would be obtained, for, under sect 7, that 'price' is the value of the shares, as Lord Justice FitzGibbon points out in his judgment in *Jameson's Case*.

13 There was some argument as to the practical effect of the restriction of the transfer contained in article 25. That is made clear in *Hanlon v North City Mining Company*, from which it appears that the directors have the power to refuse to register a transfer so long as that power is exercised bona fide in the interests of the company, and no Court will examine into their conclusion if satisfied that it has been so exercised. This power would, I think, be a further barrier in the way of the block purchaser or the rival trader, who purchases for a controlling *(pg655)* interest, if the directors, as is likely in this case, were of opinion that such a sale I was not for the benefit of the company. In my opinion, this restriction on transfer is to an extent a clog on the shares by reason of which some diminution in value will ensue, save in the hands of the family, and that it is an element that would influence an ordinary, or any, purchaser, not as a sole, or perhaps even a principal, guide, but as a considerable make-weight in his price. I am of opinion that on the question of fact Mr. Brock was not shaken in his final figure of 25s as being the value of the share in relation to the capital at the date of the death of the deceased.

14 From the point of view of their pleadings each party has taken up an extreme view, and elects to stand upon one point: the petitioners, on the actual profit-earning capacity based on the past balance sheets; and the Revenue, on the value of the shares in relation to the capital, disregarding the figures in the balance sheets. In this I think both are wrong. In my opinion, in estimating the price, every advantage and disadvantage to the company, and every benefit and clog attaching to the share, as well as the nature of the particular company, must be considered. According as the facts differ more weight will be given to one element than to another. You must consider the profit-earning capacity, the return for the purchaser's investment, the general solvency of the company, the extent of the security in the shape of assets, the nature of the management, the objects of the company, its methods of business, the capital value of the assets of the company, the restrictions upon the transfer of the shares, and the amount of liabilities. On some of these elements persons accustomed to value can place a relevant figure, but the test for some of the others is merely general business experience. In my judgment, the profit-earning capacity of the share is the most important item, and would be most prominent in the mind of the purchaser in this case. When I say 'profit capacity' I mean profit-earning on a reasonable commercial basis for a company such as may be under consideration, not necessarily as appearing in the balance sheets, which may, for reasons of the proprietors, be prepared on a particular basis. But while that is in the foreground you must consider as a definite and well-marked background the capital value of the shares. It may operate either to increase or decrease the price as the case maybe.

15 I find that the shares, taking into consideration the restriction upon the transfer, are about par value on a suitable profit-earning basis; but what consideration in addition must be made for the ratio to capital value? I think the returns given in evidence for the Revenue, which are on the basis of a sale as a going concern or at break-up values, are too high. I am not sure that the purely arithmetical basis is satisfactory, as there are some elements of security that do not appear in balance sheets. Mr Brock estimated the value of the strength of the *(pg656)* company as worth an additional 25 per cent on the price of the share. Mr Walkey, the petitioners' accountant, added 3s to his 12s per share for what he called security and solvency. These percentages give me some guide, and would bring my figure over that fixed by the Commissioners, but I do not propose to alter their value, which, from every point of view, seems to me to have been carefully arrived at as a fair value on the terms of sect 7. I accordingly affirm their figure, and dismiss the petition and appeal with costs. *(pg657)*

Case 17
IRC v Crossman

(1936) 15 ATC 94

House of Lords

20 March 1936

This case provides a comprehensive valuation report made by the highest judicial authority. In the course of their lordships' judgements, the value of a minority shareholding in a fairly typical unquoted trading company is thoroughly explored. The case is particularly useful in showing how the court views the effect on valuation of the type of restrictive clauses that are typically found in the articles of association of a family company.

Percy Crossman died on 17 August 1929. In his estate was a holding of 1,000 ordinary shares in Mann Crossman and Paulin Limited, each with the nominal value of £100. This represented 10 per cent of the ordinary share capital of the company, there being also preference shares in issue.

The articles of the company restricted the transfer of shares. The articles also gave a valuation formula, on the basis of which an ordinary share was valued at £221 4s 5d. The Revenue issued an assessment to estate duty based on a value of £475 per ordinary share.

The case was eventually heard, seven years after the date of death, by the House of Lords. The case gives the judgement of the House of Lords on five important principles in share valuation.

1. The effect on the value of a shareholding of restrictions on transfer imposed by the articles of association.
2. Confirmation that the concept of a hypothetical unconnected purchaser includes any possible purchaser.
3. The effect of a special purchaser on the value of a shareholding.
4. The concept that the valuation must be undertaken under the statutory hypothesis that the hypothetical unconnected purchaser will be entered on the register and thereby accepted as a shareholder.
5. The meaning of a share in a company.

The effect on the value of a shareholding of restrictions on transfer imposed by the articles of association

The House of Lords declared that the statutory valuation provision requires the valuation to be performed on the basis that any restriction on the transfer of the shares to the hypothetical unconnected purchaser is set aside but that purchaser takes the shares subject to the articles in their entirety. In the words of Lord Roche:

> 'The language of the Act requires, in a case where no actual sale is either possible or contemplated, that a sale in the open market of a notional character is to be assumed.
>
> Upon a notional sale there must be a notional or assumed passing of property. Insofar as the passing or transfer of property is thus notional or hypothetical, no restriction upon actual passing or transfer comes into question, and the article as to the prescribed price which is to rule under certain circumstances, though it is no doubt a constituent part of the bundle of rights which constitutes a share, does not, as I think, govern such a notional transfer so as to make the notional purchaser no more than a person who acquires an obligation to offer the shares to others at the prescribed price.
>
> In assessing the value to the notional purchaser, regard is to be had to the provisions of the articles relating to alienation and transfer of the shares.'
>
> ((1936) 15 ATC 94 at 119 **case 17 para 89**)

Confirmation that the concept of a hypothetical unconnected purchaser includes any possible purchaser

One judge in the Court of Appeal said that in considering the value of the shareholding, he excluded the possibility that a particular person would be willing to give more than the price offered by the generality of potential purchaser. This approach was criticised and declared to be wrong in the judgement of the Lord Chancellor, who said that all possible purchasers must be considered when applying the statutory hypothesis of a notional sale ((1936) 15 ATC 94 at 102/103 **case 17 paras 11–12**).

The effect of a special purchaser on the value of a shareholding

The evidence in this particular case that there was a certain identifiable trust company that for special reasons of its own would be prepared to pay a higher price than others for a shareholding in Mann Crossman Paulin Limited because of certain particular attractions which the prospect of getting upon the share register would hold out for such a company. The Lord Chancellor held that the price the special purchaser would be expected to offer must be considered in valuing the shareholding ((1936) 15 ATC 94 at 113 **case 17 para 11**); see also the judgement of Lord Blanesburgh ((1936) 15 ATC 94 at 108 **case 17 para 58**).

The concept that the valuation must be undertaken under the statutory hypothesis that the hypothetical unconnected purchaser will be entered on the register and thereby accepted as a shareholder

A valuation is undertaken on the basis that any purchaser will be recognised as having full ownership rights of the shares. In the words of Lord Blanesburgh:

'... if the notional sale is to be a sale of the entire share just as it belonged to the deceased immediately before his death, then registration of the share in the name of the notional purchaser must also be offered.'

((1936) 15 ATC 94 at 109 **case 17 para 37**)

'That is to say, the preventive provisions of the article are to be ignored, whether they provide for the other shareholders' rights of pre-emption or for the approval by the directors of every transfer.'

((1936) 15 ATC 94 at 115 **case 17 para 39**)

The meaning of a share in a company

Lord Rosale of Killowen described the fundamental characteristic of a share in a limited company:

'A share in a limited company is a property the nature of which has been accurately expounded by Mr Justice Farwell in *Borland's Trustee v Steel* ([1901] 1 Chancery page 279). It is the interest of a person in the company, that interest being composed of rights and obligations which are defined by the Companies Act and by the memorandum and articles of association of the company. A sale of a share is a sale of the interest so defined, and the subject matter of the sale is effectively vested in the purchaser by the entry of his name in the register of members.'

(case 17 para 72)

In the words of Lord MacMillan:

'My lords, a share in a joint stock company is an entirely conventional creation; the congeries of rights and liabilities of which it consists is the creature of the Companies Acts and the memorandum and articles of the particular company. Within the law the rights and liabilities appurtenant to a share may vary widely. But it cannot exist independently of the inherent attributes with which it has been created.

When therefore the legislature directs that these shares are to be conceived as being exposed for sale in the open market, in order to see what price they would fetch, I conceive them as being offered to purchasers with all their attributes. If they are subject to conditions which restrict either the rights or enjoyment of the rights of alienation of the holder, then the sale must be of the shares as so restricted. The Finance Act confers no power to strip the shares of any of their inherent attributes. The sale, no doubt, is a hypothetical sale, but the hypothesis is that the thing itself is being sold as it stands with all its qualities and all its disabilities.'

((1936) 15 ATC 94 at 117/118 **case 17 paras 82–83**)

As in *Salvesen's Trustees v IRC* (1930) 9 ATC 43 **case 15**, this case gives a full account of the way in which the process of valuing a shareholding is a matter of balancing the many different elements and is a model for a share valuation report. The particular value of *IRC v Crossman* is that the analysis of the elements in a valuation is undertaken by the highest court. The authority of the House of Lords is given to the concept that the valuation must be undertaken under the statutory hypothesis that the hypothetical unconnected purchaser will be entered on the register and thereby accepted as a shareholder.

Judgement

References, example '(pg96)', are to (1936) 15 ATC 94.

1 THE LORD CHANCELLOR: My lords, these two appeals involve the same question, namely, what is the proper basis of valuation for purposes of estate duty of shares in a limited company where the right of transfer is restricted by the articles of association. The company involved in these two cases is named Mann, Crossman & Paulin Ltd. It was incorporated in 1901 to take over and carry on an old family business of brewers. It has a paid-up capital of £2,250,000, divided into 125,000 5 per cent preference shares of £10 each and 10,000 ordinary shares of £100 each. The shares with which we are concerned in these two cases are ordinary shares. The relevant article is in the following terms: -

'Article 34(1) A male holder may at any time transfer any one or more of his said ordinary shares to any of his sons daughters or grandsons (being sons of sons) or brother or nephews (being sons of brothers) and being of the age of 25 years at the least, and being in other respects in the opinion of the directors duly qualified for membership. (2) A male holder may by his will or any codicil thereto appoint any one or more of his ordinary shares to. any of his sons daughters or grandsons (being sons of sons) or brothers or nephews (being sons of brothers) and, being at the time of his death of the age of 25 years at the least; and any such appointee shall be entitled to a transfer of the shares from the legal personal representatives of the appointor, provided that the directors within three months after the death of the appointor signify their approval of the transferee. (3) A male holder may by his will or any codicil thereto appoint any one or more of his ordinary shares to any of his sons daughters or grandsons (being sons of sons) or brothers or nephews (being sons of brothers (and who may at the time of his death be under the age of 25 years on the footing that the appointment is only to take effect as and when the appointee attains the age of 25 years, and may in like manner make provision as to the application of the interim income arising from such shares for the benefit of the appointor's widow (if any) and any child or children or remoter issue or brother or nephew (being a son of a brother) of the appointor or some or one of them. And in default of and subject to any such provision such interim income shall be applied in such manner as the legal personal representatives of the appointor shall think fit for the benefit of any such persons as aforesaid. Any such appointee shall on attaining the age of 25 years be entitled to a transfer of the shares from the legal personal representatives of the appointor, provided that the directors within three months after he becomes so entitled signify their approval of him as transferee. (3a) The ordinary shares held by any person who shall have acquired his holding under sub-clause (1), (2) or (3) of this clause and (a) who has no issue, or (b) who dies without having disposed of his ordinary shares pursuant to sub-clause (2) or (3) hereof, may, and in the case of the death of such holder without having disposed thereof shall, be offered to the company pursuant to sub-clauses (6) to (14), (c) hereof inclusive or such of the same sub-clauses as may be applicable. Provided always that in the case of ordinary shares held by any person who shall have acquired his holding under sub-clause (1), (2) or (3) of this clause, and who is a daughter of any ordinary shareholder such ordinary shares shall be transferable only pursuant to the provisions contained in the said sub-clauses (6) to (14) (c) or such of them as may be applicable.

Sub-clauses (4) and (5) are not relevant.

'*Notice of intention to transfer.* (6) Except where the transfer is made pursuant to paragraphs 1, 2, 3 or 5 of this clause, a member proposing to transfer any ordinary share (hereinafter called "the proposing transferor") shall give notice in writing (hereinafter called "the transfer notice") to the company that he desires to transfer the same. Such notice shall constitute the company his agent for the sale of the share at par value to any member of the company holding an ordinary share or ordinary shares. (7) The transfer notice may include several ordinary shares, and in such case shall operate as if it were a separate notice in respect of each. The transfer notice shall not be revocable except with the sanction of the directors. *Company's power.* (8) If the company shall, within the space of three months after being served with such notice, find a member holding an ordinary share or ordinary shares willing to purchase the share (hereinafter called "the purchasing member") and shall give notice thereof to the proposing transferor, he shall be bound, upon payment of the par value, to transfer the share to the purchasing member. *Par value.* (9) In these regulations the par value of any share means a sum equal to the capital paid up thereon. *Default by proposing transferor.* (10) If in any case the proposing transferor, after having become bound as aforesaid, makes default in transferring the share, the company may receive the purchase-money and shall thereupon cause the name of the purchasing member to be entered in the register as the holder of the share, and shall hold the purchase-money in trust for the proposing transferor. *Receipt.* (11) The receipt of the company for the purchase-money shall be a good discharge to the purchasing member, and, after his name has been entered in the register, in purported exercise of the aforesaid power, the validity of the proceedings shall not be questioned by any person. *Default by company.* (12) If the company shall not, within the space of three months after being served with the transfer notice, find a member holding an ordinary share or ordinary shares willing to purchase the shares and give notice in manner aforesaid, the proposing transferor shall, at any time within three calendar months afterwards, be at liberty (subject to paragraph 14 hereof) to sell and transfer the shares (or those not placed) to any person and at any price. *How shares to be offered to members.* (13) If, and so far as, practicable, the shares comprised in a transfer notice shall be offered by the company to the members holding an ordinary share or ordinary shares in proportion as nearly as may be to the ordinary shares held by them respectively, and any shares not accepted in response to such offer shall be offered to the remaining said members in the like proportion. Any share which it is impracticable thus to offer, may be offered to such member or members, whether a director or not, as the directors think fit. (14) Subject to paragraphs (2) and (3) of this clause the legal personal representatives of a deceased holder of an ordinary share or ordinary shares shall within three calendar months after the death of such holder, serve the company with a transfer notice in respect of the ordinary shares of the deceased, and if default is made in serving such notice within the time aforesaid, the directors shall be at liberty to appoint any person to sign and serve such notice on behalf of the legal personal representatives of the deceased, and a transfer notice signed and served by such person shall be effective. (14*a*) Provided nevertheless that where under any of the paragraphs (6), (7) and (14) of this clause a transfer notice by or *(pg97)* on behalf of any member or legal personal representatives of a member is given to the company as aforesaid in regard to any ordinary share or shares the purchase-money for such ordinary share or shares or for such of them as shall be purchased under this clause shall, in addition to the par value thereof be -

(*a*) A sum bearing the same ratio to the amount of the company's reserve fund at the date of the giving of the transfer notice as the number of shares purchased as aforesaid bears to the whole number of the then issued ordinary shares and (*b*) a sum bearing the same ratio to the full amount of the profits of that portion of the financial year current at the date of the giving of the transfer notice which shall have elapsed at the date of the giving of such notice as the number of the ordinary shares purchased as aforesaid shall bear to the full amount of the issued ordinary shares and (*c*) A sum bearing the same ratio to the full amount or value of any other undivided or unapplied profits of any preceding financial year or years (whether or not such profits shall have been carried forward) as the number of the ordinary shares purchased as aforesaid bears to the full amount of the issued ordinary shares and it shall be sufficient in such notice to specify the amount of the purchase money per share by stating it to be a sum to be fixed in accordance with this clause (No 34). The certificate of the auditor of the company as to the amount of purchase money per ordinary share which in his opinion is payable in any particular case where this clause (No 34) applies, shall be conclusive as to the amount in that case payable. The reserve fund named and referred to in sub-paragraph (a) of this clause is hereby declared to be the general reserve only (standing on the books of the company on 25th July 1907 at £110,000) less the sum of £34,467 7s on the same date forming part thereof. *General power to refuse transfer.* (15) The directors may refuse to register any transfer of a share, (A) where the company has a lien on the share; (B) where, in the case of shares not fully paid up, it is not proved to their satisfaction that the proposed transferee is a responsible person; (C) where the directors are of an opinion that the proposed transferee is not a desirable person to admit to membership, and that without being bound to assign any reason for such opinion. But paragraphs (B) and (C) of this clause shall not apply where the proposed transferee is already a member holding more than 250 ordinary shares. (16) The company may, by special resolution, repeal or alter any of the provisions of this clause, and the last preceding clause, but at the meetings to pass such special resolution, no member shall be entitled to be present or to vote, who is not a holder of an ordinary share or ordinary shares, and the quorum of each such meeting shall be members holding one-fifth at least of the issued ordinary shares.'

2   The respondents in the first appeal are the executors of one Percy Crossman, deceased; the respondents in the second appeal are the executors of Sir William Thomas Paulin, deceased. Mr Crossman died on the 17 August 1929; he was at that time the registered holder of 1,000 ordinary shares in the company. By his will he had disposed of all these shares in favour of relatives under the provisions of Article 34 (2) and these persons have since become the registered holders

of these shares. Sir William Paulin died on the 26 February 1931; at the time of his death he was the registered holder of 1,600 ordinary shares in the company. By his will Sir William Paulin gave 500 of these shares to each of his two daughters, who have since become registered holders of these shares. The remaining 600 shares formed part of his residuary estate, and on the 14 May 1931 his executors served a transfer notice in respect of those 600 shares on the company, in accordance with the provisions of sub-clause (14) of Article 34. The price fixed under the provisions of sub-clause (14*a*) of Article 34 was £209 13s 8d, and Sir William Paulin's executors accordingly sold and transferred these 600 shares to other members of the company at that price. The *(pg98)* price fixed in accordance with Article 34(14a) in the case of Mr Percy Crossman would have been £221 4s 5d. The company is a very prosperous one and had been paying a dividend at the rate of 45 per cent annually for some years.

3 The Commissioners of Inland Revenue fixed the value of the shares for estate duty purposes at £475 per share. In each case the executors presented petitions under the provisions of Section 10 of the Finance Act 1894, and claimed that the shares ought to have been valued at a price fixed in accordance with sub-clause (14*a*) of Article 34. The petitions were heard before Mr Justice Finlay; the learned Judge considered himself bound by a previous decision of the Irish Court of Appeal in a case of the *Attorney-General v Jameson* (1905, 2 Irish Reports 218) to accept the basis for which the Commissioners of Inland Revenue contended. Subject to a subsidiary point with regard to trust companies as possible purchasers, with which I will deal separately, the learned judge fixed the price at £351 in the case of Mr Crossman's executors and £355 in the case of Sir William Paulin's executors. From that decision the executors appealed in each case; the Court of Appeal gave judgment on the 27 July 1934 and by a majority decided that the proper basis of valuation was the price for which the executors contended and allowed the appeal. From that decision the present appeals are brought.

4 My lords, before expressing my own opinion, it is, I think, convenient to remind your lordships of the views expressed in Ireland in *Jameson's* case. That case dealt with shares in a limited company known as John Jameson Ltd in which there were restrictions upon the transfer of shares very similar to those which are involved in the present case. The case was commenced by an information laid by the Attorney-General in Ireland, in which a declaration was asked as to the measure of value of the shares for estate duty purposes. The case was heard originally in the King's Bench Division before Chief Baron Palles, Mr Justice Kenny, and Mr Justice Boyd. Chief Baron Palles took the view that the restrictions upon the right to transfer contained in the articles were to be disregarded altogether in assessing the value of the shares, and that they were to be valued on the basis that these restrictions were merely collateral and that the shares were to be treated as freely transferable. This view was not accepted by the other two judges who held that the shares must be valued on the basis that any purchaser in the open market would take subject to the risk of the shares being claimed by existing shareholders at the price fixed, by the articles. From this latter view there was an appeal to the Court of Appeal in Ireland, which was heard by Lord Ashbourne, the Lord Chancellor, and Lords Justices FitzGibbon, Walker and Holmes. The Court of Appeal rejected both the views which had found acceptance in the Court below, and they declared that the value of the shares was to be estimated at the price which they would fetch if sold in the open market on the terms that the purchaser should be entitled to be registered as holder of the shares and should take and hold, them subject to the provisions of the articles of association, including the articles relating to alienation, and transfer.

5 In Scotland the same point arose for discussion in the case of *Salvesen's Trustees v The Commissioners of Inland Revenue* (1930 Scottish Law Times 387, 9 ATC 43), and Lord Fleming took the same view as that which had been taken in the Irish Court of Appeal.

6 In view of this conflict of judicial authority, a conflict which, I am sorry to say, prevails even in your lordships' House, I think it is convenient to begin *(pg99)* by referring to the exact language of the Finance Act 1894, since it is upon the construction of that statute that the question ultimately depends. Section 1 of that statute provides that: -

> 'In the case of every person dying after the commencement of this Part of this Act, there shall, save as hereinafter expressly provided, be levied and paid, upon the principal value ascertained as hereinafter provided of all property real or personal, settled, or not settled, which passes on the death of such person a duty, called "estate duty," at the graduated rates hereinafter mentioned.'

Section 2 provides that property passing on the death of the deceased shall be deemed to include certain property therein specified; and it has been settled ever since the case of *Earl Cowley v The Commissioners of Inland Revenue* (1899 AC 198) that these two sections are mutually exclusive. Sections 1 to 5 together form a group of sections which deal with the grant of estate duty. There follow five sections, 6–10, dealing with the collection and recovery of duty and value of property. Section 6 (2) imposes a liability to pay the duty in respect of all personal property of which the deceased was competent to dispose at his death upon the executor. Section 7 deals with the value of the property and by Subsection 5 provides that -

> 'the principal value of any property shall be estimated to be the price which, in the opinion of the Commissioners, such property would fetch if sold in the open market at the time of the death of the deceased.'

It is upon the meaning to be attached to this subsection that the whole controversy turns.

7 In order to reach the right conclusion upon the construction to be placed upon the subsection and its application to the facts of the present case, it seems to me essential to determine what is the property which has to be valued. The respondents contended that the property fell under Section 2 and not under Section 1. The argument was that since the rights of the deceased to enjoy the produce of the shares and to dispose of them ceased with his death, the proper view was that no property actually passed on death but that upon the death there came into existence a fresh set of rights, determined by the terms of the article and belonging either to the executors or legatees or other shareholders in the company, which might be deemed to pass under Section 2, but which did not form part of the property actually passing under Section 1. I have arrived at a very definite view that this argument is unsound. I think further that it is inconsistent with the decision in your lordships' House in the case of *Cowley v The Commissioners of Inland Revenue.* As Lord Macnaghten pointed out in that case, what the Act has in view for the purpose of taxation is property passing on death, not the interest of the deceased which, if it be a limited interest, can never pass (1899 AC at 213). In my view, the property which passed at the death of the deceased consisted of the shares in the company, and this is not the less true because the terms of the articles limited the rights of the deceased shareholder or of his executors to deal with the shares, and gave certain privileges and rights of preemption on his death. If I am right so far, it follows that the Commissioners have to estimate the price which the shares would fetch if sold in the open market at the time of the death of the deceased. The Court of Appeal have cited the well-known passage in the judgment of Mr Justice Farwell, as he then was, in *Borland's Trustee v Steel Brothers & Co Ltd* (1901 1 Ch 279 at 288) as to the nature of a share. It is, as the learned judge there states – *(pg100)*

> 'the interest of a shareholder in the company measured by a sum of money, for the purpose of liability in the first place, and of interest in the second, but also consisting of a series of mutual covenants entered into by all the shareholders inter se in accordance with Section 16 of the Companies Act 1862. The contract contained in the articles of association is one of the original incidents of the share.'

8 This definition seems to me to show, with all respect to the opinion of a very learned judge, that the view entertained by Chief Baron Palles cannot be supported. And, indeed, the Crown did not seek to support it in the present case. To value the shares on the basis that the restrictions contained in the articles were to be ignored would be to value a property which the deceased never owned and which did not pass on his death. But it seems to me that the same reasoning is fatal to the conclusion reached by the majority in the Court of Appeal. Under the articles it is not possible to sell the shares in the open market until they have been offered to and refused by the existing shareholders. In order, therefore, to comply with the provisions of Section 7(5) of the Finance Act, it is necessary either to assume a sale in the open market of the shares, or else to limit the property to be valued to that which could be sold in the open market. The latter is the alternative which the Court of Appeal have preferred. Since the articles forbid a sale in the open market until the rights of pre-emption have been exhausted, all that the executors could sell in the open market at the time of the death was the right to receive the restricted price fixed by Article 34(14*a*) from any shareholder exercising his right of pre-emption. Obviously the value of this could not exceed the sum which such a shareholder would have to pay, and, accordingly, the Court of Appeal have held that that sum, that is the restricted price, is the value in the open market.

9 My lords, it seems to me that this construction involves treating the provisions of Section 7 (5) as if their true effect were to make the existence of an open market a condition of liability instead of merely to prescribe the open market price as the measure of value. The right to receive the price fixed by the articles in the event of a sale to existing shareholders under sub-clause (14a) is only one of the elements which went to make up the value of the shares. In addition to' that right, the ownership of the share gave a number of other valuable rights to the holder, including the right to receive the dividends which the company was declaring, the right to transmit the shares in accordance with Article 34 (1), (2) and (3), and the right to have the shares of other holders who wished to realise offered on the terms of Article 34 (14*a*). All these various rights and privileges go to make up a share and form ingredients in its value. They are just as much part of the share as the restriction upon the sale. The construction placed upon the statute by the Court of Appeal seems to me to ignore all these elements in the value of the share and to treat as its value what, in truth, is only the value of one of the factors which go to make up that share. But the purpose of Section 7 (5) is not to define the property in respect of which estate duty is to be levied, but merely to afford a method of ascertaining its value. If the view entertained by the Court of Appeal were correct, it would follow that any property which could not be sold in the open market would escape estate duty altogether. That seems to me quite an unnecessary and unnatural construction to place upon the language of that statute. In the words of Lord Buckmaster (*Poplar Assessment Committee v Roberts* [1922] 2 AC 103)) – *(pg101)*

> 'so to interpret the statute would be to deal with something which was nothing but a measure of value in such a manner as completely to destroy the very object for which that measure was set up.'

10 On the other hand, I can see no difficulty in treating the subsection as meaning that the Commissioners of Inland Revenue are to assume that the property which is to be valued is being sold in the open market and to fix its value for estate duty purposes upon that hypothesis. A somewhat similar problem is familiar in rating cases. There the Legislature has fixed the rateable value as the rack rent on a yearly tenancy. It has long since been established that the fact that the premises cannot actually be let on a yearly tenancy does not exempt them from liability for rates. Indeed, in those cases, in order to arrive at the rateable value the Courts have had to embark upon speculations far more difficult and artificial than any involved in the present case. I think that full justice is done to the meaning of the subsection if the property to be valued is determined by the earlier sections and Section 7 is treated as being merely a statutory direction as to the method by which the value is to be ascertained. In order to comply with that statutory direction, it is necessary to make the assumptions which the statute directs. This is not to ignore the limitations attached to the share. In the present case a share in such a company as this with an unrestricted right of transfer would probably be worth at least twice as much as the £355, which is fixed by Mr Justice Finlay. On the other hand, the effect of the construction which I am putting upon the section seems to me to be the only one which does enable the provisions of Sections 1 and 2 of the statute to be carried into effect and which ensures that the property in respect of which estate duty is levied shall include all that property which passes on the death of the deceased and not merely such part of that property as could be disposed of in open market. For these reasons I think the decision of the majority of the Court of Appeal was wrong, and that the cases of *Jameson* and *Salvesen* were rightly decided. This is sufficient to dispose of the principal point in the case.

11 There is, however, a subsidiary point upon which I must now say a few words. Before the learned judge at the hearing of the petitions, evidence was given on each side as to the value which ought to be placed upon the shares upon various hypotheses. The evidence which the learned judge seems to have accepted was that of Lord Plender, who was called on behalf of the petitioners; upon the basis of his figures, the learned judge fixed the value, on the hypothesis which I have held to be the correct one, at £351 in the *Crossman* case and £355 in the other. In fixing those figures, it appears from the judgment that Lord Plender 'did not exclude anybody or include anybody in particular; he considered the matter generally.' In my opinion that is the right way in which to arrive at the value in the open market. But the learned judge goes on to say that evidence was called for the Crown which indicated that a particular trust company would be willing to give a good deal more than the ordinary market price, because of certain particular attractions which the prospect of getting upon the share register would hold out for such a company. The learned judge says that he excluded trust companies from the possible buyers because he had evidence to satisfy him that the directors would not have consented to put them upon the register. I cannot think that this is a proper reason in the view which I have taken as to the construction to be put upon the subsection of the Act. On the other hand, I think it is a fair construction *(pg102)* to put upon the learned judge's judgment that the extra sum which could be obtained from trust companies was not an element of the value in the open market, but rather a particular price beyond the ordinary market price which a trust company would give for special reasons of its own. I do not think that it would be right to appreciate the value of the shares because of this special demand for a special purpose from a particular buyer.

12 I accept the principle upon which Lord Plender gave his evidence as the correct one to apply, and I think, therefore, that the figure which the learned judge reached of £351 and £355 respectively is the correct measure of value. It follows that in my opinion the judgment of the learned judge ought to be restored, the order of the Court of Appeal should be discharged, except in so far as it dismisses the cross-appeal of the Crown with costs, and that the costs of the appeal to the Court of Appeal and to your lordships' House should be paid by the petitioners.

13 LORD BLANESBURGH: My lords, the company of Mann, Crossman & Paulin Ltd, with some of the ordinary shares in which your lordships are, on a question of estate duty, here concerned, was incorporated as a public company in 1901 to take over and carry on an old family business of brewers. Its paid-up capital of £2,250,000 is divided into 125,000 5 per cent preference shares of £10 each, and 10,000 ordinary shares of £100 each. The preference shares are quoted on the London Stock Exchange. The regulations of the company with reference to these shares have not been printed in the record, but, doubtless, they enjoy an unfettered privilege of transfer and transmission incident to shares so favoured. The ordinary shares, of course, are not quoted. Article 34, with which we have become so familiar, effectually prevents anything of that kind. The difficulty of the case, indeed, is traceable to the fact that the effect of that article, coupled with the company's exceeding prosperity, makes it practically certain that just as there has never been, so, for many a day, there will never be, any of these ordinary shares available for any actual sale or transfer to any outsider anywhere. Not that the price that would be offered for the shares in the open market if any were there available is impossible of estimate. The fact that the preference shares are quoted is, of course, helpful. The position of the company is well known in consequence. And the prices there obtainable for ordinary shares at the relevant dates have been here ascertained by Mr Justice Finlay. The only question is whether the inquiry to which the learned judge then found the answer was one authorised by the provisions of the statute.

14 The terms of Article 34 are in detail before your lordships. The article is of a type, as will have been seen, more frequently discovered in the regulations of a private company than in those of a public company like this. In a business sense, no doubt, the ordinary shareholders here, and not for the first time, have, as a result of the article, become in effect a controlling private association within the frame of a public company. But in the sphere of company law – it is convenient to say so – the ordinary shares remain shares in a public company in no way distinguishable juridically from its preference shares.

15 I have thought it helpful to the solution of the problem before the House that if only for the purpose of illustration and contrast the capitalisation of the company and the existence of its preference shares publicly quoted should be pointedly brought to your lordships' notice. *(pg103)*

16 To no more than two characteristics of Article 34 need I specially refer now.

17 The first, somewhat unusual, is that the article discriminates between the male and the female holders of ordinary shares. The privileges by way of transfer and transmission to favoured transferees and appointees extended to male holders by subclauses (1), (2) and (3) are withheld from female holders of shares. The latter are with the male holders entitled to participate in the pre-emption privilege under subclause (13), but they can only dispose of their own shares under subclause (6); while their executors after death must do so under subclause (14).

18 This first characteristic of the article is perhaps now curious only; the second is important. The article, the pre-emption clause particularly, although that because, as is now on all hands accepted, is tainted with no illegality and is binding both upon the ordinary shareholders and the company, is not fundamental in the sense that provisions of the memorandum of association or some provisions with reference to shares contained in the Companies Act are fundamental. This has been appositely pointed out by Chief Baron Palles in his judgment in *Jameson's* case. The article is and remains binding only by agreement. It may at any time by special resolution, as indeed is in terms provided by subsection (16), be altered in any and every particular. An inalienable characteristic of the regulations of the article, all-important, as will be seen presently, when its relation to the Finance Act comes to be considered, is that they are maintained and can at any time be abrogated by the agreement of not necessarily more than three-fourths in interest of the holders of the ordinary shares affected.

19 We are concerned here with the proper charge for estate duty on 2,600 of these ordinary shares, 1,000 of them passing, by bequest, to the respondent, Douglas Crossman, on the death of his father, Mr Percy Crossman; and 1,600 passing on the death of Sir William Paulin. With reference to Mr Crossman's shares it is necessary only to say that they have been duly registered in the name of the respondent, Mr Douglas Crossman, who is also one of his father's executors.

20 In what follows I will for convenience of statement direct attention mainly to the ordinary shares passing on the death of Sir William Paulin, the questions of principle at issue being identical in the two cases.

21 Five hundred of those shares were bequeathed by the deceased to each of his two daughters. The shares like those bequeathed by Mr Crossman to his son, have been registered in their respective names. The remaining 600 shares have been duly registered in the names of other ordinary shareholders in the company, to whom, under Article 34 (13), the pre-emption clause, they had to be offered within three months of Sir William's death, and by whom they have been acquired at a price which must be taken to have been not less than £146 a share below their 'principal value' as ascertained by Mr Justice Finlay. This figure may be taken to represent the value of the pre-emption rights and suggests considerations to which attention will later be directed. The 1,000 shares – so destined by the deceased that their transit was not impeded by any restriction in Article 34 – have passed directly to the daughters, just as preference shares of the company would have passed under the regulations applicable to them had preference shares, in place of ordinary shares, been the subject of the specific bequest. And had that been the case the method to be adopted for ascertaining the 'principal value' of these preference shares would not *(pg104)* have been open to controversy. It being an accepted fact that the entire legal and beneficial interest in these shares had, under Section 1 of the Finance Act, passed on the death of the deceased, their 'principal value,' ascertained by the Commissioners under Section 7 (5), would have been taken to be the quotation for the shares current on the day of the death – a sufficient and perhaps the best criterion of the price which, had he been given the opportunity, a purchaser in the open market would have offered for the registration of the shares in his own name as successor to the deceased.

22 And this at once suggests the question whether in this matter of estate duty there is any essential difference between a preference share with its public quotation and an ordinary share with none. Why, although not saleable in the open market, should not shares passing on death be valued as if they were? Is there more in it than this, that the proof of market value when in neither case are any shares of the deceased actually sold, is more difficult in one case than in the other? The Commissioners' question in each case is in effect the same. That for the preference shares has already been indicated; for ordinary shares in substance it would be, 'assuming the deceased's shares to be saleable in the open market at his death, what price would they fetch?' The Commissioners here have answered with a figure of £475 a share, and Mr Justice Finlay on appeal with a figure of £355, an answer which, subject to a qualification not in this connection relevant, has been accepted on all hands as reliable. Is there any valid reason why it should not be accepted as the 'principal value' of these shares? I have been unable to find one. And there are cogent reasons in its favour. It is almost a case of *stet decisis*. The figure embodies what Mr Justice Finlay calls the *Jameson* principle, now 30 years old, approved since in Scotland and in the Irish Free State, nowhere questioned, and acted upon by the Revenue authorities all along, their invariable practice having been to treat the sum analogous to Mr Justice Finlay's £355 as the 'principal value' of such a share as are the ordinary shares in this case.

23 Now, however, the Court of Appeal in England, declining to follow the *Jameson* case, has held that the 'principal value' of each of Sir William Paulin's 1,600 ordinary shares is for the purposes of estate duty not £355 but £209 13s 8d only – their pre-emption price already referred to.

24 My lords, it can, I believe, be shown that this sum of £209 for each share thus arrived at, so far from being its 'principal value' is by the Finance Act itself denied that description. But as the *Jameson* principle is, in my judgment, sound, and as Mr Justice Finlay's £355 ought not, I think, to have been displaced, it may be most convenient that, reserving that point, I should trace, and where necessary seek to justify, the course which led to that valuation. There will as a result be clearly disclosed the point at which, and the justification of want of it with which, the Court of Appeal separates itself from a principle and subsequent practice so well authenticated, so uniform, and so thoroughly established.

25 But may I, by way of introduction, say one or two things, general in character. The question at issue between the Crown and the respondents should be reviewed. It has been happily stated by Lord Justice Romer as follows: -

'Are the shares to be valued' [under Section 7 (5) of the Act] 'on the footing that a purchaser would in spite of the Articles of Association be forthwith entitled to be put upon the company's register in respect of them or are they to be valued upon the footing that the purchaser would only obtain such *(pg105)* right in respect of the shares as Sir William Paulin could at the time of his death have conferred upon him consistently with those articles.'

26 The first of the Lord Justice's alternatives embodies the *Jameson* principle, applied by Mr Justice Finlay. The second is that finally adopted by Lord Justice Slesser and himself, and I would at once emphasise with regard to it the fact that the value so arrived at was in the Lord Justice's view the 'principal value' of the only property in the shares which passed on the death of the deceased – the duty as he explained at the commencement of his judgment being chargeable only under Section 1 of the Act. The seriousness of the difference in this respect between the two alternatives will emerge as we proceed.

27 I would next observe that the working of Section 7 (5) of the Finance Act, in some respects at least, is now well ascertained. Some principles governing its application generally are either accepted or are, as I think, easily justified. If these are borne in mind in this case the issue of the appeal, otherwise confused and involved, becomes, as I venture to think, relatively clear if not indeed inevitable.

28 Here are some of the fundamentals on which the working of Section 7 (5) must now, in my judgment, be taken to proceed.

(1)   The 'property,' the 'principal value' of which is thereunder to be estimated by the Commissioners, is the whole property brought into charge by the Act, and not a part of it only.

(2)   That 'property' may include many items over which the deceased had no power of disposition while he lived and over which his executor has none after his death.

(3)   If the duty of the Commissioners is, as I think, to estimate the price the 'property' as at the time of the deceased's death would fetch in the open market, if it were there to be offered for sale, it is unnecessary to inquire by whom the property would hypothetically have to be offered. It must not, however, be assumed that even the property passing under Section

1, whose price in the market is to be estimated by the Commissioners, is necessarily or even relevantly confined to property at the disposition there either of the deceased or his executor. A consideration of the circumstances surrounding the notional sale under the section of the corpus of settled property passing on death under Section 1, displaces of itself any such assumption. In that case the deceased normally never had in the corpus of the property any interest at all, while his interest in the income had ceased with his death. In other words any finding which would confine property passing under Section 1 of the Act to property of which the deceased or his executor could dispose in the open market must be otherwise justified, if it is to be accepted. Is that limitation of the Court of Appeal justified in the present case? That is the question the respondents have to face.

(4)   Except in cases within Section 3 of the Finance Act it is quite immaterial to whom the property has actually passed, whether to purchasers, legatees, or, in the case of the pre-empted shares, other members of the company issuing them. The question for the Commissioners is not to whom has the property passed. The question is whether it has passed at all. If it has passed, then subject only to a case covered by Section 3, no existing contract with reference to the property, although it be binding on the deceased's estate, has any influence upon the Commissioners' estimate of the price which in the open market it would fetch. In this connection Section 3 of the Act, quite neglected by the *(pg106)* Court of Appeal, and with its importance so far emphasised only by Chief Baron Palles, will be found to be illuminating. For the moment, however, I pass it by; observing as I conclude this general survey how it seems to indicate that the solution of the difficulty between the Crown and the respondents here will ultimately turn upon the answer to two questions: (1) What was the property in his ordinary shares which passed upon the death of each deceased; and (2) what influence, if any, does the pre-emption clause in Article 34 exercise over the parcels to be included in the notional sale of the property envisaged by Section 7 (5) of the Act.

29 Proceeding now to deal with the case presented by the Crown, my answer to the first question is that the property which so passed here was the deceased's entire legal and equitable interest in his ordinary shares; each share a separate entity – a 'property' within the meaning of the Act, charged to duty as it passed 'in the ordinary sense of the term from the deceased into the possession and property of another person after his death'; see per Lord Watson in *Attorney-General v Beech* ([1899] AC 53 at 58). And, my lords, I desire to emphasise the fact that the property which so passed was an entire 'indivisible piece of property,' as Lord Justice FitzGibbon described it to be in *Jameson's* case. *Borland's Trustee v Steel Brothers*, outstanding decision that it is in its proper sphere, had as its purpose an analysis of the nature and effect of the different rights and incidents attached to a share, so as to enable a decision to be taken as to their legality in instances in which legality was questioned. But the judgment does not suggest that a share in a joint-stock company may not properly be described in Lord Justice FitzGibbon's words or by others to the life effect. A tribunal would be rash indeed to deny that description to things which pass as such by transfer in myriads, I suppose, every month, if not every week, and pass only less frequently by transmission, surrender, or on forfeiture. As such a piece of property a share may be the subject of lien, and in the case of the *Bradford Banking Co v Briggs* (12 AC 29) the shares over which the lien there extended were not once only referred to by Lord Blackburn as 'property.' Again, in the *Colonial Bank v Whinney* (11 AC 426), where shares in a railway company were held to be included in the expression 'choses in action' in the proviso to the order and disposition section of the Bankruptcy Act, Lord Blackburn, in his judgment, speaking of the shares in question in that very case, said that they were also personal chattels the property in which did not pass by mere delivery but did pass by a deed of transfer duly stamped. I can myself feel no doubt that it is in this sense and in this sense only that shares in joint-stock companies are 'property' within the meaning of the Finance Act charged to duty under Section 1 as therein stated.

30 To all the shares here in question I would apply the words already referred to used by Lord Justice FitzGibbon in *Jameson's* case.

31 Each of the 750 shares there in question, he says, 'with all rights and liabilities, and all advantages and disadvantages, incident in its ownership, passed on Henry Jameson's death to his executors as one indivisible piece of property. In conveyancing phraseology, the executors took each share "to hold in as full and ample a manner as the same was held by Henry Jameson at his death".' And later the Lord Justice adds:

> 'The basis of my construction of the Act is the unity and indivisibility of Henry Jameson's property in the shares. I cannot adopt any procedure or accept any solution of the question in dispute, which splits up that interest for any purpose.' *(pg107)*

32 And at this point, my lords, and for two reasons, I venture to insist upon the soundness of the above views of the Lord Justice as applied to the shares in the present case.

33 First, it is, I think, of quite major importance to the whole commercial community that these views should be upheld. The troubles which would follow any departure from them were well illustrated by Mr Radcliffe's argument on behalf of the respondents. Applied to the ordinary shares of this company, the analytical method advocated by counsel would attribute one quality and character to the shares held by women, and another to the shares held by men. And in varying degrees, no one share of an issue would be like another. The truth, indeed, is that *Borland's* case – most apposite in, for instance, *Jameson's* case in the Divisional Court, where the legality of the restrictions on the shares was the main question at issue – ceases to be important (I had almost said that it ceases to be relevant) in a case like this where the complete legality of Article

34 is in every particular fully recognised. And my second reason is like unto the first. I venture to insist upon the view of the Lord Justice in order that, with its support, I may meet in advance a view presented by Chief Baron Palles, in his judgment in *Jameson*, one which, although not accepted by the Irish Court of Appeal then, nor alluded to by either Lord Justice Slesser or Lord Justice Romer now, was, at least partially, revived at your lordships' Bar by learned counsel for the respondents. The view, as expressed by the Chief Baron, was that while the whole legal and beneficial interest in each of such shares as are now in question has passed on the death of the deceased, it has so passed in what may be called two parts: (1) The share subject to the right of pre-emption – 'property' within Section 1 of the Act; and (2) the right of pre-emption itself – 'property,' that is, under Section 2 (b), in which the deceased had an interest ceasing on his death 'in respect of which a benefit accrued or arose by the cesser of such interest,' and which was, therefore, 'deemed to pass.'

34 It was on this point alone that Lord Justice FitzGibbon differed from the Chief Baron, and upon it for the reasons I have given I find myself entirely at one with the Lord Justice.

35 Later I must refer to this matter again. But if, passing it by for the moment, I may now assume that the entire property of the deceased in his ordinary shares did pass on his death under Section 1 of the Act, then the ascertainment of the 'principal value' of these shares becomes, on the *Jameson* principle, simple and entirely consistent with the scheme of the Act in this regard.

36 First, as would be in the case of the quoted preference shares of the company, it is the price in the open market obtainable for the shares as at the date of the death which has to be estimated, the shares each as an entire thing which have passed to their present registered holders in succession to the deceased.

37 And, next, if the Commissioners' notional sale is to be a sale of the entire share just as it belonged to the deceased immediately before his death, then registration of the share in the name of the notional purchaser must also be offered. Lord Justice Romer concedes this fully. With reference to the property to be valued 'it is obvious,' he says, 'that the Commissioners just assume that the property can be transferred to the hypothetical purchaser.'

38 The same conclusion is thus put by the Chief Baron in *Jameson*. The hypothetical sale and purchase, he says (1904 2 Irish Reports 683) must -

> 'be a sale of the property which the deceased had in the shares at the time of his *(pg108)* death – that is, of the entire legal and equitable interest therein of that interest by virtue of which the deceased had been, and had been 'entitled to be, "a member" of the company in respect of such shares; a sale by virtue of which the purchaser thereat would have been entitled to have had that which he had bought vested in him in the same manner as it had been vested in the

deceased, and consequently under which he would, be entitled to be registered as a member of the company in respect of those shares,'

and later (page 689), after saying that the supposed sale is being made in the open market on the assumption that the open market is available, the Chief Baron proceeds:

'And upon this assumption, which is the supposition the statute directs us to make, we must exclude the consideration of such provisions in the articles of association as would prevent a purchaser at the sale from becoming a member of the company, registered as such in respect of the shares purchased by him at such supposed sale. If we do not, we do not give effect to the assumption the statute coerces us to make.'

39 That is to say, the preventive provisions of the article are to be ignored, whether they provide for the other shareholders' rights of pre-emption or for the approval by the directors of every transfer.

40 Had this principle been remembered or accepted at the hearing of this case the difficulty created by the directors' proved objection to a trust company as shareholder could never have arisen. It would have been seen at once to be quite irrelevant to the question before the Court.

41 But the pre-emption rights definitely withdrawn from interference by that general principle are – a most important aspect of the case – separately ruled out by Section 3 of the statute, to which now attention must again be directed.

42 Once more I return to the judgment of Chief Baron Palles in *Jameson* for a lucid statement of the position, so regarded: 'The substance of the argument for the defendant was,' he says (page 682) 'that the executors were, on the death of the deceased, under an enforceable obligation to sell the shares at £100 each' (here at £209 each) 'and that this obligation ascertained and fixed their maximum value for the purposes of the Finance Act. During the argument I asked Mr Ronan whether he contended that the provisions in the articles amounted to, or contained, "a bona fide contract of purchase of the shares from the deceased for full consideration in money or money's worth, paid to him for his own use or benefit," within Section 3 of the Finance Act; or that the case was otherwise within that section. He replied that he did not; and consequently, I leave this third section out of consideration altogether.'

43 Now it is plain that, with reference to the pre-emption rights here – at £209 13s 8d for each share – no other answer could be given. It is stated, indeed by Lord Justice Romer, in his judgment, that each of these shares in the name of either of Sir William Paulin's daughters was worth £355. The result, therefore, is that, it not being possible to rely on Section 3, the existence of the pre-emption right here must be ignored so far as the parcels of the Commissioners' notional sale are concerned.

44 May I elucidate the position as I see it by an illustration, so drawn as to have regard to the regulations in this respect governing the ordinary and preference shares of the company respectively. Let it be supposed that a deceased person had in his lifetime purchased two valuable jewels from a dealer in Hatton Garden; one a diamond brooch; the other, shall we say, a string of pearls, the pearls an out-and-out purchase but the brooch on the terms that if the deceased retained the jewel at his death and died without making it the *(pg109)* subject of a specific bequest, the dealer was to have the right to purchase it from his legal personal representative for, shall we say, £1,000. The deceased died intestate, retaining both jewels. At his death the price obtainable for the brooch in the open market was £3,000. And this, too, was the value of the pearls. The dealer claimed the brooch, as he was entitled to do, at £1,000, and it was handed over to him on payment of that price. In these circumstances, what was the 'principal value' of the brooch? Like the value of the pearls, it was, I suggest, undoubtedly £3,000, and for the reason that the dealer's pre-emption price was not one protected by Section 3 of the Act. So far, the analogy between the brooch and the ordinary shares here is complete, just as is that between the pearls and preference shares in the company. But there, so far as concerns the ordinary shares and the brooch, the analogy ends. The pre-emption right over the brooch never comes within the purview of the Commissioners at all. The right does not burden the brooch in the hands of its notional purchaser. But to the ordinary shares in the purchaser's hands the pre-emption rights still attach and must be duly discounted by the Commissioners in their estimate of the price the shares will fetch.

45 And, my lords, it is at this point, more perhaps than at any other, that I find myself in accord with the *Jameson* principle and in fundamental difference with the views of the majority of the Court of Appeal. The Lords Justices have forgotten Section 3 of the Act, the application of which to the pre-emption clause, reduced in consequence to a mere agreement is, I hope, made clearer by the illustration just offered.

46 The resulting misapprehension appears most clearly in the judgment of Mr Justice Kenny in *Jameson's* case, which is approved by Lord Justice Romer. The learned judge actually assumes that a right of pre-emption with the price payable thereunder will of itself prevail against a Section 7 (5) valuation. 'There is nothing,' he says (page 671), 'to prevent a man from agreeing for a purchase of property, and giving a right of pre-emption as part of his contract.' That is so, and nothing in the Finance Act will interfere with the full exercise of the right. The Act has not in the present case interfered with the exercise of the pre-emption rights over 600 of Sir William Paulin's ordinary shares. But unless the pre-emption price is a full price under Section 3 the right of pre-emption will not be operative to withdraw the property from the operation of Section 7 (5) of the Act.

47 And, my lords, it was by the application of the *Jameson* principle, as just traced, to the facts of the case, that Mr Justice Finlay's price of £355 for each ordinary share of the deceased was reached. And that principle and its application here I have in this judgment sought to justify.

48 I have done so, largely as will have been seen by quotations, too copious perhaps, from the judgment of the Chief Baron in *Jameson's* case. I have made these quotations copious in order that they might appeal to your lordships by their own inherent strength. The whole judgment of the Chief Baron I have found to be a masterly presentment of the *Jameson* principle, a judgment which must always have been regarded as the most vital of any delivered in the case, had it not been consistently discounted by what I cannot help thinking has been a serious misapprehension as to the conclusions actually reached by the Chief Baron. The Chief Baron's real conclusion is expressed in the terms of the declaration with which he prefaces his judgment. That declaration, it will be found, is followed almost textually by the Court of Appeal (1905 2 Irish Reports), *(pg110)* the concluding words of their declaration, 'and should take and hold them subject to the provisions of the articles of association, including the articles relating to alienation and transfer of the shares of the company' being added not because of any difference with the Chief Baron, but because the Attorney-General, abandoning his previous contention, admitted in the Court of Appeal (see per Lord Justice Holmes) without reserve the legality of the articles and their binding effect upon the company and all its members.

49 In the Court below, the Chief Baron, instead of ignoring, as has been supposed, the restrictive regulations, attributing to them full force as an agreement which, as above shown, they were, and not because they were fundamental provisions like those required by statute, which they were not. As to Borland, he did not then, it is true, accept the decision of Mr Justice Farwell as to the legality of the regulations. Upon them he reserved his final opinion. But for the purposes of his judgment he could and did assume the regulations to be valid. The suggestion, which appears in the judgment of Lord Justice Slesser, that he treated the shares in the hands of the notional purchaser as being free from any of the conditions governing the other shares of the company, I believe to be completely mistaken. If this judgment has no other result, it will at least, I hope, direct the attention of the profession to a pronouncement which, although with one part of it I do not agree, ought justly to have its proper place amongst the notable deliverances of a very great judge.

50 I now turn to the judgment of the Lords Justices and the views enunciated by them. My answer to these will really be found in what has preceded. The process of reasoning by which Lords Justices Slesser and Romer reached their conclusion is made specially clear in the judgment of Lord Justice Romer, who deals in detail with each aspect of the problem.

51 First of all, as I have already noted, the case was in his judgment a Section 1 case. Upon Sir William Paulin's death his ordinary shares, the Lord Justice says, passed 'within the meaning of Section 1 of the Finance Act'. And what so passed under the designation of a share which had to be valued for the purposes of estate duty, the Lord Justice describes as 'nothing more than the totality of (the deceased's) "rights and liabilities as they exist under the provisions of the Companies Act and the constitution of the … company"'. There was nothing in Section 7 (5) of the Act to suggest to his mind even remotely 'that what is to be treated as being sold is something other than the property that passes upon the death'. And this next statement of his reduces most usefully the limits of the controversy.

> 'If a share in Mann, Crossman and Paulin Ltd, be regarded merely as a right to get placed on the register of members with the rights and subject to the liabilities that would result from such registration, the principal value of such share must of course be ascertained upon the footing that the right can be conferred upon a purchaser in the open market. If, on the other hand, as I think is the case, the inability to confer upon such a purchaser a right of registration is a part of the essence of a share, its value must be ascertained with a due recognition of that fact.'

52 My lords, these statements show how narrow are the limits of the controversy. For, no one suggests, I think, that there can under the Act be any valuation or estimate of the price of any property which has neither passed nor been deemed to pass thereunder. On the other hand, the Lord Justice agrees that if the view *(pg111)* of the Crown is correct as to the extent of the property in the shares which passed here, then the Jameson principle is rightly applicable to the very end. The Lord Justice in short makes it clear that the real controversy is over the question, what was the 'property' which, under the Act, passed when on Sir William Paulin's death his ordinary shares passed to his daughters and the pre-empting shareholders. Was there anything more left for the Commissioners to do in reference to these shares than to estimate the highest price which in the open market would be offered for the privilege of being registered as their holders? That is the view of the Crown. It is, perhaps, only by stating the question in that objective form that the strength of its position and the essential simplicity of its case are realised.

53 On the other hand, the opposite views of the Lords Justices above set forth are, I think, correctly interpreted by the respondents in the third reason of their printed case, where they describe the price in the open market to be estimated by the Commissioners under Section 7 (5) as being the price of ordinary shares in the company offered

> 'upon terms that a transfer notice giving the holders of the remaining ordinary shares a right of pre-emption at the prescribed price was to be duly served in accordance with Article 34 and that the hypothetical purchaser in the open market was to have the right to become the registered holder of the shares sold to him in the event of such right of pre-emption not being exercised or, in the event of such right of pre-emption being exercised, to receive the prescribed price payable for such shares under Article 34 by the member or members purchasing the same.'

54 I do not know, my lords, why, on the principle there invoked, the pre-emption rights should have been so carefully safeguarded and the directors' veto on any transfer should have been so completely ignored. It may have been felt that with that veto also interposed there would not be left for offer in the open market even the 'restricted and fettered thing' described by Mr Justice Kenny. To me the omission is eloquent as illustrating the length to which the respondents are necessarily driven by this process of analysis, to which for the purpose of its valuation they subject a share which passes under the Finance Act. If it was a share which passed, it was certainly not a share, as the Attorney-General strongly insisted it should be, which was being valued or notionally sold.

55 The positive objections to which, as I think, the views of the Lords Justices are open, I can, in view of what has been already said, state summarily: -

(1)   Their order does not treat each share as a single entity, which for reasons already given I believe to be essential; also, with, as I think, no justification, it makes the power of the deceased or his executors to dispose of a share on the open market the test of the extent of the property in it which passes under the Act.

(2)   Dividing the shares, it would seem, as Chief Baron Palles divided them, an operation without justification, the Lords Justices have no regard to the second interest indicated by the Chief Baron, viz the value of the pre-emption right 'deemed to pass' but have regard only to the first which 'passed' under Section 1 of the Act. Upon the principle adopted by them, over one-third of the ascertained 'principal value' of each ordinary share escapes duty.

(3)   The order fails to recognise that while the pre-emption clause of *(pg112)* Article 34 is valid and binding upon every holder of ordinary shares, it is, in view of Section 3 of the Finance Act, ineffective to prevent a notional offer of the shares for sale in the open market, although effective to reduce the price they will fetch there. In truth, the result of the order of the Court of Appeal is to give to the respondents the benefit of Section 3 of the Act in a case to which that section has no application.

56 My lords, learned counsel for the respondents, seeking for safety, perhaps, raised at your lordships' bar for the first time the contention that in this case the duty was not chargeable under Section 1 of the Act, but in large measure, if not altogether, under Section 2, and that for no duty beyond that on the pre-emption price were the executors, as such, chargeable. The order of the Court of Appeal, therefore, on that ground alone should be affirmed, for that it was only as an executor that any respondent had been sued.

57 The answer I would make to that contention is, and for the reasons I have given, that the whole duty on the £355 a share is chargeable under Section 1. But if, on the Chief Baron's view, any part of it had to be borne under Section 8 (2), then it was, I think, too late for the executors to raise that objection for the first time at your lordships' bar. The case, from the outset, is concerned with the amount payable in respect of estate duty, and not as to its ultimate incidence. I have no doubt that throughout the proceedings the executors allowed themselves to be treated as liable for any estate duty chargeable in respect of these shares.

58 I agree with, I believe, all your lordships in thinking that any possible bid for the shares by a trust company was allowed for by Lord Plender in his estimate of £355 a share accepted by the learned judge as reliable. Had that not been so the Crown's contention on this point would have been, I think, unanswered.

59 But, with that fact in view, it fails.

60 My lords, on the whole case, I am in complete agreement with the motion just made by the Lord Chancellor.

61 LORD RUSSELL OF KILLOWEN (read by Lord Macmillan): My lords, the question at issue in these cases is how, under the provision of the Finance Act 1894, are the ordinary shares in a company called Mann, Crossman and Paulin Ltd to be valued. It is not a question of ascertaining their actual value, or their true value, or their intrinsic value, or their value in some particular person's ownership. The value to be ascertained is their statutory value. I emphasise this at the outset, because the only tax imposed by Section 1 of the Finance Act, 1894, is, to quote the words of the Act, 'upon the principal value ascertained as hereinafter provided' of property passing on death.

62 The relevant section for the purpose of ascertaining the value of such property is Section 7; and in particular subsection (5) thereof. The matter resolves itself therefore into the true construction of that subsection.

63 Before referring to its terms, let me mention briefly the relevant facts as they relate to the shares owned by the testator, Sir William Paulin. It is conceded that the same principles apply to the case of both testators, and that a decision in one case will govern the other. *(pg113)*

64 The company's articles contain special provisions as to ordinary shares, the effect of which (so far as they apply to Sir William Paulin's shares) I can state briefly, but I hope accurately, thus: A male holder can transfer *inter vivos* to persons falling within a defined class and being in other respects in the opinion of the directors duly qualified for membership. A male holder can by testamentary disposition appoint to any of the same class, and such appointee will be entitled to a transfer of the shares from the legal personal representatives of the appointor, if within three months of his death the directors signify approval of the transferee. Except where a transfer is made pursuant to the above powers and certain other immaterial cases a member proposing to transfer shares can only do so after a period of three months, and then only if no member has been willing to purchase them at par plus certain additions defined by the articles. During the three months, the other members have the overriding right of pre-emption at this fixed price. It is only if and to the extent to which this right is not exercised, that the proposing transferor can sell and transfer shares to any person and at any price. The shares of a deceased member, which have not been appointed by his will under the powers indicated above, are similarly subject to an overriding right of pre-emption in the other members at the fixed price; and it is only if and to the extent to which this right is not exercised that the member's legal personal representatives can sell and transfer the shares to any person and at any price.

65 Finally the directors may refuse to register any transfer of a share (amongst other cases) where they are of opinion that the proposed transferee is not a desirable person to admit to membership and that without being bound to assign any reason for such opinion; but this power does not apply where the proposed transferee is already a member holding more than 250 ordinary shares.

66 Sir William Paulin was the owner and registered holder of 1,600 fully paid ordinary shares of £100 each in the company. By his will he appointed 500 of these shares to each of his two daughters, leaving the remaining 600 shares to become subject to a residuary trust for sale. He died on the 26 February 1931. Thereupon the 1,600 ordinary shares passed to the executors appointed by his will and in order to 'ascertain as hereinafter provided' the principal value of all property which so passed, recourse must be had to Section 7 of the Finance Act 1894. By subsection (5) of that section, it is provided that the principal value of any property shall be estimated to be the price which in the opinion of the Commissioners such property would fetch if sold in the open market at the time of the death of the deceased. The crucial question in this appeal is, what price would these 1,600 shares fetch in the circumstances specified?

67 There can, I think, be no doubt, and indeed it was conceded, that in estimating the value of Sir William Paulin's shares in accordance with this provision, no difference can be drawn between the 1,000 shares appointed to his daughters and the 600 shares which form part of his residuary estate. The yardstick is the same for each; the shares are imagined to be the subject matter of a sale in the open market at the time of the death of Sir William Paulin and an opinion must be formed as to the price which they would fetch. The whole process is hypothetical, but the parcels to be hypothetically sold are the shares. Further, since the hypothetical sale takes place at the time of the death, the hypothetical vendor must be either the dying shareholder or his legal personal representative, *(pg114)* probably the former, so as to meet the case where no legal personal representative exists. But for the purposes of this case it matters not which, because both in the case of the dying shareholder and of his legal personal representative, the subject matter of the sale would be shares over which under the articles of association, the other members of the company had an overriding right of pre-emption.

68 It is the existence of this right of pre-emption which is the foundation of the dispute between the parties, the appellants contending that it must be disregarded in estimating the price under Section 7(5), the respondents contending that it cannot be disregarded and that its existence in the circumstances of the present case controls and limits the price which the shares would fetch in the open market.

69 A similar dispute has been the subject of decision in the Irish Courts. In the case of *Attorney-General v Jameson* (1904 2 Irish Reports at page 644), it was held by a majority in the King's Bench Division in Ireland that in applying the provisions of Section 7(5) of the Finance Act 1894, regard must be had to the special provisions in a company's articles of association with reference to alienation and transfer of the shares of the company and as to 'fair value', but that the amount of the principal value was not necessarily limited to the par or fair value of the share. In that case the shares were £100 shares and the right of pre-emption was at £100 or such other sum as should from time to time be fixed as the fair value by resolution of the company in general meeting. On appeal the Court of Appeal (1905 2 Irish Reports at page 218) held that the price should be estimated upon the footing that the purchaser would be entitled to be registered as holder of the shares, but would take and hold the shares subject to the provisions of the articles of association, including the articles relating to alienation and transfer of the shares of the company. This decision has been followed by Lord Fleming in Scotland. *Salvesen's Trustees v The Commissioners of Inland Revenue* (1930 Scottish Law Times, page 387; 9 ATC 43).

70 Your lordships have to determine which of these divergent views is the correct interpretation of Section 7 (5).

71 Mr Justice Finlay, as I think he was in comity bound to do, followed, in the present cases, the decision of the Court of Appeal in Ireland. On appeal from him the Court of Appeal here have by a majority reversed his decision, and have adopted the views and reasoning of the majority in the King's Bench Division in Ireland. Where such a conflict of judicial opinion exists, the question must obviously be no easy one to answer; but for myself I feel bound to concur in the views expressed by Mr Justice Kenny and Mr Justice Boyd in Ireland and by Lords Justices Slesser and Romer in the present case.

72 A share in a limited company is a property the nature of which has been accurately expounded by Mr Justice Farwell in *Borland's Trustee v Steel* ([1901] 1 Chancery page 279). It is the interest of a person in the company, that interest being composed of rights and obligations which are defined by the Companies Act and by the memorandum and articles of association of the company. A sale of a share is a sale of the interest so defined, and the subject matter of the sale is effectively vested in *(pg115)* the purchaser by the entry of his name in the register of members. It may be that owing to provisions in the articles of association the subject matter of the sale cannot be effectively vested in the purchaser, because the directors refuse to and cannot be compelled to register the purchaser as shareholder. The purchaser could then secure the benefit of the sale by the registered shareholder becoming a trustee for him of the rights with an indemnity in respect of the obligations. In the case of the sale of such a share the risk of a refusal to register might well be reflected in a smaller price being obtainable than would have been obtained had there been no such risk. The share was property with that risk as one of its incidents.

73 But a further restriction may exist, as in the present case. The articles may stipulate that a shareholder must first give existing shareholders the chance of buying his shares at a price fixed and not competitive. In such a case a sale to an outsider of the shareholder's interest in the company must and can only be made subject to that obligation, which is one of the incidents which attach to and are part of the subject matter of the sale; and the sale to the outsider must necessarily include as an incident of the subject matter of the sale, the right to receive the fixed price if the right of pre-emption is exercised by the other shareholders. The consequence is that by reason of the nature and incidents of the subject matter of the sale, neither Sir William Paulin nor his executors, at the time of the death, could have sold these shares in the open market to anyone otherwise than subject to the right of pre-emption at the fixed price. The result of the existence of this right of pre-emption must inevitably be that no one at an actual sale in the open market would be prepared to offer more than the fixed price if even that.

74 How can any higher price be, in the Commissioners' opinion, the price which the shares would fetch at the hypothetical sale envisaged by Section 7 (5)? What justification is there for saying that the shares to be sold at the hypothetical sale are to be free from the rights of pre-emption; that they are in other words to be hypothetical shares? I can find none in the language used. The subsection is perfectly general in its terms, dealing with 'any property' and therefore covering all property which passes on the death; and the Commissioners have to form an opinion as to the highest price which a person in the 'open market' would be prepared to pay for the particular property under consideration. That I conceive is the price which 'such property would fetch.' But the property must surely be the property which is being valued, with all the rights and obligations which attach to it and are inherent in it. I can see no word in the subsection which justifies a different view. If the property in question is that bundle of rights and obligations known as a share in a limited company, the entirety of the bundle must surely be the subject-matter of the sale and not part only. The requirement that property be sold in the open market cannot alter the nature or character of the property which is there offered for sale. The words 'open market' postulate freedom of access to the market, not freedom from restrictions attaching to the subject matter of the sale.

75 I find myself in agreement with the views expressed by Mr Justice Kenny and Mr Justice Boyd in the *Jameson* case and by Lords Justices Slesser and Romer in the present case. I can find nothing in the subsection which would justify me in holding that the vendor on the hypothetical sale is to be considered as selling something which is affected by fewer restrictions than those to which it was subject in the testator's hands. So to hold would be, as pointed out by Mr Justice Boyd, to trespass on the province of the legislature and add words to the subsection. Neither can I see any logical basis for treating the *(pg116)* property offered at the hypothetical sale as being free from some of the restrictive features attaching to it, but remaining subject to others. Nor have I heard any satisfactory answer to the difficulty stated by Lord Justice Romer when he said: 'I can find nothing in Section 7 (5) to warrant the Commissioners in estimating the value of a property passing on death by reference to the price that would be paid in the open market for property that did not so pass.'

76 One of your lordships professes to derive some assistance, or comfort, from a decision of my own in the case of *Re Cassel.* I myself am not so fortunate. I have recently explained in *Christie v Lord Advocate* (15 ATC 146) how very special that case was in its facts; and that all that I did was to indicate, as best I could, the lines upon which a valuation might fairly be reached of a benefit which (being purely personal) could not be offered for sale at all. The soundness of the decision in the *Jameson* case never came under consideration in *Re Cassel.*

77 My lords, I end as I began. The only tax imposed is on the principal value of property passing on the death, to be ascertained according to the statutory provision. It is the statutory value and no other value which has to be ascertained. Upon the facts of these cases the value *according to the provisions of the statute,* cannot exceed £209 13s 8d in the case of the Paulin shares, and £221 4s 5d in the case of the Crossman shares.

78 I would dismiss the appeals.

79 In the view which I take, the question as to the exclusion of any class of possible purchasers from the open market does not arise; but I feel a difficulty in understanding how, if Lord Plender's figure is accepted, as it was by Mr Justice Finlay, any higher figure could rightly be substituted for it. As I read the learned Judge's judgment, Lord Plender in arriving at his figure had treated the market as open, and had excluded no one from it. The whole world was hypothetically there, making hypothetical bids.

80 LORD MACMILLAN: My lords, in common with my noble and learned friend Lord Russell of Killowen, I find myself constrained to take a different view of these cases from that which has commended itself to the majority of your lordships. The problem is one of a type with which your lordships are only too familiar, the problem of applying a statutory enactment to circumstances which were manifestly not in the contemplation of the legislature, when it was enacted. That in the discharge of such a task differences of judicial opinion should emerge may be matter of regret, but is scarcely surprising.

81 I begin, however, by agreeing with all your lordships that the shares with which these appeals are concerned are, within the meaning of Section 1 of the Finance Act 1894, property which passed on the death of the shareholders. The controversial question relates to the ascertainment of the principal value of these shares for estate duty purposes. The statute enacts that it is to be ascertained as provided in Section 7 (5), which directs that it 'shall be estimated to be the price which, in the opinion of the Commissioners, such property would fetch if sold in the open market at the time of the death of the deceased.'

82 My lords, a share in a joint stock company is an entirely conventional creation; the congeries of rights and liabilities of which it consists is the creature of the Companies Acts and the memorandum and articles of the particular *(pg117)* company. Within the law the rights and liabilities appurtenant to a share may vary widely. But it cannot exist independently of the inherent attributes with which it has been created.

83 When therefore the legislature directs that these shares are to be conceived as being exposed for sale in the open market, in order to see what price they would fetch, I conceive them as being offered to purchasers with all their attributes. If they are subject to conditions which restrict either the rights or enjoyment of the rights of alienation of the holder, then the sale must be of the shares as so restricted. The Finance Act confers no power to strip the shares of any of their inherent attributes. The sale, no doubt, is a hypothetical sale, but the hypothesis is that the thing itself is being sold as it stands with all its qualities and all its disabilities. If the analogy of the hypothetical tenant is invoked, I may pray in aid the words of Lord Buckmaster in the case of the *Port of London Authority v Assessment Committee of Orsett Union* (1920) Appeal Cases 271 at page 305, where he says: -

'The actual hereditament of which the hypothetical tenant is to be determined must be the particular hereditament as it stands, with all its privileges, opportunities and disabilities created or imposed either by its natural position or by the artificial conditions of an Act of Parliament.'

84 My lords, in the present case, I am of opinion that neither the right of pre-emption nor any of the other conditions and restrictions inherently affecting the alienation of these shares can justifiably be left out of account when conceiving them to be exposed for sale in the open market. The purchaser of them in the open market would speedily experience their efficacy. I cannot bring myself to believe that these shares, if sold in the open market, would fetch a price of over £300 each, yet that is what the House is about to decide.

85 It may be unfortunate for the Revenue that the legislature has chosen a method of measuring value for estate duty purposes which may not in the present instance yield the real value of these shares. But that is not your lordships' concern. It is not the value of the shares as they were held and enjoyed by the deceased shareholders or their value as they are now held and enjoyed by their successors that is in question. It is simply and solely on their market value that the toll of estate duty is to be levied.

86 For the reasons which I have thus briefly indicated and which have been more fully developed by my noble and learned friend Lord Russell of Killowen and in the opinions of Lord Justice Slesser and Lord Justice Romer in the Court of Appeal, my vote is for the dismissal of these appeals.

87 LORD ROCHE: My lords, I have had the very great advantage of reading in advance the opinions prepared by the Lord Chancellor and by my noble and learned friend Lord Russell of Killowen. The case is one of manifest difficulty, but I have arrived at a definite conclusion that the appeals should be allowed for the reasons expressed by the Lord Chancellor.

88 I think it right, however, to refer to certain additional considerations which have led me to this conclusion.

89 The effect of the decision of the Court of Appeal in Ireland in *Jameson's* case (Law Reports, Ireland, 1905 2 King's Bench 218) has been sufficiently *(pg118)* stated by others of your lordships' House. The question is whether that decision was right, or was wrong as the Court of Appeal (Lord Hanworth, Master of the Rolls, dissenting) in the present cases decided that it was. It is to be observed that the part of the judgment of Chief Baron Palles in *Jameson's* case, which went beyond the decision of the Court of Appeal in Ireland, forms no part of the contention for the present appellants. They do not question the correctness of that part of the judgment and declaration of the Court of Appeal in Ireland which directs that, in assessing the value to the notional purchaser, regard is to be had to the provisions of the articles relating to alienation and transfer of the shares. It is said, however, that, having gone so far, it is illogical not to go further or to start earlier and pay regard to the articles rendering transfer to a purchaser who is a member of the public impossible or unlikely at a price higher than that arrived at by virtue of Article 34, subclause (14a). I am unable to agree with this contention for reasons which I will presently state. I would like first, however, to consider the results which seem to follow from the contrary view. If the price so arrived at (which for convenience I call the prescribed price) is the decisive price, then, as it seems to me, however valuable a share may be intrinsically and however wide a range of disposition may have been allowed to a shareholder by the articles of a company, and however low a price may be prescribed upon a transfer outside that range of disposition, it follows that upon the shareholder's death the shares may pass to executors and then to persons appointed by will and be to them of great value, yet the values for estate duty purposes can be no higher than the prescribed price, though it be entirely inadequate, or even negligible, in amount. It is said that though this may be so, it needs legislation to prevent the happening of such a result. My lords, with all respect to those who think otherwise, in my judgment the Statute of 1894 has already provided against and prevented the happening of any such result. In this respect, I agree with the Court of Appeal in Ireland that the language of the Act requires, in a case where no actual sale is either possible or contemplated, that a sale in the open market of a notional character is to be assumed. By a sale, I mean and understand a transaction which passes the property in the thing sold. It must always be borne in mind that the Finance Act of 1894 is dealing with all descriptions of property and not expressly with shares, and I regard the word 'sold' in Section 7 (5) of this Act as having the same meaning as the word 'sale' in the Sale of Goods Act 1893; (see Section 1(3) of that Act). Shares with many other kinds of property are, of course, not within the ambit of the Sale of Goods Act; but I am of opinion that for the purposes of the Finance Act, 1894, for shares to be sold the property in them, by which I mean the legal property, must pass. Upon an actual sale there must be an actual passing of property. Upon a notional sale there must be a notional or assumed passing of property. In so far as the passing or transfer of property is thus notional or hypothetical, no restriction upon actual passing or transfer comes into question, and the article as to the prescribed price which is to rule under certain circumstances, though it is no doubt a constituent part of the bundle of rights which constitutes a share, does not, as I think, govern such a notional transfer so as to make the notional purchaser no more than a person who acquires an obligation to offer the shares to others at the prescribed price.

90 Two things are, however, said with regard to this matter. It is said that the statute does not require or impel to this conclusion. I am referring more *(pg119)* particularly to the very closely reasoned judgment of Lord Justice Romer. The passing in the open market of the interest of the testator in the company, which is described by the Lord Justice and is held by him to be sufficient to satisfy the conditions of Section 7, subsection (5), does not, as it seems to me, satisfy such conditions. It follows from that which I have said above, as to my view of the nature of a sale and the meaning of the language of this section, that I am unable to regard the transactions the Lord Justice there describes as sales within the meaning of the section. I should regard them, as at most, agreements for sale which, having regard to the subject-matter and the articles, would have to be of a conditional character.

91 It is also said that the shares to be valued are shares which, owing to their essential nature as created or defined by the articles, are worth no more to a buyer than the prescribed price, and that they must be valued at that price. With all respect to those who hold this view, I think, with the Lord Chancellor, that a great deal more passed on the deaths of the deceased shareholders than the obligation to transfer shares at the prescribed price. For example, the right to hold them and the right to leave them to others so that they in their turn might enjoy the prosperity of the company were rights of great value, and the notional purchaser must, in my opinion, be regarded as notionally acquiring on his purchase those rights amongst the other rights connected with and going to make up the shares.

92 It seems to me to be important to remind oneself that Section 7, subsection (5), of the Act is simply a provision for estimating by means of an hypothesis the value of property which has passed otherwise than by an actual sale and transfer and may be incapable of so passing. But the section has to be applied and can be applied to all such cases. As to property which, by its inherent or essential nature, cannot be actually sold or transferred, the application of the section was explained, as I should like to explain it, by my noble and learned friend, then Mr Justice Russell, in the case of *In re Cassel*, Law Reports 1927, 2 Chancery, at page 281. The learned judge says: 'Next, how is the principal value of that property to be ascertained? The machinery provided by the Act is Section 7, subsection (5), supplemented to some extent by Section 7, subsection (8). That machinery does not exactly fit the present case, because from the personal nature of the provision, the benefit of it could not be sold at all; an outside purchaser would not obtain delivery of the goods. Nevertheless, the machinery must be made to fit, and I think it can be made to fit. It was made to fit in the Irish case of *Attorney-General v Jameson*. The value cannot be ascertained by reference to market price because there can be no market.' The learned judge then proceeded to suggest or direct how a hypothetical market price should be arrived at. In substance, the process suggested seems to have amounted to an estimation or assessment on general business lines of the value of the thing or property in question to a person who could enjoy it. The judgment of Mr Justice Finlay in the present case indicates that by similar processes often adopted and quite businesslike, the witnesses on both sides were able to provide him with proper material to arrive at a notional or hypothetical market price. Indeed, the fact that the decision of the Court of Appeal of Ireland in *Jameson's* case had been acted upon for some thirty years until challenged in the present case is of itself evidence that the method of valuation then formulated was well capable of practical application. I have *(pg120)* already given my reasons for holding that it was also the method required by the statute.

93 I concur in the opinion which is, I think, held by all your lordships, that the property here in question was property falling under Section 1 of the Act of 1894. The contention to the contrary seemed to me not to be strongly pressed, and it is no disrespect to the very able argument for the respondents to say that the point appeared to be presented, not so much for its inherent merits as for the opportunity it afforded for drawing attention to the fact that some of the shares left by one of the deceased shareholders would, on the appellants' contention, be valued for taxation at a higher price than the executors would receive for them. But, as a matter of law, regard cannot be had to the particular mode of disposition adopted by a shareholder, and, as a matter of fact, the reflection presents itself to the mind that any apparent inequality in the result is due to the voluntary choice of the testator, combined with the fact that though the material subsection of the articles had been amended at some previous date, the shareholders had not chosen to amend it so as to keep pace with the prosperity of the company. At the prescribed price the shares show a return of about 20 per cent per annum and even at the price adopted by the learned judge of about 121/2 per cent per annum.

94 As to the figures, for the reasons given both by the Lord Chancellor and by Lord Russell of Killowen, I think no higher figures than the figures adopted by Mr Justice Finlay should be substituted for his figures, and the contention of the Crown in this respect fails.

95 My lords, for these reasons I am for allowing the appeals, so far as the restoration of the judgments of Mr Justice Finlay is asked for, but not further. *(pg121)*

Case 18
Findlay's Trustees v IRC

(1938) 22 ATC 437

High Court

15 July 1938

This case concerns the valuation of goodwill. It is, thus, of seminal importance when valuing a shareholding in a company that has significant generated goodwill, which needs to be considered in addition to the tangible assets shown on the balance sheet.

The case concerns a partner's share of a partnership goodwill. As noted by the judge, it is surprising that the particular business was carried on in partnership and would normally be in the ownership of a limited company. Hence, the judgement is of direct relevance to a valuation of a shareholding in a limited company that owns goodwill.

Within the decision, important comments are made on the following principles.

1.   The nature of goodwill as being a consequence of 'super profits'. This is equated with capitalised earnings less tangible assets.
2.   The necessity to carefully analyse the state of the industry as seen at the valuation date in order to form a view as to the value of goodwill.
3.   A discussion of the characteristics of the likely hypothetical purchaser of the asset being valued, particularly in relation to the risk that is being assumed by that purchaser.
4.   The influence of the means used to finance the business on the value of the businesses' goodwill.

Sir John Ritchie Findlay died on 13 April 1930. In the estate at death was a 16/20ths interest in the goodwill, copyrights, etc of the publications of John Ritchie & Co, of which Sir John Findlay had been a partner. The firm of John Ritchie & Co published three major newspapers: *The Scotsman*, *Evening Dispatch* and *Weekly Scotsman*. Estate duty at a rate of 30 per cent was payable on the estate, giving a tax liability (in 1938) of £313,286 1s 9d (at the executors' valuation).

The Revenue and the executors agreed that the tangible assets of the partnership had a value of £707,680. The executors valued the goodwill of the partnership as an additional £334,185; the Revenue valued the goodwill as an additional £426,780.

In his judgement, Lord Fleming first identifies the asset to be valued as a partner's interest in the goodwill of the business carried on in partnership ((1938) 22 ATC 437at 439 **case 18 para 1**).

Lord Fleming then considers the effect that the financing of the partnership business may have on the value of its goodwill. The newspaper publishing business was financed by £300,000 of debentures, on which interest was paid at 3.5 per cent. This interest rate was substantially below market rates at the valuation date, which led Lord Fleming to comment:

'It seems to me clear that the circumstance that a considerable part of the capital required to run the business can be raised at a comparatively low rate of interest … might have some effect in increasing its value. There is, however, no evidence to this effect and I take it that the existence of the debentures is an immaterial circumstance insofar as the ascertainment of the value of the goodwill is concerned. But this does not mean that their existence is to be disregarded in fixing the value of the interest of the partners.'

((1938) 22 ATC 437at 439 **case 18 para 2**)

After quoting the statutory valuation provision, Lord Fleming then considered the nature of the assets being valued of a partner's share in the goodwill of a substantial business:

'The deceased's interest in the partnership of John Ritchie and Company is obviously an asset of a quite exceptional character. It is, I should think, rather unusual for an undertaking of this magnitude to be carried on by a private partnership. Shares in such a partnership are subject to disadvantages and liabilities as contrasted with shares in a public company with limited liability. Thus the liability of the individual partners for the debts of a firm is unlimited and the shares in a firm, even when very valuable, may not be easily realised.'

((1938) 22 ATC 437 at 440 **case 18 para 3**)

The characteristics of the hypothetical unconnected purchaser postulated by the statutory provision are explored:

'It must therefore be assumed that, while the estimate of the value of the deceased's interest is to be made on the footing that it is sold in the open market, the hypothetical purchaser will take the interest subject to all its rights and liabilities, and all its advantages and disadvantages, just as it was held by the deceased.'

((1938) 22 ATC 437 at 440 **case 18 para 3**)

'It is to be presumed that the hypothetical purchaser having obtained all the relevant information would consider in the first place the risks which are involved in carrying on the business, and would fix the return which he considered he ought to receive on the purchase price at a rate per cent. The only other factor which he would then require to determine would be the annual profits which he would derive from the carrying on of the business. The determination of these two factors would enable him to fix the capital value of the business. A seller looking at the matter from the opposite point of view would deal with it on similar lines.'

((1938) 22 ATC 437at 440 **case 18 para 5**)

After recording the profits made by the partnership, Lord Fleming then considers, in reasonable detail, the condition of the newspaper publishing industry at the valuation date, and the view taken by the market of the prospects for *The Scotsman*, in particular:

'1930 ... was a period of general depression, which had begun in 1929, and it was certainly not a time at which sellers could expect to get good prices. Trade is said to go in cycles, and "booms" follow "slumps". But there were a number of factors which, apart from the slump, were not favourable to this business in 1930. The competition by what are called the national newspapers with their headquarters in London was in an increasing degree affecting the prospects of the morning newspapers published in the provinces of England and in Scotland. According to the evidence of Sir Bertram Ford and Mr Scott the "structure" of the *Scotsman* business was not well suited to withstand such competition.

Another factor which they regarded as unfavourable was that the *Scotsman* newspapers circulated mainly in a non-industrial area, in which the population was not increasing or increasing slowly; and that there was little scope for expansion or development. It was maintained by the appellants that the figures .indicated that the business was declining, and reference was made in particular to the figures with regard to newspaper sales, advertising revenue and expenses. The decrease in the volume of newspaper sales, though not great, is certainly not a favourable feature, especially as a reduction in circulation may tend to diminish the advertising revenue. The figures in relation to advertising revenue were the subject of a good deal of discussion.

The expenses show an increase year after year without a single exception for a period of ten years, and I do not think the respondents were able to show that this was due to a factor which was likely to be eliminated in the future.

The question, however, remains: what effect as regards the *quantum* of the price is to be given to the considerations to which I have been referring? I reject as being altogether exaggerated the idea that this business falls to be regarded as moribund in 1930. The Solicitor-General criticised with much force the evidence adduced by the appellants, because no witness had been brought from the *Scotsman* office to speak directly to the effect which the alleged adverse circumstances had upon the business. I am certainly not surprised to find that no one has come from the *Scotsman* office to say that this was a moribund business. I think, however, it is impossible to avoid coming to the conclusion that the outlook in 1930 could not be regarded as favourable for the newspaper industry, or for the *Scotsman* business in particular, and I think it is unreasonable to suppose that a buyer would expect to earn profits from this business amounting to the figure of £147,000, or anything approximating to that figure in the immediate future. A prudent buyer would, I think, proceed upon the view that the business would not recover from the serious setback which it had sustained in 1930 for some years.'

((1938) 22 ATC 437at 441/442 **case 18 paras 8 and 9**)

Having considered the evidence given by the expert witnesses as to the view that could be taken on future profits and, also, the differing approach of the two witnesses as to the capitalisation factor that should be applied to these profits, Lord Fleming then gave the valuation of the goodwill, as follows:

Assumed expected profits	£135,000
Capitalised value of earnings	
Expected profits 3 multiplier	
£135,000 × 8	1,080,000
Less: Tangible assets	(707,680)
	372,320
Share thereof in estate of Sir John Findlay	
£372,320 3 16/20	£297,856

((1938) 22 ATC 437at 441/442 **case 18 para 9**)

The other two judges agreed with Lord Fleming's analysis and conclusion, in its entirety ((1938) 22 ATC 437at 441/442 **case 18 paras 11 and 12**). This case, thus, gives an important precedent on the manner of valuing goodwill.

Judgement

References, example '(pg439)', are to (1938) 22 ATC 437.

1 LORD FLEMING: This appeal relates to the value for estate duty purposes of the interest of the late Sir John Findlay, Baronet, in the firm of John Ritchie & Company, the proprietors and publishers of the *Scotsman, Evening Dispatch and Weekly Scotsman* newspapers. The deceased was a partner of the firm, holding 16/20ths of its shares. The controversy between the parties is with regard to the value of the goodwill of the business, and of the deceased's interest therein. They are agreed that the tangible assets are to be taken to be of the value of £707,680. The goodwill was valued by the appellants, in the accounts which they lodged of the property passing on the deceased's death, at the sum of £334,185, whereof the deceased's interest was £267,343. Thereafter correspondence took place between the Commissioners of Inland Revenue and the appellants with regard to the value of the goodwill, but these negotiations did not result in any agreement. The Commissioners ultimately estimated the value of the goodwill at £426,780, and on this basis they claimed an additional assessment of estate duty which with interest amounted to £25,940 5s 5d. The appellants have appealed against this additional assessment, and the only question which we have to determine is the value of the goodwill.

2 Two of the witnesses for the appellants, namely, Sir Bertram Ford and Mr Scott dealt with the problem on the footing that the value of the goodwill fell to be ascertained as if it were a quite separate asset, whereas Mr Goeghegan for the appellants, and Mr Robson for the respondents, considered that the proper method of solving the problem was to ascertain the value of the business and all its assets as a whole, and then deduct therefrom the agreed-on value of the tangible assets, and to treat the balance as the value of the goodwill. At one stage of the hearing the parties appeared to be in dispute with regard to the manner in which debentures issued by the firm to the amount of £300,000 fell to be dealt with. At the date of the deceased's death the interest payable thereon was $3\frac{1}{2}$ per cent, but it was subsequently increased to $5\frac{1}{2}$ per cent. Mr Geoghegan and Mr Robson took the view that the existence of these debentures had no effect upon the value of the goodwill of the business, and their opinion was ultimately accepted by both sides. It seems to me clear that the circumstance that a considerable part of the capital required to run the business can be raised at a comparatively low rate of interest on the security of the assets cannot have any effect in depreciating the value of the goodwill. On the contrary it would rather appear to me that it might have some effect in increasing its value. There is, however, no evidence to this effect and I take it that the existence of the debentures is an immaterial circumstance in so far as the ascertainment of the value of the goodwill is concerned. But this does not mean that their existence is to be disregarded in fixing the value of the interest of the partners. The debentures are a debt of the business and must be deducted from its value before the interest of the partners can be determined. That has been done in the present case by deducting the amount of the debentures, namely, £300,000, from the value of the tangible assets, namely, £707,680, leaving a balance of £407,680, which is taken to be the value of the interest of the partners in the tangible assets.

3 The method by which the Commissioners are directed to estimate the value of property for estate duty purposes is prescribed by Section 7 (5) of the Finance Act 1894 as follows:

'The principal value of any property shall be estimated to be the price which in the *(pg439)* opinion of the Commissioners such property would fetch if sold in the open market at the time of the death of the deceased.'

Now it may be that under the contract of co-partnery it would not have been possible to sell the deceased's interest in the open market, but I understood the parties to be agreed that the case was ruled by the *Commissioners of Inland Revenue v Crossman* ([1937] AC 26), in which the cases of the *Attorney-General for Ireland v Jameson* ([1905] 2 IR 218), and *Salvesen's Trustees v Commissioners of Inland Revenue* (1930 SLT 387, 9 ATC 43) were approved. It must therefore be assumed that, while the estimate of the value of the deceased's interest is to be made on the footing that it is sold in the open market, the hypothetical purchaser will take the interest subject to all its rights and liabilities, and all its advantages and disadvantages, just as it was held by the deceased. The deceased's interest in the partnership of John Ritchie and Company is obviously an asset of a quite exceptional character. It is, I should think, rather unusual for an undertaking of this magnitude to be carried on by a private partnership. Shares in such a partnership are subject to disadvantages and liabilities as contrasted with shares in a public company with limited liability. Thus the liability of the individual partners for the debts of a firm is unlimited and the shares in a firm, even when very valuable, may not be easily realised. In estimating the price which might be fetched in the open market for the goodwill of the business it must be assumed that the transaction takes place between a willing seller and a willing purchaser; and that the purchaser is a person of reasonable prudence, who has informed himself with regard to all the relevant facts such as the history of the business, its present position, its future prospects and the general conditions of the industry; and also that he has access to the accounts of the business for a number of years.

4 But making all these assumptions, on what basis is the price to be estimated? Two methods have been suggested. The first method is that adopted by the appellants' witnesses, Sir Bertram Ford, general manager of the *Birmingham Post and Mail* and kindred newspapers, and Mr Scott, chairman and managing director of the *Manchester Guardian and Evening News Limited*. Shortly after the deceased's death these two gentlemen made a valuation of the goodwill for estate duty purposes, bringing out its value at £334,185, which was the basis of the figure entered in the appellants' accounts as the value of the interest of the deceased in the goodwill. There can be no question that these two gentlemen were extremely well qualified to speak of the conditions affecting the newspaper industry, particularly outside of London, and its prospects for the future. In their evidence they express the view that in general the goodwill of a newspaper business was worth three years' purchase of its net average profits; and that the average profits fell to be ascertained by taking an average of the profits for three years preceding the date of the valuation. They were, however, of opinion that in 1930 there were a number of circumstances affecting newspaper business adversely, and the *Scotsman* business in particular, which required that the average profits should in this case be multiplied by two and one half. I find myself unable to regard the method of valuation adopted by these gentlemen as entirely satisfactory. They did not attempt to justify their multiplier of three by the examination of any figures, nor did they give any evidence of the existence of a rule of practice under which valuations of newspapers were made according to the method which they adopted. They proceeded almost entirely on their own general knowledge of the trade and with one exception were not able to give particulars of instances in which their method had been followed. It is no doubt true that in some businesses and professions the value of goodwill is usually expressed in terms of some multiplier of net profits or of gross drawings. If as regards any particular kind of business a rule to that effect has been adopted in practice, it would of course be entitled to respect, but we have no evidence of that character as regards the newspaper industry.

5 It is to be presumed that the hypothetical purchaser having obtained all the relevant information would consider in the first place the risks which are involved in carrying on the business, and would fix the return which he considered he ought to receive on the purchase price at a rate per cent. The only other factor which he would then require to determine would be the annual profits which he would derive from the carrying on of the business. The determination of these two factors would enable him to fix the capital value of the business. A seller looking at the matter from the opposite point of view would deal with it on similar lines. Here we are fortunate in this respect that Mr Geoghegan and Mr Robson are in substantial agreement with regard to the first factor, ie the rate per cent of profit. Mr Geoghegan says it must not be less than $12\frac{1}{2}$ per cent, and Mr Robson *(pg440)* is prepared to concede that figure. This figure takes account of all the advantages and disadvantages of the interest which passed on the deceased's death.

6 The only factor still in dispute is the figure of net profit which the purchaser may reasonably expect to earn from the business. Mr Geoghegan and Mr Robson are agreed with regard to the methods by which the net profits should be ascertained. They both take the view that for this purpose the net profits must include income tax and also the interest payable on debentures. They are also agreed that, when the figure of profits which the purchaser may expect to earn from the business is fixed, it should be multiplied by eight in order to ascertain the *cumulo* value of the whole business. The difference between them is that Mr Robson takes as his figure of expected profits the average of the three years prior to the deceased's death, whereas

Mr Geoghegan takes the actual profits for the last of these years. Mr Robson takes the average for three years at £147,510, and multiplies it by eight, which gives him £1,180,080. From that he deducts the value of the tangible assets, £707,680, leaving a balance of £472,400, which he takes to be the goodwill of the whole business. Mr Geoghegan takes the profits for the year ended 1930 as £124,721, and multiplies it by eight, which brings out a figure of £977,768. From this he deducts the value of the tangible assets as before, £707,680, leaving £290,088 as the value of the goodwill. The only point of difference between them is whether Mr Robson's figure of £147,510 or Mr Geoghegan's figure of £124,721 should be multiplied by eight in order to ascertain the value of the business. It is to be observed that Mr Robson's valuation of £472,400 contrasts with the value estimated by the Commissioners, and on which the assessment is based, namely, £426,780. On the other hand Mr Geoghegan's figure of £290,088 contrasts with the sum of £334,185 (now adjusted to £327,525), which the appellants entered in the accounts given up by them. The Commissioners justify their assessment by Mr Robson's figure, and the appellants their valuation by Mr Geoghegan's figure. Neither can criticise the other, as each is seeking to justify the figure on which they rely by a valuation which brings out a more favourable figure.

7 The decision of this case must accordingly depend upon the figure which is to be adopted for expected profits. I do not doubt that, when one is seeking to ascertain the profits which will probably be earned by a business in the future, it is quite usual to do so by taking an average of the profits actually earned for the three preceding years. This probably operates quite equitably when one is dealing with a well established business, which has normal ups and downs, but has no violent fluctuations in either direction. But if there is a definite trend upwards or downwards, it may be different. If, for example, profits are increasing year by year by large figures, an average of three years may be unfair to the seller. If there is a similar movement downwards, it may be unfair to the purchaser. The relevant figures as regards this business are to be found in No 14 of Process, and the figures of adjusted net profit are in column 7. In order to find the figures actually used by Mr Geoghegan and Mr Robson, it is necessary to add to each of the figures in that column a sum of £16,500 representing debenture interest. But the actual figures in the column sufficiently indicate the movements of the business upwards and downwards, so far as profits are concerned, and the remarkable fact is that you have in 1930 a drop in profits of not less than £36,000, which is greater than any other increase or decrease in the column. There are large increases in the years 1922 and 1923, but it is apparent that these increases are explained by the reduction on the amount of one item of expense, namely, the cost of the newsprint. *Prima facie* the drop in profits in 1930 is of such a large amount as to suggest that it cannot properly be dealt with by the application of what is at best merely a rule of thumb.

8 This *prima facie* view is, I think, confirmed by a consideration of the position of the newspaper industry in the year 1930. That year was a period of general depression, which had begun in 1929, and it was certainly not a time at which sellers could expect to get good prices. Trade is said to go in cycles, and 'booms' follow 'slumps'. But there were a number of factors which, apart from the slump, were not favourable to this business in 1930. The competition by what are called the national newspapers with their headquarters in London was in an increasing degree affecting the prospects of the morning newspapers published in the provinces of England and in Scotland. According to the evidence of Sir Bertram Ford and Mr Scott the 'structure' of the *Scotsman* business was not well suited to withstand such competition. In their view the morning newspapers are much more amenable to competition from London than the evening newspapers, and it is accordingly a great advantage to a morning paper to have a strong evening paper associated *(pg441)* with it, and this business was criticised on the ground that the *Scotsman* was the *(pg442)* predominant partner in the group. Though the *Evening Dispatch* was increasing its circulation at this time, their view was that it was not a sufficiently strong evening paper to counteract any retrograde movement on the part of the *Scotsman*, especially as it had to face competition from a well-established rival newspaper. Another factor which they regarded as unfavourable was that the *Scotsman* newspapers circulated mainly in a non-industrial area, in which the population was not increasing or increasing slowly; and that there was little scope for expansion or development. It was maintained by the appellants that the figures in the other columns in No 14 of Process indicated that the business was declining, and reference was made in particular to the figures with regard to newspaper sales, advertising revenue and expenses. The decrease in the volume of newspaper sales, though not great, is certainly not a favourable feature, especially as a reduction in circulation may tend to diminish the advertising revenue. The figures in relation to advertising revenue were the subject of a good deal of discussion. There is a drop of £27,000 in the year 1930, which might give a buyer some uneasiness, but otherwise the tendency is rather upwards, and I do not think that the figures relating to this matter give much assistance to either side. Admittedly, however, a disquieting feature as regards the future is the increase in expenses other than the cost of newsprint. The expenses show an increase year after year without a single exception for a period of ten years, and I do not think the respondents were able to show that this was due to a factor which was likely to be eliminated in the future.

9 The question, however, remains: what effect as regards the *quantum* of the price is to be given to the considerations to which I have been referring? I reject as being altogether exaggerated the idea that this business falls to be regarded as moribund in 1930. The Solicitor-General criticised with much force the evidence adduced by the appellants, because no witness had been brought from the *Scotsman* office to speak directly to the effect which the alleged adverse circumstances had upon the business. I am certainly not surprised to find that no one has come from the *Scotsman* office to say that this was a moribund business. I think, however, it is impossible to avoid coming to the conclusion that the outlook in 1930 could not be regarded as favourable for the newspaper industry, or for the *Scotsman* business in particular, and I think it is unreasonable to suppose that a buyer would expect to earn profits from this business amounting to the figure of £147,000, or anything approximating to that figure in the immediate future. A prudent buyer would, I think, proceed upon the view that the business would not recover from the serious setback which it had sustained in 1930 for some years. The respondents, however, argued that ample allowance had been made for this, as they were willing to accept a valuation over £45,000 less than Mr Robson had brought out; and they pointed out, quite correctly, that this was equivalent to diminishing the average annual profit which they had taken, by a sum of over £5,000. I am not satisfied, however, that this is a sufficient allowance. There is still left a wide gap amounting to about £15,000 between their reduced figures and the actual profits earned in 1930, and I suggest to your lordships that we should take as the figure of expected profits a sum of £135,000, which exceeds by more than £10,000 the actual profits in 1930. If the figure of £135,000 be multiplied by eight, and the value of the tangible assets, namely, £707,680 be deducted, there is left to represent the value of the goodwill £372,320.

10 I should add that I have not found it necessary to deal in detail with the figures and computations which are set out in Nos 15 and 16 of Process. The shares there dealt with are all shares of public companies with limited liability, whose shares are quoted on the stock exchange, and they do not afford any satisfactory basis for the calculation of the deceased's interest in a business of a quite different character. As regards No 15 of Process the figures which it contains could not be regarded as being of any value, unless a careful analysis and examination had been made of the book values of the tangible assets, and, as I read Mr Robson's evidence, he did not really attach much value to them.

11 LORD CARMONT: I concur and have nothing to add.

12 THE LORD PRESIDENT (LORD NORMOND): I concur.

Case 19
Raja VN Gajapatiraju v Revenue Divisional Officer Vizagapatam

[1939] AC 303

Privy Council

23 February 1939

When valuing land (and, by implication, a shareholding) the valuation should not be restricted to the current use of the asset; a possible alternative use must be taken into account.

Although this case is concerned with the valuation of land and not the valuation of shares, the principles of valuation given in the decision of the Privy Council apply equally to a valuation of a shareholding. These principles are particularly clearly stated in the leading judgement of Lord Romer.

Raja Gajapatiraju owned land adjoining a site designated for a harbour. The harbour authority exercised its compulsory purchase powers to acquire the land from Raja Gajapatiraju. The tribunal in India awarded a compensation payment to the landowner on the basis of the value of the land as partly waste and partly cultivated. Raja Gajapatiraju appealed, claiming higher compensation on the basis of a valuation of the land to reflect its potentiality as a building site.

Giving the judgement of the Privy Council, Lord Romer said:

'… it has been established by numerous authorities that the land is not to be valued merely by reference to the use to which it is being put at the time at which its value has to be determined … but also by reference to the uses to which it is reasonably capable of being put in the future. No authority indeed is required for this proposition. It is a self-evident one. No one can suppose in the case of land which is certain, or even likely, to be used in the immediate or reasonably near future for building purposes, but which at the valuation date is waste land or is being used for agricultural purposes, that the owner, however willing a vendor, will be content to sell the land for its value as waste or agricultural land as the case may be. It is plain that, in ascertaining its value, the possibility of its being used for building purposes would have to be taken into account. It is equally plain, however, that the land must not be valued as though it had already been built upon, a proposition that is embodied in s24, sub-s 5, of the Act and is sometimes expressed by saying that it is the possibilities of the land and not its realised possibilities that must be taken into consideration.'

([1939] AC 303 at 313 **case 19 para 4**)

The Privy Council also dealt with the point that there was a special purchaser for this land, being the harbour authority. Lord Romer said:

'It has been suggested that in order to ascertain it, the arbitrator is to hold an imaginary auction. But with all respect to those who have made the suggestion, their Lordships are unable to see how this is going to help the arbitrator.'

([1939] AC 303 at 314 **case 19 para 8**)

'The truth of the matter is that the value of the potentiality must be ascertained by the arbitrator on such materials as are available to him and without indulging in feats of the imagination.'

([1939] AC 303 at 316 **case 19 para 10**)

'Upon the question of the value of the potentiality where there is only one possible purchaser, there are some authorities to which their Lordships will have to refer. But dealing with the matter apart from authority it would seem that the value should be the sum which the arbitrator estimates a willing purchaser will pay and not what a purchaser will pay under compulsion ...

The fact is that the only possible purchaser of a potentiality is usually quite willing to pay for it.'

([1939] AC 303 at 316/317 **case 19 para 12**)

'It is said that the matter assumes a totally different complexion when the only possible purchaser is the one who has obtained the compulsory powers of purchase, and that this has been established by authorities that should be followed by this Board.'

([1939] AC 303 at 318 **case 19 para 14**)

'Any enhanced value attaching to the land by reason of the fact that it has been compulsorily acquired for the purpose of the acquiring authority must always be disregarded.'

([1939] AC 303 at 318 **case 19 para 15**)

'For these reasons, their Lordships have come to the conclusion that, even where the only possible purchaser of the land's potentiality is the authority that has obtained the compulsory powers, the arbitrator in awarding compensation must ascertain to the best of his ability the price that would be paid by a willing purchaser to a willing vendor of the land with its potentiality in the same way that he would ascertain it in a case where there are several possible purchasers and that he is no more confined to awarding the land's "poramboke" [the highest value that would be offered by a purchaser who is not a special purchaser] value in the former case than he is in the latter.'

([1939] AC 303 at 323 **case 19 para 18**)

In the context of a share valuation, the author suggests that the *ratio decidendi* in this land valuation case requires the valuer of a shareholding to consider any alternative use to which the directors could put the assets of the company. This could be of particular relevance, for example, when valuing a shareholding in a trading company that suffers from low earnings but owns freehold property. If the company could pass greater value to its shareholders by letting the property to others and receiving a rent, that fact must be brought into the valuation. The arithmetic influence could be large in the case of a majority shareholding; there could also be a significant influence in the valuation of a minority shareholding if it is reasonable to assume that sufficient of the other shareholders could influence the board of directors in changing the business of the company.

Judgement

References, example '(pg308)', are to [1939] AC 303.

1 LORD ROMER: This appeal is concerned with the question of what is the proper sum to be awarded to the appellant by way of compensation in respect of the compulsory acquisition by the Vizagapatam Harbour Authority of certain land of his adjoining the harbour, the respondent being the representative of such authority for the purposes of this appeal. The circumstances in which the land was acquired are as follows:

2 The Vizagatapam Harbour, the construction of which appears to have been begun in the year 1920, was formed by making excavations in swampy land situate to the south-west of the town of Vizagatapam and by dredging a deep water channel in the creek to the south of that town that led from the swampy land into the Bay of Bengal. On the south of the land acquired by the Harbour Authority for the purpose of these works is situated the property of the appellant known as the Lova Gardens. These gardens are formed by a valley which runs down from high ground on the south-west to low ground on the north-east adjoining the land of the Harbour Authority on the south of the above-mentioned creek. The upper portion of this valley consists of a shallow basin in the hills which forms the catchment area of a spring of water that emerges from the ground at the north-east end of the basin. This spring, which appears to yield even in the dry season an average flow of 50,000 gallons a day of excellent drinking water, is situated at a height of 150 feet above sea level. Until a part of it was diverted by the Harbour Authority, as narrated hereafter, the whole of the water from *(pg308)* this spring ran down the valley to the lower end of Lova *(pg309)* Gardens and from thence discharged itself into the creek. By the early part of the year 1926 the construction of the harbour had made considerable progress and it was hoped that it would be ready for opening by the end of 1929. With that end in view a portion of the harbour site had been allocated by the Harbour Authority for the purpose of being used by oil companies and other industrial concerns. The entire south side of the harbour had indeed been allocated for industrial purposes. But the harbour land was very malarious, and so, too, was much of the land to the south of the harbour, including the lower part of the Lova Gardens; a circumstance that gave rise to some anxiety in the minds of the Harbour Authority. They accordingly consulted Mr Senior White, who is an expert upon the subject, and upon May 1, 1926, that gentleman, after making an 'anti-malarial survey' of the area, embodied the results of his survey in a report. This report disclosed a serious state of affairs in the villages situated in the area of which there appear to have been at that time no less than thirty-two of which nine were on the south side of the creek. These villages, or many of them, seem to have been dependent upon wells for their water supply, and these wells formed breeding grounds for the malaria-bearing mosquitoes. It is plain from the report that persons carrying on business at the harbour would run a serious risk of contracting malaria as matters then stood, and this would greatly hamper the development of the harbour site for industrial purposes. Further, as Mr White pointed out, there was the possibility of shipping at the quays becoming infected, and the mere possibility, which had already been suggested in the Indian press, was detrimental to the interest of the port. It appears from a letter written by Mr Rattenbury, the Deputy Engineer in Chief to the Harbour Authority, dated July 14, 1926, that in these circumstances, Mr White was 'very keen on closing the wells along the south side,' and this, the letter adds, could be done if a gravity water supply were provided instead. Such a supply could be furnished by the spring at the upper end of Lova Gardens, and accordingly the Harbour Authority conceived the idea of using the water from the spring for the purpose of freeing the harbour from malaria. But apart altogether from the assistance that this supply of water would give to the prevention of malaria, there was much to justify its acquisition on its own merits, as was pointed out in a letter of October 2, 1926, written by one of the harbour officials. For the water could be made available as a supply to the oil companies and other industrial concerns that might be established in the southern part of the harbour area. The method of utilising the water for these purposes that was ultimately adopted was this: The water was to be diverted from the lower part of the valley to which reference has been made and led from a short distance below the spring directly to the harbour area by means of a tunnel to be made through the hilly land to the north-west of the valley. This scheme, which was in due course carried out and is now in operation, involved the acquisition from the appellant of the shallow basin forming the catchment area of the spring, the site of the spring itself, and a narrow strip of land below the spring. In due course the necessary steps were taken for the compulsory acquisition of this land under the provisions of the Land Acquisition Act, 1894, the notification under s4, sub-s 1, of the Act being given on February 13, 1928. The public purpose for which the land was needed was stated in the notification to be the execution of anti-malarial works, the total area to be acquired from the appellant being 108.9 acres. Of this acreage the catchment area, including the site of the spring referred to as 2–1D and 2–1E, accounted for 105.92 acres, and the land below the spring referred to as 2–1B (0.53 acres), 2–1C (0.48 acres) and 2–3B (1.97 acres) accounted for the rest.

3 After the giving of the notification, and the procedure laid down in ss 6, 7 and 8 of the Act having been followed, the Collector took the steps prescribed by ss 9, 10 and 11 to determine the compensation that ought to be allowed to the appellant for his land. It is provided by s15 of the Act that in so doing, the Collector shall be guided by the provisions contained in ss 23 and 24, and it will be convenient before *(pg310)* continuing this narrative to turn to these provisions. So far as material to the present purpose they are as follows:

'23. – (1.) In determining the amount of compensation to be awarded for land acquired under this Act, the Court shall take into consideration -

first, the market-value of the land at the date of the publication of the declaration relating thereto under section 6;

secondly, the damage sustained by the person interested, by reason of the taking of any standing crops or trees which may be on the land at the time of the Collector's taking possession thereof;

thirdly, the damage (if any) sustained by the person interested, at the time of the Collector's taking possession of the land, by reason of severing such land from his other land;

fourthly, the damage (if any) sustained by the person interested, at the time of the Collector's taking possession of the land, by reason of the acquisition injuriously affecting his other property, moveable or immoveable, in any other manner, or his earnings.

24. But the Court shall not take into consideration -

first, the degree of urgency which has led to the acquisition;

secondly, any disinclination of the person interested to part with the land acquired;

. ....

fifthly, any increase to the value of the land acquired likely to accrue from the use to which it will be put when acquired.'

4 The general principles for determining compensation that are specified in these sections differ in no material respect from those upon which compensation was awarded in this country under the Lands *(pg311)* Clauses Act of 1845 before the coming into operation of the Acquisition of Land (Assessment of Compensation) Act of 1919. As was said by Wadsworth J when giving judgment in the High Court in the present case, 'It is well settled that English decisions under the Lands Clauses Act of 1845 lay down principles which are equally applicable to proceedings under the Indian Act.' The compensation must be determined, therefore, by reference to the price which a willing vendor might reasonably expect to obtain from a willing purchaser. The disinclination of the vendor to part with his land and the urgent necessity of the purchaser to buy must alike be disregarded. Neither must be considered as acting under compulsion. This is implied in the common saying that the value of the land is not to be estimated at its value to the purchaser. But this does not mean that the fact that some particular purchaser might desire the land more than others is to be disregarded. The wish of a particular purchaser, though not his compulsion, may always be taken into consideration for what it is worth. But the question of what it may be worth, that is to say, to what extent it should affect the compensation to be awarded, is one that will be dealt with later in this judgment. It may also be observed in passing that it is often said that it is the value of the land to the vendor that has to be estimated. This, however, is not in strictness accurate. The land, for instance, may have for the vendor a sentimental value far in excess of its 'market value.' But the compensation must not be increased by reason of any such consideration. The vendor is to be treated as a vendor willing to sell at 'the market price,' to use the words of s23 of the Indian Act. It is perhaps desirable in this connection to say something about this expression 'the market price.' There is not in general any market for land in the sense in which one speaks of a market for shares or a market for sugar or any like commodity. The value of any such article at any particular time can readily be ascertained by the prices being obtained for similar articles in the market. In the case of land, its value in general can also be measured by a consideration of the prices that have been obtained in the past for land of similar quality and in similar positions, and this is what must be meant in general by 'the market value' in s23. But sometimes it happens that the land to be valued possesses some unusual, and it may be, unique features, as regards its *(pg312)* position or its potentialities. In such a case the arbitrator in determining its value will have no market value to guide him, and he will have to ascertain as best he may from the materials before him, what a willing vendor might reasonably expect to obtain from a willing purchaser, for the land in that particular position and with those particular potentialities. For it has been established by numerous authorities that the land is not to be valued merely by reference to the use to which it is being put at the time at which its value has to be determined (that time under the Indian Act being the date of the notification under s4, sub-s 1), but also by reference to the uses to which it

is reasonably capable of being put in the future. No authority indeed is required for this proposition. It is a self-evident one. No one can suppose in the case of land which is certain, or even likely, to be used in the immediate or reasonably near future for building purposes, but which at the valuation date is waste land or is being used for agricultural purposes, that the owner, however willing a vendor, will be content to sell the land for its value as waste or agricultural land as the case may be. It is plain that, in ascertaining its value, the possibility of its being used for building purposes would have to be taken into account. It is equally plain, however, that the land must not be valued as though it had already been built upon, a proposition that is embodied in s24, sub-s 5, of the Act and is sometimes expressed by saying that it is the possibilities of the land *(pg313)* and not its realised possibilities that must be taken into consideration.

5 But how is the increase accruing to the value of the land by reason of its potentialities or possibilities to be measured? In the case instanced above of land possessing the possibility of being used for building purposes, the arbitrator (which expression in this judgment includes any person who has to determine the value) would probably have before him evidence of the prices paid, in the neighbourhood, for land immediately required for such purposes. He would then have to deduct from the value so ascertained such a sum as he would think proper by reason of the degree of possibility that the land might never be so required or might not be so required for a considerable time. In the case, however, of land possessing potentialities of such an unusual nature that the arbitrator has not similar cases to guide him, the value of the land must be ascertained in some other way. In such a case, moreover, there will, in all probability, be only a very limited number of persons capable of turning the potentialities of the land to account.

6 If the owner of the land is the only person who can do so, the value to him must be ascertained by reference to what profit he might thereby have been able to derive from the land in the future. Take as an example the case of an owner of vacant land that adjoins his factory. The land possesses the potentiality of being profitably used for an extension of the factory. But the owner is the only person who can turn that potentiality to account. In valuing the land, however, as between him and a willing purchaser, the value to him of the potentiality would necessarily have to be included.

7 The same consideration will apply to cases where the owner is not the only person but merely one of the persons able to turn the potentiality to account. The value to him of the potentiality will not be less than the profit that would accrue to him by making use of it had he retained it in his own possession. But now take the case where the owner is himself unable to turn the potentiality to account whether by promotion of a company or otherwise. In such a case there may be several other persons who would be able to do so, or there may be only one. If there are more than one, it is recognized by all the authorities that have been cited to their Lordships, and seems to be consistent with common sense, that the owner is entitled to be paid the value to him of the potentiality, though the ascertainment of its value may in many cases be a matter of considerable difficulty.

8 It has been suggested that in order to ascertain it, the arbitrator is to hold an imaginary auction. But with all respect to those who have made the suggestion, their Lordships are unable to see how this is going to help the arbitrator. *(pg314)* At such imaginary auction, all possible purchasers must, no doubt, be imagined as attending. They will include, therefore, persons who are in no way interested in the land's potentialities, and such persons will bid no higher price than the value of similar land without its potentialities. This value in this judgment is referred to as the 'poramboke' value. But they will also include what may be called the purchasers of the potentialities. There may also be present some speculative buyers who will be willing to bid more than the 'poramboke' value upon the chance of being able to resell to a purchaser of the potentiality at a profit. It would seem, however, logically, that such purchasers should be disregarded. For the object of the imaginary auction is to discover what a purchaser of the potentiality will be willing to pay for it, and this cannot depend upon the presence at the auction of persons willing to pay less, unless it be that such ultimate purchaser is to be considered willing to pay whatever fantastic price he may be forced up to by competition. And no one suggests this.

9 Proceeding, therefore, with the imaginary auction at which are present two classes of buyers – namely, the 'poramboke buyers' and the 'potentiality buyers' – the former will disappear from the bidding as soon as the 'poramboke' value has been reached, and the bidding will thereafter be confined to the 'potentiality buyers.' But at what figure will this bidding stop? As already pointed out it cannot be imagined as going on until the ultimate purchaser has been driven by the competition up to a fantastic price. For he is *ex hypothesi* a willing purchaser and not one who is by circumstances forced to buy. Nor can the bidding be imagined to stop at the first advance on the 'poramboke' value. For the vendor is a willing vendor and not one compelled by circumstances to sell his potentiality for anything that he can get. The arbitrator will, therefore, continue the imaginary bidding until a bid is reached which, in the arbitrator's estimate, represents the true value to the vendor of the potentiality. The auction will, therefore, have been an entire waste of the arbitrator's imagination. If the value *(pg315)* of the potentiality be Rs.X, the imaginary auction will have taken place to ascertain the value of X from the imaginary bidding, and all that can be said is that the bidding will stop at Rs.X.

10 The truth of the matter is that the value of the potentiality must be ascertained by the arbitrator on such materials as are available to him and without indulging in feats of the imagination.

11 Their Lordships would not have thought it necessary to deal with this question of the imaginary auction at such length, were it not for the fact that in the argument before them the respondent's counsel endeavoured to show, by reference to such an auction, that when there was only one possible purchaser of the potentiality the value of it to the vendor was nil – that is to say that the value of the land with the potentiality was substantially nothing in excess of its value without it. This argument, it may be observed, commended itself to Lord Cullen in the Scottish case of *Glass v Inland Revenue*, referred to below, but was rejected by the majority of the Court.

12 Upon the question of the value of the potentiality where there is only one possible purchaser, there are some authorities to which their Lordships will have to refer. But dealing with the matter apart from authority it would seem that the value should be the sum which the arbitrator estimates a willing purchaser will pay and not what a purchaser will pay under compulsion. It was contended on behalf of the respondent that, at an auction where there is only one possible purchaser of the potentiality, the bidding will only rise above the 'poramboke' value sufficiently to enable the land to be knocked down to that purchaser. But if the potentiality is of value to the vendor if there happen to be two or more possible purchasers of it, it is difficult to see why he should be willing to part with it for nothing merely because there is only one purchaser. To compel him to do so is to treat him as a vendor parting with his land under compulsion and not as a willing vendor. The fact is that the only possible *(pg316)* purchaser of a potentiality is usually quite willing to pay for it. An instance of this is to be found in the case of *Inland Revenue Commissioners v Clay*. That was a case under s25, sub-s 1, of the Finance (1909–1910) Act 1910, and is not perhaps strictly relevant to the present case. The facts of it, however, are worth recalling. There was a house of which the value to anyone except certain trustees was no more than £750. These trustees were the owners of a nurses' home which adjoined the house, and they were desirous of extending their premises. They accordingly purchased the house for £1000, the owner thus receiving £250 for the potentiality his house possessed by reason of its position adjoining the nurses' home. It was held by the Court of Appeal that £1000 was the value of the house to a willing seller. 'To say,' said Lord Cozens Hardy MR, 'that a small farm in the middle of a wealthy landowner's estate is to be valued without reference to the fact that he will probably be willing to pay a large price, but solely with reference to its ordinary agricultural value, seems to me absurd.' Had the house in that case been acquired compulsorily by a railway company, or local authority under the provisions of the Lands Clauses Consolidation Act 1845, before its purchase by the trustees, the house ought, in their Lordships' opinion, and for the reasons already given, to have been valued at £1000 and not merely at £750.

13 A case in many respects similar to *Clay's* case, is that of *Glass v Inland Revenue*. That also was a case arising under the Finance (1909–1910) Act 1910, and was one where land of an agricultural value of £3379 had been sold in 1911 to certain Water Commissioners for £5000, they being the only possible purchasers of the land for other than agricultural purposes. It was held that in valuing the land as on April 30, 1909, the possibility that the Commissioners might give more than the agricultural value for the land must be taken into consideration. In Lord Johnston's words, it was necessary in order to fix the value of the land on April 30, 1909, to *(pg317)* ascertain 'what is to be attributed to the probability of the Water Commissioners, in the circumstances, desiring to acquire the property, and what figure, in a friendly negotiation, they would be expected to pay for it.'

14 But however this may be, it is said that the matter assumes a totally different complexion when the only possible purchaser is the one who has obtained the compulsory powers of purchase, and that this has been established by authorities that should be followed by this Board. Of these authorities, the first one to which reference need be made is that of *In re Gough and The Aspatria, Silloth and District Joint Water Board.* In that case it was not proved that the acquiring authority was the only possible purchaser and it may be that all that the Court of Appeal decided was that it was not incumbent upon the claimant for compensation to specify that any particular body of persons were possible purchasers, though the judgment of Lord Alverstone LCJ seems quite consistent with the view that the potentiality must be valued, even if the acquiring authority be its only possible purchaser. But it is contended that Sir Richard Henn Collins MR expressed the contrary view. After referring to the particular adaptability of the land that was in question and that it ought to find a place in the estimate of the amount of compensation, he said: 'That view is supported by authority and long practice; but underlying it is the question, which is one of fact for the arbitrator, whether there is a possible market for the site, and in determining that the statutory purchase is not to be considered.'

15 But the Master of the Rolls said that the purchase, not the purchaser, was to be left out of consideration. Any enhanced value attaching to the land by reason of the fact that it has been compulsorily acquired for the purpose of the acquiring authority must always be disregarded, and the Master of the Rolls meant no more than that. The case of *Lucas and Chesterfield Gas and Water Board,* must, however, be considered in greater detail, for it is on certain *(pg318)* dicta of Fletcher Moulton LJ in that case that the respondent chiefly relies. The land that had been compulsorily acquired in that case had potentialities for which the acquiring authority was not the only possible purchaser. The point now being considered did not therefore arise for decision. But in the Court below, Bray J had said this:

'I come back to the question whether the fact that no buyer for reservoir purposes can be found, except a buyer who has obtained parliamentary powers, prevents the special value of the land being marketable. In my opinion the answer I ought to give to that question is "No".'

In the Court of Appeal, Vaughan Williams LJ said:

'I agree with Bray J that the fact that no buyer for reservoir purposes can be found except a buyer who has obtained parliamentary powers does not prevent the special value being marketable,' and stated that one of his reasons for so agreeing was that the fact that the board (who were the acquiring authority) might themselves become possible purchasers who would give a special price for the land, ought to be considered. Fletcher Moulton LJ, however, said that the decided cases to his mind laid down the principle that, when the special value exists only for the particular purchaser who has obtained powers of compulsory purchase, it cannot be taken into consideration in fixing the price, because to do otherwise would be to allow the existence of the scheme to enhance the value of the land to be purchased under it. He added that where there were other possible purchasers there would be competition among them and this fact would enhance the market price. The learned Lord Justice did not specify the authorities which laid down the principle in question and their Lordships are not aware of any that would justify it. It must, of course, be conceded that the existence of the scheme must not be allowed to enhance the price, if by 'scheme' is meant the fact that compulsory powers of acquisition have been obtained for the purpose of carrying into effect a particular scheme for the profitable use of the potentiality. The valuation must *(pg319)* always be made as though no such powers had been acquired, and the only use that can be made of the scheme is as evidence that the acquiring authority can properly be regarded as possible purchasers. But their Lordships have some difficulty in seeing why the taking into consideration of the fact that the special value exists for those purchasers only should be said to be allowing the existence of the scheme to enhance the value of the lands. The only difference that the scheme has made is that the acquiring authority, who before the scheme were possible purchasers only, have become purchasers who are under a pressing need to acquire the land; and that is a circumstance that is never allowed to enhance the value. If, on the other hand, the Lord Justice meant by 'the scheme' the intention formed by the acquiring authority of exploiting the potentiality of the land, his statement can only mean that the value of the land is not to be enhanced by the fact that they are possible purchasers. The result of this would be that, even in a case where there are two or more possible purchasers, their existence must not be allowed to enhance the value. For each purchaser must be deemed to have a scheme in the sense supposed, and the enhancement of value due to their competition which the Lord Justice envisages will in fact be due to the 'schemes.' In these circumstances their Lordships are not prepared to follow the dictum of Fletcher Moulton LJ in the *Lucas* case, and prefer the opinion there expressed by Vaughan Williams LJ. It is said, however, that the dictum of Fletcher Moulton LJ has already received the approval of this Board on more than one occasion. But in no case to which their Lordships' attention has been called was the question of the effect of there being only one possible purchaser of the land being considered by the Board, and any approval of the statement of the law by the Lord Justice must be regarded merely as an approval of such statement so far as it affected the particular question then before the Board. It is sufficient in this connection to refer to two of such cases. In *Cedars Rapids Manufacturing and Power Co v Lacoste*, Lord Dunedin, *(pg320)* in delivering the judgment of the Board, said this:

'The law of Canada as regards the principles upon which compensation for land taken is to be awarded is the same as the law of England and it has been explained in numerous cases, nowhere with greater precision than in the case of *In re Lucas and Chesterfield Gas and Water Board*, where Vaughan Williams and Fletcher Moulton LJJ deal with the whole subject exhaustively and accurately.'

As has already been pointed out, the opinions of the two Lords Justices upon the question now being considered were diametrically opposed to one another. The other case is that of *Fraser v City of Fraserville*, where Lord Buckmaster, in delivering the judgment of the Board, said:

'The principles which regulate the fixing of compensation of lands compulsorily acquired have been the subject of many decisions, and among the most recent are those of *In re Lucas and Chesterfield Gas and Water Board*, *Cedars Rapids Manufacturing and Power Co v Lacoste*, and *Sidney v North Eastern Railway Co*. The principles of those cases are carefully and correctly considered in the judgments the subject of appeal, and the substance of them is this: that the value to be ascertained is the value to the seller of the property in its actual condition at the time of expropriation with all its existing advantages and with all its possibilities, excluding any advantage due to the carrying out of the scheme in which the property is compulsorily acquired, the question of what is the scheme being a question of fact for the arbitrator in each case.'

16 It will be observed that Lord Buckmaster makes no reference whatsoever to the present question. But in one of the cases to which the noble and learned Lord referred – namely, *Sidney v North Eastern Ry Co*, Rowlatt J is thought to have said much the same as had been said by Fletcher Moulton LJ. In that case certain land possessed the potentiality of being used for the purposes of a railway. That potentiality was capable of being turned to account by *(pg321)* a railway company who had obtained compulsory powers of acquiring it and by the proprietor of an adjoining colliery. In assessing the compensation to be paid by the railway company for the land, the arbitrator took into account the possibility that, but for its acquisition by the railway company, the colliery proprietor might have purchased it, but he did not take into consideration the possibility that the company might in friendly negotiation have been willing to pay more for it than the colliery proprietor. In their Lordships' opinion he was wrong in this. The Divisional Court, however, on a case stated, upheld the decision of the arbitrator. In the course of his judgment Rowlatt J said this:

'Now if and so long as there are several competitors including the actual taker who may be regarded as possibly in the market for purposes such as those of the scheme, the possibility of their offering for the land is an element of the value in no respect differing from that afforded by the possibility of offers for it for other purposes. As such it is admissible as truly market value to the owner and not merely value to the taker. But when the price is reached at which all other competition must be taken to fail to what can any further value be attributed? The point has been reached when the owner is offered more than the land is worth to him for his own purposes and all that any one else would offer him except one person, the promoter, who is now, though he was not before, freed from competition. Apart from compulsory powers the owner need not sell to that one and that one would need to make higher and yet higher offers. In respect of what would he make them? There can only be one answer – in respect of the value to him for his scheme. And he is only driven to make such offers because of the unwillingness of the owner to sell without obtaining for himself a share in that value. Nothing representing this can be allowed.'

17 If and so far as this means that the value to be ascertained is the price that would be paid by a willing purchaser to a willing vendor, and not the price that would be paid by a 'driven' purchaser to an unwilling vendor, their Lordships *(pg322)* agree. But so far as it means that the possibility of the promoter as a willing purchaser being willing to pay more than other competitors, or in cases where he is the only purchaser of the potentiality, more than the value of the land without the potentiality is to be disregarded, their Lordships venture respectfully to differ from the learned judge.

18 For these reasons, their Lordships have come to the conclusion that, even where the only possible purchaser of the land's potentiality is the authority that has obtained the compulsory powers, the arbitrator in awarding compensation must ascertain to the best of his ability the price that would be paid by a willing purchaser to a willing vendor of the land with its potentiality in the same way that he would ascertain it in a case where there are several possible purchasers and that he is no more confined to awarding the land's 'poramboke' value in the former case than he is in the latter.

19 It is now necessary to take up once more the narrative of the events that have led up to this appeal.

20 On January 5, 1929, the appellant filed his claim for compensation. It was certainly not lacking in courage but it was lacking strangely enough in any suggestion that the land had a potential value as a source from which water might be supplied to persons or corporations outside Lova Gardens. He did, however, allege that Lova Gardens had a valuable potentiality as a building site and that such potentiality would be destroyed if he were deprived of the spring. He accordingly claimed Rs2,50,000 in this respect, calling it 'Damages sustained by severance,' though in strictness it should have been called damages sustained by reason of the acquisition injuriously affecting his other property. He also claimed Rs1200 per acre in respect of the land and Rs16,050 as the value of the masonry structures, roads, and trees on the land, the total claim amounting to Rs3,96,730.

21 On January 18, 1929, the Land Acquisition Officer made his award. He allowed in all a sum of Rs17,745–1-3 including the 15 per cent addition prescribed by s23, *(pg323)* sub-s 2, of the Act. It appears from the grounds of award bearing the same date that he thought nothing of the potentiality of Lova Gardens as a building site, and the existence of any such potentiality has now disappeared from the case and need not be referred to again. He valued the land at Rs50 an acre with the exception of the land numbered 2–3B, which he valued at Rs300 an acre. As to the claim in respect of 'Damages sustained by severance,' he thought that the rest of the appellant's land was probably better off without the water from the spring than with it. The lower part of the gardens, which was marshy and malarious, had too much water as it was. In any case he considered that the appellant would be amply compensated for the loss of the spring water by the Rs5000 that he awarded under this head. The appellant's claim of Rs2,50,000 was, he said, preposterous. He also awarded a sum of Rs4493 in respect of trees and buildings. The appellant thereupon required that the matter should be referred to the Court for determination under s18 of the Act and in due course it came on for hearing before the Subordinate Judge of Vizagapatam. It was then claimed on the appellant's behalf that the spring could, but for its acquisition, have been used by him as a source of water supply either to the Harbour Authority or to the oil companies and others residing or carrying on business in the harbour area; and the appellant claimed to be compensated upon this footing. After a lengthy hearing before him in the course of which many questions of law and fact not now in issue were discussed, the learned judge made his award. He found as a fact, and the fact cannot be disputed, that the water of the spring was on February 13, 1928, capable of being used as a source of water supply to persons outside the plaintiff's land. He also found that the only possible buyers of the water at that date were the Harbour Authority itself and the oil companies and labour camps that might be established as a result of the development of the harbour and stated that this fact would be taken into consideration in fixing the amount of compensation. But, after considering the *(pg324)* authorities on the subject, he came to the conclusion as a matter of law that the value to a vendor of a potentiality of his land can be assessed even though there are no other possible purchasers beyond the acquiring authority. Other principles of law stated by him for his guidance in making his award were that it was the contingent possibility of the user that had to be taken as the basis of valuation and not the realized possibility, and that the use to which the acquiring authority had actually put the property could be taken as a strong piece of evidence to show that the property acquired could be put to such use by the owner at the date of acquisition. Applying these principles, he found that the value of the land acquired, including the spring, was Rs1,05,000, which, with the addition of the 15 per cent under s23, sub-s 2, of the Act, amounted to Rs1,20,750. The Rs17,745–1–3 awarded by the Land Acquisition Officer had been paid to the appellant and received by him under protest, and deducting this sum from the Rs1,20,750, there remained Rs1,03,004–14–9 due to the appellant. This sum he decreed in favour of the appellant with certain interest. The valuation of Rs1,05,000 was arrived at in this way. Evidence had been given before the learned judge by two witnesses on behalf of the appellant as to what would be a proper charge for water supplied to the harbour area from the spring, and they estimated the charge at Re1–8-0 per 1000 gallons. The learned judge, however, said that taking into consideration the conclusions arrived at by him, which were presumably the conclusions of law and findings of fact referred to above, he thought it would be reasonable and proper to fix the value of the acquired property, ie the water source on the date of the acquisition on the basis of Re1 per 1000 gallons. Taking the normal supply of water at 50,000 gallons a day, this gave as the gross annual value of the water the sum of Rs18,250. He estimated that maintenance charges, depreciation of machinery, and interest on the capital outlay, would come to Rs12,273; but taking these items at the round figure of Rs13,000, the net annual income from the spring would be Rs5250. This he capitalized at twenty years' purchase and so arrived at the Rs1,05,000. *(pg325)* Having regard, amongst other things, to the extravagant claims put forward by the appellant in the first instance he awarded him no costs.

22 From this decision an appeal was taken by the present respondent to the High Court at Madras, the appellant lodging a memorandum of cross-objections to the valuation of the Subordinate Judge which need not be specified. The appeal was heard by Wadsworth and Stodart JJ and judgment allowing the appeal was delivered on May 4, 1937. The reasons for this decision given by Wadsworth J, in whose judgment Stodart J concurred, may be summarized as follows:

23 The scheme for utilization of the water and the carrying-out of anti-malarial operations in the valley (ie, the Lova Gardens) was not really an independent scheme. It was linked up with a bigger scheme for getting rid of breeding places of mosquitoes all round the southern side of the harbour so as to make the whole of that area fit for development. At the time when this scheme was promulgated the whole of that area was undeveloped. It was full of malaria and was incapable of any profitable use apart from the success of the anti-malarial campaign of which this acquisition was part. It was not conceivable that the present appellant himself would ever have been able to develop a water supply scheme, carrying out the necessary anti-malarial works and thereby encouraging business concerns to occupy the harbour land and buy water from him. The conclusion, therefore, must be that the special adaptability of the land for the supply of drinking water had no value apart from the scheme for which the acquisition was made.

24 The Harbour Authority, therefore, was at the date of the notification the only reasonably possible purchaser for the drinking water supply on the appellant's land and this being so the Subordinate Judge had erred in awarding compensation for the special adaptability of the land to supply drinking water to persons outside the appellant's land. After referring to the authorities and in particular the dictum of Fletcher Moulton LJ in the *Lucas* case, he said:

'There *(pg326)* can be little doubt that this exposition of the law when applied to the facts of the present case as we have found them would justify the conclusion that no value can be awarded to the special adaptability of this land for supplying drinking water to the harbour alone, if it can be shown that the land cannot have any value as a source of drinking water to anyone else.'

25 By the harbour the learned judge meant, of course, the Harbour Authority. Stodart J, who, as already stated, concurred in the judgment of Wadsworth J, added that: 'It is not contended that any other public authority or private undertaker except the Harbour Authority would ever have come forward to develop this area and make it habitable. Thus the value of the . spring as a source of drinking water . arose entirely from the Anti-Malarial Scheme carried out by the Harbour Authority and depended on the success of that scheme. To my hand section 24, sub-section 5, of the Land Acquisition Act is completely applicable to the facts of this case.'

26 The appeal was accordingly allowed with costs there and below and the award of the Land Acquisition officer was restored in toto. The memorandum of cross-objections was dismissed with costs. From that judgment, the necessary leave having been obtained, the appellant now appeals to His Majesty in Council.

27 Their Lordships agree with the High Court that on February 13, 1928, the only really possible purchasers of the special adaptability of the appellant's land as a water supply was the Harbour Authority. The position at that time was that the harbour was so far advanced that its opening in a few years was in contemplation. It was expected that, when that had taken place, oil companies and other industrial concerns, with their attendant labour camps, would be attracted to the harbour area, and they would all require to be supplied with water. It is plain that neither the appellant nor any purchaser from him would encounter any engineering difficulties in conducting the water from *(pg327)* the spring to the southern boundary of the harbour area. Nor would they encounter any engineering difficulty in conducting the water from that boundary to the premises of the oil companies and other concerns. They would, however, have had to obtain the consent of the Harbour Authority to lay the necessary pipes in the harbour area itself and the possibility of such consent being refused would have to be taken into consideration in estimating the value to the appellant of the special adaptability of his land, though the risk of such consent being refused was not a serious one, assuming that there was no other source from which the water could be profitably supplied by the Harbour Authority itself. There was, however, on February 13, 1928, a much more serious matter to be taken into consideration. As already pointed out, the harbour area was at that date a highly malarious place, little calculated to prove attractive as a site for any industrial concern. Unless, therefore, this state of affairs was remedied, there would be no customers for the appellant's water and the value to him of the special adaptability was nil. Now it is true that there was a practical certainty of the Harbour Authority taking steps to render the site as free as possible from malaria; for, if they did not, the harbour would not be used to any great extent even as a port of call. But, in order to carry out the necessary anti-malarial works, it was essential for the Harbour Authority to obtain a supply of drinking water from some source other than the wells in the area which were largely responsible for the malarious condition of the area and were going to be closed. The appellant on February 13, 1928, would therefore have been in this dilemma. If the only other source of water were the appellant's spring, the Harbour Authority would be the only possible purchaser. If, on the other hand, the Authority could obtain water from other sources sufficient both for the anti-malarial work and the supply of the traders in the harbour area, the appellant would almost certainly be refused permission to carry his competing supply over the Authority's land. In point of fact there *(pg328)* was at one time an alternative scheme on foot for obtaining water known as the Meghadrigedda Scheme. The scheme was to be for the benefit of the Municipality of Vizagapatam, the Bengal Nagpur Railway and the harbour. The scheme aimed at a supply of one million gallons a day of which the harbour was to have 150,000 gallons a day. The scheme has not been proceeded with, but it is impossible to say what would have been done about it had the spring in the Lova Gardens not been acquired. In these circumstances the possibility of the appellant's water being made available for the harbour by anyone other than the Harbour Authority was altogether negligible, and the only enhancement in the value to the appellant of his land by reason of its special adaptability as a water supply was the sum that the Harbour Authority, as a willing purchaser, would have been willing to give in excess of the land's 'poramboke' value.

28 Their Lordships have given their reasons for thinking, contrary to the view taken by the High Court, that such sum must be taken into consideration in fixing the compensation payable to the appellant, and that such sum is not to be treated as being a negligible one merely because the Harbour Authority was the only possible purchaser.

29 It remains to deal with s24, sub-s 5, of the Land Acquisition Act. That subsection as applied to the present case means no more than this: that in valuing the appellant's land on February 13, 1928, it must be valued as it then stood, and not as it would stand when the land had been acquired and the water on it used for ridding the harbour area of malaria. The Harbour Authority would otherwise be made to pay for the water twice over. But the sub-section does not mean that the possibility that a particular purchaser of land will give a higher price for it by reason of its possessing a special adaptability must be disregarded merely because the land will be more valuable in his hands when he exploits that adaptability than it would be if left in the hands of the vendor who was unable to exploit it. In *Clay's* case, for instance, the house after being added to the nurses' home was no doubt *(pg329)* more valuable than it was before. That, indeed, was the reason why the trustees of the home paid £250 more than any other purchaser would have paid. The house in that case was held to be of the value of £1000, not because that was its value after being put to the use for which it was acquired, but because that was the price which the willing purchaser was prepared to pay for its acquisition. In the present case the land must be valued not at the sum it would be worth after it had been acquired by the Harbour Authority and used for anti-malarial purposes, but at the sum that the Authority 'in a friendly negotiation' (to use Lord Johnston's words) would be willing to pay on February 13, 1928, in order to acquire it for those purposes.

30 Returning to the award made in the present case by the learned Subordinate Judge, it is to be observed that, in valuing the land with its special adaptability as being worth Rs1,05,000 to the appellant, he did so on the footing that the appellant would himself have been in a position to supply the water to the harbour but for its compulsory acquisition by the Harbour Authority. He would also seem to have so valued it upon the footing that the spring could have been made an income-earning concern on February 13, 1928. He would otherwise have made a substantial discount from the Rs1,05,000. It is plain, therefore, that in view of the fact that the water could not be exploited by the appellant himself and that it would necessarily be some years before the water would become a profit-earning asset in their hands, the Harbour Authority, however willing purchasers they might be, would not have agreed to pay anything like that sum. In these circumstances the matter should in strictness be referred back to the Subordinate Judge to revise his award. Both the parties to this appeal, however, have asked their Lordships, with a view to saving expense, to state what should be the proper amount of the award, and this their Lordships have consented to do. Giving the matter the best consideration they can, their Lordships are of opinion that the total price which the Harbour Authority would have been willing to pay on February 13, 1928, for the land *(pg330)* acquired, is the sum of Rs40,000, and this sum with the additional 15 per cent amounts to Rs46,000. In their Lordships' judgment the order of the High Court of May 4, 1937, should be discharged except in so far as it dismissed the present appellant's memorandum of objections with costs. The amount decreed by the Subordinate Judge in favour of the appellant should be reduced from Rs1,03,004–14–9 to Rs28,254–14–9 with interest as stated in his award. His order as to costs must stand. But the respondent must pay the appellant's costs before the High Court and his costs of this appeal. Their Lordships will humbly advise His Majesty accordingly. *(pg331)*

Case 20
Gold Coast Selection Trust Ltd v Humphrey

(1948) 30 TC 209

House of Lords

3, 4, 5, 6 and 9 February and 14 July 1948

This is an income tax case. (Prior to 1 April 1965, companies were subject to income tax on their profits.)

A trading company received a shareholding as payment for a sale; that is, as a trading receipt. The shareholding had to be valued in order to compute the trading profit of the company which was subject to income tax.

The statutory valuation provisions for capital gains tax and inheritance tax did not apply. Thus, the value of the shareholding was to be judged without any regard to the special statutory provisions that apply to a valuation for inheritance tax or capital gains tax (IHTA 1984, ss 160 and 168(1); TCGA 1992, ss 272(2) and 273(3)). If the sale of a shareholding of the size to be valued would flood the market, that fact is to be ignored when valuing for inheritance tax and capital gains tax purposes. Whether or not this is to be ignored when valuing for income tax purposes, depends on the statutory formulation for the particular income tax purpose. Valuing shares received by an employee on a share option, for example, imports the valuation provision for capital gains tax and, hence, the depressing effect of flooding the market is to be ignored (ITEPA 2003, s 421(1), which imports the definition from TCGA 1992, ss 272–274). Similarly, information not actually available at the valuation date can be assumed to be available when valuing for inheritance tax and capital gains tax purposes but a valuation for most income tax purposes only assumes such information to be available if the statutory provisions for capital gains tax are imported into the valuation provision for the particular income tax charge. This is not the case where, as here, the valuation is required in order to compute the consideration received by the taxpayer company.

This case, thus, differs from the majority of share valuation cases in that it disapplies principles specific to a valuation for capital gains tax and inheritance tax purposes.

The first question addressed by the House of Lords is the manner of taxing a trading receipt that is not cash, but is received in kind. Viscount Simon said:

> 'In my view the principle to be applied is the following. In cases such as this, when a trader in the course of his trade receives a new and valuable asset, not being money, as the result of sale or exchange, that asset, for the purpose of computing the annual profits or gains arising or accruing to him from his trade, should be valued as at the end of the accounting period in which it was received, even though it is neither realised nor realisable till later. The fact that it cannot be realised at once may reduce its present value, but that is no reason for treating it, for the purposes of income tax, as though it had no value until it could be realised. If the asset takes the form of fully paid shares, the valuation will take into account not only the terms of the agreement but a number of other factors, business of the company which has allotted the shares, the result of contemporary prospectus offering similar shares for subscription, the capital position of the company, and so forth. There may also be an element of value in the fact that the holding of the shares gives control of the company. If the asset is difficult to value, but is none the less of a money value, the best valuation possible must be made. Valuation is an art, not an exact science. Mathematical certainty is not demanded, nor indeed is it possible. It is for the Commissioners to express, in the money value attributed by them to the asset, their estimate, and this is a conclusion of fact to be drawn from the evidence before them.'
>
> ([1948] 30 TC 209 at 240 **case 20 para 19**)

It is interesting that the valuation date is the date of the end of the accounting period, not the date of the sale for which the shares provide consideration, nor the date of receipt of those shares.

The effect of there being no statutory provision requiring the valuer to ignore the flooding of the market was explored by Somervell LJ in the Court of Appeal:

> 'The trust called a number of witnesses of experience in Stock Exchange transactions and financial dealings. They gave evidence that an attempt to sell these large blocks of shares on the Stock Exchange "would probably kill the market altogether".
>
> If the trust suddenly tried to place the whole block of shares on the market everyone would want to know why. We are prepared to accept the view that there might in practice have been great difficulty in disposing of the whole block shortly after the purchase at a price which reflected the intrinsic value of the shares.

We have come to the conclusion that when there has been, as is now admitted here, a realisation of a trading asset and the receipt of another asset, and when that latter asset is marketable in its nature and not some merely personal advantage which by its nature cannot be turned into money, the profits and gains must be arrived at for the year in which the transaction took place by putting a fair value on the asset received. The fact that it could, as we will assume here, owing to its size be disposed of in the market in that year does not mean that no profit or gain for income tax purposes has been made out of the transaction.'

([1948] 30 TC 209 at 229)

In the House of Lords, this approach was approved by Viscount Simons:

'The Commissioners, as it seems to me, in fixing what money equivalent should be taken as representing the asset, must fix an appropriate money value as at the end of the period to which the Appellant's accounts are made up, by taking all the circumstances into consideration.'

([1948] 30 TC 238 **case 20 para 12**)

If a valuation is required for the purpose of a charge to income tax, where the value is not of an employee share option, of a charge to VAT or of a charge to stamp duty, this case is of particular value.

Judgement

References, example '(pg235)', are to [1948] 30 TC 209.

1 VISCOUNT SIMON.-My Lords, these are two appeals from Orders of the Court of Appeal (Scott, Somervell and Cohen, L.JJ.) dismissing appeals by the Appellant from Orders of the King's Bench Division of the High Court (Wrottesley, J.), whereby (1) an appeal by the Appellant upon a Case stated by the Commissioners for the General Purposes of the Income Tax for the City of London was dismissed and the determination of the said Commissioners affirmed, and (2) an appeal by the Respondent upon the said Case Stated was allowed. The main question involved is one of substantial importance and of considerable difficulty.

2 The Appellant, the Gold Coast Selection Trust, Ltd. (hereinafter called 'the Trust'), has at all material times carried on the trade of a dealer in stocks and shares, and an exploiter of and dealer in gold mining concessions in the Gold Coast Colony. Its practice has been to acquire concessions for land considered to have gold bearing possibilities. Concessions so acquired were exploited by the Trust to the extent necessary for the ascertaining of their potentialities. If a concession was proved to be gold *(pg235)* bearing, and if it appeared to the Trust that further development might result in the profitable production of gold, the Trust transferred such concession to a company, the business of which was to work the concessions and market the gold produced. The transferee company was in every case a public company; its directors were drawn from the directorate of the Appellant Company, and the consideration for the transfer of the concession was in each case satisfied by an issue of fully paid up shares in the transferee company.

3 The shares so issued (hereinafter called 'vendor shares') were of a par value equal to the price named in the agreement for the sale of the concessions as the sale price. Permission to deal in the shares of the transferee companies was, in due course, accorded by the London Stock Exchange in each case, and dealings in these shares in limited quantities in fact took place. The vendor shares issued to the Trust, together with other holdings acquired by it, were large enough to give the Trust control over the company which was acquiring the concession from it. So large a block of shares could not be readily disposed of in the stock market without killing the market, and there was evidence before the Commissioners that the proper way to deal with them, if it was desired to turn the block of shares into cash, would be to approach trust companies or financial houses and endeavour to place them. The evidence is of somewhat ambiguous effect, for while it indicates that a successful operation of this sort might be accomplished in reference to a substantial fraction of the total holding, it was not clearly stated that the whole block could be realised in this way, at any rate within a short time.

4 Three sales of a concession by the Trust are involved. One by an agreement made on 28 July, 1934, with the Marlu Gold Mining Areas, Ltd. (hereinafter called 'Marlu'); the second by an agreement made on 9 July, 1935, with the Gold Coast Main Reef, Ltd., and the third by agreement made on 2 December, 1936, with the Bremang Gold Dredging Co., Ltd. The main question of law is the same in all three cases, and it will be convenient to take the Marlu case as an example. Marlu had been incorporated on 26 July, 1934, with an authorised capital of £2,000,000 divided into eight million shares at 5s. each. The consideration moving from Marlu to the Trust for the sale and transfer of the concession was stated in the agreement of 28 July, 1934, to be 'the sum of Eight Hundred Thousand Pounds which shall be paid and satisfied by the allotment and issue to the Vendor or its nominees of Three million two hundred thousand shares of Five Shillings each … credited as fully paid up'. The purchase was completed and the fully paid shares allotted on 30 November, 1934. On 30 July, 1934, two days after the agreement, Marlu issued a prospectus offering for subscription at par 2,000,000 shares of 5s. each. The Trust underwrote 1,600,000 of these shares at par in consideration of an option to subscribe for 1,200,000 shares of 5s. each at the price of 6s. up to 31 July, 1936. The whole of the shares offered were subscribed; the Trust itself took up and paid for 10,759. The Trust purchased some additional shares in the market, and later bought 545,939 shares at 6s. under its option.

5 The question is whether fully paid shares acquired under the agreement of 28 July by the Trust, should, for Income Tax purposes, be valued at any and what figure in money and thus enter into the computation of *(pg236)* the profits and gains of the Trust for the year ending 5 April, 1935, so as to justify a corresponding assessment to Income Tax for the year ending 5 April, 1936. A similar question arises, with a difference in figures and amounts, in the other two cases.

6 The books of the Trust entered the cost to the Trust of the concessions sold to Marlu, viz., £107,875, as the purchase price for the 3,200,000 fully paid shares allotted under the sale agreement. It seems obvious that when the concession has been proved to be auriferous, its value cannot be limited to this. Then, year by year, as shares were sold, the profit on such sales was brought to account.

7 The Commissioners found: '1. That when the Marlu, Main Reef and Bremang shares were allotted to the Trust there was a realisation of the assets sold to those companies. 2. That at the date of the allotment the value of the shares received by the Trust was par, the price agreed to be paid by the purchasing companies.'

8 The Appellant does not dispute the first finding. But it challenges the second which, in the case of the Marlu shares, has the result that the 3,200,000 shares credited as fully paid up, which were received by the Trust as the consideration for parting with the relevant concession to Marlu, must be valued for Income Tax purposes in the year 1934–35 at the figure of £800,000.

9 The Appellant's argument comes to this, that no asset such as a block of shares fully paid up can, for Income Tax purposes, be represented by a figure of cash in the year of account in which the transaction takes place unless the asset is readily convertible into money in that year. If it was not, no money value could be attributed to it, because realisation was not presently possible. The Appellant further contended that, upon examining the material set out in the Case Stated, the Commissioners' conclusion as to value was vitiated since they had proceeded on the assumption that the block of shares must be valued at £800,000 because they were allotted as the agreed method of satisfying a consideration of £800,000.

10 The Respondent concedes that if the Commissioners had arrived at their figure on the view that the block of shares must necessarily be valued at the figure named, this was an error, and that the fact that the contract stipulated for an allottment of fully paid shares to an amount which at par was equivalent to the money figure might raise a presumption that this was the correct value, but was not conclusive. If, for example, at the time of the purchase of the concession the shares of the company stood at a high premium, an allotment of 5s. shares as fully paid as the method of discharging the consideration might confer on the company an asset worth more than the par equivalent of the shares. Equally, if contemporary dealings indicated a fall, the money value of the new asset might be less than par. But the Respondent argues that it is all a question of valuation, which is a matter for the Commissioners to determine, provided they do not proceed on a wrong view of the law, and that the Commissioners in this case arrived at the figure, not because they were bound to do so, in view of the terms of the agreement, but because, after having considered all the circumstances in the case, they reached the conclusion that this was the right figure. *(pg237)*

11 We are left, therefore, with two issues, and I must express my opinion on both. One is what is the proper way of treating an asset not immediately realisable. The other is whether the Commissioners have proceeded on the correct principle.

12 It seems to me that it is not correct to say that an asset, such as this block of shares, cannot be valued in money for Income Tax purposes in the year of its receipt because it cannot, in a commercial sense, be immediately realised. That is no reason for saying that it is incapable of being valued, though, if its realisation cannot take place promptly, that may be a reason why the money figure set against it at the earlier date should be reduced in order to allow for an appropriate interval. Supposing, for example, the contract conferring the asset on the taxpayer included a stipulation that the asset should not be realised by the transferee for five years, and that if an attempt was made to realise it before that time the property in it should revert to the transferor. This might seriously reduce the value of the asset when received, but it is no reason for saying that when received it must be regarded as having no value at all. The Commissioners, as it seems to me, in fixing what money equivalent should be taken as representing the asset, must fix an appropriate money value as at the end of the period to which the Appellant's accounts are made up, by taking all the circumstances into consideration. It is a relevant circumstance that £800,000 was the figure fixed upon as the appropriate consideration to be satisfied by fully paid shares. But it is also a relevant consideration that the asset could not be realised at once.

13 I adopt the conclusion expressed in the judgment of Somervell, L.J., where he says: 'When there has been, as is now admitted here, a realisation of a trading asset and the receipt of another asset, and when that latter asset is marketable in its nature and not some merely personal advantage which by its nature cannot be turned into money, the profits and gains must be arrived at for the year in which the transaction took place by putting a fair value on the asset received. The fact that it could not, as we will assume here, owing to its size be disposed of in the market in that year does not mean that no profit or gain for Income Tax purposes has been made out of the transaction.'

14 Cohen, L.J., who delivered a separate judgment, reached the same conclusion, saying, with reference to the case of *John Cronk & Sons, Ltd. v. Harrison*, [1937] A.C. 185; 20 T.C. 612; 'That case is, I think, clear authority for the view that, if an asset is capable of valuation, it should be valued and brought

into the account, even though that value may not be presently realisable in the accounting year … It is admitted that the profit and loss account must include assets which have to be valued, and I can see no reason why, if valuation is possible, an artificial value, whether high or low, should be placed on an asset merely because that value cannot be wholly realised in the accounting year. The fact that it cannot be realised in the accounting year is no doubt an element which the Commissioners should take into account in estimating the value, but it is not a reason for attributing to the asset a value far below that which other facts – e.g., the terms of the sales agreement, the market quotation, the prices at which the Appellant Company itself acquired shares in the market and its own statements to its shareholders about their value- show that the asset should rightly bear.' By 'artificial value' in *(pg238)* this passage the Lord Justice meant the figure of £107,875 which was the amount the Trust had spent in acquiring the site and proving the concession before they could ascertain that it was auriferous.

15 Counsel for the Appellant called the attention of the House to a number of reported cases in which the valuing of an asset was simplified because the asset was readily realisable, but this circumstance, though dwelt upon when deciding that the unrealised asset must none the less be given a money value, is nowhere declared to be the ground of the decision. Thus, in *Californian Copper Syndicate v. Harris*, 5 T.C. 159, where the syndicate was engaged in acquiring and reselling mining property, and it was held that the difference between the purchase price of such property and the value of the shares for which the property was exchanged is a profit assessable to Income Tax, Lord Trayner dealt with the contention that there was no realised profit since the shares had not been sold. He said (at page 167): 'A profit is realised when the seller gets the price he has bargained for. No doubt here the price took the form of fully paid up shares in another company, but, if there can be no realised profit, except when that is paid in cash, the shares were realisable and could have been turned into cash, if the Appellants had been pleased to do so.' I read this last sentence as rejecting the syndicate's contention that it could not be liable because the shares had not been realised; it should not be understood to mean that the crucial test is prompt realisability.

16 In *Scottish and Canadian General Investment Co., Ltd. v. Easson*, 1922 S.C. 242, at page 246; 8 T.C. 265, at page 271, the Lord President (Clyde) upheld the conclusion of the Commissioners that the profits of the company in the year in which it had received certain debentures should be assessed at a sum equal to 75 per cent. of the face value of those debentures, as representing their actual value. The Lord President said: 'The question is just one of ascertaining the profits and gains of the Company, and if instead of receiving cash the Company get a saleable security, that saleable security is just part and parcel of the Company's profits and gains.' The Lord President pointed out that the debentures themselves were saleable and had a value on the market, but he nowhere suggests that the true test is whether they could be sold immediately.

17 Neither in *Royal Insurance Co., Ltd. v. Stephen*, 14 T.C. 22, nor in *Westminster Bank, Ltd. v. Osler*, [1933] A.C. 139; 17 T.C. 381, do I find the proposition laid down which is essential to the Appellant's main argument, that an asset in kind cannot be valued for the purpose of entering into the computation of profits and gains unless it is immediately realisable.

18 In *John Emery & Sons v. Commissioners of Inland Revenue*, 1935 S.C. 802; 1936 S.C. (H.L.) 36; 20 T.C. 213, where a firm of builders erected dwelling-houses and thereafter sold them for a cash payment, subject to the ground annuals which they had created and retained in their possession, it was held in the Court of Session, and the decision was approved in the House of Lords, that the realisable value of the ground annuals should be accounted for in ascertaining the firm's trading profits. The judgments point out that ground annuals could be readily realised, but the test of immediate realisability is nowhere declared to be the essential point of the case. There is indeed authority to the contrary effect *(pg239)* contained in, or at any rate implied by, the decisions of this House in *Cronk's* case (above referred to) (1) and in *Absalom v. Talbot*, [1944] A.C. 204; 26 T.C. 166.

19 In my view the principle to be applied is the following. In cases such as this, when a trader in the course of his trade receives a new and valuable asset, not being money, as the result of sale or exchange, that asset, for the purpose of computing the annual profits or gains arising or accruing to him from his trade, should be valued as at the end of the accounting period in which it was received, even though it is neither realised nor realisable till later. The fact that it cannot be realised at once may reduce its present value, but that is no reason for treating it, for the purposes of Income Tax, as though it had no value until it could be realised. If the asset takes the form of fully paid shares, the valuation will take into account not only the terms of the agreement but a number of other factors, such as prospective yield, marketability, the general outlook for the type of business of the company which has allotted the shares, the result of a contemporary prospectus offering similar shares for subscription, the capital position of the company, and so forth. There may also be an element of value in the fact that the holding of the shares gives control of the company. If the asset is difficult to value, but is none the less of a money value, the best valuation possible must be made. Valuation is an art, not an exact science. Mathematical certainty is not demanded, nor indeed is it possible. It is for the Commissioners to express, in the money value attributed by them to the asset, their estimate, and this is a conclusion of fact to be drawn from the evidence before them.

20 I therefore reject the main contention of the Appellant, and agree with the Court of Appeal. This would lead to a dismissal of the first appeal without further enquiry were it not that I entertain considerable doubt whether the Commissioners' second finding is not, as its language might imply, a conclusion reached on the view that the shares must be valued at par because the price agreed to be paid for the concession was a sum of £800,000 to be satisfied by an allotment and issue to the Appellant of shares which at par would be equivalent to that amount. One of the contentions of the Inland Revenue set out in the Case is that numbered (f): 'that the price of the concessions as agreed between the parties was the par value of the shares', and if the Commissioners arrived at the figure of £800,000 on the view put forward in (f) that this must be the one and only proper figure of valuation, they were mistaken. The best course seems to be to refer the case back to the Commissioners and request them to fix a proper figure of valuation in the light of the material before them as set out in the Case and of any facts disclosed by further evidence before them. It may be that they will still arrive at the same figure, but if so this will be because the relevant factors, such as I have indicated above, lead them to this conclusion of fact, but the correct conclusion is not a figure inevitably forced upon the Commissioners by the terms of the agreement taken alone, but is a question of fact to be answered after taking into account the relevant surrounding circumstances at the time of the transaction.

21 This view of the matter also determines the question of the second appeal. *(pg240)*

22 I therefore move that the appeals be allowed, but only to the extent that the matter be referred back to the Commissioners to reconsider and fix the proper figure in the light of these directions. There will be no costs awarded in respect of the appeals to this House.

23 The late Lord Thankerton, who took part in the hearing of these appeals, expressed to me, before his death, his agreement with this conclusion.

24 LORD UTHWATT.-My Lords, I have had the advantage of reading in print and considering the opinion which has just been delivered by the noble and learned Lord on the Woolsack. I find myself in complete agreement with his conclusions and with his reasoning, and I am content to express my adherence to his opinion.

25 My Lords, my noble and learned friend **LORD DU PARCQ**, who is unable to be present here, desires me to say that he also agrees with the opinion which has just been expressed by the noble and learned Lord on the Woolsack.

26 LORD OAKSEY.-My Lords, in my opinion the appeal should be allowed and the case remitted to the Commissioners on the ground that they appear to have thought that they were bound, as matter of law, to assume that the shares in question were worth their par value. It remains to consider what is the true test for the Commissioners' decision.

27 It has been argued on behalf of the Crown that the fact, if it be the fact, that all the shares retained by the Appellant could not be sold in the years in question is irrelevant, and that the Commissioners may put a valuation upon the shares regardless of whether they could be realised at that value in the years of computation. In my opinion this argument is unsound.

28 In the first place it is, I think, important to consider what is meant by an Income Tax on annual profits and gains. In my view it is a tax in money on profits in money which arise to the taxpayer in the year of computation. Income must not be confused with the source of the income. A taxpayer's obligation cannot be satisfied except by money: he has no option to offer other forms of property. The reason why he is not permitted to contend that he has made no profit in a transaction if he has made a profit but taken it not in money but in other forms of property, is that the property is the equivalent of money because it can be sold for money in the year. The word annual must at least connote 'in the year' if it is to have any meaning at all, and that it has this meaning was laid down in *Ryall v. Hoare*, [1923] 2 K.B. 447; 8 T.C. 521, and approved in *Martin v. Lowry*, [1927] A.C. 312; 11 T.C. 297. It follows, in my opinion, that what the Commissioners had to decide in the present case is what profit in money, if any, was or could be derived by the Appellant Company in the years in question from the transaction by which they transferred the concessions to the Marlu, Gold Coast Main Reef and Bremang companies for shares in the companies.

29 Now it is, of course, true that the concessions had an actual or intrinsic value at the time of the transactions, but that value lay in the future and was unknown. It is also true that the Appellant Company was prepared to part with the concessions on the terms of the prospectuses, that is to say, in the hope of getting capital from the public sufficient to develop the concessions, whilst retaining the shares in question, but the par value of *(pg241)* the shares retained was not an estimate of the actual value of the concessions either at that time or in the future, for both the Appellant Company and the public who subscribed for shares must have estimated the value of their shares both at the time and in the future at a higher figure. But the fact that the Appellant Company parted with the concessions does not mean that they realised or could realise at the time the money value of the concessions, for they did not receive cash but still retained in the shares their interest in the concessions. The Appellant Company will, of course, ultimately realise the value of the concessions to the company by selling their shares or holding them and receiving dividends on them. But all that the Commissioners have to do in this case is to assess the profit on the transactions in the years in question, and for that purpose to bring into the Appellant Company's accounts the money value of the shares in the years of computation. The only true test of the money value of an article at a certain time is what can be got for it in money at that time: if it cannot be sold at that time or exchanged for something which can be sold at that time, no one can make a profit out of it which can be stated in terms of money at that time.

30 If a picture dealer exchanges a picture for another picture and it is proved that the picture taken in exchange cannot be sold in the year, not for want of time, but because having been put up at auction there is no bid, can the Revenue claim that a profit has been made on that transaction? I am assuming, of course, in this illustration that it is proved that the picture cannot be sold in the year. In the present case there was evidence that some of the shares could have been sold, and the figure which they might have realised should, of course, be brought into the Appellant's accounts. Moreover it is not a question whether they could be sold in any particular market such as the London Stock Exchange. But if the Commissioners are satisfied that the shares could not have been sold for money in Paris, New York or London or anywhere in the world in the years in question, then to bring in a cash figure for those shares is, in my opinion, attributing to the years in question profits which might or might not be realised in future years. It is, in my opinion, unsound accounting and unsound law to lay down that the Commissioners should value the shares by estimating what they may bring in by way of dividends and sales in future years, and then discounting that figure so as to arrive at their present value. There are no facts upon which the Commissioners can base such an estimate: it is simple guesswork and as a matter of fact has probably been entirely falsified by the course of events which has included the recent war. If one assumes that the Commissioners are satisfied as a matter of fact that the shares could not have been sold in the years in question, such a valuation must either be a contradiction of the fact or an estimate of future value. The Commissioners should, in my opinion, come to a conclusion on the evidence how many of the shares in question could have been sold in the years of computation, and at what price, and should bring into the Appellant Company's account that figure as against the cost of the concessions to the Appellant Company. To adopt this principle appears to me to be in accord with every case which has been cited to your Lordships' House on this appeal, and with the fundamental principles of the Income Tax Acts.

Case 21
Short v Treasury Commissioners

[1948] 1 All ER 509

House of Lords

28, 29 June, 29 July 1948

A shareholder who owns a share owns a bundle of rights in relation to the company. This is not the same as owning a proportionate part of the company's assets. Hence, even in an asset based valuation, a discount will always be appropriate. Even a holder of a 100 per cent interest in the company would have to pay costs, and usually a tax charge, to transfer assets from the ownership of the company to his personal ownership.

On 17 March 1943 Short Brothers (Rochester and Bedford) Ltd was nationalised. In consequence of an order under reg 55(4) of the Defence (General) Regulations 1939, all shares in Short Brothers (Rochester and Bedford) Ltd were transferred from the individual shareholders to a nominee of the Minister of Aircraft Production. Each shareholder was entitled to compensation, measured as the market value of his shareholding. The shareholders argued that, as the entire share capital was transferred into state ownership, the compensation paid to each shareholder should be a proportionate part of the value of the company's assets at that date.

In this case, the essential nature of a shareholding, as opposed to a proportionate share of the company's assets, was expressed by Evershed LJ in the Court of Appeal:

'Shareholders are not, in the eye of the law, part owners of the undertaking. The undertaking is something different from the totality of the shareholdings. The claimants recognised this difficulty, and in this court their main argument was, we think, addressed to an alternative statement of their case, that is, that the value of their shares must be calculated on the basis of an apportionment of the value of the totality of the shares in one hand, so as to comprehend the value of the complete control thereby conferred. This alternative is not in terms set out in the award; but, as we have already indicated, the real issues between the parties are, in our judgement, sufficiently raised by the award.

It is said on the one hand that it is of the essence of the matter that the Crown is, as it is bound to do, acquiring all the shares of the company. That is true; but, on the other hand, it is also the fact that the Crown is acquiring shares from a number of individual shareholders. *Prima facie*, as it seems to us, and apart from any special words in the regulation, each shareholder is entitled to get, and to get only, the value of what he possesses; for that is all that he has to sell or transfer. If an individual shareholder in a company owns such a number of shares in that company as gives him effective control of the company's affairs, it may well be that the value to be attributed to that holding, on a sale of it as a separate transaction, is a figure greater than the sum arrived at by multiplying the number of his shares by the "market" value for the time being of a single share. In such a case the shareholder in question, it may be said, has and is able to sell something more than a mere parcel of shares, each having the rights as to dividend and otherwise conferred upon it by the company's regulations.'

([1948] 1 All ER 509 at 122/123)

This is echoed in the House of Lords by Lord Porter:

'As to the alternative argument that the value of the business as a going concern should first be ascertained and then that global sum should be divided in due proportions between the different classes of shareholders, no doubt, if the regulation had stated that the shareholders were to receive the value of their shares calculated on their value on the sale of their business as a going concern, the appellants' claim would be correct, but, to my mind, the regulation makes quite a different stipulation. It is true that under the order all the shares are to be transferred, but though all are transferred to the nominees of the Treasury, all are not transferred from one person, and it is the value of the willing seller of his holding which has to be ascertained, not a potentiality of control which he does not possess. The paragraph speaks of the price of "any shares" which naturally refers to those embraced in any individual parcel and it is those shares, not the shares as a whole, the value of which is to be ascertained as between a willing buyer and a willing seller, a phrase which, in my mind, means a willing buyer and a willing seller of those shares. If it were not so, there would be great difficulty, if not impossibility, in distributing the total sum obtained as the price of the undertaking among the various classes of beneficiaries in cases where there were a number of different classes of shares, and even in the present case where the preference shareholders are only entitled to the nominal value of their shares on a winding-up the question might arise as to their value when they were being paid off, but the company was not being wound up.'

([1948] 1 All ER 509 at 511/512 **case 21 para 5**)

Thus, unless a commercial valuation is being undertaken of a shareholding in a company that is a quasi-partnership (see *Re Yenidje Tobacco Co Ltd* [1916–17] All ER Rep 1050 **case 10** and *Ebrahimi v Westbourne Galleries Ltd* [1972] 2 All ER 492 **case 31**), a discount from the full asset value is always required.

Judgement

References, example '(pg509)', are to [1948] 1 All ER 509.

1 LORD PORTER (29 July 1918): My Lords, this is an appeal from a judgment of the Court of Appeal affirming a decision of Morris J in the High Court. The question at issue involves a consideration of the sum to be paid to certain shareholders in Short Brothers (Rochester and Bedford) Ltd, whom I shall call Short Brothers, by the Treasury when taking over the shares in that company. *(pg509)*

2 The issued capital of the company consisted of three classes of shares, viz, 230,475 redeemable preference shares of £1 each (as to which no question arises), 250,000 A ordinary shares of 5s each, and 581,302 ordinary shares also of 5s each. The voting power was concentrated in the ordinary shares and each A ordinary share entitled its holder to four votes as against one vote in the case of each ordinary share. No distinction, however, has been made or is claimed to exist between these two types of share for the purpose of this case, though it is clear that any one possessing 200,000 A shares would have control of the company. The appellants have, I understand, been chosen so as to represent the interests concerned, Mr Short holding 22,958 A ordinary and Lonsdale Investment Trust Ltd, the second appellant, 3,000 ordinary shares. The claim arises in the way as appears in the printed Case for the respondents:

'3.– (1) By the Defence (General) Regulations 1939, reg 55(4), a competent authority was empowered for (*inter alia*) the efficient prosecution of the war to appoint by order an authorised controller of any undertaking to exercise with respect to the undertaking such functions of control on behalf of His Majesty as might be provided by the order.

(2) By reg 78(1) of the said regulations where an order appointing an authorised controller had been made in the case of an undertaking carried on by a company, the competent authority, if satisfied that it was necessary for the purpose of securing effective control, was empowered with the consent of the Treasury by order to transfer the shares of the company to such transferees as might be specified in the order.

(3) By reg 78(4) it was provided that where an order had been made under para (1) thereof the shares should on such date as might be specified in the

order vest in the transferees on behalf of the competent authority free from any mortgage, pledge or charge.

(4) By reg 78(5) the price to be paid in respect of any shares transferred by virtue of such an order was to be such price as might be specified in an order made by the Treasury, being a price which, in the opinion of the Treasury, was not less than the value of the shares as between a willing buyer and a willing seller on the date of the order made appointing the authorised controller.

(5) By reg 78(7) if any person who immediately before the date of transfer had an interest in any of the shares claimed that the price specified by the Treasury was less than the value aforesaid the value of the shares in which that person had an interest should be determined by the arbitration of a qualified accountant nominated by the Lord Chief Justice of England.

4. By an order entitled Short Brothers (Rochester and Bedford) Limited Control Order 1943, dated 17 Mar 1943, the Minister of Aircraft Production, in exercise of his powers under reg 55(4), appointed an authorised controller of the undertaking of the company.

5. By an order entitled Short Brothers (Rochester and Bedford) Limited (Transfer of Shares) Order 1943, dated 22 Mar 1943 (hereinafter referred to as the 'transfer order'), the said Minister, with the consent of the Treasury, transferred as at 23 Mar 1943, all the shares in the company to his nominees.

6. By an order entitled Short Brothers (Rochester and Bedford) Limited (Price of Shares) Order 1943, dated 31 May 1943 (hereinafter referred to as the 'prices order'), the respondents specified the following prices: (*a*) 22s 3d per share in the case of the five per cent redeemable cumulative preference shares; (*b*) 29s 3d per share in the case of the A ordinary shares; (*c*) 29s 3d per share in the case of the ordinary shares.

7. Both appellants gave notice that they were dissatisfied with the prices fixed for their shares by the prices order and Mr Sydney John Pears, a qualified accountant, was nominated by the Lord Chief Justice of England to act as arbitrator and to assess the value of the said A ordinary and ordinary shares. For convenience it was agreed that the claims of the appellants should be treated as test cases and that, if the arbitrator held that the prices to be paid by the Treasury to the appellants should be in excess of those specified in the order, the Treasury would pay those revised prices in respect of all shares of these classes, irrespective of whether other former holders had themselves claimed arbitration.

8. The arbitration was held on 15, 16, 17, 18 Oct 1946 and on 30 Oct 1946, the arbitrator stated his award in the form of a Special Case for the opinion of the court.'

3 As appears from the award itself the respondents contended that the proper basis of valuation under reg 78(5) was to assume that the shares had been purchased in individual blocks from individual shareholders on the date of transfer and to fix the value accordingly, and that, in fact, that value was best ascertained from the prices ruling on the Stock Exchange on the relevant date, viz, the date on which the controller was appointed. The appellants, on the other hand, contended that, the transfer being a transfer of all the shares, *(pg510)* the Stock Exchange value was not a true criterion inasmuch as no order transferring *(pg511)* the shares under reg 78(1) was authorised unless it provided for the expropriation of all the shares. As they maintained, the proper method for fixing the price was first to ascertain the value of the whole undertaking and then to determine the proportionate value of each class of shares. They stressed the argument that the Crown was taking, and could only take, the whole of the shares, and, therefore, must acquire the whole undertaking. No one, they contended, could acquire all the shares in a company except by paying for the business as a whole, and if the business as a whole is acquired, its value should be paid for. That, they say, was the view of the arbitrator, and he has stated what that value amounts to when the appropriate division among the ordinary shares has been made. Even if, however, the shares be treated as purchased in individual blocks the same result, so the appellants contend, is arrived at, because the potential value which is attributable to the opportunity of acquiring complete control must be taken into account.

4 My Lords, as I understood the argument of the appellants, no point was made that an inaccurate principle had been adopted or untrue figures accepted if the true method of ascertaining the shares was to value them share by share. Admittedly, the Stock Exchange price was not necessarily the value of shares calculated on this principle, but it was cogent evidence of their value and the appellants acknowledged that it would be useless to send the case back to the arbitrator unless their method of ascertaining the values were adopted. In deciding which of the views presented to your Lordships is right, it is plain that regard must be had to, and the result reached by a consideration of, the language of reg 78, and, primarily, of para 5 of that regulation. That paragraph can, I think, be expressed in shortened form so as to exhibit its essential quality. In that case it would run:

> 'The price of any shares transferred shall be not less than the value of those shares as between a willing buyer and a willing seller on the date of the order made by the authority under reg 55(4).'

The date of an order made under reg 55(4) is the date on which a controller of the business is appointed, and in the present case that date was 17 Mar 1943. The value, then, which the arbitrator must put on the shares is that which they had on 17 Mar 1943, and, in my view, that which they had before the controlling order was made, whether the effect of making it decreased or increased their value, that date being chosen, as I think, in order to make sure that no fictitious value should be placed on the shares by reason of the fact that the government were taking control and might expropriate them. At that time it was not, in fact, known that the undertaking was to be taken over or the shares transferred. They were not, in fact, transferred until 22 Mar and the Prices Order did not come into force until 23 Mar. In such circumstances it is difficult to see why the shares, if bought in individual blocks, should have any increased value attributed to them because the whole were transferred at a subsequent date. Nor do I think their value would be enhanced because there was a possibility of the government subsequently taking them over. That factor must have been well known to both brokers and jobbers, and would be a circumstance which would affect the value on the Stock Exchange. There is, therefore, no reason for attributing an increase in value to such a possibility.

5 As to the alternative argument that the value of the business as a going concern should first be ascertained and then that global sum should be divided in due proportions between the different classes of shareholders, no doubt, if the regulation had stated that the shareholders were to receive the value of their shares calculated on their value on the sale of their business as a going concern, the appellants' claim would be correct, but, to my mind, the regulation makes quite a different stipulation. It is true that under the order all the shares are to be transferred, but though all are transferred *to* the nominees of the Treasury, all are not transferred *from* one person, and it is the value of the willing seller of his holding which has to be ascertained, not a potentiality of control which he does not possess. The paragraph speaks of the price of 'any shares' which naturally refers to those embraced in any individual parcel and it is those shares, not the shares as a whole, the value of which is to be ascertained as between a willing buyer and a willing seller, a phrase which, in my mind, means a willing *(pg571)* buyer and a willing seller of those shares. If it were not so, there would be great difficulty, if not impossibility, in distributing the total sum obtained as the price of the undertaking among the various classes of beneficiaries in cases where there were a number of different classes of shares, and even in the present case where the preference shareholders are only entitled to the nominal value of their shares on a winding-up the question might arise as to their value when they were being paid off, but the company was not being wound-up.

6 This is the conclusion I should come to on the wording of para 5 above, but such a construction is supported when one finds the phrase 'any shares' used in paras 6 and 7 as applicable to individual shares and not to the shares as a whole. It is true that that phrase is used in those paragraphs in reference to individual interests in particular shares, and, therefore, it is necessary to interpret its use as applying in those paragraphs to the shares or parcels of shares individually, but the phrase is the same in each case, and I see no reason for interpreting it in a different sense in three successive paragraphs. It is used, I think, of individual shares in paras 6 and 7 because that is its natural meaning, and the fact that it is so used is a ground for refusing to attribute a less natural meaning to it in para 5.

7 My Lords, in reaching this conclusion I do not find myself assisted by the provisions of other statutes or regulations dealing with the price to be paid for expropriated shares. Each contains its own terms and deals with questions incidental to the transfer of the particular interest taken over by the government in specified industries. They follow no general principle and have no bearing the one on the other. Nor, when dealing with shares, do I find any useful analogy in the principles on which the value of land compulsorily acquired is to be determined. If the principles adopted in *Vyricherla Narayana Gajapatiraju (Raja) v Revenue Divisional Officer, Vizagapatam*, (1) be accepted as correct (which for the purposes of this case I am prepared to assume), viz, that land compulsorily acquired must be valued not merely by reference to the use to which it is being put at the time at which its value has to be determined, but also to the uses to which it is reasonably capable of being put in the future, still, in the first place, in the case of land the owner possesses a tangible asset whereas a shareholder has no direct share in the assets of a company. He has such rights as the memorandum and articles give him and nothing more. In the second place, as has already been pointed out, there is no reason to suppose that the potentialities of the shares as existing before the control order was made were not fully represented in the Stock Exchange price. My Lords, for these reasons, which are substantially those which influenced the learned judge and the Court of Appeal I would dismiss the appeal and order the apellants to pay the respondents' costs.

8 LORD UTHWATT: My Lords, the point which the appellants seek to make good is that the appropriate method of fixing the price to be paid for shares acquired under reg 78 is to ascertain the whole value of the undertaking of the company, and then in light of that value to determine the proportionate value of the separate classes of shares and of individual shares within each class.

9 The matter is put in two ways – first, on the construction of the regulation, and, secondly, (assuming the appellants to be wrong on the question of construction) as a necessary consequence of the value to be attributed to the potentialities of any share acquired pursuant to the regulation. The first argument rests on the undoubted fact that the competent authority exercising the power conferred by reg 78 must buy all the shares of the company. Paragraph 5 is, it is urged, to be constructed against this background. All the shares taken as a single *(pg512)* block are worth the value of the undertaking and each share must as a matter of construction of the regulations have a price allotted to it on the basis of that value.

10 My Lords, I agree that in constructing para 5 the background must be borne in mind, but I fail to see that this fact in any way assists the appellants. The transaction provided for by paras 1 and 4 of the regulation is in form and substance the acquisition of shares by means of separate dealings with each shareholders. Paragraph 5 follows up this conception. On its plain language it is concerned with the fixing of a price as respects each and every share acquired. It is not concerned with fixing a price as respects all the shares taken as a single block or, as respects any share, a price based on the value of all the shares taken as a single block. There is nothing in para 4 to suggest that in fixing a price the nature of the dealing in respect of which a price is to be fixed – an individual dealing – is to be thrust out of consideration, and the simple language used in this paragraph is not capable of being twisted into the complicated formula embodied in the appellants' contention. The picture painted on the background is clear and definite. I desire only to add that, if some one shareholder held a number of shares sufficient to carry control of the company, it might well be that the value proper to be attributed to his holding under the regulation was greater than the sum of the values that would be attributed to the shares comprised in that holding if they were split between various persons. The reason is that he has something to sell – control – which the others considered separately have not. The contention of the appellants, if accepted, would, as the Court of Appeal point out, deny him the real value of his holding.

11 The second argument, as I understood it in its final form, was as follows. In an enquiry as to the value of the shares as between a willing buyer and a willing seller, all possible buyers are to be taken into account. Among those buyers here was the competent authority, which, if it became a buyer, was necessarily committed to buying all the shares, and was, on the face of the regulation, buying for the purpose of obtaining control. In each individual transaction with a shareholder, therefore, the competent authority must be assumed to be ready to bargain in light of the potentialities of the share or its special adaptability to his purpose, namely the forwarding of the acquisition of control by him. Its value to him for that purpose was to be considered. My Lords, I do not think the phrases 'potentialities of the share' or 'special adaptability' carry one anywhere, or, indeed, have any particular meaning in relation to a share. A share always has the same qualities and potentialities. The appearance of a buyer needing the share for his particular purposes does not add to or detract from those qualities. But the argument does not rest on the aptness of these phrases. The substance of it is that the competent authority is to be included among the possible willing buyers, and that, wanting control, he must be taken as prepared to pay for it up to the hilt. Its value is, therefore, to be determined by the proportionate interest in the company's undertaking which it represents. There are, I think, more answers than one to this argument. I choose the easiest of them. That answer is that the argument disregards the facts. The competent authority can acquire under the regulation according to its true construction and not otherwise. One is, therefore, thrown back on the regulation. Under the regulation, though all the shares were to be acquired, they were to be acquired only through the machinery of a compulsory transaction with each shareholder. The price was to be not less than the value as between a willing buyer and a willing seller on the date of the order appointing an authorised controller – which must be read as on that date immediately before the appointment of a controller took effect. That I call the critical date. The conclusion desired by the appellants – that, in valuing the individual blocks of shares, their proportionate share in the assets of the company measures the value between a willing buyer and a willing seller – cannot, therefore, be reached unless it be assumed that on the critical date – before any steps had been taken to bring the company in any form under control – there was a certainty that the competent authority would apply to the company a regulation in possibility applicable to all companies, and a certainty that the competent authority would ultimately step in and buy all the shares. The making of the assumption is obviously out of the question. Without that assumption the argument produces no result. I would dismiss the appeal.

12 LORD DU PARCQ: My Lords, I find myself in complete agreement with the opinions of my noble and learned friends who have just addressed your Lordships, and also with the opinion of my noble and learned friend, Lord Morton of Henryton which I have had an opportunity of reading in advance. I do not desire to add any words of my own. I am authorised by my noble and learned friend, Lord Normand, whose public duties require his attendance elsewhere, to say that he agrees with those opinions and has nothing to add.

13 LORD MORTON OF HENRYTON: My Lords, the respondents contend that the proper basis of valuation of the shares in Short Brothers (Rochester *(pg513)* and Bedford) Ltd, under reg 78 is to assume that the Minister has acquired all the shares in the company in individual blocks from individual shareholders on the date of the control order of 17 Mar 1943, and on this assumption to fix the value of all the shares on the basis of the prices ruling on the Stock Exchange on that date. It is common ground between the parties that there is nothing in reg 78 which compels the arbitrator to fix the value of the shares on the basis of the Stock Exchange prices. On the facts of this case, however, if the respondents' contention on the main question of construction is correct, I think that the Stock Exchange prices afford a fair criterion of the value of each block of shares, as between a willing buyer and a willing seller, on the relevant date.

14 For my part, I feel no doubt that the respondents' contention is correct. The regulation contemplates that the competent authority shall acquire all the shares in the company at one and the same time, but it also contemplates that he shall obtain these shares from the individual shareholders and that each shareholder shall be paid for his shares in accordance with the provisions of para (5) of the regulation, which has already been read. The phrase 'the price to be paid' assumes a seller and a buyer, and the 'shares transferred' belong to the individual shareholders in the company. Each shareholder is a seller and in each case the competent authority is the buyer. The price is to be 'not less than the value of those shares as between a willing buyer and a willing seller' on the relevant date. These words mean, to my mind, that each shareholder is to be assumed to be a willing seller of his shares on that date, and the competent authority is assumed to be a willing buyer of these shares on that date. This is, in my view, the natural meaning of the words used in para (5), and if that paragraph is read, as it ought to be read, in conjunction with paras (6) and (7), it becomes still more clear that the price is to be fixed on the basis of sales of their respective holdings by individual shareholders. Paragraph (6) is clearly dealing with the case in which a block of shares belonging to an individual shareholder is subject to a mortgage, pledge or charge, and para (7) gives each individual shareholder a right to go to arbitration if he thinks that the price to be paid for his shares is less than their true value.

15 The contention of the appellants gives rise to many difficulties. I shall mention only one. If they are right, the phrase 'those shares' in para (5) means all the shares in the company, and the regulation is providing for a valuation of all the shares in the company, as one mass, on the basis of the value of the whole undertaking. If this is so, the regulation contains no provisions for apportioning this lump sum among the holders of various classes of shares. It is extremely unlikely that any regulation would be framed in such a way, and paras (6) and (7) seem to me quite inconsistent with the view that only such a 'mass' valuation has been dealt with in para (5). In my view, the Court of Appeal and Morris J rightly construed reg 78, and this appeal should be dismissed. *(pg514)*

Case 22
Re Press Caps Ltd

[1949] 1 All ER 1013

Court of Appeal

8, 11, April 1949

A company draws up its balance sheet for the purpose of its annual financial statements. A balance sheet is not a statement of the value of the shares at its date.

On 10 December 1947, the Metal Box Company Ltd made an offer to the shareholders of Press Caps Ltd based on a value of 7s for each Press Caps Ltd ordinary share, when the market price at the time was 6s 3d. The offer was accepted by 95.5 per cent of the shareholders of Press Caps Ltd, who held a total of 96.8 per cent of the company's issued share capital. Metal Box Ltd issued a notice to dissenting shareholders, informing them that, unless they assented, their shares would be compulsorily acquired, by virtue of Companies Act 1948, s 209(1) (now Companies Act 1985, s 429). A dissenting shareholder applied to the court for an order that his shares should not be compulsorily acquired as the price offered was less than the proportionate part of the published balance sheet of Press Caps Ltd at the relevant date.

In the Court of Appeal, Somervell LJ said:

'... I cannot regard this figure in the balance sheet as a valuation. It does not purport to be ... this figure [for freehold property] in the balance sheet in accordance with what is very common practice does not appear as a valuation of the property as at the date of the balance sheet, but is cost less depreciation.'

([1949] 1 All ER 1013 at 1015 **case 22 para 4**)

Judgement

References, example '(pg1013)', are to [1949] 1 All ER 1013

1 SOMERVELL LJ: This case turns on an originating summons taken out under s209 (1) of the Companies Act 1948, which confers a power to acquire the shares of shareholders who dissent from a scheme by which one company desires to obtain the transfer to itself of the shares or a class of shares in another company. In its application to offers made before the Companies Act 1948 was passed, certain amendments are made by sub-s (6) which makes s209(1) read in precisely the same words as s155(1) of the Companies Act 1929, which was the section in operation at the time when the offer which we have to consider was made. The relevant parts of s155(1) are as follows:

> 'Where a scheme or contract involving the transfer of shares or any class of shares in a company (in the section referred to as "the transferor company") to another company, whether a company within the meaning of this Act or not (in this section referred to as "the transferee company"), has, within four months after the making of the offer in that behalf by the transferee company been approved by the holders of not less than nine-tenths in value of the shares affected, the transferee company may, at any *(pg1013)* time within two months after the expiration of the said four months, give notice in the prescribed manner to any dissenting shareholder that it desires to acquire his shares, and where such a notice is given the transferee company shall, unless on an application made by the dissenting shareholder within one month from the date on which the notice was given the court thinks fit to order otherwise, be entitled and bound to acquire those shares on the terms on which under the scheme or contract the shares of the approving shareholders are to be transferred to the transferee company.'

2 In the present case the Metal Box Co, the transferee company, put forward a scheme for acquiring the total shareholding of Press Caps Ltd, the transferor company, the offer being contained in a document dated 10 Dec 1947 in the following terms:

> 'The Metal Box Co Ltd offers to acquire from the respective holders thereof the 17,232 fully paid 10% cumulative participating preference shares of 5s each and the 500,000 fully paid ordinary shares of 5s each issued by Press Caps Ltd upon the following terms. (2) Ordinary shares. For every hundred fully paid ordinary shares of 5s each held by the holder thereof in the undertaking of Press Caps Ltd, the Metal Box Co Ltd, is prepared to allot and issue to such holder in exchange therefor seven fully paid ordinary shares of £1 each in the undertaking of the Metal Box Co Ltd. The exchange of shares in the proportion before mentioned is based on a value of 7s each for the ordinary shares of Press Caps Ltd, being ninepence above the estimated market value and a value of £5 each for the ordinary shares of the Metal Box Co Ltd the mean market quotation of which on 1 Dec 1947 was £5 5s 0d. The holders of the said preference and ordinary shares of Press Caps Ltd will be entitled to receive and retain all dividends of Press Caps Ltd in respect of the year ended 30 June 1947, declared at the 1947 annual general meeting.'

As a result of that document, some 95.5 per cent in number and 96.8 per cent in value of the shareholding accepted the offer. There followed a notice to dissenting shareholders, informing them that, unless they assented, their shares would be compulsorily acquired. Some of them voluntarily accepted the offer, and other shares were compulsorily acquired without applying to the court under s155(1) of the Act of 1929, but the present applicant, a dissenting shareholder, applied to the court under that part of the section which enables the court to order that their shares shall not be compulsorily acquired.

3 The case in which the broad general principle was laid down and was decided by Maugham J, in 1933 is *Re Hoare & Co Ltd* (1). That was an application of a similar kind in respect of a scheme. In the course of his judgment, Maugham J, after referring to the fact that an application of this kind can only come before the court when ninety per cent or more of the shareholders have accepted the offer, said (150 LT 375):

'Accordingly, without expressing a final opinion on the matter, because there may be special circumstance in special cases, I am unable to see that I have any right to order otherwise in such a case as I have before me, unless it is affirmatively established that, notwithstanding the views of a very large majority of shareholders, the scheme is unfair.'

4 I accept that criterion and, therefore, I turn to the reasons which are submitted on behalf of the applicants for saying that the offer here is unfair. The main point made, which was dealt with by Vaisey J is based on the balance sheet of 1947 which has this item: 'Freehold property – at cost, less depreciation, as at 1 July 1946, £29,708 17s 0d.' There is a small addition during the year, a sum of £458 is written off, and a figure of £29,349 13s 6d appears as the freehold property at cost, less depreciation. It is common ground that the value of that freehold property was a very much larger figure, and was actually in *(pg1014)* the neighbourhood of £90,000. As I read the learned judge's judgment, it was because of that under-valuation that he made an order in favour of the applicant, and where I differ from the learned judge is that I cannot accept his view of the inference that should be drawn from this entry in the balance sheet. He says, and I think this is the key to the difference between the view I take and the view that he took:

'If you find admitted so large a discrepancy as an under-valuation of the most important asset in the balance sheet of this company, an admitted under-valuation of no less than £60,000, 1 should have thought that threw a great deal of doubt on the appropriateness of the balance sheet as an estimate of value, and through that, therefore, it also threw doubt on the market prices of the shares.'

With respect, 1 cannot regard this figure in the balance sheet as a valuation. It does not purport to be. If, in making this offer, the Metal Box Co Ltd had said: 'The freehold property of this company is worth today £30,000,' all the strictures which the learned judge makes and all the conclusions which he draws would have had the greatest possible force, but this figure in the balance sheet in accordance with what is very common practice does not appear as a valuation of the property as at the date of the balance sheet, but is cost less depreciation. Therefore, it does not seem to me that there is anything misleading about it. That being so, the reasons which led the learned judge to the conclusion which he formed really go. It was said that certain expressions in his judgment suggested that he was applying what I may call a subjective test rather than an objective test, that is to say, whether the shareholder was being reasonable, or acting on a reasonable ground, in not wanting his shares purchased. The learned judge referred to the decision of Maugham J, but I do not think that the words which he relied on could really be taken out of the general setting of his judgment and repeated as the principle which he applied.

5 I am strengthened in that by a sentence from the judgment of Vaisey J, in *Re Evertite Locknuts Ltd* (2), to which the learned judge himself referred, and in which he said ([1945] 1 All ER 403):

'At the same time, if I were to accede to this present application, it seems to me that the whole matter would be left in a condition of quite intolerable uncertainty, and that it cannot be right that one shareholder owning one-seven-hundredth part of the shares affected by the proposal should be entitled to stand out against the decision of the 699/700ths of the share capital, merely because he has, as he thinks, been left somewhat in the dark in regard to the material facts.'

6 In addition to the points to which I have referred, counsel for the transferee company also relied on these matters. He said that the valuation paid was more favourable, having regard to the Stock Exchange prices, than appeared in the offer. The offer referred to mean prices, whereas if you sought to sell a share in the transferor company you would get 5s 9d only. Therefore the 7s was 1s 3d above the selling price; and, with regard to the Metal Box Co, the five guineas again was the mean price, and if you sought to buy a share in the Metal Box Co you would have to pay £5 7s 6d. He also relied on the evidence of Mr Ryan, a director of the respondent company who was cross-examined on his affidavit. Mr Ryan said that the figure for patents and goodwill was an over-valuation, because the patents were running out and the position, at any rate as regards a considerable part of the business of Press Caps Ltd was that they were marketing articles manufactured for them by the Metal Box Co. That contract was running out shortly and it was a matter for the directors of the Metal Box Co to consider whether they should or should not renew it. He also relied on the fact that the directors of Press Caps Ltd, who at that time had no common director with the Metal Box Co, *(pg1015)* sent a letter which was enclosed with the offer, strongly recommending the offer:

'Your directors have very carefully considered the offer and they are unanimous in their strong recommendation for its acceptance.' No doubt could possibly be thrown on the *bona fides* of that recommendation. Counsel for the applicant pointed out that, as appears from the last paragraph of the document, the directors were getting compensation, some of which had been agreed and some of which was left outstanding, but I think counsel for the transferee company is entitled to rely on that as supporting the view that this was a fair offer. On these matters, therefore, the onus being on the applicant, he has not satisfied me that this offer was not a fair offer. I say that assuming that it has got to be fair to each individual shareholder, and each individual shareholder of small or moderately small parcels of shares. There is no evidence here that any one shareholder held a controlling interest.

7 Counsel for the applicant submitted that to take the Stock Exchange valuation was wrong, because s155(1) refers to a scheme or contract in the singular. He said it contemplated a transaction other than that which, in fact, took place or would normally take place, but a transaction in which the shareholders as a body (no-one on this argument, having a controlling interest) were entitled to receive their proportions of what it might be assumed a purchaser would give for getting a controlling interest. I cannot myself see anything in the section which justifies that submission, but it is unnecessary to decide that point, because, assuming such a construction is possible, I am satisfied here that, having regard to the amount – some 25 per cent or thereabouts – by which the sum offered was above the Stock Exchange relative buying and selling values, counsel for the applicant has failed to discharge the onus of showing that the offer was unfair, even on that assumed construction of the Act. There was no evidence which would enable the court to put any figure on what extra amount, in the case of a company of this kind and in the condition in which it was, would have been given by somebody getting control. If the contract to which Mr Ryan referred was an important part of their business and was just running out, it might be very difficult to find anybody who would be willing to purchase a controlling interest.

8 Counsel's second submission was that in a case of this sort more detailed information should be given than was given here. I do not think that that submission helps him, partly, perhaps, because of the way in which I regard the item against which most complaint was made. It seems to me that if in the year 1947 someone sees a freehold property valued at cost, that is the plainest possible indication, unless there are some exceptional circumstances, that it will be worth in the market more than the figure that appears in the balance sheet, and if any of the people who received this offer were interested in following up the matter, a perusal of back balance sheets would show when the property was bought and what it cost. The broad relation between that figure and its valuation today would have been readily apprehended.

9 Counsel finally took the point that this is a matter of discretion and that we ought not to interfere with the learned judge's exercise of his discretion. That is an important consideration, but I think that it is a case in which it is right to come to a different conclusion, because I take a different view of the facts and the evidence on affidavit as it has been put before the court by the applicant.

It is true there was the oral evidence of Mr Ryan, but on that there is no difference and the learned judge did not refer to it in any detail, but I have come to the conclusion that the documents which have been put forward do not justify a conclusion that the offer was unfair. For these reasons, I think it is right that this court should allow the appeal and make the appropriate order on that basis.

10 EVERSHED LJ: I agree. This is a case in which an offer was made, pursuant to what is now s209(1) of the Companies Act 1948 to acquire *(pg1016)* 500,000 ordinary shares at 5s from 1,116 holders. It is, of course, of the first importance to note that, of that 1,116, 1,115 have by now regarded the offer as one which they could fairly and properly accept. One has held out. In those circumstances, I regard as the appropriate guide to providing the answer to the application the language of Maugham J, which my brother has already read. In the light of that language, I, first of all, fail to find any such special circumstances in the present case as I think the learned judge had there in mind, with the result that, in my judgment, the onus on the single recusant is a heavy one. But counsel for the applicant has said that, nevertheless, in the end it is a matter for the discretion of the learned judge and that we ought not to disturb the exercise by him of his discretion. With the greatest respect to the learned judge, I do not think in this case that is a satisfactory answer, for I think that the learned judge took a view which was not justified on one particular matter in evidence, namely, the figure appearing in the Press Caps Co's last balance sheet as representing cost plus additions, less depreciation, of the freehold property. On the evidence it appeared that the property, in fact, is worth some three times the sum so arrived at in the balance sheet. I agree with what Somervell LJ has said, that the figure in the balance sheet does not purport to be a valuation. I think, the learned judge misdirected himself by regarding it as being a valuation which was put to the shareholders as a relevant matter of fact for their consideration in determining whether or not to accept the offer. He was, therefore, led to conclude that that figure represented (and I use his own words) a gross under-valuation of the most important asset in the Press Cap Co's undertaking. Of course, one can well understand that, if a contract has been secured by some gross under-valuation on a material matter represented to the transferee, the court would be likely enough to say: 'This contract is not one which I will enforce on an unwilling seller,' but without repeating what has fallen from Somervell, LJ, I venture to think that is not the right approach to this particular case. Indeed, counsel for the applicant has somewhat shifted his ground before this court, because the main burden of his argument has been that, in the circumstances of this case, to have taken as the basis of the offer the Stock Exchange valuations of the shares in the respective companies was unfair because this is an offer in which it is necessary, on the face of it, for the offeror to say: 'I wish to acquire the entire shareholding of the transferor company,' so that all the shareholders in that company are invited to join together in transferring to the transferee company the entire issued share capital and with it the control of the transferor company which that entire shareholding confers. Since, it is said, the Stock Exchange valuation neglects the element of control, it is in such a case not a fair approach or a fair basis for the offer. I would prefer to express no view whether in cases of this kind it is right that no element of control should be taken into account in making the offer, because in this case it seems to me the answer is provided in two ways – first, by a return to what I have already said, that since 1,115 shareholders out of 1,116 have accepted the offer, *prima facie* we should take it as fair and, to borrow the language of Maugham J, the court ought not to set up its own view of the fairness of the scheme in opposition to so very large a majority of the shareholders who are concerned, and, secondly, the figures do give a substantial, or, at least, by no means a negligible, addition to the price which would be arrived at by a simple calculation on Stock Exchange prices. I, therefore, think that counsel for the applicant, assuming in his favour that his premise is correct, fails to discharge the onus laid on him of showing that this scheme is not fair, and that the court, accordingly, ought to 'order otherwise' within the terms of the section.

11 Counsel for the applicant invited the court to impose a greater stringency in the matter of disclosure on companies when an objector such as his client in the present case applies under the present section. The question of disclosure *(pg1017)* of documents is not one which is directly raised in this case and I do not think it would be right for me or for the court in the present circumstances to express any view on that matter. I am satisfied that there is no such absence of disclosure in the present case as would justify the court in saying that counsel has discharged the onus of showing the scheme unfair. For those reasons, as well as those already given, I think the learned judge was in error, and I would, therefore, allow the appeal.

12 WYNN-PARRY J: I agree. I think, with respect, Maugham J stated the correct test in *Re Hoare & Co Ltd* (1), namely, that where the statutory majority have accepted the offer, the onus must rest on the applicant to satisfy the court that the price offered is unfair. He says (150 LT 375):

'The other conclusion I draw is this, that again *prima facie* the court ought to regard the scheme as a fair one inasmuch as it seems to me impossible to suppose that the court, in the absence of very strong grounds, is to be entitled to set up its own view of the fairness of the scheme in opposition to so very large a majority of the shareholders who are concerned. Accordingly, without expressing a final opinion on the matter, because there may be special circumstances in special cases, I am unable to see that I have any right to order otherwise in such a case as I have before me, unless it is affirmatively established that, notwithstanding the views of a very large majority of the shareholders, the scheme is unfair.'

Vaisey J accepted this test, but, with all respect, in my view he failed to apply it. He says:

'... I think all I have to be satisfied is that there is a reasonable ground to suppose that these shares are being taken over at less than what the shareholder, at any rate, thinks is their proper price, and I have further, I think, to make up my mind that the shareholder's belief in the inadequacy of the price is one which is not a mere matter of doubt or speculation but is based upon some reason and some intelligible ground.'

It is true that later the learned judge says:

'I think all I should say is I take the view here that there was an inadequacy of price, which may be quite small, but, in my judgment, is not really a trifle,'

but, again, that is linked up with his view that the real test is what the shareholder says, because he continues and refers to something 'which justifies this shareholder in saying: "I will not be coerced. I will not have my shares expropriated. I will stand where I am. I know more about this property and the value of it than the other shareholders who have walked into this scheme like a flock of sheep."'

13 In my view, he is substituting the view of the shareholder for the view of the court. A valuation is only an expression of opinion. It may be made on one of a number of bases, but the final test of what is the value of a thing is what it will fetch if sold. In some cases a sale has to take place, as one knows who exercises the administrative jurisdiction of the Chancery Division, but if there exists a market, as, for instance, the Stock Exchange in the case of shares in respect of which there is a quotation or in respect of which there is permission to deal, there may be no need to sell, and *prima facie* the Stock Exchange markings can be taken as a satisfactory indication of the value of the shares in question. For that reason alone it appears to me, with respect, that the view of Maugham J, as to where the onus lies under the section is justified. It, therefore, follows that to succeed the applicant must go behind the Stock Exchange prices, and that, undoubtedly, is a heavy task. *(pg1018)*

14 It is alleged here that the balance sheet does not represent the true position. The learned judge seems to treat the balance sheet as containing a valuation of the freehold property. I do not so read it. The statement in the balance sheet does no more than accurately represent the state of the freehold property account in the books of the company. It is no more a valuation than the items: 'Patents and goodwill – at cost less amounts written off as at 1 July 1946, £45,113 5s 0d.' The evidence on that item satisfies me that there is ground for saying that that asset was not, at the date of the balance sheet, worth anything like £45,000. The result, therefore, is that if one has to write up the one item, one must write down the other. Thus, it seems to me that when one regards the balance sheet in the light of the evidence, it affords the applicant no sufficient ground for saying that he has discharged the onus which lies on him.

15 It was argued by counsel for the applicant that Vaisey J had exercised his discretion and that we should not interfere with that exercise, but, as I have said, in my view, the learned judge misdirected himself because he treated the balance sheet as containing a valuation of the freehold property and, with all respect to him, I think that his whole judgment is coloured by this. In my view, the applicant has failed to discharge the admittedly heavy onus which lies on him. As regards counsel's argument on the question of control, I agree with what has been said by Somervell LJ, and I do not desire to add anything on that point. For these reasons, I agree that the appeal should be allowed. *(pg1019)*

Case 23
Re The Isle of Thanet Electricity Supply Co Ltd

[1950] 1 Ch 161

Court of Appeal

1, 18 November 1949

A shareholding is a bundle of rights and liabilities. A share valuation is, thus, a valuation of those rights and liabilities. The rights are set out in the company's articles of association. This case establishes that the articles are to be regarded as an exhaustive statement of the rights of the shareholder. Thus, an agreement between shareholders that does not feature in the articles is not binding on the hypothetical vendor nor the hypothetical purchaser postulated by the statutory fiction of a sale in the open market at the valuation date. It is important to fully appreciate the subtlety of the point. The existence of a shareholders' agreement may influence the value to be placed on shares in that it may give a ready market for the ultimate sale of the shares obtained by the hypothetical purchaser. However, the agreement, if it is not contained within the articles, is not directly binding on the hypothetical persons postulated in an open market valuation.

It is important to note the distinction between the facts in *Re The Isle of Thanet Electricity Supply Co Ltd* and those in *Borland's Trustee v Steel Brothers & Co Ltd* [1901] 1 Ch 279 **case 3**. In the *Borland's* case, the agreement between the shareholders is contained within the articles; in the *Isle of Thanet* case, it is not.

The Isle of Thanet Electricity Supply Co Ltd was incorporated on 3 November 1896. In 1946, the company was subject to a voluntary winding-up and the electricity supply business was passed into state ownership.

Seventeen years previously, the company had adopted new articles of association. Article 3 stated:

'The capital of the company is now £500,000 divided into 282,000 preference shares of £1 each, and 150,000 ordinary shares of £1 each, all of which have been issued, and 68,000 shares of £1 each, which have not been issued, and which may be issued as preference or ordinary shares as may be determined … the preference shares shall confer the right in a winding up of the company to repayment of capital together with arrears (if any) and whether earned or not of the preferential dividend to the date of the commencement of the winding up in priority to the ordinary shares.'

The holders of preference shares claimed a proportion of the substantial balance remaining in the hands of the liquidator in addition to the payment made to them by virtue of article 3.

The Court of Appeal rejected the application. Wynn Parry J said:

'It is for the holders of preference shares to satisfy the court that, on the true construction of the particular document, they are entitled to share in the surplus assets, at any rate in a case where a right to participate in surplus assets in a liquidation is conferred on the holders of preference shares.'

([1950] 1 Ch 161 at 167 **case 23 para 5**)

'In construing an article which deals with rights to share in profits, that is, dividend rights, and rights to share in the company's property in a liquidation, the same principle is applicable; and, second, that that principle is that, where the article sets out the rights attached to a class of shares to participate in profits while the company is going concern or to share in the property of the company in liquidation, *prima facie*, the rights so set out are in each case exhaustive.'

([1950] 1 Ch 161 at 171 **case 23 para 13**)

'With those considerations in mind I turn back to art. 3 of the articles of association in this case. As regards the rights as to profits, the whole of the distributable profits are expressly dealt with. They are to be applied first in paying the holders of the preference stock "a fixed cumulative preferential dividend at the rate of 6 per cent per annum on the amounts for the time being paid up or credited as paid up thereon respectively in priority to the ordinary shares", and, secondly, in paying a non-cumulative dividend at the rate of 6 per cent a year calculated on the same basis to the holders of the ordinary shares; and the balance is then distributable between the two classes of shares *pari passu*. Nothing could be more plainly exhaustive than that language. Then, as regards the rights in a winding-up, the holders of the preference shares are stated to be entitled to certain payments in priority to the ordinary shares. Those payments are, first of all, repayment of capital paid up on the preference stock, and, second, any arrears of dividend whether earned or not. The question, then, is: is there anything to suggest that the language regarding the rights of the holders of the preference stock in a winding up is not exhaustive? I can find nothing. The onus now, as I have said, is in my view on the holders of the preference stock to show that the provision is not exhaustive; and in my view they have failed to discharge that onus.'

([1950] 1 Ch 161 at 171/172 **case 23 para 14**)

'It was urged on us that in construing art. 3 we must have regard to the whole of the articles of association and to the surrounding circumstances. I accept that. It was urged on us that a relevant circumstance was that in this case the voting control rests in the hands of the holders of the preference stock; and from that it was sought to be argued that it is really impossible to conclude that the holders of the preference stock, the controllers of the company should have contemplated that in a liquidation they would get no more than any arrears of dividend on their preference stock, together with the capital on it. I am unable to accept that argument. It involves speculation and therefore uncertainty. The bargain as regards rights of participation, whether in profits or assets, appears to me to be contained in article 3. Nor can I find any context affecting the construction of that article to be derived from any other article in the articles of association.'

([1950] 1 Ch 161 at 173/174 **case 23 para 18**)

Judgement

References, example '(pg166)', are to [1950] 1 Ch 161.

1 **EVERSHED MR:** I will ask Wynn-Parry J to deliver the first judgment.

2 **WYNN-PARRY J:** This is an appeal from the judgment of Roxburgh J on an originating summons which raises the question how the surplus property of the company should be distributed as between the preference stockholders and the ordinary stockholders of the company in its liquidation. [His Lordship stated the facts and continued:] Roxburgh J felt himself bound by authority and, with a reluctance which appears on the face of his judgment, was constrained to make a declaration to the effect that the holders of the preference stock were entitled to participate with the holders of the ordinary stock rateably in proportion to the nominal amount of the stocks held by them respectively in this sum. The two authorities which the judge mentions in his judgment are *In re Fraser and Chalmers Ltd* and *In re John Dry Steam Tugs Ltd.* He does not in terms refer to *In re William Metcalfe & Sons Ltd*, but it is plain that he must have had that case in mind, for it is a judgment of the Court of Appeal, and at the time when the present case was before him it was good authority.

3 In *In re William Metcalfe & Sons Ltd* the Court of Appeal, while accepting that each case must be regarded as one of construction turning on the terms of the particular document, approved the statement of Astbury J in *In re Fraser and Chalmers Ltd*, where he said that all shareholders are entitled to equal treatment unless and to the extent that their rights in this respect are modified by the contract under which they hold their shares. He proceeded on the view that that was the correct principle to apply when considering the construction of articles or resolutions regulating the rights of classes of shareholders inter se. I think that the effect of *In re William Metcalfe & Sons Ltd* can, stated shortly, *(pg166)* be said to be that, in questions between preference shareholders and ordinary shareholders as to the right of the preference shareholders to share in what has been many times described as surplus assets, the onus of showing that the preference shareholders are not entitled to share in those surplus assets lies upon the ordinary shareholders.

4 Since the matter was before Roxburgh J, the position has been materially altered by the decision of the House of Lords in *Scottish Insurance Corporation Ltd v Wilsons & Clyde Coal Co Ltd.* For the purposes of the present case I do not think that it is necessary to embark upon a detailed analysis of that case or the opinions of the members of the House of Lords who heard it; but, as appears from the head-note, the facts were that the colliery assets of a coalmining company had been transferred to the National Coal Board under the Coal Industry Nationalisation Act 1946, and that in consequence it was the intention of the company to go into voluntary liquidation. Meanwhile the company proposed to reduce its capital by returning their capital to the holders of the preference stock, which would be thereby extinguished. The reduction was opposed by certain preference stockholders on the ground, *inter alia*, that it deprived them of the right to participate in the liquidation and the division of the company's surplus assets. It was held by Viscount Maugham, Lord Simonds and Lord Normand, Lord Morton of Henryton dissenting, 'that the proposed reduction was not unfair or inequitable and should be confirmed, because, even without it, the preference stockholders would not be entitled in a winding up to share in the surplus assets or to receive more than a return of their paid-up capital. Accordingly, they could not object to being paid, by means of the reduction, the amount which they would receive in the proposed liquidation.'

5 For reasons which I shall endeavour to show, it appears to me that the effect of the decision of the majority in that case is not merely to remove the onus in cases such as this from the holders of ordinary shares, but to throw the onus upon the holders of preference shares; and it is for the holders of preference shares to satisfy the court that, on the true construction of the particular document, they are entitled to share in the surplus assets, at any rate in a case where a right to participate in surplus assets in a liquidation is conferred on the holders of preference shares. *(pg167)*

6 Perhaps the point emerges more clearly from the speech of Lord Normand, where he quotes from the speech of Lord Haldane LC in *Will v United Lankat Plantations Co Ltd.* Lord Normand said, quoting the Lord Chancellor:

' "Shares are not issued in the abstract and priorities then attached to them; the issue of shares and the attachment of priorities proceed *uno flatu*; and when you turn to the terms on which the shares are issued you expect to find all the rights as regards dividends specified in the terms of the issue." With this opinion Earl Loreburn and Lord Atkinson agreed. My Lords, the *ratio decidendi* applies with equal force to priorities of participation in the company's property, and I see no ground on which it may be supposed that the declaration of rights as regards dividends is exhaustive, but the declaration of rights as regards property is not exhaustive. There is as good reason and it is equally easy to define exhaustively the one set of rights as the other. Sargant J in *In re National Telephone Co* said: "… it appears to me that the weight of authority is in favour of the view that, either with regard to dividend or with regard to the rights in a winding up, the express gift or attachment of preferential rights to preferential shares, on their creation, is, *prima facie*, a definition of the whole of their rights in that respect, and negatives any further or other right to which, but for the specified rights, they would have been entitled." The decision of this House in *Will v United Lankat Plantations Co Ltd* had not been pronounced when Sargant J decided *In re National Telephone Co* and his opinion reflects his construction of the judgment of the Court of Appeal.'

7 In my view, it follows from what I have read that Lord Normand considered that the same principle applies to the construction of rights in a winding up as applies to the construction of dividend rights, and that he approved the extract from the judgment of Sargant J in *In re National Telephone Co Ltd*, which he cites. It is, therefore, I think, plain from consideration of what I have read from Lord Normand's speech that he takes the view, and expresses it, that the onus in such a case as this lies on the holders of preference shares. *(pg168)*

8 I think that the same view is, in effect, expressed both by Viscount Maugham and by Lord Simonds, the other members of the majority. Viscount Maugham said: Much reliance is placed on behalf of the appellants on the case of *In re William Metcalfe & Sons Ltd*. I must say that in my opinion that case was wrongly decided; and it should be noted that it is expressly stated that the bulk of the sum of £21,000 there in dispute was attributable to accumulated profits. It seems to me difficult to reconcile that case with the decision of this House in *Will v United Lankat Plantations Co Ltd*, and impossible to reconcile it on sound grounds with the decision of *In re Bridgewater Navigation Co*.'

9 It appears to me from that statement of Viscount Maugham that he could not reconcile the decision in *In re William Metcalfe & Sons Ltd* with the decision of the House of Lords in *Will v United Lankat Plantations Co Ltd*, and that he was ranging himself on the same side as Lord Normand in taking the view that the onus in such cases is upon the holders of preference shares.

10 Lord Simonds, having discussed the relevant words in the relevant article in that case, said: 'I do not ignore that in the same case' – that is *Will v United*

Lankat Plantations Co Ltd – 'in the Court of Appeal the distinction between dividend and capital was expressly made by both Lord Cozens-Hardy MR and Farwell LJ, and that in *In re William Metcalfe & Sons Ltd*, Romer LJ reasserted it. But I share the difficulty, which Lord Keith has expressed in this case, in reconciling the reasoning that lies behind the judgment in *Will's* case and *In re William Metcalfe & Sons Ltd* respectively.' He proceeds: 'In *Collaroy Co Ltd v Gifard* Astbury J, after reviewing the authorities, including his own earlier decision in *In re Fraser and Chalmers*, said "But whether the considerations affecting them (*scilicet* capital and dividend preference respectively) are 'entirely different' is a question of some difficulty," and approved the proposition there urged by the ordinary shareholders that a fixed return of capital to shareholders in a winding up is just as artificial as a *(pg169)* provision for a fixed dividend and that if the latter is regarded as exhaustive, there is no *prima facie* reason why the former should not be similarly regarded.'

11 It was urged upon us that the true rule is to be found in the language of Lord Macnaghten in *Birch v Cropper*. Mr Gray, on behalf of the preference stockholder, who in effect represents all the holders of preference stock, read a passage from Lord Macnaghten's speech which is as follows:

'Every person who becomes a member of a company limited by shares of equal amount becomes entitled to a proportionate part in the capital of the company, and, unless it be otherwise provided by the regulations of the company, entitled, as a necessary consequence, to the same proportionate part in all the property of the company, including its uncalled capital. He is liable in respect of all moneys unpaid on his shares to pay up every call that is duly made upon him. But he does not by such payment acquire any further or other interest in the capital of the company. His share in the capital is just what it was before. His liability to the company is diminished by the amount paid. His contribution is merged in the common fund. And that is all.'

That passage proceeds over the next three pages, ending with these words: 'There was an express bargain made as to their rights in respect of profits arising from the business of the company. But there was no bargain – no provision of any sort – affecting their rights as shareholders in the capital of the company.' So that, both at the beginning and at the end of the passage relied on, there is this vital qualification, that the rule which was stated by Lord Macnaghten only applies if the articles are silent as to any right in the preference shareholders to participate in surplus assets.

12 That rule, as it appears to me, is in no way impinged upon by the later cases, and in particular by the case of *Scottish Insurance Corporation Ltd v Wilsons & Clyde Coal Co Ltd*. And indeed Lord Simonds, in a passage which I shall read, brings the statement by Lord Macnaghten in *Birch v Cropper* into true perspective in the light of the subsequent authorities. He says: 'Finally on this part of the case I ought to deal *(pg170)* with an observation made by Lord Macnaghten in *Birch v Cropper*, upon which counsel for the appellants relied. "They," he said, "[*scilicet* the preference shareholders] must be treated as having all the rights of shareholders, except so far as they renounced these rights on their admission to the company." But in my opinion, Lord Macnaghten can have meant nothing more than that the rights of the parties depended on the bargain that they had made and that the terms of the bargain must be ascertained by a consideration of the articles of association and any other relevant document, a task which I have endeavoured in this case to discharge. I cannot think that Lord Macnaghten intended to introduce some new principle of construction and to lay down that preference shareholders are entitled to share in surplus assets unless they expressly and specifically renounce that right.'

13 Having regard to the view which I take of the opinions of the majority of the House of Lords in the *Scottish Insurance Corporation cases*, it appears to me to be unnecessary to embark upon any review of the earlier authorities, all of which were considered in that case; and in my judgment the effect of the authorities as now in force is to establish the two principles for which Mr Christie contended: first, that, in construing an article which deals with rights to share in profits, that is, dividend rights, and rights to share in the company's property in a liquidation, the same principle is applicable; and, second, that that principle is that, where the article sets out the rights attached to a class of shares to participate in profits while the company is a going concern or to share in the property of the company in liquidation, *prima facie*, the rights so set out are in each case exhaustive.

14 With those considerations in mind I turn back to art 3 of the articles of association in this case. As regards the rights as to profits, the whole of the distributable profits are expressly dealt with. They are to be applied first in paying to the holders of the preference stock 'a fixed cumulative preferential dividend at the rate of 6 per cent per annum on the amounts for the time being paid up or credited as paid up thereon respectively in priority to the ordinary shares,' and, secondly, in paying a non-cumulative dividend at the rate of 6 per cent a year calculated on the same basis to the holders of the ordinary shares; and the balance is then distributable between *(pg171)* the two classes of shares *pari passu*. Nothing could be more plainly exhaustive than that language. Then, as regards the rights in a winding-up, the holders of the preference shares are stated to be entitled to certain payments in priority to the ordinary shares. Those payments are, first of all, repayment of the capital paid up on the preference stock, and, second, any arrears of dividend whether earned or not. The question, then, is: is there anything to suggest that the language regarding the rights of the holders of the preference stock in a winding-up is not exhaustive? I can find nothing. The onus now, as I have said, is in my view on the holders of the preference stock to show that the provision is not exhaustive; and in my view they have failed to discharge that onus.

15 There is present in this case a circumstance which, in my judgment, makes that conclusion *a fortiori*, namely, the express right conferred on the holders of the preference stock while the company remains a going concern to participate in the profits remaining after providing for the fixed non-cumulative dividend on the ordinary stock. A somewhat similar provision was contained in the articles of association of the National Telephone Co which Sargant J had to construe in the case of that name. The relevant article, which was introduced by a resolution, was as follows:

> 'That the capital of the company be increased by the issue of 15,000 new shares of £10 each. That such shares be called second preference shares, and that the holders thereof (subject to the payment of the preferential dividend of the original preference shares) be entitled to a cumulative preferential dividend at the rate of 6 per cent per annum. After the ordinary shares have received a dividend at the rate of 6 per cent per annum out of the profits of each year, the second preference shares and the ordinary shares shall participate rateably, according to the amounts paid up thereon, in any surplus profits. The second preference shares shall not confer any right of voting at any general meeting of the company, and, in the event of the company being wound up, the surplus assets thereof shall be applied in the first place in repaying to the holders of the original preference shares the full amount paid up thereon, and, subject thereto, in repaying to the holders of the second preference shares the full amount paid up thereon, in priority *(pg172)* to any payment in respect of the ordinary shares of the company.'

So that it will be seen that in almost every material respect art. 3 in this case is comparable with the provision which I have just read.

16 On that Sargant J says this:

> 'The question upon that clause, as in the previous case, is whether there is an implied negativing of any right on the part of the holders of the second preference shares to receive more in the winding up of the company than the repayment of the whole of their capital. In my opinion there is. I am speaking now, on first impression, on my own construction of these articles, apart from authority, which I shall allude to hereafter. In my judgment the fact that an express right was given, in respect of dividend, to receive more than the amount of the preferential dividends in certain events strengthens the inference that the silence as regards return of capital in a winding-up indicates that there was to be no return of capital beyond the return of the nominal amount of the capital of the shares. I should have felt disposed to come to that conclusion even without the assistance to be derived from a consideration of the terms of the rights to dividend, but with that assistance it seems to me that any business man reading that resolution would come to the conclusion that the holders of the second preference shares were not entitled on a winding-up to get more than their return of capital.'

17 I accept entirely the proposition, as indeed one is directed to do throughout the authorities, that each case must, in the end, be a question of construction of the particular document in question, and it can be but infrequently that in the construction of a particular document one obtains such almost direct aid in that construction as I obtain in this case from the remarks of Sargant J which I have just quoted. In my humble opinion they are good sense, and I would apply them in their full force to the art 3 before the court in this case.

18 It was urged on us that in construing art 3 we must have regard to the whole of the articles of association and to the surrounding circumstances. I accept that. It was urged on us that a relevant circumstance was that in this case the voting control rests in the hands of the holders of the preference stock; and from that it was sought to be argued that it is really impossible to conclude that the holders of the preference *(pg173)* stock, the controllers of the company should have contemplated that in a liquidation they would get no more than any arrears of dividend on their preference stock, together with the capital on it. I am unable to accept that argument. It involves speculation and therefore uncertainty. The bargain as regards rights of participation, whether in profits or assets, appears to me to be contained in art 3. Nor can I find any context affecting the construction of that article to be derived from any other article in the articles of association. Finally, it was urged on us that we ought to have regard to the state of the law as it existed when the articles were adopted in the year 1929, and that the relevant art 3 should be construed in the light of the law as then obtaining. There might – I say no more – perhaps have been some force in that argument had *In re William Metcalfe & Sons Ltd* been decided before the adoption of these articles; but the argument appears to me to be completely without weight when one considers what was the position of the law on this point in the year 1929. It is, I think, sufficient to say that there was then a conflict of judicial opinion on this point, which was only resolved, and then only for the time being, by the decision of the Court of Appeal in *In re William Metcalfe & Sons Ltd*. For these reasons I would allow this appeal.

19 ASQUITH LJ: I agree.

20 EVERSHED MR: I also agree. At the end of his judgment Roxburgh J stated his conclusion thus: 'It is quite clear that if, on a fair construction of the article, I cannot find that the preference shareholders are excluded from participation in the surplus assets, then they are entitled to participate.' The conclusion was based on the decision of this court in *In re William Metcalfe & Sons Ltd*, which governed this case when it was before Roxburgh J. Since then the law has been substantially affected by the decision of the House of Lords in *Scottish Insurance Corporation Ltd v Wilsons & Clyde Coal Co Ltd*. In those circumstances I shall not be thought disrespectful to the judge if I do not state at length the reasons for taking a view different from that which he reached. I agree with my brother Wynn-Parry that, as a result of *Scottish Insurance Corporation Ltd v Wilsons & Clyde Coal Co Ltd*, the two propositions for *(pg174)* which Mrs Christie contended should now be taken as established.

21 Out of respect, however, for the careful and forceful argument of Mr Gray, I will state in a few sentences why I reach that conclusion. At the end of his speech dealing with this point in *Scottish Insurance Corporation Ltd v Wilsons & Clyde Coal Co Ltd*, Lord Normand said: 'It is, I think, not possible to distinguish *Metcalfe's* case from the present case, and I have therefore come to the conclusion that it should be overruled and that the *ratio* of *Will v United Lankat Plantations Co Ltd* was correctly applied in *Collaroy Co Ltd v Giffard* and *In re National Telephone Co Ltd.'* It is true, as Mr Gray has pointed out, that the language of Lord Normand in this respect is perhaps somewhat less qualified than the language which fell from Viscount Maugham and Lord Simonds on the same matter. But the disapprobation which both Viscount Maugham and Lord Simonds expressed for *In re William Metcalfe & Sons Ltd* is found in a context in which reference was made to the fact that Lord Keith in the Court of Session had found it impossible to reconcile *Will v United Lankat Plantations Co Ltd* and *Metcalfe's* case. It seems to me, therefore, that the result of the majority speeches is to treat as established and as good law the statement of Sargant J in *In re National Telephone Co Ltd*, which Wynn-Parry J has read, and to do so notwithstanding any observations of Lord Macnaghten in *Birch v Cropper*, which must be construed as applicable only to the case where the articles are wholly silent as regards particular or specific rights.

22 I think, for myself, that during the sixty years which have passed since *Birch v Cropper* was before the House of Lords the view of the courts may have undergone some change in regard to the relative rights of preference and ordinary shareholders, and to the advantage of the preference shareholders, whose position has, in that interval of time, become somewhat more approximated to the role which Sir Horace Davey attempted to assign to them, but which Lord Macnaghten rejected in *Birch v Cropper*, namely, that of debentureholders. *(pg175)*

23 In his dissenting opinion in *Scottish Insurance Corporation Ltd v Wilsons & Clyde Coal Co Ltd*, Lord Morton of Henryton, after citing a passage from Lord Macnaghten's speech in *Birch v Cropper*, based this conclusion upon it: 'Thus in the present case the preference stockholders are entitled to share in the surplus assets with the ordinary stockholders in proportion to their respective holdings, unless the articles of the company otherwise provide.' But that view and that interpretation of Lord Macnaghten's speech were rejected by the majority of the House of Lords. It is the duty of the Court of Appeal to follow loyally the result and not to seek by minute analysis to perceive fine distinctions between the opinions of the concurring Lords, more especially when the effect might be to produce a condition of perhaps inconvenient uncertainty.

24 I therefore on the point of law conclude that, after the *Wilsons & Clyde* case, the onus is, so to speak, on the preference stockholders. It is, of course, quite true that the matter in the last resort is one of the construction of the articles. For reasons which Wynn-Parry J has already stated, and with which I agree, I think that the onus has not been discharged. It is true that this case possesses in some respects notable features: for example, the facts that the preference shareholders have a majority of the voting powers and that they have at the end of art 3 a position in regard to reduction of capital which is (I agree with Wynn-Parry J) unique in my experience; nor do I forget that they are given earlier in the article a right to participate with the ordinary shareholders in surplus profits. But I cannot come, on any of those matters or on all of them together, to a conclusion which would discharge the onus placed upon the preference stockholders, even if (without saying that it is right to do so) regard is had to the state of the law as it was thought to be when the article was first adopted.

25 I think that there may be this further difficulty: Mr Gray said that one would expect to find some kind of parallelism between the rights *inter se* of the preference shareholders and the ordinary shareholders as to dividend and their rights *inter se* in a winding up. Having regard to the nature of the right of participation, it would, I think, be difficult to reproduce a true parallel between the two classes 176 in a winding up and still more difficult to read into the *(pg176)* provisions of the article appropriate language to produce such a result. Even if one did, one would still be left with some anomaly having regard to the rights on a reduction of capital.

26 I think, for these reasons as well as those that have already been stated, that this appeal should be allowed, and that the appropriate declarations should be to the effect that the surplus assets are now distributable exclusively among the ordinary shareholders. *(pg177)*

Case 24
Attorney-General of Ceylon v Mackie & Another

[1952] 2 All ER 775

Privy Council

7, 8, 9, July, 6 October 1952

This case is important for share valuation as two fundamental principles are very clearly stated in the judgement of the Privy Council. The principles are:

1. Where the estate at death includes more than one class of share in any particular company, the valuation is of the aggregate holding; that is the market value is the highest amount that the hypothetical unconnected purchaser would pay for the two or more classes of shares, if purchased together. (The equivalent principle applies if there is a lifetime chargeable transfer.)
2. When a prospective purchaser makes an offer, he is looking to what he may be entitled to receive in the future. The price he offers is based on his assessment of future performance. Past results are only relevant insofar as they provide evidence for the future.

At his death on 7 September 1940, CW Mackie held 5,000 'management shares' (all the shares of this class in issue) and also 9,201 8 per cent cumulative preference shares (46 per cent of the shares of this class) in CW Mackie & Co Ltd. In 1940, at a time when the course of the Second World War was going badly for the British Empire, the future of the rubber trade was unpredictable and it was difficult to find anyone willing to invest large sums of money on speculation. The company carried on business as a business in Ceylon as a rubber merchant. The market price of rubber fluctuated widely from year to year. From 1908 to 1913 very large profits were made, amounting in aggregate to over Rs 3,000,000. During the next six years to 1932 large losses were incurred, amounting in aggregate to over Rs 1,800,000. During the next six years there were profits in four years and losses in two, the figures varying from a profit of Rs 443,161 in 1933 to a loss of Rs 281,907 in 1935. Finally in 1939 and 1940 there were profits of Rs 787,641 and Rs 501,878. No dividend had been paid on the preference shares since 1930 and no dividend had been paid on the management shares since 1926. The company found it necessary to borrow large sums from time to time on overdraft. The expert witness for the appellant said that he did not know of a more speculative business in Ceylon.

The valuer instructed by the executors valued the shares on a balance sheet basis. He approached the valuation by saying that a buyer would ask, first, what dividends had been paid but would quickly conclude that as no dividend had been paid for many years it was impossible to value the shares on a yield basis. He would then see that earnings had fluctuated greatly and were, thus, not a reliable indicator of future performance. He would then look at the rubber industry and the position of the company in that industry. He would see that 20–30 per cent of all rubber exported from Ceylon was handled by CW Mackie & Co Ltd. The company operated by holding large stocks and the price of rubber is subject to large and rapid fluctuations. Looking at the industry in 1940, it was an industry in a world that was devastated by a war, the length of which could not be guessed by the man in the street. When asked in cross examination whether a buyer would not have taken into account the probability that the high profits of 1940 would last for some time, he said:

> 'If a purchaser could have guessed that there was going to be a long war, no government interference, no form of increased taxation, and that he was not going to have competition from others, he might take that view. He would be a brave man. It would possibly be a gamble. In his view, no goodwill attached to the business.'
>
> ([1952] 2 All ER 775 at 778 **case 24 para 4**)

The valuer instructed by the executors of WG Mackie valued the shares at the value of the balance sheet; that is, break-up value.

The valuers for the Revenue took a more theoretical approach. They assumed that it was possible to estimate the future average maintainable profit by means of an arithmetical calculation from past profits and losses, and that a purchaser could have been found who would have paid a price for the shares determined by a further arithmetical calculation from that average maintainable profit. One witness said that 'a buyer would concentrate on the last five years' profits because that is mostly likely to represent what would happen in the future'; and the other witness went so far as to say that a prudent buyer would take it for granted that conditions would remain the same.

Aggregating holdings

The Privy Council held that the value required was the value to one person of holding both classes of share, together. Lord Reid said:

'In addition to restrictions of a usual character, the articles also contained a provision to the effect that holders of not less than nine-tenths of the share capital could at any time call for a transfer of any other shares at a fair value to be fixed by the auditors of the company. It was admitted for the appellant that no purchaser would have paid anything like Rs 250 per shares for the management shares in face of the company's articles unless he could buy at the same time a large block of the preference shares so have a majority of votes. But the appellant contends that the respondents must be supposed to have taken the course which would get the largest price for the combined holding of management and preference shares and to have offered for sale together with the management shares the whole or at least the greater part of the preference shares owned by the deceased. In their Lordships' judgment this contention is correct.'

([1952] 2 All ER 775 at 777/778 **case 24 para 3**)

This principle was re-enunciated by the Court of Appeal 42 years later in *IRC v Gray* [1994] STC 360 **case 37**, where the valuation necessitated aggregating a partnership share and a freehold subject to a lease where the partnership was the tenant.

A valuation looks to the future

It is always necessary to look at known past results of a company, both in terms of earnings and assets. However, this exercise is undertaken in order to provide a basis on which to judge the future performance of the company. Share valuation is not simply a arithmetic exercise; a share value is not simply the average of five years' profits multiplied by a P/E ratio.

The necessity to judge the future was given, in the context of this case, when Lord Reid rejected the approach of the Attorney-General, saying:

'Where the past history of a business shows consistent results or a steady trend and where there has been no disruption of general business conditions it may well be possible to reach a fair valuation by a theoretical calculation. But in this case neither condition was satisfied. The profits and losses of the company had fluctuated so violently in the past that, as the second witness for the appellant admitted, it is impossible to choose any five consecutive years in the company's history the result of which would be reflected in the next year's profits. It is, therefore, in their Lordships' judgement, not possible in this case to derive by an arithmetical calculation from past results anything which could properly have been regarded in 1940 as an average maintainable profit, and in addition there were extremely uncertain conditions in 1940. The appellant's witnesses made no allowance for these facts, and were not able to give informed evidence on the question whether a purchaser could have been found in 1940 willing to lay out the large sum required on their valuation.'

([1952] 2 All ER 775 at 778/779 **case 24 para 5**)

'No doubt, the value of an established business as a going concern generally exceeds and often greatly exceeds the total value of its tangible assets. But that cannot be assumed to be universally true. If it is proved in a particular case that at the relevant date the business could not have been sold for more than the value of its tangible assets, then that must be taken to be its value as a going concern. In their Lordships' judgement it has been proved in this case that the deceased's holding could not have been sold in September, 1940, at a price based on any higher figure than the value of the tangible assets of the company. Their Lordships will, therefore, humbly advise Her Majesty that this appeal should be dismissed.'

([1952] 2 All ER 775 at 779 **case 24 para 8**)

This case is an important corrective to the too easy attitude that a share valuation is an arithmetic exercise performed on past results.

Judgement

References, example '(pg776)', are to [1952] 2 All ER 775.

1 LORD REID (October 6): This is an appeal from a decree of the Supreme Court of Ceylon dated May 25, 1950, which allowed an appeal from an order of the District Court of Colombo dated Aug 31, 1949. The question at issue is the valuation for the purpose of estate duty of five thousand management shares of CW Mackie & Co Ltd (hereinafter called 'the company') which belonged to the late Mr CW Mackie (hereinafter called 'the deceased') at his death on Sept 7, 1940. The respondents are his executors. The District Court of Colombo held that the value of these shares at that date was Rs 250 per share. On appeal *(pg776)* the Supreme Court reduced that valuation to Rs 40.6188 per share. The appellant maintains that the valuation of the District Court should be restored.

2 The deceased had carried on business in Ceylon as a rubber merchant since about 1908, and his business was acquired by the company as a going concern on its incorporation in Ceylon in 1922. The capital of the company, which remained unchanged throughout, was Rs 1,000,000 divided in 19,800 eight per cent cumulative preference shares of Rs 50 each and five thousand management shares of Rs 2 each. The deceased was life director of the company with extensive powers, and from the beginning he had a large part of the share capital and taken the leading part in the management of the company. He left Ceylon about 1930, but continued thereafter to exercise some supervision. At his death he held 9,201 preference shares and all the management shares. The practice of the company was to buy rubber and grade it for re-sale. Its graded rubber, known as Mackie standard, had a high reputation in important foreign markets, and it appears that some twenty per cent or thirty per cent of the whole of the rubber exported from Ceylon was handled by the company. The policy of the company was to hold large stocks, and, as the price of rubber has for long been subject to large and rapid fluctuations, the company's profits varied to an extreme degree. During its first five years very large profits were made amounting in all to over Rs 3,000,000. During the next six years to 1932 large losses were incurred amounting to over Rs 1,800,000. During the next six years there were profits in four years and losses in two, the figures varying from a profit of Rs 443,161 in 1933 to a loss of Rs 281,907 in 1935. Finally in 1939 and 1940 there were profits of Rs 787,641 and Rs 501,878. No dividend had been paid on the preference shares since 1930 and no dividend had been paid on the management shares since 1926, the company having found it necessary to borrow large sums from time to time on overdraft. The leading witness for the appellant admitted that he did not know of a more speculative business in Ceylon.

3 The statute in force at the time of the deceased's death was the Estate Duty Ordinance 1938. By s20 of that ordinance it was provided that the value of any property should be estimated to be the price which, in the opinion of an assessor, such property would fetch if sold in the open market at the time of the death of the deceased. Section 20 contains a proviso to the effect that if the value of the property has been depreciated by the death of the deceased such depreciation is to be taken into account. The respondents originally sought to rely on this proviso, but they do not now do so. It is now common ground that the shares must be valued at the price which they would have fetched if sold in the open market on Sept 7, 1940. The articles of association of the company contained restrictions on transfer of a type often found in private companies, but it is admitted that the decision in *Inland Revenue Comrs v Crossman* (1) applies to this case. So the shares must be valued on the footing that the highest bidder in the open market would have been registered as a shareholder, but that he would then become subject to the restrictions in the articles. In addition to restrictions of a usual character, the articles also contained a provision to the effect that holders of not less than nine-tenths of the share capital could at any time call for a transfer of any other shares at a fair value to be fixed by the auditors of the company. It was admitted for the appellant that no purchaser would have paid anything like Rs 250 per shares for the management shares in face of the company's articles unless he could buy at the same time a large block of the preference shares and so have a majority of votes. But the appellant contends that the respondents must be supposed to have taken the course which would get the largest price for the combined holding of management and preference shares and to have offered for sale together with the management shares the whole or at least the greater part of the preference shares owned by the deceased. In their Lordships' *(pg777)* judgment this contention is correct. But it means that the valuation for which the appellant contends depends on the possibility of having been able to find in September 1940 a single purchaser prepared to venture a very large sum of money. The agreed valuation of the deceased's preference shares is Rs 806,017 and the valuation of the management shares for which the appellant now contends is Rs 1,250,000. So a purchaser who wished to acquire a sufficiently large holding to be in a dominant position would have had, on this valuation, to pay some Rs 2,000,000 in all.

4 Evidence was given in the District Court as to the value of the shares. The leading witness for the respondents was Mr Lander, a chartered accountant, who had experience of rubber companies. The gist of his evidence was that a buyer would first ask what was the last dividend and when was it paid, but, as no dividend had been paid for many years, it was impossible to value the shares on a yield basis. He then pointed out that in 1940 the future was unpredictable and it was difficult to find anyone who was willing to invest large sums of money on speculation. He valued the shares on a balance sheet basis because, in his view, no one would have paid more than that at the time. When asked in cross-examination whether a buyer would not have taken into account the probability that the high profits of 1940 would last for some time, he said that the buyer 'would have needed to know precisely what was going to happen in the world which was devastated by a war the length of which could not be guessed by the man in the street. In other words, if a purchaser could have guessed that there was going to be a long war, no government interference, no form of increased taxation, and that he was not going to have competition from others, he might take that view. He would be a brave man. It would possibly be a gamble.' In his view, no goodwill attached to the business. Similar evidence was given by other witnesses for the respondents.

5 There was really no contradictory evidence for the appellant on what their Lordships regard as some of the most important points. Neither of the appellant's witnesses professed to have been familiar with the market for shares of rubber companies or to have any direct knowledge about the possibility in 1940 of finding a purchaser for this large block of shares although they admitted that no one would pay the price on their valuation without acquiring such an interest. The respondents' case was that if the shares had been offered at prices corresponding to the value of the tangible assets held by the company they might have been sold. A purchaser would not then have been gambling on a continuance of the high rate of profit at the beginning of the war. But a purchaser could not have been found to venture Rs 2,000,000 on a speculation. The appellant's witnesses hardly dealt with these matters. Their approach was more theoretical. They assumed that it was possible to estimate the future average maintainable profit by means of an arithmetical calculation from past profits and losses, and that a purchaser could have been found who would have

paid a price for the shares determined by a further arithmetical calculation from that average maintainable profit. One witness said that 'a buyer would concentrate on the last five years' profits because that is most likely to represent what would happen in the future'; and the other witness went so far as to say that a prudent buyer would take it for granted that conditions would remain the same. It may be that these assumptions would be justified in many cases. Where the past history of a business shows consistent results or a steady trend and where there has been no disruption of general business conditions it may well be possible to reach a fair valuation by a theoretical calculation. But in this case neither condition was satisfied. The profits and losses of the company had fluctuated so violently in the past that, as the second witness for the appellant admitted, it is impossible to choose any five consecutive years in the company's history the result of which would be reflected in the next year's profits. It is, therefore, in their Lordships' judgment, not possible in this case to derive by *(pg778)* an arithmetical calculation from past results anything which could properly have been regarded in 1940 as an average maintainable profit, and in addition there were extremely uncertain conditions in 1940. The appellant's witnesses made no allowance for these facts, and were not able to give informed evidence on the question whether a purchaser could have been found in 1940 willing to lay out the large sum required on their valuation.

6 The learned judge of the District Court founded on two lists of rubber companies' shares quoted in 1939 and 1940 as showing that in 1940 the investing public were not pessimistic. Their Lordships are unable to draw any conclusion from these lists. No evidence was given about them by the appellant's witnesses. A few questions about them were put to one of the respondents' witnesses, Mr Cuming, in cross-examination. He said:

> 'There was business in buying rubber shares in 1940, but not considerable business. There was a feeling that government was going to take over the buying of rubber and as a result there was a certain amount of business.'

7 As the company's business depended on its ability to buy rubber, any such feeling could not have helped the sale of its shares. It may be that these share lists show that there were more buyers in the market in 1940 than in 1939, but they do not show whether those buyers were prepared to buy large blocks of shares or whether the price offered exceeded the break-up value of the shares. Their Lordships cannot agree with the district judge that these lists diminish the value of the evidence of the respondents' witnesses. And there are other matters where the learned judge appears to have gone beyond the evidence. For example, he said that it was quite evident to the other directors at the death of the deceased that large profits were to be made in the near future, and that there is always a goodwill attached to a company of this character.

8 In their Lordships' judgment the value of these shares at the date of the deceased's death is a question of fact which must be decided on the evidence which was led. That evidence has been very fully considered by the learned judges of the Supreme Court, and their Lordships cannot find that these learned judges have in any way misdirected themselves. It was argued for the appellant that the Supreme Court erred in law in accepting the balance sheet method of valuation because that can only give break-up value and in this case it is necessary to find the value of the business as a going concern. It is true that a purchaser of the shares held by the deceased could have obtained a controlling interest in the company as a going concern, and in their Lordships' judgment it is right to value these shares by reference to the value of the company's business as a going concern. No doubt, the value of an established business as a going concern generally exceeds and often greatly exceeds the total value of its tangible assets. But that cannot be assumed to be universally true. If it is proved in a particular case that at the relevant date the business could not have been sold for more than the value of its tangible assets, then that must be taken to be its value as a going concern. In their Lordships' judgment it has been proved in this case that the deceased's holding could not have been sold in September, 1940, at a price based on any higher figure than the value of the tangible assets of the company. Their Lordships will, therefore, humbly advise Her Majesty that this appeal should be dismissed. The appellant must pay the costs of the appeal. *(pg779)*

Case 25
Re Holt

(1953) 32 ATC 402

High Court

25 November 1953

Re Holt is the first case where the judgment gives, in effect, a full share valuation report. By contrast, the judgement of the court in each of the previous cases in this book is a judgement on one or more questions of principle. In *Re Holt*, at the end of a ten-day hearing, Danckwerts J takes the evidence given by the expert witnesses and then, himself, produces a share valuation. He goes through the various aspects, records the evidence given to him, weighs up the relative importance of the different aspects and concludes by specifying a price per share.

Matters considered by Danckwerts J include the following:

1. The concept that a purchaser will be entered on the register but will then hold the shares subject to the articles.
2. The relevance of value of the company's cash resources and liabilities.
3. The relevance of the possibility of shares being floated on the stock market.
4. The extent to which, in a valuation, accounts prepared after the valuation date can be considered.
5. A discount for the shares not being marketable.
6. The effect on the valuation of the country's economic and political situation at the time of valuation.
7. The effects on the valuation of the company's dividend record.
8. The extent to which an unquoted share can be valued by comparison with prices of quoted company shares.
9. The influence on valuation of the company's record of earnings.
10. The principle that events subsequent to the valuation date that are not forecastable on that date cannot be taken to affect the value.
11. A discussion of the nature of an prudent investor who would purchase the shares in a private company.
12. The influence a minority shareholder has on the directors.

John Holt & Co (Liverpool) Ltd carried on a trade of shipping and running stores in West Africa. On 7 January 1947 Robert Langstaff Holt created a settlement into which he transferred 43,698 John Holt & Co (Liverpool) Ltd £1 ordinary shares and also 11,643 6.5 per cent £1 preference shares. The shares settled represented 6 per cent of the ordinary shares in issue; the preference shares represented 8 per cent of the preference shares in issue. Robert Langstaff Holt died 14 months after creating the trust, on 11 March 1948. Estate duty, thus, became payable on the shares settled.

The Revenue and the executors agreed on a value of 21s for each preference share.

The Revenue assessed estate duty on the ordinary shares at a valuation of £3 per share; the executors valued the ordinary shares at 11s 3d per share. Prior to the hearing, the Revenue reduced their valuation to 25s per share and the executors increased their valuation to 17s 2d per share.

The approach taken by Danckwerts J provides a model for a valuation report. The judge's decision can be summarised as follows.

First, the shareholding is specified and the valuation date identified. The purpose of the valuation is stated at (1953) 32 ATC 402 at 403 **case 25 para 1** as being for the assessment of estate duty.

The share capital of the company is stated and the relevant articles of association that affect valuation are identified at (1953) 32 ATC 402 at 403 **case 25 paras 1 and 2**. The relevance of the articles is then given by reference to a decided case of a superior court:

> 'The principles, on which the value of shares in a private company are to be valued for the purpose of estate duty, have been settled by the House of Lords in the case of *Commissioners of Inland Revenue v Crossman*. The House of Lords decided in that case (by a majority of three to two) that the facts that a shareholder by the articles of a company may be compelled to sell his shares at the "fair value" ascertained in accordance with the articles, and that by the articles the directors may have power to refuse to register a transfer, must be ignored; but none the less it must be assumed that a purchaser will be bound by the company's articles once he is upon the register of members.'
>
> ((1953) 32 ATC 402 at 403 **case 25 para 5**)

At this point, Danckwerts J makes his oft-quoted remark:

> 'The result is that I must enter into a dim world peopled by the indeterminate spirits of fictitious or unborn sales.'
>
> ((1953) 32 ATC 402 at 403 **case 25 para 5**)

Less quoted is the equally seminal comment that the judge makes after having heard Counsel's submissions and the evidence of expert witnesses for the previous 10 days:

'In my task I have had the assistance of a number of experts on each side, who differ in their opinions in the manner in which experts normally do, and the frankest of them admitted that certain of his calculations were simply guesswork. It seems to me that their opinions are indeed properly described as guesswork, though of course it is intelligent guesswork, aided by the experience which they have gained by their work as stockbrokers or accountants. No possible suggestion can be made against the honesty of these witnesses, but their methods of calculation appear to me to be inevitably uncertain and controversial ... my remarks must not be taken to belittle the efforts which have been made by them to provide an answer to a question to which no certain answer is possible.'

((1953) 32 ATC 402 at 403 **case 25 para 6**)

The past is knowable; the future is not. We cannot bring into consideration what is unknowable at the valuation date, but the price that is offered is the price for the benefits arising from the shareholding in the future, not the past. The essential tension between these two concepts is neatly stated by Danckwerts J:

'It is necessary to assume the prophetic vision of a prospective purchaser at the moment of the death of the deceased, and firmly to reject the wisdom which might be provided by the knowledge of subsequent events.'

((1953) 32 ATC 402 at 403 **case 25 para 5**)

The history of the company is then outlined, from its incorporation on 25 March 1897 over the subsequent 50 years up to the valuation date, noting the nature of the company and the nature of the shareholders ((1953) 32 ATC 402 at 404, **case 25 paras 9 and 10**).

The earnings of the company over a 36-year period from 1912 to 1947 are analysed, giving reasons for the very large profits during the years of the First World War (£797,437 in 1919; equivalent to £5.1 million at 2003 prices) and the very large profits, again, at the end of the Second World War (£1,110,928 profit for the year spanning the valuation date; equivalent to £24.1 million at 2003 prices). The use of the results for this last year is justified by Danckwerts J's comment:

'When the deceased died on 11 March 1948, the accounts for this last year were not finally completed, but it is fair to assume that information as to the approximate results of the year's trading would have been ascertained by a prospective purchaser.'

((1953) 32 ATC 402 at 404 **case 25 para 10**)

The dividends paid are then noted and the dividend cover commented upon ((1953) 32 ATC 402 at 404 **case 25 para 11**).

The cash requirements of the company and the necessity to finance replacement ships if trading was to continue was noted as reducing the cash available for distribution to shareholders ((1953) 32 ATC 402 at 404 **case 25 para 11**).

One of the expert witnesses sought assistance in the valuation of the shares for this unquoted company by a comparison with the prices of shares quoted on the London Stock Market. Danckwerts J commented:

'Mr Benson supported his evidence with various tables containing the figures relating to various companies whose shares had a quotation on the Stock Exchange , and other figures obtained from the Actuaries' Investment Index. Such tables are not without a value, as they provide some possible basis of comparison for the purpose of checking the calculations of a witness, but it is easy to attack them on the ground that the varying circumstances of the companies, and the difficulty of applying the prices of quoted shares to the shares of a private company not quoted on the Stock Exchange, may render the comparison of little value.'

((1953) 32 ATC 402 at 405 **case 25 para 15**)

The judge then considered the information that would be available to a hypothetical prospective unconnected purchaser of the shareholding. Evidence had been given by a director of the company as to the board's view of the financial weakness in the company at that time. Danckwerts J stresses the importance to the valuation of the availability of such information. He records:

'Mr Holt said that all the information which he had given in evidence would not have been given directly to a buyer of a small quantity of shares, but it would have been made available, in confidence, to a reputable firm of accountants, acting on behalf of a buyer and approved by the board of directors, with the result, as I understood the position, that the information so revealed would not be passed on to the buyer, but that his accountant would be in a position to advise him as to the prudence of the purchase and the price which could reasonably be offered for the shares.'

((1953) 32 ATC 402 at 406 **case 25 para 18**)

The statutory assumption of an open market was noted:

'... in a company in which the family are determined to retain control, it is obvious that a member or person selected by the directors would be bound to enforce a transfer at "the fair value" under article 25 of the Company's Articles of Association. I am bound to assume, however, that this provision in the articles was not being enforced, and that the shares were thrown open for purchase by anyone who was willing to buy them ... he will, when registered as a shareholder, be subject to the provisions of the articles restricting transfer.'

((1953) 32 ATC 402 at 409/410 **case 25 para 33**)

Danckwerts J then comments on the characteristic of the hypothetical unconnected purchaser specified by statute:

'I think the kind of investor who would purchase shares in a private company of this kind ... would, in my view, be the kind of investor who would not rush hurriedly into the transaction, but would consider carefully the prudence of the course, and would seek to get the fullest possible information about the past history of the company, the particular trade in which it was engaged and the future prospects of the company. I think that such a purchaser would consider the inter-war results of the company, the effect of the 1914 War on the company's trading and the heavy losses sustained in the years which followed that War. In my view, therefore, the evidence of the witnesses for the Commissioners of Inland Revenue is open to criticism in so far as it ignores or minimises unduly (as it seem to me) the history of that period in the company's trading.'

((1953) 32 ATC 402 at 410 **case 25 paras 33 and 34**)

Danckwerts J notes that the influence of a shareholder with a 6 per cent shareholding is minimal ((1953) 32 ATC 402 at 410 **case 25 para 33**).

In the concluding part of his judgement, Danckwerts J stands back and looks at the matter in the round stating:

'Taking the most intelligent guess that I can, I have come to the conclusion that these shares of John Holt & Co (Liverpool) Limited, if sold on the hypothetical open market which the authorities and the section in the Act require me to assume, would fetch a price of 19s a share.'

((1953) 32 ATC 402 at 410 **case 25 para 36**)

As an indicator of the feelings of the judge, the following exchange is illuminating:

Junior Revenue Counsel – 'The very fact that is hypothetical takes it out of the ordinary reason of fact.'

((1953) 32 ATC 402 at 413)

Danckwerts J – 'Of course it does. I will not say what I think about it. It might be rather rude!'

((1953) 32 ATC 402 at 413)

The judgement of Danckwerts J can be taken as a useful model for a valuation report. The scheme of the judgement is as follows.

1. Identify the shareholding and date.
2. Specify principles.
3. Summarise financial information.
4. State how the different pieces of information influence the valuation.
5. Conclude by giving a numerical value.

This model was quickly followed in subsequent cases, notably *McNamee v IRC* [1954] IR 214 **case 26** and *In re Lynall deceased* [1971] 3 All ER 914 **case 29**.

Judgement

References, example '(pg403)', are to (1953) 32 ATC 402.

1 **MR JUSTICE DANCKWERTS:** This is an appeal under Section 10 of the Finance Act 1894, against the decision of the Commissioners of Inland Revenue as to the value for the purposes of estate duty of ordinary shares in the capital of a private company known as John Holt & Co (Liverpool) Limited. The shares had been settled by a voluntary settlement dated 7 January 1947, made by Robert Longstaff Holt, who died on 11 March 1948, with the result that estate duty became payable, under Section 2 (1) (*c*) of the Finance Act 1894, on his death upon the principal value of the shares, and the appellants are the trustees of the settlement. The shares were 43,698 ordinary shares of £1 each. The settlement also included 11,643 6½ per cent preference shares of £1 each, but the value of these for the purposes of estate duty has been agreed at 21s a share. At the date of the settlement, and at the date of the death of Robert Longstaff Holt, the capital of the company was, £1,150,000 divided into 150,000 preference shares and one million ordinary shares of £1 each, of which 139,140 preference shares and 697,680 ordinary shares had been issued, so that the 43,698 ordinary shares included in the settlement formed a minority holding.

2 The articles of association of the company contain restrictions on the transfer of shares on more or less familiar lines, the essential features being that

unfettered transfer to non-members is prohibited as long as a member or person approved by the directors is willing to purchase the shares at the fair value to be certified (in the case of difference) by the company's auditor in accordance with article 26 of the articles of association. By article 31 the directors are given a general power to refuse to register a transfer.

3 Under Section 7 (5) of the Finance Act 1894, the principal value of any property is to be estimated for the purposes of duty

'to be the price which, in the opinion of the Commissioners, such property would fetch if sold in the open market at the time of the death of the deceased.'

But in this case the decision of the Commissioners of Inland Revenue is not final and conclusive on the question, as by Section 10 a right of appeal is given to any person who is aggrieved by the amount of any duty claimed by the Commissioners, whether on the ground of the value of any property or otherwise.

4 There was no quotation for any of the company's shares on the Stock Exchange, and they were all held by members of the Holt family or by trustees of family trusts.

5 The principles, on which the value of shares in a private company are to be valued for the purpose of estate duty, have been settled by the House of Lords in the case of *Commissioners of Inland Revenue v Crossman*. The House of Lords decided in that case (by a majority of three to two) that the facts that a shareholder by the articles of a company may be compelled to sell his shares at the 'fair value' ascertained in accordance with the articles, and that by the articles the directors may have power to refuse to register a transfer, must be ignored; but none the less it must be assumed that a purchaser will be bound by the company's articles once he is upon the register of members. The result is that I must enter into a dim world peopled by the indeterminate spirits of fictitious or unborn sales. It is necessary to assume the prophetic vision of a prospective purchaser at the moment of the death of the deceased, and firmly to reject the wisdom which might be provided by the knowledge of subsequent events.

6 In my task I have had the assistance of a number of experts on each side, who differ in their opinions in the manner in which experts normally do, and the frankest of them admitted that certain of his calculations were simply guesswork. It seems to me that their opinions are indeed properly described as guesswork, though of course it is intelligent guesswork, aided by the experience which they have gained by their work as stockbrokers or accountants. No possible suggestion can be made against the honesty of these witnesses, but their methods of calculation appear to me to be inevitably uncertain and controversial, and, in my view, statements by several of them that they would be ready to buy the shares at the price reached by them if they had had the opportunity some five years ago, must be discounted accordingly. None the less, I could not have approached my task without their valuable assistance, and my remarks must not be taken to belittle the efforts which have been made by them to provide an answer to a question to which no certain answer is possible.

7 By the terms of the Section I have to imagine the price which the property would fetch if sold in the open market. This does not mean that a sale by auction (which would be improbable in the case of shares in a company) is to be assumed, but simply that a market is to be assumed from which no buyer is excluded: see *(pg403)* Lord Justice Swinfen Eady in *Commissioners of Inland Revenue v Clay* at page 475. At the same time, the Court must assume a prudent buyer, who would make full inquiries, and have access to accounts and other information which would be likely to be available to him: see *Findlay's Trustees v Commissioners of Inland Revenue.*

8 With those principles in mind I approach the history of the company and the evidence of the witnesses in this case.

9 The company was incorporated on 25 March 1897, to take over the business of trading in West Africa, started in 1867 by John Holt with the assistance of two younger brothers. The company also owned ships, this side of the business having been started in 1869 with a 65-ton schooner, and in the period with which I am concerned the company owned five cargo ships, which also had accommodation for some passengers. The company was, during the material period, a private company, and all the shares were held by members of the Holt family or were vested in Holt family trusts, and there was a strong desire in the family to retain control of the company and the ordinary shares. The company, however, did become a public company on 15 September 1950, (which, of course, is two-and-a-half years after the death of the deceased) in connection with an issue to the public of 650,000 5 per cent first cumulative redeemable preference shares of £1 each.

10 The company owned a number of trading stores in West Africa, and the business consisted of purchasing and carrying to West Africa goods for sale there, and purchasing and re-selling the products of West Africa, the goods being carried in both directions in the ships owned by the company. The company's results have fluctuated considerably, apparently because of the variations in price of the commodities in which the company dealt, and the West African trade has been described as a particularly hazardous trade. The company has maintained a settled policy of 'making provision in the good years for the bad ones which must inevitably follow sooner or later.' Since 1921 the practice of the company has been to limit distributions on the ordinary shares to 5 per cent less tax, and to build up its reserves by accumulating surplus profits in good years. An exceptional cash capital bonus of $1\frac{1}{4}$ per cent was, however, paid in February 1948, out of the realisation of an investment. Figures which are available for the thirty-six years from 1912 to the year ending on

30 September 1947 enable the fluctuations in the company's profits to be appreciated. In 1914 there was a loss of £132,993, but in the war years 1915 to 1919 (inclusive) very large profits rising in 1919 as high as £797,437 were made. In the years 1920 to 1923, however, when the post-war slump occurred, very severe losses were incurred, eg £597,768 in 1921. It appears that the company was able to tide over this difficult period by means of the reserves accumulated during the profitable war years, when there was not the same confiscatory taxation that was adopted during the Second World War. In the subsequent years between the wars, except for a loss of £134,593 in the unfortunate year 1931, a modest profit, averaging not more than £45,000 a year, was made until 1937 and 1938, which were very successful years, including in one year a profit of £211,000. The war years again brought very large profits, but the policy of making provision by means of reserves for a post-war slump was severely handicapped by the heavy taxation of 'excess profits', so that though the profits reached the high figure of £762,285 in 1943 and the other years were little short of this, comparatively small sums were available for dividends and reserves after provision for such taxation. Some relief from taxation came in 1946 when the profit was £681,745 and in the year ending 30 September 1947, the profits reached the very high figure of £1,011,928. When the deceased died on 11 March 1948, the accounts for this last year were not finally completed, but it is fair to assume that information as to the approximate results of the year's trading would have been ascertained by a prospective purchaser.

11 The figures to which I have referred are partly taken from the table prepared by Mr HA Benson (one of the witnesses for the petitioners) from the company's profit and loss accounts, and partly from the figures given in the 1950 share issue prospectus, on which the witnesses for the Commissioners of Inland Revenue based their calculations. There are certain variations in these figures, but these are not large enough to affect the general picture which I have stated. A dividend of 5 per cent on the ordinary shares (which had not been exceeded in the years in question) required only some £22,000, and so the company's earnings during the years immediately prior to 1948 were amply sufficient to allow a much larger distribution to the shareholders, if large sums were not set aside for other purposes, such as reserves, including the cost of new ships. At this date two of the five ships owned by the *(pg404)* company were of an age which demanded their replacement. The company had a large overdraft at its bank which approached £1 million in 1947. It was really common ground that the company was overtrading, and that the large figures for profits in the years 1946 and 1947 reflected the contemporary inflation.

12 After beginning at as high a figure as £3 0s 0d a share, the value claimed by the Commissioners of Inland Revenue is now 25s per share, though the value formally determined by them was not that figure, but 34s per share. The figures given on behalf of the petitioners started at 11s 3d as the fair value stated by the company, and rose to the value of 17s 2d per share put forward in the petition and at the hearing. I am entitled, therefore, to assume that the principle value of the shares is one or other of these figures of 25s and 17s 2d, or some other value somewhere in between. It appears that a value of 17s 6d per share was agreed on the occasion of a death on 5 April 1943, and a value of 20s per share was agreed on the occasion of other deaths which occurred on 15 November 1945, and 3 June 1946, but a period of one-and-three-quarter years had elapsed since the later of those dates when Robert Longstaff Holt died on 11 March 1948.

13 I now turn to the evidence of the witnesses. The first witness on behalf of the petitioners was Mr Henry Alexander Benson of the firm of Cooper Brothers & Company, a chartered accountant with a knowledge of conditions in Africa as well as experience in this country. He said that the West African trade had had a very bad reputation in the last thirty or forty years, and referred to the riots following a boycott of European traders, which occurred in February 1948, shortly before the death of the deceased. He also referred to the devaluation of the French Colonial franc which occurred in January 1948, as another depressing factor. He considered that a purchaser of the company's shares would be interested primarily in the profits made by the company and the dividends likely to be paid in the future. In his view the war-time and post-war profits represented an artificial prosperity which in no circumstances would continue indefinitely, and he thought that a purchaser would observe the heavy losses suffered by the company after the First World War, and would be apprehensive that such a phase might be repeated. Mr Benson thought that the position in regard to the assets and liabilities of the company in 1946 and 1947 was very vulnerable, having regard to the large amount of the company's assets represented by stocks and the size of the company's overdraft. He said that a ratio of assets to liabilities of two to one was too low for a company of this character. The company's accounts showed the ratio to be 1.73 to 1 in 1946 and 1.55 to 1 in 1947.

14 Mr Benson thought that having regard to the steady dividend policy of the company a purchaser would count on a dividend at the rate of 5 per cent not being reduced, but on the other hand he would not expect it to be increased. Mr Benson thought that the absence of any quotation of the shares on the Stock Exchange and the restrictions on transfer to which the purchaser would be subject when he got on the register, were factors which would make a purchaser require a further $1\frac{1}{2}$ per cent of income yield in reaching the appropriate price for the shares.

15 Mr Benson supported his evidence with various tables containing the figures relating to various companies whose shares had a quotation on the Stock Exchange, and other figures obtained from the Actuaries' Investment Index. Such tables are not without a value, as they provide some possible basis of comparison for the purpose of checking the calculations of a witness, but it is easy to attack them on the ground that the varying circumstances of the companies, and the difficulty of applying the prices of quoted shares to the shares of a private company not quoted on the Stock Exchange, may render the comparison of little value. On this basis Mr Benson reached a figure of 15s

2d per share, and to this he added the sum of 1s 6d, making a figure of 16s 8d. The addition of 1s 6d represented Mr Benson's estimate of the allowance which a purchaser might make in his offer for the possibility sooner or later of the company's shares being offered to the public, with a resulting capital accretion in some way to the shares held by a previous purchaser. Mr Benson considered that the time for this event would be later rather than sooner, and this was one of the points on which his evidence differed considerably from that of the witnesses for the Commissioners of Inland Revenue, who considered that the issue of shares to the public would be sooner rather than later, and attributed a much greater value to this factor. Finally, Mr Benson added a further sixpence to his estimated price as representing the amount of the net dividend likely to be declared in respect of the year 1947. Thus the value which he placed upon the shares was 17s 2d a share.

16 Mr Benson expressed the view that the *(pg405)* prices of ordinary shares tended to follow the price of consols, and produced a graph which recorded the rise of consols to a peak in 1946, when ordinary shares in the company were valued for estate duty at 20s a share, and a subsequent fall in the price of consols which, if followed by the company's shares, would bring the price of these to less than 16s 8d by March 1948. Mr Benson's view was not accepted by the witnesses for the Commissioners of Inland Revenue in this respect.

17 Mr John Alphonse Holt is one of the petitioners, and he is a director and, at the present time, the chairman of the company. He had, of course, a complete knowledge of the affairs of the company, and he had lived in West Africa. His description of the company's business was that the company exported from West Africa all the products which West Africa produces, so far as possible, and imported into West Africa most of the merchandise which was required by the inhabitants of West Africa. Mr Holt made it plain that no increase on the dividend of 5 per cent on the ordinary shares of the company was contemplated by the board of directors in March 1948. He regarded the financial position of the company at that time as 'very unsafe'. The liquid condition of the company's assets had not improved since the accounts for 1946 had been published, and the company's overdraft had substantially increased. The stocks carried by the company had increased by 50 per cent. The company was in the position of having to restore practically the whole of its buildings in West Africa, and to replace before long the two of their five ships which had been built in 1929. But the company had no plans for putting the company's ordinary shares on the market in the foreseeable future.

18 One question of some importance dealt with by Mr Holt was how far a prospective purchaser would have been able to obtain information as to the company's position and prospects by inquiry from the directors. Mr Holt said that all the information which he had given in evidence would not have been given directly to a buyer of a small quantity of shares, but it would have been made available, in confidence, to a reputable firm of accountants, acting on behalf of a buyer and approved by the board of directors, with the result, as I understood the position, that the information so revealed would not be passed on to the buyer, but that his accountant would be in a position to advise him as to the prudence of the purchase and the price which could reasonably be offered for the shares.

19 Mr John Holt said that the large profits which the company had been making were frightening, because they represented the effect of inflation, and in March 1948, he thought the sellers' market was virtually disappearing, and a recession in trade was expected at any moment. In his view, as the company's reserves were in the form of the company's current trading assets the company was extremely vulnerable.

20 I take the evidence of Mr Frank Samuel next, because his evidence had some features in common with that of Mr Holt. Mr Samuel is chairman of the United Africa company, a very much larger company than John Holt & Company (Liverpool) Limited, carrying on trade in West Africa, and a subsidiary of Unilever Limited. Mr Samuel has had long experience of West African trading, and this led him to describe the trading risks in West Africa as immensely greater than in any other part of the world. These risks, he explained, were due to the prosperity of these territories being based on agriculture, and in some cases on some particular kind only, such as the culture of cocoa or ground nuts, so that they were affected by the wide fluctuations in the prices of the products and by growing conditions. In his view the necessity of traders in West Africa carrying heavy stocks at times of high prices represented a tremendous danger, because it was only a question of time when a break in prices would come. In 1946, 1947 and 1948 Mr Samuel expected that a break in prices was imminent, and his opinion was generally shared in the West African trade. Another adverse factor in his view was the growing tendency in West African countries to try to get trade away from European firms. Mr Samuel thought that the company might appear to be earning more money while in fact having 'a much worse time', because of the cost of replacing the company's assets and the level of taxation. He was of opinion that a buyer would not expect increased dividends to be paid by the company, because of the company's earnings in 1946 and 1947, if he knew anything about West African trade. He could not see how the company's shares could be attractive to a sur-tax payer or other purchaser looking forward to capital accretion.

21 By comparison with the quoted prices of shares in other companies Mr Samuel reached a percentage yield of 4.89, to which he added $1\frac{1}{4}$ per cent for weaknesses in the company's position compared with those companies, making a total required yield of 6.14 per cent. To this he thought *(pg406)* it was necessary to add a further 2.05 per cent to compensate for the lack of a quotation and difficulties of transfer, thus producing a yield figure of 8.19 per cent. This was equal to a value of 12s 2d ex dividend. Mr Samuel could not see any real possibility of capital appreciation sufficient to bring into account, and added nothing for this factor.

22 It was suggested in cross-examination to Mr Samuel, and I think it is a fair point, that an ordinary buyer would not have all the information on West African conditions which led him to take such a depressing view. Consequently, in my view, Mr Samuel's estimate of the value of the shares, so far as based on the unattractiveness of the company's ordinary shares to him, must be discounted by this consideration.

23 Mr Mark Richard Norman is a partner in Edward Stein & Company, merchant bankers, who are also managers of and advisers to investment trusts. He was provided with copies of the company's balance sheets and accounts, and extracts from the chairman's speeches and from the company's articles of association. He made inquiries from Mr Benson (who asked him to make a valuation) and also outside inquiries, but he said that if he had really been faced with the problem of buying these shares, he would have made longer inquiries. He was asked at what price he would have been willing to purchase 43,698 ordinary shares of the company on 11 March 1948, and his answer was that the highest price he would have paid was 15s per share ex dividend. His view was confirmed by all he had heard since March 1952, when he asked to make his valuation. Mr Norman thought that in March 1948, it was generally expected that a fall in prices was going to follow the post-war boom, and the reason it did not occur was the outbreak of the Korean War in 1950. In 1948 he would not have expected the dividend to be increased, because he did not think that the profits retained by the company after taxation were adequate – by a long way. After looking at the yield of other companies and the Actuaries' Investment Index, Mr Norman thought that, on an expected dividend of 5 per cent, a yield of half as much again – $2\frac{1}{2}$ per cent – would be looked for. This produced a required yield of $7\frac{1}{2}$ per cent and a price of 13s $4\frac{1}{2}$d per share. As this was an awkward figure, and he would have been anxious to help if the company had come to his firm in 1948 for help, he increased the price of 15s, which is equivalent to 6˘!˘T per cent yield on a 5 per cent dividend, and, therefore, he considered 15s per share a favourable price. He thought 25s an absurd price, and would not have paid anything like it.

24 Mr Roger Anthony Hornby is a director of Cazenove, Akroyds & Greenwood, an unlimited company carrying on business as stockbrokers, which specialises in the underwriting of new issues of capital, and in fact acted as London brokers to the issuing house of Baring Brothers when the issue of preference shares to the public was made by John Holt & Company (Liverpool) Limited in September 1950. Anticipating that a 5 per cent dividend was likely to be paid by the company, Mr Hornby deducted from a price of 20s, according to the practice of his firm when making valuations, 20 per cent for the absence of quotation on the Stock Exchange and marketability and for the restrictions on transfer, thus reducing the price to 16s cum dividend. Mr Hornby thought that 11 March 1948, following so closely upon the boycott and riots in West Africa, could not have been a worse time to try to place the company's shares.

25 Sir Harold Montagu Barton was the first witness called on behalf of the Commissioners of Inland Revenue. He is a very experienced chartered accountant with a long experience of the valuation of shares in public and private companies. Sir Harold Barton agreed that the company was, trading in a somewhat dangerous way, but he was not alarmed by the size of the company's overdraft in 1947, nor by the company's liquid assets being very much locked up in debtors and stocks and so forth. He considered that in this way the company's assets were profitably invested, and he even said that he regarded an overdraft as a healthy sign. In Sir Harold Barton's opinion, the predominant circumstance in arriving at the price for the shares would be the question of dividend yield and prospective dividend yield, and after that the earnings and the relation of the dividends to the earnings. Another factor which Sir Harold Barton took into consideration was the effective management of this old-established business. Sir Harold Barton took the extremely low yield figure of 3 per cent and on this basis reached a price of 33s 4d to which he added eightpence for the dividend expected for the year 1947, making a price of 34s.

26 Apparently Sir Harold Barton was impressed by the evidence of the petitioners' witnesses, and in particular Mr Holt's emphasis on the policy of restricting the dividends, to the extent of increasing his yield figure to 4 per cent, producing a price of 25s. On the other hand, Sir Harold Barton was *(pg407)* inclined to discount the danger of a post-war slump, and he said that everyone had learnt lessons from the experience after the First World War. But when I questioned him as to the steps which business men would take to avoid the difficulties experienced after the First World War, he was only able to suggest a more cautious dividend policy and the keeping of more money in reserve, which seem to be measures tending to reduce the price of the shares, as contended by the petitioners. Sir Harold Barton thought Mr Holt's and Mr Samuel's expectations of a severe fall in prices unduly pessimistic, and considered that purchasers would not necessarily take a similar view. A great many of Sir Harold Barton's answers seemed to me somewhat vague, and it would appear that he had not examined the position of the company in any great detail. It is not at all clear that Sir Harold Barton considered the effect which the restrictions on transfer of shares contained in the company's articles of association would have on the purchaser.

27 Mr Charles Ian Ritchie Hutton is another experienced chartered accountant. In his view, the main factors affecting a prospective purchaser were the rate of dividend which he expected to receive on the shares, the prospects of capital appreciation and the restrictions on transfer. He thought that a purchaser would expect to secure a dividend of not less than 5 per cent, and would expect to receive a larger dividend, but in view of the statements made by the board of directors he might expect to wait a year or so before he had a substantial increase. Mr Hutton approached the question of capital appreciation on the basis of the strong probability that in the near future the company would have to go to the public for money in one shape or another. He would make some allowance for restrictions on marketability. Mr Hutton's method was to divide his valuation into two parts: (1) a fixed element representing a dividend of 5 per cent and (2) a contingent element, in which he attempted to give effect to his estimates of contingencies affecting the price of the shares. He reached a price of 18s for his fixed element on the basis of a yield figure of just under 4 per cent from the Actuaries' Investment Index in respect of 5 per cent preference shares and an addition of $1\frac{1}{2}$ per cent for restrictions on transfer, thus assuming a 5 per cent yield. But having regard to the price of 21s, which had been agreed between the parties for the $6\frac{1}{2}$ per cent preference shares of the company he reduced his figure from 18s to 16s 2d. It appeared that this corresponded, in his view, with the figure of 15s 8d reached by Mr Benson (before he added 1s 6d for the contingencies) and with the 16s reached by Mr Hornby, and consequently, so far, there was very little difference between the respective valuations.

28 But then Mr Hutton proceeded to assume that the dividend must rise to 10 per cent, and in his calculations the additional 5 per cent represented a further 16s 2d. This (contingent) 16s 2d Mr Hutton discounted by 25 per cent to compensate for delay and uncertainty, and allowing against these contingencies (on the credit side) the prospects of a further issue of shares by the company. It appeared that this deduction of 25 per cent could not have any mathematical or scientific basis, and was purely guess-work. This reduced the second or contingent 16s 2d to 12s 1d, and made Mr Hutton's valuation 28s 3d. He said that in March 1948, he would have advised a purchaser to buy at that price, and if offered the shares at 25s, he would have marshalled the resources of his family and friends in order to purchase. Mr Hutton discounted the effects of the boycott and riots in West Africa in February 1948, and the apprehensions for the future expressed by Mr Holt and Mr Samuel, and Mr Hutton actually said that 'there are no bad risks in the Commonwealth these days', which I find a very surprising statement.

29 Mr Thomas Austin Hamilton Baynes, another chartered accountant, had made a special study of the valuation of shares in private companies, and had read papers on the subject at meetings in many parts of England. He was a frank and attractive witness. The first thing that Mr Baynes looked at was the 5 per cent dividend, and he looked at the profits for a period of ten years up to and including 1947, because that happened to include two pre-war years and two post-war years. He found that the average profits for this period were £524,744. This figure he discounted by 25 per cent, because, as I understood, the very high profits of 1947 were not likely to be maintained, and this gave him a figure of £393,558, which he regarded as approximately twice the pre-war profit. He admitted that the deduction of one quarter from the average of ten years was made for no particular reason, but he was trying to get at some kind of guesswork figure for the future profits. It seems to me, moreover, that the years to which Mr Baynes confined his average might well produce a misleading result, because the years selected were the war years of exceptionally high profits and the years of post-war inflation; and the two pre-war years, 1937 and 1938, were years of *(pg408)* unusually high profits not at all typical of the years between the two wars.

30 Mr Baynes thought that the dividend paid by the company was quite unrealistic, having regard to the profits earned, but he thought it very unlikely that the company would remain a private company for long. He reached the conclusion that an investor would require an $8\frac{1}{2}$ per cent yield. He thought that the company would be likely to distribute a third of its profits with a view to a forthcoming issue of shares to the public. This represented a sum of £131,000, which was subject to the preference dividend of £9,004, leaving a figure of £122,000 and possible dividend on the ordinary shares of $17\frac{1}{2}$ per cent. This gave Mr Baynes, on an $8\frac{1}{2}$ per cent yield, a price of £2 1s per share. He thought that the type of investor who would be attracted was the sur-tax payer, looking for a capital profit. Apparently, he thought that such an investor would be prepared to pay 30s 9d in the expectation of a rise to £2 1s and a capital accretion of 10s 3d or about 33`!`S per cent on his investment. So he took a price of 30s, which included the prospective dividend for the year 1947. It is clear that, if the figure taken by Mr Baynes for the average profit, £393,558, was unreasonable for any reason, all his calculations, by which he reached his selling price of 30s per share, would be affected. It appears, also, that he had not paid any attention to the way in which heavy war-time taxation had affected the ability of the company to place money to reserve to meet future capital expenditure and the possibility of a post-war slump. Mr Baynes made no allowance for the lack of a quotation on the Stock Exchange and restrictions on transfer, because, he said, he had approached the problem of valuation in such a way that these considerations did not really affect the position.

31 Mr Henry Samuel Loebl is the senior partners in the firm of Montagu, Loebl, Stanley & Company, stockbrokers, and he had been a member of the Stock Exchange since 1904. Mr Loebl was very much affected by the personalities of those connected with the management of a company. He said that if he were satisfied with the integrity and ability of the men who ran the company, he would go no further. He appeared to have a touching confidence in the likelihood of business ability being reproduced in successive generations of Holts, as in the case of the Brookes in Brooke, Bond & Co Limited, the tea producers and dealers. When he looked at the company's balance sheets, he looked particularly at the assets in relation to capital and the reserves, and, one other thing, cover for the dividend which was being paid. He did not anticipate particularly increased dividends in the case of John Holt & Co (Liverpool) Limited. It appeared that he thought that a conservative policy of limitation of dividends was likely to benefit the shareholders in some form or another. He was not troubled with abstruse calculations. The question he asked himself was 'Is this a firm in which I would like to be a sleeping partner?' Having answered that in the affirmative, he reached a price of 28s to 29s per share, as far as I can see, by some process of intuition. Then it occurred to him that the Commissioners of Inland Revenue, by whom he was instructed, would want something more than this, and so he looked for some other company to form a guide, and took Brooke, Bond & Co Limited. He admitted that many people might think that there was no real basis for comparison in the companies, but it was 'the nearest thing in which he held shares'. He came to the conclusion that Brooke, Bond & Co represented a better investment, and so lowered his figure for the shares of John Holt & Co (Liverpool) Limited to 25s per share. He said that he himself would have been prepared to purchase the shares at 25s or a bit more in case of competition; and if Mr Benson had offered him the shares at 17s 2d he would probably have fainted. Matters like the boycott and riots in West Africa, in Mr Loebl's view, would not affect the price, and non-marketability or restrictions on transfer did not worry him at all. Dividend yield was a matter of indifference to him. He dismissed Mr Samuel's anxieties as to the future with the remark 'Personally I never think there is a risk of falling prices'.

32 That really completes the evidence, for I need not deal with the evidence of Mr Frederick William Gower, an accountant of the Board of Inland Revenue, who was merely called to deal with some disputed matters of detail in regard to the figures appearing in certain tables.

33 As I have already indicated, the problem to be decided is purely hypothetical, because, in a company in which the family are determined to retain control, it is obvious that a member or person selected by the directors would be bound to enforce a transfer at 'the fair value' under article 25 of the Company's Articles of Association. I am bound to assume, however, that this provision in the articles was not being enforced, and that the shares were thrown open for purchase by anyone who was *(pg409)* willing to buy them. Now, it is plain that the shares do not give a purchaser the opportunity to control the company, or to influence the policy of the directors to any great extent, as the shares available only represent 43,698 shares out of 697,680 ordinary shares which had been issued. Any purchaser, therefore, would be dependent upon the policy of the directors, so long as they should have the support of the general body of the shareholders. I think the kind of investor who would purchase shares in a private company of this kind, in circumstances which must preclude him disposing of his shares freely whenever he should wish, (because he will, when registered as a shareholder, be subject to the provisions of the articles restricting transfer) would be different from any common kind of purchaser of shares on the Stock Exchange, and would be rather the exceptional kind of investor, who had some special reason for putting his money into shares of this kind. He would, in my view, be the kind of investor who would not rush hurriedly into the transaction, but would consider carefully the prudence of the course, and would seek to get the fullest possible information about the past history of the company, the particular trade in which it was engaged and the future prospects of the company. I think that such a purchaser would consider the inter-war results of the company, the effect of the 1914 War on the company's trading and the heavy losses sustained in the years which followed that war.

34 In my view, therefore, the evidence of the witnesses for the Commissioners of Inland Revenue is open to criticism in so far as it ignores or minimises unduly (as it seems to me) the history of that period in the company's trading. The possibility of losses due to some severe fall in prices emphasises the importance of reserves, and I do not see how anyone considering the financial situation of the company could properly ignore the effects of inflation on the value of money and the way in which the building-up of adequate reserves to meet the difficulties likely to be caused by a slump in prices had been handicapped by the enormous sums required to be taken from profits for taxation in the years of the Second World War, and the way in which the provision for the replacement of capital assets, such as ships, had been made more difficult by allowances for depreciation being made on the basis of original cost and not the expense of replacement. In my view these matters, as well as the fluctuating nature of West African trading, would be likely to have a greater effect upon the mind of the hypothetical purchaser than was admitted by the witnesses for the Commissioners of Inland Revenue. I rule out of consideration the knowledge provided by the passage of time since 11 March 1948, that the company's dividend on ordinary shares has not been increased from 5 per cent and that the company has been able to avoid a public issue of ordinary shares by launching an exceedingly successful issue of new preference shares in September, 1950.

35 But I think that the witnesses for the Commissioners of Inland Revenue have over-valued the prospects of an increased dividend and of the issue of ordinary shares in the future on 11 March 1948. On the other hand, owing to the fall in the value of money, 5 per cent on the ordinary shares did represent a much smaller return in fact to the members of the family than that dividend represented to pre-war years, and there might have been pressure by the family in 1948 or later to increase the dividend having regard to the ample earnings of the company. Moreover, some possible hypothetical purchaser might well have thought that the company would be forced to raise further capital by an issue of ordinary shares to the public instead of adopting the method of an issue of preference shares, or debentures, or unsecured notes. Any such anticipation could have no more certainty than a guess. But I think that the petitioners' witnesses have undervalued this element in the price which the hypothetical purchaser might pay in this hypothetical open market.

36 Having carefully considered the evidence which has been given, including such assistance as may be gained from the various tables which have been put in and the various comparisons with the prices of shares of other companies quoted on the Stock Exchange (so far as any useful deductions can be made from these), and making the most intelligent guess that I can, I have come to the conclusion that these shares of John Holt & Co (Liverpool) Limited, if sold on the hypothetical open market which the authorities and the section in the Act require me to assume, would fetch a price of 19s a share. Accordingly, I determine the principal value of the 43,698 ordinary shares in the company to which this appeal relates to be 19s multiplied by the number of shares, and the resulting figure is, I think, £41,513 s. The amount of the estate duty payable on this sum can, no doubt, easily be determined. *(pg410)*

Case 26
McNamee v IRC

[1954] IR 214

High Court

12 January, 5 February 1954

The price at which shares are actually sold is not automatically the market value to be used for a valuation for a fiscal purpose.

Where there are actual sales of shares, the sale price achieved can be of use in the valuation but is only one of a number of items of information that require to be analysed in determining a value under the provisions of the statutory hypothesis.

Thomas McNamee died on 17 October 1950. In his estate were 175 Convoy Woollen Company Ltd ordinary shares, which he had purchased in 1946 for £1 per share. The shares were sold by the executors three months after the death of Thomas McNamee at a price of £1 10s per share. Other transactions in the company's shares between persons acting at arm's length had taken place at prices ranging between £1 and £1 5s.

Estate duty was payable. The Revenue valued the shares at £4 per share. The executors valued the shares at £1 10s per share.

In the High Court of Ireland, the judge, in what he referred to as 'this troublesome case', analyses the evidence of the expert witnesses.

Maguire J outlines the situation of the company around the valuation date and the shareholdings in issue ([1954] IR 214 at 216 **case 26 para 2**).

He notes that the articles restrict transfer but that in valuing the shares, it must be assumed that the purchaser should be entitled to be registered as a shareholder but take the shares subject to the articles of association ([1954] IR 214 at 217 case 26 para 5).

Maguire J described the circumstances of the hypothetical sale that is the subject of the valuation in these words:

> 'I have imagined a sale in the open market at which this small lot of shares would be offered, the number of prospective purchasers,

prudent and cautious, these share would attract, the exhaustive enquiries into the history of the company they would make, their examination of the balance sheets, the dividends, the dividend earning capacity of the company, the dividend policy of the directors, the capital resources and liabilities of the company, the company's reserves, the necessity of making provision for worn-out machinery and plant, and the replacement of machinery and plant that was out of date and obsolete, the business difficulties of the company, its new and vigorous competitors in changing markets, the uncertainties of the woollen trade, the rise and fall of the prices of wool in world markets, the effect of these prices upon the company's stocks of raw material and manufactured goods, the continuance of the company's export business, not to speak of other things that might occur to a prudent and cautious investor willing to consider a purchase of these shares with the clog as to alienation attaching to them when the purchase and registration is complete. Strange as it may seem, these topics have been the subject of evidence before me.'

([1954] IR 214 at 219 **case 26 para 9**)

The business of the company is then described, with reference to changing prices and the cost of works necessary to continue the company's business ([1954] IR 214 at 220 **case 26 para 10**).

The dividend policy is identified ([1954] IR 214 at 220 **case 26 para 10**).

The evidence of two expert witnesses as to the financial performance of the company was considered ([1954] IR 214 at 222/223 **case 26 paras 11 and 12**).

The circumstances and prices of actual sales were noted ([1954] IR 214 at 224 **case 26 para 13**).

The break-up value is computed ([1954] IR 214 at 225 **case 26 para 15**).

The judge concludes by valuing the shares at £1 12s 6d ([1954] IR 214 at 229 **case 26 para 21**).

The judgement in this case follows the scheme notes above in *Re Holt*. The judge's decision is, in effect, a valuation report which concludes by stating a numerical value.

Judgement

References, example '(pg215)', are to [1954] IR 214.

1 **MAGUIRE J:** 5 February. This is a petition pursuant to s10 of the Finance Act 1894 by Jeremiah McNamee, executor of the above-named Thomas McNamee, deceased, by way of appeal from an assessment of valuation for estate duty of the value of 175 £1 ordinary shares in the Convoy Woollen Company, Limited. The Revenue Commissioners estimated and assessed the value of the shares at £4 per share. The *(pg215)* petitioner claims a declaration that the value of each share be determined at £1 10s 0d.

2 The facts in so far as they are not in controversy are simple enough. Thomas McNamee was a retired mill-worker in the Convoy Mills. He died on the 17 October 1950, possessed of 175 ordinary shares in the Convoy Woollen Company Limited. By his will, he bequeathed all his property to his three children, his two daughters and his son, the petitioner. Probate of his will was granted to the petitioner forth of the Principal Registry of the High Court of Justice on the 3 August 1951. The value of the estate for estate duty purposes was stated to be approximately £1,000, but its final valuation awaits the determination of this appeal. The Convoy Woollen Company Limited was incorporated on the 19 December 1904, under the Companies Acts 1862 to 1900, as a public company limited by shares with a share capital of £50,000 in 50,000 ordinary shares of £1 to carry on the business *inter alia* of manufacturers of woollen cloth and woollen goods. It acquired and took over the business of an earlier company which had been incorporated in 1887. At the date of the death of Thomas McNamee, the issued capital of the Company consisted of 15,000 5 per cent preference shares of £1 each and 50,000 ordinary shares of £1 each. Clause 25 of the articles of association of the Company provides: – 'The directors may decline to register any transfer of shares without assigning any reason therefor.' Clause 28 of the articles provides for the registration of transferees 'if the transferee be first approved by the directors.' The shares of the Company are not dealt with on any stock exchange. They have no market quotation.

3 The 175 shares, the value of which is in issue, were purchased by Thomas 3 McNamee, deceased, in 1938 at £1 each. The transfer to him was registered on the 13 December 1938. They were sold in 1951 by the petitioner through his solicitor. Mr McNulty, to a Mr Kilpatrick at £11 10s 0d each. The sale was negotiated early in the year 1951 and the transfer to Mr Kilpatrick was registered on the 19 September 1951. Mr Kilpatrick had some short time before been appointed a director of the Company.

4 The Finance Act 1894, s1, enacts that estate duty shall be levied and paid upon the principal value, ascertained as thereinafter provided, of all property which passed on the death of every person after the commencement of the Act at the rates thereinafter mentioned. Sect 7 enacts the manner of 'determining

the value of any estate for the purpose of estate duty.' Sub-sect 5 converts value into price, and enacts that the principal value of any property *(pg216)* shall be estimated to be the price which, in the opinion of the Commissioners, such property would fetch if sold in the open market at the time of the death of the deceased,' that is to say, the price estimated to be obtainable on an assumed sale. The Commissioners have exclusive jurisdiction to estimate that price in the first instance. Sect 10, sub-s 1, provides that any person aggrieved by the amount of duty claimed by the Commissioners, on the ground of the value of any property, may appeal to the High Court, and the amount of duty shall be determined by the High Court; with a further appeal by leave under sub-s 2.

5 The legal considerations which must govern the determination of the value of the property for the purposes of the Act were laid down by the Court of Appeal in Ireland in *Attorney-General v Jameson*. It was held in that case that the principal value of the shares ought to be estimated at the price which, in the opinion of the Commissioners of Inland Revenue, they would fetch if sold in the open market on the terms that the purchaser should be entitled to be registered and should be registered as the holder of the shares, and should take and hold them subject to the articles of association, including the articles relating to the alienation and transfer of the shares of the Company. That case did not come before the Court on an appeal under s10 of the Finance Act 1894, but on an information by the Attorney-General for the determination of the manner in which such value was to be ascertained.

6 *Jameson's Case* was followed by Mr Justice Hanna in *Smyth v Revenue Commissioners*. It was approved of in the House of Lords in *Inland Revenue Commissioners v Crossman and Others*. In Scotland, the same point arose in *Salvesen's Trustees v Commissioners of Inland Revenue* and Lord Fleming took the same view as that which had been taken in the Irish Court of Appeal. In *In re Holt, Deceased; Holt v Inland Revenue Commissioners* the principles already laid down were applied by Mr Justice Danckwerts. The learned judge accepted the law as laid down in *Inland Revenue Commissioners v Crossman and Others*. At p 1492, he says: – 'By the terms of section 7, I have to imagine the price which the property would fetch if sold in the open market. This does not mean that a sale by auction (which would be improbable in the case of shares in a company) is to be assumed, but simply that a market is to be assumed from which no buyer is excluded: see *Inland (pg217) Revenue Commissioners v Clay*, per Swinfen Eady LJ. At the same time, the Court must assume a prudent buyer who would make full inquiries and have access to accounts and other information which would be likely to be available to him: see *Findlay's Trustees v Inland Revenue Commissioners*.'

7 While the law on the construction of s7, sub-s 5, of the Finance Act 1894, may now be regarded as settled, it is noteworthy that it has caused acute legal controversy and a great divergence of judicial opinion. In 1904, the Court of King's Bench in Ireland, consisting of Palles CB and Justices Boyd and Kenny, in *Jameson's Case*, held by a majority that in estimating such principal value

regard was to be had by the Commissioners to the special provisions in the articles of association with reference to alienation and transfer of shares of the company and as to the 'fair value' thereof. Palles CB dissenting held that the valuation of the shares should be based upon a fictitious, not an actual, sale in the open market excluding the consideration of such provisions in the articles of association as would prevent a purchaser at the sale from becoming a member of the company and registered as such in respect of the shares purchased by him at such suppositious sale. Neither of these views was accepted by the Court of Appeal in Ireland in their decision in 1905 already mentioned. In 1934, the Court of Appeal in England in *Crossman's Case*, reversing Mr Justice Finlay, a very distinguished judge in revenue cases, held by a majority (Lord Hanworth dissenting) that every ordinary share of the company must be regarded as containing as a necessary incident the obligation (when it was being sold) to offer it through the agency of the company to the shareholders at the articles price. The hypothetical sale in the open market required by s7, sub-s 5, of the Finance Act 1894, for the purpose of estimating the principle value of shares on the death of a shareholder did not justify the fixing of a price without reference to that necessary incident. The articles price as at the date of the death of the shareholder must, therefore, be taken as the value of the shares for the purpose of estate duty. The House of Lords in *Crossman's Case* by a majority (Lord Russell of Killowen and Lord MacMillan dissenting) reversed this decision, approved of the decision in *Attorney-General v Jameson* and *Salvesen's Trustees v Inland Revenue Commissioners* and laid down the law as I have already *(pg218)* stated. The preamble to the Act of 1894 (if one may look at it merely from the point of view of historic interest) follows traditional verbiage and refers to the grant of estate duty to her Most Gracious Majesty from her most dutiful and loyal subjects the Commons 'freely and voluntarily resolved to give and to grant unto Your Majesty the several duties hereinafter mentioned.' But the draftsmen of the Act itself have used words and terms which have puzzled, if not baffled, the minds of great legal authorities over two generations.

8 In the result, the translation of 'value' into 'price' has brought about this strange formula, which has been aptly described by various judges as an imaginary sale, to a hypothetical purchaser, in a hypothetical open market. The duty of determining the value of the property on this basis falls upon the Revenue Commissioners in the first instance in every case of this kind. It is an onerous duty. One may sympathise with them in their task.

9 As Lord Ashbourne said in *Jameson's Case*: – 'An actual sale in open market is out of the question. A feat of imagination has to be performed.' I have imagined a sale in the open market at which this small lot of shares would be offered, the number of prospective purchasers, prudent and cautious, these shares would attract, the exhaustive enquiries into the history of the Company they would make, their examination of the balance sheets, the dividends, the dividend earning capacity of the Company, the dividend policy of the directors, the capital resources and liabilities of the Company, the Company's reserves, the necessity of making provision for worn-out machinery and plant, and the replacement of machinery and plant that was out of date and obsolete, the business difficulties of the Company, its new and vigorous competitors in changing markets, the uncertainties of the woollen trade, the rise and fall of the prices of wool in world markets, the effect of these prices upon the Company's stocks of raw material and manufactured goods, the continuance of the Company's export business, not to speak of other things that might occur to a prudent and cautious investor willing to consider a purchase of these shares with the clog as to alienation attaching to them when the purchase and registration is complete. Strange as it may seem, these topics have been the subject of evidence before me. I have in my imagination a large number of interested would-be purchasers having made these exhaustive enquiries, competing for these shares. But l cannot entirely obliterate another viewpoint in this imaginative effort, *(pg219)* namely, that when all these enquiries are made, and the purchase of this lot of 175 shares is considered worth while, there might be few purchasers, some of whom would wish to secure the shares on very favourable terms.

10 The evidence for the petitioner is as follows: – Marshall T Cromie is managing director of the Company for four years and secretary since 1945. He produced and handed in the list of transfers of shares since July 1946, and the transfers. The highest price paid on any transfer was £1 10s 0d. Articles and memorandum of association handed in. 'We buy our raw materials wool and worsted yarn. We process the wool and manufacture it into cloth. We might purchase wool to the value of £350,000, sometimes as high as £400,000. Payment is in cash in fourteen days for wool, one month from date of invoice for worsted yam. No discounts in either case. In certain times of the year we have to run an overdraft. We have to hold reserves against possible stock losses; that we regard as essential. Fluctuations in the price of raw materials make this necessary. Before the Korean War prices rose steeply – from 90 pence per lb to 350 pence per lb within one year. They dropped from 350 pence to 120 pence per lb within six to nine months. In any period like that, the tendency is for customers to hold off buying for a further fall. The man-in-the-street stops buying. This leaves large stocks on our hands and in the hands of our customers. Customers find it difficult to dispose of stocks. The tendency is for customers to hold up delivery of goods on order.' He explains the difficulties of the business. 'We could quite easily have wiped out our complete capital and reserves in one year. Since 1883 we have been working in the same premises with various additions. We have had to make improvements in buildings and machinery. Electric wiring was done piecemeal over a number of years. We had to consider a complete re-wiring of the mills at a cost of £45,000.' A list of machinery replacements was put in evidence and totals £60,000; also, a list of work done and contemplated. £45,000 of this has been spent on wiring. Work on the boilers has cost £26,000 to replace old Lancashire boilers. The articles of association contain power to restrict the transfer of shares. No case has occurred of a refusal, but in one case the Company did not consent to transfer of shares. There are just three holdings of shares where the persons concerned

are not related to the original founders. There are 71 shareholders altogether. The three non-family shareholders would not exceed 3,000 shares. The present capital is: *(pg220)*

Issued 50,000 ordinary shares of £1.00 each
Issued 5,000 5 per cent cumulative preference shares of £1.00 each
Authorised 60,000 ordinary shares of £1.00 each
Authorised 20,000 5 per cent cumulative preference shares of £1.00 each

The shares were never quoted on the Stock Exchange. The dividend policy is to maintain its dividend at 15 per cent and to maintain its reserves. That policy has been operated for a great many years. Prior to the 15 per cent dividend, a $12\frac{1}{2}$ per cent dividend was paid. That was paid for a number of years also. Policy of directors is to maintain and increase reserves. Same policy was in force when the dividend was $12\frac{1}{2}$ per cent. The overdraft is £60,000 at present. There are no circumstances in the trade to-day to justify a departure from the Company's policy. Very definitely not at the time of the death of McNamee. There was no reason to anticipate a change in that policy or to expect an increase in dividend. There is necessity for replacements given rise to by wear. There is the necessity to keep in touch with modern trends. There is increasing competition at home and in exports. 'We are pressed to increase exports. All these steps are necessary to enable us to do so. Failure to expend these monies would render us unable to compete with more modern establishments inside and outside the country. It is a recurring necessity due to technical advances, both in process and machinery. Costs are four times as much as original. There will not be any appreciable reduction in the price of machinery – the tendency is the other way. There are a half-dozen families or more (owners of the shares). There have been extensions due to marriages. The transfers are limited to people who have business connections, suppliers of worsted yarns – not customers merely. I suggest that McNamee transfer is of value for purpose of assessment. The following numbers from list are of assessment value: 203, 248, 261, 266, 267, 269, 270. Owner could have tried to sell to anyone he liked. No case has arisen of a refusal of the Board to register a transfer. IB Carless was a daughter of JB Weir Johnston. John Moffat was an existing shareholder, Kilpatrick a director. I don't think any outsiders have come in. The Raphoe Electric Lighting shares may have been offered to outsiders; I cannot say. Fluctuations are reflected in the profits of the Company. Fluctuations in the price of wool are reflected in the profits of the Company. The profits in the three years before the death of McNamee *(pg221)* are stable. In those years there were not the violent fluctuations of 1950/1951. In general you make more profits during a war. The after-effects of a war can lead to a disaster. In 1950 our reserves were higher. Aftermaths of war are 1, great risk of stock loss, 2, spare parts, or new machinery not available. It has to be made good. We did not replace them after the first Great War. The Company was smaller during the first war and after. Machinery and plant were considerably extended between the two World Wars. Additional machinery was put in. The Company has always paid a dividend. The electric wiring is merely replacement and machinery is replacement. Machinery is worn out and run down. Some of it is out of date. New machines will be better. Technical advances are more rapid now. It is a protected industry. It is a measure of protection we have to justify. New mills have been set up, and new machinery. This we have to compete with.' Annual accounts and balance sheets 1944/45 to 1949/50 were handed in.

11 Mr Eustace Shott, accountant, of Messrs Craig, Gardner and Co, has great experience. He has known this Company for a long time and has been doing its audit for fifteen years. He gave the following figures from the accounts: -

Profits from 1945 to 1950: -

Dividend		
To 31 March	1945 – £11,352	10 per cent
To	1946 – 11,719	10 per cent
To	1947 – 11,833	10 per cent
To	1948 – 25,423	$12\frac{1}{2}$ per cent
To	1949 – 21,116	15 per cent
To	1950 – 22,774	15 per cent
Reserves:		
1945	General reserve was	£47,000
1946		£50,000
1947		£55,000
1948		£60,000
1949		£65,000
1950		£75,000
The stock-in-trade was:		
March 1945	£94,921	
March 1950	£73,950	
March 1951	£168,189 **(pg222)**	

He examined the accounts and balance sheets of the Company over many years, its earning capacity,: the dividends policy of the directors, the conservation of reserves against losses, renewals and replacements of worn-out and out-of-date plant. He says 'a buyer or investor would be principally interested in return. He would certainly want a highish rate of dividend. The ordinary investor would not be interested. I wouldn't have advised clients of mine to purchase them at all. The clause requiring consent of the directors, would prevent purchasers reselling readily. I think the price he got was very full and fair value for his shares considering my own intimate knowledge of the affairs of this Company, and the ordinary certainty that looking into the future this Company will have to adhere to the policy it has so long maintained in regard to dividend distribution and ploughing back profits for the maintenance of the business. A protective tariff can have more disadvantages than advantages. It has all kinds of obligations. This Company always had a certain amount of export trade; tariff protection limits your profit all the time. My figure for the share is £1 10s 0d.'

12 Mr Patrick Butler, of the firm of Butler Chance and Co, an accountant, and President of the Institute of Chartered Accountants, says he is not connected with the Company. He has examined and summarised the accounts of the Company from 1944/45 to 1951. He knew of the conservative manner in which the Company was run. He was aware of their conservative dividend policy. The information from the printed accounts bore out that view. 'In the textile industry the replacement of plant is very important. It is subject to obsolescence. It may have to be scrapped to provide for improvements in the process, also stock position has to be considered very carefully. Raw materials have to be stocked; if not stocked, the management is running grave risk. In 1948 the management was frightened of stock position. There was a reserve of £15,000 for stock that year; £5,000 in 1949; £5,000 in 1950. What a purchaser would ask is what is the security for my investment, and return on investment and liquidity of investment. I would say the security was very good on the balance sheet. He could look forward to a dividend of 15 per cent, but he couldn't look forward to an increased dividend. As to disposal of the investment, there is the control. The greatest price was £1 5s 0d prior to the death of deceased. I would have to advise him as to the apparent difficulty of realisation. 10 per cent is a reasonable rate to look for in companies of this kind. A dividend of 15 per cent would put £1 10s 0d *(pg223)* on the shares. That is reasonable. If it was a question of gaining control it might be worth more. But I wouldn't put more than a few shillings on that. It is difficult to be dogmatic as to the maintenance of its profits, a recession in world trade would affect this Company.' He was cross-examined at length by Mr Liston, but his evidence did not vary. At the conclusion of his evidence he said that taking all these matters into account, he put a valuation of £1 10s 0d on these shares.

13 Mr John McNulty, solicitor, of the firm of David Wilson and Co, Solicitors, Raphoe, says: – 'I purchased 150 of these shares in 1946 at £150. Registration no. 248. The parties were at arm's length. The dividend was 10 per cent. Registration no 261. That was a sale at arm's length. Weir to Carless, May 1949; JR Weir to IB Carless 777 ordinary shares for £971 5s 0d. Registration no 266, 19 March 1951, Raphoe Electric Light Co, John Moffat, 100 ordinary shares for £125. They were at arm's length. 19 September 1951, the McNamee sale was registered. In January, 1951, the McNamee sale was negotiated by me. It was not registered until the September following, registration no 269. It was the best price I could get. Mr Kilpatrick had recently been appointed a director. He wanted shares. He knew of the sale to Carless and he offered the same price.

I am certain he couldn't have got them at that price. This sale at £1 10s 0d was at arms' length. It was a completely commercial transaction. I am solicitor to the Company and I know a fair amount about its affairs. In ordinary cases I would consult the secretary as to the sale. That didn't happen in this case. I knew Mr Kilpatrick wanted the shares. We had a bit of a haggle. I pushed him up to £1 0s 0d. I couldn't get any more at all. The most I could get was the £1 10s 0d. I did not hawk them around. It was a sale to the most probable purchaser. The directors knew the shares were for sale. I got the highest price in the history of the Company.' That concluded Mr McNulty's evidence.

14 The evidence for the respondents was as follows: -

15 Mr Francis Cave, a chartered accountant of many years' experience in company work and seventeen years' experience in the Office of the Revenue Commissioners, was examined for the respondents. He examined carefully the accounts and balance sheets of the Company for six years. For the three years ending the 31 March 1950, there was a net profit of £69,314, an average profit of £23,105, which would provide a profit of 46.2 per cent. The total profit for three years after providing for the preference dividend would be *(pg224)* £22,605 for distribution or 45.21 per cent on the ordinary capital. He put in Tables 'B' and 'C'. He showed that the Company had built up its reserves from March 1944, £58,328 to £139,354 in March 1950. He came to the conclusion this was a highly successful Company worked on cautious lines. It is one of the few companies he has met in such a strong position. He tested it with the other companies mentioned by him and listed on the lists put in. On the assets on the balance sheets in March 1950 the value of the shares was £3 15s 9d. Nothing in the balance sheet for goodwill. This is sometimes called break-up value. It is not really so. This Company could pay 28.74 per cent dividend; on that basis the market price of the shares would be £5 17s 2d. The acid value is £315s 9d. That is a minimum. A reasonable figure for the price of the ordinary share is £4. This is a very reasonable figure. He agrees that a realisation of the assets might be postponed, but the value of the assets is still there and the allowance for a postponed sale would be small. He has not reviewed the history of the Company. There is not likely to be a sale of the assets in the foreseeable future. The Company might have made a public issue in 1950. It has been capably managed. The policy has been that the directors have been conservative. The management must have been very capable. The companies which he has compared are not woollen companies. There are twenty-two private companies in this industry. All are private companies or not quoted on the stock exchange. 'I try to put the Convoy Woollen Company on the stock exchange as of October 1950.' 'Do you agree there is nothing to show there is any likelihood of the Company distributing 28 per cent?' 'it is financially capable of doing it. There is a likelihood.' He does not say why or how he forms this opinion which appears to be contrary to the definite dividend-paying policy of the Company. He is trying to do his best to get the valuation to the best of his ability.

16 Mr Thomas H Scanlan, Chief Examiner in the Estate Dury Office, was the next witness. He is an experienced officer of the Department for many years –

some forty years in the Estate Duty Office. The dividend-earning capacity is the most important factor, following *Smyth's Case.* 'We considered all the surroundings and the background of the Company. With Mr Cave we picked out the lists of other companies.' He agrees with Mr Cave's figures. The other companies distribute 43 per cent of the balance available. He agrees with Mr Cave's figures and his figures *(pg225)* are the same figures. 'In the case of [JK] we had no stock exchange price for "B" shares. This industry is kept out of the hands of the public. There are some thirty-three or thirty-four private companies.' 'Have you dealt with the shares of these private companies?' he is asked. 'I am only four years dealing with this branch and I have not registered any of these cases.' He took this case over from his predecessor six months ago. 'In the case of a stock exchange share we accept the stock exchange price. This Company could pay 28 per cent.' 'Did you pay any regard to the policy of the directors?' 'If they do not distribute at 28 per cent it goes back into the Company. Inadequacy of dividends is an ordinary feature of private companies. The price we arrived at is unreal but very nearly correct, I agree. We do our best to evaluate the sale with all the facts of the case.'

17 Mr Maurice Abrahamson, member of the firm of Messrs Solomons, stockbrokers, Dublin Stock Exchange, gave evidence. He was consulted four weeks ago. He examined the accounts and balance sheets of the Company. 'The percentage of earnings the year before the death was 65 per cent. 15 per cent was paid in dividend. The general conditions of trade were then favourable. The Government floated a loan at $3\frac{1}{2}$ per cent successfully. Industrial stocks were standing high. The outlook generally was favourable. The increase in the price of wool was causing some concern. We thought it was going up too sharply. We were able to make a valuation of the shares on general principles, including conditions of trade and dividends. We extracted the figures of two companies, [JK] and [LM]. We found the position of the Convoy Woollen Company was superior to either of them – very much superior. We made allowance for the fact that those shares were readily saleable. We came to the conclusion that the shares of the Convoy Woollen Mills would have fetched on an open market £2 18s 0d. It is difficult to generalise the policy of Irish companies. The directors generally pay half of the profits available.' He explains to Mr McGonigal why he picked 'J K' only the 'A' ordinary shares. 'The 'B' ordinary are all held by the Industrial Credit Company. In the year after the death [JK] distributed a quarter of its profits. [JK] shares do not change hands frequently. They are well held. We had to assume that Convoy Woollen Company's shares would be available on the open market. It is a hypothetical approach and not a realistic approach. In October 1950 there was anxiety about the wool trade generally. The price of wool went up very high and then slumped. The *(pg226)* events as we now know them justified the policy of the directors of the Convoy Woollen Company. An investor would anticipate a similar policy in the directors. He would anticipate an increase in dividend. I did not take into account that a large sum would have to be spent on renewals and replacements. That would have affected a purchaser's decision. The figures on which we based our view contained no reference to capital commitments. I did not consider £45,000 for wiring at all. These figures would have depreciated the value of the shares by some shillings. They would have affected the buyer's mind. I was not told of the previous sales. Those were in a restricted market. Those shares might have been advertised in Donegal by word of mouth. I never heard of this Company until I was asked to advise about it. I then went into the history of the Company and its balance sheets as best I could. I have not known an investor to go into that. They are not capable. I would try to get the shares as cheaply as I could. There is always a margin between what the purchaser would give and what the vendor wants.'

18 I have considered carefully this evidence. I have had the advantage of seeing and hearing the witnesses. Without their assistance, without this evidence, I could not determine this case. On the view that I have formed, it will not be necessary to review this evidence at length. I do not propose to do so.

19 The Convoy Woollen Company is a well-managed concern with a long record of successful business. I have learnt its history. I am much impressed by its consistent tradition of sound business. It has always paid a dividend. Its profit-earning capacity, its conservative business policy, the conservative dividend-paying policy of its directors in the distribution of its profits, the somewhat rigid limitation of its dividends, its appropriation each year of large sums to reserves, its businesslike provision for contingencies and the uncertainties of trade, its careful outlook to the future are all established in the evidence of Mr Cromie, whose evidence I fully accept. Mr Cromie has given me the various dealings in the Company's shares. He has appraised their value at the time of Mr McNamee's death. Mr Shott is not merely an accountant of great experience; he is a particularly shrewd businessman whose opinion on these matters is entitled to the highest respect. I fully accept his evidence. Mr Patrick Butler impressed me much as a witness. He was very careful and cautious in considering and expressing his opinions. His evidence was of great assistance to me. I fully accept it. Mr McNulty's evidence deals with important *(pg227)* facts. He had a duty to discharge to his client, the petitioner, to obtain the highest price he could for the shares. His evidence is not challenged on cross-examination. It is not suggested that the sale to which he deposes was related in any way to an effort to reduce, or evade, the liability for estate duty. I formed the opinion that Mr McNulty was a trustworthy and reliable witness. It is only fair that I should say I am satisfied he fully discharged his duty to his client by obtaining the best price he could for the shares. I am satisfied that the sale by him of these shares to Mr Kilpatrick was a bona fide business transaction at the best price obtainable by him at the time and in the circumstances.

20 The evidence of Mr Francis Cave, Mr Thomas H Scanlan and Mr Abrahamson, who were examined on behalf of the Revenue Commissioners, was given with conspicuous fairness and propriety. It is mostly evidence of opinion and as such I have approached and considered it with the highest respect. It is based on the expectation of a much greater distribution of profits, a much higher dividend, a much smaller appropriation of profits to reserves than has hitherto appeared in any of the annual accounts and balance sheets in the Company's history. It has emphasised the profit-earning capacity of the Convoy Woollen Company. In that respect it is sound. The profit-earning capacity of the Company is and must always be of great importance. But its importance must be related to the consistent policy of this Company in relation to the limitation of dividends, the conservation of assets, and the appropriation each year of large sums from profits to reserves. It has, I think, overlooked many other, but very important matters, covered by the evidence of Mr Cromie and Mr Shott. Accepting, as I do, without qualification the evidence of Mr Cromie and Mr Shott, I regret that the evidence of the witnesses for the Revenue Commissioners cannot be reconciled with that evidence, which I have set out at length. It cannot be reconciled with the consistent history, dividend-paying policy, conservative policy as to reserves, and cautious provision for the future running through the whole of the Company's accounts. Mr Cave, Mr Scanlan and Mr Abrahamson have gone to great trouble to prepare comparative tables of other companies carrying on somewhat similar businesses, having stock exchange quotations for their shares. Those have been examined and explained. I am satisfied without going into details, but having considered all the evidence, that the analogies they have drawn from these other companies are far from complete, and that they are misleading. I am satisfied too that the inferences they ask me to draw *(pg228)* cannot fairly be drawn in the case of these shares in the Convoy Woollen Company. The affairs of each company must be considered in relation to its own position, its own difficulties, and its own domestic control. The affairs of the Convoy Woollen Company on the evidence before me are unique. I have no evidence of exactly similar companies before me. It would appear that such evidence is not available. I recognise fully that Mr Cave, Mr Scanlan and Mr Abrahamson were doing their best in the difficult circumstances of this case to appraise the value of these shares. If they have failed, as in my opinion they have failed in this case, to convince me on their evidence, they are not at fault. I cannot accept their valuations, and I cannot by any effort on my part approximate my valuation of these shares anywhere approaching the figures they have given.

21 Accepting Mr McNulty's evidence as to the bona fides of the sale of these shares to Mr Kilpatrick, and granting that this price of £1 10s 0d is the highest ever paid for these shares in the history of the Company, I still must bear in mind that this was not a sale in any real or imaginary open market. I must make allowance for a sale in an imaginary open market. It is here I find the evidence of Mr Shott and Mr Butler of great value. I have given anxious thought and consideration to this, perhaps, in some ways, the most difficult part of my task. I am satisfied that not more than £1 12s 6d – certainly not more than that – might have been obtained in the open market, an imaginary open market, for this lot of 175 shares. Accordingly I fix and determine the value of these shares at £ 1 12s 6d each.

22 I wish to add that I am greatly indebted to the learned counsel on each side for the assistance they have given me in this troublesome case. *(pg229)*

Case 27
Winter (Sutherland's Trustees) v IRC

(1961) 40 ATC 361

House of Lords

26 October 1961

In an asset based valuation, the valuer must consider the tax charge that would arise in the company if the company were to dispose of the assets for a consideration equal to the asset values used in the calculation.

An asset based valuation normally requires the current value of assets held by the company to be substituted for the historic cost that is recorded on the balance sheet. If the company were to dispose of such assets at their current value, it is commonly the case that a tax charge would arise to the company on the disposal (which may be tax payable on the capital gain or may be a clawback of capital allowances). This case considers the extent to which such a contingent liability should be brought into the calculation in order to estimate the market value of the shareholding.

Lord Guest states that the concept of market value is a price in the open market between a willing seller and a willing buyer ((1961) 40 ATC 361 at 369 **case 27 para 43**). Rather too much has been made of this statement. Lord Guest is simply stating a self-evident truth. Under the statutory hypothesis, the seller must be willing to sell, otherwise no sale price would be achieved. This is not the same as saying that the price must be high enough to make a reluctant seller into a willing seller and Lord Guest is most certainly not saying that the market value is a price between that offered by a willing buyer and that acceptable to make a seller willing to sell. It is on this point that English case law is distinguished from US case law. In the statute construed by the US courts the phrase 'willing seller' appears; UK statute does not have these words in any of the statutory valuation provisions.

Sir AM Sutherland died on 29 March 1953. In his estate were 98,700 ordinary shares of BJ Sutherland & Co Ltd, a controlling interest in a ship-owning company.

The company owned five ships, with an aggregate value at the valuation date of £1,150,000. Capital allowances had been claimed on the purchase cost of these ships, there being a capital allowance pool remaining of

£290,749 in aggregate. Hence, if the ships had been sold at their market value, there would have been a balancing charge leading to tax payable by the company of £270,079.

In his leading judgement in the House of Lords, Lord Reid outlines the statutory provision for the deduction of liabilities in assessing value for the purposes of estate duty ((1961) 40 ATC 361 at 361/362 **case 27 paras 2 and 3**).

He continued:

'The company would only have to pay tax if the law had not been altered, and if when the question arose there was in existence a Finance Act determining the rate of income tax. So there were two contingencies which had to be fulfilled, or conditions which had to be purified, before tax could be demanded from the company: the sums received for the ships must exceed the unallowed expenditure and there must be no relevant change in the law and no failure to enact a Finance Act. The question is whether in these circumstances there was a contingent liability of the company to pay tax. I cannot doubt that if a statute says that a person who has done something must pay tax, that tax is a "liability" of that person. If the amount of tax has been ascertained and it is immediately payable, it is clearly a liability; if it is only payable on a certain future date, it must be a liability which has "not matured at the date of the death, within the meaning of section 50(1)". If it is not yet certain whether or when tax will be payable or how much will be payable, why should it not be a contingent liability under the same section?'

((1961) 40 ATC 361 at 362 **case 27 paras 5 and 6**)

As the company was in Scotland, Lord Reid then states the meaning of 'obligations' as given in *Erskine's Institutes of the Law of Scotland*, published in the eighteenth century, noting that the statement had never been questioned during the two centuries since it was written.

'Section 50(1) of the Finance Act 1940 .directs the Commissioners to make an allowance for (or deduction in respect of) all liabilities of the company, and it divides liabilities, as one might expect, into three classes. First, where the liability is a sum immediately payable ... Secondly, the liability may be one which has not matured ... The third class is "contingent liabilities", which must mean sums, payment of which depends on a contingency, ie sums which will only become payable if certain things happen, and which otherwise will never become payable. Their calculation is impossible, so the Commissioners are to make such estimation as appears to be reasonable.'

((1961) 40 ATC 361 at 363 **case 27 para 9**)

In valuing shares on an asset basis, regard must, thus, be given to the tax liability that would arise on the gain that would be triggered if the assets were sold by the company at the values used in the valuation, as well as any other contingent liabilities.

Judgement

References, example '(pg361)', are to (1961) 40 ATC 361.

1 LORD REID: My lords, the appellants are the executors of the deceased Sir AM Sutherland who died on 29th March 1953. He owned 98,700 shares in BJ Sutherland & Co Ltd, and he controlled that company. Accordingly these shares had to be valued for estate duty purposes by reference to the value of the assets of the company, and not by reference to the market value of the shares at the date of his death. The company owned five ships, of which the value at that date is agreed to have been £1,150,000. The cost of these ships had been considerably less, and the company had received large capital and annual allowances so that the expenditure unallowed within the meaning of Section 297 of the Income Tax Act 1952, was only £290,749. Accordingly, if these ships had been sold when the deceased died, there would have been a balancing charge, which would have given rise to liabilities for income tax and profits tax amounting to £270,079. In fact the ships were sold somewhat later, and then the balancing charge gave rise to a liability of £370,000 for income tax and profits tax.

2 The question in this case is whether any account has to be taken of the fact that if these ships were sold for a price exceeding the unallowed expenditure, the excess would be subject to a balancing charge, I *(pg361)* need not consider profits tax, because the argument is the same as for income tax with a minor difference, which in my view is not material in this case. The question depends ultimately on the proper construction of the words 'contingent liabilities' in Section 50(1) of the Finance Act 1940, but before coming to that subsection I must briefly refer to certain other provisions.

3 Section 55 of that Act provides by subsection (1) that, where there pass shares of a company of which the deceased had control, the principal value of the shares

'... shall be estimated by reference to the net value of the assets of the company in accordance with the provisions of the next succeeding subsection.

(2) For the purposes of such ascertainment as aforesaid:

(a) the net value of the assets of the company shall be taken to be the principal value thereof estimated in accordance with the said subsection (5) [of Section seven of the Finance Act 1894], less the like allowance for liabilities of the company as is provided by subsection (1) of Section fifty of this Act in relation to the assets of a company passing on a death by virtue of Section forty-six of this Act, but subject to the modification that allowance shall be made for such a liability as is mentioned in paragraph (b) of that subsection unless it also falls within paragraph (a) thereof; ... '

Section 50 (1) provides:

'In determining the value of the estate for the purpose of estate duty the provisions of subsection (1) of Section seven of the Finance Act, 1894, as to making allowance for debts and incumbrances shall not have effect as respects any debt or incumbrance to which assets of the company passing on the death by virtue of Section forty-six of this Act were liable, but the Commissioners shall make an allowance from the principal value of those assets for all liabilities of the company (computed, as regards liabilities which have not matured at the date of the death, by reference to the value thereof at that date, and, as regards contingent liabilities, by reference to such estimation as appears to the Commissioners to be reasonable) other than:

(a) liabilities in respect of shares in or debentures of the company; and
(b) liabilities incurred otherwise than for the purposes of the business of the company wholly and exclusively.'

4 I need not set out the section of the Income Tax Act, 1952, dealing with balancing charges, because there was no dispute about their nature. If a trader claims and receives an initial allowance or annual allowances in respect of anything which he uses in his trade, there must be a reckoning with the Revenue when for any reason he ceases to use it in his trade. He may sell or scrap it, it may perish, or he may cease to carry on his trade. In any of these events the expenditure unallowed must be compared with any 'sale, insurance, salvage or compensation moneys' received. If the latter exceed the former, that shows that he has been allowed too much, and a balancing charge will be made. If the former exceeds the latter, he has been allowed too little, and he will get a balancing allowance.

5 So the position of the company at the date of the deceased's death was that, by applying for and accepting allowances in respect of these ships, it had become bound by the statute to pay tax under a balancing charge when it ceased to use these ships in its trade, if the moneys which it received for them exceeded any expenditure on them which was still unallowed. And I should add, because importance was attached to this in argument, the company would only have to pay tax if the law had not been altered, and if when the question arose there was in existence a Finance Act determining the rate of income tax. So there were two contingencies which had to be fulfilled, or conditions which had to be purified, before tax could be demanded from the company: the sums received for the ships must exceed the unallowed expenditure and there must be no relevant change in the law and no failure to enact a Finance Act. The question is whether in these circumstances there was a contingent liability of the company to pay tax.

6 No doubt the words 'liability and 'contingent liability' are more often used in connection with obligations arising from contract than with statutory obligations. But I cannot doubt that if a statute says that a person who has done something must pay tax, that tax is a 'liability' of that person. If the amount of tax has been ascertained and it is immediately payable, it is clearly a liability; if it is only payable on a certain future date, it must be a liability which has 'not matured at the date of the death, within the meaning of Section 50 (1). If it is not yet certain whether or when tax will be payable or how much will be payable, why should it not be a contingent liability under the same section?

7 It is said that where there is a contract, there is an existing obligation, even if you must await events to see if anything ever becomes payable, but that there is no comparable obligation in a case like the present. But there appears to me to be a close similarity. To take the first stage, if I see a watch in a shop window and think of buying it, I am not under a contingent liability to pay the price; similarly if an Act *(pg362)* says that I must pay tax if I trade and make a profit, I am not, before I begin trading, under a contingent liability to pay tax in the event of my starting trading. In neither case have I committed myself to anything. But if I agree by contract to accept allowances on the footing that I will pay a sum if I later sell something above a certain price, I have committed myself, and I come under a contingent liability to pay in that event. This company did precisely that, but its obligation to pay arose not from contract but from statute. I find it difficult to see why that should make all the difference.

8 It would seem that the phrase contingent liability may have no settled meaning in English law because in this case Mr Justice Danckwerts thought it necessary to resort to a dictionary and in *In re Duffy* (a case much relied on by the respondents) the Court of Appeal regarded its meaning as an open question. But the Finance Acts are United Kingdom Acts, and there is at least a strong presumption that they mean the same in Scotland as in England. A case precisely similar to this case could have come from Scotland, and your lordships would then have considered the meaning of this phrase in Scots law. So I need make no apology for reminding your lordships of its meaning there. Perhaps the clearest statement is in *Erskine's Institutes of the Law of Scotland*, Volume 2, when he says, Book III, title I, Section 6:

> 'Obligations are either pure, or to a certain day, or conditional. ... Obligations *in diem* ... are those in which the performance is referred to a determinate day. In this kind ... a debt becomes properly due from the very date of the obligation, because it is certain that that day will exist; but its

effect or execution is suspended till the day be elapsed. A conditional obligation, or an obligation granted under a condition the existence of which is uncertain, has no obligatory force till the condition be purified; because it is in that event only that the party declares his intention to be bound, and consequently no proper debt arises against him till it actually exist: so that the condition of an uncertain event suspends not only the execution of the obligation, but the obligation itself. ... Such obligation is therefore said in the Roman law to create only the hope of a debt. Yet the granter is in so far obliged that he hath no right to revoke or withdraw that hope from the creditor which he had once given him.'

So far as I am aware, that statement has never been questioned during the two centuries since it was written, and later authorities make it clear that conditional obligation and contingent liability have no different significance. I would, therefore, find it impossible to hold that in Scots law a contingent liability is merely a species of existing liability. It is a liability which, by reason of something done by the person bound, will necessarily arise or come into being, if one or more of certain events occur or do not occur. If English law is different – as to which I express no opinion – the difference is probably more in terminology than in substance.

9 I must now turn back to the provisions of Section 50 (1) of the Finance Act 1940. It directs the Commissioners to make an allowance for (or deduction in respect of) all liabilities of the company, and it divides liabilities, as one might expect, into three classes. First, where the liability is a sum immediately payable, there is no need for computation, and the whole is deducted. Secondly, the liability may be one which has not matured; that would include a sum payable at a definite future date or a sum payable on an event which must occur some time, eg the death of A. There the Commissioners are to take the present value of the debt. The third class is 'contingent liabilities', which must mean sums, payment of which depends on a contingency, ie sums which will only become payable if certain things happen, and which otherwise will never become payable. There calculation is impossible, so the Commissioners are to make such estimation as appears to be reasonable.

10 The last class appears to me to cover exactly the conditional obligation dealt with by *Erskine* in the passage I have quoted. I agree with the respondents' argument to this extent, that this class can only include liabilities which in law must arise if one or more things happen, and cannot be extended to include everything that a prudent business man would think it proper to provide against. That is the distinction which I have already tried to explain. But I cannot agree with the respondents for their argument that there must be an existing obligation, because that would exclude at least all Scottish conditional obligations.

11 This argument was based on certain observations in the Court of Appeal in *In re Duffy*, so I must now examine that case, as to which I may say at once that

I am satisfied that the decision was right, although I cannot accept all the reasons given. There, as in this case, Section 50 of the Act of 1940 had to be applied.

12 Duffy died on 24th June 1942, and therefore his company's assets had to be valued at that date. But instead of doing that the parties adopted the convenient course of valuing those assets at the end of the financial year of the company on 31st January 1942, *(pg363)* and adding a proportion of the company's profits for the year 1942–43. This artificial method of valuation led to trouble. The taxpayer sought to bring in as a contingent liability of the company a proportion of its income tax for the year 1943–44, because the earning of profits during the year 1942–43 had engendered a contingent liability for tax for 1943–44. As pointed out by Mr Justice Roxburgh, in a judgment which I find convincing, it had done nothing of the kind. Whether the company would have to pay tax for the year 1943–44 depended entirely on whether it chose to carry on trade during that year, and the profits for 1942–43 were merely the measure of the company's tax liability if it chose to do so. I doubt if the taxpayer could even have stated a plausible case if the old three years average rule had still applied. It seems to me to be verging on the absurd to say that a trader had in June 1942 incurred a contingent liability to pay tax for a year which only began nine months later.

13 But the importance of *Duffy's* case to the respondents lies in certain general observations of Lord Greene in the Court of Appeal. Dealing with Section 50 (1) he said:

'... the words in brackets ... deal with two sub-classes of liabilities. Neither of those sub-classes can go beyond the head class of liabilities',

and then he went on to consider the 'natural and ordinary meaning' of the words apparently on the assumption that 'contingent liabilities' is not a phrase of known meaning in the law of England. Then he went on to say:

'... taking the construction of these words, I find it impossible to give them a meaning extending beyond what is always ascertainable without any doubt whatsoever, namely, an existing legal liability – a liability actually existing in law at the relevant date. The words cannot be stretched so as to cover something which in a business sense is morally certain and for which every business man ought to make provision, but which in law does not become a liability until a subsequent date'.

I agree with the last sentence of this quotation, and it applied to the facts of *Duffy's* case. The taxpayer had already been allowed to deduct tax for 1942–43, and he sought in addition a deduction of something which was only 'morally certain' to become the measure of taxation in the next year – if indeed it could be said to be morally certain that the company would continue trading. But as a general statement of the law I think that the passage is inadequate, because it appears to me to deprive the category of contingent liabilities of all content. That this category is in a special position is made clear by the Act, which, in contrast to the provision for computing other kinds of liability, only requires for a contingent liability 'such estimation as appears to the Commissioners to be reasonable'. I cannot reconcile this with a requirement that such a liability must always be perfectly ascertainable as a legal liability actually existing in law at the relevant date.

14 The essence of a contingent liability must surely be that it may never become an existing legal liability because the event on which it depends may never happen.

15 There appears to me to be no further difficulty, and therefore I am not bound to hold that no deduction can be made in respect of the company's contingent liability to pay tax under a balancing charge, and not bound to hold that estate duty has to be paid on a fictitious sum. I say a fictitious sum, because in fact it was impossible for the company to realize the value of the ships without having immediately to pay away as tax a large proportion of what it received. So it would be a fiction to say that the full value of the ships could be regarded as swelling the assets of the company.

16 But the deduction will not be the sum of £270,079 which would have been payable in tax if the ships had been sold at the date of the death of the deceased. I agree with your lordships and the Court of Appeal in rejecting the appellants' arguments for this. In my view the case must go to the Commissioners of Inland Revenue in order that they may make the estimation required by Section 50 on the footing that at the date of death liability to pay under a balancing charge was a contingent liability, which would become an immediate liability of the company, if it sold or otherwise ceased to trade with the ships and received sums exceeding the expenditure still unallowed. It would not be right for me to suggest to the Commissioners how they should carry out their task; they will no doubt have regard to all relevant facts. In my judgment this appeal should be allowed, and the case remitted to a judge of the Chancery Division to proceed as accords.

17 LORD TUCKER: My lords, I have had the advantage of reading in print the speech which is to be delivered by my noble and learned friend Lord Hodson. I am in complete agreement with the conclusion he has reached that this *(pg364)* appeal should be dismissed, and the reasoning by which he has arrived at that result. In particular, I would wish to emphasise and adopt what he says with regard to the meaning of the words 'contingent liabilities' in Section 50 (1) of the Finance Act 1940. To construe these words as wide enough to include a prospective or foreseeable liability, there being at the material date no contract or statute in existence under which such liability could or would in certain contingencies arise, cannot, in my opinion, be justified and would be contrary to the reasoning of Lord Greene in *In re Duffy* which should, I think, be applied in the present case.

18 I would dismiss this appeal.

19 LORD BIRKETT: My lords, I have had the opportunity of reading and considering the speeches of my noble and learned friend on the Woolsack, Lord Reid, and of my noble and learned friend Lord Guest. I agree with their conclusions, and would allow the appeal and remit the case to the Commissioners of Inland Revenue to make the estimation referred to in Section 50 (1) of the Finance Act 1940. The facts of the case, and the relevant sections of the various statutes, have been so fully set out in the speech of my noble and learned friend, Lord Reid, that there is no necessity to repeat them, and I can confine myself to stating quite briefly the reasons which have led me to the conclusion that the appeal ought to be allowed.

20 The decisive question is whether in the circumstances of this case there was a 'contingent liability' within the meaning of Section 50 (1) of the Finance Act 1940. When Sir Arthur Sutherland died in March 1953, he had controlled the company of BJ Sutherland & Co Ltd for some years, and owned 98,700 shares in the company. To ascertain the value of these shares for estate duty purposes it was necessary, first of all, to ascertain the net value of the assets of the company at the date of his death, in accordance with the provisions of Section 55 (1), (2) of the Finance Act 1940. Section 55 (2) of the Act of 1940 expressly provides that in estimating the value of the assets, the allowance for the liabilities referred to in Section 50 (1) of the Finance Act 1940, must be taken into account. Those liabilities include contingent liabilities which are to be computed by the Commissioners on a reasonable estimation.

21 It is clear that these contingent liabilities are of a very special kind, which are not capable of precise ascertainment, but are capable of reasonable estimation. The contingent liability for which the appellants contend in this case arises in this way. At the date of Sir Arthur Sutherland's death the assets of the company which fell to be valued included five ships, which had cost the company £847,907, but were then worth over £1 million. The company had received capital allowances under the provisions of the Income Tax Act 1952, and the amount of the capital expenditure still unallowed was £290,749. In the light of the provisions of Section 292 of the Act of 1952 it was clear that if the ships were sold for anything like their true value, a balancing charge would be imposed, and a liability for income tax and profits tax would follow as a matter of course. The ships were not sold at the date of the death of Sir Arthur, but were sold some months later. A balancing charge was imposed with the result that an assessment was made for income tax and profits tax amounting to £370,114 13s. The question is: Was this liability to pay tax arising out of the balancing charge a contingent liability within the meaning of Section 50 (1) of the Finance Act 1940? It was clearly in accordance with the provisions of the Income Tax Act 1952, and I am of opinion that it was a contingent liability within the meaning of Section 50 (1) of the Finance Act 1940, and that the Commissioners should have made the reasonable estimation authorised by the Act.

22 It was argued that an existing legal liability was essential to the creation of a contingent liability, and that no such legal liability existed in this case at the date of Sir Arthur's death. In my view this is to take too narrow a view of the true meaning of contingent liability. It must have been apparent to everybody concerned with the calculation of estate duty in this case that on the sale of the ships a balancing charge was certain to arise, and that additional duty would have to be paid. The appellants had raised the question with the Commissioners of Inland Revenue before any legal proceedings were begun, for it was clear to them that on the happening of a certain event, ie the sale of the ships, the provisions of the Act of 1952 would come into operation, as the event later proved. They never doubted the existence of a liability, but it was a contingent liability. It was no less a contingent liability because the sale of the ships might not take place. The true legal position was that from the moment the appellants accepted capital allowances they were at once under a liability to pay tax in the circumstances *(pg365)* provided for in the Income Tax Act 1952. That liability was a contingent liability, and was within the meaning of those words in Section 50 (1) of the Finance Act 1940. I am confirmed in this view by the citations from the law of Scotland made by my noble and learned friends, Lord Reid and Lord Guest. I also agree with their observations on *In re Duffy*, and I would allow the appeal.

23 LORD HODSON: My lords, at his death on 29th March 1953, the deceased, Sir Arthur Munro Sutherland, was the owner of 98,700 £1 shares in the capital of BJ Sutherland & Co Ltd, of which company he had had control during the five years ending with his death. Consequently, for purposes of estate duty the shares had to be valued by reference to the net value of the assets of the company in accordance with the provisions of Section 50 and Section 55 of the Finance Act 1940, instead of by reference to the then open market value of the shares pursuant to Section 7 (5) of the Finance Act 1894.

24 The assets of the company at the date of the deceased's death included five ships, the value of which at that date had been agreed with the Estate Duty Office to be £1,150,000. The cost of these ships to the company for income tax purposes had been agreed to be £847,907, and at the date of the deceased's death the company had received capital allowances under the provisions of Part 10 of the Income Tax Act 1952, leaving 'expenditure unallowed' (as defined by Section 297 of the same Act) of £290,749. In the event of a sale of the ships for a sum in excess of the amount of such expenditure unallowed under Section 292 of the Income Tax Act 1952, a balancing charge would be imposed of an amount equal to such excess, resulting in an assessment to income tax and profits tax at the rates appropriate to the year in respect of which such assessment was made.

25 The ships were in fact sold between November 1953 and February 1954, for sums amounting in the aggregate to £1,070,505. This gave rise to balancing charges of £548,318, resulting in an additional income tax assessment on the company for the year 1953–54 at 9s in the £, amounting to £246,743 2s, and an additional profits tax assessment at the rate of $22\frac{1}{2}$ per cent for the chargeable accounting period ending on March 31st, 1953, amounting to £123,371 11s. The aggregate of this additional tax liability was £370,114 13s.

26 The question for decision is whether in valuing the assets of the company at the date of the deceased's death any deduction ought to be made in respect of a claim for additional income tax and profits tax, which might arise on a sale of the ships for an amount in excess of the expenditure unallowed having regard to the manner in which this event afterwards happened.

The following statutory provisions are material:

Finance Act 1894, Section 7 (5):

'The principal value of any property shall be estimated to be the price which, in the opinion of the Commissioners, such property would fetch if sold in the open market at the time of the death of the deceased; ... '

Finance Act 1940, Section 55:

'(1) Where for the purposes of estate duty there pass, on the death of a person dying after the commencement of this Act, shares in or debentures of a company to which this section applies, then if:

(a) the deceased had the control of the company at any time during the [five] years ending with his death; ... the principal value of the shares or debentures, in lieu of being estimated in accordance with the provisions of subsection (5) of Section seven of the Finance Act 1894, shall be estimated by reference to the net value of the assets of the company in accordance with the provisions of the next succeeding subsection.

'(2) For the purposes of such ascertainment as aforesaid:

(a) the net value of the assets of the company shall be taken to be the principal value thereof estimated in accordance with the said subsection (5), less the like allowance for liabilities of the company as is provided by subsection (1) of Section fifty of this Act in relation to the assets of a company passing on a death by virtue of Section forty-six of this Act, but subject to the modifications that allowance shall be made for such a liability as is mentioned in paragraph (b) of that subsection unless it also falls within paragraph (a) thereof;

(b) the aggregate value of all the shares and debentures of the company issued and outstanding at the death of the deceased shall be taken to be the same as the net value of the assets of the company; ...

(d) the value of any share, or of any debenture, or of a share or debenture of any class, shall be a rateable proportion, ascertained by reference to nominal amount, of the net value of the assets of the company as determined under paragraph (a) of this subsection, or, in the case mentioned in paragraph (c) of this subsection ... as the case may be.'

Section 50 (1):

'In determining the value of the estate for the purpose of estate duty the provisions of *(pg366)* subsection (5) of Section seven of the Finance Act 1894, as to making allowance for debts and incumbrances shall not have effect as respects any debt or incumbrance to which assets of the company passing on the death by virtue of Section forty-six of this Act were liable, but the Commissioners shall make an allowance from the principal value of those assets for all liabilities of the company (computed, as regards liabilities which have not matured at the date of the death, by reference to the value thereof at that date, and, as regards contingent liabilities, by reference to such estimation as appears to the Commissioners to be reasonable) other than:

(a) liabilities in respect of shares in or debentures of the company; and
(b) liabilities incurred otherwise than for the purposes of the business of the company wholly and exclusively.'

27 The appellants claim that they are entitled to make a deduction in respect of 'balancing charges' as being 'contingent liabilities' within Section 50 (1) of the Finance Act 1940. Their claim does not relate to the balancing charges which were levied on the sale of the ships after the death of the deceased, but to a sum of £270,000, which is an agreed figure representing the balancing charges which would have been paid if the ships had been sold at the time of the death.

28 The time of the death is the relevant moment, and the appellants have contended that when the statute directs property to be valued at the price which it would fetch if sold in the open market, a sale at the moment of death should be assumed. On this hypothesis of a notional sale they argue that the liability to a balancing charge was contingent on the sale, because at the date of the death the ships were worth much more than their written-down value.

29 The answer to this argument is that to apply the statutory test of value it is necessary to ascertain what the property would fetch at the time of death on a sale, not on a sale by a particular individual. Section 7 (5) of the Act of 1894 does not put the appellants in the same position as they would have been if the ships had been sold at the death. The ships were not sold, and there is nothing in the section to introduce the artificial conception that they must be deemed to have been sold. I agree therefore with the judgments delivered in the Court of Appeal, that the appellants' case fails *in limine*, since the whole basis of the argument is a notional or hypothetical sale bringing in its train a contingent liability.

30 The appellants have, however, maintained in this House, as I understand their argument, that even if they cannot succeed in upholding their hypothesis of a sale, they are entitled to make the deductions claimed as 'contingent liabilities' having regard to the wide meaning which can be given to these words. It is true that, from the accountancy point of view, any provisions which the directors of a company as business men think it prudent to make for something which may not happen can be entered in a balance sheet as a liability. In ordinary speech no doubt one often uses the words 'contingent liabilities' in this sense. I do not think in their context these words can have such an extended meaning, nor indeed do the appellants contend that they should, for they expressly disclaimed that they would seek to take into account liabilities which may exist in the future; but they have endeavoured to say that there is as it were *in gremio* a liability which was contingent, since once the voluntary allowances have been accepted, the acceptor runs the risk of attracting liability to refund the allowances.

31 This is no doubt true, but in my judgment the risk of attracting liability is not enough, and the argument involves a misconception of what is meant by 'contingent liabilities' in their context. There may be no day of reckoning; the ships may never be sold; if there is a sale, there may be a balancing allowance not a balancing charge. It is only when Section 292 of the Income Tax Act 1952, which provides for balancing charges and balancing allowances, comes into operation that any question can arise.

32 One must start with the word 'liability' which *prima facie* connotes a legal liability. When one adds to it the adjective 'contingent', one is not entitled to sail into an uncharted sea, and to take into account not only contingent liabilities but all other kinds of liabilities which may be prospective or foreseeable as likely to be incurred.

33 There can be no true contingent liability unless there is an existing legal obligation, under which a payment will become due on the happening of a future unascertained event or events. There must always be an underlying obligation. It does not matter whether one regards the obligation as suspended pending the arising of the contingency, or whether one regards the performance of the obligation as suspended. The result to my mind is the same. In the ordinary case no doubt the contingent liability is imposed by contract. A common example is a contract of insurance, when the insurance company promises to make a payment to the assured on the happening of a contingency. A car owner may have an accident and be liable to meet an award of *(pg367)* damages. If he is insured the contingency is provided for. In some cases the contingent liability may be imposed by statute. An illustration is to be found in *Southern Railway of Peru Ltd v Owen*. No doubt other examples can be found.

34 The distinction between a future liability which has not yet matured and a contingent liability is marked in Section 50 (1) itself. Those which have not matured are certain as to maturity, whereas those which are contingent are uncertain as to maturity. The value of each is capable of estimation by the Commissoners as the statute directs.

35 *In re Duffy* is authority for the proposition that the words 'contingent liabilities' in Section 50 mean legal liabilities actually existing in law at the relevant date, and cannot be stretched so as to cover something which in a business sense is morally certain, and for which every business man ought to make provision, but which in law does not become a liability until a subsequent date. That also was an estate duty case. It concerned the basis of valuation of the shares of a company on the death of the deceased, Joseph Duffy. The shares had to be valued for the purpose of calculating duty in the manner laid down in Section 55 of the Finance Act 1940. The executors sought to deduct as a contingent liability a sum equivalent to income tax on the proportion of the profits of the company applicable to that part of the company's financial year which preceded the death of the deceased. Two points were taken by the Crown: first that the tax was imposed annually, secondly, that the trader is liable only if he carries on his trade into the next year. The tax not having been imposed, although admittedly there was a moral certainty that it would be, there was no liability, and the Court of Appeal decided the case on this ground. Mr Justice Roxburgh in his judgment, which the Court of Appeal upheld, based himself on the second point taken by the Crown. He put the matter in this way:

'Mr Stamp gave a graphic illustration which really seems to me to illuminate the problem. It was this. The fact that you have got a live dog on December 31st, 1947, does not make you liable, contingently or otherwise, to pay for a dog licence in 1948. Of course, the probability is very great that you will not kill your dog overnight. Likewise, the probability was very great that this company would not go out of business immediately after the testator's death. But the fact that you are unlikely to kill your dog before January 1st cannot convert into a liability that which otherwise is not a liability, and it is quite plain that if you did kill your dog before January 1st, 1948, you would not be liable for a dog licence for the year 1948.

'It seems to me that that was just the position of this company with regard to the financial year beginning April 6th, 1943. It was unlikely that it would not carry on business, but there was nothing to compel it to do so. It was unlikely that income tax would be abolished, but there was nothing to prevent Parliament from abolishing it. But, to my mind, it is impossible to believe that a state of affairs, which you can terminate if you like by your own choice and without the intervention of anybody or anything, can properly be described as a liability. If you can go out of business and, thereby, escape from any liability to tax then, in my judgment, you are not under a liability for the tax in question.'

In my opinion the reasoning of these judgments is sound. True that to treat the passing of the next Income Tax Act as the crucial moment when liability attaches is to rest on rather an artificial basis, since it is as certain as can be that year by year income tax will be imposed. This criticism cannot, however, be levelled against the ground on which Mr Justice Roxburgh decided the case. There as here the liability could have been avoided at the volition of the company. Money for duty had to be raised, but not necessarily by the sale of the ships, though no doubt this was the convenient course to follow, and a decision was taken to sell the ships rather than shares of the company. I agree with Mr Justice Roxburgh in regarding a state of affairs which can be terminated of one's own choice without outside intervention as being inconsistent with the imposition of a liability contingent or otherwise.

36 I see no room for an intermediate kind of liability between the contingent liability which I have tried to describe and the prospective liability which may or may not come into existence, and which is admittedly outside the scope of a contingent liability for the purposes of the section; and I find it impossible to define or limit the scope of a liability such as is contended for by the appellants. They have established vulnerability no doubt but not contingent liability.

37 I will not deal at length with the subsidiary arguments presented on behalf of the appellants. Accepting the distinction between liability and assessment drawn by Lord Dunedin in *Whitney v Commissioners of Inland Revenue*, I see no distinction between section 1 and Section 292 of the Act of 1952, which enables the appellants to say that here there was a liability existing at the date of death. Further, I think that *mutatis mutandis* the same arguments apply to profits tax, and there is no *(pg368)* distinction to be drawn between profits tax and income tax. Annual imposition is necessary for both. Reliance was also placed on *British Transport Commission v Gourley*, which shows that a prospective tax burden should be taken into account in assessing damages in an action of tort. No assistance can be gained from the speeches delivered in that case, which had to do with prospective earnings, and not with liabilities actual or contingent.

38 I would dismiss the appeal.

39 LORD GUEST: My lords, on the death of Sir Arthur Sutherland on 29th March 1953, the property passing for the purposes of estate duty included 98,700 shares of £1 each in BJ Sutherland & Co Ltd. The deceased had control of the company during the five years ending with his death and the principal value of the shares had therefore to be valued according to the provisions of Section 55 (1) of the Finance Act 1940, by reference to the net value of the assets of the company. Section 55 (2) of the Act of 1940 provides that the value of the assets is to be taken to be the principal value estimated in accordance with Section 7 (5) of the Finance Act 1894, less the allowance for liabilities provided for by Section 50 (1) of the Act of 1940.

40 Section 50 (1) is in the following terms:

'In determining the value of the estate for the purpose of estate duty the provisions of subsection (1) of Section seven of the Finance Act 1894, as to making allowances for debts and incumbrances shall not have effect as respects any debt or incumbrance to which assets of the company passing on the death by virtue of Section forty-six of this Act were liable, but the Commissioners shall make an allowance from the principal value of those assets for all liabilities of the company (computed, as regards liabilities which have not matured at the date of the death, by reference to the value thereof at that date, and, as regards contingent liabilities, by reference to such estimation as appears to the Commissioners to be reasonable) other than:

(a) liabilities in respect of shares in or debentures of the company; and
(b) liabilities incurred otherwise than for the purposes of the business of the company wholly and exclusively.'

At the date of Sir Arthur's death the assets of the company included five ships. At that date the company had received in respect of those ships, which cost the company £847,907, capital allowances under Chapter II of Part X of the Income Tax Act 1952, to the amount of £557,158. The ships had at the deceased's death a greatly increased value, and if they had been sold then, the company would have sustained a balancing charge under Section 292 of the Income Tax Act 1952, giving rise to additional income tax and profits tax liability. The five ships were in fact sold during the year of assessment 1953–54 for £1,070,505, and a balancing charge arose on the sum of £548,318 giving rise to additional income tax liability and profits tax liability respectively of £246,743 and £123,371.

41 The appellants claimed that in arriving at the value for estate duty purposes of the shares, they were entitled to receive an allowance under Section 50 (1) of the Finance Act 1940, by taking into account the balancing charges attaching to the sale of the ships. In the Courts below the appellants' claim has been refused, but it is not unfair to say, at any rate so far as Mr Justice Danckwerts is concerned, that if they had not considered themselves bound by authority to decide otherwise, they might have decided in the appellants' favour.

42 The argument presented by the appellants was presented from two angles. First, it was argued that Section 7 (5) of the Finance Act 1894, envisaged a notional sale of the ships as at, the date of the deceased's death, and that from the price in the open market as provided for in Section 7 (5) the balancing charges must be deducted. The second aspect of the argument was that the liability for balancing charges was a 'contingent liability' within the meaning of Section 50 (1) of the Finance Act, 1940, and that the Commissioners of Inland Revenue must make an allowance for the balancing charges from the principal value of the assets.

43 The first argument was, in my opinion, rightly rejected by the Court of Appeal. The purpose of Section 7 (5) of the Finance Act 1894 is to value the property. As Lord Evershed said:

'It does not require it to be assumed that the sale ... has occurred. ...'

It simply prescribes, as the criterion for value, price in the open market as between a willing seller and a willing buyer, which is a familiar basis of valuation. I therefore agree with all that fell from the Master of the Rolls and Lord Justice Upjohn on this aspect of the matter. But both these learned judges appeared to think that this concluded the case in favour of the Inland Revenue, and that if you did not assume a notional sale under Section 7 (5) of the Act of 1894, there was no room for the operation of Section 50 (1) of the Finance Act 1940. With great respect to these learned judges this seems to me to fail to appreciate the *(pg369)* second limb of the appellants' argument. By section 55 (2) of the Act of 1940 you are directed to Section 7 (5) of the Act of 1894 for the method of valuation of the assets of the company, but in calculating the allowance for liabilities of the company you are directed to Section 50 (1). And among the allowances which the Commissioners are directed to make are 'contingent liabilities'. Contingent liabilities, therefore, remain as deductions from the open market value of the assets of the company.

44 If this be the correct interpretation of these sections, the only question is whether the liability to pay balancing charges was a 'contingent liability' under Section 50 (1). If the question were untrammelled by authority, I should have little difficulty in holding that the liability for these balancing charges was a contingent liability. It is plain from the terms of Section 50 (1) that the liability contemplated is different from a debt or incumbrance, because the ordinary provisions of Section 7 (1) of the Act of 1894 regarding debts and incumbrances are not to apply. Section 50 (1) refers both to liabilities which have not matured at the date of death and to contingent liabilities. Contingent liabilities must therefore be something different from future liabilities which are binding on the company, but are not payable until a future date. I should define a contingency as an event which may or may not occur, and contingent liability as a liability which depends for its existence on an event which may or may not happen.

45 A contingent obligation has in Scots law a perfectly well-known meaning. I quote from *Erskine's Institutes of the Law of Scotland*, Volume 2, Book III, title 1 Section 6:

> 'A conditional obligation, or an obligation granted under a condition the existence of which is uncertain, has no obligatory force till the condition be purified; because it is in that event only that the party declares his intention to be bound, and consequently no proper debt arises against him till it actually exist; so that the condition of an uncertain event suspends not only the execution of the obligation, but the obligation itself. ... '

In *Gloag on Contract* (second edition, pages 271, 272), future obligations are contrasted with contingent obligations. An obligation is future when, though not presently exigible, it is dependent on no other condition than the arrival of the day of payment. An obligation is contingent:

'if its enforceability is dependent on an event which may or may not happen'.

I see no reason why these principles should not be applicable to a United Kingdom statute, and no authority was quoted to show that English law differed in any way.

46 The Crown argued that *In re Duffy* was a barrier to the appellants' success, and the learned judges of the Court of Appeal considered themselves bound by that decision. In particular, reliance was placed on the construction placed by Lord Greene on the words 'contingent liabilities' when he said:

'... but, taking the construction of these words, I find it impossible to give them a meaning extending beyond what is always ascertainable without any doubt whatsoever, namely, an existing legal liability – a liability actually existing in law at the relevant date. The words cannot be stretched so as to cover something which in a business sense is morally certain and for which every business man ought to make provision, but which in law does not become a liability until a subsequent date.'

With great respect to Lord Greene, if a liability must be an existing legal liability to comply with Section 50 (1), that would appear to give no content to the adjective 'contingent'. The liability is not a legal liability until the contingency has arrived and the section cannot therefore be restricted to 'existing legal liabilities'.

47 *In re Duffy* concerned the point whether income tax payable at the standard rate for the financial year 1943–44 assessed by reference to the profit of the year 1942–43 during which the deceased died on 24 June 1942, was a contingent liability of the company for the purposes of Section 50 and Section 55 of the Finance Act 1940. The Court of Appeal decided that it was not a contingent liability, on the view that there was no present liability for income tax, and that it was not certain that income tax would be imposed in the Finance Act for the next year. Mr Justice Roxburgh, whose judgment was affirmed by the Court of Appeal, approached the matter from a slightly different angle. He held that as the company was free not to carry on business in the relevant year, and that as the company could terminate its liability to income tax by its own voluntary act by not trading, it could not be described as a liability. It is not necessary to come to a conclusion whether *In re Duffy* was rightly decided. The facts of the present case are different and more favourable to the taxpayer than they were in *In re Duffy*. The claim for initial allowances for what has been described as depreciation is the voluntary choice of the taxpayer, but once he has obtained such allowances, he is automatically involved by the operation of *(pg370)* law in the payment of balancing charges, if the assets are parted with at a price greater than the written-down value in the certain circumstances defined in Section 292 of the Income Tax Act 1952.

48 In the present case as at the date of the deceased's death the ships in question had a value on the open market considerably in excess of that written-down value. The liability for such a balancing charge was, in my view, a 'contingent liability' within the meaning of Section 50 (1) of the Act of 1940, the liability being contingent on the ships being sold at a price in excess of their written-down value. The Courts below have, in my opinion, put too narrow a construction on the words 'contingent liabilities'.

49 The Commissioners of Inland Revenue will, under Section 50 (1), require to make an estimation of the contingent liabilities as appears to them to be reasonable. The allowances to be made will not be the full extent of the balancing charges.

50 I therefore agree that the appeal should be allowed and the case dealt with in the way in which my noble and learned friend on the Woolsack proposes. *(pg371)*

Case 28
Duke of Buccleuch v IRC

[1967] 1 AC 506, HL

House of Lords

24, 25, 26 October, 20 December 1967

In this case, the judgements made in the House of Lords state some of the central concepts for share valuation.

1.   When statute requires the price in the open market, this is a price that would be achieved between a willing seller and willing buyer.
2.   A sale on the open market does not necessitate an auction being postulated. The phrase requires that the seller must have taken such steps that are reasonable and this can be a sale by advertising and awaiting offers.
3.   The statement in statute that the value is 'at the time of death' requires a sale postulated to occur at the moment of death.
4.   The sale postulated is the one that obtains the best price available for the assets. This may necessitate splitting property into parcels but does not require the valuer to assume that the last ounce of value is extracted from the property, if it would not be economic to sub-divide the property.
5.   The fact that it may be impossible, in the real world, to have a sale on the valuation date is irrelevant.
6.   When postulating the proceeds of a hypothetical sale, there is no scope for the deduction of costs that would be incurred if property were sold in the real world.

The 10th Duke of Devonshire died on 26 November 1950. Included in the Duke's estate at death were ten English landed estates, covering 186 sq miles in total, plus one Scottish landed estate.

The parties agreed that the value of the Hardwick estate should be the subject of an appeal, the principles applied in the judgement would then be applied to ascertaining the value of the other landed estates.

The Hardwick estate, 20,635 acres in area, comprised principally farms, but also included smallholdings, allotments, gardens, agricultural and industrial land, woodlands, residential properties, sporting rights, ground rents and licensed houses. The Revenue valued the estate by dividing it into 532 separate units, and the total valuation of £868,129 was made on the assumption that each unit had been sold in the open market on the date of the Duke's death at the best price which a purchaser might then reasonably have been expected to pay, irrespective of whether it would or would not have been possible to put the property on the market or of actually realising the open market price at that time. The trustees, while agreeing the value attributed to the individual units on that basis, contended that it would be impossible to sell an estate of this complexity within a reasonable period of the death (which they put at one year) unless the bulk of it were sold in one block.

The Land Tribunal accepted the approach of the Revenue and judged the value of the ten English estates to be, on this approach, £3,176,646. The Land Tribunal stated that, if the valuation were undertaken on the basis submitted by the executors, the value would be £2,743,760.

Nature of the seller and the buyer in the hypothetical open market

The Court of Appeal noted that the statutory hypothesis does not require an assumption that the sale has occurred. Instead, the statutory hypothesis simply prescribes the criteria for valuation, being the price that would be achieved between a willing seller and a willing buyer in the open market.

Is the open market an auction?

Lord Reid observed:

> 'There was some argument about the meaning of "in the open market". Originally no doubt when one wanted to sell a particular item of property one took it to a market where buyers of that kind of property congregated. Then the owner received offers and accepted what he thought was the best offer he was likely to get. And for some kinds of property that is still done. But this phrase must also be applied to other kinds of property where that is impossible. In my view the phrase requires that the seller must take – or here be supposed to have taken – such steps as are reasonable to attract as much competition as possible for the particular piece of property which is to be sold. Sometimes this will be by sale by auction, sometimes otherwise. I suppose that the biggest open market is the Stock Exchange where there is no auction. And there may be two kinds of market commonly used by owners wishing to sell a particular kind of property. For

example, it is common knowledge that many owners of houses first publish the fact that they wish to sell and then await offers: they only put the property up for auction as a last resort. I see no reason for holding that in proper cases the former method could not be regarded as sale in the open market.'

([1967] 1 AC 506 at 524 **case 28 para 7**)

The timing of the sale

Lord Reid stated:

'What must be envisaged is sale in the open market on a particular day. So there is no room for supposing that the owner would do as many prudent owners do – withdraw the property if he does not get a sufficient offer and wait until a time when he can get a better offer. The commissioners must estimate what the property would probably have fetched on that particular day if it had then been exposed for sale, no doubt after such advance publicity as would have been reasonable.'

([1967] 1 AC 506 at 525 **case 28 para 8**)

This was made even more specific in the judgement of Lord Guest:

'"At the time of the death" means at the moment of death, not within a reasonable time after the death.'

([1967] 1 AC 506 at 541 **case 28 para 56**)

How much sub-division?

The principle of sub-division is at the core of this case.

Lord Reid described the amount of sub-division required by statute as follows:

'Generally the estate will consist of what one may call natural units – units or parcels of property which can be easily identified without there being any substantial difficulty or expense in carving them out of the whole estate. In my opinion it is implicit in the scheme of the Act that section 7(5) should be applied to each of such units, and there is no justification for requiring elaborate subdivision of natural limits on the ground that if that had been done before the hypothetical sale the total price for the natural unit would have been increased. We must take the estate as it was when the deceased died.

A library was instanced by Winn LJ. Generally there would be little difficulty, delay or expense in getting someone knowledgeable to pick out valuable books for separate valuation and I would therefore regard such books as natural units. But suppose that the deceased had bought a miscellaneous and mixed lot of surplus stores intending to sort out and arrange them in saleable lots. That might involve a great deal of work, time and expense and I see no justification for requiring the supposition that had been done and then valuing the saleable lots that would have emerged.

> It is sometimes said that the estate must be supposed to have been realised in such a way that the best possible prices were obtained for its parts. But that cannot be a universal rule. Suppose that the owner of a wholesale business dies possessed of a large quantity of hardware or clothing or whatever he deals in. It would have been possible by extensive advertising to obtain offers for small lots at something near retail prices. So it would have been possible to realise the stock at much more than wholesale prices. It would not have been reasonable and it would not have been economic, but it would have been possible. Counsel for the respondents did not contend that that would be a proper method of valuation. But that necessarily amounts to an admission that there is no universal rule that the best possible prices at the date of death must be taken.
>
> I have said that this Act applies rough and ready methods. It is vain to apply theoretical logic. The question of what units to value is a practical question to be solved by common sense.'
>
> ([1967] 1 AC 506 at 525/526 **case 28 paras 10, 11 and 12**)

The impossibility, in reality, of a sale is no barrier to ascertaining a market value

Expert witnesses had stated that the Hardwick Estate would have taken several years to sell were it to have been sold in 532 separate units, as postulated by the Revenue.

In his judgement, Lord Morris of Borth-y-Gest dismissed this evidence as being 'quite irrelevant'. It would have been impossible to sell the estate on the day of death as a whole, or in 46 units or in 532 units. The statutory direction to consider a sale at that moment is a valuation provision:

> 'It points to a time by reference to which and a basis upon which values are to be estimated. When the section speaks of the value of "any property" or of "the property" an indication is, perhaps, given that each

item of property in an estate must be valued. The principles upon which value is estimated do not vary according as to whether an estate consists of one item of property or several items of property or of tens of thousands of items of property.'

([1967] 1 AC 506 at 535 **case 28 paras 36 and 37**)

Deduction of the cost of sale

The actual costs that would be incurred on an actual sale form no part of the statutory hypothesis. As Lord Guest stated:

'The words "price the property would fetch" in section 7(5) mean that it is not the price which the vendor would have received but what the purchaser would have paid to be put into the shoes of the deceased. This means that the costs of realisation do not form a legitimate deduction in arriving at the valuation. Such a result must follow from the provisions of section 7(3), which allows a deduction of 5 per cent in arriving at the value of foreign properties. The doctrine *expressio unius exclusio alterius* applies and indicates that cost of realisation are not permissible deductions in arriving at the valuation of properties within the United Kingdom.'

([1967] 1 AC 506 at 540 **case 28 para 53**)

The distinction between a UK-situs asset and a foreign situs asset should be noted. For a UK-situs asset, there is no provision for the deduction of the cost of sale. For property located outside the UK, an allowance is made for the actual cost of 'administering or realizing' the property, capped at 2 per cent of the value of the property (IHTA 1984, s 173).

Sub-division of the property to achieve higher sale proceeds

Perhaps the most important principle declared by the House of Lords in *Duke of Buccleuch v IRC* is that a sub-division of the asset is to be assumed if that would achieve a higher value. (The corollary of this is the principle declared by the Court of Appeal in *IRC v Gray* [1994] STC 360 **case 37** that separate assets in the estate must be assumed to be aggregated if that achieves a higher value.) Applying this principle to a share valuation, a valuer is required to consider all possible potential purchasers of the shareholding and this can include the sale of the holding in parts to a number of separate purchasers. Hence, if, for example, 25 per cent of the shares in a company are held by each of four shareholders and one holding falls to be valued, the valuer must consider the possibility of the remaining three shareholders each wishing to purchase one-third of the holding and, thereby, each shareholder ensures that no fellow shareholder obtains a 50 per cent holding.

Judgement

References, example '(pg523)', are to [1967] 1 AC 506, HL.

1 **LORD REID:** My Lords, the appellants are trustees of a settlement made by the 10th Duke of Devonshire in 1946. The Duke died on November 26, 1950, within five years of making the settlement and estate duty is admittedly payable on the whole of the settled property. This case is concerned with shares of the Chatsworth Estates Company and admittedly they must be valued with reference to the company's assets. These included 119,000 acres of land in England.

2 In 1961 the respondents determined the value of this land to be £3,176,64. The appellant appealed to the Lands Tribunal, maintaining that the valuation ought to be £2,743,760. The tribunal upheld the determination of the respondents and stated a case for the decision of the Court of Appeal, the question of law being: 'Whether upon the findings of fact we came to a correct decision in law.' On July 23, 1965, the Court of Appeal by a majority dismissed the appeal.

3 It is not very easy to determine what were the findings of fact of the tribunal or to state precisely the question of law which must now be decided. I think it best first to state the relevant law as I understand it and then to attempt to discover whether and if so where the tribunal misdirected themselves.

4 Section 7 of the Finance Act, 1894, provides that in determining the value of 'an estate' certain deductions are to be made. Estate there means the whole estate. Then section 7 (5) provides:

> '(5) The principal value of any property shall be estimated to be the price which, in the opinion of the commissioners, such property would fetch if sold in the open market at the time of the death of the deceased;'

5 In my view 'any property' does not refer to the whole estate of the deceased. His estate generally consists of a wide variety of different kinds of property – land, chattels, and incorporeal rights – and it would clearly be impossible to value it as a whole. The *(pg523)* context shows that 'any property' must mean any part of the estate which it is proper to treat as a unit for valuation purposes. This case turns on the determination of what are the correct principles to apply in subdividing an estate into units for valuation purposes, and it shows how greatly the total value of estate may differ according to how it has been subdivided. The statute is silent as to the proper methods of division.

6 Subsection (5) only applies after the division has been made but I think that it throws some light on this matter. It requires an estimate of the price which a particular unit would fetch if sold in a certain way, so one must envisage a hypothetical sale of the actual unit. And that sale must be supposed to have taken place 'in the open market' and 'at the time of the death.' The section must mean the price which the property *would have fetched* if sold at the time of the death. I agree with the argument of the respondents that 'at the time of death' points to a definite time – the day on which the death occurred: it does not mean within a reasonable time after the death. No doubt the words 'at the time of' are capable of such a meaning but I see nothing to recommend this meaning in this context. The value of some kinds of property fluctuates from day to day and there at least a particular day must be taken.

7 There was some argument about the meaning of 'in the open market.' Originally no doubt when one wanted to sell a particular item of property one took it to a market where buyers of that kind of property congregated. Then the owner received offers and accepted what he thought was the best offer he was likely to get. And for some kinds of property that is still done. But this phrase must also be applied to other kinds of property where that is impossible. In my view the phrase requires that the seller must take – or here be supposed to have taken – such steps as are reasonable to attract as much competition as possible for the particular piece of property which is to be sold. Sometimes this will be by sale by auction, sometimes otherwise. I suppose that the biggest open market is the Stock Exchange where there is no auction. And there may be two kinds of market commonly used by owners wishing to sell a particular kind of property. For example, it is common knowledge that many owners of houses first publish the fact that they wish to sell and then await offers: they only put the property up for auction as a last resort. I see no reason for holding that in proper cases the former method could not be regarded as sale in the open market. *(pg524)*

8 But here what must be envisaged is sale in the open market on a particular day. So there is no room for supposing that the owner would do as many prudent owners do – withdraw the property if he does not get a sufficient offer and wait until a time when he can get a better offer. The commissioners must estimate what the property would probably have fetched on that particular day if it had then been exposed for sale, no doubt after such advance publicity as would have been reasonable.

9 I am confirmed in my opinion by the fact that the Act permits no deduction from the price fetched of the expenses involved in the sale (except in the case of property abroad under subsection (3)). It is notorious that the rough and ready provisions of many sections of this Act can lead to great injustice with estate duty at its present level. But one must construe the Act keeping in mind that the maximum rate of duty which it provided was eight per cent. Parliament – or the Liberal Government of the time – seems to have thought that it was best to keep the scheme simple and to omit things which justice would seem to require if the practical difference with a low rate of duty would in most cases be negligible or would at worst be small. I find it impossible to suppose that they can have contemplated that the kinds of hypothetical sale which they envisaged would involve heavy expenses. In applying the provisions of any Act one must always try to find a construction which is not unreasonable.

10 With these matters in view I turn to consider the main question of law in this case – how the whole estate of the deceased should be divided into units for separate valuation. Generally the estate will consist of what one may call natural units – units or parcels of property which can be easily identified without there being any substantial difficulty or expense in carving them out of the whole estate. In my opinion it is implicit in the scheme of the Act that section 7 (5) should be applied to each of such units, and there is no justification for requiring elaborate subdivision of natural limits on the ground that if that had been done before the hypothetical sale the total price for the natural unit would have been increased. We must take the estate as it was when the deceased died; often the price which a piece of property would fetch would be considerably enhanced by small expense in minor repair or cleaning which would make the property more attractive to the eye of the buyer. But admittedly that cannot be supposed to have been done. And I see no more justification for requiring the supposition that natural units have been subdivided. This subsection applies to all kinds of property. A library was instanced by Winn LJ. Generally *(pg525)* there would be little difficulty, delay or expense in getting someone knowledgeable to pick out valuable books for separate valuation and I would therefore regard such books as natural units. But suppose that the deceased had bought a miscellaneous and mixed lot of surplus stores intending to sort out and arrange them in saleable lots. That might involve a great deal of work, time and expense and I see no justification for requiring the supposition that that had been done and then valuing the saleable lots that would have emerged.

11 It is sometimes said that the estate must be supposed to have been realised in such a way that the best possible prices were obtained for its parts. But that cannot be a universal rule. Suppose that the owner of a wholesale business dies possessed of a large quantity of hardware or clothing or whatever he deals in. It would have been possible by extensive advertising to obtain offers for small lots at something near retail prices. So it would have been possible to realise the stock at much more than wholesale prices. It would not have been reasonable and it would not have been economic, but it would have been possible. Counsel for the respondents did not contend that that would be a proper method of valuation. But that necessarily amounts to an admission that there is no universal rule that the best possible prices at the date of death must be taken.

12 I have said that this Act applies rough and ready methods. It is vain to apply theoretical logic. The question of what units to value is a practical question to be solved by common sense. So if the commissioners apply the right criteria there is no appeal. But in this case it is difficult to discover whether the commissioners or the tribunal have applied the right criteria.

13 The matter has been made more difficult by misconceptions about what seems to be the only authority, *Ellesmere (Earl of) v Inland Revenue Commissioners.* We were invited to consider the report in the Law Times series. But I find that there is a notable discrepancy between the two reports, which I feel sure that counsel would have drawn to our attention had they been aware of it. I find that in the Court of Appeal Lord Denning MR adopted and gave great weight to a passage from the judgment of Sankey J. as reported in the Law Times which is absent from the report in the Law Reports. I do not know what the practice was in 1918, but I suspect that the judgment in the Law Reports may have been *(pg526)* revised by the learned judge and that the judgment in the Law Times was not. The report in the Law Reports appears over the initials of the senior King's Bench reporter named in the title page of the volume and I cannot believe that an experienced reporter would have cut out this passage without the authority of the judge himself. I think that it goes too far and on second thoughts Sankey J may well have thought the same.

14 The facts were that on the death of the late Earl his successor was advised by an eminent firm to sell as one lot an estate of 2,200 acres which comprised a variety of agricultural holdings, business premises and woodlands. In 1915 it fetched £68,000. The purchaser resold in lots. By 1917 he had realised £65,000 and he still had unsold parts worth £16,000. The referee held the value at the date of death to be £75,618. Before Sankey J the commissioners contended that having regard to the varied character of the property and the fact that it did not all lie together the price realised by a sale in one lot could not represent the true value. Sankey J said that there might be many cases where a sale to a single purchaser could not realise the price which the property would fetch in the open market. He instanced an owner selling as one lot a colliery and a draper's shop, and gave instances where the owner sold in one lot because he wanted money quickly. Then he said:

> 'But it does not at all follow that the price which he obtains under such circumstances is "the price which it would fetch if sold in the open market."

What is meant by those words is the best possible price that is obtainable, and what that is is largely, if not entirely, a question of fact. I can readily conceive cases in which a sale of the whole property in one lot would realise the true market price, but I can equally imagine cases in which it would not. Here the referee held that because the property was of a miscellaneous character and not lying in a ring fence the price paid by the single purchaser was not the true value. I think he was entitled so to hold, and that the contention as to misdirection fails.'

15 I see nothing wrong with the decision, and, subject to what I have said about the best possible price, I would quarrel with nothing in the passage which I have quoted from the Law Reports. But in the Law Times there is interpolated in that passage the passage, quoted by Lord Denning, that the property must be sold 'in such a manner and subject to such conditions as might reasonably be calculated to obtain for the vendor the best price for the property' and this has been taken to justify elaborate and expensive subdivision of natural units if that course would increase the gross price. If *(pg527)* Sankey J did delete this passage when he revised his judgment I think he was wise. But it was strongly founded on by the respondents in argument and it may well have misled the tribunal. They quote it in full in their interim decision.

16 The property assessed includes ten estates in England and the respondents did not determine their valuation until 11 years after the Duke's death. They proceeded on the basis that these 10 estates had to be notionally divided into some 3,500 units and that each of these units had to be valued separately. All that we learn from the tribunal about the way in which the estates were so divided is contained in a sentence in a letter from the respondents and in a short paragraph in the interim decision. The letter states that the valuation had. been made on the basis of such lotting of the whole property as was calculated to produce the best price. Before the tribunal was the Hardwick estate (some 20,000 acres) alone was investigated, it being taken as typical. With regard to it the tribunal say:

> 'For the purposes of arriving at the valuation, 'the estate had been divided into some 532 separate units, each unit representing a lot which, in the Revenue's view, would have commanded the best market price if sold on the date of the Duke's death.'

17 If the dubious passage in the judgment of Sankey J were right if given the meaning for which the respondents contend there would be no need to say more. And it must be said in fairness to the tribunal that the argument as then presented for the appellant did not raise the method of lotting. So we do not know whether or not substantially all the units which were valued separately were what I have called natural units nor do we know how much time, work or expense was involved in the lotting or would have been involved if the owner of these estates had decided to sell them in these units. What we do know is that the tribunal quote and apparently accept evidence of one of the appellants' witnesses 'that it would have been impossible to sell all the individual units within a reasonable time of the date of death, and [he] took the view it would take at least seven years.' The respondents' witness said that it would have been impossible to sell all the units within a year, but he did not say how long he thought it would take. The argument for the appellants before the tribunal and their first argument before your Lordships was that this by itself was enough to show that the respondents' method must be wrong. For reasons which I shall state in a moment I cannot accept that argument. Before I could *(pg528)* reach any decision in favour of the appellants I should at least have to know how far this delay of seven years would have been caused by initial difficulties of lotting and drawing up conditions of sale for these numerous lots, how far it would have been caused by the lack of sufficient professional men with the necessary skill, and how far it would have been caused by a desire not to flood the market.

PART 2   Cases

18 The 10 estates to be valued were each managed as a separate unit at the time of the Duke's death and the appellants maintain that each should now be valued as a single unit subject to the excision and separate valuation of a number of outlying parts which were easily severable. The tribunal have found that, if that is the proper method of dividing the property for valuation, the total value of these estates would be some £433,000 lower than the respondents' valuation based on separate valuation of smaller units. The reason for this large difference is that only speculators or property developers or investors would be interested in buying entire estates. A buyer who intended to resell the estate in small lots would have to incur the trouble and expense involved in dividing up the estate, he would have to lay out his money for a long time, and he would expect to make a reasonable profit. He might therefore only pay for the estate some 80 per cent. of the total amount which he would expect to realise from re-selling it in small lots.

19 The appellants say that the true value of these estates at the date of death must be the amount which would be realised within a reasonable time. If the respondents' values could only be realised over a period of seven years and after incurring much expense which is not a permissible deduction, then the basis of their valuation must be wrong.

20 But we cannot approach the problem in that general way, however just and attractive it may seem. And if we could look at the problem broadly there is another side to it. If the deceased only owned two or three farms then it could not be disputed that the proper method of valuation would be to suppose each farm to have been sold as a separate unit; so what justification can there be for valuing a particular farm in one way if the deceased -had owned few others but in another way if he had owned a great many. I do not think that we can decide the question on general arguments of this kind. We must go back to section 7 (5).

21 If I am right in thinking that section 7 (5) is dealing one by one with the units into which the estate has already been divided then the hypothetical sale which it envisages must be a supposed sale of *(pg529)* one unit in the conditions which in fact existed at the date of the death. To add one unit to those which in fact were then for sale would not have disturbed the market. But if we had to suppose that a large number of the units owned by the deceased had been put on the market simultaneously, the conditions which in fact existed would have been materially altered and prices would have dropped: This is expressly dealt with by section 60 (2) of the Finance, (1909–40) Act, 1910, but I doubt whether this subsection did more than express what was already implicit in the Act of 1894.

22 It must follow that the fact that it would have taken a long time to sell separately the units of a large estate is irrelevant in so far as that delay would have been caused by the need to avoid flooding the market. And in so far as delay would have been caused by there not being enough qualified professional men to make the necessary preparations for a very large number of separate sales within a short period, that factor .must, I think, be equally irrelevant. So in my view we come back to the question with which I have already dealt – whether the estates were so easily separable into large numbers of units that these units can be regarded as what I have called natural units.

23 This matter was never separately investigated by the tribunal because the appellants did not raise it as a separate point. I think that the problem could be approached in this way. Suppose that each of these 532 units had been separately owned, Then if the owner of, one of them had died it would have cost his executors an appreciable percentage of its value to sell it – say on the average X per cent. But that would not have been a permissible deduction. So if the owner of 532 units dies his executors cannot reject in so far as the cost of realisation amounts to X per cent of the total value of the units. But in so far as it exceeds that amount they have a legitimate grievance. As the Act deals with such problems in a rough and ready way, they would have to tolerate a moderate excess. But if there were a great excess caused by initial difficulty and cost in dividing the estate into lots, that would be evidence – it might be strong evidence – that these units were not truly natural units.

24 In a case such as the present I would not regard it as fatal to the appellants' case that this point was taken before the tribunal: I would be prepared to consider whether justice required a remit for further findings. But in this case it seems to me obvious from the facts already in the case that the factor which I have tried to describe could not have accounted for the greater part of the *(pg530)* difference between the valuations of the appellants and the respondents. So I do not think that this is a case in which the exceptional course of making such a remit would be justified. I must therefore move that the appeal be dismissed.

25 LORD MORRIS OF BORTH-Y-GEST: My Lords, after the death of the 10th Duke of Devonshire, who died on November 26, 1950, it became necessary for estate duty purposes to value as at that date the shares in the Chatsworth Estates Company. By virtue of section 55 of the Finance Act, 1940, the principal value of the shares fell to be estimated by reference to the net value of the assets of the company. Amongst the many and various assets were real and leasehold properties. The principal value of the assets had to be estimated in accordance with the provisions of section 7 (5) of the Finance Act, 1894.

26 By letter dated November 3, 1961, the Commissioners of Inland Revenue informed the trustees of the Chatsworth Settlement of the values as determined by the commissioners. Included in the figures which in the aggregate gave the principal value of the shares there was a figure of £3,450,874 which was the principal value of the real and leasehold property. The real and leasehold properties were (save as to property in Scotland valued at £274,228) in various parts of England. The value of the properties in England was, therefore, determined to be £3,176,646.

27 Pursuant to section 1 (3) of the Lands Tribunal Act, 1949, the trustees (the appellants) exercised their right to appeal to the Lands Tribunal against the commissioners' determination. The appeal appears to have been limited to a consideration of the values of those assets which consisted of real and leasehold properties. In England those properties amounted to some 119,000 acres or 186 square miles. In a schedule sent by the commissioners with their letter of November 3, 1961, the properties were divided into 10 estates. The values had been arrived at by adding together the separate valuations of the various units comprising the various estates. In all there were in England some 3,521 units into which the commissioners had divided the estates. One of the 10 estates was called the Hardwick estate. Its total acreage was 20,635. Its valuation was fixed at £868,129. That sum represented the total of the separate valuations of 532 separate units. For the purposes of argument before the tribunal and parties agreed to consider that estate in particular in the hope that, if an interim decision were given in relation to that estate, it might be possible to agree values *(pg531)* in respect of the other estates in dispute. After a hearing on five days in February, 1964, the Lands Tribunal gave an interim decision on May 4, 1964. In the course that they recorded the points raised and their findings. On the basis of that decision and in the light of it the parties agreed the values of the other English properties. That enabled the Lands Tribunal to give their decision. The decision was dated January 15, 1965. By that decision they fixed the value of the English real and leasehold properties under the statutory provisions as being £3,176,646 – which was the figure as determined by the commissioners. They held, however, that if on appeal the basis should be accepted alternative to that which they upheld then the total valuation should be £2,743,760 rather than £3,176,646. Those figures exclude the property in Scotland. By section 3 (4) of the Lands Tribunal Act, 1949, a decision of the Lands Tribunal is final but a person aggrieved by the decision as being erroneous in point of law may require a case to be stated. The tribunal were asked to state a case. They did so on April 12, 1965. It is important to endeavour to ascertain what is the point of law which is raised. In the case stated the tribunal record and set out the grounds of appeal which the appellants had raised against the determination by the commissioners of £3,450,874 and they referred to their interim award (dated May 4, 1964) as containing the facts proved or admitted and the contentions advanced. The point of law was stated as being whether on their findings of fact they came to the correct decision in law.

28 It becomes necessary, therefore, to study the interim decision of May 4, 1964, in order to see what were the findings of fact and to see what were the contentions advanced which raised any question of law and to see from their interim and final decisions what their findings were.

29 The facts as found beyond those to which I have already referred appear to be as follows:

(a)   The Hardwick estate comprised principally farms with farm buildings but there were also smallholdings, allotments, gardens, agricultural land, woodlands, residential property, sporting rights, ground rents, licensed houses, leases of quarries and collieries and the land upon which the Staveley Ironworks stand.

(b)   The area of the Hardwick estate was 20,635 acres.

> 'For the purposes of arriving at the valuation, the estate had been divided into some 532 separate units, each unit representing a lot which, in the Revenue's view, would have commanded the best market price if sold on the date of the duke's death. *(pg532)*
>
> Detailed tables showing the particulars in respect of each unit were produced in evidence before the Lands Tribunal.'

30 I can find nothing in the decision of the Lands Tribunal which suggests that the units were artificial or unnatural or irrational or which suggests that it was contended that the actual division into units which was adopted was objectionable or was objected to. In the case of properties having a total area of 20,635 acres which were being managed and looked after as one estate it would be reasonable to assume that any division into separate units or lots would be made so as to accord with the realities affecting the features of and the locations of the properties. If it had been desired to suggest that the method of division into separate units had been arbitrary or unreasonable a finding to that effect would have been sought from the Lands Tribunal. The decisions of the Lands Tribunal contained no such suggestion.

(c)   The valuations of the units as assessed by the Revenue were sound and were correct provided always that the units were to be separately valued. The valuation on the Revenue basis was made on the assumption that each of the units had been sold in the open market at the time of death at a price which might reasonably have been expected to be paid for that lot at that time. Such prices were based on prices obtained on the sale of comparable properties and the general level of prices for lots of the particular kind as at the date of the death.

31 The contentions raised by the trustees would appear to have been as follows:

(i)   The basis of valuation was wrong in that the sum of £3,450,874 represented the aggregate of the individual values of each separate unit on the basis that there would have been a purchaser prepared at the time of death to give the full open market value for each such unit.

(ii)   The £3,450,874 should be reduced so as to take account of the impossibility of offering for sale at the time of death all the real and leasehold property except as a whole or as individual estates. The only purchaser on a sale in the open market at the time of death would have been an investor or a speculator: and such person would only have paid a reduced price because he would have to safeguard himself against the risks and delays and uncertainties affecting re-sale or re-sales, would also have to provide for the costs of re-sale or re-sales and would have to provide for his profit on re-sale or re-sales.

(iii)   The sum of £3,450,874 could only have been realised by an orderly disposal of the units over a considerable period of time and, *(pg533)* to arrive at a price which the. property would be expected to fetch at the time of death, deductions would have to be made to cover deferment to probable dates of sales and to cover uncertainties as to conditions. at the dates of such sales and to cover the costs of preparing for such sales.

(iv)   'The time of death' should be construed as meaning -within a reasonable period after the date of death. In fact and in practice the sale of an estate such, for example, as the Hardwick estate could only have been realised within a reasonable period (which it was said would be one year) if the bulk of the estate were sold in one block.

32 The findings of the tribunal would appear to have been as follows:

1.   The price which would have been obtained for the Hardwick estate would have been higher if it were sold in separate lots than if sold as a whole to an investor or speculator.

2.   The price to be ascertained is that which the property would fetch at the time at which the death occurred and not that which would have resulted from a sale consequent on death.

3.   The valuations as at the time of death of the various separate items were correct.

33 Accordingly, the Lands Tribunal decided that the value of the Hardwick estate arrived at under the statutory provisions was £868,129. On that basis the value of the real and leasehold property in England was £3,176,646.

34 In the event of their being wrong in law the Lands Tribunal proceeded to fix the value of the Hardwick estate on an alternative basis. On the alternative basis the value of the Hardwick estate was £733,637: on that basis the value. of the real and leasehold property in England was £2,743,760.

35 The point of law which emerges, therefore, is whether the basis taken was correct or whether the alternative basis was correct. To appreciate precisely the point of law raised it is important to quote what the Lands Tribunal state was the alternative basis which was put forward. They say:

'If we are wrong in law and what ought to be assumed are the circumstances of an actual sale taking place within a reasonably short time from the time of the death, and, that preparations for this sale would be commenced at the time of the death, then we agree that in order to secure the best open market price within such a time the properties would have to be sold in the manner put forward by the appellants, that is to say; each estate would have to be sold as a whole, and the only properties extracted would be those which could, thereby, *(pg534)* individually produce a higher price and yet at the same time leave the large unit no less attractive for sale.'

36 My Lords, I think that the Lands Tribunal were right in not accepting such a basis. In a number of respects it disobeys the directions given by section 7 (5). The value of any property must be estimated to be the price which, in the opinion of the commissioners, the property would fetch if sold in the open market at the time of the death of the deceased. 'At the time of the death' must not be paraphrased or altered so as to read 'within a reasonably short time of the death.' It follows from this that the section is envisaging a hypothetical sale at the time of the death. This is quite inconsistent with a notion that the value of a piece of property is to be estimated by postulating that preparations for an actual sale would be commenced at but after the time of death and that a sale would later follow after such preparations. This is not what the section, which is in effect a valuation section, envisages. The section prescribes the criterion for valuation.

37 The case stated contains a summary of some of the evidence given before the Lands Tribunal. There was evidence to the effect that with an estate of the size of the Hardwick estate, containing, as it did, some 20,000 acres, it would in practice take several years to effect the sale of it by selling 532 separate units. There was evidence that if it were desired to sell the whole estate within a period of about a year the only way in which in practice this could be achieved would be (after separating a few easily disposable units) to sell the main part of the property as a whole with the result that the only purchaser would be one out of a limited class of investors or speculators. Such a person would only pay a sum which would be some 20 per cent. less than the aggregate amount which he would consider that he would be able to secure at later dates after arranging for the division of the property into units and after allowing for all the expenses to which he would be put and after allowing for his profit.

38 In my view, the considerations to which this evidence pointed were quite irrelevant. It stands to reason that it would have been impossible in fact to sell the Hardwick estate after the death of the Duke but on the day of his death, it November 26, 1950. It would have been impossible there and then to sell it either as a whole or in separate units: equally, it would have been impossible there and then to sell some 46 separate units and to sell the remainder as one entity. Furthermore, it would have been quite impossible there and then to sell either as an entity or as a series of entities *(pg535)* all the various estates in England. Their total area was just under 119,000 acres or 186 square miles. All this merely serves to emphasise that section 7 (5) is a valuation section in that it points to a time by reference to which and a basis upon which values are to be estimated. When the section speaks of the value of 'any property' or of 'the property' an indication is, perhaps, given that each item of property in an estate must be valued. The principles upon which value is estimated do not vary according as to whether an estate consists of one item of property or several items of property or of tens of thousands of items of property.

39 The basis propounded by the appellants before the Lands Tribunal was, I think, rightly rejected for a further reason. The value of a property is to be estimated to be the price which it would 'fetch' if sold in the open market at the time of the death of the deceased. This points to the price which a purchaser would pay. The net amount that a vendor would receive would be less. There would be costs of and incidental to a sale. It would seem to be harsh or even unjust that allowances cannot be made in respect of them. But the words of the statute must be followed. A valuation would be on an entirely different basis if related to such figure as would be likely to be realised in fact and in practice if there was a sale at as early a date after the death as was practicable and if the units of property comprising what had been administered as a large estate could only at such time be sold to an investor or speculator.

40 It was submitted that the valuation ought to have been made on the basis of taking the property as it was at the time of death and not on some altered basis. For management purposes the properties now being considered were doubtless referred to as an estate. When all in one ownership they could conveniently and no doubt desirably all be looked after as one estate. But by being divided into separate viable units the properties were not physically altered. The fact that in the section there is a reference to 'the property' cannot mean that if many properties are in one ownership then they must only be conceived of as one property. It must be beyond question that it would take a very considerable time with an 'estate' of 20,000 acres to arrange for sales in the open market of the units or items or lots comprising it and to arrange for their separate descriptions. Unless, however, the units as arranged for valuation purposes can be characterised as unreal or spurious or artificial their classification becomes a reasonable and necessary and essential part of the process of valuing. That in reality and in practice sales of nearly 120,000 acres could not *(pg536)* suddenly have been arranged to take place on November 26, 1950, is irrelevant. Equally is it irrelevant that fair prices could not be obtained if the property market were suddenly deluged. Section 60 of the Finance (1909–1910) Act, 1910, postulates that an estimate of value 'according to the market price at the time of the death' is not to be reduced on account of the estimate being made on the assumption that the whole property (which I think must mean all the properties) is to be placed on the market at one and the same time. The stipulation that an estimate must be made of the value which a property would fetch if sold in the open market does not, in my view, require an assumption that the highest possible price will be realised. It involves that an estimate should be made of the price which would be realised under .the reasonable competitive conditions of an open market on a particular date. I see no fault in what the Lands Tribunal found had been the assumption of the Revenue in making their valuations, ie, that each of the units had been sold in the open market at the time of death at a price which might reasonably have been expected to be paid for that lot at that time, such expectation being based on prices obtained on the sale of comparable properties and the general level of prices for lots of the particular kind at the date of death.

41 On the point of law raised I consider that the Lands Tribunal were right in rejecting the alternative basis that they set out and I consider that on their findings of fact they came to a correct decision in law.

42 I would dismiss the appeal.

43 LORD HODSON: My Lords, the question at issue between the parties relates to the valuation of the Hardwick estate, part of. the real and leasehold property owned by the Chatsworth Estate Company, for the purpose of ascertaining the estate duty payable in consequence of the death of the 10th Duke of Devonshire, who died on November 26, 1950.

44 The appellants, who are the trustees of the Chatsworth Settlement, maintain that the Lands Tribunal were wrong in law is taking as a basis for the valuation of the estate a division into some 532 separate units (less 46 'hived-off' in one piece), each unit representing a lot which, in the Revenue's view, would have commanded the best market price if sold at the date of the Duke's death. The appellants agreed the value attributed to the individual units if valued on the basis adopted by the Revenue but contended that the Revenue's basis was wrong, in that it was not legitimate to divide *(pg537)* the estate into separate lots. Their contention was that the Hardwick estate and the other nine English estates subject to the settlement must be regarded as being offered for sale without lotting in the condition in which they were at the. time of death. On this assumption the only purchasers would be investors or speculators and the price which such persons would be willing to pay would be much lower. The separation into lots had never been made or contemplated and, although the lots could properly be valued individually, to do so, including making ready for sale, etc, would take several years and involve considerable expense. Accordingly, the assumption should be one of a sale in one unit, as the Hardwick estate physically was, so that a price would be obtainable of some 20 per cent. less than the price obtainable by the valuation of the commissioners.

45 The question depends on the construction of section 7 (5) of the Finance Act 1894. It is to be observed that the section does not contemplate an actual sale or even the possibility of sale. Notional sale only is envisaged, as was made plain by the decision of your Lordships in *Inland Revenue Commissioners v Crossman.*

46 It is further to be observed from the terms of the section itself that no deductions permissible to cover the expenses of sale or of making ready for sale. If there were doubt about this it is set at rest by the language of section 7 (3) of the Act, which permits an allowance to be made where additional expense in realising property has been incurred because of the property being situate out of the United Kingdom.

47 This, in my opinion, makes inadmissible the argument of the appellants that the method of valuation adopted by the Revenue should not be accepted because of the expense involved in making ready for sale and in selling in lots. Further, no deduction can be made in respect of the length of time which an actual orderly disposal of the various units might take. This, in my opinion, follows from the language of section 7 (5) which speaks of 'the time of the death of the deceased' as the moment of the hypothetical sale. I cannot, therefore, accept the argument for the appellants that these reductions should be made so as to reflect the price which could be obtained within a reasonable time of death. This involves an extended construction of the words 'the time of the death' which I do not think is admissible in the context in which they appear. *(pg538)*

48 In my opinion, the Lands Tribunal were entitled to find as a fact, as they did, that the permissible units of valuation were those which, in the case of the Hardwick estate, were 532 in all. If they were entitled to sub-divide and were not compelled to treat the English estates as indivisible, there is no objection taken to the figures reached, for the appellants agree the values attributed to the individual units if valued upon the basis adopted by the Revenue.

49 The case for the appellants has never been that the sub-division into units was artificial. On the contrary, they have argued that the valuation was objectionable owing to the impossibility of realisation within a reasonable time. I agree with my noble and learned friend Lord Wilberforce that the fact that one estate may be capable of division into 100 units and another not is not to be taken into account simply because of the practical difficulty of organising sales. This would be to treat an owner of a large estate more favourably than the owner of a small one. Accepting as I do the Revenue's contention that no deduction in respect of the expenses of sale or making ready for sale is permissible I do not see any room for further inquiry as to the way in which the value of each individual unit was reached. The Revenue rely on *Ellesmere (Earl of) v Inland Revenue Commissioners*, but I do not think it should be taken as laying down any principle according to which a particular estate ought to be regarded as one whole for valuation or regarded as divisible into portions. My noble and learned friend Lord Reid has drawn attention to the variation in the report of the case in the Law Reports as compared with that in the Law Times, but upon either version I remain of the same opinion.

50 I would dismiss the appeal.

51 LORD GUEST: My Lords, the 10th Duke of Devonshire died on November 26, 1950. The duke had some four years and eight months previously transferred to the appellant trustees nearly all his shares in the Chatsworth Estates Company, which owned a considerable amount of real and leasehold property in England. By virtue of section 55 of the Finance Act, 1940, the value of the shares in the company falls to be estimated by reference to the net value of the assets of the company. The estates are, therefore, to be treated as if they had passed on the death of the duke in terms of section 1 of the Finance Act, 1894. *(pg539)*

52 At the date of the duke's death the company owned some 186 square miles or 119,000 acres of real and leasehold property divided into 10 estates. The Commissioners of Inland Revenue determined the value of the real and leasehold property at £3,176,646, the value attributable to the Hardwick estate consisting of 20,635 acres being £868,129. The values were arrived at by the addition of separate valuations for each of 3,787 units, the division of the Hardwick estate being into 532 units. The appeal of the appellants against the determination of the commissioners was dismissed by the Lands Tribunal, but the tribunal stated that if the tribunal were wrong in law the alternative value would be £2,743,760. The tribunal stated a question of law for the Court of Appeal who sustained the determination of the tribunal.

53 Before the Lands Tribunal the Hardwick estate was taken by the parties as a typical example on the facts of which the correct principle could be decided and then applied to the other estates. The figure contended for by the appellants for the valuation of the Hardwick estate was £732,637 whereas the figure in the commissioners' determination was £868,129.

54 Owing to the agreement of the parties to take the Hardwick estate as typical the difference between the Revenue and the appellants as to the value of all the estates belonging to the company amounts to £432,886.

55 The statutory provisions governing the principal value for estate duty purposes are contained in section 7 (5) of the Finance Act, 1894. Before discussing the construction of the subsection it is necessary to appreciate the way in which the case was conducted before the Lands Tribunal. The estate was of a miscellaneous and varied character consisting principally of farms with farm buildings, but there were also smallholdings, allotments, gardens, agricultural land, woodlands, residential property, sporting rights, ground rents, licensed houses, leases of quarries and colliery lands and the land upon which the Staveley Ironworks stand. Out of the 532 units upon which the commissioners' determination had been based the appellants agreed that 46 were separate and could easily and expeditiously be disposed of separately. As regards the remaining 486 units the respondents contended that the total value of these units should be the aggregate of the valuations of each of these units. The appellants, while conceding that the 46 separate units could properly be valued separately by themselves, contended that the division and making ready for sale of the remaining block would take several years and involve considerable expense and that accordingly for the purpose of estimating the *(pg540)* principal value the whole of this block should be assumed to be sold as one unit. Sold in this way the price obtainable, it was argued, would be some 20 per cent. less than the price obtainable by the method of sale contended for by the Revenue.

56 The terms of section 7 (5) of the Finance Act, 1894, have already been quoted. The value of property under this section is to be taken to be at its market value at the date of the death of the deceased. Some things, I think, are reasonably clear The words 'price the property would fetch' in section 7 (5) mean that it is not the price which the vendor would have received but what the purchaser would have paid to be put into the shoes of the deceased. This means that the costs of realisation do not form a legitimate deduction in arriving at the valuation. Such a result must follow from the provisions of section 7 (3), which allows a deduction of 5 per cent. in arriving at the value of foreign properties. The doctrine *expressio unius exclusio alterius* applies and indicates that cost of realisation are not permissible deductions in arriving at the valuation of properties within the United Kingdom. 'At the time of the death' means at the moment of death, not within a reasonable time after the death. Further, the section does not require the envisagement of an actual sale. In fact it is irrelevant in arriving at the valuation to consider what would have been the circumstances attending an actual sale. So far the construction of section 7 (5) is, I think, reasonably clear.

57 But the contest between the appellants and the Revenue before the Lands Tribunal was whether the full value of the aggregate of the values of each unit should be taken or whether the aggregate should be reduced by some percentage deduction. This was the only issue before the Lands Tribunal, as is shown by the table of figures produced. Section 7 (5) of the Act of 1894 prescribes a method valuation in order to ascertain the 'principal value' of the estate in section 1. I do not find any assistance from section 1 in deciding into what units an estate is to be divided for purposes of valuation. This is a question of circumstances. Different properties will require different methods of valuation under the section. Different properties may require to be split into different units. A man owns a manor house, agricultural land, leases of farms, pictures, a library, a factory and some villages. To decide the market value of such an estate the property may have to be split up into several separate units of valuation. There may have to be sub-units for instance, the library may require to be examined in order to see whether the whole should be valued together or whether some individual books possess a value which necessitates *(pg541)* their separate valuation. Similarly, a village might require the separate valuation of each house, each licensed house, each hall, as these would normally be sold separately. These are entirely questions of fact to be decided upon by the Lands Tribunal. The question of law is, what is the proper method of valuation of each of these units of valuation? It was argued before this House that the Lands Tribunal had in the present case artificially divided the Hardwick estate into 532 mythical lots and then valued each lot, the addition of the individual values making up an aggregate valuation. If I had thought that such method had been adopted, I should have come to the conclusion that the Lands Tribunal had erred in law in their valuation and that this method of valuation was not in accordance with section 7 (5) of the Act of 1894. But I am not so satisfied.

58 The commissioners having issued their determination of value, it was for the appellants to displace this valuation before the Lands Tribunal. I can detect no evidence in the interim decision of the Lands Tribunal that the commissioners had divided the estate into artificial lots or that the Lands Tribunal had done so in arriving at their valuation; there was no evidence that the units into which the estate had been divided were other than proper units of valuation. The revenue basis of valuation was made.

'on the assumption that each of the units had been sold in the open market at the time of death at a price which might reasonably have been expected to be paid for that lot at that time. Such prices being based on prices obtained on the sale of comparable properties and the general level of prices for lots of that kind at that time.'

59   There was in fact no dispute between the parties as to what units were to be taken as, nor as to the valuation of, the individual units of valuation. The appellants' basis of valuation is not very easy to understand. Mr Strathon, a valuer called for the appellants, expressed the view that it would be impossible within a year after death to sell all the individual units separately and that the only way to sell such an estate within a reasonable period would be to 'hive-off' certain individual units which could be sold readily as separate units and to offer the remainder of the estate as one unit which would attract an investor. He had deducted 20 per cent. from 'the sum of the prices agreed on the Revenue basis for the units comprised in the larger unit.' His calculation of the figure of 20 per cent. is not clear. Mr Strutt, another valuer for the appellants, said it would have been impossible to sell all the individual units within a period of seven years of the date of death. *(pg542)* His valuation was based on the view that a 'speculator' would be the most likely buyer and the result of his calculations approximated very closely to Mr Strathon's. Neither of these witnesses indicated that the division into units which they accepted for their valuation was unnatural or artificial. In fact it was the basis of their valuation in arriving at the aggregate figure which they then reduced to provide for the 'investor' or 'speculative element.'

60   The only question for this House appears to me whether the Lands Tribunal erred in law in not accepting the appellants' methods of valuation and in preferring the Revenue's method. The appellants' method of valuation was, in my opinion, not in accordance with the terms of section 7 (5). It is not necessary to assume an actual sale: a hypothetical market must be assumed for all the items, of property at the date of death. The impossibility of putting the property on the market at the time of death or of actually realising the open market price is irrelevant. In other words, you do not have to assume that the property had actually to be sold; the assumption is that it is sold at the moment of death.

61   The authorities relied upon by the Revenue included *Inland Revenue Commissioners v Crossman*. This case is important because it shows that items of property must be valued even though there is no open market for them. The existence of an open market is not a condition of liability: section 7 (5) merely prescribes the open market as the measure of value (Viscount Hailsham). *Ellesmere (Earl of) v Inland Revenue Commissioners* was strongly relied on by the Crown and also finds a place in the interim decision of the Lands Tribunal and in the judgment of Lord Denning MR. This was the case of the valuation of a miscellaneous property of some 2,000 acres where the successor to the 3rd Earl of Ellesmere, contrary to advice received by him from surveyors, sold his estate to a speculator in one lot for £68,000. The surveyors had advised him that he would obtain less for the estates if he sold in one lot than if he sold it in individual lots. The speculator re-sold a portion of the property for £65,000 and the remainder was worth about £16,000. The commissioners valued the property at £77,000 on the principle that the market price was the price the property would have realised if it had been divided up and sold in lots. The referee upheld the commissioners' contention with a slight reduction on the valuation. An appeal to Sankey J failed. It will be seen that *(pg543)* on its facts this case closely resembles the present. A property of a varied and miscellaneous character actually sold as one lot, but the price obtained was not taken as the value but the value was the aggregate of the values of the separate lots. The decision of Sankey J was that the referee had acted upon the correct principle in arriving at his decision and that there was evidence upon which he could properly find the principal value of the property at the sum which he had fixed. Sankey J said:

'Now the Act of 1894 says that the value of the property shall be estimated to be the price which it would fetch if sold in the open market. That, in my opinion, does not necessarily mean the price which it would fetch if sold to a single purchaser. There may be many cases where a sale to a single purchaser cannot realise 'the price which it would fetch if sold in the open market.' Take the case of an owner having property including a colliery and a draper's shop. It is conceivable that if the colliery and the draper's shop were sold separately the best possible price might be obtained for each. On the other hand a purchaser who was anxious to buy the draper's shop might not wish to be encumbered with a colliery, and vice versa, and consequently if the owner insisted upon selling the whole property to one purchaser he would not obtain the market price which the Act contemplates. So, too, with regard to property of the same character situate in different areas. It may well be that if in such case the vendor insists upon the different parts being all sold to the same person he will not get as good a price as if he allowed different persons to buy the portions situate in the different districts. No doubt a sale in one lot of a varied property such as that in the present case may be highly convenient to the vendor. He may want to get the money quickly; he may not care to risk an auction. He may be going abroad, or may be called up to serve in the Army, and it may be of great importance to him to sell at once. But it does not at all follow that the price which he obtains under such circumstances is 'the price which it would fetch if sold in the open market.' What is meant by those words is the best possible price that is obtainable, and what that is is largely, if not entirely, a question of fact. I can readily conceive cases in which a sale of the whole property in one lot would realise the true market price, but I can equally imagine cases in which it would not. Here the referee held that because the property was of a miscellaneous character and not lying in a ring fence the price paid by the single purchaser was not the true value. I think he was entitled so to hold, and that the contention as to misdirection fails.'

62 With respect to the learned judge I entirely agree. The market *(pg544)* value of property is the best price that can be obtained for the property in the open market.

63 My noble and learned friend Lord Reid has discovered that the passage in the judgment of Sankey J which occurs in the Law Times to this effect:

'I am of opinion that according to the true construction of section 7 (5) of the Finance Act 1894, and section 60 (2) of the Finance (1909–10) Act 1910, the principal value means the price which the property would have fetched on the death of the deceased in the open market if it had been then sold in such a manner and subject to such conditions as might reasonably be calculated to obtain for the vendor the best price for the property; but I am satisfied that this is largely, if not entirely, a question of fact for the referee.'

does not appear in the official report. In fact the entire judgment appears to have been substantially re-written. It is true that the passage excised from the Law Times is referred to by the Lands Tribunal, and by the Court of Appeal and is founded on by the Revenue in support of their contention that the property must be divided into saleable lots to arrive at its value. As I have said there is, in my opinion, no justification for an artificial division of the property into separate lots in order to arrive at a higher value and the passage quoted from Sankey J in the Law Times would not afford justification for such a method of valuation. I do not, however, think that the *Ellesmere* case was a case of artificial division and I can find no suggestion in the present case that any such artificial division of the Hardwick estate was made.

64 I would dismiss the appeal.

65 LORD WILBERFORCE: My Lords, the Finance Act, 1894, requires that for the assessment of estate duty a valuation must be made of all the property passing or deemed to pass on the death. The Act lays down the principles of valuation: when the valuations have been completed and all the necessary adjustments made, the duty is levied at the appropriate rate. Although the basis for valuation is the market price at the time of death, the Act does not require that any property forming part of the estate should actually be sold: in fact, some sales will be necessary, but this is no concern of the Revenue. The Act does not require the valuers to step as it were into the shoes of the deceased or of his executors, or take account of the practical difficulties or delays inherent in *(pg545)* any realisation except to the extent that these may help to fix the market price at the time of death.

66 When, as is usually the case, the estate consists of an aggregate of items of property, each item must be separately valued, and it is not difficult to see that problems may arise as to the manner in which the separate units of valuation are to be ascertained or in which individual items are to be grouped into units of valuation. These problems must necessarily be resolved, as they are in practice, in a common sense way. The estate is to be taken as it is found: it is not to be supposed, in order to obtain higher figures of valuation, that any substantial expense is to be incurred or work done in organising the estate into units: on the other hand, some practical grouping or classification, such as can reasonably be carried out without undue expenditure of time or effort, by a prudent man concerned to obtain the most favourable price, may be supposed.

67 Questions of subdivisions or grouping must commonly occur in relation to the larger landed estates, which may consist of farms, houses, allotments, woodlands, accommodation lands and incorporeal rights. *Ellesmere (Earl of) v Inland Revenue Commissioners*, decided in 1918, was concerned with such an estate and it appears that the method there approved by the court has been adopted and followed generally as a working rule. The decision can be accepted as a sound and useful decision in the kind of situation to which it relates, but the limits of its application must be understood. The estate there was an aggregate of separate units, the division of which was apparent and which had been accepted immediately after the owner's death by his successors: the question for decision was whether the Revenue was bound to accept for valuation purposes the figure obtained through the actual sale of the estate as a whole or whether it was permissible to value the units. It did not involve and does not assist upon any question whether a particular 'estate' ought to be regarded as one whole, or whether, for valuation, it may be regarded as divisible into portions and, if the latter, how many portions, or how they may be grouped. The judgment of Sankey J, with or without the passage quoted by Lord Denning MR, and, as my noble and learned friend Lord Reid points out, omitted from the Law Reports, must be read in this light.

68 Another illustration of the working of this principle but of a kind converse to the Ellesmere case is the Scottish decision of *(pg546) Inland Revenue Commissioners v Marr's Trustees*. This related to a herd of cattle. A valuation had been made of the herd as a whole and it was objected that a separate value should have been taken for each head. The Lord Ordinary rejected the objection on the basis that a choice between herd valuation and head valuation was a pure finding of fact.

69 The Act of 1894 entrusts the task of valuation to the Commissioners of Inland Revenue, from whom an appeal lies, in matters affecting land, to the Lands Tribunal. It is for these bodies to fix the units of valuation according to the principles I have endeavoured to indicate, and then to value each unit. Their decisions, being findings of fact, can only be reviewed for misdirection or other error in law. I now proceed to examine the findings in this case.

70 This appeal relates to the Hardwick estate, selected as a case typical of the other estates belonging to the Chatsworth Estates Company. But the term 'Hardwick estate' is merely a term of convenience used to describe a considerable aggregate of separate and disparate properties. In their interim decision the Lands Tribunal describe it in these terms:

> 'The estate comprises principally farms with farm buildings, but there are also small holdings, allotments, gardens, agricultural land, woodlands, residential property, sporting rights, ground rents, licensed houses, leases

of quarries and colliery lands and the land upon which the Staveley Ironworks stand.'

They continue with the following passage:

'For the purposes of arriving at the valuation, the estate had been divided into some 532 separate units, each unit representing a lot which, in the Revenue's view, would have commanded the best market price if sold on the date of the duke's death.

Detailed tables showing the particulars in respect of each unit were produced in evidence and summarised tables were also produced at the hearing.

The appellants agree the values attributed to the individual units if valued upon the basis adopted by the Revenue, a basis which they do not accept as that which should be applied.

The dispute between the parties is as to the basis of valuation to be adopted in the light of the statutory provisions which are inapplicable.'

71 Together with a subsequent reference to unity of management which I do not find of assistance this is all the finding the decision *(pg547)* contains. There is a reference in a letter written by the Solicitor of Inland Revenue on February 14, 1962, to 'such lotting of the whole property as was calculated to produce the best price.' This is scanty material indeed and I have anxiously considered whether the whole case ought not to be remitted for further findings – a depressing result 15 years after the relevant date. In the end, however, I have come to the conclusion that this course should not have to be taken. The finding states the divisibility, in the opinion of the Lands Tribunal, of the 'estate' into 532 units; a figure arrived at, it is seen, after inspection of maps and other data as well as of the locality. It was open to the appellants to contest the appropriateness of this division and to submit either that the 'estate' should be regarded as one whole or that any division of it should be into fewer or different units: for example, that it should be regarded as consisting of outlying portions – of which there were 46 identifiable parcels – plus a central indivisible nucleus.

72 But, as the interim decision shows, they did not do this. Their case was quite a different one. It was that it was impossible to realise the estate, as so divided, within a 'reasonable time': that, if one is to suppose disposition within a 'reasonable time' (of the order of 12 months from the death) the only disposition which could be made was of the outlying portions in lots, and of the remainder as a whole. And the alternative basis of valuation suggested by them is on this hypothesis, treating the remainder as suitable for sale only to a speculator or investor. The evidence given by their two experts, as recorded in the interim decision, was to this effect: it was directed to the impossibility of realisation of the individual units within a year or a reasonable time. Neither is recorded as saying that the suggested division into 532 units was artificial, or that it did not correspond with reality or with the state of affairs actually existing at the date of death. So, unsatisfied though I must remain as to the completeness of the factual findings presented to us, I think that we are obliged to deal with this case on the footing that the Hardwick estate as existing at the date of death may properly and reasonably be regarded as composed of 532 units of valuation.

73 The next stage is to inquire what figure or figures result from this. The Revenue's valuation is stated to be

'on the assumption that each of the units had been sold in the open market at the time of death at a price which might reasonably have been expected to be paid for that lot at that time. Such prices being based on prices obtained on the sale of comparable properties and the general level of prices for lots of that kind at that time.' *(pg548)*

74 After so arriving at the values of individual units, the Revenue simply aggregates them to form a total figure for the 'estate.' The appellants' objection is that the aggregation takes no account of the impossibility of offering all the 'estate' at the time of death except as a whole, or as a whole after 'hiving-off' outlying portions. The Revenue's figure, they contend, could only have been achieved 'by an orderly disposal of the various units which would have taken a very considerable time' and so deductions should be allowed to cover 'deferment to probable dates of sales, uncertainties as to conditions at the dates of such sales and costs of preparing for such sales.'

75 The evidence of their experts, as recorded in the interim decision, was directed to showing the impossibility of disposal by lots in 'a reasonable time' and the Revenue's expert agreed with this. Both the appellants' experts said that the only sale possible in a reasonable time was by 'hiving-off' outlying portions and selling the core as one unit to an investor or speculator. The evidence did not establish positively what a 'reasonable time' would be, nor did the Lands Tribunal make any finding as to this matter.

76 My Lords, it must be clear that, if the principles of statutory valuation are as I have stated earlier in this opinion, the appellants' argument cannot succeed, based as it is upon a suppositions relevant to some actual sale which may have to be made. This is in conflict with the scheme of the Act. Once a figure has been arrived at for the value of a unit, that is the relevant 'principal' value: the Act does not provide for any reduction in the value either of any one unit or of the total of their values on account of the multiplicity of similar units: indeed, in section 60 (2) of the Finance Act, 1910, it contains an explicit prohibition of any reduction to take account of any lower price which might result from placing them all on the market at one and the same time. The nature of the 'impossibility' of disposing of the units of this estate in a reasonable time is not explained in the evidence, but whatever it is I am of opinion that no allowance for it is warranted by the legislation. If it is a matter of mere numbers and the practical or administrative difficulty in organising sales, to allow a deduction would mean treating differently the owner of 100 units (say, separate farms) from the owner of one, and that cannot be right. If it is a matter of flooding the market, that is something which under positive enactment cannot be taken account of (Finance Act 1910, s60 (2)). If it is a matter of finding a purchaser for any individual property, which may take time, that is something which ought to be reflected *(pg549)* in the individual valuations of that property. We were not informed about this one way or the other and I am left with some uneasiness whether due allowance has been made for this factor. Again the issue was not joined on this point but upon the admissibility or otherwise of a deduction on account of the time which, it was claimed, would be involved in disposing of so many units of property. This, in my view, is inadmissible.

77 There remains one other matter as to which I feel much difficulty. The appellants claim, in general terms, that, even if the Revenue's basis of valuation is correct, a deduction should be allowed for the extra expense of realisation in individual lots. The Revenue dispute this, contending that expenses of sale are in law not deductible. The wording of the Finance Act, 1894, s7 (5), adequate perhaps when it was passed, but with the great increase of rates of duty now severe and even unjust, requires the gross open market price, ie what the purchaser pays, and not what the vendor ultimately receives, to be taken as the valuation figures. Moreover, as I have already stated, in making the valuation it is not legitimate to arrive at a higher price by supposing that expenditure, by way, for example, of repair or improvement on the property, has been made. But I do not think that this is the end of the matter, or that the section necessarily prevents account being taken of the cost of lotting an estate, by which I mean preparing adequate separate particulars of existing units, or, in relation to moveables, cataloguing a collection. These are matters which may very well enter directly into the value of the property: an uncatalogued collection may be worth less than a catalogued collection: an estate as to which no particulars exist as to the individual units may be worth less than one fully equipped with maps, valuations and records. The injustice of making no allowance for the difference can be seen if one supposes that the deceased had himself caused the catalogue or particulars to be made before his death: in such a case the expense of so doing, which may be quite considerable, would have been withdrawn from his estate. So I would see no reason why, in a suitable case, the commissioners might not treat that aggregate as worth somewhat less than the total of the individual values on account of the absence of a catalogue or of necessary particulars. In referring to a suitable case, I have in mind an estate which, taking it as it is found at the date of death, can fairly be said to be made up of an aggregate of units or items, suitable for separate disposal: if, in order for this to be possible, expenditure on the estate itself is required, then it *(pg550)* would not be right to treat the estate as anything but an indivisible whole.

78 We do not know in the present case whether there was or was not such an absence of detailed description of the individual units as would fairly be reflected in diminution of value of the aggregate: the appellants, whose interest it would have been so to contend, do not seem to have called any specific evidence to the point. But in general terms they made the claim and I would have thought it appropriate to remit the matter to the Lands Tribunal for a finding of fact on this limited point. Apart from it – and I understand that this step does not commend itself to your Lordships – I have come to the conclusion that the appeal must be dismissed. *(pg551)*

Case 29
In re Lynall deceased

(1968), (1969) & (1971) 47 TC 375

High Court

17, 18, 19, 20, 21, 24, 25, 26, 27 and 28 July and 1, 2 and 17 July 1968

Court of Appeal

17, 18, 19, 20 and 23 June and 29 July 1969

[1971] 3 All ER 914, HL

House of Lords

5, 6, 7, 8, 12 and 13 July and 27 October 1971

In this case, the judge in the High Court gives a very thorough analysis of the different criteria influencing share price. The judgement of Plowman J is a useful example for a valuation report, containing many points both of legal principle and also methodology for a fiscal valuation.

The decision is made of even greater value by the fact that appeal was made ultimately to the House of Lords, which approved and restored the judgement of Plowman J.

Mrs Nellie Lynall died on 21 May 1962. In her estate was a holding of 67,980 Linread Limited £1 ordinary shares (28 per cent of issued share capital of the company). The Revenue valued the shareholding at £5 10s per share. The executors valued the shareholding at £2 per share.

Following her death, one year later in July 1963, there was a public issue of 27.5 per cent of the company's shares at £7 16s per share, the issue being 22 times over-subscribed.

Plowman J commences his judgement by identifying the shareholding to be valued and the valuation date. He then gives the statutory provisions requiring valuation.

Plowman J states the areas of dispute between the parties:

'Two important questions, however, are in dispute: first, what evidence is admissible, in relation to the likelihood at Mrs Lynall's death of a public issue? And, secondly, what was the true value of Mrs Lynall's shares at that time in the light of the admissible evidence? The latter is an exercise in the art, which I do not profess, of valuation, but I have had a great deal of expert evidence and my task is to make the most intelligent guess that I can.'

((1968) 47 TC 375 at 377 **case 29 para 5**)

Plowman J then states the history of the share capital of the company, from its incorporation 37 years before the valuation date onwards up to the valuation date ((1968) 47 TC 375 at 377 **case 29 para 7**). He notes the relevant articles that prohibit transfer other than at a fair value with pre-emptive rights (at para 8).

The business of the company, which was a manufacturer of screws, bolts and rivets, is stated, with the turnover and profits being recorded ((1968) 47 TC 375 at 378 **case 29 para 9**).

The dividend policy of the board is given ((1968) 47 TC 375 at 379 **case 29 para 10**).

The capital position of the company and the value of its fixed assets are noted ((((1968) 47 TC 375 at 379 **case 29 para 11**).

Plowman J concludes that Linread Limited was a substantial high-class private company with a successful profit record, even in a difficult year for the industry like 1961. The company showed growth, a strong liquid position, a high dividend cover and a very satisfactory cash flow. Linread Limited was undoubtedly likely to do well if it went public. To go for a public quotation required the directors to conclude that a quotation would be in the best interests of all parties ((1968) 47 TC 375 at 379 **case 29 para 12**).

The judgement now turns to the question of information, Plowman J notes:

'All the matters to which I have referred up to this point are matters of information which would have been available to the hypothetical seller and the hypothetical buyer of Mrs Lynall's shares, either from a consideration of the company's accounts up to the date of death or from other easily accessible sources. I must now mention certain additional facts which were not of that character, and which, had they been known to the hypothetical seller and the hypothetical buyer, would have influenced the purchase price and therefore the value of Mrs Lynall's shares.'

((1968) 47 TC 375 at 379 **case 29 para 13**)

The information that was not available from easily accessible sources was:

1.   The year that finished two months after the valuation date was a financially highly successful year, turnover and profit having risen substantially with the dividend declared being covered over eight times.
2.   The chairman's speech at the annual general meeting shortly after Mrs Lynall's death gave financial information that supported a high share valuation.
3.   Without making a statement to the shareholders or the public at large, the board was making investigations into ways in which money could be raised. Before the valuation date, Cazenove had reported on a method for floating the company which would have put a value of £1.3 million to £1.6 million on the business (£5.38 to £6.62 per ord).

Plowman J reviews the authorities on availability of information in this context. The judge referred to three documents as 'Category B documents'. He identified these and gave his comments on each, as follows:

'(1)   The accounts for the year ending 31 July 1962, being post-death documents, are not admissible as evidence of the value of Mrs Lynall's shares at the date of her death, except possibly to the limited extent that they record information on the period up to the date of death.

(2)   The chairman's speech is a post-death document and is not admissible. In any event, in my view, it added nothing of any material significance to the 1961 accounts themselves.

(3)   Mr Alan Lynall, whose evidence was tendered and accepted as being the evidence of the board, said in evidence that if, at the date of his mother's death, he had been asked by a prospective purchaser of her shares to forecast the profits for the year ending 31 July 1962, his answer, being as helpful as possible, would have been: "Roughly in line with the preceding year"; and if asked by the same enquirer to forecast the dividend for the year ending 31 July 1962 he would have said that he expected it to be the same as that for the preceding year ...

In the light of that evidence, which I see no reason to reject, my conclusion is that the category B documents are not admissible, since the information contained in them is neither published information nor information which would have been elicited from the board on inquiry ...'

((1968) 47 TC 375 at 386 **case 29 paras 22 and 23**)

The nature of a likely potential purchaser was then identified ((1968) 47 TC 375 at 386 **case 29 para 24**).

Plowman J then gave principles on which he proposed to value the shareholding as:

'In the ten years prior to Mrs Lynall's death there had been no transactions for value in the company's shares which would afford any guide to their value at the date of her death. In these circumstances there are, I think, three principal factors which affect valuation: (1) the appropriate dividend yield; (2) the prospective dividend; and (3) the possibility of capital appreciation.'

((1968) 47 TC 375 at 387 **case 29 para 24**)

He then dealt with each of these three points in turn, first, by means of outline summary and then by recording the relevant parts of the evidence given by the expert witnesses ((1968) 47 TC 375 at 387 to 390 **case 29 paras 24–31**).

Standing back, and looking at all the information in the round, Plowman J gave his conclusion:

'For these reasons I have reached the conclusion that, while the valuations put forward by the plaintiffs' experts are on the low side, those of the Crown's experts are on the high side. Making the best estimate I can in all the circumstances, I fix the value of Mrs Lynall's shares at £3 10s. If I am wrong in my view that the category B documents are not admissible, then I would add £1 to £3 10s, bringing the value up to £4 10s per share.'

((1968) 47 TC 375 at 391 **case 29 para 33**)

Following *In re Lynall deceased*, Parliament enacted in FA 1973, s 51(3) which states:

'For the purposes of a determination [for capital gains tax or, now, for inheritance tax], it shall be assumed that, in the open market which is postulated for the purposes of that determination, there is available to any prospective purchaser of the asset in question all the information which a prudent prospective purchaser of the asset might reasonably require if he were proposing to purchase it from a willing vendor by private treaty and at arm's length.'

(Now TCGA 1992, s 273(3) and IHTA 1984, s 168(1))

Hence for a death (for inheritance tax) or a disposal (for capital gains tax) on or after 6 July 1973, the valuer must consider what information, in all the particular circumstances of the particular case, would be available to the statutory hypothetical unconnected purchaser making an offer to purchase on the valuation date. In making the valuation, this information must be brought into consideration, as well as information that is actually available. There are very useful comments from the evidence of Bruce Sutherland in *Caton's administrators v Couch* [1995] STC (SCD) 34 at 51b **case 38 para 72** in which he gives his expert opinion (which was accepted by the Special Commissioner) of the information that directors of a large private company would be expected to provide where the prospective purchase was of a significant monetary value. The judgement as to what information would be available is not easy. In *Re Holt* (1953) 32 ATC 402 at 406 **case 25 para 15**, Danckwerts J reports the evidence given by a director of the company as regards the financial position of the company at the valuation date. The director stated in his evidence that the information he had given the court would not have been given to a buyer of shares as it was commercially sensitive. The director stated, however, that if an accountant acting for a prospective buyer of a significant number of shares had requested the commercially sensitive information, he would have supplied that information to the accountant in exchange for an undertaking that it would not be passed to the prospective buyer but would be used by the accountant to advise his client on the prudence of the purchase and the price that could reasonably be offered for the share ((1953) 32 ATC 402 at 406 **case 25 para 18**).

The evidence of value can include sale prices actually achieved and values that have already been agreed by other taxpayers or for other purposes with HMRC Share Valuation (*IRC v Stenhouse's Trustees* [1992] STC 103 at 110c–f **case 36 para 11**).

Where the valuation is in respect of an employee's share option and subject to income tax under Sch E by virtue of TA 1988, s 135, statute directs that the valuation is made in accordance with the rules that apply for capital gains tax (see ITEPA 2003, s 421(1)) and, hence, it must be assumed in valuing the shares acquired by the employee that all information would be available that one would expect to have available to a hypothetical unconnected purchaser of the number of shares that is being valued. By contrast, where the valuation is for any other purpose of income tax (such as valuing a trading receipt which consists of shares) or is undertaken for the rare purposes of VAT or stamp duty, the statutory provision deeming information to be available has no effect. Hence, for a valuation under any of these provisions, the principle enunciated in *In re Lynall deceased* is to be followed; that is, only information actually available is to be considered.

Judgement in the High Court

References, example '(pg376)', are to (1968), (1969) & (1971) 47 TC 375.

1   PLOWMAN J – This is an appeal by the executors of the late Mrs Nellie Lynall under s10 of the Finance Act 1894 against the determination by the Commissioners of Inland Revenue of the value, for the purposes of estate duty, of 67,980 £1 ordinary shares (representing a 28 per cent interest) in the capital of Linread Ltd., which at all material times was a private family company. The Commissioners of Inland Revenue originally fixed the value at £4 per share, but they have since redetermined the value at £5 10s. The Plaintiffs, on the other hand, contend for a value of somewhere between £2 and £2 15s. If the Crown is right, the rate of estate duty payable on Mrs Lynall's death will be increased from 50 per cent to 65 per cent, and something like £175,000 in duty is at stake. *(pg376)*

2   Mrs Lynall died on 21st May 1962, and in essence the dispute centres round the question how likely was it, at the time of her death, that the company would go public in the foreseeable future? It is common ground that the greater that likelihood, the higher the value to be attributed to Mrs Lynall's block of shares. In fact there was a public issue of $27\frac{1}{2}$ per cent of the company's shares in July 1963 at the equivalent of £7 16s. per share, the issue being 22 times over-subscribed. But it is again common ground that the knowledge of after-events must be disregarded in fixing the value of Mrs Lynall's shares at the date of her death.

3   There is no dispute as to the basic principles on which a minority holding in an unquoted private company falls to be valued. Section 7(5) of the Finance Act 1894, provides:

> 'The principal value of any property shall be estimated to be the price which, in the opinion of the Commissioners, such property would fetch if sold in the open market at the time of the death of the deceased.'

4   It is common ground that the shares must be valued on the basis of a hypothetical sale on 21st May 1962 in a hypothetical open market between a hypothetical willing vendor (who would not necessarily be a director) and a hypothetical willing purchaser, on the hypothesis that no one is excluded from buying and that the purchaser would be registered as the holder of his shares but would then hold them subject to the articles of association of the company, including the restrictions on transfer: see *Commissioners of Inland Revenue* v *Crossman* [1937] A.C. 26.

5   Two important questions, however, are in dispute: first, What evidence is admissible, in relation to the likelihood at Mrs Lynall's death of a public issue? and, secondly, What was the true value of Mrs Lynall's shares at that time in the light of the admissible evidence? The latter is an exercise in the art, which I do not profess, of valuation, but I have had a great deal of expert evidence and my task is to make the most intelligent guess that I can.

6 Faced with a similar problem, Danckwerts J in *Holt* v *Commissioners of Inland Revenue* [1953] 1 W.L.R. 1488, at page 1492, said this:

'The result is that I must enter into a dim world peopled by the indeterminate spirits of fictitious or unborn sales. It is necessary to assume the prophetic vision of a prospective purchaser at the moment of the death of the deceased, and firmly to reject the wisdom which might be provided by the knowledge of subsequent events. In my task I have had the assistance of a number of experts on each side who differ in their opinions in the manner in which experts normally do, and the frankest of them admitted that certain of his calculations were simply guesswork. It seems to me that their opinions are indeed properly described as guesswork, though, of course, it is intelligent guesswork, aided by the experience which they have gained by their work as stockbrokers or accountants. No possible suggestion can be made against the honesty of these witnesses, but their methods of calculation appear to me to be inevitably uncertain and controversial, and, in my view, statements by several of them that they would have been ready to buy the shares at the price reached by them if they had had the opportunity some five years ago must be discounted accordingly. Nonetheless, I could not have approached my task without their valuable assistance, and my remarks must not be taken to belittle the efforts which have been made by them to provide an answer to a question to which no certain answer is possible.' *(pg377)*

In all that, I respectfully concur.

7 So much by way of introduction. I must now say something about the company. It was incorporated in the year 1925 with an authorised capital of £1,000. At the times with which I am concerned its issued capital was £241,700, divided into 241,700 shares of £1 each. All those shares, with the exception of 200, were held within the Lynall family. Mrs Lynall's husband, Mr Ezra Lynall, who was one of the founders of the company and its chairman, held 77,040, representing approximately 32 per cent Mrs Lynall, as I have said, held 67,980, representing approximately 28 per cent; their two sons, the present Plaintiffs, each held 48,240, or approximately 20 per cent The remaining 200 were held by a Mr Ellis, the general manager, who had been in the company's service for many years. Those five persons were also the directors of the company, and except for Mrs Lynall were executive directors, Mr Ezra Lynall being managing director, Mr Alan Lynall technical director, and Mr Donald Lynall sales director.

8 Mr Ezra Lynall survived his wife and died in the year 1966. At the time of her death she was 76 years of age and her husband 69. Their elder son was 44 and their younger 39. By her will Mrs Lynall appointed her sons to be the executors and bequeathed to them equally her shares in the company. The articles of association of the Company contain stringent restrictions on transfer, in particular Article 8, which is as follows:

> 'The Directors may in their absolute and uncontrolled discretion refuse to register any proposed transfer of shares and Regulation 24 of Part I of Table "A" shall be modified accordingly and no Preference or Ordinary Share in the Company shall be transferable until it shall (by letter addressed and delivered to the Secretary of the Company) have been first offered to Ezra Herbert Lynall so long as he shall remain a Director of the Company and after he shall have ceased to be a Director of the Company to the Members of the Company at its fair value. The fair value of such share shall be fixed by the Company in General Meeting from time to time and where not so fixed shall be deemed to be the par value. The Directors may from time to time direct in what manner any such option to purchase shares shall be dealt with by the Secretary when communicated to him.'

At the time of Mrs Lynall's death a fair value never had been fixed. A prospective purchaser of Mrs Lynall's shares might well have taken the view, rightly or wrongly (and I am not really concerned which), that, on the true construction of this article, if he wished later to dispose of his shares by transfer he would be unlikely to obtain more than their par value, and that his chances of obtaining an accretion to his holding from other members of the company were remote.

9 The business of the company, which is based in Birmingham, is principally the manufacture of what are called 'cold-forged fasteners', which include such things as screws, bolts and rivets. The company is a leading manufacturer in that field. In the year 1962 about half its business was with the motor industry, and a quarter with the aircraft industry. At the time of Mrs Lynall's death the company was a very flourishing company. Its profit and dividend record can be seen from an agreed document, P.1, which was prepared by Sir Henry Benson, who gave evidence for the Crown. This shows, among other things, that between the year ending 31st July 1957 and the year ending 31st July 1961 (the last completed financial year before the death) the turnover *(pg378)* had risen from £979,000 to £1,607,000; the profits before depreciation and taxation had risen from £112,798 to £300,905; and the profits available for dividend had risen from £35,456 to £135,496. The trend between those years was upward, the most dramatic increase being between 1959 and 1960, when sales rose from £1,267,000 to £1,604,000; the profits before depreciation and taxation from £180,299 to £309,516; and the profits available for dividend from £90,697 to £141,343.

10 The policy of the board was always to pay a small dividend and retain the major part of the profits in the business in order to finance the expansion of the company and the replacement of its assets. For 1957 and 1958 a dividend at a rate of 5 per cent was paid; for 1959 10 per cent; and for 1960 and 1961 15 per cent. On average, each of those dividends was covered over six times. Even the 5 per cent. dividend for 1957 and 1958 was ten times the equivalent rate for 1952 and 1953. But in the background were the Special Commissioners. Under threat of surtax directions under s245 of the Income Tax Act 1952 additional net dividends totalling £27,798 were declared and paid in the year ended 31st July 1957 in respect of the years 1949 to 1953 inclusive, and from that time on the board's dividend policy was influenced by the desire to avoid the possibility of a surtax direction. In that they were completely successful. In June 1961 clearance was obtained down to 31st July 1959, and, although clearance was not sought in Mrs Lynall's lifetime for the years 1960 and 1961, it was obtained after her death.

11 Another agreed document prepared by Sir Henry Benson, P.2, shows a strong capital position. Between the years 1957 and 1961 the fixed assets at cost less depreciation had risen from £259,376 to £396,753. This development had been financed entirely out of accumulated profits, with the result that the capital reserves, which stood at £127,102 in 1957, had disappeared in 1961. On the other hand, the company's cash resources (including tax reserve certificates) had risen from £218,783 to £263,200. Its only liability for borrowed money was a small mortgage reducing by £2,000 per annum, which in 1957 stood at £20,000 and in 1961 at £12,000. The ratio of its current assets to its current liabilities had gone up from 1.7 : 1 in 1957 to 2.4 : 1 in 1961. The company's balance sheet as at 31st July 1961 shows that it was then committed to capital expenditure estimated at £105,000. Up to that time the increase in profits had been roughly proportional to capital expenditure.

12 This, then, was a substantial high-class private company with a successful profit record, even in a difficult year in industry like 1961, showing growth, a strong liquid position, a high dividend cover and a very satisfactory cash flow (that is to say, aggregate of depreciation and retained profits). It was undoubtedly likely to do well if it went public. But that, of course, depended on the volition of the directors.

13 All the matters to which I have referred up to this point are matters of information which would have been available to the hypothetical seller and the hypothetical buyer of Mrs Lynall's shares, either from a consideration of the company's accounts up to the date of death or from other easily accessible sources. I must now mention certain additional facts which were not of that character, and which, had they been known to the hypothetical seller and the hypothetical buyer, would have influenced the purchase price and therefore the value of Mrs Lynall's shares. The first concerns the company's accounts for the year ending 31st July 1962. Mrs Lynall died with two months of that year still to go, and at her death the accounts were not, of course, in existence. What they ultimately showed was this: sales had risen to £1,801,000; *(pg379)* profits before depreciation and taxation had risen to £400,295; and profits available for dividend had risen to £180,067. The dividend, however, remained the same at 15 per cent. This was covered over eight times. The fixed assets had risen to

£484,727, cash resources to £289,136, and the ratio of current assets to current liabilities to 3 : 1. When Mrs Lynall died the directors must have had a fairly good idea of this general trend. The 1962 accounts would have confirmed an optimistic profits forecast, but frustrated an optimistic dividend forecast.

14 The second is the chairman's speech at the annual general meeting of the company on 7th June 1962, that is to say, shortly after Mrs Lynall's death. The speech was not circulated before the meeting, and there is no evidence that it was in existence at the date of death. (At this point I should mention, parenthetically, that although the accounts for the year ending 31st July 1961 were not passed until 7th June 1962, they had been audited and signed in Mrs Lynall's lifetime and it is common ground that they ought to be taken into account.)

15 Thirdly, there are what have been called the category B documents. These are documents which came into being in Mrs Lynall's lifetime, and which record the investigations which the board was making into possible ways and means of raising money to pay prospective death duties. They are, in their nature, private documents. They show that in July 1959 Mr Ezra Lynall began to show concern with the question of estate duty on the death of himself or his wife, and consulted solicitors, who prepared a memorandum on the subject suggesting various alternatives, including a flotation. In December 1959 the board asked Messrs. Thomson McLintock to carry out a survey of the company's undertakings with a view to a public issue. In July 1960 Thomson McLintock made a preliminary report and the matter stood over until the 1960 accounts were available. In February 1962, as a result of further discussions, Thomson McLintock expressed the view that the board should consider a flotation at the earliest possible moment, either in May 1962, based on the 1961 accounts, or at the end of the year when the 1962 accounts were available. They also suggested that Messrs. Cazenoves should be consulted in order to obtain the reaction of the City. Mr Ezra Lynall replied noting Thomson McLintock's views and stating that the board did not wish to rush into a flotation without studying the situation from every angle. He agreed that Thomson McLintock should consult Cazenoves, without, however, committing the board to any course of action. In March 1962 Cazenoves made a report to Thomson McLintock suggesting the method of flotation. They thought that a minimum of 25 per cent of the shares might be sold on a $5\frac{1}{2}$ per cent to 6 per cent dividend yield basis with a minimum earnings cover of $2\frac{1}{4}$ to $2\frac{1}{2}$ times. This would put a value of £1,300,000 to £1,600,000 on the business. Copies of this report were sent to the company in April 1962, but nothing had been decided when, in May, Mrs Lynall died.

16 What knowledge of these matters is to be imputed to the hypothetical vendor and the hypothetical purchaser? And by what criterion is the answer to this question to be judged? There are a number of possibilities. At one end of the scale is the proposition for which Sir Milner Holland contended on behalf of the Crown, that the Court, in valuing the shares, should have regard to all

facts which are proved before it to have been facts at the relevant time. This would include all the facts deducible from the category B documents. At the other end of the scale is the proposition that the Court ought not to impute to the parties knowledge of anything more than the company's accounts *(pg380)* and any other information which has been made available to the shareholders or was available to the public at large. I will refer to this as 'the published information'. Between the extremes of omniscience on the one hand and the published information on the other lie two further possibilities. The first is that the hypothetical vendor and the hypothetical purchaser must be deemed to be in possession, not only of the published information, but also of any information which the directors would have given in answer to any reasonable question likely to be asked by any vendor-shareholder or intending purchaser. This is the proposition for which Mr Bagnall contends on behalf of the Plaintiffs, basing himself on *Holt v Commissioners of Inland Revenue*. The second is the proposition, for which no one has hitherto contended, that the parties must be taken to know any additional facts which a hypothetical reasonable board of directors would have disclosed in answer to any reasonable inquiries which the vendor or the intending purchaser or his advisers might have made.

17 I will consider the relevant authorities in a moment, but apart from authority there are, to my mind, two objections to the proposition for which the Crown contends. In the first place, it seems to me to substitute an intrinsic value test for 'the price which, in the opinion of the Commissioners, such property would fetch if sold in the open market', to quote s7(5) of the 1894 Act. To take an example, suppose the deceased to have been the owner of a picture which had been authenticated by the world's leading experts as being the work of some old master. In fact it is the work of a forger, but at the time of the deceased's death that fact is known only to the forger himself and possibly a small number of associates. The price the picture would fetch in the open market at the date of death might be enormous, though it might be almost nothing if the fact of the forgery were known to the buyer. On the wording of the subsection it appears to me to be plain that the higher value is the value for estate duty purposes even if the forger later confesses. Secondly, once the door is opened to let in evidence over and above the published information, and particularly if all the knowable facts are admissible, an intolerable burden of investigation would be laid upon the Commissioners, and I can see no warrant in the language of the subsection for subjecting them to it. I do not therefore accept the test suggested by Sir Milner Holland.

18 Had I felt entirely free to choose between the other alternatives, I should have preferred the 'published information' criterion, partly for the practical reason that I have already indicated, namely, the administrative difficulties of the Commissioners in applying any other, and partly because it is, in my view, wrong to assume, as a matter of law, that a board of directors would disclose to any individual member or to an intending purchaser or his advisers any information which it was under no duty to disclose, such as a contemplated flotation: see *Percival v Wright* [1902] 2 Ch. 421. In the first place, this would mean that the value of the shares, in respect of which the known financial facts remained constant, would be liable to vary at the whim of the board. Secondly, once such an assumption is made, a whole new field of inquiry is opened: What would be reasonable questions to ask? What would reasonable answers to those questions be? What would this particular board have answered if asked? – and so on. None of the answers to these questions is likely to be conclusive or even very satisfactory, and the only safe assumption is that the board would disclose what it was bound to disclose and no more.

19 I turn now to authority. Three cases were cited to me, the first of which was *Salvesen's Trustees v Commissioners of Inland Revenue* (1930) 9 ATC 43 , *(pg381)* a case in the Court of Session concerned with the depreciatory effect of restrictions on transfer contained in the company's articles of association. Lord Fleming's judgment contains a number of passages which refer to the question of the buyer's knowledge. At page 45 he said this:

"The estimation of the value of a share in a company, whose shares cannot be bought and sold in the open market, and with regard to which there have not been any sales on ordinary terms, is obviously one of difficulty. There has been one transfer by Mr Theodore Salvesen of 5,000 shares to his son at their par value, but the petitioners did not found upon this transaction as being any real guide to the value of the shares. The problem can only be dealt with by considering all the relevant facts so far as known at the date of the testator's death and by determining what a prudent investor, who knew these facts, might be expected to be willing to pay for the shares. Counsel for both the petitioners and respondents accordingly assumed that the prospective buyer would inform himself of all the relevant facts and, in particular, would have made available to him the accounts of the company. The relevant facts may, I think, be classified under the following heads: (1) The history of the whaling industry; (2) the history of the company from its inception to the date of the testator's death and particularly its position at that date; (3) the prospects of the whaling industry generally at that date and of this company in particular; and (4) to what extent the restrictions in the articles might be expected to depreciate the value of the shares." At page 49 he said: "It appears from the evidence of the chairman of the company that he has had a long and intimate knowledge and experience of the industry. The hypothetical buyer would see from the accounts that he and the other directors were quite willing year after year to embark the large profits, which they had already made from the industry, in another year's trading and would draw his own conclusions from that circumstance." Then, at page 50: "Apart from any conclusion which an intending investor might draw from the break-up value of the undertaking, he would, I feel sure, especially when he was informed that it was intended to continue the company's trading operations, examine the most recent balance sheet carefully with a view to obtaining some indication of the value of the concern as a going undertaking. A person who was being invited to acquire a third of the shares of a private company which imposed stringent conditions on the right of transfer would certainly wish to ascertain the value at which the assets had been entered in the last balance sheet. As a prudent person he would, of course, keep in view that he was purchasing the shares in October 1926 and that the balance sheet shows the affairs of the company as at July 1926 and he would make inquiry as to the alterations in its financial position which had taken place between these two dates." Finally, at page 51: "I quite recognise that the problem I have to deal with must be solved in the light of the information available at or about the time of the testator's death, but I think that, however, does not debar me completely from making any reference to the balance sheet at 31st July 1927, which includes a period of nearly three months prior to the testator's death. The profit made in that year was £171,122 and the directors set aside £400,000 as a dividend reserve. This seems to indicate that the directors must have considered that the undistributed profits that they had in hand at the end of the previous year were far more than was necessary for trading purposes and might have been used by them to maintain the rate of dividend in bad years." *(pg382)*

There is nothing in those passages which leads me to think that the judge had in mind the problem of the various categories of knowledge with which I am concerned. The facts which he regarded as relevant appear to have been what I have called the published information, particularly the accounts of the company, plus some information as to whether there had been any alteration at the date of death in the position as disclosed by the last published accounts. He permitted himself a look at the accounts for the year in which the death occurred, but as this was a document which was not in existence at the date of death he can, I think, have done so only in the context of a check on the profit and dividend forecast which might have been made at the date of death.

20 The second case, also in the Court of Session, is *Findlay's Trustees v Commissioners of Inland Revenue* (1938) 22 ATC 437. That case concerned the value to be put upon a share in the goodwill of a partnership. The hypothetical vendor would necessarily be a partner, and the relevant information would therefore include information in the possession of the vendor as a partner. At page 440, Lord Fleming said:

"In estimating the price which might be fetched in the open market for the goodwill of the business it must be assumed that the transaction takes place between a willing seller and a willing purchaser; and that the purchaser is a person of reasonable prudence, who has informed himself with regard to all the relevant facts such as the history of the business, its present position, its future prospects and the general conditions of the industry; and also that he has access to the accounts of the business for a number of years." And a little later on on the same page: "It is to be presumed that the hypothetical purchaser having obtained all the relevant information would consider in the first place the risks which are involved in carrying on the business, and would fix the return which he considered he ought to receive on the purchase price at a rate per cent."

I do not regard either of those cases as authority for the proposition that the relevant information was anything more than the information which would be known to any vendor; indeed, as far as one can see the contrary had never been suggested.

21   In the third of the three cases, *Holt v Commissioners of Inland Revenue*, which, like the present case, concerned the value for estate duty of a minority holding in a private company, Danckwerts J went further than Lord Fleming, and I must refer to a number of passages from his judgment. I have already quoted the passage at [1953] 1 WLR 1492, where he stated that it was necessary firmly to reject the wisdom which might be provided by the knowledge of subsequent events. At page 1493, he said:

> 'At the same time, the court must assume a prudent buyer who would make full inquiries and have access to accounts and other information which would be likely to be available to him: see *Findlay's Trustees v Commissioners of Inland Revenue.*'

Somewhat surprisingly, the *Salvesen* case does not appear to have been cited to Danckwerts J. At page 1495, Danckwerts J said:

> 'One question of some importance dealt with by Mr Holt was how far a prospective purchaser would have been able to obtain information as to the company's position and prospects by inquiry from the directors. Mr Holt said that all the information which he had given in *(pg383)* evidence would not have been given directly to a buyer of a small quantity of shares, but that it would have been made available, in confidence, to a reputable firm of accountants, acting on behalf of a buyer and approved by the board of directors, with the result, as I understood the position, that the information so revealed would not be passed on to the buyer, but his accountant would be in a position to advise him as to the prudence of the purchase and the price which could reasonably be offered for the shares.'

That passage should be read in the light of the fact that the information in the possession of the board was depreciatory of the value of the shares. It related to the difficulties of trading in West Africa. The executors were saying it should be taken into account; the Crown were saying it should not. The Judge then refers to the evidence of a Mr Samuel, the chairman of another company, who dealt with the difficulties of trading in West Africa, and at page 1496 he said this:

> 'It was suggested in cross-examination to Mr Samuel, and I think that it is a fair point, that an ordinary buyer would not have all the information on West African conditions which led him to take such a depressing view. Consequently, in my view, Mr Samuel's estimate of the value of the shares, so far as based on the unattractiveness of the company's ordinary shares to him, must be discounted by this consideration.'

At this point I should mention an interlocutory observation of Danckwerts J. which is not in the report, but which I quote from the transcript of the proceedings (day 3, 22nd October 1953, page 56):

> 'The Solicitor-General: My Lord, the witness is being asked about the confidence of the board, and matters of that sort. If we are going into what the board considered as a board, I should like to see the minutes of the company showing that these matters were ever discussed by the board as a board. Danckwerts J: This is, of course, of historical interest, but we are getting away from the point that it is not so much what the board thought as what other people could find out. The Solicitor-General: If this gentleman likes to express his opinion, my Lord, I certainly would not express the slightest objection, but if it is going to be represented throughout as the opinion of the board after mature consideration, then I should like to be satisfied that they did, in fact, have board meetings to consider these matters. Danckwerts J: I do not think it matters what they did so much as what information the outsider would be likely to get.'

That passage, in my judgment, reinforces the opinion which I have already expressed that facts which would be unknown to the purchaser must be left out of account in valuing the shares. Finally, at page 1501, Danckwerts J said:

> 'I think that the kind of investor who would purchase shares in a private company of this kind, in circumstances which must preclude him from disposing of his shares freely whenever he should wish (because he will, when registered as a shareholder, be subject to the provisions of the articles restricting transfer) would be different from any common kind of purchaser of shares on the Stock Exchange, and would be rather the exceptional kind of investor who had some special reason for putting his money into shares of this kind. He would, in my view, be the kind of investor who would not rush hurriedly into the transaction, but would *(pg384)* consider carefully the prudence of the course, and would seek to get the fullest possible information about the past history of the company, the particular trade in which it was engaged and the future prospects of the company.'

It appears from those passages that Danckwerts J regarded as relevant to the question of value knowledge which a prospective buyer would have obtained from the board on inquiry, and I do not think it would be right for me to dissent from that view, particularly as the information which the hypothetical purchaser would have obtained in the present case would probably not have materially affected the value of the shares. Mr Bagnall, for the Plaintiffs, accepted that the difference between what I may paraphrase as the published information value and the *Holt* information value would lie within the 10 per cent margin of error which some of the expert witnesses regarded as inherent in the operation anyway.

22 I therefore come back to the documents with the admissibility of which I am concerned, and my conclusions are as follows.

(1) The accounts for the year ending 31st July 1962, being post-death documents, are not admissible as evidence of the value of Mrs Lynall's shares at the date of her death, except possibly to the limited extent I have already mentioned.

(2) The chairman's speech is a post-death document and is not admissible. In any event, in my view, it added nothing of any material significance to the 1961 accounts themselves.

(3) Mr Alan Lynall, whose evidence was tendered and accepted as being the evidence of the board, said in evidence that if, at the date of his mother's death, he had been asked by a prospective purchaser of her shares to forecast the profits for the year ending 31st July 1962, his answer, being as helpful as possible, would have been: 'Roughly in line with the preceding year'; and if asked by the same enquirer to forecast the dividend for the year ending 31st July 1962 he would have said that he expected it to be the same as that for the preceding year. I should, perhaps, quote *verbatim* his evidence about the answers he would have given to questions about the likelihood of a public issue. At vol. 1 of the evidence, page 17D, he was asked:

> 'What was your attitude towards the possibility of the company having a public issue? (A) Could you tell me at what time? (Q) During the whole of the period from 1959 to the day before your mother died in 1962. (A) I started with an open mind on the matter, knowing practically nothing about it. As we got information from Thomson McLintock, which gave us a basis for seeing what the effects of a public issue would be on the company, I myself became very much more dubious about the correctness of such an action, and I would say that my attitude really eventually became adverse. (Q) What was it about the project that made you dubious and then subsequently adverse? (A) I felt that the way in which we would have had to have conducted the company as a public company, which would have involved distributing very much more of the company's funds in profits, would have been likely to prevent us continuing to promote the growth of the company from our own resources; so that we would either have had to stagnate or raise money by borrowing – an idea which was most unwelcome, to say the least. (Q) Again wait *(pg385)* and see if there is any objection to this question: Do you know what your father's view was on the project? (A) I believe that he started, as I did, with an open mind about it, but I think that his views changed very much in the same way as mine did. Indeed, I think they would probably have been stronger, because, in all honesty, he could see the implications I think very much more clearly than I could. (Q) Supposing that on 21 May, 1962, again my gentleman came in and said he was proposing to buy a block of shares in your Company – first of all supposing he said he was a banker and that he was proposing to buy a block of shares in your Company and he asked you whether the Directors

would give him an undertaking to have a public issue within say four or possibly five years, what would have been your attitude to that request? (A) We would not have given such an undertaking. (Q) Supposing that the person we have been talking about, the potential or hypothetical purchaser, asked you what was the likelihood of the Company having a public issue in the foreseeable future, what answer would you have given to that question? (A) That I find a very difficult one. I would certainly prefer to say nothing at all; but to say nothing at all I am afraid would have created an impression, so I would have tried then to give as accurate a view as I could of the state of affairs as I saw them, and I would have said then that I regarded the prospect as doubtful and remote. (Q) If the gentleman had said: "Well, look, let me see any minutes of the Board of Directors or other documents in the possession of the Company which might throw any light on the question of whether there would or would not be a public issue", what would you have done in answer to that request? (A) I would have said that all Board minutes and other documents were completely confidential and I would certainly not disclose anything. (Q) Supposing that it was not the gentleman who said he was negotiating a purchase of the shares who asked you the question but that it was a partner in a firm of chartered accountants who said: "We are advising a client who is negotiating a purchase of shares in your Company", and he had asked the same question about minutes and other documents of the Company, what would have been your answer to the partner in the chartered accountants? (A) It would have been the same so far as I am concerned, it would have been a breach of confidence.'

23 In the light of that evidence, which I see no reason to reject, my conclusion is that the category B documents are not admissible, since the information contained in them is neither published information nor information which would have been elicited from the board on inquiry.

24 I turn now to the troublesome question of valuation. The following matters are, I think, common ground, namely, that the sale envisaged by s7(5) of the 1894 Act would be likely to be a sale to a single purchaser, with a corporate rather than an individual existence, who would be advised by lawyers and accountants. Such a purchaser would be looking, either for a lock-up investment with an appropriate return on his money and the hope of an ultimate capital profit as the result of a public issue, or for a quick capital profit as the result of an early public issue. It is also common ground that the possibility of liquidation or a takeover can, in the circumstances of the present case, be left out of account. In the ten years prior to Mrs Lynall's death there had been no transactions for value in the company's shares which would afford any guide to their value at the date of her death. In these circumstances there are, I think, *(pg386)* three principal factors which affect valuation: (1) the appropriate dividend yield; (2) the prospective dividend; and (3) the possibility of capital appreciation. The evidence suggests certain general observations which may be made about them.

(1) *Dividend yield.* Two approaches to the problem of an appropriate yield have emerged during the course of this case. The first is to take a purely arbitrary figure based on experience and expertise and work from that. The other is to ascertain the yield which can be obtained on investments in companies in the same general field of industry in the public sector, and then to apply an arbitrary figure of discount for the fact that one is dealing not with a public company but with a private company. The latter method has the advantage over the former that it at least starts on a factual basis, but it is open to criticism on a number of counts. For example, dividend policy in a private company is likely to be entirely different from dividend policy in a public company; and the regulations affecting the transfer of shares are likely to be entirely different in the two cases. Moreover, it is in the company, Linread Ltd., and its management and not in the industry that the hypothetical purchaser is likely to be interested. These are only examples, and there are no doubt numerous other factors which influence the stock market but are irrelevant in considering the value of shares in a private company, and in particular this company. It can, however, I think, safely be said that any method of calculation involves the introduction of at least one arbitrary figure somewhere along the line.

(2) *Prospective dividend.* A number of factors enter into any assessment of the dividend which a company is likely to pay in the future. Past dividends are obviously an important consideration. In the case of the present company the profit and dividend record, the dividend policy of the board and the capital position would have suggested that, at the lowest, a 15 per cent dividend would be maintained. The likelihood of an increase would have to be judged in the light of the known policy of the directors, but that would not rule out the probability of an increase. A number of factors pointed in that direction, such as the upward trend of profits, the high dividend cover, the risk of surtax directions, the employment of surplus profits in the expansion of the business which itself might well lead to an increase of profits.

(3) *The possibility of capital appreciation.* It is common ground that in the present case this need only be considered in the context of a possible flotation. The probability of such a flotation was a matter depending primarily, but not entirely, on the wishes of the board. The board's hypothetical known assessment of the position at Mrs Lynall's death was that the prospect of a flotation was 'doubtful and remote'. But against that attitude must be set the fact that it was at least a tenable view on the published information, including the family nature of the business and the ages of the family shareholders, that the board would be forced willy-nilly to go public sooner or later in order to provide for death duties, or for some other financial reason urged upon them by their advisers, such as the fear (justified by the event) of the imposition of a general capital

gains tax. Mr Lynall's subjective view of the situation must be discounted accordingly.

25 I come now to the expert evidence. The witnesses called on behalf of the Plaintiffs were: (1) *Mr Rose*, a Fellow of the Institute of Chartered Accountants, who qualified in 1948 and from 1952 to 1960 was a partner in a firm of chartered accountants practising in Birmingham and London. Since 1960 he has been an executive director of a well-known issuing house, Neville Industrial *(pg387)* Securities Ltd., of Birmingham. He is also a director of other companies, quoted and unquoted. (2) *Mr Hamilton-Baynes*, also a Fellow of the Institute of Chartered Accountants, who has specialised in the valuation of shares in private companies and has written a standard textbook on the subject. He is a well-known expert witness in this field and gave evidence in the *Holt* case. (3) *Mr Hill-Wood.* He is a young man who has been in the City for twelve years, the first four of which were spent with stockbrokers and the last eight of which have been with Hambros Bank. He is now second in charge, under a director, of the department of industrial services, which, among other things, is concerned with investing money in private companies on the bank's own account. Two experts were called on behalf of the Crown: (1) *Sir Henry Benson*, a past President of the Institute of Chartered Accountants, and a senior partner in the firm of Cooper Bros. He is another well-known expert in this field, and he too gave evidence in the *Holt* case. (2) *Mr Andrews*, a Fellow of the Institute of Chartered Accountants, and a director of Samuel Montagu & Co., well-known merchant bankers, and experienced in advising on and negotiating the acquisition of majority and minority holdings in public and private companies. All, of course, were honest witnesses, expressing their professional opinions in the light of their experience, and, as is the way with experts, differing from each other.

26 *Mr Rose* said that he would have expected what he called an 'effective return' of 15 per cent on his money. That expression is comparable with the concept of a yield to redemption in another context. Mr Rose explained it by saying that it meant that he would require an immediate yield of 10 per cent in the expectation that the dividend would double over a 10-year cycle. He would not expect a rise in dividend for some time, because so long as profits were being applied in acquiring assets employed in the business a modest dividend would be enough to satisfy the Special Commissioners. Applying his required 10 per cent to an actual dividend of 15 per cent he reached a price of 30*s.* a share, ignoring up to that point the possibility of a public issue. He took the view that a public issue would be an aggravation rather than a solution of the estate duty problem, but nevertheless came to the conclusion that he would have advised a purchaser to pay another 20*s.* having regard to the possibility of a public issue. In reaching the figure of 20*s.* he took into account the burden of article 8. Neither he nor any other witness put a specific value on the depreciatory effect of article 8, though all agreed that it was depreciatory. The principal effect that Mr Rose attributed to it was to exclude from the category of potential investors all private individuals. In the result Mr Rose arrived at a valuation of £2 10*s.*

after taking into account the answers which Mr Lynall said he would have given in reply to questions about the profit, dividend and flotation prospects. He was not asked what effect knowledge of the category B documents would have had on his valuation.

27 *Mr Hamilton-Baynes* thought that the basic assumption to be made was that price depended on what the hypothetical purchaser was going to get out of his investment, basically in dividends. He started his process of valuation by assuming as an appropriate dividend yield a yield of 12 per cent in a case where a small private company can satisfactorily pass twelve tests set out on pages 116 – 117 of his book on *Share Valuations*. These tests are as follows: 1. If there is not at the time a political or financial crisis. 2. If the industry is not on the decline. 3. If there are no unusual clauses in the articles. 4. If the company has no pronounced trend of profits, either upward or downward. *(pg388)* 5. If the management is adequate and reasonably remunerated. 6. If the profits have not widely fluctuated. 7. If regular dividends have been paid and the dividend cover is reasonable but not excessive. 8. If the company does not depend on one customer or one supplier. 9. If the gearing is satisfactory. 10. If the company is financed without recourse to temporary loans and overdrafts; that is, if the liquid position is satisfactory. 11. If the company's fixed assets are properly maintained. 12. If one shareholder does not personally control the company, or the purchase of these shares will not give him control. He then adjusted the figure of 12 per cent to 7 per cent in order to reflect the high marks with which the present company would pass his examination paper, including the probability that sooner or later the risk of surtax directions would necessitate an increase in the dividend. Then, relating that figure of 7 per cent to the actual dividend of 15 per cent, he arrives at a figure of 43s. per share. He said that he would not in fact expect an increase of dividend for two or three years. He then reduced the 7 per cent to 6 per cent to reflect the possibility of a public issue, and so increased the share price by 7s. to 50s. He reached these figures after taking into account Mr Lynall's views as to the prospects of a public issue. His view of the depreciatory effect of article 8 was that it cancelled out the nuisance value, or 'negative control', attaching to a 28 per cent minority holding. Knowledge of the category B documents might, in his view, have added another £1 to the value of the shares.

28 *Mr Hill-Wood* approached the problem of valuation as if the transaction to be considered was an entirely different transaction from what it in fact is. He visualised it as a case of the type he was used to, where Hambros Bank was going to inject money into the company with a view to accelerating expansion and nursing it to the point where the bank itself would be able to float it. The transaction would be one between the board (not an outside shareholder) on the one side and Hambros on the other. This type of transaction is so different from that with which I am concerned that I do not think that Mr Hill-Wood's evidence helps me in arriving at a value for Mrs Lynall's shares, and accordingly, with no disrespect at all to Mr Hill-Wood, I propose to disregard it.

29 I come now to the witnesses for the Crown.

30 *Sir Henry Benson* started his process of valuation by considering dividend yields earned on shares in quoted companies at the time of Mrs Lynall's death in the same class of industry. He found that the answer lay between 5 per cent and 6 per cent. He then adjusted this figure for the private company factor (including restrictions on transfer) and considered that the yield to apply was $7\frac{1}{2}$ per cent. Sir Henry then considered what figure he should take as the prospective dividend, and taking into account the dividend record of the company, the rising trend of profits, the expectation of further increases, and the pressure likely to be exerted by the Special Commissioners, he concluded that a fair distribution and one which would satisfy the Special Commissioners would be 35 per cent of the available profits. He showed that this is the equivalent of an actual dividend of 33 per cent for 1960 or 32 per cent for 1961. On the basis of these dividends and a $7\frac{1}{2}$ per cent yield he reached share values of £4 8s. and £4 5s. 4d. respectively. He then reconsidered these figures in the light of the possibility of capital profit. He thought that the buyer and seller would have wanted to know the price at which the shares would have been quoted if the company had gone public at the date of death, and said that he would have advised that it would have been on the basis of a yield of $5\frac{1}{2}$ per cent to 6 per cent twice covered. This produced a share value on the basis of the 1961 profits and a dividend yield of 6 per cent of £7 13s. 4d. That figure had, *(pg389)* however, to be discounted to allow for an estimated period of one to five years between death and flotation and the buyer's profit. Sir Henry said that it was impossible to arrive at a precise figure, but he thought that the price agreed between buyer and seller would be £5 per share. If he was entitled to take the category B documents into account he would have taken the view that a public issue was more imminent than he had assumed, and would raise his valuation from £5 to £6 a share. As regards article 8, Sir Henry took the view that its practical effect was not material or significant, as the buyer whom he contemplated was a long-term investor and almost certainly a company.

31 *Mr Andrews* produced a novel basis of valuation. He started by postulating a figure of £300,000 (which he arrived at by jobbing back from the 1962 accounts) as a maintainable profit level. His next step was to establish a relationship between profits and capital value. He calculated that the maximum earnings available for distribution by way of dividend on the ordinary shares would be £226,000, or 18s 8d per share. He then took a figure, which the 'little man inside' (as he put it) told him ought to be 20 per cent, as an appropriate earnings yield (that is to say, 18s 8d expressed as a percentage of the share price), and arrived at a valuation of £4 13s 4d, which he rounded off at £4 10s. As a cross-check on his calculation, he asked himself at what price he would have been prepared to underwrite the shares in May 1962. In his view he could have floated the company on a dividend yield of $6\frac{1}{4}$ per cent twice covered – that is to say, an earnings yield of $12\frac{1}{2}$ per cent – and on that basis the shares would have been worth £7 10s. He then discounted that sum by 40 per cent to take account of the depreciatory factors (shares unquoted, directors' dividend policy, article 8 and minority interest), and arrived back at the figure of £4 10s. He did not regard article 8 as having any significant effect on value. If he was entitled to take the category B documents into account he would add another 30s to the £4 10s, making £6, the same figure as that proposed by Sir Henry Benson.

32 That, then, in bare outline, was the evidence of the experts, and I must now venture a few brief comments. 1. *Mr Rose.* I regard his valuation as being on the low side. I think that his figure of 10 per cent as the appropriate immediate yield is high and that he has underestimated the dividend prospects. 2. *Mr Hamilton-Baynes.* He fastened on Mr Lynall's forecast of the chances of a public issue as 'doubtful and remote', and in my view underestimated the possibility that the company would be forced to go public. Moreover, by applying his 6 per cent figure to the actual dividend of 15 per cent, I think that he underestimated the prospects of an increase in dividend, although in arriving at a figure of 6 per cent he had no doubt to some extent taken into account the prospects of an increase. In my view his valuation also is too low. 3. *Sir Henry Benson.* By applying his $7\frac{1}{2}$ per cent yield to a dividend of 32 per cent or 33 per cent Sir Henry has, in my view, overestimated the risk of a surtax direction and the probability of a large immediate increase of dividend. As I have said, the Special Commissioners were always in the background, but I do not think they were knocking at the front door. Mr Bagnall submitted that the $7\frac{1}{2}$ per cent ought to have been applied to the actual dividend of 15 per cent (which would have given a share value of £2) on the ground that the element of 'yield in the public sector' which it comprised itself took into account future dividend prospects. I think that there is some force in this criticism, though I do not think that it sufficiently takes into account the dividend prospects of this particular company. In another respect too I think that Sir Henry was perhaps over-optimistic, namely, in regarding a public issue as inevitable within a period of one to five years. In the light of Mr Lynall's evidence I regard this as *(pg390)* conjectural. 4. *Mr Andrews.* His evidence too, in my view, overrates the prospects of a public issue and disregards the effect of the views of the Lynall family. Indeed, he stated that he would have wanted the board and its advisers to tell him, as part of the deal, that it was their intention to go public. I have misgivings about a valuation which regards the immediate dividend policy of the board as irrelevant and proceeds on the basis that the whole of the profits available for distribution ought to be taken into account.

33 For these reasons I have reached the conclusion that, while the valuations put forward by the Plaintiffs' experts are on the low side, those of the Crown's experts are on the high side. Making the best estimate I can in all the circumstances, I fix the value of Mrs Lynall's shares at £3 10s. If I am wrong in my view that the category B documents are not admissible, then I would add £1 to £3 10s., bringing the value up to £4 10s. per share.

34 If anyone asks for it, I give leave to appeal.

Appeal allowed, with costs.

Judgement of the Court of Appeal

35 HARMAN LJ. – Mrs Nellie Lynall, with whose estate this appeal is concerned, died on 21st May 1962. Her age was in the middle 70s. Her principal asset was a large holding representing about 28 per cent of the issued capital of a private limited company called Linread Ltd. This was an old-established and prosperous concern havings its headquarters in Birmingham and being engaged in the manufacture of what are known as cold-forged fasteners – things in the nature of screws, nuts and bolts used in the aircraft and motor industries. The company was a private company and the shares were held entirely in the family, the chairman, Mrs Lynall's husband, owning 32 per cent and two sons owning 20 per cent each. All four were directors of the company, though Mrs Lynall was not an executive director.

36 Under the articles of association the shares of the company were very severely restricted in transfer; the directors had an absolute right to refuse to register, and a would-be seller must first offer his shares to Mr Lynall and, after he ceased to be chairman, to the other members of the company, at the fair value, which at all material times was fixed at par. At the very lowest estimate the shares were worth double that figure, but in effect a would-be transferor had nothing to sell but the par value. In these circumstances a familiar difficulty arose of valuing the shares for estate duty purposes under s7(5) of the Finance Act 1894, which is in these terms:

> 'The principal value of any property shall be estimated to be the price which, in the opinion of the Commissioners, such property would fetch if sold in the open market at the time of the death of the deceased.' *(pg391)*

It has been the law since *Attorney General v Jameson* [1905] 2 I.R. 218, the decision of a very strong Court of Appeal in Ireland, which was followed and confirmed in the House of Lords in *Commissioners of Inland Revenue v Crossman* [1937] AC 26, that the meaning to be given to this section is that for the purpose of estimating the price of such shares, price being under the section the criterion of value, it must be assumed that a purchaser would be entitled notwithstanding the restrictions to be registered as the holder, but would take his holding subject to the restrictions on transfer imposed by the articles of association. This view of the law is admittedly binding on this Court, but the Respondent taxpayer desired to reserve the point, in case the matter went to the House of Lords, that the minority view expressed by Lords Russell and Macmillan in *Crossman's* case was the right one and that the true value of shares such as these is par and no more.

37 The company had a conservative dividend record, but during the last two years of Mrs Lynall's life a dividend of 15 per cent had been paid, no doubt under the pressure exercised by the Revenue, which of course had in its hands the weapon of a surtax direction on the members. Moreover, this was a company in which two persons holding 60 per cent of the capital were about 70 years old, and inevitably the question must arise how the very heavy estate duties which would become payable on their deaths could be found. It is notorious that in order to raise the duty many such companies have been obliged to offer a certain proportion of their shares by an issue to the public, which of course involves the sweeping away of the restrictions on transfer and becoming a public company. This would have the result of very much enhancing the price which the shares would fetch, and the chance of its happening must necessarily be in the mind of any purchaser, who would so long as the company remained a private company in effect be locking up his capital.

38 The sale envisaged by the section is, as is agreed, not a real but a hypothetical sale, and must be taken to be a sale between a willing vendor and a willing purchaser: see, for instance, the speech of Lord Guest in *In re Sutherland* [1963] AC 235, at page 262. It is true that the so-called willing vendor is a person who must sell: he cannot simply call off the sale if he does not like the price; but there must be on the other side a willing purchaser, so that the conditions of the sale must be such as to induce in him a willing frame of mind.

39 The controversy which has arisen here is extraordinarily free from authority, which is strange, as valuations under the section have been going on since 1894. The dispute is, what information about the company and its past history and future prospects is to be assumed to be in the possession of the purchaser at the date of the sale. Three possibilities were canvassed. First, that which was reached by the learned judge below, namely, that the purchaser must be taken to be in possession, apart from what I call published documents, of all such further information (if any) as on the evidence in this case a member of the board applied to would have afforded. This evidence was given by one of the two sons of the family, who alleged that the board if asked would have been extremely uncommunicative. The judge himself did not favour this result, but he felt constrained to it by a decision of Danckwerts J, In *re Holt* [1953] 1 WLR 1488. The second view, which the judge would have preferred had he felt himself free, is the 'published information' footing, namely, that the purchaser would have had only such information as had before the date of the death been communicated by the board to the shareholders and no confidential information such as was within the knowledge of the board. The third possibility, which was, at any rate in this Court, supported by the Crown, was that the purchaser *(pg392)* must be supposed to have in addition to the published information such further information as would in practice, on a sale of an important block of shares such as these, have been confided by the board either to the purchaser or perhaps more probably in confidence to his financial advisers.

40 As a matter of history what happened was that the executors, in the Inland Revenue affidavit upon which probate was obtained, put in a valuation of the shares made by the secretary, who stated the value at £2 a share. The Commissioners, having considered the matter, formed the opinion that the true value following the *Jameson* principle was £4 a share. This the executors were unwilling to pay, and, being aggrieved by the decision, appealed to the High Court under s10 of the 1894 Act. The Crown then applied for discovery of documents. Now of course the executors, being directors themselves, had in their possession or power material beyond the published information and would have been bound to include it in their affidavit on discovery. By way of compromise the documents which have been called the 'B' documents were disclosed by the executors without prejudice to the question whether they would have been bound to make them available to the Crown or whether they could have objected to disclosing their contents on the ground that they only had this information as members of the board and were entitled to withhold it. This information was of two kinds: first, the interim monthly statements in the possession of the members of the board showing the progress of the company during the nine months which had passed since the period covered by the last information in the hands of the shareholders, which was that contained in the accounts for 1961; second, such facts as there were in the knowledge of the board to show the prospects or the likelihood of the company going public. Both these matters would have been of the utmost importance to a purchaser, but it was said that, not being published information, that is to say, information available to the shareholders at the date of death, they must be ignored.

41 Before Plowman J there was elaborate evidence of experts giving their opinions as to the value of the shares. None of these questions arose before us and this judgment is shortened accordingly. Plowman J, weighing the opinions on the two sides, came to the conclusion that the proper price was £3 10s. With this the taxpayer is content. The experts, however, all agreed that if the buyer was entitled to be informed upon the two points, namely the last nine months' profits and the indications of the board's intentions as to a public offer, there would have to be added a pound to the value of each share. Before us, therefore, only one point was argued, namely, whether Plowman J's valuation of £3 10s. should stand or whether it should have a pound added to it, as, on the evidence, would happen if the further information were disclosed.

42 There is an extraordinary dearth of authority on this point. In *Jameson's* case no question of valuation arose because the Commissioners had not arrived at a valuation: the only thing settled was the basis of the valuation. That case, therefore, is of no help. *Attorney-General v Jameson* was followed in Scotland by Lord Fleming in *Salvesen's Trustees v Commissioners of Inland Revenue* (1930) 9 ATC 43 in the Outer House of the Court of Session. The shares in question were shares in a private company with a restricted right of transfer and the judge made a valuation following *Jameson*. He said this, at page 46:

'The problem can only be dealt with by considering all the relevant facts so far as known at the date of the testator's death and by determining what a prudent investor, who knew these facts, might be expected to be *(pg393)* willing to pay for the shares. Counsel for both the petitioners and respondents accordingly assumed that the prospective buyer would inform himself of all the relevant facts and, in particular, have made available to him the accounts of the company.'

Then he goes into the question of what the relevant facts were. This assumes that the purchaser knew 'of the relevant facts so far as known' but does not say to whom they would be known. Later, at page 50, the learned Lord said this:

'As a prudent person, he' – that is, the buyer – 'would, of course, keep in view that he was purchasing the shares in October 1926 and that the balance sheet shows the affairs of the company as at July 1926 and he would make inquiry as to the alterations in its financial position which had taken place between these two dates. But he would first examine the balance sheet and I think that he would be very favourably impressed by the fact that the assets showed a surplus of upwards of £900,000 over its capital.'

Then he calculates the value of the shares on that footing. The judge therefore assumed that the purchaser would know all that he wanted to know, in particular the state of the company's business since the date of the last published balance sheet. In fact he felt himself entitled to look at the later published balance sheet to see what in fact happened during the last three months before the death, and this I think was only because he assumed that the purchaser would obtain that information: he could obtain it only from the board.

43 The next case is *Findlay's Trustees v Commissioners of Inland Revenue* (1938) 22 ATC 437. There the property was a share in a partnership. Here again the judge assumed that the purchaser was informed of all the facts which he required to know: see at page 440, where he said this:

'In estimating the price which might be fetched in the open market for the goodwill of the business it must be assumed that the transaction takes place between a willing seller and a willing purchaser; and that the purchaser is a person of reasonable prudence, who has informed himself with regard to all the relevant facts such as the history of the business, its present position, its future prospects and the general conditions of the industry; and also that he has access to the accounts of the business for a number of years.'

Once again the judge assumes that all relevant facts are disclosed; but there was no argument on the subject of how or from whom the purchaser must be taken to have obtained them.

44 The third case is that already mentioned, *In re Holt*. There the information in the hands of the directors was of a depreciatory character, and evidence was given by one of them of the adverse factors. He said that he would if enquiry had been made have disclosed all these facts to the prospective purchaser: see [1953] 1 WLR at page 1495:

'One question of some importance dealt with by Mr Holt was how far a prospective purchaser would have been able to obtain information as to the company's position and prospects by inquiry from the directors. Mr Holt said that all the information which he had given in evidence would not have been given directly to a buyer of a small quantity of shares, but that it would have been made available, in confidence, to a reputable firm of accountants, acting on behalf of a buyer *(pg394)* and approved by the board of directors, with the result, as I understood the position, that the information so revealed would not be passed on to the buyer, but his accountant would be in a position to advise him as to the prudence of the purchase and the price which could reasonably be offered for the shares.'

The judge in the end based his valuation on the facts so disclosed. This appears from page 1501.

'It is plain', he says, 'that the shares do not give a purchaser the opportunity to control the company, or to influence the policy of the directors to any great extent, as the shares available only represent 43,698 shares out of 697,680 ordinary shares which had been issued. Any purchaser would, therefore, be dependent on the policy of the directors, so long as they should have the support of the general body of the shareholders. I think that the kind of investor who would purchase shares in a private company of this kind, in circumstances which must preclude him from disposing of his shares freely whenever he should wish (because he will, when registered as a shareholder, be subject to the provisions of the articles restricting transfer) would be different from any common kind of purchaser of shares on the Stock Exchange, and would be rather the exceptional kind of investor who had some special reason for putting his money into shares of this kind. He would, in my view, be the kind of investor who would not rush hurriedly into the transaction, but would consider carefully the prudence of the course, and would seek to get the fullest possible information about the past history of the company, the particular trade in which it was engaged, and the future prospects of the company.'

45 None of these cases, as it seems to me, decides the point here at issue. They all, I think, assume full knowledge of all relevant facts by the purchaser, including facts not published to the shareholders before the date of death.

46 Neither side was enamoured of the basis on which Danckwerts J decided, although the taxpayer preferred it to the Crown's view. In my judgment, it is not a satisfactory basis, for it seems to depend on the whim of the board of directors in question and is uncertain and depends on whether the directors were favourably disposed to the seller or no. I think this view must be rejected. As I have said, Plowman J felt bound to follow the *Holt* decision, but stated that if free to express his own view he would decide in favour of the taxpayer's submission that published information alone ought to be taken into account and that in particular the 'B' documents were inadmissible. As to the second view, which is the taxpayer's view, it seems to me that in the end the taxpayer found he could not maintain it in its logical form, for he was constrained to admit that it was legitimate to take into account the financial results of the company for the nine months after the last published balance sheet. The reason given was that this information would eventually come into the hands of shareholders; but that cannot be made to accord with the principle that the knowledge of the shareholders at the date of death is the only relevant consideration. It seems to me, therefore, that the taxpayer's contention breaks down at this point and it is legitimate that the hypothetical purchaser should know matters which at the date of death were only known to the board. The more important information is, of course, facts which tend to show the likelihood of a public issue. Now the 'B' documents show that this had been *(pg395)* in fact under consideration by the board since 1959, and that Messrs. Thomson McLintock & Co. had been called in to report and advise on this very subject and had advised an immediate issue to the public. They show, moreover, that the board had sanctioned the taking of advice from Messrs. Cazenove & Co., well-known stockbrokers, who had at the beginning of 1962 reported in favour of a public issue and discussed ways and means.

47 This leaves the Crown's contention. Very strong evidence was produced from two leading experts that, where substantial blocks of shares in private companies are in the market, as from time to time they are, it is the invariable practice among boards of directors to answer reasonable questions in confidence to the advisers of the purchaser. In fact, it was said that if such questions are not answered no sale would ever go through, because a purchaser would fight shy if he felt he were being left in ignorance of material facts. This, then, would not produce the willing purchaser which the formula postulates. It was said, further, that where a substantial shareholder was minded to dispose of his shares in such a company the directors would feel a moral duty to assist him by answering reasonable questions. It was argued by the taxpayer that this solution was impracticable because it would depend on the availability of members of the board who could in the last resort, if unwilling to make a proper disclosure, be called into the witness box on *subpoena duces tecum* to produce some reasonable information. I suppose such circumstances might conceivably arise, but I am content to leave the matter where it is, relying on the almost unchallenged evidence that boards of directors do not behave in that way and that reasonable answers would be forthcoming.

48 No such difficulty of course arises here, for the vendors were in fact directors in possession of the information in question and the only question is whether in a normal case they would have obtained their father's leave to disclose it. Now if in fact it were necessary for the vendors to sell some of the shares in order to pay their mother's debts – as is most likely – it is clear that the father would have been only too ready to permit disclosure of facts which would enhance the purchase price. It was the taxpayer's argument that directors must be excluded from amongst possible purchasers because they would be 'special' purchasers. I do not accept this, and am of opinion that this is not an ingredient in the *Crossman* decision. In *Crossman's* case it was decided that the fact that a 'special' purchaser, namely a trust company, would have offered a special price must be ignored, but this was because that particular purchaser had a reason special to him for so doing. So, here, a director who would give an enhanced price because he would thus obtain control of the company would be left out of account. But that is not to say that directors as such are to be ignored. *All* likely purchasers are deemed to be in the market. What the Act says is that the sale is to be treated as an open market sale, that is to say, the restrictions on transfer are to be ignored for the purpose of the hypothetical sale which is to fix the price, but I cannot see why the hypothetical sellers are not to be treated as being what they are, namely, directors in possession of the information which a purchaser would reasonably require and which on the evidence he would have obtained if he were to be a willing purchaser.

49 It is agreed here, as I have said, that if information such as is contained in the 'B' documents were available to the hypothetical purchaser a pound must be added to the value of the shares, and I am accordingly of opinion that the *(pg396)* Crown's appeal succeeds and that the proper price for these shares for the purpose of estate duty ought to be set at £4 10*s*.

50 I would allow the appeal accordingly.

51 WIDGERY LJ. – The facts of this case are fully set out in the judgment in the Court below and I find it unnecessary to repeat them in full.

52 When Mrs Lynall died on 21st May 1962 she was the registered holder of 67,980 ordinary shares in Linread Ltd. This holding represented approximately 28 per cent of the issued share capital, the other substantial shareholders being her husband (32 per cent) and her two sons (each 20 per cent). Mrs Lynall's shareholding passed on her death for the purposes of the Finance Act 1894, and must be valued for the purposes of estate duty under s7(5), which my Lord has read and I will not repeat.

53 The business of the company was a family business which had started from small beginnings and had prospered. The accounts of the company for the years preceding 1962 showed a steady and rapid increase in both turnover and profits, much of the latter being retained in the business and not distributed as dividends. Both the deceased and her husband were elderly, and the possibility that the company might be minded to make a public issue of shares would have occurred to anyone who had made a careful study of the accounts and the structure of the company in 1962. It is common ground that the effect of a successful public issue would have been to enhance the price of the shares, and that as the prospect of such an issue increased the market price would increase also. The directors had in fact been giving serious thought to the possibility of a public issue since 1959, but this was known only to the members of the board. Messrs. Thomson McLintock were commissioned by the board to carry out a survey of the company's undertaking with a view to a public issue, and made their first report in July 1960. In February 1962 McLintocks were advising that the board should consider a flotation at the earliest possible moment, and in March 1962 the board received a report from stockbrokers (Messrs. Cazenoves) suggesting the method by which this might be carried out. A public issue was in fact made in 1963. It is further common ground that the price which would have been paid for these shares in the open market on the date of the death of the deceased would have been markedly affected by the extent to which the buyer was aware of these developments and of the imminence of a public issue which they indicated. This appeal is concerned only with the extent of the knowledge which is to be attributed to such a purchaser, the Judge having made alternative valuations on two hypotheses and there being no appeal in regard to his figures.

54 Three alternatives have been put forward. First, that the vendor and purchaser concerned in the hypothetical sale should be deemed to be in possession of no information as to the financial position and prospects of the company beyond that contained in the company's accounts prepared prior to the relevant date, and any other information which had then been made available to the shareholders or was available to the public at large. The Judge referred to this by the convenient label of 'the published information'. Mr Bagnall contended that the published information should also include that to be derived from the company's accounts for the financial year in which the death occurred even though these were not available until a later date. The second alternative contended for was that in addition to the published information the vendor and purchaser should be deemed to have any information *(pg397)* which the board of directors of this company would in fact have provided to a prospective purchaser on enquiry made on the relevant date. This has been referred to as the 'subjective test', since it involves an investigation of the state of mind of the board and of its probable response to such an enquiry. Thirdly, that in addition to the published information the vendor and purchaser should be deemed to have all information which would normally be made available to a genuine intending purchaser of property of the kind in question, this being information which a purchaser would expect to have and without which he would be unwilling to buy. Sir Milner Holland, who argues for this third alternative, put his proposition in a number of different ways, and the words I have used are my own paraphrase of his submission.

55 The learned Judge rejected Sir Milner's submission, and indicated a preference for the 'published information' test. He was constrained, however, to follow the decision of Danckwerts J in *In re Holt* [1953] 1 WLR 1488, and accordingly adopted the second alternative as the principle to be applied in this case. Having heard evidence from a director of the company as to the information which would have been made available to a prospective purchaser on 21st May 1962, he concluded that the confidential reports from Messrs. McLintock and Messrs. Cazenoves would not have been disclosed and fixed £3 10s. as the value of each share. He further held that if the purchaser was to be deemed to have seen this confidential information the price would have been £4 10s. per share. Neither party in this Court has shown any enthusiasm for the subjective test, though Mr Bagnall supports it as an alternative to the published information test if the latter is not acceptable. In either event he is content with the judge's valuation of £3 10s. Sir Milner, for the Crown, contends for the third alternative and a valuation of £4 10s.

56 Section 7(5) of the Act of 1894 applies to all forms of property passing on a death. It makes the hypothetical market price the test of value, and prescribes only two of the conditions to which the sale is subject, namely, that it must be a sale in the open market and conducted at the time of the death of the deceased. In so far as other conditions need to be inferred, the Court must supply those which will give effect to the intention of the section. Thus, it is established that the sale is a wholly hypothetical one conducted between hypothetical parties. As Lord Hailsham said in *Commissioners of Inland Revenue v Crossman* [1937] AC 26, at page 43: 'Lord Plender' (a witness) '"did not exclude anybody or include anybody in particular; he considered the matter generally". In my opinion that is the right way to arrive at the value in the open market.' It is also clear that quite drastic departures from the so-called reality of the situation must be made when this is necessary to give effect to the intention of the Statute. In the *Crossman* case itself a majority of the House of Lords held that, when shares in a private company are to be valued, it must be assumed that the hypothetical purchaser will have a right to be entered on the share register notwithstanding restrictions on transfer or rights of pre-emption contained in the articles, which would have precluded an open market sale in practice. A further example of such departure from reality is to be seen in *Duke of Buccleuch v Commissioners of Inland Revenue* [1967] 1 AC 506, where Lord Reid, at page 525, said:

'But here what must be envisaged is a sale in the open market on a particular day. So there is no room for supposing that the owner would do as many prudent owners do – withdraw the property if he does not get a sufficient offer and wait until a time when he can get a better offer.' *(pg398)*

It is desirable, in my opinion, that when the Court is constructing the conditions under which the hypothetical sale is deemed to take place it should build upon a foundation of reality, so far as this is possible, but it is even more important that it should not defeat the intention of the section by an undue concern for reality in what is essentially a hypothetical situation.

57 The intention underlying s7(5) is to produce a fair basis of valuation between the Crown and the subject. The same principles must govern its application whatever the nature of the property concerned, and the resultant value should not depend on the whim of any individual. A sale between a vendor and a purchaser who are fully informed on all relevant matters affecting the value of the property is a more accurate guide to value than is a sale between parties who are denied such information. As a matter of first impression these considerations lead me to support the third alternative, which is the one for which Sir Milner contends and which is also consistent with the view adopted by Lord Fleming in *Salvesen's Trustees v Commissioners of Inland Revenue* (1930) 9 A.T.C. 43, at pages 46 and 50.

58 What are the arguments to the contrary? So far as the subjective test is concerned, I can see none. Once it is accepted that the directors are to be deprived of their rights of pre-emption under the articles, and are bound to register the purchaser whether they like it or not, the transaction is so far removed from reality that they cannot usefully be asked to say how they would have responded to a request for information. In any event, I do not think that the valuation should depend upon the attitude of members of the particular board. The real contest, in my opinion, therefore, is between the first and the third alternatives. Mr Bagnall supports the published information test as one which is consistent with the Act, simple and certain in operation, and productive of consistent results in all cases. He cites the analogy of quoted shares in a public company, and says that the quoted price (which is accepted for the purposes of s7(5)) is derived from the effect of published information upon the market; but in my judgment this is not so. The validity of the quoted price derives from the fact that when other identical shares are available at that price no vendor of the shares in question will accept less, and no purchaser need pay more, whatever the state of his individual knowledge. Mr Bagnall's main argument is concerned with the practical difficulties which he says will arise if the hypothetical purchaser is assumed to have confidential information in the possession of the directors. He says (and with the support of the Judge below) that this would involve protracted enquiries which would make the Commissioners' task impossible, but the Commissioners do not take this view. He asks, rhetorically, what is to happen if the directors decline to provide the information to the Commissioners, and concludes that the result would be to force the parties to litigate, so that the information could be obtained on subpoena, and points out that even then the result would depend on whether the person in possession of 'the information' was amenable to the jurisdiction of the Court. I think that these difficulties are exaggerated. If, as a result of our decision, it is accepted that evidence is admissible of facts in the directors' knowledge which a prudent purchaser would wish to discover, the likely consequence is that such information will be made available. I would not expect a marked increase in litigation. Nor am I unduly disturbed by the fact that in a minority of cases the parties may be unable to discover confidential information which was in the directors' possession, because in these cases the assessment will be made on the basis of 'published information', which is precisely what Mr Bagnall contends for. The fact that in these cases the assessment falls to be made on what I would regard as inadequate information does not mean that a similar error must be *(pg399)* built into all other cases merely for conformity. In this connection it is useful to remember that, although the 'published information' test is favourable to the subject in the present case, it could easily favour the Crown in another. In the course of argument some concern was expressed for the small shareholder whose executors might have difficulty in persuading the directors to make the effort to supply information necessary for an assessment under s7(5). Such a case, if it arises at all, is merely another example of the class to which I have just referred. If the directors are uncooperative but there is no real reason to suppose that they have anything vital to disclose, and the amount at stake does not justify litigation, the parties will no doubt reach agreement on the basis that the published information is comprehensive.

59 Being unable to accept either of the first two alternatives, I return to the third. The Crown have led expert evidence below to the effect that a purchaser of such a substantial block of shares would require to know the state of the company's trading since the last published accounts, and what progress had been made towards a public issue, and would not conclude a deal without such information. The judge expressed no view upon this evidence, and Mr Bagnall submits, with force, that it is of no value because the transactions envisaged by the witnesses were transactions designed to assist the company, in which the directors would be cooperative, and were not transactions in which the seller might be a private shareholder at odds with the directors. This evidence satisfies me that a prudent purchaser of shares in this company would wish to have this information whether he was buying a large block of shares or a small one, but I need not decide whether he would refuse to deal if the information were not forthcoming. I would prefer to state Sir Milner's proposition somewhat differently and say that, whatever the nature of the property in question, it must be assumed that the purchaser would make all reasonable enquiries, from all available sources, which a prudent purchaser of that property would wish to make, and it must further be assumed that he would receive true and factual answers to all such enquiries.

60 In the present case a prudent purchaser would have made enquiries of the directors which, if truthfully answered, would have disclosed the confidential reports of McLintocks and Cazenoves. Accordingly I would allow this appeal and declare that the value of the shares is £4 10s. each.

61 CROSS LJ. – The question at issue in this appeal is, What degree of knowledge of matters affecting the value of the shares is to be imputed to the parties to the hypothetical sale postulated by s7(5) of the Finance Act 1894?

62 Three different possibilities were suggested in argument both in the Court below and before us, which I will call, for short, the 'published information standard', the 'Holt standard' and the 'Crown's standard'. 1. The 'published information standard' imputes to the parties to the hypothetical sale knowledge of what is shown in the company's accounts and of any other information which has in fact been made available to the shareholders or was available to the public at large. 2. The 'Holt standard' imputes to them, in addition to what they are taken to know by the published information standard, knowledge of any information which the directors of the particular company would have given in answer to any reasonable question likely to be asked by the vendor shareholder or the intending purchaser at the date of the sale. 3. The 'Crown's standard', as put in argument to, or at all events as understood by, the Judge below, was that the Court in valuing the shares should have regard to all relevant facts which were proved to have been facts at the date of the death. But in this Court counsel for the Crown submitted that the knowledge *(pg400)* to be imputed to the parties to the hypothetical sale was merely possession of the information which a willing vendor would normally require before he was prepared to sell and a willing purchaser would normally require before he was willing to purchase.

63 Plowman J considered – I think rightly – that the *Holt* standard had been adopted by Danckwerts J in *In re Holt* [1953] 1 WLR 1488 and that he ought to follow that decision. If he had felt himself free to do so he would have opted for the published information standard, which would in fact have yielded the same result, since Mr Lynall said that he would not have disclosed the information contained in the category B documents. In my judgment, however, the procedure adopted by Danckwerts J of enquiring what information the particular board would have disclosed was not supported by any earlier case and was wrong – though, as Mr Holt said that he would in fact have disclosed the information in question, and the Judge consequently took it into account, the result arrived at may well have been right. To my mind there are at least three objections to the Court enquiring what information the board in question would in fact have disclosed. In the first place, a director of a private company cannot sensibly be asked what his reactions would have been to questions put to him by a prospective vendor or purchaser of shares in his company unless he is told who the vendor was and – even more important – who the purchaser was. But as the sale is purely hypothetical he cannot be told that. Secondly, the time at which the Court is called upon to ascertain what the attitude of the board towards disclosure would have been may be many years after the death when the composition of the board may have changed. In this connection it is not irrelevant to observe that the criterion of value prescribed for estate duty purposes by s7(5) of the Finance Act 1894 has been adopted by the Finance Act 1965, s44(1), for the purpose of capital gains tax, where the chargeable disposition may be made many years after the basic date in April 1965. Thirdly, it would be very unsatisfactory if the amount of estate duty payable in cases such as this were to depend on evidence, which in the nature of the case cannot easily be challenged, given by persons who may be personally interested in the result. I do not suggest for a moment that the directors in question would give evidence which they knew to be false, but in this sort of situation the wish may easily be father to the thought, and one cannot help observing that in the *Holt* case the information which Mr Holt said that he would have disclosed was depreciatory of the value of the shares, whereas the information which Mr Lynall said that he would not have disclosed tended to enhance the value.

64 If one rejects the *Holt* test, one is left to choose between the published information test and the Crown's test. As the judge pointed out, the Crown's test as presented to him can hardly be right, since there may be all sorts of facts affecting the value of the shares which are known to some people at the relevant date but which are unknown to the board and knowledge of which cannot reasonably be imputed to the hypothetical vendor and purchaser. For example, an important customer of the company might have decided the day before the death not to renew some contract on which the company's prosperity largely depended, but might not have communicated the sad news to the company until the day after the death. As he understood them, therefore, the Judge can hardly be blamed for rejecting the Crown's contentions and saying that had he felt free to do so he would have adopted the 'published information' test. We, however, have to choose between the published information test and the Crown's test as submitted to us, and I have no doubt that the latter is to be preferred to the former. The case in favour of the published information test, *(pg401)* which was cogently argued by Mr Bagnall, started from the premise – which I think is correct – that one must not envisage a vendor who is a director as well as a shareholder. Of course, the hypothetical vendor may be a director, but he equally well may not be a director. One must, therefore, only endow him with the characteristic which must necessarily belong to all hypothetical vendors, namely, that of owning the block of shares in question. From this Mr Bagnall went on to submit that the published information test had the great merit of securing that the hypothetical vendor and purchaser should have and have only the information to which the vendor was entitled as a shareholder or which they could obtain as members of the public. But to my mind this second step in the argument was unwarranted. It is true, of course, that the accounts of the company when they have been audited and approved by the board are presented to the shareholders. Further, under s158(2) of the Companies Act 1948, any shareholder is entitled to be supplied with a copy of the last accounts. But it does not follow from this that the hypothetical vendor would have as of right at the time of the assumed sale all the information which the published information test assumes that he will have. In the first place, as one does not know when the vendor became a shareholder, one cannot predicate of him that he will be in possession of the company's accounts over a reasonable number of years before the sale. In this case the witnesses who gave evidence had before them the accounts back to 1951–52. Secondly, although the accounts for the year July 1960 to July 1961 had been audited and approved by the directors before Mrs Lynall died on 21st May 1962, they had not yet been sent to her. These two points may of course be said – and fairly said – to be comparatively trivial, for it would be a very unreasonable board of directors which refused to supply a shareholder with copies of the accounts for a few years back or with information as to the contents of accounts a copy of which was due to be sent to him. But the third difficulty in Mr Bagnall's way – namely, the fact that the accounts for the year 1961–62 (ten months of which had expired at the date of Mrs Lynall's death) were not available for the shareholders until long after death – is far more formidable. Obviously no one would give a proper price, or anything like a proper price, for the shares if he was refused all information as to the company's fortunes between the date to which the last published accounts were made up and the date of his purchase, and in fact the witnesses who gave evidence and the judge himself all assumed that the parties to the sale had some information about the ten months in question which they could only have obtained from the directors. But the assumption that the parties to the sale will have information as to the trading results for this broken period which the vendor has no right as a shareholder to require the directors to give him is inconsistent with Mr Bagnall's argument, and prompts one to ask whether there is any difference in principle between the board supplying a shareholder with information as to the current trading results and supplying him with information bearing on the likelihood of the company 'going public'. Mr Bagnall submitted that it made all the difference that the current trading results were raw material for the preparation of the company's accounts for the year which would eventually come into the hands of the shareholders, whereas the steps which the directors were taking in the direction of 'going public' might never contribute anything to any material which was published to the shareholders. This does not, however, appear to me to be a very substantial difference.

65 Another point which was urged in favour of the published information test was that the price of shares quoted on the Stock Exchange depends on the market's assessment of published as opposed to confidential information, and that it was desirable that the same standard should be applied to the valuation *(pg402)* of every sort of share. I cannot follow this argument at all, for the market for the sale of quoted shares is completely different from the market for the sale of holdings in private companies. No one will be a 'willing' purchaser of shares quoted on the Stock Exchange at a price higher than the quoted price, and if he happens to have confidential information showing that the shares are worth less than the quoted price he will not be willing to buy at all.

66 On the other hand, the uncontradicted evidence of the experts called by the Crown, Sir Henry Benson and Mr Andrews, shows that substantial minority holdings of shares in private companies are often bought and sold, and that before a price is agreed the purchaser invariably asks the vendor or the board to supply him, or alternatively to supply his advisers, in confidence with information possibly affecting the value of the shares which is not to be found in the accounts – as, for example, the trading results from the date to which the last accounts were made up and information, such as is contained in the category B documents in this case, bearing on the likelihood of a capital appreciation and the time at which one might hope to realise it. Further, the evidence showed that such information is in practice always given to enable the sale to go through. It is, of course, true – as Mr Bagnall pointed out – that the sales of which Sir Henry Benson and Mr Andrews were speaking were sales sponsored, or at least approved, by the board of the company in question. This is necessarily so, for if the board did not wish the shareholder in question to dispose of his holding they would make it clear that they would refuse to register the purchaser. It is in fact a condition of the market for the sale of minority holdings in private companies that the directors co-operate with the vendor. But that is the very condition which the *Crossman* decision obliges one to impose on the hypothetical sale envisaged by s7(5) of the Finance Act 1894, for the restrictions on transfer can only be got out of the way if the board will waive them. One can see that in certain cases the *Crossman* decision may work hardly, since it may oblige the estate of a deceased shareholder to pay estate duty on an assumed price which the shareholder could not in fact have obtained. But accepting, as we must, the principle of the *Crossman* case, the Crown's test as to the knowledge to be imputed to the parties to the sale appears to me to follow logically and not itself to involve any hardship, since the confidential information in the possession of the board is just as likely to depreciate as to enhance the value of the shares. Moreover, in a case such as this, where the executors are themselves directors, an acceptance of the published information test would involve the very odd result that if the executors, acting with the approval of their father, had sold Mrs Lynall's shares to raise money to pay duty and had disclosed the category B documents to the purchaser in order to obtain a higher price, they would, nevertheless, pay estate duty on the footing that on the hypothetical sale envisaged by s7(5) the category B documents would not have been disclosed to the purchaser.

67 The published information test has indeed the practical advantage that it would make the Commissioners' task easier than would the test for which they contend. Although the company's accounts for the year in which the death occurred might not be available for some time – possibly as much as a year or 18 months – after the death, the executors would eventually be able to make them available to the Commissioners, who could then, if the published information test be correct, determine the value of the shares without having to ask the executors to obtain information from the board which the board might refuse to give. But in those cases – and they would probably be the *(pg403)* majority – in which the executors were either directors themselves or closely connected with the board, they would be able to obtain the information if they wished. Therefore the Commissioners, if it was not forthcoming, might fairly draw the inference that there were facts unknown to them which made the shares worth more than the accounts alone would suggest, and to determine the value accordingly. On any appeal by the executors the Commissioners could of course obtain the evidence by discovery or subpoena. There may, of course, be exceptional cases in which the executors could not obtain the information, however hard they tried to do so. To take an example pressed on us by Mr Bagnall, the deceased holder of a substantial number of shares might have been a member of the family who had quarrelled with the others and had been expelled from the board. Again, one might have the case of a small holding – such as the 200 shares held by Mr Ellis in this case – which had passed into the hands of someone who was completely out of touch with the board. But I think that in such cases the Commissioners can be trusted to act reasonably and not to draw unfavourable inferences from a failure of the executors to produce information which they are not in a position to produce. At all events, the disadvantages – such as they are – of the Crown's test as compared with the published information test appear to me to weigh very lightly in the balance against the considerations telling in favour of the Crown's test which I have tried to set out.

68 In the event, therefore, I agree with my Lords that this appeal should be allowed and the figure of £4 10*s*. be substituted for £3 10*s*. as the value of each share in the company held by Mrs Lynall.

Judgement of the House of Lords

69 LORD REID – My Lords, Mrs Lynall died on 21st May 1962. At her death she owned 67,886 shares in Linread Ltd., a private company whose articles contained restrictions on the right of shareholders to sell their shares. The question at issue in this case is the proper value of these shares for estate duty purposes. At first the executors suggested £2 per share. The Revenue claimed on the basis of a value of £4 per share, which figure on obtaining further information they increased to £5 10*s*. Plowman J. fixed a value of £3 10*s*. On appeal the Court of Appeal increased this to £4 10*s*. Now the Appellants claim that the value should be fixed at £1 or alternatively £3 10*s*. per share. *(pg404)*

70 Linread began on a very modest scale in 1925. It prospered greatly but remained a family concern. At Mrs Lynall's death there were only five shareholders. She held 28 per cent of the share capital: her husband held 32 per cent: each of their two sons held 20 per cent: and the manager only held 200 shares. All five were directors. Both she and her husband were elderly, and it had been realised that there would be financial difficulties if they died without steps being taken to avoid that. So in 1959 Messrs. Thomson McLintock were asked to carry out a survey with a view to a public issue. They recommended that course, and in March 1962 a report was obtained from Messrs. Cazenoves as to the best method of flotation. No decision about this had been taken by Linread before Mrs Lynall's death, but the company was then ripe for 'going public'. The shares must be valued as provided by s7(5) of the Finance Act 1894:

71 '(5) The principal value of any property shall be estimated to be the price which, in the opinion of the Commissioners, such property would fetch if sold in the open market at the time of the death of the deceased.'

But neither Mrs Lynall nor her executors were entitled to sell these shares in the open market. Linread's articles of association provided:

'8. The Directors may in their absolute and uncontrolled discretion refuse to register any proposed transfer of shares and Regulation 24 of Part I of Table "A" shall be modified accordingly and no Preference or Ordinary Share in the Company shall be transferable until it shall (by letter addressed and delivered to the secretary of the Company) have been first offered to Ezra Herbert Lynall so long as he shall remain a Director of the Company and after he shall have ceased to be a Director of the Company to the Members of the Company at its fair value. The fair value of such share shall be fixed by the Company in General Meeting from time to time and where not so fixed shall be deemed to be the par value. The Directors may from time to time direct in what manner any such option to purchase shares shall be dealt with by the Secretary when communicated to him.'

72 No fair value had been fixed by the Company. So the position at Mrs Lynall's death was that the shares were not transferable until they had been first offered to her husband at £1 per share, and even if he did not want them they were only transferable to a purchaser accepted by the directors.

73 A similar situation occurred in *Commissioners of Inland Revenue v Crossman* [1937] AC 26. The Appellants asked us to reconsider that decision. I have done so, and I agree with the decision of the majority in this House. They followed the Irish case of *Attorney-General v Jameson* [1905] 2 I.R. 218. The most succinct statement of the ground of decision is that of Holmes L. J., at page 239:

'Turning to the 7th section of the Act, I find therein the very test of value which I should have applied in its absence. "The principal value shall be estimated to be the price which, in the opinion of the Commissioners, such property would fetch if sold in the open market at the time of the death of the deceased". The Attorney-General and the defendants agree in saying that in this case there cannot be an actual sale in open market. Therefore, argues the former, we must assume that there is no restriction of any kind on the disposition of the shares and estimate that would be given therefor by a purchaser, who upon registration would have complete control over them. My objection to this mode of *(pg405)* ascertaining the value is that the property bought in the imaginary sale would be a different property from that which Henry Jameson held at the time of his death. The defendants, on the other hand, contend that the only sale possible is a sale at which the highest price would be £100 per share, and that this ought to be the estimated value. My objection is that this estimate is not based on a sale in open market as required by the Act. Being unable to accept either solution, I go back to my own, which is in strict accordance with the language of the section. I assume that there is such a sale of the shares as is contemplated by article 11, the effect of which would be to place the purchaser in the same position as that occupied by Henry Jameson. An expert would have no difficulty in estimating their value on this basis. It would be less than the Crown claims, and more than the defendants offer; but I believe that it would be arrived at in accordance not only with the language of the Act, but with the methods usually employed in valuing property.'

74 The Appellants urged your Lordships to accept the view of the minority in *Crossman's* case. They appear to assume that there could be a sale by a shareholder of shares subject to a right of pre-emption. In my view it is legally impossible for the shareholder to sell such shares in the open market or otherwise without first obtaining from the holder of the right of pre-emption an agreement not to exercise that right. I agree with Lord Roche that sale means a transaction which passes the property in the thing sold. All that the shareholder could offer would be an undertaking that if the right of pre-emption was exercised he would assign to the 'purchaser' his right to receive the pre-emption price, and that if the right of pre-emption was not exercised he would transfer the shares to the purchaser, so that if the directors registered the transfer the property in the shares would pass but if they did not he would hold the shares in trust for the purchaser. In my view that would not be a sale. I support the view of the majority on the ground that s7(5) is merely machinery for estimating value, that it will not work if s7(5) is read literally, that it must be made to work, and that the only way of doing that is the way adopted in *Crossman's* case. If *Crossman's* case stands then the first submission of the Appellants fails. The parties admit that then the choice is between the valuation of £3 10s. and £4 10s. per share.

75 We must decide what the highest bidder would have offered in the hypothetical sale in the open market, which the Act requires us to imagine took place at the time of Mrs Lynall's death. The sum which any bidder will offer must depend on what he knows (or thinks he knows) about the property for which he bids. The decision of this case turns on the question what knowledge the hypothetical bidders must be supposed to have had about the affairs of Linread. One solution would be that they must be supposed to have been omniscient. But we have to consider what would in fact have happened if this imaginary sale had taken place, or at least – if we are looking for a general rule – what would happen in the event of a sale of this kind taking place. One thing which would not happen would be that the bidders would be omniscient. They would derive their knowledge from facts made available to them by the shareholder exposing the shares for sale. We must suppose that, being a willing seller and an honest man, he would give as much information as he was entitled to give. If he was not a director he would give the information which he could get as a shareholder. If he was a director and had confidential information, he could not disclose that information without the consent of the board of directors. *(pg406)*

76 In the present case, if we are to suppose that the bidder only had information which he could obtain himself or which could be given without the consent of the board, then admittedly £3 10s. is the correct estimate of what the highest bid would have been. But the Crown maintains, and the Court of Appeal would seem to have held, that it must be supposed that the board would have authorised the hypothetical seller to communicate highly confidential information to all who might come forward as bidders. Bidders would know that both Mrs Lynall and her husband were elderly and that they held most of the shares. Their general experience would tell them that in such circumstances it is common for a private company to make a public issue and remove restrictions on the transfer of its shares. The successful bidder would have to lock up a sum of £200,000 or more until there was a free market in the shares. If there was a prospect of an early public issue he would be prepared to pay considerably more than if it were uncertain whether or when the company would 'go public'. I have said that the board had reports which made it very probable that a public issue would be made in the near future. If bidders must be supposed to have known about these reports then it is agreed that there would have been a bid of £4 10s. per share.

77 The case for the Crown is based on evidence as to how large blocks of shares in private companies are in fact sold. There is no announcement that the shares are for sale and no invitation for competitive bids. The seller engages an expert who selects the person or group whom he thinks most likely to be prepared to pay a good price and to be acceptable to the directors. If that prospective purchaser is interested he engages accountants of high repute, and the directors agree to co-operate by making available to the accountants on a basis of strict confidentiality all relevant information about the company's affairs. Then the accountants acting in an arbitral capacity fix what they think is a fair price. Then the sale is made at that price. Obviously the working of this scheme depends on all concerned having complete confidence in each other, and I do not doubt that in this way the seller gets a better price than he could otherwise obtain. In my view this evidence is irrelevant because this kind of sale is not a sale in the open market. It is a sale by private treaty made without competition to a selected purchaser at a price fixed by an expert valuer. The 1894 Act could have provided – but it did not – that the value should be the highest price that could reasonably have been expected to be realised on a sale of the property at the time of the death. If that had been the test then the Crown would succeed, subject to one matter which I need not stop to consider. But the framers of the Act limited the enquiry to one type of sale – sale in the open market – and we are not entitled to rewrite the Act. It is quite easily workable as it stands.

78 No doubt sale in the open market may take many forms. But it appears to me that the idea behind this provision is the classical theory that the best way to determine the value in exchange of any property is to let the price be determined by economic forces – by throwing the sale open to competition when the price will be the highest price that anyone offers. That implies that there has been adequate publicity or advertisement before the sale, and the nature of the property must determine what is adequate publicity. Goods may be exposed for sale in a market place or place to which buyers resort. Property may be put up to auction. Competitive tenders may be invited. On the Stock Exchange a sale to a jobber may seem to be a private sale, but the price has been determined, at least within narrow limits, by the actions of the investing public. In a particular case it may not always be easy to say whether there has been a sale in the open market. But in my judgment the method on which *(pg407)* the Crown rely cannot by any criterion be held to be selling in the open market. If the hypothetical sale on the open market requires us to suppose that competition has been invited, then we would have to suppose that steps had been taken before the sale to enable a variety of persons, institutions or financial groups to consider what offers they would be prepared to make. It would not be a true sale in the open market if the seller were to discriminate between genuine potential buyers and give to some of them information which he withheld from others, because one from whom he withheld information might be the one who, if he had had the information, would have made the highest offer.

79 The Crown's figure of £4 10s. per share can only be justified if it must be supposed that these reports would have been made known to all genuine potential buyers, or at least to accountants nominated by them. That could only have been done with the consent of Linread's board of directors. They were under no legal obligation to make any confidential information available. Circumstances vary so much that I have some difficulty in seeing how we could lay down any general rule that directors must be supposed to have done something which they were not obliged to do. The farthest we could possibly go would be to hold that directors must be deemed to have done what all reasonable directors would do. Then it might be reasonable to say that they would disclose information provided that its disclosure could not possibly prejudice the interests of the company. But that would not be sufficient to enable the Crown to succeed. Not all financiers who might wish to bid in such a sale, and not even all the accountants whom they might nominate, are equally trustworthy. A premature leakage of such information as these reports disclose might be very damaging to the interests of the company, and the evidence in this case shews that in practice great care is taken to see that disclosure is only made to those of the highest repute. I could not hold it right to suppose that all reasonable directors would agree to disclose information such as these reports so widely as would be necessary if it had to be made available to all who must be regarded as genuine potential bidders or to their nominees. So in my opinion the Crown fail to justify their valuation of £4 10s. I would therefore allow this appeal.

80 LORD MORRIS OF BORTH-Y-GEST – My Lords, the first submission that was made on behalf of the Appellants was one that was not open to them in the Courts below. It was that we should depart from the decision of this House in *Commissioners of Inland Revenue v Crossman* [1937] A.C. 26 by preferring the opinions expressed by the minority in that case to those expressed by the majority. Even if we were persuaded that the minority opinions were to be preferred, the question would arise whether it would be right to depart from the decision. It was given as long ago as March 1936, and it must on numerous occasions have been acted upon. It was in accord with the decision of the Court of Appeal in Ireland in *Attorney-General v Jameson* [1905] 2 I.R. 218 and the reasoning in that case had guided practice in subsequent years: see also *Salvesen's Trustees v Commissioners of Inland Revenue* 1930 S.L.T. 387. It has been open to Parliament at any time since 1936 to amend s7(5) of the Finance Act 1894 if it had been considered that that section (as interpreted in this House) ought to be amended or supplanted. But, having considered the arguments attractively presented on behalf of the Appellants, I have not been persuaded that the decision in *Crossman's* case was erroneous. Section 7(5) requires an estimate to be made of the price which the property would fetch 'if sold' in the open market. So a sale in the open market must be assumed, and this in some cases will involve an assumption of the satisfaction of such conditions as would have to be satisfied to enable such a sale to take place. *(pg408)*

81 On the basis of an acceptance of the *Crossman* decision it was for the learned Judge on the appeal from the decision of the Commissioners to decide what price the shares would have fetched if sold in the open market at the time of the death of the deceased. In his careful judgment the learned Judge summarised the evidence which he had heard. It became common ground that the price to be decided upon was that which would have been paid (*a*) by a hypothetical willing purchaser (*b*) to a hypothetical willing vendor (*c*) in the open market (*d*) on 21st May 1962. The issue which was raised turned largely on the question as to what knowledge and information would be available for and would be at the command of a purchaser. There were certain documents in existence the contents of which would have influenced a purchaser who had access to them. Referred to as 'category B documents', they included (i) documents having relevance to investigations 83. made by the board into possible ways and means of raising money to pay prospective death duties which would be payable on the death of a shareholder, and showing that the board were actively contemplating a public issue; (ii) a report made in July 1960 by Messrs. Thomson McLintock (who had been asked to carry out a survey of the company's undertakings with a view to a public issue) and papers recording their views as to a possible flotation; (iii) a report made in March 1962 by Messrs. Cazenove & Co. in regard to the method of flotation, and (iv) various kindred documents and also statements showing month by month the progress made by the company. The learned Judge decided that, as the information contained in these documents was not published information, it would not have been available to a purchaser: he further decided, in view of the evidence given by a director (Mr Alan Lynall), that had an enquiry been made of the board by a prospective purchaser the information contained in the documents would not in fact have been made available by the board.

82 On the evidence which he heard the learned Judge decided that the valuation should be £3 10*s*. He held that if he were wrong in his view that the category B documents were not admissible he would have fixed the valuation at £4 10*s*. The Court of Appeal concluded, on the basis of certain evidence given at the hearing as to the practice of directors where blocks of shares in private companies are in the market, that a purchaser would have made enquiry of the board which would have resulted in the information contained in the category B documents being made available (even if only in confidence to the advisers of a purchaser). They held that the valuation figure should be that of £4 10*s*.

83 Questions also arose in regard to the availability for a prospective purchaser on 21st May 1962 of certain other information. The company's accounts for the year ending 31st July 1961 had before 21st May 1962 been drawn up and audited, but they were not passed until 7th June 1962. By 21st May 1962 some ten months trading within the year ending 31st July 1962 had taken place. The accounts for that year when drawn up revealed that sales had risen and that profits had increased. In fixing the price which would be paid by a hypothetical purchaser in the open market on 21st May 1962 to what extent should he be regarded as having information as to the current financial position of the company?

84 In argument before your Lordships counsel agreed that if the decision in the *Crossman* case stood the figure to be decided upon should be either £3 10s. or £4 10s., and that it should be the latter figure only on the basis that a *(pg409)* hypothetical purchaser would be in possession of the information contained in the category B documents as well as of information concerning the current financial position of the company. Argument turned considerably on the question whether a hypothetical purchaser in the open market would have available to him the contents of or the information contained in the category B documents, and in particular the documents in relation to the possibility of the company going public.

85 Before the learned Judge several possible classifications of the knowledge to be imputed to the hypothetical purchaser and the hypothetical vendor were canvassed. Should it comprise the published information available from published accounts or statements to all who sought it? Should it comprise all the circumstances relevant to value which in fact existed at the relevant time? Should it include such information additional to the published information which would have been supplied by the directors if they had reasonably been asked for information by a shareholder wishing to sell or by a member of the public wishing to buy? Should the test be what a reasonable board of directors would communicate?

86 At the date of her death (21st May 1962), Mrs Lynall was the registered holder of 67,886 ordinary shares in the company: her holding was about 28 per cent of the issued share capital. Accepting the *Crossman* decision the hypothetical purchaser would purchase on the basis that he would become a holder but would be subject to the restrictions on transfer imposed by the articles. If, however, the company became a public company and these restrictions were removed it is clear that the value of the shares would greatly increase. Any information relating to the prospects of the company becoming a public company, and in particular of the timing of such a change, would therefore be calculated to have very considerable effect upon the price of the shares.

87 The sum required to purchase the shares now in question would be very large. On the learned Judge's valuation of £3 10s. a share a sum of nearly £250,000 would be involved. It is obvious that no purchaser would expend so much money unless he had such reasonable information as would give him confidence. He would certainly wish to make all reasonable enquiries. In *Salvesen's Trustees* Lord Fleming pointed out the difficulty of estimating the value of shares in a company whose shares could not be bought and sold in the open market, and with regard to which there had not been any sales on ordinary terms and said: 'The problem can only be dealt with by considering all the relevant facts so far as known at the date of the testator's death, and by determining what a prudent investor, who knew these facts, might be expected to be willing to pay for the shares'. Lord Fleming proceeded to indicate what in that case were 'the relevant facts'. In *Findlay's Trustees v Commissioners of Inland Revenue* (1938) 22 A.T.C. 437 (at page 440) Lord Fleming spoke of the willing purchaser as being 'a person of reasonable prudence', who would inform himself of all relevant facts such as the history of the business being carried on and its present position and future prospects, and who would have access to the accounts of the business for a number of years.

88 In the present case it is clear that the information contained in what have been called the category B documents would be highly relevant, but the question arises whether that information would be available. In particular, the question arises whether that information would be available not just to *(pg410)* some possible purchasers and vendors, but whether it would be available to hypothetical purchasers and vendors 'in the open market'. This must mean whether it would be openly available to all potential purchasers and vendors in the market or markets in which the relevant purchases and sales take place. There may be different markets or types of markets for differing varieties of property, but in the operation of s7(5) of the Finance Act 1894 the market which must be contemplated, whatever its form, must be an 'open' market in which the property is offered for sale to the world at large so that all potential purchasers have an equal opportunity to make an offer as a result of its being openly known what it is that is being offered for sale. Mere private deals on a confidential basis are not the equivalent of open market transactions.

89 The somewhat limited issue as between the two figures of £3 10s. or £4 10s. mainly depends upon the question whether knowledge of the category B documents and of the information which they contain would be 'open market' knowledge. The conclusion of the learned Judge was that, as such information was not published information, and as (on Mr Alan Lynall's evidence, which the learned Judge accepted) it would not in fact have been elicited on enquiry, it ought not to enter into the calculation of price and value. The differing view of the Court of Appeal was based on the evidence, above referred to, of the practice of boards of directors to answer reasonable questions in confidence to the advisers of an interested potential purchaser. If this is the practice, and even if the sought-for information may be given 'in confidence' to an interested potential purchaser himself, I cannot think that this equates with open market conditions. It was said that it should be assumed that a purchaser would make reasonable enquiries from all available sources and that it must further be assumed that he would receive true and factual answers. If, however, the category B documents and the information contained in them were confidential to the board, as they were, the information could not be made generally available so that it became open market knowledge. On this somewhat limited issue I therefore prefer the figure of £3 10s. and I would restore the decision of the learned Judge.

90 On the wider issues, I doubt whether it is possible to define with precision the extent or the limits of the information on the basis of which a hypothetical purchaser of shares on a sale in the open market might purchase. There may be cases where prudent and careful potential purchasers of a large block of shares will be unwilling to purchase unless they have the inducement of being given confidential information which is not generally known. If in practice some large deals take place on the basis that some information is given which must be kept secret, then any such practice is the practice not of an open market but of a special market operating in a special way. I would see great difficulties if the Commissioners or a Court had to assess the extent to which a particular board of directors would or would not have been likely or willing to answer some particular enquiries – though there may be some enquiries of which it can with certainty be said that they would readily and properly and openly have been answered. A purchaser in the open market would probably not be content merely with what would be published information in the sense of information which had been in print in some documents sent out by a company to its shareholders. He would form his own idea as to the company's prospects having regard to trends and developments which are matters of public knowledge. Furthermore, on known facts in regard to a private company and its directors and its management he would form his own reasonable deductions.

91 I would allow the appeal. *(pg411)*

92 VISCOUNT DILHORNE – My Lords, two questions have to be decided in this appeal; first, whether the decision of this House in *Commissioners of Inland Revenue v Crossman* [1937] A.C. 26 should be adhered to; and, secondly, whether it is to be assumed that the hypothetical purchaser of shares in Linread Ltd., a private company, would have had knowledge at the time of the hypothetical sale of reports by Messrs. Thomson McLintock and by Messrs. Cazenove & Co. as to the advisability of making a public issue of shares and converting the company into a public company.

Section 7(5) of the Finance Act 1894 is in the following terms:

'(5) The principal value of any property shall be estimated to be the price which, in the opinion of the Commissioners, such property would fetch if sold in the open market at the time of the death of the deceased.'

93 Mrs Lynall died on 21st May 1962. She then held 67,886 £1 shares in the company, of which the issued share capital was £241,700 divided into 241,700 £1 shares. The price which the shares she held would have fetched if sold in the open market has therefore to be determined.

94 Article 8 of the company's articles of association contains restrictions on transfers of shares in the company. It gives the directors power in their absolute and unfettered discretion to refuse to register any proposed transfer of shares. That article also provided that no shares in the company should be transferable until they had first been offered to Mr Lynall, Mrs Lynall's husband, if he was a director of the company, at their fair value. The article went on to say that the fair value was to be fixed by the company in general meeting from time to time and where not so fixed should be deemed to be the par value. The fair value had not been fixed, and so, if Mrs Lynall had been in a position to sell her shares on 21st May 1962 and had wished to do so, she would have had to offer them in the first place to her husband at £1 a share; and if he did not want to buy them the directors could by withholding consent to registration of the transfer have prevented a sale to anyone else.

95 The question of the application of s7(5) to shares in a private company has arisen before and given rise to some conflict of judicial authority. The problem was considered in this House in *Commissioners of Inland Revenue v Crossman*, in *Attorney-General v Jameson* [1905] 2 I.R. 218 and in *Salvesen's Trustees v Commissioners of Inland Revenue* 1930 S.L.T. 387. The House was invited to reconsider the majority decision in *Crossman* and to depart from it. In my view the decision in that case was right. Parliament has enacted that the price the shares would fetch if sold in the open market has to be assessed. There could be no sale on the open market on 21st May 1962 unless the directors agreed to the registration of the transfer of the shares and Mr Lynall refused to purchase the shares at £1 a share. Therefore, for the price the shares would fetch if sold in the open market to be assessed, it must be assumed that the directors had so agreed and Mr Lynall had refused to buy. As Mr Harman said in the course of his argument for the Crown, if property is only saleable in the open market in certain circumstances, then when the Act requires the property to be valued at the price which it would fetch if sold in the open market, one must proceed on the basis that those circumstances exist. This does not mean that the shares change their character. The shares bought by the hypothetical purchaser will be subject to the restrictions imposed by article 8.

96 Turning to the second question, it was said that the normal way in which a block of shares in a private company is sold is for the vendor to find a potential purchaser, and then if the directors approve of him they will authorise their *(pg412)* accountants to furnish confidential information to an accountant acting for the purchaser who will in the light of his advice make an offer for the shares. On such a sale no doubt all or nearly all the relevant information, whether confidential or otherwise, will be disclosed to the purchaser's accountant, and a higher price will be obtainable than would be the case in the absence of such information. If the shares in Linread were sold in this way, presumably McLintocks' reports and that of Cazenoves would have been disclosed to the purchaser's accountant. The Crown contend that, as this is the normal way of selling such shares in a private company, it constitutes a sale in the open market. In my opinion it is the antithesis of a sale in the open market. Only a person or persons selected by the vendor will be able to make an offer. It is, I think, an essential feature of a sale in the open market that persons interested should have an opportunity to purchase, not just those selected by the vendor. This method of selling shares in a private company is not a sale in the open market but one by private treaty.

97 On a sale in the open market is it to be assumed that possible purchasers would have information as to the contents of the reports of McLintocks and Cazenoves? They were confidential to the directors. All the shareholders in Linread were directors, but it is not to be assumed that they would disclose confidential information they possessed to the public without the consent of the board; nor is it to be supposed that the board would have given its consent to the disclosure of the contents of those reports. In the light of the evidence given by Mr Alan Lynall, whose evidence was tendered and accepted as being the evidence of the board, and accepted by Plowman J. (set out on pages 1068–9 of his judgment in [1968] 3 W.L.R. 1056) it is clear that that would not have been given. It was agreed that, if it were held that it is to be assumed that purchasers would have knowledge of those reports in a sale on the open market, the shares were to be valued at £4 10s. a share, but that if no such assumption was to be made, their value was £3 10s. a share.

98 Some discussion took place on whether it was to be assumed that a purchaser in the open market would only have knowledge of information about the company which had been published, or whether he was to be assumed to have such information as a board of directors would have disclosed if asked for it. It is not necessary to express in this case an opinion on the point as it does not really arise. In support of the contention that he must be assumed to have such information as a board would, if asked, have disclosed *In re Holt* [1953] 1 W.L.R. 1488 was cited, but this question was never in issue in that case.

99 For the reasons I have given, in my opinion it must be held that the price a share in the company would have fetched if sold in the open market on 21st May 1962 was £3 10s., and so this appeal should be allowed.

100 LORD DONOVAN – My Lords, I would not accede to the request that this House should depart from the decision reached in 1937 in *Commissioners of Inland Revenue v Crossman* [1937] A.C. 26. The effect of that decision was to uphold the view of the Court of Appeal in Ireland in *Attorney-General v Jameson* [1905] 2 I.R. 218, so that for nearly 70 years the valuation of shares subject to a restriction on alienation has been made for estate duty purposes on the basis laid down in the latter case. It would, therefore, need to be clearly demonstrated that that basis was erroneous if it were now to be supplanted. So far from being shewn to be wrong, I think the two decisions quoted have emerged from the further examination to which they have been subjected with enhanced authority. *(pg413)*

101 I concur in the view that confidential information ought not to be regarded as available to a hypothetical purchaser under s7(5), Finance Act 1894; though I would think it right not to treat as confidential information for this purpose accounts of the company already prepared and awaiting presentation to the shareholders. I have in mind the accounts of the present company for the year to 31st July 1961.

102 I have been a little perturbed about the procedure adopted in this case, apparently as an innovation, that discovery should be applied for as a means of prising out of the Appellants the secrets of the board room. The corresponding procedure, had not the Appellants been directors of the company as well as executors, would presumably have been the service of a *subpoena duces tecum* upon an officer of the company with the like end in view. I think it would be wrong to try and compel such a witness to disclose, under pain of committal if he refused, information of a confidential character, the publication of which might do the company (which is not even a party to the proceedings) immense harm. The Revenue, following I suppose their own notions of what is permissible and what is not, have hitherto efficiently performed their duties under the Act of 1894 without resort to any such procedure. They are now proved to have been in the right, since the effect of your Lordships' decision is that such confidential information is irrelevant to the determination of the value of shares under s7(5); and being irrelevant is, therefore, inadmissible.

103 I also would allow the appeal.

104 LORD PEARSON – My Lords, the deceased Mrs Lynall at the time of her death on 21st May 1962 was the owner of 67,886 shares of £1 each in Linread Ltd. (which I shall call 'the company'), and these shares passed on her death and have to be valued for the purposes of estate duty. The statutory method of ascertaining the value is laid down by s7(5) of the Finance Act 1894, which provides:

'The principal value of any property shall be estimated to be the price which, in the opinion of the Commissioners, such property would fetch if sold in the open market at the time of the death of the deceased.'

105 Plowman J. assessed the principal value at £3 10*s*. (now £3.50) per share, but the Court of Appeal assessed it at £4 10*s*. (now £4.50) per share. The Appellants, however, have put forward to your Lordships a contention, which was not open to them in the Court of first instance or in the Court of Appeal, that *Commissioners of Inland Revenue v Crossman* [1937] A.C. 26 was wrongly decided, and that, by reason of article 8 of the company's articles of association, the deemed price of the shares in the hypothetical sale which has to be assumed under s7(5), and therefore the principal value as defined in that section, can only be £1 per share. Article 8 provides:

'The directors may in their absolute and uncontrolled discretion refuse to register any proposed transfer of shares and regulation 24 of Part 1 of Table "A" shall be modified accordingly and no preference or ordinary share in the company shall be transferable until it shall (by letter addressed and delivered to the secretary of the company) have been first offered to Ezra Herbert Lynall so long as he shall remain a director of the company and after he shall have ceased to be a director of the company to the members of the company at its fair value. The fair value of such share shall be fixed by the company in general meeting from time to time and where not so fixed shall be deemed to be the par value. The directors may from time to time direct in what manner any such option to purchase shares shall be dealt with by the secretary when communicated to him.' *(pg414)*

The company in general meeting had never fixed the fair value of its shares for the purposes of article 8, and accordingly a shareholder wishing to sell his shares would have been obliged to offer the shares to Ezra Herbert Lynall at the par value of £1 per share.

106 The question, therefore, arises whether in a case such as this the hypothetical sale in the open market under s7(5) is in itself subject to or free from the restrictions imposed by the articles of association. The question was one of difficulty and gave rise to a conflict of judicial opinions, but, in my view, it has been authoritatively and correctly decided by the majority in this House in *Commissioners of Inland Revenue v Crossman*, and though it would now be possible, it would not be right, to depart from that decision. Originally a decision on this question was given by the Irish Court of Appeal in *Attorney-General v Jameson* [1905] 2 I.R. 218, unanimously overruling the majority decision of the Irish Court of King's Bench [1904] 2 I.R. 644. The decision of the Irish Court of Appeal, as stated in the declaration proposed by Holmes L.J., at page 240, was that

> 'the principal value of the shares is to be estimated at the price which, in the opinion of the Commissioners, they would fetch if sold in the open market, on the terms that the purchaser should be entitled to be registered as holder of the shares, and should take and hold them subject to the provisions of the articles of association, including the articles relating to alienation and transfer of the shares of the company.'

107 Then in the Scottish case of *Salvesen's Trustees v Commissioners of Inland Revenue* 1930 S.L.T. 387 Lord Fleming, at page 391, while not bound by the decision and reasoning of the Irish Court of Appeal, expressed his agreement with them and followed their judgment, but also gave his own reasons. He said:

> 'If the articles of association be complied with, a sale in the open market in a reasonable sense seems to be impossible. The petitioners argued that the maximum price the shareholder can obtain for his shares in the open market is determined by the best price he can obtain in the closed market, viz. £1. But it appears to me that if this argument is well founded, it merely demonstrates that there cannot be a real sale in the open market under the articles. The Act of Parliament requires, however, that the assumed sale, which is to guide the Commissioners in estimating the value, is to take place in the open market. Under these circumstances I think that there is no escape from the conclusion that any restrictions which prevent the shares being sold in an open market must be disregarded so far as the assumed sale under section 7(5) of the Act of 1894 is concerned. But, on the other

hand, the terms of that subsection do not require or authorise the Commissioners to disregard such restrictions in considering the nature and value of the subject which the hypothetical buyer acquires at the assumed sale. Though he is deemed to buy in an open and unrestricted market, he buys a share which, after it is transferred to him, is subject to all the conditions in the articles of association, including the restrictions on the right of transfer, and this circumstance may affect the price which he would be willing to offer.'

108 To my mind, that is a clear and convincing statement.

In *Crossman's* case Finlay J. followed the decisions in the *Jameson* case and the *Salvesen* case; then the majority of the Court of Appeal took the other view; and then this House by a majority restored Finlay J.'s order. *(pg415)* I find the reasoning of the majority in this House, especially that of Lord Roche, preferable to that of the minority, and I think their decision should be followed in the present case – not only because it is an authoritative decision which has stood intact and been frequently applied over a substantial period, but also on the merits of the question involved. Accordingly, the Appellants' first contention should be rejected.

109 The Appellants' alternative contention is that Plowman J.'s assessment of £3 10s. per share should be restored, whereas the Crown contend that the Court of Appeal's assessment of £4 10s. should be upheld. It is common ground for the purposes of this appeal that, if the suggested assessment of £1 per share in accordance with the Appellants' primary contention is rejected, the choice then lies between £3 10s. per share and £4 10s. per share, and the choice depends on the extent of the information which must be deemed to have been available to participants in the hypothetical open market.

110 At the material time the company was highly prosperous, though distributing small dividends. One of the shareholders, Mrs Lynall, was 76 years of age. Another of them, her husband Ezra Herbert Lynall, was 69 years of age. There was an evident general probability that before very long the company would have to 'go public', i.e., make a public issue of shares and cease to be a private company. If that happened there would be a prospect of larger dividends and of the restrictions on transfer of shares being removed. That general probability for the fairly near future would be known in the hypothetical market, and when taken in conjunction with the prosperity of the company would justify a price of £3 10s. per share. But there was in fact more than that general probability. The facts are set out in the judgment of the learned Judge in [1968] 3 W.L.R. 1056, at page 1062 . It can be said shortly that, while the board maintained throughout a cautious and uncommitted attitude, they had instructed Messrs. Thomson McLintock to carry out a survey of the company's undertaking with a view to a public issue, and had received Messrs. Thomson McLintock's report and subsequent advice that the board should consider a flotation at the earliest possible moment, and had authorised consultation with Messrs. Cazenove & Co. in order to obtain the reaction of the City, and Messrs. Cazenove had suggested a method for the flotation. The importance of this information, if it could be deemed to be available to participants in the hypothetical market, would be that it would substantially advance the time at which a public issue of shares in the company could be expected, and therefore would enhance the price of the shares to an extent agreed to be £1 per share, making a price of £4 10s. per share.

111 The crucial question, therefore, is whether this information should be deemed to be available to participants in the hypothetical market. I should agree with what was said by Lord Fleming in the *Salvesen* case and by Danckwerts J. in *In re Holt* [1953] 1 W.L.R. 1488 to the effect that a purchaser of shares in a private company subject to restrictions on transfer would be diligent in his enquiries. Danckwerts J. said, at page 1501:

'I think that the kind of investor who would purchase shares in a private company of this kind, in circumstances which must preclude him from disposing of his shares freely whenever he should wish (because he will, when registered as a shareholder, be subject to the provisions of the articles restricting transfer) would be different from any common kind of purchaser of shares on the Stock Exchange, and would be rather the *(pg416)* exceptional kind of investor who had some special reason for putting his money into shares of this kind. He would, in my view, be the kind of investor who would not rush hurriedly into the transaction, but would consider carefully the prudence of the course, and would seek to get the fullest possible information about the past history of the company, the particular trade in which it was engaged and the future prospects of the company.'

112 In the imaginative exercise in which s7(5) requires the courts to engage, that passage seems to me to be well imagined.

113 In the present case, however, the company's board of directors had received reports and advice which were obviously of a confidential character, and the board had come to no decision as to whether they would act on the advice or not but were maintaining their cautious and uncommitted attitude. It is reasonable to imagine that in that situation the board would have kept these matters confidential, and would have been unwilling to disclose the reports and advice which they had received, and in particular unwilling to make them available to participants in the open market. *Prima facie* the information would not have been available.

114 It is, however, suggested that it would have been available in two ways. First, it is said that the likely purchasers might have included a director of the company, and he would have had the information *ex officio*. But unless others also knew it his possession of the information would not materially affect the market price which he or any other purchaser would have to pay. The situation differs from that in *Commissioners of Inland Revenue v Clay* [1914] 3 K.B. 466, at pages 471–2, where the special fact enhancing the price of the property was assumed to be a matter of local knowledge. Secondly, it is said that the directors of the company might have been willing to impart the information confidentially to a chartered accountant or other expert acting as agent for a purchaser, though the information would be imparted on the terms that it would not be passed on to the purchaser himself. But in such a case the transaction would be in the nature of a private placing and not a sale in the open market such as has to be envisaged under s7(5). In my opinion the reasonable supposition is that the information would not be available in the hypothetical open market, and so the assessment should be £3 10*s.* and not £4 10*s.*; and therefore the appeal should be allowed and the judgment of Plowman J. should be restored. *(pg417)*

Case 30
Hinchcliffe v Crabtree

(1971) 47 TC 419

House of Lords

13, 14, 15 and 19 July and 27 October 1971

TCGA 1992, s 272(3) gives the rule for the valuation, for capital gains tax purposes, of a share or security that is quoted on the London Stock Market. The price is calculated from the Stock Market Daily Official List 'except where in consequence of special circumstances prices quoted in that List are by themselves not a proper measure of market value'.

This case concerns the interpretation of that proviso.

Peter Neville Crabtree was the joint managing director of RW Crabtree & Sons Ltd, a quoted company. On 18 August 1965, Vickers made an offer to take over RW Crabtree & Sons Ltd. Peter Crabtree accepted the offer for his shareholding and received cash.

The capital gain on which he was to be assessed fell to be calculated by reference to the market value at 6 April 1965 being taken as the base cost.

Negotiations for the takeover by Vickers had commenced on 4 November 1964, having commenced at a lunch at that date between the chairman of Vickers, Sir Charles Dunphie, Peter Crabtree and others. At the valuation date of 6 April 1965, Peter Crabtree was, therefore, in possession of a significant amount of information regarding the offer that he confidently expected to be made for his shares. This information was not, however, known to the Stock Market.

In this case, the House of Lords unanimously declared that these circumstances are not 'special circumstances' for the purpose of the valuation rule in TCGA 1992, s 272(3). Hence, the base cost for the sale of shares was the price in the Stock Exchange Daily Official List (with the alternative being available by reference to bargains: see s 272(3)(b)). A valuation undertaken on the principles that would apply were the shares unquoted was not available to the taxpayer.

It would appear that the price in the Stock Exchange Daily Official List can only be ignored where there was no trading in the market or for some reason, a particular parcel of shares would not be sold on the Stock Exchange at all. For Lord Morris of Borth-y-Gest ((1971) 47 TC 419 at 447 **case 30 para 20**), if information was wrongly withheld from the market, this could be a 'special circumstance'.

Statute requires us to use the stock market price unless there are 'special circumstances'. Lord Reid construed this provision by saying:

> '"Special" must mean unusual or uncommon – perhaps the nearest word to it in this context is "abnormal".'
>
> ((1971) 47 TC 419 at 443 **case 30 para 8**)

On the basis of this decision, the Stock Market published price must be taken as the value of a shareholding quoted on that market, in all but the most exceptional circumstances. This is the case, even if the Stock Market price is demonstrably drastically different from that which would be determined by applying the principles used in valuing a holding in an unquoted company.

Judgement

References, example '(pg440)', are to (1971) 47 TC 419.

1 **LORD REID**: My Lords, the Appellant was assessed to capital gains tax in the sum of £65,695 for the year 1965–66. The Special Commissioners reduced this assessment to £20,819. Pennycuick J. dismissed an appeal from their decision, but on appeal the Court of Appeal reversed his decision. The Appellant now seeks to have the decision of the Special Commissioners restored.

2 Section 22 (10) of the Finance Act 1965 provides that gains accruing after 6th April 1965 shall be chargeable gains. So when any property is sold after that date it is necessary to find its value at that date in order to find what part of the price realised was a gain which accrued after that date. Paragraph 22 (2) of Sch. 6 requires us to assume that the property was sold on that date and immediately reacquired by its owner at its then market value. At that date the Appellant owned 98,604 ordinary stock units of R.W. Crabtree & Sons Ltd., together with a small number of preferred ordinary and preference stock units. These latter I shall not consider separately. Later in that year Vickers acquired the whole issued capital of the company: they paid 55*s.* for each ordinary stock unit. The question in this case is what was the market value of these units on *(pg440)* 6th April. They were quoted on the London Stock Exchange at 42*s.* 6*d.* on that date and the assessment which the Crown defends is based on the chargeable gains being the difference between those two figures, i.e. 12*s.* 6*d.* per stock unit.

3 The Appellant relies on s44 (3) of the Act. Section 44 provides:

'(1) Subject to the following subsections, in this Part of this Act "market value" in relation to any assets means the price which those assets might reasonably be expected to fetch on a sale in the open market. (2) In estimating the market value of any assets no reduction shall be made in the estimate on account of the estimate being made on the assumption that the whole of the assets is to be placed on the market at one and the same time: Provided that where capital gains tax is chargeable, or an allowable loss accrues, in consequence of death and the market value of any property on the date of death taken into account for the purposes of that tax or loss has been depreciated by reason of the death the estimate of the market value shall take that depreciation into account. (3) Subject to paragraph 22 (3) of Schedule 6 to this Act the market value of shares or securities quoted on the London Stock Exchange shall, except where in consequence of special circumstances prices so quoted are by themselves not a proper measure of market value, be as follows – (*a*) the lower of the two prices shown in the quotations for the shares or securities in the Stock Exchange Official Daily List on the relevant date plus one-quarter of the difference between those two figures, or (*b*) halfway between the highest and lowest prices at which bargains, other than bargains done at special prices, were recorded in the shares or securities for the relevant date, choosing the amount under paragraph (*a*) if less than that under paragraph (*b*), or if no such bargains were recorded for the relevant date, and choosing the amount under paragraph (*b*) if less than that under paragraph (*a*): Provided that – (i) this subsection shall not apply to shares or securities for which some other stock exchange in the United Kingdom affords a more active market; and (ii) if the London Stock Exchange is closed on the relevant date the market value shall be ascertained by reference to the latest previous date or earliest subsequent date on which it is open, whichever affords the lower market value.'

Subsection (3) makes it clear that the Appellant can only escape from the Stock Exchange quotation if on the relevant date there were 'special circumstances'. Whatever that expression may mean, it must refer to facts which existed at the relevant time. We must take the facts from the Case Stated by the Special Commissioners.

4 The Case has been stated in a form which makes it difficult to determine just what were the facts which the Commissioners found. Paragraph 5 of the Case is as follows:

'5. As a result of the evidence, both oral and documentary, adduced before us we find the facts set out in para. 6 below proved or admitted. Evidence given by Mr Gillum and Mr Chandler as to takeover and valuation matters is set out in paras. 7 and 8 below.'

Paragraphs 6, 7 and 8 are set out in full in [1970] Ch., at pages 628–33. For present purposes it is sufficient to summarise para. 6 very briefly. As early as September 1964 there were discussions between representatives of Vickers and Crabtrees. Opinions were expressed that there should be a merger. In January 1965 statements regarding Crabtrees' affairs were handed to Vickers. They included a calculation that the value of Crabtrees' ordinary stock units was then £3 per unit. In February the view was expressed that the only practicable *(pg441)* course was for Vickers to make a cash offer. Thereafter for various reasons negotiations proceeded slowly until the end of July. On 11 August agreement was reached. Crabtrees' board approved and on 18 August a public statement was made. An appendix to the Case shows that as a result there was an immediate increase of about 10*s.* in the price at which business was done on the London Stock Exchange. The first argument submitted by the Appellant was that these facts constituted special circumstances because if the public had been aware of the true position at or before the beginning of April the Stock Exchange quotation on 6 April would have been considerably higher. For reasons which I shall give later I reject that argument. It then becomes necessary for the Appellant to rely on statements made in paras. 7 and 8. I have quoted from para. 5, where these paragraphs are said to set out evidence as to takeover and valuation matters. Paragraph 7 begins: 'Mr Gillum gave evidence before us (which we accepted) to the following effect.' Mr Gillum was a financial expert, being connected with Kleinwort, Benson Ltd. He only came into the negotiations in August. The crucial passage in para. 7 is:

'The Stock Exchange had not in his view been given at that time information as to the negotiations which should have been supplied to it, and he thought that because of this current quotations did not afford any true measure of the value of the stock units in question.'

If the Appellant could say that the Commissioners found as a fact that information had been withheld when it ought to have been made public, he might well be able to say that that was a special circumstance.

5 It is most regrettable that the Commissioners framed the Case in this way. It is their function to find the facts, i.e. all the facts which emerge from the evidence led and which are relevant to the contentions of the parties. Expert evidence is no different from any other. They must say what facts they hold that it has proved. They have to narrate evidence if there is a contention that there was no evidence to prove a particular fact which they have found. And it may sometimes be useful to narrate some evidence in other cases, provided that the Commissioners make clear what is narration and what is a finding of fact. But here it is not at all clear what parts if any of paras. 7 and 8 are intended to be findings of fact. I would infer from para. 5 that no part is so intended. The words in brackets at the beginning of para. 7 seems to indicate that the whole of that paragraph is finding of fact, but when in para. 12 the Commissioners are summing up, they pointedly refrain from saying that matters had reached a stage when a public announcement would

have been appropriate; they only say that a stage had been reached at which in Mr Gillum's view a public announcement would have been appropriate. And in giving their reasons for their decision they do not appear to found on this. It cannot be said that the question whether information ought to have been disclosed is a question of law. It must depend on the custom of the City and the Stock Exchange and the practice observed by other companies in like circumstances. So in my judgment there is no finding of fact that information which ought to have been disclosed to the public before 6 April was withheld.

6 I would have been surprised if there had been such a finding. Counsel very properly agreed to our seeing 'Revised notes on company amalgamations and mergers' of date 31 October 1963. It is therein stated that the original edition was drawn up by the Executive Committee of the Issuing Houses Association in co-operation with a number of important financial bodies including the Stock Exchange. These notes contain the following passage:

'When talks are proceeding which may lead to an offer being made, it is important to do everything possible to maintain secrecy in order to *(pg442)* avoid disturbance in the normal price level of shares until the relevant information can simultaneously be made available to all shareholders. In particular, Directors, or others who have close associations with them, should avoid any dealings in the shares likely to be affected and should exercise great care in connection with any transactions which may have been initiated but not completed when the talks begin. It is not easy for a Board to decide when to make a public announcement. It is usually unwise to make any announcement until it is reasonably certain that an offer will in fact be forthcoming, but once this stage in negotiations has been reached an announcement should be made with the minimum of delay. Whilst the ideal must be that the first announcement should include the terms of the offer, it may nevertheless be necessary, if there are signs that the normal relationship of the price of the shares in the offeree company to the market in general is being disturbed, for a preliminary announcement to be made.'

Plainly, if that is right the conduct of the boards of Vickers and Crabtrees was proper and normal. So it would seem that if Mr Gillum gave the evidence attributed to him that must have been only his personal opinion differing from the views generally held.

7 Senior counsel for the Appellant moved in his final speech that there should be a remit to the Special Commissioners directing them to state whether or not they found the statements of Mr Gillum to be proved as facts. I would not oppose such a remit if some points arose in argument which could not reasonably have been foreseen, but it must have been apparent to counsel that this matter was likely to arise, and no doubt they exercised a wise discretion in keeping silent about it in their printed Case. I would refuse this motion.

8 Now I must turn to the interpretation of s44 (3). As might be expected, it takes the Stock Exchange quotation as reflecting market value in all normal cases. Stock Exchange prices are more liable than most open market prices to large and rapid fluctuations. But the taxpayer must take the risk of that unless there are 'special circumstances'. 'Special' must mean unusual or uncommon – perhaps the nearest word to it in this context is 'abnormal'. I see no reason to exclude any kind of abnormality. 'Rigging the market' was discussed in argument. This exception of cases where there are special circumstances must be intended to provide that a fair value is to be taken where they exist: generally a fair value could only be reached by enquiring what the market value would have been if the special circumstances had not existed. I think that that is what the section is contemplating when it says that in consequence of special circumstances the Stock Exchange quotation is not by itself a proper measure of market value. If it is not then some other measure must be found.

9 The Crown argue that this provision has a very limited application. Indeed, they say that it can only apply in two cases: first, in the very few cases where on the day in question the Stock Exchange quotation was 'stale', and secondly when in practice a particular parcel of shares would not be sold on the Stock Exchange at all. With regard to the latter I would refer to the very recent decision in this House of In re *Lynall*. It would then be necessary to imagine some other form of open market sale of that parcel on that day if the Crown's submission on this point is correct. It is unnecessary to reach any decision on that matter in this case. I can see nothing in the phraseology or in the apparent object of this provision to justify so narrow a reading of it. *(pg443)*

10 The question then is whether there were in this case any special circumstances on 6 April 1965. The Special Commissioners stated their ground of decision in these terms:

> 'we thought that, as it had been put in argument, the Stock Exchange was, in relation to the stocks at 6 April 1965, "working in blinkers". A horse in blinkers was shut off from seeing a good deal. When a market was shut off, as we thought the London Stock Exchange here had been, from information vital to a realistic assessment of the true value of the assets in question, was it right to refer to that market as "the open market" envisaged in s44 (1)? Having weighed the matter, we thought that it was not. Accordingly we held that the appeal succeeded in principle.'

They do not appear to rely on any impropriety in withholding the vital information: they seem to have regarded it as sufficient that in fact the Stock Exchange was 'working in blinkers' without considering whether this was unusual. Their apparent view that the Stock Exchange was not an open market because it lacked vital information was not supported in argument. It must happen every day that directors of many companies have in their possession confidential information which very properly they do not make public but which if made public would lead to a substantial alteration of the quoted prices of their companies' shares. That could not possibly be a 'special circumstance' and in my opinion that is all that happened here.

11 I would dismiss this appeal.

12 LORD MORRIS OF BORTH-Y-GEST: My Lords, the Appellant disposed of his stock units in R.W. Crabtree & Sons Ltd. He did so in August 1965 as a result of his acceptance of an offer then made by Vickers Ltd. to acquire for cash the whole of the issued capital of Crabtrees. He made a capital gain which was chargeable to tax. His stock units had quoted market values on 6 April 1965 on the London Stock Exchange (see para. 22 (1) (*a*) of Part II of Sch. 6 to the Finance Act 1965). In computing the amount of his gain it is first to be assumed that his shares were sold by him and immediately re-acquired by him at their market value on 6 April 1965 (see para. 22(2)). The provisions of s44 (3) of the Act (which is subject to the provisions of para. 22 (3) of Part II of the above Schedule) show how the 'market value' of shares or securities is to be arrived at if such shares or securities were quoted on the London Stock Exchange on the relevant date. There was no difficulty, as a matter of calculation on ascertained figures, in arriving at the market value (see s44 (1) of the Act) of the Appellant's stock units provided that s44 (3) applied. The subsection contains an exception from its applicability 'where in consequence of special circumstances' the prices quoted on the London Stock Exchange were 'by themselves not a proper measure of market value'.

13 The Appellant contended that the words of exception applied, and so he appealed against the assessment to capital gains tax made upon him in respect of chargeable gains for the year 1965–66. There were two questions raised before the Special Commissioners, viz. (*a*) were there 'special circumstances' and (*b*) if there were, what was the 'market value' on 6 April 1965. As the Special Commissioners held that there were special circumstances, with the result that the London Stock Exchange quotations did not govern, they proceeded to fix the 'market value' of the Appellant's stock units. The point of law which they stated in the Case Stated was 'whether on the facts found herein we were entitled to arrive at our decision set out in para. 12 above.'

14 It becomes necessary, therefore, to see what was their decision (para. 12) and what were the facts found. As to the latter the Case records that the facts *(pg444)* found are in one paragraph (para. 6) and that they are found as a result of the evidence both oral and documentary that was adduced. Then in somewhat puzzling segregation it is recorded that 'evidence given by Mr Gillum and Mr Chandler as to takeover and valuation matters' is set out in two other paragraphs. Included in para. 6 is a history of the discussions and events which, after various intervals and interludes, culminated in an announcement in the press on 17 August 1965 that Vickers would offer to acquire the whole of the issued capital of Crabtrees. The formal offer was made on 18 August 1965 by Morgan Grenfell & Co. Ltd. on behalf of Vickers. The discussions had begun informally in November 1964, after the then chairman of Crabtrees, the late

Mr C.H. Crabtree (the father of the Appellant), had received a letter from Mr Hird of Vickers inviting him to lunch at Vickers House. Following that lunch (when Mr Crabtree met the chairman of Vickers and others) there were various meetings and discussions between Mr Crabtree and Mr Hird. Discussion proceeded on the basis that there might be a merger between Vickers and Crabtrees. On 14 January 1965 detailed facts and figures concerning Crabtrees were handed over. Crabtrees calculated that the value of its stock units was £3 – the market quotation then being 47s. 6d. In February 1965 at a further meeting, when it was thought that an offer by Vickers would have to be a cash offer involving about £7,000,000, Vickers explained that an agreement they had with an American company would have to be terminated before there could be a takeover. A director of Vickers went to America in March to negotiate matters. Later on both companies were concerned with some matters of mutual interest, but on 18 June 1965 Vickers indicated that matters were progressing satisfactorily and that they did not expect that it would be long before they could proceed. Then on 30th July 1965 the chairman of Vickers (in a letter which was before the Special Commissioners and which they stated was available for inspection by the Court) wrote to the late Mr Crabtree in these terms:

"I am afraid that the unofficial discussions which we have had have taken an undue time to reach the stage at which we can begin serious talks. I am most grateful to you for being so patient during this period." In this letter he also added: "I would, therefore, just like to tell you how glad I am that we now see our way sufficiently clear to be able to start talks with you and I hope that we may conclude them satisfactorily."

15 A meeting followed on 6h August 1965, and on the Vickers side someone was present from Messrs. Morgan Grenfell & Co. who were advising Vickers. At that meeting it was agreed that 55s. should be the appropriate figure (rather than the figure of £3 mentioned in January) for the ordinary stock units. At a meeting on 11 August Mr Gillum, of Messrs. Kleinwort Benson – who in August and not before was called in to advise Crabtree – was present. At a further meeting, after 16 August, with the Vickers representatives, documents relating to the merger were signed. I have referred to these matters so that the state of affairs on 6 April may be appreciated in perspective. At that date there had been 'unofficial discussions', but over three months were to elapse before the chairman of Vickers announced that he could see the way sufficiently clear to be able to 'start talks'.

16 On those facts as found, and before referring to Mr Gillum's evidence, I do not consider that it could be held that there were special circumstances which would result in the Stock Exchange prices not being a proper measure of the price which the stock units might reasonably be expected to fetch on a sale in the open market on 6 April 1965. It is to be remembered that what is denoted by the provisions of s44 is not the intrinsic value of shares *(pg445)* but the price that they will fetch in the open market, and that as a matter of practical and

administrative convenience the London Stock Exchange quotations (i.e. the quotations in the Stock Exchange Official Daily List) are accepted as the basis to be used in following the directions given by s44 (3). But in the very nature of things Stock Exchange prices have to be arrived at without full and complete and up to the minute knowledge of all the circumstances which, if they were known, might affect prices. The Legislature has nevertheless decided that Stock Exchange prices are to be used.

17 Numerous examples could be given. Directors of a company might have improved trading figures presented to them as a result of which they decide to increase a dividend: the announcement of this might cause a rise in the price of the shares. I do not think that it could be said that in the days before the directors met the circumstance that good trading figures were coming in was a special circumstance within the contemplation of s44 (3). Similarly, a company might be in confidential negotiations for a very valuable contract. If there were knowledge that there was the possibility or prospect of securing the contract prices might rise. The circumstance that such knowledge could not be broadcast would not be a 'special' circumstance. There are very many matters in the day-to-day running of a big business which might if publicised affect prices. The Stock Exchange may be very sensitive to the merest breeze of change. Yet many such matters ought not, and many by accepted standards need not, be made public. Their mere existence does not constitute a 'special' circumstance.

18 Mr Gillum gave evidence. As he was only called in to advise Crabtrees in August 1965, when what the chairman of Vickers called the 'talks' began, his assessment of the position as at 6 April 1965 was naturally based upon what he learned as to what had taken place and as to how far matters had gone. The Commissioners accepted the evidence of Mr Gillum, which was to this effect: (*a*) that had he been advising before April 1965 he would have 'favoured' an announcement being made that discussions were in progress which might lead to a cash offer for the shares but that discussions were expected to be of some duration and that no early further announcement was to be expected; (*b*) that had there been such an announcement on 14 January 1965 the Stock Exchange prices would have risen; (*c*) that as at 6 April 1965 the position was that since the February meeting the negotiations were in a state of suspended animation, but that they were serious negotiations into which Vickers would not have entered if they had not had every expectation of being able to implement them and that the only unsettled matters were the final determination of the prices to be paid and Vickers' ability to finance the purchase; and (*d*) that in his view the Stock Exchange should have been informed of the negotiations, and because they were not the quotations did not give a true measure of the 'value' of the shares.

19 Though the Commissioners accepted that Mr Gillum held the views that he expressed, it by no means followed, had the question of making an announcement been raised sometime before April 1965, and possibly on or about 14 January, that the others concerned would have agreed that the time had come when it would be either proper or advisable to make some announcement in regard to the discussions. It is to be noted that no other evidence – such as that of some witness who could express an opinion on behalf of the Stock Exchange – was called. No one from the Stock Exchange suggested that they 'should' have been given information at any time before April 1965. *(pg446)* It is to be remembered also that a premature announcement in regard to discussions which, however promising, do not in fact materialise may bring about injustice: estate duty might in some cases become payable on the basis of prices needlessly inflated.

20 The conclusion of the Special Commissioners as expressed in para. 12 of the Case Stated may fairly be summarised as follows: (i) the negotiations before 6 April 1965 were serious negotiations; (ii) though not by then carried to a point of finality, they had reached 'a stage at which, in Mr Gillum's view, it would have been appropriate for the directors of R.W. Crabtree & Sons Ltd. to have made a public announcement.'; (iii) the consequences of an announcement would have been that the London Stock Exchange prices at 6th April would have been substantially greater than the prices that were then in fact quoted; (iv) those were 'special circumstances' within the meaning of s44 (3). Here may I say that I see no reason for acceding to a somewhat belated application that was made that the case should be remitted to the Special Commissioners. If the first three of these are accepted as findings of fact I am quite unable as a matter of law to accept that they constitute special circumstances. In regard to the findings of fact it is to be noted that there is no finding that there was any impropriety or that anyone was at fault or that there was some duty or obligation to make an announcement. There is merely an acceptance of the fact that, had Mr Gillum been advising Crabtrees in January and February 1965 (which of course he was not), he would have 'favoured' an announcement being made by Crabtrees that discussions were in progress. If Kleinwort Benson Ltd. had at that stage been advising Crabtrees, then presumably at that date Morgan Grenfell & Co. Ltd. would have been advising Vickers. It must be a matter for speculation as to what their view at that date would have been or what Vickers' view would have been or as to how Vickers would have reacted if the directors of Crabtrees had made an announcement. I would have thought that either a joint announcement or an announcement by agreement would, when the time came, have been appropriate. I need not, however, pursue these reflections, because in the absence of a finding that there ought to have been and should have been some public announcement the basis of the finding of the Special Commissioners is that because a circumstance which in fact existed (i.e., that discussions were taking place) was unknown to the public it was a 'special' circumstance within s44 (3) if public knowledge of it would have affected prices. But unless there was some impropriety or irregularity or wrongful withholding of information that the public (including members of the Stock Exchange) ought to have had, the situation was no different from that which must constantly exist, i.e., that directors of a company are in possession of information (either gratifying or disappointing) in advance of the time when it can become generally known.

21 The Special Commissioners considered that on 6 April 1965 the Stock Exchange was 'working in blinkers' in relation to the stocks. This must mean that possible buyers or sellers of the shares did not have up-to-date information of all matters that, if known, would have affected purchases or sales. But this is no more than one of the commonly existing facts of business life. It is a feature or circumstance of everyday commercial activity in the buying or selling of shares that full and complete information of every matter that might affect prices cannot in the nature of things be known. That is an ordinary circumstance. It is not a special one. I cannot accept that there is a special circumstance whenever directors have more information (that might affect prices) than stockbrokers have. It may well be that if some information is not made available to the public, and therefore to potential buyers or sellers, which would affect the *(pg447)*price of the shares in a company and if it is clearly proved that such information ought to have been made available then a special circumstance under s44 (3) might be shown. Each case must depend upon its particular facts, but a finding that information ought to have been given which was wrongly withheld would have to be based upon definite evidence given by those well qualified to speak with authority as to accepted standards and well established practices. Beyond saying this I do not consider that it would be helpful in the present case to seek to identify or to categorise the situations or circumstances which might be held to be 'special' within the meaning and contemplation of s44 (3).

22 I would dismiss the appeal.

23 VISCOUNT DILHORNE: My Lords, the Finance Act 1965, by s44 (1), provides that for the purposes of capital gains tax 'market value' in relation to any assets means the price which those assets might reasonably be expected to fetch on a sale in the open market. That is the general rule, but special provision is made for shares and securities quoted on the London Stock Exchange. They have ordinarily to be valued in accordance with the formula prescribed by s44 (3), amended, if their value on 6 April 1965 has to be ascertained, by para. 22 (3) of Sch. 6 to the Act. This formula is to be applied in relation to such shares and securities 'except where in consequence of special circumstances prices so quoted are by themselves not a proper measure of market value' or when some other stock exchange in the United Kingdom affords a more active market in the shares or securities: s44 (3).

24 In this appeal the Appellant, Mr Crabtree, contends that the prices quoted on 6 April 1965 on the London Stock Exchange for the ordinary stock units in R.W. Crabtree & Sons Ltd. (hereafter called 'the company') in consequence of special circumstances were by themselves not a proper measure of market value. He alleges that their market value was higher than the quoted price, and if he is right his liability to capital gains tax will be materially reduced.

25 Paragraph 5 of the Case Stated is in the following terms:

"As a result of the evidence, both oral and documentary, adduced before us we find the facts set out in para. 6 below proved or admitted. Evidence given by Mr Gillum" [a director of Kleinwort, Benson, merchant bankers] "and Mr Chandler" [a partner in Cazenove & Co., stockbrokers] "as to takeover and valuation matters is set out in paras. 7 and 8 below."

The facts found and set out in para. 6 may be summarised as follows. The company manufactured printing machinery. In the autumn of 1964 meetings took place between the late Mr Crabtree, the Appellant's father, and Mr Hird of Vickers, as a result of which the general conclusion was reached that the only satisfactory way of achieving the strengthening of the printing machinery industry in this country would be by a merger between Vickers and the company. Mr Rayner, a chartered accountant, was asked to prepare some statistical information for Mr Crabtree relating to the Crabtree group of companies. He produced a number of documents, including a report of the profits of the group from 1954 to 1963, an analysis of turnover, a summary of balance sheets showing the calculation of current assets less liabilities, a list of freehold properties and a calculation of the value of the company's ordinary stock. On the basis of this calculation the company assessed the value of its ordinary stock units at £3 per unit. The Stock Exchange middle market quotation for *(pg448)* such a unit was on 14 January 1965 47s. 6d. These documents were handed over to Mr Hird at a meeting on 14th January 1965. At a meeting on 24 February the conclusion was reached that the only practicable way of effecting the merger would be by a cash offer. Discussion proceeded on this footing and on the basis that the figure would be about £7,000,000. Vickers then said that they would have to terminate a licensing agreement with an American company before the takeover could be effected, and that, in view of other commitments, they would have to look into ways and means of raising the amount of cash required. On 30 July Sir Charles Dunphie, the chairman of Vickers, wrote to Mr C.H. Crabtree saying that:

"the unofficial discussions which we have had have taken an undue time to reach the stage at which we can begin serious talks", and that: "we now see our way sufficiently clear to be able to start talks with you and I hope that we may conclude them satisfactorily."

The Case Stated refers to this letter, but its full contents were not quoted. The letter was available for inspection at the hearing of the appeal. Its contents show that Vickers at least did not regard the discussions that had taken place before that date as other than unofficial, and this is relevant in relation to the question whether prior to 6 April 1965 there should have been an announcement that talks about a merger were in progress. At a meeting on 6 August it was agreed that the price to be paid for an ordinary stock unit of the company should be 55s., and a printer's draft of the offer to acquire the whole of the company's issued share capital was considered. A further meeting was held on 11 August, at which Mr Gillum was present. The documents were again considered, and on 16 August a board meeting of the company was held to approve the merger.

A press release was issued by Vickers for publication on the following day and the offer was issued on 18 August. So the first public intimation of the proposed merger was on 17 August. It was open to the Commissioners, in the light of the evidence given by Mr Gillum which is summarised in para. 7 of the Case, to have found as a fact that the public should have been informed of the discussions long before 17 August and prior to 6 April 1965. No such finding of fact is recorded in para. 6.

26 At the beginning of para. 7 the Commissioners state that they accepted Mr Gillum's evidence, the material parts of which are as follows:

'He considered that it would have been appropriate for the share-holders of R.W. Crabtree & Sons Ltd. to have been advised by or before the beginning of April 1965 of the position generally as regards the approach made by Vickers. If he had then been advising the directors of the company, he would have favoured a statement being made to the effect that they announced that discussions were in progress which might lead to a cash offer being made for the whole of the issued capital, but that the discussions were expected to be of some duration and that no further announcement should therefore be expected at an early date. Had such an announcement been made he had no doubt that the Stock Exchange quotation for the ordinary stock units would then have gone up. As to how much the price would have risen, he thought that the middle market quotation of 47s. 6d. on 14 January might reasonably have been expected on such an announcement to go up by, say, 5s. to 52s. 6d. Thereafter he would have expected the price to have remained relatively stable, but perhaps owing to interest waning somewhat in the period up to 6 April 1965, to have fallen back by then by a shilling or so. So approaching the matter, he thought that if an appropriate announcement had been made the middle market quotation on 6 April 1965 *(pg449)* would probably have been, say, 51s. 6d. or 51s. instead of 42s. 6d.. The Stock Exchange had not in his view been given at that time information as to the negotiations which should have been supplied to it, and he thought that because of this current quotations did not afford any true measure of the value of the stock units in question.'

It would seem from this that it was Mr Gillum's view that such an announcement should have been made on or before 14 January 1965, the day on which the statistical information had been given to Vickers for their consideration and before it had been considered by them, when the discussions were unofficial and when Vickers had made no offer to purchase the units. Mr Chandler did not give any evidence supporting Mr Gillum's view that such an announcement should have been made before 6 April 1965.

27 The Commissioners stated their conclusions at some length. They thought that it was clear on the evidence that prior to 6 April 1965 Vickers had entered into serious negotiations and had envisaged making a takeover bid by a cash offer. That the matter had not gone very far is shown by the terms of Sir Charles

Dunphie's letter of 30 July. The Commissioners said that matters had not been carried to a point of finality, but that they had been carried 'to a stage at which in Mr Gillum's view' it would have been appropriate for a public announcement to have been made. They then posed the question: 'Were there in those circumstances special circumstances in consequence of which the quoted prices were not a proper measure of market value as defined in s44 (1)?' On the facts they were of opinion that there were 'special circumstances' within the meaning of those words in s44 (3), and they were 'satisfied that the London Stock Exchange prices on 6 April 1965 were substantially less than they would have been if an announcement of the kind which Mr Gillum considered should have been made had been made before that date.' They thought that

> 'the Stock Exchange was, in relation to the stocks at 6 April 1965, "working in blinkers". A horse in blinkers was shut off from seeing a good deal. When a market was shut off, as we thought the London Stock Exchange here had been, from information vital to a realistic assessment of the true value of the assets in question, was it right to refer to that market as "the open market" envisaged in s44 (1)? Having weighed the matter, we thought that it was not.'

28 The question they had to consider was, not whether the market on the London Stock Exchange was on 6 April 1965 an open market within the meaning of s44 (1), but whether in consequence of special circumstances the prices quoted were by themselves not a proper measure of market value. There must be many occasions on which the directors of a company are in possession of information which if made public would affect the prices quoted on the London Stock Exchange and where it could be said that in the absence of such information the London Stock Exchange is 'working in blinkers', but the fact that directors have such information and the Stock Exchange has not cannot ordinarily by itself amount, in my opinion, to 'special circumstances' within the meaning to be given to those words in s44 (3). For circumstances to be special must be exceptional, abnormal or unusual and the mere fact that directors have knowledge which would affect the prices quoted if made public cannot, in my view, be regarded as an unusual circumstance. If, however, it clearly was the duty of the directors to make public such information, and there was failure to do so, with the result that the prices quoted were less or higher than they *(pg450)* would have been if the duty had been discharged, it might well be that that would amount to special circumstances.

29 Having heard the evidence it was for the Commissioners to state what facts they found proved or admitted. They made no finding in para. 6 of the Case that the directors were under a duty to inform the shareholders and the public before 6 April 1965 of the talks with Vickers. They accepted the evidence given by Mr Gillum, but he did not suggest that there had been any breach of duty by the directors. He merely said that he would have been in favour of an announcement being made. No attempt appears to have been made to ascertain the views of Vickers on this question. It is not likely that they would have agreed with Mr Gillum when they had not by 6 April commenced serious discussions, nor is it likely that they would have agreed that an announcement should have been made on or before 14 January, the date on which they received statistical information about the company. If such an announcement had been made, Vickers might have felt to some extent committed to make an offer for the shares. They made no offer for them until after 6 April. It is to be noted that the Commissioners did not base their conclusion on the fact that the company estimated that the intrinsic value of the ordinary stock units was £3 on 14 January 1965, when the middle market quotation was 47*s*. 6*d*. I do not consider that the facts found by the Commissioners and the evidence given by Mr Gillum suffice to justify the conclusion that there were in this case special circumstances. At a late stage in the hearing of the appeal, an application was made that the case should be sent back so that the Commissioners could make a finding on the question of fact whether there should have been an announcement before 6 April by the directors. On the evidence given before the Commissioners such a finding would not be justified. Far more evidence would be wanted to justify the conclusion that the directors had failed in their duty, and it was said that if the case was sent back no further evidence would be called.

30 During the hearing of the appeal, with the consent of counsel, reference was made to a document entitled 'Revised notes on company amalgamations and mergers' dated 31 October 1963, for which the Executive Committee of the Issuing Houses Association, the Accepting Houses Committee, the Association of Investment Trusts, the British Insurance Association, the Committee of London Clearing Bankers and the London Stock Exchange were responsible. The notes 'set out certain general principles which the organisations believe to be fundamental to the proper conduct of these transactions' (takeovers and mergers), and contain the following passages:

> 'When talks are proceeding which may lead to an offer being made, it is important to do everything possible to maintain secrecy in order to avoid disturbance in the normal price level of shares until the relevant information can simultaneously be made available to all shareholders ... It is not easy for a Board to decide when to make a public announcement. It is usually unwise to make any announcement until it is reasonably certain that an offer will in fact be forthcoming, but once this stage in negotiations has been reached an announcement should be made with the minimum of delay.'

On the facts stated in para. 6 of the Case it could not, in my view, be asserted that by 6 April 1965 it was reasonably certain that an offer would be made. On those facts I see no ground for concluding that the quoted prices of the ordinary stock units were not a proper measure of their market value on *(pg451)* 6 April 1965. The prices quoted might have been higher if an announcement such as Mr Gillum favoured had been made, but that does not show that the prices quoted were not a proper measure of their market value. That no such announcement was made does not, as I have said, amount to special circumstances within s44 (3).

31 For these reasons I would dismiss the appeal. *(pg452)*

Case 31
Ebrahimi v Westbourne Galleries Ltd

[1972] 2 All ER 492

House of Lords

8, 9, 13, 14 March, 3 May 1972

This case is one of a series of cases on a type of company that is referred to as a 'quasi-partnership'. The first valuation case to be considered by the courts on this basis is *Re Yenidje Tobacco Co Ltd* [1916–17] All ER Rep 1050 **case 10**. The concept of 'quasi-partnership' is used, and developed, in *Ebrahimi v Westbourne Galleries Ltd*, *Re Bird Precision Bellows Ltd* [1985] 3 All ER 523, CA **case 35**, *CVC v Demarco Almeida* [2002] UKPC 16, PC **case 45** and *Strahan v Wilcock* [2006] EWCA Civ 13, CA **case 49**. The last of these cases is particularly important in that the Court of Appeal gives a definition of a 'quasi-partnership' company.

The principle established by *Ebrahimi v Westbourne Galleries Ltd* is that there is a certain type of company in which the relationships between the parties are akin to that of partners. This type of company is then dubbed a 'quasi-partnership'. When looking for a fair division of value in order to compensate a director/shareholder in a quasi-partnership, the correct approach is to borrow the principles of a partnership valuation, by dividing the total assets of the company rateably amongst the shareholdings.

In around 1945, Shokrollah Ebrahimi and Asher Nazar Achoury established a partnership, Westbourne Galleries, to carry on their trade as carpet dealers. In 1958 the business was incorporated under the name Westbourne Galleries Ltd, but the commercial conduct of the business was unchanged. Trading decisions were made by Ebrahimi and Nazar, who were the directors and shareholders. Soon after the corporation, Asher Nazar's son, George Alexander Nazar Achoury was brought into the business. He was made a director and shares were passed to him. Thereafter, the shareholding were:

	Ordinary Shares
Shokrollah Ebrahimi	400
Asher Nazar Achoury	400
George Alexander Nazar Achoury	200
Total:	1,000

The majority of votes was, therefore, held by Asher Nazar and his son.

There would appear to have been a dispute between the two families as to the future conduct of the company's trade and on 12 August 1969 an ordinary resolution was passed by the company in general meeting, by the votes of Mr Nazar and Mr George Nazar, removing Shokrollah Ebrahimi from the office of director, a resolution which was effective in law by virtue of the Companies Act 1948, s 184 and Article 96 of Part I of Table A.

Shokrollah Ebrahimi presented a petition to the court under Companies Act 1948, s 222(f) (now Insolvency Act 1986, s 122(1)(g)) that his shareholding should be purchased by the other shareholders for a sum calculated as 40 per cent of the value of the assets of the company, with no discount.

Plowman J granted the order requested by Shokrollah Ebrahimi. The order was set aside by the Court of Appeal. The House of Lords reinstated the winding-up order.

Lord Wilberforce, in his leading judgement in the House of Lords, noted that the court has the power to grant a winding-up order where the granting of the order 'is just and equitable', this power having existed in statute since the Joint Stock Company's Winding Up Act 1848. In his Lordship's judgement, it is wrong to create categories or headings under which cases must be brought if the requested order is to be granted.

The same words 'just and equitable' appear in the Partnership Act 1892, s 25, as a ground for dissolution of a partnership. The Partnership Act was intended to be a codification of the case law on partnerships; Lord Wilberforce commented that he had no doubt the considerations which they reflect formed part of the common law of partnership before its codification ([1972] 2 All ER 492 at 496 **case 31 para 5**). Lord Wilberforce considers that this is of importance in that it provides a bridge between cases for an order under the 'just and equitable' provisions of the Companies Act and the principles of equity developed in relation to partnerships:

'The winding-up order was made following a doctrine which has developed in the courts since the beginning of this century. As presented by the appellant, and in substance accepted by the learned judge, this was that in a case such as this, the members of the company are in substance partners, or quasi-partners, and that a winding up may be ordered in such facts are shown as could justify a dissolution of partnership between them. The common use of the words "just and equitable" in the company and partnership law supports this approach.'

([1972] 2 All ER 492 at 496 **case 31 para 6**)

Lord Wilberforce reviewed the decision of the Court of Appeal in *Re Yenidje Tobacco Co Ltd* [1916–17] All ER 1050 **case 10**. That case concerned two shareholders. Each had an equal number of shares in the company and the two shareholders were also the two directors of the company. The articles of the company contained an arbitration provision in the event that a state of deadlock came into existence. Lord Wilberforce ruled that the authority of the case is not limited to true deadlock cases but this is merely an example of the reasons why it would be just and equitable to wind the company up.

Lord Wilberforce then reviewed decided cases and concluded:

'My Lords, in my opinion these authorities represent a sound and rational development of the law which should be endorsed. The foundation of it all lies in the words "just and equitable" and, if there is any respect in which some of the cases may be open to criticism, it is that the courts may sometimes have been too timorous in giving them full force. The words are a recognition of the fact that a limited company is more than a mere judicial entity, with a personality in law of its own: that there is room in company law for recognition of the fact that behind it, or amongst it, there are individuals, with rights, expectations and obligations *inter se* which are not necessarily submerged in the company structure ... The "just and equitable" provision does not, as the respondents suggest, entitle one party to disregard the obligation he assumes by entering a company, nor the court to dispense him from it. It does, as equity always does, enable the court to subject the exercise of legal rights to equitable considerations; considerations, that is, of a personal character arising between one individual and another, which may make it unjust, or inequitable, to insist on legal rights, or to exercise them in a particular way.'

([1972] 2 All ER 492 at 499/500 **case 31 para 16**)

He then considered the circumstances in which the court would regard a company as a 'quasi-partnership'. He refused to define the circumstances but said:

'The superimposition of equitable considerations requires something more, which typically may include one, or probably more, of the following elements: (i) an association formed or continued on the basis of a personal relationship, involving mutual confidence – this element will often be found where a pre-existing partnership has been converted into a limited company; (ii) an agreement, or understanding, that all, or some (for there may be "sleeping" members), of the shareholders shall participate in the conduct of the business; (iii) restriction on the transfer of the members' interest in the company – so that if confidence is lost, or one member is removed from management, he cannot take out his stake and go elsewhere.

It is these, and analogous, factors which may bring into play the just and equitable clause, and they do so directly, through the force of the words themselves.'

([1972] 2 All ER 492 at 500 **case 31 paras 17 and 18**)

We have to wait a further 34 years before a court defines what is meant by the term 'quasi-partnership' when applied to a company, see, for example, the judgement of Lady Justice Arden on 19 January 2006 in the Court of Appeal in *Strahan v Wilcock* [2006] EWCA Civ 13 **case 49**.

This is a case that is frequently of very great significance in a commercial valuation, where it is necessary to fix a fair value at which a director shareholder sells his shareholding on retirement to a fellow director.

Where the company whose shares are to be valued is correctly identified as a 'quasi-partnership', in the author's view, the effect of this judgement on the share valuation is twofold.

1.   Where the purpose of the valuation is to identify a fair price to be paid for a shareholding surrendered by a retiring director/share-holder, the price is computed by a valuation of the whole company (or, more precisely, of a 100 per cent shareholding in the company) without any discount.

2.   Where a valuation is required for a capital gains tax purpose or an inheritance tax purpose, one or more of the other shareholders in the company may constitute a 'special purchaser' who would be expected to pay a proportionate part of the company's full value. The extent to which this consideration bears on the resultant valuation, will depend on the particular circumstances of the company at that time and the particular characteristics of the remaining shareholders.

Judgement

References, example '(pg495)', are to [1972] 2 All ER 492.

1 LORD WILBERFORCE: My Lords, the issue in this appeal is whether the respondent company, Westbourne Galleries Ltd, should be wound up by the court on the petition of the appellant who is one of the three shareholders, the personal respondents being the other two. The company is a private company which carries on business as dealers in Persian and other carpets. It was formed in 1958 to take over a business founded by the second respondent (Mr Nazar). It is a fact of cardinal importance that since about 1945 the business had been carried on by the appellant and Mr Nazar as partners, equally sharing the management and the profits. When the company was formed, the signatories to its memorandum were the appellant and Mr Nazar and they were appointed its first directors. Of its issued share capital, 500 shares of £1 each were issued to each subscriber and it was found by the learned judge, after the point had been contested by Mr Nazar, that the appellant paid up his shares out of his own money. Soon after the company's formation the third respondent (Mr George Nazar) was made a director, and each of the two original shareholders transferred to him 100 shares, so that at all material times the appellant held 400 shares, Mr Nazar 400 and Mr George Nazar 200. The Nazars, father and son, thus had a majority of the votes in general meeting. Until the dispute all three gentlemen remained directors. The company made good profits, all of which were distributed as directors' remuneration. No dividends have ever been paid, before or after the petition was presented.

2 On 12th August 1969 an ordinary resolution was passed by the company in general meeting, by the votes of Mr Nazar and Mr George Nazar, removing the appellant from the office of director, a resolution which was effective in law by virtue of s184 of the Companies Act 1948 and art 96 of Part I of Table A. Shortly afterwards the appellant presented his petition to the court.

3 This petition was based in the first place on s210 of the Companies Act 1948, the relief sought under this section being an order that Mr Nazar and his son be ordered to purchase the appellant's shares in the company. In the alternative it sought an order for the winding-up of the company. The petition contained allegations of oppression and misconduct against Mr Nazar which were fully explored at the hearing before Plowman J. The learned judge found that some were unfounded and others unproved and that such complaint as was made out did not amount to such a course of oppressive conduct as to justify an order under s210. However, he made an order for the winding-up of the company under the 'just and equitable' provision. I shall later specify the grounds on which he did so. The appellant did not appeal against the rejection of his case under s210 and this House is not concerned with it. The company and the individual respondents appealed against the order for winding-up and this was set aside by the Court of Appeal. The appellant now seeks to have it restored. *(pg495)*

4 My Lords, the petition was brought under s222 (*f*) of the Companies Act 1948, which enables a winding-up order to be made if 'the court is of opinion that it is just and equitable that the company should be wound up'. This power has existed in our company law in unaltered form since the first major Act, the Companies Act 1862. Indeed, it antedates that statute since it existed in the Joint Stock Companies Winding-up Act 1848. For some 50 years, following a pronouncement by Lord Cottenham LC in 1849, the words 'just and equitable' were interpreted so as only to include matters *ejusdem generis* as the preceding clauses of the section, but there is now ample authority for discarding this limitation. There are two other restrictive interpretations which I mention to reject. First, there has been a tendency to create categories or headings under which cases must be brought if the clause is to apply. This is wrong. Illustrations may be used, but general words should remain general and not be reduced to the sum of particular instances. Secondly, it has been suggested, and urged on us, that (assuming the petitioner is a shareholder, and not a creditor) the words must be confined to such circumstances as affect him in his capacity as shareholder. I see no warrant for this either. No doubt, in order to present a petition, he must qualify as a shareholder, but I see no reason for preventing him from relying on any circumstances of justice or equity which affect him in his relations with the company, or, in a case such as the present, with the other shareholders.

5 One other signpost is significant. The same words 'just and equitable' appear in the Partnership Act 1892, s25, as a ground for dissolution of a partnership and no doubt the considerations which they reflect formed part of the common law of partnership before its codification. The importance of this is to provide a bridge between cases under s222 (*f*) of the Companies Act 1948 and the principles of equity developed in relation to partnerships.

6 The winding-up order was made following a doctrine which has developed in the courts since the beginning of this century. As presented by the appellant, and in substance accepted by the learned judge', this was that in a case such as this, the members of the company are in substance partners, or quasi-partners, and that a winding-up may be ordered if such facts are shown as could justify a dissolution of partnership between them. The common use of the words 'just and equitable' in the company and partnership law supports this approach. Your Lordships were invited by the respondents' counsel to restate the principle on which this provision ought to be used; it has not previously been considered by this House. The main line of his submission was to suggest that too great a use of the partnership analogy had been made; that a limited company, however small, essentially differs from a partnership; that in the case of a company, the rights of its members are governed by the articles of association which have contractual force; that the court has no power or at least ought not to dispense parties from observing their contracts; that, in particular, when one member has been excluded from the directorate or management, under powers expressly conferred by the Companies Act 1948 and the articles, an order for winding-up whether on the partnership analogy or under the just and equitable provision, should not be made. Alternatively, it was argued that before the making of such an order could be considered the petitioner must show and prove that the exclusion was not made bona fide in the interests of the company.

7 My Lords, I must first make some examination of the authorities in order to see how far they support the respondents' propositions and, if they do not, how far they rest on a principle of which this House should disapprove. I will say at once that, over a period of some 60 years, they show a considerable degree of consistency, and that such criticism as may be made relates rather to the application of accepted principle to the facts than to the statements of principles themselves. *(pg496)*

8 The real starting point is the Scottish decision in *Symington v Symingtons Quarries Ltd*. There had been a partnership business carried on by two brothers who decided to transfer it to a private limited company. Each brother was to hold half the shares except for a small holding for a third brother to hold the balance for voting. A resolution was passed in general meeting by the votes of one brother together with other members having nominal interests that he should be sole director. The other two brothers petitioned for a winding up under the just and equitable provision and the court so ordered. The reasons for so doing, given by some of their Lordships of the First Division, are expressed in terms of lost substratum or deadlock – words clearly used in a general rather than a technical sense. The judgment of Lord M'Laren, which has proved to be the most influential as regards later cases, puts the ground more generally. He points out that the company was not formed by appeal to the public: it was a domestic company, the only real partners being the three brothers. Lord M'Laren said:

> 'In such a case it is quite obvious that all the reasons that apply to the dissolution of private companies, on the grounds of incompatibility between the views or methods of the partners, would be applicable in terms to the division amongst the shareholders of this Company … '

In England, the leading authority is the Court of Appeal's decision in *Re Yenidje Tobacco Co Ltd*. This was a case of two equal director shareholders with an arbitration provision in the articles between whom a state of deadlock came into existence. It has often been argued, and was so in this House, that its authority is limited to true deadlock cases. I could, in any case, not be persuaded that the words 'just and equitable' need or can be confined to such situations. But Lord Cozens-Hardy MR clearly puts his judgment on wider grounds. Whether there is deadlock or not, he says –

> '… the circumstances are such that we ought to apply, if necessary, the analogy of the partnership law and to say that this company is now in a state which could not have been contemplated by the parties when the company was formed …'

Warrington LJ adopts the same principle, treating deadlock as an example only of the reasons why it would be just and equitable to wind the company up.

9 In 1924 these authorities were reviewed, approved and extended overseas by the Judicial Committee of the Privy Council in an appeal from the West Indian Court of Appeal (Barbados), *Loch v John Blackwood Ltd*. The judgment of the Board delivered by Lord Shaw of Dunfermline clearly endorses, if not enlarges, the width to be given to the just and equitable clause. The case itself was one of a domestic company and was not one of deadlock. One of the directors had given grounds for loss of confidence in his probity and (a matter echoed in the present case) had shown that he regarded the business as his own. His Lordship quotes with approval from the judgments of Lord M'Laren in *Symington v Symington* and Lord Cozens-Hardy MR in *Re Yenidje Tobacco Co Ltd*.

10 I note in passing the Scottish case of *Thomson v Drysdale* where a winding up was ordered under the just and equitable clause at the instance of a holder of one share against the only other shareholder who held 1,501 shares, clearly not a case of deadlock, and come to *Re Cuthbert Cooper & Sons Ltd*, a case which your Lordships must *(pg497)* consider. The respondents relied on this case which carries the authority of Simonds J as restricting the force of the just and equitable provision. The company was clearly a family company, the capital in which belonged to a father and his two elder sons. After the death of the father, leaving his shares to his younger sons and appointing them his executors, his elder sons, exercising the powers given to directors by the articles, refused to register the executors as shareholders and dismissed them from employment. The executors' petition for winding-up of the company was dismissed. My Lords, with respect for the eminent judge who decided it, I must doubt the correctness of this. Whether on the facts stated a case of justice and equity was made out, is no doubt partly a question of fact on which, even though my own view is clear enough, I should respect the opinion of the trial judge: but, this matter apart, I am unable to agree as to the undue emphasis he puts on the contractual rights arising from the articles, over the equitable principles which might be derived from partnership law, for in the result the latter seem to have been entirely excluded in the former's favour. I think that the case should no longer be regarded as of authority.

11 There are three recent cases which I should mention since they have figured in the judgments below. *Re Lundie Brothers Ltd* was, like the present, a decision of Plowman J. This was a case where the petitioner, one of three shareholders and directors, was excluded from participation in the management and from directors' remuneration. Plowman J applying partnership principles made a winding-up order under the just and equitable clause. If that decision was right it assists the present appellant. The Court of Appeal in the present case disagreed with it and overruled it, insofar as it related to a winding-up. The respondents argue that this was the first case where exclusion of a working director, valid under the articles, had been treated as a ground for winding-up under the just and equitable clause and that as such it was an unjustifiable innovation.

12 *Re Expanded Plugs Ltd* was, on the other hand, approved by the Court of Appeal in the present case. The case itself is a paradigm of obscure forensic tactics and, as such, of merely curious interest: its only importance lies in the statement, contained in the judgment, that since the relevant decisions were carried out within the framework of the articles, the petitioner must show that they were not carried out bona fide in the interests of the company. I shall return, insofar as it limits the scope of the just and equitable provision, to this principle but I should say at once that I disagree with it.

13 In *re K/9 Meat Supplies (Guildford) Ltd* there was a company of three shareholder/directors one of whom became bankrupt: the petitioner was his trustee in bankruptcy. It was contended that the company was a quasi-partnership and that since s33 of the Partnership Act 1890 provides for dissolution on the bankruptcy of one of the partners, a winding-up order on this ground should be made. Pennycuick J rejected this argument on the ground that since the 'partnership' had been transformed into a company and since the articles gave no automatic right to a winding-up on bankruptcy, bankruptcy of one member was not a ground for winding-up of itself. He then proceeded to consider whether the just and equitable provision should be applied. In my opinion, this procedure was correct and I need not express an opinion whether, on the facts, it was right to refuse an order.

14 Finally I should refer to the Scottish case of *Lewis v Haas* where the two main shareholder directors each held 49 per cent of the shares, the remaining two per cent being held by a solicitor. Lord Fraser, in the Outer House, while accepting the *(pg498)* principle that exclusion from management might be a ground for ordering a winding-up, did not find the facts sufficient to support the use of the just and equitable clause.

15 This series of cases (and there are others: *re Davis and Collett Ltd, Baird v Lees, Elder v Elder & Watson Ltd, re Swaledale Cleaners Ltd, re Fildes Bros Ltd, re Leadenhall General Hardware Stores Ltd*) amounts to a considerable body of authority in favour of the use of the just and equitable provision in a wide variety of situations, including those of expulsion from office. The principle has found acceptance in a number of Commonwealth jurisdictions. Although these were not cited at the Bar I refer to some of them since they usefully illustrate the principle which has been held to underlie this jurisdiction and show it applicable to exclusion cases.

In *re Straw Products Pty Ltd* Mann CJ said:

> '... all that Hinds has done in the past in exercise of his control has been within his legal powers. The question is whether he has used those powers in such a way as to make it just and equitable that Robertson should be allowed by the Court to retire from the partnership. The analogy of a partnership seems to me to clarify discussion.'

Re Wondoflex Textiles Pty Ltd was a case where again the company was held to resemble a partnership. The petitioner, owner of a quarter share, was removed from office as director by the governing director exercising powers under the articles. Thus the issue, and the argument, closely resembled those in the present case. The judgment of Smith J contains the following passage:

'It is also true, I think, that, generally speaking, a petition for winding up, based upon the partnership analogy, cannot succeed if what is complained of is merely a valid exercise of powers conferred in terms by the articles ... To hold otherwise would enable a member to be relieved from the consequences of a bargain knowingly entered into by him ... But this, I think, is subject to an important qualification. Acts which, in law, are a valid exercise of powers conferred by the articles may nevertheless be entirely outside what can fairly be regarded as having been in the contemplation of the parties when they became members of the company; and in such cases the fact that what has been done is not in excess of power will not necessarily be an answer to a claim for winding up. Indeed, it may be said that one purpose of [the just and equitable provision] is to enable the Court to relieve a party from his bargain in such cases.'

The whole judgment is of value. In New Zealand, the Court of Appeal has endorsed the potential application of the principle to exclusion cases: *Tench v Tench Brothers Ltd.* See also *re Modern Retreading Co Ltd*, also a case of exclusion from management and *re Sydney and Whitney Pier Bus Service Ltd* and *re Concrete Column Clamps Ltd.*

16 My Lords, in my opinion these authorities represent a sound and rational development of the law which should be endorsed. The foundation of it all lies in the words *(pg499)* 'just and equitable' and, if there is any respect in which some of the cases may be open to criticism, it is that the courts may sometimes have been too timorous in giving them full force. The words are a recognition of the fact that a limited company is more than a mere judicial entity, with a personality in law of its own: that there is room in company law for recognition of the fact that behind it, or amongst it, there are individuals, with rights, expectations and obligations *inter se* which are not necessarily submerged in the company structure. That structure is defined by the Companies Act 1948 and by the articles of association by which shareholders agree to be bound. In most companies and in most contexts, this definition is sufficient and exhaustive, equally so whether the company is large or small. The 'just and equitable' provision does not, as the respondents suggest, entitle one party to disregard the obligation he assumes by entering a company, nor the court to dispense him from it. It does, as equity always does, enable the court to subject the exercise of legal rights to equitable considerations; considerations, that is, of a personal character arising between one individual and another, which may make it unjust, or inequitable, to insist on legal rights, or to exercise them in a particular way.

17 It would be impossible, and wholly undesirable, to define the circumstances in which these considerations may arise. Certainly the fact that a company is a small one, or a private company, is not enough. There are very many of these where the association is a purely commercial one, of which it can safely be said that the basis of association is adequately and exhaustively laid down in the articles. The superimposition of equitable considerations requires something more, which typically may include one, or probably more, of the following elements: (i) an association formed or continued on the basis of a personal relationship, involving mutual confidence – this element will often be found where a pre-existing partnership has been converted into a limited company; (ii) an agreement, or understanding, that all, or some (for there may be 'sleeping' members), of the shareholders shall participate in the conduct of the business; (iii) restriction on the transfer of the members' interest in the company – so that if confidence is lost, or one member is removed from management, he cannot take out his stake and go elsewhere.

18 It is these, and analogous, factors which may bring into play the just and equitable clause, and they do so directly, through the force of the words themselves. To refer, as so many of the cases do, to 'quasi-partnerships' or 'in substance partnerships' may be convenient but may also be confusing. It may be convenient because it is the law of partnership which has developed the conceptions of probity, good faith and mutual confidence, and the remedies where these are absent, which become relevant once such factors as I have mentioned are found to exist: the words 'just and equitable' sum these up in the law of partnership itself. And in many, but not necessarily all, cases there has been a pre-existing partnership the obligations of which it is reasonable to suppose continue to underlie the new company structure. But the expressions may be confusing if they obscure, or deny, the fact that the parties (possibly former partners) are now co-members in a company, who have accepted, in law, new obligations. A company, however small, however domestic, is a company not a partnership or even a quasi-partnership and it is through the just and equitable clause that obligations, common to partnership relations, may come in.

19 My Lords, this is an expulsion case, and I must briefly justify the application in such cases of the just and equitable clause. The question is, as always, whether it is equitable to allow one (or two) to make use of his legal rights to the prejudice of his associate(s). The law of companies recognises the right, in many ways, to remove a director from the board. Section 184 of the Companies Act 1948 confers this right on the company in general meeting whatever the articles may say. Some articles may prescribe other methods, for example a governing director may have the power to remove (see *re Wondoflex Textiles Pty Ltd*). And quite apart from removal powers, *(pg500)* there are normally provisions for retirement of directors by rotation so that their re-election can be opposed and defeated by a majority, or even by a casting vote. In all these ways a particular director-member may find himself no longer a director, through removal, or non-re-election: this situation he must normally accept, unless he undertakes the burden of proving fraud or *mala fides*. The just and equitable provision nevertheless comes to his assistance if he can point to, and prove, some special underlying obligation of his fellow member(s) in good faith, or confidence, that so long as the business continues he shall be entitled to management participation, an obligation so basic that if broken, the conclusion must be that the association must be dissolved. And the principles on which he may do so are those worked out by the courts in partnership cases where there has been exclusion from management (see *Const v Harris*) even where under the partnership agreement there is a power of expulsion (see *Blisset v Daniel* and *Lindley on Partnership*).

20   I come to the facts of this case. It is apparent enough that a potential basis for a winding-up order under the just and equitable clause existed. The appellant after a long association in partnership, during which he had an equal share in the management, joined in the formation of the company. The inference must be indisputable that he, and Mr Nazar, did so on the basis that the character of the association would, as a matter of personal relation and good faith, remain the same. He was removed from his directorship under a power valid in law. Did he establish a case which, if he had remained in a partnership with a term providing for expulsion, would have justified an order for dissolution? This was the essential question for the judge. Plowman J dealt with the issue in a brief paragraph in which he said:

> '... while no doubt the petitioner was lawfully removed, in the sense that he ceased in law to be a director, it does not follow that in removing him the respondents did not do him a wrong. In my judgment, they did do him a wrong, in the sense that it was an abuse of power and a breach of good faith which partners owe to each other to exclude one of them from all participation in the business on which they have embarked on the basis that all should participate in its management. The main justification put forward for removing him was that he was perpetually complaining, but the faults were not all on one side and, in my judgment, this is not sufficient justification. For these reasons, in my judgment, the petitioner therefore has made out a case for a winding-up order.'

Reading this in the context of the judgment as a whole, which had dealt with the specific complaints of one side against the other, I take it as a finding that the respondents were not entitled, in justice and equity, to make use of their legal powers of expulsion and that, in accordance with the principles of such cases as *Blisset v Daniel*, the only just and equitable course was to dissolve the association. To my mind, two factors strongly support this. First, Mr Nazar made it perfectly clear that he did not regard the appellant as a partner; but did regard him as an employee. But there was no possible doubt as to the appellant's status throughout, so that Mr Nazar's refusal to recognise it amounted, in effect, to a repudiation of the relationship. Secondly, the appellant, through ceasing to be a director, lost his right to share in the profits through directors' remuneration, retaining only the chance of receiving dividends as a minority shareholder. True that an assurance was given in evidence that the previous practice (of not paying dividends) would not be continued, but the fact remains that the appellant was henceforth at the mercy of the Messrs Nazar as to what he should receive out of the profits and when. He was, moreover, unable *(pg501)* to dispose of his interest without the consent of the Nazars. All these matters lead only to the conclusion that the right course was to dissolve the association by winding up.

21 I must deal with one final point which was much relied on by the Court of Appeal. It was said that the removal was, according to the evidence of Mr Nazar, bona fide in the interests of the company, that the appellant had not shown the contrary, that he ought to do so or to demonstrate that no reasonable man could think that his removal was in the company's interest. This formula, 'bona fide in the interests of the company' is one that is relevant in certain contexts of company law and I do not doubt that in many cases decisions have to be left to majorities or directors to take which the courts must assume had this basis. It may, on the other hand, become little more than an alibi for a refusal to consider the merits of the case, and in a situation such as this it seems to have little meaning other than 'in the interests of the majority'. Mr Nazar may well have persuaded himself, quite genuinely, that the company would be better off without the appellant but if the appellant disputed this, or thought the same with reference to Mr Nazar, what prevails is simply the majority view. To confine the application of the just and equitable clause to proved cases of *mala fides* would be to negative the generality of the words. It is because I do not accept this that I feel myself obliged to differ from the Court of Appeal.

22 I would allow the appeal and restore the judgment of Plowman JS. I propose that the individual respondents pay the appellant's costs here and in the Court of Appeal.

23 VISCOUNT DILHORNE: My Lords, I have had the advantage of reading the opinion of my noble and learned friend, Lord Wilberforce. I agree with all he has said, and he has dealt with the matter so comprehensively that there is nothing I wish to add.

24 I agree that the appeal should be allowed and that the individual respondents should be ordered to pay the appellant's costs here and in the Court of Appeal.

25 LORD PEARSON: My Lords, I have had the advantage of reading the opinion of my noble and learned friend, Lord Wilberforce, and for the reasons given by him I would allow the appeal and restore the judgement of Plowman J.

26 I agree that the individual respondents should be ordered to pay the appellant's costs here and in the Court of Appeal.

27 LORD CROSS OF CHELSEA: My Lords, the 'just and equitable' clause first appeared in s5 of the Joint Stock Companies Winding-Up Act 1848. Subsections (1) to (6) of that section gave the court jurisdiction to wind up a company in various circumstances indicative of insolvency; sub-s(7) gave jurisdiction if the company had been dissolved or should have ceased to carry on business or should be carrying on business only for the purpose of winding-up its affairs; and sub-s(8) added 'or if any other matter or thing shall render it just and equitable that the company shall be dissolved'. The meaning of the subsection was considered by Lord Cottenham LC in 1849 in *re Agriculturist Cattle Insurance Co, ex parte Spackman.* In that case the company, which was a cattle insurance company, was not insolvent and was carrying on business; but the petitioners who held shares which were not fully paid up considered that its prospects were bad and that it might well become insolvent. The fact that some shareholders in a company take a pessimistic view of its prospects does not make it 'just and equitable' to wind it up against the wishes of the majority who take a more optimistic view and it is not surprising that the petition was dismissed, but in the course of his judgment Lord Cottenham LC expressed an opinion *(pg502)* as to the scope of the subsection which had for many years an unfortunate influence on the practice of the Companies Court. He said:

> 'This clause was, no doubt, thus worded in order to include all cases not before mentioned; but of course it cannot mean that it should be interpreted otherwise than in reference to matters *ejusdem generis,* as those in the previous clauses. There must be something in the management and conduct of the Company which shews the Court that it should be no longer allowed to continue, and that the concern ought to be wound up.'

It is not in fact easy to see what precisely Lord Cottenham LC had in mind – for there may well be matters arising in the management of a company's affairs which make it 'just and equitable' that it should be wound up but which have no relation whatever either to insolvency or a cessation of business. Nevertheless, when the sub-section reappeared as s79 (5) of the Companies Act 1862, the courts, with Lord Cottenham LC's words 'ejusdem generis' in mind, for many years interpreted it very narrowly and only made orders under it if the substratum of the company had disappeared or it was a 'bubble' company which had never had a genuine substratum at all. Towards the end of the century the idea that the 'just and equitable' clause only covered situations which could be said to be somehow 'ejusdem generis' with the situations envisaged in the preceding subsections was gradually given up, but even in recent time judges have displayed a certain unwillingness to take the words at their face value and to apply them to new situations, which may well be an unconscious reflection of the restrictive interpretation which was put on them for so many years. In the present century, when the subsection became in turn s129 (vi) of the Companies (Consolidation) Act 1908, s168 (6) of the Companies Act 1929 and s222 (*f*) of the Companies Act 1948, petitions brought under it have generally related to disputes between rival shareholders or groups of shareholders in private companies; and in many cases the parties to the dispute have stood to one another in a relationship analogous to that of partners in an unincorporated business. In some of the reported cases in which winding-up orders have been made those who opposed the petition have been held by the court to have been guilty of a 'lack of probity' in their dealings with the petitioners. Thus in *Loch v John Blackwood Ltd* the managing director and majority shareholder was deliberately keeping the minority in ignorance of the company's financial position in order to acquire their shares at an undervalue, and in *re Dave and Collett Ltd* the holder of half the shares had used his casting vote as chairman in order to bring in an additional director who would vote as he wished and then proceeded to oust the owner of the other half of the shares from any participation in the management of the company's business. But it is not a condition precedent to the making of an order under the subsection that the conduct of those who oppose its making should have been 'unjust or inequitable'. This was made clear as early as 1905 by Lord M'Laren in his judgment in *Symington v Symingtons' Quarries Ltd*.

28 To the same effect is the judgment of Lord Cozens-Hardy MR in *re Yenidje Tobacco Co Ltd*. It is sometimes said that the order in that case was made on the ground of 'deadlock'. That is not so. As the Hon Frank Russell KC, who was counsel for the appellant, pointed out, although Mr Rothman and Mr Weinberg were not on speaking terms they communicated through third parties, the company's business was flourishing, and the articles contained a provision for arbitration to which resort could be had in the event of their failing to agree on any point. The reason why the petitioner succeeded was that the court thought right to make the order which it would have made had Mr Rothman and Mr Weinberg been carrying on business under articles of partnership which contained no provision for dissolution at the instance of either of them. People do not become partners unless they have confidence in one another *(pg503)* and it is of the essence of the relationship that mutual confidence is maintained. If neither has any longer confidence in the other so that they cannot work together in the way originally contemplated then the relationship should be ended – unless, indeed, the party who wishes to end it has been solely responsible for the situation which has arisen. The relationship between Mr Rothman and Mr Weinberg was not, of course, in form that of partners. They were equal shareholders in a limited company; but the court considered that it would be unduly fettered by matters of form if it did not deal with the situation as it would have dealt with it had the parties been partners in form as well as in substance.

29 The 'just and equitable' clause is, as I see it, an equitable supplement to the common law of the company which is to be found in the memorandum and articles; but there are some reported decisions which I find difficult, if not impossible, to square with this view. The most notable of these is that of Simonds J in *re Cuthbert Cooper & Sons Ltd*. The company there was a private company founded in 1913 to take over the business then being carried on by a father and his two elder sons. The capital was £10,000 divided into £1 shares of which 5,000 were held by the father and 2,500 each by the two sons. The three of them were the directors of the company. In 1930 the father died having appointed his three younger sons who were employed by the company his executors and having bequeathed them his shares equally. The articles gave the directors an absolute discretion to refuse to register as members any person to whom a member executed a transfer of shares or any person who became entitled to shares by transmission on the death of a member. Such a person had a right to receive any dividends declared on his shares and a right to share in the surplus assets on a winding-up, but no right to attend meetings or to receive accounts. No share could be transferred either by a member or by a person entitled by transmission to a person not a member so long as a member was prepared to buy them at a price based on the average rate of dividends over the preceding three years. After the father's death the younger sons asked their brothers – now the sole directors, to register them as members but they refused to do so. Dividends were, however, declared and the younger sons – although not entitled to them as of right – received copies of the accounts. In 1936 dissensions arose. The younger sons were dismissed from their employment; the dividend payable for the year ending June 1936 was reduced; and the directors refused to supply them with the balance sheet for that year. The directors offered to buy their brothers' shares but only at a price which, so the younger brothers alleged, was far below their real value. In view of the right of the directors to refuse to register transfers a sale to an outsider was not possible. In these circumstances the younger sons petitioned to have the company wound up. They did not complain that they had no share in the management of the company but simply that they were not put on the register, the suggestion being that the directors were trying to force them to sell their half interest in the company at an undervalue by reducing the rate of dividend and refusing to let them see the accounts. In dismissing the petition the judge said that although he must be guided by the principles applied by the court in deciding whether or not to dissolve a partnership, even in a partnership case the court would be guided by the partnership articles which one must in this case assume to correspond – *mutatis mutandis* – with the articles of the company. He also said that he was not prepared to assume that the directors were not acting in good faith in refusing to register the executors as shareholders and he refused to order them to attend for cross-examination. In effect he simply applied the common law, as laid down in the company's constitution and told the petitioners that if they wished to impugn their brothers' good faith they must prove their case by bringing an action against them. One naturally hesitates to dissent from any decision of Lord Simonds; but I cannot help thinking that on this occasion he took too narrow a view. It is not right to say that in a partnership case the court is tied by the terms of the partnership articles, for it will decree a dissolution of a partnership for a fixed *(pg504)* term if it is 'just and equitable' to do so. Further, he appears to have taken no account of the fact that the petitioners had made out a prima facie case against their brothers. Of course, the directors might have been able to show that they had respectable reasons for refusing to register their brothers as members and were not in the least influenced by any wish to induce them to sell their shares to them at a price which might be less than their true value; but on the undisputed facts it was for them to establish their good faith. The proper way to deal with the case would, I venture to think, have been to say that if the directors did not wish to give evidence and submit to cross-examination the company would have to be wound up. It is to be observed that the judge himself said that he had found the case a difficult one – and in *re Swaledale Cleaners Ltd* Danckwerts LJ expressed the view that it was wrongly decided. It is true that in the earlier case of *Charles Forte Investments Ltd v Amanda* the Court of Appeal – of which Danckwerts LJ and I myself were members – had accepted the *Cuthbert Cooper* decision as correct, but it was not in any way necessary for our decision in that case to approve it and I think that we were wrong to do so.

30 What the minority shareholder in cases of this sort really wants is not to have C) the company wound up – which may prove an unsatisfactory remedy – but to be paid a proper price for this shareholding. With this in mind Parliament provided by s210 of the Companies Act 1948 that if a member of a company could show that the company's affairs were being conducted in a manner oppressive to some of the members including himself, that the facts proved would justify the making of a winding-up order under the 'just and equitable clause, but that to wind up the company would unfairly prejudice the 'oppressed' members the court could, *inter alia*, make an order for the purchase of the shares of those members by other members or by the company. To give the court jurisdiction under this section the petitioner must show both that the conduct of the majority is 'oppressive' and also that it affects him in his capacity as a shareholder. The appellant was unable to establish either of these preconditions. But the jurisdiction to wind up under s222 (*f*) continues to exist as an independent remedy and I have no doubt that the Court of Appeal was right in rejecting the submission of the respondents to the effect that a petitioner cannot obtain an order under that subsection any more than under s210 unless he can show that his position as a shareholder has been worsened by the action of which he complains.

31 The facts of this case are set out in detail in the judgment of Plowman J and I need not repeat them. The essence of the matter is that Mr Nazar and the appellant had been carrying on business as partners at will in equal shares; that the business was transferred to the company in which each had 40 per cent of the capital and Mr Nazar's son George the remaining 20 per cent; that it was not contemplated that any dividends would be paid but that the profits of the company should be distributed by way of directors' fees; and that the result of the appellant's removal from the directorship was that instead of his having a share in the management of the business and an income of some £3,000 a year he was excluded from the management and deprived of any share in the profits save such dividend as might be paid on his shares if the Nazars thought fit to declare a dividend. The Court of Appeal held that the appellant could not obtain a winding-up order under the 'just and equitable' clause unless he could show that the Nazars had not exercised the power to remove him from his directorship 'bona fide in the interest of the company' or that their grounds for exercising the power were such that no reasonable man could think that the removal was in the interest of the company. With all respect to them I cannot agree that this is an appropriate test to apply. If one assumes that the company is going to remain in existence it may very well be that a reasonable man would say that it was in the *(pg505)* interest of the company that the appellant should cease to be a director. 'These two men' he might say 'are hopelessly at loggerheads. If the business is to prosper one or other must go and the company is likely to do better without [the appellant] than without Mr Nazar'. But these considerations have not, to my mind, anything to do with the question whether in the circumstances it is right that the company should continue in existence if the appellant wishes it to be wound-up. The argument on which counsel for the respondents chiefly relied in support of the decision of the Court of Appeal was quite different. The appellant, he said, consented to the conversion of the partnership into a limited company. Even though he became, because George Nazar was taken in, only a minority shareholder he could have safeguarded his position by procuring the insertion in the articles of a provision 'weighting' the voting power of his shares on any question touching his retention of office as director: see *Bushell v Faiths.* He must, therefore, be taken to have accepted the risk that if he and Mr Nazar fell out he would be at Mr Nazar's mercy. There might be force in this argument if there was any evidence to show that the minds of the parties were directed to the point; but there is no such evidence and the probability is that no one gave a moment's thought to the change in relative strength of their respective positions brought about by the conversion of the partnership into a company. It was not suggested that the appellant had been guilty of any misconduct such as would justify one partner in expelling another under an expulsion clause contained in partnership articles. All that happened was that without one being more to blame than the other the two could no longer work together in harmony. Had no company been formed the appellant could have had the partnership wound up and although Mr Nazar and his son were entitled in law to oust him from his directorship and deprive him of his income they could only do so subject to the appellant's right to obtain equitable relief in the form of a winding-up order *(pg506)* under s222 (*f*). I would, therefore, allow the appeal.

32 In conclusion, I would refer briefly to three recent decisions under the subsection. *Re Lundie Brothers Ltd* was, like this, an 'exclusion' case. Plowman J was I think right in that case, as in this, to make a winding-up order. In *re K9 Meat Supplies (Guildford) Ltd* the company had an issued share capital of 11,001 shares, 3,667 of which were held by each of three men who were the sole directors and each of whom took part in the running of the business. It was arranged between them that the profits should be divided equally by way of directors' fees. One of the three, a Mr Darrington, got into financial difficulties. He resigned his directorship in January 1965, and in April was adjudicated bankrupt. Shortly afterwards the two remaining directors sold the business for £18,000 and placed the purchase price on deposit. They offered to buy Mr Darrington's shares from his trustee in bankruptcy at par but the trustee, taking the view that Mr Darrington ought to receive a third share of the purchase price, petitioned under s222 (*f*). Pennycuick J came with regret to the conclusion that he must dismiss the petition. He thought it deplorable that the two other quasi-partners should retain in their hands assets to which Mr Darrington's creditors were in common fairness entitled but he held that as the three had elected to trade together through the medium of a company instead of as partners there was no ground on which he could properly make the order. In coming to this conclusion he was, I think, much influenced by the case of *re Cuthbert Cooper*. I think that a winding-up order should have been made since in the absence of any other explanation the inevitable inference was that the two remaining directors in resisting a winding-up and distribution of the surplus assets among the shareholders were putting pressure on the trustee in bankruptcy to sell them Mr Darrington's share at an undervalue. The last case is the unreported decision of Brightman J in *re Leadenhall General Hardware Stores Ltd*. His decision not to make a winding-up order was, I think, justifiable – although I cannot agree with the reasons which he gave for it. If the respondents were telling the truth – and the judge held that they were – the almost inevitable inference was that the petitioner had been stealing the company's money. A petitioner who relies on the 'just and equitable' clause must come to court with clean hands, and if the breakdown in confidence between him and the other parties to the dispute appears to have been due to his misconduct he cannot insist on the company being wound up if they wish it to continue. But the judge dealt with the case on the footing that the respondents' loss of confidence in the petitioner might have been due to a tragic and inexplicable misunderstanding. If it was right in the light of the evidence to deal with the case on that basis then I would have thought that a winding-up order should have been made.

33 I agree with the order proposed by my noble and learned friend, Lord Wilberforce, with regard to costs.

34 LORD SALMON: My Lords, I concur and would allow the appeal. I agree that the individual respondents should be ordered to pay the appellant's costs here and in the Court of Appeal. *(pg507)*

Case 32
Battle v IRC

[1980] STC 86

High Court

22, 23, 24, 25 October, 9 November 1979

The manner of valuing a shareholding in an investment company differs from that method utilised for valuing a trading company shareholding. The importance of this case is, in part, that this is one of the very few cases that have been before the courts where the subject matter has been the valuation of shares in an investment company. The points of principle in this judgment are of general application when valuing investment company shares.

However, care must be taken with the arithmetic calculation as the company had three highly unusual characteristics. First, only one investment was held by the company, being a holding of government stock. Secondly, the investment risk was, thus, significantly lower than would be the case in a conventional investment company. Thirdly, being government stock, no charge to corporation tax would arise on the sale by the company of its investment.

In the summer of 1971 Mrs Muriel Nancy Battle, knowing she had terminal cancer, consulted her lawyers to see if anything could be done to lessen the amount of estate duty which would be payable on her death. As a result of the advice she was given the following events took place:

1.   On 29 July 1971, Mrs Battle bought £99,687.10 4.5 per cent British Gas Stock 1969–72.
2.   On 4 August 1971, a private company, Potterhanworth Investments Ltd, was incorporated, with Mrs Battle's nephews, Anthony Newsum Battle and Robin Maxwell Battle, as the directors and shareholders. The articles gave the directors the power to decline to register any transfer of any share.
3.   On 10 August 1971, Mrs Battle transferred £49,843.55 nominal of the Gas Stock to Anthony and £49,843.55 nominal of the Gas Stock to Robin.
4.   On 10/11 August 1971, Anthony and Robin transferred their holdings of Gas Stock to Potterhanworth in exchange for 49 shares to each of Anthony and Robin.

5.   On 12 August 1971, at an extra-ordinary general meeting of Potterhanworth, the shares numbered 1 and 2 were designated ordinary shares and the remaining 98 shares of £1 each numbered 3 to 100 were converted into preference shares.

Mrs Battle died on 19 October 1971. On 3 December 1971, Potterhanworth was put into a member's voluntary liquidation. Its assets were then valued at £102,658.94. On 14 February 1972 the liquidator repaid the preference shares (ie the shares numbered 3 to 100) at par and paid the remaining funds of Potterhanworth, after provision for liabilities and costs, to Anthony and Robin as the holders of the two ordinary shares.

Anthony and Robin each contended that the property to be treated as comprised in the gift to each by Mrs Battle was 49 shares of Potterhanworth, which at the date of her death were only worth par or less.

After outlining the facts, Balcombe J stated the general principle that valuation for estate duty purposes (and similarly for capital gains tax and inheritance tax) postulates a hypothetical vendor and a hypothetical purchaser; not particular persons and no link can be assumed between a sale made by one person and another:

> 'Once it is established that the method of valuation is on the basis of a sale in the open market what is contemplated is a notional sale between a notional vendor and a notional purchaser: one does not postulate a particular vendor or a particular purchaser. One cannot assume that the hypothetical vendor of a minority holding of shares in a company would only sell his holding in conjunction with the other holders so that its value should be assessed on the basis of a sale of all the shares.'
>
> ([1980] STC 86 at 90/91 **case 32 para 12**)

Balcombe J noted that the evidence of two expert witnesses was that a substantial discount on the asset value was necessary in order to estimate the price that would be paid for a minority holding of 49 shares ([1980] STC 86 at 91 **case 32 para 14**).

One expert witness put the discount at 10 per cent to 15 per cent ([1980] STC 86 at 91 **case 32 para 14**); the other at 15 per cent ([1980] STC 86 at 92 **case 32 para 15**).

Looking at the value of shares as relating to the break-up value of the shares, the cost of liquidation must be brought into account, with a discount also required for the risk of the other shareholders not agreeing to a liquidation ([1980] STC 86 at 91 **case 32 para 14(c)**).

Judgement

References, example '(pg88)', are to [1980] STC 86.

1 **BALCOMBE J**: In the summer of 1971 Mrs Muriel Nancy Battle, knowing she had terminal cancer, consulted her lawyers to see if anything could be done to lessen the amount of estate duty which would be payable on her death. As a result of the advice she was given the following events took place. (1) On 29th July 1971 Mrs Battle bought for cash in the stock market £99,687.10 4½% British Gas Stock 1969–72 at a price (inclusive of stamp duty and commission) of £98,087.82. (2) On 4th August 1971 a private company, Potterhanworth Investments Ltd, was incorporated, with a capital of £100 divided into 100 shares of £1 each. Mrs Battle's nephews, Anthony Newsum Battle and Robin Maxwell Battle, who are brothers, were the subscribers to the memorandum of association. Potterhanworth's articles of association incorporated by reference Part II of Table A in Sch 1 to the Companies Act 1948, including the power of the directors to decline to register any transfer of any share. (3) On 10th August 1971 Mrs Battle transferred £49,843.55 nominal of the Gas Stock to Anthony and £49,843.55 nominal of the Gas Stock to Robin. (4) On 10th August 1971 Anthony and Robin, as the subscribers to the memorandum of Potterhanworth, appointed themselves to be its first directors. (5) Also on 10th August 1971 the first meeting of the directors of Potterhanworth was held. At that meeting (*inter alia*): (a) Anthony was allotted one £1 share (share no 1) in the capital of Potterhanworth, having subscribed the sum of £1,000 (ie the share was allotted at a premium of £999). (b) Robin was similarly allotted (and at a similar premium) one £1 share (share no 2) in the capital of Potterhanworth. (c) It was resolved to enter into a transfer agreement between (1) Potterhanworth, (2) Anthony and (3) Robin, which provided for Anthony and Robin each to transfer their holdings of the Gas Stock to Potterhanworth at a value of £49,000 each in consideration of the issue to each of them of 49 shares in Potterhanworth. (In fact the valuation of each of their holdings of the Gas Stock on 10th August 1971 was £49,095.89). The transfer agreement further provided that Potterhanworth should bear the costs of all parties incurred in connection with the preparation and completion of the agreement and the stamping of the transfers to Potterhanworth of the Gas Stock. (6) After that meeting, but still on 10th August 1971, the transfer agreement was executed and Anthony and Robin duly transferred their holdings of Gas Stock to Potterhanworth. (7) On 11th August 1971, at a further meeting of the directors of Potterhanworth, it was resolved to issue 49 shares to each of Anthony and Robin in pursuance of the transfer agreement and such shares were then duly issued. Anthony's shares were numbered 3–51 and Robin's shares were numbered 52–100. (8) On 12th August 1971, at an extra-ordinary general meeting of Potterhanworth, the shares numbered 1 and 2 were designated ordinary shares and the remaining 98 shares of £1 each numbered 3 to 100 were converted into preference shares carrying the right to a 10% cumulative preferential dividend and in a winding up to a return of the nominal capital paid up thereon together with any arrears of dividend, but with no further right of participation in the profits or assets of Potterhanworth.

2 Pausing there, the effect of what had been done at the meeting of 12th August 1971 was to reduce the value of the 98 shares (which had been issued as consideration for the transfer to Potterhanworth of the Gas Stock) to a nominal sum, and to concentrate the whole value of the company, which had net assets of the order of £98,000, in the two subscribers' shares. *(pg88)*

3 Mrs Battle died on 19th October 1971. On 3rd December 1971 Potterhanworth was put into a member's voluntary liquidation. Its assets were then valued at £102,658.94. On 14th February 1972 the liquidator repaid the preference shares (ie the shares numbered 3 to 100) at par and paid the remaining funds of Potterhanworth, after provision for liabilities and costs, to Anthony and Robin as the holders of the two ordinary shares.

4 By their originating summons issued on 28th July 1978 Anthony and Robin as plaintiffs claim against the Commissioners of Inland Revenue a declaration that in ascertaining their liability to estate duty in respect of the gifts made to them by Mrs Battle the value of the gifted property in the case of each plaintiff should be taken as £48 and not as £49,095.89 as contended by the Revenue. The answer to the question raised by this claim depends on a consideration of the provisions of s38 of the Finance Act 1957, to which I now turn. Section 38(1) is, so far as material, in the following terms:

'Where property comprised in a gift *inter vivos* … is treated for purposes of estate duty as passing on the death of the donor [and the two sums of Gas Stock are so treated] and at some time before the death of the donor the donee has ceased to have the possession and enjoyment of any of the property so comprised, then *subject to the provisions of this section* the enactments relating to estate duty in respect of gifts *inter vivos* (including this section) shall apply as if the property, if any, received by the donee in substitution for that property had been comprised in the gift instead of that property …' (Emphasis mine.)

5 Anthony and Robin each contends, in reliance on this subsection, that the property to be treated as comprised in the gift to him by Mrs Battle is the 49 shares of Potterhanworth, which at the date of her death were only worth par or less. The Crown resists this contention in reliance on the qualification introduced by the words 'subject to the provisions of this section', which leads me to consider the provisions of sub-s 3. Section 38(3) provides:

'Where at a time before the death of the donor the donee … voluntarily divests himself of any … property [comprised in the gift to him] otherwise than for a consideration in money or money's worth not less than the principal value of the property at that time, then … he shall be treated for the purpose of subsection (1) of this section as continuing to have the possession and enjoyment of that property, and the principal value aforesaid shall be taken as the principal value of that property as property comprised in the gift …'

6 The Crown contends that Anthony and Robin voluntarily divested themselves of their holdings of Gas Stock for a consideration worth less than the value of those holdings on 10th August 1971 and accordingly that the value of each holding as at that date (£49,095.89) is the value of the property comprised in the gift made by Mrs Battle for estate duty purposes.

7 Finally I mention s38(15), which provides:

'For the purpose of this section the principal value of any property at a time before the death of the deceased shall be ascertained as it would be for the purposes of estate duty chargeable on his death if he had died immediately before that time … '

8 Accordingly the following questions need to be answered: (1) What was the consideration which Anthony and Robin each received for their transfers of *(pg89)* the Gas Stock to Potterhanworth on 10th August 1971? (2) How should that consideration be valued? (3) Was that consideration worth not less than £49,095.89 on 10th August 1971? I propose to consider these questions separately.

1. The nature of the consideration

9 There can be no doubt that the 49 shares in Potterhanworth which Anthony and Robin each received on 11th August 1971 constituted consideration for their transfers of the Gas Stock. But counsel for Anthony and Robin contends that in addition, and as part of the consideration, there was the benefit of a collateral agreement between Anthony and Robin that neither would deal with his shares in Potterhanworth independently of the other, with the result that each holding of 49 shares should be valued on the basis that it formed part of a single parcel of 98 shares. It is not suggested that there was any express written agreement to this effect. Nor did Anthony in his affidavit evidence, or Robin in his affidavit and oral evidence, allege that there was an express oral agreement. The highest that their evidence went was that each understood that they would together follow through the scheme which had been recommended to them by their lawyers. I am quite satisfied that there was no agreement between Anthony and Robin of the kind for which counsel contends: indeed, I never fully understood what were said to be the terms of this alleged agreement. If, as at one time appeared to be the case, the alleged agreement was no more than an obligation by each of the brothers not to deal with his 49 shares in Potterhanworth without the consent of the other, it would seem that the restrictions on transfer in the articles of Potterhanworth provided the necessary degree of restraint. But if there were any agreement wider than this, and I have already said that I am satisfied that there was not, the only agreement which on the evidence I could find had existed would have been an agreement by the brothers that each would take all steps necessary to implement the scheme proposed to them by their lawyers. But such an agreement would not suit counsel's book. He seeks to rely on the alleged agreement as establishing that the two blocks of 49 shares would always be dealt with together and, accordingly, that neither should be valued as a separate, minority holding but that each should be valued as representing 49% of the total net assets of Potterhanworth. But if the agreement was to implement the scheme as a whole, it was an essential ingredient of the scheme that at an appropriate time each holding of 49 shares should be converted into preference shares and stripped of all but a nominal value. Accordingly, such an agreement, far from enhancing the value of the 49-share holding, would effectively render it valueless.

10 Counsel for the Crown submitted that even if there had been some collateral agreement between Anthony and Robin which had the effect of ensuring that the two holdings of 49 shares could only be dealt with together, nevertheless the benefit of such an agreement would not form part of the consideration received by the brothers for the transfers of their holdings of Gas Stock to Potterhanworth. As I am satisfied that there was no such agreement, I do not find it necessary to deal further with this submission.

2. The method of valuation of the consideration

11 The 49 shares which Anthony and Robin each received as consideration for the transfer of the Gas Stock to Potterhanworth constitute an item of property. As such they come within the words 'any property' in s38(15) and so fall to be valued as they would be for the purposes of estate duty chargeable on the death of Mrs Battle if she had died immediately before 10th August 1971. That valuation is on the basis of a sale in the open market: see s7(5) of the Finance Act 1894. Even if this were not the case I find compelling the further submission by counsel for the Crown that since, by the combined effect of sub-ss 3 and 15 of s38, the holding of Gas Stock has to be valued on the basis of a sale in the open market as at 10th August 1971, the value of any consideration given for the transfer of the Gas Stock should be valued on a similar basis, otherwise one would not be comparing like with like, and there would be no true basis for the comparison of values which sub-s 3 requires to be made. In any event, in default of some other method of valuation being expressly provided, 'worth' will normally be determined by reference to the open market: see *McIlquham v Taylor* per Lindley LJ and *Attorney-General v Jameson* per Holmes LJ.

12 Once it is established that the method of valuation is on the basis of a sale in the open market what is contemplated is a notional sale between a notional vendor and a notional *(pg90)* purchaser: one does not postulate a particular vendor or a particular purchaser: see *Inland Revenue Comrs v Crossman* per Lord Blanesburgh and *Lynall v Inland Revenue Comrs*. One cannot assume that the hypothetical vendor of a minority holding of shares in a company would only sell his holding in conjunction with the other holders so that its value should be assessed on the basis of a sale of all the shares, cf *Short v Treasury Comrs*.

13 However, it was not counsel's primary contention for Anthony and Robin that there were here special factors to be taken into account which would affect what could otherwise be the open market value of the 49 shares: It was his main submission that the 49 shares should not be valued on the basis of a sale of such a holding in the open market but rather that they should be valued on the basis of what could be realised for them by means of a share exchange scheme, whereby the whole of the share capital of Potterhanworth might have been exchanged for shares in turn converted into cash. For the reasons already given, I reject that submission. In the next section of this judgment I consider what effect, if any, the availability of such a scheme would have on the open market valuation of a block of 49 shares in Potterhanworth as at 10th August 1971.

3. The value of 49 Potterhanworth shares on 10th August 1971

14 The evidence for the Crown was that the value of a minority holding of shares in a private company, even a company such as Potterhanworth, with no liabilities and its assets in a readily realisable form, would represent a substantial discount on the asset value of those shares. Convincing reasons are given for that conclusion. Mr Marriott, a partner in Mullens & Co, the stockbrokers, set out his reasons as follows, and I quote from his affidavit:

'I do not consider, however, that a hypothetical purchaser of 49 shares of Potterhanworth would have been prepared to pay as much as the asset value for such a holding. There was no doubt whatsoever of the quality of the assets but a potential purchaser of 49 shares would argue that unless he were offered some inducement in the form of a discount on the asset value he would be better off investing directly in a British Government stock for the following reasons: (a) He could buy British government stock without incurring the transfer stamp payable on a purchase of Potterhanworth shares. (b) He could subsequently sell his British Government stock without any difficulty whereas a sale of Potterhanworth shares would be subject to the onerous restrictions on transfer in the Articles of Association of Potterhanworth. (c) Should he invest in a short-dated British Government stock such as 4% British Gas 1969–72 he would be assured of receiving his redemption proceeds on a fixed date (not later than 8 August 1972 in the case of the British Gas Stock) whereas a liquidation of Potterhanworth would take time and incur some expense which would deplete the ultimate proceeds. (d) He would have complete control over his holdings of British Government stock whereas he would be a minority holder in Potterhanworth and could find himself locked in should the other shareholders decide not to liquidate the company on the repayment of 4% British Gas stock 1969–72. Having regard to all these factors, I consider that a potential purchaser of 49 shares in Potterhanworth would require a substantial discount on asset value before he would be prepared to complete his purchase. It is impossible to arrive at such a discount by a precise mathematical calculation but my experience in the market and in the valuation of unquoted shares suggests that the discount should be in the region of 10 to 15%. Taking a midpoint of $12\frac{1}{2}$%, I would value the holding of 49 shares at £42,886.53.'

15 Mr Booth, an assistant controller of death duties at the Capital Taxes Office, with considerable experience of valuing unquoted shares, gave evidence to the like effect. He *(pg91)* considered that an appropriate discount would be in the region of 15 per cent and valued a holding of 49 shares in Potterhanworth on 10th August 1971 at £41,661.20. On this point neither witness was shaken in cross-examination. Indeed, Mr Pinsent, the principal valuation witness for Anthony and Robin, an investment manager with some 15 years' experience, in general accepted the principles indicated by Mr Marriott and Mr Booth as to the way in which shares in a private investment company ought to be valued for purposes of estate duty, ie on the basis of a sale in the open market. But it was the evidence of Mr Pinsent, supported by that of Mr Harford, a Bristol stockbroker, and Mr Leighton, a Bath chartered accountant and company director with a considerable experience of investment management, that in the 'bull market' conditions of August 1971 it would have been possible to realise the shares in Potterhanworth advantageously by means of a share exchange scheme. *(pg92)*

16 The essence of such a scheme may be summarised as follows. In a 'bull market' there will be companies whose shares are quoted in the market at a premium over the asset value of those shares. Such a company might wish to take advantage of the premium by issuing new shares for cash or assets. One way in which it might do so would be to issue shares by way of a 'rights' issue to existing shareholders at a premium, but less than the premium at which the shares were quoted in the market. A rights issue could not be repeated at too frequent intervals, while a small rights issue might involve disproportionate expense, so that this was not always a suitable method of realising the premium value of the shares. Another way would be to 'place' a block of new shares, again at a suitable premium, with a merchant bank or institution, but I was told in evidence that the Stock Exchange imposed restrictions on the use of this method. A third way would be to issue shares as consideration for the purchase of all the shares in another company (the offeree). As the first company (the offeror) is paying for the shares in the offeree with new shares which stand at a premium over their own net asset value it can, in an appropriate case, afford to pay the shareholders of the offeree a premium over the asset value of their shares because notwithstanding this payment it can still increase the net asset value of its own shares. This last method, called a share exchange scheme, is particularly appropriate where the assets of the offeree consist of realisable investments.

17 To support his evidence of the availability of a share exchange scheme in August 1971 Mr Pinsent cited as examples a number of cases in which investment companies had been taken over at a premium, although he accepted that there were also many cases where the shares of the offeree were acquired at less than their net asset value. But none of the examples given was directly comparable with the case of Potterhanworth. In almost every case the portfolio of the offeree contained a large proportion of equities and one of the attractions of the takeover could be the acquisition of equities not readily available in the market. In every case but one, and that one case proved to be so exceptional as to be valueless as an example, the consideration for the acquisition of shares in the offeree was the issue of shares or other securities in the offeror, and if the shareholders of the offeree wished to obtain cash for the securities so issued to them such cash was to be provided by an outside third party, usually a merchant bank, and the terms of the offer were usually pitched so as to discourage the exercise of the cash alternative. None of the witnesses who gave evidence before me was able to cite a case where the offeree was a company similar to Potterhanworth, viz, whereby only assets consisted of gilt-edged securities. Counsel for the Crown suggested that if a company such as Potterhanworth could have been acquired at a premium, then everybody would have been going out, borrowing £100,000 from their bankers, buying £100,000 worth of gilt edged securities in the market, putting those securities into a private company acquired 'off the peg' for some £35–40, and then disposing of the shares in this company, by means of a share exchange scheme, at a premium. It was common ground amongst the witnesses that no such 'cottage industry' then existed and I can see the force of counsel's submission than I should not therefore accept the evidence for Anthony and Robin that it would have been possible for the shares of Potterhanworth to have been disposed of, at not less than their net asset value, by means of a share exchange scheme.

18 However, I am not prepared to reject the evidence of Mr Pinsent, Mr Leighton and Mr Harford, that it would, in the conditions which existed in August 1971, have been possible to find a 'purchaser', by means of a share exchange scheme, of a company having no other assets than a substantial holding of gilt edged stock. The rationale of such an acquisition, as was pointed out with force and frequency by Mr Pinsent, was that for the offeror it was an alternative to a rights issue. However I am far from satisfied that the shareholders in the offeree could have expected to receive a premium on the net asset value of their shares. The explanation given by Mr Pinsent and Mr Harford for the absence of a 'cottage industry' in the creation of companies to satisfy this demand for cash-rich companies which they said then existed was because of the element of risk involved, the market might suddenly change. I accept the evidence of Mr Harford who said that the 'cottage industry' did not exist because there was not enough in it: the only premium obtainable would have been sufficient to cover expenses, but not to provide a profit on the assets acquired for the purpose. On the evidence I find as a fact that if, on 10th August 1971, there was a company willing and able to acquire all the shares in Potterhanworth through the medium of a share exchange scheme, it would have been a special 'purchaser' who would have entered into the transaction solely for the purpose of taking advantage of the premium on its shares because no more attractive way of realising that premium was readily available, and on terms which were unlikely to have afforded to the shareholders of Potterhanworth any significant premium over the net asset value of those shares.

19 In my judgment such a finding does not help the plaintiffs in this case. Such a 'purchaser' would only have been interested in acquiring all the shares in Potterhanworth, whereas the relevant holding in the present case is a minority holding of 49 shares. I have already considered and rejected the submission that there was here a collateral agreement between Anthony and Robin which would have ensured that the two holdings of 49 shares would always be dealt with as one parcel.

20 However, the evidence of Anthony and Robin was to the effect that, whether or not there was a legally enforceable contract, nevertheless there was an understanding between them that neither would deal with his holding of shares in Potterhanworth in isolation, so that in practice the two holdings would have been dealt with together and (so the argument proceeds) should be valued on that basis. In my judgment such a valuation would not be in accordance with the principles set out above on which an open market valuation must be made and accordingly I also reject that argument.

21 Even if I were wrong on this last point, and the value of each brother's holding of 49 shares in Potterhanworth falls to be valued on the basis of a sale of a single block of 98 shares, I am still not satisfied that a holding of 49 shares was on 10th August 1971 worth not less than £49,095.89. The evidence was that, even on such a sale, a purchaser would require a discount of some $2\frac{1}{2}\%$ from the net assets value of Potterhanworth, because of the disadvantages of holding shares in a private company as compared with a direct holding of the Gas Stock. Even though it may have been possible, in the special conditions existing in August 1971, to have found a 'purchaser', by means of a share exchange scheme, of 98 shares in Potterhanworth, the evidence does not satisfy me that the possibility of such a 'purchaser' being found would have had any effect on the open market value of these shares. Accordingly in my judgment the Crown succeeds in its contentions. *(pg93)*

Case 33
Williamson v Dalton

[1981] STC 753

High Court

15 July 1981

Two points arise from the decision in this case:

1. Where there is no approved share option scheme, an employee who is granted an option is subject to income tax under Sch E at the time of the grant on the difference between the option price and the market price.
2. Even if the option cannot be exercised for many years, the option has a value. The Sch E charge is computed as the difference between the market value of the shares comprised in the option at the time when it was granted and the aggregate of the price payable for the shares under the option and the consideration for the option (see, now, ITEPA 2003, ss 476(1) and 477(3)(a)).

Alan Norman Dalton was an employee of National Westminster Bank Ltd. On 10 July 1974, he acquired an option under the scheme to purchase 960 ordinary shares of the bank at £1.83 per share. Assessment for 1974/75 in the amount of £4,592 was raised on Alan Dalton, this being the difference between the market value of 960 shares at the date of the grant of option and the sum payable for the exercise of the option.

Alan Dalton appealed stating that the option was subject to so many restrictions and contingent conditions, including a bar on transfer ability, that, at the date of the grant, it had no value and, hence, there was no Sch E liability arising.

The Special Commissioners upheld the taxpayer's argument and discharged the assessment.

In the High Court, Vinelott J held that the option was assessable under TA 1970, s 186(1) as modified by FA 1972, s 77(1) and (2) (now ITEPA 2003, ss 476(1) and 477(3)(a)).

On the question whether there is a value in an option, Vinelott J said:

'No doubt it would have been very difficult for the taxpayer to have realised the value of the option when it was first granted, but an option to acquire shares at less than the then market price, albeit after a period of time and, in broad terms, conditionally on remaining in the employment of a company in the group and maintaining the save-as-you-earn contract for seven years, must *prima facie* be taken to be a right of a kind which has a monetary value. It could have been realised, by an arrangement with a third part; that is in the context of this case, an arrangement under which the taxpayer agreed to exercise the option in accordance with the direction of the third party and to transfer any shares obtained on the exercise of the option to him, the third party undertaking to maintain the save-as-you-earn contract although no doubt there would have to have been some provision for the return of the consideration paid to the taxpayer under the arrangement and any moneys paid by the third party under the save-as-you-earn contract with interest if the option lapsed before it was exercised.'

([1981] STC 753 at 759 **case 33 para 16**)

The decision does not include any discussion as to the calculation of the amount of the Sch E assessment, which has been agreed for the purpose of the appeal, other than the comment by Vinelott J:

'The arithmetical process by which this figure is arrived at is, to say the least, obscure.'

([1981] STC 753 at 756 **case 33 para 4**)

Judgement

References, example '(pg756)', are to (1981) STC 753.

1 **VINELOTT J:** This appeal raises a short question as to the construction and effect of s77 of the Finance Act 1972. The Respondent, Alan Norman Dalton, has been at all material times an employee of the National Westminster Bank Ltd. (which I will call 'the Bank'). In 1974 the Bank introduced an earnings related savings scheme (which I will call 'the scheme') for the benefit of the employees of the Bank and its subsidiaries (which I will refer to collectively as 'the Group').

2 The scheme was complex, but a short description will suffice for the purposes of this judgment. Under the scheme an employee of the Group who entered into a save-as-you-earn contract under arrangements made by the Company in the Group which employed him by which he agreed to make regular monthly payments as personal savings over a period of seven years, was entitled to call on the Bank to grant him an option to acquire a specified number of ordinary

shares in the Bank. The consideration for the option was £1. The number of shares comprised in the option was determined by the amount of the monthly payments which the employee had agreed to make under the save-as-you-earn contract, the number of shares being the number which could be bought at the option price with the aggregate of the monthly payments over the period of seven years. The option price was 90 per cent of the mid-market price of the shares of the Bank of the relevant class quoted on the Stock Exchange on the day on which the option was granted. The option was exercisable within six months after the expiry of seven years from the grant of the option.

3 The scheme provided that the option should lapse automatically if the employee failed to maintain his monthly payments under his save-as-you-earn contract or if he ceased to be employed by a company in the Group, save in certain specified circumstances which included injury or disability and, (after three years had elapsed from the grant of the option) retirement. If the employee stopped making monthly payments under his save-as-you-earn contract he could either withdraw the moneys paid under that contract, in which event the option lapsed, or leave the moneys in the savings account, in which event the number of shares comprised in the option would be reduced to the number which could be bought at the option price with the moneys left in the savings account. If the employee died within the seven-year period his personal representatives could exercise the option within 12 months from his death, whether that 12-month period commenced before the expiry of the seven-year period or ended after six months from the expiry of the seven-year period, but the option could only be exercised up to the number of shares which could be bought with the moneys then credited to the savings account. The option was expressed to be personal and could not be assigned, except with the consent of the Bank, and lapsed on the employee's bankruptcy.

4 The Respondent took part in the scheme, and on 10 July 1974, an option was granted to him by the Bank to acquire a specified number of its shares at a price 10 per cent. below the then mid-market price. He was assessed to tax in respect of the year 1974–75 (that is the year in which the option was granted), in the sum of £147, that being agreed to be the difference between the option price and the mid-market price of the shares comprised in the option. The arithmetical process by which this figure is arrived at is, to say the least, obscure, but, as I have said, that figure has been agreed for the purposes of this appeal.

5 Section 186(1) of the Income and Corporation Taxes Act 1970 (which I will call 'the Taxes Act'), provides that:

> 'Where a person realises a gain by the exercise, or by the assignment or release, of a right to acquire shares in a body corporate obtained by that person as a director or employee of that or any other body corporate, he shall be chargeable to tax under Schedule E on an amount equal to the amount of his gain, as computed in accordance with this section.

(2) Where tax may by virtue of this section become chargeable in respect of any gain which may be realised by the exercise of a right, tax shall not be chargeable under any other provision of the Tax Acts in respect of the receipt of the right.'

6 The option granted to the Respondent clearly fell within s186(1). However, s186 was modified by s77 of the Finance Act 1972, subss (1) and (2) of which read as follows:

'(1) Where, on or after 11 April 1972, such a right as is mentioned in subsection *(pg756)* (1) of section 186 of the Taxes Act is obtained as mentioned therein and the right is capable of being exercised later than seven years after it is obtained, subsection (2) of that section shall not prevent the charging of tax under any other provisions of the Tax Acts in respect of the receipt of the right; but where tax is charged under any of those provisions, it shall be deducted from any tax which, under that section, is chargeable by reference to the gain realised by the exercise, assignment or release of the right. (2) For the purpose of any charge to tax enabled to be made by virtue of this section, the value of a right shall be taken to be not less than the market value at the time the right is obtained of the shares which may be acquired by the exercise of the right or the shares for which shares so acquired may be exchanged, reduced by the amount or value (or, if variable, the least amount or value) of the consideration for which the shares may be so acquired.'

7 I should mention at this stage that s78 of the Finance Act 1972, contained provisions exempting from tax under s77, a sum which would have been chargeable to tax on the grant of option in a case where the option was granted under an approved share option scheme. The scheme introduced by the Bank in 1974 was so approved. But s78 was repealed by the Finance Act 1974, save as regards cases where the option was exercised before 27 March 1974, which this option was not. The Bank apparently entered into arrangements with the Inland Revenue, the effect of which was to relieve employees from the charge under s77 if they switched from the 1974 scheme to a new scheme introduced by the Bank which was similar to the 1974 scheme except that the period after which the option became exercisable was reduced from seven to five years. However, those arrangements only applied to employees who switched to the five-year scheme before 14 February 1975. The Respondent did not avail himself of these arrangements.

8 In these circumstances the General Commissioners came to the conclusion that 'the option granted to the Respondent was chargeable to tax at the time of its acquisition as an emolument of his employment, nevertheless we were of the opinion that at that date it had no assessable value'.

9 It seems to me the Commissioners must have overlooked s77(2). If the option was chargeable as an emolument of the Respondent's employment, then clearly the amount of the charge must be governed by s77(2) and must accordingly extend to the difference between the market value of the shares comprised in the option at the time when it was granted and the aggregate of the price payable for the shares under the option and the consideration for the option. *Prima facie* the market value of the shares comprised in the option on the date of the grant of the option must be taken to be the mid-market price of the ordinary shares of the Bank quoted on the Stock Exchange on that date. The difference between that price and the option price is the agreed figure of £147.

10 The real question that arises in this appeal is whether the benefit of the option was a taxable perquisite of the Respondent's employment. Before turning to that question there are two subsidiary matters I should mention. The Respondent submitted that in s77(1) the words 'the right is capable of being exercised later than seven years after it is obtained' mean that this right must be one capable of being exercised before or after seven years have elapsed since the right was obtained. I doubt whether that construction would assist the Respondent, even if it were well-founded, because the option granted to him was one which might have become exercisable before the expiry of the seven-year period if he died or, in certain circumstances retired before the expiry of that period at least as regards some of the shares comprised in the option (and perhaps all of them if he or his personal representatives had accelerated payment under his save-as-you-earn contract). But this construction is, in my judgment, in any event unsound. In my judgment the words 'capable of being exercised later than seven years' are apt to describe a right which is capable of being exercised after seven years whether or not the right is also capable of being exercised before the expiry of that period.

11 Mr Carnwath submitted, though making it clear it was only a subsidiary part *(pg757)* of his case, that the words 'under any other provisions of the Tax Acts' in s77(1) include the provisions of s77(2) and that accordingly the option must be treated as having a realisable value, that is the value placed on it by subs (2), and, therefore, as having been, apart from s186, a perquisite and accordingly an emolument of the Respondent's employment. I do not think that that is a permissible construction of s77(1). Section 77(2) is not a charging section, but applies 'for the purpose of any charge to tax enabled to be made by virtue of this section'. The charge to tax must be found before s77(2) comes into operation. If it comes into operation it provides the measure of the charge. The real issue, as I have said, is whether the option granted to the Respondent was a perquisite of his employment of a kind which, apart from s186 and the statutory provisions it replaced, would have been taxable as an emolument received in the year in which the option was granted.

12 In *Abbott v Philbin* 39 TC 82, the taxpayer, a secretary of a company, was given an option in October 1954, to acquire shares of the company at the then market price. He paid £20 for the option, which was expressed to be non-transferable and was exercisable only for ten years or until the taxpayer's earlier death or retirement. The Crown sought to tax a sum equal to the difference between the market price at the date when the option was exercised, which was some two years after it was granted, and the price payable under the option. In the House of Lords it was held that the option was a perquisite of the taxpayer's employment when it was granted and that the benefit he obtained from the subsequent increase in the value of the shares stemmed from the rights conferred by the option and not from his employment.

13   The argument for the Crown was that the option was something which, like the right to occupy the bank house in *Tennant v Smith* [1892] AC 150, could not have been turned to pecuniary account when it was granted, and that the advantage the taxpayer got when he exercised his option was a perquisite of his employment. As I have indicated these arguments were rejected by a majority in the House of Lords. I do not propose to cite extensively from the speeches in the House of Lords. Lord Reid said on page 120 :

14   'I agree that the question is whether this option was a right of a kind which could be turned to pecuniary account. I do not use these words as a definition, but it is undesirable to invent a new phrase if an old one of high authority fits this case, and the parties agree that it does. But the test must be the nature of the right and not whether this particular option could readily have been turned to pecuniary account in October, 1954. Whether this option could then have been turned to pecuniary account is a question of fact, and there is no finding about it. It is true that the option was not transferable, but there are other ways of turning such a right to pecuniary account than assigning it or calling for immediate performance of the obligation to allot the shares. Even taking this particular option, I find nothing to indicate that there would have been much difficulty in finding someone who would have paid a substantial sum for an undertaking by the Appellant to apply for the shares when supplied with the purchase money and called upon to exercise the option, and thereupon to transfer the shares. It is not an unreasonable inference from the whole circumstances that both the Appellant and his employers must have thought the option worth a good deal more than £20, and others may have thought the same. No doubt a person who wished to acquire an option on the shares would pay less for an undertaking such as I have indicated than he would pay for an assignable option because of the risks involved, but that only goes to valuation of the right which the Appellant acquired. And if it is asked, why buy such an undertaking instead of buying shares on the market, the answer is that people often do prefer buying options to buying shares. I am not prepared to assume, in the absence of a finding, that this option could not have been turned to pecuniary account when it was granted.' *(pg758)*

Lord Radcliffe said at page 125:

'I think that the Crown are right in saying that a line has to be drawn somewhere between convertible and non-convertible benefits and that somehow we have to put a general meaning on the not very precise language used in *Tennant v Smith*. What I do not think, however, is that a non-assignable option to take up freely assignable shares lies on that side of the line which contains the untaxable benefits in kind. The option, when paid for, was thereafter a contractual right, enforceable against the company at any time during the next ten years so long as the holder paid the stipulated price and remained in its service. That right is, in my opinion, analogous for this purpose to any other benefit in the form of land, objects of value, or legal rights. It was not incapable of being turned into money or of being turned to pecuniary account within the meaning of these phrases in *Tennant v Smith* merely because the option itself was not assignable. What the option did was to enable the holder, at any time at his choice, to obtain shares from the company which would themselves be pieces of property or property rights of value, freely convertible into money. Being in that position he could also, at any time at his choice, sell or raise money on his right to call for the shares, even though he could not put anyone he dealt with actually into his own position as option holder against the company. I think that the conferring of a right of this kind as an incident of service is a profit or perquisite which is taxable as such in the year of receipt, so long as the right itself can fairly be given a monetary value; and it is no more relevant for this purpose whether the option is exercised or not in that year than it would be if the advantage received were in the form of some tangible form of commercial property.'

15 The Respondent points out that the option granted to him differs from the option granted to the taxpayer in *Abbott v Philbin* in that, (save to a limited extent on death or retirement and in certain other analogous circumstances) it was not exercisable for seven years and was only exercisable while he remained in employment in a company within the group and maintained payments under the save-as-you-earn contract. That being so the option, he says, was purely personal and incapable of being turned to pecuniary account. This argument was very persuasively developed by the Respondent in his written and oral submissions, but although I do not find the point an easy one, I have reached the conclusion on balance that the option granted to the Respondent was a taxable perquisite of his employment at the time it was granted.

16 Lord Reid in the passage I have cited poses the question, whether 'this option was a right of a kind which could be turned to pecuniary account' and stresses that 'the test must be the nature of the right and not whether this particular option could readily have been turned to pecuniary account'. In the present case the Commissioners have found that the option granted to the Respondent taxpayer 'was chargeable to tax at the time of its acquisition as an emolument', and it is, I think, important in this finding that they were satisfied that the option had a monetary return although they also took the view that on the evidence before them they could not form an estimate of its value. That is a conclusion of fact, but I should say on the evidence before the Commissioners that conclusion was to my mind inevitable. No doubt it would have been very difficult for the Respondent to have realised the value of the option when it was first granted, but an option to acquire shares at less than the then market price, albeit after a period of time and, in broad terms, conditionally on remaining in the employment of a company in the Group and maintaining the save-as-you-earn contract for seven years, must *prima facie* be taken to be a right of a kind which has a monetary value. It could have been realised, as Lord Reid and Lord Radcliffe point out by an arrangement with a third party under which the Respondent agreed to exercise the option in accordance with the direction of the third party and to transfer any shares obtained on the exercise of the option to him, the third party undertakes to maintain the save-as-you-earn contract although no doubt there would have to have been some provision for the return of the consideration paid to the Respondent under the arrangement and the moneys paid under the save-as-you-earn contract with interest if the option lapsed before it was exercised. Such provision would have been necessary in an arrangement entered into by the taxpayer in *Abbott* v *Philbin* to realise the value of his option and given the small number of shares in question the small discount on market value and the period which would have to elapse before the option could be exercised, it would no doubt have been difficult to find a third party willing to pay a sum for, in effect, the right to stand in the shoes of the Respondent. But the question whether rights conferred by an option are of a kind which brings them into charge as a perquisite cannot it seems to me turn an assessment of the degree of difficulty in finding a third party willing to enter into such an arrangement, unless possibly, the taxpayer can establish by positive evidence that it would have been not merely difficult but practically impossible to find a third party willing to enter into such an arrangement so that (in the words of Lord Radcliffe) the option was not a right which could 'fairly be given a monetary return'. There was no such evidence before the Commissioners.

17 For the reasons I have given I think the Commissioners were justified in their conclusion that the benefit of this option was a perquisite for the year when it was received but wrong in their conclusion that it had no assessable value. The value must be assessed in accordance with s77(2). I must accordingly allow this appeal.

Case 34
Stanton v Drayton

[1982] STC 585

House of Lords

4, 5, 6 May and 8 July 1982

This case considers when it is necessary to value shares.

Where unconnected persons make a bargain at arm's length the consideration is the sum that actually passes from the purchaser to the vendor. The market value of the shares is not substituted as deemed consideration.

On 21 September 1972, Drayton Commercial Investment Co Ltd purchased a portfolio of investments from Eagle Star Insurance Company Ltd for £3,937,962. The price was satisfied, in accordance with the agreement between the companies, by the allotment by the taxpayer company to Eagle Star of 2,461,226 ordinary shares of 25p each in the taxpayer company, the issue price of each share being 160p.

The Eagle Star ords were allotted on 11 October, and were first quoted on the Stock Exchange on 12 October 1972. The opening price on the Stock Market was 125p per ord.

Subsequently, Drayton Commercial Investment Co Ltd sold the investments it had acquired. In order to compute the gain arising on the sale, it was necessary to determine the acquisition cost. The taxpayer company submitted that the acquisition cost was the sum of £3,937,962, as this was the sum specified in a commercial agreement between unconnected parties. The Revenue submitted that the base cost was the market value of the shares issued as consideration. Initially, the Revenue contended that the market value was 125p per share, being the opening price of the London Stock Exchange; subsequently, the Revenue conceded that the market price of a single holding of 2.4 million shares may be higher than the price at which small parcels of shares trade on the Stock Market.

The House of Lords declared there is no authority for using the market value as consideration when there is an agreed sum of consideration between the parties. Hence, the base cost for the portfolio investments purchased by Drayton Commercial Investment Co Ltd was £3,937,962 and not the lower figure for which the Revenue argued.

In the leading judgement in the House of Lords, Lord Fraser of Tulleybelton said:

> 'The consideration was the taxpayer company's shares. That is, I think, how any businessman would have seen the transaction, and it is the commercial reality. Counsel for the taxpayer company argued that the correct legal analysis was not for businessmen, but for lawyers and I agree, subject to this, that the lawyer must have regard to the businessman's view. From the lawyer's point of view, it seems plain beyond argument that what Eagle Star received as consideration for its portfolio was the taxpayer company's shares. It may be possible for the taxpayer company to have given something different from that which Eagle Star received although that seems *prima facie* unlikely. I would only accept such a comparatively complicated analysis if it was the only satisfactory way of explaining what had occurred. But in this case I do not think it is. It is stated in the agreement that the price of 3.9 million pounds will be satisfied by the allotment of 2.4 million shares and that seems entirely consistent with the view that the shares were the consideration.'
>
> ([1982] STC 585 at 588e–g case 34 para 9)

To which Lord Roskill added:

> 'What then is the value of the shares? The Crown contended that it must be determined by reference to Stock Exchange prices on the day after the shares were first dealt in. I ask, why?
>
> The agreement was concluded on 21 September 1972. It became unconditional on 11 October 1972. My Lords, by virtue of para 10(2) of Sch 10 to the Finance Act 1971, I think it was on the latter date that the acquisition by the taxpayer company is to be treated as having been made. But I am quite unable to regard the evidence of some Stock Exchange dealings at or about the time as sufficient evidence to displace what I would regard as the almost overwhelming evidence of the value of the consideration in money's worth on 11 October 1972, afforded by the agreement of 21 September 1972.
>
> On the facts of the instant case, I can see no basis on which it would be legitimate to go behind the figure of 160p per share.'
>
> ([1982] STC 585 at 595d–g case 34 paras 33 and 34)

Judgement

References, example '(pg586h)', are to [1982] STC 585.

1 Lord Fraser of Tullybelton: My Lords, this appeal concerns the *(pg586h)* computation of chargeable gains for the purpose of Corporation Tax. They have to be computed in accordance with the rules for Capital Gains Tax, although they are actually assessed to Corporation Tax, because the taxpayer is a company – see Income and Corporation Taxes Act 1970, sec. 238 and sec. 265.

2 The respondent is Drayton Commercial Investment Company Limited ('Drayton'). In 1972 Drayton (then called Union Commercial *(pg586j)* Investment Company Limited) acquired from the Eagle Star Insurance Company Limited ('Eagle Star') a portfolio of investments at the price of £3,937,962 (which I shall refer to as £3.9 million). The price was satisfied, in accordance with the agreement between the companies, by the allotment by Drayton to Eagle Star of 2,461,226 ordinary shares of 25p each in Drayton, the issue price of each share being 160p. I shall refer to the number of shares allotted as 2.4 million. Drayton subsequently disposed of some of the investments, so that it became material, in order to ascertain the amount of its capital gains, to determine *(pg587a)* the amount or value of the consideration which it had given for the investments. Drayton contends that the value of the consideration was the issue price of the shares allotted to Eagle Star (160p) multiplied by the number of shares allotted (2.4 million). The appellant, on behalf of the Inland Revenue, originally contended that the consideration was the market price of the Drayton shares allotted on the day when they were first quoted, which was the day after their allotment, multiplied by 2.4 million. *(pg587b)* That price was 125p. During the hearing in your Lordships' House the appellant departed from that contention to some extent and submitted that the value of the consideration fell to be ascertained by the best evidence, and that, although the market value on the day the shares were first quoted would be some evidence, it was not conclusive. The market value was probably the price paid for comparatively small parcels of shares, and evidence might well show that the price *(pg587c)* that could have been obtained for 2.4 million shares, if they had all been offered for sale on the day they were first quoted, would have been substantially lower. It was common ground between counsel that the only question for decision at this stage was whether Drayton's contention was sound in principle, and that, if not, (i.e. if the appeal succeeds on the question of principle) the matter must be remitted to the Special Commissioners to ascertain the true value of the consideration *(pg587d)* and to make any necessary amendment in the assessment consequent thereupon.

3 The Special Commissioners upheld Drayton's contention. Vinelott J reversed their decision and remitted the case to them to value the consideration. The Court of Appeal (Waller, Oliver, and Fox LJJ) allowed the appeal and restored the decision of the Special Commissioners. *(pg587e)*

4 The agreement under which the portfolio was acquired by Drayton was dated 21 September 1972. By cl. 1 it provided *inter alia* as follows:

'1. The vendor [Eagle Star] will sell and the purchaser [Drayton] will purchase all the securities in the said portfolio at the price of £3,937,962 to be satisfied by the allotment by [Drayton] to [Eagle Star] of *(pg587f)* 2,461,226 ordinary shares of 25p each in [Drayton] the issue price of each such share for the purpose of satisfying the consideration being 160p. The said ordinary shares in [Drayton] when issued will be credited as fully paid up ...'

5 The agreement was subject to two conditions set out in cl. 2 which provides as follows: *(pg587g)*

'This agreement is conditional upon:
(i) the members of [Drayton] passing the necessary resolution of the company in general meeting creating the new shares in [Drayton] required to satisfy the consideration above mentioned
(ii) the Stock Exchange London granting permission to deal in and quotation for such new shares (subject to allotment) before 31 October 1972.' *(pg587h)*

6 The necessary resolution was passed at a general meeting of Drayton's shareholders on 9 October 1972, and Stock Exchange permission was granted on 11 October. The new shares were allotted on 11 October, and were first quoted on the Stock Exchange on 12 October 1972. I should mention that the portfolio had been valued at middle market quotation on 31 August 1972, and that *(pg587j)* is stated in cl. 4 of the agreement.

7 The statutory provision which is directly applicable is the Finance Act 1965, Sch. 6, para. 4(1)(a) which provides as follows:

'4(1) Subject to the following provisions of this Schedule, the sums allowable as a deduction from the consideration in the computation under this Schedule of the gain accruing to a person on the disposal of an asset shall be restricted to–

(a) the amount or value of the consideration, in money or money's worth, given by him or on his behalf wholly and exclusively for the acquisition of the asset, together with the incidental costs to him of the acquisition ...' *(pg588a)*

The appellant also relied on the Finance Act 1971, Sch. 10, para. 10 on the question of the date on which the consideration should be valued. I shall refer to that matter separately later.

8 In my opinion, para. 4(1)(a) means that the allowable deduction is to be restricted to 'the amount of the consideration, if it is in money, or the value in money's worth *(pg588b)* if it is not in money'. In the present case the consideration was in money's worth and it is therefore necessary to ascertain its value. The first stage is to ascertain exactly what was the consideration given by Drayton. This has been the subject of acute controversy at all stages of the appeal. Vinelott J held that the consideration was the shares in Drayton allotted to Eagle Star. The Court of Appeal held that it was not the shares but 'the benefit of an agreement by *(pg588c)* Drayton (i) to issue and allot the shares and (ii) to credit them as fully paid'. They added 'We should mention here that, as we understand it, the new shares did not exist at the time when the agreement became unconditional (and when, therefore, the acquisition took place). They were issued later on the same day'. When the appeal reached this House counsel for Drayton, while still vigorously rejecting the view that the consideration was the Drayton *(pg588d)* shares, did not fully accept the Court of Appeal's view but submitted that the consideration was 'the credit of £3,937,962 allowed to Eagle Star by [Drayton], which was offset against and extinguished Eagle Star's liability to pay [Drayton] £3,937,962 in consideration of the issue of the new shares in [Drayton] at 160p each'.

9 In my opinion, the consideration was the Drayton shares. That is, I *(pg588e)* think, how any businessman would have seen the transaction, and it is the commercial reality. Counsel for Drayton argued that the correct legal analysis was not for businessmen, but for lawyers and I agree, subject to this, that the lawyer must have regard to the businessman's view. From the lawyer's point of view, it seems plain beyond argument that what Eagle Star received as consideration for its portfolio was the Drayton shares. It may be possible for *(pg588f)* Drayton to have *given* something different from that which Eagle Star *received* although that seems *prima facie* unlikely. I would only accept such a comparatively complicated analysis if it was the only satisfactory way of explaining what had occurred. But in this case I do not think it is. It is stated in the agreement that the price of 3.9 million pounds will be satisfied by the allotment of 2.4 million shares and that seems entirely consistent with the view that the shares were the *(pg588g)* consideration. The view contended for by Drayton, and substantially accepted by the Court of Appeal, was based mainly on two decisions on questions of company law, namely *Osborne v Steel Barrel Co. Ltd.* [1942] 1 All E.R. 634 *and Craddock v Zevo Finance Co. Ltd.* (1944) 27 T.C. 267. Neither of these cases was concerned with the question which arises here.

10 In *Osborne* a new company had acquired stock in trade for a consideration *(pg588h)* consisting partly of cash and partly of shares which it issued as fully paid. The Crown's contention was that the shares had cost the company nothing and that the stock should be entered in its books simply at the amount of cash paid for it. It is perhaps not surprising that that contention failed. In the Court of Appeal Lord Greene MR said at p. 638 G that 'on the facts of [that] case' the issue of the fully paid shares represented a payment in cash equal to the par value of the *(pg588j)* shares, mainly because the only alternative would have been that the shares had been issued at a discount which would have been illegal, and no illegality was alleged. In the present appeal no question of issuing shares at discount arises and neither party contends that Drayton's shares should be valued at par. The only part of Lord Greene's opinion which seems to bear upon the present appeal is at p. 638 A where he said this:

'A company cannot issue £1,000 nominal worth of shares for stock of the market value of £500, since shares cannot be issued at a discount. Accordingly, *(pg589a)* when fully paid shares are properly issued for a consideration other than cash, the consideration moving from the company must be at the least equal in value to the par value of the shares *and must be based on an honest estimate by the directors of the value of the assets acquired.*' (Emphasis added.)

As regards the nature of the consideration moving from the company, the decision was that the price paid for the stock was cash plus shares and it is thus entirely *(pg589b)* consistent with the contention of the Crown in the present case that the consideration moving from (which is the same as given by) Drayton was the shares themselves. But on the question of value, it supports the contention of Drayton that the value must be based on an honest estimate by the directors of the value of the assets acquired, which in this case was £3.9 million, and not upon the market value of the shares allotted. *(pg589c)*

11 The other case, much canvassed in argument, was *Craddock* where there had been a reconstruction of a family company which dealt in investments. A new company had been formed to take over and hold some of the investments of the former company, and the question was as to the basis on which these investments should be valued for income tax purposes in the books of the new company. The decision of the Court of Appeal, which was upheld by this House, was that the value *(pg589d)* of the investments was their purchase price, which was the price that the new company had agreed to pay, and that the amount paid in shares of the new company should be taken to be the par value of the shares. The following passage in the judgment of Lord Greene MR at p. 277 was relied on by counsel for Drayton: *(pg589e)*

'The fallacy, if I may respectfully so call it, which underlies the argument [for the Crown in that case] is to be found in the assertion that where a company issues its own shares as consideration for the acquisition of property, these shares are to be treated as money's worth as though they were shares in another company altogether, transferred by way of consideration for the acquisition. This proposition amounts to saying that consideration in the form of fully paid shares allotted by a company must be treated as being of the value of the shares, *(pg589f)* no more and no less. Such a contention will not bear a moment's examination where the transaction is a straightforward one and not a mere device for issuing shares at a discount.'

In this House Lord Simonds said this: (27 T.C. 267 at p. 295) *(pg589g)*

'I cannot distinguish between consideration and purchase price, and ... I find that, acquiring the investments "under a bona fide and unchallengeable contract" they paid the price which that contract required, a price which, whether too high or low according to the views of third parties, was the price upon which these parties agreed.'

From these judgments I extract the following propositions relevant to the present *(pg589h)* appeal. 1. A company can issue its own shares 'as consideration for the acquisition of property' – as Lord Greene said. 2. The value of consideration given in the form of fully paid shares allotted by a company is not the value of the shares allotted but, in the case of an honest and straightforward transaction, is the price upon which the parties agreed – as Lord Simonds said. The latter point was expressed even more forcibly in the House of Lords by Lord Wright at p. 290 where he said: 'No authority *(pg589j)* was cited for the claim of the Revenue in a case like this to go behind the *agreed consideration* and substitute a different figure' (emphasis added).

12 The Court of Appeal in the passage I have quoted from their decision seems to have thought that the fact that the new shares issued by Drayton were not in existence at the time when the agreement with Eagle Star became unconditional was a further reason why they were not the consideration given by Drayton. I confess that I do not follow their reasoning on this point. At the time when the agreement became unconditional Drayton came *(pg590a)* under an unconditional obligation to hand over the consideration (whatever it might be) to Eagle Star and they did so later the same day. The fact that the consideration in the form of shares did not come into existence until some hours after the obligation had become unconditional seems to me irrelevant. Indeed, if the view of the Court of Appeal is right it might lead to the consequence that the 'benefit' or the 'credit' given by Drayton must either have been transmuted into the new *(pg590b)* shares before it was received by Eagle Star, or must have been received by Eagle Star and subsequently disposed of by Eagle Star in exchange for the new shares. Such a double disposal seems quite unrealistic and I see no reason for importing it.

13 Accordingly, I am of opinion that the consideration given by Drayton was the same as that received by Eagle Star and was the new shares. The next step is to ascertain the value of that consideration. The argument for the *(pg590c)* Crown, which was accepted by Vinelott J, was that 'value' in para. 4(1)(a) of Sch. 6 to the Finance Act 1965 meant 'market value' and might be different from the price agreed between the parties. It was said that the value of consideration was something to be determined by reference to an objective standard, and not by reference to the cost to a particular party. I was at first attracted by this argument. But further reflection has convinced me that it is erroneous for two reasons. First, as a pure *(pg590d)* matter of construction of para. 4(1)(a), I see no indication that value is used as meaning market value. The paragraph is part of the general provisions for computing the amount of gain accruing on the disposal of an asset in the ordinary case – see sec. 22(9) of the Act. It is to be contrasted with sec. 22(4) of the Act which makes provision for some special cases, including the case where a person acquires an asset 'otherwise than by way of a bargain made at arm's length and in *(pg590e)* particular where he acquires it by way of gift'. Section 22(4) shall be deemed to be for a consideration equal to the 'market value' of the asset, and the obvious reason is that no agreed value, arrived at by an arm's length transaction, is available. But in the ordinary case under para. 4(1)(a) such a value is available – namely the price agreed between the parties. Consequently there is no need to look to the market value, and no need to read in the word 'market' *(pg590f)* before value where Parliament has not seen fit to use it. Further, the deduction permitted by para. 4(1)(a) includes 'the incidental costs *to him* [the taxpayer] of the acquisition' (emphasis added). The words that I have emphasised show that, at least so far as the costs of acquisition are concerned, it is the costs to the particular taxpayer that are relevant and they are some indication that the value of the consideration given by him is to be calculated on the same basis. *(pg590g)*

14 Secondly, the cases of *Osborne* and *Craddock supra* are ample authority for saying, in the words of Lord Wright in the latter case, that the Revenue is not entitled to go behind the agreed consideration in a case where, as in the present case, the transaction is not alleged to be dishonest or otherwise not straightforward.

15 If I am right in thinking that the agreed value of the newly allotted shares, in a bargain at arm's length, is conclusive, no question arises about the date at which the *(pg590h)* value of the shares should be ascertained. It is therefore unnecessary to refer to the contentions of the parties on that matter, or to the provisions of the Finance Act 1971, Sch. 10, para. 10, which was relied on by the Crown.

16 One consequence of taking the agreed value of the shares as conclusive is that cases may occur in which that value may seem surprising, because the market value of the newly allotted shares on the day when they are first quoted proves to be much *(pg590j)* higher or much lower than their value agreed between the parties. That might happen, for example, because of some unexpected political event occurring between the date of the agreement and the date of the first quotation. But, provided the agreed value has been honestly reached by a bargain at arm's length, it must, in my opinion, be final and it is not open to attack by the Inland Revenue. Not only is that right in principle, but it is very much in accordance with practical convenience. Once it is accepted, as it was (rightly in my opinion) by counsel appearing for the Crown, that market value could not necessarily be ascertained almost instantly by reference to *(pg591a)* the Stock Exchange price list, but might have to be proved by the evidence of accountants and other financial experts, the practical inconvenience of leaving agreements liable to be reopened to such enquiry becomes clear. I do not believe that Parliament can have intended to permit that inconvenience in cases where bargains have been made at arm's length.

PART 2 Cases

17 For these reasons, which are somewhat different from those of the Court of *(pg591b)* Appeal, I would dismiss this appeal.

18 Lord Russell of Killowen: My Lords, I have had the advantage of reading in draft the speeches prepared by my noble and learned friends, Lord Fraser of Tullybelton and Lord Roskill. I concur with their opinions that this appeal be dismissed. *(pg591c)*

19 Lord Keith of Kinkel: My Lords, I have had the benefit of reading in draft the speech prepared by my noble and learned friend, Lord Fraserof Tullybelton. I agree with it, and for the reasons which he gives I, too, would dismiss the appeal.

20 Lord Roskill: My Lords, this appeal from a decision of the Court of Appeal *(pg591d)* (Waller, Oliver and Fox LJJ) dated 25 June 1981, raises a short but to my mind difficult question under para. 4(1) of Sch. 6 to the Finance Act 1965. The essential facts are simple and have been fully set out in the judgments in the courts below. I need only restate them in outline. On 21 September 1972 the respondents – I shall call them 'Drayton' though they bore a different name at that date – concluded a conditional agreement with Eagle Star Insurance Company Limited – 'Eagle Star' – for the purchase by the respondents of a large portfolio of securities belonging to Eagle Star. The price was *(pg591e)* £3,937,962. That price was to be satisfied by the allotment by Drayton to Eagle Star of 2,461,226 Ordinary Shares of 25p each. Those shares were to be issued by Drayton and credited as fully paid, the issue price of each share being 160p. The agreement was subject to two conditions, first, the passing of the necessary resolution by Drayton creating those shares, and second, the grant by the Stock Exchange of permission to deal in them and of a *(pg591f)* quotation for them before 31 October 1972. The necessary resolution was passed by Drayton on the 9 October 1972. The requisite Stock Exchange permissions were granted on 11October 1972. On that date the agreement became unconditional. It was common ground that the agreement was an arm's length transaction. Later, Drayton sold some of the securities so purchased, and became liable to corporation tax on the resultant gains. That corporation tax *(pg591g)* is chargeable in accordance with the law relating to capital gains tax by virtue of sec. 236 and 265 of the Income and Corporation Taxes Act 1970. The question which arises is how those capital gains are to be calculated.

21 My Lords, the Revenue made an assessment to tax on Drayton on the basis that the value of the consideration given by Drayton was to be taken as a sum equal to the market value of the new shares, determined by reference *(pg591h)* to Stock Exchange quoted prices on the day after those shares were first quoted after their allotment. Drayton appealed to the Special Commissioners, contending that the relevant figure was the price at which those shares were issued, namely their par value plus the premium, amounting in all to £3,937,962. Since that figure was based on the issue price of 160p per share, and the first quoted price was said to be only 125p per share, the difference was considerable, and was stated *(pg591j)* in the courts below to involve some £800,000.

22 My Lords, the Special Commissioners upheld Drayton's contentions. Before them it was argued, on Drayton's behalf, that as a matter of law they must hold that the value of the consideration given by Drayton was 160p per share, and the Special Commissioners were invited, first, to determine whether or not that contention was correct, it apparently being agreed that if it were held thereafter to be incorrect, the matter should be remitted to the Special Commissioners for determination of the value of the consideration in *(pg592a)* accordance with whatever might be held to be the correct principles.

23 My Lords, the Special Commissioners stated a case at the request of the Revenue. Vinelott J reversed their decision. His judgment is reported at [1980] 1 W.L.R. 1162. Drayton appealed to the Court of Appeal who restored the decision of the Special Commissioners. Their decision is reported at [1981] STC 525. The Court of Appeal gave leave to appeal to your Lordships' House on condition that the Revenue did not seek to disturb the order as to costs which that court had made. *(pg592b)*

24 My Lords, the relevant statutory provision is to be found in para. 4(1) of Sch. 6 to the Finance Act 1965. It reads, so far as relevant, as follows:

'Subject to the following provisions of this Schedule, the sums allowable as a deduction from the consideration in computation under this Schedule of the *(pg592c)* gain accruing to a person on the disposal of an asset shall be restricted to–

(a) the amount or value of the consideration, in money or money's worth, given by him or on his behalf wholly and exclusively for the acquisition of the asset, together with the incidental costs to him of the acquisition.'.

'Incidental costs' are defined in subpara. (b) which it is not necessary to quote. My *(pg592d)* Lords, I think the opening words of subpara. (a) must be read as meaning 'the amount in money or the value in money's worth of the consideration'. On this view the question is what is 'the value in money's worth of the consideration given' by Drayton for the acquisition of the new shares issued to Eagle Star and credited as fully paid.

25 The Revenue strenuously contended that the price specified in the agreement was *(pg592e)* not the value in money's worth of the consideration but was the cost. Value, it was said, was different from cost and was to be determined – at one time it was faintly suggested to be determined objectively – but at any rate not exclusively by reference to the cost, even though the transaction was an arm's length transaction.

26 My Lords, the argument for Drayton which found favour both with the Special Commissioners and the Court of Appeal for, as I read their respective *(pg592f)* reasoning, substantially the same reasons, was that the consideration which was given by Drayton was not the new shares themselves, but Drayton's agreement to issue and allot them and, most important, to credit them as fully paid. Drayton, it was said, had the right to require payment of the price of 160p per share but forewent that right, giving credit for that amount instead. It was the value of that credit which Drayton so provided to *(pg592g)* Eagle Star which was the consideration, and the value of that credit was 160p per share. The Revenue were not entitled to go behind that figure in the case of an arm's length transaction unless they 'impeached' the agreement of 21 September 1972, which the Revenue accepted they could not do in the instant case.

27 My Lords, the submission was that it was the value of the credit given by Drayton which was in truth the consideration the value of which had to *(pg592h)* be determined, and was founded upon authority. In his speech in your Lordships' House in *Ooregum Gold Mining Co. Ltd. of India v Roper* [1892] A.C. 125, Lord Watson in a well-known passage said:

> 'A company is free to contract with an applicant for its shares; and when he pays in cash the nominal amount of the shares allotted to him, the company may at once return the money in satisfaction of its legal indebtedness for goods *(pg592j)* supplies or services rendered by him. That circuitous process is not essential. It has been decided that under the Act of 1862, shares may be lawfully issued as fully paid up, for considerations which the company has agreed to accept as representing in money's worth the nominal value of the shares. I do not think any other decision could have been given in the case of a genuine transaction of that nature where the consideration was the substantial equivalent of full payment of the shares in cash. The possible objection to such an arrangement is that the company may overestimate the value of the consideration and, *(pg593a)* therefore, receive less than nominal value for its shares. The court would doubtless refuse effect to a colourable transaction, entered into for the purpose or with the obvious result of enabling the company to issue its shares at a discount; but it has been ruled that, so long as the company honestly regards the consideration given as fairly representing the nominal value of the shares in cash, its estimate ought not to be critically examined.' *(pg593b)*

This statement of the law was subsequently applied both by Vaughan Williams J and the Court of Appeal in *In re Wragg Ltd.* [1897] 1 Ch. 796 at pp. 813–4, and 831 and 835 respectively. Those decisions are also clear authority for the proposition that unless the agreement in furtherance of which the shares were issued for a consideration other than cash can be successfully impeached as, for example, colourable, the courts will not go behind it and consider whether or not it was commercially *(pg593c)* prudent, or whether a more advantageous bargain might have been made, since to do so would be to question the honest commercial judgment of the directors of the company concerned in the ordinary management of that company's business.

28 My Lords, a similar question arose in two later cases in the Court of Appeal, *Osborne* v *Steel Barrel Co. Ltd.* [1942] 1 All E.R. 634, and *Craddock* v *Zevo Finance Co. Ltd.* [1944] 1 All E.R. 566, the latter decision having been *(pg593d)* affirmed by your Lordships' House at (1946) 27 T.C. 267 at p. 284.

29 Both those cases involved the determination of the cost to the taxpayer of 'stock' – in the second case the 'stock' was a number of investments – for the purpose of calculating the taxpayer's trading profit in connection with his liability to income tax. In both cases the 'stock' had been acquired in whole or in part in return for the allotment of shares credited as fully paid, the shares being issued for a consideration *(pg593e)* other than cash. In both cases the taxpayer contended that the cost was what the taxpayer had paid. In both cases the Revenue sought to go behind the agreement pursuant to which those shares were so issued, and to contend that the issue of the shares credited as fully paid had cost the taxpayer either nothing, or at any rate, less than the price for which the taxpayer contended. In both cases the Revenue failed. *(pg593f)* They failed for substantially the same reason, namely, that their contention ignored the true nature of the issue of shares credited as fully paid for a consideration other than *(pg593h)* cash. In the former case Lord Greene MR at pp. 637–38, said:

> 'The argument really rests on a misconception as to what happens when a company issues shares credited as fully paid for a consideration other than cash. The primary liability of an allottee of shares is to pay for them in cash; but when shares are allotted credited as fully paid, this primary liability is satisfied by a consideration other than cash passing from the allottee. A company, therefore, when, in pursuance of such a transaction, it agrees to credit the shares as fully paid, is giving up what it would otherwise have had – namely, the right to call on the allottee for payment of the par value in cash. A company cannot issue £1,000 nominal worth of shares for stock of the market value of £500, since shares cannot be issued at a discount. Accordingly, when fully-paid shares are properly issued for a consideration other than cash, the consideration moving from the company must be at the least equal in value to the par value of the shares and must be based on an honest estimate by the directors of the value of the assets acquired.' *(pg593j)*

In the latter case, Lord Greene MR at pp. 569–70 said of the Revenue's argument:

> 'This proposition amounts to saying that consideration in the form of fully paid shares allotted by a company must be treated as being the value of the shares, no more and no less. Such a contention will not bear a moment's examination where the transaction is a straightforward one and not a mere device for issuing shares at a discount. In the everyday case of reconstruction, *(pg594a)* the shares in the new company allotted to the shareholders of the old company as fully paid will often, if not in most cases, fetch substantially less than their nominal value if sold in the market. But

this does not mean that they are to be treated as having been issued at a discount; or that the price paid by the new company for the assets which it acquires from the old company ought to be treated as something less than the nominal value of the fully-paid shares. The *(pg594b)* Crown in this case is in fact attempting to depart from the rule (the correctness of which it itself admits) that the figure at which stock-in-trade is to be brought in is its cost to the trader and to substitute the alleged market value of the stock for its cost. Of course, in a case where stock which a company proposes to acquire for shares is deliberately over-valued for the purpose of issuing an inflated amount of share capital, very different considerations apply. But *(pg594c)* nothing of the kind is present in this case which, as I have already pointed out, is a perfectly proper and normal reconstruction. The propriety of the course adopted is manifest when the uncertainty as to the value of the investments, which is pointed out by the Commissioners, is borne in mind. It is, I think, true as a general proposition that, where a company acquires property for fully-paid shares of its own, the price paid by the company is, *prima facie*, the nominal *(pg594d)* value of the shares. It is for those who assert the contrary to establish it, as could be done, for example, in the suggested case of a deliberately inflated valuation.'

This passage was expressly approved in your Lordships' House – see Viscount Simon LC at (1946) 27 T.C. 267 at p. 287, and Lord Simonds at p. 294.

30 My Lords, it is thus established beyond question, that in ascertaining the cost of acquiring 'stock' for the purpose of arriving at the taxpayer's trading profit when *(pg594e)* that stock has been acquired in return for shares credited as fully paid, being issued for a consideration other than cash, it is the cost to the taxpayer of that stock which is, at least *prima facie*, the relevant figure, and that unless the agreement can for some reason be 'impeached', the Revenue are not entitled to go behind the price which the taxpayer has paid whatever the means by which that obligation to pay that price has by agreement between the parties been discharged. *(pg594f)*

31 My Lords, in those circumstances, the crucial question is how far these well-established principles are to be applied to the ascertainment of 'the value of the consideration … in money's worth given by [the taxpayer] … wholly and exclusively for the acquisition of the asset' for the purposes of para. 4(1)(a) of Sch. 6 to the 1965 Act. For the taxpayer it is forcibly argued that there is no logical reason why its liability for corporation tax on its gains should be determined in some different way *(pg594g)* from its liability to corporation tax on its trading profits. For the Revenue it is forcibly argued that the decisions to which I have referred are decisions concerning the ascertainment of the cost of 'stock' for the purpose of arriving at the taxpayer's trading profit for income tax purposes, that that cost has been held in the circumstances in question to be the price which the taxpayer paid, that cost is different from value, and that value has to be determined by reference to matters *(pg594h)* other than cost, though ultimately it was conceded by learned counsel for the Revenue before your Lordships though not, I think, in the courts below, that cost might be relevant to the determination of value.

32 But, my Lords, if it be correct as both the Special Commissioners and the Court of Appeal thought, to say that in the present case the consideration given by Drayton was Drayton's agreement to issue and allot the *(pg594j)* shares and to credit them as fully paid, the respondents must unquestionably succeed, for it is obvious, since the agreement between Eagle Star and Drayton cannot be impeached, that the value of that credit was 160p per share. But in the passages of the judgments of Lord Greene MR to which I have referred, he was explaining the nature of an agreement to issue shares credited as fully paid and otherwise than for cash, in order to lay the foundation for the rejection of the Revenue's argument that the 'stock' in question had cost the taxpayer nothing. I do *(pg595a)* not think that the learned Master of the Rolls was intending to lay down a rule that in every case where there is an arm's length transaction, such as that now in question, the consideration must always be taken to be the value of the credit given by the company whose shares are being issued and credited as fully paid, and not the shares themselves. What the consideration is in any particular case must be determined by reference to the contract which the parties concerned have *(pg595b)* concluded. If one looks at paragraph 1 of the agreement of 21 September 1972, it seems to me plain that the consideration was the shares themselves. I do not think that any business man if asked would say that the consideration was the giving of the credit by Drayton of 160p per share, and if it be permissible to see how the parties themselves regarded the matter, Drayton in their next annual report informed their shareholders that the authorised share capital of Drayton had been increased and that the new shares had been allotted to Eagle Star *(pg595c)* at '160p per share in exchange for a portfolio of investments … '.

33 My Lords, I think that this statement reflects both the commercial reality of this arm's length transaction and the true nature of the consideration given by Drayton. Accordingly, I think in respectful disagreement with the Court of Appeal and the Special Commissioners, that the consideration in money's worth *(pg595d)* which has to be valued is the value of the shares and not the value of the credit of which I have spoken. This was, I think, the view of Vinelott J [1980] 1 W.L.R. at p.1170. But, my Lords, to reach that conclusion is not, with respect, to accept the rest of the learned judge's judgment. What then is the value of the shares? The Revenue contended that it must be determined by reference to Stock Exchange prices on the day after the shares *(pg595e)* were first dealt in. I ask, why? Lord Greene himself in *Craddock's case*, at p.569, said:

> 'Published market quotations, which often relate to quite small and isolated transactions, are notoriously no guide to the value of investments of this character, particularly when the amounts involved are large.' *(pg595f)*

Lord Greene's warning is particularly apposite in the present case, and is as much applicable today as forty years ago when it was uttered.

34 My Lords, as I have already said, the agreement was concluded on 21 September 1972. It became unconditional on 11 October 1972. My Lords, by virtue of para. 10(2) of Sch. 10 to the Finance Act 1971, I think it was on the latter date that the acquisition by Drayton is to be treated as having been made. But I am *(pg595g)* quite unable to regard the evidence of some Stock Exchange dealings at or about that time as sufficient evidence to displace what I would regard as the almost overwhelming evidence of the value of the consideration in money's worth on 11 October 1972, afforded by the agreement of 21 September 1972. For myself I would not go as far as to say that in every case of this kind the value of the consideration in money's worth must always be determined by reference to the price at which the *(pg595h)* shares credited as fully paid were issued, for it is possible that there might be a very long delay between the conclusion of the conditional agreement and the agreement becoming unconditional, during which period some catastrophic event might occur gravely affecting the value on the latter date. I would wish to reserve for future consideration whether in such a case it might not be legitimate to adduce evidence, if the evidence were available, pointing to the conclusion that the value of the *(pg595j)* consideration in money's worth was less than the price previously agreed between the parties. But on the facts of the instant case, I can see no basis on which it would be legitimate to go behind the figure of 160p per share. I think this conclusion is strongly reinforced by the finding of the Special Commissioners in para. 10 of the Special Case:

> 'It is not disputed by the Crown that there were *bona fide* commercial reasons for the figure of 160p being somewhat in excess of the price at which the *(pg596a)* appellant's shares were currently being dealt in on the Stock Exchange.' *(pg596a)*

35 My Lords, for the reasons which I have endeavoured to give I agree that this appeal fails and should be dismissed.

36 Lord Brandon of Oakbrook: My Lords, I have had the advantage of reading in draft the speech prepared by my noble and learned friend, Lord Fraser *(pg596b)* of Tullybelton. I agree with his conclusion that the appeal should be dismissed and with the reasons which he gives for arriving at that conclusion.

Case 35
Re Bird Precision Bellows Ltd

[1985] 3 All ER 523

Court of Appeal

1, 2, 3, July 1985

This case is one of a series of cases on a type of company that is referred to as a 'quasi-partnership'. The first valuation case to be considered by the courts on this basis is *Re Yenidje Tobacco Co Ltd* [1916–17] All ER Rep 1050 **case 10**. The concept of 'quasi-partnership' is used, and developed, in *Ebrahimi v Westbourne Galleries Ltd* [1972] 2 All ER 492 **case 31**, *Re Bird Precision Bellows Ltd*, *CVC v Demarco Almeida* [2002] UKPC 16, PC **case 45** and *Strahan v Wilcock* [2006] EWCA Civ 13, CA **case 49**. The last of these cases is particularly important in that the Court of Appeal gives a definition of a 'quasi-partnership' company.

When a shareholder is required to surrender his shares, the amount he should be paid is to be computed on partnership principles, if, and only if, the company is correctly regarded as a 'quasi-partnership'. Where this is the case, the amount paid is a proportionate part of the value of the entire company, without a discount being applied for the size of the shareholding.

In *Re Yenidje Tobacco Co Ltd* [1916–17] All ER Rep 1050 **case 10** and in *Ebrahimi v Westbourne Galleries Ltd* [2006] All ER (D) 106 **case 49**, the court recognised the nature of the company concerned as a 'quasi-partnership' and granted an order to one individual director/shareholder. In *Re Bird Precision Bellows Ltd*, the principle is extended from the two previous cases, in that the order is given by the court is an order for a group of shareholders constituting the majority to pay a fair market price for the shares of a minority; in the previous two cases, the court order was for the winding-up of the company.

In August 1975, EA Armstrong, ST Nin, PA Bird and S Rowden incorporated a company, Bird Precision Bellows Ltd, for the exploitation of certain processes. PA Bird was an expert in the processes exploited by the company. The contribution of EA Armstrong and SD Nin was that they performed substantially in the role of consultants and gave their services to the company in the early stages of its career at very much less than the value which would properly be attributed to those services. The parties fell out in August 1981. EA Armstrong and SD Nin were then removed from the board of directors of the company and in October 1981 they presented a petition under Companies Act 1980, s 75 [now Companies Act 1985, s 459], in which they claimed that they should be bought out. There appears to have been considerable correspondence between the parties with regard to the possibility that the respondents, the majority shareholders, should buy out the petitioners and there was some disagreement over how the price of a purchase ought to be computed.

The Court of Appeal approved the order made in the High Court by Nourse J in which he declared the price to be paid to the minority for the purchase of the shares was to be the pro rata fraction of the value of the entire company, without a discount:

> 'I would expect that in a majority of cases where purchase orders are made under s75 in relation to quasi partnerships the vendor is unwilling in the sense that the sale has been forced on him. Usually he will be a minority shareholder whose interests have been unfairly prejudiced by the manner in which the affairs of the company have been conducted by the majority. On the assumption that the unfair prejudice has made it no longer tolerable for him to retain his interest in the company, a sale of his shares will invariably be his only practical way out short of winding up. In that kind of case it seems to me that it would not merely not be fair, but most unfair, that he should be bought out on the fictional basis applicable to a free election to sell his shares in accordance with the company's articles of association, or indeed on any other basis which involved a discounted price. In my judgement the correct course would be to fix the price pro rata according to the value of the shares as a whole and without any discount, as being the only fair method of compensating an unwilling vendor of the equivalent of a partnership share.'
>
> ([1985] 3 All ER 523 at 527f–h **case 35 para 8**)

Judgement

References, example '(pg525e)', are to [1985] 3 All ER 523.

1 OLIVER LJ: This is an appeal against an order of Nourse J made on 28 October 1983 determining, pursuant to an order previously made by Vinelott J on 23 November 1981, that shares in a private company were to be purchased by the appellants in this appeal, who were the respondents to a petition (hereafter called 'the respondents'), at a price of £18.25 each. I read at this stage only the last three lines of the judge's judgment, where he concluded this part of his judgment in these terms ([1984] 3 All ER 444 at 458, [1984] Ch 419 at 436): *(pg525e)*

'I value the shares of the company as a whole at £547,500. I determine the price at which the respondents are jointly and severally to purchase the shares of the petitioners at £18.25 each'.

2 The way in which this matter came before the court was this. The company was a *(pg525f)* private company, Bird Precision Bellows Ltd, which had been incorporated in 1975. The petitioners, Mr Armstrong and Mr Nin, were the holders of some 7,800 shares out of the total issued capital of 30,000 shares. Nourse J found that the company had been incorporated in the first instance as a sort of quasi partnership between the petitioners and the respondents, who were the majority shareholders, for the exploitation of certain processes with which the principal respondent, Mr Bird, was very much concerned and *(pg525g)* in which he was very expert. The two petitioners were there substantially, I think, in the role of consultants and gave their services to the company in the early stages of its career at very much less than the value which was properly to be attributed to those services.

3 It is unnecessary to go in any great depth into the facts. The parties fell out in August 1981. The petitioners were then removed from the board of directors of the company and in October 1981 they presented a petition under s75 of the Companies Act 1980, *(pg525h)* in which they claimed that they should be bought out. There was also at that stage, although it was subsequently dropped by amendment, an alternative claim to have the company wound up.

4 I think I should read the material parts of s75 because that section has some bearing on what subsequently occurred:

'(1) Any member of a company may apply to the court by petition for an order *(pg525j)* under this section on the ground that the affairs of the company are being or have been conducted in a manner which is unfairly prejudicial to the interests of some part of the members (including at least himself) or that any actual or proposed act or omission of the company (including an act or omission on its behalf) is or would be so prejudicial ...

(3) If the court is satisfied that a petition under this section is well founded it may make such order as it thinks fit for giving relief in respect of the matters complained *(pg526a)* of.

(4) Without prejudice to the generality of subsection (3) above, an order under this section may [and then there are various things which can be done, terminating with] ... (*d*) provide for the purchase of the shares of any members of the company by other members or by the company itself and, in the case of a purchase by the company itself, the reduction of the company's capital accordingly ...' *(pg526b)*

5 What happened in this case was that there appears to have been considerable correspondence between the parties with regard to the possibility that the respondents, the majority shareholders, should buy out the petitioners and there was some disagreement how the price of a purchase ought to be arrived at. Ultimately, when the matter came before the Companies Court, as it did on 23 November 1981, it was dealt with by agreement, and a consent order (although it is not expressed as such) was made *(pg526c)* by Vinelott J on 23 November 1981.

6 The order recites the petition and the evidence which had been filed on it up to that point, and it went on in these terms:

> 'THIS COURT DOTH ORDER pursuant to Section 75 of the Companies Act 1980 that the Respondents [and then it names them] do jointly and severally purchase the *(pg526d)* 3900 shares [it is common ground that that was a mistake for 7,800] shares of the Company registered in the name of the Petitioners [and then it names the petitioners] at such price as the Court shall hereafter determine provided that such purchases may subject to the approval of this Court be effected by means of a reduction of the Share Capital of the Company. AND IT IS ORDERED that on the question of the appropriate purchase price for the said Shares the evidence of the *(pg526e)* Petitioners be filed within 14 days of the date of this order the evidence of the Respondents be filed within 21 days thereafter discovery by exchange of lists do take place on or before the 11th January 1982 with inspection within 14 days thereafter and exchange of reports by experts within 28 days after inspection.'

Then there is another paragraph as regards costs, which I need not read, which provides in effect that the respondents should pay the petitioners' costs of the petition down to *(pg526f)* and including the foot of the order. Then there is a final paragraph, as follows:

> 'Liberty to all parties to apply (1) for further and better particulars of the allegations in the Affidavits (2) for directions as to the payment of the purchase price and interest if appropriate and (3) generally.'

7 Following that order there was a substantial amount of evidence filed; experts were *(pg526g)* engaged and their reports were, as I understand it, duly exchanged and the matter came on for hearing before Nourse J. It appears to have proceeded, up to the date of the hearing before Vinelott J and at least for a month or so thereafter, with commendable celerity, but thereafter it adopted a somewhat molasses-like speed, and it finally terminated in the matter coming before the court on 25 November 1983. As I have already said, the judge, *(pg526h)* having considered all the evidence and the reports of the valuers, concluded in the way which I have read.

8 The basis of the judge's valuation is to be found in, I think, these passages from the judgment. In the first passage Nourse J said ([1984] 3 All ER 444 at 449, [1984] Ch 419 at 429–430):

'Although both ss210 [of the Companies Act 1948, which of course was the predecessor of s75] and 75 are silent on the point, it is axiomatic that a price fixed *(pg526j)* by the court must be fair. While that which is fair may often be generally predicated in regard to matters of common occurrence, it can never be conclusively judged in regard to a particular case until the facts are known. The general observations which I will presently attempt in relation to a valuation of shares by the court under s75 are therefore subject to that important reservation. Broadly speaking, shares in a small private company are acquired either by allotment on its incorporation or by *(pg527a)* transfer or devolution at some later date. In the first category it is a matter of common occurrence for a company to be incorporated in order to acquire an existing business or to start a new one, and in either event for it to be a vehicle for the conduct of a business carried on by two or more shareholders which they could, had they wished, have carried on in partnership together. Although it has been pointed out on the high authority to which I will soon refer that the description *(pg527b)* may be confusing, it is often convenient and it is certainly usual to describe that kind of company as a quasi partnership. In the second category, irrespective of the nature of the company, it is a matter of common occurrence for a shareholder to acquire shares from another at a price which is discounted because they represent a minority holding. It seems to me that some general observations can usefully be made in regard to each of these examples.' *(pg527c)*

Then he referred to the well-known passage in the speech of Lord Wilberforce in *Ebrahimi v Westbourne Galleries Ltd* [1972] 2 All ER 492 at 500, [1973] AC 360 at 379 where, as Nourse J continued –

'his Lordship [ie Lord Wilberforce], having observed that it is not enough that the company is a small one, or a private company, identifies three typical elements, *(pg527d)* one, or probably more, of which will characterise the company as a quasi partnership. They are, firstly, an association formed or continued on the basis of a personal relationship involving mutual confidence, secondly, an agreement or understanding that all or some of the shareholders shall participate in the conduct of the business, and, thirdly, restrictions on share transfers. No doubt [Nourse J went on] these three elements are the most familiar, and perhaps the most important, but they were not *(pg527e)* intended to be exhaustive. In my view there may be other typical and important elements, in particular the provision of capital by all or some of the participants.'

Nourse J continued with a passage which I think has assumed some importance in the argument, so perhaps it is worth reading ([1984] 3 All ER 444 at 449–450, [1984] Ch 419 at 4.30: *(pg527f)*

'I would expect that in a majority of cases where purchase orders are made under s75 in relation to quasi partnerships the vendor is unwilling in the sense that the sale has been forced on him. Usually he will be a minority shareholder whose interests have been unfairly prejudiced by the manner in which the affairs of the company have been conducted by the majority. On the assumption that the unfair prejudice has made it no longer tolerable for him to retain his interest in the *(pg527g)* company, a sale of his shares will invariably be his only practical way out short of winding up. In that kind of case it seems to me that it would not merely not be fair, but most unfair, that he should be bought out on the fictional basis applicable to a free election to sell his shares in accordance with the company's articles of association, or indeed on any other basis which involved a discounted price. In my judgment the correct course would be to fix the price pro rata according to the value of the *(pg527h)* shares as a whole and without any discount, as being the only fair method of compensating an unwilling vendor of the equivalent of a partnership share. Equally, if the order provided, as it did in *Re Jermym Street Turkish Baths Ltd* [1971] 3 All ER 184, [1971] 1 WLR 1042, for the purchase of the shares of the delinquent majority, it would not merely not be fair, but most unfair, that they should receive a price which involved an element of premium.' *(pg527j)*

Then in a second passage Nourse J said ([1984] 3 All ER 444 at 450, [1984] Ch 419 at 431):

'Next, I must consider the example from the second category of cases in which, broadly speaking, shares in a small private company are acquired. It is not of direct relevance for present purposes, but I mention it briefly in order finally to refute the suggestion that there is any rule of universal application to questions of this kind. *(pg528a)* In the case of the shareholder who acquires shares from another at a price which is discounted because they represent a minority it is to my mind self-evident that there cannot be any universal or even a general rule that he should be bought out under s75 on a more favourable basis, even in a case where his predecessor has been a quasi partner in a quasi partnership. He might himself have acquired the shares purely for investment and played no part in the affairs of the company. In that *(pg528b)* event it might well be fair, I do not know, that he should be bought out on the same basis as he himself had bought, even though his interests had been unfairly prejudiced in the mean time. *A fortiori*, there could be no universal or even a general rule in a case where the company had never been a quasi partnership in the first place.'

Then he said, 'In summary', that there is no general rule. *(pg528c)*

Next comes a passage to which particular criticism has been directed; Nourse J said ([1984] 3 All ER 444 at 450–451, [1984] Ch 419 at 431):

'On the other hand, there is a general rule in a case where the company is at the material time a quasi partnership and the purchase order is made in respect of the shares of a quasi partner. Although I have taken the case where there has in fact *(pg528d)* been unfairly prejudicial conduct on the part of the majority as being the state of affairs most likely to result in a purchase order, I am of the opinion that the same consequences ought usually to follow in a case like the present where there has been an agreement for the price to be determined by the court without any admission as to such conduct. It seems clear to me that, even without such conduct, that is in general the fair basis of valuation in a quasi partnership case, and that it should be *(pg528e)* applied in this case unless the respondents have established that the petitioners acted in such a way as to deserve their exclusion from the company.'

And he went on to conclude that they had not in fact deserved their exclusion on the facts of this case.

9 I have read those passages because they serve to indicate the approach of the judge to *(pg528f)* the problem with which he was confronted under the terms of the order. That approach has been criticised by counsel for the respondents on two grounds: first of all, on the general ground that it was a wrong order in any event, or a wrong approach in any event, under s75; and, secondly, on the ground that it was a wrong order, or a wrong approach, having regard to the specific terms of the consent order in this case, which, as counsel for the respondents rightly says, has to be looked at as a contract between the parties agreeing *(pg528g)* to the consent order.

10 What counsel for the respondents suggests is this. I take the two points which he makes in inverse order, that is to say I am taking his second point first. He suggests that an order made under sub-s (4) of s75 is simply an order for a purchase, without any discretion in the court to give directions which might have the effect of increasing or reducing the value of the shares in the open market, as shares in a private company. If *(pg528h)* the shares with which the purchase order is concerned are a majority holding, they are to be valued as such; if they are a minority holding, they are to be valued as such, and in his submission the court is not entitled to look behind the company and to reflect, in the order for purchase or for sale, the actual relationship between the parties. According to this approach, any agreement which has been made between the parties as to the basis on which they were to participate in the company's affairs, or as to the way in which the *(pg528j)* company's affairs were to be conducted, any contribution which the petitioner may have made to the company's success, any absence of any contribution at all by the respondent, apart from the mere fact of his shareholding, is to be ignored. The court, in other words, is to be rigidly restricted, if it is to make an order under sub-s (4)(d) at all, to making an order for a purchase at a market price of the holding being purchased, to be arrived at only by the ordinary valuation principles, which will take into account the proportionate size of the holding in relation to the issued capital as a whole and to the control of the *(pg529a)* company.

11 For my part I find myself quite unable to accept this submission. It seems to me that the whole framework of the section, and of such of the authorities as we have seen, which seem to me to support this, is to confer on the court a very wide discretion to do what is considered fair and equitable in all the circumstances of the case, in order to put right and cure for the future the unfair prejudice which the petitioner has suffered at the hands *(pg529b)*of the other shareholders of the company; and I find myself quite unable to accept that that discretion in some way stops short when it comes to the terms of the order for purchase in the manner in which the price is to be assessed. It has been pointed out, and I mention it again, that sub-s (4) is merely a collection of possible methods of giving effect to sub-s (3), and it is expressed to be without prejudice to the generality of sub-s (3), which gives the court a very wide discretion as to the granting of relief in general terms *(pg529c)* in respect of the matters of which complaint has been made.

12 We have been referred to the speech of Lord Cross in *Ebrahimi v Westbourne Galleries Ltd* [1972] 2 All ER 492 at 505, [1973] AC 360 at 385, where he says this in a very short passage, to which counsel for the petitioners drew attention:

'What the minority shareholder in cases of this sort really wants is not to have the company wound up – which may prove an unsatisfactory remedy – but to be paid *(pg529d)*a proper price for his shareholding.'

It is on the question of a 'proper' price that the parties here divide. So on the second submission of counsel for the respondents, which I have dealt with first, I find myself quite unable to accept it. In my judgment the 'proper' price is the price which the court in its discretion determines to be proper having regard to all the circumstances of the *(pg529e)* case.

13 I come now to the first submission, which is that as a matter of interpretation of the order, which, as counsel says and as I mention again, is a consent order, there is to be implied a contractual obligation that the shares should be purchased at the market value as a minority holding. The basis for this submission is that the consequence which I have outlined is one which flowed simply from the use of the order of the word 'purchase'; *(pg529f)* and it is said that 'purchase' ordinarily means purchase at market value, and therefore one reads into the order the words 'a purchase at market value to be determined by the court'. I confess that I am entirely unable to see why that should be. In my judgment 'purchase' ordinarily means no more than purchase for a money consideration; what that consideration is, is at large, and the order is one which only makes sense, and indeed can only be given any operative life, if the purchase price is fixed in the exercise of the full *(pg529g)* discretion vested in the court by s75. The court has no jurisdiction, as it seems to me, to act as a sort of arbitrator between experts, and if Vinelott J had been told that that was what was intended, and that all that was intended was simply that there should be submitted to the court the decision of the issue of what was the market value of the petitioners' holding, I confess that I doubt very much whether he would have made the order in that form, or indeed would have considered that he had any jurisdiction to do *(pg529h)* so. Essentially what is suggested is that in assessing the price Nourse J was wrong to consider the evidence which had been filed in support of the petition, and indeed subsequently, or to enter into any consideration of the merits of the case, the inception of the relationships between the parties and so on. I would find that a difficult submission to accept in any event, but the submission might have had more force, I think, if, as might at first be supposed from the terms of the order, the court was simply being asked *(pg529j)* to embark on an inquiry into the value of the shares on the assumption that it had been conceded in some unspecified way that the petitioners had been subjected to unfair prejudice and that it was therefore irrelevant to consider the manner in which they had in fact been unfairly prejudiced.

14 But it is the respondents' own case, and it was so put to the judge, that no such admission had in fact been made. As I have pointed out, the terms of sub-s (3) are perfectly clear. They simply provide that, if the court is satisfied that a petition under *(pg530a)* s75 is well founded, it may, make such order as it thinks fit for giving relief in respect of the matters complained of. If, of course, it is not so satisfied, then it has no jurisdiction to give the relief which is referred to in sub-s (3) or in sub-s (4). As it seems to me, this only has to be read for it to be seen straight away that the court, in making a valuation of the shares, can only do so if it is satisfied that the petition is well founded.

15 The judge therefore had to go into these questions, because it was expressly said that *(pg530b)* there was no admission of any unfair prejudice, and so the judge had to go into the question of whether there had been unfair prejudice to the petitioners and how it had taken place, in order to see whether he had any jurisdiction at all to embark on the inquiry which he was invited to undertake. Nourse J referred to the question of whether he ought to inquire into these matters ([1984] 3 All ER 444 at 446–447, [1984] Ch 419 at 426): *(pg530c)*

> 'The first question which arose was whether the respondents, by consenting to the order of 23 November 1981 and, I suppose, by agreeing to pay the petitioners' costs to date, had effectively admitted that they had been conducting the affairs of the company in a manner unfairly prejudicial to the petitioners as members. There was some disagreement between counsel as to what was or was not said on the *(pg530d)* respondents' side at the hearing before Vinelott J, but on what I saw and heard I was satisfied that there had been no admission to that effect. The respondents had merely agreed to buy out the petitioners at a price to be determined by the court. Assuming that unfair prejudice might sometimes affect the price which ought to be paid for the shares, I was nevertheless unable to see how, in the absence of some explicit statement of the respondents' position, they could be taken to have made any admission as to that matter.' *(pg530e)*

Then he went on ([1984] 3 All ER 444 at 447, [1984] Ch 419 at 427):

'It was unfortunate that the hopes and expectations of both sides for a shorter hearing should have been disappointed, but that was made inevitable by my decision on the first of the preliminary points and by the positions which the parties adopted *(pg530f)* in regard to the second and third. I myself suggested certain ways in which the hearing might be shortened by agreement, but without success. In future, parties who wish to limit the issues or the evidence in a case of this kind would be well advised to go further than a mere agreement that the price of the shares shall be determined by the court.'

Then he said ([1984] 3 All ER 444 at 454, [1984] Ch 419 at 434) *(pg530g)*

'I have to say that I regard the evidence of both Mr Bird and Mr Rowden on the bribery question as having been extremely unsatisfactory. If it had been necessary for me to make any finding on that question, I would have rejected their evidence in its entirety and accepted that of Mr Nin and Mr Armstrong. Having said that, I do not think that it is either necessary or desirable that I should go into this or any *(pg530h)* of the many other matters which were made the subject of allegations and counter-allegations between the parties, both at the time and in evidence in this court. Having considered all the material evidence, I am satisfied that the exclusion of Mr Armstrong and Mr Nin was wrongful and that, in that and certain other respects into which I need not go, the affairs of the company were conducted in a manner unfairly prejudicial to the interests of them and the other petitioners as members. *(pg530j)* That finding, although strictly speaking unnecessary on the view which I take of the case, is one which I feel that I ought to make, if only in fairness to Mr Armstrong and Mr Nin and after a full and exhaustive investigation of the merits.'

16 If I have any criticism of the judge's judgment, it is only that he based his inquiry on the supposition that the merits might affect only the question of the basis of the valuation of the shares, as indeed in my judgment they clearly can. But it was, I think, much more fundamental than that. Unless unfair prejudice was proved, the court was simply being *(pg531a)* asked to undertake a sort of arbitration *in vacuo*, which it had no jurisdiction to do. It seems to me quite unreasonable that the judge, having perforce considered the merits and having heard evidence from the parties, should be expected, or indeed required, by the terms of this order, then to put that entirely out of his mind when it came to the question of the terms of the purchase.

17 We have been referred to a number of authorities, first of all to a decision of *(pg531b)* Pennycuick J in *re Jermyn Street Turkish Baths Ltd* [1970] 3 All ER 57 at 67, [1970] 1 WLR 1194 at 1208, and I read an extract from his judgment. He said:

'Section 210 gives the court an unlimited judicial discretion to make such order as it thinks fit with a view to bringing to an end the matters complained of, including an order for buying out one faction by the other. It is not disputed on behalf of the respondents that, in prescribing the basis on which the price of such a *(pg531c)* sale is to be calculated, the court can in effect provide compensation for whatever injury has been inflicted by the oppressors.'

18 In *Scottish Co-op Wholesale Society Ltd v Meyer* [1958] 3 All ER 66 at 89, [1959] AC 324 at 369 Lord Denning said:

'One of the most useful orders mentioned in the section – which will enable the *(pg531d)* court to do justice to the injured shareholders – is to order the oppressor to buy their shares at a fair price; and a fair price would be, I think, the value which the shares would have had at the date of the petition, if there had been no oppression. Once the oppressor has bought the shares, the company can survive. It can continue to operate. That is a matter for him. It is, no doubt, true that an order of this kind *(pg531e)* gives to the oppressed shareholders what is, in effect, money compensation for the injury done to them; but I see no objection to this. The section gives a large discretion to the court, and it is well exercised in making an oppressor make compensation to those who have suffered at his hands.'

19 What I think is being suggested here is that these citations in some way support the respondents' arguments because it is said that what in effect the judge was seeking to do *(pg531f)* was to compensate the oppressed shareholders, and that that was not within the terms of the order. I do not read what the judge did as doing that at all. Speaking for myself, I have been quite unable to see why these two authorities should be supposed to support the arguments which the respondents have advanced. They seem to me to be entirely against them because, as it seems to me, they indicate as clearly as can be the wide discretion which the court has in directing the basis on which shares should be valued *(pg531g)* for the purpose of a purchase ordered under this section. It may be true that it can be compensatory, but what the court is required to do, in the exercise of its very wide discretion, is to do what is just and equitable between the parties.

20 It does not seem to me in any event that the matter ends simply with the mere fact that the order, to be effective as an order under s75, necessarily has to invoke the discretionary jurisdiction of the court, because there are in fact, as it seems to me, positive *(pg531h)* pointers in the order that that is exactly what was intended.

21 Going back to the terms of the order, it starts, as I have already pointed out, with the words 'THIS COURT DOTH ORDER pursuant to Section 75 of the Companies Act 1980'. I have already said that I do not for a moment think that the mere use of the word 'purchase' which then follows ('that the Respondents

... do jointly and severally purchase') contains any implication at all that they should purchase necessarily at market value. It seems to *(pg531j)* me that quite the contrary is imported by the words 'pursuant to Section 75'. What they are doing is purchasing pursuant to s75, and it is pursuant to that section that the court is to determine price. That brings in, as it seems to me, by necessary implication the general discretion of the court to do what is fair and equitable.

22 Secondly, one wonders, if all that was being asked for was an order for purchase at market price, what was the purpose, as counsel for the petitioners says, of involving the court in the matter at all? A market price could quite easily be determined outside the *(pg532a)* court by arbitration, or by submitting the matter to two valuers and their umpire. It seems to me to be quite evident from the first paragraph of the order, which I have read, that what was intended was that the matter should be approached in the full sense as an application under s75 of the 1980 Act, and that the court was expected, in arriving at the price to be paid, to take into account all the circumstances of the case.

23 That, as it seems to me, is underlined by the next part of the order, where it goes on *(pg532b)* with the question of the 'appropriate' purchase price for the shares, and proceeds with directions as to evidence. The evidence is quite clearly intended to be general evidence with regard to all the circumstances: there are provisions for discovery.

24 So far as the accountancy aspect of it is concerned, that is dealt with by the last words this section of the order: ' ... and exchange of reports by experts within 28 days after inspection.' *(pg532c)*

25 So quite clearly, as it seems to me, the whole concept of the order was that there would be a full investigation into the circumstances, with evidence filed on both sides; and, indeed, that is what took place.

26 Finally we come to the liberty to apply:

'Liberty to all parties to apply (1) for further and better particulars of the allegations in the Affidavits (2) for directions as to the payment of the purchase price *(pg532d)* and interest if appropriate and (3) generally.'

27 So they were to have liberty to apply for further and better particulars, and again it seems to me that that could only be on the footing that the judge was to inquire fully into the circumstances of the case and into the affidavits that were directed to be filed.

28 Speaking for myself, I am quite satisfied, as a matter of construction of the terms of *(pg532e)* the order, that the judge was entitled to exercise in full his discretion under s75(3) and (4). As I have already said, in my judgment those subsections give him a very wide discretion, and I am quite satisfied that no ground has been shown for interference by this court with the actual manner in which the judge in fact exercised the discretion which was vested in him by the section, and by which he concluded that this seas a quasi partnership case, and that being so it would be appropriate that the shares of the company *(pg532f)* should be valued as a whole and that the petitioners should then simply be paid the proportionate part of that value which was represented by their shareholding, without there being made a discount for the fact that this was a minority shareholding.

29 In my judgment the judge was perfectly entitled to arrive at the conclusion at which he did. I myself, certainly on a reading of the judgment and on such material as we have had, would not, I think, have come to any other conclusion, and I am fortified in the *(pg532g)* view that I have taken by an additional point which counsel for the petitioners takes on the articles of association of the company. This company, as one might expect, had articles of association which contained a pre-emption provision in the ordinary form. It was one which had this perhaps unusual feature, that it had a specific provision relating to the way in which a transfer notice was to be treated. I can read the relevant paragraphs very simply; it is the usual form of article which enables shares to be transferred to other *(pg532h)* members, or to members of their family, and then provides that apart from that no share shall be transferred until the pre-emption rights have been exhausted. Sub-article (c) of art 21 provides as follows:

'Except where the transfer is made pursuant to Sub-Article (a) hereof, the person proposing to transfer any Share (hereinafter called "the proposing transferor") shall *(pg532j)* give notice in writing (hereinafter called "the transfer notice") to the Company that he desires to transfer the same, and such notice shall specify the sum he fixcs as the fair value, and shall constitute the Company his agent for the sale of the Share to any Member of the Company (or to any person selected by the Directors as one whom it is desirable in the interests of the Company to admit to Membership) at the price so fixed or, at the option of the purchaser, at the fair value to be fixed by the Auditor in accordance with Sub-Article (e) of this Article. [Then there is this important *(pg533a)* sentence:] The transfer notice may include two or more Shares, and in such case shall operate as if it were a separate notice in respect of each … '

Then, in sub-art (e) of art 21, we have the valuation:

'In case any difference arises between the proposing transferor and the purchaser as to the fair value of a Share the Auditor shall, on the application of either party, *(pg533b)* certify in writing the sum which in his opinion is the fair value, and such sum shall be deemed to be the fair value, and in so certifying the Auditor shall be considered to be acting as an expert and not as an arbitrator; and accordingly the Arbitration Act, 1950, shall not apply.'

Counsel for the petitioners has referred us to *Dean v Prince* [1954] 1 All ER 749, [1954] Ch 409. The two passages to which he has referred us are in these terms.

Denning LJ said *(pg533c)* ([1954] 1 All ER 749 at 759, [1954] Ch 409 at 427–428):

> '*The right to control the company.* The judge [Harman J] said that the auditor should have taken into account the fact that the one hundred and forty shares were a majority holding and would give the purchaser the right to control the company. I do not think that the auditor was bound to take that fact into account. Test it in this *(pg533d)* way. Supposing it had been Mr. Prince who had died, leaving only thirty shares, those thirty shares, being a minority holding, would fetch nothing in the open market. But does that mean that other directors would be entitled to take his shares for nothing? Surely not. No matter which director it was who happened to die, his widow should be entitled to the same price per share, irrespective of whether her husband's holding was large or small. It seems to me that the fair thing to do would *(pg533e)* be to take the whole two hundred shares of the company and see what they are worth, and then pay the widow a sum appropriate to her husband's holding. At any rate, if the auditor was of opinion that that was a fair method, no one could say that he was wrong. The right way to see what the whole two hundred shares were worth, would be to see what the business itself was worth, and that is what the auditor proceeded to do.' *(pg533f)*

Then Wynn-Parry J referred to a particular article in the company's articles in these terms ([1954] 1 All ER 749 at 761, [1954] Ch 408 at 430–431):

> '... "the fair value shall be the auditor's valuation of the current worth of the company's shares." That language appears to me to preclude the auditor from placing any extra value on a block of shares because it constitutes or will in the *(pg533g)* hands of the particular transferee constitute a controlling interest.'

30 It is of course true that in the instant case the articles did not contain that rather important provision; but they did have this extraordinary provision for each share to be treated separately, as if it had been comprised in a separate transfer notice. As I have said, one does not have an express provision to the company's shares as a whole, but one has *(pg533h)* an express provision that, if a transfer notice is given in respect of more than one share, it is to be treated as a separate notice in respect of each. So the valuer has, theoretically, to go through the process of ascertaining the value separately in relation to each share concerned, and I am bound to say that it is difficult to see then how there could be any room for any account to be taken of whether the shares comprised in a transfer notice as a whole formed a minority or a majority holding. Without expressing any concluded *(pg533j)* view on the *(pg534a)* matter, I am very much inclined to the view that the valuation of a share. under the pre-emption articles in this case ought to be on the same basis as that held by this court to be appropriate in *Dean v Prince*, and that if the valuer were unwise enough to give his reasons for valuation, and to indicate in those reasons that he had taken into account the fact that all the shares which were being offered by all the deemed separate transfer notices together constituted a majority or minority holding, I think his valuation could be upset. But, as I say, it is unnecessary to express any concluded view on the matter, because in a sense this is a makeweight submission. If it is right it would, to say the least, have a very odd result if the effect of an order designed to enable the court to do what is just and equitable between the parties under s75 should result in a minority holding being bought out at a price which is less than that which it would be expected to achieve on a sale under the articles of association.

31 For all the reasons I have given, therefore, I have no hesitation in dismissing the *(pg534b)* respondents' appeal.

32 I turn now to the petitioners' cross-appeal, which arises in this way. As I have pointed out, under the last paragraph of the order there was liberty to apply in relation to interest and, the judge having determined the price at which the shares were to be bought out, application was then made for an award of interest on the amount of the purchase price when ascertained, as from a date which I think was not actually specified at that time, *(pg534c)* because argument then proceeded on whether in principle interest could or could not be awarded. That argument was adjourned and it came before the judge again on 25 November 1983, when he determined that there could be no award of interest on the purchase money.

33 The petitioners challenge that, and they seek an order that interest should be paid up to 9 December 1983. There was, as the result of a hearing before the judge, an agreed *(pg534d)* order as to the way in which, subject to this appeal, the purchase was to be carried into effect, and that provided for interest; no question of interest arises after 9 December 1983. But by their notice of cross-appeal the petitioners asked for interest, either from 31 August 1980 or, if that is rejected, from the date of the presentation of the petition, which was 12 October 1981, or, if that is rejected, from the date of the judge's order, or again, if that be wrong, from Vinelott J's order, and, if that be wrong, from 7 August 1981, *(pg534e)* when the petitioners were removed from the board.

34 The judge rejected the claim; he did so on two grounds. First of all it was argued that, although it was, I think, conceded that there was no orthodox ground for payment of interest, nevertheless interest could be paid under the general discretion which is contained in sub-s (3) of s75, in effect as a means of awarding damages in respect of matters which had occurred in the course of the carrying on of the company's business *(pg534f)* constituting the unfair prejudice. The judge rejected that, saying ([1984] 3 All ER 444 at 459, [1984] Ch 419 at 437):

'I have never heard of interest being payable before there is an obligation to pay principal. On analysis, it appears that what counsel for the petitioners is really saying is that the court has power under s75(3) to award something equivalent to interest. *(pg534g)* That must, I think, be damages for loss of the use of the purchase moneys during a period when they ought to have been in hand. As will appear, the view which I take of this case makes it unnecessary for me to express a view on that point and I do not do so.'

He then went to what was the real ground of his decision, saying ([1984] 3 All ER 444 at 459–460, [1984] Ch 419 at 437): *(pg534h)*

'In the present case there was an agreement that the respondents should buy out the petitioners on a certain basis, ie at such price as the court should determine. That price was held to be a sum equivalent to the fair value of the shares. There was no agreement that the price should bear interest from some date prior to its determination or, indeed, from any date. An agreed liberty to apply for directions *(pg534j)* as to the payment of interest (if appropriate) is not an agreement that the price should bear interest. There was no agreement that the petitioners should receive damages for loss of the use of the purchase moneys. Moreover, even if, which I emphatically refute, such an agreement could be implied, it is far too late to make that claim. A claim for damages, even of that limited character, would have entitled the respondents to adduce evidence and make submissions to the effect that the petitioners' loss was by no means what it might have seemed. Counsel for the petitioners says that the order has not yet been drawn up. That may be so, but it is *(pg535a)* no reason for allowing the petitioners to reopen the trial under the guise of a claim for interest. I am of the clear opinion that there is no case for interest or so-called interest before judgment in the present case and I therefore do not propose to enter into any questions of date or rate.'

35 Counsel for the petitioners has submitted that the true construction of the order, in giving liberty to apply for interest, in giving liberty to apply on the hearing before the *(pg535b)* judge, in effect for damages for all the things of which the petitioners complain, and that therefore the judge was wrong in refusing to entertain, as he did, the claim as being in effect a sort of disguised claim for damages.

36 I find myself quite unable to accept that submission. It seems to me as plain as can be that the liberty to apply for directions as to payment of interest on the purchase price was *(pg535c)* simply inserted for the purpose of enabling the court, when it fixed the terms of the purchase, to provide, if the purchase price was not paid, for interest to be paid on it as from a certain date. It seems to me that the judge was perfectly right in refusing to allow any question to be ventilated as to the payment of interest, as it were, in lieu of damages. I would therefore dismiss the cross-appeal.

37 So in my judgment the appeal fails, and so does the cross-appeal. *(pg535d)*

38 PURCHAS LJ: I agree that this appeal should be dismissed. Out of respect to the able argument of counsel for the respondents, I propose to add a few words of my own.

39 The short issue raised is whether, in valuing the shares that were to be transferred, the valuer should apply a discount in recognition of the fact that the holdings being transferred were minority holdings in the company. *(pg535e)*

40 The starting point is an order made by Vinelott J on 23 November 1981. The material parts of that order have already been cited by Oliver LJ, but I propose for the sake of convenience to repeat the critical words, namely:

'THIS COURT DOTH ORDER pursuant to Section 75 of the Companies Act 1980 that the Respondents [who are there named] do jointly and severally purchase the [7,800] shares of the Company registered in the name of the Petitioners ... at such price as the Court shall hereafter determine ... [the rest is not relevant].' *(pg535f)*

41 Counsel for the respondents submits that the phrase 'at such price as the Court shall hereafter determine' can only mean the price, being the fair market price, which would have been agreed between a willing buyer and a willing seller in the open market, include the discount which stems from the very nature of the holding being sold. *(pg535g)* It must ignore the concept of the authority to which Oliver LJ has already referred in *Dean v Prince* [1954] 1 All ER 749, [1954] 1 Ch 409.

42 It would also exclude the basis on which the powers under s75 of the Companies Act 1980 arise as defined in sub-s (1), and further would exclude the whole basis on which the parties came together in the commercial enterprise and on which the petitioners accepted their respective minority shareholdings. The judge found that the basis of this *(pg535h)* was fairly described as a 'quasi partnership' as considered in the leading case of *Ebrahimi v Westbourne Galleries Ltd* [1972] 2 All ER 492 esp at 500, [1973] AC 360 esp at 379 per Lord Wilberforce.

43 Counsel for the respondents submitted that to do otherwise would in effect be to award compensation either in respect of the prejudicial conduct which was the basis, albeit not admitted by the respondents, of the jurisdiction under s75, and/or the *(pg535j)* determination of the quasi partnership, that is the loss of the continuing rights, if they were of any value, attributable to the minority shareholders for the loss of their future participation. Counsel for the respondents submitted that to grant such an extra element of consideration to the purchase price would therefore be outside the terms of the consent order itself. Put another way, his submission was that under the terms of that consent order the function of the judge, or the court, envisaged in the future by that order would be merely one of an arbitrator, namely to determine the quantum of the price regardless of the other aspects which would be considered by the court were it acting in the ordinary *(pg536a)* way under the provisions of s75 of the 1980 Act.

44 I think counsel for the respondents conceded that had this petition been fought trough (rather than concluded, partly at least, by consent) under the provisions of s75, and particularly sub-s (3), the relief ordered by the court in its discretion could have been such as to effect the transfer of shares at a consideration valued on a pro rata distribution of the whole value of the company. But, whether he made that concession or not, I am *(pg536b)* for my part quite unable to make the distinction which counsel for the respondents attempted to import into the existence of the consent order in the terms restricting the power of the court to s75(4), as he would interpret that section, that is the purchase of the shares at a market value.

45 I agree with all that has been said by Oliver LJ, that the effect of sub-s (4) of s75 is merely to expand the wide powers granted under sub-s (3) of s75, and not in any way to *(pg536c)* restrict them. Moreover, the use of the expression in the consent order "purchase' [of the] shares' is not, in my judgment, intended in any way to restrict the powers otherwise enjoyed by the court. If it were, as counsel for the petitioners has submitted and as Oliver LJ has already commented, the purpose of the order and the purpose of the future involvement of the court would be negatived.

46 In my judgment the proper interpretation of this order, importing, as it does, the *(pg536d)* consent between the parties, was to leave in the discretion of the court the full jurisdiction which it would have enjoyed had the matter been fought, and the effect of the consent order was merely to exclude the earlier part of the process under s75, and to select the means by which the court, being certainly hypothetically satisfied of the sound basis of the petition for this purpose (and, of course, that is the only basis on which the court could act), would choose the particular course provided by sub-s (4)(*d*) to give relief in the *(pg536e)* terms of sub-s (3) in respect of the matters complained of in the petition.

47 For those reasons, therefore, in my judgment the judge was right to accept the submission that the powers were unfettered and that therefore, taking into account the quasi-partnership nature of the interests held by the petitioners in this particular instance, the method of valuation should be that on a pro rata basis, which he accepted.

48 For these reasons, and for the reasons already given by Oliver LJ, I agree that this *(pg536f)* appeal should be dismissed.

49 I also agree that, so far as the cross-appeal is concerned, that also should be dismissed. I echo only the words of the judge ([1984] 3 All ER 444 at 459, [1984] Ch 4 19 at 437):

'The first point to be made is that in a normal s75 case, where there has been no agreement of any kind, I cannot see how there can be any questions of interest being payable before a purchase order is made.' *(pg536g)*

And the order is not completed in this case until the judgment of the court, which is the judgment at present under appeal.

50 The reliance placed by counsel for the petitioners on the final paragraph of the order made by Vinelott J in my judgment takes his submission no further. The liberty to apply which was given to all parties was clearly for the further carrying out of the order, and *(pg536h)* certainly could not form the basis of a jurisdiction, or a consent, on the part of the parties that the court should proceed to calculate an award of interest as a matter of general jurisdiction.

51 For those reasons I also agree that the cross-appeal should be dismissed. *(pg536j)*

Case 36
IRC v Stenhouse's Trustees

[1992] STC 103

High Court

5, 6, 26 November 1991

The principle is established in this case that the parties to the proceedings before the Commissioners are entitled to put forward evidence of both actual prices achieved on actual sales and also prices agreed with the Inland Revenue Share Valuation Division.

The price at which actual transactions in shares took place is, potentially, a relevant factor in determining the market value for fiscal purposes. Equally, agreements reached by the Revenue in respect of other transactions in the company's shares may also be a relevant factor. Whether these matters are relevant for any particular valuation, is a question of fact for the Commissioners.

The facts from which this case arises are commonplace but the manner in which the case proceeded before the Special Commissioner is most unusual.

On 17 March 1978, HC Stenhouse settled into trust shares in three companies, namely, Haddockston Holdings Ltd, Scottish Western Trust Holdings Ltd and Second Haddockston Holdings Ltd. HC Stenhouse died following his lifetime transfer and capital transfer tax was levied on the value of the shares settled into trust.

The Revenue and the executors could not agree the value to be attributed to the holding in Haddockston Holdings Ltd. The matter was heard by a Special Commissioner.

At the hearing, Professor JS Macleod, the expert witness for the executors, gave evidence as to the value of the shares and explained that in arriving at his estimate of the value he had relied on the accounts of the companies to 31 March 1977, the latest available date, and on information in the public domain, such as information available through Stock Exchange sources, showing the general approach of stock market investors to investment trust companies and the level of yield which such investors might expect. Professor Macleod did not take account of any actual transactions in shares of Haddockston or Scottish Western Trust Holdings Ltd. In cross-examination, counsel for the Crown asked him whether he had taken into account actual transactions in, or agreements on value in respect of, shares of the two companies. Counsel for the trustees objected to that question.

The Commissioner ruled that evidence on actual transactions was not admissible in the hearing and evidence on agreements valued reached with the Revenue was, similarly, not admissible.

The Revenue appealed to the High Court and the Commissioners' hearing was halted pending a direction from the High Court as to the correctness of the Commissioners' ruling.

In the High Court, Lord Coulsfield quashed the Commissioners ruling on admissibility of evidence saying:

'The general rule of law, which is not in doubt, is that evidence which is relevant to the issue in the case is admissible unless it is excluded by some peremptory rule of law. Evidence is relevant if it is in some way logically connected with the matters in dispute or if it is consistent or inconsistent with, or gives rise to a logical inference regarding, the facts in issue. No peremptory rule of law of evidence was referred to in the present case and the question was argued as one of relevance of evidence. Put shortly, the Crown's contention was that evidence of agreements as to the open market value of shares in the companies and evidence of actual transactions in those shares must be relevant to the issue in the present dispute, even if such evidence might not be determinative or even of very great weight.'

([1992] STC 103 at 109d–f–k **case 36 para 9**)

Counsel for the executors argued that the determining of market value under the statutory provisions was the determination of a hypothetical transfer and, hence, evidence of actual transfers was not relevant.

Lord Coulsfield had no sympathy with this argument stating:

'In the case of a hypothetical sale, the calculation made by the trustees' witnesses are, in my view, only evidence of the value, and cannot be regarded as, in themselves, conclusive. I therefore do not understand why it is said to follow from the fact that value has to be ascertained on a hypothesis that any evidence of actual transactions should be ruled out as so irrelevant as to be inadmissible. Whether it is correct to start, as the trustees' witnesses did, with the accounts of the companies and information available in the public domain, is, in my opinion a question of fact and opinion, not one of law. Similarly, the question whether any weight, and if so how much, is to be attached to evidence of transactions seems to me to be a question fact and opinion. Some of the transactions on which the Crown relies may be of no use: but there may be others which took place between parties who were genuinely trying to strike an open market value, and I do not see why such cases should simply be ignored. As I understand the position, it is relevant to lead evidence of some transactions, albeit in a secondary role, as a check or sounding board for a conclusion reached on the basis of their preferred approach.'

([1992] STC 103 at 110c–f **case 36 para 11**)

Judgement

References, example '(pg106d)', are to [1992] STC 103.

1 **LORD COULSFIELD:** This is an appeal under sec. 17 of the Court of Exchequer (Scotland) Act 1856 by the Commissioners of Inland Revenue against a decision of a special commissioner dated 27 March 1990. The decision was made in the course of proceedings to determine the value for capital *(pg106d)* transfer tax purposes of certain shares included in a capital distribution made by the respondents on 17 March 1978. The respondents are the trustees of the *inter vivos* trust of the late HC Stenhouse. The distribution consisted of shares in three companies, namely Haddockston Holdings Ltd ('Haddockston'), Scottish Western Trust Holdings Ltd ('SWTH') and Second *(pg106e)* Haddockston Holdings Ltd, but, by the time of the hearing, the values attributable to the shares in SWTH and Second Haddockston Holdings Ltd for the purposes of assessment of tax on the transfer had been agreed. Haddockston was an investment company and on 17 March 1978 its investments consisted principally of shares in SWTH. SWTH itself was an investment company whose assets included shares in a quoted company, Stenhouse Holdings Ltd.

Haddockston and SWTH were both unquoted companies and, as I understand the position, the articles of each company contained restrictions on the *(pg106f)* transfer of shares in the companies. The respondents were not, as trustees, involved in the management of either Haddockston or SWTH.

2 The value of any property for the purposes of capital transfer tax was at the relevant date defined by sec. 38 of the Finance Act 1975, which provides:

'(1) Except as otherwise provided by this part of this Act, the value at any time of any property shall for the purposes of capital transfer tax be the price *(pg106g)* which the property might reasonably be expected to fetch if sold in the open market at that time; but that price shall not be assumed to be reduced on the ground that the whole property is to be placed on the market at one and the same time.

(2) Schedule 10 to this Act shall have effect with respect to the valuation of property for the purposes of capital transfer tax and the determination of the *(pg106h)* value transferred by a transfer of value.'

3 Paragraph 13 of Sch. 10 provides:

'(1) In determining the price which unquoted shares or securities might reasonably be expected to fetch if sold in the open market it shall be assumed that in that market there is available to any prospective purchaser of the shares *(pg106j)* or securities all the information which a prudent prospective purchaser might reasonably require if he were proposing to purchase them from a willing vendor by private treaty and at arms length.

(2) In this paragraph "unquoted shares or securities" means shares or securities which are not quoted on a recognised stock exchange.'

4 Paragraph 13 was, it appears, designed to alter the law laid down in *re Lynall deceased* (1971) 47 TC 375. *(pg107a)*

5 At the hearing on 27 March 1990, before a single commissioner, the respondents led evidence first. One of their principal witnesses, Professor JS Macleod, gave evidence as to the value of the shares and explained that in arriving at his estimate of the value he had relied on the accounts of the companies to 31 March 1977, the latest available date, and on information in the public domain, such as information available through Stock Exchange sources, showing the general approach of stock market *(pg107b)* investors to investment trust companies and the level of yield which such investors might expect. Professor Macleod did not take account of any actual transactions in shares of Haddockston or SWTH. In cross-examination, counsel for the appellants asked him whether he had taken into account actual transactions in, or agreements on value in respect of, shares of the two companies. Counsel for the respondents objected to that question. After hearing a short argument and retiring briefly to consider it, *(pg107c)* the Special Commissioner made the determination which is the subject of this appeal. One of the issues in the appeal is what the precise effect of the determination was but, on any view, it indicates some limitation on the extent to which cross-examination would be permitted, or evidence allowed to be led as to actual transactions in, or agreements relating to the value of, shares in the two companies. It was, it appears, the intention of the appellants to lead evidence of, *inter alia*, a number of transactions *(pg107d)* in the shares both of Haddockston and SWTH, at known values, involving members of the family of the late Mr Stenhouse or trusts or companies in which they had an interest. Further, there had been earlier capital distributions from the *inter vivos* trust and agreements had been reached between the appellants and the respondents as to the appropriate formula to be adopted in valuing the shares of Haddockston and SWTH for tax purposes. The formula involved discounting the net asset value of *(pg107e)* each company and represented a materially different approach to valuation from that adopted by Professor Macleod in his evidence. After the determination of the special commissioners was announced, the appellants took the view that their ability to lead appropriate evidence would be unduly restricted. Nothing further was done at the hearing and this appeal was then taken. As a result, the special commissioner was never asked to rule on the admissibility or relevance of any question or any item of evidence *(pg107f)* relating to any particular transaction or agreement and never had before him any detailed information about any such transaction or agreement.

6 In his determination, the special commissioner explained the question which had arisen and referred to sec. 38 of the 1975 Act and also to sec. 52 of the Taxes Management Act 1970 which imposes a duty on appeal commissioners to hear lawful evidence. Strictly speaking, that reference was in error because sec. 52 of the 1970 Act *(pg107g)* applies to proceedings in relation to income tax assessments and the relevant provision for the purposes of the present proceedings is contained in para. 9 of Sch. 4 to the Finance Act 1975, which is in slightly different terms, but nothing turns on the difference. After some other introductory remarks, the determination continued:

'It seems to me that the question I have to deal with is of fundamental *(pg107h)* importance in the valuation of shares in a private company for which there is no actual market. The function of the commissioners, or, if the matter comes before the court at first instance, of the court, is, to adopt so much as I can remember of a phrase of *Danckwerts* J in *Holt v IR Commrs*[1953] 1 WLR 1488 at p. 1492, "a dim world peopled by the indeterminate spirits of fictitious or unborn sales".

Fundamentally it seems to me that the question *(pg107j)* which I have to determine is wholly hypothetical. Where there is a market one looks at values in the market. When there is no market, one has to indulge in the sort of calculations that are fundamental to the present appeal.

With that background I approach this present case. The relevance of other actual transactions is limited first by the consideration that they must be transactions which both as regards time and quantity resemble this particular asset, namely a holding on this particular date. The relevance to my mind of any actual *(pg108a)* transaction which may have taken place is as a sounding board for the hypothetical calculations.

Now the hypothetical calculation is, as we know, of a sale in a notional open market between an notionally willing vendor and a notionally willing purchaser. I would add a rider that the articles of association of two of the companies with which I am concerned contain embargoes on transfers of shares. I make the assumption that there is no embargo on the *(pg108b)* hypothetical purchaser in the hypothetical sale but that the purchaser will thereafter take subject to the embargoes. I therefore have to consider what is admissible as a test of the calculations which the experts make. For my part I rule out entirely what other experts in other cases even of similar holdings of shares on the same day have said. I also rule out agreements arrived at between taxpayers and the Inland Revenue. To accept such evidence would be – to some *(pg108c)* extent – to substitute for my jurisdiction the "horse trading" negotiations of other taxpayers with the Inland Revenue. However, I do not rule out as necessarily irrelevant such real open market transactions (if any) as may be shown to have existed at this time or shortly before or shortly afterwards of similar amounts of holdings of shares in these companies. In order to be admissible such evidence must be of sales for cash between vendors and purchasers at arms length *(pg108d)* and, as I have said, of similar quantities of the same shares. If pressed as to the time I would be inclined (although I make no ruling on this particular point) having regard to the fact that 1978 was a year of great inflation and great economic turbulence, to rule out evidence of transactions separated by more than a few months from March 1978.

I am conscious that my jurisdiction is limited in a number of ways. In particular there is no interlocutory appeal. A rider to that *(pg108e)* is that there could be an application to the Court of Session by way of judicial review. I am also conscious of the fact that the appeal allowed by statute is by way of case stated. With these facts in mind I must err on the side of admitting evidence which is in doubt. Even bearing that in mind, I rule out as irrelevant everything except sales between actual parties for cash at arms length which are similar both as regards amount and time, as I have mentioned, and I so decide.' *(pg108f)*

7 An appeal under sec. 17 of the 1856 Act is competent where at the date of passing of the Act a Writ of *habeas* or of *certiorari* might competently have been issued from the Court of Exchequer. There was some discussion of the circumstances in which *certiorari* is competent but there was, in the end, no real dispute on this issue. As I understand the position, it is accepted that *certiorari* is competent where an error in *(pg108g)* law is patent on the record of the proceedings of an inferior tribunal or authority and it is not necessary that the error should be one going to the jurisdiction of the tribunal or, in other words, one which renders its proceedings *ultra vires*. There must, however, be an error of law, not merely one relating to matters of fact or in the exercise of discretion, within the limits of reasonableness.

8 The first question which has to be considered is, I think, what the effect of the *(pg108h)* special commissioner's determination is. As I have explained, the determination was made on an objection to a very broad question. At one stage of the argument, I was inclined to think that all that the commissioner had done was to assist the parties, as would be appropriate in proceedings of the character in question, by indicating in broad terms the attitude which he would be disposed to take to particular issues as they arose. The commissioner did not, as I read his determination, give an express *(pg108j)* ruling on the objection to the question which had actually been asked. Further, since the commissioner did not have the opportunity to apply the views which he had formed to particular instances, and could not be expected, in an extempore ruling of this kind, to consider instances or examples in detail, there is some difficulty in appreciating the precise effect of his determination. I am still inclined to think that it might have been more satisfactory if the appellants had gone a stage further with the hearing and endeavoured to put some questions about specific instances, before taking the matter to appeal. I have, however, come to the view that, at least in *(pg109a)* certain respects, the determination is sufficiently precise to allow me to consider whether it is correct in law. In the first place, the special commissioner has, I think, positively ruled out evidence of agreements reached between the respondents and the Inland Revenue arising out of previous distributions of, or including, shares in the same companies. Secondly, he has indicated that evidence of transactions will be admissible only if the transactions were 'sales for cash between vendors and purchasers at arms length…of similar quantities of the same shares'. Although it would have been particularly helpful to have had the benefit of the special commissioner's views on individual transactions in order to appreciate how he intended to apply these requirements, I think that, in view of the emphasis put on 'sales for cash at arm's *(pg109b)* length', it is fair to take the ruling as intended to exclude at least the bulk of the transactions on which the appellants intended to rely. All these transactions involved relatives of the late *(pg109c)* Mr Stenhouse or trusts or companies in which they were involved, and, in that respect, could be said not to be at arm's length. These were the transactions with which the parties were concerned in the debate before the commissioners and it is reasonable to conclude that the ruling was intended to deal with them. Certainly, the appellants seem to have understood that their ability to lead evidence of these transactions was at least severely limited. *(pg109d)*

9 I heard a full argument and was referred to a number of authorities, but in the end of the day the issue, for the present purposes, seems to me to become quite narrow. The general rule of law, which is not in doubt, is that evidence which is relevant to the issue in the case is admissible unless it is excluded by some peremptory rule of law (see *Walkers Evidence* p. 1). Evidence is relevant if it is in some way logically connected with the matters in dispute or if it is consistent or inconsistent with, or gives rise to a logical *(pg109e)* inference regarding, the facts in issue (*Walkers* pp. 5–6). No peremptory rule of law of evidence was referred to in the present case and the question was argued as one of relevance of evidence. Put shortly, the appellants' contention was that evidence of agreements as to the open market value of shares in the companies and evidence of actual transactions in those shares must be relevant to the issue in the present dispute, even if such evidence might not be determinative or even of very great weight. The respondents *(pg109f)* argued that the issue between the parties was a hypothetical one, namely the price which would be paid in the open market for the shares under valuation, and that it followed from the nature of that issue that it was correct to take the approach of their witnesses as the primary approach; that regard could only be had to any transactions in the shares to the limited extent allowed by the special commissioner; and that evidence of agreements was not relevant at all. Reference was made to *re Holt* [1953] 1 WLR 1488, *McNamee v IR Commrs* [1954] IR 214 and *(pg109g)* *re Lynall* as showing the nature of the issue, the approach to valuation and the information which might be taken into account.

10 *Re Lynall* was concerned with an open market valuation under sec. 7(5) of the Finance Act 1894 and Lord Reid remarked (at p.406) that sec. 7(5) was merely machinery for estimating value. He also pointed out that *(pg109h)* sale in the open market may take many forms. It is true, as the respondents argued, that the objective is to ascertain the hypothetical value of the property in a hypothetical sale between hypothetical vendor and purchaser. It is also true that it is necessary to define, as a matter of law, the assumptions which the valuer must make. For example, in the case of *re Lynall* itself, it was necessary to define the type of information which, the purchaser is to be assumed to have. Beyond that, however, *(pg109j)* valuation seems to me to be a matter of fact and expert opinion. The appellants referred to *Duke of Portland v Woods' Trustees* 1926 SC 640 where Lord President Clyde said, at pp. 651–652:

> 'The measures employed to estimate the money value of anything (including the damage flowing from a breach of contract) are not to be confounded with the value which it is sought to estimate; and the true value may only be found *(pg110a)* after employing more measures than one – in themselves all legitimate, but none of them necessarily conclusive by itself – and checking one result with another. As Lord Stair puts it in the section quoted above "it is rather in the arbitrament of the judge to ponder all circumstances".'

11 That was a case of damages for breach of contract, but the observations seem to me to be applicable more generally. I do not see why, in the present case, the type of *(pg110b)* evidence admissible should be restricted by the nature of the issue in the way suggested by the respondents. No doubt the best evidence of open market value is evidence of sales of the same or similar property on the open market. It is not, however, necessarily the case that where evidence of open market sales is available, other evidence is excluded. If it is suggested that conditions have changed, in some material respect, the evidence of market sales may have to be qualified by taking *(pg110c)* account of other evidence. The evidence of market sales is only evidence of value, and is not necessarily conclusive by itself. Similarly, in the case of a hypothetical sale, the calculation made by the respondent's witnesses are, in my view, only evidence of value, and cannot be regarded as, in themselves, conclusive. I therefore do not understand why it is said to follow from the fact that value has to be ascertained on a hypothesis that any evidence of actual transactions should be ruled out as so *(pg110d)* irrelevant as to be inadmissible. Whether it is correct to start, as the

respondents' witnesses did, with the accounts of the companies and information available in the public domain, is, in my opinion a question of fact and opinion, not one of law. Similarly, the question whether any weight, and if so how much, is to be attached to evidence of transactions seems to me to be a question of fact and opinion. Some of the transactions on which the appellants rely may be of no use: but there may be others *(pg110e)* which took place between parties who were genuinely trying to strike an open market value, and I do not see why such cases should simply be ignored. As I understand the position, the special commissioner accepted, as the respondents also did in argument, that it is relevant to lead evidence of some transactions, albeit in a secondary role, as a check or sounding board for a conclusion reached upon the basis of their preferred approach. Once that concession is made, it seems to me to be difficult *(pg110f)* to rule out *ab ante* the evidence which the appellants seek to lead as necessarily inadmissible. Whether any particular part of that evidence is of assistance must, in my view, be a question of fact and circumstance.

12 The same line of argument is, in my view, applicable with regard to the agreements. The basis on which it is sought to lead the evidence is that is concerns cases in which the taxpayers did agree values as open market values. That evidence *(pg110g)* may not be of much strength as against other types of evidence, but I am unable to see that it is so valueless as not to be admissible at all. In other fields, such as valuation for rating, evidence *(pg110h)* of agreements reached is regularly admitted as evidence of the value which would be arrived at in hypothetical transactions and I do not see that there is any reason to regard such evidence as inadmissible in the field with which this case is concerned. The commissioner's particular reason for rejecting evidence of agreements is that to accept it would be to substitute for his jurisdiction the 'horse trading' negotiations of other taxpayers with the Inland Revenue. With all respect to his views, it seems to me that the conclusion that a particular value, or a particular method of valuation, was appropriate in those particular cases, as a measure of or a means of reaching the market value, is a consideration which cannot be regarded as necessarily irrelevant. There may be every reason for treating such evidence with *(pg110j)* care but the reasons are not sufficient, in my view, to form a legal barrier to admitting the evidence at all. Again, I am assisted by the fact that the respondents conceded that it would be open to the appellants to cross-examine expert witnesses who had adopted a different approach in a previous valuation with regard to the reasons why they had done so. If that is correct, it seems to me that it follows that the whole circumstances of the previous occasion must be open for consideration in order to assess the significance of any answers that may be given in cross-examination. I can see *(pg111a)* difficulties in dealing with evidence concerning previous agreements if the appellants are not prepared to reveal the approach which they themselves took in arriving at the value in question, but that is a problem which requires to be dealt with as the evidence is heard.

13 The special commissioners are a specialist tribunal, following a relatively informal procedure, and it is a valuable feature of that procedure that the commissioners *(pg111b)* should employ their expertise and experience to regulate the proceedings by, *inter alia,* indicating what evidence may or may not, in their view, assist them in determining the question at issue before them. In the present case, however, I feel obliged to conclude that the commissioner went too far and gave a ruling which would have the effect of preventing the appellants from leading evidence which, as a matter of law, is admissible. In all the circumstances, therefore, I shall sustain *(pg111c)* the appeal, quash the ruling and remit to the special commissioners to proceed as accords.

Case 37
IRC v Gray

[1994] STC 360

Court of Appeal

19, 20 January and 9 February 1994

This case establishes the principle that where there are two assets in the estate at death, the value for inheritance tax purposes is the value of the two taken together, if this is greater than the value of the two assets taken separately.

This principle was previously enunciated by the Privy Council in *A-G of Ceylon v Mackie & Another* [1952] 2 All ER 775 **case 24**. In that case, the court was considering liability to tax in Ceylon where the deceased had a shareholding of ordinary shares and shareholding of preference shares in the same company. The court held that the correct approach to valuation was to consider the market value of the two classes of shares, taken together. The decision of the Court of Appeal in *IRC v Gray* establishes that the same principle applies for a charge under UK inheritance tax.

Lady Fox died on 27 March 1981. She was freehold owner of the 3,000 acre Croxton Park Estate in Cambridgeshire, which was let to a farming partnership in which she had a 92.5 per cent interest. The question for the Lands Tribunal was whether the freehold estate should be valued as if it had been let to strangers or whether the valuation should take into account Lady Fox's interest in the partnership which held the tenancy.

The value of the Croxton Park Estate at the date of Lady Fox's death was £2,751,000 if subject to a tenancy but £6,125,000 with vacant possession. The surrender value of the tenancy was £1,500,000 (valued as 45 per cent of the additional value created by adding it to the freehold, a basis which was put in the evidence at the hearing of the Lands Tribunal). Thus, a hypothetical purchaser who bought the freehold and the partnership together could obtain vacant possession by paying £100,000 to the minor partners in the partnership. The tenancy was not assignable and, hence, the share in the partnership was of limited value.

The executors' case was that the 3,000 acre land holding was to be valued, on its own, at £2,751,000. The Revenue's case was that the value of this landholding must take into account the partnership interest in Lady Fox's estate at death. After discounts being applied, this gave a value for the land holding of £4,280,768.

In his leading judgement Hoffmann LJ said:

'The principle is that the hypothetical vendor must be supposed to have "taken the course which would get the largest price" provided that this does not entail "undue expenditure of time and effort". In some cases this may involve the sale of an aggregate which could not reasonably be described as a "natural unit". Suppose, for example, there is evidence that at the relevant time a prudent seller would have discovered that a higher price could be obtained by the combined sale of two items which might otherwise have been though entirely unrelated to each other. Such circumstances might arise from the peculiar demands of a small number of potential buyers or even those of a single one. In my view the hypothetical seller would in those circumstances have been, subject to the caveat I have mentioned, willing to sell the items together. The fact that no one would have described them as a "natural unit" is irrelevant ...

The tribunal here misdirected itself as to the true principle which it had to apply. The share in the farming partnership, with or without other property, was plainly not a "natural" item of commerce. Few people would want to buy the right to farm in partnership with strangers. Nevertheless, s38 [now IHTA1984, s 160] requires one to suppose that it was sold. The question for the tribunal was whether, on this assumption, it would have been more advantageous to sell it with the land.'
([1994] STC 360 at 377g – 378b **case 37 paras 31 and 33**)

The decision in the case can readily be transmuted to the valuation of a shareholding. If in the estate of the deceased, there are holdings of, say, ordinary shares and also of preference shares in the same company, the valuation required for inheritance tax purposes must be the value of the two holdings combined, if this is greater than the aggregate of the values of the two shareholdings considered separately. The same principle applies where an estate has holdings in two or more companies in a group.

Judgement

References, example '(pg371c)', are to [1994] STC 360.

1 **HOFFMANN LJ**: This is an appeal by way of case stated from the Lands Tribunal. It concerns the valuation of agricultural land for the purposes of what

is now called inheritance tax but was *(pg371c)* at the material time called capital transfer tax on death. Lady Fox died on 27 March 1981. She was freehold owner of the 3,000 acre Croxton Park Estate in Cambridgeshire, which was let to a farming partnership in which she had a 92½ per cent interest. Shortly stated, the question for the Lands Tribunal was whether the freehold estate should be valued as if it had been let to strangers or whether the valuation should take into account Lady Fox's interest in the partnership which *(pg371d)* held the tenancy.

1. The statutory hypothetical sale

2 Section 19(1) of the Finance Act 1975 said that capital transfer tax should be charged on 'the value transferred by a chargeable transfer'. Section 22(1) said that on the death of any person, tax should be charged:

> 'as if, immediately before his *(pg371e)* death, he had made a transfer of value and the value transferred by it had been equal to the value of his estate immediately before his death.'

Thus Lady Fox's personal representatives were liable to capital transfer tax on the value of her estate immediately before her death.

3 The estate consisted of a number of different items of property and its value was the aggregate of the values of all those items. 'Property' is defined in s51(1) as *(pg371f)* 'rights and interests of any description'. The valuation of each *(pg371g)* item must be made in accordance with s38, which says that:

> 'the value at any time of any property shall for the purposes of capital transfer tax be the price which the property might reasonably be expected to fetch if sold in the open market at that time.'

The section thus predicates a hypothetical sale immediately before Lady Fox's death of each item of property in her estate.

4 The only express guidance which s38 offers on the circumstances in which the hypothetical sale must be supposed to have taken place is that it was 'in the open market'. But this deficiency has been amply remedied by the courts during the century since the provision first made its appearance for the purposes of estate duty in the Finance Act 1894. Certain things are necessarily entailed by the statutory *(pg371h)* hypothesis. The property must be assumed to have been capable of sale in the open market, even if in fact it was inherently unassignable or held subject to restrictions on sale. The question is what a purchaser in the open market would have paid to enjoy whatever rights attached to the property at the relevant date: *IR Commrs v Crossman* [1937] AC 26. Furthermore, the hypothesis must be applied to the property as it actually existed and not to some other property, even if in real life a *(pg371j)* vendor would have been likely to make some changes or improvements before putting it on the market: *Duke of Buccleuch & Anor v IR Commrs* [1967] 1 AC 506 at p. 525G. To this extent, but only to this extent, the express terms of the statute may introduce an element of artificiality into the hypothesis.

5 In all other respects, the theme which runs through the authorities is that one assumes that the hypothetical vendor and purchaser did whatever reasonable people buying and selling such property would be likely to have done in real life. The *(pg372a)* hypothetical vendor is an anonymous but reasonable vendor, who goes about the sale as a prudent man of business, negotiating seriously without giving the impression of being either over-anxious or unduly reluctant. The hypothetical buyer is slightly less anonymous. He too is assumed to have behaved reasonably, making proper inquiries about the property and not appearing too eager to buy. But he also reflects reality in that he embodies whatever was actually the demand for that property at the relevant time. It cannot be too strongly emphasised that *(pg372b)* although the sale is hypothetical, there is nothing hypothetical about the open market in which it is supposed to have taken place. The concept of the open market involves assuming that the whole world was free to bid, and then forming a view about what in those circumstances would in real life have been the best price reasonably obtainable. The practical nature of this exercise will usually mean that although in principle no one is excluded from consideration, most of the world will *(pg372c)* usually play no part in the calculation. The inquiry will often focus upon what a relatively small number of people would be likely to have paid. It may have to arrive at a figure within a range of prices which the evidence shows that various people would have been likely to pay, reflecting, for example, the fact that one person had a particular reason for paying a higher price than others, but taking into account, if appropriate, the possibility that through accident or whim he might not actually *(pg372d)* have bought. The valuation is thus a retrospective exercise in probabilities, wholly derived from the real world but rarely committed to the proposition that a sale to a particular purchaser would definitely have happened.

6 It is often said that the hypothetical vendor and purchaser must be assumed to have been 'willing', but I doubt whether this adds anything to the assumption that they must have behaved as one would reasonably expect of prudent parties who had *(pg372e)* in fact agreed a sale on the relevant date. It certainly does not mean that having calculated the price which the property might reasonably have been expected to fetch in the way I have described, one then asks whether the hypothetical parties would have been pleased or disappointed with the result; for example, by reference to what the property might have been worth at a different time or in different circumstances. Such considerations are irrelevant. *(pg372f)*

2. Splitting and joining

7 In *Duke of Buccleuch & Another v IR Commrs* the House of Lords applied what I might call the reality principle to the question at issue in this case, namely, whether it should be assumed that items of property in an estate were sold separately or together. The case concerned the valuation of the Chatsworth estate for the *(pg372g)* purposes of estate duty on the death of the tenth Duke of Devonshire. It comprised 119,000 acres. The Revenue said that a certain part of the Duke's estate should be assumed to have been sold in 532 separate units. The taxpayer said it should be assumed to have been sold as a whole, in which state it would have appealed only to speculators hoping to make a profit by breaking it up. *(pg372h)*

8 The problem and the principle according to which it should be solved were stated by Lord Wilberforce as follows at p. 546A–C:

'When, as is usually the case, the estate consists of an aggregate of items of property, each item must be separately valued, and it is not difficult to see that problems may arise as to the manner in which the separate units of valuation are to be ascertained or in which individual items are to be grouped into units *(pg372j)* of valuation. These problems must necessarily be resolved, as they are in practice, in a common sense way. The estate is to be taken as it is found: it is not to be supposed, in order to obtain higher figures of valuation, that any substantial expense is to be incurred or work done in organising the estate into units: on the other hand, some practical grouping or classification, such as can reasonably be carried out without undue expenditure of time or effort, by a prudent man concerned to obtain the most favourable price, may be supposed.'

9 The House of Lords was willing to infer from some cryptic remarks of the Lands *(pg373a)* Tribunal that the division of the property into 532 units would not have involved undue expenditure of time and effort. They were 'natural units' corresponding with reality, such as farms, small holdings, houses, quarries, public houses and so forth. Accordingly the Revenue's valuation was affirmed. But the House refused to accept the Revenue's more extreme proposition that the hypothetical vendor must be *(pg373b)* supposed to have divided up the estate into whatever units would have produced the best possible price. A further division of the 'natural units', requiring substantial further work, would not have been a valuation of the property as it actually was. Lord Reid drew the analogy of a wholesaler's stock, which might realise the best prices if divided up and sold retail. But that is not a reasonable hypothesis upon which to value wholesale stock *(pg373c)* (see pp. 525–526).

10 *Buccleuch* was a case about splitting up the estate and the remarks about 'natural units' as the basic particles of valuation, which cannot be further split, must be read in that context. *A-G of Ceylon v Mackie & Anor* [1952] 2 All ER 775 was a case about putting things together. The deceased was a shareholder in a company with an issued share capital of Rs1,000,000 divided into 19,800 Rs50 preference shares and 5,000 Rs2 management shares. The articles gave the holders of 90 per cent *(pg373d)* of the share capital the right compulsorily to acquire the remaining shares. The deceased held all the management shares (which constituted one per cent of the share capital) and 9,201 preference shares. Lord Reid said at pp. 777–778:

> 'It was admitted for the appellant that no purchaser would have paid anything like Rs 250 per share for the management shares in face of the company's articles unless he could buy at the same time a large block of the preference shares and so have a majority of votes. But the appellant contends *(pg373e)* that the respondents must be supposed to have taken the course which would get the largest price for the combined holding of management and preference shares and to have offered for sale together with the management shares the whole or at least the greater part of the preference shares owned by the deceased. In their Lordships' judgment this contention is correct.' *(pg373f)*

11 This shows that whether one is taking apart or putting together, the principle is that the vendor must be supposed to have 'taken the course which would get the largest price for the combined holding', subject to the caveat in *Buccleuch* that it does not entail 'undue expenditure of time and effort'. *(pg373g)*

3. The Revenue's case on aggregation

12 In the present case the Revenue's view was that the prudent vendor would have sold the freehold of the Croxton Park Estate together with Lady Fox's interest in the partnership. Tenanted farming land is worth a good deal less than the same land with vacant *(pg373h)* possession. In the present case the parties agreed that the estate would have been worth £2,751,000 tenanted but £6,125,000 with vacant possession. The Cambridge District Valuer, Mr Michael Clegg, thought that Lady Fox's interest in the partnership would in practice have enabled her (or anyone else in her place) to obtain vacant possession for a relatively modest additional payment to acquire the interests of the other partners. These were a Major Fraser, a retired Army officer aged 61, and Mr Edward Cress, a partner in Strutt and Parker aged 57 who also farmed on his own account. *(pg373j)*

13 The partnership deed provided that the death or retirement of any partner should not determine the partnership as to the others, but that any partner could give six months' notice of dissolution to dissolve the partnership with regard to himself. Major Fraser had a $2\frac{1}{2}$ per cent interest in the profits, Mr Cress 5 per cent and Lady Fox the remaining $92\frac{1}{2}$ per cent. The principal asset of the partnership was the lease. This was unassignable, so that its value lay in what the freeholder might be willing to pay for a surrender. In addition, the partnership owned the usual paraphernalia of a farming business.

14 Mr Clegg's view was that upon a dissolution of the partnership at the instance of *(pg374a)* the hypothetical purchaser who had succeeded to the share of Lady Fox, neither of the other partners would in practice wish to succeed to the partnership business. This would involve having to pay the hypothetical purchaser his $92\frac{1}{2}$ per cent share of the value of the partnership assets, including the surrender value of the tenancy. Since neither partner was particularly young and Mr Cress had a farm and profession of *(pg374b)* his own, the overwhelming likelihood was that they would prefer to sell their shares.

15 What would they have to be paid? Mr Clegg estimated that the surrender value of the tenancy was £1,500,000, being about 45 per cent of the additional value created by adding it to the freehold. Mr Clegg valued the $7\frac{1}{2}$ per cent interest in this asset at £100,000. Thus a hypothetical purchaser who bought the freehold and the partnership share could reasonably reckon on obtaining vacant possession by laying out an additional £100,000. To allow for the possibility that there might be delay *(pg374c)* or that Major Fraser and Mr Crees might hold out for more or some other unexpected hitch occur, Mr Clegg deducted another £460,000 or $7\frac{1}{2}$ per cent of the vacant possession value. On this basis he concluded that as the estate with vacant possession was agreed to be worth £6,125,000, a hypothetical purchaser would have been willing to pay £560,000 less for the tenanted freehold and Lady Fox's interest in the partnership so far as it was attributable to the tenancy. This produced *(pg374d)* a figure of £5,565,000, of which Mr Clegg thought that £4,280,768 should be apportioned to the freehold interest.

16 As £5,565,000 was a great deal more than could have been obtained by separate sales of the freehold reversion (£2,751,000) and a share in a partnership holding an unassignable tenancy, the Revenue contended that a prudent hypothetical seller would have sold the two interests together. The taxpayer thought otherwise. It was *(pg374e)* clear that the dispute would have to be resolved in accordance with the statutory appeal process.

4. The problem of jurisdiction

17 At this point a question of jurisdiction raised its head. By para. 6 of Sch. 4 to the Finance Act 1975 the Revenue may be notice determine *(pg374f)* the value of any property to which a transfer of value is wholly or partly attributable, or (among other things) any other matter which appears to them to be relevant for the purposes of a charge to capital transfer tax. Under para. 7, a person upon whom a notice of determination has been served may appeal. The appeal is ordinarily to the special commissioners or, in some cases involving a question of law, to the High Court. But by para. 7(4), neither of these tribunals may determine any question 'as *(pg374g)* to the value of land in the United Kingdom'. On any such question the appeal is to the Lands Tribunal.

18 A dispute over the valuation of the freehold reversion was undoubtedly a matter for the Lands Tribunal. But what of a dispute over a composite asset consisting of the freehold and the partnership share? The partnership assets included personalty. In fact, the taxpayer was contending that the whole partnership interest was *(pg374h)* personalty. In order to avoid any suggestion that the Lands Tribunal was being asked to value assets over which it had no jurisdiction, the Revenue devised a complicated notice of determination. Taking advantage of para. 6(2)(f) of Sch. 4, which says that the Revenue may determine any matter which appears to them relevant for the purpose of capital *(pg374j)* transfer tax, they determined the following matters:

(1)   that the value of Lady Fox's freehold interest in the estate was an 'appropriate proportion' of the value of the freehold and her interest in the farming partnership aggregated as a single unit of valuation;

(2)   that the 'appropriate proportion' should be calculated by first determining what part of the value of the aggregated asset was attributable to the freehold and her partnership interest in the tenancy, and then apportioning that figure between the two interests; *(pg375a)*

(3)   that the value attributable to the two interests in the land was £5,565,000 and the value to be attributed to the freehold was £4,280,768.

5. The issues before the Lands Tribunal

19 The taxpayer appealed to the Lands Tribunal. He contended that a process of valuation which aggregated the freehold with an indirect interest in the tenancy and *(pg375b)* then apportioned the result was not permissible. Even if it was, the Crown's methodology and resulting valuations were wrong. The parties agreed that the following issues fell to be determined:

(1)   Should the freehold reversion and the partnership share be treated as one unit of property for the purposes of s38 of the Finance Act 1975?

(2)   If the freehold reversion and the partnership share are to be so treated, *(pg375c)* should the value to be attributed to the freehold reversion be ascertained in the manner and in the amount contended for by the Crown or in some other, and if so, what manner and/or amount?

(3)   In any event, is the value of (or to be attributed to) the freehold reversion for the purposes of s38 of the Act of 1975 the sum of £4,280,768 or £2,751,000 or some other and if so what sum? *(pg375d)*

20 The case stated to this court frames the questions rather differently, but the issues as agreed at the hearing provided the framework for the Lands Tribunal's findings and helps one to interpret them.

6. First issue: can the two interests be aggregated for the purposes of valuation? (pg375e)

21 Mr Bramwell, who appeared for the taxpayer, said that there were three separate reasons why the Revenue were not entitled to aggregate the two

interests. The Lands Tribunal accepted all three. In his submissions to us, he rearranged their order and I shall take them in that order.

(a) *The attribution point* (pg375f)

22 Section 38 requires one to consider what a particular item of property would have fetched if sold on the open market. The *Buccleuch* principle may require one to suppose that it was sold alone, split into parts or together with something else. But Mr Bramwell says the process must be one of valuation, not the attribution of part of the value of something else. In this case he says that the notice of determination did not value any actual item of property. It proceeded by a 'notional *(pg375g)* lotting' of the freehold interest with an item of property which had never had a separate existence, namely Lady Fox's interest in the partnership's tenancy to the exclusion of her interest in the other partnership assets, and then attributed part of the value of this imaginary asset to the freehold. Mr Bramwell says that this exercise is far removed from the practical and common sense conduct of the hypothetical *(pg375h)* seller postulated by Lord Wilberforce in *Buccleuch*. The tribunal agreed. It said that:

> 'if it was permissible to lot the freehold interest and the share in the partnership together as being a single unit of property, then s38 requires that that single unit be valued as a single unit and that apportionment is neither admissible nor appropriate.'

23 I do not think that this fairly reflects what the notice of determination was doing. *(pg375j)* The only assumption it makes about how the hypothetical sale would have been conducted is that the freehold and Lady Fox's entire interest in the partnership would have been sold together: para. 3(1). I shall return in due course to whether such an assumption could be justified under the *Buccleuch* principle, but there is no doubt that it involves the aggregation of two assets which each had a real existence at the relevant date. Since the two assets are supposed to have been sold together because this would realise a greater price than selling them separately, the value of each asset must necessarily be an apportioned part of the price which would have been realised *(pg376a)* for both. In most cases the Revenue would not be concerned to determine separate values. But there are situations in which it is necessary: for example, when one aggregated asset is part of the free estate and the other is settled property. Similarly, I think that the Revenue were entitled to determine a separate value for the freehold interest in this case in order to avoid jurisdictional problems.

24 In my judgment, therefore, the notice does assume a value for a single unit *(pg376b)* consisting of the two interests. It does not quantify that value because for the purpose of determining the value of the one item of property undoubtedly within the jurisdiction of the Lands Tribunal, namely the freehold interest, it was not necessary to do so. The notice determines the method by which that interest should be valued. That method must, as I have said, necessarily involve apportionment of the price which the composite asset would fetch. And there was no criticism of the *(pg376c)* formula which the Revenue used for the purposes of apportionment. In my judgment, therefore, the exercise performed by the notice was in accordance with s38.

(b) The jurisdiction point (pg376d)

25 Mr Bramwell's next point was that the division of jurisdiction as to the valuation of land and property other than land meant that for the purposes of s38, land could never be supposed to have been sold in conjunction with some other form of property. The Lands Tribunal also accepted this argument but I think it is wrong.

26 When s38 first appeared as s7(5) of the Finance Act 1894, there was a single appeal to the High Court. The division between land and other property was *(pg376e)* introduced by s60(3) of the Finance (1909–1910) Act 1910 which said that 'where the question in dispute is the value of any real (including leasehold) property' the appeal was to be to a panel of referees. Section 1(3)(a)(ii) of the Lands Tribunal Act 1949 substituted the Lands Tribunal for the referees. I do not think that the procedural change introduced in 1910 was intended to change the basis upon which duty was to be assessed. *(pg376f)*

27 One can easily think of cases in which it would be artificial in the extreme to value land and other property on the basis that they are sold separately from each other. In the case of a successful business comprising premises, fixtures and fittings, book debts, stock and goodwill, it would be remarkable if the hypothetical vendor had to be supposed to have sold the premises and any fixtures forming part of the realty as one unit and the remaining assets as another, as if on a liquidation. The natural unit *(pg376g)* of valuation is the assets of the business as a going concern.

28 There are other provisions of the capital taxes legislation which expressly require the aggregation of assets for the purposes of valuation. Paragraph 7 of Sch. 10 says that where the value of any property in a person's estate would be less than the appropriate portion of the value of the aggregate of that and any 'related property', *(pg376h)* it shall be taken to be that appropriate portion. 'Related property' includes the property of a spouse. So, for example, if the tenancy had been vested in Lady Fox's husband, the freehold reversion would have been valued at the appropriate portion of the value of the estate with vacant possession. In such a case, of course, both interests are land. But what if the husband had held the entire issued share capital in a company which held the tenancy? Paragraph 7 of Sch. 10 would still have *(pg376j)* required aggregation and it would have been no answer that the Lands Tribunal had no jurisdiction over part of the combined assets. Why then should the jurisdictional divide be an obstacle to aggregation in cases in which the courts have held that it is required by the terms of s38?

29 In my judgment, therefore, jurisdiction was no objection to an aggregation required by the principle stated in *Buccleuch*. I need not decide which tribunal would have had jurisdiction if the Revenue had simply determined the total value of the composite asset, except to say that the statute cannot be construed to *(pg377a)* produce the result that the Revenue can make a determination in accordance with s38 but against which no one has jurisdiction to hear an appeal. In this case, the Lands Tribunal in my judgment had jurisdiction because the entire determination raised questions 'as to the value of land'. So far as the Lands Tribunal had to consider the value of assets which were not land, this was only part of the process of reasoning by which it arrived at an answer to the substantial *(pg377b)* question in the determination, namely the value of the freehold interest.

30 For this purpose I do not think it matters whether or not Lady Fox's partnership interest included an interest in the tenancy which was itself 'land'. The Lands Tribunal rejected the Crown's argument that it was land and that accordingly there was no jurisdictional barrier to valuing it together with the freehold. For my part, I think that the Crown was right. As between themselves, partners are not entitled *(pg377c)* individually to exercise proprietary rights over any of the partnership assets. This is because they have subjected their proprietary interests to the terms of the partnership deed which provides that the assets shall be employed in the partnership business, and on dissolution realised for the purposes of paying debts and distributing any surplus. As regards the outside world, however, the partnership deed is irrelevant. The partners are collectively entitled to each and *(pg377d)* every asset of the partnership, in which each of them therefore has an undivided share. It is this outside view which identifies the nature of the property falling to be valued for the purpose of capital transfer tax, although in accordance with the *Crossman* principle the restrictions imposed by the partnership deed must be taken into account in assessing its value: see *Burdett-Coutts* v *IR Commrs* [1960] 1 WLR 1027. In my judgment, therefore, Lady Fox had for the purposes of s38 a $92\frac{1}{2}$ per cent interest *(pg377e)* in the tenancy which the Lands Tribunal had jurisdiction to value as an interest in land.

(c) The 'natural unit' point

31 Mr Bramwell's third submission was that even if the Lands Tribunal had jurisdiction to value both interests, the aggregate did not fall within the principle in *(pg377f)* *Buccleuch* because it was not a 'natural unit'. This, as we have seen, is a term derived from the speech of Lord Reid, where it is used in the context of a landed estate to mean parts having at the relevant date a separate commercial identity. It was a helpful way of describing the basic unit of valuation in that particular case. But I think it would be dangerous to elevate the term 'natural unit' to a universal touchstone for the application of the *Buccleuch* principle. The principle is that the *(pg377g)* hypothetical vendor must be supposed to have 'taken the course which would get the largest price' provided that this does not entail 'undue expenditure of time and effort'. In some cases this may involve the sale of an aggregate which could not reasonably be described as a 'natural unit'. Suppose, for example, there is evidence that at the relevant time a prudent seller would have discovered that a higher price could be obtained by the combined sale of two items which might otherwise have *(pg377h)* been thought entirely unrelated to each other. Such circumstances might arise from the peculiar demands of a small number of potential buyers or even those of a single one. In my view the hypothetical seller would in those circumstances have been, subject to the caveat I have mentioned, willing to sell the items together. The fact that no one would have described them as a 'natural unit' is irrelevant. *(pg377j)*

32 In dealing with this point, the tribunal said that the fact that one might obtain a higher value by lotting the items together 'does not convert the two parts into a natural unit of property'. In deciding that the aggregate was not a natural unit, it relied upon the evidence of the taxpayer's valuer Mr Reeves, who said that the two items together 'would not appeal to any known sector of the market'. He had never heard of land being sold together with a share in a partnership holding a tenancy in such land. Indeed, he had never heard of a sale of a share in a farming partnership at all. *(pg378a)*

33 In my judgment the tribunal here misdirected itself as to the true principle which it had to apply. The share in the farming partnership, with or without other property, was plainly not a 'natural' item of commerce. Few people would want to buy the right to farm in partnership with strangers. Nevertheless, s38 requires one to suppose that it was sold. The question for the tribunal was whether, on this assumption, it would have been more advantageous to sell it with the land. *(pg378b)*

34 The answer which the tribunal would have given to this question appears clearly enough from the answer which it gave to the second issue, namely whether, assuming that aggregation was permissible, the method of valuation adopted by Mr Clegg (which I have described above) was correct. Mr Reeve had said that purchasers would not give any more for the land because of also being able to 'step into the shoes of Lady Fox' and exercise her rights as a partner. 'In reality' he said, *(pg378c)* 'this reversion was no different from that of any other let farm and purchasers in the market would bid accordingly'.

35 On this point, however, the tribunal preferred the approach of Mr Clegg. It said at (1991) 1 CTC pp. 460–461:

'On the assumption that in law the respondent may lot or sell together the freehold reversion and the 92.5 per cent share in the farming partnership as a single *(pg378d)* unit of property, we are persuaded that the approach to valuation adopted by Mr Clegg pays a realistic regard to the circumstances actually prevailing and likely to have been within the knowledge of the hypothetical purchaser at the valuation date. Whilst the general basis of value to be adopted is prescribed by statute as open market value there is no prescription of the method of valuation to be applied. If adjustment of the agreed value with vacant possession by *(pg378e)* deductions and/or apportionment is adopted it falls to be considered on the criterion of whether it produces a realistic answer when judged against the prevailing factual circumstances. On the evidence before us the most likely prospect in March 1981 was that the minority shareholders would negotiate a surrender of the tenancies: as indeed they in fact did during the years 1982–1984.' *(pg378f)*

This passage in my judgment shows that the tribunal were persuaded that in real life, selling the freehold and the partnership share would have produced a greater combined price than selling them separately. There was no evidence that this would have required undue effort or expense. Accordingly I think that if the tribunal had not considered it necessary to find that the aggregate was a 'natural unit', they would *(pg378g)* have decided this point in favour of the Crown. As the tribunal were also in my view wrong in rejecting aggregation on the basis of the attribution and jurisdiction points, I think that the Crown should have succeeded on the first issue as a whole.

7. The second issue: Mr Clegg's method of valuation

36 I have already quoted the views of the tribunal on this point. They are findings *(pg378h)* of fact which on the evidence the tribunal was entitled to make.

8. The case stated

37 The tribunal stated the case in the following terms:

'The questions upon which the decision of the Honourable Court is desired *(pg378j)* are:

1.(1)   Whether as a matter of law a unit of "property" for the purposes of valuation under s38 Finance Act 1975 can comprise two or more component parts where at least one of those parts is "land" (within the meaning of Paragraph 7 Schedule 4 Finance Act 1975) and at least one of those parts is not "land".

1.(2)   If the answer to question 1(1) is "No", whether, as a matter of law, Lady Fox's partnership share ("the Share") includes "land" for this purpose. *(pg379a)*

2.   If the answer to either of Questions 1(1) and 1(2) is "Yes", what as a matter of law is the correct test for determining whether Lady Fox's reversion ("the Reversion") and the Share should be valued as one unit of property for the purposes of s38 Finance Act 1975.

3.   Whether the Lands Tribunal could, as a matter of law and on the facts found, have reached the conclusion that the Reversion and the Share did not *(pg379b)* form a unit of property for the purposes of valuation under s38 Finance Act 1975.

4.   Whether, on the footing that the Reversion and the Share did form a unit of property for the purposes of valuation under s38 Finance Act 1975, it is permissible to apportion the value of that unit between the Reversion and the Share for any of the purposes of the Finance Act 1975.' *(pg379c)*

38 As will appear from what I have said so far, I would answer these questions as follows:

1.(1)   Yes.

1.(2)   Does not arise, but in my view Yes.

2.   The principle in *Buccleuch* as explained above.

3.   No. *(pg379d)*

4.   Yes.

9. Conclusion

39 Where do these answers leave the Revenue's notice of determination? In my judgment, intact. The Lands Tribunal, although it found under the second issue that Mr Clegg had adopted the correct method of valuation, expressed some doubt *(pg379e)* as to whether his deduction of £100,000 for the shares of the other partners and his allowance of about £460,000 for risk and profit was in all the circumstances enough. But on this point they had no evidence to weigh against that of Mr Clegg. The taxpayer's valuer, Mr Reeve, took his stand on the proposition that Mr Clegg's method was wrong in principle because, quite apart from the technical objections, a purchaser of the freehold would not have paid any more because he was also *(pg379f)* getting the partnership share. In fact Mr Reeve thought he would have paid rather less. It followed that Mr Reeve saw no point in supposing a sale of the combined items and offered no formal valuation or other evidence of what they might have fetched. This was a high-risk strategy because it seems clear that if Mr Reeve had contended in the alternative for a combined valuation lower than that of Mr Clegg, the tribunal would have been sympathetic. In the event however, Mr Bramwell *(pg379g)* submitted to the tribunal (in my view correctly) that they were faced with an all or nothing choice. If they accepted Mr Clegg's methodology, they had also to accept his valuation. Before this court, both sides have adhered to this position and neither has asked for the case to be remitted to the Lands Tribunal to hear further evidence. I would therefore simply allow the appeal and confirm the Revenue's notice of determination. *(pg378h)*

Case 38
Caton's Administrators v Couch

[1995] STC (SCD) 34

Special Commissioners

5, 6, 7, 8, 9 December 1994 and 28 February 1995

This case is a very useful, modern illustration of the approach taken by the Special Commissioners in valuing a shareholding. The structure of the Special Commissioners' decision can usefully be adopted in a report by a share valuer.

Philip Caton died on 7 September 1987. In his estate was a holding of 2,495,552 ordinary shares in Yorkshire Switchgear Group Ltd, being 14.02 per cent of the totalled issued share capital of that company. On 15 April 1988 the shares were sold and a charge to capital gains tax arose on the administrators of the estate, the base value being the market value of the shares at the date of death. (It appears likely that 100 per cent business property relief applied and, hence, there was no inheritance tax charge on the value of the shares.)

The administrators valued the shares at the date of death at 88p per share. The Revenue valued the shares at the date of death at 35p per share.

Dr AN Brice, the Special Commissioner, commenced her decision by recording the establishment of the company in 1907 and the history of the issued share capital of the company, noting that 79.9 per cent of the shares in issue were held by three families, the Caton family holding 38 per cent of the issued share capital ([1995] STC (SCD) 34 at 38d–h **case 38 paras 2–4**).

The articles of association that are relevant to the value of the shares were noted, reference being made to the restrictions on transfer and provisions about confidentiality ([1995] STC (SCD) 34 at 38j–39a **case 38 paras 5–6**).

The Commissioner then looked at the composition of the board of directors and the management of the company, noting that by the valuation date the board consisted largely of non-family, full-time directors ([1995] STC (SCD) 34 at 39b–d **case 38 paras 7–8**).

A summary of the company's trade then followed and the dominance of the company as a manufacturer of high voltage current breakers noted, by 1987 the company being the sole significant independent company in its market, which was dominated by a small number of major groups. Its customers included the public supply authorities and large industrial organisations ([1995] STC (SCD) 34 at 39f–j **case 38 paras 9–10**).

The Special Commissioner then considered the balance sheet value ([1995] STC (SCD) 34 at 40b–f **case 38 paras 12–14**), the trading results of the four years up the valuation date ([1995] STC (SCD) 34 at 40g–j **case 38 paras 15–16**) and the dividend history of the company over that period ([1995] STC (SCD) 34 at 41a–c **case 38 paras 17–18**).

It was noted that a number of approaches had been made by major companies for a takeover of Yorkshire Switchgear Limited, but these approaches had been consistently rebuffed. However, early in 1987 the board had arrived at the view that they intended to sell the company before May 1988. Mr Dickinson and Mr Hargreaves had discussed the position which would arise on Mr Dickinson's retirement and had discussed a programme which would lead to a sale before such retirement. The decision to embark on such a programme was taken before the death of Mr Philip Caton. Mr Dickinson was asked to approach General Electric Company to request them to put their interest in writing. He thought that he was asked to make the approach in August 1987. The programme for sale was not recorded in the minutes and Mr Hargreaves had asked for all correspondence relating to it to be sent to another office in order to preserve confidentiality. Mr Dickinson considered that this programme had the consent of the majority of the shareholders.

On 24 August 1987 a letter was received from the vice-president of the Joslyn Corporation of Chicago in the United States, requesting discussions leading to the acquisition of an equity interest in the company. Following the valuation date of 7 September 1987, on 17 September 1987 General Electric Company wrote to confirm that it would like to acquire the company if the shareholders wished to dispose of their interests. On 25 September 1987 Merlin Gerin of France wrote to say that they understood that it was the intention to sell the company and wanted to register a firm interest with the intent of making a bid.

Discussion took place at the board meeting on 25 September 1987 about future trends affecting the company, including the possibility of permitting the group to be acquired. The board agreed that discussions should take place to explore the options. On 29 September 1987 letters were sent to the three companies which had expressed an interest with a view to opening discussions.

The Special Commissioner then specified the information available to the board as at the valuation date ([1995] STC (SCD) 34 at 41j–42d **case 38 paras 22–27**) and the information that was sent to shareholders ([1995] STC (SCD) 34 at 42f–j **case 38 paras 28–31**).

The prices paid on the actual three transfers of shares that occurred during 1987 prior to the valuation date were then noted ([1995] STC (SCD) 34 at 43b, **case 38 para 31**).

The fact that the company was taken over and all shares sold for cash on 15 April 1988, seven months after the valuation date, is recorded. The value of the shares held by the Administrators on that disposal was £3,269,173 ([1995] STC (SCD) 34 at 43b **case 38 para 33**).

The expert witnesses differed in their respective views as to the information that would be available to a hypothetical unconnected purchaser of the shareholding and, hence, in the values they respectively placed on the shareholding ([1995] STC (SCD) 34 at 44d–47h **case 38 paras 39–52**).

> Dr AN Brice gives her decision on the information assumed to be available:
>
> 'In my view, CGTA1979, s152(3) [now TCGA 1992, s 273(3)] is effective to provide that any information, including unpublished confidential information, and even information which might prejudice the interests of the company, is assumed to be available in the hypothetical sale if it would be reasonably required by a prudent prospective purchaser of the asset in question. It is therefore necessary to consider, in each case, what information a prudent prospective purchaser of the asset in question would reasonably require. In the context of s152(3) I understand the word "require" to mean "demand as a condition of buying"; information is "required" if the purchaser would not proceed without it.'
>
> ([1995] STC (SCD) 34 at 50d–e **case 38 para 68**).

The decision records the evidence given by the expert witness for the administrators on the question of the information that a prudent prospective purchaser would reasonably have required:

> 'Mr Sutherland's evidence was that, if the outlay were substantial then, whatever the size of the shareholding, the purchaser would always inquire about approaches for sale because the restrictions on transfer would lock him into his investment and he would only have an exit if the company were sold. Such an enquiry would have been made by

a reasonable purchaser of this holding in this company and such a purchaser would have been informed that a sale was being considered and that approaches had been received from three sources. Such a purchaser would also have made inquiries about the up-to-date management accounts and budget forecasts and that information would have been supplied.

The evidence of Mr Richardson was that, in view of the outlay, a reasonable purchaser of this holding would have required some unpublished information relating to profitability and how maintainable that was. In his view the directors would have provided some information about profits (although not the complete information available to them). He also thought that a purchaser might well enquire about the possibility of a proposed sale but that the directors might not release that information.'

([1995] STC (SCD) 34 at 50f–h **case 38 paras 69–70**)

This was accepted by the Special Commissioner:

'I find that a prudent prospective purchaser of this holding of shares in this company of this proposed outlay would reasonably have required up to date information about the management accounts and budget forecast as at 7 September 1987. In my view that information would include the published accounts up to and including the year ending 31 August 1986; the dividend yield to that date and the dividend policy of the directors as set out in the two letters sent to the shareholders of 13 February 1987 and 1 April 1987. It would also include the information known to the board on 7 September 1987 about profits for the year ending 30 August 1987 and about the budget projections for the following year. Finally, it would include information about the restructuring of the board in December 1986, the revaluation of the company's assets which had been completed at the end of July 1987, and the other changes which would appear in the balance sheet for the year ending 30 August 1987 relating to the cash balances and the discharge of the company's debts. In my view it is reasonable to assume that the management accounts as at 7 September 1987 would have shown a figure above £2,030,000 but below £2.6m and the directors would have had enough information to allow them to make a guess as to the figure for the year end. On the information available on 7 September 1987, a figure of £2.25m might well have been supplied ...

It has been emphasised on a number of occasions that a prudent prospective purchaser is always interested in the future prospects of the company. Such a purchaser would reasonably require up-to-date information about such budget forecasts and would require these to be accurate. A budget of £3m for the year ending on 31 August 1988 had been set in July 1987. In my view it is reasonable to assume that this information would be available to a purchaser.'

([1995] STC (SCD) 34 at 52b–g **case 38 paras 80–81**)

The Special Commissioner then considers the alternative valuations by the two parties and determines the value of the shares at 56p each ([1995] STC (SCD) 34 at 54g **case 38 para 93**).

Decision

References, example '(pg38d)', are to [1995] STC (SCD) 34.

The facts

1 From the evidence before me I find the following facts.

The company

2 The predecessor of the company was established in 1907 and at that time, or later, it was incorporated under the name of Yorkshire Switchgear & Engineering Co. Ltd. (YSE). On 30 December 1978 the company was incorporated and *(pg38d)* acquired all the issued share capital of YSE. In 1985 the company had four subsidiary companies with responsibilities for the United Kingdom market, the overseas market, property and investments and the Netherlands market. The first, second and fourth subsidiaries had subsidiaries of their own. At the end of 1986 and during 1987 there was a restructuring of the group structure. *(pg38e)*

The shareholdings

3 The memorandum of association of the company records that the share capital of the company is £5,000,000 divided into 5,000,000 ordinary shares of £1 each. On 27 July 1987 the £1 ordinary shares were divided into four ordinary shares of 25p each and, on the same date, three new shares were allotted fully paid for each share held. This meant that a shareholder received 16 25p shares for each £1 *(pg38f)* share previously held. On 7 September 1987 the issued share capital of the company comprised 17,804,880 ordinary shares of 25p each. These were held by members of the Turner family, by members of the Caton family, by members of the Holroyd family, and by certain directors and employees who had purchased shares from time to time. The various holdings may be summarised as follows: *(pg38g)*

PART 2 Cases

Caton family and family trusts	6,775,456
Holroyd family and family trusts	5,396,368
Turner family and family trusts	2,046,624
Other shareholders	3,586,432
Total	17,804,880

(pg38h)

4 On 7 September 1987 the holding of 2,495,552 shares, which is the subject of this appeal, comprised 14.02 per cent of the total issued share capital as at that date and was the largest single shareholding, the next largest holding being of 8 per cent.

The restrictions in the articles of association

5 The articles of association of the company contained restrictions on the transfer *(pg38j)* of shares. Unfettered transfer to non-members was prohibited so long as a member or person approved by the directors was willing to purchase the shares at a fair value to be certified (in the case of difference) by the company's auditor. Article 32(i) gave the directors a general power to refuse to register any transfer, other than a transfer to a member.

6 The articles of association also contained a number of provisions about confidentiality. These included Article 92(g) which provided that the office of director should be vacated if the director disclosed to any third party matters relating to the business and financial status of the company, other than those matters already *(pg39a)* published in compliance with statutory and other requirements, unless such disclosure had been previously approved by a directors' meeting.

The board and management

7 YSE was founded by a Mr W. H. Turner and, in its early years, capital was invested by a Mr Holroyd. In 1938 Mr Turner recruited Mr George Caton as technical director. Mr George Caton was a talented designer of switchgear and related *(pg39b)* equipment and owned a number of patents covering his designs. He became managing director of YSE in 1947, on the death of Mr Turner, and he became chairman in 1976. He sold a number of his patents to YSE in return for the issue of shares. In 1984 Mr George Caton was succeeded by his son, Mr Philip Caton, as chairman and managing director of the company. Mr George Caton remained a member of the board until his death in June 1986. Until October 1986 most *(pg39c)* members of the board were also members of the controlling families.

8 However, in late 1986 there were significant changes in the composition of the board. In November 1986 Mr Philip Caton left the board and Mr David Hargreaves was appointed as non-executive chairman. Mr Dickinson, who had intended to retire in April 1987, was asked to remain in order to provide continuity and stability pending any sale of the company. He was appointed managing *(pg39d)* director and initially agreed to defer his retirement until the end of 1987 but ultimately remained until the sale of the company in April 1988. Five directors of the operating subsidiaries were also appointed to the board in December 1986. As a result of these changes the board then consisted largely of non-family, full-time directors. *(pg39e)*

The company's trade

9 YSE was established to manufacture the equipment which transmitted electrical power from overhead cables to the motors of tramcars. Later YSE also manufactured other types of electrical power distribution equipment. YSE was based in Leeds. During the Second World War YSE set up a second plant in Scarborough for the manufacture of radar equipment components and established *(pg39f)* a subsidiary company, Electro-Mechanical Manufacturing Co. Ltd (EMMCO) for this purpose. In the period after the Second World War YSE expanded and established branches and subsidiaries in South Africa, Australia and Singapore to supply equipment in those markets. Also, YSE became a major supplier to the Electricity Boards and other large customers. In the early 1960's, YSE was one of about 20 independent companies operating in the market of high voltage electrical switchgear in the *(pg39g)* United Kingdom.

10 I n the 1960's demand in the domestic market substantially declined. YSE acquired Lindley Thompson Ltd., a manufacturer of transformers; it expanded its activities overseas; and it also continued its policy of investing in research and development which led to reduced profits in earlier years but to improved results later. This enabled the company to maintain a competitive position at a time when *(pg39h)* other small companies were disappearing and larger groupings were being formed, both in the United Kingdom and internationally. By 1987 the company was the sole significant independent company in its market, which was dominated by a small number of major groups. The company was unique in the manufacture of high voltage current breakers. Its customers included the public supply authorities *(pg39j)* and large industrial organisations.

Information about the financial position of the company

11 The agreed bundle of documents contained copies of the minutes of the meetings of the board from 2 October 1986–26 November 1987. It also contained copies of the consolidated accounts of the company for the eight months ending on 1 September 1985; the year ending on 31 August 1986; and the year ending on 30 August 1987. The accounts for the eight months ending on 1 September 1985 compared those results with the year ending on 31 December 1984 and in that way information about the year ending on 31 December 1984 was *(pg40a)*available. The accounts for the year ending on 30 August 1987 were dated 16 November 1987.

The assets of the company

12 The balance sheet for the year ending on 31 August 1986 showed shareholders' funds of £6,874,000. On 13 January 1987 the board resolved to revalue the *(pg40b)* company's land and buildings 'in order to reflect the current property values in the presentation to shareholders'. A preliminary report of the values was made at the board meeting on 16 March 1987 which indicated a 'surplus of £1.7m over net book value'. At the board meeting on 25 September 1987 the chairman reported that, although no balance sheet was available, shareholders' funds, following revaluation, would be in the region of £10m. *(pg40c)*

13 The balance sheet for the year ending on 30 August 1987 showed shareholders' funds of £9,773,000 and a substantial increase in the values of the fixed assets. The value of freehold property rose from £230,000 in 1986 to £1,883,000 as at 30 August 1987 'reflecting the fact that the company's freehold properties had been professionally revalued as at 31 July 1987'. The value of plant and machinery rose from £475,000 in 1986 to £1,407,000 in 1987 reflecting much greater investment *(pg40d)* in the latter year. The balance sheet also showed that bank borrowings and overdrafts had been consistently reduced since 1984 so that by 30 August 1987 all such debts, which had amounted to £1,718,000, had been discharged. Finally, the balance sheets also showed that cash balances had been consistently increased over the same period so that at 30 August 1987 cash at the bank amounted to £1,590,000. *(pg40e)*

14 Mr Dickinson's evidence was that the revaluations were undertaken to prepare for a sale of the company as both the directors and the shareholders were agreed that the company should be prepared for a sale. The possibility of a sale was kept confidential. He said that the valuations were completed at the end of July and that most of the information relating to the value of the assets would have been available at the board meeting on 27 July 1987. *(pg40f)*

The trading results of the company

15 The profit and loss accounts showed a substantial increase in profits for the year ending on 30 August 1987. In 1984 pre-tax profits had been £295,000; for the eight months ending on 1 September 1985 the figure was £334,000; and for the year ending on 31 August 1986 the figure was £445,000. At the board meeting held *(pg40g)* on 27 July 1987 it was reported that, on the basis of the internal accounts up to the end of June, pre-tax profits of £2,030,000 would be achievable. At the board meeting on 25 September 1987 the chairman reviewed the accounts for the year ending on 30 August 1987; no balance sheet was available but a pre-tax profit of £2.6m (which after tax would be £1.7m) was then anticipated. When the audited accounts were published on 16 November 1987 the figure for pre-tax profits was *(pg40h)* shown as £2,352,000.

16 The evidence of Mr Dickinson was that the increase in profits in 1987 was a result of a number of factors. First, there had been changes from oil technology to gas which meant that new designs could use new moulding techniques; the designs could be smaller and could be produced with less labour, resulting in higher margins relative to costs, while at the same time giving higher performance and *(pg40j)* quality assurance which led to additional business. Other factors included: the solution of certain problems with EMMCO; the establishment of a new company in Australia in 1983 which yielded profits in 1987; improved productivity generally; and a record year from Lindley Thompson Ltd.

The dividend record of the directors

17 Mr Dickinson's evidence was that the dividend policy of the directors changed gradually after the retirement of Mr George Caton in 1984. In the year ending on 31 December 1984 no dividend was paid. In the eight-month period ending on *(pg41a)* 1 September 1985 a dividend of £166,921 was paid which was 15p per £1 share and which represented 65 per cent of post-tax profits. The same dividend was paid for the year ending on 31 August 1986 and represented 76 per cent of post-tax profits. The minutes of the board meeting on 27 July 1987 indicated that statistics were tabled giving comparisons from 1982 to the 1988 budget with dividend estimates for 1987 and 1988. These assumed dividends were covered three times by after-tax profits. A *(pg41b)* dividend level of 35 per cent of after tax profits for the then current financial year was considered and it was agreed that there would be a detailed discussion at the following meeting when more precise figures would be tabled. In the event, a dividend of 3p for each 25p share was recommended for the year ending on 30 August 1987. This amounted to £534,146 which was just over 35 per cent of the after-tax profits of £1,485,000. *(pg41c)*

The acquisition offers

18 Mr Dickinson gave evidence that Mr George Caton consistently rebuffed approaches from major companies who wished to acquire YSE and, later, the company. However, early in 1987 the board had arrived at the view that they intended to sell the company before May 1988. He and Mr Hargreaves had *(pg41d)* discussed the position which would arise on his (Mr Dickinson's) retirement and had discussed a programme which would lead to a sale before such retirement. The decision to embark on such a programme was taken before the death of Mr Philip Caton. Mr Dickinson was asked to approach GEC to request them to put their interest in writing. He thought that he was asked to make the approach in August 1987. The programme for sale was not recorded in the *(pg41e)* minutes and Mr Hargreaves had asked for all correspondence relating to it to be sent to another office in order to preserve confidentiality. Mr Dickinson considered that this programme had the consent of the majority of the shareholders as Mr JA Holroyd, Mr RC Holroyd and Mr Philip Caton, whose families together represented more than 50 per cent of the shareholdings, had been present at the board meeting on 2 October 1986 when it was confirmed that there would be a significant *(pg41f)* shareholder interest in a sale if an appropriate price were offered.

19 On 24 August 1987 a letter was received from the vice-president of the Joslyn Corporation of Chicago, in the United States of America requesting discussions leading to the acquisition of an equity interest in the company. On 17 September 1987 General Electric Company wrote to confirm that it would like to acquire the company if the shareholders wished to dispose of their interests. On 25 September 1987 Merlin Gerin of France *(pg41g)* wrote to say that they understood that it was the intention to sell the company and wanted to register a firm interest with the intent of making a bid.

20 Discussion took place at the board meeting on 25 September 1987 about future trends affecting the company, including the possibility of permitting the group to be acquired. The board agreed that discussions should take place to explore the options. On 29 September 1987 letters were sent to the three companies which had *(pg41h)* expressed an interest with a view to opening discussions.

21 Thus no offers for the purchase of the company had been received by 7 September 1987. Discussions about a possible sale had taken place. Only one letter expressing an interest had been received from the Joslyn Corporation.

The information available to the board (pg41j)

22 In 1986 board meetings were held monthly but in 1987 they were held about six times each year. The board minutes revealed that meetings of the board received regular reports from the finance director and regular information about budget forecasts and management accounts. The evidence of Mr Dickinson was that budget forecasts, in the form of projected trading accounts, with details taken from the order books, were prepared for each company with a consolidated budget for the group. The budgets dealt with all trading activity and all expenditure including maintenance and overheads. A budget was prepared in advance of each financial year and revised on 'a rolling

12-month basis' so that a revised budget would be *(pg42a)* prepared in the week prior to the board meeting which looked forward to the next twelve months. The budgets were considered at every board meeting. The budgets were prepared on a realistic and conservative basis and were not over-optimistic. The forecasting was 'reasonably close'. The minutes showed that financial progress was generally in line with the forecasts made. *(pg42b)*

23 Mr Dickinson also gave evidence that management accounts in the form of trading statements, which recorded what had actually been achieved, were also available at each board meeting. These were prepared seven days after the end of each four-weekly (or monthly) accounting period. At the meeting on 27 July 1987 the board would have had the management accounts for a minimum of 44 weeks of the financial year beginning on 1 September 1986. From that the position for the full year could have been anticipated. The management accounts after 48 weeks to *(pg42c)* 2 August 1987, would have been circulated on about 9 August 1987. The management accounts for the year ending on 30 August 1987 would, in the normal course, have been circulated on 7 September 1987 but Mr Dickinson could not say whether they had been circulated before or after that date.

24 At the board meeting on 27 July 1987 it was noted that pre-tax profits of £2,030,000 should be achievable for the year ending on 31 August 1987. At the *(pg42d)* same meeting the budget for 1987–88 was discussed and Mr Dickinson said that a pre-tax profit of £3m was being projected for the year ending on 31 August 1988.

25 Mr Dickinson's evidence was that the outlook of the company in 1987 was good; turnover had been forecasted to increase and did in fact do so. *(pg42e)*

The information sent to shareholders

26 On 13 February 1987 Mr Hargreaves wrote to all shareholders. He said that the 1986 financial performance was barely adequate and the dividend recommended had not been covered by the trading profits earned during the period. However, a number of initiatives had been taken and the directors recommended a dividend of 15p per share for the year ending on 31 August 1986. Mr Hargreaves invited all *(pg42f)* members to attend the annual general meeting on 17 March 1987 when the directors would review the progress the group had made and would look forward to the future.

27 On 1 April 1987 the finance director wrote to all shareholders to inform them of the results of the annual general meeting. The new directors appointed in December 1986 had been introduced to the meeting. The bank borrowings had *(pg42g)* been cleared and the bank was to be asked to remove the charge on the company's assets. The chairman had advised that the profit for the first half of the year showed a substantial increase over the similar period in the previous year and concluded by saying that a continuation of that trend would enable the directors to recommend the payment of a significantly higher dividend than had been possible in recent years. *(pg42h)*

28 On 1 October 1987 Mr Hargreaves wrote again to all shareholders to say that trading for the year ending on 30 August 1987 had been very much improved. He went on to say that the level of profits indicated by the management accounts was such that a dividend of 3p per share would be paid.

29 In November 1987 Mr Hargreaves wrote again to all shareholders and sent the *(pg42j)* accounts for the year ending on 30 August 1987. He said that these were most satisfactory and the company was budgeting for a substantial increase in profit for the year ending on 31 August 1988. In the longer term the outlook was encouraging. A total dividend of 3p per share was confirmed.

Other valuations

30 The minutes of the board meetings contained resolutions authorising the transfers of shares at the price of £2.05 per £1 ordinary share on 2 February 1987, 27 February 1987 and 18 May 1987. A valuation of 62p per 25p share was agreed *(pg43a)* by the Shares Valuation Division in December 1987 for the purposes of the company's share option scheme. This valuation did not take account of any prospect of a sale of the company.

The sale of the company

31 On 15 April 1988 all the issued share capital of the company was sold to *(pg43b)* Merlin Gerin of France at the price of £1.31 for each 25p ordinary share. The value of the shares held by the taxpayers on that disposal was thus £3,269,173.

The agreed submissions

32 A number of the submissions of law were agreed by the parties. As a result of s32 of the 1979 Act the allowable deductions for the purposes of computing capital *(pg43c)* gains tax were the value of the consideration given for the acquisition and the incidental costs of the acquisition and the disposal. As a result of s49(1) the shares owned by Mr Philip Stuart Caton at the date of his death on 7 September 1987 were deemed to be acquired by the taxpayers for a consideration equal to their market value at that date. As a result of s150(1), 'market value' meant the price which the shares might reasonably be expected to fetch on a sale in the open market *(pg43d)* and, as a result of s150(2), no reduction was to be made for placing all the shares on the market at the same time. Following the decisions in *IR Commrs* v *Crossman* [1937] AC 26 and *Lynall* v *IR Commrs* [1971] 47 TC 375 AC 680, the shares must be valued on the basis that no-one was excluded from purchasing the shares and that the purchaser would be registered as the holder of the shares but would thereafter hold the shares subject to the restrictions on transfer and other provisions *(pg43e)* in the articles of association of the company. Finally, as a result of s152(3), it had to be assumed that there was available to any prospective purchaser of the shares all the information which a prudent prospective purchaser might reasonably require if he were proposing to purchase from a willing vendor by private treaty and at arm's length. *(pg43f)*

The submissions of the taxpayers

33 On behalf of the taxpayers, Mr Massey submitted that it had to be assumed that the information which a prospective purchaser might reasonably require would be made available to him, regardless of whether it was confidential information and also regardless of whether that particular board would in fact have made that information available. The private treaty standard of information included *(pg43g)* unpublished confidential information known to the board but not in the public domain. Section 152(3) had been introduced by s51 of the Finance Act 1973 and Mr Massey referred to the Official Report of the Parliamentary Debates on 10 July 1973 cols 1348–1350. In col 1349 it was stated that the new clause provided that unpublished information could be taken into account in arriving at a valuation. *(pg43h)*

34 Secondly, Mr Massey submitted that the information which a prudent prospective purchaser of this holding of shares in this company would reasonably require was a question of fact on which there had been expert evidence. A purchaser of this holding would be investing in the region of £1m or more for a 14.2 per cent minority holding and would require the fullest possible information about *(pg43j)* the company including, but not limited to, its past history, its trade, and its future prospects. He referred to the decision of Widgery L.J. in the Court of Appeal in *Lynall*, to *Holt* v *IR Commrs* [1953] 1 WLR 1488 and *McNamee* v *IR Commrs* [1954] IR 214. He also cited *Dymond's Capital Taxes* at para 23.327. Specifically, the information which would have been required included: changes in the net asset position since the last balance sheet (of 1986); an anticipated *(pg44a)* profit to 30 August 1987 of £2.25m; the budget forecasts for 1988 of £3m; the view that future profit would increase after 1988; anticipated dividends of 35 per cent of post-tax profits for 1987 and 1988; and the prospects of a sale.

35 Thirdly, Mr Massey relied upon Mr Sutherland's valuation of 50p if no information about a sale was available and 88p if such information were available. He submitted that other valuations of the shares in the company, which had been agreed with the Revenue, were admissible although they should be treated with care. He cited *IR Commrs v Stenhouse's Trustees* [1992] BTC 8,017. *(pg44b)*

36 Finally, Mr Massey submitted that the expenses incurred by the Taxpayers in appealing the assessment to capital gains tax, where the sole substantive issue for determination was the market value of the asset, should be an allowable deduction in computing the chargeable gain as they fell within the provisions of s32(2)(b) as being 'expenses reasonably incurred in ascertaining market value where required by this Act'. *(pg44c)*

The expert evidence for the taxpayers

37 Mr Sutherland's evidence was that the information properly required by a prudent purchaser of any minority holding would depend on the amount of money he would have to pay. A purchaser spending £1m would make more inquiries than *(pg44d)* a purchaser spending £1,000. It was a matter of commonsense as to what would be 'reasonable' in any particular case. The purchaser would be an investor wanting a return on his investment. If a reasonable amount of money were at stake a prudent purchaser would require more than published information and it would be obtained. Some purchasers commissioned independent accountants to obtain the information for them. In particular, such a prudent purchaser would inquire about *(pg44e)* approaches for sale and future prospects of sale because a purchaser of unquoted shares would be subject to the restrictions on transfer in the Articles of association and would effectively be locked into his investment and would only have an exit if the company were sold. This applied to any size of shareholding if the outlay were large. Although the directors might be bound by rules of confidentiality, the valuation in the present case had to proceed on the basis of a hypothetical sale *(pg44f)* following the enactment of s51 in the Finance Act 1973 (now s153(3) of the 1979 Act).

38 Mr Sutherland expressed the view that any prudent prospective purchaser of this holding of shares in this company would reasonably require all information about the history and current business of the company: the changes in the structure of the board in the last year before the relevant date; the profit record and the results and *(pg44g)* dividend for the year ending on 30 August 1987; the asset backing and the cash balances which were being generated; and the prospects for future profits and dividend. That information would have revealed that the company was an attractive acquisition for most major international groups in the industry; that, although in the past approaches with a view to acquisition had been rebuffed, there was a *(pg44h)* general agreement from about 1986 that the company would be sold if an acceptable price could be obtained; that approaches had actually been received in 1987 from three sources and that a revaluation of the company's assets had taken place in July 1987 with the sale of the company in mind.

39 In valuing the shares the price paid would have been based on a number of factors including: expected profits of 2.25m before tax in the year ending on *(pg44j)* 31 August 1987 and expected profits of £3m before tax in the following year with further increases thereafter; dividends of 3p per share net in the year ending on 31 August 1987 and of 3.65p net for the following year with further increases later; the approaches which had been received with a view to acquisition and the attitude of the board and shareholders to such sale; and the fact that the company could expect to command a significant premium over its net asset value.

40 Mr Sutherland's first valuation of the shares assumed that no information about a proposed sale of the company was available and was based on expected dividends. *(pg45a)* The board meeting of 27 July 1987 had considered a dividend of 35 per cent of post-tax profits. On a basis of pre-tax profits of £2.25m and corporation tax of 35 per cent this would give a post-tax profit of £1,462,500. Thirty-five per cent of that figure was £511,875 which gave a dividend of 3p net, 4.11p gross. A profit of £3m in the year ending on 31 August 1988 would give post-tax profits of £1.95m and a dividend of *(pg45b)* one-third of post-tax profits would be £650,000 or 3.65p net per share or 5p gross per share. Because a purchaser of these shares could not readily realise them he would require a yield of at least three times that obtainable on quoted shares. At the relevant date the yield on quoted shares was about 3 per cent so a purchaser of these shares would require a yield of between 9 per cent and 10 per cent. If expected gross future dividends were to be 5p per share, and dividend yield was 10 per cent, then the value of each share would be 50p. *(pg45c)*

41 Mr Sutherland's second valuation assumed that information about a sale was available and was based on the returns a purchaser could reasonably expect on such a sale. In his experience companies of this type realised prices on sale of multiples of pre-tax profits of six or even higher. Accordingly, if annual maintainable profits were £3m, a purchaser would pay £18m. With the addition of cash balances of *(pg45d)* £2m the price would come to £20m. After costs of sale this would be about £1.10 per share. However, there was always a risk that a sale would not take place so that figure would be discounted by 20 per cent to give a final figure of 88p per share.

Views of the Revenue

42 Mr Richardson disagreed with Mr Sutherland's first valuation which, he said, *(pg45e)* was based on the assumption that the budgeted profit for the year ending on 31 August 1988 of £3m would be achieved. This was no more than an estimate of a period which had just started. The valuation also assumed a dividend of 5p in 14 months' time. He agreed that a yield of three times that of quoted shares would be required to compensate for unmarketability, restrictions on transfer etc. Mr Richardson also disagreed with Mr Sutherland's second valuation. He did *(pg45f)* not disagree with a figure of £20m for the company but he did not agree with the proposed discount of 20 per cent for delay and risk and thought that such discount should be in the region of 50 per cent or more.

The submissions of the Revenue

43 Mr Griffiths submitted that unpublished information about a sale of the
(pg45g) company, and full information about profits and budget forecasts,
could not be assumed to be available. The 'private treaty' standard of
information did not include unpublished confidential information known to
the board but not in the public domain. Such information was not available in
Lynall and so that decision could not be authority for the view that it should be
made available. He referred to *(pg45h) Findlay's Trustees* v *IR Commissioners of
Inland Revenue* (1938) 22 ATC 437 but distinguished that case on the grounds
that it concerned an 80 per cent stake in a company where a very high standard
of information would be required. He also referred to *Salvesen's Trustees* v *IR
Commissioners* of Inland revenue (1930) 9 ATC 43 but distinguished that case
on the grounds that the facts adduced were a common assumption between
the parties. In *Lynall* both decisions were treated as being authority for no
(pg45j) more than the 'published information' standard.

44 Mr Griffiths further submitted that the phrase 'reasonably requires' in
s152(3) was objective and implied that there could be information which a
purchaser could not reasonably require. What a purchaser reasonably required
must be the same as what a supplier of the information would reasonably
provide. The company's attitude was an important consideration and could not
be ignored. A balance had to be struck between the purchaser and other
interested parties. There was a difference between what a person sought and
what he would get. No regard should *(pg46a)* be paid to hindsight. He cited
Holt v *IR Commissioners of Inland Revenue* [1953] 2 All ER 1499.

45 He submitted that the level of the information available would depend on
the circumstances. There was no warrant in the statutory provisions for
disregarding confidentiality; the board had kept the prospect of sale
confidential and certain matters were even kept out of the board minutes. The
budget and management accounts were circulated only to the board and not
to other shareholders. *(pg46b)*

46 Dealing with the value of the shares, Mr Griffiths submitted that the values
of 50p produced by Mr Sutherland (on the basis that no information about a
sale was available) and 35p produced by Mr Richardson (on the same basis)
were not far apart. The difference arose because each had started with a
different figure for profits. The major difference between the parties was the
relevance of the prospect of a sale. *(pg46c)*

47 Finally, Mr Griffiths submitted that any costs had to be wholly and
exclusively incurred for the purposes of the disposal. He cited *Smith's Potato
Estates Ltd* v *Bolland* (1948) 30 TC 267 [1948] AC 508, and *Rushden Heel Co Ltd*
v *Keene* (1948) 30 TC 298. The view of the Inland Revenue was that any
reasonable costs incurred in making the valuation so that the gain could be
calculated and returned, could be deducted. However, any costs subsequently

(pg46d) incurred, for example in negotiating with the District Valuer or with the Shares Valuation Division, or in litigating the matter before any tribunal or in the courts were not allowable.

The evidence for the Revenue

48 In reaching his valuation Mr Richardson summarised the statutory provisions *(pg46e)* as providing that market value was the price paid on a sale at arm's length between a hypothetical willing seller and a hypothetical willing but prudent purchaser. He did not mention the concept of a private treaty. In his view, a holding of 14.2 per cent was uninfluential and the directors would not release information about a proposed sale to such a purchaser. Even if a purchaser were spending a considerable amount, the directors did not have a lot of information to release. *(pg46f)*

49 Mr Richardson assumed that the purchaser would have been aware of: the sub-division of the shares in July 1987; the restrictions on transfer in the articles of association; the contents of the annual accounts for the trading period ending on 31 August 1986; and the letters to shareholders from the chairman on 13 February 1987 and from the finance director on 1 April 1987 which indicated a substantial *(pg46g)* increase in profits and the possibility of a 'significantly higher dividend'. That was published information. He also assumed that, in view of the outlay to be made by the purchaser, some unpublished information would be required. He assumed that a purchaser on 7 September 1987 would require an estimate of profitability for the year ending on 31 August 1987 and would be informed that a pre-tax profit of *(pg46h)* £2.03m would be achievable and would also be informed that the 1988 budget suggested that this level of profits would be maintained. A purchaser would also require some general information about the company's business. However, the directors would keep information about a proposed sale confidential until the date of any announcement.

50 Mr Richardson valued the shares on an earnings multiple basis. He took an *(pg46j)* amount for earnings per share and applied the appropriate price/earnings ratio to produce the price of the share. In calculating earnings he took the estimated pre-tax profit of £2,030,000 and deducted corporation tax to produce post-tax profits of £1,319,500. This represented earnings of 7.4p per share. In oral evidence he said that, if the purchaser knew of profits of £2.25m and a budget estimate of £3m, then earnings would be 8.2p per share. For the price/earnings ratio Mr Richardson looked at the Financial Times Actuaries Share Index on 7 September 1987 which gave the following price/earnings ratios: *(pg47a)*

Capital goods	17.66
Mechanical Engineering	16.33
500 Share Index	18.28

He thought the ratio rather high at between 16.33 and 18.28. He therefore used *(pg47b)* a ratio of 12–14. With earnings of 7.4p per share this yielded a price in the range of 85p–£1. He then discounted that price by 60–70 per cent to allow for the fact that the holding was uninfluential and unmarketable and reached a value of 35p per share. He agreed that if earnings were 8.2p, if a ratio of 14 were used, and if the discount were 60 per cent, then the value would be 46p per share.

51 Mr Richardson also considered an alternative approach and looked at the *(pg47c)* dividend yield. He assumed a net dividend of 2.5–3p net and 3.42–4.11p gross and earnings of 7.4p per share. A price of 35p per share gave a dividend yield of 9.8– to 11.7 per cent which was not unreasonable.

The views of the taxpayers

52 Mr Sutherland disagreed with Mr Richardson's calculations in a number of respects. *(pg47d)* He did not agree that the price/earnings ratios for the quoted market were high at 16.33 and 18.28. He referred to the *Investors Chronicle* for 4 September 1987 and 11 September 1987 and to an extract from *Eastaway and Booth* (2nd edn.) which gave a price/earnings ratio for capital goods as 18.41 on 31 July 1987, although this fell to 12.27 by 31 October 1987 after 'Black Monday'. He also did not agree that the price should be discounted by 60 to 70 per cent *(pg47e)* for unmarketability and other factors. That discount might be appropriate for a company which did not pay dividends but the present company paid dividends of 35 per cent of post-tax profits. In his view the discount should be 20 to 25 per cent. He referred to *Dymond on Capital Taxes*, para 23.374 which stated:

> 'It is therefore not unreasonable … to begin with the P/E ratio of comparable *(pg47f)* quoted companies and deduct the usual 20 per cent or so for unmarketability. If the price so obtained is significantly more or less than the price calculated by reference to dividend yield, the market value is likely to be a compromise between the two. Even with quoted companies, the dividend policy usually has an important effect on the P/E ratio.' *(pg47g)*

Reasons for decision

53 In considering the submissions of the parties I first consider what information should be assumed to be available to a prudent prospective purchaser of this holding of shares in this company. I then consider the value of the shares in the light of those principles and in the light of the evidence. (pg47h)

(1) What information should be assumed to be available?

54 In considering what information should be assumed to be available I start with the words of s152(3). That subsection provides:

'… it shall be assumed that, in the open market which is postulated for the *(pg47j)* purposes of that determination, there is available to any prospective purchaser of the asset in question the information which a prudent prospective purchaser of the asset might reasonably require if he were proposing to purchase it from a willing vendor by private treaty and at arm's length.'

This section was first enacted in s51 of the Finance Act 1973 and I was informed that it has not been judicially interpreted since that date. Accordingly I have approached its interpretation by considering the decision in *Lynall*, which preceded the enactment of s51, to see if it is possible to identify the mischief which the *(pg48a)* section was designed to cure and to see if I can identify the general intention of Parliament.

55 The decision in *Lynall* concerned a valuation for estate duty purposes under s7(5) of the Finance Act 1894 which provided that the value should be the price that the property would fetch if sold in the open market at the time of death. A holding of shares in a family company, which holding amounted to 28 per cent of the total, *(pg48b)* fell to be valued as at 21 May 1962. At the time of the relevant death the company was likely to go public in the very near future but that information was known only to the directors. If the hypothetical purchaser had known of the possible flotation he would have been prepared to pay a higher value per share; if he had not known it he would have offered a lower value.

56 At first instance Plowman J [1969] 1 Ch 421 TC 375 *(pg48c)* considered what information would have been available to a hypothetical purchaser and identified four possible tests or standards.

'The first was to assume that all the *(pg48d)* facts, which were facts at the date of death, were available. This has been called the 'omniscience' standard.

The second was to assume that the only information available was the published company's accounts together with any other information made available to all the shareholders. This has been called the 'published information' standard.

The third was to assume that the purchaser obtained both the published information and any information which the directors of that company would have given in answer to any reasonable question likely to be asked by any vendor-shareholder or intending purchaser. As this test depends on considerations of what that actual board would have supplied it has been called the 'subjective' *(pg48e)* standard.

The fourth was to assume that the purchaser obtained both the published information and any additional information which a hypothetical reasonable board would have disclosed in answer to any reasonable inquiries which the vendor or the intending purchaser or his advisers might have made. As this does not require any consideration of what the actual board would have done it has been called the *(pg48f)* 'objective' standard.'

57 Plowman J [1969] 1 Ch 421 concluded that information in the accounts for the year ending after the date of death, and the contents of a speech made by the chairman of the company after the date of death, could not be taken into account. Relying on the evidence of a witness who spoke on behalf of the board, and who said that he would not disclose any board minutes *(pg48g)* or other confidential documents and who, if asked by a purchaser about the prospect of a public issue would have replied that the prospect was doubtful and remote, he concluded that the information about the proposed flotation could not be taken into account either, since that information was neither published information nor information which would in fact have been elicited from the board on inquiry. *(pg48h)*

58 Accordingly, after the hearing at first instance, the decision in *Lynall* was authority for the 'subjective' standard.

59 On appeal, the Court of Appeal [1970] Ch 138 decided that the information about the flotation should be assumed to be available and adopted a version of the objective standard. They decided that the information deemed to be *(pg48j)* available to a purchaser did not depend upon what a particular board would do. Instead it was to be assumed that the purchaser would receive true and factual answers to all his reasonable enquiries. Also, it had to be assumed that any provisions in the articles which prohibited the directors from supplying confidential information were waived for the purposes of the hypothetical sale in the same way as any provisions in the articles restricting the transfer of shares were also waived for the same purposes.

60 The House of Lords, however, held that the objective standard should not be *(pg49a)* applied and valued the shares on the assumption that the information about the proposed flotation was not available. Lord Reid said that evidence which had been adduced, about the way in which confidential information would be disclosed by a board of directors to a purchaser's advisers in confidence, was irrelevant because that kind of sale was not a sale in the open market; it was a sale by private treaty. Also, the directors were *(pg49b)* under no legal obligation to make any confidential information available. There was difficulty in laying down a general rule that directors must be supposed to have done something which they were not obliged to do. He continued ([1972] AC 680 at 696, 47 TC 375 at 408):

> 'The farthest we could possibly go would be to hold that directors must be *(pg49c)* deemed to have done what all reasonable directors would do. Then it might be reasonable to say that they would disclose information provided that its disclosure could not possibly prejudice the interests of the company.'

61 This was the principle which was adopted by Mr Griffiths in his submissions.

62 It seems to me that following the decision of the House of Lords, the decision in *Lynall* was authority for the view that the information deemed to be available to a *(pg49d)* prospective purchaser of unquoted shares in a private company did not include confidential information as that was not information which would be available on a sale in the open market but rather it was information which might be made available on a sale by private treaty. Also, the directors were under no legal obligation to make confidential information available. *(pg49e)*

63 The year after the decision in *Lynall*, s51 of the Finance Bill 1973 was introduced to amend the legislation relating both to estate duty and capital gains tax. In introducing the new clause Mr Nott said:

> 'The new clause is concerned with the valuation of unquoted shares and securities for the purpose of estate duty and capital gains tax. In effect, it *(pg49f)* provides that unpublished information can be taken into account in arriving at the valuation. It thus ensures a more realistic basis of valuation than that which has obtained since the decision in the House of Lords in the *Lynall* case, the effect of which was to exclude unpublished information.

> Although in theory the exclusion of unpublished information could work either way, the effect in practice is normally to reduce value. Thus, the *Lynall* decision has meant that, *(pg49g)* for estate duty, duty is being paid on a lower value than before that decision, but for capital gains tax the *Lynall* decision imposed severe extra tax burdens on individual taxpayers.'

64 The provisions of the clause were enacted as s51 of the Finance Act 1973 and re-enacted in s152(3) of the 1979 Act. *(pg49h)*

65 It seems to me to be clear that the provisions of s51 (and then of s152) were not intended to restate the position which obtained after the decision of the House of Lords in *Lynall*. Section 51 was enacted to overturn that decision and to provide for a version of the objective standard similar to that applied by the Court of Appeal. *(pg49j)* In doing so, the section dealt with two difficulties identified by the House of Lords and one difficulty identified by the Court of Appeal.

66 The first difficulty identified by the House of Lords was that the release of confidential information was not appropriate to a sale in the open market but was appropriate to a sale by private treaty. The legislation deals with this by providing that the sale is to be assumed to be by private treaty. It appears to me that the inclusion of those words in the section was intended to indicate that the provision of confidential information by the directors to an intending purchaser could be assumed for the purposes of the hypothetical sale.

The second difficulty identified by the House of Lords was that there was no legal *(pg50a)* obligation on the directors to disclose confidential information and it was not right to assume that they would disclose it if it would prejudice the interests of the company. It seems to me that the section deals with this difficulty by providing that it shall be assumed that information (including confidential information) 'is available' if it is reasonably required. This gives effect to the findings of the Court of Appeal, that it has to be assumed that any provisions in the articles which prohibit *(pg50b)* the directors from supplying confidential information are waived for the purposes of the hypothetical sale in the same way that any provisions in the articles restricting the transfer of the shares are also waived for the same purposes. It also means that it is not necessary to consider, for the purposes of the hypothetical sale, whether the disclosure of the information would prejudice the interests of the company.

67 The difficulty identified by the Court of Appeal was that values should not *(pg50c)* depend upon the whim of a particular person or board. It seems to me that the section deals with this difficulty by providing that all information is to be assumed to be provided to the purchaser so long as it is reasonably required. It is no longer necessary to consider what the particular board would do.

68 Accordingly, in my view, s152(3) is effective to provide that any information, *(pg50d)* including unpublished confidential information, and even information which might prejudice the interests of the company, is assumed to be available in the hypothetical sale if it would be reasonably required by a prudent prospective purchaser of the asset in question. It is therefore necessary to consider, in each case, what information a prudent prospective purchaser of the asset in question would reasonably require. In the context of s152(3) I understand the word 'require' to *(pg50e)* mean 'demand as a condition of buying'; information is 'required' if the purchase would not proceed without it.

69 Mr Sutherland's evidence was that, if the outlay were substantial then, whatever the size of the shareholding, the purchaser would always inquire about approaches for sale because the restrictions on transfer would lock him into his investment and he would only have an exit if the company were sold. Such an enquiry would have *(pg50f)* been made by a reasonable *(pg50g)* purchaser of this holding in this company and such a purchaser would have been informed that a sale was being considered and that approaches had been received from three sources. Such a purchaser would also have made inquiries about the up-to-date management accounts and budget forecasts and that information would have been supplied.

70 The evidence of Mr Richardson was that, in view of the outlay, a reasonable purchaser of this holding would have required some unpublished information relating to profitability and how maintainable that was. In his view the directors would have provided some information about profits (although not the complete information available to them). He also thought that a purchaser might well enquire about the possibility of a proposed sale but that the directors might not *(pg50h)* release that information.

Dymonds Capital Taxes, at para 23.327, states that the amount of information required will depend on the size of the purchase. If 25 per cent or more of the issued voting capital is up for sale the buyer will want to know the figures for sales and profits up to the latest date, with corresponding figures for the previous year, and the board's views on trading prospects. He will also want to know the dividend *(pg50j)* prospects and the directors' dividend policy:

> '"He will ask whether the board contemplates any transaction likely to alter the value of the shares, such as a public issue, merger, take-over or liquidation: and, if so, whether the board has sought professional advice, with details of any advice given and any action taken."'

71 *Dymond* also says that where the holding is less than 25 per cent it may be that the buyer will expect less information but this is a matter for expert evidence. *(pg51a)* The size of the company is important and a buyer investing £200,000 would obviously be entitled to know more than one investing £2,000. Where the holding was small, say less than £50,000 and less than 5 per cent of the capital, the buyer would not normally be expected to have more than the information which was published or which he could find out without questioning the directors. *(pg51b)*

72 In reaching a decision I have borne in mind that although this is a minority holding, the size of the proposed investment is large. The hypothetical purchaser is considering an investment of something in the region of £1m. I rely upon the expert evidence of Mr Sutherland and conclude that, with that amount of outlay, a prudent purchaser would consult advisers who would advise him that information about a possible exit was important; such a purchaser could, therefore, reasonably *(pg51c)* require information about approaches for sale, about future prospects of sale, and about up-to-date information from the management accounts and budget forecasts.

73 Having reached that conclusion I now turn to consider the value of the shares.

What is the value of the shares?

74 In reaching a decision about the value of the shares I have in mind the dicta *(pg51d)* of Lord Fleming in *Salvesen* when he said (1930) 9 ATC 43 at 45:

'The estimation of the value of shares by a highly artificial standard which is never applied in the ordinary share market must be a matter of opinion and does not admit of precise scientific or mathematical calculation.'

75 I have also borne in mind certain dicta of Danckwerts J in *Holt* from which I *(pg51e)* conclude that I am entitled to find a value either of 35p, as proposed by the Revenue, or of 88p as proposed by the taxpayer, or of some other value somewhere in between. Also, after carefully considering the evidence, I must make the most intelligent guess that I can.

76 My first difficulty is that Mr Richardson did not offer a value on the basis that *(pg51f)* information about a proposed sale would be available but I can safely assume that, if he had offered such a value, it would be no lower than 35p.

77 I approach the valuation by first considering a value on the basis that no information about a sale was available. Here Mr Sutherland based his valuation on expected dividends. At the relevant date dividends on quoted shares were 3 per cent but he assumed that a purchaser of these shares would require a yield of about three times that amount to compensate for unmarketability. He would therefore expect *(pg51g)* a yield from these shares of about 9–10 per cent. Mr Sutherland also assumed that expected gross future dividends would be 5p per share. He based this *(pg51h)* figure on the fact that expected pre-tax profits for the year ending on 30 August 1987 would be £2.25m, for the year ending on 31 August 1988 would be £3m, and that profits at that level would continue to be maintainable or would increase. He also based this figure on the fact that the directors would continue to recommend dividends of 35 per cent of post-tax profits.

78 I first consider the validity of the assumptions made by Mr Sutherland. The first was the assumption that a dividend yield of three times that obtained on quoted shares would be required to compensate for unmarketability etc. This strikes me as being on the high side. *Dymond* at para 23.348 talks about an uplift of between 20 *(pg51j)* and 30 per cent depending on the provisions in the articles of association relating to unmarketability and restrictions on transfer. In *Lynall* where the restrictions were stringent an uplift of 31 per cent was used. However, as Mr Richardson agreed that a yield of three times that of quoted shares would be required I accept that figure.

79 The next assumption made by Mr Sutherland was that expected gross future dividends would be 5p per share. This in turn assumes three things. First, that up-to-date information about the management accounts and budget forecasts as at 7 September 1987 would be available. Secondly, that the budget forecast of £3m *(pg52a)* would be achieved and maintained. And, finally, that the directors would adopt a dividend policy of distributing 35 per cent of post-tax profits.

80 In view of my conclusions on the general principles governing information standards I find that a prudent prospective purchaser of this holding of shares in this company for this proposed outlay would reasonably have required up to date information about the management accounts and budget forecasts as at *(pg52b)* 7 September 1987. In my view that information would include the published accounts up to and including the year ending on 31 August 1986; the dividend yield to that date and the dividend policy of the directors as set out in the two letters sent to the shareholders of 13 February 1987 and 1 April 1987. It would also include the information known to the board on 7 September 1987 about profits for the year ending on 30 August 1987 and about the budget projections for the following year. *(pg52c)* Finally, it would include information about the restructuring of the board in December 1986, the revaluation of the company's assets which had been completed at the end of July 1987, and the other changes which would appear in the balance sheet for the year ending on 30 August 1987 relating to the cash balances and the discharge of the company's debts. Specifically, the information about profits available to the board on 7 September 1987 would include that available in July *(pg52d)* 1987, namely that pre-tax profits would be £2,030,000. That figure had changed to £2.6m by the board meeting on 25 September 1987. In my view it is reasonable to assume that the management accounts as at 7 September 1987 would have shown a figure above £2,030,000 but below £2.6m and the directors would have had enough information to allow them to make a guess as to the figure for the year end. On the information available on 7 September 1987, a figure of £2.25m might well have *(pg52e)* been supplied. I do not agree with Mr Richardson that the directors would have informed the purchaser of the figure for projected profits which was current in July 1987. The purchaser could reasonably have required the more accurate information as it existed at the date of sale.

81 The same comments apply to the figures which would have been available for budget forecasts. It has been emphasised on a number of occasions that a prudent *(pg52f)* prospective purchaser is always interested in the future prospects of the company. Such a purchaser would reasonably require up-to-date information about such budget forecasts and would require these to be accurate. We know from the evidence of Mr Dickinson that a budget of £3m for the year ending on 31 August 1988 had been set in July 1987. In my view it is reasonable to assume that this information would be available to a purchaser. The recent trading history of the *(pg52g)* company, the significant improvements which had been made in the year ending on 31 August 1987, the continuing influence of the new board which had been appointed in December 1986, and the fact that the budgets were based on the order books and were usually achieved, all point to a conclusion that a figure of £3m was not unreasonable. *(pg52h)*

82 On the basis that this information (and all other information reasonably required) was available, was it reasonable to assume that this level of profits would be maintained in the future? A number of factors are relevant here. Although the profits of the company had been stagnant before December 1986, that month saw the appointment of a new chairman and a new board. The change in direction and new policies which followed ensured that from that date the financial and trading *(pg52j)* position of the company strengthened substantially. There was a significant, but steady, improvement and no reason why it should not be maintained and possibly increased. It has to be borne in mind that the new board took office part of the way through the year ending on 30 August 1987 and the improvements which they put in hand would only have resulted in improved profits for part of that year. In my view, therefore, it was reasonable to assume that the budget forecast of £3m would be achieved and that it would also be maintained.

83 Finally I consider whether it was reasonable to assume that the directors would *(pg53a)* continue their policy of distributing 35 per cent of post-tax profits. The figures tabled at the board meeting on 27 July 1987 showed that, over a number of years, dividends were covered three times by after-tax profits, although in 1985 and 1986 a higher proportion had been distributed. The new board considered a policy of distributing 35 per cent of post-tax profits at their meeting on 27 July 1987 and I consider that it would be reasonable to assume that such a policy would be implemented (as it was) and *(pg53b)* continued.

84 It follows that, in my view, the assumptions made by Mr Sutherland, which under-lay his assumption that expected gross future dividends would be 5p per share, were reasonable.

85 However, Mr Sutherland's valuation is at the top end of his own range and it does rely upon a number of future events, not all of which might have been achieved. In *(pg53c)* my view, the advisers of a prudent purchaser may well have offered a lower price, perhaps in the region of 45p, to take account of these factors.

86 I now turn to consider the valuation proposed by Mr Richardson. He valued the shares on an earnings multiple basis by taking an amount for earnings per share and applying the appropriate price/earnings ratio to produce the price. In calculating earnings he took a figure of £2,030,000, which amounted to 7.4p per share. However, *(pg53d)* for the reasons stated above, in my view the earnings figure known to a purchaser would have been more than £2,030,000 but less than £2.6m and I have treated a figure of 2.25m as reasonable. Mr Richardson agreed that earnings of this figure would increase the earnings per share to 8.2p. Mr Richardson then looked at price/earnings ratios for quoted *(pg53e)* shares which on that date varied between 16.33 and 18.28. He thought these rather high and reduced them to 12–14 on the basis that the shares in this company would not have the '"highs and lows' of quoted shares. With earnings of 7.4p this yielded a price in the range of 85p to £1. Next

Mr Richardson discounted the price of 85p to £1 by 60–70 per cent to allow for the fact that the shares were unmarketable and that the holding was uninfluential and reached his value of 35p per share. He agreed that if earnings were 8.2p, if a ratio of 14 were used, and if the discount were *(pg53f)* 60 per cent, then the price would be 46p per share.

87 It seems to me that Mr Richardson's valuation has two main defects, namely, that it starts by assuming a level of earnings which is too low and it assumes a price/earnings ratio which is too low. Higher earnings of 8.2p per share, and a higher price/earnings ratio of, say 15, would yield a price of £1.23 which, if discounted by 60 per cent for unmarketability, etc, would give a price of 49.2p which is *(pg53g)* close to Mr Sutherland's valuation.

88 Having considered the figures as carefully as I can I conclude that a value of 45p would be appropriate if up-to-date information about the management accounts and budget forecasts were made available but if there were no information about a sale. *(pg53h)*

89 I have referred to the other valuations in the light of the decision in *Stenhouse's Trustees* which decided that evidence of actual transactions was admissible but that the question as to whether any weight and, if so, how much was to be attached to such transactions was a matter of fact. The evidence before me of other transactions related to some transfers of shares at the price of £2.05 per £1 share *(pg53j)* (equivalent to 12.8p per 25p share) in February and May 1987 and a value of 65p in December 1987. In my view very little weight can be attached to the earlier valuations. There was no evidence as to how the values had been reached, nor upon what information they had been based. In any event the information available in February, and possibly also in May, about the assets and profits of the company must have differed significantly from the information available on 7 September 1987. Perhaps a little more weight could be placed on the December valuation. However, I must assume that information about that valuation was not available to the hypothetical purchaser buying on 7 September 1987. Also, by December quite *(pg54a)* different information may have been available about the profits and future prospects of the company (ignoring the possibility of a sale). I have, therefore, reached a view about the value of the shares in this holding on the relevant date without any reference to these other valuations. However, I find some comfort from the fact that the value I have reached is not out of line with the value reached in December and that the higher value reached in December 1987 is consistent with the steady *(pg54b)* improvement in the financial position of the company which began in December 1986.

90 I now turn to consider the valuation on the basis that a sale would take place. Here, Mr Sutherland based his valuation on the assumption that a purchaser would pay six times or higher the value of pre-tax profits. Assuming pre-tax profits of £3m that would *(pg54c)* amount to £18m which, with the addition of cash balances would amount to £20m. This figure was agreed by Mr Richardson.

Mr Sutherland then discounted that price by 20 per cent for delay and risk to reach his figure of 88p. Mr Richardson, however, thought that the discount should be in the region of 50 per cent or more.

91 In considering the appropriate level of the discount I have borne in mind that this shareholding is only 14.2 per cent and its owner could not insist on a sale. Also, this *(pg54d)* company was trading successfully at the relevant date and it was not inevitable that it would be sold. Further, the information about a sale as at 7 September was that only one letter had been received 'requesting discussions leading to the acquisition of an equity interest'. Although discussions had also taken place with one or two other companies which had shown an interest in a purchase and, in principle, offers would be considered by the board and the shareholders sympathetically if the price *(pg54e)* was right, there were, at that date, very many uncertainties. In the light of those factors I am inclined to agree with Mr Richardson that the discount should be in the region of 50 per cent or even more.

92 If I take a figure for the worth of the company as £20m, which was agreed by Mr Richardson, that gives a price of £1.12 per share. Although I take no account of the fact that on the actual sale in April 1988 a value of £1.31 per share was realised, *(pg54f)* that transaction does give some reassurance that the price of £1.12 is within the right region. If I then discount the price of £1.12 by 50 per cent I reach a figure of 56p per share. That figure is in line with the value of 45p reached on the basis that no information about a sale was in prospect and, in my view, the difference between the two correctly reflects the added value which that information would give, bearing in mind the fact that, at 7 September 1987, there was no certainty that a *(pg54g)* sale would take place at all.

93 Accordingly I determine the value of the shares at 56p each.

[The next section of the Special Commissioners' decision was reversed by the Court of Appeal and has been omitted.]

94 My decisions on the issues for determination in the appeal are therefore:

(1) that, in determining the value of this holding of shares on 7 September 1987 it should be assumed that unpublished information about the profits and budget forecasts of the company, and unpublished information about a possible sale of the company, would be available to a purchaser;

(2) that the value of the shares on 7 September 1987 was 56p each; ...

The appeal is, therefore, allowed and the value of the shares determined at 56p each.

Case 39
Clark v Green

[1995] STC (SCD) 99

(1995) Sp C 5

Special Commissioners

12, 13 December 1994, 11, 12, 13 January and 28 February 1995

In both this case and in the previous case, *Caton's Administrators v Couch* [1995] STC (SCD) 34 **case 38**, the question is asked, 'What information would a reasonable prudent purchaser require?'

Dr AN Brice, the Special Commissioner, heard the evidence for *Caton's Administrators v Couch* [1995] STC (SCD) 34 **case 38** from Monday 5 to Friday 9 December 1994 and commenced hearing the evidence in *Clark v Green* the following Monday, 12 December 1994. The Special Commissioner gave her decision in both cases on the same day, 28 February 1995. The contrast between the two decisions on this point is, thus, of particular interest.

In *Caton's Administrators v Couch*, the purchase postulated was for an investment of £1.4 million. The Special Commissioner accepted the hypothetical purchaser was considering an investment of something in the region of £1 million.

> 'I rely upon the expert evidence of Mr Sutherland and conclude that, with that amount of outlay, a prudent purchaser would consult advisers who would advise him that information about a possible exit was important; such a purchaser could, therefore, reasonably require information about approaches for sale, about future prospects of sale, and about up-to-date information from the management accounts and budget forecasts.'
>
> (*Caton's Administrators v Couch* ([1995] STC (SCD) 34
> at 51c **case 38 para 74**)

In *Clark v Green*, the hypothetical prospective purchaser was considering an investment of £168,000. The decision of the Special Commissioner on the information that must be assumed to be available is:

'I conclude that, in view of the amount of the outlay, and in view of the fact that the last published accounts, for the year ending 31 August 1986, were more than one year out of date at the date of the proposed sale, and in view of the fact that the approximate results of the year's trading for the accounting year ending on 30 August 1987 were available on 28 September 1987, a prudent prospective purchaser of this holding would reasonably require up-to-date information about profits and also information as to whether that level of profits was maintainable. However, in my view the size of this holding, and the size of the outlay required to purchase this holding, are not sufficiently large to lead me to conclude that a prospective purchaser of this holding could reasonably require information about a possible sale of the company.'

([1995] STC (SCD) 99 at 111d **case 39 para 76**)

Decision

References, example '(pg101a)', are to [1995] STC (SCD) 99.

The appeal

1 The Executor of Mrs Dorothy Anne Clark deceased (the Appellant) appeals *(pg101a)* against an assessment to capital gains tax dated 4 April 1990 in the sum of £178,020.00.

2 The hearing of the appeal took place immediately after the conclusion of the hearing of the appeal of *The Administrators of PS Caton Deceased v Dr Malcolm Couch (SC 3129/94)* but before the decision in that appeal had been released. The two appeals were not consolidated. *(pg101b)*

The issues for determination

3 At the date of her death, on 28 September 1987, Mrs Clark was the registered holder of 562,112 ordinary shares of 25 pence each in Yorkshire Switchgear Group Ltd (the company). The company was not quoted on a recognised stock exchange. On 15 April 1988 all the issued share capital of the company was sold and, for the *(pg101c)* purposes of computing the liability of the Appellant to capital gains tax on that disposal, it is necessary to determine the value of the shares at the date of death. I was informed that the same value was also required for the purposes of calculating the inheritance tax payable on the death but the assessment under appeal relates only to capital gains tax.

4 The issues for determination in the appeal were: *(pg101d)*

(1)   When determining the value of the shares at the date of death should it be assumed that unpublished information relating to the profits of the company, and unpublished information relating to a possible sale of the company, would be available to a purchaser?

(2)   What was the value of the shares on 28 September 1987? Was it 18 pence per share, as proposed by the Appellant?; or 30 pence per share as proposed by the Inland Revenue **(pg101e)** on the basis that unpublished information about the profits of the company was assumed to be available? or 55–60 pence per share as proposed by the Inland Revenue on the basis that unpublished information about a possible sale of the company was assumed to be available?; or some other figure?

The statutory provisions (pg101f)

5 At the time of the disposal the relevant legislation was contained in the Capital Gains Tax Act 1979 (the 1979 Act).

6 Section 49 (1) provided:

'(1) For the purposes of this Act the assets of which a deceased person was competent to dispose *(pg101g)*

(a)   shall be deemed to be acquired on his death by the personal representatives ... for a consideration equal to their market value at the date of death, but

(b)   shall not be deemed to be disposed of by him on his death ...'
(pg101h)

7 Section 150 provided:

'(1) In this Act "market value" in relation to any assets means the price which those assets might reasonably be expected to fetch on a sale in the open market.

(2) In estimating the market value of any assets no reduction shall be made in the estimate on account of the estimate being made on the assumption that the *(pg101j)* whole of the assets is to be placed on the market at one and the same time.'

8 Section 152 provided:

'(1) The provisions of subsection (3) below shall have effect in any case where, in relation to a '(1) The provisions of subsection (3) below shall have effect in any case where, in relation to an asset to which this section applies, there falls to be determined by virtue of section 150(1) above the price which the asset might reasonably be expected to fetch on a sale in the open market. *(pg102a)*

(2) The assets to which this section applies are shares and securities which are not quoted on a recognised stock exchange ... at the time at which their market value for the purposes of tax on chargeable gains falls to be determined.

(3) For the purposes of a determination falling within subsection (1) above, it shall be assumed that, in the open market which is postulated for the purposes of that determination, there is available to any prospective purchaser of the *(pg102b)* asset in question all the information which a prudent prospective purchaser of the asset might reasonably require if he were proposing to purchase it from a willing vendor by private treaty and at arm's length.'

The evidence (pg102c)

9 An agreed statement of facts and an agreed bundle of documents were produced.

10 Mr Jacobs, who represented the Appellant at the hearing, gave oral evidence on behalf of the Appellant about the valuation of the shares. Mr Jacobs is a Senior Manager with Messrs Touche Ross & Co. He joined the Shares Valuation Division of the Capital Taxes Office in 1982. In 1990 he joined Messrs Spicer and Oppenheim which firm merged with Touche Ross later that year. Mr Jacobs produced a 'Summary of Representations' which related both to his submissions and to his valuation. *(pg102d)*

11 Oral evidence was given on behalf of the Inland Revenue by Mr Alan Edward Richardson. Mr Richardson is a Chief Examiner in the Capital Taxes Office and has worked in the Shares Valuation Division for 16 years. Mr Richardson produced a proof of his evidence.

12 Mr Griffiths produced an outline of his submissions of law and of some supplementary submissions. *(pg102e)*

The facts

13 From the evidence before me I find the following facts.

The company
14 The business of the company was established in 1907. The company was *(pg102f)* incorporated on 30 December 1978. It has a number of wholly owned subsidiaries. The company manufactures electrical switchgear and power transformers.

PART 2 Cases

The shareholdings
15 The Memorandum of Association of the company records that the authorised share capital of the company is £5,000,000 divided into 5,000,000 ordinary shares *(pg102g)* of £1 each. As at 26 July 1987 the issued share capital of the company was 1,112,805 ordinary shares of £1 each. On 27 July 1987 each £1 share was divided into four shares of 25 pence each and, on the same date, three new shares were allotted fully paid for each share held. This meant that a shareholder received sixteen 25 pence shares for each £1 share previously held. On 28 September 1987 the issued share capital of the company comprised 17,804,880 ordinary shares of 25 pence each. The *(pg102h)* holding of 562,112 shares, which is the subject of this appeal, thus comprised 3.16% of the total issued share capital.

The articles of association
16 The articles of association of the company contained restrictions on the transfer of shares. Unfettered transfer to non-members was prohibited so long as a member, *(pg102j)* or person approved by the directors, was willing to purchase the shares at a fair value to be certified (in the case of difference) by the company's auditor. Article 32(i) gave the directors a general power to refuse to register any transfer, other than a transfer to a member.

17 The articles of association also contained provisions about confidentiality. Article 92(g) provided that the office of director had to be vacated if the director disclosed to any third party unpublished matters relating to the business and financial status of the company, unless such disclosure had been previously *(pg103a)* approved by a directors' meeting. Article 131 provided that a member who was not a director had no right to inspect any account or book or document of the company, unless such right was conferred by statute or authorised by the directors or by the company in general meeting. Article 82 provided for the appointment of employees as 'Special Directors'; the persons so appointed were not entitled to copies of, or access to, the accounts or information relating to the accounts. *(pg103b)*

The board and management
18 In late 1986 there were significant changes in the composition of the board. In November 1986 Mr David Hargreaves was appointed as non-executive Chairman. In December 1986 there were other appointments to the board, as a result of which the board then consisted largely of non-family full-time directors. *(pg103c)*

Information about the financial position of the company
19 The agreed bundle of documents contained copies of the minutes of the meetings of the board from 2 October 1986 to 26 November 1987 and also minutes of the annual general meeting held on 14 December 1987.

The assets of the company
20 The balance sheet for the year ending on 31 August 1986 showed shareholders' *(pg103d)* funds of £6,874,000. On 13 January 1987 the board

resolved to revalue the company's land and buildings 'in order to reflect the current property values in the presentation to shareholders'. A preliminary report of the values was made at the board meeting on 16 March 1987 which indicated a 'surplus of £1.7m over net book value'. *(pg103e)* At the board meeting on 25 September 1987 the Chairman reported that, although no balance sheet was available, shareholders' funds, following revaluation, would be in the region of £10m.

The trading results of the company

21 In 1984 pre-tax profits were £295,000; for the eight months ending on 1 September 1985 the figure was £334,000; and for the year ending on 31 August 1986 the figure was £445,000. *(pg103f)*

22 At the board meeting held on 27 July 1987 it was reported that, on the basis of the internal accounts up to the end of June, pre-tax profits of £2,030,000 would be achievable, for the year ending on 30 August 1987. At the board meeting of 25 September 1987 consolidated trading figures were tabled, although the balance sheets had not been finalised. The consolidated trading summary showed pre-tax profit of £2.6m and after tax profit of £1.7m. *(pg103g)*

The dividend record of the directors

23 No dividend was paid for the year ending on 31 December 1984. In the eight month period ending on 1 September 1985 a dividend of £166,921 was paid which was 15 pence for each £1 share which represented 65 per cent of after tax profits of *(pg103h)* £257,000. The same dividend was paid in the year ending on 31 August 1986 when it represented 76 per cent of after-tax profits of £218,000.

24 The minutes of the board meeting on 27 July 1987 indicated that statistics were then tabled giving comparisons from 1982 to the 1988 budget with dividend estimates for 1987 and 1988. These assumed dividends were covered three times by after-tax profits. A dividend level of 35 per cent of after-tax profits for the then current *(pg103j)* financial year was considered and it was agreed that there would be a detailed discussion at the following meeting when more precise figures would be tabled. In the event, a dividend of 3 pence for each 25 pence share was recommended for the year ending on 30 August 1987.

The acquisition offers

25 On 24 August 1987 a letter was received from the Vice-President of the Joslyn Corporation of Chicago in the United States of America, requesting discussions leading to the acquisition of an equity interest in the company. On 17 September 1987 the *(pg104a)* General Electric Company wrote to confirm that it would like to acquire the company if the shareholders wished to dispose of their interests. On 25 September 1987 Merlin Gerin of France wrote to say that they understood that it was the intention to sell the company and wanted to register a firm interest with the intent of making a bid.

26 Discussion took place at the board meeting on 25 September 1987 about future *(pg104b)* trends affecting the company, including the possibility of permitting the group to be acquired. The board agreed that discussions should take place to explore the options. On 29 September 1987 letters were sent to the three companies which had expressed an interest with a view to opening discussions.

27 Thus no offers for the purchase of the company had been received by 28 September 1987 but negotiations had been opened, with at least three possible *(pg104c)* purchasers expressing an interest.

The information sent to the shareholders

28 On 13 February 1987 the Chairman, Mr Hargreaves, wrote to all shareholders. He said that the 1986 financial performance was barely adequate and the dividend recommended had not been covered by the trading profits earned during the *(pg104d)* period. However, a number of initiatives had been taken and the directors recommended a dividend of 15 pence per share for the period ending on 31 August 1986. Mr Hargreaves invited all members to attend the annual general meeting on 17 March 1987 when the directors would review the progress the group had made and would look forward to the future.

29 In 1 April 1987 the Finance Director, Mr GD Smith, wrote to all shareholders *(pg104e)* to inform them of the results of the annual general meeting. The new directors appointed in December 1986 had been introduced to the meeting. The bank borrowings had been cleared and the bank was to be asked to remove the charge on the company's assets. The chairman had advised that the profit for the first half of the year showed a substantial increase over the similar period in the previous year and concluded by saying that a continuation of that trend would enable the *(pg104f)* directors to recommend the payment of a significantly higher dividend than had been possible in recent years.

30 On 1 October 1987 Mr Hargreaves wrote again to all shareholders to say that trading for the year ending on 30 August 1987 had been very much improved. He went on to say that the level of profits indicated by the management accounts was such that a dividend of 3 pence per share would be paid. *(pg104g)*

The sale of the company

31 On 15 April 1988 all the issued share capital of the company was sold, to Merlin Gerin of France, at the price of £1.31 for each 25 pence ordinary share. The value of the shares held by the Appellant on that disposal was thus £736,366.72. *(pg104h)*

The submissions of the appellant

32 On behalf of the Appellant Mr Jacobs submitted that, in valuing this holding of shares, it should be assumed that the information available to a prospective purchaser was published information only. Statute provided that the information assumed to be available was that which a prudent prospective purchaser might reasonably require. 'Require' did not mean that which a purchaser requested, but *(pg104j)* that which a purchaser could insist upon or demand as of right. The information which a prudent purchaser might reasonably require depended on a number of factors, including the size and influence of the holding, the size of the outlay, the legal obligations of the directors, the attitude of a reasonable board of directors to the release of confidential information, and the behaviour of investors in the open market. He cited *Holt v Inland Revenue Commissioners* [1953] 2 All ER 1499; *Lynall v Commissioners of Inland Revenue* (1971) 47 TC 375; and *Dymond's Capital Taxes* at paragraph 23.327. *(pg105a)*

33 Specifically, this holding was small and uninfluential. The holder could not influence company policy nor dividend policy and had no rights under the Companies Acts. Also, the size of the outlay was small. If the price were 18 pence the outlay would be £101,180.16; if the price were 30 pence the outlay would be £168,633.60. Such an outlay would not entitle a purchaser to require more than published information. He referred to a number of publications including *(pg105b) Dymond's Capital Taxes* at paragraph 23.328. *Foster's Inheritance Tax,* 1994 Edition, at paragraph H3.11, and *Eastaway and Boothon Practical Share Valuation*, at paragraph 9.03.

34 Mr Jacobs then submitted that, as far as the legal obligations of the directors were concerned, *Percival v Wright* [1902] 2 Ch 421 was authority for the view that the directors could not release confidential information unless the board agreed to do so. In the light of Article 92(g) it was unreasonable to assume that a purchaser of this *(pg105c)* holding could demand that the directors meet and authorise the release of unpublished information. In the light of Article 131 it was reasonable to assume that the directors would not release the prospective trading results for the year ending on 30 August 1987. If, under Article 82, information was kept from 'Special Directors' then it was reasonable to assume that it would be witheld from an outside purchaser of this holding. Also, directors had a duty to act primarily for the benefit *(pg105d)* of the company, that is the shareholders, as a whole and not for the benefit of a section of the shareholders or of an outsider, such as the purchaser of this holding. Directors also owed the company a fiduciary duty and release of information to a purchaser could be a breach of trust. He cited *Pennington's Company Law* at pages 583, 584 and 591. *(pg105e)*

35 Turning to the attitude of the board of directors of this company, Mr Jacobs referred to a letter written by the Appellant to his advisers on 13 January 1992, included at pages 60–62 in the agreed bundle of documents. This indicated that the Appellant had been unable to obtain information from the board.

The evidence on behalf of the appellant

36 In evidence, Mr Jacobs said that he had considered the methods of valuation *(pg105f)* used in *Lynall, Buckingham v Francis* [1986] 2 All ER 738 and *re Courthope* (1928) 7 ATC 538 and had used three methods of valuation. His primary method had been to establish a figure for earnings and to apply an appropriate price/earnings ratio to arrive at price. He second method was based on dividend yield and his third method was based on discounted assets.

37 For the first method he had to reach a figure for earnings. He had assumed that the information available included the contents of the articles of association, the *(pg105g)* contents of the annual accounts for the four years ending on 31 August 1986, and the contents of the two letters to shareholders dated 13 February 1987 and 1 April 1987. From this information a purchaser would know that pre-tax profits for 1986 were £445,000 which represented earnings of 1.22 pence per share. He had assumed that a purchaser would make a 'best guess' at future earnings and, in his view, a prudent purchaser would assume no more than that profits for the year ending on *(pg105h)* 30 August 1987 might be double the level of profits for the year ending on 31 August 1986, that is that profits for 1987 might reach a pre-tax level of £890,000. This gave a figure for post-tax profits in 1987 of £436,000 which represented earnings of 2.44 pence per share.

38 In order to ascertain an appropriate price/earnings ratio Mr Jacobs looked at *(pg105j)* three sectors in the Financial Times Actuaries Share Index for 28 September 1987. That Index gave ratios for industrials of 18.91; for electricals of 25.39; and for GEC of 13.30. An average of these three was 19.20. Mr Jacobs discounted this figure by 35 per cent, to reflect lack of marketability and transfer restrictions, giving a ratio of 12.48. He then reduced the ratio still further to 10 to take account of the small size of the company compared with its quoted counterparts. He then increased the ratio to 15 to reflect the expectations of improved results, the strong asset backing of the company (valued at £10m), and the prospect of an improved dividend. *(pg106a)*

39 Taking earnings for 1986 as 1.22 pence per share, Mr Jacobs then applied a price/earnings ratio of 15 to get a price of 18.3 pence per share. If prospective earnings were 2.44 pence per share and the price were 18 pence the price/earnings ratio would be 7.37 which would reflect the greater risk.

40 The second method was the dividend yield approach. In 1985 dividends had been covered by profits by a factor of 1.5 and in 1986 by a factor of 1.3. Cover for *(pg106b)* unquoted companies should, in theory, be higher than for quoted companies to reflect the greater risk in the former. However, the figures for the company were low as compared with companies in the quoted sector, where cover was 2.4 for industrials, 1.9 for electricals and 2.9 for GEC. In 1986 a dividend of 15 pence for each £1 share had been paid. Each old £1 share was now represented by sixteen 25 pence shares so the 1986 dividend represented just under 1 pence per share. If prospective *(pg106c)* earnings were assumed to double then a prudent purchaser might anticipate an increase to 1.5 pence per share to allow for the dividends to be adequately covered. He produced calculations to show that a price of 18 pence per share reflected a dividend yield of 11.3 per cent which he submitted was reasonable.

41 The final method was the 'discounted assets' approach. Mr Jacobs emphasised that this was not a primary method of valuation. Assuming £10m of assets, which *(pg106d)* included £1.6m for the revaluation of the fixed assets, this represented a value of 56 pence per share. If this were discounted by 33 per cent to give a 'purchaser's profit' of 50 per cent, this gave a price of 37.52 pence per share. If this were further discounted by 60 per cent for the fact that no sale was imminent, for the small size of the holding, and for the reduced asset backing in 1986, the price would be 15 pence per share.

42 Mr Jacobs' opinion was that the value of the shares was 18 pence each. *(pg106e)*

The views of the Inland Revenue

43 The Inland Revenue did not agree with the calculations used by Mr Jacobs in his first method. He had assumed that profits for 1987 would be double the figure for 1986 and he had reached a figure of £890,000 before tax. However, the actual figures available showed a very much greater increase. Also, Mr Jacobs had reduced his *(pg106f)* pre-tax figure by corporation tax at 49%, but that was the rate for 1986. The proper rate for 1987 was 35% and, if that had been applied, the post-tax earnings would have been £578,500, which represented earnings of 3.25 pence per share. The Inland Revenue also disagreed with the addition of the premium of 50% to the price earnings ratio of 10; such an addition was unusual and was not justified. If earnings were 3.25 pence per share, and a price/earnings ratio of 10 were applied, the price of each share *(pg106g)* would be 32.5 pence.

44 The Inland Revenue pointed out that Mr Jacobs had assumed, in his third method, that the purchaser would have known about the revaluation of the fixed assets but this assumption was inconsistent with his submission that a purchaser would only have published information. Also, the discounted assets basis of valuation was only *(pg106h)* appropriate in the case of a company which was about to be wound up and that was not the case here.

The submissions of the Inland Revenue

45 On behalf of the Inland Revenue Mr Griffiths submitted that, in view of the outlay required to purchase this holding of shares, it should be assumed that a prudent *(pg106j)* prospective purchaser could reasonably require up-to-date information about the profits of the company and whether those profits were maintainable. Section 152(3) of the 1979 Act assumed that information would be available if a hypothetical reasonable board would have provided it in answer to any reasonable inquiries which the vendor or the intending purchaser or his advisers might make. This was the test adopted by Lord Reid in *Lynall* where he balanced the purchaser's need to know against possible prejudice to the company. Mr Griffiths submitted that 'require' meant demand as a condition of buying. *(pg107a)*

46 Mr Griffiths also submitted that the directors' duty of confidentiality, the directors' duty to act in the interests of the company and all the shareholders, and the directors' obligations of trust, had to be considered in the light of the statutory provisions relating to the valuation of the shares for capital gains tax purposes. Section 152(3) had the effect of providing that information reasonably required was *(pg107b)* assumed to be available. The sale was a hypothetical sale to which the actual restrictions in the Articles did not apply. Evidence as to what the actual board of directors would do was irrelevant.

47 Finally, Mr Griffiths submitted that it should not be assumed that a purchaser of this holding would be given information about a possible sale of the company. However, it was necessary to ensure consistency of treatment with the valuation in *(pg107c)* the estate of PS Caton deceased and, if it were decided in that appeal that such information would be made available, then he submitted that the same conclusion should apply in the present case.

The evidence on behalf of the Inland Revenue

48 Mr Richardson gave evidence that, in reaching his valuation, he had assumed *(pg107d)* that the purchaser would have been aware of the annual accounts covering the trading period from 1 January 1984 to 31 August 1986 and the two letters to shareholders of 13 February 1987 and 1 April 1987. He also assumed that, in view of the prospective outlay, the purchaser would require an estimate of the profitability of the company for the year ending on 31 August 1987 and confirmation, if that could be given, that the increased level of profitability was *(pg107e)* maintainable. Although he did not assume that a purchaser would be given access to the minutes of the meetings of the board, he did assume that a purchaser would have been informed of the information available to the board at their meeting on 27 July 1987, namely that a pre-tax profit of £2.03m should be achievable and that it could be maintained. *(pg107f)*

49 Mr Richardson's primary valuation method was the earnings multiple basis. To calculate earnings he took the estimated pre-tax profit figure of £2.03m and deducted corporation tax at 35%. This gave a figure for post-tax profits of £1,319,500 which represented earnings of 7.4 pence per share. He then consulted the Financial Times Actuaries Share Index to find an appropriate price/earnings ratio. On Monday 28 September 1987 the ratio for capital goods was 17.67, that for *(pg107g)* mechanical engineering was 16.92, and that for the 500 Share Index was 18.60. In his view these ratios were high and the unquoted market was likely to be less volatile. He therefore adopted a ratio between 12 and 14, which gave a price in the range of 85 pence to £1 on earnings of 7.4 pence per share. He discounted the ratio by 65% to allow for the fact that this was an uninfluential holding and for unmarketability. That gave a ratio of 4 which, on earnings of 7.4 pence per share, gave a price of 30 pence per share. *(pg107h)*

50 Mr Richardson's second approach was to look at dividend yield. He assumed earnings of 7.4 pence per share and also assumed that a net dividend of 2.5 to 3 pence could be anticipated. The gross dividend would be 3.42–4.11 pence so a price of 30 pence gave a dividend yield of 11.4–13.7%. This was not unreasonable.

51 Mr Richardson's valuation did not assume that information about a proposed *(pg107j)* sale would be available to a prospective purchaser. However, he had considered a valuation on the basis that such information would be available. He started with the figure of £1.31 per share which was achieved on the sale in April 1988, which valued the company at £23.3m. He then discounted the price of £1.31 by 50% because negotiations were at an early stage and there was a risk of failure. That gave a price of 65 pence per share. If the value of the company on 28 September 1987 were £20M, that would give a value for each share of between £1 to £1.10 which, if discounted by 50%, would give a value for each share of 50–55 pence. In his view an *(pg108a)* appropriate value would be between 55 pence and 60 pence per share.

The views of the Appellant

52 Mr Jacobs did not agree with the primary valuation made by Mr Richardson. He did not accept that the purchaser would have been aware of projected pre-tax profits of £2.03m nor that that level of profits would be maintainable. *(pg108b)*

Reasons for decision

53 In considering the submissions of the parties I first consider what information should be assumed to be available to a prudent prospective purchaser of this holding of shares in this company. I then consider the value of the shares in the light of those principles and in the light of the evidence. *(pg108c)*

(1) What information should be assumed to be available?
In considering what information should be assumed to be available I start with the words of section 152(3). That subsection provides:

> 'it shall be assumed that, in the open market which is postulated for the purposes of that determination, there is available to any prospective purchaser *(pg108d)* of the asset in question the information which a prudent prospective purchaser of the asset might reasonably require if he were proposing to purchase it from a willing vendor by private treaty and at arm's length.'

54 This section was first enacted in section 51 of the Finance Act 1973 and I was informed that it has not been judicially interpreted since that date. Accordingly I have approached its interpretation by considering the decision in *Lynall,* which preceded *(pg108e)* the enactment of section 51, to see if it is possible to identify the mischief which the section was designed to cure and to see if I can identify the general intention of Parliament.

55 The decision in *Lynall* (1972) concerned a valuation for estate duty purposes under section 7(5) of the Finance Act 1894 which provided that the value should be the price that the property would fetch if sold in the open market at the time of death. A holding of shares in a family company, which holding amounted to 28% of the total, *(pg108f)* fell to be valued as at 21 May 1962. At the time of the relevant death the company was likely to go public in the very near future but that information was known only to the directors. If the hypothetical purchaser had known of the possible flotation he would have been prepared to pay a higher value per share; if he had not known it he would have offered a lower value.

56 At first instance Plowman J considered what information would have been *(pg108g)* available to a hypothetical purchaser and identified four possible tests or standards.

57 The first was to assume that all the facts, which were facts at the date of death, were available. This has been called the 'omniscience' standard.

58 The second was to assume that the only information available was the company's accounts together with any other information made available to all the shareholders. *(pg108h)* This has been called the 'published information' standard.

59 The third was to assume that the purchaser obtained both the published information and any information which the directors of that company would have given in answer to any reasonable question likely to be asked by any vendor-shareholder or intending purchaser. As this test depends on considerations *(pg108j)* of what that actual board would have supplied it has been called the 'subjective' standard.

60 The fourth was to assume that the purchaser obtained both the published information and any additional information which a hypothetical reasonable board would have disclosed in answer to any reasonable inquiries which the vendor or the intending purchaser or his advisers might have made. As this does not require any consideration of what the actual board would have done it has been called the 'objective' standard. *(pg109a)*

61 Plowman J concluded that information in the accounts for the year ending after the date of death, and the contents of a speech made by the chairman of the company after the date of death, could not be taken into account. Relying on the evidence of a witness who spoke on behalf of the board, and who said that he would not disclose any board minutes or other confidential documents and who, if asked by a purchaser about the *(pg109b)* prospect of a public issue would have replied that the prospect was doubtful and remote, he concluded that the information about the proposed flotation could not be taken into account either, since that information was neither published information nor information which would in fact have been elicited from the board on inquiry.

62 Accordingly, after the hearing at first instance, the decision in *Lynall* was *(pg109c)* authority for the 'subjective' standard.

On appeal, the Court of Appeal found in favour of the Inland Revenue and adopted a version of the objective standard. Specifically, they decided that the information deemed to be available to a purchaser did not depend on what a particular board would do. Instead it was to be assumed that the purchaser would receive true and factual answers to all his reasonable enquiries. *(pg109d)* Also, it had to be assumed that any provisions in the articles which prohibited the directors from supplying confidential information were waived for the purposes of the hypothetical sale in the same way as any provisions in the articles restricting the transfer of shares were also waived for the same purposes.

63 The House of Lords, however, held that the objective standard should not be applied and valued the shares on the assumption that the information about the *(pg109e)* proposed flotation was not available. Lord Reid said that the evidence which had been adduced relating to the way in which confidential information would be disclosed by a board of directors to a purchaser's advisers in confidence was irrelevant because that kind of sale was not a sale in the open market. It was a sale by private treaty. Also, the directors were under no legal obligation to make any confidential information available. There was *(pg109f)* difficulty in laying down a general rule that directors must be supposed to have done something which they were not obliged to do. He continued:

> 'The farthest we could possibly go would be to hold that directors must be deemed to have done what all reasonable directors would do. Then it might be reasonable to say that they would disclose information provided that its disclosure could not possibly prejudice the interests of the company.' *(pg109g)*

64 This was the principle which was adopted by Mr Griffiths in his submissions.

65 It seems to me that, following the decision of the House of Lords, the decision in *Lynall* was authority for the view that the information deemed to be available to a prospective purchaser of unquoted shares in a private company did not include *(pg109h)* confidential information. That was not information which would be available on a sale in the open market but rather it was information which might be made available on a sale by private treaty. Also, it was confidential information which the directors were under no legal obligation to make available.

66 The year after the decision in *Lynall*, section 51 of the Finance Act 1973 *(pg109j)* was enacted. This amended the legislation relating both to estate duty and capital gains tax, and the provisions of that section have been re-enacted in section 152(3) of the 1979 Act.

67 It seems to me to be clear that the provisions of section 51 (and then of section 152) were not intended to restate the position which obtained after the decision of the House of Lords in *Lynall*. Section 51 was enacted to overturn that decision and to provide for a version of the objective standard similar to that applied by the Court of Appeal. In doing so, it dealt with two difficulties identified by the House of Lords and one difficulty identified by the Court of Appeal. *(pg110a)*

68 The first difficulty identified by the House of Lords was that the release of confidential information was not appropriate to a sale in the open market but was appropriate to a sale by private treaty. The legislation deals with this by providing that the sale is to be assumed to be by private treaty. It appears to me that the inclusion of those words in the section was intended to open the way to the provision of confidential information by the directors to an intending purchaser. *(pg110b)*

69 The second difficulty identified by the House of Lords was that there was no legal obligation on the directors to disclose confidential information and it was not right to assume that they would disclose it if it would prejudice the interests of the company. It seems to me that the section deals with this difficulty by providing that it shall be assumed that confidential information 'is available' if it is reasonably required. This gives effect to the findings of the Court of Appeal that it has to be *(pg110c)* assumed that any provisions in the articles which prohibit the directors from supplying confidential information are waived for the purposes of the hypothetical sale in the same way that any provisions in the articles restricting the transfer of the shares are also waived for the same purposes. It also means that it is not necessary to consider, for the purposes of the hypothetical sale, whether the disclosure of the information would prejudice the interests of the company. *(pg110d)*

70 The difficulty identified by the Court of Appeal was that values should not depend on the whim of a particular person or board. It seems to me that the section deals with this difficulty by providing that all information is to be assumed to be provided to the purchaser so long as it is reasonably required. It is no longer necessary to consider what the particular board would do. *(pg110e)*

71 Accordingly, in my view, section 152(3) is effective to provide that any information, including unpublished confidential information, and even information which might prejudice the interests of the company, is assumed to be available in the hypothetical sale if it would be reasonably required by a prudent prospective purchaser of the asset in question. It is therefore necessary to consider, in each case, what information a prudent prospective purchaser of the asset in question would reasonably require. *(pg110f)*

72 Mr Jacobs' evidence was that the information reasonably required by a purchaser of a 3% minority holding was published information and no more. From that information a purchaser would be able to make a 'best guess' estimate of future profits. The evidence of Mr Richardson was that, in view of the outlay, a reasonable purchaser of this holding would have required some unpublished information relating to profitability and how maintainable that was. In his view the directors *(pg110g)* would have provided some information about profits, namely the information available to them in July 1987. He also thought that a purchaser might well enquire about the possibility of a proposed sale but that the directors would not release that information to a purchaser of this holding.

73 *Dymonds Capital Taxes*, at paragraph 23.327, states that the amount of information *(pg110h)* required will depend on the size of the purchase. If 25% or more of the issued voting capital is up for sale the buyer will want to know the figures for sales and profits up to the latest date, with corresponding figures for the previous year, and the board's views on trading prospects. Where the holding is less than 25% it may be that the buyer will expect less information but that is a matter for expert evidence. The size of the company is important and a buyer investing £200,000 *(pg110j)* would obviously be entitled to know more than one investing £2,000. Where the holding was small, say less than £50,000 and less than 5 per cent of the capital, the buyer would not normally be expected to have more than the information which was published or which he could find out without questioning the directors.

74 *Foster*, at paragraph H3.11, indicates that the amount of information available will depend on the size of the holding and the value of the property; no hard and fast rules could be laid down and each case had to be decided upon its own merits. *Eastaway and Booth* indicates that, if a significant value could be placed on a *(pg111a)* shareholding of 25% or less, it could certainly be argued that anyone about to spend, say, a six figure sum on a shareholding would 'reasonably require' up-to-date information about their investment.

75 In reaching a decision I have borne in mind that, although this is a small minority holding, the size of the proposed outlay is in excess of a six figure sum.

The hypothetical purchaser is considering an investment of something in the region of *(pg111b)* £100,000–£169,000. I have also borne in mind that the date of the hypothetical sale is 28 September 1987 and that the accounting year of the company ended on 30 August 1987. Although the accounts were not finalised on 28 September, information as to the approximate results of the year's trading was available to the board at their meeting on 25 September 1987. *(pg111c)*

76 I conclude that, in view of the amount of the outlay, and in view of the fact that the last published accounts, for the year ending on 31 August 1986, were more than one year out of date at the date of the proposed sale, and in view of the fact that the approximate results of the year's trading for the accounting year ending on 30 August 1987 were available on 28 September 1987, a prudent prospective purchaser of this holding would reasonably require up-to-date information about *(pg111d)* profits and also information as to whether that level of profits was maintainable. However, in my view the size of this holding, and the size of the outlay required to purchase this holding, are not sufficiently large to lead me to conclude that a prospective purchaser of this holding could reasonably require information about a possible sale of the company.

77 Having reached that conclusion I now turn to consider the value of the shares. *(pg111e)*

What is the value of the shares?
78 In reaching a decision about the value of the shares I have in mind the *dicta* of Lord Fleming in *Salvesen v Commissioners of Inland Revenue* (1930) ATC 43 when he said:

'The estimation of the value of shares by a highly artificial standard which is *(pg111f)* never applied in the ordinary share market must be a matter of opinion and does not admit of precise scientific or mathematical calculation.'

79 I have also borne in mind certain *dicta* of Danckwerts J in *Holt*. From this I conclude that I am entitled to find a value either of 30 pence, as proposed by the Inland Revenue, or of 18 pence as proposed by the Appellant, or some other value somewhere in between. Also, after carefully considering the evidence, I must make the most *(pg111g)* intelligent guess that I can.

80 Both Mr Jacobs and Mr Richardson valued the shares on an earnings multiple basis by taking an amount for earnings per share and applying a price/earnings ratio to produce the price. I therefore I start with the information about earnings which must be assumed to be available. For the reasons mentioned above I do not agree *(pg111h)* with Mr Jacobs that this information is limited to the figure of £445,000 contained in the accounts for the year ending on 31 August 1986 doubled to £890,000 to reflect the optimism in the letters to shareholders. Neither do I agree with Mr Richardson that the information is the figure of £2.03m which was available to the board on 27 July 1987. The date of the hypothetical sale is 28 September 1987 and the information available to the board at their meeting on 25 September 1987 was *(pg111j)* that profits would be £2.6m. I accept that the financial information available on 25 September had not been audited, and there may have been some caution in releasing it, but in my view it is reasonable to assume that a figure for earnings in the region of £2.25m might have been supplied.

81 On the assumptions as to profits made by Mr Jacobs, earnings per share were 1.22 pence in 1986 and 2.44 pence in 1987 (or 3.25 pence if the proper rate of corporation tax were applied). On the assumptions as to profits made by Mr Richardson, earnings per share were 7.4 pence. If it were assumed that the information available revealed profits *(pg112a)* of £2.25m then earnings per share would be 8.2 pence.

82 Mr Jacobs applied a price/earnings ratio of 15 to the historic earnings and a ratio of 7.37 to prospective earnings. Mr Richardson applied a ratio of 4.

83 Having considered the figures as carefully as I can I prefer the valuation produced by Mr Richardson, although, in my view, it is, if anything, rather low. Accordingly I determine the value of the shares at 30 pence each. *(pg112b)*

84 I appreciate the desire of the Inland Revenue to ensure some consistency between the valuation of this holding and the valuation of the holding in the appeal of *Caton*, where a value of 45 pence per share has been determined, on the basis that no information about a sale was available. The difference between the two valuations reflects the difference in the size of the shareholdings which, in turn, reflects the amount of information assumed to be available. For example, in *Caton (pg112c)* it was assumed that information about budget forecasts would be available whereas the valuation in this appeal makes no such assumption.

Applications for costs

85 Both the Appellant and the Inland Revenue applied for an order for costs.

86 The power of the Special Commissioners to award costs is contained in Rule 21 of *(pg112d)* The Special Commissioners (Jurisdiction and Procedure) Regulations 1994 SI 1994 No 1811 (the Rules). Rule 21 provides:

'(1) Subject to paragraph (2) below, a Tribunal may make an order awarding the costs of, or incidental to, the hearing of any proceedings by it against a party to those proceedings … if it is of the opinion that the party has acted *(pg112e)* wholly unreasonably in connection with the hearing in question.

(2) No order shall be made under paragraph (1) above against a party without first giving that party an opportunity of making representations against the making of the order.

(3)   An order under paragraph (1) above may require the party against whom it is made to pay to the other party ... the whole or part of the costs incurred *(pg112f)* by the other party ... of, or incidental to, the hearing of the proceedings, such costs to be taxed if not otherwise agreed.'

(1) Application by the Appellant

87 Mr Jacobs applied for an order that the Inland Revenue should pay the Appellant's costs of the appeal from 2 November 1990 when he had made an offer of 30 pence per share. *(pg112g)* The costs amounted to about £25,000. Mr Griffiths resisted this application. The rules provided that costs could only be awarded in respect of the hearing. There had been a need to ensure consistency between the values determined in the present appeal and the values determined in the appeal of PS Caton deceased which concerned the same type of shares in the same company on dates which were only three weeks apart. The Inland Revenue had been unable to reach any agreement with the *(pg112h)* appellant in that case and the delay had not been caused by the Inland Revenue.

The facts

88 Negotiations between the Appellant's advisers and the Shares Valuation Division of the Capital Taxes Office commenced in December 1987 when the Appellant's advisers offered *(pg112j)* a price of 25 pence per share. Thereafter different values were offered by the Inland Revenue and the Appellant until, in November 1990, the Appellant offered 30 pence. On 21 December 1990 the Inland Revenue said that they would accept 30 pence if the Administrators of PS Caton deceased would accept 35 pence, as there was a need to ensure consistency between the two valuations. On 5 November 1992 the Appellant's offer of 30 pence was withdrawn. Thereafter different values were offered by the Appellant and, at a meeting between the Appellant and his advisers on 10 May 1994 the offer of 30 pence was repeated. *(pg113a)*

Decision

89 My power to make an order awarding costs is limited by Rule 21. I interpret that Rule as meaning that I may only make an order in respect of the costs of the hearing and then only if the party against whom the order is made has acted wholly unreasonably in connection with the hearing. Mr Jacobs' request relates not only to the costs of the hearing but also to the costs of negotiations after *(pg113b)* November 1990, when the Appellant first offered a price of 30 pence. Further, although Mr Jacobs implies that the Inland Revenue has acted wholly unreasonably since that date, he did not specifically submit that they have acted wholly unreasonably in connection with the hearing.

90 Having read the correspondence between the Appellant and his advisers and the Inland Revenue I have to say that I have considerable sympathy with the Appellant. More *(pg113c)* than six years ago his advisers offered to settle the matter at the price of 25 pence and more than four years ago they offered to settle at 30 pence, which is the value proposed by the Inland Revenue in this appeal. The delay in agreeing a value must have increased the costs payable by the Appellant to his advisers and has delayed the completion of the administration of the estate of Mrs Clark. I understand the point made by the Inland Revenue that they perceived a need to ensure consistency between the valuation in *(pg113d)* this appeal and that in the appeal of Caton. However, each taxpayer is entitled to have his affairs dealt with promptly and it is not a satisfactory explanation for delay that the Inland Revenue have not finalised the tax affairs of another taxpayer. Having said that, however, it is my view that, under the provisions of Rule 21, I do not have the power to make an order that the Inland Revenue should pay the Appellant's costs of the protracted negotiations. Neither do I consider that I have *(pg113e)* the power to award the costs of the hearing as, in my view, the Inland Revenue did not act wholly unreasonably in connection with the hearing.

(2) Application by the Inland Revenue

91 Mr Griffiths applied for an order that the Appellant should pay the costs of the Inland Revenue in respect of the adjournment on December 13 and that on January 11. The first adjournment had been necessary because the proof of evidence of Mr Jacobs *(pg113f)* had not disclosed the substance of his evidence. The second adjournment had been necessary because the Appellant had been unwilling to agree a statement of facts.

92 This application was resisted by Mr Jacobs. The delay in submitting his proof of evidence arose from the fact that he had been unsure of his role. He had asked if *(pg113g)* he could both present the case and give expert evidence and had received conflicting replies. He would have been willing not to give expert evidence. The delay in submitting the statement of facts arose because he understood that Mr Griffiths would prepare the document.

The facts

93 The first day of the hearing took place on Monday December 12. At the *(pg113h)* commencement of the hearing the parties informed me that they had been unable to agree a statement of facts but that it should be available the following day. Mr Jacobs commenced his submissions but called no witnesses as to fact. On the second day of the hearing, December 13, no statement of facts was available. On that day Mr Jacobs gave opinion evidence on the subject of the valuation of the *(pg113j)* shares. Prior to the hearing he had provided Mr Griffiths with a copy of his proof of evidence. The evidence he gave on December 13 was very much fuller than that outlined in his proof and contained a substantial amount of new material. Mr Griffiths asked for an adjournment to consider the new evidence and this was granted. I directed that during the adjournment a statement of facts should be lodged. The hearing reconvened on Wednesday 11 January (the third day of the hearing) when I was informed that the parties had corresponded but that no statement of facts was available. Mr Jacobs indicated that if there were to be a *(pg114a)* further adjournment it should be possible to reach agreement. The hearing was therefore adjourned to the following day. On the fourth day of the hearing, Thursday 12 January, an agreed statement of facts was produced.

Decision

94 Rule 17 of the Rules provides that, so far as appears appropriate, the *(pg114b)* tribunal should conduct the hearing in such manner as it considers most suitable to the clarification and determination of the issues before it and generally to the just handling of the proceedings and, so far as appears to it appropriate, should seek to avoid formality in the procedure. Rule 14 provides that a party to proceedings, other than the Inland Revenue, may be represented by any person whether or not legally qualified, although a tribunal may refuse to permit a person who is not legally *(pg114c)* qualified, or who is not a member of an incorporated society of accountants, to represent a party if there are good and sufficient reasons for doing so. Rule 12 provides that no expert evidence may be adduced by a party at a hearing unless the substance of the evidence has been disclosed in writing in advance of the hearing.

95 In the normal case expert evidence should be independent and uninfluenced by the exigencies of the litigation. The role of an expert witness is to provide *(pg114d)* independent assistance by way of unbiased opinion in relation to matters within his expertise. In the High Court an expert witness does not also act as advocate, Mr Jacobs represented the Appellant at the hearing and also wished to give opinion evidence concerning the valuation of the shares. However, Mr Jacobs also indicated that he was quite willing not to be regarded as an expert witness.

96 I accept that Mr Jacobs was unsure as to his role. However, the proof of his *(pg114e)* evidence which he had exchanged with Mr Griffiths before the hearing was substantially different from the evidence he gave at the hearing and, in my view, Mr Griffiths was entitled to an adjournment to consider it. Also, Mr Jacobs called no witnesses as to fact and his opening submissions, and his opinion on the valuation of the shares, assumed certain facts. In the absence of an agreed statement of facts, it was difficult to identify which facts were agreed and which were not. In my view *(pg114f)* the statement of facts which was ultimately agreed could well have been agreed before the hearing or at least during the first adjournment.

97 Having said that, however, I am aware that any award of costs has to be made against a party to the proceedings, which in this case would be the Appellant. Also, I have to ask myself whether the Appellant acted 'wholly unreasonably' in these *(pg114g)* matters. In the light of the inexperience of Mr Jacobs, and in the light of the fact that any award of costs would have to be made against the Appellant, I have concluded that no award should be made.

Decision

98 My decisions on the issues for determination in the appeal are:

(1)   that, in *(pg114h)* determining the value of this holding of shares on 28 September 1987, it should be assumed that unpublished information

about the profits of the company would be available to a purchaser but that information about a proposed sale of the company would not be so available; and

(2)   that the value of the shares on 28 September 1987 was 30 pence each. *(pg114j)*

99 The appeal is therefore dismissed. The value of the shares is determined at 30 pence each. There will be no order as to costs.

Case 40
Hawkings-Byass v Sassen

[1996] STC (SCD) 319

(1996) Sp C 88

Special Commissioners

11, 12, 13, 14, 15, 8, 19, 20 March and 16, 17, 18, 19, 30 April and 1, 10 May and 9 July 1996

This is a useful case that records a comprehensive valuation exercise, undertaken by two Special Commissioners after a hearing lasting 15 days.

The hearing concerned the valuation of three separate shareholdings, having a common valuation date. The Special Commissioners held that, in making the valuation, statute requires a purchaser to be postulated for each shareholding. It was not acceptable to assume that all three holdings were on the market at the same time, as there was no factual evidence to that effect.

On 25 March 1988, Geoffrey Hawkings-Byass and his son Nicholas Hawkings-Byass sold their shareholdings in Gonzalez Byass and Co (Cayman Islands) Ltd. John Hawkings-Byass sold his shareholding on 31 March 1988. All three taxpayers had acquired their shares before 31 March 1982, hence it was necessary to value the shares at that date to compute the capital gain arising.

The three shareholdings to be valued represented 18.16 per cent, 11.09 per cent and 9.09 per cent, respectively, of the issued share capital of the company.

The Special Commissioners decision commences with identifying the holdings for which a valuation is required at the valuation date ([1996] STC (SCD) 319 at 321 **case 40 para 4**).

The share capital in issue is then stated ([1996] STC (SCD) 319 at 321 **case 40 para 4**) and the position of the company in the group of companies noted ([1996] STC (SCD) 319 at 322b **case 40 para 7(3)**).

The history of the sherry producing business Gonzalez Byass is summarised, from its foundation in 1836, and the continuation of family ownership of the business noted ([1996] STC (SCD) 319 at 321g **case 40 para 7(1)**).

The articles of association that restrict transfer of shares were identified. The Special Commissioner notes a special article that gives the right for a shareholder to appoint one director for every 1,000 ordinary shares he/she holds and also notes the interesting provision that the articles require that the only persons who are eligible to be appointed as director are males who have the surname 'Gonzalez' or the surname 'Byass' ([1996] STC (SCD) 319 at 322j **case 40 para 7(4)(iii)**). Considerable detail is then given as to the composition of the board of directors in the years up to the valuation date and reference made to allegiances between different parts of the extended family ([1996] STC (SCD) 319 at 323c **case 40 para 7(5)**).

The difficulty in this particular case of valuing the shares as at 31 March 1982 was increased by the Special Commissioners finding that the accounts provided by the company are not reliable. Assets are undervalued. Profits for the years 1979, 1980 and 1981 are understated. If a conventional takeover bid for the whole company were made a fresh set of accounts would have had to have been drawn up ([1996] STC (SCD) 319 at 327e **case 40 para 8**).

The Special Commissioners then asked the following questions as to the hypothetical unconnected purchaser:

'(1) Who would people the market place?
(2) What homework would they have carried out before making a bid, for it is in our opinion unrealistic to suppose that potential purchasers would not have briefed themselves so far as they could any more than that Geoffrey or Nicholas or John would not have prepared himself so as to elicit the highest reasonably possible bid?'

A conventional portfolio valuation of each holding was derisory. The Special Commissioner states that Gonzalez Byass and Co (Cayman Islands) Ltd was not an ordinary company. He describes the Gonzalez Byass business as a jewel. The business was operated in Spain governed by an English constitution of a unique kind (see [1996] STC (SCD) 319 at 327f **case 40 para 8**).

The prospective purchasers for any one of the holdings notionally on offer on 31 March 1982 were identified as including the other shareholders in the company. The Special Commissioners commented:

'For the Gonzalez shareholders, the Jerez block in particular, eminently acquisitive, Geoffrey's holding would have given that block control.

Nicholas's shareholding (John's likewise) would not alone have given the Jerez block control, but in practical ... terms it would since they would have needed relatively few votes from the so-called uncommitted Spanish shareholders ... to have practical control.'

([1996] STC (SCD) 319 at 327h **case 40 para 9)**

The Special Commissioners then recorded the numerical analysis undertaken on four different bases:

1.   Earnings basis ([1996] STC (SCD) 319 at 328g **case 40 para 9(A)(1)**);
2.   Dividend yield basis ([1996] STC (SCD) 319 at 329e **case 40 para 9(A)(2)**);
3.   Turnover basis ([1996] STC (SCD) 319 at 329j **case 40 para 9(A)(3)**);
4.   Assets basis ([1996] STC (SCD) 319 at 330c **case 40 para 9(A)(4)**).

The Special Commissioners then noted the relevant case law, in particular the judgement of the Court of Appeal as given by Hoffman LJ in *IRC v Gray:*

'It cannot be too strongly emphasised that ... there is nothing hypothetical about the open market in which it is supposed to have taken place. The concept of the open market involves assuming that the whole world was free to bid, and then forming a view about what in those circumstances would in real life have been the best price reasonably obtainable. The practical nature of this exercise will usually mean that although in principle no one is excluded from consideration, most of the world will usually play no part in the calculation. The inquiry will often focus on what a relatively small number of people would be likely to have paid.'

(*IRC v Gray* [1994] STC 360 **case 37 para 5**, quoted by the Special Commissioner in *Hawkings-Byass v Sassen* [1996] STC (SCD) 319 at 331j **case 40 para 13)**

'It follows ... in our opinion, that any purchaser would have done his homework and would have assembled all the information reasonably necessary for his purpose. He would have prepared himself to make an informed bid on the basis of information he was entitled to seek and have provided to him. In our opinion, it is a material factor that each vendor is a director and that the purchaser would be entitled to appoint a director (two in the case of Geoffrey's shares). We summarise by saying that in our opinion the hypothetical market takes place in a real world but for all that we are not allowed to assume that all three holdings were on the market at the same time unless there were factual evidence to that effect of which there is none ....

Extensive submissions were made with regard to the question whether multinationals would or would not enter the hypothetical market. We take the view that they would do so but that, having read the Articles of Association, their entry would probably have to be covert. It could nevertheless be done. The attractions to a multinational of a stake in the company producing Tio Pepe as well as a profitable brandy business are obvious. The articles of GB Cayman and the divisions within the company would, however, have a restraining effect on the amount which it would be willing to pay. Gonzalez shareholders or some of them would certainly be in the market as would the other Hawkings-Byass shareholders. The former would be acquisitive. The Hawkings-Byass would strain every nerve to preserve their freedom, if necessary with the help of a multinational.'

([1996] STC (SCD) 319 at 332f/332h **case 40 paras 13 and 14**)

Any share valuer would have sympathy in the comments then made by the Special Commissioners:

'It is an invidious task to provide a valuation.

Mr Green very helpfully produced ten tables setting out calculations of value made on different bases which are explained in footnotes.'

([1996] STC (SCD) 319 at 333d/g **case 40 para 17(1) and (2)**)

After analysing the numerical evidence given by the expert witnesses, the Special Commissioners conclude:

'We determine the value of Geoffrey's shares at £307 each and Nicholas's and John's at £256 each as at 31 March 1982.'

([1996] STC (SCD) 319 at 335b **case 40 para 17(5)**)

Decision

References, example '(pg320j)', are to [1996] STC (SCD) 319.

1 We have before us appeals against assessments to capital gains tax for the year *(pg320j)* 1987/88 by Geoffrey William Hawkings-Byass ('Geoffrey'), his son Nicholas Geoffrey Edward Hawkings-Byass ('Nicholas') and his brother (Nicholas's uncle) John Arthur Hawkings-Byass ('John') arising out of the disposal by each of them of their holding of shares in Gonzalez Byass and Co (Cayman Islands) Ltd ('G B Cayman') on 25 March 1988 in the case of Geoffrey and Nicholas and on 31 March 1988 in the case of John.

PART 2 Cases

2 The appeals were heard together. Geoffrey and Nicholas were represented by Mr Brian Green of Counsel and the Crown was represented by Mr DA Griffiths *(pg321a)* of the Solicitor's office, Inland Revenue. John was not represented and did not appear.

3 The question for determination is the open market value of each holding of shares on 31 March 1982. This falls to be ascertained in order that the indexation provisions in Finance Act 1982 may be applied in computing the Appellants' chargeable gains arising from the disposal of their shares in 1988. The shares were *(pg321b)* not quoted on a recognised stock exchange. The provisions of sections 150 and 152 of the Capital Gains Tax Act 1979 apply which we shall consider later.

4(1) Geoffrey in effect disposed of 21795 ordinary shares of 70p each in GB Cayman (18.16%) for £507 per share giving a total of £11,047,530. Nicholas likewise disposed of 13305 such shares (11.09%) for the same price per share giving a total of £6,745,635. John disposed of 10908 such shares (9.09%) for *(pg321c)* £3,272,100, a price of £300 per share. The issued capital of GB Cayman consisted of 120,000 70p ordinary shares.

(2) Technically Geoffrey and Nicholas disposed of their shares by granting the purchasers an option to purchase in consideration of £50 per share followed by a sale at the price of £457 per share on the exercise of the option. John's was a straight sale.

(3) The purchasers were in each case Carlos Gonzalez Rivero, Manuel Mauricio Gonzalez-Gordon Diez and Alfredo Gonzalez Diez *(pg321d)* who all lived in Spain.

5 The Crown has agreed with John that his shares should be valued as at 31 March 1982 in proportion to the value ascribed to Nicholas's shares.

6(a) Geoffrey and Nicholas gave evidence before us. In addition, Peter Fergusson and Graham John Hines gave evidence on behalf of the Appellants. Christopher Gerrard Glover MSc FCA, gave expert evidence on their behalf. *(pg321e)* Mr Glover has practised independently as a share valuation specialist for the past fourteen years, having been an investment analyst with Phillips & Drew for ten years followed by eight years specialising exclusively in the valuation of unquoted shares with Ernst & Young. He is the author of '*Valuation of Unquoted Companies*' (1986, 1992, 2nd Edn.).

(b) The Crown called two expert witnesses, namely John Robert Baker, a Principal in the Shares Valuation Division of the Capital Taxes Office, and *(pg321f)* John Reginald Gillum who has had a career of more than 32 years in the City of London as a corporate finance merchant banker.

7(1) Putting aside, for the moment, the Cayman Islands aspect, Gonzalez Byass is the well known producer of sherry which is made in and only in a defined area in southwest Spain of which the principal towns are Jerez de la Frontera, called Jerez, El Puerto de Santa Maria and Sanlucar de Barrameda. The business was founded *(pg321g)* in 1836 by Manuel

Gonzalez. He exported sherry to England. In the 1850s his London agent was Robert Blake Byass whom he took into partnership. In 1863 the firm became Gonzalez Byass. In 1886 an English limited company was formed. The company acquired the partnership business in exchange for preference shares and 10,000 ordinary shares which were issued equally between Manuel Gonzalez *(pg321h)* and Robert Blake Byass. In 1982 the members of Gonzalez Byass were descendants of Manuel Gonzalez or Robert Blake Byass. The Byass family ceased to own 50% of the ordinary shares on or possibly before the death of Geoffrey's grandfather, Robert William Byass, who died in 1958, aged 96, since he gave some of his shares to the Marquess of Torre Soto, a descendant of Manuel Gonzalez.

(2)   Gonzalez Byass became the largest producer of sherry and its brand named *(pg321j)* Tio Pepe was the world's No.1 Fino Sherry. It produced other brands of sherry. The UK was the principal overseas market for its sherry which was imported in bulk, bottled and distributed by, in recent years, a wholly owned UK subsidiary company. Holland particularly and Germany provided other appreciative markets. The market for sherry in Spain was much lower than in the UK. Gonzalez Byass also produced and sold brandy, Soberano, a three star brandy which accounted for 25% of the Spanish market. It also produced two five star brandies. 90% of the brandy produced in *(pg322a)* Spain was consumed in Spain. The Gonzalez Byass operations centred on Jerez. There was a sales and distribution organisation in each of the provinces of Spain. It was diffuse largely owing to Spain's geography. There were few supermarkets (in 1982). Most goods were sold through smaller wholesale or retail units, individual shops and bars. *(pg322b)*

(3)   The group structure of Gonzalez Byass is set out in Mr Glover's report at page 47 and in Mr Baker's report at tab. 2 as at 31 March 1982. For the purposes of clarity we omit certain companies and confine ourselves to the main skeleton as it was in March 1982. At page 50 of Tab 2 Vol. A of the documentary evidence there is the Group Structure as it was in 1988.

Gonzalez, Byass and Co. Limited was incorporated in 1896. It was known during the proceedings as 'UK1'. It had some unique Articles of Association which are mirrored in those of its holding company, GB Cayman, which was incorporated in 1972. Gonzalez Byass & Co. Limited was the only trading company for many years. *(pg322c)* Its operations in Spain were carried out by a branch. The registered office of this company was in England. The Head Office, being the principal office of the company for the time being outside the United Kingdom, was at such place outside the United Kingdom as the directors determined. This was in Jerez.

The branch of UK1 in Spain where the sherry was produced in due course became Gonzalez Byass SA, a wholly owned Spanish subsidiary of UK1. In 1981, after several years *(pg322d)* of negotiation, the Spanish authorities finally permitted the assets of UK1 situated in Spain to be transferred to Gonzalez Byass SA ('GBSA'). The transfer took place on 1 November 1981. UK1 had another wholly owned subsidiary company formed in 1958 namely Gonzalez Byass (UK) Ltd ('UK2') which conducted the English or UK trade, that is, the importation of sherry in bulk, bottling and selling it in the UK. *(pg322e)*

(4) (i) The original ordinary shares in GB Cayman numbered 10,000 of £7 each, as did those in UK1. Pursuant to an agreement dated 24 November 1981 to which we refer later, 1000 of these shares became 10800 of 70p each. There were preference shares, but they are not material in the present context. They were redeemed in 1982. *(pg322f)*

(ii) Under the Articles of Association, there were no restrictions on the transfer of ordinary shares to other ordinary shareholders or to any lineal descendant of the Gonzalez or Byass families (article 28). Geoffrey and John, whose mother was a Byass, and their respective lineal descendants were deemed to be Byass by birth. With minor exceptions, any other type of transfer was subject to the directors' right in their absolute discretion to refuse to register such transfer. Any proposed share transfer not falling within article 28 (broadly speaking, a transfer to *(pg322g)* another member) was subject to the pre-emption provisions of article 29. Under this article a transfer notice was required and the ordinary shares were to be offered at a fixed price to the other ordinary shareholders pro rata to their existing holdings. The fixed price was to be determined every year by the Company in general meeting. If no buyers could be found among existing members, the shares could *(pg322h)* be transferred to a non-member at a price no less than the fixed price, but always subject to the directors' right to refuse to register the transfer if they saw fit. Article 29 also obliged the directors to refuse to register any transfer of shares where, in their opinion, the transferee was in any way connected with a competitor. The current fixed price was £42 per share when 10,000 were in issue.

(iii) Under article 85 of the Articles of Association the ordinary shareholders had *(pg322j)* power to appoint one director for every 1000 ordinary shares held by him or them. Only a male person whose surname was Gonzalez or Byass (including Geoffrey and John and their descendants as above) could be appointed director. The number of directors could not exceed ten.

(iv) It follows that if a shareholder held 2000 original ordinary shares, he could appoint himself and one other as directors. If he held, say, 1500 such shares, he could use 1000 for the purpose of appointing himself and use 500 to support some other shareholder or 100 shares to support five other shareholders as directors. **(pg323a)**

A schedule at p. 273B of Vol. B dated 5 July 1983 provides an illustration of the process in practice. Geoffrey supported himself with 14511 (new) shares. He also supported Manuel Maria Gonzalez Diez, who was a personal friend, with 7284 (new) shares. The trustees of the Torre Soto trust, a Tangier based trust established by the Marquess de Torre Soto for the benefit of his issue, used their shares in differing amounts to support four other directors. Voting on the board of directors followed the number of shares held by a director, or used to support him. (pg323b)

(5) (i)   Whilst there were three Byass shareholder/directors and, in the 1970s, a Byass trust (of which more later) which held 1052 original shares of £7 each, the Gonzalez shareholdings were diffusely spread. Forty seven shareholders from seven interrelated families are recorded in Mr Baker's report at tab 3. They include two sets of trustees of which one was the Torre Soto trust whereunder there were ten beneficiaries each of whom was entitled to a proportionate share of the voting rights **(pg323c)** attached to the shares comprised in the trust. Ten Gonzalez shareholders held less than 100 (new) shares, twenty two held more than 100 but less than 1000 shares, nine held over 1000 but less than 2000 shares, one held 6000 and two sisters held 3000 each. Only one held more shares and that was Carlos Maria Gonzalez Rivero ('Carlos') who held 11,880 shares. Contrast the Byass family, Geoffrey owning 21,795 shares, Nicholas 13,305 and John 10,908. **(pg323d)**

(ii)   Allegiances amongst the Gonzalez group could and did fluctuate, but not always; they could be united. There was a hard core of Gonzalez shareholders ('the Jerez block'), some who were reckoned by Geoffrey to be 'uncommitted' and a few who might be expected to side with the Byass family. Carlos headed the Jerez block. On 31 March 1982, he was a director of GB Cayman. Other Spanish directors were Manuel Mauricio Gonzalez, Gordon Diez ('Mauricio'), Manuel **(pg323e)** Maria Gonzalez Diez ('Manuel' or 'Manolo'), Alfredo Gonzalez Diez ('Alfredo') and Ricardo Enrique Gonzalez Gilbey. In addition to the directors, there were about three shareholders who were employees and looked to Gonzalez Byass for a living. Most of the Spanish shareholders held their shares purely as investments and were not employees. **(pg323f)**

(iii)   In a document known as Project 502 wherein Geoffrey in 1980, in connection with a scheme for him to acquire control of GB Cayman, gave a thumbnail sketch of groups of shareholders, Carlos is described as 'power-hungry and has formed an alliance with Alfredo exchanging power for support since he has no issue.' Alfredo, who was very wealthy, 'is the power behind the scenes, share hungry for his family and prepared to apply almost any pressure necessary to this end.' **(pg323g)**

(iv)   Appendix 2 in Mr Glover's Report which was spoken to by Geoffrey and Nicholas sets out the shareholding as at 31 March 1982 and adjusting the Byass concentration of shares by 388 (see (6) (iv) below), the Jerez block commanded 3634 (old) shares, the Byass block 4480, leaving 1886 uncommitted shares.

(6) (i) Geoffrey was invited to join the firm by his grandfather in 1947 when he was some 22 years of age. He worked and was trained in the cellars in England, **(pg323h)** the bodegas in Spain and also at a branch in Oporto, Portugal. In 1950 he was elected a director of UK1. His grandfather was chairman, Mauricio's father, Marquess of Bonanza, Carlos's father and Pedro, Marquess of Torre Soto were board members, as was Reginald Byass, the chairman's son. It was all very civilised. In 1958, when grandfather Byass died, Carlos and Mauricio who were managers in Spain became directors. Manolo, whose wife was Portuguese, became **(pg323j)** general manager of the Oporto branch and shortly afterwards joined the board of directors of UK1. John was already a director in 1958. In 1964 there was a cash crisis in Spain largely because 180 day bills were not discounted. Geoffrey recommended that a general manager be introduced. The Gonzalez shareholders supported by Geoffrey relieved Carlos and Mauricio of their executive functions. Santos Cascallana was appointed in 1965. He was a professional manager. Carlos particularly did not approve and thought that Geoffrey had stabbed him and Mauricio in the back. The seeds were sown which blossomed into the Jerez block. **(pg324a)** Nevertheless, Santos who became general manager in Jerez was very energetic and able. He was also a politician, though as events proved years later, perhaps not sufficiently so. He secured the support of Carlos and Mauricio in attacking Geoffrey. He resented the English company, its methods and profile.

(ii) In 1968 Geoffrey became chairman of all the companies in the Group. In 1974 Nicholas became a board member. So did Alfredo a son of the Marquess of **(pg324b)** Torre Soto ('a perfect executioner', he had great charm but was in Geoffrey's eyes 'devious and amoral'). He had made a fortune as a commodity trader in Madrid. He was able and a shrewd businessman. The board of five Gonzalez and three Byass was completed by Ricardo Enrique Gonzalez Gilbey. Nicholas, Alfredo and Ricardo were not 'executive directors'. They had the right only to attend and vote at board meetings. **(pg324c)**

(iii) We take from paragraphs 7.12 to 7.20 of Mr Glover's report with a few minor alterations in square brackets the account of the next events.

'The election of Nicholas Hawkings-Byass underlined the fact that the Byass family, a small compact group of shareholders, with [over 40] per cent of the shares in their hands, were likely to remain more powerful than the ever more *(pg324d)* numerous and dispersed Gonzalez shareholders and that the cycle of Byass dominance would continue indefinitely. To Carlos and Mauricio, Nicholas' election provided further evidence of Geoffrey Hawkings-Byass' continuing role and was a painful reminder of their own exclusion from management. To Santos Cascallana it was an impediment to his cause. To the remaining shareholders, some of them stuck in middle management roles with little or no *(pg324e)* prospect of further advancements, it fostered resentment of the Byass' power.

All these political machinations were disruptive but insufficient to upset the status quo. The memory of Carlos and Mauricio's ruinous time in management was still fairly recent and many Gonzalez shareholders would not countenance them in power again. Furthermore, the older generation, the family heads, still held Geoffrey Hawkings-Byass in high esteem and valued his *(pg324f)* contribution to the Company. Alfredo and his allies realised that, unless they found some cause célèbre, they were unlikely to convince the "uncommitted" Gonzalez shareholders to unite against the Byass family. The purchase by Nicholas and his uncle John of Gonzalez Byass shares from a Byass family trust in 1975 presented Alfredo with just such a common cause.

Geoffrey's uncle, Reginald Byass, had died in 1960 leaving 1052 "old" £7 *(pg324g)* ordinary shares in a will trust for the benefit of his widow during her lifetime and afterwards to his two children, Charles and Betty-Mary. In 1975, Charles and Geoffrey, the two trustees, sold 500 shares to Nicholas and John. The remaining 552 shares devolved equally to Charles and Betty-Mary on their mother's death later that year, i.e., December 1975. In March 1976, Charles *(pg324h)* sold his 276 shares to John and Nicholas; Betty-Mary retained her shares. These transfers were effected at the fixed price of £42 a share. This was the price at which members of the Company had been in the habit of transferring shares. The price was set each year by an independent firm of chartered accountants and had been approved by the shareholders at the annual general meeting. It was also the value agreed for fiscal purposes. *(pg324j)*

Alfredo saw in all this an opportunity to embarrass the Byass shareholders and, in particular, Geoffrey who had been trustee of his uncle's will trust. He portrayed the purchase of these shares as evidence of Geoffrey, Nicholas and John's intention to consolidate their power over the Gonzalez family. He conceived a plan to wrest these shares from the Byass family and distribute them amongst the Gonzalez shareholders. The first step was the offer to purchase Betty-Mary's 276 shares at £400 a share. This was formalised in January 1977. This offer was conditional on Betty-Mary and Charles initiating *(pg325a)* legal action against the trustees of the Reginald Byass will trust for the recovery of the 776 shares sold to Nicholas and John on the ground that the trustees had sold them at an under-value. The Gonzalez family undertook to finance the legal action in return for an undertaking by Charles and Betty-Mary to sell to them as many shares as were recovered. The price varied from £400 a share to £600 a share depending on the number of shares recovered. [Proceedings commenced in the High Court in England in 1977.] **(pg325b)**

The dealings with Charles and Betty-Mary were fronted by Jorgé and Alvaro, two of Alfredo's brothers. The prospect of an easy gain was sufficient to unite the Gonzalez shareholders, especially as they had been assured that their beneficial interest in the plan would not be disclosed, thus saving them any embarrassment with the Byass directors. *(pg325c)*

Alfredo had by this manoeuvre achieved the support of all the various factions within the Gonzalez camp. This gave Carlos, Mauricio and Santos Cascallana the opportunity they had been looking for. With the family united behind them, in 1977 they proceeded to relieve Geoffrey, Nicholas and John of their managerial responsibilities in the United Kingdom and in their stead, they appointed a Spanish managing director Francisco Valencia *(pg325d)* ("Paco Valencia") to GBUK (UK2). In March 1980 Geoffrey was removed from the chairmanship of the main Group boards and these jobs were allocated to other members of the Gonzalez family, such as Carlos and Mauricio. Thus Carlos and Mauricio had exacted their revenge; the professional management in Spain now controlled virtually all the day-to-day affairs of the companies in the Group; and there was the added prospect of the Gonzalez family receiving *(pg325e)* Byass shares. [Geoffrey was nevertheless relieved that Manolo became Chairman of GB Cayman, for whom he had voted, as he and Manolo were close personal friends.]

This unprecedented unity amongst the Spanish shareholders and management did not last long and cracks began to appear. Santos Cascallana, in furtherance of his ambition, turned his attention to the Oporto business *(pg325f)* where Manolo was in charge. With the backing of Carlos and Mauricio he manoeuvred his own manager into position there. In this, Carlos and Mauricio repaid Manolo for his own part in their earlier dismissal. The new manager in Oporto turned out to be a disaster and in 1979 the business had to be disposed of, leaving Manolo without a job and bitter at his cousins' betrayal. In London, the new Spanish managing director proved inept and the *(pg325g)* business deteriorated [through his failure to control profligate expenditure.]

Undeterred, Santos Cascallana proceeded with his next move, which was the takeover of an ailing competitor, Terry. GBSA was to be the vehicle for this. A bid of this size would have severely dented GBSA's resources and would have necessitated an injection of outside capital. The introduction of this new *(pg325h)* capital, arranged by Santos Cascallana, would have diluted both families' control and given Santos Cascallana the upper hand. In the event, this gamble seriously backfired and instead of having his plan approved at a specially convened board meeting in November or December 1979, he was summarily dismissed by a unanimous board.

The import of all these turbulent events was not lost on the more thoughtful *(pg325j)* Gonzalez shareholders. But as the litigation for the recovery of the shares had not been settled, they felt morally and financially bound to keep in line with the rest of the family. The legal action was eventually settled out of court on 24 November 1981. The Byass family agreed to cede 388 ordinary shares to the Gonzalez family. This reduced the combined Byass shareholdings from 42.2 per cent to 38.3 per cent. The transfer was given effect by way of renunciation of part of their entitlement under a scrip issue. The Gonzalez family made a cash payment to the successors of Charles and Betty-Mary both *(pg326a)* of whom by then had died. This was equivalent to the agreed price for the shares.'

(iv)   It was the agreement of 24 November 1981 which provided for the reorganisation of the share capital of GB Cayman. The original 10,000 ordinary shares of £7 each were to become 100,000 shares of 70p each. There was to be an *(pg326b)* issue of 20,000 new ordinary shares of 70p each on a 2 for 10 basis. The Byass Group were to renounce 4656 of the new ordinary shares to the Gonzalez Group (the equivalent of 388 original shares). So, of the 1052 shares in the will trust, the Byass Group in effect lost 276 sold by Betty-Mary and 388 (half the 776 shares sold to John and Nicholas), a total of 664.

(v)   It is not we think necessary to give a detailed account of the ebb and flow of *(pg326c)* support for the Byass family or the support that Geoffrey in particular gave to Manolo or Jorgé. Geoffrey voted against Manolo with regard to the principle of selling the Oporto branch but he voted with him against the Jerez camp when it came to the actual sale which took place to a man named Christie who lived in France and in the event failed to meet his commitments. Manolo wanted the sale to be rescinded and Geoffrey tried to interest another firm but to no avail. Manolo *(pg326d)* was appreciative. Mr Peter Fergusson who was a partner in Norton, Rose, Botterell and Roche and was closely involved with the sale of the Oporto business had no doubt that that sale drove Manolo into the Byass camp. Mr Fergusson's involvement with Gonzalez Byass extended from 1975 to 1985. Jorgé was one of the two who fronted the Jerez camp's attack on the Byass family over the will trust shares. He lived in

America. When the litigation was settled, Jorgé wanted 'to play *(pg326e)* happy families', as Geoffrey put it, and it seems that he had not realised that the trustees' sales might not have been as improper as he, briefed by the Jerez camp, had supposed. Consequently, in Geoffrey's words, after dining together in December 1981, he became contrite and thereafter tried to undo the damage he had caused.

(vi)   In March 1983 Geoffrey and John were appointed Joint Managing Directors *(pg326f)* of UK2 on a vote supported by Manolo and Jorgé against Carlos, Alfredo and Mauricio, and Paco Valencia was removed as managing director in the UK. He had overstepped the mark like Santos Cascellana in Spain in 1979 but in a different way. (Nicholas in evidence and John's statement Vol. B p.203).

(vii) Minutes taken by Mr Fergusson of proceedings in Madrid on 27 and 28 April 1983 between 'the Gonzalez Group' and 'the Byass/Manolo/Jorgé Group' (Bundle B p.262) evidence the fact that neither Manolo nor Jorgé was in the Jerez Group at that time *(pg326g)* and that pattern in their voting record continues in the documents thereafter contained in Bundle B. The voting pattern for directors on 5 July 1983 (Bundle B p.273B) shows on Geoffrey's evidence 61,536 votes cast for the Byass camp and 58,464 for the Jerez camp, including in the former Manolo and Jorgé. The Torre Soto trustees placed votes for both blocks but more for Byass than for Jerez. *(pg326h)*

(7)   We received evidence from Mr Hines. He is and has since 1984 been a director of the Sherry Institute of Spain the function of which is to promote the sale of sherry in the UK. He is an employee of the Spanish Government in London. He had worked for three companies in the wine trade including Mathews Clark & Sons, importers of Martell Cognac, sherry and other wines and spirits. He was employed by GB (UK) from 1970 until 1984, starting as a regional *(pg326j)* manager; he became a senior salesman in 1979 and was later director and general manager of the holding company for GB(UK)'s wine agencies. He thus had first hand knowledge of Gonzalez Byass. He left that firm when he was 40 years of age and went to the Sherry Institute. He knows Jerez and the sherry companies well. Focusing on March 1982, he said that Gonzalez Byass was clearly a leader in Jerez, it was the most homogenous organisation, it had two very good managers who replaced Santos Cascellana, it had the largest vineyards and provided top quality products. The quality was second to none and it was a very respected company as *(pg327a)* also was Domecq and Osborne. Harveys was the leader in the UK, Gonzalez Byass came second. Its reputation was high in the UK because of its very fine Tio Pepe, which takes five to six years to produce ready for sale. As compared with 1988 sales of sherry were greater in 1982. There had been a gentle decline partly owing to a change in UK taxation in about 1984 which made sherry more expensive. (Geoffrey attributed the decline to *(pg327b)* changing habits

in the UK, people eating lighter food and drinking less heavy wine.) Sales had peaked in 1979 but this was an artificial peak created by certain houses in Spain which exported a large amount of sherry of no great quality to qualify for a tax rebate. (Geoffrey gave evidence to the same effect). He did not think that the industry in Spain was, as was stated by Mr Baker in his report (p.12), 'in the doldrums' in March 1982. Gonzalez Byass certainly was not. It was in a *(pg327c)* very strong position: it was at its height in 1982 (an opinion held also by Nicholas and by Geoffrey who distinguished between increasing branded sales and bulk unbranded sherry which was in the doldrums). There was over-production in 1980 following the planting up of new vineyards in the 1970s. But, as Mr Hines put it, Gonzalez Byass did not subscribe to the South Sea Bubble: it had not overplanted. It was well run and financially sound; it was not over-extended like Domecq which *(pg327d)* was ripe for a bid (from a reputable suitor) : see Financial Times 27 March 1982 pp.63–64 Glover's report.

8 The apparently simple question in this appeal, what was the open market value of each of the Appellants' holding of shares in GB Cayman on 31 March 1982 is bedeviled by a number of factors. The accounts are not reliable. Assets are undervalued. Profits for the years 1979, 1980 and 1981 are understated. If a *(pg327e)* conventional take-over bid for the whole company were made a fresh set of accounts would have to have been drawn up. Each of the shareholdings was of importance, Geoffrey's specially, Nicholas's and John's not much less so. This is recognised by both experts though reflected in their valuations in a different way. Mr Baker started with a low value which he substantially increased to reflect the attraction of the shares to a special purchaser. Mr Glover opted for a pro rata value *(pg327f)* based on an entirety value. This was not an ordinary company. The Gonzalez Byass business was a jewel. It operated in Spain governed by an English constitution of a unique kind. Who would have peopled the market place? What home work would they have carried out before making a bid, for it is in our opinion unrealistic to suppose that potential purchasers would not have briefed themselves so far as they could any more than that Geoffrey or Nicholas or John would not have *(pg327g)* prepared himself so as to elicit the highest reasonably possible bid? A conventional portfolio valuation of each holding was derisory.

9 The prospective purchasers for any one of the holdings notionally on offer on 31 March 1982 obviously include the other shareholders in the company. For the Gonzalez shareholders, the Jerez block in particular, eminently acquisitive, *(pg327h)* Geoffrey's holding would have given that block control. Nicholas's shareholding (John's likewise) would not alone have given the Jerez block control, but in practical though not legal terms it would since they would have needed relatively few votes from the so called uncommitted Spanish shareholders (534 out of 1886 [*Glover* p.27]) to have practical control. On the other hand, in this theoretical market, the other Byass members would have been concerned to retain each and every holding since if they *(pg327j)* did not do so their own shareholdings would lose much of their influence and value. Such a purchase, however, would merely preserve but not increase the total Byass family holding. The evidence with regard to third party purchasers is conflicting. The practical participants who have knowledge of and experience in the sherry industry in Spain, Geoffrey, Nicholas and Mr Hines, had no doubt that a path would be beaten to the doorstep of a Byass shareholder whose shares were on offer, particularly by a purchaser from within the drinks industry, generally referred to as a multinational but also including a competitor in Spain. Geoffrey had had several *(pg328a)* enquiries over the years, specifically from Guinness and from Rumasa an acquisitive Spanish private holding company which had acquired some 17 sherry firms. It was the prospect of a sale by the Appellants to Seagrams which triggered the sale to the purchasers in 1988. Not being a shareholder, a third party, looking at the matter in practical terms, might have had some difficulty having regard to the Articles of Association but he could have acted through a trust with the vendor director as a *(pg328b)* nominee since the shares carried the right to appoint a director. Statutorily, however, one has to assume that the notional holder of the shares is entitled to be placed on the register. Mr Glover considered that a multinational would have been attracted by a Byass holding of shares since it could exploit the entrée given to it by virtue of that holding, a policy pursued by Rumasa. Mr Gillum as a merchant banker in England who had no experience whatever of Spain or the sherry industry *(pg328c)* would have advised a multinational to stay clear and make no offer, in the absence of a partnership arrangement and of a means of getting out of the company if things went wrong. Mr Baker's evidence was to similar effect.

We have no doubt that the Gonzalez shareholders would have been able to finance the purchase of shares on 31 March 1982. Carlos was a director of the Bank of Bilbao. Alfredo was wealthy in his own right. The evidence with regard to *(pg328d)* Jorgé's wealth is conflicting. Of him Geoffrey wrote in project 502 that he 'would like shares but cannot afford them'. On the other hand he was married to a very wealthy Cuban and was reputed to be a 'unit man' i.e. one who had $100m. He was 'independent, respected and wealthy'. Carlos, Alfredo and Mauricio financed their purchase in 1988 and we can see no reason why they or other members of that family group should have been unable to do so in 1982. For the Byass family, *(pg328e)* finance might have been more of a problem, but Nicholas was confident that in the last resort a multinational would have helped. Short of that, acting as a block with Manolo and Jorgé, finance could have been forthcoming from or with the backing of company assets.

(A) There are four possible bases for valuation of shares in an unquoted limited company viz, an earnings basis, a dividends basis, a turnover basis and an *(pg328f)* assets basis (entirety value). The auditors' reports on UK1 for the years 1979, 1980 and 1981 are heavily qualified.

(1) Earnings basis

Neither Mr Glover nor Mr Baker considered the earnings history as disclosed by the accounts of UK1 was satisfactory. Mr Baker said:

> 'given the fluctuations in the *(pg328g)* Company's profitability in the years immediately preceding the valuation date … it is difficult to formulate any reliable forecast of future earnings'

(Report para 20(b)(i)). The earnings record was 'erratic and modest' (ibid para 21(a)). Mr Glover's evidence at para 12.36 of his Report is that a company's earnings record and its prospects are probably the single most important consideration in arriving at a valuation of shares, an opinion with which Mr Baker *(pg328h)* agrees. But Mr Glover considered it well nigh impossible to value the shares on this basis because of the problems with the trading record. In the absence of a reliable restatement of its earnings on UK as distinct from Spanish accounting principles (over 80% of the Group's activities were not subject to audit) a valuation of shares on an earnings basis was not reliable and could not be recommended. If restated, he thought the profits of 1978 (£6.866m) would be reduced and the *(pg328j)* profits in the three succeeding years increased (£2.861m, £1.769m and £2.724m). The 1978 profits were inflated by a Spanish tax amnesty which released hidden reserves. Stocks were revalued in 1979 which had the effect of taking £3.66m gross out of the profit and loss account during the 1979–1981 period. The effective rate of tax in Spain being about 20% suggests an average understatement of £1m per year over the three years. This does not take account of a substantial revaluation upwards of fixed assets (£11.69m) in 1979 with consequential increase in depreciation charges. *(pg329a)*

Despite the deficiencies, Mr Baker adopted a straight average of the post tax earnings for the three years 1979–1981 available for ordinary shares, viz £2.438m or £20.32 per share, though in giving evidence he favoured earnings for 1981 alone, £2.716m, giving £22.63 per share. In arriving at his valuation Mr Baker said in cross examination but not in his report that he allowed a 20% uplift on what we call a hunch basis (per Mr Baker 'judgment') in order to allow for understated *(pg329b)* earnings, a percentage he adhered to after he discovered that profits had been reduced by £3.66m as mentioned above and at p. 19 of the report had stated that it was difficult to reconcile the earnings with the company's book value. Using a price/earnings ratio of 4 applied to earnings of £20.32 per share the value of minority holdings was £81.28 per share.

Mr Baker's methodology was criticised by Mr Glover. Mr Baker estimated the *(pg329c)* value of the company at £36m (page 19 Report) which implies a price/earnings ratio of 10.2, taking 1981 earnings alone. So either Mr Baker's price/earnings ratio of 4, which also included a 'hunch' element, has to give way or earnings have to be increased to justify a capitalisation of £27.69m (£36m

– 30% control premium; 1981 earnings £2.716m; £27.69m/£2.716m = 10.2). On a price/earnings ratio of 4, earnings have to be increased by 250%. Note, however, that going on 1981 figures alone, *(pg329d)* the capitalisation is not £36m but £39.6m and a price/earnings ratio of 11.2 (£2.716m 3 7.86 3 1.5 = £32.022m + £900,000 = £32.92m + Mr Baker's second 20% uplift = £39.5 which, less the control premium of 30% = £30.39m, entailing a price/earnings ratio of £30.39m/£2.716m = 11.2).

(2) Dividend yield basis (pg329e)

Mr Baker worked out a value on this basis. Mr Glover rejected this method because no one would buy shares in GB Cayman for their dividends. The dividend history was erratic and payment dilatory. Mr Glover said that if this basis were to be used the proper method to adopt is the investment rate of return. The minimum rate of return is the government bond yield, then 13.32%. This produced an *(pg329f)* absolutely safe investment which could be realised at any time. The 1981 dividend worked out at £4.166 per share (and was covered 5.43 times). £4.166 to yield 13.32% gives a basic value of £31.28 per share. Mr Baker took a gross dividend yield of 6.33% from the Brewers and Distillers sector, adjusted that downwards for various depreciatory factors and appreciated upwards for the generous cover, arriving at 4.75% (p.18 Report). Applied to a dividend of £4.166 per share the value became £87.71 per share. Subjecting that value to the government bond yield (£87.71 3 13.32%) *(pg329g)* produces a dividend of £11.70. In Mr Glover's opinion a value of £87.71 per share could not be derived from the proper application of a dividend yield calculation. Moreover there was no evidence that at 31 March 1982 a dividend of £11.70 could be expected. Mr Baker provided no cogent or methodological justification for his process of appreciation and depreciation. It was all a matter of 'judgment'. *(pg329h)*

It seems to us unrealistic to pay £87.71 per share in a private company with GB Cayman's dividend record for pure investment purposes when on a government bond yield basis the price should be £31.28.

(3) Turnover basis

This basis is not commonly used, but in Mr Glover's opinion it provided more certain data since unlike earnings, turnover figures were not subject to understatement and Spanish fiscal distortion. *(pg329j)*

Adopting this basis one can arrive at an 'Entirety Value'. Mr Glover preferred and adopted the Brewers sector criteria excluding companies not properly comparable with GB Cayman for reasons of size and diversity of products. One arrives at a multiple by comparing market capitalisation with turnover for each company in the list from which one deduces an average. That average (0.66) one applies to GB Cayman's turnover for 1981, *(pg330a)* £53.34m.

The result is a notional quoted value of £35.204m. (The same exercise was done with the whisky sector.) Mr Baker made a cross check on his valuation using the same method of calculation but he discounted the multiple by 15% for what were referred to as 'Spanish factors' a course which we do not accept since, not being an economist, Mr Baker misunderstood fundamentally the function of exchange rates (in this instance peseta/sterling) and he had no expertise with regard *(pg330b)* to the Spanish economy and the sherry industry in particular. Even on this flawed basis, an entirety value (including associated companies valued at £900,000) works out at £39.55m.

(4) Assets basis

Mr Glover used this basis together with the turnover basis, since GB *(pg330c)* had extensive real estate in Jerez and vast aging stocks of sherry and brandy. Net asset values are material in valuing investment or property holding companies and are not irrelevant in the case of an organisation like GB Cayman. Being conservative and prudent in his approach Mr Glover used a discount of 16% from net assets based on quoted brewers rather than a premium of 17% based on quoted spirits companies. Net assets of £42.13m (book value as shown in the consolidated *(pg330d)* balance sheet of UK1 at 31 December 1981) less a discount of 16% produces a notional quoted value on an asset basis of £35.389m.

(B) Mr Glover calculated the 'entirety value' as follows. He took £35.297m as the notional quoted value, being the midpoint between notional quoted value on a turnover basis and that on an assets basis. He said that that sum divided by 1981 earnings of £2,729,000 produces a price/earnings ratio of 12.9 which in the circumstances is not *(pg330e)* unreasonable as compared with whisky distillers average of 14% and brewers of 13.2%. Mr Glover then added a control premium of 30% (which Mr Baker agreed) and arrived at an entirety value of £46m.

Mr Baker's entirety value of £36m and earnings of £20.32 per share reflects a multiple of 14.76 'which is as high as any purchaser would wish to go' (p.19 Report). The multiple would be 17.7 on net book value of £43.2m (Mr Baker's figure para 21(a)) divided by £2.438m (3 years' average earnings) *(pg330f)* and 15.9 on £43.2m divided by £2.716m (1981 earnings alone). He used a price/earnings ratio of 4% on a portfolio valuation plus a premium.

For the record, since it does not appear in Mr Baker's proof, we set out Mr Baker's calculation of entirety value of £36m as distilled by Mr Green in his reply to the Crown's case.

Mr Baker

(1)   took average earnings for 1979–1981: £2.438m
(2)   multiplied that figure by 7.86 : sector average p/e ratio (Report p.17) = £19,162,680 *(pg330g)*

(3) added 50% for (i) control premium 30% (ii) understated earnings 20%
= £28,744,020
(4) added interest in associated companies at £900,000 [£954,000 accounts
31 December 1981, Vol C tab 2 p.83]
(5) equals £30m
(6) adds another 20% for undervalued assets (after estimating unfunded
pension liabilities) = £36m.

The 20% uplift for understated earnings was introduced on no reasoned basis
(see A(1) above). The additional 20% for undervalued assets is based on no
(pg330h) disclosed reason. They account for £10.2m of the £36m valuation.

11 The valuations actually made.

(A) Mr Baker valued

Geoffrey's shares at £115 per share (18.16% holding)
Nicholas's at £105 per share (11.09% holding)
John's at £105 per share (9.09% holding) *(pg330j)*

He considered that, in the light of the widespread shareholdings, each of these
holdings might have some influence as compared with the myriad Gonzalez
shareholdings and they carried the right to appoint directors (two in Geoffrey's
case). Mr Baker ruled out a multinational purchaser and a Hawkings-Byass
shareholder. He allowed for a possible demand from amongst the Gonzalez
shareholders, but no individual or family group would acquire independent
control on buying any one of the three holdings and each would cost a lot of
money, £2m or more. Mr Baker uplifted his portfolio valuation of £85 per share,
bearing in *(pg331a)* mind these considerations, to £105 per share for the two
smaller holdings (23.5% increase) and £115 in the case of Geoffrey's shares
(35% increase) whose 18.16% holding was more important in itself than the
two smaller holdings and carried the right to appoint two directors. Thus
Geoffrey's holding was worth £2,506,425, Nicholas's £1,397,025 and John's
£1,145,340. *(pg331b)*

(B) Mr Glover's valuation as at 31 March 1982
Mr Glover considered that a typical trade purchaser would have paid the pro
rata value of Geoffrey's and Nicholas's shares, i.e. £383.33 per share based on
entirety value of £46m. He considered that there was a case to be made for a
higher figure. He recognised that there were divisions amongst the
shareholders at that date and considered that a multinational would have been
attracted to buy shares in the *(pg331c)* company to exploit the internal divisions
and so eventually to obtain control. He recognised that neither holding was a
controlling interest but he considered that it would fetch its pro rata value
because of the overriding concern of the shareholders to ensure that the
holding was not acquired by a competitor or a multinational; moreover the
holding itself could alter the balance of power within the company. *(pg331d)*

12 The Statute Law

Section 150 Capital Gains Tax Act 1979 provides so far as material hereto

'(1) In this Act "market value" in relation to any assets means the price which those assets might reasonably be expected to fetch on a sale in the open market.' *(pg331e)*

Section 152

'(1) The provisions of subsection (3) below shall have effect in any case where, in relation to an assets to which this section applies, there falls to be determined by virtue of section 150 (1) above the price which the asset might reasonably be expected to fetch on a sale in the open market. *(pg331f)*

(2) The assets to which this section applies are shares and securities which are not quoted on a recognised stock exchange, within the meaning of section 535 of the Taxes Act, at the time as at which their market value for the purposes of tax on chargeable gains falls to be determined. *(pg331g)*

(3) For the purposes of a determination falling within subsection (1) above, it shall be assumed that, in the open market which is postulated for the purposes of that determination, there is available to any prospective purchaser of the asset in question all the information which a prudent prospective purchaser of the asset might reasonably require if he were proposing to purchase it from a willing vendor by private treaty and at arm's length.' *(pg331h)*

13 Authority

(1) The purchaser of any holding of shares is assumed to be entitled to be registered as the owner of shares but subject to the Articles of Association. (*IRC v Crossman* [1937] AC 26).

(2) The shareholdings in the instant appeal carry the right to appoint a director (or two directors in Geoffrey's case) but the appointee *(pg331j)* would have to be a Gonzalez or a Hawkings-Byass (deemed to be a Byass) by birth.

(3) The sale on 31 March 1982 is hypothetical but per Hoffman LJ in *IRC v Gray* [1994] BTC 8,034 at p.8,037:

> 'it cannot be too strongly emphasised that . there is nothing hypothetical about the open market in which it is supposed to have taken place. The concept of the open market involves assuming that the whole world was free to bid, and then forming a view about what in those circumstances would in real *(pg332a)* life have been the best price reasonably obtainable. The practical nature of this exercise

will usually mean that although in principle no one is excluded from consideration, most of the world will usually play no part in the calculation. The inquiry will often focus on what a relatively small number of people would be likely to have paid. It may have to arrive at a figure within a range of prices which the evidence shows that various people would have been likely to pay, *(pg332b)* reflecting, for example, the fact that one person had a particular reason for paying a higher price than others, but taking into account, if appropriate, the possibility that through accident or whim he might not actually have bought. The valuation is thus a retrospective exercise in probabilities, wholly derived from the real world but rarely committed to the proposition that a sale to a particular purchaser would definitely have happened.' *(pg332c)*

(*This was an inheritance tax appeal but the statutory provisions are similar.*)

(4)　In *Couch v Caton's Administrators* [1996] BTC 114 the Special Commissioner (Dr AN Brice) held at p.129 that:

's.152(3) is effective to provide that any information, including unpublished confidential information, and even information which might *(pg332d)* prejudice the interests of the company, is assumed to be available in the hypothetical sale if it would be reasonably required by a prudent prospective purchaser of the asset in question. It is therefore necessary to consider, in each case, what information a prudent prospective purchaser of the asset in question would reasonably require. In the context of s152(3) I understand the word "require" to mean "demand as a condition of buying"; information is *(pg332e)* "required" if the purchase would not proceed without it.'

(The Crown did not appeal against this part of the decision.)

(5)　It follows from subpara (4), in our opinion, that any purchaser would have done his homework and would have assembled all the information reasonably necessary for his purpose. He would have prepared himself to make an informed bid on the basis of *(pg332f)* information he was entitled to seek and have provided to him.

(6)　In our opinion, it is a material factor that each vendor is a director and that the purchaser would be entitled to appoint a director (two in the case of Geoffrey's shares).

(7)　We summarise by saying that in our opinion the hypothetical market takes place in a real world (cf *Walton v IRC* [1996] BTC 8,015 at pp.8,020 and 8,021) but for all that we are not allowed to assume that all three holdings were on the market at *(pg332g)* the same time unless there were factual evidence to that effect of which there is none.

14 Extensive submissions were made with regard to the question whether multinationals would or would not enter the hypothetical market. We take the view that they would do so but that, having read the Articles of Association, their entry *(pg332h)* would probably have to be covert. It could nevertheless be done. Through its nominee the multinational, if successful, would be sitting in the boardroom, although one has to assume that it would not have unfettered access to confidential information (cf. para 13(4) above). As we see it, it would know or be informed about the alliances formed and reformed between shareholders and see in them opportunities for exploiting differences and thereby provide it with avenues for its *(pg332j)* self advancement commercially.

The attractions to a multi-national of a stake in the company producing Tio Pepe as well as a profitable brandy business are obvious. The Articles of GB Cayman and the divisions within the company would however have had a restraining effect on the amount which it would be willing to pay.

The Gonzalez shareholders or some of them would certainly be in the market as would the other Hawkings-Byass shareholders. The former would be acquisitive. The Betty-Mary saga makes that plain as do Geoffrey's comments on Carlos and Alfredo contained in Project 502. The Hawkings-Byass's would strain every nerve *(pg333a)* to preserve their freedom, if necessary with the help of a multinational.

15 Mr Baker recognised that a premium should be added to the portfolio value he placed on the Appellants' shareholdings. This was referred to as the Special Purchaser Premium. The premium was 35% in Geoffrey's case and 23.5% in Nicholas's case. It was a matter of judgment taking account of the size of the holdings, the likely purchasers and the fact that the holdings entitled the owner to *(pg333b)* appoint two directors in Geoffrey's case and one in the others'. It was not based on competition which should be the justification for a premium.

16 On the evidence before us and the compelling analysis produced by Mr Green in his reply (pp.26–31), the holdings of each of Geoffrey and Nicholas could, we do not say, would, but could have conferred control on the Jerez block. So at the very least each holding was of much greater significance than its size alone would indicate. It *(pg333c)* follows from that that there were two groups of shareholders who could be called Special Purchasers, the Jerez group and the Byass group.

17 Our valuation

(1)   It is an invidious task to provide a valuation. Experts and we ourselves alike are at a serious disadvantage through the accounts of GB Cayman being so *(pg333d)* unreliable. A real potential purchaser in the market on 31 March 1982 would have had the accounts restated. We do not accept Mr Baker's valuation. It is inherently faulty. No one would bid for any of the shares on offer merely for the sake of the dividends. Such a bidder, if there were one, would in any event be outbid by a multinational or a Gonzalez or a Hawkings-Byass. Whilst we accept Mr Glover's method of arriving at an entirety value in the, we would say, unique circumstances *(pg333e)* of this appeal, giving a pro rata value of £383.33 per share, we

are not satisfied that that value would have been realised on a sale of, say, Nicholas's shares, on 31 March 1982. To our minds there must be some uncertainty with regard to the enthusiasm which would be displayed by a multinational when it had read the Articles of Association and with regard to the composition of the Byass group on 31 March 1982. Taking the latter point we conclude that on balance of *(pg333f)* probabilities that group did include Jorgé and Manolo on 31 March 1982.

(2)   Mr Green very helpfully produced ten tables setting out calculations of value made on different bases which are explained in footnotes. Column A contains Mr Baker's actual valuation. Mr Baker's value of the entirety was £36m on the basis of three year's average earnings of £2.438m. In evidence he expressed a preference for taking the recorded profits for 1981 alone, £2.716m. This produces an entirety *(pg333g)* value of £39.6m and a price/earnings ratio of 11.2. In column H allowing a deduction of 35% for unmarketability and Mr Baker's unreasoned 20% uplift for understated earnings, the earnings per share become £27.16, the 11.2 price/earnings ratio becomes 7.28 and the minority value on stock exchange principles becomes £197.72. Geoffrey's shares uplifted by 35% = £266.93 and *(pg333h)* Nicholas's £244.19 (uplift 23.5%). In our view this is the minimum value adopting in practice Mr Baker's preferences and methods. Removing the unreasoned uplift of 20% for understated earnings and substituting therefor a calculated percentage of 26.5% uplift, the minority value on stock exchange principles becomes £208.57 which we think is the fairest (Baker) valuation. It is worked out in column J. (There could be an uplift of 41% which is probably too crude. Mr Baker also thought that *(pg333j)* the stock revaluation in 1979 would have had less impact by 1981. It is assumed that stock revaluation would add to profits (net of Spanish tax of 20%) an average of £1m in each of three years. Three years average earnings are £2.438m; add £1m = £3.432m. £1m over £2.438m = 41%. The lower percentage comes from 1981 earnings £2.716m adding £1m to the 3 year average to produce £3.438m; £3.438m − £2.716 = £722k, thus entailing an uplift of £722k over £2.716 = 26.5%.) *(pg334a)*

Turning to the premium feature which Mr Baker played down on page 22 of his report, he recognised that Geoffrey's was the largest single shareholding in the company and carried the right to appoint two directors. The three shareholdings might have some unspecified influence as compared with uninfluential shareholdings. He excluded multinationals as competitors for the share holdings and he thought that Gonzalez shareholders would be interested to buy but there would be no great pressure *(pg334b)* on them to do so. Moreover he was doubtful about their ability to raise the necessary finance. Mr Baker was asked in cross examination but was unable to say what would be a suitable premium if we found on the evidence that multinationals would be interested, that members of the Gonzalez families would have been eager to purchase the shares, that the shareholdings of Geoffrey and

Nicholas had strategic importance, that one way or another finance could *(pg334c)* and would have been provided for the purchase. We do not know therefore whether Mr Baker would have applied to the £208.57 value of Geoffrey's shares his uplift of 35% or a greater percentage taking account of our findings or a lower uplift since he would have a higher value per share to start with. If the uplift of 35% were applied Geoffrey's shares on this basis would be valued at £281.57 each and Nicholas's at £257.59 (uplift 23.5%). *(pg334d)*

(3)   Whilst we accept Mr Glover's method of valuation by reference to turnover, we do not agree that on the statutory hypothesis a purchaser would have paid £383.33 per share for Geoffrey's or Nicholas's shares.

A multinational would have to be prepared to wait, possibly for some years, building up goodwill and confidence before obtaining the commercial benefits it sought. Indeed there could be no certainty that those benefits would be obtained at all. Meanwhile, the *(pg334e)* dividends received would fall far short of what would be needed to service the capital. On the other hand we consider that a multinational could have reasonable confidence that proposals which could be shown to be of benefit to GB Cayman and its shareholders would not be rejected out of hand, particularly if they gave openings to new markets. Once the shareholders became aware of the potential for higher returns there would inevitably be pressure on the directors.

The remaining *(pg334f)* Hawkings-Byass shareholders would be concerned at the substantial reduction of their family block; this would be particularly so in the case of Nicholas and John. They did not however have the resources to buy themselves though they probably would have been able to obtain financial support. Nevertheless, a lender would require a fair margin of security and, depending on who was the lender, he would only lend a proportion of what he conceived the holding to be worth. The *(pg334g)* Hawkings-Byass family might well have acted in concert either with a multinational or with a member or members of the Gonzalez family in order to protect their position.

The Gonzalez family would in all probability gain control even by acquiring Nicholas's holding. This would have made it much simpler for them to acquire finance. Indeed they would have found it easier to raise finance than the *(pg334h)* Hawkings-Byass family. All that they would have needed to do would have been to top the nearest bidder.

It seems to us that taking all uncertainties into account the Gonzalez family could have succeeded with a bid of two-thirds of entirety value for Nicholas's holding. This would give a potential appreciation of 50 per cent when entirety value could be achieved and places a value of £256 on each of Nicholas's shares. Geoffrey's larger holding would have given 'clearcut' control to the Jerez block, *(pg334j)* leaving the remaining Hawkings-Byass family with under 25 per cent. In those circumstances we consider that a premium of 20 per cent would have been appropriate giving a value of £307 per share, leaving potential appreciation of 25 per cent for the purchaser.

(4)   We now ask ourselves in view of the foregoing what price each shareholding might reasonably be expected to fetch on a sale in the open market on 31 March 1982. We do not adopt a price based even on the reworked figures of Mr Baker's valuation as we do not have the benefit of his opinion of the appropriate premium *(pg335a)* having regard to the facts we have found; furthermore it is based on earnings which even for 1981 alone must be regarded as unreliable. We prefer to follow Mr Glover's more certain approach to the problem even though we do not accept that the share should be valued on a pro rata basis (£383.33 per share).

(5)   We determine the value of Geoffrey's shares at £307 each and Nicholas's and John's at £256 each as at 31 March 1982. Accordingly the price which each *(pg335b)* holding might reasonably be expected to fetch on a sale in the open market on that date is: Geoffrey's 21,795 3 £307 = £6,691,065; Nicholas's 13,305 3 £256 = £3,406,080; John's 10,908 3 £256 = £2,792,448.

    Determination accordingly

Case 41
Caton's Administrators v Couch

[1997] STC 970

Court of Appeal

12, 19 June 1997

The costs incurred by a taxpayer in negotiating a share valuation and the cost in any appeal to the Special Commissioners are not deductible in computing a capital gains tax liability arising from the disposal of that shareholding.

Share valuation is a costly business. Significant time is required to produce a valuation. The cost of a valuation is then multiplied several times if there is significant correspondence with the HMRC Share Valuation followed by a lengthy appeal.

The appeal to determine the value of the holding of shares in the estate of Philip Caton deceased was heard by the Special Commissioners in 1995 and has been the subject of a commentary in this book.

In that case, the Special Commissioner, Dr AN Brice, gave an order that:

> 'the professional costs incurred by the taxpayers up to and including the hearing of the appeal [were] an allowable deduction in the nature of "expenses reasonably incurred in ascertaining market value" within the meaning of CGTA 1979, s 32(2)(b) [now TCGA 1992, s 38(2)(b)] for the purpose of computing the chargeable gain.'
> (*Caton's Administrators v Couch* [1995] STC (SCD) 34 at 56e omitted in the print included in this book.)

The Revenue appealed against this order. The High Court allowed the appeal and reversed the order, Rimer J stating:

> 'I ... conclude that the natural interpretation of the class of allowable costs referred to in TCGA 1992, s 38(2)(b) does not extend to or include the cost that are incurred by the taxpayers in carrying out their negotiations with the Revenue or in pursuing their appeal against the assessment.'
> ([1996] STC 201 at 229h omitted in the print included in this book.)

The administrators appealed to the Court of Appeal.

Statute specifies that the costs deducted in computing a capital gain are restricted to:

'(a)   the amount or value of the consideration, in money or money's worth, given by him or on his behalf wholly and exclusively for the acquisition of the asset, together with the incidental costs to him of the acquisition

(b)   ...

(c)   the incidental costs to him of making the disposal.'

(now TCGA 1992, s 38(1))

'Statute limits the "incidental costs" to 'expenditure wholly and exclusively incurred by him for the purposes of the acquisition or, as the case may be, the disposal, being fees, commission or remuneration paid for the professional services of any surveyor or valuer, or auctioneer, or accountant, or agent or legal adviser and costs of transfer or conveyance (including stamp duty) together –

(a)   in the case of the acquisition of an asset, with costs of advertising to find a seller; and

(b)   in the case of a disposal with costs of advertising to find a buyer and costs reasonably incurred in making any valuation or apportionment required for the purposes of the computation ... including in particular expenses reasonably incurred in ascertaining market value where required by this Act.'

(TCGA 1992, s 38(2))

In the judgement given on behalf of all three judges, Morrit JJ said:

'The material words are those appearing at the end of sub-s (2)(b) which permit the deduction of "costs reasonably incurred in making any valuation or apportionment required for the purposes of the computation under this Chapter" and "expenses reasonably incurred in ascertaining market value where required by this Act ...

A person who has realized a chargeable gain is obliged to make a return of such gains computed as required by the relevant legislation. At the material time this was provided for by ss12(1) and 8(1) pf the Taxes Management Act 1970 (the 1970 Act). In order to comply with that duty the taxpayer may incur expense in obtaining valuations or ascertaining the market value for the purpose of computing, as required by the relevant legislation, his liability to capital gains tax. It is not disputed that the costs and expenses incurred in performing those tasks for the purpose of discharging the statutory duty to make a return are allowable deductions ...

In my view the words "wholly and exclusively" do not govern paras (a) or (b) ... [TCGA 1992, s 38] falls into two parts, that which preceded the words ""together ... with" and that which follows them. The first part is concerned with the expenditure incurred in the acquisition or the disposal; such expenditure must be incurred wholly and exclusively for those purposes. But the second part included expenditure which cannot fall within the first part; though the costs of finding a buyer or a seller might, the costs of making a valuation or apportionment as required for the purposes of the requisite computation could not. Further in the latter case the text for deductibility is reasonableness which, whilst not entirely incompatible with a need to be wholly and exclusively incurred for a purpose, is different ...

A taxpayer must, in relation to each taxable disposal, make such valuations and ascertainments of market value as are required by the Act. In my judgement it follows that where reference is made in s32(2)(b) to a valuation or a ascertainment of market value it is not a reference to the final and indisputable valuation or ascertainment which may only emerge after extensive litigation ...

I conclude that the costs and expenses which a taxpayer may deduct pursuant to s32(2)(b) of the 1979 Act in respect of any particular disposal are limited to those which he incurs in complying with his obligations under s12 of the 1970 Act and do not extend to costs incurred in negotiating or contesting his liability to capital gains tax arising out of that disposal. The effect, but not the reason for, that conclusion is to preclude the deduction of costs by a taxpayer in conducting tax controversy with the Revenue.'

([1997] STC 970 at 973d, 973g, 975b, 979c and 979j
case 41 paras 5, 7, 14, 29 and 33)

The practical effect of this judgement is, of course, that a substantial proportion of the total cost incurred by a taxpayer when there is a contested valuation attracts no tax relief.

Judgement

References, example '(pg972a)', are to [1997] STC 970.

1 **MORRITT LJ:** At his death on 7 September 1987 Mr PS Caton owned 14 per cent of the issued share capital of Yorkshire Switchgear Group Ltd. For the purposes of *(pg972a)* capital gains tax, in consequence of the provisions of s49(1) of the Capital Gains Tax Act 1979, his personal representatives ('the

administrators') were deemed to have acquired that holding on his death for a consideration equal to its then market value. On 15 April 1988 the administrators sold the holding for approximately £3.27m representing £1.31 per share.

2 The question then arose whether the administrators were liable to pay capital *(pg972b)* gains tax and if so how much. The Revenue assessed them as liable for tax of £494,430 on the footing that the open market value of the shares on 7 September 1987 had been 35p. The administrators appealed to the special commissioners contending that the open market value at the date of death was 50p or 80p per share, depending on whether certain unpublished confidential information was or was not taken into account. After lengthy negotiations the appeal was heard over *(pg972c)* five days in December 1994. One of the three questions to be determined was whether–

> 'the professional costs incurred by the taxpayers up to and including the hearing of the appeal [were] an allowable deduction in the nature of "expenses reasonably incurred in ascertaining market value" within the meaning of *(pg972d)* sec. 32(2)(b) Capital Gains Tax Act 1979 for the purposes of computing the chargeable gain.'

3 The special commissioner, Dr AN Brice, answered that question in the affirmative and in the light of her answers to the other two questions determined that the open market value of the shares when deemed to have been acquired by the administrators was 56p each. The inspector of taxes appealed. In the event *(pg972e)* his appeal was confined to the question of the deductibility of professional costs. By his order made on 20 December 1995 Rimer J ([1996] BTC 114) allowed the appeal. He determined at p. 141–142 that:

> 'the ... costs both of the negotiations leading up to the appeal and of the appeal are not costs and expenses which are deductible for the purposes of [s. 32(2)(b)].' *(pg972f)*

This is an appeal of the administrators from that order. They contend that the decision of the judge was wrong in law and ask that the determination of the special commissioner be affirmed. The issue for our determination is, thus, one of the proper construction of s32(2)(b) of the Capital Gains Tax Act 1979 in the context of the Act as a whole. *(pg972g)*

4 The scheme of the legislation is to charge tax on chargeable gains arising on the disposal of an asset. The computation of such a gain involves ascertaining the consideration received on its disposal and deducting from that amount the consideration (including costs) given or deemed to have been given for its acquisition, expenditure incurred in the protection of the asset or the enhancement *(pg972h)* of its value and the incidental costs of the disposal. In this case there was no doubt as to the consideration received in respect of the

disposal of the shares. The questions arose in respect of what was deductible therefrom in computing the chargeable gain. That which may be deducted is prescribed by s32, which, so far as material, is in these terms:

'(1) Except as otherwise expressly provided, the sums allowable as a *(pg972j)* deduction from the consideration in the computation … of the gain accruing to a person on the disposal of an asset shall be restricted to–

(a)   the amount or value of the consideration, in money or money's worth, given by him or on his behalf wholly and exclusively for the acquisition of the asset, together with the incidental costs to him of the acquisition …

(c)   the incidental costs to him of making the disposal. *(pg973a)*

(2) For the purposes of this section and for the purposes of all other provisions of this Act the incidental costs to the person making the disposal of the acquisition of the asset or of its disposal shall consist of expenditure wholly and exclusively incurred by him for the purposes of the acquisition or, as the case may be, the disposal, being fees, commission or remuneration paid for the professional services of any surveyor or valuer, or auctioneer, or accountant, *(pg973b)* or agent or legal adviser and costs of transfer or conveyance (including stamp duty) together–

(a)   in the case of the acquisition of an asset, with costs of advertising to find a seller, and

(b)   in the case of a disposal with costs of advertising to find a buyer and costs reasonably incurred in making any valuation or apportionment *(pg973c)* required for the purposes of the computation … including in particular expenses reasonably incurred in ascertaining market value where required by this Act.'

5 The material words are those appearing at the end of subs. (2)(b) which permit the deduction of–

'costs reasonably incurred in making any valuation or *(pg973d)* apportionment required for the purposes of the computation under this Chapter'

and

'expenses reasonably incurred in ascertaining market value where required by this Act.'

6 To deal with cases in which an acquisition or disposal is deemed to have taken place as well as to avoid the artificial reduction of the consideration in cases of actual acquisitions or disposals the legislation contains a number of provisions *(pg973e)* which deem the consideration to have been the open market value of the asset at the relevant time. Examples are to be found in s29A (acquisitions or disposals otherwise than by a bargain made at arms length), s49(1) (deemed acquisition by personal representatives on death) and s54(1) (deemed disposal by a trustee to a beneficiary becoming absolutely entitled to settled property). All such cases involve the making of valuations in accordance with s150. Further there are *(pg973f)* special provisions for valuation in the case of assets disposed of in a series of transactions (s. 151) and unquoted shares and securities (s. 152).

7 A person who has realised a chargeable gain is obliged to make a return of such gains computed as required by the relevant legislation. At the material time this was provided for by ss12(1) and 8(1) of the Taxes Management Act 1970. In order to comply with that duty the taxpayer may incur expense in *(pg973g)* obtaining valuations or ascertaining the market value for the purpose of computing, as required by the relevant legislation, his liability to capital gains tax. It is not disputed that the costs and expenses incurred in performing those tasks for the purpose of discharging the statutory duty to make a return are allowable deductions. *(pg973h)*

8 Of course the Revenue is not obliged to accept the taxpayer's figures. The inspector may make his own valuations and raise an assessment on the basis of those figures. If the parties are unable to reach agreement then the taxpayer has a right of appeal, pursuant to s50(6) and (7) of the Taxes Management Act 1970, to the general or special commissioners. If the appeal involves questions of the value of land, leases, unquoted shares or securities then s47 provides for the determination *(pg973j)* of those questions, in the case of land and leases, by the Lands Tribunal and, in the case of unquoted shares, by the special commissioners. In the case of unquoted shares or securities the question of value is to be heard and determined in the same way as an appeal.

9 The special commissioner concluded that the permissible deductions included the costs of the appeal of the administrators to her. She said:

'I turn to consider whether the appeal process comes within the meaning of *(pg974a)* the words "ascertaining market value where required by this Act". The appeal process is regulated by s31 of the Taxes Management Act 1970 (which allows an appeal against an assessment). Section 57 of that Act refers to regulations about appeals. It provides for a procedure to ensure that, where the market value of an asset on a particular date may affect the liability to capital gains tax *(pg974b)* of two or more persons, any such person is enabled to have the matter "determined" by the tribunal having jurisdiction. It also prescribes a procedure by which the matter is not "determined" differently on different occasions.

It appears to follow from these provisions that market value is "determined" by an appeal in which case it would also follow that the appeal process is part of the determination of market value as provided by the 1979 Act. I note that s150 refers to the "estimation" of market value; s152 refers *(pg974c)* to the "determination" of market value and s32(2)(b) refers to the "ascertainment" of market value. It was not argued before me that there was any difference in meaning of these words. In any event, one meaning of "to determine" is "to ascertain" and one meaning of "to ascertain" is to "determine".

Accordingly I conclude that, in principle, the expenditure incurred up to and including the hearing of an appeal is incurred *(pg974d)* in ascertaining market value within s32(2)(b).'

10 She then considered whether the costs and expenses had been reasonably incurred and decided that they had.

11 Rimer J disagreed. After reviewing the rival arguments he said at p. 141–142: *(pg974e)*

'the costs incurred by the taxpayers for the purposes of the appeal are correctly characterised as costs incurred for the purpose of conducting a tax controversy with the Revenue. I consider that the same can also be said of any costs incurred in the course of any negotiation with the Revenue over the question of value, and regardless of whether it is successful or not. If the *(pg974f)* negotiations are abortive and no compromise is agreed, then I find it difficult to see how such costs could be said to have been incurred in ascertaining the value of the shares: the negotiations would not have ascertained anything except that the parties could not agree. But even if they are successful I agree with Mr Henderson that the exercise in which the taxpayers would have been engaged would not be one which could properly be described as "making [a] *(pg974g)* valuation" of the shares or as "ascertaining [their] value". It would be an exercise of negotiation with the Revenue as to the amount of any actual or proposed assessment, and I consider that it can make no material difference that the subject matter of the negotiation is the value of the shares.

I accordingly conclude that the natural interpretation of the class of allowable costs referred to in s32(2)(b) does not extend to or include the costs which *(pg974h)* were incurred by the taxpayers in carrying out their negotiations with the Revenue or in pursuing their appeal against the assessment. In my view the taxpayers' submissions require an unnatural meaning to be attributed to the relevant language. I see no reason to interpret s32(2)(b) in such an unnatural way.' *(pg974j)*

12 He also accepted a submission of the Revenue that to have reached the opposite conclusion would have involved the consequence, unique to the capital gains tax legislation, that the liability for the tax might depend on events occurring after the assessment had been raised.

13 Before the special commissioner there had also been an issue whether the words 'wholly and exclusively' appearing in s32(2) in relation to expenditure incurred by the taxpayer for the purposes of the acquisition governed the provisions of para. (a) and (b) which appear later in the subsection. The special commissioner appears *(pg975a)* to have thought that they did; but her decision on this point is vitiated by the fact that she seems to have thought, wrongly, that the words are included in para. (b) itself. Rimer J did not find it necessary to determine the point. In the light of the argument put forward by the administrators it is convenient to deal with this point at the outset.

14 In my view the words 'wholly and exclusively' do not govern para. (a) or (b). *(pg975b)* Section 32(2) falls into two parts, that which precedes the words 'together ... with' and that which follows them. The first part is concerned with the expenditure incurred in the acquisition or the disposal; such expenditure must be incurred wholly and exclusively for those purposes. But the second part includes expenditure which cannot fall within the first part; though the costs of finding a buyer or a seller might, the costs of making a valuation or apportionment as *(pg975c)* required for the purposes of the requisite computation could not. Further in the latter case the test for deductibility is reasonableness which, whilst not entirely incompatible with a need to be wholly and exclusively incurred for a purpose, is different.

15 The argument for each party started with the decision of the House of Lords in *Smith's Potato Estates Ltd v Bolland (HMIT)* (1948) 30 TC 267. *(pg975d)* In that case the taxpayer had appealed decisions of the Revenue in connection with its liability to excess profits tax. The appeal had been brought because of the commercial effect the decision might have on the business of the company through its liability for tax in subsequent accounting periods. The taxpayer sought to deduct the costs so incurred in the computation of its profits for the purposes of income tax and excess profits tax. The deductions were disallowed, such *(pg975e)* disallowance being upheld in the Court of Appeal and, by a majority, in the House of Lords. A similar point, with the same result, arose in *Rushden Heel Co Ltd v Keene (HMIT)* (1948) 30 TC 298.

16 The speeches of the majority in *Smith's Potato Estates* recognised that some part of the cost of preparation of trading accounts for tax purposes was, in practice, allowed as a deduction in computing profits but that the costs of conducting an *(pg975f)* appeal to ascertain the true measure of the taxpayer's liability to tax was not. Thus Lord Porter said at p. 288:

> 'I should myself draw a marked distinction between accounts made up on the purely trading basis and those which are prepared for and accepted by the Inland Revenue. If there were no obligation to ascertain and pay either of *(pg975g)* these taxes, there would be no necessity for making up accounts on Income Tax principles, it would suffice to make up the ordinary commercial accounts. The computation of accounts for tax purposes is therefore not directly associated with the carrying on of the business. It is

an obligation imposed upon the company for another and extraneous purpose, that is, for the purpose of *(pg975h)* ascertaining the tax to be paid out of profits. It is not, at any rate directly, undertaken for trade purposes but to satisfy the Revenue authorities.

It is true that as matter of convenience the cost of making up accounts for the Inland Revenue is allowed by the authorities as a deduction from profits, as is the cost of making up the strictly business accounts of the trade, but this is not a matter of principle but of expediency. The two duties overlap and in practice are *(pg975j)* almost indivisible. Moreover it is of advantage to the Revenue to have the figures required for their purposes carefully and accurately made up. Strictly, however, I think the expenses should be divided, and any additional cost of making up Revenue accounts should be disallowed in determining the allowable deduction for Income Tax purposes, but the advantages of allowing both to be deducted as a practical measure outweigh the disadvantages, though the result may not be strictly logical. But no such illogicality has to be faced when the sum which is alleged to be deductible is not the cost of *(pg976a)* accountant's work in ascertaining trading profits, but the expense of an appeal to the Board of Referees for the purpose of discovering the true measure of profits for tax purposes only. Such expenditure is incurred directly for tax purposes and for nothing else, though it may indirectly affect both the amount available for distribution to the proprietors of the business and that to be put to reserve.' *(pg976b)*

17 Lord Simmonds recognised both the general rule and the practical exception from it in these passages at p. 292–293:

'It is significant that Counsel were not able to call to the attention of the House any case in which the Appellants' present contention had been put forward. For a long period of years large sums of money have been devoted to *(pg976c)* the litigation of Income Tax claims – the most acute minds of the legal and accountancy professions have been at the service of the taxpayers – yet the claim that such money was expended wholly or exclusively for the purpose of the trade appears never to have reached a court of law. The reason is not far to seek. It is that neither the cost of ascertaining taxable profit nor the cost of disputing it with the Revenue authorities is money spent to enable the trader *(pg976d)* to earn profit in his trade. What profit he has earned, he has earned before ever the voice of the tax-gatherer is heard. He would have earned no more and no less if there was no such thing as Income Tax. His profit is no more affected by the exigibility of tax than is a man's temperature altered by the purchase of a thermometer, even though he starts by haggling about the price of it ... *(pg976e)*

I do not doubt that as a practical measure the Revenue authorities allow accountancy charges as a deduction in computing profits, both because such charges are necessary for trading as well as tax purposes and it would be vexatious to distinguish between them, and because they must find their own task an easier one if they are dealing with professional men who speak their *(pg976f)* language and understand their art. I do not think it necessary to decide how far in this direction the Revenue authorities are bound to go.'

18 Lord Normand went slightly further than Lord Porter or Lord Simmonds in accepting that the cost of negotiations with the Revenue, were, in practice, allowed as a deduction. He said at p. 295: *(pg976g)*

'Every trading company must keep books of account and these books are used by the accountants for the purpose of making up the commercial profit and loss account. The accountants may use that account by applying to it the modifications which Income Tax law requires in order to bring out the profit for Income Tax purposes, and they may have to negotiate with Inland Revenue *(pg976h)* officials in order to justify their account of profits and perhaps to obtain a correction of an assessment. It will also be necessary to prepare an account showing the amount of the distributable profits after making provision for the Income Tax liability. As the first and last of these accounts are among the purposes of the trade, the taxpayer may say that the whole accounting process, *(pg976j)* including even the prosecution of an appeal in order to determine the correct Income Tax assessment, is carried out for the purposes of the trade, and it may be added that the proper conduct of the trade requires that the assessment shall be correct. On the other hand, it may be said that there is in strictness no part of the accounting process which is not directly or indirectly concerned with Income Tax liability, and that, as the payment of Income Tax is not a purpose of the trade, none of the costs incident to the accounting process are laid out exclusively for the purposes of the trade. That would be an extreme and, I think, an untenable position. The Inland Revenue's contention in *(pg977a)* these appeals did not go nearly so far. It was that the costs and expenses of appeal proceedings before the Commissioners of Inland Revenue or the Board of Referees, and from them to the courts, are not laid out exclusively for the purposes of the trade and are, therefore not permissible deductions. The line drawn by the Inland Revenue would allow deduction of the costs incurred in negotiations with their officers before an appeal is *(pg977b)* taken, or where no appeal is taken, either as a concession to the taxpayer or as a practical and convenient settlement of a disputable point.'

19 The administrators submit that in 1965 the draftsman of the statutory predecessor of s32(2) would have been well aware of the limitations imposed by the decisions in *Smith's Potato Estates* and *Rushden Heel* on *(pg977c)* the deductibility of professional fees incurred in ascertaining the true measure of tax liability. He would have recognised that no costs could have been regarded as being incurred wholly and exclusively for the purposes of the acquisition or disposal. It was submitted that the words at the end of para. (b) were added so as to allow deduction in the case of capital gains tax as a matter of right rather than by way of concession, as is still the case for income tax. *(pg977d)*

20 From this proposition it was argued that the words used went beyond the limits in practice recognised in *Smith's Potato Estates* so that, until there was a final determination of market value as required by the legislation or for the purposes of any computation likewise required, all costs and expenses incurred in connection with valuations were deductible provided only that they were reasonably incurred. *(pg977e)* Counsel frankly accepted that the consequence of his argument would be that the costs of proceedings by way of appeal from an assessment to capital gains tax would be deductible in ascertaining the market value of the asset in question provided that the issue was one of valuation, the costs were reasonably incurred and had not been recovered under an order of the court. It was suggested that such a consequence would accord with the philosophy behind the capital gains tax legislation to the *(pg977f)* effect that it is a tax on gains not arithmetical differences, cf *Aberdeen Construction Group Ltd v IR Commrs* (1978) 52 TC 281 at p. 296; if the disposal of an asset gave rise to these liabilities then there was no gain to that extent. And, it was observed, if that had not been the intention why was not some limit imposed for it would have been so easy to write one in.

21 It was submitted that market value was not ascertained unless and until there *(pg977g)* was a final determination of market value because the figures had been agreed by the Revenue and the taxpayer, with or without intermediate negotiations, or determined by the court as part of an appeal from an assessment, whether or not, due to the nature of the asset in question, any part of s47 applied. It was accepted that some of the costs involved might fall within the description of the cost of conducting a tax controversy with the Revenue but it did not follow *(pg977h)* that on that account they were not within s32(2)(b) and therefore deductible.

22 Counsel for the administrators disputed the observation of Rimer J at p. 142 that the consequence of his argument would produce a situation unique to capital gains tax in that the correctness of the assessment would depend on subsequent events. He pointed out that s40 and 41, dealing with deferred payments of consideration *(pg977j)* and contingent liabilities, expressly allows events subsequent to the assessment to affect the liability to tax. Similarly s115 and 126, which provide for rollover and holdover relief, permit an accrued liability for capital gains tax to be discharged in the light of subsequent events. In any event, as he observed, s50(6), which provides for appeals against assessments, uses the present tense with regard to whether the appellant has been overcharged.

23 These are powerful arguments. Counsel for the Revenue accepted that as a matter of abstract English the construction of s32(2)(b) for which *(pg978a)* the administrators contend is possible. He argued that the construction advanced by the Revenue was to be preferred as being consistent with the words used and the historical background to the legislation as well as avoiding the absurdities to which the alternative propounded by the administrators gives rise. Counsel submitted that there is no reason to assume that the draftsman in 1965, who must be presumed to have been aware of *Smith's Potato Estates* intended to do more than put *(pg978b)* on a statutory basis for capital gains tax that which was allowed by concession in respect of income tax. Thus the dividing line is to be drawn at a point which precludes the deduction of the cost of maintaining the tax controversy with the Revenue. If the line is drawn where the administrators contend then, uniquely in the field of capital gains tax, the taxpayer would not only obtain tax relief for the costs incurred in disputing his liability for that tax but those costs would, to that *(pg978c)* extent, reduce the liability in dispute. It is suggested that the costs which are deductible pursuant to s32(2)(b) are limited to those incurred by the taxpayer in the initial valuation required to compute his liability for capital gains tax and the unilateral ascertainment by him of the market value as required by the Act for him to complete his tax return.

24 I prefer the arguments for the Revenue. Like both counsel I find that it is *(pg978d)* convenient to start with the *Smith's Potato Estates* case. The case was concerned with the question whether the costs of the appeal had been expended 'wholly and exclusively' for the purpose of the company's trade. In view of my conclusion on the construction of those words in s32(2) the decision has no direct application. But, in my judgment, it would have shown the draftsman of the original capital gains tax legislation contained in Finance Act 1965 that in the field *(pg978e)* of income tax and excess profits tax, in practice, the Revenue allowed the taxpayer to deduct the costs of preparing accounts from which to compute his profits for tax purposes. Thus he would have known, first, that there was no general right to deduct from a liability for tax, for example estate duty, the general costs of finally ascertaining it, and, second, that such deductions as were allowed in the field of income tax and excess profits tax depended on a concession and were not as of *(pg978f)* right.

25 The contrast between the costs of producing accounts from which to compute profits for tax purposes and the conduct of a tax controversy with the Crown, to which Rimer J referred, was first drawn by Lord Greene MR in *Rushden Heel Ltd v Keene* at p. 317 and adopted by the majority in the House of Lords in *Smith's Potato Estates*. In that context the contrast was more *(pg978g)* meaningful for if the purpose of the expenditure was in whole or in part the purpose of conducting the tax controversy it could not have been wholly and exclusively for the purpose of the taxpayer's trade. Nevertheless the draftsman of the relevant provision in Finance Act 1965 must have been aware that that was where the line had been drawn. *(pg978h)*

26 It is common ground that the draftsman intended to provide for a right in the field of capital gains tax broadly equivalent to the concession in the field of income tax. But I do not accept that he intended to go further than that and permit the deduction of all costs incurred by a taxpayer in and prior to the final determination of the market value of the asset in question. Such a right would be unique in the field of revenue law. Had it been intended the enactment would have been *(pg978j)* accorded greater prominence than that of a postscript to a definition of 'incidental costs'.

27 However the presumed intention of the draftsman is not enough; the words used must be capable of reflecting it. In my view they are. The phrase of which s32(2) is the definition is 'the incidental costs to him of making the disposal'. Thus the words 'by him' must be implied in those parts of s32(2) where they have been omitted. Accordingly the relevant part of para. (b) must be read as providing for the deduction of: *(pg979a)*

> 'costs reasonably incurred [by him] in making any valuation or apportionment required for the purposes of the computation under this chapter, including in particular expenses reasonably incurred [by him] in ascertaining market value where required by this Act.'

28 Section 12 of the Taxes Management Act 1970 applies s8 of that Act in relation to capital gains tax *(pg979b)* as it applies in relation to income tax and subject to any necessary modifications. Section 8 imposes an obligation on any person so required by a notice from an inspector of taxes to deliver to him–

> 'a return of his income, computed in accordance with the Income Tax Acts and specifying each separate source of income and the amount from each separate source.'

29 Thus to enable him to comply with that statutory obligation a taxpayer must, in *(pg979c)* relation to each taxable disposal, make such valuations and ascertainments of market value as are required by the Act. In my judgment it follows that where reference is made in s32(2)(b) to a valuation or an ascertainment of market value it is not a reference to the final and indisputable valuation *(pg979d)* or ascertainment which may only emerge after extensive litigation.

30 The argument for the administrators depends on reading the words 'valuation or apportionment required for the purposes of the computation under this Chapter' and 'ascertaining market value where required by this Act' in the opposite sense. But if that were intended one would expect there to be some reference to the valuation or ascertainment of value being 'in accordance with' the Act, as opposed to being 'required by' the Act, as well as to the valuation or ascertainment being final as between the Revenue and the taxpayer. *(pg979e)*

31 In so far as para. (b) remains ambiguous the consequences of the rival contentions show, in my judgment, that the construction advanced by the Revenue is to be preferred. It is true, as contended by the administrators, that the legislation makes provision for a tax liability to change in the light of subsequent events. But the provisions on which they rely have a different effect. Thus s40 and 41 impose tax, in the first instance, on a hypothesis. *(pg979f)* The subsequent event is one which shows the hypothesis to have been wrong and the provision in question permits the tax to be charged on a factual rather than hypothetical basis. Sections 115 and 126 provide for reliefs against tax if, subsequently, the taxpayer claims it. None of these sections has the effect, which the construction of s32(2)(b) advanced by the administrators would, of enabling the liability to tax to be diminished, and in theory extinguished altogether, by *(pg979g)* contesting the liability itself.

32 To construe the paragraph as the administrators suggest would be a positive deterrent to reaching a sensible agreement with the Revenue as to the quantum of liability. It would give rise to the absurd position that on an appeal against an assessment which had failed the assessment would nevertheless require reduction to take account of such costs of the unsuccessful appeal as had been reasonably incurred. But as appeals to the High Court, the Court of Appeal and the House of Lords lie on points of law only the factual question whether the costs had been reasonably *(pg979h)* incurred would, at each stage, have to be remitted to the commissioners for their determination. So absurd a result may be avoided by adopting the construction advanced by the Revenue. *(pg979j)*

33 For all these reasons I conclude that the costs and expenses which a taxpayer may deduct pursuant to s32(2)(b) in respect of any particular disposal are limited to those which he incurs in complying with his obligations under s12 of the Taxes Management Act 1970 and do not extend to costs incurred in negotiating over or contesting his liability to capital gains tax arising out of that disposal. The effect, but not the reason for, that conclusion is to preclude the deduction of costs by a taxpayer in conducting a tax controversy with the Revenue. I would dismiss this appeal. *(pg980a)*

SCHIEMANN LJ: I agree.

STUART-SMITH LJ: I also agree.

Case 42
Denekamp v Pearce

[1998] STC 1120

High Court

2 October 1998

In this case, a 24 per cent shareholding, a minority interest, in a trading company is valued by discounting the full asset value of the company.

Cwmbran Cash & Carry Co Ltd was incorporated in 1965 and traded as a cash and carry business in South Wales. During the 1970s it expanded rapidly. As at 31 March 1982 the company's main activity was that of wholesale cash-and-carry but it had three wholly owned subsidiaries, which carried on business in the building and catering trades.

The company mainly traded in groceries and consumable goods of every description and had its centre of operations in a leasehold property from where it sold its goods to local tradesmen. The subsidiaries were loss-making and by 1982 were proving a strain on the company.

The company was liquidated in the spring of 1988. John Charles Denekamp, who held 2,400 ordinary £1 shares (24 per cent of the issued share capital) was, thus, subject to capital gains tax on the distribution made to him. The taxpayer and the Revenue were unable to agree the market value of the shares as at 31 March 1982, that being the base cost to be taken in computing the capital gain chargeable on John Denekamp.

The early 1980s was a period of severe economic recession. The company's trading results deteriorated markedly from a net profit of £65,462 for the year ended 31 December 1978 to a net profit of £23,385 for the year ended 31 March 1981 followed by a loss of £27,850 in the year to 31 March 1982. Thereafter, losses became even larger.

In 1981 the taxpayer's father asked a firm of valuers and commercial agents to market the company as a going concern. They kept the company on its books for a considerable time but little interest was shown. In 1982 a businessman met the taxpayer and his father to discuss the possibility of purchasing the company but decided not to proceed. The taxpayer says that the price discussed was £1 million. The businessman's recollection is that the consideration required was more than anticipated and his firm had other commitments which they needed to make.

THK Everett, the Special Commissioner, postulated the approach taken by the hypothetical purchaser at 31 March 1982 and the information that would be available to him in the following terms:

'I must assume that such purchaser was given all the information available to the directors . ...

He would have known that dividends had not been paid and were unlikely to be paid ...

Even though the 1981 and 1982 accounts were not available, the knowledge available to the taxpayer and the administration director would be passed to the potential purchaser who would discover that the peak in the company's profitability was reached in or about 1978 and that since that time the company had become less profitable. Its future in the economic depression of the early 1980s did not look rosy ...

I take the view that a potential purchaser, being prudent and weighing everything in the balance, would have come to the conclusion that a sale of the company sometime in the future was the most likely outcome.'

(Reported as *Cash & Carry v Inspector of Taxes* [1998] STC (SCD) 46 reproduced in *Denekamp v Pearce* [1998] STC 1120 at 1126b, 1126c and 1126h **case 42 paras 36, 37, 40 and 41**)

The Special Commissioner then gave his valuation of the shareholding:

'Looking at all the evidence and bearing in mind the statutory provisions and the results of the decided cases I have come to the conclusion that I can accept that the total assets amounted to £598,064 as stated above, producing a share value of £59.75 per share and that I should apply to that figure a discount of 55% to recognise the status of the taxpayer's minority holding, which will produce a value of £26.89 per share.'

([1998] STC 1120 at 1126j, **case 42 para 42**)

The taxpayer applied to the High Court, appearing for himself in person, arguing two alternative submissions:

1. the court should make its own valuation of the value of the shares, including in the calculation the value of the company's goodwill,

which was not mentioned in the hearing before the Special Commissioner; and

2.   that the valuation should be remitted back to the Special Commissioner with the direction that he reconsider the value.

Parke J ruled:

'The result of the whole matter is: First, I cannot vary the decision of the Special Commissioner; and second, I cannot make any formal order that makes the effect of remitting the case to the Special Commissioner for him to consider whether he wishes to vary his decision. I must therefore affirm Mr Everett's decision and dismiss the appeal.'

([1998] STC 1120 at 1129g **case 42 para 61**)

Decision of the Special Commissioner

References, example '(pg1121h)', are to [1998] STC 1120.

1 The taxpayer appeals against assessments to capital gains tax for *(pg1121h)* the years 1988–89 and 1989–90. The assessments, made in estimated amounts, relate to distributions made to the taxpayer of 2,400 ordinary £1 shares in a company called Cash & Carry Co Ltd ('the company'). The taxpayer acquired those shares before 31 March 1982 and the issue in these appeals is the value of those shares as at that date. *(pg1121j)*

2 I received in evidence a short agreed statement of facts and several bundles of documents. Oral evidence in support of the appeals was provided by the taxpayer and by the administration director of the company from 1975 onwards.

3 Oral evidence on behalf of the Revenue was given by Mr Thomas Charles Carne, the advisory accountant to the Board of Inland Revenue and by Mr Thomas Frame Vassie, a chief examiner in the Shares Valuation Division of the Capital Taxes Office. Written statements of the evidence of both Mr Carne and Mr Vassie were produced. *(pg1122a)*

The facts

4 The company was incorporated in 1965 and traded as a cash and carry business in South Wales. During the 1970s it expanded rapidly. As at 31 March 1982 the company's main activity was that of wholesale cash and carry but it had three *(pg1122b)* wholly owned subsidiaries, which carried on business in the building and catering trades.

5 At the material time, the company mainly traded in groceries and consumable goods of every description and had its centre of operations in a leasehold property from where it sold its goods to local tradesmen. The subsidiaries were loss making and by 1982 were proving a strain on the company. *(pg1122c)*

6 The issued share capital in the company as at 31 March 1982 amounted to £10,009, divided into 10,000 ordinary £1 shares and 9 £1 'A' ordinary shares. The 'A' shares did not enjoy voting rights but otherwise ranked pari passu with the other ordinary shares. The *(pg1122d)* taxpayer's family then owned among them 100 per cent of the voting capital. The directors were: the taxpayer, the taxpayer's father and mother, and two employees, one of whom was the administration director. At the material time the shares were unquoted and there was no prospect of their becoming quoted.

7 The transfer of shares in the company was restricted by the company's articles. These permitted free transfer between the family and of the shares of deceased *(pg1122e)* shareholders but otherwise gave the directors complete discretion to refuse to register any transfer.

8 As at March 1982 the company had not paid a dividend for many years and there was no real prospect of its doing so in the foreseeable future.

9 Until 1982 the taxpayer believed that he and his wife would eventually become the owners of the majority shareholding in the company, either by purchase or by *(pg1122f)* succession on his father's death. It was therefore a shock to the taxpayer that in or about February 1982, the taxpayer's father informed him that it was his intention to transfer a sufficient number of shares to the taxpayer's brother and sister so that all three children would have an equal holding of shares in the company. Neither the taxpayer's brother nor his sister had ever been involved with the family business. Both of them had pursued their own separate careers. The taxpayer was dismayed *(pg1122g)* by his father's intended actions and informed his father that if he continued with his intended proposal, he, the taxpayer, would resign and leave the company immediately. In the circumstances, his father took no action for a period of five years.

10 In April 1987 the taxpayer's father announced at a shareholder's meeting that he *(pg1122h)* intended to transfer shares to the taxpayer's brother and sister so that they would have an equal holding of shares with the taxpayer. Thereupon the taxpayer resigned and it was agreed that the company should go into immediate liquidation. Both the taxpayer and the administration director continued working for the company until the liquidation was completed in or about the spring of 1988.

11 The early 1980s were a period of severe economic recession. The company's *(pg1122j)* trading results deteriorated markedly from a net profit of £65,462 for the year ended 31 December 1978 to a net profit of £23,385 for the year ended

31 March 1981 followed by a loss of £27,850 in the year to 31 March 1982. Thereafter losses became even larger.

12 In 1981 the taxpayer's father asked a firm of valuers and commercial agents to market the company as a going concern. They kept the company on its books for *(pg1123a)* a considerable time but little interest was shown. In 1982 a businessman met the taxpayer and his father to discuss the possibility of purchasing the company but decided not to proceed. The taxpayer says that the price discussed was £1m. The businessman's recollection is that the consideration required was more than anticipated and his firm had other commitments which they needed to make. *(pg1123b)*

13 Negotiations concerning the value of the company shares as at the material date were initially undertaken on behalf of the whole family by a taxation specialist. Subsequently a personality clash developed between the taxpayer's brother and the adviser and thereafter he acted only for the taxpayer in an advisory capacity. The taxpayer's brother (who is an accountant) thereupon took over the negotiations with the Share Valuation Division on behalf of the whole family including the taxpayer but without informing the taxpayer. *(pg1123c)* From early 1995 the taxpayer undertook negotiations with the Share Valuation Division of the Capital Taxes Office in relation to his own shareholding.

14 On 17 March 1995 the Share Valuation Division of the Capital Taxes Office wrote to the taxpayer. The letter included the following paragraph:

> 'As promised, enclosed are copies of correspondence relating to the *(pg1123d)* valuation of shares in the above company. Unfortunately, I have no written details on the early negotiations that took place between my colleague, and your adviser, as these were almost exclusively done on the telephone. Reading through the notes of these discussions, it is clear that the proposed values have been arrived at on a discounted assets basis with the book assets, as expressed in the company's balance sheet for the year ended March 1982, uplifted to *(pg1123e)* reflect market value of its property (agreed with the District Valuer's office). The total assets were agreed at £598,064 £59.75 per share to which figure a discount has been applied to account for the status and influence of a small minority shareholding in this unquoted company. No doubt your adviser will be able to shed further light on the conduct of the early negotiations should further clarification be sought.' *(pg1123f)*

15 The company's accounts for the accounting period ended 31 March 1980, 1981, 1982 and 1983 contained an item in the balance sheets referred to as 'deferred taxation'. For the accounting period ended 31 March 1980 the amount was £117,528; for 1981 it amounted to £115,840; for 1982 £113,250 and a similar amount for 1983. No such item appeared in the accounts for the accounting period ended 31 March 1984 but those accounts contained the following note: *(pg1123g)*

'Deferred Taxation

Deferred taxation is the taxation attributable to timing differences between profits computed for taxation purposes and profits as stated in financial statements.

Provision is made for deferred taxation of the liability method at the current rate of corporation tax except in respect of any reduction that can *(pg1123h)* reasonably be expected to continue in the future by reason of recurring and continuing timing differences and for losses available. For this reason, no provision is provided in these financial statements.

This represents a change in the accounting policy of the company, which have previously made provision for all timing differences.' *(pg1123j)*

16 The company's accounts for the 15-month period ended 31 March 1980 are dated 11 November 1980. The company's accounts for the years ended 31 March 1981 and 31 March 1982 were not available as at 31 March 1982. The 1981 accounts are dated 16 August 1982 and the 1982 accounts are dated 21 October 1983.

17 The taxpayer was very much a 'hands on' managing director and general *(pg1124a)* manager of the company who knew the weekly turnover of the company and kept very strict control on it. He had no control over the subsidiary companies which were managed by persons who were not members of the family. The taxpayer knew in 1982 what the assets of the company were and as he received the bank statements for the company, he was aware of the state of the company's overdraft with the bank. *(pg1124b)*

The expert evidence

18 The taxpayer accepted Mr Carne's evidence in total as supplemented by Mr Carne's oral evidence. That was to the effect that in his opinion on the balance of probability and in the absence of access to the company's accountants' working papers, the item 'deferred taxation' should not have been included in the 1982 accounts of the company and such inclusion represented an error on the part of *(pg1124c)* the company's accountants. His opinion was based on the presumption that the company's accounts showed its state as a going concern. The position would be different in the event of a liquidation.

19 When considering Mr Vassie's evidence I have to bear in mind that whilst claiming to be an independent expert he was in fact employed by the Revenue and had trained and supervised the persons who negotiated at length in correspondence *(pg1124d)* with the taxpayer and his adviser. I believe that Mr Vassie was an honest witness but nevertheless I must take account of his position which is different from that of a truly independent expert.

20 I must also record here that the figures contained in Mr Vassie's report were altered at the last minute by an addendum to his evidence, by reason of an updating of the value of land owned by one of the subsidiary companies, whereby £40,000 *(pg1124e)* was added to the value of that land increasing its value from £15,000 to £55,000.

21 In so far as Mr Vassie's evidence is at variance with Mr Carne's I prefer the evidence of Mr Carne.

22 I must also distance myself from Mr Vassie's discount of 66 2/3 per cent; which he used to produce his final valuation figure of £18.48 per share. In my judgment that discount is too large. *(pg1124f)*

The statutory provisions

23 Section 150(1) of the Capital Gains Tax Act 1979 provides:

'(1) In this Act "market value" in relation to any assets means the price which those assets might reasonably be expected to fetch on a sale in the open market.' *(pg1124g)*

24 Section 152 provides:

'(1) The provisions of subsection (3) below shall have effect in any case *(pg1124h)* where, in relation to an asset to which this section applies, there falls to be determined by virtue of section 150(1) above the price which the asset might reasonably be expected to fetch on a sale in the open market.

(2) The assets to which this section applies are shares and securities which are not quoted on a recognised stock exchange, within the meaning of section 841 of the Taxes Act 1988, at the time as at which their *(pg1124j)* market value for the purposes of tax on chargeable gains falls to be determined.

(3) For the purposes of a determination falling within subsection (1) above, it shall be assumed that, in the open market which is postulated for the purposes of that determination, there is available to any prospective purchaser of the asset in question all the information which a prudent prospective purchaser of the asset might reasonably require if he were proposing to purchase it from a willing vendor by private treaty and at arm's length.' *(pg1125a)*

Conclusions

25 I must deal first with the question as to whether the letter dated 17 March 1995 from the Capital Taxes Office constituted an agreement enforceable by the taxpayer. My answer must be that it did not constitute such an agreement. *(pg1125b)*

26 I accept the submissions of counsel for the inspector in relation to this matter. It is clear from the documentary evidence that no agreement in the sense of an offer and acceptance was ever reached. Secondly, the alleged agreement did not relate to either of the assessments under appeal. For an agreement to be enforceable between the taxpayer and the Revenue it must be in accordance with the provisions of s54 of the Taxes Management Act 1970 which provide that: *(pg1125c)*

'... where ... the Crown and the appellant come to an agreement, whether in writing or otherwise, that the assessment or decision under appeal should be treated as upheld without variation, or as varied in particular manner or as discharged or cancelled ...'

27 The letter from the Capital Taxes Office did not relate to the assessment nor did *(pg1125d)* it relate to a decision under appeal.

28 It therefore falls to me to estimate the value of the taxpayer's shares at the material date, taking into account the information available to a hypothetical purchaser at the relevant time.

29 In coming to a decision I am reminded of a dictum of Lord Fleming in *Salvesen's Trustees v IR Commrs 1930* SLT 387, where he said at p. 392: *(pg1125e)*

'The estimation of the value of shares by a highly artificial standard which is never applied in the ordinary share market must be a matter of opinion and does not admit a precise scientific or mathematical calculation.'

30 In *Holt v IR Commrs*[1953] 2 All ER 1499 Danckwerts J said at p. 1503: *(pg1125f)*

'After beginning at as high a figure as £3 a share, the value claimed by the Crown is now 25s. per share, though the value formally determined by them was not that figure but 34s. per share. The figures given on behalf of the petitioners started at 11s.3d. as the fair value stated by the company, and rose to a value of 17s.2d. per share put forward in the petition and at the hearing. I am entitled, therefore, to assume that the principal value of the shares is one *(pg1125g)* or other of these figures of 25s. and 17s.2d., or some other value somewhere in between.'

31 In the dispute before me the Crown, with the assistance of Mr Vassie, are seeking a valuation of £18.48 per share whilst the taxpayer contends for a valuation of £48.48 per share. *(pg1125h)*

32 Although there is thus a difference of some £30 between the suggested valuations put forward by the parties there are in reality only two real points of disagreement. The first relates to the question of the deferred taxation and the second, more important, relates to the level of discount to be applied to the taxpayer's holding to reflect its status as a minority shareholding. *(pg1125j)*

33 The real bone of contention in these appeals is the level of discount. The Crown's witness, Mr Vassie, contends for a discount of 66 2/3 per cent whilst the taxpayer suggests a discount of only 10 per cent.

34 The taxpayer has suggested that the company was placed on the market in 1981 and that the asking price in 1982 was £1m but he does not seek to support that valuation now. He is content to accept the figure propounded in the letter from the Capital Taxes Office of £598,064. That figure is only marginally larger than *(pg1126a)* Mr Vassie's final figure for the value of the company as a going concern in the sum of £555,000.

35 In all the circumstances and taking into account the evidence of Mr Carne I am prepared to accept the higher figure of £598,064.

36 The decision in relation to the level of discount is much more difficult, as much *(pg1126b)* depends on the information available to the hypothetical purchaser at the time. I must assume that such purchaser was given all the information available to the directors.

37 He would have known that dividends had not been paid and were unlikely to be paid. That the taxpayer was the driving force in the company. Should the taxpayer decide to leave, it was likely in the short term at least, that the company would be *(pg1126c)* less profitable. In such an event the majority shareholders might decide to liquidate.

38 Even though the 1981 and 1982 accounts were not available the knowledge available to the taxpayer and the administration director would be passed to the potential purchaser who would discover that the peak in the company's profitability was reached in or about 1978 and that since that time the company had become *(pg1126d)* less profitable. Its future in the economic depression of the early 1980s did not look rosy.

39 Three possible scenarios concerning the future of the company post-1982 would be considered by the hypothetical purchaser. First, the company might continue to trade for some time in the future. That would be unattractive to a purchaser to say the least. He would receive no dividend, could not compel the board to accept him *(pg1126e)* as a director nor could he enforce a liquidation. Secondly, the board might decide to liquidate the company (as in fact happened in 1987). Although as things happened the 1987 liquidation proved a success, owing to the efforts of the taxpayer and his colleague, I believe that the prospect of an early liquidation of the company would not be attractive to a potential purchaser of the taxpayer's shares. He would be thinking in terms of a forced sale and its likely poor outcome. *(pg1126f)*

40 Finally there was the prospect of a sale of the company. The purchaser would know that the company had been on the market since 1981 with little interest shown but it is possible that he might be made aware of the interest of the businessman. The aborted meeting between the taxpayer and his father and the businessman took place in April 1982 and arrangements for such an appointment may well have been in place by 31 March 1982. *(pg1126g)*

41 Like Mr Vassie, I take the view that a potential purchaser, being prudent and weighing everything in the balance, would have come to the conclusion that a sale of the company sometime in the future was the most likely outcome. Where I part company with Mr Vassie is that I do not believe that the uncertainties justified so large a discount as 66 2/3 per cent. In *Caton's Administrators* v *Couch (HMIT)* (1995) Sp C 6, a discount of 50 per cent was applied to a smaller minority holding *(pg1126h)* than the taxpayer's. In *Caton* the holding amounted to 14.02 per cent of the total issued share capital whereas the taxpayer's holding amounted to 24 per cent. However, in *Caton* the company was successful and profitable, unlike the taxpayer's company.

42 Looking at all the evidence and bearing in mind the statutory provisions and the results of the decided cases I have come to the conclusion that I can accept *(pg1126j)* that the total assets amounted to £598,064 as stated above, producing a share value of £59.75 per share and that I should apply to that figure a discount of 55 per cent to recognise the status of the taxpayer's minority holding, which will produce a value of 26.89p per share.

43 I understand that there is a further issue between the parties concerning the valuation of the taxpayer's wife's nine 'A' ordinary shares. It is believed that the parties may be able to agree the valuation for her small holding based on the result of these appeals. *(pg1127a)*

Judgement of the High Court

44 Park J: This is an appeal by Mr John Charles Denekamp ('the taxpayer') from a *(pg1127c)* decision adverse to him given by a special commissioner, Mr Everett, upon the taxpayer's appeals against certain capital gains tax assessments. I have listened very carefully to the taxpayer's fully prepared and well presented submissions but I am unable to accede to them. For the reasons that I will give I must dismiss the appeal. *(pg1127d)*

45 The taxpayer owned a 24 per cent shareholding in a family company named Cwmbran Cash & Carry Co Ltd ('CCC'). CCC was put into liquidation in 1987 and a number of distributions were made to the taxpayer in that year and in 1988 in respect of his shareholding. For capital gains tax purposes, the receipt by the taxpayer of each distribution constituted a part-disposal of his shares in CCC. Capital gains tax was therefore payable to the extent that the value of the

PART 2 Cases

(pg1127e) distribution exceeded the applicable base value of the taxpayer's shareholding. This case concerns what that applicable base value was.

46 In the particular circumstances of the case the base value is the open market value on 31 March 1982 of the taxpayer's 24 per cent shareholding. For the 're-basing' of capital gains tax base values to 1982 values see s96(2) of the Finance Act 1988: *(pg1127f)*

> '... in computing for the purpose of capital gains tax the gain or loss accruing on the disposal it shall be assumed that the asset was on 31 March 1982 sold by the person making the disposal, and immediately re-acquired by him, at its market value on that date.'

47 I need not go into the circumstances of CCC in great detail. As its name implies, its principal activity was a cash and carry business. *(pg1127g)*

48 Evidence was presented to the special commissioner on behalf of the Revenue about the market value of the taxpayer's 24 per cent shareholding on 31 March 1982. In circumstances which I shall explain later, the Revenue's expert witness valued the taxpayer's shares at £18.48 each. The taxpayer, who appeared in person before *(pg1127h)* the special commissioner as he did before me, submitted a value of £48.48 each. The special commissioner decided that the shares were worth £26.89 each. The practical effect of the submissions which the taxpayer has made to me, were I to accede to them, is that the shares should have been valued at £35.89 each.

49 The method which the Revenue's expert valuer adopted in arriving at the value of the taxpayer's shareholding was the familiar one of beginning with a valuation *(pg1127j)* for 100 per cent of the shares in the company and reducing that valuation in two stages. The first stage would be to reduce it to 24 per cent to reflect the taxpayer's holding in the company. The second stage would be to discount that 24 per cent valuation by a further percentage to reflect the well known-depreciatory factors which cause a minority shareholding in a private company to be worth appreciably less than the *aliquot* proportion of the value of a 100 per cent shareholding.

50 Before Mr Everett it became substantially agreed that the initial figure, that is to say, the value of 100 per cent of CCC, was £598,064. That figure was somewhat greater *(pg1128a)* than the figure originally put forward by the Revenue's expert valuer. The taxpayer accepted the £598,064 figure; indeed, he had adopted it as the starting figure in the valuation which he himself had put before the special commissioner. Mr Everett was content to accept it but, as I read his decision, he preferred the approach, though not the figure of the Revenue's valuer: while agreeing with that approach he thought that the valuer's figure was on the low side, and Mr Everett was prepared *(pg1128b)* to adjust it upwards to the taxpayer's opening figure of £598,064. The issue before him was the percentage to be applied in the second discounting exercise to which I have referred.

51 The figure of £598,064 was based on the assets of CCC shown in the balance sheet with a number of adjustments. In particular, the figure for freehold (or it may be leasehold) properties was adjusted by reference to current market values as *(pg1128c)* opposed to the historic cost at which they no doubt appeared in the balance sheet. However, no adjustment was made for the goodwill of CCC's cash and carry trade. No figure appeared in the balance sheet for the goodwill, and when I say that no adjustment was made I mean that nothing was added for the value of the asset.

52 The essential point which the taxpayer raises before me is that the special *(pg1128d)* commissioner ought not to have started with £598,064; rather, he should have started with a higher figure because the trade of CCC was such that it had a goodwill value. Thus the true market value of 100 per cent of the company was not £598,064 but that figure plus the value of the goodwill of the trade. The taxpayer has suggested to me that that value was £200,000.

53 I am unable to accept that submission or to do anything at this stage in the tax *(pg1128e)* appeal process to give effect to the point which the taxpayer now raises. It might have been different if before the special commissioner the taxpayer had adduced evidence, probably including expert evidence, to support the existence of a positive value for goodwill inherent in the underlying assets of the company. In such a case it might have been open to the taxpayer to argue on the well known principle in *Edwards (HMIT) v Bairstow* [1956] AC 14 that the only *(pg1128f)* proper conclusion that the special commissioner could have reached given the evidence before him was one in which the starting figure for the valuation exercise was greater than £598,064. The fact is however that the taxpayer did not adduce any such evidence before the special commissioner. Indeed, as I have said, the £598,064 was his own initial figure. He has explained to me that the valuation which he submitted was one which assumed a likely liquidation of the company and *(pg1128g)* on that basis, as he understood the position, there was no real scope for including a goodwill element.

54 The Revenue's expert valuation did not assume an early liquidation but rather, for the purpose of valuing 100 per cent of the company, a sale of the company with its business as a going concern. Nevertheless, the Revenue's valuer did not make an addition to the value for goodwill, and I can understand why not given the modest *(pg1128h)* profitability of the business around the relevant time. Equally, it could have been argued that, had the company as a whole been sold as a going concern, a purchaser would have been prepared to add a goodwill element to the price.

55 It was however clear on a reading of the Revenue's valuation that, upon the general approach on which Mr Everett substantially based his starting figure of *(pg1128j)* £598,064, the valuer had not included goodwill. If the taxpayer had wished to say that the valuer should have included goodwill he could and should have put material before the special commissioner to that effect at that time.

56 I sympathise with the taxpayer as a litigant in person. It is understandable that when he was before the special commissioner he did not appreciate the relevance of this point, but the fact remains that he had his opportunity to adduce evidence supporting an element of goodwill value and did not take it. The fact that he might *(pg1129a)* not fully have understood fully the nature of that opportunity cannot, given the nature of our tax appeal system, help him now.

57 The only evidence before the special commissioner which might have borne on this point was that there had been one meeting earlier in 1982 between on the one hand the taxpayer and his father (who I believe had been the founder of the business and was also a major shareholder) and on the other hand representatives *(pg1129b)* of a competitor company. The purpose of the meeting was to discuss the possibility of the competitor buying the shares in CCC. The taxpayer's father had mentioned a price for the shares which would have included an element for goodwill. However, the evidence was that the meeting led nowhere. There was a very short written statement before Mr Everett from a director of the competitor stating that virtually all he could remember was that the price asked was too high and the matter was taken no further. *(pg1129c)*

58 Plainly, that being the state of the evidence before the special commissioner, there can be no conceivable argument that he should have commenced his valuation by reference to a figure higher than £598,064. The taxpayer suggested that before the special commissioner the Revenue had in some way suppressed the possibility that there might have been a goodwill element present. I do not accept that the Revenue did anything of the sort. *(pg1129d)*

59 In so far as the taxpayer entertains hopes that I may be able to determine this appeal myself in a manner which increases the capital gains tax base value of his 24 per cent shareholding, and correspondingly reduces the capital gains tax assessments, there is no possible basis on which I can do that. *(pg1129e)*

60 A further question is whether, even if I cannot on this appeal myself reach a decision which gives a different base value for the taxpayer's shares, I can remit the case to the special commissioner for him to reconsider the matter taking into account such new material as the taxpayer may then submit in support of a goodwill valuation. There is however an overwhelming body of authority to the effect that I cannot or should not do any such thing. This is not a case where new facts have emerged since the hearing before the special commissioner; rather, it is a *(pg1129f)* case where on further reflection after that hearing the unsuccessful party, in the present case the taxpayer, now wishes to present his case differently. He wants to seek to obtain additional evidence which, if obtainable now, was equally obtainable when the original hearing took place. In my judgment it would be an improper exercise of the discretion of the court to make an order to that effect. *(pg1129g)*

61 The result of the whole matter is: first, I cannot vary the decision of the special commissioner; and, second, I cannot make any form of order which has the effect of remitting the case to the special commissioner for him to consider whether he wishes to vary his decision. I must therefore affirm Mr Everett's decision and dismiss the appeal.

62 There is one other matter which I mention in conclusion. *(pg1129h)* The taxpayer has explained to me in detail the course of negotiations between himself and the Revenue's Share Valuation Division. In the course of those negotiations offers were made by the Revenue, in most cases expressly on a 'without prejudice' basis, to resolve the matter on the basis of a value of the shares which, if agreed, would have been more favourable to the taxpayer than the figure which has resulted from Mr Everett's decision. *(pg1129j)*

63 There was a further unfortunate episode, which I shall not go into in detail, involving other members of the taxpayer's family and their capital gains tax negotiations which, like the taxpayer's, arose out of the liquidation of CCC. The taxpayer took the view that there had been an improper breach of taxpayer confidentiality on the part of the Revenue. He made a complaint about it to the Inland Revenue Adjudicator and that complaint was upheld.

64 The taxpayer feels understandably aggrieved about this aspect of the matter. *(pg1130a)* More specifically, he has suggested to me that, but for this element of mishandling of the matter by the Revenue, he would in all probability have accepted the compromise valuation which the Revenue had originally offered to him. That may or may not be so, but as I have sought to explain to him, and as I devoutly hope he will accept, it is not a matter which I can take into account on this appeal, or a matter which in any way permits me to change the valuation determined by *(pg1130b)* Mr Everett or the amount of the consequential capital gains tax liability.

65 The result of the whole matter is that, for the reasons which I have briefly indicated, I must dismiss the appeal. *(pg1130c)*

Case 43
Ward v IRC

[1999] STC (SCD) 1

Special Commissioner

5 October, 4 November 1998

The right to receive shares in the future is an asset in the estate of a deceased person.

Gwendolyn Olivia Cook died on 10 May 1997. Her estate included three accounts with Woolwich Building Society totalling £51,204. On 11 January 1996 the Society announced its intention to seek the approval of members to converting itself into a public limited company listed on the London Stock Exchange.

A special general meeting was held on 11 February 1997 and the resolution to convert to a public limited company was carried. The next step was to obtain the agreement of the Building Societies Commission. The Commission declared that any interested party had until 17 March 1997 to make any representations on the proposed incorporation. The Commission conducted a hearing on 16 April 1997. Following this, at a date after the deceased's death on 10 May 1997, the Building Societies Commission gave its consent to the proposed conversion of Woolwich Building Society into a public limited company. Flotation was expected on 7 July 1997 and did in fact take place on that date.

Under the terms of the transfer document the deceased was entitled to 450 'free shares' in Woolwich plc and an 'additional variable distribution' which brought up her total entitlement to 2,414 shares. Under the transfer document, the deceased having died before flotation, the first named executor under her will was entitled to the shares as part of her estate. The estimated trading price of the shares, if listed on the London Stock Exchange on 20 December 1996 would have been in the range 175p to 200p per share.

The executors argued that no shares in the new company Woolwich plc were in the estate at death and no value was due to be included in the estate in respect of any shareholding that would be allocated after the date of death.

The Revenue argued that there was property in the estate at death, this being the transfer document which was expected to lead ultimately to the allocation to 2,414 shares in Woolwich plc.

DA Shirley, the Special Commissioner ruled:

'It does not seem to me to be relevant, even if true, that the deceased owned nothing (under the transfer document) which could be marketed. Property may be difficult to market, but it is still property and, in the deceased's case, it would form part of her estate. In my opinion the deceased held rights under the transfer document which transcended the mere hope that she would obtain shares in Woolwich Plc. Accordingly, I hold that the rights conferred on the deceased by the transfer document were part of the property to which she was entitled, they were part of her estate and as such they fall to be valued in calculating the value transferred by the transfer of value the deceased is deemed to have made immediately before her death.'

([1999] STC (SCD) 1 at 3f **case 43 para 5**)

The taxpayer did not submit a valuation.

The Special Commissioner accepted the valuation submitted by the Revenue for the asset in the estate. This was:

Expected share price at completion (per transfer document)	187.5p
Expected increase by completion	x 1.1
	206.25p
Margin to reflect fluctuation (fall)	x 0.9
	185.625p
Number of shares	x 2,414
	£4,481.00
Discount for 2 months delay (@ 10% pa)	x 0.9842
	£4,410.00
less purchaser's costs say	£160.00
	£4,250.00

([1999] STC (SCD) 1 at 4b **case 43 para 5(2)(c)**)

Decision

References, example '(pg2d)', are to [1999] STC (SCD) 1.

1 (1) This is an appeal against a determination by the Inland Revenue Commissioners in relation to a transfer of value deemed to have taken place on the death of Gwendolen Olivia Cook (the deceased) on 10 May 1997. *(pg2d)*

(2) The commissioners determined that, firstly, the estate of the deceased included three accounts with Woolwich Building Society (the society) totalling £51,204 and, secondly, the value of the deceased's interest in the society, having regard to those accounts, was enhanced by £4,250 to reflect the anticipated benefit of the conversion of the society into a public limited company.

(3) The deceased's executors take issue with the second determination. As a matter of fact, the first determination is correct. **(pg2e)**

2 The relevant statutory provisions are succinct. Section 1 of the Inheritance Tax Act 1984 (the 1984 Act) provides that inheritance tax shall be charged on the value transferred by a chargeable transfer. Section 4 provides that on the death of any person tax shall be charged as if, immediately before his death, he had made a transfer of value and the value transferred by it had been equal to the value of his *(pg2f)* estate immediately before his death. And a person's estate is the aggregate of all the property to which he is beneficially entitled (see s5(1)). 'Property' includes rights and interests of any description (see s272). And the value at any time of any property shall be the price which the property might reasonably be expected to fetch if sold in the open market at that time (see s160).

3 The commissioners' second determination is more intelligible if it is elucidated by facts which lead up to it. *(pg2g)*

(1) On 11 January 1996 the society announced its intention to seek the approval of members to converting itself into a public limited company listed on the London Stock Exchange. The chairman, Sir Brian Jenkins GBE, MA, FCA, wrote on the same day to members (of which the deceased was one) outlining the proposals and the advantages of conversion. Towards the end of his two-page letter he wrote: *(pg2h)*

> 'Conversion and flotation are subject to a number of conditions, including the separate approvals of those investing and borrowing members eligible to vote, confirmation by the Building Societies Commission and authorisation of the Woolwich as a bank by the Bank of England. *(pg2j)*

(2) In January 1997 the society sent out, under cover of a letter, a copy of the transfer document giving full details of the proposed conversion of

the society into a public limited company authorised under the Banking Act 1987 and listed on the London Stock Exchange.

A special general meeting was to be held on 11 February 1997 at which members were to vote on the proposed conversion. The meeting duly took place and the resolution to convert was carried. Following that, the Building Societies Commission was open to representations being made to it no later than 17 March 1997 *(pg3a)* and its confirmation hearing was due to take place on 16 April 1997. The confirmation was given at an unspecified date but after the deceased's death on 10 May 1997. Flotation was expected on 7 July 1997 and did in fact take place on that day.

(3)   Under the terms of the transfer document the deceased was entitled to 450 'free shares' in Woolwich plc and an 'additional variable distribution' which *(pg3b)* brought up her total entitlement to 2,414 shares. Under the transfer document, the deceased having died before flotation, the first named executor under her will was entitled to the shares as part of her estate (see ss 5.1.1 and 5.5.1 of the transfer document). The estimated trading price of the shares, if listed on the London Stock Exchange on 20 December 1996 would have been in the range 175p to 200p per share (see the opinion of J Henry Schroder & Co Ltd and BZW Securities Ltd at p 72 of the transfer document). *(pg3c)*

4 Malcolm John Wray Ward, an executor under the deceased's will, appeared in person. He contended that the deceased had nothing which could be marketed. Her rights under the transfer document could not be valued. All she had was a mere hope that she would obtain shares in Woolwich plc. The approval by the Building Societies Commission was not a mere formality; it might not have been forthcoming. There could have been an economic depression and the conversion would have been halted. There could have been, *(pg3d)* but in fact there was not, an application made for judicial review since, so it was said, the way shares were allotted was not wholly fair. Moreover, the Stock Exchange might not agree to list shares in Woolwich plc. All that the deceased or her estate possessed was the valueless hope of acquiring new shares. *(pg3e)*

5 (1) I am not persuaded by these contentions. One bears in mind that the deceased is deemed to have made a transfer of value immediately before her death and that the value transferred thereby had been equal to the value of the deceased's estate, being the aggregate of all the property to which she was beneficially entitled. With due respect to the executor it does not seem to me to be relevant, even if true, that the deceased owned nothing (under the transfer document) which could be *(pg3f)* marketed. Property may be difficult to market, but it is still property and, in the deceased's case, it would form part of her estate. In my opinion the deceased held rights under the transfer document which transcended the mere hope that she would obtain shares in Woolwich plc. Accordingly, I hold that the rights conferred on the deceased by the transfer document were part of the property to which she was entitled, they

were part of her estate and as such they fall to be valued in *(pg3g)* calculating the value transferred by the transfer of value the deceased is deemed to have made immediately before her death.

(2) (a) In *Alexander* v *IRC* [1991] STC 112 at 125 Nicholls LJ concludes his summary of the scheme of inheritance tax as follows:

> '(3) Thus, the legislation makes it necessary to identify the "value" of an *(pg3h)* estate at a particular time. In short, value means market value: "the price which the property might reasonably be expected to fetch if sold in the open market at that time" (see [s 160]). This mode of valuation involves a notional sale ... the section is doing no more than prescribe the basis on which the valuation shall be made. The notional sale does not change the subject matter of the valuation. What is being valued is property belonging to the transferor, and it is being valued as at a time when he still owned it. The notional sale is designed merely to identify the sum which a purchaser in the open market might reasonably be expected to pay to be placed, in respect of that property, in the same position as the transferor. *(pg3j)* This interpretation of [s 160] accords with the decision of the House of Lords in *IRC v Crossman* [1937] AC 26 regarding the comparable valuation provisions in the estate duty legislation (see s7(5) of the Finance Act 1894). As Viscount Hailsham LC said (at 42–43), *(pg4a)* the notional sale is "merely a statutory direction as to the method by which the value is to be ascertained".'

(b)   The executor has submitted no valuation as such. He merely asserts that the deceased's hope was valueless and he points to possible impediments in the way of hope being rewarded. *(pg4b)*

(c)   For the Crown, a value of £4,250 is given for the 2,414 shares arrived at as follows:

Expected share price at completion (per transfer document)	187.5p
Expected increase by completion	× 1.1
	206.25p
Margin to reflect fluctuation (fall)	× 0.9
	185.625p
Number of shares	× 2,414
	£4,481.00
Discount for 2 months delay (@ 10% pa)	× 0.9842
	£4,410.00
less purchaser's costs, say	£160.00
	£4,250.00

The executor made no comment on this valuation in reply to the Crown's case or otherwise. *(pg4e)*

(d)   I reject the executors' valuation of nil. There being no other valuation apart from the Crown's, I uphold the commissioners' determination and dismiss the appeal.

Case 44
Billows v Hammond

[2000] STC (SCD) 430

Special Commissioners

26, 27 and 28 July 2000

A share valuation is never undertaken in isolation. There is always the tax calculation which provides the necessity for the valuation. In addition, practitioners will be all too aware of the common situation where a valuation is merely one part of a number of intermeshed problems relating to transactions with a family company and, perhaps, between members of the family.

Only a tiny percentage of valuation negotiations are brought before the courts. When a share valuation is the subject of a court hearing, it is usually the case that any court report is restricted to the arguments concerning the valuation and gives little of the flavour of the negotiations that have proceeded that hearing and even less of the intermeshing of commercial, domestic and physical concerns surrounding the events for which the valuation is required.

Billows v Hammond is different. Mr Leonard K Billows appeared in person to conduct the appeal on his own behalf before the Special Commissioner, THK Everett. He was keen to tell the court all the issues he had with the Revenue. He was an elderly gentleman who discovered immediately prior to the appeal hearing that he had mislaid his hearing aid. The furniture in the courtroom was rearranged so that he could hear what was being said by witnesses, by Counsel for Inland Revenue and by the Special Commissioner. In his tax return for 1986/87, Mr Billows gave details of the disposal of 20 shares in Billows Limited. For the following year, the only entry made by Mr Billows in the capital gains section of his tax return was to write the word 'none' in the section headed 'chargeable assets disposed of'. In fact, on 6 December 1986, Mr Billows gave 339 shares to his son and a further 339 shares to his daughter. The Revenue seemed to consider that the gift of these shares gave a capital gain of, perhaps, £200,000; Mr Billows thought the gain was £nil. At the time the gifts were made, there was a Revenue investigation into the company.

In January 1991 the Revenue wrote to Mr Billows asking why the entries in the company's accounts showing this reduction in his shareholdings were not reflected in his personal tax return. No reply was sent and, so, 365 days later, the Revenue sent a letter requesting a reply. This was quickly provided by Mr Billows, in which he said:

'As I did not handle the transfer I have no records of the transaction … I am not an accountant and I am not familiar with the basis of figures involved'

([2000] STC (SCD) 430 at 433f **case 44 para 23**).

Correspondence then took place over the eight years from February 1992 until the hearing in July 2000.

Mr Billows, in his witness statement, stated that, in respect of the Revenue, he 'has a deep sense of grievance' ([2000] STC (SCD) 430 at 436b **case 44 para 34**). This arose, (or, perhaps, was fuelled by) his appearance before the General Commissioners in 1987 to appeal against a Sch E income tax assessments on himself and corporation tax assessments on the company for undeclared income over a 14-year period and a determination requiring the company to operate PAYE when it had not done so. Mr Billows was particularly unhappy with the allegation by the Inspector before the Commissioners that the company's accounts were unreliable and the taxpayer's tax returns were also unreliable. In December 1989, Mr Billows (and his company) appealed to the High Court against the decision of the General Commissioners. Vinelot J, in the High Court, said that the Commissioners 'were almost bound to infer that the shortfall (by which his reported income was less than his living expenses) represented cash receipts by the company which had been improperly diverted to the taxpayer' ([1990] STC 162 at 172j). The High Court held that there had been no error of law and dismissed the appeal. In January 1991, Mr Billows appealed to the Court of Appeal, saying that he and his wife 'lived very modestly and that any shortfall that there might be was made up out of capital, of which he had plenty' ([1991] STC 127, CA at 128d). The Court of Appeal dismissed the appeal and refused Mr Billows application for leave to appeal to the House of Lords.

This, then, was the very human background to the share valuation exercise undertaken by the Special Commissioner in July/August 2000, assisted by the submissions of Mr Billows, on his own behalf, and by Counsel for the Revenue.

Mr Billows had previously expressed the view that there could be no capital gain arising as the company's profit in 1982 was £35,374 and this had fallen to £22,916 for 1986, the year in which he gave away the shares ([2000] STC (SCD) 430 at 434g **case 44 para 28**).

The approach adopted by the Shares Valuation Division (SVD) examiner is conventional and demonstrates the wealth of information held by that Revenue Division. The starting point in the valuation is recording the profit before tax and observing that, apart from one exceptional year, the profit increased year on year ([2000] STC (SCD) 430 at 437d **case 44 para 40**).

The next step taken by the SVD examiner was to consider what adjustments should be made to the reported profit to reflect the profit that would be expected to be generated if the company were run by a hypothetical third party. This required, he suggested, substituting a full market rent for the factory, being £4,000 per annum higher than that actually paid ([2000] STC (SCD) 430 at 437g **case 44 para 42**). To the earnings thus adjusted, the SVD examiner applied a multiple, which he described as 'somewhat arbitrary' ([2000] STC (SCD) 430 at 437j **case 44 para 43**). A discount was then applied to reflect the size of the holding ([2000] STC (SCD) 430 at 438f **case 44 para 50**).

Given the circumstances of this case, the task faced by the Special Commissioner is in complete contrast to that of his colleague in *Caton's Administrators v Couch*. In that case, Dr Nuala Bryce, sitting as Special Commissioner, had the benefit of a share valuation made by a very experienced, well-respected independent expert, who had been cross-examined on his opinion. In *Billows v Hammond*, there was no independent expert and the Special Commissioner noted that the SVD examiner 'although striving to be disinterested, is a long-serving employee of the Revenue and as such cannot be viewed strictly as a totally independent expert witness' ([2000] STC (SCD) 430 at 440d **case 44 para 61**), who 'had never visited the company's premises and had no experience of the particular trade' ([2000] STC (SCD) 430 at 440e **case 44 para 62**).

It is probably not an overstatement to say that the Special Commissioner considered himself to be the only independent person to have undertaken the valuation. It is, therefore, interesting to see how the Special Commissioner approached the valuation task.

The process adopted by the Special Commissioner can be summarised as follows:

Step 1
The basic facts of the incorporation of the company, the shares in issue and the assets placed into the company at incorporation are recorded ([2000] STC (SCD) 430 at 432f **case 44 para 13**).

Step 2
The nature of the company's business is described and competitors identified ([2000] STC (SCD) 430 at 436d **case 44 para 35**). Billows Limited was a specialist manufacturer of equipment for the graphic arts industry, with only one serious UK competitor and a few overseas competitors. The main commercial activity was to provide a very accurate hole-punching and plate-bending service for the photographic industry.

Step 3
The financial results of the company for the four years prior to the valuation date and also for the year in which the valuation date falls, are stated and it is noted that the Revenue allege that the company's accounts were unreliable ([2000] STC (SCD) 430 at 437b and 440h **case 44 para 38 and 64**).

Step 4
Adjustments that would be made by a prospective purchaser were estimated. In this case, there is a suggested adjustment to profits to take account of the low rent paid by the company (see above) and the adjustment to net assets to provide an allowance of 'as much as £100,000 as a deduction for the company's value for the cost of the tax investigation' into the company's affairs ([2000] STC (SCD) 430 at 440h **case 44 para 64**).

Step 5
Reported valuations in comparable situations were considered. The only case put forward in evidence was substantially rejected by the Commissioner as not being comparable ([2000] STC (SCD) 430 at 441c **case 44 para 65**).

Step 6
The availability and willingness of purchasers in the market for the particular shareholding was considered. The Commissioner noted that statute requires him to assume the existence of a willing purchaser at the valuation date ([2000] STC (SCD) 430 at 441e **case 44 para 67**).

Step 7
The final step taken by the Commissioner is when 'he stood back and considered the matter in the round'. The Commissioner records three points:

1.   This is a private company with unquoted shares.
2.   The Revenue investigation being carried on at the valuation date was a substantial problem for the company.
3.   There was rapid technological change, at the valuation date; within the industry, the manually operated pump manufactured by the company for film montage was being rapidly replaced by digital

electronic equipment. In fact, the company subsequently successfully transferred its manufacturing to the new technology, but this could not have been known at the valuation date ([2000] STC (SCD) 430 at 441j **case 44 para 70**).

Step 8
The Commissioner gave his conclusion:

'Looking at the amount in the round in the light of the evidence and taking into account the almost unique position in which the company found itself at the relevant date I have come to the conclusion that a fair open market value for the shares transferred in December 1986 would be £195 per share.'

([2000] STC (SCD) 430 at 442a **case 44 para 71**)

Decision

References, example '(pg431d)', are to [2000] STC (SCD) 430.

Mr Leonard Kay Billows ("Mr Billows") appeals against an assessment to capital gains tax for the year ended 5 April 1987 in the estimated sum of £205,000. That assessment was made more than six years after the end of the relevant tax year and accordingly was made pursuant to the provisions of section 36 Taxes Management Act 1970. *(pg431d)*

1 The assessment was made following a gift of unquoted shares in his company Billows Ltd to each of his two children in December 1986.

The questions for my determination are as follows:

2 Following the gift of the shares to his children was Mr Billows guilty of negligent conduct resulting in a loss of tax to the Crown? *(pg431e)*

3 If the answer to question one is in the affirmative, what was the value of the shares transferred by Mr Billows to his son and daughter, at the date of the transfer?

4 The evidence before me consisted of the sworn testimony of the following persons: *(pg431f)*

(a)   Mr Billows
(b)   Mrs Avril Whitfield, HM Inspector of Taxes. Whilst working at the Milton Keynes District Tax Office between March 1986 and August 1997, she dealt with Mr Billows' capital gains tax file.

(c)   Mr Michael Alan Fowler, HM Inspector of Taxes. He is an employee of the shares valuation division of the Inland Revenue's Capital Taxes Office and attended a meeting with Mr Billows at the premises of Billows Ltd in company with two *(pg431g)* colleagues from the share valuation division on 11 April 1996. His note of that meeting was annexed to his witness statement.

5 I also received sworn evidence of opinion from Mr Thomas Frame Vassie, a chief examiner in the shares valuation division of the Inland Revenue Capital Taxes Office.

6 The witness statements of each of the four witnesses will be available to the Court should this appeal proceed further. *(pg431h)*

7 In addition to the oral testimony I received two bundles of documents put in evidence by the Inland Revenue and one bundle of documents put in evidence by Mr Billows. Lengthy negotiations between the parties covering the period from 1996 to the date of the appeal hearing produced little, if any agreement between them. Mr Billows for his part maintained that the shares had very little, if any value at the date of the transfer from him to his children, whilst the Inland Revenue maintains that their intrinsic value was significant.

8 Mr Billows is an elderly gentleman who suffers from deafness. Prior to the appeal hearing he had mislaid his hearing aid. On this becoming apparent on the first morning of the appeal I indicated to him that if he wished to apply for an adjournment until such time as he had replaced his hearing aid, I would consider such an application sympathetically. I record this offer in my decision as on several occasions during his submissions Mr Billows complained that he had had very little time to prepare his case as a copy of Mr Vassie's witness statement, giving his opinion as to the value of the shares transferred reached him only a few days before the appeal hearing. On each occasion I renewed my suggestion to Mr Billows that he should apply for an adjournment, but on each such occasion he refused to make such an application and indicated that he wished the appeal hearing to continue without an adjournment. *(pg431j)*

9 Insofar as it was possible, arrangements were made within the courtroom, by a re-arrangement of the furniture, for Mr Billows to be aware of what was being said by witnesses, by Mr Tidmarsh and by myself. In addition, his daughter Mrs Buckley and the company accountant Mr Christopher Coote seated on either side of Mr Billows in the courtroom explained to him any points of difficulty which he encountered owing to his poor hearing. I am satisfied that in all the circumstances, Mr Billows was fully aware of what was taking place in the courtroom and did not suffer because of his disability and was enabled to respond to the Inland Revenue's submissions to the best of his ability.

The facts

From the evidence before me I find the following relevant facts:

10 Billows Ltd ("the Company") was incorporated on 26 September 1972. Its accounting year *(pg432d)* ends on 30 April in each year and its first period of trading covered the period from 26 September 1972 to 30 April 1973.

11 The Company capital at all times has been represented by 1,000 ordinary shares of £1 each.

12 On incorporation 700 shares were issued to Mr Billows and 200 shares were issued to his wife, Mrs MJ Billows. The remaining 100 shares remained unissued. *(pg432e)*

13 At or prior to incorporation the Company acquired the assets of an earlier company operated by Mr Billows, namely Billows Graphic Equipment. Those assets included the following:

Plant and machinery £8,995
Motor vehicles £3,340
Special tools and jigs £1,605
Office equipment fixtures and fittings £1,536 *(pg432f)*

(The above figures (which differ in some respects from those shown in Mr Billows' witness statement), are taken from the balance sheet of the Company's opening accounts to the period ended 30 April 1973.) *(pg432g)*

14 There is no evidence that Mr Billows' shares were issued partly or wholly in return for the acquisition by the Company of the assets of Billows Graphic Equipment. The Company accounts do not contain a share premium account and the Company's return of allotments shows that 898 shares were issued for cash at par. Whilst the return of allotments was made by Mr Billows' accountants, the Company accounts were approved and signed by Mr Billows and his wife. *(pg432h)*

15 Mr Billows had previously been a major shareholder in another company which carried on a similar trade to that of Billows Ltd, namely Protocol Engineering Ltd ("Protocol"). Before setting up the Company Mr Billows sold his shares in Protocol and left its employment. Some other employees left with him and joined him as employees of his new company.

16 On 28 March 1983 the 100 unissued shares in the Company were allotted to Mr Billows' children. 50 of those shares were allotted to Mrs Sandra Jean Buckley, Mr Billows' daughter and the remaining 50 to his son Mr Colin David Billows. At about the same time Mrs MJ Billows transferred her 200 shares to her children, giving 100 shares to her son and 100 shares to her daughter. Mrs Buckley and her brother are employed full-time with the Company. *(pg432j)*

17 On 4 April 1986 Mr Billows gave 10 of his shares to his son and a further 10 of his shares to his daughter. *(pg433a)*

18 In his tax return for the year 1986/87, which he signed on 5 March 1987, Mr Billows gave details of those transfers to his children on 4 April 1986 to the Inland Revenue and stated that the amount of his gains for the year was "none".

19 On 16 December 1986 Mr Billows gave a further 339 of his shares in the Company to his son and a further 339 of his shares in the Company to his daughter. Since 16 December 1986 the shareholdings in the Company have remained *(pg433b)* unaltered. Of the 1,000 issued shares, Mr Billows retains 2 shares and his son and daughter each hold 499 shares.

20 Mr Billows completed his tax return for 1987/88 on 14 August 1990 and it was received by HM Inspector of Taxes on 23 August 1990. In the section of that return dealing with "chargeable assets disposed of" Mr Billows wrote "none". He sent his return for 1987/88 under cover of his letter dated 21 August 1990 *(pg433c)* addressed to HM Inspector of Taxes Milton Keynes 1. At the same time he also enclosed his tax returns for the years 1988/89, 1989/90 and 1990/91. The covering letter makes no mention of his transfer of shares to his children on 16 December 1986 or any other date.

21 On 10 January 1991 the Inland Revenue wrote to Mr Billows, referring to his tax returns for the years 1987/88 to 1990/91 inclusive. The letter reported that the *(pg433d)* Company's accounts for the accounting period ended 30 April 1987 revealed a transfer of 698 shares in total to his children. The letter requested an explanation as to why appropriate entries were not made in Mr Billows' tax return.

22 It appears that nothing happened for a year but on 10 January 1992 the Inland Revenue sent a reminder to Mr Billows seeking a reply to the Inland Revenue's letter dated one year previously. *(pg433e)*

23 Mr Billows eventually replied on 6 February 1992 in a letter which was received by the Inland Revenue on 10 February 1992. It stated:

"I am in receipt of your letter dated 10 January.

The transfer of shares was done by my accountant of the time Everett Collins & Loosley who I understood supplied all the information to the Revenue. From your letter it appears it was either not done or the information has been misplaced.

You will *(pg433f)* appreciate that as I did not handle the transfer I have no records of the transaction. Would you therefore please supply me with details of any records of the transfer that you have with all the information necessary to make the calculations you require. I am not an accountant and I am not familiar with the basis of the figures involved." *(pg433g)*

24 On 16 March 1992 the Inland Revenue wrote again to Mr Billows stating that the Company accounts did not include any specific details regarding the transfer of the shares in question. The only information in the accounts was that at 30 April 1986 Mr Billows owned 700 shares in the Company and that a year later he owned 2 shares and that his son and daughter each owned 499 shares. The letter concluded *(pg433h)* by requesting Mr Billows to inform the Inland Revenue of the value of the shares at the date of their disposal and their original cost.

25 Having received no reply to their letter the Inland Revenue sent a reminder to Mr Billows on 18 September 1992.

26 Mr Billows eventually replied on 13 October 1992 in a letter which was received by the Inland Revenue on 15 October 1992. It states: *(pg433j)*

"Your letter of 16 March referred to in your letter dated 18 September 1992 did not fully answer my letter dated 6 February 1992.

My letter of the 6th requested from you 'all the information necessary to make the calculations you require'. This was not received.

I have no information regarding the formula to be used in assessing the value of a private company as used by the Revenue. If you supply the formula I am quite capable of using it.

I would inform you that the shares were transferred by me for which no payment was *(pg434a)* made so no sale value was obtained. Also my accountant considered the shares had no free market value so no CGT would be payable.

In view of the opinion of the accountant and my own view of the Company value I have therefore not been surprised that no correspondence was received from the Revenue at the time of the transfer or subsequently and the following year's accounts were sent to the Revenue which showed the transfer.

I do not believe that the transaction *(pg434b)* gave rise to a liability to CGT but on receipt of your basis for calculation I will respond to clear this matter which I was previously informed by my accountant had been cleared."

27 The Inland Revenue responded by letter to Mr Billows on 10 November 1992 quoting section 18 Taxation of Chargeable Gains Act 1992 and seeking further *(pg434c)* information in order to enable the Inland Revenue to assess the value of the shares transferred.

28 Mr Billows wrote again to the Inland Revenue on 2 December 1992 and for the first time he gave details of the transfers of the shares to his children in December 1986. His letter states as follows:

"I am in receipt of your letter dated 10th Nov. 1992.

I am not aware of *(pg434d)* Section 18 TGCA 1992 so cannot base any calculations on that Section you say is applicable. Would you please send me the relevant information. I have asked you twice to supply me with the necessary basis you wish me to use to comply with your request to supply a valuation.

As you are "not privy to their method of calculation" would you please request them to send the formula to me?

The answers to your questions are as under which I have extracted from *(pg434e)* the audited accounts and the filed "Annual Returns".

1.   700
2.   20 on 4.4.86 and 678 on 15.12.86
3 & 4. Please supply a basis of calculation

Referring to leaflet CGT 16 you have sent to me it would appear that the *(pg434f)* important question is what is the difference in value of the Company shares between 1982 and 1986. The Company made a profit of £35,374 in 1982 and £22,912 in 1986. On this basis of profit to value of the Company shares most people would say that there was no capital gain to be deemed on shares that returned £35,374 in 1982 and £22,912 four years later.

I would therefore on a commercial basis consider that the realisable value of my shareholding was *(pg434g)* less in 1986 than it was in 1982 – there being no capital gain in the relevant period – presumably a notation or loss.

I believe the foregoing to be a reasonable assessment of the position which is in accordance with the advice I had at the time "that no Capital Gains Tax" was applicable to the share transfer.

Other factors may be relevant i.e. my age at the time of the transfer *(pg434h)* 62–63.

I look forward to your assessment and any comment from your colleagues at the Shares Valuation Division if you think it necessary."

29 On 10 May 1994 Mr RA Knight of the Inland Revenue Shares Valuation Division wrote to the Inspector of Taxes with his estimated values per share representing his current opinion based on the Company's accounts. He had not been able to reach any *(pg434j)* consensus with Mr Billows. Mr Knight's estimated values were as follows:

20 × £1 ords @ 4 April 1986 – £15 per share
698 × £1 ords @ 4 April 1986 – £135 per share
679 × £1 ords @ 15 December 1986 – £450 per share
698 × £1 ords @ 15 December 1986 – £450 per share

30 On 6 June 1994 the Inspector of Taxes assessed Mr Billows to capital gains tax pursuant to section 36 Taxes Management Act 1970. The assessment was for the year ended 5 April 1987 *(pg435a)* and was made in the estimated sum of £205,000. In support of the assessment the Inland Revenue alleged negligent conduct on the part of Mr Billows and that the assessment was made for the purpose of making good to the Crown the loss of capital gains tax attributable to Mr Billows' negligent conduct. The Crown does not allege fraudulent conduct on the part of Mr Billows.

31 During the six years which have elapsed since the issue of the assessment *(pg435b)* negotiations have continued between the Inland Revenue and Mr Billows but it has proved impossible to reach agreement as to the value of the Company in 1986 or the value of the shares transferred during that year.

32 As part of its effort to reach agreement with Mr Billows the Inland Revenue officers attended a meeting with Mr Billows (and briefly with his daughter) at the offices and factory of the Company on 11 April 1996. The Inland Revenue was *(pg435c)* represented at that meeting by Mr Fowler who gave evidence before me, Mr Knight (the author of the letter dated 10 May 1994) and a third inspector named Mr Richardson.

The visit produced no meeting of minds between the Inland Revenue and Mr Billows. Mr Richardson made a final offer to settle at £275,000 but Mr Billows did not respond.

33 During the course of the negotiations which took place between the Inland Revenue *(pg435d)* and Mr Billows Mr Knight sought to establish the value of the Company as at 4 April 1986 on the occasion of Mr Billows' gift of 10 shares to his son and 10 shares to his daughter. Whilst pursuing that line of enquiry Mr Knight wrote to Mr Billows on 6 October 1994 and his letter contains the following:

> "My main concern however, has been to establish a whole Company value *(pg435e)* and it is in this area that we have experienced considerable difficulty. This case primarily concerns a majority shareholding of almost 70%, and I think it reasonable to assume that a prospective purchaser would have had access to virtually all relevant accounts together with any associated information. It would be in the vendor's interest to furnish him with this information if he wished a sale to progress.
>
> Further, I did not say that the shares disposed of *(pg435f)* were worth £150,000, but that the Company would have been worth in the region of

that figure based on a maintainable profit of around £20,000 and a multiple of 7.5. We cannot possibly calculate a share price until we have agreed upon a value for the entire concern.

If you believe my maintainable profit figure to be over optimistic, then perhaps we could adopt the figure of £13,819 as outlined in your letter of 3 June 1994. My adopted multiple of 7.5, *(pg435g)* very much on the low side given the averages in evidence during 1986/87, would value the Company at around £100,000."

Unfortunately, both Mr Billows' accountants and Mr Billows assumed, wrongly, that Mr Knight was offering to agree a value of the Company in the figure of £100,000 as at December 1986, and not, as Mr Knight's previous *(pg435h)* correspondence made clear, an offer to value the Company at that figure as at April 1986. That, probably genuine, misapprehension on the part of Mr Billows' accountants and the Appellant himself has muddied the waters in negotiations which have taken place between the Inland Revenue and Mr Billows. He has sought throughout to maintain a value of nil £ for each of the shares as at December 1986 although he has been willing to accept a value for the whole Company of £100,000. Such a *(pg435j)* valuation would produce no capital gains tax liability for Mr Billows.

34 Another factor which has bedevilled the negotiations between the Inland Revenue and Mr Billows is the history of the relationship between the two parties. In 1987 Mr Billows and his Company each appeared before the General Commissioners for Income Tax for the division of Bletchley in order to appeal against assessments to income tax under Schedule E, in the case of Mr Billows, for the years 1972/73 to 1985/86 inclusive and in the case of the Company assessments to corporation tax for the accounting periods ended 30 April 1973 to 1986 and a determination under *(pg436a)* Regulation 29 of the Income Tax (Employment) Regulations 1973 for 1978/79. Although the Commissioners discharged the assessments on Mr Billows up to and including 1977/78 they determined that he had received undeclared income for the years 1978/79 to 1985/86 inclusive. Most of the assessments on the Company were discharged. Mr Billows appealed both to the High Court *(pg436b)* and to the Court of Appeal unsuccessfully and his witness statement in this appeal makes plain that he "still has a deep sense of grievance". He was particularly unhappy with the allegation by the Inspector before the General Commissioners that the Company's accounts were unreliable and that Mr Billows' tax returns were also unreliable. Full details of the appeals by Mr Billows and the Company are to be found in the report of *Billows v Robinson* 64 TC 17.

35 I take the following description of the Company's business from paragraphs 11 to 15 *(pg436c)* of Mr Billows' witness statement, which paragraphs I accept, as follows:

"The business was founded, to design, manufacture and sell register equipment to the graphic arts industry. It also modified existing equipment being used by customers i.e. printing presses, cameras, step and repeat machines and other pre-press equipment to make compatible with the *(pg436d)* equipment the Company supplied.

The customers were widespread being approximately one-third overseas and two-thirds home market. A typical monthly customer list would be spread around 40. From the Company's inherited expertise it had built up a very specialised business. In the UK there was only one serious competitor being Protocol Engineering Ltd. This was the company started by LK Billows in his own home in Potters Bar in 1950 of *(pg436e)* which he was a 50% shareholder when he left and sold his entire shareholding in 1972.

The Company's business was in 1986 self-contained in that it conceived, designed and marketed its own exclusive products. The Company sold its products in the UK but direct to printers and through distributors. Overseas products were almost exclusively sold through agents. Manufacture was largely done in-house.

The Company occupied premises in Milton Keynes *(pg436f)* rented at £36,000 per annum from Kelloran Ltd a company equally owned by SJ Buckley and CD Billows." [It should be noted that the shares valuation division estimated that the rent should be £40,000. This would have the effect of reducing the Company profit by another £4,000 per annum. My comment.]

"The Company's only meaningful competitor in the UK was the former company of LK Billows, Protocol Engineering Ltd. Overseas there were a few competitors. *(pg436g)* They were insignificant in the UK but had a stronghold in their home markets in the USA and Germany."

36 In 1986 the Company's main business was film montage. It provided a very accurate hole-punching and plate-bending service for the photographic industry. *(pg436h)* The main item produced was a manually operated pump which, remarkably, the Company was able to sell throughout the world. Since then the Company has moved with the times and is now a highly technical concern and produces computer controlled graphic equipment.

37 At the meeting between the Inland Revenue and Mr Billows which took place on 11 April 1996 he was asked about his view of the trading outlook of the Company *(pg436j)* as at December 1986. The relevant paragraph of the note of the meeting prepared the following day by Mr Fowler and approved by Mr Richardson and Mr Knight and which I accept, states as follows:

"[Mr Billows] was not very specific regarding the outlook as at December 1986 but implied that with development work and customer expansion being ongoing features there was no reason not to expect the trend of increasing turnover and growth profit to continue." *(pg437a)*

38 The gross profits of the Company and its turnover for the years 1983 to 1987 inclusive as provided by the Company's accountants are as follows: *(pg437b)*

	1983	1984	1985	1986	1987
Turnover	£377,799	£470,609	£723,452	£958,315	£1,705,933
Gross profit	£141,312	£193,097	£267,604	£434,038	£548,436
Gross margin	37.4%	41.0%	37.0%	45.3%	50.9%

39 Protocol made substantial profits in the years up to and including 1989. In 1990 and 1991 it suffered very large losses (£624,623 before tax in 1991) and was put into receivership. Attempts by the receiver to sell Protocol as a going concern failed. Several companies showed interest initially but no offers to buy were made. *(pg437c)* Eventually Mr Billows purchased the assets of Protocol and also employed some of its staff.

The evidence of Mr TF Vassie

40 Mr Vassie noted the upward trend in both turnover and gross profit from 1983 to 1987 inclusive and calculated the net profit before tax and before the *(pg437d)* management charge for the directors as follows: *(pg437e)*

1983 : £69,433
1984 : – £784 (loss)
1985 : £43,972
1986 : £111,712
1987 : £178,368

41 Viewing these figures both in the light of the guarded optimism shown by Mr Billows as recorded in Mr Fowler's note of the meeting which took place on 11 April 1996 and alternatively in the light of Mr Billows' less optimistic forecast as shown in his witness statement, Mr Vassie gave it as his opinion that a purchaser would estimate the future maintainable profit for the Company before allowing for a management charge as being at least £145,000 as at 15 December 1986. *(pg437f)*

42 Taking into account the District Valuers' opinion that the rent for the factory should be £40,000 per annum rather than the actual rent paid of £36,000 Mr Vassie estimated that on commercial lines, £78,000 would be a reasonable estimate of the Company's future maintainable profit before tax as at 15 December 1986 made up as follows: *(pg437g)*

Profit, before adjustments :	£145,000
Less	
Directors' remuneration	£45,000
Directors' pension contributions	£9,000
Interest on outstanding loans	£9,000
Rental adjustment (£40,000 – £36,000)	£ 4,000
	£67,000
	£78,000

(pg437h)

43 To that figure Mr Vassie applied a multiple, a figure which he described as "somewhat arbitrary". (pg437j)

44 Mr Vassie stated in cross-examination that it was "difficult to find a comparable to Billows".

45 The only comparable figure to which Mr Vassie was able to refer was a sale in June in 1987 of an 80% holding in Dale Graphic Equipment Ltd ("Dale"). Dale was a company in the same general field of business as the Company having been set up by two ex-salesmen formerly employed by the Company.

46 From the latest results available for Dale Mr Vassie annualised the figure for turnover and pre-tax profit as at 31 December 1987 and from that produced a (pg438a) multiple of 5.43. That figure applied to the (calculated) pre-tax profit of £45,554 for Dale produced the "calculated" turnover of £833,838.

47 Mr Vassie acknowledged in his witness statement that he was unaware of the exact circumstances surrounding the sale of Dale in June 1987.

Lacking any other comparable data Mr Vassie sought support for his opinion from the cases of *Hawkings-Byass v Sassen* [1996] STC (SCD) 319 *(pg438b)*and the *Administrators of the Estate of Caton (deceased) v Couch* [1995] STC [SCD] 34. He also sought support from Mr Christopher G Glover's book entitled "*Valuation of unquoted Companies*" (second edition). The relevant paragraph in Mr Glover's book relied upon by Mr Vassie contains the following:

> "The author has a bench-mark yield for smaller private companies of 20% *(pg438c)* (i.e., a multiple of 5). This is shaded up or down to reflect positive or negative attributes of the subject company."

48 In the result Mr Vassie applied a multiple of 5 to his estimated figure of £78,000 for the maintainable profits producing a value for the Company of £390,000. From that figure he deducted a sum of £25,000 as the sort of allowance for tax liabilities arising under the Inland Revenue investigation (still ongoing at December 1986 and *(pg438d)* unresolved) that a purchaser was likely to make. Accordingly Mr Vassie's estimate of the value of the whole Company became £365,000 equivalent to the value of £365 per share. (I note that Mr Richardson, also of the Inland Revenue shares valuation division, was prepared to allow a figure of £50,000, as a deduction to cover the Company's involvement in the tax dispute, when he wrote to Mr Billows on 18 April 1986.)

49 Finally, to that share value he applied a discount of 15% to take account of the *(pg438e)* fact that the number of shares transferred amounted to slightly less than a 70% holding. Mr Vassie's final valuation therefore became £310.25 per share or £216,554 for a holding of 698 shares.

50 On the final day of the hearing I recalled Mr Vassie to the witness box in order that he might explain the reasons for what appears to be a very rapid increase in value of the Company from Mr Knights's figure of £100,000 at April 1986 to Mr Vassie's *(pg438f)* figure of £365,000 as at December of the same year, encompassing an interval of only a little over 8 months.

51 Mr Vassie gave it as his opinion that Mr Knight's figure of £100,000 was too low although he conceded that he had "done no real work" on the April 1986 valuation. He suggested what seemed to be an off-the-cuff figure of £200,000 for April 1986 but emphasised that in his view there had been a rapid increase in the value of the *(pg438g)* Company during the eight months period in question.

Conclusions

52 In coming to a conclusion as to the value of the shares transferred by Mr Billows in December 1986 I must first record that his witness statement contains several *(pg438h)* factual inaccuracies and, more seriously, allegations that the Inland Revenue lied and made allegations fraudulently. Those allegations were repeated more than once in his witness statement, accompanied by allegations of dishonesty on the part of the Inland Revenue.

53 I would like to make it abundantly clear that from the detailed evidence presented to me in this appeal there is not one iota of truth in Mr Billows' *(pg438j)* allegations. The various members of the Inland Revenue concerned in this appeal and in the previous income and corporation tax investigations were merely doing their jobs to the best of their ability and they should not have to suffer allegations of mendacity, dishonesty and fraud.

The requirements of section 36 Taxes Management Act 1970

54 The assessment laid on Mr Billows was an extended time limit assessment and in those circumstances Mr Tidmarsh accepted on behalf of the Crown that the burden of proof lay with his client, in order to establish the validity of the *(pg439a)* assessment.

Section 36 states as follows:

> "36. – (1) An assessment on any person (in this section referred to as "the person in default") for the purpose of making good to the Crown a loss of income tax *(pg439b)* or capital gains tax attributable to his fraudulent or negligent conduct or the fraudulent or negligent conduct of a person acting on his behalf may be made at any time not later than 20 years after the 31 January next following the year of assessment to which it relates."

55 The Crown does not allege fraudulent conduct but Mr Tidmarsh has submitted that in making his return for 1987/88, and stating in the section requiring him to *(pg439c)* reveal details of chargeable assets disposed of, the word "none" that Mr Billows was indeed negligent. Furthermore, there was no direct admission of the details of the transfer of total of 678 shares to his son and daughter in December 1986 until he wrote to the Inspector on 2 December 1992, almost six years after the event.

56 Mr Tidmarsh countered the accusation that it was possible for an "in-time" assessment to have been made before the expiry of the six year time limit *(pg439d)* by referring to a dictum of Carswell LCJ in Re McGuckian [2000] STC 65 at 78c–d, dealing with a similar submission in relation to Section 41. He said:

> "Any default on the part of the Revenue, if Mr Ward's failure to issue an assessment in 1985 could be so described, is only material if it could be *(pg439e)* regarded as the sole cause of the loss of tax. Once the Revenue has shown that the taxpayer's acts or omissions may have been a causative factor in causing the loss of tax, cadit quaestio and the Revenue's omissions are not material for the purposes of s41."

57 In my judgment the Crown has discharged the burden of proof laid upon it by section 36. I take into account that Mr Billows must have been aware of the obligation *(pg439f)* placed upon him by his tax return, for in the previous year in relation to his tax return for 1986/87, he had given very full details of the transfers of 20 shares in total to his children in the appropriate section of his return form.

58 The question of whether there has been a loss of capital gains tax to the Crown depends upon my eventual decision as to the value of the shares transferred but it *(pg439g)* is clear that the purpose of the assessment, once negligence has been established was to make good a loss of capital gains tax to the Crown in the light of the valuation advice received by the Inspector from the shares valuation division.

The base value of the shares transferred

59 Mr Tidmarsh, who appeared for the Inspector, very fairly pointed out that there *(pg439h)* was a possibility, to put it no higher, that Mr Billows' shares were issued to him initially in return for the assets put into the Company by Mr Billows. Unfortunately for Mr Billows there is no evidence whatsoever that that is what took place. It is possible that his advisers did not consider the possibility of issuing shares in return for the assets introduced but it is plain from the documentary *(pg439j)* evidence that the shares were issued to Mr Billows in return for cash. In addition, there was no share premium account. The evidence therefore is all in favour of an issue of shares at par and I find on the facts that Mr Billows' 700 £1 shares in the Company were issued at par.

The value of the shares transferred in December 1986

60 I can do no better in dealing with this question than to quote from a decision of my colleague Dr Nuala Brice in *Caton's Administrators v Couch* [1995] STC (SCD) 34 where she said: *(pg440a)*

> "In reaching a decision about the value of the shares I have in mind the *dicta* of Lord Fleming in *Salvesen's Trustees* when he said ((1930) 9 ATC 43 at 45):

> "the estimation of the value of shares by a highly artificial standard which is never applied in the ordinary share market must be a matter of opinion and does not admit of precise scientific or mathematical calculation." *(pg440b)*

> I have also borne in mind certain *dicta* of Danckwerts J in Holt from which I conclude that I am entitled to find a value either of 35p, as proposed by the Revenue, or 88p as proposed by the administrators, or of some other value somewhere in between. Also, after carefully considering the evidence, I must make the most intelligent guess that I can." *(pg440c)*

61 Under those perhaps less than helpful guidance comments I must first recognise that Mr Vassie, who gave evidence of opinion on behalf of the Crown, although striving to be disinterested, is a long serving employee of the Inland Revenue and as such cannot be viewed strictly as a totally independent expert witness. In coming to that conclusion I rely upon dicta in the judgment of Cresswell J in the "*Ikarian Reefer*" [1993] 2 Ll. L.Rep. 68 *(pg440d)* at page 81 where he enumerated the duties and responsibilities of expert witnesses. He laid particular stress on the independent status of expert witnesses.

62 I am also conscious that Mr Vassie had no experience of the trade and manufacturing processes carried on by the Company, that he reached his conclusions entirely from documentary evidence and that he did not visit the *(pg440e)* premises. I have some sympathy with Mr Billows' contention that at the very least Mr Vassie should have visited the offices and factory of the Company although I am well aware that by the time that Mr Vassie was instructed, the Company's operations had changed markedly from what they were in December 1986. Mr Knight did visit the premises in company with Mr Fowler and Mr Richardson but he did so only after giving his opinion that in April 1986 the Company's value was only *(pg440f)* £100,000.

63 Throughout this hearing and beforehand during the negotiations with the Inland Revenue, Mr Billows has maintained that the Company shares were valueless in December 1986 although he was willing to accept Mr Knight's valuation of £100,000 if that valuation were to be applied at December 1986 instead of April 1986. *(pg440g)*

64 Mr Billows has laid great stress upon the fact that at the time when the shares were transferred to his children the Inland Revenue investigation was still under way, for the first hearing before the General Commissioners did not take place until 30 April 1987 and the litigation which followed was not concluded until the Court of Appeal gave judgment on 31 January 1991. In the light of the Inland Revenue allegations that the *(pg440h)* Company's accounts were unreliable and that Mr Billows' tax returns were also unreliable Mr Billows contended that any intending purchaser of the Company would be unable to make reasoned judgments as to its value. As against this, it was never alleged by the Inland Revenue that the Company's profits were lower than the figures which appeared in the Company's accounts. The allegation was that the profits were understated. And Mr Tidmarsh contended that any intending purchaser would *(pg440j)* realise that it was possible that the Company's profits were understated and would therefore be able to make his valuation on the basis that the profits would certainly not be lower than shown in the Company's accounts. He would, however, have to make allowance for the very substantial costs incurred by the Company in resisting the assessments laid on it by the Inland Revenue and I suspect that such a purchaser might well make a larger allowance than the sum of £25,000 included in Mr Vassie's calculations. Mr Richardson was prepared to accept an allowance or deduction of *(pg441a)* £50,000 for this purpose when he wrote to Mr Billows on 18 April 1996. In the event, the total additional tax payable by the Company amounted to about £16,500 and no interest was paid and penalties were not levied, but the putative purchaser at December 1986 would not know the eventual outcome of the litigation and might well reasonably suppose that were the Inland Revenue to be successful, substantial interest payments could be demanded and penalties levied. He might well decide to make an allowance of as much as £100,000 as a deduction from the Company's *(pg441b)* value for the cost of the tax investigation and litigation.

65 In cross-examination Mr Vassie agreed that it was "difficult to find a comparable to Billows". It is an unusual Company with few competitors in this country. Mr Billows discounted the comparison with Dale. He submitted that Dale's trade was very different from that of the Company and that the sale of the 80% holding in Dale was exceptional, as the purchaser was a Swedish company which had been *(pg441c)* connected with Dale through its trade for some time.

66 Mr Billows contended that it would not have been possible to find a purchaser for the Company in December 1986 and cited in support the fact that when Protocol was in receivership the receiver was unable to find a purchaser for that Company. Eventually Mr Billows purchased the assets of Protocol and the Company took on some of Protocol's staff. However, it is apparent that Protocol *(pg441d)* was in dire financial straits when it went into receivership and yet, despite this fact, there were several interested enquirers when the receiver placed the Company on the market, even though those enquirers did not produce a purchaser for the Company.

67 In any event, I am required by the statute to assume the existence of a willing purchaser as at December 1986 and to arrive at a value for the shares such as would have governed the sale and purchase between an arms length vendor and purchaser *(pg441e)* in the open market.

68 Mr Billows has made much of the fact that Mr Knight offered a valuation for the whole Company of £100,000. Mr Billows believed at the time that the offer related to December 1986 but in fact it related, as the correspondence clearly shows, to April 1986 when Mr Knight was trying to establish whether the 20 shares transferred by Mr Billows in April 1986 gave rise to any chargeable gain. *(pg441f)*

69 That value of £100,000 in April 1986 has never been withdrawn insofar as I am aware, although it was criticised briefly by Mr Vassie in his evidence on being recalled to the witness stand. However, he freely admitted that he had done no real work on an April 1986 valuation and therefore I discount his criticism and his suggested value of £200,000 as a more realistic value for April 1986. *(pg441g)*

70 Although it is true that turnover and gross profits were increasing throughout the period from 1984 to 1987 it seems to me incredible that the Company's value should almost quadruple in a period of eight months. I am dealing here with a private company with unquoted shares and factors such as a possible takeover which might produce a very rapid rise in the share value of a public limited company do not arise. The suggested steep rise in the Company's value seems *(pg441h)* particularly unlikely bearing in mind the two substantial problems highlighted by Mr Billows but largely discounted by Mr Vassie. First there is the problem of the Inland Revenue investigation of the Company which was nearing its conclusion in December 1986, only three months or so before the first hearing before the General Commissioners. Secondly, there is the accepted fact that at the relevant time, towards the end of 1986, a rapid change was occurring in the Company's trade and *(pg441j)* manufacturing processes. Film Montage at that time was a dying art which was rapidly being replaced by digital electronic equipment and the Company's plate punch market was also disappearing. With the benefit of hindsight it has become apparent that the Company has successfully adapted to the new electronic age but the hypothetical purchaser would not be able to be certain of such success as at December 1986.

71 Looking at the amount in the round in the light of the evidence and taking into account the almost unique position in which the Company found itself at the *(pg442a)* relevant date I have come to the conclusion that a fair open market value for the shares transferred in December 1986 would be £195 per share.

72 I adjourn this hearing to enable the parties to agree figures and when they are reported to me I will determine the assessment formally. *(pg442b)*

Case 45
CVC v Demarco Almeida

[2002] 2 BCLC 108 PC

[2002] UKPC 16

Privy Council

15 January, 21 March 2002

This case is one of a series of cases on a type of company that is referred to as a 'quasi-partnership'. The first valuation case to be considered by the courts on this basis is *Re Yenidje Tobacco Co Ltd* [1916–17] All ER Rep 1050 **case 10**. The concept of 'quasi-partnership' is used, and developed, in *Ebrahimi v Westbourne Galleries Ltd* [1972] 2 All ER 492 **case 31**, *Re Bird Precision Bellows Ltd* [1985] 3 All ER 523, CA **case 35**, *CVC v Demarco Almeida* and *Strahan v Wilcock* [2006] EWCA Civ 13, CA **case 49**. The last of these cases is particularly important in that the Court of Appeal gives a definition of a 'quasi-partnership' company.

Where the company is a 'quasi-partnership' in respect of a shareholder who has been oppressed, the value placed on the shareholding is a proportionate part of the value of the total company, without discount.

CVC is a company incorporated in the Cayman Islands. It has 100 shares in issue. 96 shares are held by a single shareholder, Opportunity Equity Partners Ltd. The remaining four shares were held by the directors of the company. One director, with a one per cent shareholding, was Mr Demarco. Mr Demarco was dismissed as a director of the company. Under the terms of a shareholders' agreement, his dismissal had the consequence that he was required to sell his share to the majority shareholder. The agreement did not give a formula for establishing the price at which the shares should be sold.

Opportunity Equity Partners Ltd offered to purchase Mr Demarco's share for US$1, being the value of one per cent shareholding, viewed in isolation. Mr Demarco refused. Opportunity Equity Partners Ltd obtained an order from the Cayman Island court requiring Mr Demarco sell his share for US$1. Mr Demarco appealed and the Cayman Island's Court of Appeal set aside the order. Opportunity Equity Partners Ltd appealed to the Privy Council for the order to be re-established.

In his leading judgement in the Privy-Council, Lord Millett held that CVC was a 'quasi-partnership'. He provided guidance as to how such a company is to be identified:

'Companies where the parties possess rights, expectations and obligations which are not submerged in the company structure are commonly described as "quasi-partnership companies". Their essential feature is that the legal, corporate and employment relationships do not tell the whole story; and that behind them there is a relationship of trust and confidence similar to that obtaining between partners which makes it unjust or inequitable for the majority to insist on its strict legal rights. The typical characteristics of such a company are that there should be (i) a business association formed or continued on the basis of a personal relationship of mutual trust and confidence, (ii) an understanding or agreement that all or some of the shareholders should participate in the management of the business and (iii) restrictions on the transfer of shares so that a member cannot realise his stake if he is excluded from the business. These elements are typical, but the list is not exhaustive.'

([2002] 2 BCLC 108 at 117b **case 45 para 32**)

On this basis, the Privy Council held that Mr Demarco was entitled to receive in exchange for his share a pro-rated portion of the value of the total company, without discount. Opportunity Equity Partners Ltd was, thus, denied an order for acquisition for the share of US$1 ([2002] 2 BCLC 108 at 122i **case 45 para 58**).

This case is important in that it affirms that even a one per cent shareholding can be valued without discount in appropriate circumstances.

In valuing the shareholding, however, it is the circumstances that are all important. This case is concerned with an application for a winding-up order under the equivalent of the English Insolvency Act 1986, s 122. Within the context of that legislation, Lord Millett stated:

'To require Mr Demarco to submit not only to his exclusion from the company but to the acquisition of his shares at less than their going concern value by a purchaser which intends to carry on the business is hardly less unfair.'

([2002] 2 BCLC 108 at 119e **case 45 para 40**)

'Mr Demarco is not desirous of disposing of his shares; he would rather keep them and continue to participate in the management of the company. It is Opportunity's conduct in excluding him from management that has driven him, however reluctantly, to seek to realise the value of his investment. In this situation the case law in England is that normally the shares should be valued without any discount.'

([2002] 2 BCLC 108 at 118h **case 45 para 40**)

In valuing a minority shareholding for a fiscal purpose, the right a minority shareholder may have to receive the value calculated without any discount may mean that there is a special purchaser available who would be prepared to bid more than the generality of hypothetical non-connected third party purchasers. The existence of such a special purchaser is clearly a factor that needs to be taken into account in a valuation, as discussed in my comments on *IRC v Crossman* **case 17**. This does not, however, mean that a minority shareholding in a quasi-partnership is valued, for a fiscal purpose, without a discount. Rather, I suggest, that the valuer should consider whether there is, in the circumstances of the particular company, another shareholder with such potential rights as would be prepared to make an offer for the shares being valued with a view to obtaining an undiscounted value in a winding-up proceeding or under the terms of a shareholders agreement. If such a special purchaser is identified, this could increase the valuation. The increase would not take the value to the undiscounted proportional price as the offer made by the special purchaser would be on the basis, I suggest, that he would look for a profit on his onward sale.

Judgement

References, example '(pg110g)', are to [2002] 2 BCLC 108 PC.

1 LORD MILLETT: The first appellant, CVC/Opportunity Equity Partners Ltd (the company), is a private company incorporated in the Cayman Islands. *(pg110g)* The second appellant Opportunity Invest II Inc (Opportunity) is its majority shareholder. It owns all but four of the issued shares in the company. The respondent, Mr Demarco Almeida (Mr Demarco), is a minority shareholder with a single share.

2 The appellants appeal from an order of the Cayman Islands Court of Appeal dated 17 August 2000. By their order the Court of Appeal allowed *(pg110h)* Mr Demarco's appeal from an order of Graham J made on 29 July 1999 and discharged an injunction which he had granted to the appellants. The injunction had restrained Mr Demarco from presenting a petition to wind up the company on the just and equitable ground. The appellants seek to have the injunction restored. *(pg110i)*

3 The judge granted the injunction on the ground that Mr Demarco had unreasonably refused a fair offer for the purchase of his shares and was threatening to bring winding-up proceedings for an improper purpose, that is to say in order to extract a still higher offer, a course which the appellants condemn as tantamount to blackmail and an abuse of the process of the court. The Court of Appeal allowed Mr Demarco's appeal because they were not satisfied that the offer for his shares was a fair one. *(pg111a)*

4 Two interrelated questions thus lie at the heart of the present appeal. (1) Was the offer to purchase Mr Demarco's shares a fair one so that it was unreasonable for him to reject it? (2) Were the threatened proceedings brought for an ulterior purpose and thus an abuse of the process of the court? *(pg111b)*

The company's business

5 The company is a single venture vehicle which carries on business as the general manager of a venture capital limited partnership established under the law of the Cayman Islands. The limited partners, who provide the funds of the partnership, are Citibank NA and associated companies. The funds have largely been invested in Brazilian enterprises and are said to be *(pg110c)* worth in the region of $US 1 bn. They belong to the limited partners; the company has no beneficial interest in them. It derives its substantial income from fees and commissions for making deals and acquisitions on behalf of the partnership.

6 Under the arrangements between the company and the limited partners *(pg111d)* entered into in December 1997, the company can be removed as general manager for cause by a simple majority of the limited partners or without cause by a 75% majority of such partners. 'Cause' is defined to include the institution of proceedings seeking the liquidation or winding up of the company where the proceedings are not dismissed or stayed within 30 days of their institution. The partnership is to be treated as dissolved upon the removal of the general manager unless 75% in value of the limited partners agree within 90 days upon the *(pg111e)* appointment of another general manager.

7 Since the limited partners are associated companies, their Lordships consider it unnecessary to consider whether the presentation of the proposed petition would constitute 'cause' to remove the company as general manager. *(pg111f)* They propose to proceed on the footing that the company's tenure as general manager is at the will of the limited partners and so relatively precarious in any event. At the same time they would observe that, while the limited partners may be free to remove the company as general manager, it does not follow that it is open to the individuals behind Opportunity to accept the substitution of another company with different shareholders without *(pg111g)* accounting for any benefit which they might themselves obtain by the substitution: see *North Holdings Ltd* v *Southern Tropics Ltd* [1999] 2 BCLC 625 and the cases there cited.

The company's structure

8 Mr Demarco, who is resident in Brazil, became a shareholder, director *(pg111h)* and employee of the company in December 1997. The company has 100 issued ordinary shares of $1 each which are and have since then been held as follows:

Mr Demarco	1
Mr Andrade	1
Mr de Carvalho	1 *(pg111i)*
Mr Wilson	1
Opportunity	96

The four individuals were all deal-makers engaged by the company in late 1997 by written agreements on similar terms. *(pg112a)*

9 Although Mr Demarco holds only 1% of the issued shares, he claims in the draft petition to be beneficially entitled to 3.5% of the company's issued share capital pursuant to an oral agreement between him and the appellants entered into prior to his engagement. His claim is denied by the appellants, who advance a different case as to what was orally agreed between them. This dispute still remains to be resolved but is not material to the *(pg112b)* present appeal.

Mr Demarco's appointment

10 Under the terms of his engagemcnt, Mr Demarco was employed full time in the business of the company, his employment was terminable on three days' notice by either party, and upon termination of his employment he was *(pg112c)* at the company's request to resign immediately from office as a director without any claim for compensation. While his employment continued he was entitled to (1) a director's salary of US $12,000 pa, (ii) aggregate annual remuneration of US $240,000 (inclusive of director's salary) and (iii) a performance bonus by way of a share in the profits on any deal he effected for the partnership. *(pg112d)*

11 Under the terms of a shareholders' agreement to which all the members of the company were parties: (i) a director could be removed only by shareholders holding a majority of the shares in the company; (ii) a shareholder should not sell any share in the company except to Opportunity pursuant to annex A to the agreement; (iii) Opportunity granted each *(pg112e)* shareholder an irrevocable put option over his shares at a price and on the terms to be agreed pursuant to annex A; and (iv) each of the individual shareholders granted Opportunity a call option over his shares on similar terms. Annex A was left blank.

12 On 4 February 1999 Mr Demarco was dismissed by Opportunity for *(pg112f)* alleged 'bad performance'. Since then he has been excluded from any part in the management of the company. He has no longer been invited to attend board meetings or sent financial information in relation to the company or the partnership. Mr Demarco accepts that he cannot challenge his dismissal or exclusion from management of the company's business; but he does challenge Opportunity's right to exclude him therefrom without offering him *(pg112g)* a fair price for his shares.

Company law in the Cayman Islands

13 Section 94 of the Companies Act (1998 Revision) of the Cayman Islands provides that a company may be wound up by the court if: *(pg112h)*

> '... (d) the Court is of opinion that it is just and equitable that the company should be wound up.'

Corresponding provisions in identical terms have formed part of English company law since the first of the companies acts, namely the Companies Act 1862. *(pg112i)* Indeed, it made its first appearance in the Joint Stock Companies Winding-up Act 1848. The relevant provision is now contained in s122 of the English Insolvency Act 1986. Despite its presence in that Act, it is well established that a shareholder with fully paid shares has no *locus standi* to present a winding-up petition unless there is *prima facie* evidence that there would be a surplus on a winding up. *(pg113a)*

14 The statute law of the Cayman Islands contains no provision corresponding to s210 of the Companies Act 1948 (the 1948 Act) or its successors s75 of the Companies Act 1980 and s459 of the Companies Act 1985. These enable a shareholder to present a petition on the ground that the company's affairs are being or have been conducted in a manner which is *(pg113b)* oppressive (or in the later legislation unfairly prejudicial) to the interests of some part of the members including himself. They give the court wide powers to make such orders as it thinks fit with a view to bringing the matters complained of to an end, including a power to regulate the conduct of the company's affairs in the future, and a power to order the company or other members of the company to purchase the petitioner's shares. Under the 1948 Act it was necessary for the petitioner to establish facts which would justify the winding up of the company on the just and equitable ground even though that was not the remedy which he sought; but this is no longer required.

15 Section 210 of the English 1948 Act *(pg113c)* implemented a recommendation of the *Report of the Committee on Company Law Amendment* (Cmd 6659 *(pg113d)* (1945) para 60, chairman Cohen J). The Committee was anxious to strengthen the position of minority shareholders. It observed that the winding up of the company, which was the only remedy then available, would often not benefit the minority shareholder, since the break-up value of the assets might be small, and the only available purchaser might be that very majority whose conduct had driven the minority to seek redress. *(pg113e)* Accordingly, the Committee recommended that the court should have a jurisdiction which it had previously lacked to impose a just solution on the parties. In practice, the courts have generally sought to bring the matters complained of to an end by requiring one party, usually but not invariably the majority shareholders, to buy the other parties' shares at a fair price, *(pg113f)* fixed in case of dispute by the court.

16 As their Lordships have already noted, no such jurisdiction has been conferred on the court in the Cayman Islands. The only remedy available to a minority shareholder is to have the company wound up. This is likely to be contrary to his own interests and proportionately more so to the interests of *(pg113g)* the majority, and it is not normally what the minority shareholder really wants. But the risk that the company may be wound up tends to concentrate minds and encourages the parties to negotiate an acceptable compromise. This usually consists of an offer by the majority shareholders to buy out the minority at an appropriate price. *(pg113h)*

The proceedings

17 Following his dismissal Mr Demarco made repeated but unsuccessful attempts to negotiate his withdrawal from the company and the realisation of his interest. He has had numerous meetings with the persons who control Opportunity. According to his evidence, he provided them in January 1999 *(pg113i)* with a written calculation of the value of his 3.5% interest. When this was unproductive, he invited them to indicate their own assessment of the value of his interest, but received no response. Mr Demarco's lawyers were given to understand that Opportunity was not willing to acquire his interest or pay anything for it. If he was to realise his interest, he would have to resort to legal proceedings. *(pg114a)*

18 Mr Demarco was advised that, because annex A to the shareholders' agreement had not been completed, his put option was unenforceable. In those circumstances, he was told, the only remedy available to him under the law of the Cayman Islands was to present a petition to wind up the company. As he has since emphasised, this was not the remedy he wanted; but it was *(pg114b)* the only remedy he had.

19 By a letter dated 18 June 1999 Mr Demarco's lawyers alleged that there had clearly been a breakdown in the mutual trust and confidence between the participants in the business venture, and that they had advised him that the most appropriate course of action was for him to petition to wind up the company on the just and equitable ground. They gave notice of *(pg114c)* his intention to present such a petition within 14 days unless he received full payment of the value of his interest.

20 Opportunity's lawyers responded by a letter dated 29 June 1999 in which they stated that they were authorised to confirm that Opportunity would purchase Mr Demarco's shareholding 'at an appropriate price', and *(pg114d)* 'in the light of the above' they sought confirmation that he would withdraw his threat to present a petition.

21 Mr Demarco's lawyers naturally assumed that this was an offer to negotiate a realistic price for his shares, for nothing less could be expected to induce him to withdraw his threat to commence proceedings. Mr Demarco, however, rightly as it turned out, was more sceptical. On 1 July his lawyers *(pg114e)* wrote to say that as matters stood their instructions were to present a winding-up petition on the following day. If Opportunity wished to make an offer to pay 'the full value' of his interest this would have to be done and agreed that day.

22 On 2 July Graham J granted 'an interim injunction restraining Mr Demarco *(pg114f)* from presenting a winding-up petition against the company before 19 July. Although the order was made *ex parte*, Mr Demarco's lawyers were notified of the hearing in advance and the order was made in their presence. It seems unlikely that they resisted the making of the order. Mr Demarco had no desire to have the company wound up. His object was to bring Opportunity to the negotiating table, and his threat to present a winding-up petition appeared to have had the desired effect. Opportunity presented the case to the judge on the basis that it would be wrong to allow a winding-up *(pg114g)* petition to be presented when it had made an offer to buy Mr Demarco's shares at 'an appropriate price'. The judge may well have assumed that following his order the parties would open serious negotiations in relation to the price to be paid for Mr Demarco's interest. *(pg114h)*

23 Instead, as appeared from the evidence shortly afterwards filed on behalf of Opportunity and subsequently confirmed by its lawyers, by the ,appropriate price' for Mr Demarco's share Opportunity meant its par value of US $1. According to its evidence, there was an oral understanding that, if any of the individual shareholders wished to transfer his shares to *(pg114i)* Opportunity, the transfer would take place at par; and that if any of them was dismissed for misconduct or bad performance, Opportunity would exercise its call option *(pg115a)* by acquiring his shareholding at par. Opportunity deposed that annex A was not in existence when the shareholders' agreement was signed, but this failed to explain the apparent inconsistency between the alleged understanding and the express terms of the put and call options contained in the body of the shareholders' agreement. Opportunity contended that the petition was bound to fail, since Mr Demarco's participation in the management of the company was due to his position as an employee, and it had been agreed that upon his dismissal as an employee he would cease to be a director and would no longer be involved in the management of the company. *(pg115b)*

24 In his evidence in answer, Mr Demarco categorically denied the existence of any understanding that he should dispose of his shares at par. He alleged that his beneficial interest in the company was 3.5%, and not merely the 1% represented by his registered shareholding. On advice he did not deal with the contention that a petition was bound to fail, but reserved *(pg115c)* his right to file evidence in support of the petition when the time came.

25 Meanwhile, Opportunity commenced proceedings against Mr Demarco in the Grand Court in the Cayman Islands, seeking repayment of moneys lent and other relief. Although pleading the oral as well as written agreements which it claimed constituted the arrangements under which Mr Demarco *(pg115d)* had been engaged by the company, Opportunity did not allege any understanding that he would transfer his share at par if dismissed for misconduct or bad performance, but pleaded the terms of a written agreement which set out the consequences of Mr Demarco's dismissal, including the fact that his shares would remain his property in that event. When Opportunity's application to continue the injunction came before *(pg115e)* Graham J on 29 July, however, its story had changed again. According to the judge, its case now was that Mr Demarco's share had been registered in his name by mistake and belonged beneficially to Opportunity.

26 In the course of the hearing it evidently became clear that the judge was not disposed to restrain the presentation of the petition whether on the basis that it was doomed to fail or on the basis of an offer of $US 1 founded *(pg115f)* upon a disputed oral understanding. After obtaining his client's instructions, counsel for Opportunity informed the judge that it would agree to purchase Mr Demarco's shareholding in the company at a price equivalent to that which he would have obtained as a contributory on the liquidation of the company. Mr Demarco rejected the offer as inadequate. He submitted that, *(pg115g)* as Opportunity was offering to acquire his interest with the intention that the company should continue to carry on business, the price should be based on the value of the company as a going concern.

27 The judge found that Opportunity had made a bona fide and fair offer which it was unreasonable for Mr Demarco to reject, and granted the injunction as prayed. *(pg115h)*

28 Shortly afterwards, Opportunity's lawyers wrote to confirm and clarify the terms of its offer. Since Mr Demarco was seeking to wind up the company, Opportunity was prepared to calculate and pay him whatever he would receive if his petition were successful. The sum in question would represent 3.5% of the net asset value of the company together with 3.5% of *(pg115i)* the dividends which had accrued or become payable. The valuation should be carried out either by separate experts to be appointed by each party or by a jointly agreed court expert, and made on the assumption that the company had ceased to trade as the general partner of the limited partnership. In that event not only would the company's future stream of income be brought to an end, but it would also incur additional liabilities to refund some of the *(pg116a)* income it had previously received. Before the Board counsel for Opportunity indicated that the assumption should be expressed to be that the company had been ordered to be wound up. The relevant assumption, however expressed, would clearly exclude, and was intended to exclude, a valuation on the basis of a going concern. *(pg116b)*

29 The Court of Appeal allowed Mr Demarco's appeal, but continued the injunction pending the hearing of an appeal to their Lordships' Board. In the meantime, the parties exchanged valuations showing, as might be expected from the nature of the company's business, a very substantial difference between break up and going concern valuations.

30 Since the hearing in the Court of Appeal, Opportunity has amended *(pg116c)* its pleadings in the action in the Grand Court. It now pleads an oral agreement that if Mr Demarco should cease for any reason to be employed by the company as a deal-maker he would relinquish his interest in the company 'at its then value'. It also pleads that, so long as he was so employed, he would be incrementally entitled to become a 3.5% shareholder over a period of five years. Thus the company has variously alleged (1) that Mr Demarco's shareholding belongs beneficially to Opportunity, (ii) that *(pg116d)* there was an oral understanding that if he were dismissed for misconduct or bad performance he would transfer it to Opportunity at par and (iii) that it was orally agreed that if he ceased for any reason to be employed as a dealmaker he would relinquish his interest at its current value, presumably (if the *(pg116e)* company was likely to continue to carry on business in the foreseeable future) on a going concern basis. The action is due to be heard in April of this year, and accordingly their Lordships content themselves with observing that Opportunity's latest version of what was orally agreed between the parties sits uneasily with its contention that it was unreasonable of Mr Demarco to refuse its offer to buy his shares on a different and less favourable basis. *(pg116f)*

The just and equitable ground

31 In his often cited speech in *Ebrahimi* v *Westbourne Galleries Ltd* [1972] 2 All ER 492, [1973] AC 360 Lord Wilberforce explained the rationale of the 'just and equitable ground' for winding up a solvent company at the suit of a minority shareholder. He said ([1972] 2 All ER 492 *(pg116g)* at 500, [1973] AC 360 at 379):

'The words are a recognition of the fact that a limited company is more than a mere judicial entity, with a personality in law of its own: that there is room in company law for recognition of the fact that behind it, or amongst it, there are individuals, with rights, expectations and *(pg116h)* obligations *inter se* which are not necessarily submerged in the company structure. That structure is defined by the Companies Act 1948 and by the articles of association by which shareholders agree to be bound. In most companies and in most contexts, this definition is sufficient and exhaustive, equally so whether the company is large or small. The "just *(pg116i)* and equitable" provision does not, as the respondents suggest, entitle one party to disregard the obligation he assumes by entering a company, nor the court to dispense him from it. It does, as equity always does, enable the court to subject the exercise of legal rights to equitable considerations; considerations, that is, of a personal character arising between one individual and another, which may make it unjust, or *(pg117a)* inequitable, to insist on legal rights, or to exercise them in a particular way.'

32 Companies where the parties possess rights, expectations and obligations which are not submerged in the company structure are *(pg117b)* commonly described as 'quasi-partnership companies'. Their essential feature is that the legal, corporate and employment relationships do not tell the whole story; and that behind them there is a relationship of trust and confidence similar to that obtaining between partners which makes it unjust or inequitable for the majority to insist on its strict legal rights. The typical characteristics of such a company are that there should be (1) a business *(pg117c)* association formed or continued on the basis of a personal relationship of mutual trust and confidence, (ii) an understanding or agreement that all or some of the shareholders should participate in the management of the business and (iii) restrictions on the transfer of shares so that a member cannot realise his stake if he is excluded from the business. These elements are typical, but the list is not exhaustive. *(pg117d)*

33 Opportunity denies that the company is such a company or that Mr Demarco was anything more than an employee and director who was given a share as an inducement to work for the company. This was the basis of the submission, made below and repeated before the Board, that the threatened petition is doomed to fail. But Mr Demarco clearly claims that the company *(pg117e)* did possess the relevant characteristics. His case is that there was formerly a relationship of trust and confidence between the parties which has since broken down and which makes it unjust or inequitable for Opportunity to exclude him from the business without offering him an opportunity to realise his interest at a fair price. This will be a critical issue in the case if it is allowed to proceed to trial. Mr Demarco may or may not succeed in establishing it, *(pg117f)* but the petition itself has not yet been presented and the evidence in support has not yet been filed. It is impossible in the present state of the evidence to say that the petition is manifestly unfounded, and accordingly their Lordships reject this ground of appeal.

34 In *O'Neill v Phillips, Re a company* (*No 00709 of 1992*) [1999] 2 *(pg117g)* BCLC 1 at 16, [1999] 1 WLR 1092 at 1107 Lord Hoffmann explained that the unfairness did not lie in the exclusion of the petitioner from the management of the company but in his exclusion without a reasonable offer for his shares. If the respondent has plainly made a reasonable offer, he said, then the exclusion as such will not be unfairly prejudicial and he will be entitled to have the petition struck out. Their Lordships draw attention to the *(pg117h)* requirement that the offer must plainly be reasonable: a respondent is not entitled to have the petition restrained or struck out if the reasonableness of his offer is open to question.

35 As his reference to unfair prejudice shows, Lord Hoffmann was speaking in the context of a petition for relief under s459 of the Companies *(pg117i)* Act 1985, rather than a petition for a winding up on the just and equitable ground. Their Lordships will consider hereafter whether this affects what amounts to a reasonable offer; but there is no difference in principle. If the company possesses the relevant characteristics, then it is unfair for the majority to insist on their legal right to exclude the petitioner without making a reasonable offer for his shares. It is no less accurate to describe such conduct *(pg118a)* as unjust or inequitable than it is to describe it as oppressive or unfairly prejudicial to the interests of the minority. As their Lordships have already noted, a petitioner could not obtain a remedy under s210 of the 1948 Act unless he alleged facts which would justify the court in making a winding-up order. The section provided an alternative remedy but the wrong was often the same. *(pg118b)*

The basis of valuation

36 The parties cannot be expected to agree upon the monetary value of Mr Demarco's interest. This is a matter of judgment and opinion, and their respective advisers may be expected to disagree. But there should be no difficulty in agreeing the basis of valuation and the machinery for resolving any *(pg118c)* disagreement.

37 There are essentially three possible bases on which a minority holding of shares in an unquoted company can be valued. In descending order these are: (i) as a rateable proportion of the total value of the company as a going concern without any discount for the fact that the holding in question is a *(pg118d)* minority holding; (ii) as before but with such a discount; and (iii) as a rateable proportion of the net assets of the company at their break up or liquidation *(pg118e)* value.

38 Which of these should be adopted as the appropriate basis of valuation depends on all the circumstances. The choice must be fair to both parties, and it is difficult to see any justification for adopting the break up or liquidation basis of valuation where the purchaser intends to continue to carry on the business of the company as a going concern. This would give the purchaser a windfall at the expense of the seller.

39 If the going concern value is adopted, a further question arises: whether a discount should be applied to reflect the fact that the holding is a minority one. An outsider would normally be unwilling to pay a significant price for a *(pg118f)* minority holding in a private company, and a fair price as between a willing seller and a willing purchaser might be expected to reflect this fact. It would seem to be unreasonable for the seller to demand a higher price from an unwilling purchaser than he could obtain from a willing one. Small private companies commonly have articles which restrict the transfer of shares by *(pg118g)* requiring a shareholder who is desirous of disposing of his shares to offer them first to the other shareholders at a price fixed by the company's auditors. It is the common practice of auditors in such circumstances to value the shares as between a willing seller and a willing buyer and to apply a substantial discount to reflect the fact that. the shares represent a minority holding.

40 The context in which the shares fall to be valued in a case such as the *(pg118h)* present is, however, very different. Mr Demarco is not desirous of disposing of his shares; he would rather keep them and continue to participate in the management of the company. It is Opportunity's conduct in excluding him from management that has driven him, however reluctantly, to seek to realise the value of his investment. In this situation the case law in England is that normally the shares should be valued without any discount: see for example *(pg118i) re Bird Precision Bellows Ltd* [1985] BCLC 493, [1986] Ch 658, *Virdi* v *Abbey Leisure Ltd, re Abbey Leisure Ltd* [1990] BCLC 342 and *O'Neill* v *Phillips* [1999]2 BCLC 1, [1999] 1 WLR 1092. In *re Bird Precision Bellows Ltd* [1985] BCLC 493 at 498, [1986] Ch 658 at 667 Oliver LJ cited with evident approval the observations of Nourse J at first instance where he said: *(pg119a)*

> 'I would expect that in a majority of cases where purchase orders are made under s75 in relation to quasi-partnerships the vendor is unwilling in the sense that the sale has been forced on him. Usually he will be a minority shareholder whose interests have been unfairly prejudiced by *(pg119b)* the manner in which the affairs of the company have been conducted by the majority. On the assumption that the unfair prejudice has made it no longer tolerable for him to retain his interest in the company, a sale of his shares will invariably be his only practical way out short of a winding up. In that kind of case it seems to me that it would not merely not be fair, but most unfair, that he should be bought out on the fictional basis applicable *(pg119c)* to a free election to sell his shares in accordance with the company's articles of association, or indeed on any other basis which involved a discounted price. In my judgment the correct course would be to fix the price pro rata according to the value of the shares as a whole and without any discount, as being the only fair method of compensating an unwilling vendor of the equivalent of a partnership share. Equally, if the order *(pg119d)* provided, as it did in *re Jermyn Street Turkish Baths Ltd* [1971] 3 All ER 184, [1971] 1 WLR 1042, for the purchase of the shares of the delinquent majority, it would not merely not be fair, but most unfair, that they should receive a price which involved an element of premium.'

To require Mr Demarco to submit not only to his exclusion from the company *(pg119e)* but to the acquisition of his shares at less than their going concern value by a purchaser which intends to carry on the business is hardly less unfair.

41 The rationale for denying a discount to reflect the fact that the holding in question is a minority holding lies in the analogy between a quasi-partnership *(pg119f)* company and a true partnership. On the dissolution of a partnership, the ordinary course is for the court to direct a sale of the partnership business as a going concern with liberty for any of the former partners who wish to bid for the business to do so. But the court has power to ascertain the value of a former partner's interest without a sale if it can be done by valuation, and frequently does so where his interest is relatively small: *(pg119g)* see *Syers* v *Syers* (1876) 1 App Cas 174. But the valuation is not based on a notional sale of the outgoing partner's share to the continuing partners who, being the only possible purchasers, would offer relatively little. It is based on a notional sale of the business as a whole to an outside purchaser.

42 In the case of a company possessing the relevant characteristics, the majority can exclude the minority only if they offer to pay them a fair price for *(pg119h)* their shares. In order to be free to manage the company's business without regard to the relationship of trust and confidence which formerly existed between them, they must buy the whole, part from themselves and part from the minority, thereby achieving the same freedom to manage the business as an outside purchaser would enjoy. *(pg119i)*

43 The practice of striking out a petition or restraining the presentation of a threatened petition after the petitioner has unreasonably refused a fair offer for his shares is a relatively recent development in England and postdates the introduction of s210 of the 1948 Act. The cases in which the English courts have been called upon to decide what constitutes such an offer have therefore been decided in the context of a claim that the respondents should be ordered *(pg120a)* to purchase the petitioner's shares (or occasionally vice versa), or at least in a situation where the court has power to grant such relief. Opportunity submits that the position is very different where, as in the Cayman Islands, the only relief available to the petitioner is to have the company wound up. In such a case, it argues, the petitioner's shares have no value beyond the amount which could be obtained in respect of them on a winding up, and an offer to buy at a *(pg120b)* price which reflects that value cannot be stigmatised as unfair.

44 The proposition that the value of the petitioner's shares should reflect the remedy available to him if no offer is made has a superficial attraction, but their Lordships regard it as unsound. Its attraction lies in the popular notion that the value of an asset depends on what a willing purchaser would be *(pg120c)* prepared to pay for it, and that it has no value if no one is willing to buy it. In cases such as the present the respondents are normally unwilling purchasers. They do not want to buy the petitioner's shares and would not make him an offer at all were it not for their concern to have the proceedings aborted.

45 Where the court has power to order the respondents to purchase the *(pg120d)* petitioner's shares, the flaw in the proposition that the value of his shares is measured by the remedy is readily apparent. The price at which the respondents ought to offer to buy the petitioner's shares in order to have the proceedings struck out if he refuses to accept it and the price which the court will order them to pay if the petition is successful cannot be measured in terms of each other without producing a circularity. The concept of a fair price *(pg120e)* assumes that the shares have an objective value by which the fairness of the offer can be assessed.

46 Their Lordships consider that the proposition is equally unsound where the only remedy available to the petitioner is to have the company wound up. In the first place, it assumes that the fair value of the shares is to be measured by their value to the petitioner and that their value to the respondents is to be *(pg120f)* ignored. The amount which the petitioner would obtain in respect of his shares on a winding up represents the least that they can be worth to him, but it does not represent their fair value as between the parties. In the second place, the fairness of the offer should be judged by reference to what will happen if it is accepted, not if it is refused. *(pg120g)*

47 Opportunity sought to draw comfort from a passage in the judgment of Millett J in *re A company (No 003843 of 1986)* [1987] BCLC 562 at 571 where he said:

> '… it is now manifestly unreasonable for the petitioners to continue to press for a winding-up order. That would give them a financial remedy *(pg120h)* only, but it would be a financial remedy which would inevitably result in a later payment of a lesser sum than could be obtained from the offer that has been made.'

But the passage must be read in context. As it makes clear, the respondents had offered to buy the petitioners' shares at more than their break up or liquidation *(pg120i)* value. In fact they had offered to pay a price equal to a rateable proportion of the company's assets at the market value of the company as a going concern, the valuation to be made by an independent chartered accountant selected by agreement or in default nominated by the president of the Institute of Chartered Accountants. The petitioners rejected the offer because they were *(pg121a)* not interested in selling their shares at any price. They wanted to be reinstated as directors, failing which they insisted that the company should be wound up. The passage lends no support to Opportunity's submission that a fair price can be based on the company's break up or liquidation value.

48 The proposition is inconsistent with the rationale which excludes a *(pg121b)* discount to reflect the fact that the petitioner's interest represents a minority holding. In the case of a quasi-partnership company the corporate structure represents the legal medium by which a business is carried on as a joint venture. The petitioner's interest in the joint venture cannot be determined by a sale of his shareholding to his co-venturers unless the price reflects his share in the underlying business. The subject matter of the notional sale which *(pg121c)* forms the basis of valuation is, therefore, not the petitioner's minority holding but the entire share capital of the company.

49 Their Lordships are satisfied that Opportunity's offer to purchase Mr Demarco's interest at a valuation based on the company's break up or liquidation value falls far short of a fair offer and fails to remedy his complaint. *(pg121d)* It is not entitled on this ground to restrain the presentation of a winding-up petition.

Abuse of process

50 Opportunity also submits that, by presenting a winding-up petition after he has been offered the full value of the amount which he would obtain in respect of his interest if the company were wound up, Mr Demarco would *(pg121e)* be abusing the process of the court by using it for an ulterior purpose.

51 This contention, too, has a superficial attraction, for it is easy to doubt the *bona fides* of a plaintiff who commences or continues proceedings after he has been offered everything which he could hope to achieve in the proceedings even if wholly successful. In the case of an ordinary action, however, the *(pg121f)* defendant is not entitled to have the proceedings struck out on the ground that the plaintiff has been offered the full amount of his claim. The defendant's remedy is either to submit to judgment or to pay money into court, await judgment, and ask for his costs.

52 The special nature of winding-up proceedings and the loss which they *(pg121g)* may cause the company and its shareholders, however, makes it incumbent on the court to ensure that they are not brought for an improper purpose. In particular, they must not be brought simply to bring pressure on the respondents to yield to the petitioner's demands, however unreasonable, rather than suffer the losses consequent upon the presentation of a petition or the making of a winding-up order. *(pg121h)*

53 Where the petitioner can achieve his object by other means, therefore, he may be restrained from bringing winding-up proceedings. In *Charles Forte Investments Ltd* v *Amanda* [1963] 2 All ER 940, [1964] 1 Ch 240, a minority shareholder complained of the board's refusal to register transfers of his shares to a third party. He threatened to present a winding-up petition unless the *(pg121i)* board registered the transfers. He was restrained from presenting a petition. The shareholder had other and more suitable remedies available to him, namely an action for rectification of the register or proceeding by way of motion under s116 of the 1948 Act, and his threat to employ the machinery of winding up was an attempt to bring pressure on the board to reverse its decision and an abuse of the process of the court. *(pg122a)*

54 There is this similarity between that case and the present: in neither case

would the winding up of the company achieve what the minority shareholder wanted. But there the similarity ends. In that case the shareholder had other and more suitable remedies available to him: his choice to initiate winding-up proceedings was not made in good faith. In the *(pg122b)* present case Mr Demarco has no other remedy available to him. He does not want the company wound up: but he has no choice but to initiate winding-up proceedings if he is to have any hope of receiving a reasonable offer for his shares, an offer to which, if his claim is well founded, he is entitled.

55 The fact that the court lacks the necessary power to make a more suitable order does not mean that a winding-up order would be unjust if *(pg122c)* Opportunity declines to make a fair offer for Mr Demarco's shares. By presenting a winding-up petition on the just and equitable ground Mr Demarco is invoking the traditional jurisdiction of equity to subject the exercise of legal rights to equitable considerations. If he can make good his contention that the business venture which the parties carried on through the medium of the company possessed the necessary characteristics, then equity *(pg122d)* will not allow Opportunity to exploit its position to make a profit at his expense. If it wants to carry on the company's business as a going concern without him, it must offer to pay him the going concern value of his interest. If it is unwilling to pay him more than the break up or liquidation value of his interest, then the court may order that the company be wound up. This *(pg122e)* will not obtain more for Mr Demarco than he has already been offered, but it will achieve a fair and just result between the parties by ensuring that they are treated equally.

56 Their Lordships would wish to emphasise that this does not mean that a minority shareholder can use the threat of winding-up proceedings in order to bring pressure on the majority to yield to his demands however *(pg122f)* unreasonable. As *re A company (No 003843 of 1986)* [1987] BCLC 562 demonstrates, the court will be astute to prevent such conduct. In a case such as the present, it would be an abuse of the process of the court for a petitioner to commence or continue proceedings after he has plainly received a fair offer for his shares. If he holds out for more, the respondent can apply for the *(pg122g)* proceedings to be restrained or struck out. The court is fully in control and will not allow its process to be abused.

57 Their Lordships are satisfied that Mr Demarco has not acted unreasonably in rejecting Opportunity's offer to buy his interest, and that by continuing to hold out for a fair offer he is not threatening to abuse the process of the court. *(pg122h)*

Conclusion

58 Their Lordships will humbly advise Her Majesty that the appeal should be dismissed with costs. *(pg122i)*

Case 46
Marks v Sherred

[2004] STC (SCD) 362

SpC 418

Special Commissioner

10, 11 May, 23 June 2004

This case determines the market value of a majority shareholding in an unquoted trading company as at 31 March 1982.

As trading company share valuations at 31 March 1982 are very frequently required, it might be expected that this case would give valuable guidance on the approach to be approved by the court. In this respect, the case is unsatisfactory.

The factual background to the case is not particularly exceptional. During the 1990s, Ross Marks made a disposal of his 66 per cent shareholding in Ross Group Plc (formerly Ross Marks Ltd). In order to calculate the capital gain it was necessary to ascertain the market value of the 66 per cent shareholding as at 31 March 1982. At that date there were three other shareholders; two family shareholders between them owned 30 per cent of the share capital and the general manager, not a family member, held the remaining 4 per cent. The company made up its accounts at 31 March each year. Properly audited annual accounts were produced, in the usual way, after the year end, but in the 1980s Ross Marks Ltd did not have management accounts, nor did it undertake budgeting or forecasting. The accounts for the year ended 31 March 1982 were, thus, not on that date. The hypothetical purchaser would have relied, as did the taxpayer, upon information provided informally to him by the company's bookkeeper, on the company's bank statements and on his own feel for how the business was progressing.

The valuation on behalf of the taxpayer was undertaken by a former examiner of Inland Revenue Shares Valuation Division who had moved to private practice. Interestingly the valuation submitted by the Revenue was, also, undertaken by an independent valuer who had, similarly started his career in Inland Revenue Shares Valuation Division and moved to private practice. The taxpayer was represented by his solicitor; the Revenue was represented by a barrister. The solicitor representing the taxpayer submitted that the Revenue's expert was partial. The Special Commissioner rejected the contention.

In his decision, the Special Commissioner describes much evidence given by the taxpayer as 'vague', saying: 'I came to the conclusion, that the taxpayer was able to recall the good points about RML rather more easily than he could recall the bad' ([2004] STC (SCD) 362 at 365d **case 46 para 9**). It, thus, comes as no great surprise when reaching the end of the decision to discover that the Special Commissioner substantially adopted the valuation of the Revenue's expert, in preference to that of the taxpayer's expert.

Perhaps the most important distinction between the alternative valuations presented by the Special Commissioner was the starting point. The expert witness called by the taxpayer argued that the accounts for year ended 31 March 1982 could not have been available and, hence, the starting point for the arithmetic calculating was the accounts for the year ended 31 March 1981. The expert witness acting on behalf of the Revenue took the view that no purchaser would be satisfied with basing an offer on accounts a year old. The Revenue's witness said the purchaser would want details of RML's trading results for the current year; if the company's records had not been analysed to measure the profit to date, he would look at the available data and analyse it himself. ([2004] STC (SCD) 362 at 366h, **case 46 para 16**). The solicitor representing the taxpayer submitted that the Revenue's expert based his evidence upon audited accounts for the year to 31 March 1982 which, by definition, could not have been available on that date. The Special Commissioner rejected this contention, similarly, as did, interestingly, the expert for the taxpayer. The Special Commissioner said:

> 'I am satisfied that the premise from which the taxpayer's valuation proceeds is unrealistic. I readily accept that a purchaser would look closely at the 1981 results, and would regard them and those achieved in preceding years as relevant to the determination of the price. He would certainly give them proper weight in reaching his conclusion but I am not persuaded that he would use them as the starting point. I agree with the Revenue's expert that he would scrutinise all of the available information up to the last possible moment before the conclusion of his purchase.'
>
> ([2004] STC (SCD) 362 at 368b **case 46 para 21**)

The Special Commissioner ruled that for a purchase of this size of shareholding he must assume that the prospective purchaser would insist on seeing even confidential information ([2004] STC (SCD) 362 at 367i **case 46 para 20**).

The company made most purchases overseas, denominated in dollars. During 1981 and 1982 the dollar appreciated significantly against the pound. The company's trading profit, measured in pounds, for the year ending 31 March 1982 was, thus, reduced. The expert witness appearing for the taxpayer attempted to counterbalance this effect by recalculating the results as if the £/$ rate has been static. This was completely rejected by the Special Commissioner.

The Revenue's valuer added back what he considered were excessive directors' emoluments. This add back increased the share valuation but, strangely, the valuer appearing for the taxpayer disagreed with the add back.

Both experts approached the valuation as an exercise in applying an appropriate P/E ratio to adjusted earnings. Neither expert discounted the valuation by reference to the fact that the shareholding was 66 per cent and not 100 per cent. The Special Commissioner states in his decision:

> 'I was asked to take no account of any possible premium or discount which might have arisen by reason of the taxpayer's holding a controlling shareholding on the one hand, or his having to take into consideration the interests of minority shareholders on the other, but instead to value the entire company and to determine the value of the taxpayer's shares at 66% of the resulting figure.'
>
> ([2004] STC (SCD) 362 at 363h **case 46 para 2**)

The only sense I can make of this statement is that the choice of P/E, in itself, reflects the discount required for a majority holding that is less than the 75 per cent required to approve a reorganisation.

The expert for the taxpayer applied a P/E of 11 to adjusted profits of £148,190 to give a value for the 66 per cent shareholding of £1,050,000; the expert for the Revenue applied a P/E of 10 to adjusted profits of £100,000, to give a value for the shareholding of £561,000.

The Special Commissioner accepted the Revenue's multiplier and added something to the base profit to reflect some hope for the future and declared that the value of the taxpayer's shareholding was £633,000.

At the beginning of this commentary I stated that I find this decision unsatisfactory. Why is this so? Reflecting on this case, I think the reason for my finding the decision unsatisfactory is that the English adversarial system of court procedure is unsuited to the determination of market value in this type of circumstance. A better result would be achieved, I suggest, by an inquisitorial system conducted by a Special Commissioner expert in valuation. In this case, both sides said that the measure of value was capitalised earnings. In an adversarial system, it would be a bold commissioner who rejected the evidence of both parties' witnesses and investigated, himself, whether reference should be made to assets or, indeed, to the availability of a dividend yield to a purchaser who acquired a 66 per cent shareholding. The Special Commissioner was not a bold inquisitor and so this was not tested. P/E multiples of 10 and 11 appear to have been derived by comparison with the published results of listed companies in the same industry sector. In my view, the P/E ratios of listed companies are almost irrelevant in deciding on an appropriate multiple for valuing a shareholding in an unlisted family company. The Special Commissioner states that he was asked not to apply a discount. An inquisitorial commissioner would investigate whether a discount should be applied to the value of a 66 per cent shareholding. Most valuers would apply a discount. Perhaps, the discount was inherent in the P/E ratio chosen; this is not clear from the Commissioner's decision. Perhaps more seriously, the point does not seem to have been taken fully that a price paid by a prospective purchaser is the estimate that the purchaser puts on the value to him of the shareholding in the future. Year ended 31 March 1982 may have been a very bad year, but that is not the point. What we are required to do is to look at the outlook for earnings, as perceived on 31 March 1982. We have to decide whether a purchaser would envisage a return to better years, or a continuation of bad times. The approach taken by both sides to the corporation tax charge is, also, unsatisfactory, in my view. Strangely, it appears that even the Revenue did not have adequate records to show the history of corporation tax paid by the company. Neither side appears to have made the point that the history of tax paid is irrelevant. A purchaser at 31 March 1982 makes his calculations of the future based on the tax rate that he then knows for the future. It seems that the company had been paying the small company's rate of corporation tax. From 1979 to 1981 the small companies rate was at 40 per cent; for 1982 it had reduced to 38 per cent and to 30 per cent the following year, where it stayed for five years, before a further progressive reduction to its current level of 19 per cent. The rationale for attempting to calculate the effective corporation tax charge for preceding years for the purpose of calculating the value of a shareholding for the future is, thus, flawed.

Decision

References, example '(pg363f)', are to [2004] STC (SCD) 362.

1 I am required in this appeal to determine the market value, at 31 March 1982, of the taxpayer's shares in Ross Marks Ltd ('RML') which later became Ross Group plc *(pg363f)*. That value is relevant to the taxpayer's liability to capital gains tax for the years of assessment 1992/3 to 1995/6 on his disposals of the shares but I am not required at this stage to determine the amount of his liability, nor to decide some other matters which have arisen during the course of the appeal. The only matter before me is the 31 March 1982 value of the shares; the taxpayer is deemed by sections 35(2) and 55(1) of the Taxation of Capital Gains Act 1992 *(pg363g)* to have sold the shares on that day and have reacquired them immediately at their market value.

2 On that date the taxpayer, Ross Marks, owned 66% of the shares in RML. His mother and brother owned a further 30%, and the general manager of the company, who was also a director but not a member of the taxpayer's family, owned the remaining 4%. I was asked to take no account of any possible premium or *(pg363h)* discount which might have arisen by reason of the taxpayer's holding a controlling shareholding on the one hand, or his having to take into consideration the interests of minority shareholders on the other, but instead to value the entire company and to determine the value of the taxpayer's shares at 66% of the resulting figure.

3 What is meant by 'market value' is defined by section 272(1) and (2) of the 1992 Act in these terms: *(pg363j)*

'(1) In this Act 'market value' in relation to any assets means the price which those assets might reasonably be expected to fetch on a sale in the open market.

(2) In estimating the market value of any assets no reduction shall be made in the estimate on account of the estimate being made on the assumption that the whole of the assets is to be placed on the market at one and the same time.' *(pg364a)*

The principles to be applied in the valuation of unquoted shares are prescribed by section 273 as follows:

'(1) The provisions of subsection (3) below shall have effect in any case where, in relation to an asset to which this section applies, there falls to be determined by virtue of section 272(1) the price which the asset might reasonably be expected to fetch on a sale on the open market. *(pg364b)*

(2) The assets to which this section applies are shares and securities which are not quoted on a recognised stock exchange at the time as at which their market value for the purposes of tax on chargeable gains falls to be determined.

(3) For the purposes of a determination falling within subsection (1) above, it shall be assumed that, in the open market which is postulated for the purposes of that determination, there is available to any prospective purchaser of the *(pg364c)* asset in question all the information which a prudent prospective purchaser of the asset might reasonably require if he were proposing to purchase it from a willing vendor by private treaty and at arm's length.'

4 The taxpayer's evidence was that RML was incorporated in July 1972 as a private company, and it was still a private company (and correspondingly unquoted *(pg364d)* so as to come within section 273) in March 1982. The taxpayer was at all material times its managing director and, for all practical purposes, its controlling mind. Its principal business was the import and sale within the United Kingdom of small electronic equipment for the domestic consumer market, and especially headphones, although in total it dealt in about 350 different products. They were sold under the brand name 'Ross'; the company had obtained some fairly limited *(pg364e)* formal trademark protection by 1982 but I accept that, even where there was no formal protection, the company had a recognised trade name and (as later events showed) it was able to procure further protection without difficulty. I am satisfied that RML was not vulnerable to the abuse by others of its trading name.

5 Only limited financial records for the period before 1982 survive. Such as remain show that RML's turnover increased quite strongly during the 1970s. In *(pg364f)* the year to 31 March 1981, the last year for which audited accounts were available on 31 March 1982, it achieved turnover of £1,496,006. Its gross profit in that year was £594,220, just short of 40% of turnover, and its net profit before tax, after allowing for directors' emoluments, was £160,074, or 10.7% of turnover. In preceding years, those percentages had been somewhat different but there had nevertheless been steady growth in net profit. No dividends were declared in any *(pg364g)* year and the accumulated net profit was carried forward.

6 In the year to 31 March 1982, the audited accounts show, RML's turnover increased to £1,884,100 (an improvement of almost 26% on the preceding year) and gross profit was £621,264, or just under 33% of turnover although gross profit was depressed by an increase in stock. Net profit after directors' emoluments but *(pg364h)* before tax was diminished by a significant increase in overheads and, at £54,311, was a mere 2.9% of turnover.

7 It may be remembered that at that time, there was considerable speculation in the currency markets. During the early 1980s sterling fell quite sharply against most major currencies including in particular the US dollar. RML's products were almost entirely manufactured in the Far East, mainly in Hong Kong and Taiwan, *(pg364j)* and were priced (and had to be paid for) in US dollars. The sterling cost of the goods therefore increased quite considerably. In earlier years, the taxpayer said, RML had obtained some protection against currency movements by buying dollars forward but in 1981 its broker, obviously taking an optimistic view of sterling's future prospects, advised the taxpayer that RML should no longer continue that practice. The taxpayer told me he followed that advice with adverse consequences for RML's profitability, which was reflected in the reduction in gross profit as a percentage of turnover. I mention in passing that currency movements do not *(pg365a)* explain the substantial increases in overheads which were responsible for the significant fall in net profit. Within these overheads, directors' remuneration fell, but other expenditure increased, sometimes by large amounts.

8 Despite the setback in the year to March 1982, the taxpayer remained very optimistic for RML's future prospects and was, he said, already contemplating flotation on the unlisted securities market ('USM'), as it then was, within the *(pg365b)* following five years – that is, by 1987. He had also decided to protect RML from some of the adverse currency movements which had afflicted it by embarking on the manufacture of some of the company's products within the United Kingdom.

9 The taxpayer's recollection, he said, was that he had already taken advice about a possible flotation, and had also taken the first steps towards establishing a United Kingdom manufacturing base. I take into account the fact that RML did *(pg365c)* float on the USM in 1987, and that it did begin manufacturing within the UK, though a subsidiary, at some time between 1982 and 1987 – the taxpayer was vague on this point as he was in much of his evidence, though I recognise that he was giving evidence 20 years and more after the relevant events. I came to the conclusion, after listening to his evidence, that the taxpayer was able to recall the *(pg365d)* good points about RML rather more easily than he could recall the bad, and that he was inclined to play down the difficulties which RML underwent as a result of the depreciation of sterling and to ignore altogether the other factors which had depressed its net profits in the year to 31 March 1982. I concluded too that although both flotation and UK manufacturing were, by that date, very much in the taxpayer's mind, no active steps towards achieving those objectives had been taken. It was clear that he was of an optimistic disposition, and he was certainly *(pg365e)* optimistic about RML's prospects in 1982, although it can be said in his favour that his optimism was largely borne out by subsequent events.

10 In 1982 RML did not have management accounts or any equivalent, nor did it undertake budgeting or forecasting. Properly audited annual accounts were produced, in the usual way, after the year end, but as each year proceeded, the *(pg365f)* taxpayer relied upon information provided informally to him by the company's bookkeeper, on the company's bank statements and on his own feel for how the business was progressing. I do not find it surprising, nor a matter for adverse comment, that a comparatively small company, controlled on a day to day basis by its majority shareholder, was run at that time in such an informal manner.

11 Each of the parties called an expert witness, who had already provided a *(pg365g)* report. For the appellant, I heard from Maggie Mullen and for the respondent from Michael Ruse. They had each spent some time in the Inland Revenue's shares valuation division before carrying out similar work with major firms of accountants, and had then set up their own practices. Carol Fraser, the solicitor representing the taxpayer, suggested that Mr Ruse was partial but I am quite satisfied not only that there is no merit in that suggestion, but also that there is nothing in his report *(pg365h)* or his evidence to support it, and that Mr Ruse, like Miss Mullen, approached his task fairly.

12 The experts agreed that the appropriate method of valuing the company was the capitalised earnings approach, which requires the maintainable earnings of the business to be identified and then multiplied by an appropriate factor. The *(pg365j)* disagreement between them about the multiplier was relatively modest – Mr Ruse maintained that 10 was appropriate while Miss Mullen suggested 11 – but there was a much greater difference between them about the level of the company's maintainable earnings.

13 Miss Mullen began with the audited figures for the year to 31 March 1981, which she compared with the available figures for preceding years in order to establish a trend. She recognised that the audited figures for the year to 31 March 1982 showed a marked deterioration in the company's profit but, accepting the *(pg366a)* taxpayer's explanation that the deterioration was due to adverse exchange rate movements, she recalculated the figures so as to assume a steady exchange rate, at the average level of the three preceding years. By this means she determined what she described as the true maintainable earnings. The resulting figure was comparable to that achieved in the preceding years, although showing a rather slower rate of growth than had previously been achieved. She had also taken *(pg366b)* account of the increase in overheads revealed by the 1982 accounts, which I have already mentioned. She considered that by adopting this approach she was doing much as a potential purchaser would have done, if he was intending to buy the company on 31 March 1982 when, for obvious reasons, the final figures to that date could not be available. The net profit before tax, recalculated as she thought appropriate, was £190,000 for the year. She considered that conclusion was *(pg366c)* consistent with net, after tax, earnings of £148,190, the figure achieved in the year to 1981; in her opinion that was, therefore, a maintainable earnings level.

14 In order to determine a fair multiplier, she examined six quoted companies which also traded in the consumer electronics markets. Of these, only two were sufficiently similar to RML to be useful for comparison purposes. One, Amstrad plc (much larger than the appellant) had a market valuation which supported a *(pg366d)* multiplier (its price-earnings ratio) at 31 March 1982 of 11.4. (I observe that Mr Ruse had the figure at 11.6). The other comparator, Electrocomponents plc, traded in the same market as the appellant, which was in fact one of its suppliers, but that fact of itself made it necessary to treat this company with some caution when using it for comparison purposes. Its capitalisation supported a multiplier of 19.4 at 31 March 1982. The average of the electricals sector of the FT Actuaries *(pg366e)* Share Index at that time was 17.4 (which Mr Ruse put at 17.63).

15 Miss Mullen recognised that RML was not a public company, that it was comparatively small and that it had to be considered in a different light from the comparators. Taking Amstrad, Electrocomponents and the average together, she arrived at a starting point for the multiplier of 15, which she then adjusted to take account of factors which appeared to her likely to have some effect on that figure: *(pg366f)* that what was being sold was a majority shareholding and that RML had a strong brand name on the one hand, but that it lacked liquidity, was in competition with larger companies and had a less strong growth pattern than some of them on the other. She arrived – although, as she accepted, with no precision – at a range of 10 to 12 and her selected figure was in the middle of that range, that is 11. Consequently her value of the company at 31 March 1982 was 11 multiplied by *(pg366g)* £148,190 or £1.63 million; the taxpayer's shares therefore had a value, rounded down slightly, of £1,050,000 at that date.

16 Mr Ruse, while adopting a broadly similar approach to Miss Mullen, was of the view that a purchaser would be influenced much more by the company's recent trading history than Miss Mullen had conceded. He accepted that the accounts for *(pg366h)* the years up to that ending on 31 March 1981 showed reasonably strong growth but he took the view that no purchaser would be satisfied with that; he would want details of RML's trading results for the current year (and if it had not been analysed, he would look at the available raw data and analyse it himself). The hypothetical purchaser would also be aware that a company such as this made the bulk of its purchases in US dollars and was exposed to currency fluctuations. He *(pg366j)* considered that it was unrealistic to do as Miss Mullen had done, that is rework the company's figures as if the adverse currency movements had simply not occurred; and her calculation took no account of the actual sterling – dollar exchange rate at 31 March 1982. He was sure that it would not have been a difficult task to make a reasonably accurate calculation of RML's results for the first 11 months of the trading year, particularly since the bulk of its trade occurred in the period leading up to Christmas, from which it would be apparent that the results for the whole year would be much less good than those for the year to 1981. *(pg367a)*

17 On the other hand he had identified some costs which had reduced the company's profitability and which a purchaser would not need to suffer. These were the high level of directors' emoluments and the high cost of entertaining.

Adjusting those figures downwards to what he considered more reasonable levels enabled Mr Ruse to increase the pre-tax net profit available to an intending purchaser from the £54,311 shown in the 1982 accounts to as much as £82,000. *(pg367b)* He accepted too that a purchaser would not take one poor year in isolation but would recognise that the company had been adversely affected by factors which would not necessarily continue. The hypothetical purchaser would, he said, take into account that in previous years, when it had not been badly affected by adverse currency movements, RML had achieved better results. Those results too should be adjusted to take account of the excessive expenditure which he had identified. *(pg367c)* He proposed, therefore, that the sustainable profit should be determined at £100,000 per year, by adding a 'hope' factor of £18,000 to the £82,000 adjusted profit for 1982. It is worth mentioning that this figure, despite the adjustments, gives much greater weight to the results actually achieved in the year to 1982 than to the results in the preceding two years. Mr Ruse's estimate of the after tax profit was £85,000 per year. That was, he conceded, imprecise but it is (as I accept) *(pg367d)* impossible from the available accounts to determine RML's effective corporation tax rate. Miss Mullen's estimation of the tax liability is no more precise.

18 Mr Ruse's approach to determining the multiplier was very similar to that of Miss Mullen and he too took Amstrad as a comparable company, although he described a number of limitations on its use as a comparator. (He rejected Electrocomponents as only a small part of its turnover was generated by goods *(pg367e)* similar to those dealt in by RML.) Amstrad had a much higher corporation tax rate (less susceptible to change than was RML's). Its capitalisation was based upon sales of comparatively small parcels of shares while what was at issue here was the disposal of the majority shareholding. As it was a listed company, Amstrad's shares were more marketable than those in RML. There was no realistic prospect of a flotation of RML in the near future; Mr Ruse did not regard the taxpayer's *(pg367f)* prediction of flotation within 5 years from 1982 as 'the near future'. Amstrad's price-earnings multiple of 11.6 was, as he accepted, low for the industry sector but it had to be regarded as significant to RML's valuation because of the comparability of the two companies and must be given substantial weight in determining the multiplier to be used in this case.

19 He also thought it pertinent to take into account the level of prevailing *(pg367g)* interest rates. On 31 March 1982 base rate was 13%. At that time, he thought, an investor would require a return of not less than 10% and for that reason a multiplier of 10 was the maximum he thought appropriate. He accordingly put the value of the company at 10 multiplied by £85,000, that is £850,000, of which the taxpayer's 66% share amounted to £561,000. *(pg367h)*

20 What I am required to determine is the price which a willing purchaser would pay to a willing vendor for the taxpayer's shareholding in RML. It is inherent in the valuation that the parties should have equal access to

information. The prospective purchaser can insist on seeing even confidential information: see *Caton's Administrators v Couch (Inspector of Taxes)* [1995] STC (SCD) 34 (reversed on other grounds [1996] STC 201, [1997] STC 930) and I must assume that he would do so. I must *(pg367j)* also assume that the purchaser has no special reason for buying, nor the vendor a special reason for selling. The purchaser must buy at the determined price; he cannot simply walk away if he does not like it. Similarly the vendor is bound to sell; he cannot refuse to do so if he dislikes the price. The sale is of course hypothetical and the hypothesis brings with it a number of imponderables. As Lord Fleming put it in *Salvesen's Trustees v IRC* (1930) 9 ATC 43 at 45 'The estimation of the value of shares by a highly artificial standard which is never applied in the ordinary share market must be a matter of opinion and does not consist of precise scientific or *(pg368a)* mathematical calculation.' An obvious question is whether the company would suffer because the taxpayer was no longer the controlling shareholder, or would prosper better because of his absence. It seems to me I must leave such considerations out of account, and treat RML, neutrally, as a continuing business.

21 I am satisfied that the premise from which Miss Mullen proceeds is unrealistic. I readily accept that a purchaser would look closely at the 1981 results, *(pg368b)* and would regard them and those achieved in preceding years as relevant to the determination of the price. He would certainly give them proper weight in reaching his conclusion but I am not persuaded that he would use them as the starting point. I agree with Mr Ruse that he would scrutinise all of the available information up to the last possible moment before the conclusion of his purchase. A prudent prospective purchaser would be aware of the adverse currency movements at the *(pg368c)* time (he could scarcely have been unaware of them since they were extensively reported in the press) and he would know that the company was heavily exposed to purchases in dollars, and that it had failed to take any steps to hedge against the risks. I cannot accept that a prudent purchaser would regard a recalculation of the actual results in the year to 31 March 1982 by the use of historical exchange rates as a sensible basis for the determination of a fair price. He would, at the most, *(pg368d)* regard the recalculated figure as an indication of what might be achieved with better management but he would also be aware that, however successful RML might henceforth be in hedging against adverse currency movements, it could not protect itself against movements which had already occurred. It would have to buy products at the prevailing exchange rate, and not at an historical rate. On 31 March 1982 the exchange rate was $1.82 to £1, considerably lower than the rate *(pg368e)* of $2.13 to £1 which Miss Mullen had used, and it would have to be assumed that RML's purchases would be correspondingly expensive, at least in the short term until a UK manufacturing base had been established. I recognise that RML's competitors were probably also affected by currency movements, to a greater or lesser extent.

22 For the same reason, it seems to me that Mr Ruse's adjustments of the *(pg368f)* profits to take account of excessive expenditure are appropriate; I am satisfied that a prudent purchaser would examine costs of that kind and would be willing to take potential savings into account in his valuation. Rather surprisingly, Mrs Fraser attacked Mr Ruse's approach by contending that it was arbitrary. To some extent it is, but it struck me as fair, and approached in a reasonable and measured manner, as was his suggested 'hope' factor. I remark only that Miss Mullen did not suggest *(pg368g)* either adjustment, although her rather different approach made them less relevant.

23 I also reject Mrs Fraser's repeated contention (with which Miss Mullen dissociated herself) that Mr Ruse had based his evidence upon the audited accounts for the year to 31 March 1982. She argued that a prospective purchaser would not have these figures – which Mr Ruse readily agreed – and that it was *(pg368h)* unreasonable to base any calculation on the outcome for the year. Mr Ruse's point, with which I entirely agree, was that the actual figures for 1982 were the best available guide to what the hypothetical purchaser, making proper enquiries, would have been able to discover from the available information. I accept the validity of the argument advanced by Michael Gibbon, counsel for the respondent, that Miss Mullen's approach of largely ignoring what actually happened during the course of *(pg368j)* the year to 31 March 1982 cannot be right.

24 It will be apparent that I prefer Mr Ruse's approach to that of Miss Mullen. Nevertheless, I have concluded that, overall, the hypothetical purchaser would take a rather more generous view than Mr Ruse. I am satisfied that he would consider whether RML had a sound business to whose true profitability the pre-1982 figures were a realistic and reliable guide, and would ask himself whether the year to 1982 (using the information to be gleaned from the company's books) was an isolated poor year whose outcome might not be repeated. Prudently, he would be aware *(pg369a)* that RML's results could not be improved immediately – it would have to adjust to a more expensive dollar and it also seems to have been left with a good deal of highly-priced stock; but he would, in my opinion, take a view about the longer term.

25 A simple average of the results for the three years to 31 March 1982, after *(pg368b)* making the adjustments suggested by Mr Ruse, is £141,000. For the reasons I have given, I do not think a prudent purchaser would regard that as a figure on which he could realistically base his valuation; he would want to discount it to some extent. Some protection against the low value of the pound, and further currency movements, could be obtained by beginning manufacture in the UK (though that would not be immediate and would incur some cost) and by currency hedging. The purchaser would also be concerned, I think, by the significant (and, at least to *(pg368c)* me, largely unexplained) increase in overhead costs during the year. Nevertheless, Mr Ruse's suggested £100,000 seems to me to be extremely cautious, and one which attaches too much weight to one poor year, for which there is some explanation, and too little to the earlier years. There is no suggestion in Mr Ruse's report, or elsewhere, that the business itself was in decline; I am satisfied that this was a sound business which had suffered a setback. *(pg368d)*

26 Achieving a fair valuation is, to a very large extent, a question of impression; although both of the experts have proceeded upon established valuation principles, ultimately their conclusions depend on informed opinion rather than precise arithmetic. I cannot claim that my own view is based on anything more than a feel for what is right. While I am satisfied that, overall, Mr Ruse's approach is to be *(pg368e)* preferred, to my mind it takes too little account of the fact that the hypothetical purchaser, if he were to buy the shares at all, would do so only if he took an optimistic, even if cautiously optimistic, view of RML's future prospects. I am satisfied that such a purchaser would be willing to uplift the 1982 results (or, to be pedantic, what he would anticipate to be the 1982 results) by rather more than the £18,000 (after adjustment) which Mr Ruse proposes. *(pg368f)*

27 I have come to the conclusion that a fair figure for the net sustainable pre-tax annual profit of the business at 31 March 1982 is £115,000. That figure takes into account the better results, and the history of growth, to March 1981, the poor results in the year to March 1982, the cost of taking protective measures, Mr Ruse's proposed adjustments of the overheads and the comparatively high level of stock held by RML at 31 March 1982. A calculation of the effective rate of corporation *(pg368g)* tax which the company actually suffered is no longer possible, as I have mentioned. Mr Ruse suggested 15% but on the assumption that pretax profits were £100,000; Miss Mullen did not make any formal suggestion although her figures assume 22%. The effective rate of tax in the three years to 31 March 1982 was 16.6%. It seems to me that adopting a 15% rate is likely to be excessively generous to the taxpayer and I propose to adopt the average rate of 16.6%. Net after tax earnings are *(pg368h)* therefore £95,910 per year.

28 I prefer, too, Mr Ruse's arguments about the appropriate multiplier. I accept – as indeed both experts indicated – that the average rate for the electrical sector at the time was 17.6 but that sector covers a very broad range of businesses and it must, I think, be treated with great caution. If, as both experts also agreed, *(pg368j)* the most directly comparable company was Amstrad, whose price-earnings ratio at the time was 11.6, it seems to me that an investor in this company (particularly one willing to take some chance on the future) and buying less readily marketable shares, would expect to fix his price by reference to a smaller multiplier. I have concluded that I should determine this appeal on the basis that Mr Ruse is right at a multiplier of 10.

29 I accordingly conclude that the value of the entire company at 31 May 1982 was £959,100 and that the value of the taxpayer's shareholding was *(pg369a)* £633,006.

30 I am aware that that determination does not dispose of the appeal since assessments are now to be made and, if they are not agreed, further determinations will be necessary, and that there are ancillary issues outstanding. I accordingly give the parties permission to apply for directions for a continuation of the appeal in such manner as may be appropriate. *(pg369b)*

Case 47
De Jongh Weill v Mean Fiddler Holdings

[2005] All ER (D) 331

High Court

22 July 2005

This extraordinary case is included for two reasons: (1) to demonstrate that it is not only the valuation of shares that may be required but even the value of the denial of a opportunity to acquire shares; and (2) to show the judicial approach to the valuation of financial instruments.

In an earlier case, the court held that there was a contract on 26 July 1999 under which Mr Vince Power obtained the services of Mr Weill, the remuneration for which included an undertaking that Mr Power's company, Mean Fiddler Holdings Ltd, would issue warrants to Mr Weill, which, if exercised, would give him a shareholding of 2 per cent of the company. It was to be entirely at the choice of Mr Weill whether or not, and, if so, when the option was exercised.

Mr Power and Mr Weill fell out and the .com revolution fell out of favour with investors. In August 1999 the value of the company was suggested to be £33,500,000, giving a value per share of 70p. On 6 November 2001 the company was listed and shares commenced trading at 49p per share. The share price subsequently dropped to 10p per share.

No warrants were ever issued to anyone, and certainly not to Mr Weill.

The value of a warrant is, of course, the difference between the share price and the amount payable under the warrant. Warrants can have a value of £nil, which is the case when the current share price is below the warrant exercise price. As we, in this case, are not looking at a specific date of exercise, the calculation of the value of a warrant is not an easy arithmetic calculation. We have to ask: 'if the warrants had been issued to Mr Weill, at what share price would he have exercised them?'

In this case there were no warrants. There is, nevertheless, a value to be placed on the damages that fall to be paid to Mr Weill for being denied the issue of warrants due to him. The authority for this dates from 1911. In *Chaplin v Hicks* [1911] 2 KB 786 an aspiring actress, Miss Chaplin, entered a competition the prize for which was guaranteed employment for a defined period. In consequence of a mistake made by Mr Hicks, Miss Chaplin was not able to attend the selection process. Damages were awarded to Miss Chaplin calculated as the value of the employment she would have obtained had she won the competition *multiplied by* the chance that Miss Chaplin would have had of being the winner of the competition had she been correctly entered. In his judgement, Vaughan Williams LJ said:

'the fact that damages cannot be assessed with certainty does not relieve the wrong-doer of the necessity of paying damages for his breach of contract.'

It was on the basis of this judgement that Judge Bruce Cole QC computed damages payable to Mr Weill. The case gives a useful description of the lost chance in this case (**case 47 paras 40–56**).

Judge Bruce Cole QC then states:

'I think that the proper course is to proceed from the base that Mr Weill had the warrants in meanfiddler.com plc. Then, in order to be able to reach a sensible or clear base from which to proceed with the valuation exercise, I make the finding of fact that on the balance of probability Mr Weill would not have realised the underlying assets in the plc warrants. Rather, he would have held on to the warrants and sought to make money out of them by selling them – not, I should say, by hedging them himself on the FTSE-100, as he suggested at some stage. (The experts were agreed that he could not have done this.) His potential profit lay in the warrants and, in particular, in their time value and their potential volatility. The fact is, as I think Mr Lawler said, the warrants were tradeable and they were potentially more valuable than the underlying shares because of their unique character as an asset: their time value and their volatility presented for an investor a very cheap way of obtaining an interest in the company. A speculation, yes, but for investors prepared to make a speculation on what they could get from a warrant for, say, less than half the price of a share, was a right to a share which, if the warrants came 'into the money' would cost them nothing. That is, for a price based on the value of the warrant they could put themselves into the position of being able to call for the shares if and when they came 'in the money' without any net expenditure on their part. Thus, I proceed on the basis that Mr Weill had the plc warrants and would then have sought to profit from trading them in what ever way he could in order to make a profit from them.'

(case 47 para 59)

'The next step is to try to determine what sort of price Mr Weill could have got for these meanfiddler.com plc warrants on the market. It is obvious from just stating what the issue is that the task is fraught with uncertainties and difficulties in terms of reaching a precise figure. Of course, I cannot do that. The 'broad brush' requires (or enables) me to look at the matter widely, making what discounts I think are appropriate to reflect the not inconsiderable uncertainties. Not only is it an exercise in looking backwards and trying to say what would have been, but it also involves looking at a highly uncertain and rather esoteric area of speculative trading. The difficulty of my task is underlined by the emphatic manner in which the professional witnesses contradict each other and disagree with each other's conclusions and opinions. This is partly because what they are being asked to do is put themselves back in late 2001 and to speculate what might have been possible in what was an esoteric corner of the financial world. This is further reason for my reminding myself that my final decision must be one which can do no more than reach a fairly 'rough and ready' result given that I am venturing into the world of financial speculation. When I mentioned to one of the experts that it seemed to me that the best thing to do in such a situation was always to hedge one's position carefully he replied that that was not of the essence of this sort of market which was really one of speculation.'

(case 47 para 66)

'… taking into account all the available (and, at time, conflicting) evidence which I have head from the professional I have come to the conclusion that it is appropriate to value the warrants on the basis of a 50% volatility level.'

(case 47 para 72)

This remarkable case concludes with a remarkable judgement:

'It is therefore follows that the Claimant is entitled to damages to be calculated according to the following formula:

70% 3 Y (where Y = 50% of the value of the warrants as calculated on the basis of time expiring on 21 Jan 04, a share price of 40p and a volatility level of 50%).'

(case 47 para 74)

Judgement

1. Background

1 JUDGE BRUCE COLES QC: This second judgment in this matter is concerned with the issue of damages. A split trial was ordered and the question of liability was tried in 2002.1 refer to my judgment dated 26th January, 2003 and to the detailed exposition of the facts which gave rise to this claim. The issue on the trial of liability was whether there was a contract between the Claimant and the Defendant for the provision of financial consultancy services by the Claimant to the Defendant. I found that there was such a contract and that it was contained in a letter sent by the Claimant to the Defendant (and countersigned on behalf of the Defendant) dated 19.8.99. The contract provided that in return for the provision of these financial consultancy services by the Claimant, the Defendant would, inter alia, grant warrants to purchase shares in the Defendant. The issues now before the Court are whether there was a breach of that contract and, if so, what damages, if any, the Claimant has suffered as a consequence of any such breach.

2. Basic Facts

2 I have set out the terms of the letter of 19.8.99 in full at para. 23 of my first judgment, but it is convenient to set out the central terms of the letter again, here. After stating that his 'brief was to develop the internet presence of the company and to add value to its 'normal day to day operations', the letter stated that Mr. Weill's 'compensation for this activity' was to include a monthly fee and reasonable expenses for 6 months starting from 26.7.99. It then went on to state

> 'in addition, warrants to purchase shares in the Mean Fiddler Group Ltd will be granted to a company representing my family interests for 2% of the company at the current mutually agreed valuation of £22.5 million, 3% of the company at a valuation of 50% higher than the current valuation, and 5% of the company at a valuation of 100% higher than the current valuation for 4 years.'

It is common ground that the reference to the Mean Fiddler Group Ltd. was a reference to the Defendant, Mean Fiddler Holdings Ltd. (I shall hereinafter refer to Mean Fiddler Holdings Ltd. as 'Holdings')

3 It is relevant to note that at the date of this agreement the main entity in what was called the Mean Fiddler Group of companies was Holdings and it was wholly owned by Mr. Vince Power, the founder of the business. Holdings was the parent company of the group which consisted of a number of different companies all concerned with the entertainment industry. At first it was anticipated that Holdings would float on the Stock Exchange on the alternative investment market, but because of the financial state of Holdings that plan was abandoned. However, Mr. Weill then recommended that the intellectual property rights in Holdings were a valuable asset and that they be 'spun off into a separate company which would then be floated and the cash raised on this floatation could then be injected into Holdings to 'shore it up' for the intermediate future. As a result of these recommendations a new company, 'meanfiddler.com pic', was formed in April, 2000 and its shares admitted to trading on the Alternative Investment Market (A.I.M.) in May, 2000. (I am told that the use of lower case in the name of the new company was to reflect its positioning in the 'dot.com revolution') Mr. Weill obtained a 10% share in the equity of this new company. This company later became known as 'Annestown Ltd.' and then 'Mean Fiddler Music Group plc.' Although Holdings and the new meanfiddler.com plc had common shareholders, they had no relationship, inter se. Neither was the subsidiary of the other. Holdings had sold its intellectual property rights to meanfiddler.com plc and was paid £2 million for this transaction. Mr. Weill became a director of meanfiddler.com plc at the time of its incorporation and received shares in that company.

4 Mr. Weill started his consultancy at the time of the agreement and worked in that capacity until October, 2000 when there was a falling out between him and the senior management of the group. It was Mr. Power's evidence that this falling out was over a bank account which, he says, the Claimant opened and from which he paid monies belonging to Holdings to a third party, not connected with the business. Mr. Weill denied this, but it is clear that there was a falling out between them and it is also clear that there was quite a degree of animosity on Mr. Power's part towards the Claimant. This was exacerbated by the commencement of these proceedings by Mr. Weill on 21.10.01 and it seems to have been further exacerbated by the adverse finding on liability against Mr. Power's company.

5 The 'dot.com' business was not as successful as anticipated and the decision was taken that there should be a restructuring of the group of companies. To this end a decision was taken in the latter part of 2000 to affect a 'reverse takeover'. The event has been called the 'RTO' during the course of the proceedings and I shall refer to it by that acronym. The RTO was conducted in accordance with the rules of A.I.M. Each company involved in the RTO had its own professional advisers and they operated at 'arms length' during the procedure. A public announcement of the intended RTO was made to the stock market on 16.1.01. It was announced that meanfiddler.com pic was going to buy the whole of Holdings so as to bring Holdings and meanfiddler.com plc under one 'umbrella'. What was involved was that the existing listed plc (meanfiddler.com plc) would issue shares and then transfer a proportion of those shares to the Holdings' shareholders in return for the transfer to the plc of those shareholders' shares in Holdings. In other words, all the shareholders in the private company, Holdings, would get equivalent interests in the enlarged public company (which later became known as Mean Fiddler Music Group plc, hereinafter called 'MFMG plc.') and this company would be the 100% owner of Holdings.

6 Mr. Weill never had any warrants issued either to him or to any company of his nomination. It is this fact which gave rise to this claim by him for specific performance and/or damages for the loss of the opportunity, which it is claimed would otherwise have been his, to realise profits from the warrants. Mr. Weill had referred to the question of a family company having the right to purchase up to a total of 10% in Holdings in a letter which he sent to two of his fellow directors in Holdings on 25.10.00 (C/49). He said this was an 'active contingent claim'. A more formal reference was made to the claim to these warrants in the letter from Addleshaw-Booth & Co (the Claimant's solicitors) dated 20.11.00 and sent to Mr. Power. The letter says:

> '... by an agreement dated 19th August, 1999 ... our client was granted warrants to purchase shares in (Holdings). As you will appreciate, the granting of those warrants was fundamental to the business arrangement entered into between (Holdings) and its affiliated companies and our client.'

The letter went on to request

> 'confirmation by return that the warrants have been correctly reflected in the books and records of (Holdings) and that all proper and necessary disclosure of them shall be made to all and any parties and/or regulatory authorities that have or may have an interest in the corporate structure and/or share ownership of (Holdings).'

On 8.12.00 Finers, Holding's solicitors, wrote denying that the Claimant was entitled to call on Holdings to grant him warrants or that he had any other rights over its shares. It said that his receipt of the shares in meanfiddler. corn pic was the performance of that obligation. In their reply of 22.12.00 Addleshaw Booth & Co. denied that the issue of shares in the new company was a performance of the agreement of 19.8.99 and threatened to issue proceedings within 14 days if a satisfactory response was not forthcoming. As I have said, on 16.1.01 an announcement was made that there was a conditional agreement whereby meanfiddler.com plc was going to acquire the entire issued share capital of Holdings. This was the first public intimation of the RTO, although it had been discussed at meanfiddler.com plc towards the end of the previous year (2000).

The RTO and related events

7 It is, I think, necessary to look in a little more detail at the mechanics and the events surrounding the RTO and the trading history of the re-structured business following the RTO. It took some time to effect the RTO and, in particular, to find sufficient funds. It was initially decided that meanfiddler.com plc should raise £8 million by the issue of shares. The prospectus was not issued until July, 2001 and the gap in time was no doubt accounted for by negotiations for the placement of the shares.

8 It was, of course, necessary to value Holdings for the purpose of the RTO and through their independent advisers each company agreed an objective valuation of Holdings at £33.5 million. It is to be noted that this valuation was some £11 million more than the value put on Holdings at the time Mr. Weill entered into the contract with Holdings in August, 1999. It was nearly 50% more and put the value of a share in Holdings at 70p.

9 An essential step in the RTO was the agreement of the shareholders in Holdings to sell their shares to meanfiddler.com plc. This agreement was expressed in a document dated 28.9.01 which is at Bundle D2/p.98. The agreement, which is headed 'Agreement for the Sale and Purchase of the Entire Issued Share Capital of Mean Fiddler Holdings Limited', recites that 'the Sellers (shareholders in Holdings) wished to sell and the Buyer (Meanfiddler.Com PLC) wished to purchase all of the issued share capital of (Holdings)' and the total consideration for the shares was fixed at £33,5000,000. The sellers received the number of shares shown against his/her name in Schedule 5 of the Agreement 'at the price of 70p. per share.' As well as being a 'seller', Mr. Power was also a separate party to the Agreement as 'the Covenantor' and in that capacity he warranted and represented to the Buyer in Clause 6.1 that, except as fairly set out in the Disclosure Letter, each of the Warranties in Schedule 2 was true and accurate in all respect and not misleading at the date of the agreement. In Schedule 2 the following warranty was given by Mr. Power:

> '2.3 No person has the right or has claimed to have the right (whether exercisable now or at a future date and whether contingent or not) to subscribe for, or to convert any security into any shares or loan capital or other securities of the Group Company.'

The exception referred to in the Disclosure Letter was a claim by a Mr. Tony Moore, a former director of meanfiddler.com plc, to share options held by him. The disclosure stated that the company had been advised that the entitlement to the options had lapsed. The 'Group Company' was defined as meaning meanfiddler.com plc 'and each of the Subsidiaries'. 'Subsidiary' is defined as meaning 'a subsidiary as defined in s.736 of the Companies Act, 1985'. Mr. Onslow makes the point that Mr. Weill had claimed to have the right to warrants in respect of shares in Holdings through which he would have had a right to shares: i.e., the warrants had not been issued to him so he did not have the 'right' to subscribe for or to convert any security into shares, but he had nevertheless claimed to have this right in October 2000 through his solicitors' letter. At the date of the Agreement Holdings was not a subsidiary of meanfiddler.com plc – they were, as I have already observed, parallel companies in the group but Holdings was not the subsidiary of meanfiddler.com plc. Mr. Moverley Smith did not argue the point and nor was there any evidence as to the substance of the advice given to Mr. Power by the professionals. Although there may be some question as to the extent of the disclosure required in Schedule 2, Part I there is a farther representation in Schedule 2, Part IV under the heading 'Litigation'. Para 3.1 states as follows:

'The Company (i.e., Holdings) is not engaged in any material litigation, arbitration, mediation, conciliation, expert determination, adjudication or other dispute resolution process as claimant or defendant.'

Para. 3.3 provides:

'There are no disputes, claims, proceedings or other dispute resolution processes as referred to in paragraphs 3.1 and 3.2 pending or threatened by or against the Company (Holdings) and the Sellers are not aware of any circumstances which are likely to give rise to any such disputes, claims, proceedings or other dispute resolution process.'

10 I shall return to this point later, but I have set out the terms of the Agreement for the sale of these shares in Holdings in some detail because Mr. Onslow says that there was either a misrepresentation by Mr. Power or he failed to make a full declaration in terms of the Agreement. I am not so sure that he is right that the disclosure in Schedule 2, Part 1 is deficient, although I am not so doubtful about that in Part IV. The evidence from Mr. Power was that his professional advisers did not think it was necessary to disclose this claim by Mr. Weill. No evidence was given as to the basis of this advice.

11 At any rate, the Prospectus was issued on 12.7.01 and the purpose and manner of the RTO was spelt out in the Introduction to that document. It is worth noting the following points from this Introduction:

(i) It reiterated that it was the intention that meanfiddler.com plc would acquire the entire issued share capital of Holdings for a consideration of £3.5 million to be satisfied by the issue of shares in meanfiddler.com plc to Holdings's shareholders.

(ii) The purpose of the RTO was to raise additional working capital for the enlarged group of companies under the umbrella of the Meanfiddler organisation.

(iii) The aim was to raise £8 million, before expenses, by way of an offer of up to 11,428,571 shares at 70p per share, subject to the minimum amount being raised. The minimum gross amount was £5 million. The net minimum amount was £4 million, allowing for the expenses of the RTO at £1 million.

(iv) The Prospectus noted that the acquisition was classified as a 'reverse takeover' under the AIM Rules and therefore required the approval of shareholders.

(v) Meanfiddler.com plc was also seeking shareholder approval to change its name to Meanfiddler Music Group PLC ('MFG').

(vi) It referred to the Acquisition Agreement and to Mr. Power's willingness to give 'normal warranties'.

(vii) Part VI of the Prospectus document was headed 'Additional Information' and stated, inter alia, at para. 11.4.1 that all Loan Stock in Holdings would be converted into ordinary shares prior to the completion of the sale of the shares. Mr. Onslow places some reliance on this, saying that it is an indication that what neither company was prepared to contemplate was the idea that after the RTO there should be some stray holders of contingent interests. The same point is also made in relation to the heading of the Agreement for the sale of the shares – viz., 'Agreement for the Sale and Purchase of the *Entire* Issued Share Capital ... ' (see para. 9, above.) (My emphasis.) The relevance of this to the valuation of any right which the Claimant may have held will become clear later.

(viii) At para. 13, under the heading 'Litigation', it was stated that save for what was stated in para. 13.2, 'no legal ... proceedings are active, pending or threatened against ... (Holdings) which are having or may have a significant effect on the Enlarged Group's financial position.'

12 The launch of the RTO did not meet with market approval and as a result the share value of meanfiddler.com plc dropped dramatically. Then, within a few days it was discovered that a mistake was made in the valuation of meanfiddler.com plc and a Supplementary Prospectus had to be issued on 26.7.01. This postponed the RTO to 20.8.01. At the same time as the Supplementary Prospectus was being issued Mr. Weill repeated his claim to warranties. On 18.7.01 his solicitors e-mailed the Defendant's solicitors again saying that their client had little option but to issue legal proceedings and would be issuing them within 7 days. The claim was rejected by Finers (the Defendant's solicitors) on 19.7.01. On 30.7.01 (prior to the giving of the warranties in the Sale agreement of 25.9.01) Addleshaw Booth & Co. wrote a formal 'letter before action' to Finers. It concluded in these terms:

'Our client now requires Mean Fiddler Group Holdings Limited to grant the warrants to Conserve & Management SA. Absent your confirmation within the next 7 days that this will be done, our client will be left with no choice but to issue proceedings.'

As I have already observed, proceedings were in fact issued on 21.10.01. It is of some interest to note that during the course of this trial the Defendant disclosed an advice which Finers gave to them at that time. The advice is contained in a letter dated 24.10.01 (F1/37A). Contrary, in part, to their case on the liability issues, in it the solicitors acknowledge the existence of an agreement in the letter of 19.8.99, but go on to advise that this was superseded by a subsequent agreement giving the Claimant shares in meanfiddler.com plc.

13 The closing date for the new issue was 21.8.01 and the minimum amount which had to be subscribed was £5 million. They failed to raise this amount and therefore the RTO had itself failed. Eventually, however, further financial support was forthcoming from the Bass Group which subscribed for 5 million shares, thus bringing the amount subscribed overall to £5 million. The formal agreement for the purchase of the shares in Holdings was executed on 28.9.01 and on 26.10.01 the RTO was approved by an EGM of meanfiddler.com plc and on 6.11.01 shares in meanfiddler.com plc was relisted and commenced trading at 49p. per share.

3. Issues relating to the construction of the contract

The Warrants
14 Having set out the matrix of facts in the context of which this matter has to be resolved, I turn now to examine just what it was that Holdings had promised to give Mr. Weill by way of payment for the provision of his financial services. This, I think, properly comes under the heading of 'construction of the contract'. He was to get 'warrants to purchase shares' in Holdings. A substantial amount of time was spent during the hearing addressing just what this meant — or, rather, just what these warrants were to be. The Claimant contends that the warrants were to take the form of a transferable financial instruments granting the holder the right to subscribe for shares in Holdings in amounts and at prices calculable by reference to the percentages and valuations specified in the Agreement. He claims that the warrants were to have a 4 year term – i.e., they were to be exercisable at any time within 4 years of issue. Thus, the agreement provided that the holder of the warrant would have the right to subscribe to shares worth up to 10% of the value of the company. If he wanted to purchase 2% of the share capital he would have to pay 2% of the mutually agreed valuation of £225 million – i.e., £450,000. By way of observation it is worth noting here that he would obviously not pay or 'put up' the £450,000 unless the shares he was getting in Holdings were worth at least that amount. This is what is called being 'in the money'. Putting it another way, he would not exercise the option granted by the warrant unless the 'strike price' (or 'exercise price') was equal to or in excess of the share price. If he wanted to purchase another 3% of the shares he would have had to put up a further £1,012,5090 and if he wanted to purchase a farther 5% of the shares he would have to put up a further £2,250,000. Thus, if he had wanted to purchase 10% of the shares in Holdings he would have had to put up a total of £3,712,500. In his evidence Mr. Lawler, the expert called by the Defendant, after having said that the warrants referred to in this agreement were of the type which give the right to

subscribe for shares at a defined price ('strike price') at some time in the future, went on to say:

> 'Warrants are potentially valuable because if the amount that could be realised from the shares is above the exercise price then the warrant holder can exercise the options, subscribe for the shares, sell the shares on the open market, and hence make a profit. (This is often colloquially known as the warrants being "in the money"). Conversely, if the current value of the shares is below the exercise price (the warrants being "out of the money" or "under-water"), then the warrant holder would lose money if he exercised them. Clearly the warrant will be exercised only when it is "in the money".'

He then observed that if the warrants are 'out of the money' the holder will simply hold on to them in the hope that the value of the underlying shares increases, and they become valuable in the future (i.e., within the time for the exercise of the warrant). 'If', he said, 'as often happens, they lapse when they are still 'out of the money' then the holder gets nothing.' Dr Fitzgerald (the expert called by the Claimant) took this point a little further when describing how it is that warrants come to have a value. In the event that the current stock price is above the strike price, then it will have an intrinsic value. For instance, if the strike price is 500p and the stock price is 525p, then they have an intrinsic value of 25p. In addition to the intrinsic value (if any) they have what is termed a 'time value' because even if they are 'in the money' they could go even more 'in the money' in the future and this possibility gives their worth some extra premium. Thus, one could get a situation where the strike price is 500p, the shares are trading at 525p but the 500 strike call is trading in the market at 40p – for if they are assignable or transferable these rights are tradable on the market. In this situation the warrant could be described as having a premium of 40p, which consists of 25p of intrinsic value and 15p of time value. Thus, this leads Dr. Fitzgerald to conclude that 'an option which is out of the money will only have a time value. The price of such an option will be entirely determined today by the value placed by the market on potential future profits on the option (warrant) position.' (See E/1/9) When referring to the warrants contemplated by this agreement of 19.8.99 he says:

> 'The out of the money warrants would still have a positive market price, because with a four year maturity as stated in the letter, there is a good possibility that they might move to being in the money during their four year life.'

The value of a warrant partly lies in the fact that it is exercisable over a period of time and from the fact that over the life of the warrant the underlying stock may become worth more than the strike price.

15 It has never been suggested that Mr. Weill would ever have been in the position of wanting to purchase more than 2% of the shares because it was never contended that the warrants would ever have been 'in the money' to the extent of justifying the purchase of either a 5% or 10% stake. However, the Claimant further contends that the warrants would have been transferable and, further, in the event of Holdings being taken over by another Company, they would have been convertible into warrants to purchase shares in that Company. In this instance, it is said that if he had the warrants in Holdings these would have been converted into warrants to purchase shares in meanfiddler.com plc after the RTO. Thus, the main issues which have emerged in relation to these warrants are

(i) Were they assignable/transferable?

(ii) What was the date from which they were exercisable – when did the 4 year term commence?

(v) To whom were the warrants given – who can sue for any breach of contract in failure to issue warrants?

Associated with this issue is the submission by the Defendant that the Claimant has suffered no loss.

There is also a further question, namely would they have been converted into warrants in meanfiddler.com plc, or have been convertible? It is, I think, more convenient to deal with this under the heading of 'Calculation of Loss', although there is an issue of construction in this enquiry. All these questions go to the ultimate exercise which the Court has to perform, namely the valuation of the loss of the chance to have profited from the issue of the warrants in accordance with the agreement. The Claimant says that the warrants were exercisable from either January or December, 2000, that they were assignable and that they would have been converted into warrants in meanfiddler.com plc at the RTO. These maters are crucial to Mr. Weill's case. The value to him of these warrants lay in establishing that they were assignable and had a time value. A fourth point, namely convertibility, is also important to him in his quest to establish a claim of any worth because if they are/were likely to be converted into shares in the plc, they would have an enhanced value.

Were the warrants transferrable/assignable?
16 It emerged from the evidence that the term 'warrant' is used in at least two senses in commercial dealings and the two senses go to issue of their transferability. What was said is that the term 'warrant' is used to describe both employee share options and warrants (so called so as to distinguish them from options). Before determining what was the nature of the rights granted in the agreement of 19.8.99 I note that Dr. Fitzgerald, the expert called by the Claimant, made another distinction between options and warrants which may have some bearing on the case when it comes to examining what might have happened had the warrants been convertible into warrants in meanfiddler.com plc. In referring to options and warrants (properly so called), he said:

'They are both similar in that they allow the holder the right to buy the underlying security at a fixed price for a given period of time, but options are written or sold on the shares that are already issued and outstanding, meaning that when they are issued the shares simply change hands from one owner to another. Warrants, however, are securities that are issued by the company itself, and, when they are exercised, the company issues new additional shares in exchange for the agreed upon strike price. Options when exercised do not result in dilution and warrants do, therefore employee stock options are really employee stock warrants because the company has issued them and when they are exercised the company issue new additional shares, and as a dilution to existing shareholders.' (26.1.05/p.34)

Dr. Fitzgerald then went on to say that the words 'warrant' and 'option' are sometimes used inter-changeably – although I think he was saying this in the sense that the terms are often used 'loosely' and not necessarily with regard to the final but important distinctions between them.

17 Turning, then, to the distinction between employee stock options (or warrants, loosely so called) and warrants (properly so called) which are not defined in terms of the class of person who is entitled to them. The essential distinctions between employee stock options and warrants is that employee stock options are non-transferrable and come to an end at the termination of the employee's employment, whereas warrants are transferable (and therefore potentially tradable) and are usually defined in terms of a period within which they are to be exercised or called upon. Thus, the question which must be determined is whether the reference to 'warrants' in the letter of 19.8.99 was a reference to non-transferrable instruments which were equivalent to employee stock options or transferable instruments which were defined in terms of something other than by reference to the holder's employment relationship with the grantor and/or their non-transferability.

18 It is fair to say that this distinction is one which emerged quite late in the day from the Defendant. No point was taken in the pleadings as to the distinction between the two. Mr. Lawler seemed to have assumed in his Statement (E/3/115) that what Mr. Weill was promised were employee stock options. He said that these have become popular in recent years as a means of incentivising senior managers. It is also noted that Mr. Power was not aware of the distinction between employee stock options and warrants (see Day 3/25). However, he did say that he left these sorts of matters up to his CEO. In his evidence Mr. Lawler said that the term 'warrants' is , in his experience, usually used as meaning employee stock options.

19 I have concluded that when the agreement of 19.8.99 referred to the granting of 'warrants' it was referring to the granting of something different from employee stock options. It was referring to what I have referred to as 'warrants properly so called' – i.e., warrants in the sense of tradable, assignable rights to acquire shares in Holdings, which rights could be exercisable over a 4 year period at the rates set out in the letter. I have reached this conclusion taking into account the following matters:

(i) The agreement says 'warrants' and does not say 'employee share options'.

(vii) Again, Mr. Moverley-Smith says that Holdings was a closely held private company and it was unlikely that it would have welcomed the prospect of strangers acquiring shares in it. This seems to me to be conjecture and there is no real evidence to support this contention. Indeed, this runs contrary to the evidence which shows that Mr. Power and Mr. Prior both favoured Mr. Weill obtaining a share in the equity of the Company as distinct from his being given a larger consultancy fee (see para. 24, below).

(viii) As with other issues of construction or determination of the meaning of the agreement which I will address later, I have to bear in mind that this was a commercial agreement between the directors of a company which was by no means a small 'player' in the entertainment industry and a 'savvy' business man who was well aware of the potential for the Meanfiddler Group and was intent upon getting a share in this nature. Where there is such a commercial transaction it should, I think, be interpreted or viewed in a way which was commercially realistic. I shall refer later to the recent House of Lords decision in *Sirius International Insurance Co. v FM General Insurance Ltd.* and Others, The Times, December 3rd, 2004 for a recent statement approving such an approach. I mention this because it seem to me that it is much more likely that what Mr. Weill was securing for himself was a stake in the possible success of his strategy for the group as a whole, and not just something very narrowly limited to Holdings' future.

Time for exercise of warrants

20 There is an issue as to when the four year period for the exercise of the warrants would have commenced. They were not, of course, issued. The competing dates for the commencement of this four year period are:

(i) 26.7.99 – the date fixed in the letter of 19.8.99 for the commencement of the payment of the consultancy fee. It is said by the Defendant that if the consultancy fee is payable from this date, so too is the other element of the compensation i.e., the warrants.

(ii) 19.8.99 – the date of the agreement itself.

(iii) 26.1.00 – this is 6 months after the commencement of the time for payment of the consultancy fee and the day on which the entitlement to that fee ceased. It is said that thereafter the right to the warrants 'kicked in'.

(iv) 4.12.00 – two weeks from the letter of 20.11.00 in which the Addleshaw Booth & Co. wrote to the Defendants requesting confirmation that the Warrants had been issued and properly recorded in the Defendant's books and records.

21 It is, I think, a question of the construction of the contract. The words are set out in the penultimate paragraph of the letter of 19.8.99 (C/29). The first point to make is that the phrase 'for 4 years' qualifies the word 'warrants' in line 3 of that paragraph. Thus, what was to be granted by way of compensation for the services rendered were 'warrants to be exercised within 4 years', or '4 year warrants'. But, when was the 4 year period to commence? Or, to put it more crucially for the purposes of this case, when did the 4 year period for the exercise of the warrant expire? By when did Mr. Weill have to exercise his option to purchase share in Holdings? It is, of course, an important question because it goes both to the date for specific performance and also to the valuation of the warrants, given that they have, inter alia, a 'time value'.

22 The Claimant's primary submission, I think, is that the four year period starts at the point of the issue of the warrants. I am a little uncertain as to whether this is their primary submission, because upon reading the transcript I do not think that Mr. Onslow really 'nailed his colours' finally to any particular date. However, in the Claimant's Re-amended Statement of Case on Remedies the case is put that under the Agreement the Defendant was bound to issue the Warrants by 26.1.00 (the 'issue Date' being 6 months from 26.7.99) 'at the latest'. Alternatively, it is said, the date was 2 weeks from 2.11.00 (the date on which the Claimant's solicitors wrote to the Defendant requesting confirmation that the Warrants had been issued and properly recorded in the Defendant's books and records). Mr. Moverley-Smith says that the date was the commencement of the consultancy, viz., 26.7.99, alternatively, the date of the agreement itself or, alternatively, the 26.1.00. He is criticised by Mr. Onslow for being uncertain in his case, but I think that this is unfair. He is entitled to put alternative, fall-back, dates according to what argument he is advancing.

23 The problem with the interpretation which Mr. Onslow primarily submits is that it makes for uncertainty in the reading of the contract. I think that I should construe the contract in such a way, if possible, as to give it certainty. Commercially, to have the matter left in the air, as it were, would have meant that either party could have used this fact to prolong the coming into being of the right to call for the shares and to have used this as some sort of 'tactic' in their commercial bargaining. This would have been unsatisfactory and I do not believe it was the intention of the parties that this was to be the case. It is true that the Agreement refers to the fact that the warrants 'will be granted' – not necessarily 'are hereby granted' and I think regard must be had to this. I have concluded that the proper and commercial interpretation of this provision in the agreement is that the warrants were to have come into existence by the end of the first 6 months period of the consultancy – at the time when the specific fee came to and end. It therefore follows that on its true construction this contract provided for the granting of the warrants by 26.1.00 and that it is from this date that the 4 year period is to run. The right to call for the issue of shares in Holdings expired at midnight on 25.1.04.

The 'no loss' argument – For whose benefit was the contract made?

24 Before turning to the other issues pertaining to the definition or the quality of these warrants (i.e., their duration and their convertibility) I shall examine what is a fundamental next step, viz.: to whom were the rights to be given and who can sue for the failure to issue the warrants. This is what was called during argument, 'the no loss' point. It is not a privity point (as I think I first categorised it), because the Claimant was privy to the contract with the Defendant. It is, I think, a point which is properly dealt with under the main heading of 'construction of the contract'.

25 As I have already noted, the agreement provided for the issue of the warrants 'to a company representing (Mr. Weill's) family interests'. The point is taken by the Defendant that no such company was ever nominated by Mr. Weill and, in any event, the contract was not made for his benefit but for the benefit of a third party. The principle upon which the Defendant relies is that a promisee cannot sue for damages for breach of a contract which was made for the benefit of a third party because the loss is not suffered by the promisee but the third party. Mr. Moverley-Smith puts his argument as follows: 'Any award of damages is compensatory. Thus if, under the terms of an agreement between A and B, A contracts to benefit C, a third party, but in the event A fails to comply with his contractual obligations, save in exceptional circumstances B cannot recover anything other than nominal damages from A because he has himself suffered no loss.'

26 I have been referred to para. 18–042ff of *Chitty on Contracts*, 29th Edition for a discussion of the recent law on this point. At para. 18–042 it is stated as follows:

> 'Although a contract for the benefit of a third party generally does not, at common law, enable a third party to assert rights arising under it, the contract remains nevertheless binding between promisor and promisee. The fact that the contract was made for the benefit of a third party does, however, give rise to special problems so far as the promisee's remedies against the promisor are concerned. Actual performance of the contract may also lead to disputes between promisee and third party.'

Under the heading *'Promisee's Remedies'*, the learned authors note that the promisee may seek specific performance of the contract, subject to certain reservations which are discussed later in the text. It is also noted that the promisee may sue for payment of an agreed sum to himself. In relation to this it is said:

> 'It may be objected that to allow such a claim would force the promisor to do something which he never contracted to do, viz., to pay the promisee

when he contracted to pay the third party; and one view therefore is that the promisee cannot sue for the agreed sum, save in (exceptional circumstances). ... But the objection to allowing the promisee to claim payment to himself loses most of its force where the promisor would not in fact be prejudiced by having to pay the promisee rather than the third party (so long as such payment gave him a good discharge).' (para. 18–045)

The learned authors of Chitty then go on to deal with a claim by the promisee for damages for his own loss. It is said that 'the promisee might claim damages where he has suffered loss as a result of the promisor's failure to perform in favour of the third party.' (para. 18–046). The discussion then moves on to the issue of the promisee claiming damages in respect of the third party's loss and the general rule against there being any such claim is stated in the following terms:

'... in an action for damages, the claimant cannot recover more than the amount required to compensate him for his loss, so that the promisee cannot, in general, recover damages for breach of a contact made for the benefit of a third party in respect of loss suffered, not by the promisee himself, but by that third party.' (para. 18–047)

27 I was addressed by counsel and taken to the authorities in relation to this last point in order to see whether this case falls within one of the exceptions to this last stated principle. However, it seems to me that the point does not arise if, on a true reading of the facts, this is not a case where Mr. Weill is claiming damages sustained by a third party, but is really claiming damages which he himself has suffered.

28 It is, I think, necessary to examine the evidence in some detail in order to reach a view on this. It was Mr. Weill's original plan for Holdings for it to exploit the growth in internet use. He set out his 'grand scheme' in his letter of 24.5.99 – a letter which we had to examine in the first set of proceedings. His analysis was that Mean Fiddler's 'audience is already on line waiting for it to make its presence apparent' (Bundle C/l). He offered to provide his consultancy services to assist Holdings in developing this new business activity. We have examined the details of his proposals in the 'liability' proceedings, but in this letter he said that as a result of this plan he could make the company 'an attractive candidate for further equity funding from an IPO' (Initial Public Offering – i.e., the company's first offering of stock to the public when the shares would be given a market value reflecting expectations for its future growth). It was at this point that Mr. Weill then introduced the question of the consideration for his services. He said:

'To that end, I will want to be compensated largely on the commercial success of the project as a principal rather than from fee income. The market will reward the company for demonstrating brand development and scale-ability; the ability to grow profits and revenues without growing infrastructure or overheads. We can accomplish this by working together.

The terms that I have in mind are an initial retainer of £20K to insure management's full commitment and a monthly fee thereafter of £2k per month for 6 months. In addition to this, a company representing my family interests would be granted options to purchase 2% of the company at the current mutually agreed valuation, 3% of the company at a valuation 50% higher than the current valuation and 5% of the company at a valuation of 100% higher than the current valuation for 4 years.

This compensation scheme highlights a clear incentive to dramatically raise the company's market valuation and to assist it in realising the tremendous value that could be released through further commercial development.'

For what it is worth, Mr. Prior understood that what Mr. Weill was doing was putting his main 'eggs' in the equity basket and looked forward to a 'simple option agreement' being drawn up and put in place. (See his letter to Mr. Weill of 265.99 – C/4. In this letter Mr. Prior made it clear that he was very much against granting Mr. Weill any sort of substantial consultancy fee.) Mr. Weill enlarged upon his equity concept in his letter of 26.5.99 to Mr. Prior (C/6) and stated that he believed that the value to him in what was being done was to be able to share in the increase in value of the company. He said:

'From a UK compliance view, I will need to take some fee, but will waive any up front retainer if we can come up with an agreement that states Vince and the senior managers are really on board. I will work for a token monthly payment in the UK and equity options granted to the offshore company owned by the family trust. I must state in advance that I expect and fully intend that those options will cost the company literally millions of pounds, or we are both wasting our time. If we do not sincerely believe that we can increase the market value of Mean Fiddler ... by a multiple greater than three, we really should not be involved.'

Later, in a fax dated 7.8.99 addressed to Mr. Prior, Mr. Weill expanded on the idea of a trust holding the warrants. He said:

'The contract that I see is for 6 months at £2000 per month with options granted to the company owned by the trust at a valuation of Mean Fiddler at £22m. I intend to be active and associated with the company for at least a few years thereafter, and we can negotiate this and see how things evolve The monthly payment for the first 6 months is necessary under UK law for compliance, because if there isn't any payment other than the options, the authorities here can rule that the warrants were the actual compensation for working in the UK and any gain (if we are fortunate to realise a big one!) would be fully taxable in the UK. Given the nature and potential of what we are discussing here, and a company worth £22m, a payment of £12K doesn't strike me as too onerous.' (C/24)

In his fax dated 11.8.99 addressed to both Mr. Power and Mr. Prior, Mr. Weill said:

'Just to be absolutely clear, the value created by re-positioning the company into a media company as well as a media facilitator, should accrue completely to the Mean Fiddler Group. *Hence I wish to be involved, through warrants, in this entity. This is not an exercise to create wealth to third parties.*' (Italics added.)

29 When he was cross-examined by Mr. Moverley-Smith (17.1.05, pp103ff) Mr. Weill expanded on the rationale behind this method of payment. He was cross-examined about what he meant by 'compliance' and it was not very clear what he actually meant. He could not point to any specific requirement of English law or Revenue practice which would make it necessary for him to receive a consultancy fee in the UK, but what did emerge from the cross-examination was that the idea of having the warrants held by a third party trustee was something which Mr. Weill saw as a tax benefit to himself. It is clear from what he said that he envisaged that the warrants would be issued to a third party company which was independent of himself and he had identified that company as being 'Consery & Manage SA'. It was, he said, a company which was 'something separate. It is not me.' When I asked him whether it was to be done this way for 'tax purposes' he replied, 'Yes, it is for planning one's estate'. He also made it clear that he was not acting as agent for this third party company and nor was it his 'alter ego'. In re-examination Mr. Weill said that he did not believe that the Defendant company was at all concerned who would benefit from the issue of the warrants – i.e., they never expressed any interest in the identity of the beneficiary. (18.1.05/95) and it is correct to say that neither Mr. Power nor Mr. Prior when giving evidence expressed any interest in this. Indeed, as Mr. Weill said, for all they were interested, the beneficiary could well have been a company in which Mr. Weill himself had a 100% interest.

30 I have come to the conclusion that it is appropriate to take a wide view of the commercial realities of this agreement which Mr. Weill was making with Holdings. I remind myself of the judgment of Lightman J in the Court of Appeal when reviewing my earlier decision on liability. His Lordship said that it was necessary to construe the contract in its factual context: 'This requires regard to be given to the genesis of the Signed Document. It must be construed in the context of the matrix of facts in which it was entered into; and a purposive construction must be adopted.' (para.20). I am also mindful of the recent decision of the House of Lords in *Sirius International Insurance Co (Publ) v FAI General Insurance Ltd. and Others (The Times,* 3rd. December, 2004) in which Lord Steyn said that there has been a 'shift from literal methods of interpretation towards a more commercial approach'. 'The tendency', he said, 'should therefore, generally speaking, be against literalism'. When one approaches this question of who it was that this contract for services rendered by Mr. Weill was to benefit, I think it is obvious that what he was doing was making a contract with the company in which he was to be *thereat* beneficiary of the consideration which was being paid for the services which he was rendering. I have thus come to the conclusion that as this is the commercial reality of the transaction, there is no point in examining whether this case falls within one of the exceptions identified by the learned authors if Chitty. I have reached this conclusion for the following reasons:

(1) When one examines the pre-contract negotiations through the correspondence it is obvious that it was Mr Weill's purpose to benefit himself and not some third entity. Thus, he says: 'I will want to be compensated largely on the commercial success of the project **as a principal** rather than from fee income'. And, he said, 'I wish to be involved, through warrants, in this entity. (This is not an exercise to create wealth to third parties.' (My emphasis) Further, Mr. Power and Mr. Prior were much more enthusiastic about the idea of Mr. Weill being rewarded for the services he was about to render to Holdings by way of the issue of warrants (or, at least, by virtue of his obtaining an interest it the equity of the company) than by his receiving substantial payments by way of commission or retainers. No doubt they recognised the incentive element in t such a method of reward.

(2) It was of no consequence to Holdings whether Mr. Weill was to be the holder of the warrants or some third party. No third party was identified (at the stage of making the contract), so that there is no question of Holdings being compromised vis-a-vis that third party by virtue of payment to Mr. Weill.

(3) There was really no distinction as a matter of practicality between a potential third party and Mr Weill – i.e., from the point of view of the Defendant. It would, of course, have been different if, say, the contract was for the issue of the warrants to Oxfam – i.e., an organisation or entity with which he had no connection and from whom he would have received no benefit for himself.

(4) I think that it is more realistic to look on the references to nominated third parties as a method of payment – a practical rather than a substantive point. It seems clear from the correspondence that it was he who was to benefit in reality and the idea of a nominated 'off shore' company was just the way **he** was to be paid – see the fax of 11.8.99: 'I wish to be involved, through warrants, in this entity'.

(5) The fact that no third party was actually identified or nominated at this contract stage supports the point that he was doing it this way for his own benefit: it is contrary to the events as they actually were to suggest that it was someone other than Mr. Weill who was to benefit from the payment for the services. There is no question that Holdings would have been vulnerable to a claim by a third party for failure to issue the warrants.

(4) Was there a breach of contract? – The 'no breach' argument

31 Associated with the arguments advanced on what I have called the 'no loss' argument, Mr. Moverley Smith argued that there has, in fact, been no breach of contract here because Mr. Weill never nominated a third party company to whom the warrants were to be issued. Mr. Moverley Smith's argument is that all that Mr. Weill had was a simple contractual right to be issued with a certain number of shares at a certain price within a prescribed period. He says that Mr. Weill has not shown that the Defendants failed in its contractual obligation to issue shares. Indeed, no attempt was ever made to exercise the Holdings Warrants and no such claim can be made based upon a failure to honour the warrants.

32 I think that the fallacy in this argument is to mis-interpret just what it was that Mr. Weill was given under the contract. What he received was a contractual right to have warrants to purchase shares in Holdings at defined prices. The warrants themselves would give him the right (exercisable within 4 years) to shares in Holdings. What the contract of 19.8.99 said was that his 'compensation' for the rendering of his consultancy services included a monthly fee and reasonable expenses for 6 months from 26.7.99 and, 'in addition, warrants to purchase shares in' Holdings. It is true that the detailed terms of the warrants themselves had not been settled between the parties. But that does not deprive the agreement of any legal status. It is when I move on to the question of valuing the Claimant's loss that I will turn to what terms the warrants, if issued, are likely to have included – i.e., in the context of assessing just what was the nature of the 'thing' of which Mr. Weill was deprived. The key question will be the issue of 'convertibility' – would they have contained a provision for convertability into warrants in or shares in any company which might take over Holdings in this instance, meanfiddler.com plc?

33 So, there was a breach by the Defendant of its contractual obligation to issue warrants. At the earliest, Finers' e-mail of 8.12.00 (Fl/1) in reply to Addleshaw Booth and Co.'s letter of 20.11.00 was a clear denial of the claim to the warrants and at the latest, on 30.7.01 (Fl/17) Addleshaw Booth & Co (the Claimant's solicitors) wrote to Finers Stephens Innocent (the Defendant's solicitors) requiring Holdings to grant the warrants to Conseiy & Manage SA by 6.8.01. By a letter dated 3.8.01 Finers replied in the following terms:

'(Your client) should be aware that our client regards the claim as being without any merit and that no company asssociated with Mean Fiddler group will, under any circumstances, be issuing any warrants or providing any other form of consideration to your client and any action taken by him will be defended in an extremely vigorous manner. '(Fl/31)

(5) The Claimant's Loss

34 One starts with the basic proposition that what the Claimant has lost is the opportunity or chance to have made a profit from the warrants in Holdings - i.e., a profit either made by selling the warrants or by calling for the underlying shares and realising their value. It is important to bear in mind that what Mr. Weill had was a claim to a right – i.e., a claim to have warrants issued to him by Holdings which would then give him (or the holder of the warrants) the right to call for the issue of the underlying shares within the period 26.1.00 – 25.1.04. The other crucial thing for Mr. Weill to establish in this valuation 'exercise' is that what he lost in reality was the chance to make a profit from having warrants in or the right to the underlying shares in a publicly listed company–not Holdings, but meanfiddler.com plc (or MFMG). It is certainly recognised by the experts that warrants in the private company, Holdings, would have no inherent market value – although Mr. Onslow was never prepared to concede that point and argued that even this 'lowest' form of right would have some value, the chance of exploiting which Mr. Weill lost as a consequence of the breach of contract. Mr. Weill acknowledges that as at 26.1.00 warrants in Holdings would not have been of any substantial value: what he says is that if the contract had been performed and he had the warrants then, he would have held on to them because they would have been 'out of the money'. However, they (or their equivalent in meanfiddler.com. plc) came into the money at the RTO in July, 2001 and the accompanying floatation of meanfiddler.com plc on the AIM. There was agreement between the experts, Dr. Fitzgerald and Mr. Lawler, that it would have 'generally (been) illogical for the Claimant to exercise the first tranche of warrants' up to and including the time of the RTO because of the substantial time value as well as intrinsic value that would be present in the warrants. (See 'Memorandum of Discussion between Warrant Valuation Experts' 16/7/04 at E/11/174.) Mr. Weill's case is that either under the terms of the warrants as they would have been issued or by negotiations during the course of 2001 he would have obtained warrants in the publicly quoted meanfiddler.com plc. He says that if he had these warrants he would then have been in a position to either have sold them, or made a profit from 'hedging' them himself, or negotiated a buy-out by meanfiddler.com plc of his interest, or realised the intrinsic value of the Holdings warrants either by exercising them and then selling the resulting shares or sold the warrants themselves. What I am now about is determining how Mr. Weill and meanfiddler. com plc / Holdings would have dealt with each other at the time of the RTO (this being the first time when the warrants would have been worth anything of substance to Mr. Weill) and, then, if Mr. Weill would have earned a profit through the realisation of the warrants.

35 What I have to do is to value the right which Mr. Weill has lost as a consequence of the Defendant's breach of contract in failing to comply with the agreement of 19.8.99. I have to assess the value of his lost chance. Mr. Onslow submits that this is a 'classic loss of chance case' and that it qualifies as a loss of chance case by two recognised routes

(a) The warrants, if issued, would have given Mr. Weill the chance, not the certainty, of making money. Holdings was contractually bound to provide that chance, but failed to do so.

(b) The potential outcome, if the warrants had been issued, would depend upon the hypothetical acts of third parties (meanfiddler.com plc and potential purchasers of the warrants).

What I propose to do is to look first at the legal principles which govern such a claim, then to examine the evidence which has a bearing on this. This latter exercise will, of course, involve looking at the expert evidence which goes primarily to how, if at all, any value attaches in the market place to this right.

Discussion of applicable law
36 As I have said, Mr. Onslow says that this is a classic 'loss of chance' case and he says one gets there by virtue of either the principles set out in para. 35(a) or (b), above. Support for the first 'route' comes from the well known case *of Chaplin v Hicks* [1911] 2K.B. 786 – well known, that is, for the unique facts. It is the case of the actress who entered a competition to be offered a prize in the form of guaranteed employment for a defined period. The defendant failed to give her the opportunity to attend a selection process and she thereby lost the opportunity or chance to be selected as a winner in the competition. It was argued by the Defendant that the damages were of such a nature as to be impossible of assessment. It was said that the plaintiffs chances of winning a prize turned on such a number of contingencies that it was impossible for any one, even after arriving at the conclusion that she had lost her opportunity by the breach, to say that there was any assessable value to that loss. The jury had awarded her £100 damages for the loss of chance or opportunity to win the competition. In rejecting this argument Vaughan Williams L.J. said:

> 'I am unable to agree with that contention. I agree that the presence of all the contingencies upon which the gaining of the prize might depend makes the calculations not only difficult but incapable of being carried out with certainty or precision. The proposition is that, whenever the contingencies on which the result depends are numerous and difficult to deal with, it is impossible to recover damages for the loss of the chance or opportunity of winning the prize. In the present case I understand that there were fifty selected competitors, of whom the plaintiff was one, and twelve prizes, so that the average chance of each competitor was about one in four. Then it is said that the questions which might arise in the minds of the judges are so numerous that it is impossible to say that the case is one in which it is possible to apply the doctrine of averages at all. I do not agree with the contention that, if certainty is impossible of attainment, the damages for a breach of contract are unassessable. ... I wish to deny with emphasis that, because precision cannot be arrived at, the jury has no function in the assessment of damages.' (at p. 792)

His Lordship recognised that the process of assessment may involve an element of guesswork, but said that 'the fact that damages cannot be assessed with certainty does not relieve the wrong-doer of the necessity of paying damages for his breach of contract.'

37 The second proposition put by Mr. Onslow, viz., that this is a loss of chance case by virtue of the fact that the possible outcome would depend upon the hypothetical acts of third parties, is covered in the more recent Court of Appeal decision in the case of *Allied Maples Group Ltd. v Simmons & Simmons* [1995] 1 W.L.R. 1602. In this case the Plaintiff lost the opportunity of obtaining a warranty or indemnity against loss when contracting to take over the assets of the vendor, including four department stores leased by a subsidiary. The headnote sums up the central part of the judgment applicable to the present case in the following terms:

'Where the defendant's negligence consisted of an omission, causation depended on the answer to the hypothetical question of what the plaintiff would have done if the defendant had not been guilty of the omission, which was a matter of inference to be determined from all the circumstances and that where the plaintiffs loss depended on the hypothetical action of a third party he was entitled to succeed if he could show that there was a real or substantial, rather than a speculative, chance that the third party would have acted so as to confer the benefit or avoid the risk to the plaintiff.' (p1602–3).

In his judgment Stuart-Smith L.J. addressed the question of what had to be proved and to what standard. First of all he said that when it came to assessing causation as a matter of historical facts the court rightly proceeds on the basis of the balance of probability. But, the question of evaluating a lost chance is a question of quantum, not causation, and that issue does not depend upon a balance of probabilities. He said:

'Where the plaintiffs loss depends upon the actions of an independent third party, it is necessary to consider as a matter of law what it is necessary to establish as matter of causation, and where causation ends and quantification of damages begins.'

Thus, where what has to be proved is a causal link between the breach and the loss and where the breach consists of some positive act or misfeasance the question of causation is an historical fact and the court has to determine on the balance of probabilities whether the defendant's act caused the plaintiffs loss. Where the breach consists of an omission, or failure to act, causation depends not upon a question of historical fact, but on the answer to the hypothetical question, what would the plaintiff have done if ... ? Again, although the question is hypothetical, His Lordship said that 'it is well established that the plaintiff must prove on balance of probability that he would have taken action to obtain the benefit or avoid the risk.' (at p. 1610) Where, however, the question is what would a third party have done, either in addition to action by the plaintiff or independently, what the plaintiff has to show is not that on the balance of probability the third party would have acted so as to confer the benefit or avoid the risk to the plaintiff, but that there was a real or substantial chance rather than a speculative one that this would have happened. As Mr. Onslow submitted, the principle upon which the Court acts in a case of contractual failure to supply a chance is set out in the judgment of Waller LJ. in the case of *Coudert Brothers v Normans Bay Ltd.*, 27.4.04, unreported, when he said:

> 'It seems to me that one thing ought to be clear, if under their contractual obligations this is a case where the chance should have been provided unless that chance is of no real value at all or totally incapable of being quantified, damages for that loss should be recoverable.'

38 Thus, what these authorities establish for the purposes of this case is that where the Claimant says he did or would have acted in a certain way, then he must establish that on the balance of probabilities. However, when he has to show that a third party would have acted in a certain way, he has to show that there was a substantial or real chance that that would have happened. Thus, for example, in so far as he says he would have retained the warrants after they had been issued and then disposed of them in a particular way, he has to show this as a matter of the balance of probability. Where, however, he says that meanfiddler.com plc would have, for example, exchanged his warrants in Holdings for warrants in meanflddler.com plc he has to show that there was a substantial or real chance that this would have happened.

39 The next step is for the court to value the loss of the chance that a third party would have acted in a certain way. That is, once it is satisfied that the chance was a real one, one of substance and not merely negligible or fanciful, the court must evaluate that chance by applying percentage discounts to what the maximum recovery figure may be. This was the process of evaluation referred to in the solicitors' negligence case *of Mount v Barker Austin* [1998] PNLR 493 at p. 511 by Simon Brown LJ as follows:

> 'If and when the court decides that the plaintiffs chances in the original action were more than merely negligible it will then have to evaluate them. That requires the court to make a realistic assessment of what would have been the plaintiffs prospects of success had the original litigation been fought out. Generally speaking one would expect the court to tend towards a generous assessment given that it was the defendant's negligence which lost the plaintiff the opportunity of succeeding in full or fuller measure.'

The lost chance in this case
40 The next stage is to decide whether there was a real or substantial chance that the warrants which the Claimant should have obtained in Holdings under the agreement would have been converted into warrants in the publicly quoted company which was to eventually become MFMG. If the answer to this question

is in the affirmative, it is then appropriate to decide whether he had a real or substantial chance of profiting from these assets and, if so, to evaluate that chance.

41 It is Mr. Weill's case that warrants issued to him by Holdings would have contained a provision for their convertibility into warrants in meanfiddler.com plc or, if not, they would nevertheless have been converted as a matter of fact as the consequence of negotiations which were bound to have taken place between Mr. Weill and the companies during the time leading to the RTO.

42 In order to succeed in obtaining an award of damages in this case what Mr. Weill has to do is:

(i) Show that on the balance of probabilities he would have retained the warrants in Holdings until the RTO and that there was a real or substantial, rather than a speculative, chance that the plc would have converted these warrants in Holdings into warrants given by meanfiddler.com plc.

(ii) Then show that if he had had warrants issued to him in meanfiddler.com plc there was a real or substantial chance that he would he would have realised those assets and made a profit from doing so.

If I conclude in Mr. Weill's favour on the above, then I have to assess the value of his chance and in doing that I must take into account all the relevant matters, such as the uncertainties of the market, any factors which might go to reduce his percentage chances of success.

43 To summarise the Defendant's position on these points, it is as follows:

(i) The Claimant would never have obtained warrants in meanfiddler.com plc: either through the contractual provisions of the warrants themselves or as a matter of negotiation.

(ii) Even if he did obtain warrants in the plc., they would not have been tradeable.

(iii) Even if they were tradeable, he would not have made any profit out of trading them.

44 I turn, then, to examine the issue whether the Claimant would have had a real or substantial chance of obtaining warrants in meanfiddler.com plc at the time of the RTO. This issue has to be seen against the background of facts at the time. I have already examined the circumstances in which Mr. Weill came to be employed by Holdings and the expectations which were held by both him and the company as to the value which he would bring to the Company. It was his original plan that the Group (or a part of the Group) would become a public company and that this would add value to the Group as a whole. The original plan was that it would be Holdings which became a plc., but the plan was 'refined' and it was eventually decided during the course of 2001 that there would be a RTO whereby meanfiddler.com plc took over the assets of Holdings and was the 'lead' company within the Group. The point was that Mr. Weill saw himself (and was originally employed on this basis) as profiting from the growth of the Group. It is interesting to note that in his letter of 19.9.99 (which became the contract document), he actually said that he was to get warrants to purchase shares in 'the Mean Fiddler Group Ltd.'. It has been accepted and the case has proceeded on the basis that this meant Holdings, but it indicates just how the parties were thinking.

45 It was originally envisaged that Holdings would be floated as a public company, but in early 2000 the decision was taken to float a new company – meanfiddler.com plc. This was done in April 2000. In October, 2000 Mr. Weill fell out with Mr. Power. I have concluded that, on the balance of probabilities, Mr. Weill would not have taken up the shares in Holdings during 2000. They would have been of no real value to him at that time: it was a private company and the warrants would not have been 'in the money'. But in 2001 the concept of the RTO was canvassed and the situation was changing. I can not judge what Mr. Weill would actually have done as 2001 developed — although I can say that on the balance of probabilities that it seems to me he would have bided his time and waited to see what was going to happen after the RTO. He knew that an RTO was a possibility: he said in his evidence that it was being talked about before the termination of his relationship with Mr. Power. There was, of course, the initial failed attempt at the RTO in early 2001. Furthermore, the crucial point was that it was still not financially advantageous for him to have taken shares in Holdings before the RTO: the warrants would still not have been 'in the money'. The plan was that the plc would acquire the shareholding of Holdings 'in its entirety': this was the scheme declared in the RTO documents. The future was looking bright for the new venture through the RTO and I think, on the balance of probabilities, that Mr. Weill would have still been in the possession of the warrants in Holdings (had they been issued to him, of course) in the lead up to the RTO. I accept the evidence which he gave as follows:

> 'Had the Warrants been issued (in December, 1999 or January, 2000) I would have held them until there was an opportunity to realise their value. That said, I would have been keen to have realised their value as quickly as reasonably possible, as by this time I had sufficient experience of MFG to know that it was advisable. Holdings was run for the personal benefit of Vince Power and while a good business, had serious problems with management. I have little doubt that the point at which I would have sought to realise the Warrants' value was at the time of the RTO in October, 2001.' (See B2/1/5, paras. 17–18)

46 Mr. Weill said that he would have sought to have realised the value of the warrants by selling the warrants, rather than exercise the warrants and selling the underlying shares. This is understandable bearing in mind that the Claimant's meanfiddler.com plc warrants would have been 'out of the money'. I note para. 11 of Mr. Lawler's Report:

'..., if the Claimant is able to show he is entitled to warrants in Mf.com, the Claimant's Mf.com warrants were "out of the money" (i.e., the exercise price was above the value of the resulting shares) between the time of the RTO and at least February, 2004. The Claimant could not therefore have made money be exercising them before this time.'

But, of course, there would have been no profit in selling the warrants in Holdings. He would have had to have traded warrants in the plc. But would he have had warrants in the plc to trade? He would have had such warrants if the warrants as issued in Holdings (or, as they ought to have been issued in Holdings in accordance with the contract) had contained a clause to the effect that in the event of a take-over of Holdings by another company, he would have been entitled to have had his Holdings warrants exchanged for warrants in the take-over company. Alternatively, if there as no such clause, would he have been in such a position as to negotiate a conversion with the plc?

47 As I have said, at the time when the warrants ought to have been issued under the contract matters were fluid – there was discussion and debate as to how best to achieve 'the grand plan' and I believe that Mr. Weill would have been very conscious of his 'rights' and how he was going to secure his share in potential profits. Looking at the matter in the sense of assessing the value of a chance, I conclude, on the balance of probabilities, that Mr. Weill would have been at great pains to either have secured a provision in the warrants themselves for convertibility of his position into any new company which may take over Holdings in the future, or, if he had not secured such an express provision in the warrants, he would have been at great pains to negotiate himself into such a position when it became obvious that the preferred route was that of an RTO. I have made the point before and I think it is apposite here: he was very 'savvy' about what was happening and how he was going to get a 'share in the action'. He knew the potential value of warrants and how they may well be of great value to him in the event that the venture 'took off. I accept Mr. Weill's evidence (at para 22 of his second statement) which is as follows:

'Given that I was at all times aware of the potential for an RTO of Holdings by the listed entity, at the time when the warrants were actually issued it would have made sense to stipulate, and I am sure that I would have stipulated, for an 'exchange' clause to ensure that the warrants in Holdings would be transferred on a pro rata basis to equivalent interests in the publicly traded entity.'

48 But, that is only the first stage. The enquiry I am making also involves assessing what the chances were of third parties acting in a particular way – what would have been Holdings/meanfiddler.com plc's position on that? For the purpose of this exercise what I have to decide is what was the likely course they might have taken, assessed in terms of 'real or substantial' rather than 'fanciful'. Firstly, the terms of the warrants, had they been issued in accordance with the contract, would have been negotiated at a time before Mr. Weill fell out with Mr. Power. At a time when matters were proceeding as to plan. Mr. Power and his senior management had seen the merit, from their point of view, in Mr. Weill taking his 'payment' for services primarily through a device linked to the success of his advice and guidance. Secondly, I was referred to forms of warrants used in other circumstances. The ones I was referred to included a provision in their terms for convertibility in the event of a take-over or, at least, treatment of warrant holders on a par with shareholders. This is not particularly helpful because each contract will be different, depending on the circumstances. But, what is of significance is that the scheme for the RTO was that the plc would purchase 100% of the shares in Holdings. That was the intention declared in the Prospectus and that was what was done. For all practical purposes there would have been no difference between a warrant holder and a share holder. The warrant holder could have been a thorn in the side of the negotiations and would have had some 'muscle'.

49 The RTO was proving to be difficult – at least, they were having difficulty in raising funds and I think it is relevant to comment that if Mr. Weill was minded to 'stir things up' it would have reacted adversely on the RTO process and the search for funds. If Mr. Weill had held warrants in Holdings and his interest was not being properly recognised, either by being converted into warrants in meanfiddler.com plc or by Mr. Weill not being given shares in meanfiddler.com plc or some form of pay-out, then I am sure that there would have been a major dispute. Such a dispute may have been embarrassing for the plc. They were not in a very strong bargaining position. Furthermore, the value of the warrants to Mr. Weill lay in them being converted into warrants in the plc and, perhaps to a lesser extent, in their continuance given their 4 year 'life'. This would have been a strong motivation for Mr. Weill to get the best he could out of the situation.

50 The Defendant say that the warrants would not have contained a conversion clause and nor would they have converted the warrants in Holdings into warrants in the plc. When Mr. Power gave evidence he expressed some hostility towards Mr. Weill. He did not like him: not only because of his having established his case on liability, but also because of the circumstances which gave rise to the breakdown in their relationship. There is the strange evidence as to meanfiddler.com plc's failure to make a full disclosure of the on-going dispute with Mr. Weill. I do not have to make any decisions in relation to that episode, but I do observe that I was surprised that Mr. Power and his advisers had not made full disclosure of Holdings on-going dispute with Mr. Power over these very matters. What it perhaps shows is that the plc was feeling rather vulnerable about Mr. Weill's claims and this, in turn, gives rise to the consideration that perhaps there is weight in what Mr. Weill says about the company being bound to negotiate with him about his warrants.

51 The other side of the argument is that it would not have hindered the RTO were meanfiddler.com plc not prepared to convert options in Holdings to similar options in the plc. It would not have affected the plc's ability to properly manage Holdings for there to be outstanding warrants in Holdings. Furthermore, there would have been very little likelihood of Mr. Weill actually exercising his warrants in Holdings: he would have had to pay a large amount of money for a 2% holding in a subsidiary company. Not an attractive deal for Mr. Weill. Evidence was given by Mr. Dean James, the Chief Organising Officer of MFMG that 'given the relationship between the Claimant and the Board of Mf.com, there is no way that Mf.com would have given the Claimant warrants in it or have paid the Claimant for his warrants in the Defendant.' Mr. James recognised that there were contingent interests in Holdings which were 'rolled over' into the plc, viz., the options which Mr. Melvin Benn held and which he, Mr. James, also held. These were, however, employee share options which were granted as an employee and were, says Mr. James, in a different category to the warrants which Holdings had contracted to give to Mr. Weill. Mr James also makes the point that 'there would have been no reason to give Mr. Weill the right to convert his warrants into shares in meanfiddler.com plc in light of the fact that he had already been permitted to subscribe at par for founder shares in Mf.com'. I find this a less convincing point, given that this was done at a separate time from the granting of the right to the options. I should say that I do not place a great deal of reliance upon the practice recommended by the 'FSA' (the Finnish Services Authority) referred to by Dr. Fitzgerald, but I do note the view expressed by Julian Redmayne in his book on Equity Warrants (Euromoney Publications) which was as follows:

> 'It is of critical importance to warrant holders that the warrants' time value is protected as well as their intrinsic value. When the underlying share is trading below the exercise price, the warrant possesses no intrinsic value. In that event time value protection is particularly important for warrant holders as it is their only potential source of value. In the event of a company going into liquidation the warrants generally expire worthless. If the company is subject to a takeover bid, there are generally provisions protecting the interests of warrant holders.'

52 When Mr. Power gave his evidence it was clear that he was very bitter about Mr. Weill and has been for some time. In his statement he said:

> 'The Court has ruled that Mr. Weill had warrants at the time of the RTO.' (This is not quite right: the ruling was that he had a contractual right to warrants) 'However, the Defendant would not, in any circumstances, have paid a cash amount to Mr. Weill to buy out the warrants. The relationship between the Board of Directors and Mr. Weill had been completely eroded. As I explained in my first witness statement, the Board of Mf.com was extremely concerned that Mr. Weill had entered into contracts without proper Board authority Also, he had retained more than £100,000 in an account which he had opened for Mf.com without telling anyone about the

account; further, contrary to company policy, he appointed himself sole signatory.'

In his cross-examination by Mr. Onslow Mr. Power gave a further demonstration of his annoyance, or anger, over Mr. Weill. Thus, he said:

'He took the £100,000. He didn't disclose it. He disclosed it when he was threatened by myself and admitted it. He had no authority to do it and then he was sacked. It's absolute lies. He was shaking like a leaf when I actually met him in the cafe off Wigmore Street. He took the money He looked like someone who had been caught out.'

This was not put to Mr. Weill and I do not have to try this issue raised by Mr. Power about the circumstances surrounding his falling out with the Board. However, it is of significance that he says what he does because it casts light on the relationship between Mr. Weill and the Company – at least after October, 2000.

53 There were other points advanced by Mr. Moverley-Smith as to why the plc would not have converted the Holdings warrants into warrants in meanfiddler.com plc. He says that it is clear that by January 19th, 2001 Mr. Weill's claim had been rejected by Holdings and there was nothing done by Mr. Weill between then and July, 2001 to apply any leverage. He also refers to the evidence that the RTO could have taken place with Mr. Weill still holding warrants in Holdings. (Mr. James and Mr. Beaney (who was the nominated adviser to meanfiddler.com plc at the time of the RTO).) There is also the point that the Court can assume that Holdings/meanfiddler.com plc would have acted in its best interests and not out of any sense of largess towards Mr. Weill. Further, in her evidence Ms. Wharry of Seymour Pierce (who acted for the plc on the RTO) said that even if Mr. Weill had been given warrants in meanfiddler.com plc the plc would have insisted that he entered into a lock-in agreement for a period of 12 months in the same way that other directors were obliged to do. This is not something on which I am required to make a final finding of fact, but it is another factor to put into 'the melting pot' when valuing any chance Mr. Weill may have lost by not getting the warrants.

54 Having reviewed the matter in this way I have come to the conclusion that there is more than a negligible chance that Mr. Weill would have received warrants in the plc immediately before the RTO. I have concluded that the way he would have done so would have been by way of contractual terms written in the warrants themselves. I am conscious that it is not for me to sit down and write the contractual terms of the warrants. That is not the function which I have. What I have to decide is whether there was more than a negligible chance of the warrants containing a provision for the conversion of his warrants in Holdings into warrants into a company taking over Holdings by way of an RTO. At the time when the warrants should have been issued and the contractual terms settled, the parties were co-operating and working together and I doubt that Mr. Power or the other members of the Board would have seen anything untoward in Mr. Weill taking a stand on this. After all, they had agreed to him being remunerated in this way – to them it was the most satisfactory way from the company's point of view. He would only get something out of it in proportion to how much he had put into it – or, rather, by virtue of the fact that he was successful on behalf of the company.

55 I have more doubts as to whether, after the breakdown of the relationship between Mr. Weill and Mr. Power in October, 2000 and the way feelings were running so high – at least against Mr. Weill, meanfiddler.com plc would have bowed to commercial negotiations during 2001 to give Mr. Weill warrants in the plc in exchange for his warrants in Holdings.

56 What I am doing is assessing a chance: it seems to me that what I must do at this stage is to indicate the percentage of that chance because it is only after I have done this that I can go on to calculate the damage which Mr. Weill has sustained as a result of being deprived of this chance. Bearing in mind all the matters which I have canvassed and being conscious that this exercise is one which is often described as being a 'broad brush' exercise and also taking into account the fact that it was Holdings who was in breach of contract as a result of which Mr. Weill was obliged to come to Court, I have decided that the percentage to be applied to the chance is 70%. That he, Mr. Weill had a 70% chance of being in a position where he had warrants in meanfiddler.com plc. at the time of the RTO.

Assessment of damages
57 What, then, has Mr. Weill lost by being deprived of this 70% chance to obtain tradeable warrants in meanfiddler.com plc by virtue of the RTO in July, 2001? The fact is that, as Mr. Onslow submitted in his closing submissions (para 8), this is a case where there is more than one contingency to be taken into account when assessing the value of the lost chance. The first (and necessary) contingency which must be established before the other contingencies become relevant, is that Mr. Weill would have been possessed of he right to warrants in meanfiddler.com plc. I have valued that chance at a 70% chance. The next contingencies flow from this. Thus, the valuation exercise involves making findings as to the percentage chance for those contingencies to have taken place. Thus, as Mr. Onslow said, if there is 70% chance on the issue of convertibility and then I go on to assess that there is 50% chance on his actually having obtained a certain price for realising his warrants in meanfiddler.com plc, then the final figure is the product of 50% × 70%. This is the exercise which the Court must go through when assessing the value of the chance he lost to make a profit when he was deprived, by the Defendant's breach of contract, of realising the assets (i.e., the warrants).

58 Thus, the enquiry is: what would/could Mr. Weill have done with these warrants in meanfiddler.com plc? How much, if anything, could he have realised from them, given that it was his evidence that he would have realised the asset as soon as possible after the RTOT? As Mr. Onslow puts it in his submissions: 'The questions which (now) arise are:

(i) whether there was a real chance of C realising the MFMG warrants profitably;

(ii) what the value of that chance was.'

What he says is that he would have realised the value of the warrants in meanfiddler.com plc by: (i) a trade sale; or (ii) hedging; or

(iii) through a negotiated buy-out by meanfiddler.com plc or by Holdings; or

(iv) by realising the intrinsic value of the MFH warrants either by exercise (and sale of the resultant shares in the plc.) or by sale of the warrants themselves.

There is the further point made by the Claimant that even if he did not get warrants in meanfiddler.com plc in exchange for his Holdings warrants, he would still have been able to trade the warrants in Holdings. Before I examine these submissions I think it is necessary to clearly identify 'the base' from which this is done.

59 I do think it is necessary for me to make what at this stage is something of a basic finding of fact as to what Mr. Weill would have done himself with warrants in meanfiddler.com plc. at the time of the RTO. As I have previously said, when I come to make the findings of fact as to what Mr Weill, himself, would have done I do this by applying the standard of the balance of probabilities. It seems to me that Mr. Weill is indulging in something of a 'fence sitting' exercise in relation to what he would or might have done (to be distinguished from what a third party might have done). He seems to have been saying :'I might have traded the Holdings warrants, if I had not got the pic warrants and if I did get the plc warrants then . ... ' Again, he says, 'if I got the plc warrants I might either have cashed in the warrants and taken the shares in meanfiddler.com plc or I might have traded the warrants in one way or another.' Dr. Fitzgerald was clear in his opinion that the value of the warrants lay in selling them as warrants and not in exercising the warrants and taking the underlying shares. As he said at para. 4.10:

'I believe .. (that) no rational investor whether holding MFH (Holdings) or MFG (meanfiddler.com plc) warrants would have exercised them at the stock price levels present on 6.11.01.1 have examined earlier in the Report the effective strike price on the first tranche of warrants (the £223million strike MFH warrants) as 47P per Meanfiddler.Com share. Given the already mentioned need to establish a discount to the market to liquidate 972,451 shares, even those warrants would effectively be out of the money by the close on 6.11.01. Hence, I take the view that there were no circumstances in which it would be optimal for the Claimant to exercise either the MFH or the MFG warrants at the time of the completion of the RTO.'

I think that the proper course is to proceed from the base that Mr. Weill had the warrants in meanfiddler.com plc. Then, in order to be able to reach a sensible or clear base from which to proceed with the valuation exercise, I make the finding of fact that on the balance of probability Mr. Weill would not have realised the underlying assets in the plc warrants. Rather, he would have held on to the warrants and sought to make money out of them by selling them – not, I should say, by hedging them himself on the FTSE -100, as he suggested at some stage. (The experts were agreed that he could not have done this.) His potential profit lay in the warrants and, in particular, in their time value and their potential volatility. The fact is, as I think Mr. Lawler said, the warrants were tradeable and they were potentially more valuable than the underlying shares because of their unique character as an asset: their time value and their volatility presented for an investor a very cheap way of obtaining an interest in the company. A speculation, yes, but for investors prepared to make a speculation on what they could get from a warrant for, say, less than half the price of a share, was a right to a share which, if the warrants came 'into the money' would cost them nothing. That is, for a price based on the value of the warrant they could put themselves into the position of being able to call for the shares if and when they came 'in the money' without any net expenditure on their part. Thus, I proceed on the basis that Mr. Weill had the pic warrants and would then have sought to profit from trading them in what ever way he could in order to make a profit from them.

60   It is Mr. Weill's case that there was a market for warrants of this nature. The Defendant says that there was no market. What I have to assess is whether there would have been a real or substantial chance of a market existing for the sale of these warrants. It was at this point that the Court was assisted by two formidable expert witnesses: Dr. Fitzgerald who was called by the Claimant and Mr. Lawler who was called by the Defendant. Both these gentlemen came before the Court with a considerable experience of the London financial market (and, indeed, other markets around the world) and they spoke with considerable authority. Both were doing their best to assist the Court and gave their evidence in a very professional manner. Dr. Fitzgerald's experience and qualifications are set out at p.3 of his initial report dated 7.7.04. (Bundle E/1) He has a Ph.D in Finance from the University of Manchester and has an academic career as well as a career working in the markets. These markets include fixed income derivatives trading, arbitrage trading and volatility and relative value trading in equities, commodities and fixed income including convertibles and warrants. He said, and I am sure that this is the case, that 'as a consequence of my professional and academic experience, I am familiar with all forms of derivatives trading and risk management, the pricing and risk management of convertibles and equity warrants and the implementation of investment strategies.' Mr. Lawler is a partner in the forensic accounting group of Begbies,

Traynor, Chartered Accountants. He says in his Report dated 7.7.04 (Bundle E/9) that he 'has spent the majority of his working life working with and assisting companies and other stakeholders to resolve their complex financial issues, often considering questions of loss and damage.' I am grateful to both experts for the very clear way they have sort to explain the not inconsiderable difficulties in this case.

61 In one sense, given that my task is to assess the value of a lost chance, it is easier than having to reach a firm conclusion on a matter of fact and rule accordingly. What I am looking at is the concept of real or substantial chance and this is a different exercise from determining issues on the balance of probability. Thus, although I might come to accept the evidence of Dr. Fitzgerald that there was a market for warrants of this kind, I might nevertheless then go on to discount the chance of success by virtue of the qualifications and doubts which Mr. Lawler's opinion might establish. The other consideration is that one is applying this 'broad brush' approach. This is important to remember. I have heard a huge amount of technical evidence from the various witnesses called on the question of evaluation/loss and I cannot set it all out in this judgment with a view to weighing in a minute manner the various nuances, one way or the other. Thus, for example, I do not see it as my task, applying this 'broad brush' approach as I do, to make a definite finding on whether Mr. Weill would have actually indulged in a static hedge, it being agreed by both experts and Mr. Weill that it would not have been appropriate to have sought to execute a dynamic hedge on the FTSE index.

62 To remind myself of the 'key' dates, the RTO was completed at the EGM on 26.10.01 and the shares in the newly reconstituted plc were admitted to AIM trading on 6.11.01. Dr. Fitzgerald says there was a market in warrants of the sort which I have found that Mr. Weill had a real and substantial chance of obtaining. He did not develop this point in his First Report because the absence of a market was not something which was raised by the Defendant until a later stage. He did, however, deal with the point in the Joint Memorandum of the Experts dated 19.7.04 and in his Supplementary Report dated 18.8.04 (E/13/213). In this Joint Memorandum of the experts it is recorded that they were of the opinion that it would not have been possible for the Claimant to directly

> 'David Lawler has also stressed his views that such unquoted warrants, i.e., the Mf.Com warrants, would not be readily saleable at a realistic price to other market participants. Again, I would wish to express the contrary view here. As someone who has been heavily involved in equity arbitrage activities and hedge fund management, I would take the view that there is always a price at which a financial instrument issued by a public company would be purchased, whether it is a quoted security or not. Would-be purchasers such as equity marketmakers, equity arbitrage desks, warrants and convertibles trading desks, and hedged funds are always interested in picking up equity volatility and gamma exposure at an attractive price and hedging it. This would include, in my view, major equity trading houses. It would certainly

have been the case when I was Head of Arbitrage at Mitsubishi Finance International that, if a market participant had offered me four year warrants of a stock with a potential volatility of over 100% per annum at no more than their intrinsic value, then I would have purchased them without hesitation.' (El3/216)

It is important to note that Dr. Fitzgerald reaches this rather enthusiastic conclusion on the basis that the underlying stock had a potential volatility of over 100% – that is another matter and I shall have to explore it. The point would be that the lower the volatility the greater the discount which would have to be made when making the final valuation of the underlying share price. Ms. Wharry in her evidence said that there would be no formal market for warrants in this plc. She said that Mr. Weill would have had to exchange the warrants for shares and traded in those shares but, at she points out, this would have been a costly exercise for him.

65 I have come to the conclusion, having reviewed the evidence on the matter, that there was a real or substantial and not just a negligible possibility that Mr. Weill would have found a market for the warrants in meanfiddler.com plc had he sought to dispose of them (which, on the balance of probabilities, I have found he would have done). However, I think that when I come to evaluate this chance there are discounts to be made to reflect the uncertainties which arise and which have been referred to by Mr. Lawler and I shall come back to this point, below. When identifying just what the 'market' was, the view I have of the evidence is that there was not a 'formal' market, so to speak, but it would have been a matter of approaching various marketmakers and choosing what was best on offer. The evidence on this is not specific and this is, I think, as far as I can go. All of this goes into the 'pot' when making the relevant discount for contingencies which has to be made before I can 'come up with' a final monetary sum by way of evaluation, I should also emphasise that in reaching this conclusion I have taken into account the other evidence on this point, including that of Ms. Whany and Mr. Phillips. What they concentrate on is the point that there was no formal market and what Dr. Fitzgerald says is that there was an 'informal' market 'out there' where a buyer could be found.

66 The next step is to try to determine what sort of price Mr. Weill could have got for these meanfiddler.com plc warrants on the market. It is obvious from just stating what the issue is that the task is fraught with uncertainties and difficulties in terms of reaching a precise figure. Of course, I cannot do that. The 'broad brush' requires (or enables) me to look at the matter widely, making what discounts I think are appropriate to reflect the not inconsiderable uncertainties. Not only is it an exercise in looking backwards and trying to say what would have been, but it also involves looking at a highly uncertain and rather esoteric area of speculative trading. The difficulty of my task is underlined by the emphatic manner in which the professional witnesses contradict each other and disagree with each other's conclusions and opinions. This is partly because what they are being asked to do is put themselves back in late 2001 and to speculate what might have been possible in what was is an esoteric corner of the financial world. This is further reason for my reminding myself that my final decision must be one which can do no more than reach a fairly 'rough and ready' result given that I am venturing into the world of financial speculation. When I mentioned to one of the experts that it seemed to me that the best thing to do in such a situation was always to hedge one's position carefully he replied that that was not of the essence of this sort of market which was really one of speculation.

67 What it all comes down to is being able to assess what was a reasonable market price which could have been secured on a sale of meanfiddler.com plc warrants at the time of the RTO or shortly thereafter. The experts do not agree on the figure. Dr. Fitzgerald's position is summed up in the Joint Memorandum of the experts as follows:

> 'Mr. Desmond Fitzgerald's position was that a warrant valuation with a 49p share price and a 60% assumed volatility would be a realistic mid-market price. By reducing the volatility input to a very conservative 40%, he believed the resultant value would represent an attractive sale price to a marketmaker or institutional trade. This would give a rage of warrant values depending on maturity from £251,993 to £432,299. David Lawler took the view that, if a purchaser could be found, a reasonable valuation for the warrants should assume a 40% volatility and a share price discounted to 20p giving a range depending on maturity of £6,092 to £27,858,'

68 In his Report Dr. Fitzgerald said that the value of a warrant would depend upon some or all of the following 'inputs':

(a) The current level of the underlying asset – i.e., the quoted shares in meanfiddler.com plc.

(b) The interest rate or discount factor appropriate for the maturity of the warrant.

(c) The forecast level of dividends (or forecast dividend yield) on the underlying stock over the period through to the maturity of the warrant, zero in this case.

(d) The strike or exercise price of the warrant.

(e) The maturity of the warrant.

(f) The volatility of the underlying stork that is forecast for the period between the current date and the maturity of the warrant.

In this case the main concentration was on (a), (d), (e) and (f). There really seems to be two main base points to try to discover: the potential underlying share price as viewed in early November, 2001 and the potential volatility of the stock: i.e., how marketmakers might have seen the volatility. In assessing the share price, it is a fact that the shares were placed on the market at 70p. The opening price was 52p, by mid-December 2001 it had fallen to 20p and in February, 2002 it was at 17p, having fallen as low as 12p or 13p. It was mostly in the region of 40p during November, 2001. There was not very much movement on the stock and one has to make discounts to take into account the marketability of the stock and issues of liquidity. It is typical of the acute disputes in the professional evidence that the experts vary from a discount of nearly 80% (leaving the share price near to 10p) and a much lesser discount based on a higher volatility level and the ability of the warrant holder to put on a dynamic hedge against the warrants by buying or borrowing meanfiddler.com plc stock. The evidence is that this is likely to have been possible, given that Bass had as much as £3m.'s worth of the stock.

69 Doing the best I can, using my 'broad brush' approach, and bearing in mind that what I am calculating is the value of the warrants as at the beginning to middle of November, 2001, I have concluded after taking into account the not inconsiderable amount of conflicting evidence of all the professional witnesses that an appropriate value to place on a meanfiddler.com plc share for the purpose of this valuation exercise is 40p.

70 A substantial amount of evidence was given on the issue of the volatility of the plc shares – or, rather, their potential volatility as viewed from some time at the end of 2001. The principle is that the higher the volatility of the underlying shares, the higher the price an investor would be prepared to pay for a warrant. 'Volatility' refers to the potential of the shares to go up to high prices and fall to low prices. What the speculator is interested in is being able to buy low and then watch the underlying share go high, beyond the strike price. It is the potential of the underlying stock to do this which is all important and it is for this reason that considerable time was spent in the evidence in trying to assess this volatility level. Thus, this tends to make a virtue of the fall in the stock's value: the speculator being able to see that it can fall and (hopefully) rise again, thereby increasing its volatility.

71 Both Mr. Lawler and Dr. Fitzgerald were at pains to explain to me what Dr. Fitzgerald called the 'open sensitivities: Delta and Gamma'. He explained how traders and managers have their own language for describing the sensitivities of option positions to change in the major inputs and I have found that part of his Report both informative and helpful. The experts also explained to me the concept of dynamic hedging, or 'risk managing', and how this can be used to protect warrant positions and how, through a dynamic hedging strategy profits can be earned whether the market goes up or down. What is important to note is that the marketmaker's business of making a profit from warrants is not just about sitting on the warrant and hoping that the value of the underlying assets will go over the strike price before maturity of the warrant. It involves this process of hedging.

72 Again, taking into account all the available (and, at times, conflicting) evidence which I have heard from the professionals I have come to the conclusion that it is appropriate to value the warrants on the basis of a 50% volatility level.

Conclusions

73 Thus, I am now in the position of reaching a base from which the calculation of the value of the warrants can be made. My conclusion is that the warrants should be valued on the following basis: warrants the term date of which was 25.1.04, with an underlying share price of 40p and a volatility rate of 50%. The experts have applied what is known as the 'Black-Scholes' formula to arrive at a theoretical value of the warrants and gave a number of different results based upon a variety of permutations of share price/volatility/expiry date, but I do not think that they have applied this formula to the above base. What I would like is for the parties to agree what the value of the warrants would be based upon the Black-Scholes method. I then intend to make a discount for all the contingencies which arise. These contingencies include the following matters:

(i) Uncertainties as to timing and, in particular, when Mr. Weill would have actually sold the warrants.

(ii) Uncertainties as to the level of volatility.

(iii) Uncertainties as to the price of the underlying stock at the relevant time and the price which a buyer would have therefore put on the underlying stock.

(iv) Uncertainties as to actual existence of a market for these warrants.

(v) Uncertainties as to the ability of a marketmaker to borrow and then sell the stock necessary to execute a dynamic hedging strategy. (This is to be distinguished from an exercise of hedging on the FTSE-100 which Mr. Weill claimed he could have carried out as an alternative way of making a profit. I have held that such a course was not open to him on the evidence.)

(vi) Illiquidity of the stock in so far as it went to the potential slowness of being able to place stock for the dynamic hedge and also in terms of how it may have affected a potential investor's (speculator's) view of the stock.

(vii) The fact that this whole exercise is really trying to 'double-guess' what would be the position in a speculative market place – never an easy task for a Court but one which has to be done, I think, when the Court is faced with having to assess the value of a lost chance such as Mr. Weill had here.

This is not a complete list of the uncertainties for which a discount has to be given and there will be bound to be an overlap between some of the headings, but it is, I think, a fair indication of just what has to be discounted and why a discount is necessary. Taking all these matters into account I have concluded that the proper discount to make on this figure which is to be calculated according to the Black-Scholes method is one of 50%. I wish to make it clear that I have not 'double discounted' at this stage – in reaching the 'base position' of 40 p per share and 50% volatility I did so upon the evidence of the various professionals and not on the basis of discounting each heading for uncertainties. As Mr. Onslow submitted, I could have examined each head and then given a discount percentage to that particular head or I could have looked at the matter overall with the 'broad brush' and I have chosen to do the latter, really because the more one looked into each one of the possible contingencies the more conflicts arose and it just became impossible to state a definitive preference for a particular view. I had before me able and experienced financial people who often gave conflicting views about a particular matter and I have no way of concluding that one is absolutely right and the other absolutely wrong. Because it is such a speculative area, this is not surprising. Indeed, what I have done seems to me to be in line with how a Court must approach this very difficult area of assessing the value of a lost chance – and the task is made even the more difficult by virtue of the fact that the chance lost here is a chance to make money in what is, by any standards, a speculative environment.

74 It therefore follows that the Claimant is entitled to damages to be calculated according to the following formula:

70% × Y (where Y = 50% of the value of the warrants as calculated on the basis of time expiring on 21.1.04, a share price of 40p and a volatility level of 50%).

As I have said, I will leave it to the parties to make the calculations and to produce a final figure. There is also the issue of interest and as I understand it the parties agree that interest should run at the appropriate rate in favour of the Claimant. Interest should run, I think, from 15.11.01.

75 Finally, the Claimant seeks an order for specific performance and damages. I cannot see that this is a case for specific performance. The time for the exercise of the options in any warrants which ought to have been issued to the Claimant has long since expired and to make an order for specific performance would be meaningless. In those circumstances I decline to make an order for specific performance.

Case 48
Shinebond v Carrol

[2006] STC (SCD) 147

Special Commissioner

29 November 2005, 12 January 2006

In this case, the Special Commissioner rules that only an asset based valuation is relevant for determining the market value of 100 per cent shareholding in an investment company.

On 22 December 1988 Shinebond Ltd sold its 100 per cent shareholding to Chas Polsky Estates Ltd for £397,365. The gain assessable on Chas Polsky Estates Ltd was calculated by reference to the market value of a 100 per cent holding in Chas Polsky Estates Ltd as at 31 March 1982.

At 31 March 1982 the assets of the company consisted of a leasehold interest in 165–167 Commercial Road, London E1 plus current assets (mainly deposits and inter-group loans).

The value of 165–167 Commercial Road at 31 March 1982 was the subject of a hearing before the Land Tribunal, which determined the value of the leasehold interest as at 5 April 1982 at £168,000. The net current assets totalled £32,257.

The accountant representing the taxpayer at the hearing valued the 100 per cent shareholding in Chas Polsky Estates Ltd by taking the net rent and capitalising this using a yield of 10 per cent, to which a further capitalised value was added, being calculated as a yield of 7.5 per cent of the dividends historically paid. This gives a valuation of £252,257.

On behalf of the Revenue, it submitted that the valuation of the 100 per cent shareholding should be undertaken by taking the value of the leasehold interest, as determined by the Lands Tribunal and adding the net current assets, then applying a discount for the tax liability which would have arisen had the company sold the property at the valuation price. The Revenue valued the shareholding at £187,207.

The Special Commissioner stated in his decision:

'The company exists solely for the purpose of owning the property. The property has a value which is realisable independently of its use in the company's business (in contrast, for example, with the fixed assets of a trading business). The shares in question represent the entire issued share capital of the company. The owner of 100% of the shares has unfettered control over the company, and has the ability to force the company to realise and distribute the value of its assets. In these circumstances a hypothetical prospective purchaser would have valued the company by adding the value of the property to its other assets and deducting its liabilities.'

([2006] STC (SCD) 147 at 150f/g **case 48 para 12**)

The taxpayer's argument that capitalised value of dividends should be taken into account was, similarly, dismissed:

'In my view capitalising dividends is not relevant in valuing a controlling interest in an unlisted property investment company. As the appellant owns all of the shares of the company, it can control whether any dividends are paid, and if so, how much they are. To a great extent the amount paid by way of dividends is at the whim of the controlling shareholder.'

([2006] STC (SCD) 147 at 151j/152a **case 48 para 18**)

The Revenue had sought to deduct 30 per cent of the corporation tax that would have been payable if, on 31 March 1982, the company had sold the property for the market value at that date. The Revenue argued that a sale on that date would have attracted corporation tax at a rate of 30 per cent on the difference between the value and the historic cost of the property. The tax liability that would have arisen would have been £43,500. This tax liability was contingent on an actual disposal and the Revenue sought to discount by 30 per cent of this sum; that is £13,050. The Special Commissioner rejected the Revenue's discount stating:

'If the company sold the property for £168,000 at any time after 31 March 1982 the property would have been 'rebased' to its market value in the hands of the company as at 31 March 1982 by virtue of the provisions of Finance Act 1988, s 96 – which has been determined by the Lands Tribunal to be £168,000. The company would not realise any chargeable gain. Indeed, after taking account of indexation allowances, it might be treated as realising an allowable loss. I therefore consider that there is no contingent tax liability to take into account in determining the value of the company.'

([2006] STC (SCD) 147 at 152g-h case 48 para 21 with wording reordered)

It is difficult to agree with the decision of the Special Commissioner on this point. The essence of market value for capital gains tax purposes is the price that would be paid on the valuation date. A person making an offer for the shares on 31 March 1982 cannot possibly have known that a Finance Act six years later would change the method of calculating tax on a capital gain. As at 31 March 1982, the shareholding was in a company that had a contingent tax liability. The House of Lords held in *Winter (Sutherland's Trustees) v IRC* (1961) 40 ATC 361 **case 27** that, when shares are valued on an asset basis, a reduction in the value must be given to reflect the tax liability that would arise on the gain that would be triggered if the assets of the company were sold by the company at the values used in the valuation.

Decision

References, example '(pg148d)', are to [2006] STC (SCD) 147.

The Appeal

1 This is an appeal of Shinebond Limited relating to the gain realised on the disposal of its shareholding in Chas Polsky Estates Limited ('the Company') to Mr Dee of London Limited for £397,365 on 22 December 1988. An assessment for corporation tax for the accounting period ended 31 January 1989 was raised on 20 September 1989, which included a charge in respect of the gain made on the disposal of the shares in the Company. The Appellant submitted a Notice of Appeal *(pg148d)* and Postponement Application on 25 September 1989. The sole issue to be determined is the market value of Shinebond Limited's shareholding in the Company as at 31 March 1982.

2 Mr Amin of Amin, Patel and Shah, accountants, represented the Appellant. Mr Hart of the office of the Acting Solicitor of HM Revenue and Customs represented the Respondent. There was one bundle of documents. *(pg148e)* Neither party called any witnesses.

The Background Facts

3 The background facts have been agreed between the parties and are not in dispute. The Company was incorporated in England and Wales in 1958. The Appellant acquired all of the issued shares of the Company in an arm's length *(pg148f)* transaction on 27 November 1981 for a total price of £152,634. As at 31 March 1982 the entire issued share capital was owned by the Appellant. The principal asset of the Company on that date was a leasehold interest in a

property known as 165–167 Commercial Road, London E1 ('the Property'). The leasehold interest owned by the Appellant was a headlease, which at 31 March 1982 had an unexpired term of 36 years at a ground rent of £150 per annum. The whole of the Property *(pg148g)* was sublet for an aggregate rent of £16,800 on fully repairing and insuring terms. In addition to the Property, the Company had an excess of assets (mainly deposits and the benefit of inter-group loans) over liabilities of £32,257. As at 5 April 1982, the audited balance sheet of the Company showed no borrowings (other than a modest directors loan account). The Company's profit and loss account for the year *(pg148h)* ended 5 April 1982 showed only £17 expenditure on bank charges and interest. I therefore deduce that the Company had no material borrowings for the year.

4 The Appellant sold its shareholding in the Company to Mr Dee of London Limited for £397,365 on 22 December 1988. Included in the bundle of documents is a letter dated 1 May 1990 from Mr Shah, a director of Mr Dee of London Limited, to Mr Joga of Shinebond Limited. The letter confirms a recent meeting between Mr Joga *(pg148j)* and Mr Shah at which Mr Joga reminded Mr Shah that Mr Dee of London Limited offered to buy the Property sometime in 1982. Mr Shah states that he has discussed the matter with his other directors, and that they recall that such an offer was made. I note from the letterhead that the address of Mr Dee of London Limited is at 175 Commercial Road, which is not far from the Property. In addition, Mr Dee of London Limited were tenants of part of the Property.

5 On 13 October 2003, the Special Commissioners referred to the Lands Tribunal the question of the valuation of the Property pursuant to s46D(1) Taxes *(pg149a)* Management Act 1970. The Notice of Reference provided that the question as to whether or not there was a 'special purchaser' as at 31 March 1982, and the valuation effect of the 'special purchaser's' interest in acquiring the Property was to be taken to be a question of the valuation of land. By a consent order made on 17 January 2005, the Lands Tribunal ordered that the value of the Property as at 31 March 1982 was £168,000. *(pg149b)*

Issue to be determined

6 The sole issue to be determined is the value of the shareholding of the Appellant in the Company as at 31 March 1982. That value is relevant to the Appellant's liability to corporation tax for 1988/89 on its disposal of the shares in the Company, since by virtue of s96 Finance Act 1988, the Appellant is deemed to *(pg149c)* have sold those shares and immediately reacquired them at their market value on 31 March 1982.

7 'Market value' is defined for these purposes by s150(1) and (2) Capital Gains Tax Act 1979 (now s272(1) and (2) Taxation of Chargeable Gains Act 1992) as follows: *(pg149d)* 's150(1) – In this Act 'market value' in relation to any assets means the price which those assets might reasonably be expected to fetch on a sale in the open market.

(2) In estimating the market value of any assets no reduction shall be made in the estimate on account of the estimate being made on the assumption that the whole of the assets is to be place on the market at one and the same time.' *(pg149e)*

8 The principles to be applied in the valuation of unquoted shares are set out in s152 Capital Gains Tax Act 1979:

's152 – (1) The provisions of subsection (3) below shall have effect in any case where, in relation to an asset to which this section applies, there falls to be *(pg149f)* determined by virtue of section 150(1) above the price which the asset might reasonably be expected to fetch on a sale in the open market.

(2) The assets to which this section applies are shares and securities which are not quoted on a recognised stock exchange, within the meaning of section 535 of the Taxes Act, at the time as at which their market value for the purposes of tax on chargeable gains falls to be determined. *(pg149g)*

(3) For the purposes of a determination falling within subsection (1) above, it shall be assumed that, in the open market which is postulated for the purposes of that determination, there is available to any prospective purchaser of the asset in question all the information which a prudent prospective purchaser of the asset might reasonably require if he were proposing to purchase it from a willing vendor by private treaty and at arm's length.' *(pg149h)*

Valuation approaches

9 I am required to determine how these provisions are applied in the particular circumstances of this case. I am invited by the parties to choose between alternative approaches to the valuation of the Company. Mr Amin, for the *(pg149j)* Appellant, submits in essence that the Company should be valued by applying an appropriate yield percentage to its gross income. In contrast Mr Hart, for the Respondent, submits that the Company should be valued on the basis of its net assets.

10 The Appellant submits that the correct valuation of the Company's shares is £252,257. This is based on annual net rental income for the year ended 5 April 1982 of £22,218 (after adjustment to take account of voids and management expenses) and annual interest income of £4005. Capitalising these using a yield of *(pg150a)* 10% gives a valuation of £262,224. In addition, the Appellant submits that account should be taken of dividends of £3000 which were paid for each of the financial years ended 5 April 1980 and 1981. This gives £40,000 of value (adopting a yield of 7.5%) in addition to the value of the retained assets (which would, of course, have been depleted by the payment of the dividend). Mr Amin also drew my attention to the letter from Mr Dee of London Limited referred to above, in which *(pg150b)* Mr Dee of London Limited confirm that they would have purchased the Property in 1982 for £220,000. Accordingly Mr Amin submits that the valuation of £252,257 adopted in the Company's tax computations is correct.

11 In contrast, the Respondent's approach is to aggregate the net assets of the Company as at 31 March 1982 – namely £168,000 for the Property and £32,257 for its other net assets. This results in a valuation of £200,257. The Appellants *(pg150c)* submit that this valuation should be adjusted to take account of the tax liability which would arise in the hands of the Company should it dispose of the Property. If the Company disposed of the Property for £168,000, it would realise a gain of £145,000. As at 31 March 1982 the effective rate of corporation tax that would have been charged on the gain would be 30%, and the tax liability would therefore have been £43,500. Of course this tax liability is contingent. It would only arise if *(pg150d)* the Company sold the Property, which might never happen. Accordingly on the basis that the prospective purchaser acquired the Company with a view to retaining the Property as an investment, a discount should be applied to this contingent liability when valuing the Company's shares. The Respondent suggests that a 30% discount is appropriate (namely 30% of £43,500, which equals £13,050). Taking all these factors into account, the Respondent values the Company at £187,207. *(pg150e)*

12 I find that the Respondent's approach to the valuation of the Company to be the more appropriate in these circumstances. The Company is an investment company whose sole business activity is the ownership of the Property. Its only other assets are modest amounts of cash (or assets similar to cash – such as short term deposits and inter-group loans) and it had no material borrowings. The Company exists solely for the purpose of owning the Property. The Property has a *(pg150f)* value which is realisable independently of its use in the Company's business (in contrast, for example, with the fixed assets of a trading business). The shares in question represent the entire issued share capital of the Company. The owner of 100% of the shares has unfettered control over the Company, and has the ability to force the Company to realise and distribute the value of its assets. In these circumstances a hypothetical prospective purchaser would have valued the *(pg150g)* Company by adding the value of the Property to its other assets and deducting its liabilities.

13 I am supported in this view by Christopher Glover's book, 'Valuation of Unquoted Companies' (Gee, 2nd Edition, 1992). Mr Glover says: *(pg150h)*

'The asset basis should not be used to determine the value of a company, other than one whose assets have a readily realisable exchange value, such as property investment companies, investment trust companies and so-called 'money-box' businesses. Such companies are investment intermediaries and not economic enterprises. These remarks apply to controlling interests. Where minority interests are concerned, the asset basis is generally *(pg150j)* inappropriate, even when the company is an investment intermediary. This is because asset values are out of the reach of the minority shareholder.' (page 244)

He goes on to conclude that:

'Majority interests in investment intermediaries will usually be valued on the assets basis. The reason for this is simple. The assets of such companies are *(pg151a)* marketable and have a value independent of the earnings of the company. They are purchased by the company precisely because they are marketable and the dealing in such assets is the main object of the company.' (page 265)

14 I was also referred to the unreported decision of the Hong Kong Supreme Court (Appellate Jurisdiction: Full Court): *In re Harry Charrington deceased* (26 November 1975) *(pg151b)* 1 HKTC 723, in which the Hong Kong court determined that an approach based on 'asset backing' was appropriate in determining the value of a minority shareholding in a trading company which did not pay dividends, but which owned a valuable tenanted building. I find the decision of limited assistance, as many of the key factors influencing the Hong Kong court in *Charrington* are not applicable in this case. In particular the decision was influenced by the 'peculiar atmosphere of Hong Kong' at the time where the ordinary investor is attracted more readily by *(pg151c)* the possibility of capital gain than by the probability of secure annual returns.

15 I am not persuaded that the use of the gross yield basis of valuation is appropriate in the circumstances of this case. No justification was given by the Appellant for this approach which results in a valuation for the shares in the Company which exceeds the aggregate value of the Property and the other net assets by some £52,000. *(pg151d)*

16 The Appellant ascribes this difference to goodwill inherent in the site which arises because of its central location in the garment district of London. I find this explanation unconvincing, as the attractiveness of the location would have been one of the factors taken into account in the negotiation of the value of the Property in the course of the Lands Tribunal proceedings (the District Valuer in his expert witness report in the Lands Tribunal proceedings refers to the location and to *(pg151e)* rentals paid in comparable properties in the neighbourhood). Mr Amin further justifies this additional value by reference to the premium Mr Dee of London Limited was prepared to pay for the property in 1982, as the Property was close to their other premises in Commercial Road and as they were an existing tenant in the building. I also find this argument unconvincing. The only evidence that Mr Dee of London Limited was prepared to purchase the property in 1982 for £220,000 is a *(pg151f)* letter written some eight years later. There is no contemporaneous evidence (such as correspondence or minutes) of any such offer having been received. In any event, the impact of a 'special purchaser' (such as Mr Dee of London Limited) would have been taken into account in the Lands Tribunal determination of the value of the Property given the terms of the Notice of Reference to that Tribunal. To take the impact of a 'special purchaser' into account as further addition to the valuation *(pg151g)* would give rise to double counting.

17 Insofar as yields are relevant to the valuation of the Property, they are one of a number of factors which would have already have been taken into account in establishing an agreed value for the Property in the course of the Lands Tribunal reference. This is apparent from the expert witness report of the District Valuer *(pg151h)* mentioned above, in which he refers to historic as well as expected future rental income, the wasting nature of the asset, the repairing covenants under the leases, the ground rent payable and the price paid by the Appellant for the Company in 1981. Insofar as they are appropriate to valuing the Company's other assets (such as cash and debtors), the yield percentage cannot be applied directly to the Company's interest income for the year, as this would depend on its fluctuating *(pg151j)* balances throughout the year, and would not correspond to the balance actually held on the relevant date (31 March 1982).

18 In my view capitalising dividends is not relevant in valuing a controlling interest in an unlisted property investment company. As the Appellant owns all of the shares of the Company, it can control whether any dividends are paid, and if so, how much they are. To a great extent the amount paid by way of dividends in any year by a company which is profitable and has significant distributable reserves (such as the Company) is at the whim of the controlling shareholder. *(pg152a)*

19 It is interesting to note that when the Appellant responded on 26 September 1991 to the standard questionnaire issued by the Shares Valuation Division, it gave as the explanation for the value of £252,225 placed on the shares: *(pg152b)*

Value of leasehold interest	£220,000
+ Net current assets	£32,225
	£252,225 *(pg152c)*

Thus the Appellant originally valued the Company on an assets basis, but has given no reasons for the subsequent change in its methodology.

20 On the question of the deduction for the contingent tax liability, I was referred by Mr Hart to Eastaway, Booth and Eamer, 'Practical Share Valuation' (Butterworths, 4th Edition, 1998): *(pg152d)*

'When the company's assets have been calculated by direct valuation it will be necessary to make an adjustment for taxation in respect of the chargeable gains ... which would be taxable if the assets were to be disposed of at the realised value. This adjustment is normally only made in respect of interests *(pg152e)* in property and, unless the company is being valued on a break-up basis, it will be necessary to take account of the fact that such taxation would not be immediately payable as there would be no actual disposal. It could normally be appropriate to discount the potential tax charge to take account both of the fact that it would be over stating the net asset value of the company to ignore the tax charge, but also to recognise the fact that there is no immediate *(pg152f)* intention to dispose of the properties concerned and therefore no actual crystallisation of the tax charge.' (page 134)

21 However, the Property would have been 'rebased' to its market value in the hands of the Company as at 31 March 1982 by virtue of the provisions of s96 Finance Act 1988 – which has been determined by the Lands Tribunal to be *(pg152g)* £168,000. In other words, if the Company sold the property for £168,000 at any time after 31 March 1982, the Company would not realise any chargeable gain. Indeed, after taking account of indexation allowances, it might be treated as realising an allowable loss. I therefore consider that there is no contingent tax liability to take into account in determining the value of the Company. *(pg152h)*

Decision

22 The value of the Appellant's shareholding in the Company as at 31 March 1982 is therefore calculated as follows: *(pg152j)*

Market value of the Property as determined by Lands Tribunal £168,000
(pg153a)

plus

Other net assets at agreed amount	£32,257
	£200,257

(pg153b)

23 I therefore determine that the market value of the Appellant's shareholding in the Company as at 31 March 1982 for the purposes of s150 Capital Gains Tax Act 1979 is £200,257.00, or £200.257 per share. *(pg153c)*

Case 49
Strahan v Wilcock

[2006] All ER (D) 106

[2006] EWCA Civ 13

Court of Appeal

19 January 2006

This case gives a robust definition of a 'quasi-partnership company', the defining of which has eluded judicial comment previously. The case is, thus, in the string of 'quasi-partnership' cases reported in this book, starting with *Re Yenidje Tobacco Co Ltd* [1916–17] All ER Rep 1050 **case 10**. The concept of 'quasi-partnership' is used, and developed, in *Ebrahimi v Westbourne Galleries Ltd* [1972] 2 All ER 492 **case 31**, *Re Bird Precision Bellows Ltd* [1985] 3 All ER 523, CA **case 35** and *Strahan v Wilcock*.

Unlike the other cases using the concept of a 'quasi-partnership', in *Strahan v Wilcock*, the plaintiff who is awarded damages based on an undiscounted portion of the full market value was not an original shareholder of the company. The case is, thus, a development of the *dicta* of Lord Wilberforce in *Ebrahimi v Westbourne Galleries Ltd*:

'The superimposition of equitable considerations requires something more, which typically may include one, or probably more, of the following elements: (i) an association formed **or continued** on the basis of a personal relationship, involving mutual confidence – this element will often be found where a pre-existing partnership has been converted into a limited company; (ii) an agreement, or understanding, that all, or some (for there may be 'sleeping' members), of the shareholders shall participate in the conduct of the business; (iii) restriction upon the transfer of the members' interest in the company – so that if confidence is lost, or one member is removed from management, he cannot take out his stake and go elsewhere.'
([1973] AC 360 at 371 **case 31 para 17** (author's emphasis))

Plan-It Welding Services Ltd was formed by Mr Wilcock in 1987. Its business was light and heavy engineering. 900 shares were issued to Mr Wilcock and the 100 remaining were registered in the name of his wife. Mr Strahan joined the company in spring 1991 as a production consultant, but within a short time, Mr Wilcock asked Mr Strahan to take over the running of the company and to become the deputy managing director. Mr Strahan agreed. By 1991 Mr Wilcock was devoting considerably less time to the company's business and affairs. Mr Strahan was in day-to-day control of the running of such business and affairs and Mr Wilcock, when he was not on holiday, was calling at the premises of the company at regular intervals. After about a year, Mr Strahan was made the managing director of the company and Mr Wilcock became the chairman.

The parties also agreed that, initially for a period of five years, Mr Strahan would have an option to purchase all Mr Wilcock's shares at a price per share based on a valuation of the company at £1.25 million.

In 1997 Mr Strahan's remuneration was increased to £30,000 per annum with a bonus dependent on profits. Mr Wilcock agreed that Mr Strahan could purchase up to 10 per cent of the share capital of the company out of his bonuses.

On 20 September 2001, Mr Strahan was dismissed from his employment with the company. Mr Strahan then asked Mr Wilcock to buy his shares at their full value on a non-discounted basis. Mr Wilcock declined, and Mr Strahan presented a petition for relief from unfair prejudice under the Companies Act 1985, s 459 based on his exclusion from management and Mr Wilcock's failure to buy out his shares at their non-discounted value.

Lady Justice Arden, in the Court of Appeal, quoted, with approval, the judgement of HHJ Howarth in the High Court on the general principle to be adopted when identifying a quasi-partnership:

'What is a quasi partnership? In my judgement it is an association of shareholders in a company where if they were conducting the same business without having formed or acquired a limited liability company, they would in law be joint proprietors of that business and would thus be partners in accordance with the Partnership Act 1890. Thus mere investment in the company will not create a quasi partnership any more than it will constitute the investor as a partner if the business is run by an unincorporated body. There has to be both investment as a co-owner and participation in the decision making processes connected with the running of the business.'

([2006] All ER (D) 106 **case 49 para 14**)

Lady Justice Arden continued:

'The question whether the relationship between shareholders constitutes a 'quasi-partnership' is relatively easy to answer if the company's business was previously run by a partnership in which the shareholders were partners. It is indeed common for partnerships to be converted into companies for tax or other reasons. It is also relatively easy to establish whether a relationship between shareholders constitutes a 'quasi-partnership' when a company was formed by a group of persons who are well known to each other and incorporation of the company was with a view to them all working together in the company to exploit some business concept which they have. It is much less easy to determine whether a company is a 'quasi-partnership' in a case such as this. Mr Strahan did not know Mr Wilcock when the company was formed. He joined the company as an employee. It was only subsequently that he acquired some of its shares from Mr Wilcock and became a director. However it is clear on the authorities that a relationship of 'quasi-partnership' may be acquired after the formation of the company. Lord Wilberforce specifically refers to an association 'formed or continued' on the basis of a personal relationship.'

([2006] All ER (D) 106 **case 49 para 19**)

'The difficulty, however, about this question as such is that it assumes what it sets out to prove, namely the relationship between the parties was a form of partnership ie that is rested on the type of a personal relationship which is an ingredient of a 'quasi-partnership'. In addition, the assumption is counter-factual: there never was a partnership between Mr Wilcock and Mr Strahan. Their relationship was only ever in or through the company. Logically, the appropriate question is whether, if the company had been formed (viz incorporated) at the time the company is alleged to have become a 'quasi-partnership' (that is, in this case, at the time when Mr Strahan acquired his shares), the company would have qualified as a 'quasi-partnership', applying the guidance set out by Lord Wilberforce. Thus, it is important to ask whether at that point in time the company would have been formed on the basis of a personal relationship involving mutual confidence. It would also be appropriate to ask whether, under the arrangements agreed between the parties. Likewise it would be appropriate to ask whether there was a restriction on the transfer of the members' interests in the company.'

([2006] All ER (D) 106 **case 49 para 21**)

Lady Justice Arden then looked at the detail of the arrangements between Mr Wilcock and Mr Strahan (**case 49 para 23**). It is interesting to note that she considered the absence of any written agreement between the parties as reinforcing the conclusion that there was a personal relationship involving mutual trust and confidence and, hence, strengthening the argument for the company being a quasi partnership.

She comments:

> 'In truth, the relationship between Mr Wilcock and Mr Strahan was multi-layered and multi-faceted, involving aspects arising from Mr Strahan's employment, his right under the options and his participation in the management of the company's business. Moreover, the terms of the option agreements did not inevitably mean that the parties adopted the position of vendor and purchaser under a commercial contract. On the contrary, Mr Wilcock considered that, under the terms of the second option agreement, he was giving Mr Strahan the opportunity to acquire shares in the company at a price representing about half their value, something he was most unlikely to have done if the relationship was a purely commercial one.'
>
> **(case 49 para 25)**

The Court of Appeal, unanimously, approved the finding that the relationship was one of quasi-partnership and that Mr Wilcock was obliged to make payment to Mr Strahan on the basis of the company's full value, without discount (**case 49 paras 31–34**).

Judgement

1 **LADY JUSTICE ARDEN:** This is an appeal from the order of HHJ Howarth (sitting as an additional judge of the Chancery Division) dated 22 March 2005. By his order, the judge ordered Mr Wilcock to purchase all the ordinary shares in Plan-It Welding Services Ltd ('the company') held by Mr Strahan at their full value with no discount for the fact that those shares represented a minority shareholding. This appeal concerns a situation that often arises in a closely-held company. The sole or principal shareholder of the company brings in a person ('the new participant') to help him run the company. The new participant is given an executive role. The parties get on well, and the principal shareholder gives him or sells him an equity stake. Then, after some time, the parties fall out and the principal shareholder causes the dismissal of the new participant. He and the principal shareholder part company. In these circumstances, should the principal shareholder purchase the shares of the new participant and if so, should he do so on terms that the new participant receives the full value of the shares, i.e. their non-discounted value, or should those shares be valued on the basis that they represent a minority shareholding, i.e. on terms that their value is discounted to reflect their non-saleability in the open market? The general principle is well settled. Normally, in 'quasi-partnership' companies the appropriate basis of valuation is on a non-discounted basis. This is established by the decision of this court in *Re Bird Precision Bellows* Ltd [1984] 1 Ch. 419 and the speech of Lord Hoffmann in

O'Neill v Phillips [1999] 1 WLR 1092, at 1107 with which the other members of the House agreed. But Lord Hoffmann added:

> 'That is not to say that there may not be cases in which it will be fair to take a discounted value. But such cases will be based upon special circumstances … '

2 Is the normal principle excluded by showing that the parties had, or also had, purely commercial arrangements about the participant's acquisition of shares in the first place? Do these circumstances constitute 'special circumstances' for the purposes of Lord Hoffmann's dictum?

3 The jurisdiction of the court to make the order in this case derives from the statutory remedy for unfair prejudice contained in sections 459 to 461 of the Companies Act 1985 ('the 1985 Act'). The material parts of sections 459 and 461 of the 1985 Act are as follows:

> '459 (1) A member of a company may apply to the court by petition for an order under this Part on the ground that the company's affairs are being or have been conducted in a manner which is unfairly prejudicial to the interests of its members generally or of some part of its members (including at least himself) or that any actual or proposed act or omission of the company (including an act or omission on its behalf) is or would be so prejudicial …
>
> 461 (1) If the court is satisfied that a petition under this Part is well founded, it may make such order as it thinks fit for giving relief in respect of the matters complained of.
>
> (2) Without prejudice to the generality of subsection (1), the court's order may –
> …
> (d)   provide for the purchase of the shares of any members of the company by other members or by the company itself and, in the case of a purchase by the company itself, the reduction of the company's capital accordingly.'

Background and the judge's judgment

4 The company was formed by Mr Wilcock in 1987. Its business was light and heavy engineering. The authorised and issued share capital of the company was £1,000 divided into 1000 shares of £1 each, of which 900 shares had been issued to Mr Wilcock and were registered in his name and the remainder were registered in the name of his wife. In due course, Mrs Wilcock's shares were acquired by Mr Wilcock.

5 Mr Strahan did not join the company until 1991. The judge found that:

'The Petitioner ('Mr Strahan') joined the company in the spring of 1991 as a production consultant, but within a short time, Mr Wilcock asked Mr Strahan to take over the running of the company and to become the deputy managing director, which Mr Strahan agreed. At this time Mr Wilcock and his wife were separated and divorce proceedings were under way. Mr Wilcock had two young children, who were taking up a lot of his time. As a result, Mr. Wilcock was devoting considerably less time to the company's business and affairs. Mr Strahan was in day-to-day control of the running of such business and affairs and Mr Wilcock, when he was not on holiday, was calling at the premises of the company at regular intervals. After about a year, Mr Strahan was made the managing director of the company and Mr Wilcock became the chairman.' (judgment, paragraph 3).

6 At some point, the parties also agreed that, initially for a period of five years, Mr Strahan would have an option to purchase all Mr Wilcock's shares at a price per share based on a valuation of the company at £1.25m. I will call this option 'the first option'. There is some uncertainty about its precise terms, which were never ultimately recorded in a written agreement between the parties, but that uncertainty does not matter for the purposes of this appeal. In December 1996, Mr Strahan was advised by his own accountant that the option price under the first option was high.

7 In 1997 Mr Strahan's remuneration was increased to £30,000 per annum with a bonus dependent on profits. The judge found that at about the same time Mr Strahan was given another option to buy up to 10 per cent of Mr Wilcock's shares, which I will call 'the second option'. The circumstances leading to the second option were as follows. The judge found that Mr Strahan was unable to buy the company at the option price of £1.25m. Accordingly, he went back to Mr Wilcock in 1996. His evidence was as follows: 'I approached Bill [Mr Wilcock] and told him that in return for my part in the company's renewed success I would like a further incentive for my efforts. I suggested the possibility of me acquiring shares in the company, thinking that this would reduce the total funds that I would then have to produce to buy the company from him.' (witness statement, paragraph 17).

8 The judge held:

'Part of these new terms was that Mr Strahan was to have an option to acquire shares in the company from Mr Wilcock. The purchase price for such shares was to be paid out of the bonus due to Mr Strahan. The purchase price was to be £625 for each share ...' (judgment, paragraph 6)

9 Mr Wilcock agreed that Mr Strahan could purchase up to 10 per cent of the share capital of the company out of his bonuses. However, his case was that the reason for this arrangement was simply that Mr Strahan took the view that he might wish to make a further attempt to purchase the business and that if he acquired some shares in the business this might have the effect of reducing the overall sum to be paid in the event of exercising the option (witness statement paragraph 26). Mr Strahan was advised that the option price fixed by the second option placed a value on the company in excess of its true value, which he was advised was only £600,000. Mr Wilcock, however, took the view that the company was worth £1.25m and so he perceived the option price under the second option agreement to be generous to Mr Strahan.

10 By exercising the second option, Mr Strahan acquired 21, 25 and 4 ordinary shares in the company from Mr Wilcock in respectively 1998, 1999 and 2000. In 2000, however, he invested only part of his bonus in buying shares from Mr Wilcock. He said that he was advised that it would be better to put the remaining monies into his pension scheme.

11 However, on 20 September 2001, Mr Strahan was dismissed from his employment with the company. Negotiations took place between the solicitors for Mr Strahan and the solicitors for the company as a result of which Mr Strahan compromised his claim against the company arising out of his dismissal and resigned as a director.

12 Mr Strahan then asked Mr Wilcock to buy his shares at their full value on a non-discounted basis. Mr Wilcock declined, and Mr Strahan presented a petition for relief from unfair prejudice under Section 459 of the 1985 Act based on his exclusion from management and Mr Wilcock's failure to buy out his shares at their non-discounted value. In his petition he also relied on the creation and issue of further classes of ordinary share capital on which dividends were paid and from which Mr Strahan was excluded. The judge found in favour of Mr Strahan on those matters, but it is not necessary to consider those findings on this appeal.

13 On Mr Strahan's case based on his exclusion from management and Mr Wilcock's failure to purchase his shares, Miss Lesley Anderson, for Mr Strahan, submitted to the judge that equitable obligations were owed to him as the company was a 'quasi-partnership'. (I will examine the meaning of that term below.) The judge's conclusions on this submission were as follows:

'48. What is a quasi partnership? In my judgment it is an association of shareholders in a company where if they were conducting the same business without having formed or acquired a limited liability company, they would in law be joint proprietors of that business and would thus be partners in accordance with the Partnership Act 1890. Thus mere investment in the company will not create a quasi partnership any more than it will constitute the investor as a partner if the business is run by an unincorporated body. There has to be both investment as a co-owner and participation in the decision making processes connected with the running of the business. If prior to March 1998 Mr Wilcock had been a sole trader running the business and he took Mr Strahan into the ownership of that business by selling him a 2% interest in the business, Mr Strahan would have become a partner in the business. This partnership interest would have increased in 1999 to a 4% interest and in 2000 to a 5% share. I appreciate that the above percentages are approximate only, but they are not far wrong.'

14 Having found that the company was a 'quasi-partnership', the judge turned to consider whether, given that on his findings the company was a 'quasi-partnership', Mr Wilcock owed Mr Strahan an obligation in equity to purchase his shares on a non-discounted basis upon Mr Strahan ceasing to participate in the management of the business.

15 The judge held as follows:

'49. By holding out an expectation to Mr Strahan that he could purchase the remaining shares in the company at any time up to 5 June 2002, Mr Wilcock must be taken as having given Mr Strahan to understand that he would continue in the employment of the company until at least that date. No doubt he could have been dismissed for misconduct during that time, but that has nothing to do with this case. Mr Strahan was, of course, dismissed before that date. After that date, if Mr Strahan had not purchased the other shares in the company from Mr Wilcock, the parties would have had to sit down and come to a new arrangement which would have involved either the further purchase of shares by Mr Strahan and the sale of shares by Mr Wilcock, or the severance of his relations between Mr Strahan and the company, including the repurchase of his shares. This does not directly help me save that I find it impossible to conceive that if by June 2002, Mr Strahan had not purchased the shares of Mr Wilcock at a price agreed by both of them, then he would be dismissed from the employment of the company and Mr Wilcock would have bought back the shares of Mr Strahan at a price of at least the price paid by Mr Strahan when he bought them. Clearly the expectation that Mr Strahan could purchase the shares of Mr Wilcock in the company at any time until 5 June 2002 would be of little interest to Mr Strahan if he was no longer employed by the company. I cannot see how Mr Strahan would want to buy shares in the company out of his bonus if he thought that he could be left with those shares which he might well not be able to sell and which might never pay him any dividend. At the very least he must have expected that he could sell those shares back at the price he paid for them, or may be more or less, depending on the financial health of the company at the relevant time. If Mr Wilcock had thought about matters when the understanding had been reached in 1997 or when the first shares were being bought in 1998, he too would have come to the same conclusion. This is sufficient to amount to a mutual understanding.

50. Mr Strahan purchased his shares with money to which he was entitled. The contentions of Mr Wilcock lead to the result that Mr Strahan has

received only a temporary benefit from that money and the risk is all one way. Either Mr Strahan buys at least 90% of the shares in the company at a price which is considerably more than he has been professionally advised they are worth or he is likely to be left with valueless shares on his hands. It is difficult to imagine circumstances which do not more obviously affect the conscience of Mr Wilcock.

51. For these reasons I find that Mr Wilcock has conducted the company's affairs in a manner which is unfairly prejudicial to the interests of Mr Strahan. He has caused the employment of Mr Strahan to be terminated prior to June 2002 without offering to buy back the shares of Mr Strahan at a fair price. In my view it is hard to find a clearer case where the court would exercise its powers under Section 459. This is clearly a case where obligations of good faith apply. Mr Strahan clearly had legitimate expectations that his shares would be purchased if his employment came to an end before June 2002. The dealings of Mr Wilcock and Mr Strahan in relation to the shares in the company which were acquired by Mr Strahan clearly affected the conscience of Mr Wilcock in the manner I have indicated. All the other elements of the law summarised above are clearly satisfied. Even if I should be wrong in my conclusion as to the existence of a quasi partnership, I would still have reached the same conclusion for the reasons set out above. This is a plain case where a court of equity would intervene in the way I have indicated.'

16 Accordingly, the judge held that Mr Wilcock's failure to offer to buy Mr Strahan's shares at their non-discounted value following his dismissal by the company amounted to unfair prejudice for the purposes of section 459 of the 1985 Act. As I have said, the judge held that the appropriate form of order was an order that Mr Wilcock purchase Mr Strahan's shares in the company at their non-discounted value. This is often called a 'buy out order'.

Was there a 'quasi-partnership' relationship?

17 The burden of the dispute between the parties on this appeal is as to the basis of valuation in the buy out order. Shares are generally ordered to be purchased on the basis of their valuation on a non-discounted basis where the party against whom the order is made has acted in breach of the obligation of good faith applicable to the parties' relationship by analogy with partnership law, that is to say where a 'quasi-partnership' relationship has been found to exist. It is difficult to conceive of circumstances in which a non-discounted basis of valuation would be appropriate where there was unfair prejudice for the purposes of the 1985 Act but such a relationship did not exist. However, on this appeal I need not express a final view on what those circumstances might be.

18 In general, the relationship between shareholders is governed exclusively by the terms of the memorandum and articles of association of the company of which they are shareholders. Their rights and obligations are derived from those documents and those documents alone. In some circumstances, however, equitable obligations will arise between shareholders. The relationship where such equitable obligations exist is often labelled, not always helpfully, as a 'quasi-partnership'. The classic statement of the law as to when such a relationship will arise is set out in the speech of Lord Wilberforce in *Ebrahimi v Westbourne Galleries Ltd* [1973] AC 360 at 371. Although this was a case involving the court's discretion to order the winding-up of a company on the 'just and equitable' ground (now section 122 (1) (g) of the Insolvency Act 1986), the same principles apply to claims for relief from unfair prejudice under section 459 of the 1985 Act. Lord Wilberforce held:

> 'My Lords, in my opinion these authorities represent a sound and rational development of the law which should be endorsed. The foundation of it all lies in the words 'just and equitable' and, if there is any respect in which some of the cases may be open to criticism, it is that the courts may sometimes have been too timorous in giving them full force. The words are a recognition of the fact that a limited company is more than a mere legal entity, with a personality in law of its own: that there is room in company law for recognition of the fact that behind it, or amongst it, there are individuals, with rights, expectations and obligations inter se which are not necessarily submerged in the company structure. That structure is defined by the Companies Act and by the articles of association by which shareholders agree to be bound. In most companies and in most contexts, this definition is sufficient and exhaustive, equally so whether the company is large or small. The 'just and equitable' provision does not, as the respondents suggest, entitle one party to disregard the obligation he assumes by entering a company, nor the court to dispense him from it. It does, as equity always does, enable the court to subject the exercise of legal rights to equitable considerations; considerations that is, of a personal character arising between one individual and another, which may make it unjust, or inequitable, to insist on legal rights, or to exercise them in a particular way.

> It would be impossible, and wholly undesirable, to define the circumstances in which these considerations may arise. Certainly the fact that a company is a small one, or a private company, is not enough. There are very many of these where the association is a purely commercial one, of which it can safely be said that the basis of association is adequately and exhaustively laid down in the articles. The superimposition of equitable considerations requires something more, which typically may include one, or probably more, of the following elements: (i) an association formed or continued on the basis of a personal relationship, involving mutual confidence – this element will often be found where a pre-existing partnership has been converted into a limited company; (ii) an agreement, or understanding, that all, or some (for there may be 'sleeping' members), of the shareholders shall participate in the conduct of the business; (iii) restriction upon the transfer of the

members' interest in the company – so that if confidence is lost, or one member is removed from management, he cannot take out his stake and go elsewhere.

It is these, and analogous, factors which may bring into play the just and equitable clause, and they do so directly, through the force of the words themselves. To refer, as so many of the cases do, to 'quasi-partnerships' or 'in substance partnerships' may be convenient but may also be confusing. It may be convenient because it is the law of partnership which has developed the conceptions of probity, good faith and mutual confidence, and the remedies where these are absent, which become relevant once such factors as I have mentioned are found to exist: the words 'just and equitable' sum these up in the law of partnership itself. And in many, but not necessarily all, cases there has been a pre-existing partnership the obligations of which it is reasonable to suppose continue to underlie the new company structure. But the expressions may be confusing if they obscure, or deny, the fact that the parties (possibly former partners) are now co-members in a company, who have accepted, in law, new obligations. A company, however small, however domestic, is a company not a partnership or even a quasi-partnership and it is through the just and equitable clause that obligations, common to partnership relations, may come in.'

19 The question whether the relationship between shareholders constitutes a 'quasi-partnership' is relatively easy to answer if the company's business was previously run by a partnership in which the shareholders were the partners. It is indeed common for partnerships to be converted into companies for tax or other reasons. It is also relatively easy to establish whether a relationship between shareholders constitutes a 'quasi-partnership' when a company was formed by a group of persons who are well known to each other and the incorporation of the company was with a view to them all working together in the company to exploit some business concept which they have. It is much less easy to determine whether a company is a 'quasi-partnership' in a case such as this. Mr Strahan did not know Mr Wilcock when the company was formed. He joined the company as an employee. It was only subsequently that he acquired some of its shares from Mr Wilcock and became a director. However, it is clear on the authorities that a relationship of 'quasi-partnership' may be acquired after the formation of the company. Lord Wilberforce specifically refers to an association 'formed or continued' on the basis of a personal relationship.

20 The question then is: in what circumstances should the courts determine that such a company constitutes a 'quasi-partnership'? At the end of paragraph 48 of his judgment (set out above), the judge in effect approached this issue by asking whether, if Mr Wilcock had been a sole trader running the business prior to Mr Strahan first acquiring an interest in it, Mr Strahan would have become a partner upon acquiring that interest. He answered that question affirmatively.

21 The difficulty, however, about this question as such is that it assumes what it sets out to prove, namely the relationship between the parties was a form of partnership i.e. that it rested on the type of a personal relationship which is an ingredient of a 'quasi-partnership'. In addition, the assumption is counter-factual: there never was a partnership between Mr Wilcock and Mr Strahan. Their relationship was only ever in or through the company. Logically, the appropriate question is whether, if the company had been formed (viz incorporated) at the time the company is alleged to have become a 'quasi-partnership' (that is, in this case, at the time when Mr Strahan acquired his shares), the company would have qualified as a 'quasi-partnership', applying the guidance set out by Lord Wilberforce. Thus, it is important to ask whether at that point in time the company would have been formed on the basis of a personal relationship involving mutual confidence. It would also be appropriate to ask whether, under the arrangements agreed between the parties, all the parties, other than those who were to be 'sleeping' members, would be entitled to participate in the conduct of the business. Likewise it would be appropriate to ask whether there was a restriction on the transfer of the members' interests in the company. That last requirement is in fact met by the articles of association in the present case, which restrict the transfer of shares. With limited exceptions, the directors can refuse to register the transfer of shares. The articles would therefore enable the directors to prevent Mr Strahan from transferring his shares to a third party.

22 Was the company a 'quasi-partnership'? Mr Strahan joined the company initially in 1991 but as I have explained, the judge found that he rapidly took over day-to-day control and became first deputy managing director and then managing director. It was Mr Wilcock who became the 'sleeping' member of the company. In 1994 Mr Wilcock gave Mr Strahan the first option. Under this option, Mr Strahan could acquire the entire share capital of the company exercisable within a five-year period. The condition of that offer was that Mr Strahan should be in full time employment of the company at the date when the option was exercised. This option was not committed to writing and appears to have been for a rolling five-year period.

23 As I have said, the judge held that the company was a 'quasi-partnership'. The factors which support the judge's conclusion are as follows. First, pursuant to the second option, Mr Strahan bought 5 per cent of the company's shares, a not insignificant percentage. The only other shareholder was Mr Wilcock. Secondly, the evidence showed that Mr Wilcock agreed to the second option as a reward for Mr Strahan's efforts in the company and as an incentive to him and this is confirmed by the fact that under the second option Mr Strahan had to pay for the shares he acquired out of his bonuses. Thirdly, at the relevant time Mr Strahan was participating in management decisions of the company. Indeed, as I have said, Mr Wilcock had in effect become a sleeping partner. Mr Strahan became a signatory and possibly the only signatory on the mandate for the company's bank account. Fourthly, the terms of the option agreement were informally agreed between them. The terms were never committed to writing, and this reinforces the conclusion that there was a personal relationship involving mutual trust and confidence between the parties. Fifthly, while Mr Strahan was rewarded by the payment of remuneration, he also received a share of the profits in the form of his bonus. In addition, it was in effect agreed that Mr Wilcock should receive his return from the company in the form of dividends. In point of fact those dividends were substantially greater than Mr Strahan's remuneration. Mr Wilcock's case is that his return was in reality no more than a tax-efficient way to pay remuneration. The judge made no finding on that but he found as a fact that Mr Strahan had waived his right to receive any dividend on his shares whilst he was an employee of the company. The fact that Mr Wilcock and Mr Strahan came to an understanding or agreement as to the form of the return they were each to obtain from the company's profits is indicative that their relationship was more a 'quasi-partnership' relationship than a relationship between a majority shareholder and company executive. All these factors can be found among the findings of fact made by the judge in his judgment.

24 Mr Anthony Elleray QC, for Mr Wilcock, submits that the judge drew the wrong inferences from the facts and that the relationship between Mr Wilcock and Mr Strahan was a commercial one, stemming originally from Mr Strahan's status as a mere employee of the company. On Mr Elleray's submission, the first option was a purely commercial arrangement between parties dealing at arm's length. He submits that Mr Strahan was given the second option merely as a stepping stone to facilitate his acquisition of the whole of the share capital of the company under the first option. He also submits that Mr Strahan saw the second option in that light. On that basis, Mr Strahan's expectation that he could exercise the option in the second option agreement was no more and no less than as a prospective purchaser of shares. Further, the real reason why Mr Strahan did not proceed to use all his bonus to acquire shares in 2000 was that as from 2000 the company had started to make losses: his motivation in this respect confirmed the commercial basis on which he took the benefit of the option arrangements. In addition, Mr Elleray submits that, if Mr Strahan is entitled to a buy out order on a non-discounted basis, he takes all the benefits and none of the risks of share ownership.

25 In my judgment, the judge was entitled to draw the inferences that he did from the evidence and to conclude that the relationship between Mr Wilcock and Mr Strahan developed into the relationship of 'quasi-partnership'. Mr Elleray's submissions do not take sufficient account of the five factors listed in paragraph 23 above, which as I have said were all consistent with the existence of a 'quasi-partnership' between the parties. In truth, the relationship between Mr Wilcock and Mr Strahan was multi-layered and multi-faceted, involving aspects arising from Mr Strahan's employment, his right under the options and his participation in the management of the company's business. Moreover, the terms of the option agreements did not inevitably mean that the parties adopted the position of vendor and purchaser under a commercial contract. On the contrary, Mr Wilcock considered that, under the terms of the second option agreement, he was giving Mr Strahan the opportunity to acquire shares in the company at a price representing about half their value, something he was most unlikely to have done if the relationship was a purely commercial one. Moreover, the second option opened the door to Mr Strahan becoming a shareholder without acquiring all the shares under the first option. Again, this is something that Mr Wilcock is hardly like to have wanted to do under a purely commercial contract of purchase and sale. Mr Wilcock must have contemplated that in that half-way house Mr Strahan and he would run the company together. Seen overall the relationship between the parties met the description laid down by Lord Wilberforce in the *Westbourne Galleries* case.

26 In addition, like the judge (judgment, paragraph 50), I do not accept the argument that Mr Strahan bore no risk by acquiring shares in the company. He bore the risk that the company might go into liquidation or that (as happened) Mr Wilcock might be unwilling to repurchase his shares at their full value if he caused the removal of Mr Strahan from the company or that he (Mr Strahan) might be unable to find a purchaser for his shares in the company because he held a minority shareholding or that if he did find a purchaser Mr Wilcock would cause the directors to refuse to register the share transfer.

27 The next question is whether there are equitable considerations which bind Mr Wilcock to purchase Mr Strahan's shares on a non-discounted basis once Mr Strahan had been dismissed by the company. In determining what equitable obligations arise between the parties, the court must look at all the circumstances, including the company's constitution, any written agreement between the shareholders, and the conduct of the parties. These matters were explained by Lord Hoffmann in *O'Neill v Phillips* at page 1099 to 1102:

> '...there will be cases in which equitable considerations make it unfair for those conducting the affairs of the company to rely upon their strict legal powers. Thus unfairness may consist in a breach of the rules or in using the rules in a manner which equity would regard as contrary to good faith.

> This approach to the concept of unfairness in section 459 runs parallel to that which your Lordships' House, in *In re Westbourne Galleries Ltd.* [1973] AC 360, adopted in giving content to the concept of 'just and equitable' as a ground for winding up. After referring to cases on the equitable jurisdiction to require partners to exercise their powers in good faith, Lord Wilberforce said, at p. 379:

>> "The words ['just and equitable'] are a recognition of the fact that a limited company is more than a mere legal entity, with a personality in law of its own: that there is room in company law for recognition of the fact that behind it, or amongst it, there are individuals, with rights, expectations and obligations inter se which are not necessarily submerged in the company structure. That structure is defined by the Companies Act [1948] and by the articles of association by which

shareholders agree to be bound. In most companies and in most contexts, this definition is sufficient and exhaustive, equally so whether the company is large or small. The 'just and equitable' provision does not, as the respondents [the company] suggest, entitle one party to disregard the obligation he assumes by entering a company, nor the court to dispense him from it. It does, as equity always does, enable the court to subject the exercise of legal rights to equitable considerations; considerations, that is, of a personal character arising between one individual and another, which may make it unjust, or inequitable, to insist on legal rights, or to exercise them in a particular way."

...In the Australian case of *In re Wondoflex Textiles Ltd.* [1951] VLR 458, 467, Smith J also contrasted the literal meaning of the articles with the true intentions of the parties:

"It is also true, I think, that, generally speaking, a petition for winding up, based upon the partnership analogy, cannot succeed if what is complained of is merely a valid exercise of powers conferred in terms by the articles ... To hold otherwise would enable a member to be relieved from the consequences of a bargain knowingly entered into by him ... But this, I think, is subject to an important qualification. Acts which, in law, are a valid exercise of powers conferred by the articles may nevertheless by entirely outside what can fairly be regarded as having been in the contemplation of the parties when they became members of the company; and in such cases the fact that what has been done is not in excess of power will not necessarily be an answer to a claim for winding up. Indeed, it may be said that one purpose of [the just and equitable provision] is to enable the court to relieve a party from this bargain in such cases."

I cite these references to 'the literal construction of these articles' contrasted with good faith and 'the plain general meaning of the deed' and 'what the parties can fairly have had in contemplation' to show that there is more than one theoretical basis upon which a decision like *Blisset v Daniel* can be explained. Nineteenth century England law, with its division between law and equity, traditionally took the view that while literal meanings might prevail in a court of law, equity could give effect to what it considered to have been the true intentions of the parties by preventing or restraining the exercise of legal rights. So Smith J speaks of the exercise of the power being valid 'in law' but its exercise not being just and equitable because contrary to the contemplation of the parties. This way of looking at the matter is a product of English legal history which has survived the amalgamation of the courts of law and equity. But another approach, in a different legal culture, might be simply to take a less literal view of 'legal' construction and interpret the article themselves in accordance with what Page Wood V-C called 'the plain general meaning of the deed.' Or one might, as in Continental systems, achieve the same result by introducing a general requirement of good faith into contractual performance. These are all different ways of doing the same thing. I do not suggest there is any advantage in abandoning the traditional English theory, even though it is derived from arrangements for the administration of justice which were abandoned over a century ago. On the contrary, a new and unfamiliar approach could only cause uncertainty. So I agree with Jonathan Parker J when he said in *Re Astec (BSR) plc* [1998] 2 BCLC 556 at 588:

> "… in order to give rise to an equitable constraint based on 'legitimate expectation' what is required is a personal relationship or personal dealings of some kind between the party seeking to exercise the legal right and the party seeking to restrain such exercise, such as will affect the conscience of the former."

This is putting the matter in very traditional language, reflecting in the word 'conscience' the ecclesiastical origins of the long-departed Court of Chancery. As I have said, I have no difficulty with this formulation. But I think that one useful cross-check in a case like this is to ask whether the exercise of the power in question would be contrary to what the parties, by words or conduct, have actually agreed. Would it conflict with the promises which they appear to have exchanged? In *Blisset v Daniel* the limits were found in the 'general meaning' of the partnership articles themselves. In a quasi-partnership company, they will usually be found in the understandings between the members at the time they entered into association. But there may be later promises, by words or conduct, which it would be unfair to allow a member to ignore. Nor is it necessary that such promises should be independently enforceable as a matter of contract. A promise may be binding as a matter of justice and equity although for one reason or another (for example, because in favour of a third party) it would not be enforceable by law.

I do not suggest that exercising rights in breach of some promise or undertaking is the only form of conduct which will be regarded as unfair for the purposes of s 459. For example, there may be some event which puts an end to the basis upon which the parties entered into association with each other, making it unfair that one shareholder should insist upon the continuance of the association. The analogy of contractual frustration suggests itself. The unfairness may rise not from what the parties have positively agreed but from a majority using its legal powers to maintain the association in circumstances to which the minority can reasonably say it did not agree: non haec in foedera veni. It is well recognised that in such a case there would be power to wind up the company on the just and equitable ground (see *Virdi v Abbey Leisure Ltd* [1990] BCLC 342) and it seems to me that, in the absence of a winding up, it could equally be said to come within s 459. But this form of unfairness is also based upon established equitable principles and it does not arise in this case.'

28 Lord Hoffmann went on to explain that the concept of legitimate expectation was unnecessary in this context. The crucial question is whether, as explained in the passage already cited, equitable principles arose which made it unfair for a party to exercise rights conferred by the articles. He went on to hold on the facts of the case that there was no unfair prejudice. However, at page 1107 he held that where a majority shareholder prevents a minority shareholder from continuing to participate in the management of the company it would almost always be unfair for the minority shareholder to be excluded without an offer to buy his shares:

> 'Usually, … the majority shareholder will want to put an end to the association. In such a case, it will almost always be unfair for the minority shareholder to be excluded without an offer to buy shares or make some other fair arrangement. The Law Commission Report on *Shareholder Remedies*, at pp. 30–37, paras. 3.26 has recommended that in a private company limited by shares in which substantially all the members are directors, there should be statutory presumption that the removal of a shareholder as a director, or from substantially all his functions as a director, is unfairly prejudicial conduct. This does not seem to me very different in practice from the present law. But the unfairness does not lie in the exclusion alone but in exclusion without a reasonable offer. If the respondent to a petition has plainly made a reasonable offer, then the exclusions as such will not be unfairly prejudicial and he will be entitled to have the petition struck out. It is therefore very important that participants in such companies should be able to know what counts as a reasonable offer.
>
> In the first place, the offer must be to purchase the shares at a fair value. This will ordinarily be a value representing an equivalent proportion of the total issued share capital, that is, without a discount for its being a minority holding. The Law Commission (paragraphs 3.57–62) has recommended a statutory presumption that in cases to which the presumption of unfairly prejudicial conduct applies, the fair value of the shares should be determined on a pro rata basis. This too reflects the existing practice. This is not to say that there may not be cases in which it will be fair to take a discounted value. But such cases will be based upon special circumstances and it will seldom be possible for the court to say that an offer to buy on a discounted basis is plainly reasonable, so that the petition should be struck out.'

29 It follows from these passages that it is appropriate to ask whether the relationship between Mr Wilcock and Mr Strahan was such as to make it unfair in the sense given above for Mr Wilcock to decline to buy Mr Strahan's shares on a non-discounted basis after his dismissal, alternatively the test is whether Mr Wilcock's failure to buy out Mr Strahan's shares on a non-discounted basis after he had been dismissed from the company is fairly to be regarded as having been outside the parties' reasonable contemplation when Mr Strahan's acquired his shares. If so, Mr Wilcock's failure in this regard would constitute unfair prejudice.

30 The judge considered these questions in paragraphs 49 to 51 of his judgment (leaving to one side the last two sentences which, as I have said, do not need to be considered on this appeal). In my judgment, he also came to the correct conclusion. Mr Strahan's departure from the company was involuntary: he did not take a unilateral decision to leave nor is it said that he was guilty of misconduct. He had been involved in the management of the company. Once he left the company, he was no longer able to do that which the parties anticipated that he should have the opportunity to do, namely to purchase the shares of the company held by Mr Wilcock pursuant to the first option. Indeed he was no longer interested in doing so because of the company's financial position and because the price was too high. However, that is not the end of the matter. He retained his existing shares. Mr Wilcock rightly recognised that once Mr Strahan left the company he (Mr Wilcock) should buy his shares. However, he contended that he should do so only on a discounted basis. In my judgment, the judge was right to reject that contention. Mr Strahan had been prevented from continuing to participate in management. Moreover he had invested his bonuses in buying the shares. He was not able to benefit from any increase in the value of those shares by staying in the company and contributing to its profitability (if such was achievable). In those circumstances, the expectation reasonably to be imputed to the parties, given their previous relationship, was that he should receive the true value of those shares. He had invested in the company. In those circumstances fairness demanded that he should be entitled to claim back not simply the cost of acquiring the shares (viz the value of the bonuses foregone), but their value at the date of the buy out order.

31 It will be seen from this judgment that the terms of the first and second options principally throw light on whether the relationship between the parties was one of 'quasi-partnership'. Those options are an essential part of the background and require careful consideration for a proper understanding of the parties' relationship. Once, however, the question of 'quasi-partnership' was answered in Mr Strahan's favour, those options have little role to play. They were certainly arrangements of a commercial nature between the parties and such as might have been negotiated by parties who were not in a 'quasi-partnership'. However, that does not mean that they constitute 'special circumstances' justifying a buy out order other than on a full, non-discounted basis. On the contrary, the existence of the 'quasi-partnership' cannot be ignored and the fact that the shares were paid for out of bonuses which Mr Strahan had earned strengthens the conclusion as to the appropriateness in this case of the basis of valuation which normally flows from the fact of exclusion from management in the case of 'quasi-partnership' company. Mr Elleray rightly did not suggest that the prejudice which Mr Strahan suffered by using his bonus to buy the shares from Mr Wilcock should be left out of account on the grounds that it was prejudice suffered by him only in his capacity as a director. The statutory requirement that the unfair prejudice complained of should be suffered by the petitioner in his capacity as a member is satisfied by Mr Wilcock's failure to purchase Mr Strahan's shares on appropriate terms.

32 Accordingly I would dismiss the appeal.

LORD JUSTICE RICHARDS: I agree.

LORD JUSTICE MUMMERY: I also agree.

Case 50
Irvine v Irvine

PART 2 Cases

[2006] 4 All ER 102

[2006] EWHC 583 (Ch)

High Court

16, 23 March 2006

A 49.96 per cent shareholding is to be valued as a minority shareholding, with the discount appropriate to a minority.

This short case is included as a corrective for any mistaken belief on valuation of a minority shareholding that may arise from the quasi-partnership cases (see *Re Yenidje Tobacco Co Ltd* [1916–17] All ER Rep 1050 **case 10**, *Ebrahimi v Westbourne Galleries Ltd* [1972] 2 All ER 492 **case 31**, *Re Bird Precision Bellows Ltd* [1985] 3 All ER 523, CA **case 35** and *Strahan v Wilcock* [2006] All ER (D) 106 **case 49**).

Unless there is, in fact, a quasi-partnership, a discount is necessary when valuing a minority holding. In this case, Patricia Irvine's effective holding is only a minority one because one more share was given to her brother-in-law, Ian Irvine, than to her. The court held that this history is irrelevant. The question is simply: 'What is the number of shares held?'

Similarly, the reason for the valuation cannot negate the discount for a minority. In this case, the court has found that Patricia was an oppressed minority; the manner in which the company's affairs were managed was unfairly prejudiced against Patricia, the minority shareholder. Again, when valuing Patricia's shareholding, this is not relevant. A discount is applied to the sum of money payable to her.

Judgement

References, example '(pg103)', are to [2006] 4 All ER 102.

1 BLACKBURNE J: On 10 March 2006 I handed down judgment on this section 459 petition. I found that unfair prejudice had been established and ordered the first respondent ('Ian') to buy or procure the purchase of the

petitioners' shares in the second respondent ('CIHL'). I expressed the view that in valuing the shares there should not be any minority discount but stressed that I had not heard argument on the point. The matter has since been argued.

2 The petitioners' shares together represent 49.96% of the issued shares in CIHL. Of that 49.96% just under half are held by the first petitioner ('Patricia') and the balance by the second petitioner ('the Trust'). The shares were acquired from the 50% holding in CIHL formerly owned by Malcolm Irvine ('Malcolm'), Patricia's late husband and Ian's younger brother. Malcolm died on 1 March 1996. In August 1994 Malcolm had given half of his shareholding to the Trust. By his will, Malcolm had given one share to Ian and the remainder to Patricia. Patricia is one of the two trustees of the Trust. The other trustee, Michael Thatcher, has 'delegated' his powers as a trustee to Patricia in relation to the Trust. The Trust is for the benefit of Patricia's three sons who are all now adults. For all practical purposes Patricia and the Trust speak as one voice.

3 The question which I have to decide is whether in the working out of the buy-out order the 49.96% shareholding (as effectively it is) is to be valued on a pro-rata *(pg103)*, non-discounted basis to reflect the fact that it is a minority holding. Miss Catherine Roberts, appearing on behalf of the petitioners, submitted that it should; Mr Nigel Dougherty, appearing on behalf of Ian, submitted that it should be valued on a discounted basis.

4 Most, if not all, of the authorities in which the question has been raised whether the shares in a company which is the subject of a section 459 petition should be valued on a pro-rata or on a discounted basis have been cases where the company is or is alleged to be a quasi-partnership. Certainly, Miss Roberts was unable to draw my attention to any in which a non-discounted basis of valuation has been applied to a minority holding in a company which is not a quasi-partnership.

5 The legislation does not stipulate how the matter is to be approached. On the other hand, the courts have repeatedly emphasised that the overriding requirement in quasi-partnership cases is that the price to be paid, where a buy-out order is made, should be fair. In *Re Bird Precision Bellows Ltd* [1984] Ch 419 (a case under section 75 of the Companies Act 1980, the predecessor to section 459) Nourse J said (at 431D):

> 'In the case of the shareholder who acquires shares from another at a price which is discounted because they represent a minority it is to my mind self-evident that there cannot be any universal or even a general rule that he should be bought out under section 75 on a more favourable basis, even in a case where his predecessor has been a quasi-partner in a quasi-partnership. He might himself have acquired the shares purely for investment and played no part in the affairs of the company. In that event it might well be fair – I do not know – that he should be bought out on the same basis as he himself had bought, even though his interests had been

unfairly prejudiced in the meantime. A fortiori, there could be no universal or even a general rule in a case where the company had never been a quasi-partnership in the first place.

In summary, there is in my judgment no rule of universal application. On the other hand, there is a general rule in a case where the company is at the material time a quasi-partnership and the purchase order is made in respect of the shares of a quasi-partner ... It seems clear to me that ... that is [namely, a valuation on a non-discounted basis], in general, the fair basis of valuation in a quasi-partnership case, and that it should be applied in this case unless the respondents have established that the petitioners acted in such a way as to deserve their exclusion from the company.'

6 In *Strahan v Wilcock* [2006] EWCA Civ 13 (at [17]) Arden LJ stated that:

'Shares are generally ordered to be purchased on the basis of their valuation on a non-discounted basis where the party against whom the order is made has acted in breach of the obligation of good faith applicable to the parties' relationship by analogy with partnership law, that is to say where a 'quasipartnership' relationship has been found to exist. It is difficult to conceive of circumstances in which a non-discounted basis of valuation would be appropriate where there was unfair prejudice for the purposes of the 1985 Act but such a relationship did not exist. However, on this appeal I need not express a final view on what those circumstances might be.' *(pg104)*

7 The reason for so treating the valuation of shares on a buy-out order in a quasi-partnership case was offered by Lord Millett in *CVC/Opportunity Equity Partners Ltd v Demarco Almeida* [2002] UKPC 16; [2002] 2 BCLC 108 (at [41]):

'The rationale for denying a discount to reflect the fact that the holding in question is a minority holding lies in the analogy between a quasi-partnership company and a true partnership. On the dissolution of a partnership, the ordinary course is for the court to direct a sale of the partnership business as a going concern with liberty for any of the former partners who wish to bid for the business to do so. But the court has power to ascertain the value of a former partner's interests without a sale if it can be done by valuation, and frequently does so where his interest is relatively small: see Syers v Syers (1876) 1 App Cas 174. But the valuation is not based on a notional sale of the outgoing partner's share to the continuing partners who, being the only possible purchasers, would offer relatively little. It is based on a notional sale of the business as a whole to an outside purchaser.

In the case of a company possessing the relevant characteristics, the majority can exclude the minority only if they offer to pay them a fair price for their shares. In order to be free to manage the company's business without regard to the relationship of trust and confidence which formerly existed between them, they must buy the whole, part from themselves and part from the minority, thereby achieving the same freedom to manage the business as an outside purchaser would enjoy.'

8 Is there any reason in the present case for concluding that, although it is a minority holding and although CIHL is not a quasi-partnership, fairness requires the petitioners' shares to be valued on a non-discounted basis? Or, taking up the comment of Arden LJ, are there present in this case circumstances (which she considered difficult to conceive) that would make it appropriate for the petitioners to receive a non-discounted valuation for their shares?

9 Miss Roberts advanced the following considerations for submitting that such circumstances do exist. Although, since Malcolm's death CIHL had not been a quasi-partnership, the company remained nevertheless a 'family company' in that all the shares were held by or for the benefit of members of the Irvine family. The articles contained restrictions on the transfer of shares and there is no open market for their disposal. Treating the shareholdings of Patricia and the Trust as a combined holding the difference between that holding and Ian's is only one share (in that the petitioners' holding is 50% less one share and Ian's is 50% plus one share). If only proper dividends had been paid and Ian had been less greedy in the remuneration which he drew for himself the petitioners would have been content to remain shareholders of the Company. It is only because over several years Ian has behaved in the way that he has that the petitioners have been driven to seek an exit from the company by means of a buy-out order. If this was not a case where a pro-rata basis of valuation should apply, it would be difficult to think that any such case would ever arise, and there would be a risk therefore that the court's discretion in fixing the basis of valuation for a minority holding in a company which was not a quasi-partnership would be atrophied.

10 Mr Dougherty submitted that the matter was one of principle. CIHL was not a quasi-partnership. As a result of the gift by Malcolm to Ian of the single share, control of CIHL passed to Ian. No conditions were attached to the gift of that share. Ian was not subject to any restrictions, over and above those contained in CIHL's articles, against disposing of his majority holding to an *(pg105)* external purchaser. The petitioners' shareholdings constituted a minority holding even though the difference between them and Ian's is so small. There were no circumstances which could be described as exceptional so as to justify a departure from the ordinary assumption that a minority shareholding is valued as such. The fact that the court has found that the manner in which Ian has conducted CIHL's affairs was unfairly prejudicial to the interests of the petitioners so as to establish their entitlement to a buy-out order cannot, of itself, determine the basis of valuation of the petitioners' shares.

11 I accept Mr Dougherty's submissions. A minority shareholding, even one where the extent of the minority is as slight as in this case, is to be valued for what it is, a minority shareholding, unless there is some good reason to attribute

to it a pro-rata share of the overall value of the company. Short of a quasi-partnership or some other exceptional circumstance, there is no reason to accord to it a quality which it lacks. CIHL is not a quasi-partnership. There are no exceptional circumstances. The shareholdings must therefore be valued for what they are: less than 50% of CIHL's issued share capital. The extent of the discount to be applied will be a matter for the valuers.

Index to Part 1